University Casebook Series

March, 1991

ACCOUNTING AND THE LAW, Fourth Edition (1978), with Problems Pamphlet (Successor to Dohr, Phillips, Thompson & Warren)

George C. Thompson, Professor, Columbia University Graduate School of Business.
Robert Whitman, Professor of Law, University of Connecticut.
Ellis L. Phillips, Jr., Member of the New York Bar.
William C. Warren, Professor of Law Emeritus, Columbia University.

ACCOUNTING FOR LAWYERS, MATERIALS ON (1980)

David R. Herwitz, Professor of Law, Harvard University.

ADMINISTRATIVE LAW, Eighth Edition (1987), with 1989 Case Supplement and 1983 Problems Supplement (Supplement edited in association with Paul R. Verkuil, Dean and Professor of Law, Tulane University)

Walter Gellhorn, University Professor Emeritus, Columbia University.
Clark Byse, Professor of Law, Harvard University.
Peter L. Strauss, Professor of Law, Columbia University.
Todd D. Rakoff, Professor of Law, Harvard University.
Roy A. Schotland, Professor of Law, Georgetown University.

ADMIRALTY, Third Edition (1987), with Statute and Rule Supplement

Jo Desha Lucas, Professor of Law, University of Chicago.

ADVOCACY, see also Lawyering Process

AGENCY, see also Enterprise Organization

AGENCY—PARTNERSHIPS, Fourth Edition (1987)

Abridgement from Conard, Knauss & Siegel's Enterprise Organization, Fourth Edition.

AGENCY AND PARTNERSHIPS (1987)

Melvin A. Eisenberg, Professor of Law, University of California, Berkeley.

ANTITRUST: FREE ENTERPRISE AND ECONOMIC ORGANIZATION, Sixth Edition (1983), with 1983 Problems in Antitrust Supplement and 1990 Case Supplement

Louis B. Schwartz, Professor of Law, University of Pennsylvania.
John J. Flynn, Professor of Law, University of Utah.
Harry First, Professor of Law, New York University.

BANKRUPTCY, Second Edition (1989), with 1990 Case Supplement

Robert L. Jordan, Professor of Law, University of California, Los Angeles.
William D. Warren, Professor of Law, University of California, Los Angeles.

BANKRUPTCY AND DEBTOR–CREDITOR LAW, Second Edition (1988)

Theodore Eisenberg, Professor of Law, Cornell University.

i

BUSINESS CRIME (1990)

Harry First, Professor of Law, New York University.

BUSINESS ORGANIZATION, see also Enterprise Organization

BUSINESS PLANNING, Temporary Second Edition (1984)

David R. Herwitz, Professor of Law, Harvard University.

BUSINESS TORTS (1972)

Milton Handler, Professor of Law Emeritus, Columbia University.

CHILDREN IN THE LEGAL SYSTEM (1983) with 1990 Supplement (Supplement edited in association with Elizabeth S. Scott, Professor of Law, University of Virginia)

Walter Wadlington, Professor of Law, University of Virginia.
Charles H. Whitebread, Professor of Law, University of Southern California.
Samuel Davis, Professor of Law, University of Georgia.

CIVIL PROCEDURE, see Procedure

CIVIL RIGHTS ACTIONS (1988), with 1990 Supplement

Peter W. Low, Professor of Law, University of Virginia.
John C. Jeffries, Jr., Professor of Law, University of Virginia.

CLINIC, see also Lawyering Process

COMMERCIAL AND DEBTOR–CREDITOR LAW: SELECTED STATUTES, 1990 EDITION

COMMERCIAL LAW, Second Edition (1987)

Robert L. Jordan, Professor of Law, University of California, Los Angeles.
William D. Warren, Professor of Law, University of California, Los Angeles.

COMMERCIAL LAW, Fourth Edition (1985), with 1990 Case Supplement

E. Allan Farnsworth, Professor of Law, Columbia University.
John Honnold, Professor of Law, University of Pennsylvania.

COMMERCIAL PAPER, Third Edition (1984), with 1990 Case Supplement

E. Allan Farnsworth, Professor of Law, Columbia University.

COMMERCIAL PAPER, Second Edition (1987) (Reprinted from COMMERCIAL LAW, Second Edition (1987))

Robert L. Jordan, Professor of Law, University of California, Los Angeles.
William D. Warren, Professor of Law, University of California, Los Angeles.

COMMERCIAL PAPER AND BANK DEPOSITS AND COLLECTIONS (1967), with Statutory Supplement

William D. Hawkland, Professor of Law, University of Illinois.

COMMERCIAL TRANSACTIONS—Principles and Policies, Second Edition (1991)

Alan Schwartz, Professor of Law, Yale University.
Robert E. Scott, Professor of Law, University of Virginia.

COMPARATIVE LAW, Fifth Edition (1988)

Rudolf B. Schlesinger, Professor of Law, Hastings College of the Law.
Hans W. Baade, Professor of Law, University of Texas.
Mirjan P. Damaska, Professor of Law, Yale Law School.
Peter E. Herzog, Professor of Law, Syracuse University.

UNIVERSITY CASEBOOK SERIES—Continued

COMPETITIVE PROCESS, LEGAL REGULATION OF THE, Fourth Edition (1990), with 1989 Selected Statutes Supplement

Edmund W. Kitch, Professor of Law, University of Virginia.
Harvey S. Perlman, Dean of the Law School, University of Nebraska.

CONFLICT OF LAWS, Ninth Edition (1990)

Willis L. M. Reese, Professor of Law, Columbia University.
Maurice Rosenberg, Professor of Law, Columbia University.
Peter Hay, Professor of Law, University of Illinois.

CONSTITUTIONAL LAW, Eighth Edition (1989), with 1990 Case Supplement

Edward L. Barrett, Jr., Professor of Law, University of California, Davis.
William Cohen, Professor of Law, Stanford University.
Jonathan D. Varat, Professor of Law, University of California, Los Angeles.

CONSTITUTIONAL LAW, CIVIL LIBERTY AND INDIVIDUAL RIGHTS, Second Edition (1982), with 1989 Supplement

William Cohen, Professor of Law, Stanford University.
John Kaplan, Professor of Law, Stanford University.

CONSTITUTIONAL LAW, Eleventh Edition (1985), with 1990 Supplement (Supplement edited in association with Frederick F. Schauer, Professor, Harvard University)

Gerald Gunther, Professor of Law, Stanford University.

CONSTITUTIONAL LAW, INDIVIDUAL RIGHTS IN, Fourth Edition (1986), (Reprinted from CONSTITUTIONAL LAW, Eleventh Edition), with 1990 Supplement (Supplement edited in association with Frederick F. Schauer, Professor, Harvard University)

Gerald Gunther, Professor of Law, Stanford University.

CONSUMER TRANSACTIONS, Second Edition (1991), with Selected Statutes and Regulations Supplement

Michael M. Greenfield, Professor of Law, Washington University.

CONTRACT LAW AND ITS APPLICATION, Fourth Edition (1988)

Arthur Rosett, Professor of Law, University of California, Los Angeles.

CONTRACT LAW, STUDIES IN, Third Edition (1984)

Edward J. Murphy, Professor of Law, University of Notre Dame.
Richard E. Speidel, Professor of Law, Northwestern University.

CONTRACTS, Fifth Edition (1987)

John P. Dawson, late Professor of Law, Harvard University.
William Burnett Harvey, Professor of Law and Political Science, Boston University.
Stanley D. Henderson, Professor of Law, University of Virginia.

CONTRACTS, Fourth Edition (1988)

E. Allan Farnsworth, Professor of Law, Columbia University.
William F. Young, Professor of Law, Columbia University.

CONTRACTS, Selections on (statutory materials) (1988)

CONTRACTS, Second Edition (1978), with Statutory and Administrative Law Supplement (1978)

Ian R. Macneil, Professor of Law, Cornell University.

UNIVERSITY CASEBOOK SERIES—Continued

COPYRIGHT, PATENTS AND TRADEMARKS, see also Competitive Process; see also Selected Statutes and International Agreements

COPYRIGHT, PATENT, TRADEMARK AND RELATED STATE DOCTRINES, Third Edition (1990), with 1989 Selected Statutes Supplement and 1981 Problem Supplement

Paul Goldstein, Professor of Law, Stanford University.

COPYRIGHT, Unfair Competition, and Other Topics Bearing on the Protection of Literary, Musical, and Artistic Works, Fifth Edition (1990), with 1990 Statutory Supplement

Ralph S. Brown, Jr., Professor of Law, Yale University.
Robert C. Denicola, Professor of Law, University of Nebraska.

CORPORATE ACQUISITIONS, The Law and Finance of (1986), with 1990 Supplement

Ronald J. Gilson, Professor of Law, Stanford University.

CORPORATE FINANCE, Third Edition (1987)

Victor Brudney, Professor of Law, Harvard University.
Marvin A. Chirelstein, Professor of Law, Columbia University.

CORPORATION LAW, BASIC, Third Edition (1989), with Documentary Supplement

Detlev F. Vagts, Professor of Law, Harvard University.

CORPORATIONS, see also Enterprise Organization

CORPORATIONS, Sixth Edition—Concise (1988), with 1990 Case Supplement and 1990 Statutory Supplement

William L. Cary, late Professor of Law, Columbia University.
Melvin Aron Eisenberg, Professor of Law, University of California, Berkeley.

CORPORATIONS, Sixth Edition—Unabridged (1988), with 1990 Case Supplement and 1990 Statutory Supplement

William L. Cary, late Professor of Law, Columbia University.
Melvin Aron Eisenberg, Professor of Law, University of California, Berkeley.

CORPORATIONS AND BUSINESS ASSOCIATIONS—STATUTES, RULES, AND FORMS (1990)

CORRECTIONS, SEE SENTENCING

CREDITORS' RIGHTS, see also Debtor-Creditor Law

CRIMINAL JUSTICE ADMINISTRATION, Fourth Edition (1991)

Frank W. Miller, Professor of Law, Washington University.
Robert O. Dawson, Professor of Law, University of Texas.
George E. Dix, Professor of Law, University of Texas.
Raymond I. Parnas, Professor of Law, University of California, Davis.

CRIMINAL LAW, Fourth Edition (1987)

Fred E. Inbau, Professor of Law Emeritus, Northwestern University.
Andre A. Moenssens, Professor of Law, University of Richmond.
James R. Thompson, Professor of Law Emeritus, Northwestern University.

CRIMINAL LAW AND APPROACHES TO THE STUDY OF LAW, Second Edition (1991)

John M. Brumbaugh, Professor of Law, University of Maryland.

iv

CRIMINAL LAW, Second Edition (1986)

Peter W. Low, Professor of Law, University of Virginia.
John C. Jeffries, Jr., Professor of Law, University of Virginia.
Richard C. Bonnie, Professor of Law, University of Virginia.

CRIMINAL LAW, Fourth Edition (1986)

Lloyd L. Weinreb, Professor of Law, Harvard University.

CRIMINAL LAW AND PROCEDURE, Seventh Edition (1989)

Ronald N. Boyce, Professor of Law, University of Utah.
Rollin M. Perkins, Professor of Law Emeritus, University of California, Hastings College of the Law.

CRIMINAL PROCEDURE, Third Edition (1987), with 1990 Supplement

James B. Haddad, Professor of Law, Northwestern University.
James B. Zagel, Chief, Criminal Justice Division, Office of Attorney General of Illinois.
Gary L. Starkman, Assistant U. S. Attorney, Northern District of Illinois.
William J. Bauer, Chief Judge of the U.S. Court of Appeals, Seventh Circuit.

CRIMINAL PROCESS, Fourth Edition (1987), with 1990 Supplement

Lloyd L. Weinreb, Professor of Law, Harvard University.

DAMAGES, Second Edition (1952)

Charles T. McCormick, late Professor of Law, University of Texas.
William F. Fritz, late Professor of Law, University of Texas.

DECEDENTS' ESTATES AND TRUSTS, Seventh Edition (1988)

John Ritchie, late Professor of Law, University of Virginia.
Neill H. Alford, Jr., Professor of Law, University of Virginia.
Richard W. Effland, late Professor of Law, Arizona State University.

DISPUTE RESOLUTION, Processes of (1989)

John S. Murray, President and Executive Director of The Conflict Clinic, Inc., George Mason University.
Alan Scott Rau, Professor of Law, University of Texas.
Edward F. Sherman, Professor of Law, University of Texas.

DOMESTIC RELATIONS, see also Family Law

DOMESTIC RELATIONS, Second Edition (1990)

Walter Wadlington, Professor of Law, University of Virginia.

EMPLOYMENT DISCRIMINATION, Second Edition (1987), with 1990 Supplement

Joel W. Friedman, Professor of Law, Tulane University.
George M. Strickler, Professor of Law, Tulane University.

EMPLOYMENT LAW, Second Edition (1991), with Statutory Supplement

Mark A. Rothstein, Professor of Law, University of Houston.
Andria S. Knapp, Visiting Professor of Law, Golden Gate University.
Lance Liebman, Professor of Law, Harvard University.

ENERGY LAW (1983) with 1986 Case Supplement

Donald N. Zillman, Professor of Law, University of Utah.
Laurence Lattman, Dean of Mines and Engineering, University of Utah.

UNIVERSITY CASEBOOK SERIES—Continued

FEDERAL COURTS AND THE FEDERAL SYSTEM, Hart and Wechsler's Third Edition (1988), with 1989 Case Supplement, and the Judicial Code and Rules of Procedure in the Federal Courts (1989)

Paul M. Bator, Professor of Law, University of Chicago.
Daniel J. Meltzer, Professor of Law, Harvard University.
Paul J. Mishkin, Professor of Law, University of California, Berkeley.
David L. Shapiro, Professor of Law, Harvard University.

FEDERAL COURTS AND THE LAW OF FEDERAL–STATE RELATIONS, Second Edition (1989), with 1990 Supplement

Peter W. Low, Professor of Law, University of Virginia.
John C. Jeffries, Jr., Professor of Law, University of Virginia.

FEDERAL PUBLIC LAND AND RESOURCES LAW, Second Edition (1987), with 1990 Case Supplement and 1990 Statutory Supplement

George C. Coggins, Professor of Law, University of Kansas.
Charles F. Wilkinson, Professor of Law, University of Oregon.

FEDERAL RULES OF CIVIL PROCEDURE and Selected Other Procedural Provisions, 1990 Edition

FEDERAL TAXATION, see Taxation

FOOD AND DRUG LAW (1980), with Statutory Supplement

Richard A. Merrill, Dean of the School of Law, University of Virginia.
Peter Barton Hutt, Esq.

FUTURE INTERESTS (1970)

Howard R. Williams, Professor of Law, Stanford University.

FUTURE INTERESTS AND ESTATE PLANNING (1961), with 1962 Supplement

W. Barton Leach, late Professor of Law, Harvard University.
James K. Logan, formerly Dean of the Law School, University of Kansas.

GOVERNMENT CONTRACTS, FEDERAL, Successor Edition (1985), with 1989 Supplement

John W. Whelan, Professor of Law, Hastings College of the Law.

GOVERNMENT REGULATION: FREE ENTERPRISE AND ECONOMIC ORGANIZATION, Sixth Edition (1985)

Louis B. Schwartz, Professor of Law, Hastings College of the Law.
John J. Flynn, Professor of Law, University of Utah.
Harry First, Professor of Law, New York University.

HEALTH CARE LAW AND POLICY (1988)

Clark C. Havighurst, Professor of Law, Duke University.

HINCKLEY, JOHN W., JR., TRIAL OF: A Case Study of the Insanity Defense (1986)

Peter W. Low, Professor of Law, University of Virginia.
John C. Jeffries, Jr., Professor of Law, University of Virginia.
Richard C. Bonnie, Professor of Law, University of Virginia.

INJUNCTIONS, Second Edition (1984)

Owen M. Fiss, Professor of Law, Yale University.
Doug Rendleman, Professor of Law, College of William and Mary.

INSTITUTIONAL INVESTORS, (1978)

David L. Ratner, Professor of Law, Cornell University.

UNIVERSITY CASEBOOK SERIES—Continued

INSURANCE, Second Edition (1985)

William F. Young, Professor of Law, Columbia University.
Eric M. Holmes, Professor of Law, University of Georgia.

INSURANCE LAW AND REGULATION (1990)

Kenneth S. Abraham, University of Virginia.

INTERNATIONAL LAW, see also Transnational Legal Problems, Transnational Business Problems, and United Nations Law

INTERNATIONAL LAW IN CONTEMPORARY PERSPECTIVE (1981), with Essay Supplement

Myres S. McDougal, Professor of Law, Yale University.
W. Michael Reisman, Professor of Law, Yale University.

INTERNATIONAL LEGAL SYSTEM, Third Edition (1988), with Documentary Supplement

Joseph Modeste Sweeney, Professor of Law, University of California, Hastings.
Covey T. Oliver, Professor of Law, University of Pennsylvania.
Noyes E. Leech, Professor of Law Emeritus, University of Pennsylvania.

INTRODUCTION TO LAW, see also Legal Method, On Law in Courts, and Dynamics of American Law

INTRODUCTION TO THE STUDY OF LAW (1970)

E. Wayne Thode, late Professor of Law, University of Utah.
Leon Lebowitz, Professor of Law, University of Texas.
Lester J. Mazor, Professor of Law, University of Utah.

JUDICIAL CODE and Rules of Procedure in the Federal Courts, Students' Edition, 1989 Revision

Daniel J. Meltzer, Professor of Law, Harvard University.
David L. Shapiro, Professor of Law, Harvard University.

JURISPRUDENCE (Temporary Edition Hardbound) (1949)

Lon L. Fuller, late Professor of Law, Harvard University.

JUVENILE, see also Children

JUVENILE JUSTICE PROCESS, Third Edition (1985)

Frank W. Miller, Professor of Law, Washington University.
Robert O. Dawson, Professor of Law, University of Texas.
George E. Dix, Professor of Law, University of Texas.
Raymond I. Parnas, Professor of Law, University of California, Davis.

LABOR LAW, Eleventh Edition (1991), with 1991 Statutory Supplement

Archibald Cox, Professor of Law, Harvard University.
Derek C. Bok, President, Harvard University.
Robert A. Gorman, Professor of Law, University of Pennsylvania.
Matthew W. Finkin, Professor of Law, University of Illinois.

LABOR LAW, Second Edition (1982), with Statutory Supplement

Clyde W. Summers, Professor of Law, University of Pennsylvania.
Harry H. Wellington, Dean of the Law School, Yale University.
Alan Hyde, Professor of Law, Rutgers University.

UNIVERSITY CASEBOOK SERIES—Continued

LAND FINANCING, Third Edition (1985)

The late Norman Penney, Professor of Law, Cornell University.
Richard F. Broude, Member of the California Bar.
Roger Cunningham, Professor of Law, University of Michigan.

LAW AND MEDICINE (1980)

Walter Wadlington, Professor of Law and Professor of Legal Medicine, University of Virginia.
Jon R. Waltz, Professor of Law, Northwestern University.
Roger B. Dworkin, Professor of Law, Indiana University, and Professor of Biomedical History, University of Washington.

LAW, LANGUAGE AND ETHICS (1972)

William R. Bishin, Professor of Law, University of Southern California.
Christopher D. Stone, Professor of Law, University of Southern California.

LAW, SCIENCE AND MEDICINE (1984), with 1989 Supplement

Judith C. Areen, Professor of Law, Georgetown University.
Patricia A. King, Professor of Law, Georgetown University.
Steven P. Goldberg, Professor of Law, Georgetown University.
Alexander M. Capron, Professor of Law, University of Southern California.

LAWYERING PROCESS (1978), with Civil Problem Supplement and Criminal Problem Supplement

Gary Bellow, Professor of Law, Harvard University.
Bea Moulton, Professor of Law, Arizona State University.

LEGAL METHOD (1980)

Harry W. Jones, Professor of Law Emeritus, Columbia University.
John M. Kernochan, Professor of Law, Columbia University.
Arthur W. Murphy, Professor of Law, Columbia University.

LEGAL METHODS (1969)

Robert N. Covington, Professor of Law, Vanderbilt University.
E. Blythe Stason, late Professor of Law, Vanderbilt University.
John W. Wade, Professor of Law, Vanderbilt University.
Elliott E. Cheatham, late Professor of Law, Vanderbilt University.
Theodore A. Smedley, Professor of Law, Vanderbilt University.

LEGAL PROFESSION, THE, Responsibility and Regulation, Second Edition (1988)

Geoffrey C. Hazard, Jr., Professor of Law, Yale University.
Deborah L. Rhode, Professor of Law, Stanford University.

LEGISLATION, Fourth Edition (1982) (by Fordham)

Horace E. Read, late Vice President, Dalhousie University.
John W. MacDonald, Professor of Law Emeritus, Cornell Law School.
Jefferson B. Fordham, Professor of Law, University of Utah.
William J. Pierce, Professor of Law, University of Michigan.

LEGISLATIVE AND ADMINISTRATIVE PROCESSES, Second Edition (1981)

Hans A. Linde, Judge, Supreme Court of Oregon.
George Bunn, Professor of Law, University of Wisconsin.
Fredericka Paff, Professor of Law, University of Wisconsin.
W. Lawrence Church, Professor of Law, University of Wisconsin.

LOCAL GOVERNMENT LAW, Second Revised Edition (1986)

Jefferson B. Fordham, Professor of Law, University of Utah.

UNIVERSITY CASEBOOK SERIES—Continued

MASS MEDIA LAW, Fourth Edition (1990)

Marc A. Franklin, Professor of Law, Stanford University.
David A. Anderson, Professor of Law, University of Texas.

MUNICIPAL CORPORATIONS, see Local Government Law

NEGOTIABLE INSTRUMENTS, see Commercial Paper

NEGOTIATION (1981) (Reprinted from THE LAWYERING PROCESS)

Gary Bellow, Professor of Law, Harvard Law School.
Bea Moulton, Legal Services Corporation.

NEW YORK PRACTICE, Fourth Edition (1978)

Herbert Peterfreund, Professor of Law, New York University.
Joseph M. McLaughlin, Dean of the Law School, Fordham University.

OIL AND GAS, Fifth Edition (1987)

Howard R. Williams, Professor of Law, Stanford University.
Richard C. Maxwell, Professor of Law, University of California, Los Angeles.
Charles J. Meyers, late Dean of the Law School, Stanford University.
Stephen F. Williams, Judge of the United States Court of Appeals.

ON LAW IN COURTS (1965)

Paul J. Mishkin, Professor of Law, University of California, Berkeley.
Clarence Morris, Professor of Law Emeritus, University of Pennsylvania.

PENSION AND EMPLOYEE BENEFIT LAW (1990)

John H. Langbein, Professor of Law, University of Chicago.
Bruce A. Wolk, Professor of Law, University of California, Davis.

PLEADING AND PROCEDURE, see Procedure, Civil

POLICE FUNCTION, Fifth Edition (1991)

Reprint of Chapters 1–10 of Miller, Dawson, Dix and Parnas's CRIMINAL JUSTICE ADMINISTRATION, Fourth Edition.

PREPARING AND PRESENTING THE CASE (1981) (Reprinted from THE LAW-YERING PROCESS)

Gary Bellow, Professor of Law, Harvard Law School.
Bea Moulton, Legal Services Corporation.

PROCEDURE (1988), with Procedure Supplement (1989)

Robert M. Cover, late Professor of Law, Yale Law School.
Owen M. Fiss, Professor of Law, Yale Law School.
Judith Resnik, Professor of Law, University of Southern California Law Center.

PROCEDURE—CIVIL PROCEDURE, Second Edition (1974), with 1979 Supplement

The late James H. Chadbourn, Professor of Law, Harvard University.
A. Leo Levin, Professor of Law, University of Pennsylvania.
Philip Shuchman, Professor of Law, Cornell University.

PROCEDURE—CIVIL PROCEDURE, Sixth Edition (1990)

Richard H. Field, late Professor of Law, Harvard University.
Benjamin Kaplan, Professor of Law Emeritus, Harvard University.
Kevin M. Clermont, Professor of Law, Cornell University.

UNIVERSITY CASEBOOK SERIES—Continued

PROCEDURE—CIVIL PROCEDURE, Fifth Edition (1990)

Maurice Rosenberg, Professor of Law, Columbia University.
Hans Smit, Professor of Law, Columbia University.
Rochelle C. Dreyfuss, Professor of Law, New York University.

PROCEDURE—PLEADING AND PROCEDURE: State and Federal, Sixth Edition (1989), with 1990 Case Supplement

David W. Louisell, late Professor of Law, University of California, Berkeley.
Geoffrey C. Hazard, Jr., Professor of Law, Yale University.
Colin C. Tait, Professor of Law, University of Connecticut.

PROCEDURE—FEDERAL RULES OF CIVIL PROCEDURE, 1990 Edition

PRODUCTS LIABILITY AND SAFETY, Second Edition, (1989), with 1989 Statutory Supplement

W. Page Keeton, Professor of Law, University of Texas.
David G. Owen, Professor of Law, University of South Carolina.
John E. Montgomery, Professor of Law, University of South Carolina.
Michael D. Green, Professor of Law, University of Iowa

PROFESSIONAL RESPONSIBILITY, Fifth Edition (1991), with 1991 Selected Standards on Professional Responsibility Supplement

Thomas D. Morgan, Professor of Law, George Washington University.
Ronald D. Rotunda, Professor of Law, University of Illinois.

PROPERTY, Sixth Edition (1990)

John E. Cribbet, Professor of Law, University of Illinois.
Corwin W. Johnson, Professor of Law, University of Texas.
Roger W. Findley, Professor of Law, University of Illinois.
Ernest E. Smith, Professor of Law, University of Texas.

PROPERTY—PERSONAL (1953)

S. Kenneth Skolfield, late Professor of Law Emeritus, Boston University.

PROPERTY—PERSONAL, Third Edition (1954)

Everett Fraser, late Dean of the Law School Emeritus, University of Minnesota.
Third Edition by Charles W. Taintor, late Professor of Law, University of Pittsburgh.

PROPERTY—INTRODUCTION, TO REAL PROPERTY, Third Edition (1954)

Everett Fraser, late Dean of the Law School Emeritus, University of Minnesota.

PROPERTY—FUNDAMENTALS OF MODERN REAL PROPERTY, Second Edition (1982), with 1985 Supplement

Edward H. Rabin, Professor of Law, University of California, Davis.

PROPERTY, REAL (1984), with 1988 Supplement

Paul Goldstein, Professor of Law, Stanford University.

PROSECUTION AND ADJUDICATION, Fourth Edition (1991)

Reprint of Chapters 11–26 of Miller, Dawson, Dix and Parnas's CRIMINAL JUSTICE ADMINISTRATION, Fourth Edition.

PSYCHIATRY AND LAW, see Mental Health, see also Hinckley, Trial of

PUBLIC UTILITY LAW, see Free Enterprise, also Regulated Industries

UNIVERSITY CASEBOOK SERIES—Continued

REAL ESTATE PLANNING, Third Edition (1989), with Revised Problem and Statutory Supplement (1991)

Norton L. Steuben, Professor of Law, University of Colorado.

REAL ESTATE TRANSACTIONS, Revised Second Edition (1988), with Statute, Form and Problem Supplement (1988)

Paul Goldstein, Professor of Law, Stanford University.

RECEIVERSHIP AND CORPORATE REORGANIZATION, see Creditors' Rights

REGULATED INDUSTRIES, Second Edition, (1976)

William K. Jones, Professor of Law, Columbia University.

REMEDIES, Second Edition (1987)

Edward D. Re, Chief Judge, U. S. Court of International Trade.

REMEDIES, (1989)

Elaine W. Shoben, Professor of Law, University of Illinois.
Wm. Murray Tabb, Professor of Law, Baylor University.

SALES, Second Edition (1986)

Marion W. Benfield, Jr., Professor of Law, University of Illinois.
William D. Hawkland, Chancellor, Louisiana State Law Center.

SALES AND SALES FINANCING, Fifth Edition (1984)

John Honnold, Professor of Law, University of Pennsylvania.

SALES LAW AND THE CONTRACTING PROCESS, Second Edition (1991)

(Reprinted from Commercial Transactions, Second Edition (1991)
Alan Schwartz, Professor of Law, Yale University.
Robert E. Scott, Professor of Law, University of Virginia.

SECURED TRANSACTIONS IN PERSONAL PROPERTY, Second Edition (1987) (Reprinted from COMMERCIAL LAW, Second Edition (1987))

Robert L. Jordan, Professor of Law, University of California, Los Angeles.
William D. Warren, Professor of Law, University of California, Los Angeles.

SECURITIES REGULATION, Sixth Edition (1987), with 1990 Selected Statutes, Rules and Forms Supplement and 1990 Cases and Releases Supplement

Richard W. Jennings, Professor of Law, University of California, Berkeley.
Harold Marsh, Jr., Member of California Bar.

SECURITIES REGULATION, Second Edition (1988), with Statute, Rule and Form Supplement (1988)

Larry D. Soderquist, Professor of Law, Vanderbilt University.

SECURITY INTERESTS IN PERSONAL PROPERTY, Second Edition (1987)

Douglas G. Baird, Professor of Law, University of Chicago.
Thomas H. Jackson, Dean of the Law School, University of Virginia.

SECURITY INTERESTS IN PERSONAL PROPERTY (1985) (Reprinted from Sales and Sales Financing, Fifth Edition)

John Honnold, Professor of Law, University of Pennsylvania.

SELECTED STANDARDS ON PROFESSIONAL RESPONSIBILITY, 1991 Edition

UNIVERSITY CASEBOOK SERIES—Continued

TAXATION, FUNDAMENTALS OF CORPORATE, Second Edition (1987), with 1989 Supplement

Stephen A. Lind, Professor of Law, University of Florida and University of California, Hastings.
Stephen Schwarz, Professor of Law, University of California, Hastings.
Daniel J. Lathrope, Professor of Law, University of California, Hastings.
Joshua Rosenberg, Professor of Law, University of San Francisco.

TAXATION, FUNDAMENTALS OF PARTNERSHIP, Second Edition (1988)

Stephen A. Lind, Professor of Law, University of Florida and University of California, Hastings.
Stephen Schwarz, Professor of Law, University of California, Hastings.
Daniel J. Lathrope, Professor of Law, University of California, Hastings.
Joshua Rosenberg, Professor of Law, University of San Francisco.

TAXATION, PROBLEMS IN THE FEDERAL INCOME TAXATION OF PARTNER-SHIPS AND CORPORATIONS, Second Edition (1986)

Norton L. Steuben, Professor of Law, University of Colorado.
William J. Turnier, Professor of Law, University of North Carolina.

TAXATION, PROBLEMS IN THE FUNDAMENTALS OF FEDERAL INCOME, Second Edition (1985)

Norton L. Steuben, Professor of Law, University of Colorado.
William J. Turnier, Professor of Law, University of North Carolina.

TORT LAW AND ALTERNATIVES, Fourth Edition (1987)

Marc A. Franklin, Professor of Law, Stanford University.
Robert L. Rabin, Professor of Law, Stanford University.

TORTS, Eighth Edition (1988)

William L. Prosser, late Professor of Law, University of California, Hastings.
John W. Wade, Professor of Law, Vanderbilt University.
Victor E. Schwartz, Adjunct Professor of Law, Georgetown University.

TORTS, Third Edition (1976)

Harry Shulman, late Dean of the Law School, Yale University.
Fleming James, Jr., Professor of Law Emeritus, Yale University.
Oscar S. Gray, Professor of Law, University of Maryland.

TRADE REGULATION, Third Edition (1990)

Milton Handler, Professor of Law Emeritus, Columbia University.
Harlan M. Blake, Professor of Law, Columbia University.
Robert Pitofsky, Professor of Law, Georgetown University.
Harvey J. Goldschmid, Professor of Law, Columbia University.

TRADE REGULATION, see Antitrust

TRANSNATIONAL BUSINESS PROBLEMS (1986)

Detlev F. Vagts, Professor of Law, Harvard University.

TRANSNATIONAL LEGAL PROBLEMS, Third Edition (1986) with 1991 Revised Edition of Documentary Supplement

Henry J. Steiner, Professor of Law, Harvard University.
Detlev F. Vagts, Professor of Law, Harvard University.

TRIAL, see also Evidence, Making the Record, Lawyering Process and Preparing and Presenting the Case

UNIVERSITY CASEBOOK SERIES—Continued

TRUSTS, Fifth Edition (1978)

George G. Bogert, late Professor of Law Emeritus, University of Chicago.
Dallin H. Oaks, President, Brigham Young University.

TRUSTS AND ESTATES, SELECTED STATUTES ON, 1991 Edition

TRUSTS AND SUCCESSION (Palmer's), Fourth Edition (1983)

Richard V. Wellman, Professor of Law, University of Georgia.
Lawrence W. Waggoner, Professor of Law, University of Michigan.
Olin L. Browder, Jr., Professor of Law, University of Michigan.

UNFAIR COMPETITION, see Competitive Process and Business Torts

WATER RESOURCE MANAGEMENT, Third Edition (1988)

The late Charles J. Meyers, formerly Dean, Stanford University Law School.
A. Dan Tarlock, Professor of Law, IIT Chicago-Kent College of Law.
James N. Corbridge, Jr., Chancellor, University of Colorado at Boulder, and
    Professor of Law, University of Colorado.
David H. Getches, Professor of Law, University of Colorado.

WILLS AND ADMINISTRATION, Fifth Edition (1961)

Philip Mechem, late Professor of Law, University of Pennsylvania.
Thomas E. Atkinson, late Professor of Law, New York University.

WRITING AND ANALYSIS IN THE LAW, Second Edition (1991)

Helene S. Shapo, Professor of Law, Northwestern University
Marilyn R. Walter, Professor of Law, Brooklyn Law School
Elizabeth Fajans, Writing Specialist, Brooklyn Law School

University Casebook Series

CASES AND MATERIALS

ON

CORPORATIONS

CONCISE SIXTH EDITION

By

WILLIAM L. CARY
Late Dwight Professor of Law, Columbia University

and

MELVIN ARON EISENBERG
Koret Professor of Law, University of California at Berkeley

Westbury, New York
THE FOUNDATION PRESS, INC.
1988

Library of Congress Cataloging-in-Publication Data

Cary, William Lucius, 1910–
    Cases and materials on corporations / by William L. Cary, Melvin
A. Eisenberg. — 6th ed., concise.
       p. cm. — (University casebook series)
    Includes index.
    ISBN 0–88277–662–2
    1. Corporation law—United States—Cases.   I. Eisenberg, Melvin
Aron. II. Title. III. Series.
KF1413.C35 1988
346.73'066—dc19
[347.30666]

88–18693
CIP

Cary & Eisenberg Corp. 6th Ed. Concise UCB
2nd Reprint—1991

PREFACE

This edition reflects both substantial continuity and substantial change. The continuity is to be found in the carryover of many cases from the fifth edition, in much of the organization, and in the preservation of the traditional character. The changes are more diffuse.

One major change is the addition of chapters on agency and partnership. Chapter 1 provides a brief sketch of those agency-law principles that are most salient to the study of business organizations—authority, and the agent's duty of loyalty. Chapter 2 is a somewhat fuller introduction to the law of partnership. Since not all teachers may want to include coverage of these subjects, the casebook is written to be self-contained even if these chapters are omitted.

This edition emphasizes the statutory nature of corporation law, and unlike earlier editions focuses on both the Delaware statute and the Revised Model Business Corporation Act. These statutes are integrated into the text by copious cross-references to a new Statutory Supplement. (There are also numerous cross-references to the California and New York statutes—particularly where they differ materially from Delaware and the RMBCA—and to relevant federal statutes and rules.[1]) Students should refer to the Statutory Supplement whenever such cross-references appear. Where a cross-referenced statutory provision is followed in the Supplement by the Official Comment to that provision, the Comment should be read as well.

In many areas of corporate law, it is difficult to fully understand the issues and the legal rules without some background knowledge of the underlying business and market mechanics. Accordingly, this edition includes extensive descriptions of such matters as the basic markets for securities, data on shareholdership, the structure of the board and its committees in the modern publicly held corporation, and the mechanics of the proxy voting process and proxy solicitation. This edition has also added selected introductory materials on corporate finance and the economics of corporate law. These materials have been chosen and edited with an eye toward ensuring that they will be accessible to students who do not have a background in these areas. Among the subjects covered by these materials are agency costs, the efficient market hypothesis, elementary principles of valuation, limited liability, derivative actions, and dividends. The materials on valuation, drawn from Brealy & Myers, Principles of Corporate Finance (3d ed. 1988), are set out in Chapter XI, Section 1(c). Some teachers may wish to introduce these materials earlier in the course. A natural location would be Chapter IV, Section 1. This Section deals with the separation of owner-

---

1. In a few cases, a statute or rule is printed in the casebook itself. Usually, this is done where a statute or rule is both relatively short and central to the Chapter or Section (for example, Rule 10b–5 and section 16(b)), or where a state statutory provision is drawn from a statute other than the four state statutes included in the Supplement.

ship and control, and the materials on valuation speak directly to that issue.

———————

In the preparation of this edition, the following conventions have been used: Where a portion of the text of an original source (such as a case) has been omitted, the omission is indicated by ellipses (. . .). The omission of footnotes from original sources is not indicated, but the original footnote numbers are used for those footnotes that are retained. American Law Institute, Principles of Corporate Governance: Analysis and Recommendations, is cited simply as ALI, Principles of Corporate Governance.

MELVIN A. EISENBERG

July, 1988

ACKNOWLEDGMENTS

A number of people provided extremely valuable assistance in the preparation of this edition. Michael Colantuono, Kevin Coyle, Andrew Gross, Marina Hsieh, Harry Litman, and Margaret Meriwether all did outstanding work as research assistants in connection with the preparation of this edition. Robert A.G. Monks and Bruce A. Reznik generously assembled very important data on institutional shareholdings. My secretary, Vickie Parker, as usual turned baroque drafts into highly polished manuscripts, did three days' worth of work in single afternoons, reminded me countless times of things that had slipped between the cracks, and was generally invaluable.

I also thank the authors, publishers, and copyrightholders who permitted me to reprint portions of the following works:

Ad Hoc Subcommittee on Merit Regulation of the State Regulation of Securities Committee, Section of Corporations, Banking and Business Law, American Bar Association, Report of State Merit Regulation of Securities Offerings, 41 Business Lawyer 785 (1986). Copyright 1986 by the American Bar Association.

Alison Grey Anderson, Conflicts of Interest: Efficiency, Fairness and Corporate Structure, 25 U.C.L.A. Law Review 738 (1978) (with permission of Fred B. Rothman & Co.).

William D. Andrews, The Stockholder's Right to Equal Opportunity in the Sale of Shares, 78 Harvard Law Review 505 (1965).

Adolf A. Berle, The Theory of Enterprise Entity, 47 Columbia Law Review 343 (1947). Copyright 1947 by the Directors of the Columbia Law Review Association, Inc. All rights reserved.

Phillip I. Blumberg, Corporate Groups and Enterprise Liability: Procedural and Substantive Issues Pertaining to the Liability of Multinational Corporations for the Activities of Subsidiaries, derived from P. Blumberg, The Law of Corporate Groups: Tort, Contract and Other Common Law Problems in the Substantive Law of Parent and Subsidiary Corporations, ch. 1 (1987) (Little, Brown & Co.).

Richard Brealy & Stewart C. Myers, Principles of Corporate Finance (3d ed. 1988), McGraw-Hill Book Company.

Victor M. Brudney & Marvin A. Chirelstein, Cases and Materials on Corporate Finance (3d ed. 1987), Foundation Press, Inc.

Committee on Federal Regulation of Securities, Section of Corporations, Banking and Business Law, American Bar Association, Report of the Task Force on Regulation of Insider Trading, Part I: Regulation under the Antifraud Provisions of the Securities Exchange Act of 1934, 41 Business Lawyer 223 (1985). Copyright 1985 by the American Bar Association.

Committee on Federal Regulation of Securities, Section of Corporations, Banking and Business Law, American Bar Association, Report of the Task Force on Regulation of Insider Trading, Part II: Reform of Section 16, 42 Business Lawyer 1087 (1987). Copyright 1987 by the American Bar Association.

Committee on Federal Regulation of Securities, Section of Corporations, Banking and Business Law, American Bar Association, The SEC and Corporate Disclosure, 36 Business Lawyer 118 (1980). Copyright 1980 by the American Bar Association.

Frank H. Easterbrook & Daniel R. Fischel, Corporate Control Transactions, 91 Yale Law Journal 698 (1982) (with permission of The Yale Law Journal Company and Fred B. Rothman & Co.), and Limited Liability and the Corporation, 52 University of Chicago Law Review 89 (1985).

Francis J. Feeney, Jr., The Saga of Rule 415: Registration for the Shelf, 9 Corporation Law Review 1 (1986).

Janet Gamer Feldman & Richard L. Teberg, Beneficial Ownership under Section 16 of the Securities Exchange Act of 1934, 17 Case Western Reserve Law Review 1054 (1966).

Scott Thomas FitzGibbon, Professional Ethics and the Lawyer Organizing a Corporation, 25 Corporate Practice Commentator 198 (1983) (with permission of Callaghan & Co., 155 Pfingsten Rd., Deerfield, IL 60015).

William P. Hackney & Tracey G. Benson, Shareholder Liability for Inadequate Capital, 43 University of Pittsburgh Law Review 837 (1982).

Robert W. Hamilton, Private Sale of Control Transactions: Where We Stand Today, 36 Case Western Reserve Law Review 248 (1985).

James Heard, Esq., Conflicts of Interest in the Proxy Voting System (1987). Copyright 1987 Investor Responsibility Research Center, Inc.

Alan M. Hoffman, Israels on Corporate Practice (4th ed. 1983), Practising Law Institute.

George B. Javaras, Equal Opportunity in the Sale of Controlling Shares: A Reply to Professor Andrews, 32 University of Chicago Law Review 420 (1965).

Richard W. Jennings & Harold Marsh, Jr., Securities Regulation—Cases and Materials (6th ed. 1987), Foundation Press, Inc.

Michael Jensen & William H. Meckling, Theory of the Firm: Managerial Behavior, Agency Costs and Ownership Structure, 3 Journal of Financial Economics 305 (1976).

W. Page Keeton, Robert E. Keeton, Dan B. Dobbs & David G. Owen, Prosser & Keeton on The Law of Torts (5th ed. 1984), West Publishing Company.

Richard O. Kummert, State Statutory Restrictions on Financial Distributions by Corporations to Shareholders (pt. I), 59 Washington Law Review 185 (1984) (with permission of Fred B. Rothman & Co.).

ACKNOWLEDGMENTS

Jonathan M. Landers, A Unified Approach to Parent, Subsidiary, and Affiliate Questions in Bankruptcy, 42 University of Chicago Law Review 589 (1975).

Louis M. Loss, Fundamentals of Securities Regulation (2d ed. 1988), Little, Brown & Co.

Bayless A. Manning, The Business Judgment Rule and the Director's Duty of Attention: Time for Reality, 39 Business Lawyer 1477 (1984). Copyright 1984 by the American Bar Association.

Harold Marsh, Jr., California Corporation Law (2d ed. 1987), Prentice Hall Law & Business, reprinted with the permission of Prentice Hall Law & Business. Copyright 1987. All rights reserved.

David L. Ratner, Securities Regulation in a Nutshell (2d ed. 1982), West Publishing Company.

Roberta Romano, The State Competition Debate in Corporate Law, 8 Cardozo Law Review 709 (1987).

Joel Seligman, The Future of the National Market System, 10 Journal of Corporate Law 79 (1984).

Larry W. Sonsini, Regulation A, 16 The Review of Securities Regulation 781 (1983).

Subcommittee on Executive Compensation, Section of Corporations, Banking and Business Law, American Bar Association, Executive Compensation: A Road Map for the Corporate Advisor, 40 Business Lawyer 221 (1984). Copyright 1984 by the American Bar Association.

Paul Halpern, Michael J. Trebilcock & Stuart Turnbull, An Economic Analysis of Limited Liability in Corporation Law, 30 University of Toronto Law Journal 117 (1980).

Detlev F. Vagts, Challenges to Executive Compensation: For the Markets or the Courts?, 8 Journal of Corporate Law 231 (1983).

*

SUMMARY OF CONTENTS

ANALYTICAL TABLE OF CONTENTS

CHAPTER V. SHAREHOLDER INFORMATIONAL RIGHTS AND PROXY VOTING

CHAPTER VI. THE SPECIAL PROBLEMS OF CLOSE CORPORATIONS

CHAPTER XI. STRUCTURAL CHANGES: COMBINATIONS, TENDER OFFERS, RECAPITALIZATIONS

CHAPTER XII. CORPORATE DISTRIBUTIONS

TABLE OF CASES

Principal cases are in italic type. Nonprincipal cases are in roman type. References are to Pages.

CASES AND MATERIALS
ON
CORPORATIONS

*

Chapter I

AGENCY

SECTION 1. INTRODUCTION

Courses in corporations or business associations are, in large part, courses in organizational law. The most common forms of business organization in this country are the sole proprietorship, the corporation, and the partnership. A sole proprietorship is a business owned by one individual. It might be thought that the term "organization" is an inappropriate characterization of a form that involves only a single owner. That terminology can, however, be justified on at least two grounds. First, a business enterprise owned by an individual is likely to have a degree of psychological and sociological identity separate from that of the individual. This separateness is often expressed by giving the enterprise its own name, like "Northside Travel" or "Cambridge Office Supplies." [1] (The separate identity of the enterprise is also likely to be expressed by separate financial records. An individual who owns a sole proprietorship has unlimited personal liability for obligations incurred in the conduct of the business, so that in one sense all of his assets are invested in the business and there is no legal distinction between his business and nonbusiness liabilities. Typically, however, a sole proprietor will consider only a certain portion of his property and cash as invested in the business, and will keep a separate set of records that reflect the assets, liabilities, and income of the business as if its finances were separate from his own.)

A second reason for calling a sole proprietorship an organization is that a sole proprietor typically will not conduct the business by himself, but will engage various people—salespersons, mechanics, managers—to act on his behalf in conducting the business. The employment by one person of another to act on his behalf brings us to the most elementary form of organizational law, known as the law of agency. An agent is a person who by mutual assent acts on behalf of another and subject to the other's control. Restatement, Second, Agency § 1. The person for whom the agent acts is a principal. Id. Agency law governs the relationship between agents and principals, and among agents, principals, and third parties with whom the agent deals on the principal's behalf. Although agency is a consensual relationship, whether an agency relationship has been created does not turn on whether the parties think of themselves as agent and principal.

---

1. Most states have Fictitious (or Assumed) Name Statutes, which require a person who does business in a name other than his own to register his name, the name under which he will do business, and his business and residence address in the office of a designated official such as the County Clerk.

1

"Agency is a legal concept which depends upon the existence of required factual elements: the manifestation by the principal that the agent shall act for him, the agent's acceptance of the undertaking and the understanding of the parties that the principal is to be in control of the undertaking. The relation which the law calls agency does not depend upon the intent of the parties to create it, nor their belief that they have done so. To constitute the relation, there must be an agreement, but not necessarily a contract, between the parties; if the agreement results in the factual relation between them to which are attached the legal consequences of agency, an agency exists although the parties did not call it agency and did not intend the legal consequences of the relation to follow. Thus, when one . . . asks a friend to do a slight service for him, such as to return for credit goods recently purchased from a store, neither one may have any realization that they are creating an agency relation or be aware of the legal obligations which would result from performance of the service." Restatement (Second) of Agency § 1, Comment b.

SECTION 2. AGENCY AND AUTHORITY

A. GAY JENSON FARMS CO. v. CARGILL, INC.
Supreme Court of Minnesota, 1981.
309 N.W.2d 285.

Heard, considered, and decided by the court en banc.

OPINION

PETERSON, Justice.

Plaintiffs, 86 individual, partnership or corporate farmers, brought this action against defendant Cargill, Inc. (Cargill) and defendant Warren Grain & Seed Co. (Warren) to recover losses sustained when Warren defaulted on the contracts made with plaintiffs for the sale of grain. After a trial by jury, judgment was entered in favor of plaintiffs, and Cargill brought this appeal. We affirm.

This case arose out of the financial collapse of defendant Warren Seed & Grain Co., and its failure to satisfy its indebtedness to plaintiffs. Warren, which was located in Warren, Minnesota, was operated by Lloyd Hill and his son, Gary Hill. Warren operated a grain elevator and as a result was involved in the purchase of cash or market grain from local farmers. The cash grain would be resold through the Minneapolis Grain Exchange or to the terminal grain companies directly. Warren also stored grain for farmers and sold chemicals, fertilizer and steel storage bins. In addition, it operated a seed business which involved buying seed grain from farmers, processing it and reselling it for seed to farmers and local elevators.

Lloyd Hill decided in 1964 to apply for financing from Cargill.[1] Cargill's officials from the Moorhead regional office investigated Warren's operations and recommended that Cargill finance Warren.

Warren and Cargill thereafter entered into a security agreement which provided that Cargill would loan money for working capital to Warren on "open account" financing up to a stated limit, which was originally set as $175,000.[2] Under this contract, Warren would receive funds and pay its expenses by issuing drafts drawn on Cargill through Minneapolis banks. The drafts were imprinted with both Warren's and Cargill's names. Proceeds from Warren's sales would be deposited with Cargill and credited to its account. In return for this financing, Warren appointed Cargill as its grain agent for transaction with the Commodity Credit Corporation. Cargill was also given a right of first refusal to purchase market grain sold by Warren to the terminal market.

A new contract was negotiated in 1967, extending Warren's credit line to $300,000 and incorporating the provisions of the original contract. It was also stated in the contract that Warren would provide Cargill with annual financial statements and that either Cargill would keep the books for Warren or an audit would be conducted by an independent firm. Cargill was given the right of access to Warren's books for inspection.

In addition, the agreement provided that Warren was not to make capital improvements or repairs in excess of $5,000 without Cargill's prior consent. Further, it was not to become liable as guarantor on another's indebtedness, or encumber its assets except with Cargill's permission. Consent by Cargill was required before Warren would be allowed to declare a dividend or sell and purchase stock.

Officials from Cargill's regional office made a brief visit to Warren shortly after the agreement was executed. They examined the annual statement and the accounts receivable, expenses, inventory, seed, machinery and other financial matters. Warren was informed that it would be reminded periodically to make the improvements recommended by Cargill.[3] At approximately this time, a memo was given to the Cargill official in charge of the Warren account, Erhart Becker, which stated in part: "This organization [Warren] needs *very strong* paternal guidance."

In 1970, Cargill contracted with Warren and other elevators to act as its agent to seek growers for a new type of wheat called Bounty

---

1. Prior to this time, Atwood Larson had provided working capital for Warren, and Warren had used Atwood Larson as its commission agent for the sale of market grain on the grain exchange.

2. Loans were secured by a second mortgage on Warren's real estate and a first chattel mortgage on its inventories of grain and merchandise in the sum of $175,000 with 7% interest. Warren was to use the $175,000 to pay off the debt that it owed to Atwood Larson.

3. Cargill headquarters suggested that the regional office check Warren monthly. Also, it was requested that Warren [Cargill?] be given an explanation for the relatively large withdrawals from undistributed earnings made by the Hills, since Cargill hoped that Warren's profits would be used to decrease its debt balance. Cargill asked for written requests for withdrawals from undistributed earnings in the future.

208. Warren, as Cargill's agent for this project, entered into contracts for the growing of the wheat seed, with Cargill named as the contracting party. Farmers were paid directly by Cargill for the seed and all contracts were performed in full. In 1971, pursuant to an agency contract, Warren contracted on Cargill's behalf with various farmers for the growing of sunflower seeds for Cargill. The arrangements were similar to those made in the Bounty 208 contracts, and all those contracts were also completed. Both these agreements were unrelated to the open account financing contract. In addition, Warren, as Cargill's agent in the sunflower seed business, cleaned and packaged the seed in Cargill bags.

During this period, Cargill continued to review Warren's operations and expenses and recommend that certain actions should be taken.[4] Warren purchased from Cargill various business forms printed by Cargill and received sample forms from Cargill which Warren used to develop its own business forms.

Cargill wrote to its regional office in 1970 expressing its concern that the pattern of increased use of funds allowed to develop at Warren was similar to that involved in two other cases in which Cargill experienced severe losses. Cargill did not refuse to honor drafts or call the loan, however. A new security agreement which increased the credit line to $750,000 was executed in 1972, and a subsequent agreement which raised the limit to $1,250,000 was entered into in 1976.

Warren was at that time shipping Cargill 90% of its cash grain. When Cargill's facilities were full, Warren shipped its grain to other companies. Approximately 25% of Warren's total sales was seed grain which was sold directly by Warren to its customers.

As Warren's indebtedness continued to be in excess of its credit line, Cargill began to contact Warren daily regarding its financial affairs. Cargill headquarters informed its regional office in 1973 that, since Cargill money was being used, Warren should realize that Cargill had the right to make some critical decisions regarding the use of the funds. Cargill headquarters also told Warren that a regional manager would be working with Warren on a day-to-day basis as well as in monthly planning meetings. In 1975, Cargill's regional office began to keep a daily debit position on Warren. A bank account was opened in Warren's name on which Warren could draw checks in 1976. The account was to be funded by drafts drawn on Cargill by the local bank.

In early 1977, it became evident that Warren had serious financial problems. Several farmers, who had heard that Warren's checks

---

4. Between 1967 and 1973, Cargill suggested that Warren take a number of steps, including: (1) a reduction of seed grain and cash grain inventories; (2) improved collection of accounts receivable; (3) reduction or elimination of its wholesale seed business and its speciality grain operation; (4) marketing fertilizer and steel bins on consignment; (5) a reduction in withdrawals made by officers; (6) a suggestion that Warren's bookkeeper not issue her own salary checks; and (7) cooperation with Cargill in implementing the recommendations. These ideas were apparently never implemented, however.

were not being paid, inquired or had their agents inquire at Cargill regarding Warren's status and were initially told that there would be no problem with payment. In April 1977, an audit of Warren revealed that Warren was $4 million in debt. After Cargill was informed that Warren's financial statements had been deliberately falsified, Warren's request for additional financing was refused. In the final days of Warren's operation, Cargill sent an official to supervise the elevator, including disbursement of funds and income generated by the elevator.

After Warren ceased operations, it was found to be indebted to Cargill in the amount of $3.6 million. Warren was also determined to be indebted to plaintiffs in the amount of $2 million, and plaintiffs brought this action in 1977 to seek recovery of that sum. Plaintiffs alleged that Cargill was jointly liable for Warren's indebtedness as it had acted as principal for the grain elevator.

The matter was bifurcated for trial in Marshall County District Court. In the first phase, the amount of damages sustained by each farmer was determined by the court. The second phase of the action, dealing with the issue of Cargill's liability for the indebtedness of Warren, was tried before a jury.

The jury found that Cargill's conduct between 1973 and 1977 had made it Warren's principal.[6] Warren was found to be the agent of Cargill with regard to contracts for:

1. The purchase and sale of grain for market.
2. The purchase and sale of seed grain.
3. The storage of grain.

The court determined that Cargill was the . . . principal of Warren. It was concluded that Cargill was jointly liable with Warren for plaintiffs' losses, and judgment was entered for plaintiffs.

Cargill seeks a reversal of the jury's findings. . . . Northwestern County Elevator Association, North Dakota Grain Dealers Association and Northwestern National Bank of Minneapolis have all filed briefs on appeal as amici curiae, seeking to have the jury verdict reversed.

1. The major issue in this case is whether Cargill, by its course of dealing with Warren, became liable as a principal on contracts made by Warren with plaintiffs. Cargill contends that no agency relationship was established with Warren, notwithstanding its financing of Warren's operation and its purchase of the majority of Warren's grain. However, we conclude that Cargill, by its control and influence over Warren, became a principal with liability for the transactions entered into by its agent Warren.

Agency is the fiduciary relationship that results from the manifestation of consent by one person to another that the other shall act on his behalf and subject to his control, and consent by the other so to act. Jurek v. Thompson, 308 Minn. 191, 241 N.W.2d 788 (1976);

---

6. At trial, plaintiffs sought to establish actual agency by Cargill's course of dealing between 1973 and 1977 rather than "apparent" agency or agency by estoppel, so that the only issue in this case is one of actual agency.

Lee v. Peoples Cooperative Sales Agency, 201 Minn. 266, 276 N.W. 214 (1937); Restatement (Second) of Agency § 1 (1958). In order to create an agency there must be an agreement, but not necessarily a contract between the parties. Restatement (Second) of Agency § 1, comment b (1958). An agreement may result in the creation of an agency relationship although the parties did not call it an agency and did not intend the legal consequences of the relation to follow. *Id.* The existence of the agency may be proved by circumstantial evidence which shows a course of dealing between the two parties. *Rausch v. Aronson,* 211 Minn. 272, 1 N.W.2d 371 (1941). When an agency relationship is to be proven by circumstantial evidence, the principal must be shown to have consented to the agency since one cannot be the agent of another except by consent of the latter. *Larkin v. McCabe,* 211 Minn. 11, 299 N.W. 649 (1941).

Cargill contends that the prerequisites of an agency relationship did not exist because Cargill never consented to the agency, Warren did not act on behalf of Cargill, and Cargill did not exercise control over Warren. We hold that all three elements of agency could be found in the particular circumstances of this case. By directing Warren to implement its recommendations, Cargill manifested its consent that Warren would be its agent. Warren acted on Cargill's behalf in procuring grain for Cargill as the part of its normal operations which were totally financed by Cargill.[7] Further, an agency relationship was established by Cargill's interference with the internal affairs of Warren, which constituted de facto control of the elevator.

A creditor who assumes control of his debtor's business may become liable as principal for the acts of the debtor in connection with the business. Restatement (Second) of Agency § 14 O (1958). It is noted in comment a to section 14 O that:

> A security holder who merely exercises a veto power over the business acts of his debtor by preventing purchases or sales above specified amounts does not thereby become a principal. However, if he takes over the management of the debtor's business either in person or through an agent, and directs what contracts may or may not be made, he becomes a principal, liable as a principal for the obligations incurred thereafter in the normal course of business by the debtor who has now become his general agent. The point at which the creditor becomes a principal is that at which he assumes de facto control over the conduct of his debtor, whatever the terms of the formal contract with his debtor may be.

A number of factors indicate Cargill's control over Warren, including the following:

(1) Cargill's constant recommendations to Warren by telephone;

---

7. Although the contracts with the farmers were executed by Warren, Warren paid for the grain with drafts drawn on Cargill. While this is not in itself significant—see Lee v. Peoples Cooperative Sales Agency, 201 Minn. 266, 276 N.W. 214 (1937)—it is one factor to be taken into account in analyzing the relationship between Warren and Cargill.

(2) Cargill's right of first refusal on grain;

(3) Warren's inability to enter into mortgages, to purchase stock or to pay dividends without Cargill's approval;

(4) Cargill's right of entry onto Warren's premises to carry on periodic checks and audits;

(5) Cargill's correspondence and criticism regarding Warren's finances, [officers'] salaries and inventory;

(6) Cargill's determination that Warren needed "strong paternal guidance";

(7) Provision of drafts and forms to Warren upon which Cargill's name was imprinted;

(8) Financing of all Warren's purchases of grain and operating expenses; and

(9) Cargill's power to discontinue the financing of Warren's operations.

We recognize that some of these elements, as Cargill contends, are found in an ordinary debtor-creditor relationship. However, these factors cannot be considered in isolation, but, rather, they must be viewed in light of all the circumstances surrounding Cargill's aggressive financing of Warren.

It is also Cargill's position that the relationship between Cargill and Warren was that of buyer-supplier rather than principal-agent. Restatement (Second) of Agency § 14K (1958) compares an agent with a supplier as follows:

> One who contracts to acquire property from a third person and convey it to another is the agent of the other only if it is agreed that he is to act primarily for the benefit of the other and not for himself.

Factors indicating that one is a supplier, rather than an agent, are:

> (1) That he is to receive a fixed price for the property irrespective of price paid by him. This is the most important. (2) That he acts in his own name and receives the title to the property which he thereafter is to transfer. (3) That he has an independent business in buying and selling similar property.

Restatement (Second) of Agency § 14K, comment a (1958).

Under the Restatement approach, it must be shown that the supplier has an independent business before it can be concluded that he is not an agent. The record establishes that all portions of Warren's operation were financed by Cargill and that Warren sold almost all of its market grain to Cargill. Thus, the relationship which existed between the parties was not merely that of buyer and supplier.

A case analogous to the present one is Butler v. Bunge Corporation, 329 F.Supp. 47 (N.D.Miss.1971). In *Butler,* the plaintiff brought an action to recover the price of a soybean crop sold to an elevator that was operated by Bayles, a purported agent of the defendant Bunge Corporation. Bayles had agreed to operate a former Bunge elevator pursuant to an agreement in which Bayles was designated as manager. Although Bunge contended that Bayles was an independent contractor, the court determined that the elevator was an agent of Bunge.

In this case, as in *Butler,* Cargill furnished substantially all funds received by the elevator. Cargill did have a right of entry on Warren's premises, and it, like Bunge, required maintenance of insurance against hazards of operation. Warren's activities, like Bayles' operations, formed a substantial part of Cargill's business that was developed in that area. In addition, Cargill did not think of Warren as an operator who was free to become Cargill's competitor, but rather conceded that it believed that Warren owed a duty of loyalty to Cargill. The decisions made by Warren were not independent of Cargill's interest or its control.

Further, we are not persuaded by the fact that Warren was not one of the "line" elevators that Cargill operated in its own name. The Warren operation, like the line elevator, was financially dependent on Cargill's continual infusion of capital. The arrangement with Warren presented a convenient alternative to the establishment of a line elevator. Cargill became, in essence, the owner of the operation without the accompanying legal indicia.

The amici curiae assert that, if the jury verdict is upheld, firms and banks which have provided business loans to county elevators will decline to make further loans. The decision in this case should give no cause for such concern. We deal here with a business enterprise markedly different from an ordinary bank financing, since Cargill was an active participant in Warren's operations rather than simply a financier. Cargill's course of dealing with Warren was, by its own admission, a paternalistic relationship in which Cargill made the key economic decisions and kept Warren in existence.

Although considerable interest was paid by Warren on the loan, the reason for Cargill's financing of Warren was not to make money as a lender but, rather, to establish a source of market grain for its business. As one Cargill manager noted, "We were staying in there because we wanted the grain." For this reason, Cargill was willing to extend the credit line far beyond the amount originally allocated to Warren. It is noteworthy that Cargill was receiving significant amounts of grain and that, notwithstanding the risk that was recognized by Cargill, the operation was considered profitable.

On the whole, there was a unique fabric in the relationship between Cargill and Warren which varies from that found in normal debtor-creditor situations. We conclude that, on the facts of this case, there was sufficient evidence from which the jury could find that Cargill was the principal of Warren within the definitions of agency set forth in Restatement (Second) of Agency §§ 1 and 140. . . .

Affirmed.

SIMONETT, J., took no part in the consideration or decision of this case.

NOTE ON AUTHORITY

The primary issue in *Cargill* was whether an agency relationship existed. In many agency cases it is admitted that an agency relationship exists, but the question is, what liabilities arose out of a certain transaction between the agent and a third party? Most of the issues implicated by that question are addressed by the legal rules governing authority. This Note will emphasize the liability of the principal to the third party, but will also consider the liability of the third party to the principal, the liability of the agent to the third party, and the liabilities of the agent and the principal to each other. Although the law of agency encompasses liabilities in tort as well as in contract, this Note will address only issues that relate to contractual transactions.

1. *Liability of Principal to Third Party.* A principal becomes liable to a third party as a result of an act of the principal's agent if the agent had actual, apparent, or inherent authority.

a. *Actual authority.* An agent has actual authority to act in a given way on a principal's behalf if the principal's words or conduct would lead a reasonable person in the agent's position to believe that the principal had authorized him to so act.

> *Restatement (Second) of Agency § 26, Illustration 2:* P goes to an office where, as he knows, several brokers have desks, and leaves upon the desk of A, thinking it to be the desk of X, a note signed by him, which states: "I authorize you to contract in my name for the purchase of 100 shares of Western Union stock at today's market." A comes in, finds the note and, not knowing of the mistake, immediately makes a contract with T in P's name for the purchase of the shares. A had [actual] authority to make the contract.[1]

Actual authority may be either *implied* or *express:* "It is possible for a principal to specify minutely what the agent is to do. To the extent that he does this, the agent may be said to have express authority. But most authority is created by implication. Thus, in the authorization to 'sell my automobile', the only fully expressed power is to transfer title in exchange for money or a promise to give money. In fact, under some circumstances . . . there may or may not be power to take or give possession of the automobile or to extend credit or to accept something in partial exchange. These powers are all implied or inferred from the words used, from customs and from the relations of the parties. They are described as 'implied authority.'" Restatement (Second) of Agency § 7, Comment c.[2]

A common type of implied actual authority is *incidental authority,* which is the authority to do acts that are reasonably necessary to accomplish an authorized transaction or that usually accompany it.

---

1. The Restatement (Second) of Agency uses the term "authority" to mean what is conventionally called "actual authority." The conventional terminology is easier to work with, since it sets up a clear opposition between authority of various types.

2. Occasionally, courts use the term "implied authority" to mean apparent authority, but this is bad usage and is not often encountered.

> *Restatement (Second) of Agency § 35, Illustration 4:* P directs A to sell goods by auction at a time and place at which, as P and A know, a statute forbids anyone but a licensed auctioneer to conduct sales by auction. Nothing to the contrary appearing, A's authority includes authority to employ a licensed auctioneer.

> *Restatement (Second) of Agency § 26, Illustration 5:* P authorizes A, a local broker, to sell and convey land. At the time and place it is the custom to make such sales with a warranty of title. A has implied authority to execute and deliver a proper deed to the purchaser and to insert in the deed the usual covenants as to title.

Incidental authority is a type of implied actual authority, because if the principal has authorized the agent to engage in a given transaction, and certain acts are reasonably necessary to accomplish the transaction, or usually accompany it, a reasonable person in the agent's position would interpret the authority to engage in the transaction as also conferring authority to engage in the incidental acts.

b. *Apparent authority.* An agent has apparent authority to act in a given way on the principal's behalf in relation to a third party, T, if the words or conduct of the principal would cause a reasonable person in T's position to believe that the principal had authorized the agent to so act.

> *Restatement (Second) of Agency § 8, Illustration 1:* P writes to A directing him to act as his agent for the sale of Blackacre. P sends a copy of this letter to T, a prospective purchaser. A has [actual] authority to sell Blackacre and, as to T, apparent authority.

> *Illustration 2:* Same facts as in Illustration 1, except that in the letter to A, P adds a postscript, not included in the copy to T, telling A to make no sale until after communication with P. A has no [actual] authority to sell Blackacre but, as to T, he has apparent authority.

> *Illustration 3:* Same facts as in Illustration 1, except that after A and T have received the letters, P telegraphs a revocation to A. A has no [actual] authority but, as to T, he has apparent authority to sell Blackacre.

In most cases, actual and apparent authority go hand in hand, as Restatement (Second) of Agency § 8, Illustration 1 suggests. For example, if P Bank appoints A as cashier, and nothing more is said, A will reasonably believe he has the authority that cashiers normally have, and third parties who deal with A will reasonably believe the same thing. Apparent authority becomes salient in such a case if P Bank does not actually give A all the authority that cashiers usually have, and T deals with A knowing that A is a cashier but not knowing that P Bank has placed special limits on A's authority.

The authority of A in the cashier hypothetical is a special type of apparent authority known as power of position. " . . . [A]pparent authority can be created by appointing a person to a position, such as that of manager or treasurer, which carries with it generally recognized duties; to those who know of the appointment there is apparent authority to do the things ordinarily entrusted to one occupying such a position, regardless of unknown limitations which are imposed upon the particular agent. . . . If a principal puts an agent into, or knowingly permits him to occupy, a position in which according to the ordinary habits of persons in the locality, trade or profession, it is usual for such an agent to have a particular kind of authority, anyone dealing with him is justified in inferring that he has such authority, in the absence of reason to know otherwise." Restatement (Second) of Agency § 27, Comment a, § 49, Comment c.

> *Restatement (Second) of Agency § 49, Illustration 4:* The P bank appoints A as an information clerk, with authority only to answer questions of depositors. During alterations, however, the bank directs A to occupy the space normally occupied by one of the receiving tellers, a sign indicating that it is the "information" window. The sign becomes displaced and T, a depositor in the bank, makes a cash deposit with A, believing that he is a teller. P is bound by this transaction.

c. *Inherent authority.* The concept of inherent authority is neither as well-defined nor as widely recognized as the concepts of actual and apparent authority, but it is adopted in Restatement (Second) of Agency § 8A, and has support in a handful of important cases. Restatement (Second) of Agency § 8A states that:

> Inherent agency power is a term used . . . to indicate the power of an agent which is derived not from authority, apparent authority or estoppel, but solely from the agency relation and exists for the protection of persons harmed by or dealing with . . . [an] agent.

Section 8A purports to be a definition, but isn't. It states that inherent authority is an agency power that is not derived from actual authority, apparent authority, or estoppel. It states reasons for according legal recognition to a power that is not derived from those concepts. But it doesn't state what inherent authority *is.* The commentary to § 8A, however, gives examples of cases that illustrate inherent authority. Of these, the two most important are the power of an agent to subject his principal to liability in tort based on activity by the agent within the scope of his employment, and the power of a "general agent" to subject his principal to liability based on contract. (A "general agent" is "an agent authorized to conduct a series of transactions involving a continuity of service." Restatement (Second) of Agency § 3(1).)

Section 161 of the Restatement concerns the inherent authority of general agents of disclosed or partially disclosed principals. (A principal is "disclosed" if at the time of the transaction the third party knows that the agent is acting on behalf of a principal and knows the principal's identity. A principal is "partially disclosed" if at the time of the transaction the third party knows that the agent is acting on behalf of a principal, but does not know the principal's identity.) Under Section 161, a disclosed or partially disclosed principal is liable for an act done on his behalf by a general agent, even if the principal had *forbidden* the agent to do the act, if (i) the act usually accompanies or is incidental to transactions that the agent is authorized to conduct, and (ii) the third party reasonably believes the agent is authorized to do the act. This rule is probably not too important, since most of the cases it covers would undoubtedly fall within an agent's apparent authority based on power of position.

More striking is Section 194, which concerns general agents for undisclosed principals. (A principal is "undisclosed" if the agent, in dealing with the third party, purports to be acting on his own behalf. An undisclosed principal is liable for his agent's authorized activities, even though, because the agent does not disclose his agency, the third party believes the agent is acting strictly on his own behalf. One reason the undisclosed principal is liable is that he set the transaction in motion and stood to gain from it. A second reason is this: Even if the undisclosed principal was not directly liable to the third party, the agent would be. Therefore, the third party could sue the agent, and the agent could then sue the principal for indemnification of the damages he had to pay the third party. Accordingly, allowing the third party to sue the undisclosed principal does not materially enlarge the principal's liability, and collapses two lawsuits into one.) Section 194 parallels Section 161, by making an undisclosed principal liable for certain acts of his general agent even if the acts were forbidden. However, Section 194 has a much sharper bite than Section 161, because in the cases covered under Section 194 there would normally be neither actual authority (since the act is forbidden) nor apparent authority (since the agent purports to be acting on his own behalf).

The weight given by the Restatement, and some cases, to whether an agent is "general" or "special" has been criticized. Why should the question whether a principal may be bound even in the absence of actual or apparent authority turn on whether the agent is "general" or "special"? It is instructive, in this regard, to consider the Restatement's rationale for the concept of inherent authority:

> The principles of agency have made it possible for persons to utilize the services of others in accomplishing far more than could be done by their unaided efforts. Although the agency relation may exist without reference to mercantile affairs . . . its primary function in modern life is to make possible the commercial enterprises which could not exist otherwise. . . . Partnerships and corporations, through which most of the work of the world is done today, depend for their existence upon agency principles. . . . It is inevitable that in doing their work, either through negligence or excess of zeal, agents will harm third persons or will deal with them in unauthorized ways. It would be unfair for an enterprise to have the benefit of the work of its agents

without making it responsible to some extent for their excesses and failures to act carefully.

Restatement (Second) of Agency § 8A comment a. See also § 161 comment a. This rationale extends beyond general agents, but it too gives little in the way of either a definition of inherent authority or a test for when the principal will be liable for the acts of an agent who has neither actual nor apparent authority.

The concept that an agent who has no apparent authority may bind his principal, even though he engages in a forbidden act, may be supported by a different rationale, which does lead to a definition and a test. Experience tells us that agents will sometimes act in violation of their instructions with perfect good faith, either because they fail to remember a certain instruction or because they believe that in a given case their principal's objective is best served by violating the instruction. As between the principal and the third party, the principal should bear the burden if the violation was reasonably foreseeable.

The reasonable-foreseeability rationale leads to a definition: Inherent authority is authority to take an action that a reasonable person in the principal's position should have foreseen the agent would be likely to take, even though the action would be in violation of the agent's instructions. The reasonable-foreseeability rationale also leads to a test for inherent authority that complements the tests for actual and apparent authority: Would a reasonable person in the principal's position have foreseen that, despite his instructions, there was a significant likelihood the agent would act as he did? In answering this question, it is relevant but not dispositive that a "general agent" is involved.

The reasonable-foreseeability rationale, definition, and test explain the relevant cases better than the Restatement, and would bring the rules governing a principal's liability in contract close to those governing the principal's liability in tort.

d. *Ratification.* Even if an agent has neither actual, apparent, nor inherent authority, the principal will be bound to the third party if the agent purported to act on the principal's behalf and the principal, with knowledge of the material facts, either (1) affirmed the agent's conduct by manifesting an intention to treat the agent's conduct as authorized, or (2) engaged in conduct that was justifiable only if he had such an intention.

Manifesting an intention to treat the agent's conduct as authorized is sometimes known as express ratification.

Restatement (Second) of Agency § 84, Illustration 1: Without power to bind P, A purports to represent him in buying a horse from T. P affirms. P is now a party to the transaction.

Engaging in conduct that is justifiable only if the principal intends to treat the agent's conduct as authorized is sometimes known as implied ratification. The most common example is the case where, as a result of the purported agent's transaction, the principal knowingly receives or retains something to which he would not otherwise be entitled:

> *Restatement (Second) of Agency § 98, Illustration 1:* P authorizes A to sell a refrigerator at a specified price without a warranty. A, purporting to have authority to do so, contracts with T for the sale of the refrigerator at a lower price than that specified and with a warranty of performance for two years, T paying part of the purchase price. P receives the check given by T, knowing all the facts. The contract as made between A and T is affirmed.

> *Restatement (Second) of Agency § 98, Illustration 2:* P authorizes A to sell a typewriter for $50 in cash. A, purporting to have authority to do so, contracts to sell it to T for $25 and T's old typewriter, which T delivers to A. P receives T's old typewriter, knowing the facts. The transaction between T and A is affirmed.

Ratification need not be communicated to the third party to be effective, although it must be objectively manifested. Restatement (Second) of Agency § 95. However, it must occur before the third party has withdrawn, the agreement has otherwise terminated, or the situation has so materially changed that it would be inequitable to hold the third party. See Restatement (Second) of Agency §§ 88, 89.

Ratification should be distinguished from a related concept: the creation of actual or apparent authority by acquiescence. "[I]f the agent performs a series of acts of a similar nature, the failure of the principal to object to them is an indication that he consents to the performance of similar acts in the future under similar conditions." Restatement (Second) of Agency § 43, Comment b. Suppose, for example, an agent engages in a series of comparable purchases on the principal's behalf. Prior to the first purchase, a reasonable person in the agent's position would not have thought he had authority to enter into such a transaction. Nevertheless, the principal did not object either to that purchase or to a later such purchase. At that point, a reasonable person in the agent's position would assume that the principal approved the agent's engaging in such purchases. Accordingly, the principal's acquiescence gives rise both to actual authority and, as to third persons who know of the acquiescence, apparent authority.

    e. *Termination of agent's authority.* A principal normally has the *power* to terminate an agent's authority, even if doing so violates a contract between the parties, and even if the authority is expressed to be irrevocable. Accordingly, a contractual provision that an agent's authority cannot be terminated by either party is normally effective only to create liability for wrongful termination. The rule rests largely on the ground that contracts relating to personal services will not be specifically enforced.

> *Restatement (Second) of Agency § 118, Illustration 1:* In consideration of A's agreement to advertise and give his best energies to the sale of Blackacre, its owner, P, grants to A "a

power of attorney, irrevocable for one year" to sell it. A advertises and spends time trying to sell Blackacre. At the end of three months P informs A that he revokes. A's authority is terminated.

2. *Liability of Third Party to Principal.* The general rule is that if an agent and a third party enter into a contract under which the agent's principal is liable to the third party, the third party is liable to the principal as well. Restatement (Second) of Agency § 292. The major exception is that the third party is not liable to an undisclosed principal if the agent or the principal knew that the third party would not have dealt with the principal. Id. comment c.

3. *Liability of Agent to Third Party.* The liability of an agent to a third party depends in part on whether the principal was disclosed, partially disclosed, or undisclosed.

a. *Partially disclosed principal.* If the principal is partially disclosed (that is, if at the time of the transaction the third party knows that the agent is acting on behalf of a principal, but does not know the principal's identity), the general rule is that the agent is bound to the third party even though the principal is bound too. Restatement (Second) of Agency § 321. The theory is that if the third party did not know the identity of the principal, and therefore could not investigate the principal's credit or reliability, he probably expected that the agent would be liable, either solely or as a co-promisor or surety. Id., comment a.

b. *Undisclosed principal.* If the principal is undisclosed (that is, if at the time of the transaction the agent purported to act on his own behalf), the general rule is also that the agent is bound even though the principal is bound too. Restatement (Second) of Agency § 322. The theory is that the third party must have expected the agent to be a party to the contract, since that is how the agent presented the transaction. However, there is a quirk in the law here. Under the majority rule, if the third party, after learning of an undisclosed principal's identity, obtains a judgment against the principal, the agent is discharged from liability even if the judgment is not satisfied. (A counterpart rule discharges the undisclosed principal if the third party gets a judgment against the agent.) Under the minority rule, which is more rational, neither the agent nor the principal is discharged by a judgment against the other, but only by satisfaction of the judgment.

c. *Disclosed principal.* Assume now that the principal was disclosed (that is, at the time of the transaction the third party knew that the agent was acting on behalf of a principal and knew the principal's identity). If the principal *is* bound by the agent's act, because the agent had actual, apparent, or inherent authority, or because the principal ratified the act, the general rule is that the agent is not bound to the third party. Restatement (Second) of Agency § 320. The theory is that in such a case the third party does not expect the agent to be bound, does expect the principal to be bound, and gets just what he expects.

If the principal is *not* bound by the agent's act, because the agent did not have actual, apparent, or inherent authority, the general rule is that the agent is liable to the third party, either for breach of an implied warranty of authority, Restatement (Second) of Agency § 329, or, under some cases, on the contract itself. In principle, the difference in the two theories might lead to a difference in the measure of damages. Under the liability-on-the-contract theory, the third party will recover gains that would have been derived under the contract—essentially, expectation damages. In contrast, under the implied-warranty theory it might seem that the third party would recover only losses suffered by having entered into the transaction—essentially, reliance damages. However, Restatement (Second) of Agency § 329, while adopting the implied-warranty theory, provides for an expectation measure of damages, just as if it had adopted the contract theory: "The third person can recover in damages not only for the harm caused to him by the fact that the agent was unauthorized, but also for the amount by which he would have benefitted had the authority existed." Id. at Comment j.

4. *Liability of Agent to Principal.* If an agent takes an act that he has no actual authority to perform, but that binds the principal because the agent had apparent authority, the agent is liable to the principal for any resulting damages. Restatement (Second) of Agency § 383, comment e. Whether an agent is liable to the principal for an act that binds the principal by virtue of the agent's inherent authority is an unsettled point.

5. *Liability of Principal to Agent.* If an agent has acted within his actual authority, the principal is under a duty to indemnify the agent for payments authorized or made necessary in executing the principal's affairs. This includes authorized payments made by the agent on the principal's behalf, payments on contracts upon which the agent was authorized to make himself liable (as where the agent acted on behalf of a partially disclosed or undisclosed principal), payments of damages to third persons that the agent incurs because of an authorized act that constituted a breach of contract, and expenses in defending actions brought against the agent by third persons because of the agent's authorized conduct. Restatement (Second) of Agency §§ 438, 439.

SECTION 3. THE AGENT'S DUTY OF LOYALTY

TARNOWSKI v. RESOP
Supreme Court of Minnesota, 1952.
236 Minn. 33, 51 N.W.2d 801.

KNUTSON, Justice.

Plaintiff desired to make a business investment. He engaged defendant as his agent to investigate and negotiate for the purchase of a route of coin-operated music machines. On June 2, 1947, relying upon the advice of defendant and the investigation he had made, plaintiff purchased such a business from Phillip Loechler and Lyle Mayer of Rochester, Minnesota, who will be referred to hereinafter as the sellers. The business was located at LaCrosse, Wisconsin, and throughout the surrounding territory. Plaintiff alleges that defendant represented to him that he had made a thorough investigation of the route; that it had 75 locations in operation; that one or more machines were at each location; that the equipment at each location was not more than six months old; and that the gross income from all locations amounted to more than $3,000 per month. As a matter of fact, defendant had made only a superficial investigation and had investigated only five of the locations. Other than that, he had adopted false representations of the sellers as to the other locations and had passed them on to plaintiff as his own. Plaintiff was to pay $30,620 for the business. He paid $11,000 down. About six weeks after the purchase, plaintiff discovered that the representations made to him by defendant were false, in that there were not more than 47 locations; that at some of the locations there were no machines and at others there were machines more than six months old, some of them being seven years old; and that the gross income was far less than $3,000 per month. Upon discovering the falsity of defendant's representations and those of the sellers, plaintiff rescinded the sale. He offered to return what he had received, and he demanded the return of his money. The sellers refused to comply, and he brought suit against them in the district court of Olmsted county. The action was tried, resulting in a verdict of $10,000 for plaintiff. Thereafter, the sellers paid plaintiff $9,500, after which the action was dismissed with prejudice pursuant to a stipulation of the parties.

In this action, brought in Hennepin county, plaintiff alleges that defendant, while acting as agent for him, collected a secret commission from the sellers for consummating the sale, which plaintiff seeks to recover under his first cause of action. In his second cause of action, he seeks to recover damages for (1) losses suffered in operating the route prior to rescission; (2) loss of time devoted to operation; (3) expenses in connection with rescission of the sale and his investigation in connection therewith; (4) nontaxable expenses in connection with prosecution of the suit against the sellers; and (5) attorneys' fees in connection with the suit. The case was tried to a jury, and plaintiff recovered a verdict of $5,200. This appeal is from the judgment entered pursuant thereto. . . .

1. With respect to plaintiff's first cause of action, the principle that all profits made by an agent in the course of an agency belonging to the principal, whether they are the fruits of performance or the violation of an agent's duty, is firmly established and universally recognized. Smitz v. Leopold, 51 Minn. 455, 53 N.W. 719; Crump v. Ingersoll, 44 Minn. 84, 46 N.W. 141; Kingsley v. Wheeler, 95 Minn. 360, 104 N.W. 543; Goodhue Farmers' Warehouse Co. v. Davis, 81 Minn. 210, 83 N.W. 531; Snell v. Goodlander, 90 Minn. 533, 97 N.W. 421; City of Minneapolis v. Canterbury, 122 Minn.

301, 142 N.W. 812, 48 L.R.A.,N.S., 842; Doyen v. Bauer, 211 Minn. 140, 300 N.W. 451; Magee v. Odden, 220 Minn. 498, 20 N.W.2d 87.

It matters not that the principal has suffered no damage or even that the transaction has been profitable to him. Raymond Farmers Elevator Co. v. American Surety Co., 207 Minn. 117, 290 N.W. 231, 126 A.L.R. 1351.

The rule and the basis therefor are well stated in Lum v. McEwen, 56 Minn. 278, 282, 57 N.W. 662, where, speaking through Mr. Justice Mitchell, we said: "Actual injury is not the principle the law proceeds on, in holding such transactions void. Fidelity in the agent is what is aimed at, and, as a means of securing it, the law will not permit him to place himself in a position in which he may be tempted by his own private interests to disregard those of his principal. . . . It is not material that no actual injury to the company [principal] resulted, or that the policy recommended may have been for its best interest. Courts will not inquire into these matters. It is enough to know that the agent in fact placed himself in such relations that he might be tempted by his own interests to disregard those of his principal. The transaction was nothing more or less than the acceptance by the agent of a bribe to perform his duties in the manner desired by the person who gave the bribe. Such a contract is void. This doctrine rests on such plain principles of law, as well as common business honesty, that the citation of authorities is unnecessary."

The right to recover profits made by the agent in the course of the agency is not affected by the fact that the principal, upon discovering a fraud, has rescinded the contract and recovered that with which he parted. Restatement, Agency, § 407(2). Comment e on Subsection (2) reads: "If an agent has violated a duty of loyalty to the principal so that the principal is entitled to profits which the agent has thereby made, the fact that the principal has brought an action against a third person and has been made whole by such action does not prevent the principal from recovering from the agent the profits which the agent has made. Thus, if the other contracting party has given a bribe to the agent to make a contract with him on behalf of the principal, the principal can rescind the transaction, recovering from the other party anything received by him, or he can maintain an action for damages against him; in either event the principal may recover from the agent the amount of the bribe."

It follows that, insofar as the secret commission of $2,000 received by the agent is concerned, plaintiff had an absolute right thereto, irrespective of any recovery resulting from the action against the sellers for rescission.

2. Plaintiff's second cause of action is brought to recover damages for (1) losses suffered in the operation of the business prior to rescission; (2) loss of time devoted to operation; (3) expenses in connection with rescission of the sale and investigation therewith; (4) nontaxable expenses in connection with the prosecution of the suit against the sellers; and (5) attorneys' fees in connection with the suit.

The case comes to us on a bill of exceptions. No part of the testimony of the witnesses is included, so we must assume that the evidence establishes the items of damage claimed by plaintiff. Our inquiry is limited to a consideration of the question whether a principal may recover of an agent who has breached his trust the items of damage mentioned after a successful prosecution of an action for rescission against the third parties with whom the agent dealt for his principal.

The general rule is stated in Restatement, Agency, § 407(1), as follows: "If an agent has received a benefit as a result of violating his duty of loyalty, the principal is entitled to recover from him what he has so received, its value, or its proceeds, and also the amount of damage thereby caused, except that if the violation consists of the wrongful disposal of the principal's property, the principal cannot recover its value and also what the agent received in exchange therefor."

In Comment a on Subsection (1) we find the following: ". . . In either event, whether or not the principal elects to get back the thing improperly dealt with or to recover from the agent its value or the amount of benefit which the agent has improperly received, he is, in addition, entitled to be indemnified by the agent for any loss which has been caused to his interest by the improper transaction. Thus, if the purchasing agent for a restaurant purchases with the principal's money defective food, receiving a bonus therefor, and the use of the food in the restaurant damages the business, the principal can recover from the agent the amount of money improperly expended by him, the bonus which the agent received, and the amount which will compensate for the injury to the business."

The general rule with respect to damages for a tortious act is that "The wrong-doer is answerable for all the injurious consequences of his tortious act, which according to the usual course of events and the general experience were likely to ensue, and which, therefore, when the act was committed, he may reasonably be supposed to have foreseen and anticipated." 1 Sutherland, Damages (4 ed.) § 45, quoted with approval in Sargent v. Mason, 101 Minn. 319, 323, 112 N.W. 255, 257.

The general rule is given in Restatement, Torts, § 910, as follows: "A person injured by the tort of another is entitled to recover damages from him for all harm, past, present and prospective, legally caused by the tort."

Bergquist v. Kreidler, 158 Minn. 127, 196 N.W. 964, involved an action to recover attorneys' fees expended by plaintiffs in an action seeking to enforce and protect their right to the possession of real estate. Defendant, acting as the owner's agent, had falsely represented to plaintiffs that they could have possession on August 1, 1920. It developed after plaintiffs had purchased the premises that a tenant had a lease running to August 1, 1922, on a rental much lower than the actual value of the premises. Defendant (the agent) conceded that plaintiffs were entitled to recover the loss in rent, but contended that attorneys' fees and disbursements expended by plaintiffs in testing the validity of the tenant's lease were not recoverable. In affirming plaintiffs' right to recover we said, 158 Minn. 132, 196 N.W. 966: ". . . the litigation in which plaintiffs became involved was the direct, legitimate, and a to be expected result of appellant's misrepresentation. The loss sustained by plaintiffs in conducting that litigation 'is plainly traceable' to appellant's wrong and he should make compensation accordingly."

So far as the right to recover attorneys' fees is concerned, the same may be said in this case. Plaintiff sought to return what had been received and demanded a return of his down payment. The sellers refused. He thereupon sued to accomplish this purpose, as he had a right to do, and was successful. His attorneys' fees and expenses of suit were directly traceable to the harm caused by defendant's wrongful act. As such, they are recoverable.

. . . The general rule applicable here is stated in 15 Am.Jur., Damages, § 144, as follows: "It is generally held that where the wrongful act of the defendant has involved the plaintiff in litigation with others or placed him in such relation with others as makes it necessary to incur expense to protect his interest, such costs and expenses, including attorneys' fees, should be treated as the legal consequences of the original wrongful act and may be recovered as damages."

The same is true of the other elements of damage involved. See, generally, 15 Am.Jur., Damages, § 138. . . .

Affirmed.

RESTATEMENT (SECOND) OF AGENCY §§ 387–390

§ 387.   General Principle

Unless otherwise agreed, an agent is subject to a duty to his principal to act solely for the benefit of the principal in all matters connected with his agency.

§ 388.   Duty to Account for Profits Arising Out of Employment

Unless otherwise agreed, an agent who makes a profit in connection with transactions conducted by him on behalf of the principal is under a duty to give such profit to the principal.

Comment:

a. Ordinarily, the agent's primary function is to make profits for the principal, and his duty to account includes accounting for any unexpected and incidental accretions whether or not received in violation of duty. Thus, an agent who, without the knowledge of the principal, receives something in connection with, or because of, a transaction conducted for the principal, has a duty to pay this to the principal even though otherwise he has acted with perfect fairness to the principal and violates no duty of loyalty in receiving the amount. . . .

Illustrations:

1. A, a real estate broker acting for P, the seller, in order to assure himself of his commission, makes a contract with T, a purchaser, by which, if T cancels the contract with P, as he is given the right to do, T is to pay A the amount of A's commission. T repudiates the contract with P but pays A. A holds his commission as a constructive trustee for P.

2. P authorizes A to sell land held in A's name for a fixed sum. A makes a contract to sell the land to T, who makes a deposit which is to be forfeited if the transaction is not carried out. T forfeits the amount. A sells the land to another person at the price fixed by P. A is under a duty to account to P for the amount received from T. . . .

Comment:

b. Gratuities to agent. An agent can properly retain gratuities received on account of the principal's business if, because of custom or otherwise, an agreement to this effect is found. Except in such a case, the receipt and retention of a gratuity by an agent from a party with interests adverse to those of the principal is evidence that the agent is committing a breach of duty to the principal by not acting in his interests.

Illustrations:

4. A, the purchasing agent for the P railroad, purchases honestly and for a fair price fifty trucks from T, who is going out of business. In gratitude for A's favorable action and without ulterior motive or agreement, T makes A a gift of a car. A holds the automobile as a constructive trustee for P, although A is not otherwise liable to P. . . .

Comment:

c. Use of confidential information. An agent who acquires confidential information in the course of his employment or in violation of his duties has a duty not to use it to the disadvantage of the principal. . . . He also has a duty to account for any profits made by the use of such information, although this does not harm the principal. Thus, where a corporation has decided to operate an enterprise at a place where land values will be increased because of such operation, a corporate officer who takes advantage of his special knowledge to buy land in the vicinity is accountable for the profits he makes, even though such purchases have no adverse effect upon the enterprise. So, if he has "inside" information that the corporation is about to purchase or sell securities, or to declare or to pass a dividend, profits made by him in stock transactions undertaken because of his knowledge are held in constructive trust for the principal. He is also liable for profits made by selling confidential information to third persons, even though the principal is not adversely affected.

§ 389. Acting as Adverse Party Without Principal's Consent

Unless otherwise agreed, an agent is subject to a duty not to deal with his principal as an adverse party in a transaction connected with his agency without the principal's knowledge.

§ 390. Acting as Adverse Party with Principal's Consent

An agent who, to the knowledge of the principal, acts on his own account in a transaction in which he is employed has a duty to deal fairly with the principal and to disclose to him all facts which the agent knows or should know would reasonably affect the principal's judgment, unless the principal has manifested that he knows such facts or that he does not care to know them.

Comment:

a. *Facts to be disclosed.* One employed as agent violates no duty to the principal by acting for his own benefit if he makes a full disclosure of the facts to an acquiescent principal and takes no unfair advantage of him. Before dealing with the principal on his own account, however, an agent has a duty, not only to make no misstatements of fact, but also to disclose to the principal all relevant facts fully and completely. A fact is relevant if it is one which the agent should realize would be likely to affect the judgment of the principal in giving his consent to the agent to enter into the particular transaction on the specified terms. Hence, the disclosure must include not only the fact that the agent is acting on his own account (see § 389), but also all other facts which he should realize have or are likely to have a bearing upon the desirability of the transaction from the viewpoint of the principal. This includes, in the case of sales to him by the principal, not only the price which can be obtained, but also all facts affecting the desirability of sale, such as the likelihood of a higher price being obtained later, the possibilities of dealing with the property in another way, and all other matters which a disinterested and skillful agent advising the principal would think reasonably relevant.

If the principal has limited business experience, an agent cannot properly fail to give such information merely because the principal says he does not care for it; the agent's duty of fair dealing is satisfied only if he reasonably believes that the principal understands the implications of the transaction.

Illustrations:

1. P employs A to sell Blackacre for $1,000. A, having sought a customer, is unable to find one and reports such fact to P. He then states that he is willing to pay $1,000, telling P truthfully that he believes that a better sale might be made later in view of the chance that the locality

will develop. A pays P $1,000. A month later, A sells the land for $1,500. In the absence of other facts, A has violated no duty to P.

2. P employs A to purchase a suitable manufacturing site for him. A owns one which is suitable and sells it to P at the fair price of $25,000, telling P all relevant facts except that, a short time previously, he purchased the land for $15,000. The transaction can be rescinded by P. . . .

Comment:

c. Fairness. The agent must not take advantage of his position to persuade the principal into making a hard or improvident bargain. If the agent is one upon whom the principal naturally would rely for advice, the fact that the agent discloses that he is acting as an adverse party does not relieve him from the duty of giving the principal impartial advice based upon a carefully formed judgment as to the principal's interests. If he cannot or does not wish to do so, he has a duty to see that the principal secures the advice of a competent and disinterested third person. An agent who is in a close confidential relation to the principal, such as a family attorney, has the burden of proving that a substantial gift to him was not the result of undue influence. Even though an agent employed to sell is not in such a position, payment of less than the reasonable market value for property he buys from the principal is evidence that the bargain was unfair. If the principal is not in a dependent position, however, and the agent fully performs his duties of disclosure, a transaction of purchase and sale between them is not voidable merely because the principal receives an inadequate price or pays too great a price.

Illustrations:

4. P, a young physician with some inherited wealth and no business experience, places his property in charge of A to manage. Desiring a particular piece of land which represents a large share of P's assets, A waits until there is a slump in the price of land and, believing correctly that the slump is only temporary, suggests to P that it be sold, offering as an incentive that P's income from his profession will increase and that, although the price to be obtained is low, P can well afford to get more enjoyment from the proceeds now than from a larger amount later. P thereupon agrees to sell to A at a price which is as much as could be obtained at that time for the property. It may be found that A violated his duty of dealing fairly with P.

5. Same facts as in Illustration 4, except that A provides P with an independent experienced adviser, who gives disinterested advice, setting out the possibilities of accretion in values. It may be found that A has satisfied his duty of loyalty.

JENSEN & MECKLING, THEORY OF THE FIRM: MANAGERIAL BEHAVIOR, AGENCY COSTS AND OWNERSHIP STRUCTURE

3 J. Financial Economics 305, 308 (1976).

We define an agency relationship as a contract under which one or more persons (the principal(s)) engage another person (the agent) to perform some service on their behalf which involves delegating some decision making authority to the agent. If both parties to the relationship are utility maximizers there is good reason to believe that the agent will not always act in the best interests of the principal. The *principal* can limit divergences from his interest by establishing appropriate incentives for the agent and by incurring monitoring costs designed to limit the aberrant activities of the agent. In addition in some situations it will pay the *agent* to expend resources (bonding costs) to guarantee that he will not take certain actions which would harm the principal or to ensure that the principal will be compensated if he does take such actions. However, it is generally impossible for the principal or the agent at zero cost to ensure that the agent will make optimal decisions from the principal's viewpoint. In most agency relationships the principal and the agent will incur positive monitoring and bonding costs (non-pecuniary as well as pecuniary), and in addition there will be some divergence between the agent's decisions and those decisions which would maximize the welfare of the principal. The dollar equivalent of the reduction in welfare experienced by the principal due to this divergence is also a cost of the agency relationship, and we refer to this latter cost as the "residual loss". We define *agency costs* as the sum of:

(1) the monitoring expenditures by the principal,

(2) the bonding expenditures by the agent,

(3) the residual loss.

Chapter II

PARTNERSHIP

SECTION 1. PARTNERSHIP FORMATION

Although partnership has a rich history under the common law, in this country general partnerships are now governed by the Uniform Partnership Act. This Act was promulgated by the National Conference of Commissioners on Uniform State Laws in 1914, and has since been adopted in every state, except Louisiana. The Act will be cited in this book either by its full name or as the "U.P.A."

UNIFORM PARTNERSHIP ACT §§ 6, 7

[See Statutory Supplement] *

MARTIN v. PEYTON
New York Court of Appeals, 1927.
246 N.Y. 213, 158 N.E. 77.

Appeal from Supreme Court, Appellate Division, First Department.

Action by Charles S. Martin against William C. Peyton and others. A judgment of the Special Term, entered on the report of a referee in favor of the defendants was affirmed by the Appellate Division (219 App.Div. 287, 220 N.Y.S. 29), and plaintiff appeals. Affirmed.

ANDREWS, J. Much ancient learning as to partnership is obsolete. Today only those who are partners between themselves may be charged for partnership debts by others. (Partnership Law [Cons. Laws, ch. 39], sec. 11.) There is one exception. Now and then a recovery is allowed where in truth such relationship is absent. This is because the debtor may not deny the claim. (Sec. 27.)

Partnership results from contract, express or implied. If denied it may be proved by the production of some written instrument; by testimony as to some conversation; by circumstantial evidence. If nothing else appears the receipt by the defendant of a share of the profits of the business is enough. (Sec. 11.)

---

* Corporations and Business Associations—Statutes, Rules, and Forms (M. Eisenberg, ed.).

25

Assuming some written contract between the parties the question may arise whether it creates a partnership. If it be complete; if it expresses in good faith the full understanding and obligation of the parties, then it is for the court to say whether a partnership exists. It may, however, be a mere sham intended to hide the real relationship. Then other results follow. In passing upon it effect is to be given to each provision. Mere words will not blind us to realities. Statements that no partnership is intended are not conclusive. If as a whole a contract contemplates an association of two or more persons to carry on as co-owners a business for profit a partnership there is. (Sec. 10.) On the other hand, if it be less than this no partnership exists. Passing on the contract as a whole, an arrangement for sharing profits is to be considered. It is to be given its due weight. But it is to be weighed in connection with all the rest. It is not decisive. It may be merely the method adopted to pay a debt or wages, as interest on a loan or for other reasons.

An existing contract may be modified later by subsequent agreement, oral or written. A partnership may be so created where there was none before. And again, that the original agreement has been so modified may be proved by circumstantial evidence—by showing the conduct of the parties.

In the case before us the claim that the defendants became partners in the firm of Knauth, Nachod & Kuhne, doing business as bankers and brokers, depends upon the interpretation of certain instruments. There is nothing in their subsequent acts determinative of or indeed material upon this question. And we are relieved of questions that sometimes arise. "The plaintiff's position is not," we are told, "that the agreements of June 4, 1921, were a false expression or incomplete expression of the intention of the parties. We say that they express defendants' intention and that that intention was to create a relationship which as a matter of law constitutes a partnership." Nor may the claim of the plaintiff be rested on any question of estoppel. "The plaintiff's claim," he stipulates, "is a claim of actual partnership, not of partnership by estoppel. . . ."

Remitted then, as we are, to the documents themselves, we refer to circumstances surrounding their execution only so far as is necessary to make them intelligible. And we are to remember that although the intention of the parties to avoid liability as partners is clear, although in language precise and definite they deny any design to then join the firm of K.N. & K.; although they say their interests in profits should be construed merely as a measure of compensation for loans, not an interest in profits as such; although they provide that they shall not be liable for any losses or treated as partners, the question still remains whether in fact they agree to so associate themselves with the firm as to "carry on as co-owners a business for profit."

In the spring of 1921 the firm of K.N. & K. found itself in financial difficulties. John R. Hall was one of the partners. He was a friend of Mr. Peyton. From him he obtained the loan of almost

$500,000 of Liberty bonds, which K.N. & K. might use as collateral to secure bank advances. This, however, was not sufficient. The firm and its members had engaged in unwise speculations, and it was deeply involved. Mr. Hall was also intimately acquainted with George W. Perkins, Jr., and with Edward W. Freeman. He also knew Mrs. Peyton and Mrs. Perkins and Mrs. Freeman. All were anxious to help him. He, therefore, representing K.N. & K., entered into negotiations with them. While they were pending a proposition was made that Mr. Peyton, Mr. Perkins and Mr. Freeman or some of them should become partners. It met a decided refusal. Finally an agreement was reached. It is expressed in three documents, executed on the same day, all a part of the one transaction. They were drawn with care and are unambiguous. We shall refer to them as "the agreement," "the indenture" and "the option."

We have no doubt as to their general purpose. The respondents were to loan K.N. & K. $2,500,000 worth of liquid securities, which were to be returned to them on or before April 15, 1923. The firm might hypothecate them to secure loans totalling $2,000,000, using the proceeds as its business necessities required. To insure respondents against loss K.N. & K. were to turn over to them a large number of their own securities which may have been valuable, but which were of so speculative a nature that they could not be used as collateral for bank loans. In compensation for the loan the respondents were to receive 40 per cent of the profits of the firm until the return was made, not exceeding, however, $500,000 and not less than $100,000. Merely because the transaction involved the transfer of securities and not of cash does not prevent its being a loan within the meaning of section 11. The respondents also were given an option to join the firm if they or any of them expressed a desire to do so before June 4, 1923.

Many other detailed agreements are contained in the papers. Are they such as may be properly inserted to protect the lenders? Or do they go further? Whatever their purpose, did they in truth associate the respondents with the firm so that they and it together thereafter carried on as co-owners a business for profit? The answer depends upon an analysis of these various provisions.

As representing the lenders, Mr. Peyton and Mr. Freeman are called "trustees." The loaned securities when used as collateral are not to be mingled with other securities of K.N. & K., and the trustees at all times are to be kept informed of all transactions affecting them. To them shall be paid all dividends and income accruing therefrom. They may also substitute for any of the securities loaned securities of equal value. With their consent the firm may sell any of its securities held by the respondents, the proceeds to go, however, to the trustees. In other similar ways the trustees may deal with these same securities, but the securities loaned shall always be sufficient in value to permit of their hypothecation for $2,000,000. If they rise in price the excess may be withdrawn by the defendants. If they fall they shall make good the deficiency.

So far there is no hint that the transaction is not a loan of securities with a provision for compensation. Later a somewhat closer connection with the firm appears. Until the securities are returned the directing management of the firm is to be in the hands of John R. Hall, and his life is to be insured for $1,000,000, and the policies are to be assigned as further collateral security to the trustees. These requirements are not unnatural. Hall was the one known and trusted by the defendants. Their acquaintance with the other members of the firm was of the slightest. These others had brought an old and established business to the verge of bankruptcy. As the respondents knew, they also had engaged in unsafe speculation. The respondents were about to loan $2,500,000 of good securities. As collateral they were to receive others of problematical value. What they required seems but ordinary caution. Nor does it imply an association in the business.

The trustees are to be kept advised as to the conduct of the business and consulted as to important matters. They may inspect the firm books and are entitled to any information they think important. Finally they may veto any business they think highly speculative or injurious. Again we hold this but a proper precaution to safeguard the loan. The trustees may not initiate any transaction as a partner may do. They may not bind the firm by any action of their own. Under the circumstances the safety of the loan depended upon the business success of K.N. & K. This success was likely to be compromised by the inclination of its members to engage in speculation. No longer, if the respondents were to be protected, should it be allowed. The trustees, therefore, might prohibit it, and that their prohibition might be effective, information was to be furnished them. Not dissimilar agreements have been held proper to guard the interests of the lender.

As further security each member of K.N. & K. is to assign to the trustees their interest in the firm. No loan by the firm to any member is permitted and the amount each may draw is fixed. No other distribution of profits is to be made. So that realized profits may be calculated the existing capital is stated to be $700,000, and profits are to be realized as promptly as good business practice will permit. In case the trustees think this is not done, the question is left to them and to Mr. Hall, and if they differ then to an arbitrator. There is no obligation that the firm shall continue the business. It may dissolve at any time. Again we conclude there is nothing here not properly adapted to secure the interest of the respondents as lenders. If their compensation is dependent on a percentage of the profits still provision must be made to define what these profits shall be.

The "indenture" is substantially a mortgage of the collateral delivered by K.N. & K. to the trustees to secure the performance of the "agreement." It certainly does not strengthen the claim that the respondents were partners.

Finally we have the "option." It permits the respondents or any of them or their assignees or nominees to enter the firm at a later date if they desire to do so by buying 50 per cent or less of the interests therein of all or any of the members at a stated price. Or a corporation may, if the respondents and the members agree, be formed in place of the firm. Meanwhile, apparently with the design of protecting the firm business against improper or ill-judged action which might render the option valueless, each member of the firm is to place his resignation in the hands of Mr. Hall. If at any time he and the trustees agree that such resignation should be accepted, that member shall then retire, receiving the value of his interest calculated as of the date of such retirement.

This last provision is somewhat unusual, yet it is not enough in itself to show that on June 4, 1921, a present partnership was created nor taking these various papers as a whole do we reach such a result. It is quite true that even if one or two or three like provisions contained in such a contract do not require this conclusion, yet it is also true that when taken together a point may come where stipulations immaterial separately cover so wide a field that we should hold a partnership exists. As in other branches of the law a question of degree is often the determining factor. Here that point has not been reached. . . .

The judgment appealed from should be affirmed, with costs.

CARDOZO, Ch. J., POUND, CRANE, LEHMAN, KELLOGG and O'BRIEN, JJ., concur.

Judgment affirmed, etc.

ZAJAC v. HARRIS

Supreme Court of Arkansas, 1967.
241 Ark. 737, 410 S.W.2d 593.

GEORGE ROSE SMITH, Justice. The appellee, George Harris, brought this suit to compel the appellant, Carl A. Zajac, to account for the profits and assets of a partnership that assertedly existed between the parties for some two years. Zajac denied that a partnership existed, insisting that Harris was merely an employee in a business owned by Zajac. The chancellor concluded that Harris had met the burden of proving the partnership relationship. The court accordingly referred the case to a master for a statement of the partnership accounts. The essential question here is whether the chancellor's recognition of the partnership is against the weight of the evidence. [ISSUE]

At first blush the testimony appears to be in such hopeless conflict that the controlling issue at the trial must have been one of credibility. Upon reflection, however, we arrive at a somewhat different view of the case. The business association that is known in the law as a partnership is not one that can be defined with precision. To the [K relationship] contrary, a partnership is a contractual relationship that may vary, in form and substance, in an almost infinite variety of ways. The draftsmen of the controlling statute, the Uniform Partnership Act, tacitly acknowledged that fact by stating only in the most general language an assortment of rules that are to be considered in determining whether a partnership exists.   Ark.Stat.Ann. § 65–107 (Repl. 1966).

In the case at bar there is the additional consideration that these two laymen went into business together without consulting a lawyer or attempting to put their agreement into writing.   It is apparent from the testimony that neither man had any conscious or deliberate intention of entering into a particular legal relationship.   When the testimony is viewed in this light the conflicts are not so sharp as they might otherwise appear to be.   Our problem is that of determining from the record as a whole whether the association they agreed upon was a partnership or an employer-employee relationship.

Before the two men became business associates Zajac had conducted a combination garage-and-salvage company, filling station, and grocery store in the Marche community in Pulaski county.   This dispute relates only to the salvage branch of the enterprise.

In the salvage operation now in controversy the parties bought wrecked automobiles from insurance companies and either rebuilt them for resale or cannibalized them by reusing or reselling the parts. Harris, the plaintiff, testified that he and Zajac agreed to go into business together, splitting the profits equally—except that Harris was to receive one fourth of the proceeds from any parts sold by him. Harris borrowed $9,000 from a bank, upon the security of property that he owned, and placed the money in a bank account that he used in buying cars for the firm.   The profits were divided from time to time as the cars were resold, so that Harris's capital was used and reused.   He identified checks totaling more than $73,000 that he signed in making purchases for the business.

Zajac, by contrast, took the position that Harris was merely an employee working for a commission of one half the profits realized from cars that Harris himself had bought.   Zajac denied that he had ever agreed that Harris would spend his own money in buying cars. "I told him, when you go out there, when you bid on a car, make a note that I will pay for it."   We have no doubt, however, that Harris *did* use his own money in the venture and that Zajac knew that such expenditures were being made.

Counsel for Zajac put much stress upon their client's controlling voice in the management of the business.   Zajac and his wife and their accountant had charge of the books and records.   No partnership income tax return was ever filed.   Harris was ostensibly treated as an employee, in that federal withholding and Social Security taxes were paid upon his share of the profits.   The firm also carried workmen's compensation insurance for Harris's protection.   In our opinion, however, any inferences that might ordinarily be drawn from these bookkeeping entries are effectively rebutted by the undisputed fact that Harris, apart from being able to sign his name, was unable to read or write.   There is no reason to believe that he appreciated the significance of the accounting practices now relied upon by Zajac. They were unilateral.

We attach much weight to Zajac's candid admissions, elicited by the chancellor's questions, that Zajac paid Harris one half of the profits derived from cars that Zajac bought with his own money and sold by his own efforts. Zajac has insisted from the outset that Harris was working upon a commission basis, but that view cannot be reconciled with Harris's admitted right to receive his share of the profits derived from business conducted by Zajac alone.

There is no real dispute between the parties about the governing principles of law. The ultimate question is whether the two men intended to become partners, as that term is used in the law. Brandenburg v. Brandenburg, 234 Ark. 1117, 356 S.W.2d 625 (1962). Harris's receipt of a share of the net profits is prima facie evidence that he was a partner, unless the money was paid to him as wages. Ark.Stat.Ann. § 65–107. Unlike the fact situation in Morrow v. McCaa Chevrolet Co., 231 Ark. 497, 330 S.W.2d 722 (1960), Harris's position does not rest upon the bare fact that he received a share of the profits. He invested, as we have seen, substantial sums of his own money in the acquisition of cars for the firm. Zajac concedes that Harris was entitled to a share of the profits from transactions that Harris certainly did not handle on a commission basis. When the testimony is reconciled, as we have attempted to do, it does not appear that the chancellor was wrong in deciding that a partnership existed.

Affirmed.

BYRD, J., not participating.

SECTION 2. THE LEGAL NATURE OF A PARTNERSHIP

NOTE ON THE LEGAL NATURE OF A PARTNERSHIP: ENTITY OR AGGREGATE STATUS

1. Individuals may associate in a wide variety of forms, and the issue often arises whether a given form of association has a legal status separate from that of its members. Frequently, this issue is stated in terms of whether or not a form of association is a "separate entity" or a "legal person" (as opposed to a natural person, that is, an individual). A variety of issues may turn on the answer to this question—for example, whether the association can sue and be sued in its own name, and whether it can hold property in its own right.

In the history of English and American law this issue arose in the context of many different kinds of associations, such as universities, charitable institutions, and even municipalities. In most cases the issue was eventually resolved in a straightforward way, but in the case of partnerships it continued to be vexing. The predominant although not exclusive view under the common law was that a partnership was not an entity, but merely an aggregate of its members; that, as it was sometimes put, a partnership was no more a legal person than a friendship.

In 1902, the Conference of Commissioners on Uniform State Laws determined to promulgate a Uniform Partnership Act. Dean James Barr Ames of Harvard Law School was appointed to draft the Act. Subsequently, the Commissioners instructed Dean Ames, at his own urging, to draft the Act on the theory that a partnership is a legal entity. Accordingly, in the drafts submitted by Dean Ames a partnership was defined as "a legal person formed by the association of two or more individuals for the purpose of carrying on business with a view to profit," and various provisions of the drafts reflected the entity theory. Dean Ames died before the work was completed, however, and his successor, Dean William Draper Lewis of the University of Pennsylvania Law School, was distinctly unfriendly to the entity view. Ultimately, Dean Lewis convinced the Commissioners to instruct him to draft the Act on the aggregate theory. U.P.A. Section 6 therefore provides that "A partnership is an association of two or more persons to carry on as co-owners a business for profit." Although the language of this provision does not render the issue completely free from doubt, there is little doubt that the Act was intended to adopt the aggregate theory.

That is not, however, the end of the story. Having adopted the aggregate theory, the U.P.A. nevertheless deals with a number of issues *as if* the partnership were an entity. This may seem to be a pragmatic solution, and for many purposes the U.P.A. does work pretty well. On the whole, however, the use of an aggregate theory in the U.P.A. was unfortunate. Generally speaking, the entity theory of a partnership is much more functional than the aggregate theory. In those cases where the U.P.A. does not treat the partnership as if it were an entity, the result tends to be bad, and in need of legislative revision. In those cases where the U.P.A. does treat the partnership as if it were an entity, the result is good, but the statutory approach is often made needlessly complex by the mechanics of reconciling the entity result with the aggregate theory.[1]

2. The question often arises whether a partnership is to be treated as an aggregate or an entity for the purpose of some statute other than the U.P.A. This question is a matter of legislative intent under the particular statute. As in all such matters, the answer will depend on the language employed and the purposes manifested in the statute at hand. The fact that the U.P.A. adopted the aggregate theory will be relevant, but not dispositive, in answering that question. A legislature may choose to treat a partnership as an entity for purposes of another statute even though a partnership is defined as an

1. On the common law background and the statutory history of the entity/aggregate debate, see Commissioners' Prefatory Note to the Uniform Partnership Act, 6 Uniform Laws Ann. 5 (1969); Lewis, The Uniform Partnership Act, 24 Yale L.J. 617 (1915); Crane, The Uniform Partnership Act—A Criticism, 28 Harv.L.Rev. 762 (1915); Crane, The Uniform Partnership Act and Legal Persons, 29 Harv.L.Rev. 838 (1916); Jensen, Is a Partnership Under the Uniform Partnership Act an Aggregate or an Entity?, 16 Vand.L.Rev. 377 (1963).

association under the U.P.A.   See, e.g., United States v. A & P Trucking Co., 358 U.S. 121, 79 S.Ct. 203, 3 L.Ed.2d 165 (1958).

3.   As you proceed through the balance of this Chapter, consider whether the legal rules that are the subject of each Section reflect an aggregate or an entity approach.

REPORT OF THE ABA SUBCOMMITTEE ON REVISION OF THE U.P.A., 43 Bus.Law. 121, 124 (1987).   "Because the 'entity theory' avoids a number of technical problems, such as the authority of a general partnership to sue or be sued in its partnership name, the subcommittee determined that it should be incorporated into any revision of the UPA whenever possible and that the 'aggregate theory' should be retained only where it appears to be essential, e.g., because of tax considerations."*

SECTION 3.   THE ONGOING OPERATION OF PARTNERSHIPS

(a) MANAGEMENT

UNIFORM PARTNERSHIP ACT
§§ 18(a), (e), (g), (h), 19, 20

[See Statutory Supplement]

SUMMERS v. DOOLEY
Supreme Court of Idaho, 1971.
94 Idaho 87, 481 P.2d 318.

DONALDSON, Justice.

This lawsuit, tried in the district court, involves a claim by one partner against the other for $6,000.   The complaining partner asserts that he has been required to pay out more than $11,000 in expenses without any reimbursement from either the partnership funds or his partner.   The expenditure in question was incurred by the complaining partner (John Summers, plaintiff-appellant) for the purpose of hiring an additional employee.   The trial court denied him any relief except for ordering that he be entitled to one half $966.72 which it found to be a legitimate partnership expense.

---

* The title of this Report, as used here and elsewhere in this text, is an abbreviation.   The full title is UPA Revision Subcommittee of the Partnership Committee of the ABA Corporation, Banking and Business Law Section, Should the Uniform Partnership Act be Revised?

FACTS

The pertinent facts leading to this lawsuit are as follows. Summers entered a partnership agreement with Dooley (defendant-respondent) in 1958 for the purpose of operating a trash collection business. The business was operated by the two men and when either was unable to work, the non-working partner provided a replacement at his own expense. In 1962, Dooley became unable to work and, at his own expense, hired an employee to take his place. In July, 1966, Summers approached his partner Dooley regarding the hiring of an additional employee but Dooley refused. Nevertheless, on his own initiative, Summers hired the man and paid him out of his own pocket. Dooley, upon discovering that Summers had hired an additional man, objected, stating that he did not feel additional labor was necessary and refused to pay for the new employee out of the partnership funds. Summers continued to operate the business using the third man and in October of 1967 instituted suit in the district court for $6,000 against his partner, the gravamen of the complaint being that Summers has been required to pay out more than $11,000 in expenses, incurred in the hiring of the additional man, without any reimbursement from either the partnership funds or his partner. After trial before the court, sitting without a jury, Summers was granted only partial relief [1]

PC.

and he has appealed. He urges in essence that the trial court erred by failing to conclude that he should be reimbursed for expenses and costs connected in the employment of extra help in the partnership business.

ISSUE

The principal thrust of appellant's contention is that in spite of the fact that one of the two partners refused to consent to the hiring of additional help, nonetheless, the non-consenting partner retained profits earned by the labors of the third man and therefore the non-consenting partner should be estopped from denying the need and value of the employee, and has by his behavior ratified the act of the other partner who hired the additional man.

ISSUE

The issue presented for decision by this appeal is whether an equal partner in a two man partnership has the authority to hire a new employee in disregard of the objection of the other partner and then attempt to charge the dissenting partner with the costs incurred as a result of his unilateral decision.

The State of Idaho has enacted specific statutes with respect to the legal concept known as "partnership." Therefore any solution of partnership problems should logically begin with an application of the relevant code provision.

In the instant case the record indicates that although Summers requested his partner Dooley to agree to the hiring of a third man, such requests were not honored. In fact Dooley made it clear that he was "voting no" with regard to the hiring of an additional employee.

An application of the relevant statutory provisions and pertinent case law to the factual situation presented by the instant case indicates

1. The trial court did award Summers one half of $966.72 which it found to be a legitimate partnership expense.

that the trial court was correct in its disposal of the issue since a majority of the partners did not consent to the hiring of the third man. I.C. § 53–318(8) provides:

> "Any difference arising as to ordinary matters connected with the partnership business may be decided by a *majority of the partners. . . .*"   (emphasis supplied)

It is the opinion of this Court that the preceding statute is of a mandatory rather than permissive nature. This conclusion is based upon the following reasoning. Whether a statute is mandatory or directory does not depend upon its form, but upon the intention of the legislature, to be ascertained from a consideration of the entire act, its nature, its object, and the consequences that would result from construing it one way or the other. In re McQuistons Adoption, 238 Pa. 304, 86 A. 205 (1913).

The intent of the legislature may be implied from the language used, or inferred on grounds of policy or reasonableness. See Barnett v. Prairie Oil & Gas Co. et al., 19 F.2d 504 (8th Cir.1927); Motorcoach Operators Ass'n. v. Board of Street Railway Commissioners of the City of Detroit, 267 Mich. 568, 255 N.W. 391 (1934); 3 Sutherland, Statutory Construction, § 5803, p. 79. A careful reading of the statutory provision indicates that subsection 5 bestows *equal rights in the management and conduct of the partnership business* upon all of the partners. The concept of equality between partners with respect to management of business affairs is a central theme and recurs throughout the Uniform Partnership law, I.C. § 53–301 et seq., which has been enacted in this jurisdiction. Thus the only reasonable interpretation of I.C. § 53–318(8) is that business differences must be decided by a majority of the partners provided no other agreement between the partners speaks to the issues.

A noted scholar has dealt precisely with the issue to be decided.

> ". . . if the partners are equally divided, those who forbid a change must have their way." Walter B. Lindley, A Treatise on the Law of Partnership, Ch. II, § III, ¶ 24–8, p. 403 (1924). See also, W. Shumaker, A Treatise on the Law of Partnership, § 97, p. 266.

See also, Clarke et al. v. Slate Valley R. Co., 136 Pa. 408, 20 A. 562 (1890) for a discussion of this rule.

In the case at bar one of the partners continually voiced objection to the hiring of the third man. He did not sit idly by and acquiesce in the actions of his partner. Under these circumstances it is manifestly unjust to permit recovery of an expense which was incurred individually and not for the benefit of the partnership but rather for the benefit of one partner.

Judgment affirmed. Costs to respondent.

McQUADE, C.J., and McFADDEN, SHEPARD and SPEAR, JJ., concur.

QUESTION

Suppose that A, B, and C form a partnership. A contributes 90% of the capital, and by agreement is entitled to 90% of any profits and is responsible for 90% of any losses. B and C each contribute 5% of the capital and by agreement are each entitled to 5% of any profits and are responsible for 5% of any losses. Nothing is said in the agreement concerning how decisions will be made. If, on an ordinary matter connected with the partnership, A votes one way, and B and C another, who prevails?

———

NOTE ON THE MANAGEMENT OF PARTNERSHIPS

1. The cases and authorities are divided on the issue raised in Summers v. Dooley. In accord with *Summers* is Covalt v. High, 100 N.M. 700, 675 P.2d 999 (App.1983). But see National Biscuit Co. v. Stroud, 249 N.C. 467, 106 S.E.2d 692 (1959), noted, 1960 Duke L.J. 150 (where one of two partners transacts with a third party on a matter that is otherwise within the ordinary business of the partnership, the other partner is liable even though he had put the third party on notice that the partners were divided on the matter).

2. Since U.P.A. Section 18(h) provides that partnership action requires a majority vote, what is added by U.P.A. Section 18(e), which provides that all partners have equal rights in the management and conduct of the partnership business? Presumably, the effect of this Section is to require that, absent contrary agreement, every partner be provided on an ongoing basis with information concerning the partnership business, and be consulted in partnership decisions. See Hillman, Power Shared and Power Denied: A Look at Participatory Rights in the Management of General Partnerships, 1984 U.Ill.L.Rev. 865 (1984); E. Scamell & R. Banks, Lindley on the Law of Partnership, 427 (14th ed. 1979).

> For a majority of partners to say; We do not care what one partner may say, we, being the majority, will do what we please, is, I apprehend what this Court will not allow. So, again, with respect to making Mr. *Robertson* the treasurer, Mr. *Const* had a right to be consulted; his opinion might be overruled, and honestly over-ruled, but he ought to have had the question put to him and discussed: In all partnerships . . . the partners are bound to be true and faithful to each other: They are to act upon the joint opinion of all, and the discretion and judgment of anyone cannot be excluded: What weight is to be given to it is another question. . . .

Const v. Harris, 37 Eng.Rep. 1191, 1202 (Ch.1824) (Lord Chancellor Eldon). Thus a majority of partners who made decisions without consulting a minority partner would violate § 18(e), absent contrary agreement.

———

(b) DISTRIBUTIONS AND INDEMNIFICATION

UNIFORM PARTNERSHIP ACT §§ 18(b), (c), (d), (f)

[See Statutory Supplement]

QUESTION

Suppose A, B, and C form a partnership. A contributes 90% of the capital, and B and C each contribute 5%. All work full-time in the partnership business, with roughly equal responsibilities. Nothing is said in the partnership agreement concerning how partnership profits will be divided. If the partnership makes a profit in a given year, how is it to be divided?

NOTE ON PARTNERSHIP DISTRIBUTIONS AND INDEMNIFICATION

1. Section 18(f), which provides that no partner (other than a surviving partner) is entitled to remuneration for acting in the partnership's business, is subject to any contrary agreement between the partners. Such an agreement may be implied rather than express, and the courts often find an implied agreement to pay compensation for services. See A. Bromberg, Crane & Bromberg on Partnership 375–79 (1968).

2. As shown in the next Section, each partner is individually liable to a partnership creditor for partnership obligations. As between the partners, however, each partner is liable only for his share of a partnership obligation. Thus if one partner pays off a partnership obligation in full (or, for that matter, if he simply pays more than his share), he is entitled to indemnification from the other partners for the difference between what he paid and his share of the liability.

SECTION 4. THE AUTHORITY OF A PARTNER

UNIFORM PARTNERSHIP ACT §§ 3, 4(3), 9, 10, 11, 12, 13, 14

[See Statutory Supplement]

OWENS v. PALOS VERDES MONACO

California Court of Appeal, 1983.
142 Cal.App.3d 855, 191 Cal.Rptr. 381.

FEINERMAN, P.J.—Appellants appeal from a judgment ordering specific performance of an agreement for the purchase and sale of 57 acres of unimproved land in Palos Verdes.

The subject property was owned by Monaco Land Holders (MLH), a general partnership. At the time of trial, the three general partners of MLH were Seymour Owens (Owens), Albert Fink (Fink), and Pearl A. Borinstein (Pearl) as trustee under certain trust agreements for the benefit of her daughter Joan Nancy Borinstein (Joan).

Suit was originally brought by one of the partners of MLH, Owens, for declaratory relief and injunctive relief seeking to prevent the sale of the subject property. Kajima International Inc., a California Corporation (Kajima), the proposed buyer of the property, cross-complained for specific performance. . . .

By stipulation of the parties, the suit was bifurcated and issues at trial were limited to Owens' claim for declaratory and injunctive relief and Kajima's claim for specific performance. . . .

P.C. After a court trial, judgment for specific performance was rendered in favor of Kajima. . . . Owens' complaint for declaratory relief and injunction was also dismissed with prejudice.

Owens, . . . MLH, Fink, Pearl, Joan, etc. appeal from the judgment. . . .

FACTS

The subject property was originally acquired by MLH in 1959. At that time Owens, Herbert Kronish (Kronish) and Manny Borinstein (Borinstein) acquired 250 acres of unimproved land in the Palos Verdes area. The three men formed four different partnerships and divided the 250 acres among the partnerships. One hundred and twenty-eight acres were transferred to MLH, and the 57–acre parcel which is the subject of this action was part thereof. The original partners of MLH were Owens, Kronish and Borinstein. . . .

In 1963, Fink became a partner in all four partnerships. In 1969 or 1970 Kronish withdrew from all the partnerships and died a year later. Borinstein died in 1974 and, thereafter, his wife, Pearl, assumed his interests as trustee of various trusts for the benefit of their daughter Joan.

In late 1976 . . . Owens told [Paul Walker, a real estate broker,] to show the 57–acre parcel which is the subject of this lawsuit, to "pursue the sale," and "keep him informed."

John Sogorka (Sogorka), a salesman for Walker, showed the subject property to [Arthur Strouse, Kajima's real estate manager]. . . . Owens', Fink's and Borinstein's names were mentioned in connection with the property, and the asking price for the property was stated to be $2 million.

In November 1976, Kajima made two offers on the property. Each of the offers was hand-delivered to both Owens and Fink by Sogorka. After Owens read the first Kajima offer, he told Sogorka, "Al Fink will be handling this from now on; just keep me apprised of what's going on." Both of Kajima's initial offers were rejected. Fink told Sogorka that he had had a meeting with Owens about the second offer, that the proposed purchase price was too low, that they had suggested some changes in the offer, and that Owens did not like some of the paragraphs and had crossed them out completely. From November 1976, through February 1977, Sogorka continued to try to put a package together to effect a sale of the property.

On March 2, 1977, a meeting was arranged to discuss the possible sale of the subject property to Kajima. . . . Joan and Fink [were present]. . . . Walker had phoned Owens and invited him to be present at the March 2 meeting. Walker testified that Owens asked if Fink was going to attend the meeting, and when he told Owens that Fink had indicated he would attend, Owens "said that Al was going, then he didn't intend to be there." No agreement was reached at the March 2 meeting.

Another meeting to discuss the sale was set for March 25, 1977. . . . Prior to the meeting, Fink phoned Owens and told him about the meeting and "that we were possibly close to selling the property." Fink testified, "And he [Owens] asked me to then attend the meeting, make the best possible deal we could for ourselves." Walker also telephoned Owens prior to the March 25 meeting and invited him to attend. Walker testified, "Mr. Owens told me he would not be in attendance since Al [Fink] was there and he spoke for the two of them."

At the March 25 meeting. . . . [t]he seller was represented by Fink, Joan, and the selling partnership's attorney. . . . At this meeting the parties reached an oral agreement on the price, terms and conditions of a sale.

During the course of the March 25 meeting, Fink stated, in response to a question concerning his authority to act, that he was authorized to negotiate the sale on behalf of the partnership.

The next working day after March 25, Joan and Fink placed a telephone call to Owens. Joan and Fink were each on extension phones. Fink explained to Owens the terms of the sale which had been agreed upon at the March 25 meeting. Joan testified that "Mr. Owens in a very enthusiastic way said he thought it was a great deal and that he was very, very pleased with everything that had been negotiated. And his words were something 'let's proceed' or 'let's go ahead'—was very enthusiastic about it." Fink replied, "Fine; we'll proceed," or "We'll go ahead and have the papers drawn up." Joan testified that she understood the terms and conditions and had indicated to Fink that she approved of the sale. With respect to the telephone call to Owens, Fink testified, "Mr. Owens was—seemed satisfied and approved the terms, conditions, price, and, overall, over the telephone seemed happy about it." Fink also talked with Pearl after the March 25 meeting. He discussed the agreed-upon price, terms and conditions of sale with her. He told her he approved of the transaction. Fink testified that Pearl said, "[s]he approved of the proposal only if Mr. Owens had also approved," and that he told her that Owens had approved the sale.

On April 1, 1977, a meeting was held at Title Insurance & Trust Company to open escrow and to sign the documents which had been prepared by [Kajima's attorney, who] had worked with Sigel, MLH's attorney, in the drafting of the papers.

Some time after the March 25 meeting and before the April 1 meeting, Sogorka hand-delivered a document to Owens. He testified, "It was a rather lengthy document. All I did was hand it to him and . . . I said, 'This is a meeting coming up.' And he said, 'I was aware of that, I won't be there, . . .' but that Al Fink would be handling it and just keep him aware of what's going on."

Prior to the April 1 meeting, Fink called Owens to tell him that the meeting would be at Title Insurance & Trust Company and that the documents were ready to be signed. Fink testified that Owens ". . . told me that he didn't have the time that day, and couldn't be there; however, if I would pick up the papers and bring them back, he would sign them." Owens also told Fink to go to the meeting and see that escrow was opened and that Kajima deposited the money in escrow.

Pearl broke her leg on March 31, and, as a result, she and her daughter, Joan, were unable to attend the April 1 meeting.

Escrow was opened at the meeting on April 1, 1977. . . . [Kajima's attorney, Boss,] testified that prior to the April 1 meeting he had been advised that three partners of the selling partnership would attend the meeting. When the meeting commenced, Boss inquired as to the whereabouts of the other two partners. He was advised that they would not be able to attend the meeting. Boss testified that he asked, "given the fact that there was no—only one partner, Mr. Fink, present at the meeting, whether he was authorized to sign for and bind the partnership." Both Fink and Sigel [MLH's attorney] responded that Fink was authorized.

Fink signed the April 1 agreement for conveyance of real property and escrow instructions on behalf of the selling partnership. Ikeda signed the agreement as the authorized representative of Kajima. Kajima paid $15,000 into escrow at the April 1 meeting, and the escrow was opened.

On the evening of April 1, Fink took a signed original of the agreement to Pearl's house. Joan was with Pearl. Pearl signed the agreement. Fink brought the signed document to Sigel.

Fink first learned that Owens did not want the sale to go forward on April 13 or 14, 1977. Pearl testified that she was surprised and upset when she learned that Owens did not want to go forward with the sale.

* * *

DISCUSSION

The seminal issue in this appeal is whether Fink's signature alone was sufficient to bind MLH to the terms of the April 1 agreement. The resolution of that question depends upon the conclusion we reach regarding Fink's authority to act for the partnership. The trial court found that Fink had actual authority to bind the partnership under the terms of paragraph XIV(A) of the partnership agreement.[6] The court also found that Fink had apparent, or ostensible authority under Corporations Code section 15009, subdivision (1) and that "[t]he sellers are estopped to deny that Fink had authority to sell the land to Kajima."

In our view of the matter, the provisions of Corporations Code section 15009 [UPA § 9], subdivision (1) are dispositive of the issue of Fink's authority to bind the partnership. . . .

* * *

The Supreme Court in analyzing section 15009 in Ellis v. Mihelis (1963) 60 Cal.2d 206, at pages 217–218 [32 Cal.Rptr. 415, 384 P.2d 7], stated: "[¶] These provisions distinguish between acts of a partner which bind the partnership because of his status as a partner without any express authority being required and acts binding on the partnership only after express authorization by all partners. Under the express terms of subdivision (1) of the section all acts of a partner which are apparently within the usual course of the particular business bind the partnership. The effect of the provision is that the status of a partner, without more, serves as a complete authority with respect to such acts, obviating the necessity of any express authority, either oral or written, from the other members of the firm.

"*It necessarily follows that insofar as a partner limits his conduct to matters apparently within the partnership business, he can bind the other partners without obtaining their written consent.* Subdivision (2), however, provides that there must be express authority for acts of a partner which do not appear to be in the usual course of the business. . . .

"The distinction made by subdivisions (1) and (2) between acts which are apparently in the usual course of business and those which are not is in accord with the cases in other jurisdictions which have held, without mention of any statutory requirement for written authority of an agent, that *a contract executed by one partner alone to sell partnership real estate is binding on the other partners provided the partnership is in the business of buying or selling real estate and the property covered by the contract is part of the stock held for sale.*" (Italics added.)

Corporations Code section 15010 provides in part: "Where title to real property is in the partnership name, any partner may convey title to such property by a conveyance executed in the partnership name; but the partnership may recover such property unless the

---

6. Paragraph XIV(A) of the MLH partnership agreement provided, "Sales of all or any portion of the partnership real property may be effected by the decision of partners having a majority in interest in the profits of the partnership."

partner's act binds the partnership under the provisions of paragraph (1) of Section 15009, . . ."

In the case before us, Fink's signature alone was sufficient to bind the partnership if the sale of the subject property was an act "for apparently carrying on in the usual way the business of the partnership."

"The apparent scope of the partnership business depends primarily on the conduct of the partnership and its partners and what they cause third persons to believe about the authority of the partners. Ostensible agency or acts within the scope of the partnership business are presumed 'where the business done by the supposed agent, so far as open to the observation of third parties, is consistent with the existence of an agency, and where, as to the transaction in question, the third party was justified in believing that an agency existed.' [Citations.]" (Blackmon v. Hale (1970) 1 Cal.3d 548, 557 [83 Cal. Rptr. 194, 463 P.2d 418].)

The trial court found that "[t]he sale of the land to Kajima was apparently in the ordinary course of the selling partnership's business." This finding was supported by the evidence. The sole purpose of the MLH partnership was the holding and sale of the subject property. The partnership agreement provided: "The general character and nature of business of this partnership shall be the holding of the real property described in Exhibit 'A' [of which the 57–acre subject property was a part] with the view to the appreciation in value thereof and *the ultimate sale of said real property* in its unimproved state." (Italics added.) The only dealings which Kajima and the people who represented it had with MLH concerned the sale of the subject property. There is no indication in the record that MLH had any business other than the sale of the subject property.

The trial court found that: "Fink was the only partner who ever attended meetings with representatives of Kajima regarding this transaction up to and including April 1, 1977. Fink conducted the negotiations on behalf of the sellers.

"In the context of the negotiations for the sale of the land, Fink's role as sale negotiator for the sellers, and Owens' statements to Walker and Sogorka to the effect that Fink would handle the deal on behalf of the sellers, which were reported to Kajima, were two factors in reasonably leading Kajima to believe that Fink had authority to sell the land."

. . . The conduct of the partnership and its partners in this case was sufficient to sustain the findings that the partnership was in the business of selling property and that Fink, a partner, was authorized to act for the partnership.

Appellants argue that sale of the subject property cannot be considered to be within the apparent scope of the partnership business because sale of said property would make it impossible to carry on the partnership business.

Section 15009, subdivision (3) specifies certain acts which are not within the scope of the usual course of business. It provides: "Unless authorized by the other partners or unless they have abandoned the business, one or more but less than all the partners have no authority to: . . . (b) Dispose of the good will of the business. (c) Do any other act which would make it impossible to carry on the ordinary business of a partnership."

Historically, partnerships were divided into two types, commercial or trading partnerships and noncommercial or nontrading partnerships. Though this distinction has been rejected in California, it is clear that a nontrading partnership (such as MLH) has no good will to dispose of. In the 20 years prior to the transaction at issue, MLH had never engaged in commerce. MLH had no customers, its name was not known to the public, and it had no value in excess of the value of its sole asset. Therefore, Fink could not rightly be said to have exceeded his authority under section 15009, subdivision (3) by disposing of the good will of MLH.

[handwritten margin note: MLH – a non-trading partnership had no good will]

The trading/nontrading distinction is also valuable in considering whether Fink exceeded his statutory authority by making it impossible to carry on the ordinary business of the partnership. A number of reported decisions, including Petrikis v. Hanges (1952) 111 Cal.App. 2d 734 [245 P.2d 39], cited by appellants, hold that the sale of a partnership's only asset is beyond the scope of usual partnership business and thus cannot be effected by a single partner. In *Petrikis,* the seller of real property, Mr. Petrikis, sold the partnership's only asset, a cocktail lounge, without written authority from his partners. The Court of Appeal held that Petrikis had not bound the partnership because he had acted beyond the scope of usual business in selling the partnership's only asset. *Petrikis* is distinguishable from the present case in that *Petrikis* involved a trading partnership. Petrikis' partnership was in the business of running a bar, not the business of holding a bar in anticipation of its eventual sale. (See also, Ellis v. Mihelis, supra, 60 Cal.2d 206.) In the case at bench, MLH had a singular purpose. It existed solely to hold and sell a piece of real property. The business of MLH was selling its land. Thus, the sale was in the ordinary course of MLH's business.

* * *

The evidence is sufficient to support the trial court's findings with respect to Fink's agency and the findings and conclusions of law support the trial court's determination that specific performance of the April 1 agreement is appropriate.

* * *

ASHBY, J., and HASTINGS, J., concurred.

A petition for a rehearing was denied May 31, 1983, and the petition of . . . appellant for a hearing by the Supreme Court was denied August 10, 1983. MOSK, J., was of the opinion that the petition should be granted.

NOTE ON OWENS v. PALOS VERDES MONACO

The court in Owens v. Palos Verdes Monaco went to some lengths to establish that the sale of land was in the ordinary course of the partnership business and therefore fell within the California counterpart of U.P.A. § 9(1). Since it is at least arguable that all the partners either authorized or ratified Fink's execution of the April 1 agreement, why didn't the court avoid the problem of interpretating U.P.A. § 9(1) by holding that even if the agreement was not in the ordinary course of the partnership business, it was "authorized by the other partners" under U.P.A. § 9(2)? One possible answer, of course, is that the court did not think that the actions of the other partners constituted an authorization or ratification of the agreement. There is a more likely answer. Some states, including California, have a provision in their Statute of Frauds known as the "equal-dignity rule." Under that rule, where a contract that must be in writing is made by an agent, the contract is unenforceable against the principal, even if it is in writing, unless the agent's authority is also in writing. In Ellis v. Mihelis, 60 Cal.2d 206, 32 Cal.Rptr. 415, 384 P.2d 7 (1963), referred to in *Owens,* the California Supreme Court held that the California equal-dignity rule applied to U.P.A. § 9(2), but not to § 9(1). The following passage from *Ellis,* most of which is quoted in *Owens,* is worth repeating here against that background.

> Under the express terms of subdivision (1) . . . all acts of a partner which are apparently within the usual course of the particular business bind the partnership. The effect of the provision is that the status of a partner, without more, serves as complete authority with respect to such acts, obviating the necessity of any express authority, either oral or written, from the other members of the firm [thereby making the lack of written authority irrelevant].

> It necessarily follows that insofar as a partner limits his conduct to matters apparently within the partnership business, he can bind the other partners without obtaining their written consent. Subdivision (2), however, provides that there must be express authority for acts of a partner which do not appear to be in the usual course of the business. This subdivision . . . contains no language which would justify a conclusion that written authority is not necessary in situations where the statute of frauds would ordinarily be applicable.

Thus the court in *Owens* may have avoided deciding the case under U.P.A. § 9(2) because even if Fink was actually authorized by the other partners to make the April 1 agreement, so that the substantive test of Section 9(2) was satisfied, the authority did not meet the formal requirement overlaid on Section 9(2) by the equal-dignity rule as interpreted in *Ellis.*

––––––––

BURNS v. GONZALEZ, 439 S.W.2d 128 (Tex.Civ.App.1969). Bosquez and Gonzalez were partners in a business that sold broadcast time on a radio station located in Mexico. The station was owned and operated by a Mexican corporation, Radiodifusora. Bosquez and Gonzalez each owned 50% of Radiodifusora's stock, and Bosquez was its president. In 1957, Radiodifusora made a contract with Burns, which it failed to perform. Subsequently, Bosquez, purporting to act on his own behalf and on behalf of the partnership, executed a $40,000 promissory note payable to Burns, partly in exchange for Burns's promise not to sue Radiodifusora. Burns sued Bosquez and Gonzalez on the note, as partners, and Gonzalez argued that Bosquez had no authority to execute the note on the partnership's behalf. In reviewing a jury verdict in favor of defendants, the court stated:

> [Since the] express limitation on the authority of Bosquez was unknown to Burns, then, under the language of Sec. 9(1), his act in executing the note would bind the partnership if such act can be classified as an act "for apparently carrying on in the usual way the business of the partnership."
>
> As we interpret Sec. 9(1), the act of a partner binds the firm, absent an express limitation of authority known to the party dealing with such partner, if such act is for the purpose of "apparently carrying on" the business of the partnership in the way in which other firms engaged in the same business in the locality usually transact business, or in the way in which the particular partnership usually transacts its business. In this case, [however,] there is no evidence relating to the manner in which firms engaged in the sale of advertising time on radio stations usually transact business.

SECTION 5. LIABILITY FOR PARTNERSHIP OBLIGATIONS

UNIFORM PARTNERSHIP ACT §§ 9, 13, 14, 15, 16, 17, 36

[See Statutory Supplement]

NOTE ON LIABILITY FOR PARTNERSHIP OBLIGATIONS

1. The provisions of the Uniform Partnership Act governing liability for partnership obligations reflect an amalgam of the entity and aggregate theories. On the one hand, Sections 9, 13, and 14 make "the partnership" liable for defined acts of the partners. It might seem to follow that this liability could be enforced by a suit against the partnership. However, the U.P.A. does not authorize such a suit, since it does not recognize a partnership as an entity, and

unless authorized by statute, suit normally cannot be brought against an association that is not recognized as an entity.

Indeed, the U.P.A. goes to the opposite extreme. Under Section 15, the partners are liable only jointly, rather than jointly and severally, for most nontortious partnership obligations. At common law, if an obligation owed by more than one person is "several" the obligors can be sued separately. If an obligation is "joint and several" the obligors can be sued either separately or jointly. If, however, an obligation is only "joint" the obligee must join all the obligors, subject to a few exceptions where jurisdiction over all cannot be obtained. See C. Clark, Handbook of the Law of Code Pleading 373–74 (2d ed. 1947). Thus under the U.P.A., not only can an action not be brought against a partnership, but if a partnership obligation falls within Section 15(b), and one partner is not joined, the action can be dismissed on motion by the partners who were joined. (If the partners who were joined don't move to dismiss, the defense is waived. However, the plaintiff's cause of action is usually considered to be merged into the judgment, thereby extinguishing his claim against the unjoined partners.)

2. This state of affairs is obviously undesirable, and many states have statutorily patched it up. The legislative action falls into several categories.

a. At least one statute, Nebraska §§ 67–304(4), 67–306(1), varies the U.P.A. by treating partnerships as entities rather than associations. See Horn's Crane Serv. v. Prior, 182 Neb. 94, 152 N.W.2d 421 (1967); In re Svoboda and Hannah, 180 Neb. 215, 142 N.W.2d 328 (1966). Under such a statute, the partnership can be sued on a partnership obligation.

b. Many states have adopted Common Name Statutes, which explicitly allow a partnership to be sued. An example is N.Y.Civ. Prac.L. & R. § 1025: "Two or more persons conducting a business as a partnership may sue or be sued in the partnership name. . . ."

c. Some states either vary U.P.A. Section 15(a) by making all partnership liabilities joint and several, or have adopted Joint Debtor Statutes, which provide that a suit against joint obligors can proceed even if some of the obligors are not joined. An example is Cal.Civ. Proc.Code § 410.70: "In an action against two or more persons who are jointly, jointly and severally, or severally liable on a contract, the court in which the action is pending has jurisdiction to proceed against such of the defendants as are served as if they were the only defendants." These approaches do not allow suit against a partnership, but do make it easier to sue the partners.

SECTION 6. PARTNERSHIP PROPERTY AND PARTNERSHIP INTERESTS

UNIFORM PARTNERSHIP ACT §§ 8, 18, 24, 25, 26, 27, 28

[See Statutory Supplement]

NOTE ON PARTNERSHIP PROPERTY AND PARTNERSHIP INTERESTS

1. As a business matter, there will almost invariably be a separation between the property of a partnership and the property of the individual partners (although in partnerships that operate very informally, it may sometimes be difficult to determine whether a given asset is partnership property or individual property that the partner allows the partnership to use). If the aggregate theory were strictly applied, however, a partnership could not own property as a matter of law. Rather, the property that the partners think of as partnership property would as a matter of law be held by the individual partners as joint tenants or tenants in common. For a variety of reasons, such a regime would be wholly impracticable. Accordingly, in the matter of partnership property, as in several other matters, the U.P.A. lays down rules that effectively treat the partnership *as if* it were an entity. This objective is accomplished largely with mirrors. U.P.A. Section 8 recognizes the concept of "partnership property," and explicitly permits real property to be held in the partnership's name. (Even before the U.P.A. it was well settled that personal property could be so held.) However, U.P.A. Section 25(1) provides that "partnership property" is owned by the *partners,* under the ingenuous nomenclature, "tenant in partnership." U.P.A. Section 25(2) then systematically strips from the individual partners every incident normally associated with ownership. Under Section 25(2)(a), a partner has no right to possess partnership property as an individual. Under Section 25(2)(b), a partner cannot individually assign his rights in specific partnership property. Under Section 25(2)(c), a partner's rights in specific partnership property cannot be subject to attachment or execution by a creditor of the partner in the latter's individual capacity. Under Section 25(2)(d), when the partner dies his right in specific partnership property does not devolve on his heirs or legatees. Under Section 25(2)(e), widows, heirs, and next of kin cannot claim dower, courtesy, or allowances in the partner's right to specific partnership property.

In short, under the U.P.A. individual partners own the partnership property in theory, but all the incidents of ownership are vested in the partnership. As aptly put in A. Bromberg, Crane & Bromberg on Partnership 230 (1968):

The U.P.A. draftsmen first embraced, then shrank from a complete entity treatment of the firm. They reached workable results consistent with the entity theory, but not identical, by creating a newly labelled "tenancy in partnership" in which the partners are said to own the partnership property. In this tenancy, the co-ownership rules developed at common law are codified and stiffened in their entity features. The net effect is self-contradictory. Although stating that each partner is a co-owner of partnership property, the Act systematically destroys the usual attributes of ownership. . . . Functionally, despite the literal language, the partnership owns its property and the partners do not. The Act would be better if it conceded this rather than accomplishing it by indirection.

2. Although a partner does not own partnership property under the U.P.A., except in some metaphysical sense, he does own his interest in the partnership, that is, his share of the partnership. The net result is a functional two-level ownership structure somewhat comparable to the legal two-level ownership structure in a corporation. A corporation is the owner of corporate property and a shareholder is the owner of his shares in the corporation. A partnership is the functional owner of partnership property and a partner is the owner of his interest in the partnership.

As compared to ordinary property interests, a partnership interest is conditioned in one very important respect. Normally, the owner of a property interest can freely sell it, and a creditor can freely levy on it. Under U.P.A. Section 18(g), however, no person can become a partner without the consent of all the partners. It follows that unless the partnership agreement otherwise provides, a partner cannot make a transfer of his partnership interest that would substitute the transferee as a partner in the transferor's place. Correspondingly, a creditor can neither levy on a partnership interest in such a way as to be substituted as a partner, nor recover his debt by selling the interest to a third party who will be substituted as a partner. Nevertheless, a partnership interest is assignable. The assignee does not become a partner (unless all the other partners consent), and has no right to information about the partnership and no right to inspect the partnership books. However, while the partnership continues the assignee has a right to receive the profits to which the assigning partner would otherwise be entitled, and on dissolution the assignee has a right to receive the assigning partner's interest. According to A. Bromberg, supra, at 240, partnership interests have a fairly high degree of assignability despite the limitations on the rights of an assignee.

———

SECTION 7. THE PARTNER'S DUTY OF LOYALTY

UNIFORM PARTNERSHIP ACT §§ 20, 21

[See Statutory Supplement]

π   Δ
MEINHARD v. SALMON
New York Court of Appeals, 1928.
249 N.Y. 458, 164 N.E. 545.

Appeal from a judgment of the Appellate Division of the Supreme Court in the first judicial department, entered June 28, 1928, *P.C.* modifying and affirming as modified a judgment in favor of plaintiff entered upon the report of a referee.

CARDOZO, Ch. J. On April 10, 1902, Louisa M. Gerry leased *FACTS* to the defendant Walter J. Salmon the premises known as the Hotel *Lease—* Bristol at the northwest corner of Forty-second street and Fifth avenue *hotel 20 yrs* in the city of New York. The lease was for a term of twenty years, *to a* commencing May 1, 1902, and ending April 30, 1922. The lessee *to change* undertook to change the hotel building for use as shops and offices at *to offices &* a cost of $200,000. Alterations and additions were to be accretions to *shops* the land. *(200,000)*

Salmon, while in course of treaty with the lessor as to the execution of the lease, was in course of treaty with Meinhard, the *π= loaned* plaintiff, for the necessary funds. The result was a joint venture with *lessee the* terms embodied in a writing. Meinhard was to pay to Salmon half of *funds →* the moneys requisite to reconstruct, alter, manage and operate the *lessee to* property. Salmon was to pay to Meinhard 40 per cent of the net *pay π 40%* profits for the first five years of the lease and 50 per cent for the years *of net profits* thereafter. If there were losses, each party was to bear them equally. *first 5 yrs* Salmon, however, was to have sole power to "manage, lease, underlet *+ 50% after* and operate" the building. There were to be certain pre-emptive *losses= to* rights for each in the contingency of death. *bear equally*
Δ to have
sole mgmt
rights

The two were coadventurers, subject to fiduciary duties akin to those of partners (King v. Barnes, 109 N.Y. 267). As to this we are all agreed. The heavier weight of duty rested, however, upon *early* Salmon. He was a coadventurer with Meinhard, but he was manager *years =* as well. During the early years of the enterprise, the building, *a loss* reconstructed, was operated at a loss. If the relation had then ended, Meinhard as well as Salmon would have carried a heavy burden. *later =* Later the profits became large with the result that for each of the *large profits* investors there came a rich return. For each, the venture had its phases of fair weather and of foul. The two were in it jointly, for better or for worse.

When the lease was near its end, Elbridge T. Gerry had become the owner of the reversion. He owned much other property in the neighborhood, one lot adjoining the Bristol Building on Fifth avenue and four lots on Forty-second street. He had a plan to lease the entire tract for a long term to some one who would destroy the buildings then existing, and put up another in their place. In the latter part of 1921, he submitted such a project to several capitalists and dealers. He was unable to carry it through with any of them. Then, in January, 1922, with less than four months of the lease to run, he approached the defendant Salmon. The result was a new lease to the Midpoint Realty Company, which is owned and controlled by Salmon, a lease covering the whole tract, and involving a huge outlay. The term is to be twenty years, but successive covenants for renewal will extend it to a maximum of eighty years at the will of either party. The existing buildings may remain unchanged for seven years. They are then to be torn down, and a new building to cost $3,000,000 is to be placed upon the site. The rental, which under the Bristol lease was only $55,000, is to be from $350,000 to $475,000 for the properties so combined. Salmon personally guaranteed the performance by the lessee of the covenants of the new lease until such time as the new building had been completed and fully paid for.

The lease between Gerry and the Midpoint Realty Company was signed and delivered on January 25, 1922. Salmon had not told Meinhard anything about it. Whatever his motive may have been, he had kept the negotiations to himself. Meinhard was not informed even of the bare existence of a project. The first that he knew of it was in February when the lease was an accomplished fact. He then made demand on the defendants that the lease be held in trust as an asset of the venture, making offer upon the trial to share the personal obligations incidental to the guaranty. The demand was followed by refusal, and later by this suit. A referee gave judgment for the plaintiff, limiting the plaintiff's interest in the lease, however, to 25 per cent. The limitation was on the theory that the plaintiff's equity was to be restricted to one-half of so much of the value of the lease as was contributed or represented by the occupation of the Bristol site. Upon cross-appeals to the Appellate Division, the judgment was modified so as to enlarge the equitable interest to one-half of the whole lease. With this enlargement of plaintiff's interest, there went, of course, a corresponding enlargement of his attendant obligations. The case is now here on an appeal by the defendants.

Joint adventurers, like copartners, owe to one another, while the enterprise continues, the duty of the finest loyalty. Many forms of conduct permissible in a workaday world for those acting at arm's length, are forbidden to those bound by fiduciary ties. A trustee is held to something stricter than the morals of the market place. Not honesty alone, but the punctilio of an honor the most sensitive, is then the standard of behavior. As to this there has developed a tradition that is unbending and inveterate. Uncompromising rigidity has been the attitude of courts of equity when petitioned to undermine the rule of undivided loyalty by the "disintegrating erosion" of particular exceptions (Wendt v. Fischer, 243 N.Y. 439, 444). Only thus has the level of conduct for fiduciaries been kept at a level higher than that trodden by the crowd. It will not consciously be lowered by any judgment of this court.

The owner of the reversion, Mr. Gerry, had vainly striven to find a tenant who would favor his ambitious scheme of demolition and construction. Baffled in the search, he turned to the defendant Salmon in possession of the Bristol, the keystone of the project. He figured to himself beyond a doubt that the man in possession would prove a likely customer. To the eye of an observer, Salmon held the lease as owner in his own right, for himself and no one else. In fact he held it as a fiduciary, for himself and another, sharers in a common venture. If this fact had been proclaimed, if the lease by its terms had run in favor of a partnership, Mr. Gerry, we may fairly assume, would have laid before the partners, and not merely before one of them, his plan of reconstruction. The pre-emptive privilege, or, better, the pre-emptive opportunity, that was thus an incident of the enterprise, Salmon appropriated to himself in secrecy and silence. He might have warned Meinhard that the plan had been submitted, and that either would be free to compete for the award. If he had done this, we do not need to say whether he would have been under a duty, if successful in the competition, to hold the lease so acquired for the benefit of a venture then about to end, and thus prolong by indirection its responsibilities and duties. The trouble about his conduct is that he excluded his coadventurer from any chance to compete, from any chance to enjoy the opportunity for benefit that had come to him alone by virtue of his agency. This chance, if nothing more, he was under a duty to concede. The price of its denial is an extension of the trust at the option and for the benefit of the one whom he excluded.

No answer is it to say that the chance would have been of little value even if seasonably offered. Such a calculus of probabilities is beyond the science of the chancery. Salmon, the real estate operator, might have been preferred to Meinhard, the woolen merchant. On the other hand, Meinhard might have offered better terms, or reinforced his offer by alliance with the wealth of others. Perhaps he might even have persuaded the lessor to renew the Bristol lease alone, postponing for a time, in return for higher rentals, the improvement of adjoining lots. We know that even under the lease as made the time for the enlargement of the building was delayed for seven years. All these opportunities were cut away from him through another's intervention. He knew that Salmon was the manager. As the time drew near for the expiration of the lease, he would naturally assume from silence, if from nothing else, that the lessor was willing to extend it for a term of years, or at least to let it stand as a lease from year to year. Not impossibly the lessor would have done so, whatever his protestations of unwillingness, if Salmon had not given assent to a project more attractive. At all events, notice of termination, even if not necessary, might seem, not unreasonably, to be something to be looked for, if the business was over and another tenant was to enter. In the absence of such notice, the matter of an extension was one that would naturally be attended to by the manager of the enterprise, and not neglected altogether. At least, there was nothing in the situation to give warning to any one that while the lease was still in being, there had come to the manager an offer of extension which he had locked within his breast to be utilized by himself alone. The very fact that Salmon was in control with exclusive powers of direction charged him the more obviously with the duty of disclosure, since only through disclosure could opportunity be equalized. If he might cut off renewal by a purchase for his own benefit when four months were to pass before the lease would have an end, he might do so with equal right while there remained as many years (cf. Mitchell v. Reed, 61 N.Y. 123, 127). He might steal a march on his comrade under cover of the darkness, and then hold the captured ground. Loyalty and comradeship are not so easily abjured.

[margin handwriting: Salmon had a duty to Disclose to π]

Little profit will come from a dissection of the precedents. None precisely similar is cited in the briefs of counsel. What is similar in many, or so it seems to us, is the animating principle. Authority is, of course, abundant that one partner may not appropriate to his own use a renewal of a lease, though its term is to begin at the expiration of the partnership (Mitchell v. Read, 61 N.Y. 123; 84 N.Y. 556). The lease at hand with its many changes is not strictly a renewal. Even so, the standard of loyalty for those in trust relations is without the fixed divisions of a graduated scale. There is indeed a dictum in one of our decisions that a partner, though he may not renew a lease, may purchase the reversion if he acts openly and fairly (Anderson v. Lemon, 8 N.Y. 236; cf. White & Tudor, Leading Cases in Equity [9th ed.], vol. 2, p. 642; Bevan v. Webb, 1905, 1 Ch. 620; Griffith v. Owen, 1907, 1 Ch. 195, 204, 205). It is a dictum, and no more, for on the ground that he had acted slyly he was charged as a trustee. The holding is thus in favor of the conclusion that a purchase as well as a lease will succumb to the infection of secrecy and silence. Against the dictum in that case, moreover, may be set the opinion of DWIGHT, C., in Mitchell v. Read, where there is a dictum to the contrary (61 N.Y. at p. 143). To say that a partner is free without restriction to buy in the reversion of the property where the business is conducted is to say in effect that he may strip the good will of its chief element of value, since good will is largely dependent upon continuity of possession (Matter of Brown, 242 N.Y. 1, 7.) Equity refuses to confine within the bounds of classified transactions its precept of a loyalty that is undivided and unselfish. . . .

[margin handwriting: Partner may purchase a reversion on lease if does so openly & fairly]

We have no thought to hold that Salmon was guilty of a conscious purpose to defraud. Very likely he assumed in all good faith that with the approaching end of the venture he might ignore his coadventurer and take the extension for himself. He had given to the enterprise time and labor as well as money. He had made it a success. Meinhard, who had given money, but neither time nor labor, had already been richly paid. There might seem to be something grasping in his insistence upon more. Such recriminations are not unusual when coadventurers fall out. They are not without their force if conduct is to be judged by the common standards of competitors.

That is not to say that they have pertinency here. Salmon had put himself in a position in which thought of self was to be renounced, however hard the abnegation. He was much more than a coadventurer. He was a managing coadventurer (Clegg v. Edmondson, 8 D.M. & G. 787, 807). For him and for those like him, the rule of undivided loyalty is relentless and supreme (Wendt v. Fischer, supra; Munson v. Syracuse, etc., R.R. Co., 103 N.Y. 58, 74). A different question would be here if there were lacking any nexus of relation between the business conducted by the manager and the opportunity brought to him as an incident of management (Dean v. MacDowell, 8 Ch. D. 345, 354; Aas v. Benham, 1891, 2 Ch. 244, 258; Latta v. Kilbourn, 150 U.S. 524). For this problem, as for most, there are distinctions of degree. If Salmon had received from Gerry a proposition to lease a building at a location far removed, he might have held for himself the privilege thus acquired, or so we shall assume. Here the subject-matter of the new lease was an extension and enlargement of the subject-matter of the old one. A managing coadventurer appropriating the benefit of such a lease without warning to his partner might fairly expect to be reproached with conduct that was underhand, or lacking, to say the least, in reasonable candor, if the partner were to surprise him in the act of signing the new instrument. Conduct subject to that reproach does not receive from equity a healing benediction.

A question remains as to the form and extent of the equitable interest to be allotted to the plaintiff. The trust as declared has been held to attach to the lease which was in the name of the defendant corporation. We think it ought to attach at the option of the defendant Salmon to the shares of stock which were owned by him or were under his control. The difference may be important if the lessee shall wish to execute an assignment of the lease, as it ought to be free to do with the consent of the lessor. On the other hand, an equal division of the shares might lead to other hardships. It might take away from Salmon the power of control and management which under the plan of the joint venture he was to have from first to last. The number of shares to be allotted to the plaintiff should, therefore, be reduced to such an extent as may be necessary to preserve to the defendant Salmon the expected measure of dominion. To that end an extra share should be added to his half.

Subject to this adjustment, we agree with the Appellate Division that the plaintiff's equitable interest is to be measured by the value of half of the entire lease, and not merely by half of some undivided part. A single building covers the whole area. Physical division is impracticable along the lines of the Bristol site, the keystone of the whole. Division of interests and burdens is equally impracticable. Salmon, as tenant under the new lease, or as guarantor of the performance of the tenant's obligations, might well protest if Meinhard, claiming an equitable interest, had offered to assume a liability not equal to Salmon's, but only half as great. He might justly insist that the lease must be accepted by his coadventurer in such form as it had been given, and not constructively divided into imaginary fragments. What must be yielded to the one may be demanded by the other. The lease as it has been executed is single and entire. If confusion has resulted from the union of adjoining parcels, the trustee who consented to the union must bear the inconvenience (Hart v. Ten Eyck, 2 Johns. Ch. 62). . . .

[Three judges dissented. Andrews, J., who wrote the dissenting opinion, agreed that "(w)ere this a general partnership I should have little doubt as to the correctness of this result assuming the new lease to be an offshoot of the old," but concluded that the parties joint venture "had in view a very limited object and was to end at a limited time."]

SECTION 8. DISSOLUTION (I): DISSOLUTION BY RIGHTFUL ELECTION

UNIFORM PARTNERSHIP ACT
§§ 29, 30, 31(1), 38(1), 40

[See Statutory Supplement]

LEWIS, THE UNIFORM PARTNERSHIP ACT, 24 Yale L.J. 617, 626–27 (1915). "The subject of the dissolution and winding up of a partnership is involved in considerable confusion principally because of the various ways in which the word 'dissolution' is employed. The term sometimes designates the completion of the winding up of partnership affairs. This, the end of the association, should be called the termination of the partnership. Again the term is sometimes used to designate the process of liquidation or winding up. . . . Lastly, the term is employed as designating a change in the relation of the partners caused by any partner ceasing to be associated in the carrying on of the business. As thus used 'dissolution' does not terminate the partnership, it merely ends the carrying on of the business in that partnership. The partnership continues until the winding up of partnership affairs is completed. This last is the sense in which the term 'dissolution' is used in the Act."

DREIFUERST v. DREIFUERST

Wisconsin Court of Appeals, 1979.
90 Wis.2d 566, 280 N.W.2d 335.

Before BROWN, P.J., BODE, J., and ROBERT W. HANSEN, Reserve Judge.

 BROWN, P.J. The plaintiffs and the defendant, all brothers, formed a partnership. The partnership operated two feed mills, one located at St. Cloud, Wisconsin and one located at Elkhart Lake,

Wisconsin. There were no written Articles of Partnership governing this partnership.

On October 4, 1975, the plaintiffs served the defendant with a notice of dissolution and wind-up of the partnership. The action for dissolution and wind-up was commenced on January 27, 1976. The dissolution complaint alleged that the plaintiffs elected to dissolve the partnership. There was no allegation of fault, expulsion or contravention of an alleged agreement as grounds for dissolution. The parties were unable, however, to agree to a winding-up of the partnership.

Hearings on the dissolution were held on October 18, 1976 and March 4, 1977. Testimony was presented regarding the value of the partnership assets and each partner's equity. At the March 4, 1977 hearing, the defendant requested that the partnership be sold pursuant to sec. 178.33(1), Stats., and that the court allow a sale, at which time the partners would bid on the entire property. By such sale, the plaintiffs could continue to run the business under a new partnership, and the defendant's partnership equity could be satisfied in cash.

On February 20, 1978, the trial court, by written decision, denied the defendant's request for a sale and instead divided the partnership assets in-kind according to the valuation presented by the plaintiffs. The plaintiffs were given the physical assets from the Elkhart Lake mill, and the defendant was given the physical assets from the St. Cloud mill. The defendant appeals this order and judgment dividing the assets in-kind.

Under sec. 178.25(1), Stats., a partnership is dissolved when any partner ceases to be associated in the carrying on of the business. The partnership is not terminated, but continues, until the winding-up of partnership is complete. Sec. 178.25(2), Stats. The action started by the plaintiffs, in this case, was an action for dissolution and wind-up. The plaintiffs were not continuing the partnership and, therefore, secs. 178.36 and 178.37, Stats.,[3] do not apply. The sole question in this case is whether, in the absence of a written agreement to the contrary, a partner, upon dissolution and wind-up of the partnership, can force a sale of the partnership assets.

At the outset, we note, and the parties agree, that the appellant was not in contravention of the partnership agreement since there was no partnership agreement. The partnership was a partnership at will. They also agree there was no written agreement governing distribution of partnership assets upon dissolution and wind-up. The dispute, in this case, is over the authority of the trial court to order in-kind distribution in the absence of any agreement of the partners.

Section 178.33(1), Stats., provides:

> When dissolution is caused in any way, except in contravention of the partnership agreement, each partner, as against his copartners and all persons claiming through them in respect to their interests in the partnership, *unless otherwise agreed*, may have

---

3. Sections 178.36 and 178.37 deal with cases where the partnership is not wound up, but continues after one partner leaves.

the partnership property applied to discharge its liabilities, and the surplus applied to pay *in cash* the net amount owing to the respective partners. [Emphasis supplied.]

The appellant contends this statute grants him the right to force a sale of the partnership assets in order to obtain his fair share of the partnership assets in cash upon dissolution. He claims that in the absence of an agreement of the partners to in-kind distribution, the trial court had no authority to distribute the assets in-kind. He is entitled to an in-cash settlement after judicial sale.

The respondents contend the statute does not entitle the appellant to force a sale and grants the trial court the power to distribute the assets in-kind if in-kind distribution is equitably possible and doesn't jeopardize the rights of creditors.

We do not believe that the statute can be read in any way to permit in-kind distribution unless the partners agree to in-kind distribution or unless there is a partnership agreement calling for in-kind distribution at the time of dissolution and wind-up.

A partnership at will is a partnership which has no definite term or particular undertaking and can rightfully be dissolved by the express will of any partner. Sec. 178.26(1)(b), Stats.; J. Crane and A. Bromberg, Law of Partnership § 74(b) (1968) [hereinafter cited as Crane and Bromberg]. In the present case, the respondents wanted to dissolve the partnership. This being a partnership at will, they could rightfully dissolve this partnership with or without the consent of the appellant. In addition, the respondents have never claimed the appellant was in violation of any partnership agreement. Therefore, neither the appellant nor the respondents have wrongfully dissolved the partnership.

Unless otherwise agreed, partners who have not wrongfully dissolved a partnership have a right to wind up the partnership. Sec. 178.32, Stats. Winding-up is the process of settling partnership affairs after dissolution. Winding-up is often called liquidation and involves reducing the assets to cash to pay creditors and distribute to partners the value of their respective interests. Crane and Bromberg, supra, §§ 73 and 80(c). Thus, lawful dissolution (or dissolution which is caused in any way except in contravention of the partnership agreement) gives each partner the right to have the business liquidated and his share of the surplus paid *in cash.* Young v. Cooper, 30 Tenn.App. 55, 203 S.W.2d 376 (1947); sec. 178.33(1), Stats.; Crane and Bromberg, supra, § 83A. In-kind distribution is permissible only in very limited circumstances. If the partnership agreement permits in-kind distribution upon dissolution or wind-up or if, at any time prior to wind-up, all partners agree to in-kind distribution, the court may order in-kind distribution. Logoluso v. Logoluso, 43 Cal.Rptr. 678 (1965); Gathright v. Fulton, 122 Va. 17, 94 S.E. 191, 194 (1917). While at least one court has permitted in-kind distribution, absent an agreement by all partners, Rinke v. Rinke, 330 Mich. 615, 48 N.W.2d 201 (1951), the court's holding in that case was limited. In *Rinke,* the court stated:

The decree of the trial court provided for dividing the assets of the partnerships rather than for the sale thereof and the distribution of cash proceeds. Appellants insist that such method of procedure is erroneous and [not] contemplated by the uniform partnership act. Attention is directed to Section 38 of said act, C.L. 1948, § 449.38, Stat.Ann. § 20.38. Construing together pertinent provisions of the statute leads to the conclusion that it was not the intention of the legislature in the enactment of the Uniform Partnership Act to impose a mandatory requirement that, under all circumstances, the assets of a dissolved partnership shall be sold and the money received therefor divided among those entitled to it, particularly so, as in the case at bar, where there are no debts to be paid from the proceeds. *The situation disclosed by the record in the present case is somewhat unusual in that no one other than the former partners is interested in the assets of the businesses. In view of this situation and of the nature of the assets, we* think that the trial court was correct in apportioning them to the partners. There is no showing that appellants have been prejudiced thereby. [Emphasis supplied.] 330 Mich. at 628, 48 N.W.2d at 207.

The Michigan court's holding was limited to situations where: (1) there were no creditors to be paid from the proceeds, (2) ordering a sale would be senseless since no one other than the partners would be interested in the assets of the business, and (3) an in-kind distribution was fair to all partners.

That is not the case here. There was no showing that there were no creditors who would be paid from the proceeds, nor was there a showing that no one other than the partners would be interested in the assets. These factors are important if an in-kind distribution is to be allowed. Section 178.33(1) and § 38 of the Uniform Partnership Act are intended to protect creditors as well as partners. In-kind distributions may affect a creditor's right to collect the debt owed since the assets of the partnership, as a whole, may be worth more than the assets once divided up. Thus, the creditor's ability to collect from the individual partners may be jeopardized. Secondly, if others are interested in the assets, a sale provides a more accurate means of establishing the market value of the assets and, thus, better assuring each partner his share in the value of the assets. Where only the partners are interested in the assets, a fair value can be determined without the necessity of a sale. The sale would be merely the partners bidding with each other without any competition. This process could be accomplished through negotiations or at trial with the court as a final arbitrator of the value of the assets. With these policy considerations in mind, we think the Michigan court's holding in *Rinke* was limited to the facts of that case. Those facts not being present in this case, we do not feel an in-kind distribution in this case was proper.

However, even assuming the respondents in this case can show that there are no creditors to be paid, no one other than the partners are interested in the assets, and in-kind distribution would be fair to all partners, we cannot read § 38 of the Uniform Partnership Act or sec.

[handwritten margin note: all partners must agree to in-kind distribution]

178.33(1), Stats. (the Wisconsin equivalent), as permitting an in-kind distribution under any circumstances, unless all partners agree. The statute and § 38 of the Uniform Partnership Act are quite clear that if a partner may force liquidation, he is entitled to his share of the partnership assets, after creditors are paid *in cash.* To the extent that Rinke v. Rinke, supra, creates an exception to cash distribution, we decline to adopt that exception. We, therefore, must hold the trial court erred in ordering an in-kind distribution of the assets of the partnership.

[handwritten margin note: can he force a sale?]

The last question that arises is whether the appellant can force an actual sale of the assets or whether the trial court can determine the fair market value of the assets and order the respondents to pay the appellant in cash an amount equal to his share in the assets.

[handwritten margin note: yes — to find true mkt value unless otherwise agreed]

As discussed above, a sale is the best means of determining the true fair market value of the assets. Generally, liquidation envisions some form of sale. Since the statutes provide that, unless otherwise agreed, any partner who has not wrongfully dissolved the partnership has the right to wind up the partnership and force liquidation, he likewise has a right to force a sale, unless otherwise agreed. Fortugno v. Hudson Manure Co., 51 N.J.Super. 482, 144 A.2d 207, 218–19 (1958); Young v. Cooper, 30 Tenn.App. 55, 203 S.W.2d 376 (1947). See also Crane and Bromberg, supra, § 83A; 4 Vill.L.Rev. 457 (1959). While judicial sales in some instances may cause economic hardships, these hardships can be avoided by the use of partnership agreements.

By the Court.—Judgment reversed and cause remanded for further proceedings not inconsistent with this opinion.

A. BROMBERG, CRANE & BROMBERG ON PARTNERSHIP 476–77 (1968).

"A partner may compel liquidation after dissolution 'unless otherwise agreed.' The agreement may be made at the time of dissolution, although this presents practical obstacles. Or it may be embodied in the partnership agreement, where dissolution can usually be considered long in advance and therefore treated with more detachment.

"[Agreements to continue the partnership after dissolution, which are usually referred to as continuation agreements] are most commonly drawn for dissolution by death. . . . [b]ut they can be made equally applicable to any kind of dissolution, and even to a partnership at will. The main elements in such an agreement are the events on which it comes into effect, the method of disposition of the outgoing partner's interest, and the compensation to him.

"An agreement of this sort is the only reliable way of assuring the preservation of a partnership business. It is likely to offer the best price to the outgoing interest. In addition, it can have important income tax effects, and can (contrary to general impression) provide almost any desired degree of continuity for the partnership entity."

SECTION 9. DISSOLUTION (II): DISSOLUTION BY JUDICIAL DECREE AND WRONGFUL DISSOLUTION

UNIFORM PARTNERSHIP ACT §§ 31(2), 32, 38

[See Statutory Supplement]

DRASHNER v. SORENSON

Supreme Court of South Dakota, 1954.
75 S.D. 247, 63 N.W.2d 255.

SMITH, P.J.   In January 1951 the plaintiff, C.H. Drashner, and defendants, A.D. Sorenson and Jacob P. Deis, associated themselves as co-owners in the real estate, loan and insurance business at Rapid City. For a consideration of $7500 they purchased the real estate and insurance agency known as J. Schumacher Co. located in an office room on the ground floor of the Alex Johnson Hotel building.   The entire purchase price was advanced for the partnership by the defendants, but at the time of trial $3,000 of that sum had been repaid to them by the partnership.   Although, as will appear from facts presently to be outlined, their operations were not unsuccessful, differences arose and on June 15, 1951 plaintiff commenced this action in which he sought an accounting, dissolution and winding up of the partnership.   The answer and counterclaim of defendants prayed for like relief.

The cause came on for trial September 4, 1951.   The court among others made the following findings.   VII.   "That thereafter the plaintiff violated the terms of said partnership agreement, in that he demanded a larger share of the income of the said partnership than he was entitled to receive under the terms of said partnership agreement; that the plaintiff was arrested for reckless driving and served a term in jail for said offense;   that the plaintiff demanded that the defendants permit him to draw money for his own personal use out of the moneys held in escrow by the partnership; that the plaintiff spent a large amount of time during business hours in the Brass Rail Bar in Rapid City, South Dakota, and other bars, and neglected his duties in connection with the business of the said partnership. . . .   That the plaintiff, by his actions hereinbefore set forth, has made it impossible to carry on the partnership."   The conclusions adopted read as follows: I "That the defendants are entitled to continue the partnership and have the value of the plaintiff's interest in the partnership business determined, upon the filing and approval of a good and sufficient bond, conditioned upon the release of the plaintiff from any liability arising out of the said partnership, and further conditioned upon the payment by the defendants to the plaintiff of the value of plaintiffs' interest in the partnership as determined by the Court."   II

"That in computing the value of the plaintiff's interest in the said partnership, the value of the good will of the business shall not be considered." III "That the value of the partnership shall be finally determined upon a hearing before this Court, ..." and IV "That the plaintiff shall be entitled to receive one-third of the value of the partnership property owned by the partnership on the 12th day of September, 1951, not including the good will of the business, after the payment of the liabilities of the partnership and the payment to the defendants of the invested capital in the sum of $4,500.00." Judgment was accordingly entered dissolving the partnership as of September 12, 1951.

After hearing at a later date the court found: I "That the value of the said partnership property on the 12th day of September, 1951, was the sum of Four Thousand Four Hundred Ninety-eight and 90/100 Dollars ($4498.90), and on said date there was due and owing by the partnership for accountant's services the sum of Four Hundred Eighty Dollars ($480.00), and that on said date the sum of Four Thousand Five Hundred Dollars ($4500.00) of the capital invested by the defendants had not been returned to the defendants." and II "That there is not sufficient partnership property to reimburse the defendants for their invested capital." Thereupon the court decreed "that the plaintiff had no interest in the property of the said partnership", and that the defendants were the sole owners thereof.

The assignments of error are predicated upon insufficiency of the evidence to support the findings and conclusions. Of these assignments, only those which question whether the court was warranted in finding that (a) the plaintiff caused the dissolution wrongfully, and (b) the value of the partnership property, exclusive of good will, was $4498.90 on the 12th day of September, 1951, merit discussion. A preliminary statement is necessary to place these issues in their framework.

The agreement of the parties contemplated an association which would continue at least until the $7500 advance of defendants had been repaid from the gross earnings of the business. Hence, it was not a partnership at will. Vangel v. Vangel, 116 Cal.App.2d 615, 254 P.2d 919; Zeibak v. Nasser, 12 Cal.2d 1, 82 P.2d 375. In apparent recognition of that fact, both plaintiff and defendants sought dissolution in contravention of the partnership agreement, see SDC 49.0603(2) under SDC 49.0604(1)(d) on the ground that the adverse party had caused the dissolution wrongfully by willfully and persistently committing a breach of the partnership agreement, and by so conducting himself in matters relating to the partnership business as to render impracticable the carrying on of the business in partnership with him.

[The court here quoted U.P.A. Section 38(2)].

From this background we turn to a consideration of the evidence from which the trial court inferred that plaintiff caused the dissolution wrongfully.

The breach between the parties resulted from a continuing controversy over the right of plaintiff to withdraw sufficient money from the partnership to defray his living expenses. Plaintiff was dependent upon his earnings for the support of his family. The defendants had other resources. Plaintiff claimed that he was to be permitted to draw from the earnings of the partnership a sufficient amount to support himself and family. The defendants asserted that there was a definite arrangement for the allocation of the income of the partnership and there was no agreement for withdrawal by plaintiff of more than his allotment under that plan. Defendants' version of the facts was corroborated by a written admission of plaintiff offered in evidence. From evidence thus sharply in conflict, the trial court made a finding, reading as follows: "That the oral partnership agreement between the parties provided that each of the three partners were to draw as compensation one-third of one-half of the commissions earned upon sales made by the partners; that the other one-half of the commissions earned on sales made by the partners and one-half of the commissions earned upon sales made by salesmen employed by the partnership, together with the earnings from the insurance business carried on by the partnership, was to be placed in a fund to be used for the payment of the operating expenses of the partnership, and after the payment of such operating expenses to be used to reimburse the defendants for the capital advanced in the purchase of the Julius Schumacher business and the capital advanced in the sum of Eight Hundred Dollars ($800.00) for the operating expenses of the business."

As an outgrowth of this crucial difference, there was evidence from which a court could reasonably believe that plaintiff neglected the business and spent too much time in a nearby bar during business hours. At a time when plaintiff had overdrawn his partners and was also indebted to one of defendants for personal advances, he requested $100 and his request was refused. In substance he then said, according to the testimony of the defendant Deis, that he would see that he "gets some money to run on", if they "didn't give it to him he was going to dissolve the partnership and see that he got it." Thereafter plaintiff pressed his claims through counsel, and eventually brought this action to dissolve the partnership. The claim so persistently asserted was contrary to the partnership agreement found by the court.

The foregoing picture of the widening breach between the parties is drawn almost entirely from the evidence of defendants. Of course, plaintiff's version of the agreement of the parties, and of the ensuing differences, if believed, would have supported findings of a different order by the trier of the fact. It cannot be said, we think, that the trial court acted unreasonably in believing defendants, and we think it equally clear the court could reasonably conclude that the insistent and continuing demands of the plaintiff and his attendant conduct rendered it reasonably impracticable to carry on the business in partnership with him. It follows, we are of the opinion, the evidence supports the finding that plaintiff caused the dissolution wrongfully. Zeibak v. Nasser, 12 Cal.2d 1, 82 P.2d 375; Owen v. Cohen, 19 Cal.

2d 147, 119 P.2d 713; Meherin v. Meherin, 93 Cal.App.2d 459, 209 P.2d 36; and Vangel v. Vangel, 116 Cal.App.2d 615, 254 P.2d 919.

This brings us to a consideration of the sufficiency of the evidence to support the finding of the court that the property of the partnership was of the value of $4498.90 as of the date of dissolution.

Bitter complaint is made because the trial court refused to consider the good will of this business in arriving at its conclusion. The feeling of plaintiff is understandable. These partners must have placed a very high estimate upon the value of the good will of this agency because they paid Mr. Schumacher $7500 to turn over that office with its very moderate fixtures and its listing of property, together with an agreement that he would not engage in the business in Rapid City for at least two years. No doubt they attached some of this good will value to the location of the business which was under only a month to month letting. Cf. 38 C.J.S., Good Will, § 3, page 951; In re Brown's Will, 242 N.Y. 1, 150 N.E. 581, 44 A.L.R. 510, at page 513. Their estimate of value was borne out by the subsequent history of the business. Its real estate commissions, earned but only partly received, grossed $21,528.25 and its insurance commissions grossed $661.21 in the period January 15 to August 31, 1951. In that period the received commissions paid all expenses, including the commissions of salesmen, retired $3,000 of the $7500 purchase price advanced by defendants, and all of $800 of working capital so advanced, allowed the parties to withdraw $1453.02 each, and accumulated a cash balance of $2221.43. In addition the partnership has commissions due. . . . Notwithstanding this indication of the great value of the good will of this business, the statute does not require the court to take it into consideration in valuing the property of the business in these circumstances. The statute provides such a sanction for causing the dissolution of a partnership wrongfully. SDC 49.0610(2)(c)(2) quoted supra. The court applied the statute. . . .

That the $1500 value placed on [the assets other than good will] was conservative we do not question. However, after mature study and reflection we have concluded that the court's finding is not against the clear weight of the evidence appearing in this record. Hence we are not at liberty to disturb it.

The brief of plaintiff includes some discussion of his right to a share in the profits from the date of the dissolution until the final judgment. It does not appear from the record that this claim was presented to the trial court, or that the net profit of the business during that period was evidenced. Because that issue was not presented below, it is not before us.

The judgment of the trial court is affirmed.

All the Judges concur.

SECTION 10. LIMITED PARTNERSHIPS

(a) THE UNIFORM LIMITED PARTNERSHIP ACTS

Over the course of time, the Commissioners on Uniform State Laws have promulgated several uniform limited partnership acts.

In 1916, the Commissioners promulgated the original Uniform Limited Partnership Act. It was adopted in every state except Louisiana.

In 1976, the Commissioners promulgated a replacement for the Uniform Limited Partnership Act, called the Revised Uniform Partnership Act. The new Act modernized the prior Act, picked up some modifications of the original Act that had been made in adopting states, and generally reflected the influence of the corporate model. It has been widely but not universally adopted.

In 1985, the Commissioners amended the Revised Uniform Limited Partnership Act in a number of important respects. The states are still in the process of adopting these amendments.

In the balance of this Section, the 1916 Act, and the 1976 Act as amended in 1985, will be referred to as the ULPA and the RULPA, respectively.

(b) FORMATION OF A LIMITED PARTNERSHIP

REVISED UNIFORM LIMITED PARTNERSHIP ACT §§ 101, 201

[See Statutory Supplement]

Unlike general partnerships, limited partnerships are basically creatures of statute, although they have nonstatutory historical antecedents. Section 1 of the ULPA defined a limited partnership as "a partnership formed by two or more persons under the provisions of Section 2, having as members one or more general partners and one or more limited partners." Section 2, in turn, provided that persons who desire to form a limited partnership must execute a certificate setting forth the name of the partnership, the names and residences of each member (including the limited partners), the contributions of the partners, and much other information, and must file the certificate in a designated state or county office.

RULPA § 101 carries forward the substance of ULPA Section 1. However, Section 201 drastically reduces the amount of information that must be contained in the certificate. Under Section 201, as amended, the certificate need only state the name of the limited partnership, the name and business address of each general partner, the latest date upon which the limited partnership is to dissolve, and the name and address of the agent for service of process. Thus under the RULPA, as amended, neither the identity of the limited partners nor the partnership's capitalization need be stated in the certificate.

(c) LIABILITY OF LIMITED PARTNERS

REVISED UNIFORM LIMITED PARTNERSHIP ACT
§§ 302, 303

[See Statutory Supplement]

NOTE ON RULPA § 303(a)

Prior to the 1985 amendments to the RULPA, § 303(a) of that Act read as follows:

> . . . [A] limited partner is not liable for the obligations of a limited partnership unless he is also a general partner or, in addition to the exercise of his rights and powers as a limited partner, he takes part in the control of the business. However, if the limited partner's participation in the control of the business is not substantially the same as the exercise of the powers of a general partner, he is liable only to persons who transact business with the limited partnership with actual knowledge of his participation in control.

This provision, or a close counterpart, is still in force in states that adopted the RULPA but have not yet adopted the 1985 amendments.

(d) NOTE ON LIMITED PARTNERSHIPS

1. In the last twenty years, many publicly held limited partnerships have been organized. The limited partnership interests in these limited partnerships were initially offered to the public through underwriters, like corporate securities, and in some cases then publicly traded on organized markets. Most or all of these enterprises were organized as limited partnerships rather than corporations so that investors could obtain the tax benefits associated with tax shelters. Although the 1986 Tax Reform Act severely limited both the availability and the benefits of tax shelters, the tax rates under that Act provide a new incentive to use limited partnerships rather than

publicly held corporations so as to avoid the so-called "double taxation" of income—once at the corporate level when the income is earned, and again at the shareholder level when the income is distributed as a dividend. However, under IRC § 7704 "publicly traded" partnerships are, with certain exceptions, taxed as corporations.

2. Section 1105 of the RULPA states that "[i]n any case not provided for in this Act the provisions of the Uniform Partnership Act govern." There are, however, several significant differences between the RULPA and the Uniform Partnership Act, beyond those required by the difference in the nature of the general and limited partnerships. For example, under Uniform Partnership Act §§ 29, 31, 32, the ceasing of any partner to be associated in carrying on the business causes dissolution, as does the death, bankruptcy, or wrongful conduct of a partner—although the business of the partnership can be continued if there was a prior agreement to that effect or if the dissolution was wrongful. In contrast, under RULPA §§ 101(3), 402, and 801(4), the death, bankruptcy, declaration of incompetence, removal, or withdrawal of a general partner does not cause dissolution if the certificate of limited partnership permits the business to be carried on by the remaining general partners and they do so.

Another difference between general and limited partnerships relates to the transferability of partnership interests. Under the Uniform Partnership Act a partner in a general partnership can assign his partnership interest, but the rights of the assignee are extremely limited, and a transferee cannot be substituted as a partner without the unanimous consent of the remaining partners, unless the partnership agreement otherwise provides. Furthermore, even if the partnership agreement does permit such a substitution, the substitution will cause a dissolution under Section 29. ULPA § 19 explicitly stated that a limited partner can make his transferee a substituted limited partner if the limited-partnership certificate so provides. RULPA § 704 carries the substance of that provision forward, and Section 702 explicitly provides that "[a]n assignment of a partnership interest does not dissolve a limited partnership. . . ." Furthermore, RULPA § 401, as amended, provides that additional general partners may be admitted as provided in writing in the partnership agreement, presumably without causing dissolution.

Chapter III

THE CORPORATE FORM

SECTION 1. DECIDING WHETHER TO INCORPORATE

(a) NONTAX CONSIDERATIONS

Most business enterprises today are organized as sole proprietorships, general partnerships, limited partnerships, or corporations. Assume that an individual or a group of individuals want to begin a business, and must select a form of organization. That decision will depend upon tax and nontax considerations. Conventionally, the most attractive nontax attributes of the corporate form are said to be limited liability, free transferability of ownership interests, continuity of existence, and centralized management. In analyzing these attributes, and their impact on the choice of form, it is useful to consider three types of cases: a business to be owned by one person, a business to be owned by a few owner-managers, and a business to be owned at least in part by members of the public, who will not participate in management.

1. *Limited liability.* Sole proprietors and general partners are personally liable for obligations that arise out of the conduct of their business. In contrast, the shareholder-owners of a corporation are not personally liable for the corporation's debts. See, e.g., Del. § 102(b)(6). This legal rule is conventionally expressed by the statement that shareholders have "limited liability." That term is something of a misnomer. Normally, shareholders have *no* personal liability for corporate obligations. "Limited liability" is a shorthand expression for the concept that a shareholder's exposure to loss is limited to the amount he paid or agreed to pay for his stock. The *managers* of a corporation also normally cannot be held personally liable for corporate obligations. As long as they act on the corporation's behalf and within their authority, with respect to liability they are treated like agents, not principals, even if they are owners as well as managers.[1] Limited partners also normally have limited liability.[2]

In practice, the difference between the various forms of business organization with respect to the attribute of limited liability may not

---

1. For purposes other than liability, however, directors may not be treated as agents, because the power to manage the corporation's business is characteristically vested in the board by statute, not merely by an act of the shareholders. See Chapter IV, Section 1, infra.

2. See Chapter II, Section 10(c), supra.

66

be quite as dramatic as it is in theory. Sole proprietors and general partners may be able to limit their contract liability through appropriate contractual provisions, and may be able to limit their tort liability through insurance. Owner-managers in a limited partnership may be able to avoid personal liability by forming a corporation to be the sole general partner. See Frigidaire Sales Corp. v. Union Properties, Inc., 88 Wash.2d 400, 562 P.2d 244 (1977).[3] Conversely, shareholders of a small corporation may find that credit won't be extended to their corporation unless they personally guarantee its debts. Shareholders may also become personally liable for corporate obligations by operation of certain common law or statutory rules. (See Section 8, infra.)

Nevertheless, it remains true that incorporation will shield owners from at least some and perhaps most or even all of the liabilities to which they would be exposed under the sole proprietorship or partnership forms. Because members of the public will normally not invest in ownership interests that carry the risk of personal liability, if a business is to be owned in part by members of the public it will almost invariably be put in either the corporate or limited partnership forms.

2. *Free transferability of interests.* The transferee of a partnership interest cannot be substituted as a partner without the unanimous consent of the remaining partners, unless the partnership agreement otherwise provides. In contrast, shares of corporate stock are freely transferable.[4] The ownership of a sole proprietorship is also freely transferable.

In practice, these legal differences may not be too significant. If a business is owned by several owner-managers, cooperation will be a very important aspect of the enterprise. Often, therefore, no one will want to purchase one owner-manager's interest if the other owner-managers object. Correspondingly, the owners themselves will typi-

3. However, if limited partners have voting rights, as they often do there may be a residual risk of personal liability. The following passage from a prospectus for the sale of limited partnership interests is typical:

It is contemplated that the Partnership will . . . conduct business in California, Colorado, Idaho, Nebraska, Oregon and Washington. Maintenance of limited liability will require compliance with legal requirements in such jurisdictions in which the Partnership . . . [conducts] business. Limitations on the liability of limited partners for the obligations of a limited partnership have not been clearly established in many jurisdictions. If it were determined that the right or exercise of the right by the limited partners as a group to remove or replace the General Partner, to make certain amendments to the Partnership Agreement or to take other action pursuant to the Partnership Agreement constituted "control" of the Partnership's business

for the purposes of the statutes of any relevant jurisdiction, a limited partner might be personally liable for Partnership obligations under the law of such jurisdiction.

Red Lion Inns Limited Partnership Prospectus, April 7, 1987, at 62.

This risk is minimized under Section 303 of the Revised Uniform Limited Partnership Act, as amended. That section provides that a limited partner who "participates in the control of the business" is liable only to those persons transacting business with the partnership who "reasonably believ[e], based on the limited partner's conduct, that the limited partner is a general partner."

4. In fact, a stock certificate—that is, a certificate evidencing that a certain person is the owner of a given number of shares—is a negotiable instrument. See U.C.C. §§ 8–102, 8–105(1). Accordingly, a transfer to a holder in due course cuts off most claims against the transferee.

cally want to restrict each others' right to transfer their interests, so as
not to risk being locked in with a colleague they haven't approved.
Thus for most businesses owned by a few owner-managers, the
partnership law restriction on the transferability of partnership interests reflects the owners' desires and expectations. Correspondingly, if
the owner-managers employ the corporate form, they can and often
will agree to restrict the transferability of their shares. See Chapter
VI, Section 5. (Conversely, if partners want to allow partnership
interests to be freely transferable, they can accomplish that objective
by a provision in the partnership agreement.)

If a business is to be owned by members of the public, free
transferability of ownership interests can be achieved by use of either
the limited partnership or the corporate form. A limited partner can
substitute his transferee in his place if the limited partnership agreement so provides, and such a provision is common in publicly held
limited partnerships.

Accordingly, the legal rules concerning the transferability of
ownership interests probably do not make very much difference in the
choice of form. However, a related business consideration may affect
that choice where an enterprise will have public investors. Public
investors prefer ownership interests that are traded on organized
markets that have depth, that is, the capability of absorbing proposed
trades more or less instantaneously. In the past, the trading markets
for limited-partnership interests have had less depth than the trading
markets for stock in comparably sized corporations. Furthermore,
most public investors probably were uncomfortable with limited partnership interests, partly because their attributes were not well-known,
and partly because of a residual threat of personal liability.[5] Historically, therefore, where public ownership was contemplated, limited
partnerships were a less attractive form than corporations, tax considerations aside.

3. *Continuity of existence.* A sole proprietorship has no legal
existence apart from that of its owner. A general partnership is
dissolved by such events as the death or bankruptcy of a partner, and
can be wrongfully dissolved by any partner at any time. In contrast,
the legal existence of a corporation is perpetual unless a shorter term
is stated in the certificate of incorporation.

On the other hand, the *business* of a partnership can continue even
after the partnership has been technically dissolved, if the partnership
agreement so provides. Continuity is even less of a problem in the
case of a limited partnership, because the death or bankruptcy of a
limited partner will not cause dissolution, and the death or bankruptcy
of a general partner will not cause dissolution if the agreement permits
the business to be carried on by the remaining general partners and
they do so. Furthermore, in considering the attribute of perpetual life
a distinction must be drawn between (i) a business enterprise and (ii)
the legal form in which the business enterprise is organized. Although the corporate legal form has perpetual existence, in practice

---

5. See note 3, supra.

the continuity of a business enterprise owned by only a few owner-managers, even if in corporate form, will depend on the continued participation of those owners.

4. *Centralized management.* Under the corporate statutes, a corporation is to be managed by, or under the direction of, a board of directors. An owner—that is, a shareholder—has no right to participate in the management of a corporation, and no power to act on its behalf. This attribute is known as *centralized management.* Centralized management, as such, is not unique to corporations. The management of a limited partnership is centralized in the general partners, and many general partnership agreements centralize management in designated partners.

There is, however, one respect in which the legal attributes of centralized management in the corporation and the partnership differ materially. A shareholder has no power to bind the corporation to a contract or to place it under other types of obligation. In contrast, a general partner does have such a power if he is acting in the usual course of the partnership business. The right of a partner to participate in the management of the partnership business can be varied by the partnership agreement, but the power of a partner acting in the usual course of business to bind the partnership cannot (although a partner who binds the partnership in violation of the partnership agreement will be obliged to indemnify his fellow partners against consequent losses).

A closely related advantage of the corporate form straddles the elements of liability and centralized management. A shareholder in a corporation can wear both an investor and a control hat without losing limited liability: By acting as an officer or director the shareholder can participate in the control of the corporation without becoming individually liable for the corporation's obligations. It is harder to accomplish that objective in a partnership. A general partner is always liable for partnership obligations. A limited partner who participates in the control of a limited partnership may become liable for the partnership's obligations.

5. *Cost and simplicity.* As a practical matter, cost and simplicity are likely to be very important considerations for a single owner or a small group of owners. Organizing a corporation or a limited partnership is a complex matter, normally requiring an attorney's services and filing fees. Furthermore, certain formalities must be observed even after organization, if the shareholders don't want to risk personal liability through disregard of the corporate form. (See Section 8, infra.) In contrast, a sole proprietorship or general partnership can be organized and maintained with little or no formalities or filing fees. Moreover, partnership law norms probably correspond more closely to the expectations of a small group of owner-managers than do corporate law norms. As a result, in the typical small enterprise a general-partnership agreement may not need to be quite as complex as a shareholders' agreement. From the perspective of cost and simplicity, therefore, the sole-proprietorship or general-partnership forms are

likely to be more attractive than the corporate or limited-partnership forms.

6. *Summary.* To summarize, a single owner or a small group of owner-managers may prefer the corporate or limited-partnership forms because they provide greater insulation from liability, and may prefer the sole-proprietorship or general-partnership forms because of their simplicity and lower cost, but are likely to be indifferent with respect to the attributes of free transferability of interests, continuity of existence, and centralized management. However, the three latter attributes, which can be achieved through either the limited-partnership or the corporate forms, are important if an enterprise expects to raise funds from the public. As between those two forms the limited partnership has the disadvantage of not being familiar, but that may change over time.[6]

(b) TAX CONSIDERATIONS

The critical difference between corporate and partnership taxation is that a corporation is normally taxed as an entity while a partnership is not. Under the entity approach a corporation's income is taxed to the corporation when it is received. If the corporation's after-tax income is later distributed as a dividend, the dividend is taxed to the shareholders as part of their income. This effect is sometimes referred to as "double taxation." In contrast, partnership income is treated on a conduit basis. Under the conduit approach partnership income is treated as if it had been personal income realized by the partners, and is taxed to the partners as individuals, not to the partnership as a separate entity.

Under the Internal Revenue Code of 1954, maximum corporate tax rates were lower than maximum individual rates, and capital gains were taxed at rates that were normally much lower than the rates on ordinary income. Under these conditions, from a tax perspective corporate status was commonly more attractive than partnership status. Under the Tax Reform Act of 1986, however, maximum corporate tax rates are higher than maximum individual tax rates, and capital gains are taxed at the same rates as ordinary income. Given these conditions, and the fact that partnership avoids the double-taxation effect, partnership-tax treatment is now usually more attractive than corporate-tax treatment.

The Internal Revenue Code provides a route through which partnership-tax treatment can be achieved by certain corporate enterprises. Subchapter S of the Code (I.R.C. §§ 1361–1379) permits the owners of qualifying corporations to elect a special tax status under which the corporation and its shareholders receive conduit-type taxa-

---

6. An attribute not discussed in the text is entity status. In theory, corporations have the status of legal entities, while partnerships do not. In practice, however, partnerships are treated as if they were entities for so many purposes that the difference between the partnership and corporate forms regarding this attribute is inconsequential.

tion that is comparable (although not identical) to partnership taxation. The taxable income of an S corporation is computed essentially as if the corporation were an individual. I.R.C. § 1363(b). Items of income, loss, deduction, and credit, with some exceptions, are then passed through to the shareholders on a pro rata basis, and added to or subtracted from each shareholder's gross income. I.R.C. § 1366. Among the conditions for making and maintaining a Subchapter S election are the following: (1) The corporation may not have more than thirty-five shareholders. (2) The corporation may not have more than one class of stock. (3) All the shareholders must be individuals or qualified estates or trusts. (4) No shareholder may be a nonresident alien. (5) The corporation may not be a member of an affiliated group of corporations. I.R.C. § 1361.[7] The amount of the corporation's assets and income is immaterial under Subchapter S.

Under Subchapter S, an electing corporation is taxed like a partnership. In some cases, a partnership—particularly a limited partnership—may be taxed like a corporation. Under I.R.C. § 7701(a)(3), the term "corporation" is defined to include "associations." The latter term is not itself defined, but may include noncorporate organizations. In Morrissey v. Commissioner, 296 U.S. 344, 56 S.Ct. 289, 80 L.Ed. 263 (1935), the Supreme Court held that whether a partnership was an "association" within the meaning of the Code depended on how closely it resembled a corporation. Subsequently, the Internal Revenue Service adopted Regulations that identify four critical "characteristics of corporations"—continuity of life, centralized management, limited liability, and free transferability of interests. The Regulations indicate that a limited partnership will be treated as an association (and will therefore be taxed like a corporation) if, but only if, it has more than two of these characteristics. See Treas.Reg. § 301.7701–2(a). Although the Regulations purport to adopt *Morrissey*'s resemblance test, they define continuity of life and limited liability in such a restrictive manner that it is almost impossible to find that a given limited partnership has those characteristics.[8] This

---

7. The term *affiliated groups* refers primarily to corporations in a parent-subsidiary relationship where the parent possesses 80% of the voting power and the stock value of the subsidiary. See I.R.C. § 1504.

8. Treas.Reg. § 301.7701–2(a)(1) provides that an organization has continuity of life if the "death, insanity, bankruptcy, retirement, resignation, or expulsion of any member" does not cause dissolution of the entity. Since both limited and general partnerships are normally dissolved upon the death, insanity, bankruptcy, retirement, resignation, or expulsion of a general partner, under this Regulation a partnership cannot possess continuity of life. Even a provision in the partnership agreement providing for continuity despite the death or other disability of a partner does not imbue the partnership with continuity of life, under the Regulation, because such a continuation will necessarily be dependent on the willingness of the remaining partners to carry on. See Glensder Textile Co. v. Commissioner, 46 B.T.A. 176 (1942), acq. 1942–1 C.B. 8.

Treas.Reg. § 301.7701–2(d)(1) provides that an organization has limited liability if under local law there is no member who is personally liable for the debts of or claims against the organization. Clearly, general partners in a limited partnership can be held personally liable for partnership debts. Under the Regulations, however, if a general partner has "no substantial assets (other than his interest in the partnership) which could be reached by a creditor of the organization" and is acting merely as a "dummy" under the direct and active control of the limited partners, the general partner will be deemed to have no personal liability. Treas.Reg. § 301.7701–2(d)(2); see Larson v. Commissioner, 66 T.C. 159, 179–82 (1976) 1979–1 C.B.1. The Regula-

means that a limited partnership will never have more than two of the four critical characteristics. Therefore, as a practical matter no limited partnership is likely to be taxed as a corporation under section 7701. See Hecker, The Tax Classification of Limited Partnerships Revisited, 88 Com.L.J. 537 (1983).[9] For example, in Larson v. Commissioner, 66 T.C. 159 (1976), 1979–1 C.B. 1, GHL, a corporation, was the sole general partner of two limited partnerships, Mai–Kai and Somis. Under *Morrissey's* resemblance test, Mai–Kai and Somis would almost certainly have qualified as "associations" that were taxable as corporations under § 7701. Effective continuity of life was assured because in each case the general partner was a corporation; management was centralized in GHL's hands; there was no effective personal liability because GHL had little capital; and the limited partnership interests were freely transferable. A majority of the Tax Court nevertheless held that Mai–Kai and Somis did not constitute associations under the restrictive tests laid down in the Regulations, because they lacked both continuity of life and personal liability, as those terms are (artificially) defined in the Regulations. While Mai–Kai and Somis did have centralized management and free transferability of interests, the majority read the Regulations to apply a mechanical test, under which a limited partnership would not constitute an association unless at least three of the four critical characteristics were present. Chief Judge Dawson, concurring, stressed that the regulations "virtually rule out the possibility that [a limited partnership formed under the ULPA] will be a taxable association within the meaning of section 7701(a) (3)," *id.* at 187, and the various opinions in the case made it clear that but for the Regulations a different result would have followed.

However, under IRC § 7704 a "publicly traded" partnership is, with certain exceptions, taxed as a corporation without regard to section 7701 and the Regulations thereunder.

SECTION 2. SELECTING A STATE OF INCORPORATION

1. Once the owners of a business decide to incorporate, they must determine in which state they should incorporate. Under traditional choice-of-law rules, a corporation's internal affairs are governed by the law of its state of incorporation even if the corporation has no

---

tions also provide that "when the limited partners act as the principals of such general partner, personal liability will exist with respect to such limited partners." Treas.Reg. § 301.7701–2(d)(2). At least one court has concluded that for purposes of these Regulations either the general or the limited partners will always have personal liability, so that a limited partnership can never possess limited liability within the meaning of the Regulations. Zuckman v. United States, 207 Ct.Cl. 712, 524 F.2d 729, 741 (1975).

9. However, the Internal Revenue Service will not issue an advance ruling that a limited partnership will be taxed like a partnership unless certain conditions, relating to such factors as the relative interests of limited and general partners, are satisfied. See Rev.Proc. 72–13, 1972–1 C.B. 735; Rev.Proc. 74–17, 1974–1 C.B. 438; Hecker, supra, at 542, 545.

other contact with that state.[1]   A corporation with only a few owners—a "close corporation"—will almost invariably incorporate locally,
that is, in the state where it has its principal place of business.
Incorporation in some other state—"out-of-state incorporation"—will
usually be unnecessary, because for most practical purposes the various
state statutes now offer fairly comparable legal regimes to close
corporations.   Out-of-state incorporation may also increase costs.   A
corporation normally must pay taxes to the state of incorporation for
the privilege of organizing within that state and maintaining its
corporate status.   It must also pay taxes to the local state for the
privilege of doing business in that state.   Elements of the manner in
which these two taxes are measured may overlap, so that total taxes
will be less if the corporation is incorporated in the state in which it
does most of its business.   Furthermore, local attorneys, familiar with
local corporate law, may be hesitant about rendering formal opinions
on the laws of other states.   The attorney for a close corporation is
therefore likely to be more comfortable if the business is incorporated
locally, and legal costs may be less because the attorney will not need
to regularly consult with out-of-state counsel.

In the case of a publicly held corporation, a different calculus
prevails.   On the corporation's side of the equation, the legal regimes
offered by various states may differ significantly.   The rules governing
such issues as what transactions require shareholder approval and
trigger appraisal rights, and how are the fiduciary duties of directors
and officers enforced, may vary dramatically across state lines.   The
extra costs attendant on out-of-state incorporation may be inconsequential in comparison with the corporation's total revenues and the
comparative advantages of a particular state's legal regime.

On the state's side of the equation, franchise-tax revenues represent a potentially enormous source of revenue to a state, like Delaware, with a small fiscal base.   Such a state therefore has a great
economic incentive to tailor its corporation-law regime in a way that
will attract incorporation.

2.   Delaware is far and away the preeminent state in terms of the
number of publicly held corporations incorporated there.   Many states
have striven to match or outmatch Delaware in attracting publicly held
corporations.   What accounts for Delaware's continued success?
First, Delaware is reliable.   Both history and structural political factors
help to assure corporations that Delaware, more than most states, will
be responsive to corporate needs on a continuing basis.   See Romano,
supra, at 721–25.   Second, Delaware offers corporations more than a
statute.   It also has an unusually well-developed case law in the
corporate area.   Its law is therefore much more predictable than that
of many states.[2]   Third, a Delaware corporate address is accepted,

1.   Statutes in some states vary this rule
under limited circumstances.   See, e.g.,
Cal.Corp.Code § 2115 (subjecting certain
foreign corporations to the state's corporate laws); N.Y.Bus.Corp.Law §§ 1317–
1320.

2.   As Romano points out, this also gives
attorneys an incentive to advise Delaware
incorporation.   Romano, The State Competition Debate in Corporate Law, 8 Cardozo
L.Rev. 709, 723 (1987).

perhaps even prestigious. The investment community does not look askance when a corporation reincorporates in Delaware to take advantage of some new provision of the Delaware statute. In contrast, reincorporation in another tiny state for the same purpose might raise eyebrows.

Because the law of the state of incorporation normally governs internal corporate affairs, and because Delaware is preeminent for publicly held corporations, the Delaware statute provides a major axis of this book. A second major axis is provided by the Revised Model Business Corporation Act, promulgated by the Committee on Corporate Laws of the ABA's Section of Business Law. Although the Model Act itself has no official status, it has served as a template for the statutes of many states.

––––––––

SECTION 3. ORGANIZING A CORPORATION

Once a decision has been made to incorporate, and the state of incorporation has been selected, the next step is to create or "organize" the corporation. The first stage of the organization process, and the most critical from a legal perspective, is to file a "certificate of incorporation" or "articles of incorporation" or "charter" (the nomenclature varies from state to state) with the relevant state official—usually the secretary of state.

––––––––

DEL. GEN. CORP. LAW §§ 101, 102, 103, 106, 107, 108, 109

[See Statutory Supplement] *

––––––––

REV. MODEL BUS. CORP. ACT §§ 2.01, 2.02, 2.03(a), 2.05, 2.06

[See Statutory Supplement]

––––––––

FORM OF CERTIFICATE OF INCORPORATION

[See Statutory Supplement]

––––––––

NOTE ON THE PURPOSE CLAUSE

Before the adoption of modern statutes which permit a corporation to engage in any lawful purpose, the clauses in certificates of

––––––––

* Corporations and Business Associations, Statutes, Rules, and Forms (M. Eisenberg, ed.).

Sec. 3
incorporation
formed an
extreme
Corp
law

...ing the purpose for which the corporation was
...powers the corporation was to have tended to be
...rate. Some clauses still are. For example, N.Y.Bus.
...01(a) permits a corporation to be organized "for any
...ss purpose," with certain limited exceptions. Section
...quires that the certificate of incorporation set forth "[t]he
...purposes for which [the corporation] is formed, it being
...to state, either alone or with other purposes, that the
...of the corporation is to engage in any lawful act or activity for
...orporations may be organized under this chapter." Nonethe-
...eading handbook on New York corporation law, A. Hoffman,
...s on Corporate Practice (4th ed. 1983) sets out the following
...ose clause in its model certificate of incorporation:

The purposes for which the Corporation is formed are as follows:

To engage in the business of manufacturing, producing, purchasing or otherwise acquiring, selling, leasing or otherwise disposing of, and generally dealing in and with, at wholesale or retail, as principal or agent, devices, equipment, materials and supplies made of wood, metal, plastics or other material, or any combination thereof, used or useful in the building, construction and contracting industries or in any other field in which such devices, equipment, materials or supplies may profitably be used. The business described in the preceding sentence shall be the primary business of the corporation and the conduct of such business shall be the primary purpose for which the corporation is formed.

To purchase or otherwise acquire, hold, own, sell, lease or otherwise dispose of real property, improved or unimproved, and personal property, tangible or intangible, including, without limitation, goods, wares and merchandise of every description and the securities and obligations of any issuer, whether or not incorporated.

To engage in any other lawful act or activity for which corporations may be organized under the Business Corporation Law of the State of New York; *provided,* that the corporation is not formed to engage in any act or activity requiring the consent or approval of any official, department, board, agency or other body of said State without such consent or approval first being obtained.

Id. at 527–29. This clause, long as it is, is still much shorter than the clauses employed before the enactment of the present statute.

———

NOTE ON INITIAL DIRECTORS

Once a corporation is under way, its board of directors is elected by the shareholders. However, there can be no shareholders until stock is issued, and the function of issuing stock is normally committed to the board. Accordingly, there must be a mecha. naming directors before stock is issued, or for issuing. directors are elected by the shareholders. There are either statutory patterns for solving this problem. Under the la before states, like New York, the corporation's incorporators have ers of shareholders until stock is issued, and the powers of di until directors are elected. N.Y.Bus.Corp.Law §§ 404(a), 6i Under such a statute, the incorporators will typically adopt by-laws, the number of directors, and elect directors to serve until the fir annual meeting of shareholders. See N.Y.Bus.Corp.Law § 404(a). Under the law of other states, like Delaware, the incorporators have the powers of shareholders and directors unless initial directors are named in the corporation's certificate of incorporation. Del.Gen. Corp.Law §§ 107, 108. If the initial directors are named in the certificate of incorporation, the functions of the incorporators pass to the directors when the certificate is filed and recorded. Del.Gen. Corp.Law §§ 107, 108(a).

Once the initial directors are named, either by the incorporators or by the certificate of incorporation, they will hold an organization meeting. A typical agenda for such a meeting is reflected in the Form of Minutes that follows.

———

FORM OF MINUTES OF ORGANIZATION MEETING
[See Statutory Supplement]

———

FORM OF BY-LAWS
[See Statutory Supplement]

———

FORM OF STOCK CERTIFICATE
[See Statutory Supplement]

———

DEL. GEN. CORP. LAW § 109
[See Statutory Supplement]

———

REV. MODEL BUS. CORP. ACT §§ 2.06, 10.20–10.22
[See Statutory Supplement]

———

SECTION 4. THE CLASSICAL ULTRA VIRES DOCTRINE

INTRODUCTORY NOTE

1. Under the classical theory of corporate existence, the corporation is regarded as a fictitious person, endowed with life and capacity only insofar as provided in its charter. Early corporate charters tended to narrowly circumscribe the activities in which a corporation could permissibly engage. Transactions outside that sphere were characterized by the courts as "ultra vires" (beyond the corporation's power) and unenforceable—unenforceable *against* the corporation because beyond the corporation's powers, and unenforceable *by* the corporation on the ground of lack of mutuality.[1] A leading example is Ashbury Railway Carriage & Iron Co. v. Riche, 7 L.R.–Eng. & Ir.App. 653, 33 L.T.R. 450 (1875). Ashbury was authorized by its charter to "to make and sell, or lend on hire, railway-carriages and wagons, and all kinds of railway plant, fittings, machinery, and rolling-stock; to carry on the business of mechanical engineers and general contractors; to purchase and sell, as merchants, timber, coal, metals, or other materials; and to buy and sell any such materials on commission, or as agents." 7 L.R.–Eng. & Ir.App. at 654. Ashbury purchased a concession to construct and operate a railway line in Belgium, and Riche contracted to do the construction. After Riche had done some of the work, Ashbury repudiated the contract. Riche brought suit. The House of Lords held for Ashbury on the ground that it lacked the power under its charter to build a railroad, and therefore lacked the power to contract for that purpose.

The original purpose of the ultra vires doctrine seems to have been to protect the public or the state from unsanctioned corporate activity. Accordingly, under classical English law even unanimous shareholder ratification would not be a bar to an ultra vires defense if the transaction was outside the objects of the corporation. See

---

1. The term "ultra vires" is best reserved for the question whether a corporation is empowered to take an action, but it is often loosely used in other contexts:

(i) In some cases, an action the corporation is empowered to take is lawful only if consent has been obtained from a public official. Corporate action without having secured such consent is sometimes labeled ultra vires. See, e.g., Texas & Pacific Ry. Co. v. Pottorff, 291 U.S. 245, 54 S.Ct. 416, 78 L.Ed. 777 (1934). However, failure to secure the consent does not make the action ultra vires; the action, if consented to, would be within the corporation's powers, and if not consented to, would be unlawful even if taken by an individual.

(ii) In other cases, a corporation can take certain action only if the action has been approved by a prescribed shareholder vote. Action without such approval is sometimes labeled ultra vires. Here too the label is inappropriate, because the action is within the corporation's powers, and the only issue is which corporate organ must authorize it.

(iii) In still other cases, an action, although within the scope of permissible corporate activity, is outside the scope of authority of the officer or agent who took it. Such an action may be "ultra vires" the officer, but it is not ultra vires the corporation.

Ashbury, supra; Frommel, Reform of the Ultra Vires Rule: A Personal View, 8 The Company Lawyer 11 (1987).

2. In theory, the classical ultra vires doctrine was applicable to two somewhat different kinds of questions. The first question was whether a corporation had acted beyond its *purposes,* that is, had engaged in a type of business activity not permitted under its certificate. The second question was whether the corporation had exercised a *power* not specified in its certificate. In practice, the two questions tended to merge. For example, certificates of incorporation commonly contained clauses describing the corporation's purposes and powers with a provision to the effect that they were to be deemed both purposes and powers. Similarly, judicial opinions would often say that a corporation had no "power" to engage in a type of business activity not permitted under the certificate.

3. A number of problems concerning specific types of powers tended to recur. See 1 Model Business Corporation Act Annotated 190–91 (3d ed. 1985). One of these recurring problems concerned the power of a corporation to guarantee a third party's debts. Early cases often held such guarantees ultra vires in the absence of a certificate provision explicitly conferring the power to guarantee. See, e.g., Brinson v. Mill Supply Co., 219 N.C. 498, 14 S.E.2d 505 (1941).[2] Present-day statutes explicitly empower a corporation to make guarantees, even without a provision to that effect in the certificate of incorporation. See, e.g., Del. Gen. Corp. Law § 123.

Another recurring issue concerned the power of a corporation to be a general partner. Early cases often held that a corporation had no power to enter into a partnership unless that power was explicitly granted by a statute or by the certificate. See, e.g., Whittenton Mills v. Upton, 76 Mass. (10 Gray) 582 (1858); Central R.R. Co. v. Collins, 40 Ga. 582 (1869). The concern was that a corporate partner would be bound by the acts and decisions of copartners who were not its duly appointed officers, thereby improperly impinging on the board's power and duty to manage the corporation.[3] Present-day statutes make this problem moot by explicitly empowering corporations to become partners. See, e.g., Del.Gen.Corp. Law § 122(11); N.Y.Bus.Corp. Law § 202(15); Rev. Model Bus.Corp. Act § 3.02(9).

4. Ultra vires was always regarded by the commentators as an unsound doctrine. For example, Ballantine, writing in 1927, argued:

> The practical question . . . is not what power or capacity or authority has the state granted to an imaginary person, but rather what authority has the group of stockholders granted to their representatives, the directors, to do business on their behalf.

---

2. Where the corporation received a direct benefit from making the guarantee, the courts often found that the guarantee was within the corporation's implied powers. See Kriedmann, The Corporate Guaranty, 13 Vand.L.Rev. 229 (1959).

3. The cases did permit corporations to enter into joint ventures, which are usually temporary in nature and created for a limited purpose.

> . . . [I]n general the objects and purposes clause of the
> articles should operate simply like by-laws or articles of
> partnership, as limitations on the actual authority of the
> directors and officers to bind the corporation, but not upon
> their ostensible or apparent authority, unless reasonably to be
> inferred or actually known.

Ballantine, Proposed Revision of the Ultra Vires Doctrine, 12 Cornell
L.Q. 453, 455 (1927). Neither the courts nor, for the most part, the
legislatures, ever went quite that far, but the history of the doctrine is
one of steady erosion by the courts and the bar, resulting in large part
from the widespread view that the doctrine was unsound. This
erosion proceeded along a variety of fronts:

(i) It was established even in early cases that corporate powers
could be implied as well as explicit. See Sutton's Hospital Case, 10
Coke 23a (1613). The courts eventually became very liberal in
finding implied powers, including implied powers to enter into business activities not specified in the certificate. Thus in Jacksonville
Mayport, Pablo Ry. & Navigation Co. v. Hooper, 160 U.S. 514, 526,
16 S.Ct. 379, 40 L.Ed. 515 (1896), the Supreme Court held that a
Florida company, whose purpose, under its charter, was to run a
railroad, could also engage in leasing and running a resort hotel.
"Undoubtedly the main business of a corporation is to be confined to
that class of operations which properly appertain to the general
purposes for which its charter was granted. But it may also enter into
and engage in transactions which are auxiliary or incidental to its main
business." See also, e.g., John B. Waldbillig, Inc. v. Gottfried, 22
A.D.2d 997, 254 N.Y.S.2d 924 (1964), aff'd 16 N.Y.2d 773, 209
N.E.2d 818, 262 N.Y.S.2d 498 (1965) (corporation organized to
"engage in the business of building, construction, and contracting"
could have incidental or implied power to practice engineering).

(ii) Generally speaking, ultra vires was not a defense at all to tort
or criminal liability, and in areas where it was a defense it could not
be used to reverse completed transactions. Accordingly, the major
impact of the doctrine was confined to executory contracts.

(iii) Even as applied to executory contracts, the ambit of the
doctrine was limited. If both parties to a contract had fully performed, ultra vires could not be used to undo the transaction. If
neither had performed, ultra vires was a defense to both the corporation and the third party. The difficult case occurred where only one
party had performed, and the nonperforming party then sought to
assert ultra vires as a defense for its nonperformance. Under the
majority view, the nonperforming party, having received a benefit
under the contract, was "estopped" from asserting the ultra vires
defense. See, e.g., Joseph Schlitz Brewing Co. v. Missouri Poultry &
Game Co., 297 Mo. 400, 229 S.W. 813 (1921). Under the minority
view—known as the "federal rule"—part performance did not raise an
estoppel, on the theory that an ultra vires contract was prohibited by
law and therefore void. Even the cases taking this view, however,
usually permitted the performing party to recover in quasi-contract for

the value of any benefit conferred. See Central Transportation Co. v. Pullman's Palace-Car Co., 139 U.S. 24, 11 S.Ct. 478, 35 L.Ed. 55 (1891).

(iv) Under American law, at least, unanimous shareholder approval barred the ultra vires defense unless creditors would be injured. See Note, 83 U.Pa.L.Rev. 479, 488–92 (1935).

(v) The final source of erosion of the ultra vires doctrine was the decreasing significance of the certificate of incorporation as a limit on the corporation's purposes and powers. Draftsmen began writing seemingly endless and crushingly boring certificate provisions that enumerated every possible business purpose and power imaginable. Eventually, most statutes made this kind of draftsmanship unnecessary by stating that the certificate of incorporation could provide simply that the corporation could engage in any lawful business, and by setting out a laundry list of powers that are conferred on every corporation without enumeration in the certificate.

Modern = Certificate could say corp can engage in any lawful business.

DEL. GEN. CORP. LAW §§ 101(b), 102(a)(3), 121, 122, 124

[See Statutory Supplement]

REV. MODEL BUS. CORP. ACT §§ 3.01(a), 3.02, 3.04

Statutes comparable to Del.Gen.Corp.Law § 124 and Rev.Model Bus.Corp. Act § 3.04 have been adopted in all but a few states. See Schaeftler, Ultra Vires—Ultra Useless: The Myth of State Interest in Ultra Vires Acts of Business Corporations, 9 J.Corp.Law 81, 81–83 & n. 6 (1983).

GOODMAN v. LADD ESTATE CO.

Supreme Court of Oregon, 1967.
246 Or. 621, 427 P.2d 102.

Before McALLISTER, C.J., and SLOAN, GOODWIN, HOLMAN * and LUSK, JJ.

LUSK, Justice.

Plaintiffs brought this suit to enjoin the defendant Ladd Estate Company, a Washington corporation, from enforcing a guaranty agreement executed by Westover Tower, Inc., a corporation, in favor of Ladd Estate. From a decree dismissing the suit plaintiffs appeal.

* Did not participate in this decision.
(Footnote by the court.)

In 1961 the defendant Walter T. Liles[1] held all the common shares of Westover and he, Dr. Edmond F. Wheatley and Samuel H. Martin were its directors.

On September 8, 1961, Dr. Wheatley borrowed $10,000 from Citizens Bank of Oregon and gave his promissory note therefor, which was endorsed by Ladd Estate. Contemporaneously with this transaction Liles, individually, and Westover, by Liles as president, and Martin, as secretary, executed an agreement in writing by which they unconditionally guaranteed Ladd Estate against loss arising out of the latter's endorsement of the Wheatley note to Citizens Bank. The agreement was also signed by Ladd Estate. It recited that it was made at the request of Liles and Westover and that Ladd Estate would not have guaranteed payment of the Wheatley note without the guarantee of Liles and Westover to Ladd Estate.

Wheatley defaulted on his note, Ladd Estate paid to Citizens Bank the amount owing thereon, $9,583.61, and demanded reimbursement from Westover. Upon the latter's rejection of the demand Ladd filed an action at law upon the guaranty agreement against Liles and Westover.

The plaintiffs Morton J. Goodman and Edith Goodman, husband and wife, came into the case in this manner: On September 27, 1963, plaintiffs purchased all the common shares of Westover from a receiver appointed by the Circuit Court for Multnomah County who was duly authorized to make such sale. At the time of such purchase, plaintiffs were fully aware of the guaranty agreement given by Westover and Liles to Ladd Estate. It is conceded that the guaranty agreement was ultra vires the corporation. Plaintiffs, as stockholders, brought this suit pursuant to the provisions of ORS 57.040. [ORS 57.040 is comparable to Del.G.C.L. § 124, supra]. . . .

It will be noticed that the court may set aside and enjoin the performance of the ultra vires contract if it deems such a course equitable. Plaintiffs argue that to deny them the relief they seek would be "shocking," because Westover executed the guaranty agreement in order to enable one of its directors, Wheatley, to obtain a loan of money to be used for purposes entirely foreign to any corporate purpose. We see nothing shocking or even inequitable about it. The corporation was organized for the purposes, among others, to engage in the business of providing housing for rent or sale and to obtain contracts of mortgage insurance from the Federal Housing Commissioner, pursuant to the provisions of the National Housing Act, 12 U.S.C.A. § 1701 et seq. Authorized capital stock comprised 30,100 shares of which 100 shares, having a par value of $1 per share and designated preferred stock, were issued to the Commissioner, pursuant to § 1743(b)(1), U.S.C.A. and 30,000 shares, having a par value of $1 per share and designated common stock, were issued to Liles. Voting rights of the shareholders were

---

1. Pursuant to stipulation, the suit was dismissed as to Liles and Westover. The stipulation provided that "this suit may proceed in the same manner as if the said Walter T. Liles and Westover Tower, Inc. were parties hereto."

vested exclusively in the holders of the common stock. The guaranty agreement recites that, at the request of Liles and Westover, Ladd Estate guaranteed payment of the Wheatley note. Ladd Estate made good on its endorsement when Wheatley defaulted and now calls upon Westover to honor its obligation. The agent of the plaintiffs, who purchased the shares for them, testified that he considered the question whether the guaranty was a valid obligation of the corporation before making the purchase and concluded that it was not. The fact that he guessed wrong does not in any way enhance plaintiffs' claim to equitable consideration.

Neither would it be inequitable to enforce the agreement because of the purpose which the guaranty was intended to serve. Even before the enactment of ORS 57.040 a corporation might properly enter into a guaranty agreement in the legitimate furtherance of its business or purposes: Depot R. Syndicate v. Enterprise B. Co., 87 Or. 560, 562, 170 P. 294, 171 P. 223, L.R.A.1918C, 1001; 19 Am.Jur. 2d 493, Corporations § 1030; that the agreement does not further such purposes is what makes it ultra vires. But the statute says the agreement is enforceable even though ultra vires, and to accept the plaintiffs' argument would be to say that because it is ultra vires the agreement is inequitable and, therefore, unenforceable. This would effectually emasculate the statute.

Moreover, plaintiffs are in no position to invoke the aid of a court of equity. Liles, the former holder of their shares—all the voting shares of Westover—induced Ladd Estate to endorse Wheatley's note by procuring Westover to execute the guaranty agreement. If a shareholder himself has participated in the ultra vires act he cannot thereafter attack it as ultra vires: 7 Fletcher, Cyc. of Corporations (perm. ed., 1964 rev.) 613, § 3453. This would seem to be emphatically so of a shareholder who exercises the entire voting power of the corporation. Plaintiffs, as purchasers of Liles' shares, are in no better position than he would have been to raise the question: McCampbell v. Fountain Head R. Co., 111 Tenn. 55, 75, 77 S.W. 1070, 102 Am. St.Rep. 731; 7 Fletcher, op. cit. 614, § 3456.

It should be added that no rights of creditors of Westover are involved and there is nothing to indicate that the security of any mortgage guaranteed by the Federal Housing Commissioner would be impaired by enforcement of the agreement here in question. . . .

We are of the opinion that plaintiffs are not entitled to equitable relief. The decree is affirmed.

INTER–CONTINENTAL CORP. v. MOODY, 411 S.W.2d 578 (Tex.Civ.App.,1966). Inter–Continental Corp., a Texas corporation, guaranteed a note given by Shively, its president, to Moody. Moody knew or should have known that the guarantee was given for Shively's personal benefit. Shively lost control of Inter-Continental and Moody brought suit on the guarantee. Texas had a statute comparable to Del.Gen.Corp.Law § 124. Inter–Continental defended on the ground of ultra vires, and also arranged for a minority shareholder to intervene for the purpose of enjoining payment of the note on the same ground. (Inter–Continental's attorney drafted the shareholder's petition, promised to pay his legal expenses, and contacted his lawyer, who testified that he had never talked to the shareholder.) The court held that a defense of ultra vires by the corporation is barred under the statute even if the third party actually knew that the corporation lacked authority to enter into the transaction. However, the court continued, a shareholder can intervene to enjoin an ultra vires act even if he has been solicited to do so by the corporation, provided the shareholder is not the corporation's agent. (On a rehearing, the court added that if on remand "it is determined that on the facts the stockholder is entitled to some relief . . . [the other party] will be entitled to a judgment against the corporation, not for the full amount of the note, but only to the extent that the stockholder is held not to be entitled to relief.") See Note, 45 Tex.L.Rev. 1422 (1967).

---

711 KINGS HIGHWAY CORP. v. F.I.M.'S MARINER REPAIR SERV., INC., 51 Misc.2d 373, 273 N.Y.S.2d 299 (Spec.Term 1966). Kings Highway leased a theater to Mariner Repair for fifteen years, beginning July 1, 1966. Before July 1, Kings Highway brought an action for a declaratory judgment to invalidate the lease, on the ground that it was void because it would be ultra vires for Mariner Repair to conduct a motion-picture theater business. The New York statute, Bus.Corp.Law § 203, was comparable to Del.Gen. Corp.Law § 124. Held, for Mariner Repair. "It is undisputed that the present case does not fall within the stated exceptions contained in Section 203. . . . Neither is there merit to the plaintiff's contention that Section 203 applies only where ultra vires is raised as a defense. Notwithstanding the fact that this section is entitled 'Defense of ultra vires' it seems that except in the three stated situations set forth in the section, which are not applicable to the instant case, ultra vires may not be invoked as a sword in support of a cause of action any more than it can be utilized as a defense. . . ."

SECTION 5. THE OBJECTIVE AND CONDUCT OF THE CORPORATION

The question considered in this Section is, to what extent may a corporation act in a manner that is not intended to maximize corporate profits. This question is often put in terms of whether a given act would be "ultra vires," but it penetrates much more deeply into the nature of the corporate institution, and its place in society, than does the classical ultra vires issue.

A.P. SMITH MFG. CO. v. BARLOW

Supreme Court of New Jersey, 1953.
13 N.J. 145, 98 A.2d 581, appeal dismissed, 346 U.S. 861, 74 S.Ct. 107, 98 L.Ed.
373 (1953).

JACOBS, J.   The Chancery Division, in a well-reasoned opinion by Judge Stein, determined that a donation by the plaintiff The A.P. Smith Manufacturing Company to Princeton University was *intra vires*. Because of the public importance of the issues presented, the appeal duly taken to the Appellate Division has been certified directly to this court under Rule 1:5–1(*a*).

The company was incorporated in 1896 and is engaged in the manufacture and sale of valves, fire hydrants and special equipment, mainly for water and gas industries.   Its plant is located in East Orange and Bloomfield and it has approximately 300 employees. Over the years the company has contributed regularly to the local community chest and on occasions to Upsala College in East Orange and Newark University, now part of Rutgers, the State University. On July 24, 1951 the board of directors adopted a resolution which set forth that it was in the corporation's best interests to join with others in the 1951 Annual Giving to Princeton University, and appropriated the sum of $1,500 to be transferred by the corporation's treasurer to the university as a contribution towards its maintenance. When this action was questioned by stockholders the corporation instituted a declaratory judgment action in the Chancery Division and trial was had in due course.

Mr. Hubert F. O'Brien, the president of the company, testified that he considered the contribution to be a sound investment, that the public expects corporations to aid philanthropic and benevolent institutions, that they obtain good will in the community by so doing, and that their charitable donations create favorable environment for their business operations.   In addition, he expressed the thought that in contributing to liberal arts institutions, corporations were furthering their self-interest in assuring the free flow of properly trained personnel for administrative and other corporate employment.   Mr. Frank W. Abrams, chairman of the board of the Standard Oil Company of New Jersey, testified that corporations are expected to acknowledge their public responsibilities in support of the essential elements of our free enterprise system.   He indicated that it was not "good business" to disappoint "this reasonable and justified public expectation," nor was it good business for corporations "to take substantial benefits from their membership in the economic community while avoiding the normally accepted obligations of citizenship in the social community." Mr. Irving S. Olds, former chairman of the board of the United States Steel Corporation, pointed out that corporations have a self-interest in the maintenance of liberal education as the bulwark of good government.   He stated that "Capitalism and free enterprise owe their survival in no small degree to the existence of our private, independent universities" and that if American business does not aid in their maintenance it is not "properly protecting the long-range interest of its stockholders, its employees and its customers." Similarly, Dr. Harold W. Dodds, President of Princeton University, suggested that if private institutions of higher learning were replaced by governmental institutions our society would be vastly different and private enterprise in other fields would fade out rather promptly. Further on he stated that "democratic society will not long endure if it does not nourish within itself strong centers of non-governmental fountains of knowledge, opinions of all sorts not governmentally or politically originated. If the time comes when all these centers are absorbed into government, then freedom as we know it, I submit, is at an end."

The objecting stockholders have not disputed any of the foregoing testimony nor the showing of great need by Princeton and other private institutions of higher learning and the important public service being rendered by them for democratic government and industry alike. Similarly, they have acknowledged that for over two decades there has been state legislation on our books which expresses a strong public policy in favor of corporate contributions such as that being questioned by them. Nevertheless, they have taken the position that (1) the plaintiff's certificate of incorporation does not expressly authorize the contribution and under common-law principles the company does not possess any implied or incidental power to make it, and (2) the New Jersey statutes which expressly authorize the contribution may not constitutionally be applied to the plaintiff, a corporation created long before their enactment. See R.S. 14:3–13; R.S. 14:3–13.1 et seq.

In his discussion of the early history of business corporations Professor Williston refers to a 1702 publication where the author stated flatly that "The general intent and end of all civil incorporations is for better government." And he points out that the early corporate charters, particularly their recitals, furnish additional support for the notion that the corporate object was the public one of managing and ordering the trade as well as the private one of profit for the members. See 3 Select Essays on Anglo–American Legal History 201 (1909); 1 Fletcher, Corporations (rev. ed. 1931), 6. See also Currie's Administrators v. The Mutual Assurance Society, 4 Hen. & M. 315, 347 (Va.Sup.Ct.App. 1809), where Judge Roane referred to the English corporate charters and expressed the view that acts of incorporation ought never to be passed "but in consideration of services to be rendered to the public." However, with later economic and social developments and the free availability of the corporate device for all trades, the end of private profit became generally accepted as the controlling one in all businesses other than those classed broadly as public utilities. Cf. Dodd, For Whom Are Corporate Managers Trustees?, 45 Harv.L.Rev. 1145, 1148 (1932). As a concomitant the common-law rule developed that those who managed the corporation could not disburse any corporate funds for philanthropic or other worthy public cause unless the expenditure would benefit the corporation. Hutton v. West Cork Railway Company, 23 Ch.D. 654 (1883); Dodge v. Ford Motor Co., 204 Mich. 459, 170 N.W. 668, 3 A.L.R. 413 (Sup.Ct. 1919). Ballantine, Corporations (rev. ed. 1946), 228; 6A Fletcher, supra, 667.

During the 19th Century when corporations were relatively few and small and did not dominate the country's wealth, the common-law rule did not significantly interfere with the public interest. But the 20th Century has presented a different climate. *Berle and Means, The Modern Corporation and Private Property* (1948). Control of economic wealth has passed largely from individual entrepreneurs to dominating corporations, and calls upon the corporations for reasonable philanthropic donations have come to be made with increased public support. In many instances such contributions have been sustained by the courts within the common-law doctrine upon liberal findings that the donations tended reasonably to promote the corporate objectives. See *Cousens, How Far Corporations May Contribute to Charity*, 35 Va.L. Rev. 401 (1949). . . .

[C]ourts, while adhering to the terms of the common-law rule, have applied it very broadly to enable worthy corporate donations with indirect benefits to the corporations. In *State ex rel. Sorensen v. Chicago B. & Q.R. Co.*, 112 Neb. 248, 199 N.W. 534, 537 (1924), the Supreme Court of Nebraska, through Justice Letton, went even further and without referring to any limitation based on economic benefits to the corporation said that it saw "no reason why if a railroad company desires to foster, encourage and contribute to a charitable enterprise, or to one designed for the public weal and welfare, it may not do so"; later in its opinion it repeated this view with the expression that it saw "no reason why a railroad corporation may not, to a reasonable extent, donate funds or services to aid in good works."

. . .

When the wealth of the nation was primarily in the hands of individuals they discharged their responsibilities as citizens by donating freely for charitable purposes. With the transfer of most of the wealth to corporate hands and the imposition of heavy burdens of individual taxation, they have been unable to keep pace with increased philanthropic needs. They have therefore, with justification, turned to corporations to assume the modern obligations of good citizenship in the same manner as humans do. Congress and state legislatures have enacted laws which encourage corporate contributions, and much has recently been written to indicate the crying need and adequate legal basis therefor. . . . In actual practice corporate giving has correspondingly increased. Thus, it is estimated that annual corporate contributions throughout the nation aggregate over 300 million dollars with over 60 million dollars thereof going to universities and other educational institutions. Similarly, it is estimated that local community chests receive well over 40% of their contributions from corporations; these contributions and those made by corporations to the American Red Cross, to Boy Scouts and Girl Scouts, to 4–H Clubs and similar organizations have almost invariably been unquestioned.

During the first world war corporations loaned their personnel and contributed substantial corporate funds in order to insure survival; during the depression of the '30s they made contributions to alleviate the desperate hardships of the millions of unemployed; and during the second world war they again contributed to insure survival. They now recognize that we are faced with other, though nonetheless vicious, threats from abroad which must be withstood without impairing the vigor of our democratic institutions at home and that otherwise victory will be pyrrhic indeed. More and more they have come to recognize that their salvation rests upon sound economic and social environment which in turn rests in no insignificant part upon free and vigorous nongovernmental institutions of learning. It seems to us that just as the conditions prevailing when corporations were originally created required that they serve public as well as private interests, modern conditions require that corporations acknowledge and discharge social as well as private responsibilities as members of the communities within which they operate. Within this broad concept there is no difficulty in sustaining, as incidental to their proper objects and in aid of the public welfare, the power of corporations to contribute corporate funds within reasonable limits in support of academic institutions. But even if we confine ourselves to the terms of the common-law rule in its application to current conditions, such expenditures may likewise readily be justified as being for the benefit of the corporation; indeed, if need be the matter may be viewed strictly in terms of actual survival of the corporation in a free enterprise system. The genius of our common law has been its capacity for growth and its adaptability to the needs of the times. Generally courts have accomplished the desired result indirectly through the molding of old forms. Occasionally they have done it directly through frank rejection of the old and recognition of the new. But whichever path the common law has taken it has not been found wanting as the proper tool for the advancement of the general good. *Cf. Holmes, The Common Law,* 1, 5 (1951); *Cardozo, Paradoxes of Legal Science, Hall, Selected Writings,* 253 (1947).

In 1930 a statute was enacted in our State which expressly provided that any corporation could cooperate with other corporations and natural persons in the creation and maintenance of community funds and charitable, philanthropic or benevolent instrumentalities conducive to public welfare, and could for such purposes expend such corporate sums as the directors "deem expedient and as in their judgment will contribute to the protection of the corporate interests." . . . In 1950 a more comprehensive statute was enacted. *L.* 1950, *c.* 220; *N.J.S.A.* 14:3–13.1 *et seq.* In this enactment the Legislature declared that it shall be the public policy of our State and in furtherance of the public interest and welfare that encouragement be given to the creation and maintenance of institutions engaged in community fund, hospital, charitable, philanthropic, educational, scientific or benevolent activities or patriotic or civic activities conducive to the betterment of social and economic conditions; and it expressly empowered corporations acting singly or with others to contribute reasonable sums to such institutions, provided, however, that the contribution shall not be permissible if the donee institution owns more than 10% of the voting stock of the donor and provided, further, that the contribution shall not exceed 1% of capital and surplus unless the excess is authorized by the stockholders at a regular or special meeting. To insure that the grant of express power in the 1950 statute would not displace preexisting power at common law or otherwise, the Legislature provided that the "act shall not be construed as directly or indirectly minimizing or interpreting the rights and powers of corporations, as heretofore existing, with reference to appropriations, expenditures or contributions of the nature above specified." N.J.S.A. 14:3–13.3. It may be noted that statutes relating to charitable contributions by corporations have now been passed in 29 states. See *Andrews, supra,* 235.

The appellants contend that the foregoing New Jersey statutes may not be applied to corporations created before their passage. Fifty years before the incorporation of The A.P. Smith Manufacturing Company our Legislature provided that every corporate charter thereafter granted "shall be subject to alteration, suspension and repeal, in the discretion of the legislature." L. 1846, p. 16; R.S. 14:2–9. A similar reserved power was placed into our State Constitution in 1875 (Art. IV, Sec. VII, par. 11), and is found in our present Constitution. . . .

. . . We are entirely satisfied that within the orbit of above authorities the legislative enactments found in *R.S.* 14:3–13 and *N.J. S.A.* 14:3–13.1 *et seq.* and applied to pre-existing corporations do not violate any constitutional guarantees afforded to their stockholders.

. . . And since in our view the corporate power to make reasonable charitable contributions exists under modern conditions, even apart from express statutory provision, its enactments simply constitute helpful and confirmatory declarations of such power, accompanied by limiting safeguards.

In the light of all of the foregoing we have no hesitancy in sustaining the validity of the donation by the plaintiff. There is no suggestion that it was made indiscriminately or to a pet charity of the corporate directors in furtherance of personal rather than corporate ends. On the contrary, it was made to a preeminent institution of higher learning, was modest in amount and well within the limitations imposed by the statutory enactments, and was voluntarily made in the reasonable belief that it would aid the public welfare and advance the interests of the plaintiff as a private corporation and as part of the community in which it operates. We find that it was a lawful exercise of the corporation's implied and incidental powers under common-law principles and that it came within the express authority of the pertinent state legislation. As has been indicated, there is now widespread belief throughout the nation that free and vigorous non-governmental institutions of learning are vital to our democracy and the system of free enterprise and that withdrawal of corporate authority to make such contributions within reasonable limits would seriously threaten their continuance. Corporations have come to recognize this and with their enlightenment have sought in varying measures, as has the plaintiff by its contribution, to insure and strengthen the society which gives them existence and the means of aiding themselves and their fellow citizens. Clearly then, the appellants, as individual stockholders whose private interests rest entirely upon the well-being of the plaintiff corporation, ought not be permitted to close their eyes to present-day realities and thwart the long-visioned corporate action in recognizing and voluntarily discharging its high obligations as a constituent of our modern social structure.

The judgment entered in the Chancery Division is in all respects Affirmed.

For affirmance—Chief Justice VANDERBILT, and Justices HEHER, OLIPHANT, WACHENFELD, BURLING and JACOBS—6.

For reversal—None.

NOTE ON DODGE v. FORD

Chapter XII, Section 1(k)(2), infra.

DEL. GEN. CORP. LAW § 122(9), (12)

[See Statutory Supplement]

REV. MODEL BUS. CORP. ACT § 3.02(12)–(14)

[See Statutory Supplement]

NOTE ON THE CONDUCT OF THE CORPORATION

1. Virtually all states have now adopted statutory provisions relating to corporate contributions comparable to Del.Gen.Corp.Law § 122(9) and Rev.Model Bus.Corp. Act § 3.02(13). Although typically these provisions do not explicitly incorporate a limit of reasonableness, the commentators generally agree that such a limit is to be implied:

> The usual location of such statutes is among the traditional recitations of general corporate powers, such as the right of perpetual succession, amenity to suit and access to the courts, the acquisition and disposition of property, the use of a corporate seal, etc. It is beyond dispute that each of these powers can be employed by corporate representatives only in the interests of the corporation. The directors and officers cannot cause a corporation to acquire property or use its seal for purposes which are foreign to it or unconnected with its interest or benefit. Nothing in the provisions relating to corporate donations changes this principle. Nor does there appear to be any need to do so by affording such statutes a unique construction.

. . . The conversion of a business corporation into an eleemosynary institution would still be improper, as would be the giving away of all or a substantial part of the corporate assets or a constant unbalanced feeding of a "pet" charity without regard for the corporate welfare.

Prunty, Love and the Business Corporation, 46 Va.L.Rev. 467 (1960). Of particular significance is the commentary of Ray Garrett, a principal figure in the drafting history of the Model Act:

Donations should be reasonable in amount in the light of the corporation's financial condition, bear some reasonable relation to the corporation's interest, and not be so "remote and fanciful" as to excite the opposition of shareholders whose property is being used. Direct corporate benefit is no longer necessary, but corporate interest remains as a motive.

Garrett, Corporate Donations, 22 Bus.Law. 297, 301 (1967). See also 6A W. Fletcher, Cyclopedia of the Law of Private Corporations § 2939 (Perm. ed. 1981).

2. There is very little direct authority on the permissibility of taking ethical considerations into account in framing corporate action where doing so might not enhance profits. However, statutory provisions like Rev.Model Bus.Corp. Act § 3.02(13) provide indirect support for doing so, since it would be anomalous to permit the corporation to donate money it has already earned for public welfare or charitable purposes, while prohibiting the corporation from forgoing a limited amount of profits in the service of generally recognized ethical principles.

3. Adams v. Smith, 275 Ala. 142, 153 So.2d 221 (1963), and Moore v. Keystone Macaroni Mfg. Co., 370 Pa. 172, 87 A.2d 295 (1952), held that payments by a corporation to the widow of an executive, in recognition of the executive's past service to the corporation, were improper. In neither case, however, was a showing made that the executive had not been fully compensated for his contributions to the company or that the widow had been left unprovided for. The authority of *Moore* is further weakened by the subsequent adoption of Pa.Bus.Corp.Law § 1316, which provides that "[e]very business corporation may, by resolution of its board of directors, grant allowances or pensions to its directors, officers and employees and, after their death, to their dependents or beneficiaries, whether or not such a grant was made during their lifetime." In Fogelson v. American Woolen Co., 170 F.2d 660 (2d Cir.1948), a corporation had created a pension plan for its employees in which the benefit level was based in part on services prior to the adoption of the plan. A shareholder brought an action challenging the plan, and the district court granted summary judgment for the corporation. The Court of Appeals reversed, on the ground that the size of the president's pension under this plan raised a triable issue of fact whether the directors had exercised their "best business judgment." However, the court of appeals did not reject the theory of funding a pension plan on the basis of past services, and stated that one of the tenable

reasons for the adoption of a pension plan is that it "accords with present day notions of justice to superannuated employees." Id. at 663.

MILTON FRIEDMAN, THE SOCIAL RESPONSIBILITY OF BUSINESS IS TO INCREASE ITS PROFITS, N.Y. Times, Sept. 13, 1970, § 6 (magazine) at 32. "In a free-enterprise, private-property system, a corporate executive is an employee of the owners of the business. He has direct responsibility to his employers. That responsibility is to conduct the business in accordance with their desires, which generally will be to make as much money as possible while conforming to the basic rules of the society, both those embodied in law and those embodied in ethical custom."

AMERICAN LAW INSTITUTE, PRINCIPLES OF CORPORATE GOVERNANCE § 2.01
Tent. Draft No. 2, 1984.

§ 2.01. The Objective and Conduct of the Business Corporation

A business corporation should have as its objective the conduct of business activities with a view to enhancing corporate profit and shareholder gain, except that, whether or not corporate profit and shareholder gain are thereby enhanced, the corporation, in the conduct of its business

(a) is obliged, to the same extent as a natural person, to act within the boundaries set by law,

(b) may take into account ethical considerations that are reasonably regarded as appropriate to the responsible conduct of business, and

(c) may devote a reasonable amount of resources to public welfare, humanitarian, educational, and philanthropic purposes.

SECTION 6.   PREINCORPORATION TRANSACTIONS BY PROMOTERS

INTRODUCTORY NOTE

The term *promoter* has an invidious sound to most of us. To quote Professor L.C.B. Gower:

> If, in a psycho-analyst's consulting room, we were asked to say what picture formed in our minds at the mention of the expression "company promoter," most of us would probably confess that we envision a character of dubious repute

and antecedents who infests the commercial *demi-monde* with a menagerie of bulls, bears, stags, and sharks as his familiars, and who, after rising to affluence by preying on the susceptibilities of a gullible public, finally retires from the scene in the blaze of a sensational suicide or Old Bailey trial.   In other words, we should envisage someone whose profession it was to form bogus companies and foist them off on the public to the latter's detriment and his own profit.   Such figures have existed and it is probably too much to hope that they will ever be entirely eradicated, but even in their Edwardian heyday they formed only the minutest fraction of those whom the law classifies as promoters.

L. Gower, J. Cronin, A. Easson, & Lord Wedderburn of Charlton, Gower's Principles of Modern Company Law 324 (4th Ed. 1979) (footnotes omitted).   See also A. Dewing, Financial Policy of Corporations 402–11 (5th ed. 1953).

The promoter, however, performs a necessary and useful economic service.   He is the person who transforms an idea into a business capable of generating a profit, who brings and holds together the persons needed, and who superintends the various steps required to bring the new business into existence.   He contributes business imagination, plus the judgment and skill to execute the idea.   As noted by Justice Rugg in Old Dominion Copper Mining & Smelting Co. v. Bigelow, 203 Mass. 159, 177, 89 N.E. 193, 201 (1909):

> In a comprehensive sense promoter includes those who undertake to form a corporation and to procure for it the rights, instrumentalities and capital by which it is to carry out the purposes set forth in its charter, and to establish it as fully able to do its business.   Their work may begin long before the organization of the corporation, in seeking the opening for a venture and projecting a plan for its development, and it may continue after the incorporation by attracting the investment of capital in its securities and providing it with the commercial breath of life.

A corporate promotion includes three stages: discovery, investigation, and assembly.   H. Guthmann & H. Dougall, Corporate Financial Policy 248 (4th ed. 1962).   The discovery stage involves the generation of an idea, such as the perception of a need for a new product or service or for another company in an existing line of business.   The investigation stage involves an analysis of what resources will be required to turn the idea into a business and whether the estimated earnings will justify the costs.   The assembly stage involves bringing property, money, and personnel together into an organization.

Often, as part of the assembly stage, contracts are made for the benefit of the corporation even before the corporation has been formed.   If, as is usually the case, the corporation is later formed, and benefits from such a contract, issues may arise regarding whether the corporation becomes liable under the contract, and whether the promoter remains liable. This Section addresses those issues.

RKO–STANLEY WARNER THEATRES, INC.
v. GRAZIANO
Supreme Court of Pennsylvania, 1975.
467 Pa. 220, 355 A.2d 830.

EAGEN, Justice.

On April 30, 1970, RKO–Stanley Warner Theatres, Inc., [RKO], as seller, entered into an agreement of sale with Jack Jenofsky and Ralph Graziano, as purchasers. This agreement contemplated the sale of the Kent Theatre, a parcel of improved commercial real estate located at Cumberland and Kensington Avenues in Philadelphia, for a total purchase price of $70,000. . . . Jenofsky and Graziano failed to complete settlement on the last scheduled date.

Subsequently, on November 13, 1970, RKO filed a complaint in equity seeking judicial enforcement of the agreement of sale. Although Jenofsky, in his answer to the complaint, denied personal liability for the performance of the agreement, the chancellor, after a hearing, entered a decree nisi granting the requested relief sought by RKO.[3] Exceptions to the decree of the chancellor were filed and dismissed by the court en banc which directed that the decree nisi be entered as a final decree. This appeal ensued.

At the time of the execution of this agreement, Jenofsky and Graziano were engaged in promoting the formation of a corporation to be known as Kent Enterprises, Inc. Reflecting these efforts, Paragraph 19 of the agreement, added by counsel for Jenofsky and Graziano, recited:

> "It is understood by the parties hereto that it is the intention of the Purchaser to incorporate. Upon condition that such incorporation be completed by closing, all agreements, covenants, and warranties contained herein shall be construed to have been made between Seller and the resultant corporation and all documents shall reflect same."

In fact, Jenofsky and Graziano did file Articles of Incorporation for Kent Enterprises, Inc., with the State Corporation Bureau on October 9, 1971; twelve days prior to the scheduled settlement date. Jenofsky now contends the inclusion of Paragraph 19 in the agreement and the subsequent filing of incorporation papers, released him from any personal liability resulting from the non-performance of the agreement.

The legal relationship of Jenofsky to Kent Enterprises, Inc., at the date of the execution of the agreement of sale was that of promoter. Dintenfass, to use v. Wirkman, 14 Pa.D. & C. 798, 799 (Phila.Com.

---

3. The chancellor ordered Jenofsky and Graziano to pay $22,500 to RKO and to execute and deliver to RKO their note and purchase money mortgage in the principal sum of $45,000 in accordance with the terms of the agreement.

Pl.1930). As such, he is subject to the general rule that a promoter, although he may assume to act on behalf of a projected corporation and not for himself, will be held personally liable on contracts made by him for the benefit of a corporation he intends to organize. Frazier v. Ash, 234 F.2d 320, 326 (5th Cir.1956); Stanley J. How and Associates, Inc. v. Boss, 222 F.Supp. 936, 939 (S.D.Iowa 1963); King Features Syndicate v. Courrier, 241 Iowa 870, 43 N.W.2d 718 (1950). See also 41 A.L.R.2d 477 et seq.; 13 Am.Jur. 252 et seq., Corporations, § 113. This personal liability will continue even after the contemplated corporation is formed and has received the benefits of the contract, unless there is a novation or other agreement to release liability. Dintenfass, to use v. Wirkman, supra. 18 C.J.S. Corporations § 132.

The imposition of personal liability upon a promoter where that promoter has contracted on behalf of a corporation is based upon the principle that one who assumes to act for a nonexistent principal is himself liable on the contract in the absence of an agreement to the contrary. See 41 A.L.R.2d 477, 485. As stated in Comment (a) under Section 326 of the Restatement of Agency, Second: "there is an inference that a person intends to make a present contract with an existing person. If, therefore, the other party knows that there is no principal capable of entering into such a contract, there is a rebuttable inference that, although the contract is nominally in the name of the nonexistent person, the parties intend that the person signing as agent should be a party, unless there is some indication to the contrary." [4]

However, even though a contract is executed by a promoter on behalf of a proposed corporation, where the person with whom the contract is made agrees to look to the corporation alone for responsibility, the promoter incurs no personal liability with respect to the contract. Frazier v. Ash, supra at 326, 327; 13 Am.Jur. 253, Corporations § 113; 18 C.J.S. Corporations § 132.

In O'Rorke v. Geary, 207 Pa. 240, 56 A. 541 (1903), wherein this Court affirmed on the basis of the opinion of the court below, there is set forth the three possible understandings that parties may have when an agreement is executed by a promoter on behalf of a proposed corporation. It is stated therein:

"When a party is acting for a proposed corporation, he cannot, of course, bind it by anything he does, at the time, but he may (1) take on its behalf an offer from the other which, being accepted after the formation of the company, becomes a contract; (2) make a contract at the time binding himself, with the stipulation or understanding, that if a company is formed it will take his place and that then he shall be relieved of responsibility; or (3) bind himself personally without more and look to the proposed company, when formed, for indemnity."

4. Although Comment (a) speaks in terms of a principal-agent relationship, it is clear that this proposition is also particularly applicable to promoters. Comment (b) of Section 326 provides: "The classic illustration of the rule stated in this Section is the *promoter*." [Emphasis supplied.]

Id. at 242, 56 A. at 542. See also In re Collins Hosiery Mills, 19 F.Supp. 500, 502 (E.D.Pa.1937).

Both RKO and Jenofsky concede the applicability of alternative No. 2 to the instant case. That is, they both recognize that Jenofsky (and Graziano) was to be initially personally responsible with this personal responsibility subsequently being released. Jenofsky contends the parties, by their inclusion of Paragraph 19 in the agreement, manifested an intention to release him from personal responsibility upon the mere formation of the proposed corporation, provided the incorporation was consummated prior to the scheduled closing date. However, while Paragraph 19 does make provision for recognition of the resultant corporation as to the closing documents, it makes no mention of any release of personal liability. Indeed, the entire agreement is silent as to the effect the formation of the projected corporation would have upon the personal liability of Jenofsky and Graziano. Because the agreement fails to provide expressly for the release of personal liability, it is, therefore, subject to more than one possible construction. Cf. Frickert v. Deiter Bros. Fuel Co., Inc., 464 Pa. 596, 347 A.2d 701 (1975).

In Consolidated Tile and Slate Co. v. Fox, 410 Pa. 336, 339, 189 A.2d 228, 229 (1963), we stated that where an agreement is ambiguous and reasonably susceptible of two interpretations, "it must be construed most strongly against those who drew it." We further stated, "if the language of the contract is ambiguous and susceptible of two interpretations, one of which makes it fair, customary and such as prudent men would naturally execute, while the other makes it inequitable, unusual, or such as reasonable men would not likely enter into, the construction which makes it rational and probable must be preferred." Cf. Frickert v. Deiter Bros. Fuel Co., Inc., supra. Instantly, the chancellor determined that the intent of the parties to the agreement was to hold Jenofsky personally responsible until such time as a corporate entity was formed and until such time as that corporate entity adopted the agreement. We believe this construction represents the only rational and prudent interpretation of the parties' intent.

As found by the court below, this agreement was entered into on the financial strength of Jenofsky and Graziano, alone as individuals. Therefore, it would have been illogical for RKO to have consented to the release of their personal liability upon the mere formation of a resultant corporation prior to closing. For it is a well-settled rule that a contract made by a promoter, even though made for and in the name of a proposed corporation, in the absence of a subsequent adoption (either expressly or impliedly) by the corporation, will not be binding upon the corporation. See 18 C.J.S. Corporations § 118; Zalewski v. Pennsylvania Rabbit Breeders Cooperative, 76 Pa.D. & C. 225, 227 (Adams Com.Pl.1950). If, as Jenofsky contends, the intent was to release personal responsibility upon the mere incorporation prior to closing, the effect of the agreement would have been to create the possibility that RKO, in the event of non-performance, would be able to hold no party accountable; there being no guarantee that the resultant corporation would ratify the agreement.[5] Without express language in the agreement indicating that such was the intention of the parties, we may not attribute this intention to them.

Hold

Therefore, we hold that the intent of the parties in entering into this agreement was to have Jenofsky and Graziano personally liable until such time as the intended corporation was formed and ratified the agreement.[6]

Decree affirmed. Costs on Jenofsky.

JONES, C.J., took no part in the consideration or decision of this case.

ROBERTS, J., filed a concurring opinion in which NIX, J., joined.

MANDERINO, J., filed a dissenting opinion.

ROBERTS, Justice (concurring).

Although I concur in the majority's result, I cannot join in most of its analysis. Well-settled principles of contract law support the chancellor's findings. Thus, there is no need for the majority's extended discussion of the doctrine of promoter's liability.

Appellee contracted to sell property to appellant. Appellant argues that a clause in the written agreement, which he drafted, relieves him of liability provided he forms a corporation before the closing date. He claims this is so regardless whether the new corporation adopts the contract.

The agreement, as drafted, does not specifically address whether appellant is relieved of liability upon the mere formation of a new corporation. Rather, it is ambiguous because it is susceptible of two possible constructions. Under appellant's proposed construction, the contract allows him to avoid liability completely, leaving appellee no rights under the contract. As the majority correctly notes, it is unlikely that appellee agreed to such unreasonable terms.

When determining the intent of the parties to an ambiguous agreement, preference should be given to that construction which is both rational and probable. . . . Additionally, an ambiguous clause in an agreement should be construed against the interest of the drafting party: appellant. . . . Thus, the chancellor's finding that the parties agreed to hold appellant liable until such time as the new corporation adopted the agreement is fully supported in the record. I therefore concur in the majority's result.

5. In this regard, we note that there is no allegation by Jenofsky that Kent Enterprises, Inc., either expressly adopted or attempted to ratify the agreement entered into with RKO.

6. We are buttressed in this conclusion by reference to alternative No. 2, set forth in O'Rorke v. Geary, supra, and conceded by both parties to represent their intentions herein. This alternative clearly envisions some affirmative action by the projected corporation before the release of the promoter's personal liability will be effected, i.e., "if a company is formed *it will take his place.*" [Emphasis supplied.] Similarly, Comment (b) under Section 326 of the Restatement of Agency, Second, provides that parties "may agree to a present contract by which the promoter is bound, but with an agreement that his liability terminates if the corporation is formed *and manifest its willingness to become a party.*" [Emphasis supplied.]

NIX, J., joins in this concurring opinion.

MANDERINO, Justice (dissenting).

I dissent. Contrary to the majority's finding that the agreement was ambiguous because of its failure to provide expressly for the release of appellant Jenofsky from personal liability, I find clear on the face of paragraph 19 of the agreement an intention to release Jenofsky from personal liability upon the mere formation of the proposed corporation, provided the incorporation was completed prior to the scheduled closing date. According to paragraph 19, once the incorporation was completed, "all agreements . . . [would] be construed to have been made between the seller and the resultant corporation. . . ."

It is inconceivable to me how the majority can agree with the Chancellor's finding that Jenofsky was to be personally responsible until the new corporation in some way adopted the agreement. There is no language anywhere in the agreement to suggest such a far-fetched interpretation. Paragraph 19 clearly states that Jenofsky was to be releasd from personal liability as soon as the corporation was formed.

Nor is it our duty to decide the logic, or lack of logic, of the parties in entering into this agreement. This was not a contract of adhesion, and, just because we might not have entered into the same contract, we nevertheless cannot read beyond its clearly intended meaning. I would therefore reverse the decision of the court en banc.

REV. MODEL BUS. CORP. ACT § 2.04

[See Statutory Supplement]

QUAKER HILL, INC. v. PARR, 148 Colo. 45, 364 P.2d 1056 (1961). Quaker Hill sold a large quantity of nursery stock to "Denver Memorial Nursery, Inc." A sales contract was executed together with a promissory note. The form of the signature on the note was as follows:

"Denver Memorial Nursery, Inc.

"E.D. Parr, Pres.

"James P. Presba, Sc'y.–Treas."

The signature on the contract was comparable.

As Quaker Hill knew, Denver Memorial Nursery, Inc. had not yet been formed when the contract was signed. Quaker Hill had insisted that the deal be consummated even before the corporation was formed, because the growing season was rapidly passing. About a week after the contract was signed, the corporation that was originally to be called Denver Memorial Nurseries, Inc. was formed under the name "Mountain View Nurseries, Inc." A new note and contract, prepared by Quaker Hill's Division Manager, and containing the name Mountain View Nurseries, Inc. as contracting party, was then submitted to Parr and Presba, signed in Mountain View's name, and returned to Quaker Hill. Quaker Hill thereafter used the designation Mountain View Nurseries in its communications. Mountain View never functioned as a going concern, and Quaker Hill brought suit under the contract and note against Parr and Presba, in their individual capacities. Held, for defendants.

"The general principle which plaintiff urges as applicable here is that promoters are personally liable on their contracts, though made on behalf of a corporation to be formed. . . . A well recognized exception to this general rule, however, is that if the contract is made on behalf of the corporation and the other party agrees to look to the corporation and not to the promoters for payment, the promoters incur no personal liability.

"In the present case, according to the trial court's findings, the plaintiff, acting through its agent, was well aware of the fact that the corporation was not formed and nevertheless urged that the contract be made in the name of the proposed corporation. There is but little evidence indicating intent on the part of the plaintiff to look to the defendants for performance or payment. The single fact supporting plaintiff's theory is the obtaining of an individual balance sheet. On the contrary, the entire transaction contemplated the corporation as the contracting party. Personal liability does not arise under such circumstances. See 41 A.L.R.2d 477, where the annotation recognizes the noted exception that personal liability does not attach where the contracting party is shown to be looking solely to the corporation for payment and not to the promoters or officers."

RESTATEMENT (SECOND) OF AGENCY § 326, Comment b (1958). "When a promoter makes an agreement with another on behalf of a corporation to be formed, the following alternatives may represent the intent of the parties:

"(1) They may understand that the other party is making a revocable offer to the nonexistent corporation which will result in a contract if the corporation is formed and accepts the offer prior to the withdrawal. This is the normal understanding.

"(2) They may understand that the other party is making an irrevocable offer for a limited time. Consideration to support the promise to keep the offer open can be found in an express or limited promise by the promoter to organize the corporation and use his best efforts to cause it to accept the offer.

"(3) They may agree to a present contract by which the promoter is bound, but with an agreement that his liability terminates if the corporation is formed and manifests its willingness to become a party. There can be no ratification by the newly formed corporation, since it was not in existence when the agreement was made. . . .

"(4) They may agree to a present contract on which, even though the corporation becomes a party, the promoter remains liable either primarily or as surety for the performance of the corporation's obligation.

"Which one of these possible alternatives, or variants thereof, is intended is a matter of interpretation on the facts of the individual case."

D. A. McARTHUR v. TIMES PRINTING CO.
Supreme Court of Minnesota, 1892.
48 Minn. 319, 51 N.W. 216.

MITCHELL, J.   The complaint alleges that about October 1, 1889, the defendant contracted with plaintiff for his services as advertising solicitor for one year; that in April, 1890, it discharged him, in violation of the contract.   The action is to recover damages for the breach of the contract.   The answer sets up two defenses: (1) That plaintiff's employment was not for any stated time, but only from week to week; (2) that he was discharged for good cause.   Upon the trial there was evidence reasonably tending to prove that in September, 1889, one C.A. Nimocks and others were engaged as promoters in procuring the organization of the defendant company to publish a newspaper; that, about September 12th, Nimocks, as such promoter, made a contract with plaintiff in behalf of the contemplated company, for his services as advertising solicitor for the period of one year from and after October 1st,—the date at which it was expected that the company would be organized; that the corporation was not, in fact, organized until October 16th, but that the publication of the paper was commenced by the promoters October 1st, at which date plaintiff, in pursuance of his arrangement with Nimocks entered upon the discharge of his duties as advertising solicitor for the paper; that after the organization of the company he continued in his employment in the same capacity until discharged, the following April; that defendant's board of directors never took any formal action with reference to the contract made in its behalf by Nimocks, but all of the stockholders, directors, and officers of the corporation knew of this contract at the time of its organization, or were informed of it soon afterwards, and none of them objected to or repudiated it, but, on the contrary, retained plaintiff in the employment of the company without any other or new contract as to his services.

There is a line of cases which hold that where a contract is made in behalf of, or for the benefit of, a projected corporation, the corporation, after its organization, cannot become a party to the contract, either by adoption or ratification of it.   Abbott v. Hapgood, 150 Mass. 248, 22 N.E. 907; Beach, Corporation, sec. 198.   This, however, seems to be more a question of name than of substance; that is, whether the liability of the corporation, in such cases, is to be placed on the ground of its adoption of the contract of its promoters, or upon some other ground, such as equitable estoppel.   This court, in accordance with what we deem sound reason, as well as the weight of authority, has held that, while a corporation is not bound by engagements made on its behalf by its promoters before its organization, it may, after its organization, make such engagements its own contracts. And this it may do precisely as it might make similar original contracts; formal action of its board of directors being necessary only where it would be necessary in the case of a similar original contract. That [is,] it is not requisite that such adoption or acceptance be expressed, but it may be inferred from acts or acquiescence on part of the corporation, or its authorized agents, as any similar original contract might be shown. Battelle v. Northwestern Cement & Concrete Pavement Co., 37 Minn. 89, 33 N.W. 327 (1887). See, also, Mor. Corp. sec. 548. The right of the corporate agents to adopt an agreement originally made by promoters depends upon the purposes of the corporation and the nature of the agreement. Of course, the agreement must be one which the corporation itself could make, and one which the usual agents of the company have express or implied authority to make. That the contract in this case was of that kind is very clear; and the acts and acquiescence of the corporate officers, after the organization of the company, fully justified the jury in finding that it had adopted it as its own.

The defendant, however, claims that the contract was void under the statute of frauds, because, "by its terms, not to be performed within one year from the making thereof," which counsel assumes to be September 12th,—the date of the agreement between plaintiff and the promoter. This proceeds upon the erroneous theory that the act of the corporation, in such cases, is a ratification, which relates back to the date of the contract with the promoter, under the familiar maxim that "a subsequent ratification has a retroactive effect, and is equivalent to a prior command." But the liability of the corporation, under such circumstances, does not rest upon any principle of the law of agency, but upon the immediate and voluntary act of the company. Although the acts of a corporation with reference to the contracts made by promoters in its behalf before its organization are frequently loosely termed "ratification," yet a "ratification," properly so called, implies an existing person, on whose behalf the contract might have been made at the time. There cannot, in law, be a ratification of a contract which could not have been made binding on the ratifier at the time it was made, because the ratifier was not then in existence. In re Empress Engineering Co., 16 Ch.Div. 128; Melhado v. Porto Alegre, N.H. & B. Ry. Co., L.R. 9 C.P. 505; Kelner v. Baxter, L.R. 2 C.P. 185. What is called "adoption," in such cases, is, in legal effect, the making of a contract of the date of the adoption, and not as of some former date. The contract in this case was, therefore, not within the statute of frauds. The trial court fairly submitted to the jury all the issues of fact in this case, accompanied by instructions as to the law which were exactly in the line of the views we have expressed; and the evidence justified the verdict.

The point is made that plaintiff should have alleged that the contract was made with Nimocks, and subsequently adopted by the defendant. If we are correct in what we have said as to the legal effect of the adoption by the corporation of a contract made by a promoter in its behalf before its organization, the plaintiff properly pleaded the contract as having been made with the defendant. But we do not find that the evidence was objected to on the ground of variance between it and the complaint. The assignments of error are very numerous, but what has been already said covers all that are entitled to any special notice.

Order affirmed.

CLIFTON v. TOMB, 21 F.2d 893 (4th Cir.1947). ". . . Since a corporation before its organization cannot have agents, and is unable to contract or be contracted with, it is not liable upon any contract which a promoter attempts to make for it, unless it becomes so by its own act after its incorporation is completed. . . . But there are cases where a corporation becomes bound for the contracts of its promoters. While there are many decisions holding corporations liable in such cases, the courts have had great difficulty in finding a scientific or rational basis for sustaining such liability. The usual grounds that have been suggested are ratification, adoption, novation, and that the proposition made to the promoters is a continuing offer to be accepted or rejected by the corporation when it comes into being, and upon acceptance becomes an original contract on its part; and the liability has also been sustained on the ground that the corporation, by accepting the benefits of a contract, takes it cum onere, and is estopped to deny its liability on the contract."

SECTION 7. CONSEQUENCES OF DEFECTIVE INCORPORATION

CANTOR v. SUNSHINE GREENERY, INC.
Superior Court of New Jersey, Appellate Division, 1979.
165 N.J.Super. 411, 398 A.2d 571.

LARNER, J.

This appeal involves the propriety of a personal judgment against defendant William J. Brunetti for the breach of a lease between plaintiffs and a corporate entity known as Sunshine Greenery, Inc., and more particularly whether there was a *de facto* corporation in existence at the time of the execution of the lease.

Plaintiffs brought suit for damages for the breach of the lease against Sunshine Greenery, Inc. and Brunetti. Default judgment was entered against the corporation and a nonjury trial was held as to the liability of the individual. The trial judge in a letter opinion determined that plaintiffs were entitled to judgment against Brunetti individually on the theory that as of the time of the creation of the contract he was acting as a promoter and that his corporation, Sunshine Greenery, Inc., was not a legal or *de facto* corporation.

The undisputed facts reveal the following: Plaintiffs prepared the lease naming Sunshine Greenery, Inc. as the tenant, and it was signed by Brunetti as president of that named entity. Mr. Cantor, acting for plaintiffs, knew that Brunetti was starting a new venture as a newly formed corporation known as Sunshine Greenery, Inc. Although Cantor had considerable experience in ownership and leasing of commercial property to individuals and corporations, he did not request a personal guarantee from Brunetti, nor did he make inquiry as to his financial status or background. Without question, he knew and expected that the lease agreement was undertaken by the corporation and not by Brunetti individually, and that the corporation would be responsible thereunder.

At the time of the signing of the lease on December 16, 1974 in Cantor's office, Brunetti was requested by Cantor to give him a check covering the first month's rent and the security deposit. When Brunetti stated that he was not prepared to do so because he had no checks with him, Cantor furnished a blank check which was filled out for $1,200, with the name of Brunetti's bank and signed by him as president of Sunshine Greenery, Inc. The lease was repudiated by a letter from counsel for Sunshine Greenery, Inc. dated December 17, 1974, which in turn was followed by a response from Cantor to the effect that he would hold the "client" responsible for all losses. The check was not honored because Brunetti stopped payment, and in any event because Sunshine Greenery, Inc. did not have an account in the bank.

The evidence is clear that on November 21, 1974 the corporate name of Sunshine Greenery, Inc. had been reserved for Brunetti by the Secretary of State, and that on December 3, 1974 a certificate of incorporation for that company was signed by Brunetti and Sharyn N. Sansoni as incorporators. The certificate was forwarded by mail to the Secretary of State on that same date with a check for the filing fee, but for some unexplained reason it was not officially filed until December 18, 1974, two days after the execution of the lease.[1]

In view of the late filing, Sunshine Greenery, Inc. was not a *de jure* corporation on December 16, 1974 when the lease was signed. See N.J.S.A. 14A:2–7(2). Nevertheless, there is ample evidence of the fact that it was a *de facto* corporation in that there was a *bona fide* attempt to organize the corporation some time before the consummation of the contract and there was an actual exercise of the corporate powers by the negotiations with plaintiffs and the execution of the contract involved in this litigation. When this is considered in the light of the concession that plaintiffs knew that they were dealing with that corporate entity and not with Brunetti individually, it becomes evident that the *de facto* status of the corporation suffices to absolve Brunetti from individual liability. Plaintiffs in effect are estopped from attacking the legal existence of the corporation collaterally

---

1. We note that the letter enclosing the certificate of incorporation is addressed to "Mortimer G. Newman, Jr., Secretary of State, State House Annex, Trenton, New Jersey." Whether this misidentification of the person holding the office of Secretary of State accounts for the filing delay we are unable to say from the record.

because of the nonfiling in order to impose liability on the individual when they have admittedly contracted with a corporate entity which had *de facto* status. . . .   In fact, their prosecution of the claim against the corporation to default judgment is indicative of their recognition of the corporation as the true obligor and theoretically inconsistent with the assertion of the claim against the individual.

The trial judge's finding that Sunshine Greenery, Inc. was not a *de facto* corporation is unwarranted under the record facts herein.   The mere fact that there were no formal meetings or resolutions or issuance of stock is not determinative of the legal or *de facto* existence of the corporate entity, particularly under the simplified New Jersey Business Corporation Act of 1969, which eliminates the necessity of a meeting of incorporators.   See N.J.S.A. 14A:2–6 and Commissioners' Comment thereunder.   The act of executing the certificate of incorporation, the *bona fide* effort to file it and the dealings with plaintiffs in the name of that corporation fully satisfy the requisite proof of the existence of a *de facto* corporation.   To deny such existence because of a mere technicality caused by administrative delay in filing runs counter to the purpose of the *de facto* concept, and would accomplish an unjust and inequitable result in favor of plaintiffs contrary to their own contractual expectations. . . .

In view of the foregoing, the judgment entered against defendant William J. Brunetti is reversed and set aside, and the matter is remanded to the Law Division to enter judgment on the complaint in favor of William J. Brunetti.

TIMBERLINE EQUIPMENT CO., INC. v. DAVENPORT

Supreme Court of Oregon, 1973.
267 Or. 64, 514 P.2d 1109.

DENECKE, Justice.

Plaintiff brought this action for equipment rentals against the defendant Dr. Bennett and two others.   In addition to making a general denial, Dr. Bennett alleged as a defense that the rentals were to a de facto corporation, Aero–Fabb Corp., of which Dr. Bennett was an incorporator, director and shareholder.   He also alleged plaintiff was estopped from denying the corporate character of the organization to whom plaintiff rented the equipment.   The trial court held for plaintiff.   Dr. Bennett, only, appeals.

On January 22, 1970, Dr. Bennett signed articles of incorporation for Aero–Fabb Co.   The original articles were not in accord with the statutes and, therefore, no certificate of incorporation was issued for the corporation until June 12, 1970, after new articles were filed.   The leases were entered into and rentals earned during the period between January 22nd and June 12th.

Prior to 1953 Oregon had adopted the common-law doctrine that prohibited a collateral attack on the legality of a defectively organized corporation which had achieved the status of a de facto corporation. See, for example, Marsters v. Umpqua Oil Co., 49 Or. 374, 377, 90 P. 151, 12 LRA(ns) 825 (1907).

In 1953 the legislature adopted the Oregon Business Corporation Act. Oregon Laws 1953, ch. 549. The Model Business Corporation Act was used as a working model for the Oregon Act. 1952 Oregon State Bar Committee Reports, p. 5.

ORS 57.321 of the Oregon Business Corporation Act provides:

"Upon the issuance of the certificate of incorporation, the corporate existence shall begin, and such certificate of incorporation shall be conclusive evidence that all conditions precedent required to be performed by the incorporators have been complied with and that the corporation has been incorporated under the Oregon Business Corporation Act, except as against this state in a proceeding to cancel or revoke the certificate of incorporation or for involuntary dissolution of the corporation."

This section is virtually identical to § 56 of the Model Act. The Comment to the Model, prepared as a research project by the American Bar Foundation and edited by the American Bar Association Committee on Corporate Laws, states:

* * *

"Under the unequivocal provisions of the Model Act, any steps short of securing a certificate of incorporation would not constitute apparent compliance. Therefore a de facto corporation cannot exist under the Model Act.

"Like provisions are made throughout the Model Act in respect of the conclusiveness of the issuance by the secretary of state of the appropriate certificate in connection with filings made in his office. . . .

"In some states, however, issuance of the certificate of incorporation and compliance with any additional requirements for filing, recording or publication is not conclusive evidence of incorporation. In those states, such action is stated to be only prima facie evidence of incorporation, and in others the effect is merely one of estoppel preventing any question of due incorporation being raised in legal actions by or against the corporation." Model Business Corporation Act Annotated § 56, p. 205 (2d ed. 1971).

ORS 57.793 provides:

"All persons who assume to act as a corporation without the authority of a certificate of incorporation issued by the Corporation Commissioner, shall be jointly and severally liable for all debts and liabilities incurred or arising as a result thereof."

This is merely an elaboration of § 146 of the Model Act. The Comment states:

"This section is designed to prohibit the application of any theory of de facto incorporation. The only authority to act as a corporation under the Model Act arises from completion of the procedures prescribed in sections 53 to 55 inclusive. The consequences of those procedures are specified in section 56 as being the creation of a corporation. No other means being authorized, the effect of section 146 is to negate the possibility of a de facto corporation.

"Abolition of the concept of de facto incorporation, which at best was fuzzy, is a sound result. No reason exists for its continuance under general corporate laws, where the process of acquiring de jure incorporation is both simple and clear. The vestigial appendage should be removed." 2 Model Business Corporation Act Annotated § 146, pp. 908–909 (2d ed. 1971).

In Robertson v. Levy, 197 A.2d 443 (D.C.Ct. of App.1964), the court held the president of a defectively organized corporation personally liable to a creditor of the "corporation." The applicable legislation was similar to Oregon's. The court held the legislation ended the common-law doctrine of de facto corporation.

The Alaska court upheld the cancellation of a special land-use permit upon the ground that the applicant had not yet been issued its certificate of incorporation at the time the permit was issued. Swindel v. Kelly, 499 P.2d 291 (Alaska 1972). Alaska has a statute similar to Oregon's. The court commented: "The concept of de facto corporations has been increasingly disfavored, and Alaska is among the states whose corporation statutes are designed to eliminate the concept." 499 P.2d at 299, n. 28.

Vincent Drug Co. v. Utah State Tax Com'n, 17 Utah 2d 202, 407 P.2d 683 (1965), cited by defendant, involved a statute similar to that of Oregon; however, the court held the de facto corporation doctrine continued to exist. No reasoning is stated and we find the case unpersuasive.

We hold the principle of de facto corporation no longer exists in Oregon.

The defendant also contends that the plaintiff is estopped to deny that it contracted with a corporation.[1]

The doctrine of "corporation by estoppel" has been recognized by this court but never fully dissected. . . . Corporation by estoppel is a difficult concept to grasp and courts and writers have "gone all over the lot" in attempting to define and apply the doctrine. One of the better explanations of the problem and the varied solutions is

1. Robertson v. Levy, supra (197 A.2d 443), held the adoption of the provisions of the Model Business Corporation Act eliminated the concept of corporations by estoppel as well as de facto corporations. Fletcher follows this view. Fletcher, supra, § 3890. However, the same court that decided Robertson v. Levy, with the same panel, held a party was estopped to deny the existence of the corporation. Namerdy v. Generalcar, 217 A.2d 109 (D.C.Ct. of App.1966). Robertson v. Levy was not mentioned.

In view of our decision that the defense of estoppel was not established, we do not need to decide the effect of the new Business Corporation Act on the doctrine of estoppel. We observe, however, that "[a]lthough some cases tend to assimilate the doctrines of incorporation *de facto* and by estoppel, each is a distinct theory and they are not dependent on one another in their application." Cranson v. International Business Machine Corp., 234 Md. 477, 200 A.2d 33, 38 (1964).

contained in Ballantine, Manual of Corporation Law and Practice §§ 28–30 (1930):

> "The so-called estoppel that arises to deny corporate capacity does not depend on the presence of the technical elements of equitable estoppel, viz., misrepresentations and change of position in reliance thereon, but on the nature of the relations contemplated, that one who has recognized the organization as a corporation in business dealings should not be allowed to quibble or raise immaterial issues on matters which do not concern him in the slightest degree or affect his substantial rights." Ballantine, supra, at 92.

As several writers have pointed out, in order to apply the doctrine correctly, the cases must be classified according to who is being charged with estoppel. Ballantine, supra, at 91; 1 Hornstein, Corporation Law and Practice § 30, p. 31, n. 6 (1959).

When a defendant seeks to escape liability to a corporation plaintiff by contending that the plaintiff is not a lawful corporate entity, courts readily apply the doctrine of corporation by estoppel. Thompson Optical Institute v. Thompson [119 Or. 252, 237 P. 965 (1925)], well illustrates the equity of the doctrine in this class of cases. R.A. Thompson carried on an optical business for years. He then organized a corporation to buy his optical business and subscribed to most of the stock in this corporation. He chaired the first meeting at which the Board resolved to purchase the business from him. The corporation and Thompson entered into a contract for the sale of the business which included a covenant by Thompson not to compete. Thereafter, Thompson sold all of his stock to another individual. Some years later Thompson re-entered the optical business in violation of the covenant not to compete. The corporation brought suit to restrain Thompson from competing. Thompson defended upon the ground that the corporation had not been legally organized. We held, "The defendant cannot be heard to challenge the validity of the contract or the proper organization of the corporation."[2] 119 Or. at 260, 237 P. at 968.

The fairness of estopping a defendant such as Thompson from denying the corporate existence of his creation is apparent.

On the other hand, when individuals such as the defendants in this case seek to escape liability by contending that the debtor is a corporation, Aero–Fabb Co., rather than the individual who purported to act as a corporation, the courts are more reluctant to estop the plaintiff from attacking the legality of the alleged debtor corporation. Ballantine, supra, at 96; 8 Fletcher, Cyclopedia of the Law of Private Corporations (perm. ed.) § 3914, p. 228.

The most appealing explanation of why the plaintiff may be estopped is based upon the intention of the parties. The creditor-plaintiff contracted believing it could look for payment only to the

---

2. The court also based its decision upon a finding that the plaintiff was a de facto corporation.

corporate entity.   The associates, whatever their relationship to the supposed corporate entity, believed their only potential liability was the loss of their investment in the supposed corporate entity and that they were not personally liable. . . .

From the plaintiff-creditor's viewpoint, such reasoning is somewhat tenuous.   The creditor did nothing to create the appearance that the debtor was a legal corporate entity.   The creditor formed its intention to contract with a debtor corporate entity because someone associated with the debtor represented, expressly or impliedly, that the debtor was a legal corporate entity.

We need not decide whether the doctrine of corporation by estoppel would apply in such a case as this.   The trial court found that if this doctrine was still available under the Business Corporation Act defendants did not prove all the elements necessary for its application, and, moreover, it would be inequitable to apply the doctrine.[3]

Under the explanation stated above for the application of the doctrine of estoppel in this kind of case, it is necessary that the plaintiff believe that it was contracting with a corporate entity.   The evidence on this point is contradictory and the trial court apparently found against defendants.

The trial court found, and its findings are supported by the evidence, that all the defendants were partners prior to January 1970 and did business under the name "Aero–Fabb Co."   Not until June 1970 were the interests in this partnership assigned to the corporation "Aero–Fabb Co." and about the same time the assumed business name "Aero–Fabb Co." was cancelled. . . .

Plaintiff's bookkeeper testified that she thought it was a corporation because, "This was the way the information was given to me."   It is uncertain whether the information was given to her by someone employed by plaintiff or by a company with whom she made a credit check.   In any event, plaintiff's salesman said Mr. Davenport, speaking for the organization, stated several times that he was in a partnership with Drs. Gorman and Bennett.   The salesman was dubious and checked the title to the land on which the debtors' operation was being conducted and found it was in the name of the three defendants as individuals.

A final question remains: Can the plaintiff recover against Dr. Bennett individually?

In the first third of this century the liability of persons associated with defectively organized corporations was a controversial and well-documented legal issue.   The orthodox view was that if an organization had not achieved de facto status and the plaintiff was not estopped to attack the validity of the corporate status of the corporation, all shareholders were liable as partners.   This court, however, rejected the orthodox rule.   In Rutherford v. Hill, 22 Or. 218, 29 P. 546, 29 Am.St.R. 596, 17 L.R.A. 549 (1892), we held that a person could not

---

3. The trial court made these as conclusions of law, but these statements are in effect general findings of fact.

be held liable as a partner merely because he signed the articles of incorporation though the corporation was so defectively formed as to fall short of de facto status. The court stated that under this rule a mere passive stockholder would not be held liable as a partner. We went on to observe, however, that if the party actively participated in the business he might be held liable as a partner.

This controversy subsided 30 or 40 years ago probably because the procedure to achieve de jure corporate status was made simpler; so the problem did not arise.

The Model Act and the Oregon Business Corporation Act, ORS 57.793, solve the problem as follows:

> "All persons who assume to act as a corporation without the authority of a certificate of incorporation issued by the Corporation Commissioner, shall be jointly and severally liable for all debts and liabilities incurred or arising as a result thereof."

We have found no decisions, comments to the Model Act, or literature attempting to explain the intent of this section.

We find the language ambiguous. Liability is imposed on "[a]ll persons who assume to act as a corporation." Such persons shall be liable "for all debts and liabilities incurred or arising as a result thereof."

We conclude that the category of "persons who assume to act as a corporation" does not include those whose only connection with the organization is as an investor. On the other hand, the restriction of liability to those who personally incurred the obligation sued upon cannot be based upon logic or the realities of business practice. When several people carry on the activities of a defectively organized corporation, chance frequently will dictate which of the several active principals directly incurs a certain obligation or whether an employee, rather than an active principal, personally incurs the obligation.

We are of the opinion that the phrase, "persons who assume to act as a corporation" should be interpreted to include those persons who have an investment in the organization and who actively participate in the policy and operational decisions of the organization. Liability should not necessarily be restricted to the person who personally incurred the obligation.

The trial court found that Dr. Bennett "acted in the business venture which was subsequently incorporated on June 12, 1970."

The proposed business of the corporation which was to be formed was to sell airplanes, recondition airplanes and give flying lessons. Land was leased for this purpose. Equipment was rented from plaintiff to level and clear for access and for other construction.

There is evidence from which the trial court could have found that while Drs. Bennett and Gorman, another defendant, entrusted the details of management to Davenport, they endeavored to and did retain some control over his management. All checks required one of their signatures. Dr. Bennett frequently visited the site and observed the activity and the presence of the equipment rented by plaintiff. He met with the organization's employees to discuss the operation of the business. Shortly after the equipment was rented and before most of the rent had accrued, Dr. Bennett was informed of the rentals and given an opinion that they were unnecessary and ill-advised. Drs. Bennett and Gorman thought they had Davenport and his management "under control."

This evidence all supports the finding that Dr. Bennett was a person who assumed to act for the organization and the conclusion of the trial court that Dr. Bennett is personally liable.

Affirmed.

NOTE ON CANTOR

At the time *Cantor* was decided, the New Jersey statute had a counterpart of Model Act § 56, but did not have a counterpart of Model Act § 146.

REV. MODEL BUS. CORP. ACT §§ 2.03, 2.04

[See Statutory Supplement]

DEL. GEN. CORP. LAW §§ 106, 329, 392

[See Statutory Supplement]

NOTE ON ESTOPPEL

The court in *Timberline* pointed out that the estoppel theory is sometimes used as an alternative to the de facto corporation theory. Neither the precise contours of the estoppel theory nor its relationship to the de facto theory has ever been entirely clear. It is sometimes said that the estoppel theory differs from the de facto theory in that it is effective for only a specific transaction. However, the de facto theory also may be effective only for a specific transaction: A decision in one suit that a corporation has de facto status will normally not be controlling in a suit brought by an unrelated plaintiff on an unrelated transaction.

A problem with the estoppel theory is that in fact it is not a single theory, but a cluster of very different rules covering cases that fall into very different categories, only one of which involves a true estoppel, that is, reliance by one party on the other's representation.

1. First is the case in which an association, or its owners, having claimed corporate status in an earlier transaction with a third party, T, later denies that status in a suit brought by T. This is a true estoppel case, at least if T relied on the initial claim.

2. Another category consists of cases in which the question of corporate status is raised in a technical procedural context. For example, the defendant in a suit brought by a would-be corporation may seek to raise the defense that the plaintiff is not really a corporation, and therefore cannot sue in a corporate name. The courts tend to regard such defenses as nonmeritorious, and to brush them off, using "estoppel" as a handy tool.

3. In the most important category of cases, a third party who has dealt with a business as a corporation seeks to impose personal liability on would-be shareholders who in turn raise estoppel as a defense. Here the issue is whether, as a matter of equity, the claimant, having dealt with a business as if it were a corporation, should be prevented—"estopped"—from treating it as anything else. A leading case in this category is Cranson v. International Business Mach. Corp., 234 Md. 477, 200 A.2d 33 (1964). Here a third party had dealt with a business as if it were a corporation. In fact, it wasn't, because, without the knowledge of the would-be shareholders, their attorney had negligently failed to file the certificate of incorporation before the transaction with the third party.

In this third category of cases the estoppel theory is comparable in its function to the de facto theory, but the two theories differ in two important ways in their application:

First, the nub of the estoppel theory in such cases is that the third party has dealt with the business as if it were a corporation. Presumably, therefore, the theory would not apply to a tort claimant, or other involuntary creditor, who was a stranger to the business before his claim arose. In contrast, the de facto theory can be applied to such claimants.

Second, the would-be shareholders would not need to resort to the estoppel theory if they could establish that their business had de facto corporate status. Presumably, therefore, less in the way of corporateness must be shown to establish a corporation by estoppel than to establish a de facto corporation. (Thus in Cranson v. International Business Mach., supra, the court applied the estoppel theory only after observing that since the certificate of incorporation had not been filed at the time of the transaction, the de facto theory might not be applicable.)

There is an obvious relationship between the first and second points. A tort claimant or other involuntary creditor has a stronger claim against would-be shareholders than a contract creditor, because a contract creditor who transacts with a would-be corporation expects only limited liability, while the expectation of a typical tort or other involuntary creditor is usually not so limited.

NOTE ON QUO WARRANTO

1. A traditional method for testing corporate status is through a quo warranto proceeding brought by the state. This proceeding

derives from an ancient prerogative writ issued on behalf of the King against one who falsely claimed an office or franchise. Such a proceeding can be maintained even against a de facto corporation, because the de facto theory is a defense only against a "collateral attack" on corporate status—in effect, only against a challenge raised by private actors—not against a challenge by the state itself.

Most states now provide by statute for proceedings in the nature of quo warranto, often without using that name. See, e.g., New York § 109; California § 1801(a).

2. An association that fails to meet all the requirements for incorporation may nevertheless be a corporation "de jure" if the noncompliance is extremely insubstantial. De jure status, unlike de facto status, is a good defense even to a quo warranto proceeding. For example, in People v. Ford, 294 Ill. 319, 128 N.E. 479 (1920), the Attorney General filed an information in the nature of quo warranto against three incorporators who had failed to comply with a statute providing that the statement of incorporation be sealed. The incorporators had filed on the Secretary of State's forms, which neither contained nor mentioned a seal. The court concluded that de jure status had been attained: the provision for a seal was only "directory," because the purpose of the statute was to make a public record, and a seal did not further that purpose.

SECTION 8. DISREGARD OF THE CORPORATE ENTITY

DEL. GEN. CORP. LAW § 102(b)(6)

§ 102. **Contents of certificate of incorporation**

* * *

(b) . . . [T]he certificate of incorporation may . . . contain any or all of the following matters: . . . .

(6) A provision imposing personal liability for the debts of the corporation on its stockholders or members to a specified extent and upon specified conditions; otherwise, the stockholders or members of a corporation shall not be personally liable for the payment of the corporation's debts except as they may be liable by reason of their own conduct or acts.

REV. MODEL BUS. CORP. ACT § 6.22

§ 6.22. **Liability of Shareholders.** . . . .

(b) Unless otherwise provided in the articles of incorporation, a shareholder of a corporation is not personally liable for the acts or debts of the corporation except that he may become personally liable by reason of his own acts or conduct.

EASTERBROOK & FISCHEL, LIMITED LIABILITY AND THE CORPORATION
52 U.Chi.L.Rev. 89 (1985).

Publicly held corporations typically dominate other organizational forms when the technology of production requires firms to combine both the specialized skills of multiple agents and large amounts of capital. The publicly held corporation facilitates the division of labor. The distinct functions of managerial skills and the provision of capital (and the bearing of risk) may be separated and assigned to different people—workers who lack capital, and owners of funds who lack specialized production skills. Those who invest capital can bear additional risk, because each investor is free to participate in many ventures. The holder of a diversified portfolio of investments is more willing to bear the risk that a small fraction of his investments will not pan out.

Of course this separation of functions is not costless. The separation of investment and management requires firms to create devices by which these participants monitor each other and guarantee their own performance. Neither group will be perfectly trustworthy. Moreover, managers who do not obtain the full benefits of their own performance do not have the best incentives to work efficiently. The costs of the separation of investment and management (agency costs) may be substantial. Nonetheless, we know from the survival of large corporations that the costs generated by agency relations are outweighed by the gains from separation and specialization of function. Limited liability reduces the costs of this separation and specialization.

First, limited liability decreases the need to monitor. All investors risk losing wealth because of the actions of agents. They could monitor these agents more closely. The more risk they bear, the more they will monitor. But beyond a point more monitoring is not worth the cost. Moreover, specialized risk bearing implies that many investors will have diversified holdings. Only a small portion of their wealth will be invested in any one firm. These diversified investors have neither the expertise nor the incentive to monitor the actions of specialized agents. Limited liability makes diversification and passivity a more rational strategy and so potentially reduces the cost of operating the corporation. . . .

Second, limited liability reduces the costs of monitoring other shareholders. Under a rule exposing equity investors to additional liability, the greater the wealth of other shareholders, the lower the probability that any one shareholder's assets will be needed to pay a judgment. Thus existing shareholders would have incentives to engage in costly monitoring of other shareholders to ensure that they do not transfer assets to others or sell to others with less wealth. Limited liability makes the identity of other shareholders irrelevant and thus avoids these costs. . . .

[Third, limited] liability reduces the costs of purchasing shares. Under a rule of limited liability, the value of shares is determined by the present value of the income stream generated by a firm's assets. The identity and wealth of other investors is irrelevant. Shares are fungible; they trade at one price in liquid markets. Under a rule of unlimited liability . . . shares would not be fungible. Their value would be a function of the present value of future cash flows *and* of the wealth of shareholders. The lack of fungibility would impede their acquisition. . . .

Fourth, limited liability makes it possible for market prices to impound additional information about the value of firms. With unlimited liability, shares would not be homogeneous commodities, so they would no longer have one market price. Investors would therefore be required to expend greater resources analyzing the prospects of the firm in order to know whether "the price is right." When all can trade on the same terms, though, investors trade until the price of shares reflects the available information about a firm's prospects. Most investors need not expend resources on search; they can accept the market price as given and purchase at a "fair" price.

Fifth, . . . limited liability allows more efficient diversification. Investors can minimize risk by owning a diversified portfolio of assets. Firms can raise capital at lower costs because investors need not bear the special risk associated with nondiversified holdings. This is true, though, only under a rule of limited liability or some good substitute. Diversification would increase rather than reduce risk under a rule of unlimited liability. If any one firm went bankrupt, an investor could lose his entire wealth. The rational strategy under unlimited liability, therefore, would be to minimize the number of securities held. As a result, investors would be forced to bear risk that could have been avoided by diversification, and the cost to firms of raising capital would rise.

Sixth, limited liability facilitates optimal investment decisions. When investors hold diversified portfolios, managers maximize investors' welfare by investing in any project with a positive net present value. They can accept high-variance ventures (such as the development of new products) without exposing the investors to ruin. Each investor can hedge against the failure of one project by holding stock in other firms. In a world of unlimited liability, though, managers would behave differently. They would reject as "too risky" some projects with positive net present values. Investors would want them to do this because it would be the best way to reduce risks. By definition this would be a social loss, because projects with a positive net present value are beneficial uses of capital.

Both those who want to raise capital for entrepreneurial ventures, and society as a whole, receive benefits from limited liability. The equity investors will do about as well under one rule of liability as another. Every investor must choose between riskless T–bills and riskier investments. The more risk comes with an equity investment, the less the investor will pay. Investors bid down the price of equity until, at the margin, the risk-adjusted returns of stock and T–bills are the same. So long as the rule of liability is known, investors will price shares accordingly. The choice of an inefficient rule, however, will shrink the pool of funds available for investment in projects that would subject investors to risk. The increased availability of funds for projects with positive net values is the real benefit of limited liability.

LANDERS, A UNIFIED APPROACH TO PARENT, SUBSIDIARY, AND AFFILIATE QUESTIONS IN BANKRUPTCY

42 U.Chi.L.Rev. 589, 620–21 (1975).

Since state corporation laws allow limited liability without any exceptions, the question may well be asked why veil piercing should be permitted in any case. It could be argued that the legislature's clear intention to be generous in according this privilege is evidenced by the minimal requirements for setting up a corporation. Unless there were an invalid incorporation or some basis for an estoppel, limited liability would be an iron-clad rule.

Although the origins of the doctrine of veil piercing are obscure, a literal application of the principle of limited liability has not been adhered to by the courts. Virtually all courts have demonstrated a willingness to depart from limited liability under some circumstances; the problem is essentially one of defining the appropriate circumstances. If one could hypothesize the legislative intent in this area, it would probably be to permit separate incorporation, with its attendant privilege of limited liability, in the following circumstances: first, to encourage an existing business to expand into a new field by limiting its risk in doing so; second, to permit the insulation of parts of a business enterprise from the risks of other parts in circumstances where the separate parts might exist as separate businesses; and third, to satisfy various legal or administrative requirements. On the other hand, it is doubtful that the legislature intended to bestow the privilege of limited liability on attempts to divide one business into a number of mutually dependent units or to divide the business so that all the assets were in one company and all the liabilities were in another.

This hypothesis assumes that there is a model of corporateness inherent in the legislative grant of corporate personality, a significant departure from which would cause the loss of that aspect of corporateness known as limited liability. The model for corporateness requires both economic viability and the observance of certain procedural formalities. While this proposed test is not precise or capable of quantification, it is possible to reconcile most of the piercing cases by reference to its criteria.

WALKOVSZKY v. CARLTON

Court of Appeals of New York, 1966.
18 N.Y.2d 414, 276 N.Y.S.2d 585, 223 N.E.2d 6.

FULD, Judge.   This case involves what appears to be a rather common practice in the taxicab industry of vesting the ownership of a taxi fleet in many corporations, each owning only one or two cabs.

The complaint alleges that the plaintiff was severely injured four FACTS years ago in New York City when he was run down by a taxicab owned by the defendant Seon Cab Corporation and negligently operated at the time by the defendant Marchese.   The individual defendant, Carlton, is claimed to be a stockholder of 10 corporations, including Seon, each of which has but two cabs registered in its name, and it is implied that only the minimum automobile liability insurance required by law (in the amount of $10,000) is carried on any one cab. Although seemingly independent of one another, these corporations are alleged to be "operated . . . as a single entity, unit and enterprise" with regard to financing, supplies, repairs, employees and garaging, and all are named as defendants.[1]   The plaintiff asserts that he is also entitled to hold their stockholders personally liable for the damages sought because the multiple corporate structure constitutes an unlawful attempt "to defraud members of the general public" who might be injured by the cabs.

The defendant Carlton has moved, pursuant to CPLR 3211(a) 7, to dismiss the complaint on the ground that as to him it "fails to state a cause of action".   The court at Special Term granted the motion but the Appellate Division, by a divided vote, reversed, holding that a P.C. valid cause of action was sufficiently stated.   The defendant Carlton appeals to us, from the nonfinal order, by leave of the Appellate Division on a certified question.

The law permits the incorporation of a business for the very purpose of enabling its proprietors to escape personal liability (see, e.g., Bartle v. Home Owners Co-op., 309 N.Y. 103, 106, 127 N.E.2d 832, 833) but, manifestly, the privilege is not without its limits. Broadly speaking, the courts will disregard the corporate form, or, to use accepted terminology, "pierce the corporate veil", whenever necessary "to prevent fraud or to achieve equity".   (International Aircraft Trading Co. v. Manufacturers Trust Co., 297 N.Y. 285, 292, 79 N.E.2d 249, 252.)   In determining whether liability should be extended to reach assets beyond those belonging to the corporation, we are guided, as Judge Cardozo noted, by "general rules of agency". (Berkey v. Third Ave. Ry. Co., 244 N.Y. 84, 95, 155 N.E. 58, 61, 50 A.L.R. 599.)   In other words, whenever anyone uses control of the corporation to further his own rather than the corporation's business, he will be liable for the corporation's acts "upon the principle of *respondeat superior* applicable even where the agent is a natural person". . . .   Such liability, moreover, extends not only to

---

1. The corporate owner of a garage is also included as a defendant.

the corporation's commercial dealings . . . but to its negligent acts as well. . . .

In the Mangan case (247 App.Div. 853, 286 N.Y.S. 666, mot. for lv. to app. den. 272 N.Y. 676, 286 N.Y.S. 666, supra), the plaintiff was injured as a result of the negligent operation of a cab owned and operated by one of four corporations affiliated with the defendant Terminal. Although the defendant was not a stockholder of any of the operating companies, both the defendant and the operating companies were owned, for the most part, by the same parties. The defendant's name (Terminal) was conspicuously displayed on the sides of all of the taxis used in the enterprise and, in point of fact, the defendant actually serviced, inspected, repaired and dispatched them. These facts were deemed to provide sufficient cause for piercing the corporate veil of the operating company—the nominal owner of the cab which injured the plaintiff—and holding the defendant liable. The operating companies were simply instrumentalities for carrying on the business of the defendant without imposing upon it financial and other liabilities incident to the actual ownership and operation of the cabs. . . .

In the case before us, the plaintiff has explicitly alleged that none of the corporations "had a separate existence of their own" and, as indicated above, all are named as defendants. However, it is one thing to assert that a corporation is a fragment of a larger corporate combine which actually conducts the business. (See Berle, The Theory of Enterprise Entity, 47 Col.L.Rev. 343, 348–350.) It is quite another to claim that the corporation is a "dummy" for its individual stockholders who are in reality carrying on the business in their personal capacities for purely personal rather than corporate ends. (See African Metals Corp. v. Bullowa, 288 N.Y. 78, 85, 41 N.E.2d 366, 469.) Either circumstance would justify treating the corporation as an agent and piercing the corporate veil to reach the principal but a different result would follow in each case. In the first, only a larger corporate entity would be held financially responsible . . . while, in the other, the stockholder would be personally liable. . . . Either the stockholder is conducting the business in his individual capacity or he is not. If he is, he will be liable; if he is not, then it does not matter—insofar as his personal liability is concerned—that the enterprise is actually being carried on by a larger "enterprise entity". (See Berle, The Theory of Enterprise Entity, 47 Col.L.Rev. 343.)

At this stage in the present litigation, we are concerned only with the pleadings and, since CPLR 3014 permits causes of action to be stated "alternatively or hypothetically", it is possible for the plaintiff to allege both theories as the basis for his demand for judgment. In ascertaining whether he has done so, we must consider the entire pleading, educing therefrom " 'whatever can be imputed from its statements by fair and reasonable intendment.' " (Condon v. Associated Hosp. Serv., 287 N.Y. 411, 414, 40 N.E.2d 230, 231. . . .) Reading the complaint in this case most favorably and liberally, we do not believe that there can be gathered from its averments the allegations required to spell out a valid cause of action against the defendant Carlton.

The individual defendant is charged with having "organized, managed, dominated and controlled" a fragmented corporate entity but there are no allegations that he was conducting business in his individual capacity. Had the taxicab fleet been owned by a single corporation, it would be readily apparent that the plaintiff would face formidable barriers in attempting to establish personal liability on the part of the corporation's stockholders. The fact that the fleet ownership has been deliberately split up among many corporations does not ease the plaintiff's burden in that respect. The corporate form may not be disregarded merely because the assets of the corporation, together with the mandatory insurance coverage of the vehicle which struck the plaintiff, are insufficient to assure him the recovery sought. If Carlton were to be held individually liable on those facts alone, the decision would apply equally to the thousands of cabs which are owned by their individual drivers who conduct their businesses through corporations organized pursuant to section 401 of the Business Corporation Law, Consol.Laws, c. 4 and carry the minimum insurance required by subdivision 1 (par. [a]) of section 370 of the Vehicle and Traffic Law, Consol.Laws, c. 71. These taxi owner-operators are entitled to form such corporations (cf. Elenkrieg v. Siebrecht, 238 N.Y. 254, 144 N.E. 519, 34 A.L.R. 592), and we agree with the court at Special Term that, if the insurance coverage required by statute "is inadequate for the protection of the public, the remedy lies not with the courts but with the Legislature." It may very well be sound policy to require that certain corporations must take out liability insurance which will afford adequate compensation to their potential tort victims. However, the responsibility for imposing conditions on the privilege of incorporation has been committed by the Constitution to the Legislature (N.Y. Const., art. X, § 1) and it may not be fairly implied, from any statute, that the Legislature intended, without the slightest discussion or debate, to require of taxi corporations that they carry automobile liability insurance over and above that mandated by the Vehicle and Traffic Law.

This is not to say that it is impossible for the plaintiff to state a valid cause of action against the defendant Carlton. However, the simple fact is that the plaintiff has just not done so here. While the complaint alleges that the separate corporations were undercapitalized and that their assets have been intermingled, it is barren of any "sufficiently particular[ized] statements" (CPLR 3013; see 3 Weinstein-Korn-Miller, N.Y.Civ.Prac., par. 3013.01 et seq., pp. 30–142 et seq.) that the defendant Carlton and his associates are actually doing business in their individual capacities, shuttling their personal funds in and out of the corporations "without regard to formality and to suit their immediate convenience." (Weisser v. Mursam Shoe Corp., 2 Cir., 127 F.2d 344, 345, 145 A.L.R. 467, supra.) Such a "perversion of the privilege to do business in a corporate form" (Berkey v. Third Ave. Ry. Co., 244 N.Y. 84, 95, 155 N.E. 58, 61, 50 A.L.R. 599, supra) would justify imposing personal liability on the individual stockholders. (See African Metals Corp. v. Bullowa, 288 N.Y. 78, 41 N.E.2d 466, supra.) Nothing of the sort has in fact been charged, and it cannot reasonably or logically be inferred from the happenstance that the business of Seon Cab Corporation may actually be carried on by a larger corporate entity composed of many corporations which, under general principles of agency, would be liable to each other's creditors in contract and in tort.[3]

In point of fact, the principle relied upon in the complaint to sustain the imposition of personal liability is not agency but fraud. Such a cause of action cannot withstand analysis. If it is not fraudulent for the owner-operator of a single cab corporation to take out only the minimum required liability insurance, the enterprise does not become either illicit or fraudulent merely because it consists of many such corporations. The plaintiff's injuries are the same regardless of whether the cab which strikes him is owned by a single corporation or part of a fleet with ownership fragmented among many corporations. Whatever rights he may be able to assert against parties other than the registered owner of the vehicle come into being not because he has been defrauded but because, under the principle of *respondeat superior*, he is entitled to hold the whole enterprise responsible for the acts of its agents.

In sum, then, the complaint falls short of adequately stating a cause of action against the defendant Carlton in his individual capacity.

The order of the Appellate Division should be reversed, with costs in this court and in the Appellate Division, the certified question answered in the negative and the order of the Supreme Court, Richmond County, reinstated, with leave to serve an amended complaint.

KEATING, Judge (dissenting).

The defendant Carlton, the shareholder here sought to be held for the negligence of the driver of a taxicab, was a principal shareholder and organizer of the defendant corporation which owned the taxicab. The corporation was one of 10 organized by the defendant, each containing two cabs and each cab having the "minimum liability"

---

3. In his affidavit in opposition to the motion to dismiss, the plaintiff's counsel claimed that corporate assets had been "milked out" of, and "siphoned off" from the enterprise. Quite apart from the fact that these allegations are far too vague and conclusory, the charge is premature. If the plaintiff succeeds in his action and becomes a judgment creditor of the corporation, he may then sue and attempt to hold the individual defendants accountable for any dividends and property that were wrongfully distributed (Business Corporation Law, §§ 510, 719, 720).

[By ed.: Cf. R. Clark, Corporate Law 84 n. 14 (1986):

The court overlooked the possibility of suit under New York's version of the [Uniform Fraudulent Conveyance Act], it having been held long before that a prior judgment is *not* a procedural prerequisite to suit under that statute. American Surety Co. v. Connor, 166 N.E. 783 (N.Y.1929). (This has also been the consistent interpretation in other states of the UFCA. . . .) Furthermore, New York fraudulent conveyance law has been applied to remedy milking and diversion of corporate assets, even where one of the devices was payment of dividends. United States v. 58th Street Plaza Theatre, Inc., 287 F.Supp. 475, 498 (S.D.N.Y. 1968). (Emphasis in original.)]

insurance coverage mandated by section 370 of the Vehicle and Traffic Law. The sole assets of these operating corporations are the vehicles themselves and they are apparently subject to mortgages.*

From their inception these corporations were intentionally under-capitalized for the purpose of avoiding responsibility for acts which were bound to arise as a result of the operation of a large taxi fleet having cars out on the street 24 hours a day and engaged in public transportation. And during the course of the corporations' existence all income was continually drained out of the corporations for the same purpose.

The issue presented by this action is whether the policy of this State, which affords those desiring to engage in a business enterprise the privilege of limited liability through the use of the corporate devise, is so strong that it will permit that privilege to continue no matter how much it is abused, no matter how irresponsibly the corporation is operated, no matter what the cost to the public. I do not believe that it is.

Under the circumstances of this case the shareholders should all be held individually liable to this plaintiff for the injuries he suffered. (See Mull v. Colt Co., D.C., 31 F.R.D. 154, 156; Teller v. Clear Serv. Corp., 9 Misc.2d 495, 173 N.Y.S.2d 183.) At least, the matter should not be disposed of on the pleadings by a dismissal of the complaint. "If a corporation is organized and carries on business without substantial capital in such a way that the corporation is likely to have no sufficient assets available to meet its debts, it is inequitable that shareholders should set up such a flimsy organization to escape personal liability. The attempt to do corporate business without providing any sufficient basis of financial responsibility to creditors is an abuse of the separate entity and will be ineffectual to exempt the shareholders from corporate debts. It is coming to be recognized as the policy of law that shareholders should in good faith put at the risk of the business unincumbered capital reasonably adequate for its prospective liabilities. If capital is illusory or trifling compared with the business to be done and the risks of loss, this is a ground for denying the separate entity privilege." (Ballantine, Corporations [rev. ed., 1946], § 129, pp. 302–303.) . . .

The policy of this State has always been to provide and facilitate recovery for those injured through the negligence of others. The automobile, by its very nature, is capable of causing severe and costly injuries when not operated in a proper manner. The great increase in the number of automobile accidents combined with the frequent financial irresponsibility of the individual driving the car led to the adoption of section 388 of the Vehicle and Traffic Law which had the effect of imposing upon the owner of the vehicle the responsibility for its negligent operation. It is upon this very statute that the cause of

---

* It appears that the medallions, which are of considerable value, are judgment proof. (Administrative Code of City of New York, § 436–2.0.) [Footnote by the court.]

action against both the corporation and the individual defendant is predicated.

In addition the Legislature, still concerned with the financial irresponsibility of those who owned and operated motor vehicles, enacted a statute requiring minimum liability coverage for all owners of automobiles. The important public policy represented by both these statutes is outlined in section 310 of the Vehicle and Traffic Law. That section provides that: "The legislature is concerned over the rising toll of motor vehicle accidents and the suffering and loss thereby inflicted. The legislature determines that it is a matter of grave concern that motorists shall be financially able to respond in damages for their negligent acts, so that innocent victims of motor vehicle accidents may be recompensed for the injury and financial loss inflicted upon them."

[handwritten margin note: Rationale of Vehicle Insurance Law.]

The defendant Carlton claims that, because the minimum amount of insurance required by the statute was obtained, the corporate veil cannot and should not be pierced despite the fact that the assets of the corporation which owned the cab were "trifling compared with the business to be done and the risks of loss" which were certain to be encountered. I do not agree.

The Legislature in requiring minimum liability insurance of $10,000, no doubt, intended to provide at least some small fund for recovery against those individuals and corporations who just did not have and were not able to raise or accumulate assets sufficient to satisfy the claims of those who were injured as a result of their negligence. It certainly could not have intended to shield those individuals who organized corporations, with the specific intent of avoiding responsibility to the public, where the operation of the corporate enterprise yielded profits sufficient to purchase additional insurance. . . .

The defendant, however, argues that the failure of the Legislature to increase the minimum insurance requirements indicates legislative acquiescence in this scheme to avoid liability and responsibility to the public. In the absence of a clear legislative statement, approval of a scheme having such serious consequences is not to be so lightly inferred.

The defendant contends that the court will be encroaching upon the legislative domain by ignoring the corporate veil and holding the individual shareholder. This argument was answered by Mr. Justice DOUGLAS in Anderson v. Abbot, [321 U.S. 349], 366–367, 64 S.Ct. p. 540, where he wrote that: "In the field in which we are presently concerned, judicial power hardly oversteps the bounds when it refuses to lend its aid to a promotional project which would circumvent or undermine a legislative policy. To deny it that function would be to make it impotent in situations where historically it has made some of its most notable contributions. If the judicial power is helpless to protect a legislative program from schemes for easy avoidance, then indeed it has become a handy implement of high finance. *Judicial interference to cripple or defeat a legislative policy is one thing; judicial interference with the plans of those whose corporate or other devices would circumvent that policy is quite another.* Once the purpose or effect of the scheme is clear, once the legislative policy is plain, we would indeed forsake a great tradition to say we were helpless to fashion the instruments for appropriate relief." (Emphasis added.)

The defendant contends that a decision holding him personally liable would discourage people from engaging in corporate enterprise.

What I would merely hold is that a participating shareholder of a corporation vested with a public interest, organized with capital insufficient to meet liabilities which are certain to arise in the ordinary course of the corporation's business, may be held personally responsible for such liabilities. Where corporate income is not sufficient to cover the cost of insurance premiums above the statutory minimum or where initially adequate finances dwindle under the pressure of competition, bad times or extraordinary and unexpected liability, obviously the shareholder will not be held liable (Henn, Corporations, p. 208, n. 7).

The only types of corporate enterprises that will be discouraged as a result of a decision allowing the individual shareholder to be sued will be those such as the one in question, designed solely to abuse the corporate privilege at the expense of the public interest.

For these reasons I would vote to affirm the order of the Appellate Division.

DESMOND, C.J., and VAN VOORHIS, BURKE and SCILEP-PI, JJ., concur with FULD, J.

KEATING, J., dissents and votes to affirm in an opinion in which BERGAN, J., concurs.

Order reversed, etc.

NOTE ON FURTHER PROCEEDINGS IN
WALKOVSZKY v. CARLTON

Following the decision in *Walkovszky,* the plaintiff amended his complaint. The Appellate Division held that "the amended complaint sufficiently alleges a cause of action against appellant, i.e., that he and the other individual defendants were conducting the business of the taxicab fleet in their individual capacities." Walkovszky v. Carlton, 29 A.D.2d 763, 287 N.Y.S.2d 546 (1968). That decision was affirmed by the Court of Appeals, 23 N.Y.2d 714, 244 N.E.2d 55, 296 N.Y.S.2d 362 (1968), noting that the amended complaint "now meets the pleading requirements set forth in [our prior] opinion and states a valid cause of action." Neither opinion stated the particulars in which the amended complaint differed from the original.

HALPERN, TREBILCOCK & TURNBULL, AN ECONOMIC ANALYSIS OF LIMITED LIABILITY IN CORPORATION LAW

30 U.Toronto L.J. 117, 145–46 (1980).

When considering imperfections in markets, the involuntary creditor—paradigmatically a tort creditor like the pedestrian who was injured by the taxi in *Walkovsky v. Carlton* —provides us with the polar case of transactions and information costs that may be prohibitively high. In this situation we are concerned with the potential for owners of a limited liability corporation to effect uncompensated transfers of the risk of business failure to this class of creditor. In the following discussion we will determine the impact on both the efficient behaviour of owners and the compensation for the involuntary creditor of the choice of a liability regime. We conclude that some form of unlimited liability regime may be justified with respect to this class of creditor. We use *Walkovsky v. Carlton* as illustrative of the relevant considerations.

First, consider the circumstances of the *Walkovsky v. Carlton* case, where the cab owner has limited liability and the legislated minimum insurance coverage. In the case of the pedestrian, it must be assumed that the taxi cab corporation is the least-cost loss avoider, otherwise it is unlikely that there would be a finding of tortious liability for negligence. Limited liability here may undermine the deterrent objectives of the tort system (because of moral hazard problems). In addition, there is no incentive for the owner to carry adequate insurance since, in the event of default, there is no cost to the owner.

Now assume that limited liability is removed in this case. The owner of the unlimited liability company will have the following major options: first, he can self-insure by having sufficient amounts of personal wealth to meet most tort claims; second, he can purchase insurance on his own account to meet most tort claims; third, he can have the corporation take out this insurance. Given the large size of the potential tort claims, it is unlikely that the first option would be taken. If either of the other two options are taken then the combination of unlimited liability and insurance results in a limited liability regime where the owner is no longer personally responsible in the event of default. Thus we are again faced with a moral hazard situation. However, there is an important difference between unlimited liability combined with insurance and limited liability. In the latter case the owners obtain insurance against third-party claims for which there is no cost. However, in the former case, the insurance premium has a market-determined price. Since the premium will depend upon the behaviour of the taxi owners, it will be in the best interests of the owners to undertake some cost-justified risk-reduction precautions (eg, hire safer drivers). Thus the incentive to efficient behaviour is increased. With respect to the compensation issue, either the second or third options will result in insurance being purchased which will cover most of the tort claims that the corporation would face.

———

BERKEY v. THIRD AVE. RY. CO., 244 N.Y. 84, 155 N.E. 58 (1926) (Cardozo, J.). "The whole problem of the relation between parent and subsidiary corporations is one that is still enveloped in the mists of metaphor. Metaphors in law are to be narrowly watched, for starting as devices to liberate thought, they end often by enslaving it. We say at times that the corporate entity will be ignored when the parent corporation operates a business through a subsidiary which is characterized as an 'alias' or a 'dummy.' All this is well enough if the picturesqueness of the epithets does not lead us to forget that the essential term to be defined is the act of operation. Dominion may be so complete, interference so obtrusive, that by the general rules of agency the parent will be a principal and the subsidiary an agent. Where control is less than this, we are remitted to the tests of honesty and justice. Ballentine, Parent and Subsidiary Corporations, 14 Cal.Law Review, 12, 18, 19, 20. The logical consistency of a juridical conception will indeed be sacrificed at times, when the sacrifice is essential to the end that some accepted public policy may be defended or upheld. This is so, for illustration, though agency in any proper sense is lacking, where the attempted separation between parent and subsidiary will work a fraud upon the law. . . . At such times unity is ascribed to parts which, at least for many purposes, retain an independent life, for the reason that only thus can we overcome a perversion of the privilege to do business in a corporate form."

NOTE ON ZAIST v. OLSON

Zaist v. Olson, 154 Conn. 563, 227 A.2d 552 (1967), employs a widely used test for disregarding the corporate entity that differs at least in form from the *Walkovszky* test. The facts in *Zaist* were extremely complex. In essence, Martin Olson controlled and substantially owned various corporations, including Olson, Inc. and East Haven. East Haven's fixed assets consisted of office furniture, cars, a truck of small value, and a few small tools. Martin Olson, Olson, Inc., and several other Olson corporations acquired three tracts of land. East Haven then contracted with the other corporations to erect shopping centers on the tracts, and engaged various contractors, including the plaintiffs, to do the construction. East Haven paid its contractors with funds supplied to East Haven by other Olson corporations out of the proceeds of bank loans secured by mortgages on the tracts. In the end, a portion of the amounts owed to the plaintiffs by East Haven remained unpaid, and the plaintiffs sued Martin Olson and Olson, Inc. for the balance. The court below held for the plaintiffs, on the theory that East Haven was the agent of Martin Olson and Olson, Inc. The Connecticut Supreme Court affirmed on a somewhat different theory:

> . . . [T]his brings us to the basic question of the plaintiffs' right to look beyond East Haven, the corporate entity with which they dealt, to Olson and Olson, Inc., for a recovery of the amount due them.

The . . . [lower] court based this right on agency. No express agency was found to exist, and, consequently, either an implied agency was meant, or the term "agency" was loosely used, as is sometimes done, to pierce the shield of immunity afforded by the corporate structure in a situation in which the corporate entity has been so controlled and dominated that justice requires liability to be imposed on the real actor. 1 Fletcher, Corporations (Perm.Ed.1963 Rev.) § 43; Ballantine, Corporations (Rev.Ed.) § 136. The complaint alleged that East Haven was "the agent or instrumentality" of Olson and Olson, Inc. We think that it was the latter.

Courts will disregard the fiction of separate legal entity when a corporation "is a mere instrumentality or agent of another corporation or individual owning all or most of its stock." Hoffman Wall Paper Co. v. City of Hartford, 114 Conn. 531, 535, 159 A. 346. . . . "Under such circumstances, the general rule which recognizes the individuality of corporate entities and the independent character of each in respect to their corporate transactions and the obligations incurred by each in the course of such transactions will be disregarded, where, as here, the interests of justice and righteous dealing so demand." Connecticut Co. v. New York, N.H. & H.R. Co., 94 Conn. 13, 26, 107 A. 646, 651. . . . The circumstance that control is exercised merely through dominating stock ownership, of course, is not enough. . . . There must be "such domination of finances, policies and practices that the controlled corporation has, so to speak, no separate mind, will or existence of its own and is but a business conduit for its principal." 1 Fletcher, op. cit., p. 205.

In the present case, Olson, Inc., owned none of the stock of East Haven. On the other hand, Olson held a dominating stock interest in both East Haven and Olson, Inc., and was president, treasurer and a director of both corporations. It is not the fact that he held these positions which is controlling but rather the manner in which he utilized them. The essential purposes of the corporate structure, including stockholder immunity, must and will be protected when the corporation functions as an entity in the normal manner contemplated and permitted by law. When it functions in this manner, there is nothing insidious in stockholder control, interlocking directorates or identity of officers. When, however, the corporation is so manipulated by an individual or another corporate entity as to become a mere puppet or tool for the manipulator, justice may require the courts to disregard the corporate fiction and impose liability on the real actor. . . . It is because of this that there have arisen what are called the "instrumentality" or "identity" rules.   Powell, Parent and Subsidiary Corporations §§ 2, 3.

The instrumentality rule requires, in any case but an express agency, proof of three elements: (1) Control, not mere majority or complete stock control, but complete domination, not only of finances but of policy and business practice in respect to the transaction attacked so that the corporate entity as to this transaction had at the time no separate mind, will or existence of its own; and (2) Such control must have been used by the defendant to commit fraud or wrong, to perpetrate the violation of a statutory or other positive legal duty, or a dishonest or unjust act in contravention of plaintiff's legal rights; and (3) The aforesaid control and breach of duty must proximately cause the injury or unjust loss complained of. . . .

Complementing the instrumentality rule is the identity rule.   Powell, op. cit. § 24.   Its application is illustrated in Luckenbach S.S. Co. v. W.R. Grace & Co., 267 F. 676 (4th Cir.)   In that case, Edgar F. Luckenbach owned 94 percent of the stock of the Luckenbach Steamship Company and almost 90 percent of the stock of the Luckenbach Company. The Luckenbach Steamship Company had a capital of $10,000 and owned no ships.   The Luckenbach Company was capitalized at $800,000 and did own ships which it leased to the steamship company.   Both corporations had the same officers and directors, and Luckenbach was president of and personally managed both.   When the steamship company defaulted on a contract with W.R. Grace and Company, the latter, in a suit against the two corporations, was allowed recovery against the Luckenbach Company.   The court said (p. 681): "For all practical purposes the two concerns are one, and it would be unconscionable to allow the owner of this fleet of steamers, worth millions of dollars, to escape liability because it had turned them over a year before to a $10,000 corporation, which is simply itself in another form." The proposition has been otherwise expressed as follows: "If plaintiff can show that there was such a unity of interest and ownership that the independence of the corporations had in effect ceased or had never begun, an adherence to the fiction of separate identity would serve only to defeat justice and equity by permitting the economic entity to escape liability arising out of an operation conducted by one corporation for the benefit of the whole enterprise."   Mull v. Colt Co., 31 F.R.D. 154, 163 (S.D.N.Y.). . . .

The facts in the present case are, beyond question, that Olson caused the creation of both East Haven and Olson, Inc., and thereafter completely dominated and controlled not only them but his other corporate creations.   All shared the same office.   All the work and material furnished by the plaintiffs went into land which, after being juggled about, came to rest in Olson or Olson, Inc. The record is significantly silent with regard to any formal corporate action by the directors or stockholders of any of the several corporations except in the insignificant instances specifically mentioned. . . . East Haven had no sufficient funds of its own and acquired no funds for the work on its own initiative. It had no proprietary interest in the property on which the work was done, and, so far as appears, it gained nothing from whatever part it played in the transaction. . . . With no showing of any responsible corporate action of its own, it was used by Olson for the benefit of Olson and Olson, Inc. On the facts established, the cause of justice would not be served by denying to the plaintiffs the amount found due them and unpaid because of the inadequate resources of East Haven. . . .

Consequently, a judgment against Olson was warranted. The court could, with equal propriety, reach the conclusion that the identity of Olson and Olson, Inc., was such that judgment against Olson, Inc., was warranted.

Two justices dissented. Justice House concluded that the facts did not "support a conclusion that the control which the defendants Martin Olson and Martin Olson, Inc., undoubtedly did exercise over The East Haven Homes, Inc., was used by them or either of them 'to commit fraud or wrong, to perpetrate the violation of a statutory or other positive legal duty, or a dishonest and unjust act in contravention of' the plaintiffs' legal rights." 227 A.2d at 560 (House, J., dissenting). Justice Cotter concluded that "[c]lose corporations, although individual entities from a legal standpoint, are normally no more than vehicles for the goals and motives of their principals. The law is not necessarily advanced by adopting a rule which includes a presumption that this kind of corporation may have a 'separate mind, will, or existence of its own.' " 227 A.2d at 561 (Cotter, J., dissenting).

For similar, more recent cases, see, e.g., Gallagher v. Reconco Builders, Inc., 91 Ill.App.3d 999, 47 Ill.Dec. 555, 415 N.E.2d 560 (1980) (undercapitalization, disregard of corporate formalities, and "an element of injustice, fraud, or fundamental unfairness" can provide a basis for individual liability); Stap v. Chicago Aces Tennis Team, Inc., 63 Ill.App.3d 23, 20 Ill.Dec. 230, 379 N.E.2d 1298 (1978).

AUTOMOTRIZ DEL GOLFO DE CALIFORNIA S.A. DE C.V. v. RESNICK, 47 Cal.2d 792, 796, 306 P.2d 1, 3 (1957) "[T]he two requirements for application of [the disregard-of-the-corporate-entity doctrine] are (1) that there be such unity of interest and ownership that the separate personalities of the corporation and the individual no longer exist and (2) that, if the acts are treated as those of the corporation alone, an inequitable result will follow."

BARBER, PIERCING THE CORPORATE VEIL, 17 Willamette L.Rev. 371, 372 (1981). "In theory, the piercing doctrine applies to publicly held and closely held or family corporations. A review of the decisional law, however, shows no case in which the shareholders of a corporation whose stock was publicly traded or widely held were found personally liable for the obligations of the corporation."

MINTON v. CAVANEY

Supreme Court of California in Bank, 1961.
56 Cal.2d 576, 15 Cal.Rptr. 641, 364 P.2d 473.

TRAYNOR, Justice. The Seminole Hot Springs Corporation, hereinafter referred to as Seminole, was duly incorporated in California on March 8, 1954. It conducted a public swimming pool that it leased from its owner. On June 24, 1954 plaintiffs' daughter drowned in the pool, and plaintiffs recovered a judgment for $10,000 against Seminole for her wrongful death. The judgment remains unsatisfied.

On January 30, 1957, plaintiffs brought the present action to hold defendant Cavaney personally liable for the judgment against Seminole. Cavaney died on May 28, 1958 and his widow, the executrix of his estate, was substituted as defendant. The trial court entered judgment for plaintiffs for $10,000. Defendant appeals.

Plaintiffs introduced evidence that Cavaney was a director and secretary and treasurer of Seminole and that on November 15, 1954, about five months after the drowning, Cavaney as secretary of Seminole and Edwin A. Kraft as president of Seminole applied for permission to issue three shares of Seminole stock, one share to be issued to Kraft, another to F.J. Wettrick and the third to Cavaney. The commissioner of corporations refused permission to issue these shares unless additional information was furnished. The application was then abandoned and no shares were ever issued. There was also evidence that for a time Seminole used Cavaney's office to keep records and to receive mail. Before his death Cavaney answered certain interrogatories. He was asked if Seminole "ever had any assets?" He stated that "insofar as my own personal knowledge and belief is concerned, said corporation did not have any assets." Cavaney also stated in the return to an attempted execution that "[I]nsofar as I know, this corporation had no assets of any kind or character. The corporation was duly organized but never functioned as a corporation."

Defendant introduced evidence that Cavaney was an attorney at law, that he was approached by Kraft and Wettrick to form Seminole, and that he was the attorney for Seminole. Plaintiffs introduced Cavaney's answer to several interrogatories that he held the post of secretary and treasurer and director in a temporary capacity and as an accommodation to his client.

Defendant contends that the evidence does not support the court's determination that Cavaney is personally liable for Seminole's debts and that the "alter ego" doctrine is inapplicable because plaintiffs failed to show that there was "(1) . . . such unity of interest and ownership that the separate personalities of the corporation and the individual no longer exist and (2) that, if the acts are treated as those of the corporation alone, an inequitable result will follow.' "

Riddle v. Leuschner, 51 Cal.2d 574, 580, 335 P.2d 107, 110; Automotriz Del Golfo De California S.A. De C.V. v. Resnick, 47 Cal. 2d 792, 796, 306 P.2d 1, 63 A.L.R.2d 1042; Minifie v. Rowley, 187 Cal. 481, 487, 202 P. 673.

The figurative terminology "alter ego" and "disregard of the corporate entity" is generally used to refer to the various situations that are an abuse of the corporate privilege. . . . The equitable owners of a corporation, for example, are personally liable when they treat the assets of the corporation as their own and add or withdraw capital from the corporation at will . . .; when they hold themselves out as being personally liable for the debts of the corporation . . .; or when they provide inadequate capitalization and actively participate in the conduct of corporate affairs. . . .

In the instant case the evidence is undisputed that there was no attempt to provide adequate capitalization. Seminole never had any substantial assets. It leased the pool that it operated, and the lease was forfeited for failure to pay the rent. Its capital was " 'trifling compared with the business to be done and the risks of loss . . .' " Automotriz Del Golfo De California S.A. De C.V. v. Resnick, supra, 47 Cal.2d 792, 797, 306 P.2d 1, 4. The evidence is also undisputed that Cavaney was not only the secretary and treasurer of the corporation but was also a director. The evidence that Cavaney was to receive one-third of the shares to be issued supports an inference that he was an equitable owner (see Riddle v. Leuschner, supra, 51 Cal.2d 574, 580, 335 P.2d 107), and the evidence that for a time the records of the corporation were kept in Cavaney's office supports an inference that he actively participated in the conduct of the business. The trial court was not required to believe his statement that he was only a "temporary" director and officer "for accommodation." In any event it merely raised a conflict in the evidence that was resolved adversely to defendant. Moreover, section 800 of the Corporations Code provides that ". . . the business and affairs of every corporation shall be controlled by a board of not less than three directors." Defendant does not claim that Cavaney was a director with specialized duties (see 5 U.Chi.L.Rev. 668). It is immaterial whether or not he accepted the office of director as an "accommodation" with the understanding that he would not exercise any of the duties of a director. A person may not in this manner divorce the responsibilities of a director from the statutory duties and powers of that office.

There is no merit in defendant's contentions that the "alter ego" doctrine applies only to contractual debts and not to tort claims . . .; that plaintiffs' cause of action abated when Cavaney died . . . or that the judgment in the action against the corporation bars plaintiffs from bringing the present action. . . .

In this action to hold defendant personally liable upon the judgment against Seminole plaintiffs did not allege or present any evidence on the issue of Seminole's negligence or on the amount of damages sustained by plaintiffs. They relied solely on the judgment against Seminole. Defendant correctly contends that Cavaney or his estate cannot be held liable for the debts of Seminole without an opportunity to relitigate these issues. . . . Cavaney was not a party to the action against the corporation, and the judgment in that action is therefore not binding upon him unless he controlled the litigation leading to the judgment. . . .

The judgment is reversed.

GIBSON, C.J., and PETERS, WHITE and DOOLING, JJ., concur.

SCHAUER, Justice (concurring and dissenting).

I concur in the judgment of reversal on the ground . . . stated in [the last paragraph of] the majority opinion. . . .

I dissent from any implication that *mere professional activity by an attorney at law, as such,* in the organization of a corporation, can constitute any basis for a finding that the corporation is the attorney's alter ego or that he is otherwise personally liable for *its* debts, whether based on contract or tort. . . .

In the process of developing an idea of a person or persons into an embryonic corporation and finally to full legal entity status with a permit issued, directors and officers elected, and assets in hand ready to begin business, there may often be delays. In such event a qualifying share of stock may stand in the name of the organizing attorney for substantial periods of time. In none of the activities indicated is the corporation actually engaging in business. And the lawyer who handles the task of determining and directing and participating in the steps appropriate to transforming the idea into a competent legal entity *ready to engage in business* is not an alter ego of the corporation. By his professional acts he has not been engaging in business in the name of the corporation; he has been merely practicing law.

McCOMB, J., concurs.

———

ARNOLD v. BROWNE, 27 Cal.App.3d 386, 396, 103 Cal. Rptr. 775, 783 (1972). "[The plaintiffs] further contend that Inter Helo Corporation was undercapitalized. They have, however, cited no cases in which an appellate court has held that a business was undercapitalized when the trial court made a contrary finding. In almost every instance where the trial court has found inadequate capitalization, there are other factors present. . . . Evidence of inadequate capitalization is, at best, merely a factor to be considered by the trial court in deciding whether or not to pierce the corporate veil (Harris v. Curtis, 8 Cal.App.3d 837, 841, 87 Cal.Rptr. 614). To be sure, it is an important factor, but no case has been cited, nor have any been found, where it has been held that this factor alone *requires* invoking the equitable doctrine prayed for in the instant case."

SECTION 9. EQUITABLE SUBORDINATION OF SHAREHOLDER CLAIMS

COSTELLO v. FAZIO

United States Court of Appeals, Ninth Circuit, 1958.
256 F.2d 903.

HAMLEY, Circuit Judge. Creditors' claims against the bankrupt estate of Leonard Plumbing and Heating Supply, Inc., were filed by J.A. Fazio and Lawrence C. Ambrose. The trustee in bankruptcy objected to these claims, and moved for an order subordinating them to the claims of general unsecured creditors. The referee in bankruptcy denied the motion, and his action was sustained by the district court. The trustee appeals.

The following facts are not in dispute: A partnership known as "Leonard Plumbing and Heating Supply Co." was organized in October, 1948. The three partners, Fazio, Ambrose, and B.T. Leonard, made initial capital contributions to the business aggregating $44,806.40. The capital contributions of the three partners, as they were recorded on the company books in September 1952, totaled $51,620.78, distributed as follows: Fazio, $43,169.61; Ambrose, $6,451.17; and Leonard, $2,000.

In the fall of that year, it was decided to incorporate the business. In contemplation of this step, Fazio and Ambrose, on September 15, 1952, withdrew all but $2,000 apiece of their capital contributions to the business. This was accomplished by the issuance to them, on that date, of partnership promissory notes in the sum of $41,169.61 and $4,451.17, respectively. These were demand notes, no interest being specified. The capital contribution to the partnership business then stood at $6,000—$2,000 for each partner.

The closing balance sheet of the partnership showed current assets to be $160,791.87, and current liabilities at $162,162.22. There were also fixed assets in the sum of $6,482.90, and other assets in the sum of $887.45. The partnership had cash on hand in the sum of $66.66, and an overdraft at the bank in the amount of $3,422.78.

Of the current assets, $41,357.76, representing "Accounts receivable—Trade," was assigned to American Trust Co., to secure $50,000 of its $59,000 in notes payable. Both before and after the incorporation, the business had a $75,000 line of credit with American Trust Co., secured by accounts receivable and the personal guaranty of the three partners and stockholders, and their marital communities.

The net sales of the partnership during its last year of operations were $389,543.72, as compared to net sales of $665,747.55 in the preceding year. A net loss of $22,521.34 was experienced during this last year, as compared to a net profit of $40,935.12 in the year ending September 30, 1951.

Based on the reduced capitalization of the partnership, the corporation was capitalized for six hundred shares of no par value common stock valued at ten dollars per share. Two hundred shares were issued to each of the three partners in consideration of the transfer to the corporation of their interests in the partnership. Fazio became president, and Ambrose, secretary-treasurer of the new corporation. Both were directors. The corporation assumed all liabilities of the partnership, including the notes to Fazio and Ambrose.

In June 1954, after suffering continued losses, the corporation made an assignment to the San Francisco Board of Trade for the benefit of creditors. On October 8, 1954, it filed a voluntary petition in bankruptcy. At this time, the corporation was not indebted to any creditors whose obligations were incurred by the pre-existing partnership, saving the promissory notes issued to Fazio and Ambrose.

Fazio filed a claim against the estate in the sum of $34,147.55, based on the promissory note given to him when the capital of the partnership was reduced. Ambrose filed a similar claim in the sum of $7,871.17. The discrepancy between these amounts and the amounts of the promissory notes is due to certain set-offs and transfers not here in issue.

In asking that these claims be subordinated to the claims of general unsecured creditors, the trustee averred that the amounts in question represent a portion of the capital investment in the partnership. It was alleged that the transfer of this sum from the partnership capital account to an account entitled "Loans from Copartners," effectuated a scheme and plan to place co-partners in the same class as unsecured creditors. The trustee further alleged, with respect to each claimant:

> ". . . If said claimant is permitted to share in the assets of said bankrupt now in the hands of the trustee, in the same parity with general unsecured creditors, he will receive a portion of the capital invested which should be used to satisfy the claims of creditors before any capital investment can be returned to the owners and stockholders of said bankrupt."

A hearing was held before the referee in bankruptcy. In addition to eliciting the above recounted facts, three expert witnesses called by the trustee, and one expert witness called by the claimants, expressed opinions on various phases of the transaction.

Clifford V. Heimbucher, a certified public accountant and management consultant, called by the trustee, expressed the view that, at the time of incorporation, capitalization was inadequate. He further stated that, in incorporating a business already in existence, where the approximate amount of permanent capital needed has been established by experience, normal procedure called for continuing such capital in the form of common or preferred stock.

Stating that only additional capital needed temporarily is normally set up as loans, Heimbucher testified that ". . . the amount of capital employed in the business was at all times substantially more than the $6,000 employed in the opening of the corporation." He also expressed the opinion that, at the time of incorporation, there was "very little hope [of financial success] in view of the fact that for the year immediately preceding the opening of the corporation, losses were running a little less than $2,000 a month. . . ."

William B. Logan, a business analyst and consultant called by the trustee, expressed the view that $6,000 was inadequate capitalization for this company. John S. Curran, a business analyst, also called by the trustee, expressed the view that the corporation needed at least as much capital as the partnership required prior to the reduction of capital.

Robert H. Laborde, Jr., a certified public accountant, had handled the accounting problems of the partnership and corporation. He was called by the trustee as an adverse witness, pursuant to § 21, sub. j of the Bankruptcy Act, 11 U.S.C.A. § 44, sub. j. Laborde readily conceded that the transaction whereby Fazio and Ambrose obtained promissory notes from the partnership was for the purpose of transferring a capital account into a loan or debt account. He stated that this was done in contemplation of the formation of the corporation, and with knowledge that the partnership was losing money.

The prime reason for incorporating the business, according to Laborde, was to protect the personal interest of Fazio, who had made the greatest capital contribution to the business. In this connection, it was pointed out that the "liabilities on the business as a partnership were pretty heavy." There was apparently also a tax angle. Laborde testified that it was contemplated that the notes would be paid out of the profits of the business. He agreed that, if promissory notes had not been issued, the profits would have been distributed only as dividends, and that as such they would have been taxable. . . .

. . . Laborde expressed no opinion as to the adequacy of proprietary capital put at the risk of the business. On the other hand, the corporate accounts and the undisputed testimony of three accounting experts demonstrate that stated capital was wholly inadequate.

On the evidence produced at this hearing, as summarized above, the referee found that the paid-in stated capital of the corporation at the time of its incorporation was adequate for the continued operation of the business. He found that while Fazio and Ambrose controlled and dominated the corporation and its affairs they did not mismanage the business. He further found that claimants did not practice any fraud or deception, and did not act for their own personal or private benefit and to the detriment of the corporation or its stockholders and creditors. The referee also found that the transaction which had been described was not a part of any scheme or plan to place the claimants in the same class as unsecured creditors of the partnership.

On the basis of these findings, the referee concluded that, in procuring the promissory notes, the claimants acted in all respects in good faith and took no unfair advantage of the corporation, or of its stockholders or creditors.

referee found F & A to have acted in good faith.

Pursuant to § 39, sub. c of the Bankruptcy Act, 11 U.S.C.A. § 67, sub. c, the trustee filed a petition for review of the referee's order. The district court, after examining the record certified to it by the referee, entered an order affirming the order of the referee.

On this appeal, the trustee advances two grounds for reversal of the district court order. The first of these is that claims of controlling shareholders will be deferred or subordinated to outside creditors where a corporation in bankruptcy has not been adequately or honestly capitalized, or has been managed to the prejudice of creditors, or where to do otherwise would be unfair to creditors.

Issue(s) on appeal

→ RULE

As a basis for applying this asserted rule in the case before us, the trustee challenges most of the findings of fact noted above.

The district court and this court are required to accept the findings of the referee in bankruptcy, unless such findings are clearly erroneous.

Where a finding of fact by the referee is based upon conflicting evidence, or where the credibility of witnesses is a factor, a district court and, on appeal, a court of appeals will seldom hold such a finding clearly erroneous. The same reluctance is not encountered with regard to a factual conclusion from given facts. In the latter case, the proper conclusion from given facts can be made by the trial judge, or the court of appeals, as well as the referee.

The factual conclusion of the referee, that the paid-in capital of the corporation at the time of its incorporation was adequate for the continued operation of the business, was based upon certain accounting data and the expert testimony of four witnesses. The accounting data, summarized above, is contained in the opening balance sheet and the comparative profit and loss statements of the corporation, and is not in dispute.

It does not require the confirmatory opinion of experts to determine from this data that the corporation was grossly undercapitalized. In the year immediately preceding incorporation, net sales aggregated $390,000. In order to handle such a turnover, the partners apparently found that capital in excess of $50,000 was necessary. They actually had $51,620.78 in the business at that time. Even then, the business was only "two jumps ahead of the wolf." A net loss of $22,000 was sustained in that year; there was only $66.66 in the bank; and there was an overdraft of $3,422.78.

Yet, despite this precarious financial condition, Fazio and Ambrose withdrew $45,620.78 of the partnership capital—more than eighty-eight per cent of the total capital. The $6,000 capital left in the business was only one-sixty-fifth of the last annual net sales. All this is revealed by the books of the company.

Partnership in precarious position & F & A w/d almost all capital

But if there is need to confirm this conclusion that the corporation was grossly undercapitalized, such confirmation is provided by three of the four experts who testified. The fourth expert, called by appellees, did not express an opinion to the contrary.

We therefore hold that the factual conclusion of the referee, that the corporation was adequately capitalized at the time of its organization, is clearly erroneous.

The factual conclusion of the trial court, that the claimants, in withdrawing capital from the partnership in contemplation of incorporation, did not act for their own personal or private benefit and to the detriment of the corporation or of its stockholders and creditors, is based upon the same accounting data and expert testimony.

Laborde, testifying for the claimants, made it perfectly clear that the depletion of the capital account in favor of a debt account was for the purpose of equalizing the capital investments of the partners and to reduce tax liability when there were profits to distribute. It is therefore certain, contrary to the finding just noted, that, in withdrawing this capital, Fazio and Ambrose did act for their own personal and private benefit.

It is equally certain, from the undisputed facts, that in so doing they acted to the detriment of the corporation and its creditors. The best evidence of this is what happened to the business after incorporation, and what will happen to its creditors if the reduction in capital is allowed to stand. The likelihood that business failure would result from such undercapitalization should have been apparent to anyone who knew the company's financial and business history and who had access to its balance sheet and profit and loss statements. Three expert witnesses confirmed this view, and none expressed a contrary opinion.

Accordingly, we hold that the factual conclusion, that the claimants, in withdrawing capital, did not act for their own personal or private benefit and to the detriment of the corporation and creditors, is clearly erroneous.

Recasting the facts in the light of what is said above, the question which appellant presents is this:

> Where, in connection with the incorporation of a partnership, and for their own personal and private benefit, two partners who are to become officers, directors, and controlling stockholders of the corporation, convert the bulk of their capital contributions into loans, taking promissory notes, thereby leaving the partnership and succeeding corporation grossly undercapitalized, to the detriment of the corporation and its creditors, should their claims against the estate of the subsequently bankrupted corporation be subordinated to the claims of the general unsecured creditors?

The question almost answers itself.

In allowing and disallowing claims, courts of bankruptcy apply the rules and principles of equity jurisprudence. Pepper v. Litton, 308

U.S. 295, 304, 60 S.Ct. 238, 84 L.Ed. 281. Where the claim is found to be inequitable, it may be set aside (Pepper v. Litton, supra), or subordinated to the claims of other creditors. As stated in Taylor v. Standard Gas Co., supra, 306 U.S. at page 315, 59 S.Ct. at page 547, the question to be determined when the plan or transaction which gives rise to a claim is challenged as inequitable is "whether, within the bounds of reason and fairness, such a plan can be justified."

Where, as here, the claims are filed by persons standing in a fiduciary relationship to the corporation, another test which equity will apply is "whether or not under all the circumstances the transaction carries the earmarks of an arm's length bargain." Pepper v. Litton, supra, 308 U.S. at page 306, 60 S.Ct. at page 245.

Under either of these tests, the transaction here in question stands condemned.

Appellees argue that more must be shown than mere under-capitalization if the claims are to be subordinated. Much more than mere undercapitalization was shown here. Persons serving in a fiduciary relationship to the corporation actually withdrew capital already committed to the business, in the face of recent adverse financial experience. They stripped the business of eighty-eight per cent of its stated capital at a time when it had a minus working capital and had suffered substantial business losses. This was done for personal gain, under circumstances which charge them with knowledge that the corporation and its creditors would be endangered. Taking advantage of their fiduciary position, they thus sought to gain equality of treatment with general creditors.

In Taylor v. Standard Gas & Electric Co., 306 U.S. 307, 59 S.Ct. 543, 83 L.Ed. 669, and some other cases, there was fraud and mismanagement present in addition to undercapitalization. Appellees argue from this that fraud and mismanagement must always be present if claims are to be subordinated in a situation involving undercapitalization.

This is not the rule. The test to be applied, as announced in the Taylor case and quoted above, is whether the transaction can be justified "within the bounds of reason and fairness." In the more recent Heiser case, supra, 327 U.S. pages 732–733, 66 S.Ct. at page 856, the Supreme Court made clear, in these words, that fraud is not an essential ingredient:

> ". . . In appropriate cases, acting upon equitable principles, it [bankruptcy court] may also subordinate the claim of one creditor to those of others in order to prevent the consummation of a course of conduct by the claimant, which, as to them, would be fraudulent *or otherwise inequitable*. . . ." (Emphasis supplied.)

The fact that the withdrawal of capital occurred prior to incorporation is immaterial. This transaction occurred in contemplation of incorporation. The participants then occupied a fiduciary relationship to the partnership; and expected to become controlling stockholders, directors, and officers of the corporation. This plan was effectuated, and they were serving in those fiduciary capacities when the corporation assumed the liabilities of the partnership, including the notes here in question.

Nor is the fact that the business, after being stripped of necessary capital, was able to survive long enough to have a turnover of creditors a mitigating circumstance. The inequitable conduct of appellees consisted not in acting to the detriment of creditors then known, but in acting to the detriment of present or future creditors, whoever they may be.

In our opinion, it was error to affirm the order of the referee denying the motion to subordinate the claims in question. We do not reach appellant's other major contention, that the notes are not provable in bankruptcy because they were to be paid only out of profits, and there were no profits.

Reversed and remanded for further proceedings not inconsistent with this opinion.

UNIFORM FRAUDULENT TRANSFER ACT § 4(a)

[See Statutory Supplement]

NOTE ON SUBORDINATION OF SHAREHOLDER CLAIMS

1. The doctrine of equitable subordination is often referred to as the "Deep Rock" doctrine, named after the subsidiary corporation in the seminal case of Taylor v. Standard Gas & Electric Co., 306 U.S. 307, 59 S.Ct. 543, 83 L.Ed. 669 (1939). The Court in this case subordinated a parent's claim as a creditor of the subsidiary to the claims of other creditors and of preferred stockholders, because of the improper management of the subsidiary by the parent for the benefit of the parent and because the subsidiary had been inadequately capitalized. Under the *Deep Rock* doctrine, when a corporation is in bankruptcy the claim of a controlling shareholder may be subordinated to other claims, including the claims of preferred shareholders, on various equitable grounds.

In Pepper v. Litton, 308 U.S. 295, 310, 60 S.Ct. 238, 246, 84 L.Ed. 281 (1939) Justice Douglas stated the rationale of the *Deep Rock* doctrine as follows:

> Though disallowance of [shareholder] claims will be ordered where they are fictitious or a sham, these cases do not turn on the existence or nonexistence of the debt. Rather they involved simply the question of order of payment. At times equity has ordered disallowance or subordination by disregarding the corporate entity. That is to say, it has treated the debtor-corporation simply as a part of the stockholder's own enterprise, consistently with the course of

conduct of the stockholder. But in that situation as well as in the others to which we have referred, a sufficient consideration may be simply the violation of rules of fair play and good conscience by the complainant; a breach of fiduciary standards of conduct which he owes the corporation, its stockholders and creditors.''

2.   In Gannett Co. v. Larry, 221 F.2d 269 (2d Cir.1955), the Gannett Company was in the newspaper publishing business. To ensure a supply of newsprint in view of a threatened shortage, Gannett purchased all the stock of Berwin Paper Manufacturing Corporation. Prior to the acquisition, Berwin had been in the business of publishing a newspaper. Gannett converted Berwin to a newsprint supplier and lent substantial sums to it for that purpose. However, the threatened newsprint shortage never materialized; by 1952 the newsprint market had changed completely and Berwin was operating at a loss. As a result, business was suspended in 1953 and Berwin became insolvent, and a trustee in bankruptcy was appointed. The court subordinated Gannett's claim to the claims of other creditors. Even assuming that Gannett's mistakes were business errors in good faith, "the fact remains that the losses suffered by Berwin were suffered, not in an attempt by Gannett primarily to make the subsidiary a financially profitable proposition, but to turn it into a source of newsprint, of no interest to the other creditors—unless financially profitable—but of distinct interest to Gannett, whether or not financially profitable, because of Gannett's newsprint shortage. Because of this factor. . . . 'It would be unfair to allow the claim of Gannett on a parity with other creditors who lacked the interest which Gannett had in Berwin's disastrous experiment in the newsprint field.' In such circumstances, proof of fraud or illegality is not necessary".

3.   Arnold v. Phillips, 117 F.2d 497 (5th Cir.1941), cert. denied 313 U.S. 583, 61 S.Ct. 1102, 85 L.Ed. 1539 (1941), raises the question of what is adequate capitalization. Wishing to engage in the brewing business, Arnold formed a company with capital stock of $50,000 paid for in cash. He then lent the company $75,000 (shortly thereafter secured by a mortgage on the plant) so that it would have enough to start operations. The business began to lose heavily, and Arnold advanced large additional sums. On bankruptcy liquidation, the mortgage held by Arnold was held invalid, on the ground of inadequate capitalization, insofar as it represented money loaned to build and equip the plant (i.e., to the extent of $75,000), but valid as to subsequent advances after the company became a going concern. The court said:

> The two series of advances differ materially as respects their nature and purpose. Those made before the enterprise was launched were, as the district court found, really capital. Although the charter provided for no more capital than $50,000, what it took to build the plant and equip it was a permanent investment, in its nature capital. . . . . There can be little doubt that what he contributed to the plant was

actually intended to be capital, notwithstanding the charter was not amended and demand notes were taken. . . .

After two years of prosperity, with the original capital thus enlarged demonstrated to be sufficient, with a book surplus of nearly $100,000 after payment of large salaries and dividends in the form of interest, there arose a situation very different from that in the beginning. Adversity then occurring raised a problem not different from that which commonly faces a corporation having losses. It may borrow to meet its needs. Had this corporation borrowed of a bank upon the security of the plant, the debt would no doubt be valid. What would render it invalid when Arnold furnished the money? . . .

We do not think a case is presented where the corporate entity ought to be disregarded as being a sham, a mere obstacle to justice, or instrument of fraud. It is not denied that a corporation, owned by one man save for qualifying shares, is lawful in Texas. That it was created to shield the owner from liability beyond the capital set up by the charter does not show an unlawful or fraudulent intent, for that is a main purpose of every incorporation. It becomes an evidence of fraud only when the capital is unsubstantial and the risk of loss great, or the contributions to capital are greatly overvalued, and the like. It would be hard to say in this case that $50,000 was not a substantial capital, and impossible so to say after holding that the real capital was $125,500, though some was irregularly paid in. There is nothing to show the enterprise was entered upon or prosecuted with a fraudulent purpose.

Id. at 501–502.

4. If a parent and a subsidiary, or two affiliated corporations, are both bankrupt, the courts sometimes consolidate the assets and liabilities of the several corporations into a common pool. See In re Seatrade Corp., 255 F.Supp. 696 (S.D.N.Y.1966), aff'd sub nom. Chemical Bank New York Trust Co. v. Kheel, 369 F.2d 845 (2d Cir.); Landers, A Unified Approach to Parent, Subsidiary, and Affiliate Questions in Bankruptcy, 42 U.Chi.L.Rev. 589, 629–51 (1975).

———

SECTION 10. THE CORPORATE ENTITY AND THE INTERPRETATION OF STATUTES AND CONTRACTS

The questions often arise (1) whether a statute or contract that applies to a corporation also applies by implication to the corporation's shareholders, or (2) whether a statute or contract that applies to an individual also applies by implication to a corporation that the individual owns. If a statute prohibits aliens from owning ships that ply the

U.S. coastal trade, does it also prohibit corporations from owning ships where all of the stock is held by aliens? If Corporation A agrees with X not to compete with X, may A's sole shareholder compete with X?

These are not questions concerning whether individual liability should be imposed despite the general rule of limited liability. Rather, they are questions of interpretation. In making such an interpretation, it must be borne in mind that, on the one hand, the law normally treats a corporation and its shareholders as distinct, but on the other, the legislature or contracting parties may not intend to treat a corporation and its shareholders as distinct for all purposes. Two of the leading cases in this area are United States v. Milwaukee Refrigerated Transit Co., 142 Fed. 247, 255 (E.D.Wis.1905), and Anderson v. Abbott, 321 U.S. 349, 64 S.Ct. 531, 88 L.Ed. 793 (1944). In the *Milwaukee* case, a statute prohibited railroads from giving rebates to shippers. The statute was held applicable to a corporation that was not itself a shipper, but had been formed by a shipper's officers and principal shareholders for the purpose of obtaining what were in substance rebates. "[A] corporation will be looked upon as a legal entity as a general rule, and until sufficient reason to the contrary appears; but, when the notion of legal entity is used to defeat public convenience . . . the law will regard the corporation as an association of persons." In the *Anderson* case, a statute made a shareholder in a national bank liable for the debts of the bank "to the amount of his stock therein, at the par value thereof in addition to the amount invested in such stock." The question was whether this statute applied to shareholders of a parent corporation with a national bank subsidiary, although technically only the parent was a shareholder in the bank. The Supreme Court concluded that the parent's shareholders would be deemed shareholders of the bank for the purpose of the statute, on the ground that to hold otherwise would permit that purpose to be undercut:

> It has often been held that the interposition of a corporation will not be allowed to defeat a legislative policy, whether that was the aim or only the result of the arrangement. . . .
>
> To allow this holding company device to succeed would be to put the policy of double liability at the mercy of corporation finance.

321 U.S. at 362–63. See also Kavanaugh v. Ford Motor Co., 353 F.2d 710, 716–17 (7th Cir.1965); Note, Efficacy of the Corporate Entity in Evasion of Statutes, 26 Iowa L.Rev. 350 (1941).

Chapter IV

CORPORATE STRUCTURE

SECTION 1. SHAREHOLDERSHIP IN PUBLICLY HELD CORPORATIONS

NOTE ON SHAREHOLDERSHIP IN PUBLICLY HELD CORPORATIONS

New concepts regarding the large publicly held corporation first received widespread recognition in 1932, with the publication of Berle & Means' classic work, *The Modern Corporation and Private Property.* One of this book's principal conclusions, almost revolutionary at the time, was that as corporate ownership became more widely dispersed, control had come to be divorced from ownership:

Frequently . . . ownership is so widely scattered that working control can be maintained with but a minority interest. . . . Separation of ownership and control becomes almost complete when not even a substantial minority interest exists, as in the American Telephone and Telegraph Company. . . . Under such conditions control may be held by the directors or titular managers who can employ the proxy machinery to become a self-perpetuating body, even though as a group they own but a small fraction of the stock outstanding. . . . [A] large body of security holders has been created who exercise virtually no control over the wealth which they or their predecessors in interest have contributed to the enterprise. In the case of management control, the ownership interest held by the controlling group amounts to but a very small fraction of the total ownership. Corporations where this separation has become an important factor may be classed as quasi-public in character in contradistinction to the private, or closely held corporation in which no important separation of ownership and control has taken place. . . .

. . . [P]arallel with the growth in the size of the industrial unit has come a dispersion in its ownership such that an important part of the wealth of individuals consists of interests in great enterprises of which no one individual owns a major part. . . .

. . . [T]he position of ownership has changed from that of an active to that of a passive agent. In place of actual physical properties over which the owner could exercise direction and for which he was responsible, the owner now holds a piece of paper representing a set of rights and expectations with respect to an enterprise. But over the enterprise and over the physical property—the instruments of production—in which he has an interest, the owner has little control. . . .

. . . [I]n the corporate system, the "owner" of industrial wealth is left with a mere symbol of ownership while the power, the responsibility and the substance which have been an integral part of ownership in the past are being transferred to a separate group in whose hands lies control. (Id. at 4–5, 66, 68.)

Following Berle & Means, it has become customary to distinguish major three categories of control:

(i) *Majority Control.* The first category consists of corporations in which a single shareholder or a compact group owns either a majority of the stock or an amount so large—say 35–40%—that it will carry a majority of votes in a normal election. This category is referred to as majority or owner control.

(ii) *Management Control.* The second category consists of corporations in which the largest block of stock owned by a single shareholder or compact group is very small—say 5%–10%. This category is referred to as management control. Why? First, because shareholders who do not own significant amounts of a corporation's stock will normally not want to spend a significant amount of time on the corporation's affairs, and management fills the vacuum. Second, and more important, because when a corporation's stock is held by thousands of shareholders living across the country, voting must be done by proxy rather than in person. Typically, in this type of corporation management controls the corporate proxy machinery, and management's access to that machinery is cost-free. In contrast, shareholders who want to unseat management must pay for the expense of a proxy campaign out of their own pockets. If a proxy fight does occur, management has in its favor not only cost-free access to the corporate proxy machinery, but the legitimacy that goes along with being management. Add the fact that shareholders who are extremely dissatisfied often prefer to sell rather than vote—so that the market siphons off many potential anti-management shareholders— and it can easily be seen that where no individual, firm, or compact group owns more than 5–10% of a corporation's stock, incumbent management will normally be protected in its control by the heavy costs and poor prospects that proxy fights involve.

(iii) *Minority or Joint Control.* The third category consists of corporations in which the largest block of stock owned by a single shareholder or compact group falls between the limits of majority control and management control. This category is referred to as minority or joint minority-management control. If in such a case the minority block is owned by management itself, unseating the minority's control is almost impossible. If the minority stock is not owned by management, management and the minority owners are likely to work together, because as a practical matter both have sources of power: management will have control of the proxy machinery and the legitimacy of management; the minority owners will have a strong base from which to begin a proxy fight (thereby reducing the number of outside votes that must be garnered) and the legitimacy of ownership.

Most of the measurement of control categories has focused on only the very largest American corporations. In their study of the 200 largest nonfinancial corporations as of 1929 (measured by value of assets), Berle & Means found 65 cases in which no outstanding block of stock as large as 5% was held by a single shareholder or a compact group, and 16 more cases in which the largest outstanding block was in the 5–20% range.[1] In a study of the 200 largest nonfinancials as of 1963, intended to bring the Berle & Means data up to date, Robert Larner found 169 cases in which no block of stock as large as 10% was so held.[2] At least among the 200 largest nonfinancials, therefore, there seems to be a marked trend toward management control.

The data collected by Berle & Means and Larner on the very largest corporations is impressive and important, but it must be kept in perspective. To begin with, management control is most likely to occur in the very largest corporations, measured by number of shareholders, and becomes increasingly less likely as the size of the corporation diminishes. There are approximately three million corporations in this country. Although there are no definitive data on the distribution of corporations by number of shareholders, Table 1 (based on 1970's data) probably gives a fair approximation:

Table 1[3]

Number of Shareholders	Percentage of Corporations
1–10	93.94
11–99	4.03
100–499	1.53
500–1499	.29
1500–2999	.10
3000–10,000	.07
Over 10,000	.03

As Table 1 shows, even corporations that are publicly held usually have a relatively small number of shareholders. Moreover, a distinction must be drawn between corporations whose shareholdership is atomistically distributed, so that few or no holders own more than an infinitesimal portion of the stock, and corporations whose shareholdership is concentrated, so that although no single person owns a 10% block, a relatively small number of persons hold a relatively large percentage of the corporation's stock. Where shareholdings are concentrated, the small number of shareholders who own a relatively

1. A. Berle & G. Means, at 69–94, 116.

2. Larner, Ownership and Control in the 200 Largest Nonfinancial Corporations, 1929 and 1963, 56 Am.Econ.Rev. 777 (1966); see also Jones, Corporate Governance: Who Controls the Large Corporation, in Symposium: Corporate Social Responsibility, 30 Hast.L.J. 1261 (1979).

3. Table 1 is derived from M. Eisenberg, The Structure of the Corporation 42, Table 5-1 (1976).

large percentage of the corporation's stock may have significant say even though they do not form a group, and therefore lack control.

The data suggests that shareholdings are concentrated even in large publicly held corporations. For example, in connection with its 1963 *Special Study,* the SEC made a survey to determine the correlation between distribution of shareholdings and number of shareholders in an extensive sample of over-the-counter corporations. In more than half of the corporations with 100 to 1000 shareholders, the ten largest record shareholders held 50 percent or more of the stock. In more than half of the sampled corporations with 1000 to 1999 shareholders, the ten largest record shareholders held at least 40 percent of the stock. In more than half of the sampled corporations with 2000 to 4999 shareholders, the ten largest record shareholders held at least 30 percent of the stock. In about 30 percent of the sampled corporations with 5000 or more shareholders, the ten largest record shareholders held over 30 percent of the stock. In about 40 percent of the sampled corporations with 5000 or more shareholders, the ten largest record shareholders held almost 20 percent of the stock.[4] Similarly, a survey of common shareholdings in 2932 publicly held corporations, conducted under the auspices of the Brookings Institution and the New York Stock Exchange, showed that as of 1951, 2.1 percent of such shareholdings accounted for over half of the total value of all shareholdings.[5]

What accounts for the concentration of shareholdings in even the very largest corporations? One factor is that holdings of stock by individuals is highly concentrated among a relatively small number of top wealthholders. For example, Butters, Thompson, and Bollinger estimated that as of 1949, the marketable stock held by individuals was owned by approximately 4.5 million spending units. Of these 4.5 million units, 1.1 percent owned approximately 65 percent of the stock by value.[6]

The second factor accounting for the concentration of shareholdership is that a great proportion of stock is held by a relatively small number of institutional shareholders, such as bank trust departments, mutual funds, insurance companies, and other financial institutions. Total shareholdings of institutional shareholders are shown in Table 2:

4. SEC, Report of Special Study of the Securities Markets, H.R.Doc. No. 95, 88th Cong., 1st Sess., pt. 3, at 30 (1963).

5. L. Kimmel, Share Ownership in the United States 42–43 (1952).

6. J. Butters, L. Thompson, & L. Bollinger, Effects of Taxation—Investments by Individuals 373–389 (1953). For a comparable analysis, see Staff of Senate Committee on Banking and Currency, 84th Cong., 1st Sess., Factors Affecting the Stock Market 90 (1955). See also Blume, Crockett & Friend, Stockownership in the United States: Characteristics and Trends, Surv. Current Bus., Nov. 1974, at 16, 27; Smith & Franklin, The Concentration of Personal Wealth, 1922–1969, Am.Econ.Rev., May 1974, at 162, 166 (Table 1).

Table 2[7]

INSTITUTIONAL OWNERSHIP OF CORPORATE STOCK
as of June 30, 1986

TYPE OF INSTITUTION- AL INVESTOR	EQUITY HOLDINGS OF THE INSTITUTIONAL INVESTOR (billions)	PERCENTAGE OF TOTAL EQUITY HOLDINGS IN THE ECONOMY
Private Pension Plans	456.4	15.5
State and Local Employee Retirement Plans	150.2	5.1
Mutual Funds	161.2	5.4
Life Insurance Companies	82.9	2.8
Foreign	167.4	5.6
Banks, as Trustee	450.8	15.3
Foundations, etc.	127.0	4.3
		54.0

The proportion of stock of large publicly held corporations held by institutional investors is higher than the proportion of all corporate stock held by institutional investors, because such investors tend to prefer the stock of large, listed corporations.

Moreover, most of these shareholdings are held by a relatively small percentage of all institutions. The SEC's *Institutional Investor Study* reported in 1971 that the 50 largest bank trust departments accounted for 72 percent of the common stock managed by all bank trust departments; the 71 investment advisers managing the largest investment-company complexes accounted for 64 percent of all common stock managed by all investment advisers; the 26 largest life insurance companies accounted for 82 percent of all common stock held by such companies; and the 25 largest property-and-liability insurance companies accounted for 71 percent of all common stock held by such insurers.[8] The net result is that a relatively small number of institutional investors hold, in the aggregate, a very substantial proportion of the stock of many or most of the country's very largest corporations.

---

7. Sources: Federal Reserve, Flow of Funds Accounts Financial Assets and Liabilities Year-End 1963–1986 (September 1987); FDIC Form 001 Filings, Annual Report of Trust Assets; National Association of College and University Business Officers; The Foundation Center, National Data Book xii (1988). Much of this data was collected by Robert A.G. Monks and Bruce A. Reznick, and some is estimated.

8. Securities and Exchange Commission, Institutional Investor Study Report, H.R. Doc. No. 64, 922 Cong., 1st Sess. pt 3, at 1309.

SECTION 2. THE ALLOCATION OF POWER BETWEEN MANAGEMENT AND SHAREHOLDERS

DEL. GEN. CORP. LAW § 141(a)

§ 141   Board of directors . . . .

(a) The business and affairs of every corporation organized under this chapter shall be managed by or under the direction of a board of directors, except as may be otherwise provided in this chapter or in its certificate of incorporation. If any such provision is made in the certificate of incorporation, the powers and duties conferred or imposed upon the board of directors by this chapter shall be exercised or performed to such extent and by such person or persons as shall be provided in the certificate of incorporation.

REV. MODEL BUS. CORP. ACT § 8.01(b)

§ 8.01   Requirement for and Duties of Board of Directors . . .

(b) All corporate powers shall be exercised by or under the authority of, and the business and affairs of the corporation managed under the direction of, its board of directors, subject to any limitation set forth in the articles of incorporation.

CHARLESTOWN BOOT & SHOE CO. v. DUNSMORE

New Hampshire Supreme Court, 1880.
60 N.H. 85.

Shareholder cannot order the board to take any particular action [handwritten marginalia]

CASE. Demurrer to the declaration in which the following facts were alleged:—The plaintiffs are a manufacturing corporation having for its object a dividend of profits, and commenced business in 1871. Dunsmore was elected director in 1871 and Willard in 1873, and entered upon the discharge of their duties, and have continued so to act by virtue of successive elections until the present time. December 10, 1874, the corporation * voted to choose a committee to act with the directors to close up its affairs, and chose one Osgood for such committee. Osgood tendered his services, but the defendants refused to act with him, and contracted new debts to a larger extent than allowed by law. By their negligence, debts due to the corporation to the amount of $2,161.23 have been wholly lost. By their negligence in disposing of the goods of the corporation, a loss has accrued of $3,300.40. By their neglect to sell the buildings and machinery of

---

* By "the corporation," in this phrase and some others, the court seems to mean the body of shareholders. (Footnote by ed.)

the corporation when they might and ought, and were urged by Osgood to sell, the same depreciated in value to the extent of $20,000.

Also for that the plaintiffs owned and possessed a certain shop of the value of $10,000, and a large amount of machinery and fixtures of the value of $10,000; "and whereas it was the duty of said defendants, directors as aforesaid, to procure sufficient and proper insurance against fire to be made on said property, and keep the same so sufficiently insured, of all which the said defendants had notice, yet they did not and would not keep the said property so insured, and afterwards, to wit, on the 28th day of April, 1878, while the said property was so remaining without insurance, the same was wholly consumed by fire and wholly lost to the plaintiff, whereby the plaintiff suffered great loss and damage, to wit, $20,000."

SMITH, J. The provision of the statute is, that the business of a dividend paying corporation shall be managed by the directors. The statute reads, "The business of every such corporation shall be managed by the directors thereof, subject to the by-laws and votes of the corporation, and under their direction by such officers and agents as shall be duly appointed by the directors or by the corporation." G.L., c. 148, s. 3; Gen.Stats., c. 134, s. 3. The only limitation upon the judgment or discretion of the directors is such as the corporation by its by-laws and votes shall impose. It may define its business, its nature and extent, prescribe rules and regulations for the government of its officers and members, and determine whether its business shall be wound up or continued; but when it has thus acted, the business as thus defined and limited is to be managed by its directors, and by such officers and agents under their direction as the directors or the corporation shall appoint. The statute does not authorize a corporation to join another officer with the directors, nor compel the directors to act with one who is not a director. They are bound to use ordinary care and diligence in the care and management of the business of the corporation, and are answerable for ordinary negligence. *March v. Railroad*, 43 N.H. 516, 529; *Scott v. Depeyster*, 1 Edw. Ch. 513, 543; Ang. & Ames Corp., s. 314. There is no difference in this respect between the agents of corporations and those of natural persons, unless expressly made by the charter or by-laws. *Ib.*, s. 315. It would be unreasonable to hold them responsible for the management of the affairs of the corporation if compelled to act with one who to a greater or less extent could control their acts. The statute not only entrusts the management of the business of the corporation to the directors, but places its other officers and agents under their direction. When a statute provides that powers granted to a corporation shall be exercised by any set of officers or any particular agents, such powers can be exercised only by such officers or agents, although they are required to be chosen by the whole corporation; and if the whole corporation attempts to exercise powers which by the charter are lodged elsewhere, its action upon the subject is void. *Insurance Co. v. Keyser*, 32 N.H. 313, 315. The vote choosing Osgood a committee to act with the directors in closing up the affairs of the plaintiff corporation was inoperative and void.

The declaration also alleges that it was the duty of the defendants, as directors, to keep the property of the corporation insured. There is no statute that makes it the duty of the directors of a corporation to keep its property insured, and there are no facts alleged from which we can say, as matter of law, that it was the duty of the defendants to insure the property of the corporation.

Demurrer sustained.

STANLEY, J., did not sit: the others concurred.

PEOPLE EX REL. MANICE v. POWELL, 201 N.Y. 194, 200–01, 94 N.E. 634, 637 (1911). " 'The board of directors of a corporation do not stand in the same relation to the corporate body which a private agent holds towards his principal . . . . In corporate bodies the powers of the board of directors are, in a very important sense, original and undelegated.' (*Hoyt v. Thompson's Executors,* 19 N.Y. 207, 216; *Beveridge v. N.Y.E.R.R. Co.,* 112 N.Y. 1, 22, 23.)

"While the ordinary rules of law relating to an agent are applicable in considering the acts of a board of directors in behalf of a corporation when dealing with third persons, the individual directors making up the board are not mere employees, but a part of an elected body of officers constituting the executive agents of the corporation. They hold such office charged with the duty to act for the corporation according to their best judgment, and in so doing they cannot be controlled in the reasonable exercise and performance of such duty. As a general rule the stockholders cannot act in relation to the ordinary business of the corporation, nor can they control the directors in the exercise of the judgment vested in them by virtue of their office.

"The relation of the directors to the stockholders is essentially that of trustee and *cestui que trust.* The peculiar relation that they bear to the corporation and the owners of its stock grows out of the inability of the corporation to act except through such managing officers and agents. The corporation is the owner of the property, but the directors in the performance of their duty possess it, and act in every way as if they owned it."

AUER v. DRESSEL

Court of Appeals of New York, 1954.
306 N.Y. 427, 118 N.E.2d 590, 48 A.L.R.2d 604.

APPEAL, by permission of the Court of Appeals, from an order of the Appellate Division of the Supreme Court in the first judicial department, entered December 28, 1953, which unanimously affirmed an order of the Supreme Court at Special Term (HAMMER,

J.), entered in Bronx County, granting a motion by petitioners-respondents for an order . . . requiring the president of R. Hoe & Co., Inc., to call a special meeting of class A stockholders of the company.

DESMOND, J. This . . . proceeding was brought by class A stockholders of appellant R. Hoe & Co., Inc., for an order in the nature of mandamus to compel the president of Hoe to comply with a positive duty imposed on him by the corporation's by-laws. Section 2 of article I of those by-laws says that "It shall be the duty of the President to call a special meeting whenever requested in writing so to do, by stockholders owning a majority of the capital stock entitled to vote at such meeting". On October 16, 1953, petitioners submitted to the president written requests for a special meeting of class A stockholders, which writings were signed in the names of the holders of record of slightly more than 55% of the class A stock. The president failed to call the meeting and, after waiting a week, the petitioners brought the present proceeding. The answer of the corporation and its president was not forthcoming until October 28, 1953, and it contained, in response to the petition's allegation that the demand was by more than a majority of class A stockholders, only a denial that the corporation and the president had any knowledge or information sufficient to form a belief as to the stockholdings of those who had signed the requests. Since the president, when he filed that answer, had had before him for at least ten days the signed requests themselves, his denial that he had any information sufficient for a belief as to the adequacy of the number of signatures was obviously perfunctory and raised no issue whatever. . . . There was no discretion in this corporate officer as to whether or not to call a meeting when a demand therefor was put before him by owners of the required number of shares. The important right of stockholders to have such meetings called will be of little practical value if corporate management can ignore the requests, force the stockholders to commence legal proceedings, and then, by purely formal denials, put the stockholders to lengthy and expensive litigation, to establish facts as to stockholdings which are peculiarly within the knowledge of the corporate officers. In such a situation, Special Term did the correct thing in disposing of the matter summarily. . . .

The petition was opposed on the further alleged ground that none of the four purposes for which petitioners wished the meeting called was a proper one for such a class A stockholders' meeting. Those four stated purposes were these: (A) to vote upon a resolution indorsing the administration of petitioner Joseph L. Auer, who had been removed as president by the directors, and demanding that he be reinstated as such president; (B) voting upon a proposal to amend the charter and by-laws to provide that vacancies on the board of directors, arising from the removal of a director by stockholders or by resignation of a director against whom charges have been preferred, may be filled, for the unexpired term, by the stockholders only of the class theretofore represented by the director so removed or so resigned; (C) voting upon a proposal that the stockholders hear certain charges preferred, in the requests, against four of the directors, determine whether the conduct of such directors or any of them was inimical to the corporation and, if so, to vote upon their removal and vote for the election of their successors; and (D) voting upon a proposal to amend the by-laws so as to provide that half of the total number of directors in office and, in any event, not less than one third of the whole authorized number of directors constitute a quorum of the directors.

The Hoe certificate of incorporation provides for eleven directors, of whom the class A stockholders, more than a majority of whom join in this petition, elect nine and the common stockholders elect two. The obvious purpose of the meeting here sought to be called (aside from the indorsement and reinstatement of former president Auer) is to hear charges against four of the class A directors, to remove them if the charges be proven, to amend the by-laws so that the successor directors be elected by the class A stockholders, and further to amend the by-laws so that an effective quorum of directors will be made up of no fewer than half of the directors in office and no fewer than one third of the whole authorized number of directors. No reason appears why the class A stockholders should not be allowed to vote on any or all of those proposals.

The stockholders, by expressing their approval of Mr. Auer's conduct as president and their demand that he be put back in that office, will not be able, directly, to effect that change in officers, but there is nothing invalid in their so expressing themselves and thus putting on notice the directors who will stand for election at the annual meeting. As to purpose (B), that is, amending the charter and by-laws to authorize the stockholders to fill vacancies as to class A directors who have been removed on charges or who have resigned, it seems to be settled law that the stockholders who are empowered to elect directors have the inherent power to remove them for cause (*Matter of Koch,* 257 N.Y. 318, 321, 322; *Abberger v. Kulp,* 156 Misc. 210, 212; 1 White on New York Corporations, pp. 558–559; 2 Fletcher's Cyclopedia Corporations [Perm. ed.], §§ 351, 356). Of course, as the *Koch* case points out, there must be the service of specific charges, adequate notice and full opportunity of meeting the accusations, but there is no present showing of any lack of any of those in this instance. Since these particular stockholders have the right to elect nine directors and to remove them on proven charges, it is not inappropriate that they should use their further power to amend the by-laws to elect the successors of such directors as shall be removed after hearing, or who shall resign pending hearing. Quite pertinent at this point is *Rogers v. Hill* (289 U.S. 582, 589) which made light of an argument that stockholders, by giving power to the directors to make by-laws, had lost their own power to make them; quoting a New Jersey case, the United States Supreme Court said: " 'It would be preposterous to leave the real owners of the corporate property at the mercy of their agents, and the law has not done so' ". Such a change in the by-laws, dealing with class A directors only, has no effect on the voting rights of the common stockholders, which rights have to do with the selection of the remaining two directors only. True, the certificate of incorporation authorizes the board of directors to remove any director on charges, but we do not consider that provision as an abdication by the stockholders of their own traditional, inherent power to remove their own directors. Rather, it provides an additional method. Were that not so, the stockholders might find themselves without effective remedy in a case where a majority of the directors were accused of wrongdoing and, obviously, would be unwilling to remove themselves from office.

We fail to see, in the proposal to allow class A stockholders to fill vacancies as to class A directors, any impairment or any violation of paragraph (h) of article Third of the certificate of incorporation, which says that class A stock has exclusive voting rights with respect to all matters "other than the election of directors". That negative language should not be taken to mean that class A stockholders, who have an absolute right to elect nine of these eleven directors, cannot amend their by-laws to guarantee a similar right in the class A stockholders, and to the exclusion of common stockholders, to fill vacancies in the class A group of directors.

There is urged upon us the impracticability and unfairness of constituting the numerous stockholders a tribunal to hear charges made by themselves, and the incongruity of letting the stockholders hear and pass on those charges by proxy. Such questions are really not before us at all on this appeal. The charges here are not, on their face, frivolous or inconsequential, and all that we are holding as to the charges is that a meeting may be held to deal with them. Any director illegally removed can have his remedy in the courts (see *People ex rel. Manice* v. *Powell*, 201 N.Y. 194).

The order should be affirmed, with costs, and the Special Term directed forthwith to make an order in the same form as the Appellate Division order with appropriate changes of dates.

[The dissenting opinion of Judge VAN VOORHIS is omitted.]

LEWIS, CH. J., DYE, FULD and FROESSEL, JJ., concur with DESMOND, J.; VAN VOORHIS, J., dissents in opinion in which CONWAY, J., concurs.

Order affirmed.

CAMPBELL v. LOEW'S INC., 36 Del.Ch. 563, 572–73, 577–79, 134 A.2d 852, 857–58, 861–62 (1957). "Plaintiff next argues that the shareholders of a Delaware corporation have no power to remove directors from office even for cause and thus the call for that purpose is invalid. The defendant naturally takes a contrary position.

"While there are some cases suggesting the contrary, I believe that the stockholders have the power to remove a director for cause. See *Auer v. Dressel*, 306 N.Y. 427, 118 N.E.2d 590, 48 A.L.R.2d 604; compare *Bruch v. National Guarantee Credit Corp.,* 13 Del.Ch. 180, 116 A. 738. This power must be implied when we consider that otherwise a director who is guilty of the worst sort of violation of his duty could nevertheless remain on the board. It is hardly to be believed that a director who is disclosing the corporation's trade secrets to a competitor would be immune from removal by the stockholders. Other examples, such as embezzlement of corporate funds, etc., come readily to mind.

"But plaintiff correctly states that there is no provision in our statutory law providing for the removal of directors by stockholder action. In contrast he calls attention to § 142 of 8 *Del.C.*, dealing with officers, which specifically refers to the possibility of a vacancy in an office by removal. He also notes that the Loew's by-laws provide for the removal of officers and employees but not directors. From these facts he argues that it was intended that directors not be removed even for cause. I believe the statute and by-law are of course some evidence to support plaintiff's contention. But when we seek to exclude the existence of a power by implication, I think it is pertinent to consider whether the absence of the power can be said to subject the corporation to the possibility of real damage. I say this because we seek intention and such a factor would be relevant to that issue. Considering the damage a director might be able to inflict upon his corporation, I believe the doubt must be resolved by construing the statutes and by-laws as leaving untouched the question of director removal for cause. This being so, the Court is free to conclude on reason that the stockholders have such inherent power.

"I therefore conclude that as a matter of Delaware corporation law the stockholders do have the power to remove directors for cause. I need not and do not decide whether the stockholders can by appropriate charter or by-law provision deprive themselves of this right. . . .

"I next consider whether the directors sought to be removed have been given a reasonable opportunity to be heard by the stockholders on the charges made.

"The corporate defendant freely admits that it has flatly refused to give the [Tomlinson faction on the board, which included two directors the opposing Vogel faction sought to remove] a stockholders' list. Any doubt about the matter was removed by the statement of defendant's counsel in open court at the argument that no such list would be supplied. The Vogel faction has physical control of the corporate offices and facilities. By this action the corporation through the Vogel group has deliberately refused to afford the directors in question an adequate opportunity to be heard by the stockholders on the charges made. This is contrary to the legal requirements which must be met before a director can be removed for cause.

"At the oral argument the defendant's attorney offered to mail any material which might be presented by the Tomlinson faction. This falls far short of meeting the requirements of the law when directors are sought to be ousted for cause. Nor does the granting of the statutory right to inspect and copy some 26,000 names fulfill the requirement that a director sought to be removed for cause must be afforded an opportunity to present his case to the stockholders before they vote.

"When Vogel as president caused the notice of meeting to be sent, he accompanied it with a letter requesting proxies granting authority to vote for the removal of the two named directors. It is true that the proxy form also provided a space for the stockholder to vote against such removal. However, only the Vogel accusations accompanied the request for a proxy. Thus, while the stockholder could vote for or against removal, he would be voting with only one view-point presented. This violates every sense of equity and fair play in a removal for cause situation.

"While the directors involved or some other group could mail a letter to the stockholders and ask for a proxy which would revoke the earlier proxy, this procedure does not comport with the legal require- ment that the directors in question must be afforded an opportunity to be heard before the shareholders vote. This is not an ordinary proxy contest case and a much more stringent standard must be invoked, at least at the initial stage, where it is sought to remove a director for cause. This is so for several reasons. Under our statute the directors manage the corporation and each has a somewhat independent status during his term of office. This right could be greatly impaired if substantial safeguards were not afforded a director whose removal for cause is sought. . . .

"There seems to be an absence of cases detailing the appropriate procedure for submitting a question of director removal for cause for stockholder consideration. I am satisfied, however, that to the extent the matter is to be voted upon by the use of proxies, such proxies may be solicited only after the accused directors are afforded an opportuni- ty to present their case to the stockholders. This means, in my opinion, that an opportunity must be provided such directors to present their defense to the stockholders by a statement which must accompany or precede the initial solicitation of proxies seeking author- ity to vote for the removal of such director for cause. If not provided then such proxies may not be voted for removal. And the corpora- tion has a duty to see that this opportunity is given the directors at its expense. Admittedly, no such opportunity was given the two direc- tors involved. Indeed, the corporation admittedly refused to supply them with a stockholders' list.

"To require anything less than the foregoing is to deprive the stockholders of the opportunity to consider the case made by both sides before voting and would make a mockery of the requirement that a director sought to be removed for cause is entitled to an opportunity to be heard before the stockholders vote. . . .

"I therefore conclude that the procedural sequence here adopted for soliciting proxies seeking authority to vote on the removal of the two directors is contrary to law. The result is that the proxy solicited by the Vogel group, which is based upon unilateral presentation of the facts by those in control of the corporate facilities, must be declared invalid insofar as they purport to give authority to vote for the removal of the directors for cause.

"A preliminary injunction will issue restraining the corporation from recognizing or counting any proxies held by the Vogel group and others insofar as such proxies purport to grant authority to vote for the removal of Tomlinson and Meyer as directors of the corporation."

DEL. GEN. CORP. LAW § 141(k)

[See Statutory Supplement]

REV. MODEL BUS. CORP. ACT §§ 8.08–8.09

[See Statutory Supplement]

CAL. CORP. CODE §§ 303, 304

[See Statutory Supplement]

N.Y. BUS. CORP. LAW § 706

[See Statutory Supplement]

NOTE ON REMOVAL OF DIRECTORS

1. Under the common law:

(i) The shareholders can remove a director for cause. See, e.g., Auer v. Dressel, supra; Campbell v. Loew's, Inc., supra.

(ii) Shareholders cannot remove a director without cause, absent specific authority in the certificate of incorporation or by-laws. See, e.g., Frank v. Anthony, 107 So.2d 136 (Fla.Dist.Ct.App.1958); Toledo Traction, Light & Power Co. v. Smith, 205 Fed. 643, 645–646 (N.D.Ohio 1913); People ex rel. Manice v. Powell, 201 N.Y. 194, 94 N.E. 634 (1911). However, a certificate or by-law provision can permit the removal without cause of directors elected after the provision has been adopted. Everett v. Transnation Development Corp., 267 A.2d 627 (Del.Ch.1970); In re Singer, 189 Misc. 150, 70 N.Y.S.2d 550 (1947), aff'd without opinion 273 App.Div. 755, 75 N.Y.S.2d 514.

(iii) The board cannot remove a director, with or without cause. See, e.g., Bruch v. National Guarantee Credit Corp., 13 Del.Ch. 180, 116 A. 738 (1922); cf. Stott v. Stott Realty Co., 246 Mich. 267, 224 N.W. 623 (1929). It is doubtful whether the certificate of incorporation can change this rule. See Dillon v. Berg, 326 F.Supp. 1214 (D.Del.1971), aff'd 453 F.2d 876 (3d Cir.); Bruch v. National Guarantee Credit Corp., supra.

(iv) The cases are split on whether a court can remove directors for cause. Compare Webber v. Webber Oil Co., 495 A.2d 1215 (Me.1985) and Harkey v. Mobley, 552 S.W.2d 79 (Mo.App.1977) (courts do not have power to remove directors) with Brown v. North Ventura Road Development Co., 216 Cal.App.2d 227, 30 Cal.Rptr. 568 (1963); Ross v. 311 North Central Avenue Building Corp. 130 Ill.App.2d 336, 264 N.E.2d 406 (1970) and Feldman v. Pennroad Corp., 60 F.Supp. 716 (D.Del.1945), aff'd, 155 F.2d 773 (3d Cir. 1946), cert. denied 329 U.S. 808, 67 S.Ct. 621, 91 L.Ed. 690 (1947) (courts have power to remove directors, at least for fraud or the like).

2. The common law rules have been significantly altered by statute in a number of states:

(i) Some statutes permit the shareholders to remove a director without cause. See, e.g., Cal.Corp.Code § 303(a); Rev.Model Bus. Corp.Act § 8.08. A few statutes permit the shareholders to remove a director without cause if the certificate or by-laws so provide. See, e.g., N.Y.Bus.Corp.Law § 706(b).

(ii) Some statutes permit the board to remove a director for cause, see, e.g., Mass.Gen.Laws ch. 156B, § 51(c), or for specified reasons such as conviction of a felony, see, e.g., Calif.Corp.Code § 302. A few statutes permit the board to remove a director for cause or for specified reasons if the certificate of incorporation so provides. See, e.g., N.J.Stat.Ann. § 14A:6–6.

(iii) Some statutes permit the courts to remove a director for specified reasons, such as fraudulent or dishonest acts. These statutes usually provide that a petition for such removal can be brought only by a designated percentage of the shareholders (most commonly 10%), by the attorney general, or in some cases, by either. See, e.g., Calif.Corp.Code § 304; N.Y.Bus.Corp.Law § 706(d); Rev.Model Bus.Corp.Act § 8.09.

SECTION 3. THE LEGAL STRUCTURE OF MANAGEMENT (I): THE BOARD OF DIRECTORS AND THE OFFICERS

NOTE ON THE LEGAL STRUCTURE OF THE CORPORATION

Until recently, corporation law reflected what might be called the traditional model of formal corporate decisionmaking. Under this model, the board of directors manages the corporation's business and makes business policy; the officers act as agents of the board and execute its decisions; and the shareholders elect the board and decide on "major corporate actions" or "fundamental" changes. The model is an inverted pyramid in form. At the top of the inverted pyramid are the shareholders, whose vote is required to elect the board of directors and to pass on other major corporate actions.   The next level down is represented by the directors, who constitute the policymaking body of the corporation and select the officers.   At the bottom of the inverted pyramid are the officers, who have some discretion but in general are limited to the execution of policies formulated by the board.

Perhaps the most striking aspect of the traditional legal model is the distinctive position of the board.   Simple business organizations are managed either by the owners or by persons who are legally agents of the owners.   Under the traditional legal model of the corporation, however, the officers are agents not of the shareholders but of the board, while the board itself is conceived of not strictly as an agent of the shareholders but as an independent institution.   For example, although the authority of an agent can normally be terminated by his principal at any time, directors are normally removable by shareholders only for good cause.   Similarly, although an agent must normally follow his principal's instructions, shareholders have no legal power to give binding instructions to the board on matters within its power.   Any study of corporate structure must therefore consider two very different interfaces: that between the shareholders and the managerial organs taken together, and that between the managerial organs themselves.

In recent times, it has become obvious that the traditional legal model is inadequate.   Under that model, the board of directors manages the corporation's business and sets business policy.   This aspect of the model was reflected in a central provision of the traditional corporate statutes: "The business and affairs of a corporation shall be managed by a board of directors."   It has become increasingly clear, however, that in practice the board rarely performs either the management or the policymaking functions.   It has always been understood that in closely held corporations the business is typically managed by owner-managers, pretty much without any regard to formal capacities.   All serious students of corporate affairs also now recognize that in the typical large publicly held corporation the management function is vested not in the board but in the executives. "Under the system of directorates which has developed in this country among large, listed companies, directors are unable to 'manage' corporations in any narrow interpretation of the word. . . .   Directors do not and cannot 'direct' corporations in the sense of operating them."   J. Baker, *Directors and Their Functions* 12 (1945).   See also R. Gordon, *Business Leadership in the Large Corporation* 79–90, 114–115, 128–134, 143–46 (2d ed. 1961).   It is often said, however, that the board *does* make business policy, and it is frequently implied that by making business policy the board fulfills the statutory command.   In fact, of course, policymaking is not equivalent to management: civilians may make policy for the Army; they certainly do not manage the Army.   In any event, the typical board no more makes business policy than it manages the business.   In the publicly held corporation, policymaking, like management, is an executive function.   As early as 1945 the economist Robert Aaron Gordon reported in *Business Leader-*

ship in the Large Corporation that in both financial and nonfinancial matters there was little or no indication that the boards of large companies initiated decisions on either specific matters or broad policies. Although the board's approval function was more important than its function of initiating activities, Gordon found that "even with respect to approval, many boards in these large companies are almost completely passive," and that the final approval function was usually exercised by the chief executive in conjunction with either his immediate subordinates, an executive or finance committee of the board, or a few influential directors acting as his informal advisors. Gordon, supra, at 128–129, 131. See also id. at 114. Similarly, John C. Baker of the Harvard Business School reported the same year that major policies in production, marketing, finance, and personnel were usually formulated by the executives and not even formally confirmed by the board (although there was often consultation with individual directors). In such matters as addition of new products, preparation of operating budget, and negotiation of collective bargaining agreements, the board's role was limited to receipt and consideration of after-the-fact reports. Baker, supra, at 18. More recent studies, particularly that of Professor Myles Mace, have confirmed these earlier findings. M. Mace, *Directors: Myth and Reality* 47–48 and passim (1971).

In short, under what might be called the modern legal model of management structure—that is, the model that embodies actual corporate practice—most of the powers supposedly vested in the board are actually vested in the executives. The drastic skew between the traditional and modern models is not simply an accident of time or temper. Rather, it is the virtually inevitable result of several critical constraints imposed by modern board practice.

1. *Constraints of time.* A board of directors normally can act only at meetings. Since boards typically meet only six to twelve times a year, and meetings usually last only a few hours, J. Bacon, Corporate Directorship Practices 127, Table 21 (1967); Heidrick & Struggles, Profile of the Board of Directors 5 (1971), few boards spend more than thirty-six hours a year in meeting time, and about half spend only eighteen hours a year or less. Since time spent preparing for meetings is roughly comparable to meeting time, it is obvious that by reason of time constraints alone the typical board could not possibly "manage" the business of a large, publicly held corporation in the normal sense of that term: Such businesses are far too complex to be managed by persons who put in the equivalent of five to ten working days a year. Furthermore, the same constraint precludes the board from making business policy: In a complex organization concerned with complex choices, policy cannot be developed on a part-time basis.

2. *Constraints of information.* Although an opportunity to consider relevant data is obviously essential to meaningful decisionmaking, of 474 industrials surveyed by Heidrick & Struggles only 17.2 percent provided directors with manufacturing data prior to the meeting, only 21.3 percent provided marketing data, only 5.7 percent provided an agenda, and 11 percent provided no information at all. Heidrick &

Struggles, supra, at 5. Furthermore, directors normally have no staff to evaluate the information they do receive or to gather information directly. Instead, the board must rely on the executives to perform those functions, either directly or through the executives' staff. Thus the amount, quality, and structure of the information that reaches the board is almost wholly within the control of the corporation's executives. This kind of power over information flow is virtually equivalent to power over decision.

3. *Constraints of composition.* The typical board includes a number of directors who are economically or psychologically tied to the corporation's executives, particularly its chief executive. Indeed, a substantial number of seats are held by inside directors, that is, by the corporation's own executives. Dependent on the chief executive for both retention and promotion, and on other executives for day-to-day support, the inside director is highly unlikely to dissent at a board meeting from the inside line determined by management prior to the meeting.

Nor is dependence on the corporation's chief executive confined to inside directors. Many of the outside directors in large publicly held corporations are lawyers or investment bankers. Probably most of these are suppliers of services to the corporation on whose boards they sit, and are therefore highly interested in maintaining a good relationship with the chief executive, who normally has control over the purchase of such services. Many other outside directors are commercial bankers, who also are often intent on retaining the corporation's business. Many of the remaining directors are psychologically tied to the chief executive by friendship, former colleagueship, or both. Furthermore, as a result of current practices on selection and tenure, even those directors who are not bound to incumbent management by economic or psychological ties are unlikely to be truly independent. Directors are typically selected not by the board, as might be expected, but by the chief executive. A new director is likely to be aligned with the chief executive simply by virtue of the fact that he owes the latter his appointment—an element reinforced by the chief executive's role in orienting new directors to the board.

AMERICAN LAW INSTITUTE, PRINCIPLES OF CORPORATE GOVERNANCE §§ 3.01–3.02

(Tent. Draft No. 2, 1984).

§ 3.01. Management of the Corporation's Business: Powers and Functions of Senior Executives

The management of the business of a publicly held corporation [§ 1.23] * should be conducted by or under the supervision of such

* Under § 1.23, the term "publicly held corporation" means "a corporation that as of the record date for its most recent annual shareholders' meeting had both 500 or more record holders of its equity securities and $3 million of total assets . . . ." (Footnote by ed.)

senior executives . . . as may be designated by the board of directors in accordance with the standards of the corporation [§ 1.27] * and by those other officers . . . and employees to whom the management function is delegated by those executives, subject to the powers and functions of the board under § 3.02.

The principle embodied in § 3.01 reflects the result a court would almost certainly reach through interpretation of the statutory language in the context of long-established practice. . . .

§ 3.02. Powers and Functions of the Board of Directors

(a) Except as otherwise provided by statute, the board of directors of a publicly held corporation [§ 1.23] should:

(1) Elect, evaluate, and, where appropriate, dismiss the principal senior executives. . . .

(2) Oversee the conduct of the corporation's business with a view to evaluating, on an ongoing basis, whether the corporation's resources are being managed in a manner consistent with the principles of § 2.01 (Objective and Conduct of the Business Corporation).

(3) Review and approve corporate plans and actions that the board or the principal senior executives consider major, and changes in accounting principles and practices that the board or the principal senior executives consider material.

(4) Perform such other functions as are prescribed by law, or assigned to the board under a standard of the corporation [§ 1.27].

(b) Except as otherwise provided by statute or by a standard of the corporation, the board of directors of a publicly held corporation should also have power to:

(1) Make recommendations to shareholders.

(2) Initiate and adopt major corporate plans, commitments, and actions, and material changes in accounting principles and practices; instruct any committee, officer [§ 1.19], or other employee; and review the actions of any committee, officer, or other employee.

(3) Manage the business of the corporation.

(4) Act as to all other corporate matters not requiring shareholder approval.

(c) Except as otherwise specifically provided by statute or by a standard of the corporation, and subject to the board's ultimate responsibility for oversight under § 3.02(a), the board may delegate to its committees authority to perform any of its functions and exercise any of its powers.

---

* Under § 1.27, the term "standard of the corporation" means "a valid certificate or by-law provision, or board or shareholder resolution, regulating corporate governance." (Footnote by ed.)

NOTE ON DIRECTORS' INFORMATIONAL RIGHTS

Under the common law, a director has a wide-ranging right to information concerning the corporation, which may be exercised through inspection of books, records, and documents. Although the right is often characterized as "absolute," the cases are split on whether the director's intent is relevant.

Under one line of authority, which finds its fullest expression in the New York cases, the director's intent is deemed irrelevant, on the theory that a director must have unqualified access to information if he is to perform his directorial duties. See, e.g., Cohen v. Cocoline Products, Inc., 309 N.Y. 119, 127 N.E.2d 906 (1955); Overland v. Le Roy Foods, Inc., 304 N.Y. 573, 107 N.E.2d 74 (1952); Dusel v. Castellani, 43 A.D.2d 799, 350 N.Y.S.2d 258 (1973); Maidman v. Central Foundry Co., 27 A.D.2d 923, 279 N.Y.S.2d 365 (1967); Edelman v. Goodman, 21 A.D.2d 786, 250 N.Y.S.2d 572 (1964); Davis v. Keilsohn Offset Co., 273 App.Div. 695, 79 N.Y.S.2d 540 (1948). But see Griffin v. Varflex Corp., 79 A.D.2d 857, 434 N.Y.S.2d 488 (1980). In Cohen v. Cocoline Products, Inc., supra, the court said, "In order properly to perform his directing duties, a corporate director must . . . keep himself informed as to the policies, business and affairs of the corporation, and as to the acts of its officers. He owes a stewardship obligation to the corporation and its stockholders, and he may be subjected to liability for improper management during his term of office. Because of these positive duties and potential liabilities, the courts of this State have accorded to corporate directors an absolute, unqualified right . . . to inspect their corporate books and records." 309 N.Y. at 123, 127 N.E.2d at 907–08. In Dusel v. Castellani, supra, the corporation resisted inspection on the ground that the director was the principal of a competitor, was hostile to the corporation, and would use the information to its detriment. The court said, "so long as petitioner remains a director and has not been legally removed from office, he cannot be denied his right of inspection. . . . If petitioner should attempt to use the information which he secures from his inspection to the damage of the Corporation, [it] could sue him for breach of his fiduciary responsibility as a director and compel him to account for his misconduct." 43 A.D. at 799, 350 N.Y.S.2d at 259. In Davis v. Keilsohn Offset Co., supra, the corporation urged that the director's sole purpose was to hamper and embarrass the corporation and that the corporation had sued the director for breach of his fiduciary duty on the ground that he had attempted to wreck the corporation for the benefit of a competitor he controlled. The court said the director's object in seeking the examination was immaterial. 273 App.Div. at 696–97, 79 N.Y.S.2d at 541–42. New Jersey takes a comparable approach, see Pilat v. Broach Systems, Inc., 108 N.J.Super. 88, 260 A.2d 13 (1969), as does California by statute, Cal.Corp.Code § 1602.

Under a competing line of authority, the director's intent is deemed relevant, on the theory that his right to information presupposes that he is not hostile to the corporation. In State v. Seiberling

Rubber Co., 53 Del. 295, 298, 168 A.2d 310, 312 (1961), the Delaware Superior Court said, "if it can be established that [the director's] motives are improper, or that they are in derogation to the interest of the corporation, then his right to inspect ceases to exist." In a later case, Henshaw v. American Cement Corp., 252 A.2d 125, 129 (Del.Ch.1969), the Delaware Chancery Court cited *Seiberling* with approval, but added, "An examination of books and records to ascertain the condition of corporate affairs and the propriety of certain actions is a proper purpose even though the one who seeks inspection may be hostile to management. . . . [The director's] purpose is not improper because of the possibility that he may abuse his position as a director and make information available to persons hostile to the Corporation or otherwise not entitled to it. If [the director] does violate his fiduciary duty in this regard, then the Corporation has its remedy in the courts." See also Paschall v. Scott, 41 Wash.2d 71, 247 P.2d 543 (1952).

Several cases have coupled the principle that a director has an absolute right to information with the principle that the order granting the right can impose protective terms and conditions on its exercise. See, e.g., Drake v. Newton Amusement Corp., 123 N.J.L. 560, 9 A.2d 636 (1939); Moore v. State Bank, 561 S.W.2d 722 (Mo.App. 1978).

SECTION 4. THE LEGAL STRUCTURE OF MANAGEMENT (II): COMPOSITION AND COMMITTEES OF THE BOARD IN PUBLICLY HELD CORPORATIONS

DEL. GEN. CORP. LAW § 141(c)

[See Statutory Supplement]

REV. MODEL BUS. CORP. ACT § 8.25

[See Statutory Supplement]

AMERICAN LAW INSTITUTE, PRINCIPLES OF CORPORATE GOVERNANCE, PART III, INTRODUCTORY NOTE AND §§ 3.03–3.07

Tent. Draft No. 2, 1984.

Introductory Note:

1. *Scope.* . . . [Provisions concerning the management of publicly held corporations should] reflect two highly important social needs regarding such corporations. One is the need to permit a

corporation to be highly flexible in structuring its operational management. The other is the need for processes that ensure managerial accountability to shareholders for accomplishing the objective of the corporation, as stated in § 2.01. . . . *

Broadly speaking, three kinds of corporate and social institutions contribute toward satisfying the need for managerial accountability: direct review by the body of shareholders; the discipline of the product and capital markets and of the market for corporate control; and oversight of management by the board of directors and its committees. Direct review by the body of shareholders, however, while perhaps effective in close corporations, is seldom efficacious in publicly held corporations, because of the disparate and shifting nature of the shareholder body and the complexity of modern management issues. The discipline of the various markets, while important in publicly held corporations, is also subject to important limitations. For example, a corporation may earn profits and survive for a long period of time despite bad management, just as it may incur losses or even fail despite good management. A corporation with a large cash flow may be able to meet its capital needs for a long period of time through internal and even external financing although its profits are lower than good management would produce. Similarly, the discipline of the market for corporate control is limited by a number of elements, including the high transaction costs of takeover bids, the necessity to offer a premium well in excess of market price, the requirements of relevant statutes, the defensive techniques available, the incentives to take over well-run rather than poorly run companies, and the time-lag often experienced by the public in ascertaining lack of managerial efficiency.

Given the inefficacy of direct shareholder review in the publicly held corporation, and the constraints on the efficacy of markets, the board of directors and its committees take on particular significance. Undoubtedly, the character and ability of directors are the most critical ingredients in the success of the board and its committees. Nevertheless, assurance of managerial accountability is also closely related to the structure of the board and its committees, and the objectivity of their members. . . .

3. *Division of corporations into three tiers.* Until the last 25–35 years, all provisions of corporate statutes—and for that matter, most case-law doctrines—were made uniformly applicable to all corporations, regardless of size. . . . However, it is often useful to distinguish between different classes of corporations, as defined principally by number of shareholders. Initially, a distinction may be drawn between those corporations whose shares are widely distributed— "publicly held corporations"—and those whose shares are not. A further distinction may then be drawn between large and small publicly held corporations. Certain practices that are appropriate for corporations with a relatively large number of shareholders and

---

* Section 2.01 is set out at p. 123, supra.
(Footnote by ed.)

significant assets might be too costly for publicly held corporations with a smaller shareholder and asset base. Furthermore, small publicly held corporations, more typically than large corporations, may be dominated by controlling shareholder groups, and such groups would normally perform the oversight functions that are best carried out in their absence by the board and its committees. Based on these principles, this Chapter adopts a three-tier division of corporations. All of its provisions are applicable to the first tier; most but not all are applicable to the second tier. . . .

(a) *First tier.* Under § 1.16, the first tier consists of corporations with at least 2,000 record holders of equity securities and $100 million of total assets—a definition that is comparable in part to the listing standards of the New York Stock Exchange. The population of this tier is estimated to be approximately 1,500–2,000 American corporations. . . .

(b) *Second tier.* Under § 1.23, the second tier consists of corporations (other than first-tier corporations) with at least 500 record holders of equity securities and $3 million of total assets—a definition that parallels to a significant extent § 12(g) of the Securities Exchange Act. . . . The population of this tier is estimated to be approximately 5,500–6,500 American corporations. . . .

Although the first and second tiers are conceptually separate, under the mechanics of this Chapter they are frequently aggregated. Accordingly, the term "publicly held corporation" (§ 1.23) covers corporations in both tiers, while the term "large publicly held corporation" (§ 1.16) covers only corporations in the first tier.

(c) *Third tier.* While Chapter 1 addresses the structure only of first- and second-tier corporations, no inference should be drawn that all corporations that fall into the third, residual, tier should be treated alike. Included in this tier are several very different subclasses, such as close corporations, with a relatively small number of shareholders, and corporations which are too large to classify as close corporations but not quite large enough to be classified as publicly held for purposes of Chapter 1. The legal structures appropriate for these subclasses may differ significantly. . . .

§ 3.03. Audit Committee in First–Tier Corporations

Every large publicly held corporation [§ 1.16] should have an audit committee, to oversee the audit process, consisting of at least three members, and composed of directors who are neither employed by the corporation nor persons who were so employed within the *two* * preceding years, including at least a majority of members who have no significant relationship [§ 1.26 **] with the corporation's senior executives.

---

* Italics are used in the black-letter of the Principles of Corporate Governance where the number recommended for a bright-line test is deemed preferable, but not clearly superior, to somewhat higher or lower numbers. (Footnote by ed.)

** Section 1.26 provides as follows:

§ 1.26. Significant Relationship

(1) Except as provided in § 1.26(2), a director has a "significant relationship" with the senior executives . . . of a corporation

§ 3.04.   Directors Who Have No Significant Relationship to the Senior Executives

It is recommended as a matter of corporate practice that:

(a) The board of every large publicly held corporation [§ 1.16] should have a majority of directors who are free of any significant relationship [§ 1.26] with the corporation's senior executives . . ., unless a majority of the corporation's voting securities . . . are owned by a single person . . ., a family group . . ., or a control group. . . .

(b) The board of a publicly held corporation [§ 1.23] that does not fall within Subsection (a) should have at least three directors who are free of any significant relationship with the corporation's senior executives.*

§ 3.05.   Audit Committee in Second–Tier Corporations; Powers and Functions of the Audit Committee

It is recommended as a matter of corporate practice that:

(a) Every publicly held corporation [§ 1.23] not falling within § 3.03 should have an audit committee, to oversee the audit process, composed in the manner described in § 3.03.

if, as of the record date for the annual meeting of shareholders:

(a) He is employed by the corporation, or was so employed within the *two* preceding years;

(b) He is a member of the immediate family . . . of an individual who (a) is employed by the corporation as an officer [§ 1.19], or (b) was employed by the corporation as a senior executive within the *two* preceding years;

(c) He has made to or received from the corporation, during either of its *two* preceding fiscal years, commercial payments . . . which exceeded *$200,000,* or he owns or has power to vote an equity interest . . . in a business organization . . . to which the corporation made, or from which the corporation received, during either of its *two* preceding fiscal years, commercial payments that, when multiplied by his percentage equity interest in the organization, exceeded *$200,000;*

(d) He is a principal manager . . . of a business organization to which the corporation made, or from which the corporation received, during either of the organization's *two* preceding fiscal years, commercial payments that exceeded *5 percent* of the organization's consolidated gross revenues for that year, or *$200,000,* whichever is more; or

(e) He is affiliated in a professional capacity with a law firm that was the primary legal adviser to the corporation with respect to general corporate or securities-law matters, or with an investment-banking firm that was retained by the corporation in an advisory capacity or acted as a managing underwriter in an issue of the corporation's securities, within the *two* preceding years, or was so affiliated with such a law or investment-banking firm when it was so retained or so acted.

(2) A director shall not be deemed to have a significant relationship with the senior executives under § 1.26(1)(c)–(e) if, on the basis of countervailing or other special circumstances, it could not reasonably be believed that the judgment of a person in the director's position would be affected by his relationship under § 1.26(1)(c)–(e). . . .   (Footnote by ed.)

---

* Section 3.04 is formulated as a recommendation of corporate practice. Account should also be taken, however, of § 3.03, which requires first-tier corporations to have an audit committee consisting of at least three members, and composed of members who are neither employed by the corporation nor persons who were employed by the corporation within the two preceding years, including a majority of members who are free of § 1.26 relationships. The indirect effect of this provision is to require first-tier corporations to include on the board itself at least enough such directors to satisfy § 3.03.

(b) The audit committee of a publicly held corporation appointed under §§ 3.03 or 3.05(a) should, subject to the board's review:

(1) Recommend the firm to be employed as the corporation's independent auditor, and review and approve the discharge of any such firm.

(2) Review and approve the independent auditor's compensation, the terms of its engagement, and the independence of such auditor.

(3) Review, in consultation with the independent auditor, the results of each external audit of the corporation, the report of the audit, any related management letter, and management's responses to recommendations made by the independent auditor in connection with the audit.

(4) Review, in consultation with the independent auditor and management, the corporation's annual financial statements, any certification, report, opinion, or review rendered by the independent auditor in connection with those financial statements, and any significant disputes between management and the independent auditor that arose in connection with the preparation of those financial statements.

(5) Consider, in consultation with the independent auditor and the chief internal auditor, if any, the adequacy of the corporation's internal accounting controls.

(6) Consider, when presented by the independent auditor, a principal senior executive, or otherwise, material questions of choice with respect to the appropriate auditing and accounting principles and practices to be used in the preparation of the corporation's financial statements. . . .

§ 3.06. Nominating Committee in First- and Second-Tier Corporations: Composition, Powers, and Functions

It is recommended as a matter of corporate practice that:

(a) Every publicly held corporation [§ 1.23], except corporations a majority of whose voting securities are owned by a single person . . ., a family group . . ., or a control group . . ., should have a nominating committee to oversee the process of nomination to the board. The committee should be composed of directors who are not officers . . . or employees of the corporation, including at least a majority of members who have no significant relationship [§ 1.26] with the corporation's senior executives.

(b) The nominating committee should:

(1) Recommend to the board candidates for all directorships to be filled by the shareholders or the board.

(2) Consider candidates for directorships proposed by the chief executive officer and, within the bounds of practicability, by any other senior executive or any director or shareholder.

(3) Recommend to the board directors to fill the seats on board committees.

§ 3.07. **Compensation Committee in First-Tier Corporations: Composition, Powers, and Functions**

It is recommended as a matter of corporate practice that:

(a) Every large publicly held corporation [§ 1.16] should have a compensation committee, to oversee the compensation of senior executives, which should be composed of directors who are not officers . . . or employees of the corporation, including at least a majority of members who have no significant relationship [§ 1.26] with the corporation's senior executives. . . .

(b) The compensation committee should, subject to the board's review:

(1) Review and approve the annual salary, bonus, stock options, and other benefits, direct and indirect, of the senior executives.

(2) Review and approve new executive compensation programs; review on a continuing basis the operation of the corporation's executive compensation programs to determine whether they are properly coordinated; establish and periodically review policies for the administration of executive compensation programs; and take steps to modify any executive compensation program that yields payments and benefits not reasonably related to executive performance or otherwise operates in a manner that was not originally contemplated.

(3) Establish and periodically review policies in the area of management perquisites. . . .

SECTION 5. FORMALITIES REQUIRED FOR ACTION BY THE BOARD

DEL. GEN. CORP. LAW §§ 141(b), (f), (i), 229

[See Statutory Supplement]

REV. MODEL BUS. CORP. ACT
§§ 8.20, 8.21, 8.22, 8.23, 8.24

[See Statutory Supplement]

NOTE ON FORMALITIES REQUIRED FOR ACTION BY THE BOARD

The validity of an action by the board of directors is governed by rules concerning the formalities required for meeting, notice, quorum, and voting.

Before turning to these rules, a preliminary question should be addressed. In the most typical case involving the validity of a board action, a third party claims to have a right against the corporation based on a contract executed by an officer and purportedly approved by the board. The corporation defends on the ground that the purported board approval was invalid because a requisite formality was not satisfied. In such a case, the third party could have foreclosed this defense by demanding, when he made the contract, that the corporation produce a certificate from its secretary attesting that the board, at a duly held meeting, duly adopted resolutions authorizing the contract. A corporate secretary normally has at least apparent authority to provide such certified resolutions, and in the normal case the corporation is bound by the secretary's certificate. See Section 6, infra. Why then should problems concerning the validity of board action ever arise? There are several reasons. Sometimes it is awkward to demand such a certificate. Sometimes the third party does not realize he is best protected by such a certificate. Sometimes the third party doesn't know about the board approval at the time of the transaction (relying, instead, on the action by the officer), and only later learns of the purported board approval. And often problems concerning the validity of board action do not involve a third party, but instead grow out of a contest between inside factions.

Let us now turn directly to the rules concerning the validity of board action. These rules can be stratified at three levels. At the first level are rules that lay down a basic model of board action. At the second level are rules that explicitly permit variations in the basic model. At the third level are rules that govern the consequence of noncompliance with rules at the first two levels. The rules at all three levels originated in the common law, but most of the issues on the first two levels are now governed by statute. Unless otherwise indicated, the following account is based on predominant statutory patterns.

Level 1: The Basic Model.

(i) *Meetings.* Under the basic model the board of directors is conceived as a collegial body. Therefore, directors can act only at a duly convened meeting at which a quorum is present. As a corollary, directors have no power to act on the corporation's behalf except at such a meeting. The theory behind the basic model is that someone—presumably, the body of shareholders—is entitled to a collegial interchange among all the directors before a board decision is made, or, at least, is entitled to insist that all the directors be given the opportunity to attend a meeting affording the opportunity for such interchange, and that a majority of the directors actually do attend.

(ii) *Notice.* Formal notice is not required for a regular board meeting; since the meeting is regular, the directors are already on notice of its date, time, and place. In the case of a special meeting, however, notice of date, time, and place must be given to every director. The notice need not state the purpose of a meeting unless the certificate of incorporation or the bylaws otherwise provide. The statutes usually provide that notice must be given a stated number of days in advance of the meeting, but then add that the stated period may be made shorter or longer by the certificate of incorporation or by-laws.

(iii) *Quorum.* A quorum consists of a majority of the full board (that is, a majority of the authorized number of directors)—not a majority of the directors then in office, which may be less than the authorized number because of board vacancies.

(iv) *Voting.* Assuming that a quorum is present when a vote is taken, the affirmative vote of a majority of those present—not a majority of those voting—is required.

Level 2: Explicitly Approved Variations.

(i) *Meetings.* Most statutes provide that a meeting of the board can be conducted by conference telephone, or by any other means of communication through which all participating directors can simultaneously hear each other. Of more importance, most permit board action to be accomplished by unanimous written consent, without a meeting of any kind. The Official Comment to Rev. Model Bus. Corp. Act § 8.21, which so provides, explains this rule as follows:

> The power of the board of directors to act unanimously without a meeting is based on the pragmatic consideration that in many situations a formal meeting is a waste of time. For example, in a closely held corporation there will often be informal discussion by the manager-owners of the venture before a decision is made. . . .
>
> In publicly held corporations, formal meetings of the board of directors may be appropriate for many actions. But there will always be situations where prompt action is necessary and the decision noncontroversial, so that approval without a formal meeting may be appropriate.
>
> Under section 8.21 the requirement of unanimous consent precludes the possibility of stifling or ignoring opposing argument. A director opposed to an action that is proposed to be taken by unanimous consent, or uncertain about the desirability of that action, may compel the holding of a

directors' meeting to discuss the matter simply by withholding his consent.[1]

(ii) *Notice.* Most statutes provide that notice can be waived in writing before or after a meeting, and that attendance at a meeting constitutes a waiver unless the director attends merely to protest against holding the meeting.

(iii) *Quorum.* A majority of statutes permit the certificate of incorporation or bylaws to require a greater number for a quorum than a majority of the full board. A substantial minority of the statutes, including the Delaware statute and the Model Act, permit the certificate or bylaws to set a lower number, but usually no less than one-third of the full board.

(iv) *Voting.* Most statutes provide that the articles or bylaws can require a greater-than-majority vote for board action.

Level 3: Consequences of Noncompliance.

The rules at Levels 1 and 2 are relatively clear. The consequences of noncompliance with those rules are not always clear. In a publicly held corporation, where bureaucratic order usually prevails and the statutory rules stand surrogate for fair shareholder expectations concerning corporate procedure, lack of a quorum, lack of the requisite affirmative vote, or an uncured lack of notice to even one director will usually render board action ineffective. In closely held corporations, where formalities are seldom followed and the shareholders tend to make their own rules, the results of a failure to observe proper formalities are much less clear-cut. Unless otherwise indicated, the balance of this Note concerns cases involving closely held corporations.

1. *Unanimous informal approval.* Some cases, most of which are quite old, have held that informal approval by directors is ineffective even if the approval is explicit and unanimous. For example, in Baldwin v. Canfield, 26 Minn. 43, 54, 1 N.W. 261, 270 (1879), the court said:

> [T]he general rule that [is] the governing body of a corporation, as such, are agents of the corporation only as a board, and not individually. Hence it follows that they have no authority to act, save when assembled at a board meeting. The separate action, individually, of the persons composing such governing body, is not the action of the constituted body of men clothed with corporate powers.

Cases like *Baldwin* are of doubtful validity today. More characteristic of modern authority is Gerard v. Empire Square Realty Co., 195 App.Div. 244, 187 N.Y.S. 306 (1921). Plaintiff brought an

---

1. Consider 1 H. Marsh, Marsh's California Corporation Law § 8.22 (2d ed. 1981):

[This procedure] should be used only for emergency or routine action, and should not be made a substitute for regular board meetings at which the directors can question the officers and exchange views with each other. If that practice of dispensing altogether with board meetings were followed, the directors might face a charge of failing to exercise the care required of them. . . .

action against several related corporations to recover damages for breach of an employment contract. The corporations' shares were owned by five persons, all of whom were directors. Owing to dissension, no shareholders' or directors' meetings were held, but there was evidence that each director had separately agreed to hire plaintiff. The court held that on these facts the corporations would be bound:

> I think that under the circumstances of the case we are considering, where the directors own all the capital stock of the corporations, where they are members of the same family but so at variance that directors' and stockholders' meetings are not held, their action, concurred in by all, although separately and not as a body, binds the corporation. We must recognize the fact that to a greater and greater degree all business, great and small, is being brought under the management of corporations instead of partnerships; that they are, in perhaps the majority of instances, conducted by officers and directors little informed in the law of corporations, who often act informally, sometimes without meetings or even by-laws. To hold that in all instances technical conformity to the requirements of the law of corporations is a condition to a valid action by the directors, would be to lay down a rule of law which could be used as a trap for the unwary who deal with corporations, and to permit corporations sometimes to escape liability to which an individual in the same circumstances would be subjected.

The results in this area are too disparate to be captured by a single clear rule. In general, however, it is fair to say that at a minimum, most modern courts would hold informal but explicit approval by all the directors to be effective where, as in *Gerard*, a person who has contracted with a corporate officer has been led to regard his transaction with the corporation as valid, and all the shareholders are directors or have acquiesced in the transaction or in a past practice of informal board action. See Anderson v. K.G. Moore, Inc., 6 Mass.App.Ct. 386, 376 N.E.2d 1238 (1978), cert. denied 439 U.S. 1116 (1979); Myhre v. Myhre, 170 Mont. 410, 422, 554 P.2d 276, 282 (1976) ("Where the directors of a corporation are the only stockholders, they may act for the corporation without formal meetings. Formal meetings can also be waived by custom or general consent"); Leslie, Semple & Garrison, Inc. v. Gavit & Co., 81 A.D.2d 950, 439 N.Y.S.2d 707 (1981); Remillong v. Schneider, 185 N.W.2d 493 (N.D.1971); cf. Rowland v. Rowland, 102 Idaho 534, 633 P.2d 599 (1981). In the balance of this Note, the concept that informal board action should be valid at least under these circumstances will be referred to as the shareholder-acquiescence model.

Where a case falls within the shareholder-acquiescence model, corporate liability is consistent with the rules at Levels 1 and 2. Those rules are designed to protect shareholder interests. Under the conditions of the shareholder-acquiescence model, all the shareholders have acquiesced, in their directorial or shareholder capacities, either to the transaction or to a practice of informal action. As stated in Lake Motel, Inc. v. Lowery, 224 Va. 553, 559–60, 299 S.E.2d 496, 500 (1983):

> Lake . . . . rests its case for reversal upon the bald proposition that, in the absence of a formal resolution of the board of directors authorizing the sale to the Lowerys, the deed effectuating the sale is void. We considered a similar argument in *Moore v. Aetna Co.,* 155 Va. 556, 155 S.E. 707 (1930):
>
>> . . . Certainly a corporation should act through its board of directors, and in accordance with the limitations imposed by its charter and by-laws; but when, with the knowledge and acquiescence of all of its stockholders, it declines so to do, it must accept the consequences. It cannot be permitted to accept all the benefits of such irregular contracts without assuming all of the resulting liabilities.
>
> 155 Va. at 570, 155 S.E. at 711. . . .
>
> . . . [This rule] is designed to protect parties who deal in good faith with close corporations that conduct their internal affairs informally.

Furthermore, where a third person has been led to regard a transaction with the corporation as valid, it is typically because he has dealt with an officer who purported to have either authority to consummate the transaction or board approval of the transaction. In such cases there is something to be said for a rule that the corporation, which appointed the officer, ought to be bound by his conduct, particularly if the third person has relied on the transaction. True, the usual rule is that a corporation is not bound by an officer's conduct in the absence of actual or apparent authority. However, the question is close enough that adding the element of informal board approval may appropriately tip the balance, particularly when reliance is present. See Morris v. Y. & B. Corp., 198 N.C. 700, 153 S.E. 327 (1930).[2]

Today, many cases involving unanimous informal approval probably fall under the statutory rule that such approval is effective if it is in writing. (Indeed, Baldwin v. Canfield, supra, which involved a form of written consent, would probably be decided differently under the modern statutes.[3]) It might be argued that these statutes by negative

---

2. An example of a modern case in which the corporation was not bound by the informal approval of all the directors is Fradkin v. Ernst, 571 F.Supp. 829 (N.D. Ohio 1983). This case did not fall within the shareholder-acquience model. There were a number of shareholders; the shareholders were not shown to have acquiesced; and the transaction did not involve a party who had been led reasonably to regard the transaction as valid (the defendant-directors were seeking to uphold the questioned transaction, and they were in a position to know of the lack of necessary formalities).

See also Greenberg v. Harrison, 143 Conn. 519, 124 A.2d 216 (1956), in which the transaction in question was a preferential transfer to an insider.

3. However, Baldwin v. Canfield may not quite fit within the shareholder-acquiescence model. In that case, one director, who was the moving force in the transaction, owned all the shares, but he had pledged his shares to a bank. Therefore, while all the shareholders had acquiesced, all parties with an economic interest in the corporation's stock had not.

implication preclude the courts from giving effect to informal unanimous approval that is not in writing. In Village of Brown Deer v. City of Milwaukee, 16 Wis.2d 206, 114 N.W.2d 493 (1962), cert. denied 371 U.S. 902, 83 S.Ct. 205, 9 L.Ed.2d 164, the court held, "The legislature has said that the corporation could act informally, without a meeting, by obtaining the consent in writing of all of the directors. In our opinion, this pronouncement has preempted the field and prohibits corporations from acting informally without complying with" the statute. In *Brown Deer,* however, apparently only a majority of the directors knew of the transaction in question, so there was no unanimous approval, formal or informal. Other cases decided in jurisdictions that have unanimous-written-consent statutes have held the corporation bound by unanimous oral consent. See Note, Corporations: When Informal Action by Corporate Directors Will Be Permitted to Bind the Corporation, 53 B.U.L.Rev. 101, 120 (1973). The intent of the statutes seems to be to protect persons dealing with a corporation, not to weaken the rights of such persons. The preferable construction of these statutes, therefore, is that they provide a safe harbor and leave the balance of the field to judicial development. Indeed, the statutes can be read to support liability under the shareholder-acquiescence model, because they manifest a legislative policy that undermines the basic model's emphasis on collegial interchange.

2. *Unanimous acquiescence.* In the type of case just considered, all the directors informally but explicitly approve a transaction. Suppose that a majority of the directors explicitly approve a transaction, and the remaining directors know of the transaction and take no steps to disavow it, so that although they do not explicitly approve, they may be said to acquiesce. The difference between this case and the case in which all the directors explicitly approve is not terribly significant—even in the latter case the approval is only informal—and the courts will normally treat the two cases alike. See, e.g., Winchell v. Plywood Corp., 324 Mass. 171, 85 N.E.2d 313 (1949). The same result will normally follow even if there is no explicit approval by a majority of the directors but all the directors acquiesce. See Juergens v. Venture Capital Corp., 1 Mass.App.Ct. 274, 295 N.E.2d 398 (1973); Wuerderman v. J.O. Lively Const. Co., 602 S.W.2d 215 (Mo.App. 1980); Pierce v. Astoria Fish Factors, Inc., 31 Wash.App. 214, 640 P.2d 40 (1982).

3. *Majority acquiescence.* Suppose, finally, that a majority of the directors approve a transaction, explicitly or by acquiescence, but the remaining directors lack knowledge of the transaction. Some courts have refused to hold the corporation liable under these circumstances. See, e.g., Hurley v. Ornsteen, 311 Mass. 477, 42 N.E.2d 273 (1942). Other courts have have held the corporation liable, at least if the shareholders acquiesced in the transaction or the shareholders or the remaining directors acquiesced in a practice of informal action by the directors. One theory is that the remaining directors would have known of the transaction if they had been properly active. Another is that the shareholders, if they have tolerated informal action by the directors over a period of time, have by that acquiescence authorized

the directors to act in this manner. See, e.g., Holy Cross Gold Mining & Milling Co. v. Goodwin, 74 Colo. 532, 223 P. 58 (1924):

> Ballard, the president, and Peck, the secretary, who executed or signed the contract sued on, were directors of the defendant. They constituted a majority of the board of directors, because there were but three directors, G.E. Stearns being the third. The directors had never held a meeting, except on October 10, 1918. Peck and Ballard came to the office of plaintiff's attorney and signed the contract involved herein on January 14, 1922. The evidence shows that it was the customary usage of the corporation to act through its directors individually. In the instant case a majority of the directors acted. The case of Longmont S.D. Co. v. Coffman, 11 Colo. 551, 19 Pac. 508, is authority for the proposition that a board of directors may act individually and the act be binding on the corporation if it has become a practice of the directors to act that way.

In some cases involving informal approval by only a majority of the directors, the courts have held the corporation liable simply because a majority of the shareholders had approved or acquiesced in the transaction. See Phillips Petroleum Co. v. Rock Creek Mining Co., 449 F.2d 664 (9th Cir.1971); Mannon v. Pesula, 59 Cal.App.2d 597, 139 P.2d 336 (1943); Mickshaw v. Coca Cola Bottling Co., Inc., of Sharon, Pennsylvania, 166 Pa.Super. 148, 70 A.2d 467 (1950).

SECTION 6. AUTHORITY OF CORPORATE OFFICERS

DEL. GEN. CORP. LAW § 142

[See Statutory Supplement]

REV. MODEL BUS. CORP. ACT §§ 8.40, 8.41

[See Statutory Supplement]

NOTE ON AUTHORITY
CHAPTER I, SECTION 2, supra

NOTE ON THE AUTHORITY OF CORPORATE OFFICERS

Legal questions concerning the authority of a corporate officer typically arise out of a transaction between a third person and the corporation in which an officer acted on the corporation's behalf. The major concepts relevant to determining such questions are the agency principles of actual and apparent authority. The application of these principles in the corporate context often rests on the officer's position, that is, his title. Apparent authority will often rest largely on position, because a third party can normally assume that an officer has the authority customarily vested in persons holding the position in question. Even actual authority may rest partly on position, because the authority an officer reasonably believes he possesses may depend in part on the authority customarily possessed by persons holding the position in question.

1. *The President.* There are a great number of cases concerning the apparent authority of a president by virtue of his position. Some cases—most but not all of them early—hold that a president does not have any apparent authority by virtue of his position; that he has only the actual authority the board confers upon him. For example, in Federal Services Finance Corp. v. Bishop Nat. Bank of Hawaii at Honolulu, 190 F.2d 442 (9th Cir.1951), supplemented, 205 F.2d 11 (9th Cir.1953), the court held that the president of an ordinary trading corporation had no presumed power by virtue of his office to cash checks payable to the company's order. See also Har-Bel Coal Co. v. Asher Coal Mining Co., 414 S.W.2d 128 (Ky.1966); Lucey v. Hero Int'l Corp., 361 Mass. 569, 281 N.E.2d 266 (1972); Nelms v. A & A Liquor Stores, Inc., 445 S.W.2d 256 (Tex.Civ.App.1969).

Some cases avoided the force of this rather unrealistic rule by holding that a special rule applies where the president also serves as general manager. See, e.g., Memorial Hospital Ass'n of Stanislaus County v. Pacific Grape Products Co., 45 Cal.2d 634, 637, 290 P.2d 481, 483 (1955): "Where the president of a corporation is also its general manager, having the power to superintend and conduct its business, he has implied authority to make any contract or do any other act appropriate in the ordinary course of its business. In such case his powers are greater than he would have as president alone." See also Flectcher Oil Co. v. City of Bay City, 346 Mich. 411, 78 N.W.2d 205 (1956); cf. Gillian v. Consolidated Foods Corp., 424 Pa. 407, 227 A.2d 858 (1967).[1] The title "general manager" is rarely

---

1. A very different view was summarized as follows by Judge Friendly in Scientific Holding Co. v. Plessey Inc., 510 F.2d 15, 23–24 (2d Cir.1974):

In two early opinions, the New York Court of Appeals stated that the president or other general officer of a corporation engaged in business activities had, by virtue of his office, prima facie power to make any contract for the corporation that the board of directors could have authorized or ratified, and that the burden of proving any lack of authorization was on those seeking to impeach the contract. *See* Patterson v. Robinson, 116 N.Y. 193, 22 N.E. 372 (1889) (president); Hastings v. Brooklyn Life Ins. Co., 138 N.Y. 473, 34 N.E. 289 (1893) (secretary who was one of corporation's general managing agents). However, a number

used today; its closest modern counterpart is "chief executive officer" (CEO), although the CEO title may carry more weight now than the GM title did in the past. The title is not inevitably conferred on the president. In many corporations, the chairman of the board is the CEO. In a few corporations, there is an "office of the chief executive" shared by several persons. There is little or no case law on the implications of the CEO title.

As reflected in Lee v. Jenkins Brothers, 268 F.2d 357 (2d Cir. 1959), cert. denied 361 U.S. 913, 80 S.Ct. 257, 4 L.Ed.2d 183 (1959), the prevalent modern rule is that the president, by virtue of his position, has apparent authority to take actions in the ordinary course of business, but not extraordinary actions. The difficulty lies in drawing a line between what is "ordinary" and what is "extraordinary." Some cases have been restrictive in determining the apparent authority of a president, perhaps influenced by statutory language that the business of the corporation shall be managed by the board. See Sacks v. Helene Curtis Industries, 340 Ill.App. 76, 91 N.E.2d 127 (1950); Parks v. Midland Ford Tractor Co., 416 S.W.2d 22, 29 (Mo. App.1967); Liebermann v. Princeway Realty Corp., 17 A.D.2d 258, 233 N.Y.S.2d 1001 (1962), aff'd, 13 N.Y.2d 999, 195 N.E.2d 57, 245 N.Y.S.2d 390 (1963). Other cases, like Lee v. Jenkins Brothers, interpret the president's apparent authority in a more expansive manner. See Three Sisters, Inc. v. Vertigo West, Inc., 18 Ill.App.3d 400, 309 N.E.2d 400 (1974); Yucca Mining & Petroleum Co. v. Howard C. Phillips Oil Co., 69 N.M. 281, 365 P.2d 925 (1961). The decisions that give the authority of officers an expansive interpretation in cases involving third persons reflect both the reality that the management of the business of the corporation is normally conducted by or under the supervision of its executives rather than its board, and a sound understanding of the normal expectations of third persons in such cases.

Any attempt at precision in determining the apparent authority of a president would almost certainly be futile, because the issue is highly dependent on the context in which it arises, and the types of business transactions that may arise are endlessly variable. Nevertheless, cer-

of subsequent New York cases indicated adherence to the narrower proposition that the presumption of the president's authority extends only to transactions in the ordinary course of the company's business. *See, e.g.,* Banker's Trust Co. v. International Ry. Co., 207 App.Div. 579, 202 N.Y.S. 561 (1st Dept. 1924), aff'm, 239 N.Y. 619, 147 N.E. 220 (1925) (mem.); Wen Kroy Realty Co., Inc. v. Public Nat'l Bank & Trust Co., 260 N.Y. 84, 183 N.E. 73 (1932).

In 1934, Judge L. Hand, speaking for this court in Schwartz v. United Merchant & Manufacturers, Inc., 72 F.2d 256 (2 Cir.1934), attempted to discern the precise content of the New York "rule." After briefly summarizing most of the applicable New York decisions, Judge

Hand concluded that "there is no absolute rule in New York that any contract which the president of a company may make, however out of the ordinary, throws upon the company the duty of showing that he was unauthorized. It is true that whatever powers are usual in the business may be assumed to have been granted; but the presumption stops there. . . ." *Id.* 72 F.2d at 258. Although certain commentators have found this holding to be inconsistent with the *Patterson–Hastings* rule . . . most subsequent New York cases, as well as federal cases applying New York law, have adopted the "ordinary business rule"

. . . [W]e believe the law of New York is what Judge Hand stated in *Schwartz.*

tain boundaries can be identified. To begin with, some matters, such as the declaration of dividends, are required by statute to be decided by the board. Typically, the statutes also enumerate certain matters that the board cannot delegate to a committee, such as approval of an action that requires approval by both the board and the shareholders pursuant to statute. By analogy, it would normally not be within the authority of the president or other senior executives to take binding action on these matters.

Beyond these boundaries, among the elements to be taken into account for purposes of determining what constitutes an "extraordinary" action, that would normally be outside the apparent authority of the president, are the economic magnitude of the action in relation to corporate assets and earnings, the extent of risk involved, the timespan of the action's effect, and the cost of reversing the action. Examples of the kinds of actions that would normally be "extraordinary" include the creation of long-term or other significant debt, the reacquisition of equity or debt securities, significant capital investments, business combinations (including those effected for cash), the disposition of significant businesses, entry into important new lines of business, significant acquisitions of stock in other corporations, and actions that would foreseeably expose the corporation to significant litigation or significant new regulatory problems. A useful generalization is that decisions that would make a significant change in the structure of the business enterprise, or the structure of control over the enterprise, are extraordinary corporate actions and therefore normally outside the president's apparent authority.[2]

Of course, the president, or any other officer, may have actual authority greater than his apparent authority. The president's actual authority may be found in the certificate of incorporation, the by-laws, or board resolutions, see, e.g., Missouri Valley Steel Co. v. New Amsterdam Casualty Co., 275 Minn. 433, 148 N.W.2d 126 (1966), or may derive from a pattern of past acquiescence by the board, see, e.g., Buxton v. Diversified Resources Corp., 634 F.2d 1313 (10th Cir.1980), cert. denied 454 U.S. 821, 102 S.Ct. 105, 70 L.Ed.2d 93 (1981); Juergens v. Venture Capital Corp., 1 Mass.App.Ct. 274, 295 N.E.2d 398 (1973); A. Schulman, Inc. v. Baer Co., 197 Pa.Super. 429, 178 A.2d 794 (1962), or from the board's acquiescence in or ratification of a specific transaction, see, e.g., De Pova v. Camden Forge Co., 254 F.2d 248 (3d Cir.), cert. denied 358 U.S. 816, 79 S.Ct. 26, 3 L.Ed.2d 59 (1958); Rachelle Enterprises, Inc. v. United States, 169 F.Supp. 266 (Ct.Cl.1959); Wuerderman v. J.O. Lively Const. Co., 602 S.W.2d 215 (Mo.App.1980); Pierce v. Astoria Fish Factors, Inc., 31 Wash.App. 214, 640 P.2d 40 (1982); Coastal Pharmaceutical Co. v. Goldman, 213 Va. 831, 195 S.E.2d 848 (1973).[3]

2. The last two paragraphs are adapted from ALI, Principles of Corporate Governance § 3.01, Reporter's Note (Tent. Draft No. 2, 1984).

3. In Boston Athletic Ass'n v. International Marathons, Inc., 392 Mass. 356, 363–365, 467 N.E.2d 58, 62–63 (1984), the court held that despite a board delegation of

2. *Chairman of the Board.* There is little case-law on the apparent authority of a chairman of the board by virtue of his position, in part because the actual authority of the chairman varies enormously. "It is an office in evolution assuming different roles in different corporations. In some it is held by a chief executive officer who has relinquished day-by-day operations to a younger man while still holding the reins of power; in others it is held by a retired chief executive officer whose counsel and advice are still valued; in still others it provides a formula for dividing up between two relatively equal principals the control of the corporation." American Express Co. v. Lopez, 72 Misc.2d 648, 340 N.Y.S.2d 82 (Civ.Ct.1973).

3. *Vice-presidents.* The case-law on the apparent authority of vice-presidents is also sparse. Under the relatively strict outlook of the earlier cases, a vice-president had little or no apparent authority. See James F. Monaghan, Inc. v. M. Lowenstein & Sons, 290 Mass. 331, 195 N.E. 101 (1935). There is some indication that the more expansive approach reflected in Lee v. Jenkins Brothers may carry over to vice-presidents, at least if they have the appearance of standing close to the top of the corporate hierarchy. Kanavos v. Hancock Bank & Trust Co., 14 Mass.App.Ct. 326, 439 N.E.2d 311 (1982).

4. *Secretary.* The secretary has apparent authority to certify the records of the corporation, including resolutions of the board. Accordingly, a secretary's certificate that a given resolution was duly adopted by the board is conclusive in favor of third party relying on the certificate. See, e.g., McMan Oil & Gas Co. v. Hurley, 24 F.2d 776 (5th Cir.1928); C.L. McClain Fuel Corp. to Use of Wayne Title & Trust v. Lineinger, 341 Pa. 364, 368, 19 A.2d 478, 480 (1941); Diamond Paint Co. of Houston v. Embry, 525 S.W.2d 529 (Tex.Civ. App.1975). The significance of the secretary's power of certification is demonstrated in In re Drive–In Development Corp., 371 F.2d 215, 219–20 (7th Cir.1966), cert. denied, Creditors' Committee of Drive– In Development Corp. v. National Boulevard Bank of Chicago, 387 U.S. 909, 87 S.Ct. 1691, 18 L.Ed.2d 626 (1967), which involved the question whether a corporation was bound by a guaranty:

> . . . [T]he referee found that Drive In's minute book did not show that a resolution authorizing Maranz to sign the guaranty was adopted by the directors and that Dick [the corporate secretary] could not recall a specific directors' meeting at which such a resolution was approved. From these findings, the referee concluded that Maranz, who signed the guaranty on behalf of Drive In, had no authority, "either actual or implied or apparent," to bind Drive In. This conclusion was erroneous. Drive In was estopped to

certain authority to the corporation's president, he did not have the authority to make an exclusive contract with an independent company to promote the Boston Marathon, stating the board cannot "delegate authority which is so broad that it enables the officer to bind the corporation to extraordinary commitments. . . ."

Certain transactions require specific authorization by the board in order to be valid." This case involved a charitable organization, and special reasons of policy may be applicable to such corporations. It seems doubtful that the same result could properly be reached in the case of a business corporation.

deny Maranz' express authority to sign the guaranty because of the certified copy of a resolution of Drive In's board of directors purporting to grant such authority furnished to the bank by Dick, whether or not such a resolution was in fact formally adopted. Dick was the secretary of the corporation. Generally, it is the duty of the secretary to keep the corporate records and to make proper entries of the actions and resolutions of the directors. Therefore it was within the authority of Dick to certify that a resolution such as challenged here was adopted. Statements made by an officer or agent in the course of a transaction in which the corporation is engaged and which are within the scope of his authority are binding upon the corporation. Consequently Drive In was estopped to deny the representation made by Dick in the certificate forwarded to National Boulevard, in the absence of actual or constructive knowledge on the part of the bank that the representation was untrue. . . .

. . . [T]he realities of modern corporate business practices do not contemplate that those who deal with officers or agents acting for a corporation should be required to go behind the representations of those who have authority to speak for the corporation and who verify the authority of those who presume to act for the corporation.[4]

Other than the very important power of certification, a secretary's apparent authority by virtue of his position is close to nil. See Hollywyle Ass'n v. Hollister, 164 Conn. 389, 324 A.2d 247 (1973) (secretary has no apparent authority to sign a deed); Ideal Foods, Inc. v. Action Leasing Corp., 413 So.2d 416, 417 (Fla.App.1982) ("The secretary of a corporation, merely as such, is a ministerial officer, without authority to transact the business of the corporation upon his volition and judgment"); Citizens Development Co. v. Kypawva Oil Co., 191 Ky. 183, 186, 229 S.W. 88, 90 (1921) (secretary is "merely a ministerial officer who keeps the books and minutes of the stockholders' and directors' meetings and has charge of the seal of the company").

5. *Treasurer.* The apparent authority of the treasurer, under the case-law, is also close to nil. See Ideal Foods, Inc. v. Action Leasing Corp., 413 So.2d 416 (Fla.App.1982); Slavin v. Passaic Nat. Bank & Trust Co., 114 N.J.L. 341, 176 A. 339 (1935); Jacobus v. Jamestown Mantel Co., 211 N.Y. 154, 105 N.E. 210 (1914).

---

4. But see Keystone Leasing Corp. v. Peoples Protective Life Insurance Co., 514 F.Supp. 841, 846, 851 (E.D.N.Y.1981) (corporation was not estopped to contradict corporate resolution certified by its secretary, because the third party "must have been aware of the suspect nature" of the certified resolutions).

SECTION 7. FORMALITIES REQUIRED FOR SHAREHOLDER ACTION

———

DEL. GEN. CORP. LAW §§ 211, 213, 214, 216, 222, 228

[See Statutory Supplement]

———

REV. MODEL BUS. CORP. ACT §§ 7.01, 7.02, 7.03–7.07, 7.21, 7.25–7.28

[See Statutory Supplement]

———

NOTE ON FORMALITIES REQUIRED FOR SHAREHOLDER ACTION

1. *Meeting and notice.* All of the statutes contemplate that a corporation will hold an annual meeting of shareholders. Notice of place, time, and date is required for the annual meeting and for any special meeting. The notice of a special meeting must also describe the purpose for which the meeting is called. Some state statutes, and the federal Proxy Rules, also require a description of purpose in the notice of an annual meeting. However, the Proxy Rules apply to only a small fraction of all corporations, and under most of the state statutes the notice of an annual meeting must describe the matters to be acted upon only in certain cases—for example, when it is proposed to amend the certificate of incorporation, sell substantially all of the corporation's assets, engage in a merger, or dissolve.

Because the identity of the shareholders in a publicly held corporation constantly undergoes change, notice of a meeting is given not to those persons who are beneficial owners of stock on the date of the meeting, but to those persons who are shareholders of record on a designated record date prior to the meeting. Correspondingly, only those persons who were record holders on the record date are entitled to vote at the meeting. The record date is normally fixed in the by-laws, or by the board, within prescribed statutory limts. If a record date is not fixed in this manner, the statutes usually provide that the record date will be the day of, or the business day preceding, the day on which the notice of meeting is sent. (Under an older, alternative procedure that is still sanctioned in many statutes, but is generally regarded as archaic, the corporation can close its share-transfer books as of a given date, and give notice only to those persons who were record holders at the time the transfer books were closed.)

2. *Quorum.* Under most of the statutes a majority of the shares entitled to vote is necessary for a quorum, unless the certificate of incorporation sets a higher or lower figure. A substantial majority of the statutes provide that the certificate cannot set a quorum lower than

one-third of the shares entitled to vote. Most of the balance of the statutes set no minimum.

3. *Voting* (i) *Ordinary matters.* Under most statutes, the affirmative vote of a majority of the shares represented at a meeting is required for shareholder action on ordinary matters. Under some statutes, however, only the affirmative vote of a majority of those voting is required. If a statute requires the affirmative vote of a majority of those present, an abstention affectively counts as a negative vote.

Virtually all the statutes permit the certificate of incorporation to set a higher vote than would otherwise be required. Under some of the statutes, a certificate amendment that adds a provision requiring a higher-than-normal vote may be adopted only by the same vote as is required under the amendment.

(ii) *Structural changes.* Structural changes, such as certificate amendment, merger, sale of substantially all assets, and dissolution, usually require approval by a majority or two-thirds of the outstanding voting shares, rather than a majority of those present or voting at the meeting. See Chapter XI.

(iii) *Election of directors.* The election of directors requires only a plurality vote—that is, those candidates who receive the highest number of votes are elected, up to the maximum number to be chosen at the election, even if they receive less than a majority of the votes present at the meeting. Some states require cumulative voting in the election of directors. See infra.

(iv) *Written consent.* All statutes permit the shareholders to act by written consent in lieu of a meeting. About three-fourths of the statutes permit shareholder action by written consent if the consent is unanimous. The remaining statutes vary in their details. Del.Gen. Corp.Law § 228 permits shareholders to act by written consent if consents are signed by the holders of a number of shares that would have been sufficient to take the action in question at a meeting at which all shareholders were present and voting. See also Del.Gen. Corp.Law § 213. On the Delaware statute, see Herzel, Davis & Harris, Consents to Trouble, 42 Bus.Law. 135 (1986); Finkelstein and Varallo, Action by Written Consent: A Reply to Messrs. Herzel, Davis, and Harris, 42 Bus.Law. 1075 (1987).

On the issues covered in this Note, see generally 2 Model Business Corporation Act Annotated 513–77, 639–685 (3d ed. 1987); 5 W. Fletcher, Cyclopedia of the Law of Private Corporations §§ 1996, 1996.1, 2006–2013, 2020 (rev. perm. ed.).

BOHANNAN v. CORPORATION COMMISSION

Supreme Court of Arizona, 1957.
82 Ariz. 299, 313 P.2d 379.

STRUCKMEYER, Justice.

Appellants petitioned the court below for a writ of mandamus to compel the filing of the articles of incorporation of a proposed domestic company.   Judgment was entered that no writ issue and this appeal followed.

On the 24th of January, 1956, appellants attempted to form a corporation to be known as the Associated Mortgage and Investment Company by filing their proposed articles of incorporation with the Arizona Corporation Commission.   The Commission rejected the articles, giving as its reason that Part 4 thereof provided for a system of staggered directors in violation of the Constitution, Article 14, Section 10, and statute Section 10–271, A.R.S.   Part 4 established a nine-member board of directors to be elected on a staggered basis in this manner: At the first meeting all nine to be elected, three to serve one year, three to serve two years, and three to serve three years; thereafter, at each annual election, three directors to be elected for terms of three years each.   The Commission's rejection of the proposed articles was based on the opinion of the Attorney General issued December 19, 1955.   He emphasized the then very recent case of Wolfson v. Avery, 6 Ill.2d 78, 126 N.E.2d 701, as authority against the practice of staggering directors by term under a constitutional provision similar to that of Arizona.   The learned trial judge leaned heavily on the same case for the proper construction of the Arizona Constitution.

As a preliminary, it is to be observed that there is nothing contrary to the public policy of this state in the practice of classification of directors by term.   It has as its aim corporate stability and continuity of experienced management.   As one of the common methods of classification of directors, it seemingly has not been questioned in Arizona prior to the Attorney General's opinion.   Cumulative voting for directors, on the other hand, as a somewhat more recent development in corporate practice is in derogation of the common law and not to be permitted unless specifically authorized by constitutional, statutory or charter provisions.   State ex rel. Swanson v. Perham, 30 Wash.2d 368, 191 P.2d 689.

Article 14, Section 10, of the Arizona Constitution provides:

> "In all elections for directors or managers of any corporation, each shareholder shall have the right to cast as many votes in the aggregate as he shall be entitled to vote in same company under its charter multiplied by the number of directors or managers *to be elected* at such election; and each shareholder may cast the whole number of votes, either in person or by proxy, for one candidate, or distribute such votes among two or more such candidates; and such directors or managers shall not be elected otherwise."   (Italics ours.)

Section 10–271, A.R.S. 1956, is merely a restatement of this article. It was adopted in the first year of statehood, and because it offers no assistance in the solution of the problem presented, will not be further considered.   Since the provisions of the Constitution are mandatory unless expressly therein declared to be otherwise, Constitution, Article 2, Section 32, State ex rel. Morrison v. Nabours, 79 Ariz. 240, 286 P.2d 752, any scheme, plan or device which completely denies the effectiveness of cumulative voting must necessarily fall. The Commission points out that at least one method of staggering directors by terms plainly denies to the stockholders this right; namely where a corporation has three directors elected one each year for a three-year term. Unquestionably such a plan is illegal and void as coming within the implied prohibition of the Constitution in that it absolutely denies the mandatory right guaranteed to cumulate votes; but merely because it is possible to circumvent the Constitution by one method of staggering directors does not mean that all schemes or plans to that end are within the implied prohibition.

It is urged by appellees that the general effect of staggering directors by term is to reduce the number of directors which can be elected by minority stockholders, dependent upon such varying factors as the number of directors to be elected, the proportion of stock that the minority controls, and the total number of shares. It is true that illustrations can be pointed to which in any system of classification of directors by term this result will follow, dependent upon a reduction in the number of shares controlled by the minority. If this argument has any validity, it must be predicated on the proposition that the Constitution demands that minority stockholders be represented on corporate boards in proportion to or at least somewhat in the ratio to the number of shares owned or controlled by such minority. In our examination into this basic predicate, we take it as axiomatic that this court does not have the right to insert in the Constitution that which is not expressed or cannot be fairly implied, Prigg v. Commonwealth of Pennsylvania, 16 Pet. 539, 41 U.S. 539, 10 L.Ed. 1060, so that if we are unable to find that the Constitution either by direct expression or fair implication requires proportionate representation, we will be compelled to render a construction which is consistent with the normal and ordinary meaning of the words. Such a construction merely guarantees that a means be provided whereby it is possible for some minority entitled to participate in the elections to secure representation on the board and would not guarantee to a minority stockholder or any particular percentage less than forty-nine per cent a director of his or their choosing.

In Wolfson v. Avery, supra, the Illinois court found that the phrase in the constitution "to be elected", S.H.A.Ill.Const. art. 11, § 3, expressed a recognition that the number of directors varied as between corporations and did not contemplate the possibility that less than the whole number of directors might be elected at any particular annual meeting. This was without extrinsic aids to assist in the formulation of constitutional intent, although later in the same opinion such aids were used to fortify the court's prior conclusion. In the dissenting opinion it was pointed out that there was no express prohibition in the Constitution against classification and the staggering of directors when the words of the Constitution are taken in their ordinary signification. We have examined both arguments advanced, which we do not repeat here, and can say that each has some element of logical plausibility. We are more inclined to agree with the dissenting justice, but do not expressly base our conclusions on this alone. Rather to the extent that Article 14, Section 10, is susceptible of two possible interpretations in that reasonable men may differ as to the import of its language, we find it to be ambiguous.

We will, therefore, look beyond the article for assistance in determining its meaning. . . ., and in so doing examine into, ascertain and give effect to the intent and purpose of the framers of the Constitution. . . . In this we are unable to conclude, as did the Illinois court, that it was the intention of the framers of the Constitution to require that minority shareholders be represented on corporate boards in proportion to the per cent of shares controlled by them.

We have been referred to the statement by Mr. E.E. Ellinwood, an illustrious attorney and member of the Bar of this state and a member of the constitutional convention. There at a meeting of the committee of the whole, he in part stated:

> "Mr. Chairman, this provision in one form or the other is in effect in California, Illinois, Idaho, Missouri, Montana, South Dakota, Pennsylvania, North Dakota, West Virginia, and it seems to me it is very essential. It gives the minority stockholder a look-in. While he cannot control the corporation he can have a member on the board so he knows what is going on, and I think if this system is adopted the minority stockholders will be protected."

Plainly there is manifested an intention to protect minority stockholders, but nothing stated imports an intention to give proportional representation to them. Rather the purpose is to make it possible to have "a member on the board so that he knows what is going on." From this the least that can be said is that it contains no comfort for the argument in favor of proportional representation.

In our conclusion, we give considerable weight to the fact as pointed out that the propriety of staggering directors is here for the first time questioned since statehood, forty-five years ago. Uniform acquiescence of meaning, if it is not manifestly erroneous, will not be disturbed, at least in cases of doubt, for injustices are likely to result after a long period of time during which many rights will necessarily have been acquired. We are convinced also because a constitution is not the beginning of law but assumes the existence of a system of laws which is to remain in force, that the framers of the Constitution will not be presumed to have intended changes or innovations on the common law. Much of the argument is addressed to the wisdom of staggering directors by terms, and we have been cited to numerous publications and articles espousing either one side or the other of this question. Ordinarily, construction by determination of the wisdom of a particular policy is not to be approved. . . .

We are not convinced by the arguments presented that Article 14, Section 10, must be construed to defeat appellants' plan for the government of this corporation. Cf. Janney v. Philadelphia Transportation Company, 387 Pa. 282, 128 A.2d 76. If abuses do arise through the classification of directors by term, they can be corrected by the legislature, since it is clearly within the sphere of action of that body. Humphrys v. Winous Co., 165 Ohio St. 45, 133 N.E.2d 780. The judgment of the court below is reversed with directions to grant the petition for peremptory writ of mandamus.

UDALL, C.J., and WINDES and PHELPS, JJ., concurring.

Nearly twenty years after the *Bohannan* decision, the Arizona legislature enacted § 10–037 of the General Corporation Law, to permit classification of directors "[w]hen the articles of incorporation [provide] for a board of directors of nine or more members."

---

2 H. MARSH, MARSH'S CALIFORNIA CORPORATION LAW § 11.2

2d ed. 1981.

In voting cumulatively, a shareholder casts for any one or more candidates a number of votes greater than the number of his shares. The number of votes a shareholder is entitled to cast cumulatively is calculated by multiplying the number of votes to which his shares are entitled by the number of directors to be elected. In other words, if there is a five-man board and the shareholder owns 100 shares (each entitled to one vote per share), then the shareholder has 100 times five or 500 votes which he may cast in the election. He may cast the entire sum, 500 votes, for one candidate or he may allocate the votes among more than one or all of the candidates. If he votes an equal number of votes for five candidates, however, he has not "cumulated" his votes; if all shareholders do this, the effect is the same as though cumulate voting did not exist.

The significant calculation in cumulative voting is the determination of the number of shares needed to elect a specified number of directors. Such a calculation may be made according to the following formula:

$$X = \frac{S \times D}{N + 1} + 1 \text{ (vote)}$$

In this formula X is the number of shares required to elect a specified number of directors (D); S is the number of shares which are voted at an election of directors; N is the total number of directors who will be elected. In an election for the entire five-man board of a corporation having 1,000 shares outstanding entitled to vote, if all of such shares are present and are voted at the meeting, the number of shares entitled to elect two directors may be calculated as follows:

$$S = 1,000; \quad N = 5; \quad D = 2.$$

$$X = \frac{1000 \times 2}{5+1} + .2 = \frac{2,000}{6} + .2 = 334 \text{ [16]}$$

---

16. The 1 *vote* in the formula is translated here into .2 share since there are *five* directors and .2 share in this particular case equals 1 *vote*. The calculation produc- es the figure 333.53, but this must be rounded off to the next higher integer, since normally no fractional shares are outstanding.

Therefore, in the example, assuming all shares which are entitled to vote do so, 334 shares are required to elect two directors. To illustrate, assume there are 1,000 shares outstanding entitled to vote in an election of directors and two shareholders, one holding 334 shares and the other holding 666 shares. In the election, the shareholders would be entitled to cast a number of votes equal to the number of shares they hold times the number of directors to be elected or, respectively, 1,670 votes and 3,330 votes. If the majority shareholder distributed his votes equally among four candidates, each candidate would receive 832+ votes. Since the minority shareholder is able to cast 1,670 votes, he would cast 835 votes for each of two candidates, resulting in the election of both of his candidates and the election of only three of those of the majority shareholder. The majority shareholder could not cumulate his votes in any manner that would produce more than 835 votes for more than three of his candidates.

On the other hand, if the majority shareholder held 667 shares (or one more) he could distribute his 3,335 votes by giving each of four candidates 833+ votes; whereas, the minority shareholder with 333 shares and 1,665 votes could give each of two candidates only 832+ votes, which would mean that he could elect only one. . . .

The formula may easily be rearranged to determine the number of directors one could elect given the ownership of a specified number of voting shares. If an individual owns 350 of the 1,000 outstanding shares entitled to vote in an election for directors, the calculation of the number of directors he could elect to a nine man board would require rearrangement of the formula to determine the value for D. The resultant formula would be expressed as follows:

$$D = \frac{(X - 1)\ (N + 1)}{S}$$

The calculation of the number of directors that could be elected with 350 shares would be as follows:

$$D = \frac{(350 - 1)\ (9 + 1)}{1,000} = \frac{349\ (10)}{1,000} = \frac{3,490}{1,000} = 3.49$$

Rounding off to the lower integer, since a fractional director cannot be elected, the number of directors that could be elected by a proper cumulation of the votes of 350 shares at an election at which all of the 1,000 outstanding shares voted would be three out of a total of nine.

The general formula assumes that all shares entitled to vote in an election of directors are voted and are properly cumulated. If the total number of shares entitled to vote in an election are not voted, the number of shares necessary to elect a director is obviously less. Therefore, a particular faction at a shareholders' meeting may be able to elect a number of directors greater than that which would ordinarily result upon the proper cumulation of votes at a meeting at which all voting shares are present and voting. Furthermore, errors in calculation and in cumulating of votes may give unexpected results.

In Pierce v. Commonwealth [19] inadvertence by the holders of a majority of the voting shares in cumulating their votes resulted in the

---

19.   104 Pa.St.Rep. 150 (1883).

election of a majority of the directors by a minority of the shareholders. In that case the majority held 3,396 shares to the 3,037 shares held by the minority, in an election of six directors. The majority cumulated its votes ($3,396 \times 6 = 20,376$) equally over six candidates (each candidate receiving 3,396 votes). The minority group cumulated its votes ($3,037 \times 6 = 18,222$) over four candidates (each candidate receiving approximately 4,555 votes). The minority group elected all four of its candidates and gained control of the board. The election was upheld by the Supreme Court of Pennsylvania.*

Note: Just over one-fourth of the states mandate cumulative voting, either by constitutional provision or by statute.

---

* For qualifications on the general formulas, see Glazer, Glazer & Grofman, Cumulative Voting in Corporate Elections; Introducing Strategy Into the Equation, 35 S.C.L.Rev. 295 (1984). (Footnote by ed.)

Chapter V

SHAREHOLDER INFORMATIONAL RIGHTS AND PROXY VOTING

SECTION 1. SHAREHOLDER INFORMATIONAL RIGHTS (I): INSPECTION OF BOOKS AND RECORDS

DEL. GEN. CORP. LAW §§ 219, 220

[See Statutory Supplement]

REV. MODEL BUS. CORP. ACT §§ 7.20, 16.01–16.04

[See Statutory Supplement]

N.Y. BUS. CORP. LAW § 624

[See Statutory Supplement]

STATE EX REL. PILLSBURY v. HONEYWELL, INC.

Supreme Court of Minnesota, 1971.
291 Minn. 322, 191 N.W.2d 406.

KELLY, Justice.

Petitioner appeals from an order and judgment of the district court denying all relief prayed for in a petition for writ of mandamus to compel respondent, Honeywell, Inc., (Honeywell) to produce its original shareholder ledger, current shareholder ledger, and all corporate records dealing with weapons and munitions manufacture. We must affirm.

The issues raised by petitioner are as follows: (1) Whether Minnesota or Delaware law determines the right of a shareholder to inspect respondent's corporate books and records; (2) whether petitioner, who bought shares in respondent corporation for the purpose of changing its policy of manufacturing war munitions, had a proper purpose germane to a shareholder's interest. . . .

Petitioner attended a meeting on July 3, 1969, of a group involved in what was known as the "Honeywell Project." Participants in the project believed that American involvement in Vietnam

186

was wrong, that a substantial portion of Honeywell's production consisted of munitions used in that war, and that Honeywell should stop this production of munitions. Petitioner had long opposed the Vietnam war, but it was at the July 3rd meeting that he first learned of Honeywell's involvement. He was shocked at the knowledge that Honeywell had a large government contract to produce anti-personnel fragmentation bombs. Upset because of knowledge that such bombs were produced in his own community by a company which he had known and respected, petitioner determined to stop Honeywell's munitions production.

On July 14, 1969, petitioner ordered his fiscal agent to purchase 100 shares of Honeywell. He admits that the sole purpose of the purchase was to give himself a voice in Honeywell's affairs so he could persuade Honeywell to cease producing munitions. Apparently not aware of that purpose, petitioner's agent registered the stock in the name of a Pillsbury family nominee—Quad & Co. Upon discovering the nature of the registration, petitioner bought one share of Honeywell in his own name on August 11, 1969. In his deposition testimony petitioner made clear the reason for his purchase of Honeywell's shares:

"Q. . . . [D]o I understand that you requested Mr. Lacey to buy these 100 shares of Honeywell in order to follow up on the desire you had to bring to Honeywell management and to stockholders these theses that you have told us about here today?

"A. Yes. That was my motivation."

The "theses" referred to are petitioner's beliefs concerning the propriety of producing munitions for the Vietnam war.

During July 1969, *subsequent* to the July 3, 1969, meeting and after he had ordered his agent to purchase the 100 shares of Honeywell stock, petitioner inquired into a trust which had been formed for his benefit by his grandmother. The purpose of the inquiry was to discover whether shares of Honeywell were included in the trust. It was then, *for the first time,* that petitioner discovered that he had a contingent beneficial interest under the terms of the trust in 242 shares of Honeywell.

Prior to the instigation of this suit, petitioner submitted two formal demands to Honeywell requesting that it produce its original shareholder ledger, current shareholder ledger, and all corporate records dealing with weapons and munitions manufacture. Honeywell refused.

On November 24, 1969, a petition was filed for writs of mandamus ordering Honeywell to produce the above mentioned records. In response, Honeywell answered the petition and served a notice of deposition on petitioner. . . .

In the deposition petitioner outlined his beliefs concerning the Vietnam war and his purpose for his involvement with Honeywell. He expressed his desire to communicate with other shareholders in the hope of altering Honeywell's board of directors and thereby changing its policy. To this end, he testified, business records are necessary to insure accuracy.

A hearing was held on January 8, 1970, during which Honeywell introduced the deposition, conceded all material facts stated therein, and argued that petitioner was not entitled to any relief as a matter of law. Petitioner asked that alternative writs of mandamus issue for all the relief requested in his petition. On April 8, 1970, the trial court dismissed the petition, holding that the relief requested was for an improper and indefinite purpose. Petitioner contends in this appeal that the dismissal was in error.

1. Honeywell is a Delaware corporation doing business in Minnesota. Both petitioner and Honeywell spent considerable effort in arguing whether Delaware or Minnesota law applies. The trial court, applying Delaware law, determined that the outcome of the case rested upon whether or not petitioner has a proper purpose germane to his interest as a shareholder. Del.Code Ann. tit. 8, § 220 (Supp. 1968). This test is derived from the common law and is applicable in Minnesota. See, Sanders v. Pacific Gamble Robinson Co., 250 Minn. 265, 84 N.W.2d 919 (1957).[1] Minn.St. c. 300, upon which petitioner relies, applies only to firms incorporated under that chapter. We need not rule on whether the lower court applied the right state law since the test used was correct.

Under the Delaware statute the shareholder must prove a proper purpose to inspect corporate records other than shareholder lists. Del.Code Ann. tit. 8, § 220(c) (Supp.1968). This facet of the law did not affect the trial court's findings of fact. The case was decided solely on the pleadings and the deposition of petitioner, the court determining from them that petitioner was not entitled to relief as a matter of law. Thus, problems of burden of proof did not confront the trial court and this issue was not even raised in this court.

2. The trial court ordered judgment for Honeywell, ruling that petitioner had not demonstrated a proper purpose germane to his interest as a stockholder. Petitioner contends that a stockholder who disagrees with management has an absolute right to inspect corporate records for purposes of soliciting proxies. He would have this court rule that such solicitation is per se a "proper purpose." Honeywell argues that a "proper purpose" contemplates concern with investment return. We agree with Honeywell.

This court has had several occasions to rule on the propriety of shareholders' demands for inspection of corporate books and records. Minn.St. 300.32, not applicable here, has been held to be declaratory of the common-law principle that a stockholder is entitled to inspection for a proper purpose germane to his business interests. While inspection will not be permitted for purposes of curiosity, speculation, or vexation, adverseness to management and a desire to gain control

1. In Sanders v. Pacific Gamble Robinson Co., 250 Minn. 265, 84 N.W.2d 919 (1957), the court referred to Minn.St. 300.32 but did not apply it since the corporation was foreign.

of the corporation for economic benefit does not indicate an improper purpose.[2]

Several courts agree with petitioner's contention that a mere desire to communicate with other shareholders is, per se, a proper purpose. Lake v. The Buckeye Steel Castings Co., 2 Ohio St.2d 101, 206 N.E.2d 566 (1965). This would seem to confer an almost absolute right to inspection. We believe that a better rule would allow inspections only if the shareholder has a proper purpose for such communication. This rule was applied in McMahon v. Dispatch Printing Co., 101 N.J.L. 470, 129 A. 425 (1925), where inspection was denied because the shareholder's objective was to discredit politically the president of the company, who was also the New Jersey secretary of state.

The act of inspecting a corporation's shareholder ledger and business records must be viewed in its proper perspective. In terms of the corporate norm, inspection is merely the act of the concerned owner checking on what is in part his property. In the context of the large firm, inspection can be more akin to a weapon in corporate warfare. The effectiveness of the weapon is considerable:

"Considering the huge size of many modern corporations and the necessarily complicated nature of their bookkeeping, it is plain that to permit their thousands of stockholders to roam at will through their records would render impossible not only any attempt to keep their records efficiently, but the proper carrying on of their businesses." Cooke v. Outland, 265 N.C. 601, 611, 144 S.E.2d 835, 842 (1965). See, also, Matter of Pierson, 28 Misc. 726, 59 N.Y.S. 1003 (Sup.Ct. 1899), affirmed, 44 App.Div. 215, 60 N.Y.S. 671 (1899). Because the power to inspect may be the power to destroy, it is important that only those with a bona fide interest in the corporation enjoy that power.

That one must have proper standing to demand inspection has been recognized by statutes in several jurisdictions. Courts have also balked at compelling inspection by a shareholder holding an insignificant amount of stock in the corporation.

Petitioner's standing as a shareholder is quite tenuous. He only owns one share in his own name, bought for the purposes of this suit. He had previously ordered his agent to buy 100 shares, but there is no showing of investment intent. While his agent had a cash balance in the $400,000 portfolio, petitioner made no attempt to determine whether Honeywell was a good investment or whether more profitable shares would have to be sold to finance the Honeywell purchase. Furthermore, petitioner's agent had the power to sell the Honeywell shares without his consent. Petitioner also had a contingent beneficial interest in 242 shares. Courts are split on the question of whether an equitable interest entitles one to inspection. See 5 Fletcher, Private Corporations, § 2230 at 862 (Perm.ed.rev.vol.1967). Indicative of

---

2. Nationwide Corp. v. Northwestern Nat. Life Ins. Co., 251 Minn. 255, 87 N.W.2d 671 (1958); Sanders v. Pacific Gamble Robinson Co. *supra;* State ex rel. G.M. Gustafson Co. v. Crookston Trust Co., 222 Minn. 17, 22 N.W.2d 911 (1946). . . .

petitioner's concern regarding his equitable holdings is the fact that he was unaware of them until he had decided to bring this suit.

Petitioner had utterly no interest in the affairs of Honeywell before he learned of Honeywell's production of fragmentation bombs. Immediately after obtaining this knowledge, he purchased stock in Honeywell for the sole purpose of asserting ownership privileges in an effort to force Honeywell to cease such production. We agree with the court in Chas. A. Day & Co. v. Booth, 123 Maine 443, 447, 123 A. 557, 558 (1924) that "where it is shown that such stockholding is only colorable, or solely for the purpose of maintaining proceedings of this kind, [we] fail to see how the petitioner can be said to be a person interested, entitled as of right to inspect . . . .." But for his opposition to Honeywell's policy, petitioner probably would not have bought Honeywell stock, would not be interested in Honeywell's profits and would not desire to communicate with Honeywell's shareholders. His avowed purpose in buying Honeywell stock was to place himself in a position to try to impress his opinions favoring a reordering of priorities upon Honeywell management and its other shareholders. Such a motivation can hardly be deemed a proper purpose germane to his economic interest as a shareholder.[5]

3. The fact that petitioner alleged a proper purpose in his petition will not necessarily compel a right to inspection. "A mere statement in a petition alleging a proper purpose is not sufficient. The facts in each case may be examined." Sawers v. American Phenolic Corp., 404 Ill. 440, 449, 89 N.E.2d 374, 379 (1949). Neither is inspection mandated by the recitation of proper purpose in petitioner's testimony. Conversely, a company cannot defeat inspection by merely alleging an improper purpose.[6] From the deposition, the trial court concluded that petitioner had already formed strong opinions on the immorality and the social and economic wastefulness of war long before he bought stock in Honeywell. His sole motivation was to change Honeywell's course of business because that course was incompatible with his political views. If unsuccessful, petitioner indicated that he would sell the Honeywell stock.

We do not mean to imply that a shareholder with a bona fide investment interest could not bring this suit if motivated by concern with the long- or short-term economic effects on Honeywell resulting

---

5. We do not question petitioner's good faith incident to his political and social philosophy; nor did the trial court. In a well-prepared memorandum, the lower court stated: "By enumerating the foregoing this Court does not mean to belittle or to be derisive of Petitioner's motivations and intentions because this Court cannot but draw the conclusion that the Petitioner is sincere in his political and social philosophy, but this Court does not feel that this is a proper forum for the advancement of these political-social views by way of direct contact with the stockholders of Honeywell Company or any other company. If the courts were to grant these rights on the basis of the foregoing, anyone who has a political-social philosophy which differs with that of a company in which he becomes a shareholder can secure a writ and any company can be faced with a rash and multitude of these types of actions which are not bona fide efforts to engage in a proxy fight for the purpose of taking over the company or electing directors, which the courts have recognized as being perfectly legitimate and acceptable."

6. See, Nationwide Corp. v. Northwestern Nat. Life Ins. Co., 251 Minn. 255, 87 N.W.2d 671 (1958).

from the production of war munitions.   Similarly, this suit might be appropriate when a shareholder has a bona fide concern about the adverse effects of abstention from profitable war contracts on his investment in Honeywell.

In the instant case, however, the trial court, in effect, has found from all the facts that petitioner was not interested in even the long-term well-being of Honeywell or the enhancement of the value of his shares.   His sole purpose was to persuade the company to adopt his social and political concerns, irrespective of any economic benefit to himself or Honeywell.   This purpose on the part of one buying into the corporation does not entitle the petitioner to inspect Honeywell's books and records.

4.   Petitioner argues that he wishes to inspect the stockholder ledger in order that he may correspond with other shareholders with the hope of electing to the board one or more directors who represent his particular viewpoint.   On p. 30 of his brief he states that this purpose alone compels inspection:

". . . [T]his Court has said that a stockholder's motives or 'good faith' are not a test of his right of inspection, except as 'bad faith' actually manifests some recognized 'improper purpose'—such as vexation of the corporation, or purely destructive plans, or *nothing specific,* just pure idle curiosity, or necessarily illegal ends, or *nothing germane to his interests.*   State ex rel. Gustafson Co. v. Crookston Trust Co. [222 Minn. 17, 22 N.W.2d 911 (1946)] . . .."   (Italics supplied.)

While a plan to elect one or more directors is specific and the election of directors normally would be a proper purpose, here the purpose was not germane to petitioner's or Honeywell's economic interest. Instead, the plan was designed to further petitioner's political and social beliefs.   Since the requisite propriety of purpose germane to his or Honeywell's economic interest is not present, the allegation that petitioner seeks to elect a new board of directors is insufficient to compel inspection. . . .

The order of the trial court denying the writ of mandamus is affirmed.

CREDIT BUREAU REPORTS, INC. v. CREDIT BUREAU OF ST. PAUL, INC.

Supreme Court of Delaware, 1972.
290 A.2d 691.

Per curiam:

The Chancery Court granted inspection of the defendant-corporation's stockholder list to the plaintiff-stockholder under 8 Del.C. § 220.

We have affirmed for the reasons stated in the opinion below. See Del.Ch., 290 A.2d 689.

The case is governed by General Time Corporation v. Talley Industries, Inc., Del.Supr., 240 A.2d 755 (1968). There we stated that, under § 220, "the desire to solicit proxies for a slate of directors in opposition to management is a purpose reasonably related to the stockholder's interest as a stockholder"; and we held that "any further or secondary purpose in seeking the list is irrelevant". Those rulings are dispositive.

The corporation erroneously argues that Northwest Industries, Inc. v. B.F. Goodrich Company, Del.Supr., 260 A.2d 428 (1969) modified the aforementioned rules of *General Time.* On the contrary, *Goodrich* gave express recognition to *General Time* and its above-stated rulings.

The *Goodrich* case furnishes guidelines for the sufficiency of the statement of purpose in a demand for inspection under § 220. Here, the sufficiency of the statement of purpose is unquestionable.

The defendant corporation also relies upon Pillsbury v. Honeywell, Inc., Minn., 191 N.W.2d 406 (1971). Insofar as the *Pillsbury* case is inconsistent herewith, it is inconsistent with 8 Del.C. § 220 as properly applied.

Affirmed.

NOTE ON THE SHAREHOLDER'S INSPECTION RIGHTS

At common law, a shareholder "acting in good faith for the purpose of advancing the interests of the corporation and protecting his own interest as a stockholder" has a right to examine the corporate books and records at reasonable times. Albee v. Lamson & Hubbard Corp., 320 Mass. 421, 424, 69 N.E.2d 811, 813 (1946). The general rule is that the shareholder has the burden of alleging and proving good faith and proper purpose. Id. But see Bennett v. Mack's Supermarkets, Inc., 602 S.W.2d 143 (Ky.1979).

Many or most legislatures have now enacted statutes governing the right of inspection. Many of these statutes are more limited in their coverage than the common law rule. For example, a statute may apply only to certain kinds of shareholders (such as those who are record holders of at least 5% of the corporation's stock or who have been record holders for at least six months) or only to certain kinds of books and records. A common problem of interpretation is whether the statutes (i) preserve the common law rule that the shareholder must prove a proper purpose; (ii) discard the proper purpose test, or (iii) preserve the proper purpose test, but place on the corporation the burden of proving that the shareholder's purpose is improper. Generally, the last interpretation is followed, at least if the language is ambiguous. Crane Co. v. Anaconda Co., 39 N.Y.2d 14, 382 N.Y.S.2d 707, 346 N.E.2d 507 (1976); Carter v. Wilson Const. Co., Inc., 83 N.C.App. 61, 348 S.E.2d 830 (1988); Rosentool v. Bonanza Oil and Mine Corp., 221 Or. 520, 352 P.2d 138 (1960). But see

Riser v. Genuine Parts Co., 150 Ga.App. 502, 258 S.E.2d 184 (1979). A second common problem of interpretation, under those statutes that are more limited in their coverage than the common law rule, is whether the statutes replace or supplement that rule. The general answer is that the statutes supplement the common law, so that a suit for inspection that does not fall within the statute can still be brought under the common law. See Tucson Gas & Electric Co. v. Schantz, 5 Ariz.App. 511, 428 P.2d 686 (1967); Bank of Heflin v. Miles, 294 Ala. 462, 318 So.2d 697 (1975); State ex rel. Lowell Wiper Supply Co. v. Helen Shop, Inc., 211 Tenn. 107, 362 S.W.2d 787 (1962). But see Caspary v. Louisiana Land & Exploration Co., 707 F.2d 785 (4th Cir.1983).

Among the purposes the courts have recognized as "proper" for purposes of exercising the shareholder's inspection right are: (i) To determine whether the corporation is being properly managed or whether there has been managerial misconduct (at least if the shareholder alleges some specific concerns). Skouras v. Admiralty Enterprises, Inc., 386 A.2d 674 (Del.Ch.1978); Briskin v. Briskin Manufacturing Co., 6 Ill.App.3d 740, 286 N.E.2d 571 (1972); State ex rel. Watkins v. Cassell, 294 S.W.2d 647 (Mo.App.1956); Hagy v. Premier Mfg. Corp., 404 Pa. 330, 172 A.2d 283 (1961). (ii) To determine the condition of the corporation. Riser v. Genuine Parts Co., 150 Ga.App. 502, 258 S.E.2d 184 (1979). (iii) To ascertain the value of the petitioner's shares. Friedman v. Altoona Pipe and Steel Supply Co., 460 F.2d 1212 (3d Cir.1972); CM & M Group, Inc. v. Carroll, 453 A.2d 788 (Del.1982); E.I.F.C., Inc. v. Atnip, 454 S.W.2d 351 (Ky.1970).

SECTION 2. SHAREHOLDER INFORMATIONAL RIGHTS (II): REPORTING REQUIREMENTS

INTRODUCTORY NOTE

Given the limitations of the shareholder's inspection right, not the least of which is the cost of going to court, it was probably inevitable that corrective action would be taken to ensure that shareholders are provided with adequate information at the corporation's expense. Two major bodies of rules evolved to alleviate the deficiencies in the inspection right—(i) the Securities Exchange Act of 1934 and the Rules promulgated by the SEC thereunder, and (ii) the rules for listed companies issued by various stock exchanges, particularly the New York Stock Exchange. To put these rules in context, this Section will begin with overviews of the Securities Exchange Act and the stock markets.

(a) AN OVERVIEW OF THE SEC AND THE SECURITIES EXCHANGE ACT

SECURITIES AND EXCHANGE COMMISSION, THE WORK OF THE SEC
3–4, 9–13 (1986).

The U.S. Securities and Exchange Commission's mission is to administer Federal securities laws that seek to provide protection for investors. The purpose of these laws is to ensure that the securities markets are fair and honest and to provide the means to enforce the securities laws through sanctions where necessary. Laws administered by the Commission are the:

- Securities Act of 1933;
- Securities Exchange Act of 1934;
- Public Utility Holding Company Act of 1935;
- Trust Indenture Act of 1939;
- Investment Company Act of 1940; and
- Investment Advisers Act of 1940. . . .

SECURITIES EXCHANGE ACT OF 1934

By this act, Congress extended the "disclosure" doctrine of investor protection to securities listed and registered for public trading on our national securities exchanges. Thirty years later, the Securities Act Amendments of 1964 extended disclosure and reporting provisions to equity securities in the over-the-counter market. This included hundreds of companies with . . . shareholders numbering 500 or more. (Today, securities of thousands of companies are traded over the counter.) The act seeks to ensure fair and orderly securities markets by prohibiting certain types of activities and by setting forth rules regarding the operation of the markets and participants.

CORPORATE REPORTING

Companies seeking to have their securities registered and listed for public trading on an exchange must file a registration application with the exchange and the SEC. If they meet the size test described above, companies whose equity securities are traded over the counter must file a similar registration form. Commission rules prescribe the nature and content of these registration statements and require certified financial statements. These are generally comparable to, but less extensive than, the disclosures required in Securities Act registration statements. Following the registration of their securities, companies must file annual and other periodic reports to update information contained in the original filing. In addition, issuers must send certain reports to requesting shareholders. Reports may be read at the

Commission's public reference rooms, copied there at nominal cost, or obtained from a copying service under contract to the Commission.

PROXY SOLICITATIONS

Another provision of this law governs soliciting proxies (votes) from holders of registered securities, both listed and over-the-counter, for the election of directors and/or for approval of other corporate action. Solicitations, whether by management or minority groups, must disclose all material facts concerning matters on which holders are asked to vote. Holders also must be given an opportunity to vote "yes" or "no" on each matter. Where a contest for control of corporate management is involved, the rules require disclosure of the names and interests of all "participants" in the proxy contest. Thus, holders are enabled to vote intelligently on corporate actions requiring their approval. The Commission's rules require that proposed proxy material be filed in advance for examination by the Commission for compliance with the disclosure requirements. In addition, the rules permit shareholders to submit proposals for a vote at the annual meetings. . . .

REGISTRATION OF EXCHANGES AND OTHERS

As amended, the 1934 Act requires registration with the Commission of:

- "National securities exchanges" (those having a substantial securities trading volume);
- Brokers and dealers who conduct securities business in interstate commerce;
- Transfer agents;
- Clearing agencies;
- Municipal brokers and dealers; and
- Securities information processors.

To obtain registration, exchanges must show that they are organized to comply with the provisions of the statute as well as the rules and regulations of the Commission. The registering exchanges must also show that their rules contain just and adequate provisions to ensure fair dealing and to protect investors.

SECURITIES EXCHANGE ACT § 12(a), (b), (g)

(a) It shall be unlawful for any member, broker, or dealer to effect any transaction in any security (other than an exempted security) on a national securities exchange unless a registration is effective as to such security for such exchange in accordance with the provisions of this title and the rules and regulations thereunder. *must be registered*

(b) A security may be registered on a national securities exchange by the issuer filing an application with the exchange (and filing with the Commission such duplicate originals thereof as the Commission may require). . . .

(g)(1) Every issuer which is engaged in interstate commerce, or in a business affecting interstate commerce, or whose securities are traded by use of the mails or any means or instrumentality of interstate commerce shall . . .

(B) within one hundred and twenty days after the last day of its first fiscal year . . . on which the issuer has total assets exceeding $1,000,000 and a class of equity security . . . held of record by five hundred or more . . . persons,

register such security by filing with the commission a registration statement (and such copies thereof as the Commission may require) with respect to such security. . . .

SECURITIES EXCHANGE ACT RULE 12g-1

Rule 12g-1. An issuer shall be exempt from the requirement to register any class of equity securities pursuant to section 12(g)(1) if on the last day of its most recent fiscal year the issuer had total assets not exceeding $5,000,000. . . .

(b) AN OVERVIEW OF THE STOCK MARKETS

SELIGMAN, THE FUTURE OF THE NATIONAL MARKET SYSTEM

10 J.Corp.Law 79, 83–86, 95–97, 114–115 (1984).

The Securities Exchanges *

The hallmark of a securities exchange is centralization of trading on an exchange floor. Wherever trading may originate, the ultimate execution of an order usually will occur at a specialist's post on the floor of one of the securities exchanges.

Currently, there are ten securities exchanges registered with the SEC. To be traded on a registered securities exchange, the issuer of a security usually must comply with the exchange's listing requirements. Exchange listing requirements typically require a minimum number of publicly-held shares and a minimum amount of market and asset value. . . .

Regardless of where in the country an order originates, usually it will be communicated to a specialist in that security on an exchange floor. Twenty years ago, before the markets were automated, a "market order" or order to execute at the market price usually would have been routed to the specialist in the following way. A customer

---

* Caption numbers are omitted throughout. [Footnote by ed.]

would telephone a broker and ask the broker to buy or sell a given number of shares in a security traded on a particular exchange. The broker then would write out an order form and forward the order to be telephoned or wired to the trading room of the broker's firm, often located in New York City. The trading room would forward the order to a floor broker on the floor of the appropriate exchange. The floor broker then would carry the order to the specialist's post. If volume in the security was sufficiently active, the floor broker could execute the order by matching it against the reciprocal order of another floor broker standing in the "crowd" in front of the specialist's post or against a reciprocal order that had been left with the specialist by another floor broker. When an order was left with the specialist, the size and price of the order would be written in the specialist's "book." When buy and sell orders could not be matched, the specialist was obligated to function as a dealer, and buy or sell sufficient stock to ensure an orderly and continuous market.

Similarly, twenty years ago, a customer would have forwarded a "limit order" or order to execute a transaction at a designated price above or below the then current market in a nearly identical way. Again, the broker would route the order to the trading room which would forward it to a floor broker who would carry it to the specialist. The specialist then would have recorded the order in the "specialist's book." The orders in the book would be executed when the market price rose or fell to the price designated in the limit order.

Today there are several different methods by which market or limit orders can be executed. However, the theoretical justification for stock exchange trading has remained essentially the same as it was before the automation of the stock markets. By centralizing all buy and sell orders in a given security, investors theoretically should receive the best execution of their orders by a continuous matching of the highest-priced buy orders against the lowest-priced sell orders. In effect, this creates a continuous "auction" in the security. Thus, exchange markets sometimes are called "auction" markets. With a regular volume of orders flowing to a single place of execution, a central market should be "orderly," without wide or abrupt price swings; "continuous," with minimum price variations between successive transactions; "liquid," with the ability to process orders immediately and have "depth" or the capacity to handle temporary imbalances in supply and demand caused by substantial volume without becoming disorderly.

Exchange trading is dominated by the NYSE [New York Stock Exchange]. As of 1981, the NYSE was responsible for 80.68% of the share volume executed on the stock exchanges and 84.74% of the dollar volume of trading on all stock exchanges. Looked at another way, the value of stocks listed on the New York Stock Exchange equalled $1,143.8 billion; the value of securities listed on the American Stock Exchange or exclusively listed on other exchanges equalled only $94.4 billion. The 2,305 companies whose securities were listed on the NYSE as of September 30, 1982, include as Professor Poser accurately has written, "most of the largest industrial and commercial enterprises in the United States."

The second largest securities exchange is the American Stock Exchange (Amex). The Amex was responsible in 1981 for 9.32% of the share volume and 5.41% of the dollar volume of all securities exchanges. The dollar value of all securities listed on the Amex was approximately one-thirteenth of the value of all securities listed on the NYSE, or $89.4 billion for the Amex to $1,143.8 billion for the NYSE. . . . Trading on the Amex . . . tends to be in a class of securities discrete from those traded on the NYSE. As of September 30, 1982, there were 961 securities listed on the Amex. Listing requirements for the Amex are easier to satisfy than those of the NYSE. The NYSE currently requires a company to have 2,000 holders of 100 shares or more, 1 million publicly held shares, a minimum market value of $8–$16 million depending on market conditions and minimum net tangible assets of $16 million before its security will be listed. The Amex requires 1,200 shareholders, 400,000 publicly held shares, $3 million in market value and net tangible assets of $2 million. The Amex traditionally served as a kind of "minor league" to the NYSE's "major league." Frequently securities would remain listed on the Amex until the number of shareholders and shares and the size of the firm satisfied the NYSE's listing requirement. At that point, securities typically would delist from the Amex and list with the NYSE.

There are eight other exchanges, euphemistically known as the "regional exchanges." In total, the eight regional exchanges were responsible in 1981 for 10.00% of the share volume and 9.75% of the dollar volume of all securities exchanges. Virtually all of this trading occurred on five regional exchanges: the Boston Stock Exchange, the Cincinnati Stock Exchange, the Midwest Stock Exchange, the Pacific Stock Exchange, and the Philadelphia Stock Exchange. . . .

The Over-the-Counter Market

All securities not trading on a national securities exchange trade in an over-the-counter (OTC) market. Several distinct types of securities trading coexist within the OTC market, ranging from United States Treasury bonds and notes, to corporate bonds, to trading in stock. As distinguished from the securities exchanges, OTC trading is not centralized on a discrete number of exchange floors. Instead, OTC dealers may become market makers in a security by signifying an intent to deal in that security. This has made the OTC market highly competitive. A 1983 study of leading over-the-counter stocks found that each security averaged approximately eleven market makers. A few securities were traded by more than twenty market makers. . . .

To be an OTC dealer no seat need be purchased on an exchange. The OTC dealers in a quite literal sense, long were unified only by a "nationwide web of telephone and telegraph wires." Primarily to

prevent fraudulent practices in OTC trading, the SEC in 1938 successfully lobbied for enactment of the Maloney Act Amendments to the
1934 Securities Exchange Act. These amendments permitted the
creation of the National Association of Securities Dealers (NASD) in
1939 to be a disciplinarian comparable in the OTC market to the
securities exchanges. . . .

Before February 1971, quotations in over-the-counter stocks were
reported exclusively in daily "pink sheets" published by the National
Quotations Bureau, listing bid and ask prices of each dealer in each
stock for the previous trading day. To obtain up-to-the-minute competitive quotations, a stockbroker or dealer had to telephone one or
more dealers in an over-the-counter security; the time and difficulty
involved in telephoning over-the-counter dealers frequently discouraged brokers or dealers placing orders from engaging in rigorous
comparative shopping. Quotations for approximately 8,000–9,000
securities today are made through the pink sheets.

NASDAQ

Quotations for most over-the-counter equity trading today is
handled through the NASDAQ OTC quotation system. To be traded
in NASDAQ, a domestic security usually must be registered with the
SEC under the 1934 Securities Exchange Act. . . . In addition,
there must be at least two OTC market makers dealing in the security;
a minimum of 100,000 publicly held shares and a minimum capital
and surplus of $1 million. NASDAQ dramatically improved the
quality of the over-the-counter securities market. At the heart of the
NASDAQ system is the Central Processing Complex, located in
Trumbull, Connecticut. The complex consists of two UNIVAC
1100/82 computers. The computers are connected by high-speed
trunk lines, regional concentrator centers, and tens of thousands of
miles of leased telephone lines to desk top terminals located throughout the country. Each terminal consists of a specially designed
keyboard and a cathode-ray tube screen capable of instantaneous
display of data. NASDAQ provides three levels of service. In the
NASDAQ Level 1 service, brokers view the highest bid and lowest
ask quotations for each NASDAQ security which has a minimum of
two registered market makers entering quotations. In 1982, approximately 81,000 terminals provided Level 1 service. On Level 2,
brokers or dealers view a montage of current bid and ask prices of
each market maker for any available NASDAQ security. As distinguished from Level 1, Level 2 identifies market makers and always
includes size. However, most market makers only nominally comply
with the size requirement, listing quotations only on a 100 share bid–
100 share asked basis. Level 3 service allows NASDAQ market
makers instantaneously to insert new quotations into the system. As
with Level 2 service, Level 3 service essentially is used only by market
makers and broker-dealer firm trading rooms. In 1982, 1,700 NAS-
DAQ terminals were operating with Level 2 and 3 service.

NASDAQ Level 2 and 3 service revolutionized the OTC market. At the touch of a few buttons, a broker or dealer could instantly see the competitive quotations of all market makers in a given security. Newspapers could be supplied with volume data concerning each over-the-counter security for the first time. Investors could obtain current quotations. Most significantly, the simultaneous availability of rival market makers' quotations narrowed price spreads. Several economic studies corroborated this result. One calculated that between 1970 and 1972, the mean market spread for a sample of over-the-counter securities fell from 0.4871 to 0.4028. Spreads on 85% of NASDAQ securities further narrowed after the SEC persuaded NASDAQ, on July 7, 1980, to begin making available to newspapers the best-bid and best-offer prices of NASDAQ securities, rather than the "median" or "representative" quotations.

In part because of the NASDAQ competitive market maker system, a number of firms whose securities were traded over-the-counter did not seek an exchange listing at the earliest possible opportunity. As of September 1983, approximately 1,600 securities eligible for trading on the American Stock Exchange and approximately 600 eligible for listing on the New York Stock Exchange remained solely traded in the NASDAQ system. Between 1974 and 1979, NASDAQ share volume as a percentage of New York Stock Exchange volume grew from 34 to 45%. During the 1980–1983 period, NASD volume as a percent of NYSE volume increased from 59 to 74%. Indeed, daily NASDAQ volume exceeded that of the NYSE for the first time on May 27, 1983. In addition to the advantages of a competitive market maker system, the NASDAQ volume surge also was aided by a substantial increase in the number of newspapers carrying NASDAQ quotations and the lower cost of initiating NASDAQ rather than NYSE or Amex trading. . . .

Block Orders

One of the most profound changes to occur in securities market trading during the past two decades has been the dramatic growth in institutional trading volume. Between 1960 and 1980, the NYSE estimates that the percent of NYSE stock held by institutional investors increased from 17.2% to 35.4%. More significantly, institutions accounted for 72% of all public NYSE dollar volume by the fourth quarter of 1980; individuals accounted for only 28%.

Much institutional trading is effected through block transactions, arbitrarily defined by the SEC to involve 10,000 or more shares or a market value of $200,000 or more. Through 1965, block trades of 10,000 or more shares were relatively unusual on the NYSE. In 1965, only 3.1% of reported share volume involved block trades, with an average of only nine block trades made a day. In contrast, some 41% of all NYSE reported share volume involved block orders in 1982, with an average of 1,007 block trades each day.

Today block orders typically are executed through highly different methods than are used by individuals to buy or sell small orders.

A block trade usually is initiated when an institution decides to sell a large quantity of shares it holds in a specific firm. If the institution believes its order is too large to be executed on a securities exchange without unduly disrupting existing prices, it will contact one or more block trading firms such as Salomon Brothers, Goldman Sachs, Merrill Lynch or Morgan Stanley. The institution ultimately will trade through the block trading firm in one of two ways. The block trader may act as an agent and operate on a straight commission basis. Alternatively, the block trader may act as a dealer and make a "firm" bid to the institution to execute the entire block at a specific minimum price. When a firm bid is made, the institution typically also is assured that the market in that security will be "cleaned up." That is, no stock will be left to be sold after the block trade. The block trader is able to make this commitment by contacting other institutions or traders and by deciding itself to purchase shares from the block for its own account. If the block trader acts as an agent, it will undertake to sell the entire block, usually to other institutions.

Most of the work done by block houses occurs away from an exchange floor. Competition in block trading occurs among the block trading houses when they attempt to secure the contract to sell the block. Often institutions will seek competitive bids before entering a transaction. Institutions are highly effective in negotiating favorable rates. One recent SEC study reported that the per share commission on trades of 10,000 or more shares for institutions is 5.5¢ compared with a per share commission for individuals of 35.9¢ for trades of 200–999 shares.

After a block trade is assembled in a listed . . . security the trade usually will be brought to an exchange for execution. . . .

Because the block trading market is not centralized, institutions and block houses rely on telephone or electronic systems to communicate trading interest. . . .

(c) PERIODIC DISCLOSURE UNDER THE SECURITIES EXCHANGE ACT

SECURITIES EXCHANGE ACT § 13(a)

Sec. 13. (a) Every issuer of a security registered pursuant to section 12 of this title shall file with the Commission, in accordance with such rules and regulations as the Commission may prescribe as necessary or appropriate for the proper protection of investors and to insure fair dealing in the security—

(1) such information and documents (and such copies thereof) as the Commission shall require to keep reasonably current the information and documents required to be included in or

filed with an application or registration statement filed pursuant to section 12 . . .

(2) such annual reports (and such copies thereof), certified if required by the rules and regulations of the Commission by independent public accountants, and such quarterly reports (and such copies thereof), as the Commission may prescribe. . . .

———

SECURITIES EXCHANGE ACT RULES 13a–1, 13a–11, 13a–13

SECURITIES EXCHANGE ACT FORMS 8–K, 10–K, 10–Q

[See Statutory Supplement]

———

NOTE ON REPORTING BY REGISTERED CORPORATIONS

The Securities Exchange Act addresses the informational deficiencies in state law by imposing reporting requirements on corporations registered under section 12. Under section 13 of the Act, and the rules promulgated thereunder, such corporations must file a Form 10–K annually, a Form 10–Q quarterly, and a Form 8–K within 15 days after the occurrence of certain specified events. Form 10–K must include audited financial statements; management's discussion of the corporation's financial condition and results of operations; and disclosure concerning legal proceedings, developments in the corporation's business, executive compensation, conflict-of-interest transactions, and other specified issues. Form 10–Q must include quarterly financial data prepared in accordance with generally accepted accounting principles; a management report; and disclosure concerning legal proceedings, defaults on senior securities, and other specified issues. Among the matters that trigger an 8–K Report are a change in control of the corporation, the acquisition or disposition of a significant amount of assets, and a change of accountants.

A limitation on the usefulness of the reporting requirements under the Securities Exchange Act is that the required reporting is not both comprehensive and timely. The 8–K, which is the most timely form, need be filed in only very limited cases and may be filed as late as 15 days after the event. The 10–Q is also limited in its coverage, and much less timely. The 10–K is more comprehensive, but not timely at all. See Brown, Corporate Communications and the Federal Securities Laws, 53 Geo.Wash. L.Rev. 741 (1985).

———

(d) DISCLOSURE UNDER STOCK EXCHANGE RULES

NEW YORK STOCK EXCHANGE, LISTED COMPANY MANUAL
§§ 202.01, 202.03, 202.05, 202.06.

Disclosure and Reporting Material Information

202.01   **Internal Handling of Confidential Corporate Matters**

. . .

Negotiations leading to mergers and acquisitions, stock splits, the making of arrangements preparatory to an exchange or tender offer, changes in dividend rates or earnings, calls for redemption, and new contracts, products, or discoveries are the type of developments where the risk of untimely and inadvertent disclosure of corporate plans are most likely to occur. Frequently, these matters require extensive discussion and study by corporate officials before final decisions can be made. Accordingly, extreme care must be used in order to keep the information on a confidential basis.

Where it is possible to confine formal or informal discussions to a small group of the top management of the company or companies involved, and their individual confidential advisors where adequate security can be maintained, premature public announcement may properly be avoided. In this regard, the market action of a company's securities should be closely watched at a time when consideration is being given to important corporate matters. If unusual market activity should arise, the company should be prepared to make an immediate public announcement of the matter.

At some point it usually becomes necessary to involve other persons to conduct preliminary studies or assist in other preparations for contemplated transactions, e.g., business appraisals, tentative financing arrangements, attitude of large outside holders, availability of major blocks of stock, engineering studies and market analyses and surveys. Experience has shown that maintaining security at this point is virtually impossible. Accordingly, fairness requires that the company make an immediate public announcement as soon as disclosures relating to such important matters are made to outsiders.

The extent of the disclosures will depend upon the stage of discussions, studies, or negotiations. So far as possible, public statements should be definite as to price, ratio, timing and/or any other pertinent information necessary to permit a reasonable evaluation of the matter. As a minimum, they should include those disclosures made to outsiders. Where an initial announcement cannot be specific or complete, it will need to be supplemented from time to time as more definitive or different terms are discussed or determined. . . .

202.03 Dealing with Rumors or Unusual Market Activity

The market activity of a company's securities should be closely watched at a time when consideration is being given to significant corporate matters. If rumors or unusual market activity indicate that information on impending developments has leaked out, a frank and explicit announcement is clearly required. If rumors are in fact false or inaccurate, they should be promptly denied or clarified. A statement to the effect that the company knows of no corporate developments to account for the unusual market activity can have a salutary effect. It is obvious that if such a public statement is contemplated, management should be checked prior to any public comment so as to avoid any embarrassment or potential criticism. If rumors are correct or there are developments, an immediate candid statement to the public as to the state of negotiations or of development of corporate plans in the rumored area must be made directly and openly. Such statements are essential despite the business inconvenience which may be caused and even though the matter may not as yet have been presented to the company's Board of Directors for consideration. . . .

202.05 Timely Disclosure of Material News Developments

A listed company is expected to release quickly to the public any news or information which might reasonably be expected to materially affect the market for its securities. . . .

202.06 Procedure for Public Release of Information

(A) Immediate Release Policy

The normal method of publication of important corporate data is by means of a press release. This may be either by telephone or in written form. Any release of information that could reasonably be expected to have an impact on the market for a company's securities should be given to the wire services and the press *"For Immediate Release."* . . .

Annual and quarterly earnings, dividend announcements, mergers, acquisitions, tender offers, stock splits, major management changes, and any substantive items of unusual or non-recurrent nature are examples of news items that should be handled on an immediate release basis. News of major new products, contract awards, expansion plans, and discoveries very often fall into the same category. . . .

News which ought to be the subject of immediate publicity must be released by the fastest available means. The fastest available means may vary in individual cases and according to the time of day. Ordinarily, this requires a release to the public press by telephone, telegraph, or hand delivery, or some combination of such methods. Transmittal of such a release to the press solely by mail is not considered satisfactory. Similarly, release of such news exclusively to the local press outside of New York City would not be sufficient for adequate and prompt disclosure to the investing public.

To insure adequate coverage, releases requiring immediate publicity should be given to Dow Jones & Company, Inc., and to Reuters Economic Services.

Companies are also encouraged to promptly distribute their releases to Associated Press and United Press International as well as to newspapers in New York City and in cities where the company is headquartered or has plants or other major facilities. . . .

See also American Stock Exchange, AMEX Company Guide, §§ 401–405 (Disclosure Policies), 2 CCH, American Stock Exchange Guide ¶ 10,121–10,125.

(e) REPORTING UNDER STATE LAW

REV. MODEL BUS. CORP. ACT §§ 16.20, 16.21

[See Statutory Supplement]

CAL. CORP. CODE § 1501

[See Statutory Supplement]

N.Y. BUS. CORP. LAW § 624

[See Statutory Supplement]

NOTE ON REPORTING UNDER STATE LAW

The reporting requirements of the Securities Exchange Act apply to only a fraction of all publicly held corporations, because they are normally applicable only if a corporation is registered under section 12, that is, if it has at least 500 record holders of a class of equity securities and meets certain other conditions. However, a corporation may have well under 500 shareholders and yet may be publicly held in the sense that its shareholders are scattered and not directly involved in managing the corporation or in monitoring management. Accordingly, there is an obvious need to require corporations that have significant public ownership, but are not registered under section 12, to report to their shareholders information on financial results and material conflict-of-interest transactions. A few modern statutes have adequately addressed that need. Under the California statute, any corporation that has 100 or more record shareholders, and is neither registered under the Exchange Act nor exempted from such registration, must send its shareholders an annual report that includes a balance sheet, an income statement, and a statement of changes in financial position for the fiscal year. Cal.Corp. Code § 1501. The financial data must be prepared in conformity with generally accepted accounting principles. The annual report must describe transactions during the previous fiscal year, involving an amount in excess of $40,000, in which a director, officer, or more-than-ten-percent shareholder had a direct or indirect material interest, and any indemnification exceeding $10,000 paid during that fiscal year to any officer or director. Corporations with less than 100 record shareholders must send their shareholders an annual report that includes a balance sheet, an income statement, and a statement of financial change. The financial data must be prepared on a reasonable basis, and the accounting basis used in the preparation of the data must be disclosed. In these smaller corporations, mandatory dissemination of an annual report may be waived in the bylaws, but if it is, any shareholder is entitled to the relevant information on request. Moreover, five-percent shareholders in any size corporation are entitled, on request, to an interim statement covering the elapsed quarters of the current fiscal year.

The Revised Model Business Corporation Act also addresses the need for reporting to shareholders, although on a more limited basis. Section 16.20 provides that every corporation must furnish to its shareholders annual financial statements, including a balance sheet and an income statement. The statements must be prepared on the basis of generally accepted accounting principles if the corporation prepares its financial statements on that basis. Section 16.21 requires the reporting of indemnification payments.

The California and Model Act provisions demonstrate the practicability of requiring reporting in smaller publicly held corporations. Nevertheless, most statutes still do not address the issue adequately. Many statutes, such as N.J. Stat.Ann. § 14A:5–28, simply provide that a corporation must furnish "its balance sheet as at the end of the preceding fiscal year, and its profit and loss and surplus statements for such fiscal year" upon a shareholder's written request. Some statutes, like that of Delaware, don't require corporations to furnish financial statements to shareholders even on written request.

——————

SECTION 3. THE PROXY RULES (I):
AN INTRODUCTION

——————

NOTE ON TERMINOLOGY

This and the next two Sections concern the Proxy Rules, which are promulgated by the SEC. The following terms are important in considering these Rules:

Proxyholder. A person authorized to vote shares on a shareholder's behalf.

Proxy, or *form of proxy.* The instrument in which such an authorization is embodied. (The term "proxy" is also sometimes used to mean a proxyholder, but for purposes of clarity that usage will be avoided in the Notes in this Chapter.)

Proxy solicitation. The process by which shareholders are asked to give their proxies.

Proxy statement. The written statement sent to shareholders as a means of proxy solicitation.

Proxy materials. The proxy statement and form of proxy.

J. HEARD & H. SHERMAN
CONFLICTS OF INTEREST IN THE PROXY
VOTING SYSTEM
74–85 (1987).

Very few contested elections are run without the aid of professional proxy solicitors. Because of their experience and personal contacts in the investment community and at proxy departments of brokerage houses and banks, professional solicitors usually are able to generate a higher vote turnout than issuer companies can do by themselves. For this reason, both management and the dissident side usually engage their own solicitors during contested elections. Even for uncontested elections, companies that are worried about not reaching a quorum count employ the services of a solicitor to guarantee a high turnout. Companies also use solicitors when they expect significant opposition to uncontested management proposals, such as antitakeover charter amendments or defensive recapitalizations.

The leading proxy solicitation firms include Georgeson and Co., the Carter Organization, D.F. King and Co., Morrow and Co. and the Kissel–Blake Organization.

By virtue of their years of experience in the business, solicitors often know how a particular shareholder, or a particular type of shareholder, will vote on different issues. For this reason, firms trying to pass proposals that they fear will be met with strong opposition often engage solicitors to determine whether or not the proposal should even be included on the ballot. For example, Georgeson and Co. prepares a best case/worst case voting scenario for clients on various types of proposals. If the likely outcome seems to be a defeat for management, based on Georgeson's analysis, the issuer company will often decide to exclude the proposal from its ballot. John Wilcox, a principal at Georgeson, told IRRC that this explains why so few antitakeover proposals are defeated. According to Wilcox, most antitakeover proposals that are likely to be defeated, based on Georgeson's or another solicitor's analysis, are never put on a ballot in the first place.

When engaged by management or a dissident during a contested election, a solicitor's services are invaluable. The solicitor handles all the physical requirements of the proxy campaign. It identifies beneficial owners, mails the proxy material to recordholders, makes sure that beneficial owners have received proxy material from the recordholder bank or broker, rounds up late votes with phone calls or follow-up mailings, and tabulates the vote for management or the dissident.

The first of these functions, identifying beneficial owners, is among the most important services a solicitor can offer. As previously explained, registration in bank nominee name often enables a beneficial owner to hide its identity and security position from the issuer company. When votes come in to a solicitor from a bank client, the proxy is signed by the bank, and the owner is identified only by an account number assigned to the client by his bank. The owner's name does not appear on the proxy card. When such votes are cast against management or a dissident, the interested party has no way of knowing who is behind the shares being voted against him. But proxy solicitors have developed their own data bases over the years that match bank account numbers with the identity of their owners. This enables a solicitor to tell a client who is behind the bank votes being cast during the proxy campaign. When the proxy vote is going against the solicitor's client, this ability becomes very important, for it allows the solicitor or the solicitor's client to contact the shareowner and ask him to reconsider his vote.

During a proxy campaign, a solicitor keeps in close contact with the proxy clerks at brokerage firms and with appropriate bank officers to make sure that their client's proxy material is being forwarded to beneficial owners. A solicitor can therefore decide if a second mailing is necessary. Such contact also enables a solicitor to tell his client how the vote is progressing, since brokers and banks usually tally votes as they are received but wait until shortly before a meeting to submit their proxies. If a solicitor determines that the final voting results may go against its client, advance information gives the solicitor's client time to exert more pressure on important shareholders to influence their vote, to resolicit shareholders who may have voted against the client, or to redouble efforts to reach shareholders who have not responded.

When final proxies arrive, the solicitor checks them to make sure that they are valid proxies, that they have been signed correctly, that they represent the appropriate number of shares, and that they are not duplicate or replacement proxies. Once done, the solicitor usually also participates in the actual tabulation at the annual meeting. The solicitor's experience can save a company much time when counting the vote, since the solicitor knows which way of sorting and collating the proxies will be the most expedient. When proxy votes are challenged by the opposing side in a proxy contest, the solicitor's knowledge of the technical requirements of valid proxies can prove invaluable. . . .

———

SECURITIES EXCHANGE ACT § 14(a), (c)

SECURITIES EXCHANGE ACT RULES
14a–1—14a–6, 14c–2, 14c–3, SCHEDULE 14A,
SCHEDULE 14C

[See Statutory Supplement]

NOTE—AN OVERVIEW OF THE PROXY RULES

1. *Background.* Proxy voting is the dominant mode of share-holder decisionmaking in publicly held corporations. There are a number of reasons for this. Shareholders in such corporations are often geographically dispersed, so that a given shareholder may not live near the site of the meeting. Shareholders often have some principal business other than investing, so that a given shareholding may not represent a substantial proportion of a shareholder's total wealth. And whether a shareholder supports or opposes the matters scheduled for action at a meeting, he may not wish to speak on the issues. Physical attendance at a shareholders's meeting is normally an uneconomical use of a shareholder's time when he can vote by proxy.

A natural outgrowth of the preference for proxy voting is proxy solicitation—the process of systematically contacting shareholders and urging them to execute and return proxy forms that authorize named proxyholders to cast the shareholder's votes, either in a manner designated in the proxy form or according to the proxyholder's discretion.

Despite these developments, as of the 1930's state law hardly regulated proxy voting, except in the extreme case in which proxies had been fraudulently solicited. Abuses were notorious and wide-spread. Accordingly, Congress entered the field in 1934 through Section 14(a) of the Securities Exchange Act, which currently pro-vides:

> It shall be unlawful for any person, by the use of the mails or by any means or instrumentality of interstate commerce or of any facility of a national securities exchange or otherwise, in contravention of such rules and regulations as the Commission may prescribe as necessary or appropriate in the public interest or for the protection of investors, to solicit or to permit the use of his name to solicit any proxy or consent or authorization in respect of any security (other than an ex-empted security) registered pursuant to section 12 of this title.

In itself, Section 14(a) has no effect on private conduct: its only effect is to authorize the SEC to promulgate rules that will govern private conduct. Pursuant to Section 14(a), the SEC has promulgated a set of Proxy Rules that serve a variety of purposes.

2. *Coverage.* Rule 14a–2 provides that the Proxy Rules "apply to every solicitation of a proxy with respect to securities registered

pursuant to section 12 of the Act," with certain exceptions. One of these exceptions is "[a]ny solicitation made otherwise than on behalf of the registrant where the total number of persons solicited is not more than ten." [1] Under Rule 14a–2, therefore, a solicitation of even one person by management falls within the Proxy Rules. A solicitation of ten persons or less by nonmanagement does not fall within the Proxy Rules. A solicitation of eleven persons or more by nonmanagement falls within the Proxy Rules even if none of the persons solicited actually grants a proxy.

The definitions of "proxy" and "solicitation" are extremely broad. Under Rule 14a–1(d), the term "proxy" means "every proxy, consent, or authorization within the meaning of section 14a of the Act. The consent or authorization may take the form of failure to object or to dissent." Under Rule 14a–1(j), the term "solicitation" includes "(i) [a]ny request for a proxy . . .; (ii) [a]ny request to execute or not to execute, or to revoke, a proxy; or (iii) [t]he furnishing of a form of proxy or other communication to security holders under circumstances reasonably calculated to result in the procurement, withholding, or revocation of a proxy." In Studebaker Corp. v. Gittlin, 360 F.2d 692 (2d Cir.1966), Gitlin, a shareholder in Studebaker, had solicited authorizations from other Studebaker shareholders to inspect Studebaker's shareholders list, for the purpose of meeting the five percent test in the relevant New York inspection statute. Judge Friendly said:

> . . . The assistant general counsel of the SEC . . . stated at the argument that the Commission believes § 14(a) should be construed, in all its literal breadth, to include authorizations to inspect stockholders lists, even in cases where obtaining the authorizations was not a step in a planned solicitation of proxies.

> We need not go that far to uphold the order of the district court. In SEC v. Okin, 132 F.2d 784 (2d Cir.1943), this court ruled that a letter which did not request the giving of any authorization was subject to the Proxy Rules if it was part of "a continuous plan" intended to end in solicitation and to prepare the way for success. This was the avowed purpose of Gittlin's demand for inspection of the stockholders list. . . .

Id. at 695–96.[2]

1. The exception does not exempt such a solicitation from Rule 14a–9, an antifraud rule.

2. Compare American Home Investments Co. v. Bedel, 525 F.2d 1022 (8th Cir. 1975).

In June 1963, Chicago & North Western Railway made a tender offer to buy control of the Rock Island railway. Shortly thereafter, the directors of Rock Island executed a plan of merger with another railroad, Union Pacific. The proposed merger required shareholder approval. On July 25, prior to the start of formal solicitation for approval for the merger, Union Pacific placed an advertisement in about 45 newspapers, addressed to Rock Island shareholders and other interested groups, which presented reasons why the North Western tender offer should be rejected by the Rock Island shareholders and why those shareholders should vote to approve the merger with Union Pacific. In October, after the formal solicitation had begun, Hayden,

3. *Remedies.*   Under Section 21 of the Securities Exchange Act, the SEC can seek an injunction against threatened or actual violations of the Act or the rules thereunder.   Under Section 32, any person who willfully violates any provisions of the Act or the rules thereunder is subject to a fine of up to $10,000 and imprisonment for up to five years.   The Proxy Rules can also be enforced by private actions. See Section 4, infra.

4. *Transactional disclosure.*   One purpose of the Proxy Rules is to require full disclosure in connection with transactions that shareholders are being asked to approve, such as mergers, certificate amendments, or election of directors.   This purpose is accomplished in the first instance by Rule 14a–3 and Schedule 14A.   Rule 14a–3 provides that no solicitation of proxies that is subject to the Proxy Rules shall be made unless the person being solicited "is concurrently furnished or has previously been furnished with a written proxy statement containing the information specified in Schedule 14A."   Schedule 14A, in turn, lists in detail the information that must be furnished when specified types of transactions are to be acted upon by the shareholders.   Rule 14a–3 and Schedule 14A are backed up by Rule 14a–9 and Rule 14a–6.   Rule 14a–9 provides that no solicitation subject to the Proxy Rules shall contain any statement that is false or misleading with respect to any material fact or omits a material fact. Rule 14a–6 requires the prior filing of preliminary copies of the proxy materials with the SEC.   Characteristically, the SEC's staff comments on these materials and the corporation then negotiates with the staff concerning changes, before the definitive proxy materials are issued. In theory, the corporation could ignore staff comments.   In practice, it is highly unlikely to do so.   For one thing, the SEC might seek to enjoin the solicitation on the ground that it violated the Proxy Rules. For another, the corporation has to deal with the staff on an ongoing basis, and therefore has an incentive to keep its relations with the staff nonadversarial.

5. *Periodic disclosure.*   The Proxy Rules also require certain forms of annual disclosure.   Much of this disclosure is only very loosely related to any specific action the shareholders are asked to vote upon. For example, Rule 14a–3 provides that the proxy statement for an annual meeting at which directors are to be elected must be accompanied by an annual report that includes audited balance sheets for each of the corporation's two most recent fiscal years, audited income

Stone & Co., Inc., a large New York brokerage firm, released and distributed 7,500 copies of a four-page letter, entitled "Progress Report," which was cast in the form of advice to Rock Island shareholders and concluded that the North Western offer was "far more attractive than . . . the Union Pacific offer."   The Report had not been preliminarily filed with the SEC under Rule 14a–6.   In Brown v. Chicago, Rock Island & Pacific Railroad Co., 328 F.2d 122 (7th Cir.1964), the court concluded that Union Pacific's advertisement did not fall under the Proxy Rules, because Union Pacific's purpose was to inform and motivate the public, not to solicit proxies.   In Union Pacific Railroad Co. v. Chicago and North Western Railway Co., 226 F.Supp. 400 (N.D.Ill.1964), the court concluded that Hayden, Stone's Progress Report did fall under the Proxy Rules, because it was "reasonably calculated to result in the procurement, withholding, or revocation of a proxy," and therefore constituted unlawful solicitation.

statements for its three most recent fiscal years, and certain other information. Under Items 7 and 8 of Schedule 14A, the proxy statement for an annual meeting at which directors are being elected must disclose the compensation of the five most highly paid executives and the executive officers as a group (including not only salary, but bonuses, deferred compensation, stock options, and the like), and significant conflict-of-interest transactions during the corporation's last fiscal year involving, among others, directors, executive officers, and five percent beneficial owners. Under Item 7, the proxy statement for such a meeting must also disclose whether the corporation has audit, nominating, and compensation committees, and if so, the number of meetings each committee held during the last fiscal year and the functions it performs. And under Section 14(c), Regulation 14C, and Schedule 14C, a corporation that is registered under Section 12 must distribute, in connection with an annual meeting at which directors are to be elected, an annual report and certain other information (such as information relating to conflict-of-interest transactions and compensation), even if the corporation is *not* soliciting proxies.

6. *Proxy contests.* Proxy Rule 14a–11 regulates proxy contests, in which insurgents try to oust incumbent directors. Basically, Rule 14a–11 is an adaptation of the salient concepts of other Proxy Rules to the special circumstances of a proxy fight. Its main bite is to require the filing of certain information by insurgents.

7. *Access to the body of shareholders.* Two Proxy Rules, 14a–7 and 14a–8, provide mechanisms through which the stockholders can communicate with each other. See Section 5, infra.

8. *Mechanics of proxy voting.* Still another purpose of the Proxy Rules is to regulate the mechanics of proxy voting itself. This is done, somewhat indirectly, through Rule 14a–4, which governs the form of proxy. See the Statutory Supplement.

SAMPLE FORM OF PROXY

UB UNIVERSAL BUSINESS CORPORATION   **Proxy**

270 Universal Center, Horizon, California 91770

This Proxy is Solicited on Behalf of the Board of Directors.

The undersigned hereby appoints John Red, Mary Blue, and Lee White as Proxies, each with the power to appoint his or her substitute, and hereby authorizes them to represent and to vote, as designated below, all the shares of common stock of Universal Business held on record by the undersigned on October 23, 1980, at the annual meeting of shareholders to be held on December 20, 1980 or any adjournment thereof.

1. ELECTION OF DIRECTORS

FOR all nominees listed below *(except as marked to the contrary below)* ☐

WITHHOLD AUTHORITY to vote for all nominees listed below ☐

(INSTRUCTION below)   To withhold authority to vote for any individual nominee strike a line through the nominees's name in the list

J. Allen, S. Brown, J. Doe, J. Green, G. Johansen, A. Jones, M. Roe, J. Smith and M. Stanton

2. PROPOSAL TO APPROVE THE APPOINTMENT OF DOLLAR AND CENTS as the independent public accountants of the corporation

☐ FOR   ☐ AGAINST   ☐ ABSTAIN

3. STOCKHOLDER PROPOSAL RELATING TO FORM AND CONTENT OF POST-MEETING REPORTS:

☐ FOR   ☐ AGAINST   ☐ ABSTAIN

[C6891]

4. In their discretion the Proxies are authorized to vote upon such other business as may properly come before the meeting.

This proxy when properly executed will be voted in the manner directed herein by the undersigned stockholder. If no direction is made, this proxy will be voted for Proposals 1, 2, and 3.

Please sign exactly as name appears below.   When shares are held by joint tenants, both should sign.   When signing as attorney, as executor, administrator, trustee or guardian, please give full title as such. If a corporation, please sign in full corporate name by President or other authorized officer. If a partnership please sign in partnership name by authorized person.

SAMPLE CARD A

DATED _____ 1980

PLEASE MARK SIGN DATE AND RETURN THE PROXY CARD PROMPTLY USING THE ENCLOSED ENVELOPE

Signature _____

Signature if held jointly _____

[C6892]

SECTION 4. THE PROXY RULES (II): PRIVATE ACTIONS UNDER THE PROXY RULES

SECURITIES EXCHANGE ACT RULE 14a–9

[See Statutory Supplement]

NOTE ON J.I. CASE CO. v. BORAK

In J.I. Case Co. v. Borak, 377 U.S. 426, 84 S.Ct. 1555, 12 L.Ed. 2d 423 (1964), the Supreme Court held that a shareholder could bring either a direct or a derivative action for violation of the Proxy Rules, although neither the 1934 Act nor the Proxy Rules themselves explicitly provide for such an action.

The injury which a stockholder suffers from corporate action pursuant to a deceptive proxy solicitation ordinarily flows from the damage done the corporation, rather than from the damage inflicted directly upon the stockholder. The damage suffered results not from the deceit practiced on him alone but rather from the deceit practiced on the stockholders as a group. To hold that derivative actions are not within the sweep of the section would therefore be tantamount to a denial of private relief. Private enforcement of the proxy rules provides a necessary supplement to Commission action. As in antitrust treble damage litigation, the possibility of civil damages or injunctive relief serves as a most effective weapon in the enforcement of the proxy requirements. The Commission advises that it examines over 2,000 proxy statements annually and each of them must necessarily be expedited. Time does not permit an independent examination of the facts set out in the proxy material and this results in the Commission's acceptance of the representations contained therein at their face value, unless contrary to other material on file with it. Indeed, on the allegations of respondent's complaint, the proxy material failed to disclose alleged unlawful market manipulation of the stock of ATC, and this unlawful manipulation would not have been apparent to the Commission until after the merger.

We, therefore, believe that under the circumstances here it is the duty of the courts to be alert to provide such remedies as are necessary to make effective the congressional purpose.

Id. at 432–33.

MILLS v. ELECTRIC AUTO–LITE CO.

Supreme Court of the United States, 1970.
396 U.S. 375, 90 S.Ct. 616, 24 L.Ed.2d 593.

Mr. Justice HARLAN delivered the opinion of the Court.

This case requires us to consider a basic aspect of the implied private right of action for violation of § 14(a) of the Securities Exchange Act of 1934,[1] recognized by this Court in *J.I. Case Co. v. Borak*, 377 U.S. 426 (1964). As in *Borak* the asserted wrong is that a corporate merger was accomplished through the use of a proxy statement that was materially false or misleading. The question with which we deal is what causal relationship must be shown between such a statement and the merger to establish a cause of action based on the violation of the Act.

I

Petitioners were shareholders of the Electric Auto–Lite Company until 1963, when it was merged into Mergenthaler Linotype Company. They brought suit on the day before the shareholders' meeting at which the vote was to take place on the merger, against Auto–Lite, Mergenthaler, and a third company, American Manufacturing Company, Inc. The complaint sought an injunction against the voting by Auto–Lite's management of all proxies obtained by means of an allegedly misleading proxy solicitation; however, it did not seek a temporary restraining order, and the voting went ahead as scheduled the following day. Several months later petitioners filed an amended complaint, seeking to have the merger set aside and to obtain such other relief as might be proper.

In Count II of the amended complaint, which is the only count before us,[2] petitioners predicated jurisdiction on § 27 of the 1934 Act, 15 U.S.C. § 78aa. They alleged that the proxy statement sent

1. 48 Stat. 895, as amended, 15 U.S.C. § 78n(a).

2. In the other two counts, petitioners alleged common-law fraud and that the merger was *ultra vires* under Ohio law.

out by the Auto–Lite management to solicit shareholders' votes in favor of the merger was misleading, in violation of § 14(a) of the Act and SEC Rule 14a–9 thereunder. (17 CFR § 240.14a–9.) Petitioners recited that before the merger Mergenthaler owned over 50% of the outstanding shares of Auto–Lite common stock, and had been in control of Auto–Lite for two years. American Manufacturing in turn owned about one-third of the outstanding shares of Mergenthaler, and for two years had been in voting control of Mergenthaler and, through it, of Auto–Lite. Petitioners charged that in light of these circumstances the proxy statement was misleading in that it told Auto–Lite shareholders that their board of directors recommended approval of the merger without also informing them that all 11 of Auto–Lite's directors were nominees of Mergenthaler and were under the "control and domination of Mergenthaler." Petitioners asserted the right to complain of this alleged violation both derivatively on behalf of Auto–Lite and as representatives of the class of all its minority shareholders.

On petitioners' motion for summary judgment with respect to Count II, the District Court for the Northern District of Illinois ruled as a matter of law that the claimed defect in the proxy statement was, in light of the circumstances in which the statement was made, a material omission. The District Court concluded, from its reading of the *Borak* opinion, that it had to hold a hearing on the issue whether there was "a causal connection between the finding that there has been a violation of the disclosure requirements of § 14(a) and the alleged injury to the plaintiffs" before it could consider what remedies would be appropriate. (Unreported opinion dated February 14, 1966.)

After holding such a hearing, the court found that under the terms of the merger agreement, an affirmative vote of two-thirds of the Auto–Lite shares was required for approval of the merger, and that the respondent companies owned and controlled about 54% of the outstanding shares. Therefore, to obtain authorization of the merger, respondents had to secure the approval of a substantial number of the minority shareholders. At the stockholders' meeting, approximately 950,000 shares, out of 1,160,000 shares outstanding, were voted in favor of the merger. This included 317,000 votes obtained by proxy from the minority shareholders, votes that were "necessary and indispensable to the approval of the merger." The District Court concluded that a causal relationship had thus been shown, and it granted an interlocutory judgment in favor of petitioners on the issue of liability, referring the case to a master for consideration of appropriate relief. (Unreported findings and conclusions dated Sept. 26, 1967; opinion reported at 281 F.Supp. 826 (1967)).

The District Court made the certification required by 28 U.S.C. § 1292(b), and respondents took an interlocutory appeal to the Court of Appeals for the Seventh Circuit. That court affirmed the District Court's conclusion that the proxy statement was materially deficient, but reversed on the question of causation. The court acknowledged that, if an injunction had been sought a sufficient time before the stockholders' meeting, "corrective measures would have been appropriate." 403 F.2d 428, 435 (1968). However, since this suit was brought too late for preventive action, the courts had to determine whether the misleading statement and omission caused the submission of sufficient proxies," as a prerequisite to a determination of liability under the Act. If the respondents could show, "by a preponderance of probabilities, that the merger would have received a sufficient vote even if the proxy statement had not been misleading in the respect found," petitioners would be entitled to no relief of any kind. *Id.,* at 436.

 Causation

The Court of Appeals acknowledged that this test corresponds to the common-law fraud test of whether the injured party relied on the misrepresentation. However, rightly concluding that "[r]eliance by thousands of individuals, as here, can scarcely be inquired into" (*id.,* at 436 n. 10), the court ruled that the issue was to be determined by proof of the fairness of the terms of the merger. If respondents could show that the merger had merit and was fair to the minority shareholders, the trial court would be justified in concluding that a sufficient number of shareholders would have approved the merger had there been no deficiency in the proxy statement. In that case respondents would be entitled to a judgment in their favor.

Claiming that the Court of Appeals has construed this Court's decision in *Borak* in a manner that frustrates the statute's policy of enforcement through private litigation, the petitioners then sought review in this Court. We granted certiorari, 394 U.S. 971 (1969), believing that resolution of this basic issue should be made at this stage of the litigation and not postponed until after a trial under the Court of Appeals' decision.[4]

II

As we stressed in *Borak,* § 14(a) stemmed from a congressional belief that "[f]air corporate suffrage is an important right that should attach to every equity security bought on a public exchange." H.R. Rep. No. 1383, 73d Cong., 2d Sess., 13. The provision was intended to promote "the free exercise of the voting rights of stockholders" by ensuring that proxies would be solicited with "explanation to the stockholder of the real nature of the questions for which authority to cast his vote is sought." *Id.,* at 14; S.Rep. No. 792, 73d Cong., 2d Sess., 12; see 377 U.S., at 431. The decision below, by permitting all liability to be foreclosed on the basis of a finding that the merger

---

4. Respondents ask this Court to review the conclusion of the lower courts that the proxy statement was misleading in a material respect. Petitioners naturally did not raise this question in their petition for certiorari, and respondents filed no cross-petition. Since reversal of the Court of Appeals' ruling on this question would not dictate affirmance of that court's judgment, which remanded the case for proceedings to determine causation, but rather elimination of petitioners' rights thereunder, we will not consider the question in these circumstances. *United States v. American Ry. Exp. Co.,* 265 U.S. 425, 435 (1924); *Langnes v. Green,* 282 U.S. 531, 535–539 (1931); *Morley Constr. Co. v. Maryland Cas. Co.,* 300 U.S. 185, 191–192 (1937); R. Stern & E. Gressman, Supreme Court Practice 314, 315 (4th ed. 1969).

was fair, would allow the stockholders to be bypassed, at least where the only legal challenge to the merger is a suit for retrospective relief after the meeting has been held. A judicial appraisal of the merger's merits could be substituted for the actual and informed vote of the stockholders.

The result would be to insulate from private redress an entire category of proxy violations—those relating to matters other than the terms of the merger. Even outrageous misrepresentations in a proxy solicitation, if they did not relate to the terms of the transaction, would give rise to no cause of action under § 14(a). Particularly if carried over to enforcement actions by the Securities and Exchange Commission itself, such a result would subvert the congressional purpose of ensuring full and fair disclosure to shareholders.

Further, recognition of the fairness of the merger as a complete defense would confront small shareholders with an additional obstacle to making a successful challenge to a proposal recommended through a defective proxy statement. The risk that they would be unable to rebut the corporation's evidence of the fairness of the proposal, and thus to establish their cause of action, would be bound to discourage such shareholders from the private enforcement of the proxy rules that "provides a necessary supplement to Commission action." *J.I. Case Co. v. Borak,* 377 U.S., at 432.[5]

Such a frustration of the congressional policy is not required by anything in the wording of the statute or in our opinion in the *Borak* case. Section 14(a) declares it "unlawful" to solicit proxies in contravention of Commission rules, and SEC Rule 14a–9 prohibits solicitations "containing any statement which . . . is false or misleading with respect to any material fact, or which omits to state any material fact necessary in order to make the statements therein not false or misleading. . . ." Use of a solicitation that is materially misleading is itself a violation of law, as the Court of Appeals recognized in stating that injunctive relief would be available to remedy such a defect if sought prior to the stockholders' meeting. In *Borak,* which came to this Court on a dismissal of the complaint, the Court limited its inquiry to whether a violation of § 14(a) gives rise to "a federal

---

5. The Court of Appeals' ruling that "causation" may be negated by proof of the fairness of the merger also rests on a dubious behavioral assumption. There is no justification for presuming that the shareholders of every corporation are willing to accept any and every fair merger offer put before them; yet such a presumption is implicit in the opinion of the Court of Appeals. That court gave no indication of what evidence petitioners might adduce, once respondents had established that the merger proposal was equitable, in order to show that the shareholders would nevertheless have rejected it if the solicitation had not been misleading. Proof of actual reliance by thousands of individuals would, as the court acknowledged, not be feasible,

see R. Jennings & H. Marsh, Securities Regulation, Cases and Materials 1001 (2d ed. 1968); and reliance on the *nondisclosure* of a fact is a particularly difficult matter to define or prove, see 3 L. Loss, Securities Regulation 1766 (2d ed. 1961). In practice, therefore, the objective fairness of the proposal would seemingly be determinative of liability. But, in view of the many other factors that might lead shareholders to prefer their current position to that of owners of a larger, combined enterprise, it is pure conjecture to assume that the fairness of the proposal will always be determinative of their vote. Cf. *Wirtz v. Hotel, Motel & Club Employees Union,* 391 U.S. 492, 508 (1968).

cause of action for rescission or damages," 377 U.S., at 428. Referring to the argument made by petitioners there "that the merger can be dissolved only if it was fraudulent or non-beneficial, issues upon which the proxy material would not bear," the Court stated: "But the causal relationship of the proxy material and the merger are questions of fact to be resolved at trial, not here. We therefore do not discuss this point further." *Id.,* at 431. In the present case there has been a hearing specifically directed to the causation problem. The question before the Court is whether the facts found on the basis of that hearing are sufficient in law to establish petitioners' cause of action, and we conclude that they are.

Where the misstatement or omission in a proxy statement has been shown to be "material," as it was found to be here, that determination itself indubitably embodies a conclusion that the defect was of such a character that it might have been considered important by a reasonable shareholder who was in the process of deciding how to vote.[6] This requirement that the defect have a significant *propensity* to affect the voting process is found in the express terms of Rule 14a–9, and it adequately serves the purpose of ensuring that a cause of action cannot be established by proof of a defect so trivial, or so unrelated to the transaction for which approval is sought, that correction of the defect or imposition of liability would not further the interests protected by § 14(a).

There is no need to supplement this requirement, as did the Court of Appeals, with a requirement of proof of whether the defect actually had a decisive effect on the voting. Where there has been a finding of materiality, a shareholder has made a sufficient showing of causal relationship between the violation and the injury for which he seeks redress if, as here, he proves that the proxy solicitation itself, rather than the particular defect in the solicitation materials, was an essential link in the accomplishment of the transaction. This objective test will avoid the impracticalities of determining how many votes were affected, and, by resolving doubts in favor of those the statute is designed to protect, will effectuate the congressional policy of ensuring that the shareholders are able to make an informed choice when they are consulted on corporate transactions. Cf. *Union Pac. R. Co. v. Chicago & N.W.R. Co.,* 226 F.Supp. 400, 411 (D.C.N.D.Ill.1964); 2 L. Loss, Securities Regulation 962 n. 411 (2d ed. 1961); 5 *id.,* at 2929–2930 (Supp.1969).[7]

---

6. . . . . In this case, where the misleading aspect of the solicitation involved failure to reveal a serious conflict of interest on the part of the directors, the Court of Appeals concluded that the crucial question in determining materiality was "whether the minority shareholders were sufficiently alerted to the board's relationship to their adversary to be on their guard." 403 F.2d at 434. An adequate disclosure of this relationship would have warned the stockholders to give more careful scrutiny to the terms of the merger than they might to one recommended by an entirely disinterested board. Thus, the failure to make such a disclosure was found to be a material defect "as a matter of law," thwarting the informed decision at which the statute aims, regardless of whether the terms of the merger were such that a reasonable stockholder would have approved the transaction after more careful analysis. See also *Swanson v. American Consumer Industries, Inc.,* 415 F.2d 1326 (C.A.7th Cir.1969).

7. We need not decide in this case whether causation could be shown where

III

Our conclusion that petitioners have established their case by showing that proxies necessary to approval of the merger were obtained by means of a materially misleading solicitation implies nothing about the form of relief to which they may be entitled. We held in *Borak* that upon finding a violation the courts were "to be alert to provide such remedies as are necessary to make effective the congressional purpose," noting specifically that such remedies are not to be limited to prospective relief. 377 U.S., at 433, 434. In devising retrospective relief for violation of the proxy rules, the federal courts should consider the same factors that would govern the relief granted for any similar illegality or fraud. One important factor may be the fairness of the terms of the merger. Possible forms of relief will include setting aside the merger or granting other equitable relief, but, as the Court of Appeals below noted, nothing in the statutory policy "requires the court to unscramble a corporate transaction merely because a violation occurred." 403 F.2d at 436. In selecting a remedy the lower courts should exercise " 'the sound discretion which guides the determinations of courts of equity,' " keeping in mind the role of equity as "the instrument for nice adjustment and reconciliation between the public interest and private needs as well as between competing private claims." *Hecht Co. v. Bowles*, 321 U.S. 321, 329–330 (1944), quoting from *Meredith v. Winter Haven*, 320 U.S. 228, 235 (1943).

We do not read § 29(b) of the Act,[8] which declares contracts made in violation of the Act or a rule thereunder "void . . . as regards the rights of" the violator and knowing successors in interest, as requiring that the merger be set aside simply because the merger agreement is a "void" contract. This language establishes that the guilty party is precluded from enforcing the contract against an unwilling innocent party, but it does not compel the conclusion that the contract is a nullity, creating no enforceable rights even in a party

---

the management controls a sufficient number of shares to approve the transaction without any votes from the minority. Even in that situation, if the management finds it necessary for legal or practical reasons to solicit proxies from minority shareholders, at least one court has held that the proxy solicitation might be sufficiently related to the merger to satisfy the causation requirement, see *Laurenzano v. Einbender*, 264 F.Supp. 356 (D.C.E.D.N.Y. 1966); cf. *Swanson v. American Consumer Industries, Inc.*, 415 F.2d 1326, 1331–1332 (C.A.7th Cir.1969); *Eagle v. Horvath*, 241 F.Supp. 341, 344 (D.C.S.D.N.Y.1965); *Globus, Inc. v. Jaroff*, 271 F.Supp. 378, 381 (D.C.S.D.N.Y.1967); Comment, Shareholders' Derivative Suit to Enforce a Corporate Right of Action Against Directors Under SEC Rule 10b–5, 114 U.Pa.L.Rev. 578, 582 (1966). But see *Hoover v. Allen*, 241 F.Supp. 213, 231–232 (D.C.S.D.N.Y.1965);

Barnett v. Anaconda Co., 238 F.Supp. 766, 770–774 (D.C.S.D.N.Y.1965); *Robbins v. Banner Industries, Inc.*, 285 F.Supp. 758, 762–763 (D.C.S.D.N.Y.1966). See generally 5 L. Loss, Securities Regulation 2933–2938 (Supp.1969).

8. Section 29(b) provides in pertinent part: "Every contract made in violation of any provision of this chapter or of any rule or regulation thereunder . . . shall be void (1) as regards the rights of any person who, in violation of any such provision, rule, or regulation, shall have made . . . any such contract, and (2) as regards the rights of any person who, not being a party to such contract, shall have acquired any right thereunder with actual knowledge of the facts by reason of which the making . . . of such contract was in violation of any such provision, rule, or regulation. . . ." 15 U.S.C. § 78cc(b).

innocent of the violation. The lower federal courts have read § 29(b), which has counterparts in the Holding Company Act, the Investment Company Act, and the Investment Advisers Act, as rendering the contract merely voidable at the option of the innocent party. . . . This interpretation is eminently sensible. The interests of the victim are sufficiently protected by giving him the right to rescind; to regard the contract as void where he has not invoked that right would only create the possibility of hardships to him or others without necessarily advancing the statutory policy of disclosure.

The United States, as *amicus curiae,* points out that as representatives of the minority shareholders, petitioners are not parties to the merger agreement and thus do not enjoy a statutory right under § 29(b) to set it aside.[11] Furthermore, while they do have a derivative right to invoke Auto–Lite's status as a party to the agreement, a determination of what relief should be granted in Auto–Lite's name must hinge on whether setting aside the merger would be in the best interests of the shareholders as a whole. In short, in the context of a suit such as this one, § 29(b) leaves the matter of relief where it would be under *Borak* without specific statutory language—the merger should be set aside only if a court of equity concludes, from all the circumstances, that it would be equitable to do so. Cf. *SEC v. National Securities, Inc.,* 393 U.S. 453, 456, 463–464 (1969).

Monetary relief will, of course, also be a possibility. Where the defect in the proxy solicitation relates to the specific terms of the merger, the district court might appropriately order an accounting to ensure that the shareholders receive the value that was represented as coming to them. On the other hand, where, as here, the misleading aspect of the solicitation did not relate to terms of the merger, monetary relief might be afforded to the shareholders only if the merger resulted in a reduction of the earnings or earnings potential of their holdings. In short, damages should be recoverable only to the extent that they can be shown. If commingling of the assets and operations of the merged companies makes it impossible to establish direct injury from the merger, relief might be predicated on a determination of the fairness of the terms of the merger at the time it was approved. These questions, of course, are for decision in the first instance by the District Court on remand, and our singling out of some of the possibilities is not intended to exclude others. . . .

For the foregoing reasons we conclude that the judgment of the Court of Appeals should be vacated and the case remanded to that court for further proceedings consistent with this opinion.

It is so ordered.

---

11. If petitioners had submitted their own proxies in favor of the merger in response to the unlawful solicitation, as it does not appear they did, the language of § 29(b) would seem to give them, as innocent parties to that transaction, a right to rescind their proxies. But it is clear in this case, where petitioners' combined holdings are only 600 shares, that such rescission would not affect the authorization of the merger.

[The opinion of Justice Black, concurring in part and dissenting in part, is omitted.]

NOTE ON FURTHER PROCEEDING IN MILLS v. ELECTRIC AUTO–LITE

On remand, the District Court held the exchange to be unfair and awarded damages of $1,233,918.35, as well as approximately $740,000 in pre-judgment interest. The Seventh Circuit reversed, concluding that the merger terms were fair and the plaintiff was therefore not entitled to damages. 552 F.2d 1239 (7th Cir.), cert. denied, 434 U.S. 922, 98 S.Ct. 398, 54 L.Ed.2d 279 (1977).

NOTE ON CAUSATION AND STANDING IN PRIVATE ACTIONS UNDER THE PROXY RULES

Suppose that a corporation issues a false or misleading proxy statement, but a majority of the stock is held by a controlling shareholder who is responsible, directly or through his agents, for the misstatements or omissions, and therefore is not deceived. Should a minority shareholder lack standing to bring an action under Rule 14a–9, on the theory that the wrong caused no loss to the minority because the majority shareholder would have effected the transaction even if the proxy statement had made full disclosure and all the other shareholders had voted against the transaction? The Supreme Court explicitly left this issue open in footnote 7 of Mills v. Electric Auto–Lite Co., supra. Some early district court decisions held that suit was barred, see, e.g., Barnett v. Anaconda Co., 238 F.Supp. 766 (S.D. N.Y.1965), but the trend of the decisions is now clearly in favor of letting such an action proceed. See, e.g. Schlick v. Penn–Dixie Cement Corp., 507 F.2d 374, 382–84 (2d Cir.1974), cert. denied 421 U.S. 976, 95 S.Ct. 1976, 44 L.Ed.2d 467 (1975).

NOTE ON THE STANDARD OF FAULT IN PRIVATE ACTIONS UNDER THE PROXY RULES

Under *Borak* and *Mills,* shareholders have standing to bring an action under Rule 14a–9, which prohibits false or misleading proxy statements. Does a plaintiff-shareholder prevail if he shows that a proxy statement was false or misleading by virtue of a material misstatement or omission, or must he also show that the misstatement or omission resulted from the defendant's fault? If the plaintiff must show fault, does negligence suffice?

In the leading case of Gerstle v. Gamble–Skogmo, Inc., 478 F.2d 1281 (2d Cir.1973), where the proxy statement was issued in connection with a proposed merger, the Second Circuit, in an opinion written by Judge Friendly, held that negligence sufficed to establish liability under Rule 14a–9.   478 F.2d at 1298–1301.   Accord: Gould v. American–Hawaiian Steamship Co., 535 F.2d 761 (3d Cir.1976).   In Adams v. Standard Knitting Mills, Inc., 623 F.2d 422 (6th Cir.), cert. denied 449 U.S. 1067, 101 S.Ct. 795, 66 L.Ed.2d 611 (1980), the Sixth Circuit held, two-one, that "scienter should be an element of liability in private suits under the proxy provisions as they apply to outside accountants."

The result reached was not necessarily inconsistent with Judge Friendly's opinion in *Gerstle*. Friendly pointed out that his analysis "does not mean that scienter should never be required in an action under Rule 14a–9," and laid much stress on the fact that in *Gerstle* the transaction redounded to the defendant's benefit.   478 F.2d at 1300.

In Shidler v. All American Life & Financial Corp., 775 F.2d 917 (8th Cir.1985), the Eighth Circuit and held there was no liability without fault in an action under Section 14(a):

> The purpose of section 14(a) is "to prevent management or others from obtaining authorization for corporate action by means of deceptive or inadequate disclosure in proxy solicitation." J.I. Case Co. v. Borak, 377 U.S. 426, 431, 84 S.Ct. 1555, 1559, 12 L.Ed.2d 423 (1964). A strict liability rule would impose liability for fully innocent misstatements. It is too blunt a tool to ferret out the kind of deceptive practices Congress sought to prevent in enacting section 14(a).

775 F.2d at 927.

TSC INDUSTRIES, INC. v. NORTHWAY, INC., 426 U.S. 438, 96 S.Ct. 2126, 48 L.Ed.2d 757 (1976). "[In] *Mills*, we attempted to clarify to some extent the elements of a private cause of action for violation of § 14(a). In a suit challenging the sufficiency under § 14(a) and Rule 14a–9 of a proxy statement soliciting votes in favor of a merger, we held that there was no need to demonstrate that the alleged defect in the proxy statement actually had a decisive effect on the voting. So long as the misstatement or omission was material, the causal relation between violation and injury is sufficiently established, we concluded, if "the proxy solicitation itself . . . was an essential link in the accomplishment of the transaction." 396 U.S., at 385, 90 S.Ct., at 622. After *Mills*, then, the content given to the notion of materiality assumes heightened significance.[7] . . .

"The question of materiality, it is universally agreed, is an objective one, involving the significance of an omitted or misrepresented fact to a reasonable investor. Variations in the formulation of a general test of materiality occur in the articulation of just how

---

7. Our cases have not considered, and we have no occasion in this case to consider, what showing of culpability is required to establish the liability under § 14(a) of a corporation issuing a materially misleading proxy statement, or of a person involved in the preparation of a materially misleading proxy statement. See Gerstle v. Gamble–Skogmo, Inc., 478 F.2d 1281, 1298, 1301 (2d Cir.1973); Richland v. Crandall, 262 F.Supp. 538, 553 n. 12 (S.D.N.Y. 1967); Jennings & Marsh, Securities Regulation: Cases and Materials 1358–1359 (3d ed. 1972). See also Ernst & Ernst v. Hochfelder, 425 U.S. 185, 207–209, 96 S.Ct. 1375, 1388, 47 L.Ed.2d 668 (1976).

significant a fact must be or, put another way, how certain it must be that the fact would affect a reasonable investor's judgment.

"The Court of Appeals in this case concluded that material facts include 'all facts which a reasonable shareholder *might* consider important.' 512 F.2d, at 330 (emphasis added). This formulation of the test of materiality has been explicitly rejected by at least two courts as setting too low a threshold for the imposition of liability under Rule 14a–9. Gerstle v. Gamble–Skogmo, Inc., 478 F.2d 1281, 1301–1302 (C.A.2 1973); Smallwood v. Pearl Brewing Co., 489 F.2d 579, 603–604 (C.A.5 1974). In these cases, panels of the Second and Fifth Circuits opted for the conventional tort test of materiality—whether a reasonable man *would* attach importance to the fact misrepresented or omitted in determining his course of action. See Restatement (Second) of Torts § 538(2)(a) (Tent.Draft No. 10, 1964). See also ALI Federal Securities Code § 256(a) (Tent.Draft No. 2, 1973). Gerstle v. Gamble–Skogmo, supra, at 1302, also approved the following standard, which had been formulated with reference to statements issued in a contested election: 'whether, taking a properly realistic view, there is a substantial likelihood that the misstatement or omission may have led a stockholder to grant a proxy to the solicitor or to withhold one from the other side, whereas in the absence of this he would have taken a contrary course.' General Time Corp. v. Talley Industries, Inc., 403 F.2d 159, 162 (C.A.2 1968), cert. denied, 393 U.S. 1026, 89 S.Ct. 631, 21 L.Ed.2d 570 (1969). . . .

"In formulating a standard of materiality under Rule 14a–9, we are guided, of course, by the recognition in *Borak* and *Mills* of the Rule's broad remedial purpose. That purpose is not merely to ensure by judicial means that the transaction, when judged by its real terms, is fair and otherwise adequate, but to ensure disclosures by corporate management in order to enable the shareholders to make an informed choice. See *Mills,* supra, at 381, 90 S.Ct., at 620. As an abstract proposition, the most desirable role for a court in a suit of this sort, coming after the consummation of the proposed transaction, would perhaps be to determine whether in fact the proposal would have been favored by the shareholders and consummated in the absence of any misstatement or omission. But as we recognized in *Mills,* supra, at 382 n. 5, 90 S.Ct., at 620, such matters are not subject to determination with certainty. Doubts as to the critical nature of information misstated or omitted will be commonplace. And particularly in view of the prophylactic purpose of the Rule and the fact that the content of the proxy statement is within management's control, it is appropriate that these doubts be resolved in favor of those the statute is designed to protect. *Mills,* supra, at 385, 90 S.Ct., at 622.

"We are aware, however, that the disclosure policy embodied in the proxy regulations is not without limit. See id., at 384, 90 S.Ct., at 621. Some information is of such dubious significance that insistence on its disclosure may accomplish more harm than good. The potential liability for a Rule 14a–9 violation can be great indeed, and if the standard of materiality is unnecessarily low, not only may the corporation and its management be subjected to liability for insignificant omissions or misstatements, but also management's fear of exposing itself to substantial liability may cause it simply to bury the shareholder in an avalanche of trivial information—a result that is hardly conducive to informed decisionmaking. Precisely these dangers are presented, we think, by the definition of a material fact adopted by the Court of Appeals in this case—a fact which a reasonable shareholder *might* consider important. We agree with Judge Friendly, speaking for the Court of Appeals in *Gerstle,* that the 'might' formulation is 'too suggestive of mere possibility, however unlikely.' 478 F.2d, at 1302.

"The general standard of materiality that we think best comports with the policies of Rule 14a–9 is as follows: an omitted fact is material if there is a substantial likelihood that a reasonable shareholder would consider it important in deciding how to vote. This standard is fully consistent with *Mills* general description of materiality as a requirement that 'the defect have a significant *propensity* to affect the voting process.' It does not require proof of a substantial likelihood that disclosure of the omitted fact would have caused the reasonable investor to change his vote. What the standard does contemplate is a showing of a substantial likelihood that, under all the circumstances, the omitted fact would have assumed actual significance in the deliberations of the reasonable shareholder. Put another way, there must be a substantial likelihood that the disclosure of the omitted fact would have been viewed by the reasonable investor as having significantly altered the 'total mix' of information made available."

NOTE ON STATE LAW

Perhaps as a result of experience under the Proxy Rules, the standards applied by state courts today, in reviewing the adequacy of disclosure to shareholders under state law in connection with a matter proposed for a shareholder vote, is likely to be close to the standards under the Proxy Rules. See Note on the Duty of Complete Candor, Chapter VIII, Section 6.

SECTION 5. THE PROXY RULES (III): COMMUNICATION BY SHAREHOLDERS

SECURITIES EXCHANGE ACT RULE 14a–7

[See Statutory Supplement]

SECURITIES EXCHANGE ACT RULE 14a–8
[See Statutory Supplement]

LOVENHEIM v. IROQUOIS BRANDS, LTD.
United States District Court, District of Columbia, 1985.
618 F.Supp. 554.

GASCH, District Judge.

I. BACKGROUND

This matter is now before the Court on plaintiff's motion for preliminary injunction.

Plaintiff Peter C. Lovenheim, owner of two hundred shares of common stock in Iroquois Brands, Ltd. (hereinafter "Iroquois/Delaware"), seeks to bar Iroquois/Delaware from excluding from the proxy materials being sent to all shareholders in preparation for an upcoming shareholder meeting information concerning a proposed resolution he intends to offer at the meeting. Mr. Lovenheim's proposed resolution relates to the procedure used to force-feed geese for production of paté de foie gras in France,[2] a type of paté imported by Iroquois/Delaware. Specifically, his resolution calls upon the Directors of Iroquois/Delaware to:

> form a committee to study the methods by which its French supplier produces paté de foie gras, and report to the share-holders its findings and opinions, based on expert consultation, on whether this production method causes undue distress, pain or suffering to the animals involved and, if so, whether further distribution of this product should be discontinued until a more humane production method is developed.

Attachment to Affidavit of Peter C. Lovenheim.

Mr. Lovenheim's right to compel Iroquois/Delaware to insert information concerning his proposal in the proxy materials turns on the applicability of section 14(a) of the Securities Exchange Act of 1934, 15 U.S.C. § 78n(a) ("the Exchange Act"), and the shareholder

---

2. Paté de foie gras is made from the liver of geese. According to Mr. Lovenheim's affidavit, force-feeding is frequently used in order to expand the liver and thereby produce a larger quantity of paté. Mr. Lovenheim's affidavit also contains a description of the force-feeding process:

Force-feeding usually begins when the geese are four months old. On some farms where feeding is mechanized, the bird's body and wings are placed in a metal brace and its neck is stretched. Through a funnel inserted 10–12 inches down the throat of the goose, a machine pumps up to 400 grams of corn-based mash into its stomach. An elastic band around the goose's throat prevents regurgitation. When feeding is manual, a handler uses a funnel and stick to force the mash down.

Affidavit of Peter C. Lovenheim at ¶ 7. Plaintiff contends that such force-feeding is a form of cruelty to animals. *Id.*

Plaintiff has offered no evidence that force-feeding is used by Iroquois/Delaware's supplier in producing the paté imported by Iroquois/Delaware. However his proposal calls upon the committee he seeks to create to investigate this question.

proposal rule promulgated by the Securities and Exchange Commission ("SEC"), Rule 14a–8. . . .

Iroquois/Delaware has refused to allow information concerning Mr. Lovenheim's proposal to be included in proxy materials being sent in connection with the next annual shareholders meeting. In doing so, Iroquois/Delaware relies on an exception to the general requirement of Rule 14a–8, Rule 14a–8(c)(5). That exception provides that an issuer of securities "may omit a proposal and any statement in support thereof" from its proxy statement and form of proxy:

> if the proposal relates to operations which account for less than 5 percent of the issuer's total assets at the end of its most recent fiscal year, and for less than 5 percent of its net earnings and gross sales for its most recent fiscal year, and is not otherwise significantly related to the issuer's business. . . .

Proposal must account for 5% of total assets

II. LIKELIHOOD OF PLAINTIFF PREVAILING ON MERITS. . . .

C. *Applicability of Rule 14a–8(c)(5) Exception*

. . . [T]he likelihood of plaintiff's prevailing in this litigation turns primarily on the applicability to plaintiff's proposal of the exception to the shareholder proposal rule contained in Rule 14a–8(c)(5).

Iroquois/Delaware's reliance on the argument that this exception applies is based on the following information contained in the affidavit of its president: Iroquois/Delaware has annual revenues of $141 million with $6 million in annual profits and $78 million in assets. In contrast, its pâté de foie gras sales were just $79,000 last year, representing a net loss on pâté sales of $3,121. Iroquois/Delaware has only $34,000 in assets related to pâté. Thus none of the company's net earnings and less than .05 percent of its assets are implicated by plaintiff's proposal. McCaffrey Affidavit ¶ 6. These levels are obviously far below the five percent threshold set forth in the first portion of the exception claimed by Iroquois/Delaware.

π's proposal = > 5%

Plaintiff does not contest that his proposed resolution relates to a matter of little economic significance to Iroquois/Delaware. Nevertheless he contends that the Rule 14a–8(c)(5) exception is not applicable as it cannot be said that his proposal "is not otherwise significantly related to the issuer's business" as is required by the final portion of that exception. In other words, plaintiff's argument that Rule 14a–8 does not permit omission of his proposal rests on the assertion that the rule and statute on which it is based do not permit omission merely because a proposal is not economically significant where a proposal has "ethical or social significance."

π relies on ethical & social significance for his proposal

Iroquois/Delaware challenges plaintiff's view that ethical and social proposals cannot be excluded even if they do not meet the economic or five percent test. Instead, Iroquois/Delaware views the exception solely in economic terms as permitting omission of any proposals relating to a de minimis share of assets and profits. Iroquois/Delaware asserts that since corporations are economic entities, only an economic test is appropriate.

The Court would note that the applicability of the Rule 14a–8(c)(5) exception to Mr. Lovenheim's proposal represents a close question given the lack of clarity in the exception itself. In effect, plaintiff relies on the word "otherwise," suggesting that it indicates the drafters of the rule intended that other noneconomic tests of significance be used. Iroquois/Delaware relies on the fact that the rule examines other significance in relation to the issuer's business. Because of the apparent ambiguity of the rule, the Court considers the history of the shareholder proposal rule in determining the proper interpretation of the most recent version of that rule.

Prior to 1983, paragraph 14a–8(c)(5) excluded proposals "not significantly related to the issuer's business" but did not contain an objective economic significance test such as the five percent of sales, assets, and earnings specified in the first part of the current version.[9] Although a series of SEC decisions through 1976 allowing issuers to exclude proposals challenging compliance with the Arab economic boycott of Israel allowed exclusion if the issuer did less than one percent of their business with Arab countries or Israel, the Commission stated later in 1976 that it did "not believe that subparagraph (c)(5) should be hinged solely on the economic relativity of a proposal." Securities Exchange Act Release No. 12,999, 41 Fed.Reg. 52,994, 52,997 (1976). Thus the Commission required inclusion "in many situations in which the related business comprised less than one percent" of the company's revenues, profits or assets "where the proposal has raised *policy questions* important enough to be considered 'significantly related' to the issuer's business."[11]

As indicated above, the 1983 revision adopted the five percent test of economic significance in an effort to create a more objective standard. Nevertheless, in adopting this standard, the Commission stated that proposals will be includable notwithstanding their "failure to reach the specified economic thresholds if a significant relationship to the issuer's business is demonstrated on the face of the resolution or supporting statement." Securities Exchange Act Release No. 19,135, 47 Fed.Reg. 47,420, 47,428 (1982). Thus it seems clear based on the history of the rule that "the meaning of 'significantly related' is not *limited* to economic significance." Comment, *1983 Amendments, supra* note 10 at 183 (emphasis in original).

9. *See* Comment, *The 1983 Amendments to Shareholder Proposal Rule 14a–8: A Retreat from Corporate Democracy?,* 59 Tulane L.Rev. 161, 183–84 (1984) (hereinafter "Comment, *1983 Amendments* ").

11. Comment, *1983 Amendments, supra* note [9] at 185 (emphasis supplied). For example, "[p]roposals requesting the cessa-

tion of further development, planning and construction of nuclear power plants and proposals requesting shareholders be informed as to all aspects of the company's business in European communist countries have been included in this way." *Id.* (footnotes omitted).

The only decision in this Circuit cited by the parties relating to the scope of section 14 and the shareholder proposal rule is *Medical Committee for Human Rights v. SEC*, 432 F.2d 659 (D.C.Cir.1970).[12] That case concerned an effort by shareholders of Dow Chemical Company to advise other shareholders of their proposal directed at prohibiting Dow's production of napalm. Dow had relied on the counterpart of the 14a–8(c)(5) exemption then in effect[13] to exclude the proposal from proxy materials and the SEC accepted Dow's position without elaborating on its basis for doing so.[14] In remanding the matter back to the SEC for the Commission to provide the basis for its decision, *id.* at 682, the Court noted what it termed "substantial questions" as to whether an interpretation of the shareholder proposal rule "which permitted omission of [a] proposal as one motivated primarily by *general* political or social concerns would conflict with the congressional intent underlying section 14(a) of the [Exchange] Act." 432 F.2d at 680 (emphasis in original).[15]

Iroquois/Delaware attempts to distinguish *Medical Committee for Human Rights* as a case where a company sought to exclude a proposal that, unlike Mr. Lovenheim's proposal, was economically significant merely because the motivation of the proponents was political. The argument is not without appeal given the fact that the *Medical Committee* Court was confronted with a regulation that contained no reference to economic significance. *See supra* note 13. Yet the *Medical Committee* decision contains language suggesting that the Court assumed napalm was not economically significant to Dow:

> The management of Dow Chemical Company is repeatedly quoted in sources which include the company's own publications as proclaiming that the decision to continue manufacturing and marketing napalm was made not *because* of business considerations, but *in spite* of them; that management in essence decided to pursue a course of activity which generated little profit for the shareholders. . . .

Id. at 681 (emphasis in original).

This Court need not consider, as the *Medical Committee* decision implied, whether a rule allowing exclusion of all proposals not meeting specified levels of economic significance violates the scope of

12. The *Medical Committee* decision was vacated as moot by the Supreme Court after the shareholder proposal at issue failed to get support from three percent of all shareholders, thereby triggering a separate basis for exclusion, Rule 14a–8(c)(4)(i), 17 C.F.R. § 240.14a–8(c)(4)(i). *See SEC v. Medical Committee for Human Rights*, 404 U.S. 403, 406, 92 S.Ct. 577, 579, 30 L.Ed.2d 560 (1972).

13. Rule 14a–8(c)(2), 17 C.F.R. § 240.14a–8(c)(2) (1970), permitted exclusion if a proposal was submitted "primarily for the purpose of promoting general economic, political, racial, religious, social or similar causes."

14. *Medical Committee* arose as a direct appeal of the Commission's formal determination. In the instant case, the propriety of excluding the shareholder proposal has not gone before the full Commission although the staff of the SEC has advised Iroquois/Delaware that it will recommend that no enforcement action be taken if the company excludes plaintiff's proposal.

15. The Court defined the purpose of section 14(a) of assuring that shareholders exercise their right "to control the important decisions which affect them in their capacity as stockholders and owners of the corporation." 432 F.2d at 680–81.

section 14(a) of the Exchange Act. *See* 432 F.2d at 680. Whether or not the Securities and Exchange Commission could properly adopt such a rule, the Court cannot ignore the history of the rule which reveals no decision by the Commission to limit the determination to the economic criteria relied on by Iroquois/Delaware. The Court therefore holds that in light of the ethical and social significance of plaintiff's proposal and the fact that it implicates significant levels of sales, plaintiff has shown a likelihood of prevailing on the merits with regard to the issue of whether his proposal is "otherwise significantly related" to Iroquois/Delaware's business.[16]

For the reasons discussed above, the Court concludes that plaintiff's motion for preliminary injunction should be granted. . . .

SECTION 6. PROXY CONTESTS

SECURITIES EXCHANGE ACT RULE 14a–11, SCHEDULE 14B

[See Statutory Supplement]

ROSENFELD v. FAIRCHILD ENGINE AND AIRPLANE CORP.

Court of Appeals of New York, 1955.
309 N.Y. 168, 128 N.E.2d 291.

FROESSEL, Judge. In a stockholder's derivative action brought by plaintiff, an attorney, who owns 25 out of the company's over 2,300,000 shares, he seeks to compel the return of $261,522, paid out of the corporate treasury to reimburse both sides in a proxy contest for their expenses. The Appellate Division, 284 App.Div. 201, 132 N.Y.S.2d 273, has unanimously affirmed a judgment of an Official Referee, Sup., 116 N.Y.S.2d 840, dismissing plaintiff's complaint on the merits, and we agree. Exhaustive opinions were written by both courts below, and it will serve no useful purpose to review the facts again.

Of the amount in controversy $106,000 was spent out of corporate funds by the old board of directors while still in office in defense of their position in said contest; $28,000 were paid to the old board by the new board after the change of management following the proxy contest, to compensate the former directors for such of the remaining expenses of their unsuccessful defense as the new board found was fair and reasonable; payment of $127,000 representing reimbursement of

16. The result would, of course, be different if plaintiff's proposal was ethically significant in the abstract but had no meaningful relationship to the business of Iroquois/Delaware as Iroquois/Delaware was not engaged in the business of importing paté de foie gras.

expenses to members of the prevailing group, was expressly ratified by a 16 to 1 majority vote of the stockholders.

The essential facts are not in dispute, and, since the determinations below are amply supported by the evidence, we are bound by the findings affirmed by the Appellate Division. The Appellate Division found that the difference between plaintiff's group and the old board "went deep into the policies of the company", and that among these Ward's contract was one of the "main points of contention". The Official Referee found that the controversy "was based on an understandable difference in policy between the two groups, at the very bottom of which was the Ward employment contract".

By way of contrast with the findings here, in Lawyers' Advertising Co. v. Consolidated Ry., Lighting & Refrigerating Co., 187 N.Y. 395, at page 399, 80 N.E. 199, at page 200, which was an action to recover for the cost of publishing newspaper notices not authorized by the board of directors, it was expressly found that the proxy contest there involved was "by one faction in its contest with another for the control of the corporation . . . a contest for the perpetuation of their offices and control." We there said by way of *dicta* that under *such* circumstances the publication of certain notices on behalf of the management faction was not a corporate expenditure which the directors had the power to authorize.

Other jurisdictions and our own lower courts have held that management may look to the corporate treasury for the reasonable expenses of soliciting proxies to defend its position in a bona fide policy contest. . . .

It should be noted that plaintiff does not argue that the aforementioned sums were fraudulently extracted from the corporation; indeed, his counsel conceded that "the charges were fair and reasonable", but denied "they were legal charges which may be reimbursed for". This is therefore not a case where a stockholder challenges specific items, which, on examination, the trial court may find unwarranted, excessive or otherwise improper. Had plaintiff made such objections here, the trial court would have been required to examine the items challenged.

If directors of a corporation may not in good faith incur reasonable and proper expenses in soliciting proxies in these days of giant corporations with vast numbers of stockholders, the corporate business might be seriously interfered with because of stockholder indifference and the difficulty of procuring a quorum, where there is no contest. In the event of a proxy contest, if the directors may not freely answer the challenges of outside groups and in good faith defend their actions with respect to corporate policy for the information of the stockholders, they and the corporation may be at the mercy of persons seeking to wrest control for their own purposes, so long as such persons have ample funds to conduct a proxy contest. The test is clear. When the directors act in good faith in a contest over policy, they have the right to incur reasonable and proper expenses for solicitation of proxies and in defense of their corporate policies, and are not obliged to sit idly by. The courts are entirely competent to pass upon their *bona fides* in any given case, as well as the nature of their expenditures when duly challenged.

It is also our view that the members of the so-called new group could be reimbursed by the corporation for their expenditures in this contest by affirmative vote of the stockholders. With regard to these ultimately successful contestants, as the Appellate Division below has noted, there was, of course, "no duty . . . to set forth the facts, with corresponding obligation of the corporation to pay for such expense". However, where a majority of the stockholders chose—in this case by a vote of 16 to 1—to reimburse the successful contestants for achieving the very end sought and voted for by them as owners of the corporation, we see no reason to deny the effect of their ratification nor to hold the corporate body powerless to determine how its own moneys shall be spent.

The rule then which we adopt is simply this: In a contest over policy, as compared to a purely personal power contest, corporate directors have the right to make reasonable and proper expenditures, subject to the scrutiny of the courts when duly challenged, from the corporate treasury for the purpose of persuading the stockholders of the correctness of their position and soliciting their support for policies which the directors believe, in all good faith, are in the best interests of the corporation. The stockholders, moreover, have the right to reimburse successful contestants for the reasonable and bona fide expenses incurred by them in any such policy contest, subject to like court scrutiny. That is not to say, however, that corporate directors can, under any circumstances, disport themselves in a proxy contest with the corporation's moneys to an unlimited extent. Where it is established that such moneys have been spent for personal power, individual gain or private advantage, and not in the belief that such expenditures are in the best interests of the stockholders and the corporation, or where the fairness and reasonableness of the amounts allegedly expended are duly and successfully challenged, the courts will not hesitate to disallow them.

The judgment of the Appellate Division should be affirmed, without costs.

DESMOND, Judge (concurring). We granted leave to appeal in an effort to pass, and in the expectation of passing, on this question, highly important in modern-day corporation law: is it lawful for a corporation, on consent of a majority of its stockholders, to pay, out of its funds, the expenses of a "proxy fight", incurred by competing candidates for election as directors? Now that the appeal has been argued, I doubt that the question is presented by this record. The defendants served were Allis who was on the old board but was reelected to the new board, McComas and Wilson, defeated members of the old board, and Fairchild, leader of the victorious group and largest stockholder in the corporation. The expenses of the old board, or management group, in the proxy fight, were about $134,000, and those of the victorious Fairchild group amounted to about $127,500. In the end, the corporation paid both those sums, and it is for the reimbursement thereof, to the corporation, that this stockholder's derivative action is brought. Of the proxy fight expenses of the management slate, about $106,000 was paid out on authorization of the old board while the old directors were still in office. The balance of those charges, as well as the whole of the expenses of the new and successful, Fairchild group, was paid by the corporation after the new directors had taken over and after a majority of stockholders had approved such expenditures. The election had been fought out on a number of issues, chief of which concerned a contract which Ward (a defendant not served), who was a director and the principal executive officer of the company, had obtained from the corporation, covering compensation for, and other conditions of, his own services. Each side, in the campaign for proxies, charged the other with seeking to perpetuate, or grasp, control of the corporation. The Fairchild group won the election by a stock vote of about two-to-one, and obtained, at the next annual stockholders' meeting and by a much larger vote, authorization to make the payments above described.

Plaintiff asserts that it was illegal for the directors (unless by unanimous consent of stockholders) to expend corporate moneys in the proxy contest beyond the amounts necessary to give to stockholders bare notice of the meeting and of the matters to be voted on thereat. Defendants say that the proxy contest revolved around disputes over corporate policies and that it was, accordingly, proper not only to assess against the corporation the expense of serving formal notices and of routine proxy solicitation, but to go further and spend corporate moneys, on behalf of each group, thoroughly to inform the stockholders. The reason why that important question is, perhaps, not directly before us in this lawsuit is because, as the Appellate Division properly held, [284 App.Div. 201, 132 N.Y.S.2d 280] plaintiff failed "to urge liability as to specific expenditures". The cost of giving routinely necessary notice is, of course, chargeable to the corporation. It is just as clear, we think, that payment by a corporation of the expense of "proceedings by one faction in its contest with another for the control of the corporation" is *ultra vires,* and unlawful. Lawyers' Advertising Co. v. Consolidated Ry., Lighting & Refrigerating Co., 187 N.Y. 395, 399, 80 N.E. 199, 200. Approval by directors or by a majority stock vote could not validate such gratuitous expenditures. Continental Securities Co. v. Belmont, 206 N.Y. 7, 99 N.E. 138, 51 L.R.A., N.S., 112. Some of the payments attacked in this suit were, on their face, for lawful purposes and apparently reasonable in amount but, as to others, the record simply does not contain evidentiary bases for a determination as to either lawfulness or reasonableness. Surely, the burden was on plaintiff to go forward to some extent with such particularization and proof. It failed to do so, and so failed to make out a prima facie case.

We are, therefore, reaching the same result as did the Appellate Division but on one only of the grounds listed by that court, that is, failure of proof. We think it not inappropriate, however, to state our general views on the question of law principally argued by the parties, that is, as to the validity of corporate payments for proxy solicitations and similar activities in addition to giving notice of the meeting, and of the questions to be voted on. For an answer to that problem we could not do better than quote from this court's opinion in the Lawyers' Advertising Co. case, 187 N.Y. 395, 399, 80 N.E. 199, 200, supra: "The remaining notices were not legally authorized and were not legitimately incidental to the meeting or necessary for the protection of the stockholders. They rather were proceedings by one faction in its contest with another for the control of the corporation, and the expense thereof, as such, is not properly chargeable to the latter. This is so apparent as to the last two notices that nothing need be said in reference to them; but a few words may be said in regard to the first one, calling for proxies. It is to be noted that this is not the case of an ordinary circular letter sent out with and requesting the execution of proxies. The custom has become common upon the part of corporations to mail proxies to their respective stockholders, often accompanied by a brief circular of directions, and such custom when accompanied by no unreasonable expenditure, is not without merit in so far as it encourages voting by stockholders, through making it convenient and ready at hand. The notice in question, however, was not published until after proxies had been sent out. It simply amounted to an urgent solicitation that these proxies should be executed and returned for use by one faction in its contest, and we think there is no authority for imposing the expense of its publication upon the company. . . . it would be altogether too dangerous a rule to permit directors in control of a corporation and engaged in a contest for the perpetuation of their offices and control, to impose upon the corporation the unusual expense of publishing advertisements or, by analogy, of dispatching special messengers for the purpose of procuring proxies in their behalf."

A final comment: since expenditures which do not meet that test of propriety are intrinsically unlawful, it could not be any answer to such a claim as plaintiff makes here that the stockholder vote which purported to authorize them was heavy or that the change in management turned out to be beneficial to the corporation.

The judgment should be affirmed, without costs.

VAN VOORHIS, Judge (dissenting). The decision of this appeal is of far-reaching importance insofar as concerns payment by corporations of campaign expenses by stockholders in proxy contests for control. This is a stockholder's derivative action to require directors to restore to a corporation moneys paid to defray expenses of this nature, incurred both by an incumbent faction and by an insurgent faction of stockholders. The insurgents prevailed at the annual meeting, and payments of their own campaign expenses were attempted to be ratified by majority vote. It was a large majority, but the stockholders were not unanimous. Regardless of the merits of this contest, we are called upon to decide whether it was a corporate purpose (1) to make the expenditures which were disbursed by the incumbent or management group in defense of their acts and to remain in control of the corporation, and (2) to defray expenditures made by the insurgent group, which succeeded in convincing a majority of the stockholders. The Appellate Division held that stockholder authorization or ratification was not necessary to reasonable expenditures by the management group, the purpose of which was to inform the stockholders concerning the affairs of the corporation, and that, although these incumbents spent or incurred obligations of $133,966 (the previous expenses of annual meetings of this corporation ranging between $7,000 and $28,000), plaintiff must fail for having omitted to distinguish item by item between which of these expenditures were warranted and which ones were not; and the Appellate Division held that the insurgents also should be reimbursed, but subject to the qualification that "The expenses of those who were seeking to displace the management should not be reimbursed by the corporation except upon approval by the stockholders." It was held that the stockholders had approved.

[margin note: It should not have to itemize to itemize his complaint]

No resolution was passed by the stockholders approving payment to the management group. It has been recognized that not all of the $133,966 in obligations paid or incurred by the management group was designed merely for information of stockholders. This outlay included payment for all of the activities of a strenuous campaign to persuade and cajole in a hard-fought contest for control of this corporation. It included, for example, expenses for entertainment, chartered airplanes and limousines, public relations counsel and proxy solicitors. However legitimate such measures may be on behalf of stockholders themselves in such a controversy, most of them do not pertain to a corporate function but are part of the familiar apparatus of aggressive factions in corporate contests. In Lawyers' Advertising Co. v. Consolidated Ry., Lighting & Refrigerating Co., 187 N.Y. 395, 399, 80 N.E. 199, 201, this court said: "This notice in question, however, was not published until after proxies had been sent out. It simply amounted to an urgent solicitation that these proxies should be executed and returned for use by one faction in its contest, and we think there is no authority for imposing the expense of its publication upon the company. It may be conceded that the directors who caused this publication acted in good faith, and felt that they were serving the best interests of the stockholders; but it would be altogether too dangerous a rule to permit directors in control of a corporation and engaged in a contest for the perpetuation of their offices and control, to impose upon the corporation the unusual expense of publishing advertisements, or, by analogy, of dispatching special messengers for the purpose of procuring proxies in their behalf."

[margin note: Expenses were frivolous]

[margin note: Should not allow directors to publish paid Ads]

The Appellate Division acknowledged in the instant case that "It is obvious that the management group here incurred a substantial amount of needless expense which was charged to the corporation," but this conclusion should have led to a direction that those defendants who were incumbent directors should be required to come forward with an explanation of their expenditures under the familiar rule that where it has been established that directors have expended corporate money for their own purposes, the burden of going forward with evidence of the propriety and reasonableness of specific items rests upon the directors. . . . The complaint should not have been dismissed as against incumbent directors due to failure of plaintiff to segregate the specific expenditures which are *ultra vires,* but, once plaintiff had proved facts from which an inference of impropriety might be drawn, the duty of making an explanation was laid upon the directors to explain and justify their conduct.

The second ground assigned by the Appellate Division for dismissing the complaint against incumbent directors is stockholder ratification of reimbursement to the insurgent group. Whatever effect or lack of it this resolution had upon expenditures by the insurgent group, clearly the stockholders who voted to pay the insurgents entertained no intention of reimbursing the management group for their expenditures. The insurgent group succeeded as a result of arousing the indignation of these very stockholders against the management group; nothing in the resolution to pay the expenses of the insurgent group purported to authorize or ratify payment of the campaign expenses of their adversaries, and certainly no inference should be drawn that the stockholders who voted to pay the insurgents intended that the incumbent group should also be paid. Upon the contrary, they were removing the incumbents from control mainly for the reason that they were charged with having mulcted the corporation by a long-term salary and pension contract to one of their number, J. Carlton Ward, Jr. If these stockholders had been presented with a resolution to pay the expenses of that group, it would almost certainly have been voted down. The stockholders should not be deemed to have authorized or ratified reimbursement of the incumbents.

There is no doubt that the management was entitled and under a duty to take reasonable steps to acquaint the stockholders with essential facts concerning the management of the corporation, and it may well be that the existence of a contest warranted them in circularizing the stockholders with more than ordinarily detailed information. . . .

What expenses of the incumbent group should be allowed and what should be disallowed should be remitted to the trial court to ascertain, after taking evidence, in accordance with the rule that the incumbent directors were required to assume the burden of going forward in the first instance with evidence explaining and justifying their expenditures. Only such as were reasonably related to informing the stockholders fully and fairly concerning the corporate affairs should be allowed. The concession by plaintiff that such expenditures as were made were reasonable in amount does not decide this question. By way of illustration, the costs of entertainment for stockholders may have been, and it is stipulated that they were, at the going rates for providing similar entertainment. That does not signify that entertaining stockholders is reasonably related to the purposes of the corporation. The Appellate Division, as above stated, found that the management group incurred a substantial amount of needless expense. That fact being established, it became the duty of the incumbent directors to unravel and explain these payments.

Regarding the $127,556 paid by the new management to the insurgent group for their campaign expenditures, the question immediately arises whether that was for a corporate purpose. . . .

In considering this issue, as in the case of the expenses of the incumbents, we begin with the proposition that this court has already held that it is beyond the power of a corporation to authorize the expenditure of mere campaign expenses in a proxy contest. Lawyers' Advertising Co. v. Consolidated Ry., Lighting & Refrigerating Co., supra. . . .

. . . The case most frequently cited and principally relied upon from among [the] Delaware decisions is Hall v. Trans-Lux Daylight Picture Screen Corp. [20 Del. Ch. 78]. There the English case was followed of Peel v. London & North Western Ry. Co. . . . which distinguished between expenses merely for the purpose of maintaining control, and contests over policy questions of the corporation. In the Hall case the issues concerned a proposed merger, and a proposed sale of stock of a subsidiary corporation. These were held to be policy questions, and payment of the management campaign expenses was upheld.

In our view, the impracticability [of distinguishing between expenses incurred merely for the purpose of maintaining control, and expenses in contests over policy questions] is illustrated by the statement in the Hall case, supra, 20 Del.Ch. at page 85, 171 A. at page 229, that "It is impossible in many cases of intracorporate contests over directors, to sever questions of policy from those of persons". This circumstance is stressed in Judge Rifkind's opinion in [Steinberg v. Adams, 90 F.Supp. 604] at page 608: "The simple fact, of course, is that generally policy and personnel do not exist in separate compartments. A change in personnel is sometimes indispensable to a change of policy. A new board may be the symbol of the shift in policy as well as the means of obtaining it."

That may be all very well, but the upshot of this reasoning is that inasmuch as it is generally impossible to distinguish whether "policy" or "personnel" is the dominant factor, any averments must be accepted at their face value that questions of policy are dominant. Nowhere do these opinions mention that the converse is equally true and more pervasive, that neither the "ins" nor the "outs" ever say that they have no program to offer to the shareholders, but just want to acquire or to retain control, as the case may be. In common experience, this distinction is unreal. It was not mentioned by this court in Lawyers' Advertising Co. v. Consolidated Ry., Lighting & Refrigerating Co., supra. As in political contests, aspirations for control are invariably presented under the guise of policy or principle. . . .

The main question of 'policy' in the instant corporate election, as is stated in the opinions below and frankly admitted, concerns the long-term contract with pension rights of a former officer and director, Mr. J. Carlton Ward, Jr. The insurgents' chief claim of benefit to the corporation from their victory consists in the termination of that agreement, resulting in an alleged actuarial saving of $350,000 to

$825,000 to the corporation, and the reduction of other salaries and rent by more than $300,000 per year. The insurgents had contended in the proxy contest that these payments should be substantially reduced so that members of the incumbent group would not continue to profit personally at the expense of the corporation. If these charges were true, which appear to have been believed by a majority of the shareholders, then the disbursements by the management group in the proxy contest fall under the condemnation of the English and the Delaware rule.

These circumstances are mentioned primarily to illustrate how impossible it is to distinguish between "policy" and "personnel" as Judge Rifkind expressed it, but they also indicate that personal factors are deeply rooted in this contest. That is certainly true insofar as the former management group is concerned. . . .

Some expenditures may concededly be made by a corporation represented by its management so as to inform the stockholders, but there is a clear distinction between such expenditures by management and by mere groups of stockholders. The latter are under no legal obligation to assume duties of managing the corporation. They may endeavor to supersede the management for any reason, regardless of whether it be advantageous or detrimental to the corporation but, if they succeed, that is not a determination that the company was previously mismanaged or that it may not be mismanaged in the future. A change in control is in no sense analogous to an adjudication that the former directors have been guilty of misconduct. The analogy of allowing expenses of suit to minority stockholders who have been successful in a derivative action based on misconduct of officers or directors, is entirely without foundation.

Insofar as a management group is concerned, it may charge the corporation with any expenses within reasonable limits incurred in giving widespread notice to stockholders of questions affecting the welfare of the corporation. Lawyers' Advertising Co. v. Consolidated Ry., Lighting & Refrigerating Co., supra. Expenditures in excess of these limits are *ultra vires.* The corporation lacks power to defray them. The corporation lacks power to defray the expenses of the insurgents in their entirety. The insurgents were not charged with responsibility for operating the company. No appellate court case is cited from any jurisdiction holding otherwise. No contention is made that such disbursements could be made, in any event, without stockholder ratification; they could not be ratified except by unanimous vote if they were *ultra vires.* The insurgents, in this instance, repeatedly announced to the stockholders in their campaign literature that their proxy contest was being waged at their own personal expense. If reimbursement of such items were permitted upon majority stockholder ratification, no court or other tribunal could pass upon which types of expenditures were "needless", to employ the characterization of the Appellate Division in this case. Whether the insurgents should be paid would be made to depend upon whether they win the stockholders election and obtain control of the corporation. It would be entirely irrelevant whether the corporation is "benefitted" by their efforts or by the outcome of such an election. The courts could not indulge in a speculative inquiry into that issue. That would truly be a matter of business judgment. In some instances corporations are better governed by the existing management and in others by some other group which supersedes the existing management. Courts of law have no jurisdiction to decide such questions, and successful insurgent stockholders may confidently be relied upon to reimburse themselves whatever may be the real merits of the controversy. The losers in a proxy fight may understand the interests of the corporation more accurately than their successful adversaries, and agitation of this character may ultimately result in corporate advantage even if there be no change in management. Nevertheless, under the judgment which is appealed from, success in a proxy contest is the indispensable condition upon which reimbursement of the insurgents depends. Adventurers are not infrequent who are ready to take advantage of economic recessions, reduction of dividends or failure to increase them, or other sources of stockholder discontent to wage contests in order to obtain control of well-managed corporations, so as to divert their funds through legal channels into other corporations in which they may be interested, or to discharge former officers and employees to make room for favored newcomers according to the fashion of political patronage, or for other objectives that are unrelated to the sound prosperity of the enterprise. The way is open and will be kept open for stockholders and groups of stockholders to contest corporate elections, but if the promoters of such movements choose to employ the costly modern media of mass persuasion, they should look for reimbursement to themselves and to the stockholders who are aligned with them. If the law be that they can be recompensed by the corporation in case of success, and only in that event, it will operate as a powerful incentive to persons accustomed to taking calculated risks to increase this form of high-powered salesmanship to such a degree that, action provoking reaction, stockholders' meetings will be very costly. To the financial advantages promised by control of a prosperous corporation, would be added the knowledge that the winner takes all insofar as the campaign expenses are concerned. To the victor, indeed, would belong the spoils.

The questions involved in this case assume mounting importance as the capital stock of corporations becomes more widely distributed. To an enlarged extent the campaign methods consequently come more to resemble those of political campaigns, but, as in the latter, campaign expenses should be borne by those who are waging the campaign and their followers, instead of being met out of the corporate or the public treasury. Especially is this true when campaign promises have been made that the expenses would not be charged to the corporation. . . .

The judgment appealed from should be reversed so as to direct respondent Fairchild to pay to the corporation the sum of $118,448.78, with appropriate interest, representing the moneys reimbursed to him by the corporation and, upon his default, the respondent, Allis should be required to pay said sum; respondents Fairchild and Allis should be required to pay to the corporation the sum of $9,107.10, with appropriate interest, representing the amount reimbursed to L.M. Bolton by the corporation; and an interlocutory judgment should be entered for an accounting to determine what part of the $133,966, representing expenses incurred by the old board, was improperly charged to the corporation and requiring the respondents Wilson and McComas to pay to the corporation the sum thereof, and the respondents Allis and Fairchild such amounts thereof as were paid out after July 15, 1949, with costs of the action to the plaintiff in all courts.

CONWAY, C.J., and BURKE, J., concur with FROESSEL, J.; DESMOND, J., concurs in part in a separate opinion; VAN VOORHIS, J., dissents in an opinion in which DYE and FULD, JJ., concur.

Judgment affirmed.

Chapter VI

THE SPECIAL PROBLEMS OF CLOSE CORPORATIONS

SECTION 1. INTRODUCTION

(a) A BRIEF LOOK AT PARTNERSHIP

NOTE ON PARTNERSHIP LAW

The title of this chapter refers to "close corporations." Exactly what constitutes a close corporation is often a matter of theoretical dispute. Some authorities emphasize the number of shareholders, some the presence of owner-management, some the lack of a market for the corporation's stock, and some the existence of formal restrictions on the transferability of the corporation's shares. For present purposes, a close corporation can be regarded as one whose shares are held by a relatively small number of persons: given that element, the remaining incidents normally follow. Viewed from this perspective, the close corporation resembles the partnership, which is also typically characterized by a small number of owners, as well as owner-management and nontransferability of ownership interests. Indeed, certain aspects of partnership law form an important backdrop to the study of close corporations, not only because the practitioner must have some acquaintance with partnership law to render intelligent advice to clients who must decide between the two forms, but also because in recent years legislators and courts have increasingly looked to partnership-law norms in solving close-corporation-law problems.

The most striking aspect of partnership law is its heavily contractual nature. For many purposes, the Uniform Partnership Act ("UPA") operates only in the absence of an agreement by the partners on a given issue. The following is a highly generalized summary of the partnership-law rules most salient to the ongoing conduct of the firm:

(1) As concerns internal decisionmaking, partnership law is essentially *suppletory,* that is, the UPA impliedly validates whatever arrangements the partners make between themselves, and provides rules to govern only those situations that the owners' arrangements fail to cover. The two basic rules are:

(a) Absent contrary agreement, all partners have equal rights in the management and conduct of the partnership business. UPA § 18(e).

(b) Absent contrary agreement, differences among the partners "as to ordinary matters connected with the partnership business" are determined by a majority of the partners, but differences as to matters that are outside the scope of the partnership business, would be in conflict with the partnership agreement, or would make it impossible to carry on the ordinary business of the partnership, require unanimous consent. U.P.A. §§ 9(3)(c), 18(h).

(2) Any partner has power to bind the partnership on a matter in the ordinary course of business, even if he has no authority in fact by virtue of the partnership's internal arrangements, unless the third party with whom he deals knows that the partner has no authority in fact. U.P.A. § 9(1).

(3) Absent contrary agreement, partnership profits are shared per capita, and no partner is entitled to a salary. U.P.A. §§ 18(a), (f).

(4) Absent contrary agreement, no person can become a member of a partnership without the consent of all the partners. U.P.A. § 18(g).

(5) Partnerships are normally created for a limited term—frequently a relatively short term—and dissolution is easy. If the partnership is not for a specified term (express or implied) any partner may cause dissolution at any time. If the partnership is for a specified term, dissolution occurs at the end of the term or on the death or incapacity of any partner, and may also be caused by any partner during the term, although in that case the dissolving partner will have acted wrongfully and will be liable to the remaining partners in damages. U.P.A. §§ 31, 38(2)(a)(II). Further demonstrating the contractual nature of partnership, partners may and often do agree that on death of a partner the partnership will continue, and the surviving partners or the firm itself will purchase the decedent's partnership interest. (A distinction should be drawn between dissolution and winding-up. U.P.A. § 29 defines dissolution as a change in the relation of the partners caused by any partner ceasing to be associated in carrying on the business. Dissolution is a *legal* event. However, the occurrence of this legal event may entail winding-up— an *economic* event, consisting of the termination of the active conduct of the business and the liquidation of assets and liabilities. Thus the partnership is not terminated on dissolution, but continues until the winding-up or liquidation of partnership affairs is completed.)

(6) Partners stand in a fiduciary relationship to each other. See, e.g., Meinhard v. Salmon, 249 N.Y. 458, 164 N.E. 545 (1928).

(7) The Internal Revenue Code generally taxes a partnership's profits and losses to the individual partners, rather than to the partnership.

Although it is often said that a close corporation is an "incorporated partnership," it will readily be seen that ordinary corporation-law norms are diametrically opposed to almost every one of these partnership-law rules:

(1) As to many aspects of internal decisionmaking, traditional corporate statutes are *regulatory* rather than suppletory. For example, under traditional corporate-law norms, shareholders, as such, have no right to participate in the management of the corporation's business.

(2) Since shareholders as such have no right to participate in the management of the corporation's business, they also have no apparent authority to bind the corporation.

(3) Corporate profits are not shared except to the extent dividends are declared, and at that point are not shared per capita, but in proportion to stock ownership.

(4) Shares of stock—and the shareholder status they carry—are freely transferable.

(5) Corporations are normally created for a perpetual term, and dissolution is relatively difficult.

(6) The traditional view was that, with certain exceptions, shareholders do not stand in a direct fiduciary relationship to each other.

(7) The Internal Revenue Code generally taxes profits and losses to the corporation, rather than to the individual shareholders.

These norms were essentially designed with an eye to the publicly held corporation, and as will be seen, their application to close corporations often leads to the frustration of legitimate expectations.

(b) AN INTRODUCTION TO THE CLOSE CORPORATION

DONAHUE v. RODD ELECTROTYPE CO.

Supreme Judicial Court of Massachusetts, 1975.
367 Mass. 578, 328 N.E.2d 505.

TAURO, Chief Justice.

The plaintiff, Euphemia Donahue, a minority stockholder in the Rodd Electrotype Company of New England, Inc. (Rodd Electrotype), a Massachusetts corporation, brings this suit against the directors of Rodd Electrotype, Charles H. Rodd, Frederick I. Rodd and Mr. Harold E. Magnuson, against Harry C. Rodd, a former director, officer, and controlling stockholder of Rodd Electrotype and against Rodd Electrotype (hereinafter called defendants). The plaintiff seeks to rescind Rodd Electrotype's purchase of Harry Rodd's shares in Rodd Electrotype and to compel Harry Rodd "to repay to the corporation the purchase price of said shares, $36,000, together with interest from the date of purchase." The plaintiff alleges that the defendants caused the corporation to purchase the shares in violation of their fiduciary duty to her, a minority stockholder of Rodd Electrotype.[4]

The trial judge, after hearing oral testimony, dismissed the plaintiff's bill on the merits. He found that the purchase was without prejudice to the plaintiff and implicitly found that the transaction had been carried out in good faith and with inherent fairness. The Appeals Court affirmed with costs. Donahue v. Rodd Electrotype Co. of New England, Inc., 1 Mass.App. 876, 307 N.E.2d 8 (1974). The case is before us on the plaintiff's application for further appellate review. . . .

[Briefly, the facts were as follows: In the mid–1930's Harry Rodd and Joseph Donahue had become employees of Royal Electrotype (the predecessor of Rodd Electrotype). Donahue's duties were confined to operational matters within the plants, and he never participated in the management aspect of the business. In contrast, Rodd's advancement within the company was rapid, and in 1946 he became general manager and treasurer. Subsequently Rodd acquired 200 of the corporation's 1000 shares and Donahue (at Rodd's suggestion) acquired 50 shares. In 1955 Rodd became president and general manager, and later that year Royal itself purchased the remaining 750 shares, so that Rodd and Donahue became Royal's sole shareholders, owning 80% and 20% of its stock, respectively. In 1960 the corporation was renamed Rodd Electrotype, and in the early 60's Harry Rodd's two sons, Charles and Frederick, took important positions with the company. In 1965 Charles succeeded his father as president and general manager.

In 1970 Harry Rodd was seventy-seven years old and not in good health, and his sons wished him to retire. Prior to 1967 Harry had distributed 117 of his 200 shares equally among his sons and his daughter, and had returned 2 shares to the corporate treasury. Harry insisted that as a condition to his retirement some financial arrangement be made with respect to his remaining 81 shares. Accordingly, Charles, acting on the corporation's behalf, negotiated for the purchase of 45 of Harry's shares for $800/share—a price which, Charles testified, reflected book and liquidating value. At a special board meeting in July 1970, the corporation's board (then consisting of Charles and Frederick Rodd and a lawyer) voted to have the corporation make the purchase at this price. Subsequently Harry Rodd sold 2 shares to each of his three children at $800/share, and gave each child 10 shares as a gift.[7] Meanwhile Donahue had died and his 50

---

4. In form, the plaintiff's bill of complaint presents, at least in part, a derivative action, brought on behalf of the corporation, and, in the words of the bill, "on behalf of . . . [the] stockholders" of Rodd Electrotype. Yet . . . the plaintiff's bill, in substance, was one seeking redress because of alleged breaches of the fiduciary duty owed *to her,* a minority stockholder, by the controlling stockholders.

We treat the bill of complaint (as have the parties) as presenting a proper cause of suit in the personal right of the plaintiff. . . .

7. An inference is permissible that the "gift" of these shares was a part of the "deal" for the stock purchase.

[handwritten margin notes: Donahue's shares passed to his wife + son. They wanted to sell at same price. Board refused.]

shares had passed to his wife and son. When the Donahues learned that the corporation had purchased Harry Rodd's shares, they offered their shares to the corporation on the terms given to Harry but the offer was rejected.[10] This suit followed.]

In her argument before this court, the plaintiff has characterized the corporate purchase of Harry Rodd's shares as an unlawful distribution of corporate assets to controlling stockholders. She urges that the distribution constitutes a breach of the fiduciary duty owed by the Rodds, as controlling stockholders, to her, a minority stockholder in the enterprise, because the Rodds failed to accord her an equal opportunity to sell her shares to the corporation. The defendants reply that the stock purchase was within the powers of the corporation and met the requirements of good faith and inherent fairness imposed on a fiduciary in his dealings with the corporation. They assert that there is no right to equal opportunity in corporate stock purchases for the corporate treasury. For the reasons hereinafter noted, we agree with the plaintiff and reverse the decree of the Superior Court. However, we limit the applicability of our holding to "close corporations," as hereinafter defined. Whether the holding should apply to other corporations is left for decision in another case, on a proper record.

[handwritten margin note: Holding limited to Close Corps]

A. *Close Corporations.* In previous opinions, we have alluded to the distinctive nature of the close corporation . . . but have never defined precisely what is meant by a close corporation. There is no single, generally accepted definition. Some commentators emphasize an "integration of ownership and management" (Note, Statutory Assistance for Closely Held Corporations, 71 Harv.L.Rev. 1498 [1958]), in which the stockholders occupy most management positions. . . . Others focus on the number of stockholders and the nature of the market for the stock. In this view, close corporations have few stockholders; there is little market for corporate stock. The Supreme Court of Illinois adopted this latter view in Galler v. Galler, 32 Ill.2d 16, 203 N.E.2d 577 (1965). . . . We accept aspects of both definitions. We deem a close corporation to be typified by: (1) a small number of stockholders; (2) no ready market for the corporate stock; and (3) substantial majority stockholder participation in the management, direction and operations of the corporation.

[handwritten margin note: def:]

As thus defined, the close corporation bears striking resemblance to a partnership. . . . Just as in a partnership, the relationship among the stockholders must be one of trust, confidence and absolute loyalty if the enterprise is to succeed. . . .

In Helms v. Duckworth, 101 U.S.App.D.C. 390, 249 F.2d 482 (1957) . . . Judge Burger, now Chief Justice Burger, writing for the court, emphasized the resemblance of the two-man close corporation to a partnership: "In an intimate business venture such as this, stockholders of a close corporation occupy a position similar to that of

10. Between 1965 and 1969, the company offered to purchase the Donahue shares for amounts between $2,000 and $10,000 ($40 to $200 a share). The Donahues rejected these offers.

joint adventurers and partners. While courts have sometimes declared stockholders 'do not bear toward each other that same relation of trust and confidence which prevails in partnerships,' this view ignores the practical realities of the organization and functioning of a small 'two-man' corporation organized to carry on a small business enterprise in which the stockholders, directors, and managers are the same persons" (footnotes omitted). Id. at 486.

Although the corporate form provides . . . advantages for the stockholders (limited liability, perpetuity, and so forth), it also supplies an opportunity for the majority stockholders to oppress or disadvantage minority stockholders. The minority is vulnerable to a variety of oppressive devices, termed "freeze-outs," which the majority may employ. . . . An authoritative study of such "freeze-outs" enumerates some of the possibilities: "The squeezers . . . may refuse to declare dividends; they may drain off the corporation's earnings in the form of exorbitant salaries and bonuses to the majority shareholder-officers and perhaps to their relatives, or in the form of high rent by the corporation for property leased from majority shareholders . . .; they may deprive minority shareholders of corporate offices and of employment by the company. . . ."

The minority can, of course, initiate suit against the majority and their directors. Self-serving conduct by directors is proscribed by the director's fiduciary obligation to the corporation. . . . However, in practice, the plaintiff will find difficulty in challenging dividend or employment policies. Such policies are considered to be within the judgment of the directors . . . [G]enerally, plaintiffs who seek judicial assistance against corporate dividend or employment policies do not prevail. . . .

Thus, when these types of "freeze-outs" are attempted by the majority stockholders, the minority stockholders, cut off from all corporation-related revenues, must either suffer their losses or seek a buyer for their shares. Many minority stockholders will be unwilling or unable to wait for an alteration in majority policy. Typically, the minority stockholder in a close corporation has a substantial percentage of his personal assets invested in the corporation. The stockholder may have anticipated that his salary from his position with the corporation would be his livelihood. Thus, he cannot afford to wait passively. He must liquidate his investment in the close corporation in order to reinvest the funds in income-producing enterprises.

At this point, the true plight of the minority stockholder in a close corporation becomes manifest. He cannot easily reclaim his capital. In a large public corporation, the oppressed or dissident minority stockholder could sell his stock in order to extricate some of his invested capital. By definition, this market is not available for shares in the close corporation. In a partnership, a partner who feels abused by his fellow partners may cause dissolution by his "express will . . . at any time" . . . and recover his share of partnership assets and accumulated profits. . . . By contrast, the stockholder in the close corporation or "incorporated partnership" may achieve dissolution and recovery of his share of the enterprise assets only by compliance with the rigorous terms of the applicable chapter of the General Laws. . . .

Thus, in a close corporation, the minority stockholders may be trapped in a disadvantageous situation. No outsider would knowingly assume the position of the disadvantaged minority. The outsider would have the same difficulties. To cut losses, the minority stockholder may be compelled to deal with the majority. This is the capstone of the majority plan. Majority "freeze-out" schemes which withhold dividends are designed to compel the minority to relinquish stock at inadequate prices. . . . When the minority stockholder agrees to sell out at less than fair value, the majority has won.

Because of the fundamental resemblance of the close corporation to the partnership, the trust and confidence which are essential to this scale and manner of enterprise, and the inherent danger to minority interests in the close corporation, we hold that stockholders [17] in the close corporation owe one another substantially the same fiduciary duty in the operation of the enterprise [18] that partners owe to one another. In our previous decisions, we have defined the standard of duty owed by partners to one another as the "utmost good faith and loyalty." Cardullo v. Landau, 329 Mass. 5, 8, 105 N.E.2d 843 (1952); DeCotis v. D'Antona, 350 Mass. 165, 168, 214 N.E.2d 21 (1966). Stockholders in close corporations must discharge their management and stockholder responsibilities in conformity with this strict good faith standard. They may not act out of avarice, expediency or self-interest in derogation of their duty of loyalty to the other stockholders and to the corporation.

We contrast this strict good faith standard with the somewhat less stringent standard of fiduciary duty to which directors and stockholders of all corporations must adhere in the discharge of their corporate responsibilities. Corporate directors are held to a good faith and inherent fairness standard of conduct (Winchell v. Plywood Corp., 324 Mass. 171, 177, 85 N.E.2d 313 [1949]) and are not "permitted to serve two masters whose interests are antagonistic." Spiegel v. Beacon Participations, Inc., 297 Mass. 398, 411, 8 N.E.2d 895, 904 (1937). "Their paramount duty is to the corporation, and their personal pecuniary interests are subordinate to that duty." Durfee v. Durfee & Canning, Inc., 323 Mass. 187, 196, 80 N.E.2d 522, 527 (1948).

---

17. We do not limit our holding to majority stockholders. In the close corporation, the minority may do equal damage through unscrupulous and improper "sharp dealings" with an unsuspecting majority. See Helms v. Duckworth, 101 U.S. App.D.C. 390, 249 F.2d 482 (1957).

18. We stress that the strict fiduciary duty which we apply to stockholders in a close corporation in this opinion governs *only* their actions relative to the operations of the enterprise and the effects of that operation on the rights and investments of other stockholders. We express no opinion as to the standard of duty applicable to transactions in the shares of the close corporation when the corporation is not a party to the transaction. Cf. Andrews, The Stockholder's Right to Equal Opportunity in the Sale of Shares, 78 Harv.L.Rev. 505 (1965). Compare Perlman v. Feldmann, 219 F.2d 173 (2d Cir.), cert. den. 349 U.S. 952, 75 S.Ct. 880, 99 L.Ed. 1277 (1955) with Zahn v. Transamerica Corp., 162 F.2d 36 (3d Cir.1947).

The more rigorous duty of partners and participants in a joint adventure, here extended to stockholders in a close corporation, was described by then Chief Judge Cardozo of the New York Court of Appeals in Meinhard v. Salmon, 249 N.Y. 458, 164 N.E. 545 (1928): "Joint adventurers, like co-partners, owe to one another, while the enterprise continues, the duty of the finest loyalty. Many forms of conduct permissible in a workaday world for those acting at arm's length, are forbidden to those bound by fiduciary ties. . . . Not honesty alone, but the punctilio of an honor the most sensitive, is then the standard of behavior." Id. at 463–464, 164 N.E. at 546. . . .

B. *Equal Opportunity in a Close Corporation.* Under settled Massachusetts law, a domestic corporation, unless forbidden by statute, has the power to purchase its own shares. . . . An agreement to reacquire stock "[is] enforceable, subject, at least, to the limitations that the purchase must be made in good faith and without prejudice to creditors and stockholders." . . . When the corporation reacquiring its own stock is a close corporation, the purchase is subject to the additional requirement, in the light of our holding in this opinion, that the stockholders, who, as directors or controlling stockholders, caused the corporation to enter into the stock purchase agreement, must have acted with the utmost good faith and loyalty to the other stockholders.

To meet this test, if the stockholder whose shares were purchased was a member of the controlling group, the controlling stockholders must cause the corporation to offer each stockholder an equal opportunity to sell a ratable number of his shares to the corporation at an identical price. Purchase by the corporation confers substantial benefits on the members of the controlling group whose shares were purchased. These benefits are not available to the minority stockholders if the corporation does not also offer them an opportunity to sell their shares. The controlling group may not, consistent with its strict duty to the minority, utilize its control of the corporation to obtain special advantages and disproportionate benefit from its share ownership. See Jones v. H.F. Ahmanson & Co., 1 Cal.3d 93, 108, 81 Cal. Rptr. 592, 460 P.2d 464 (1969); Note, 83 Harv.L.Rev. 1904, 1908 (1970). Cf. Brudney and Chirelstein, Fair Shares in Corporate Mergers and Takeovers, 88 Harv.L.Rev. 297, 334 (1974).

The benefits conferred by the purchase are twofold: (1) provision of a market for shares; (2) access to corporate assets for personal use. By definition, there is no ready market for shares of a close corporation. The purchase creates a market for shares which previously had been unmarketable. It transforms a previously illiquid investment into a liquid one. If the close corporation purchases shares only from a member of the controlling group, the controlling stockholder can convert his shares into cash at a time when none of the other stockholders can. Consistent with its strict fiduciary duty, the controlling group may not utilize its control of the corporation to establish an exclusive market in previously unmarketable shares from which the minority stockholders are excluded. See Jones v. H.F. Ahmanson & Co. . . .

The purchase also distributes corporate assets to the stockholder whose shares were purchased. Unless an equal opportunity is given to all stockholders, the purchase of shares from a member of the controlling group operates as a *preferential* distribution of assets. In exchange for his shares, he receives a percentage of the contributed capital and accumulated profits of the enterprise. The funds he so receives are available for his personal use. The other stockholders benefit from no such access to corporate property and cannot withdraw their shares of the corporate profits and capital in this manner unless the controlling group acquiesces. Although the purchase price for the controlling stockholder's shares may seem fair to the corporation and other stockholders under the tests established in the prior case law (see Spiegel v. Beacon Participations, Inc., 297 Mass. 398, 429, 8 N.E.2d 895 [1937]; Winchell v. Plywood Corp., 324 Mass. 171, 178, 85 N.E.2d 313 [1949]), the controlling stockholder whose stock has been purchased has still received a relative advantage over his fellow stockholders, inconsistent with his strict fiduciary duty—an opportunity to turn corporate funds to personal use.

The rule of equal opportunity in stock purchases by close corporations provides equal access to these benefits for all stockholders. We hold that, in any case in which the controlling stockholders have exercised their power over the corporation to deny the minority such equal opportunity, the minority shall be entitled to appropriate relief. To the extent that language in Spiegel v. Beacon Participations, Inc., 297 Mass. 398, 431, 8 N.E.2d 895 (1937), and other cases suggests that there is no requirement of equal opportunity for minority stockholders when a close corporation purchases shares from a controlling stockholder, it is not to be followed.

C. *Application of the Law to this Case.* We turn now to the application of the learning set forth above to the facts of the instant case.

The strict standard of duty is plainly applicable to the stockholders in Rodd Electrotype. Rodd Electrotype is a close corporation [under the test set out above]. . . .

. . . In testing the stock purchase from Harry Rodd against the applicable strict fiduciary standard, we treat the Rodd family as a single controlling group. . . . From the evidence, it is clear that the Rodd family was a close-knit one with strong community of interest. . . .

Moreover, a strong motive of interest requires that the Rodds be considered a controlling group. When Charles Rodd and Frederick Rodd were called on to represent the corporation in its dealings with their father, they must have known that further advancement within the corporation and benefits would follow their father's retirement and the purchase of his stock. . . .

On its face, then, the purchase of Harry Rodd's shares by the corporation is a breach of the duty which the controlling stockholders, the Rodds, owed to the minority stockholders, the plaintiff and her son. The purchase distributed a portion of the corporate assets to

Harry Rodd, a member of the controlling group, in exchange for his shares. The plaintiff and her son were not offered an equal opportunity to sell their shares to the corporation. In fact, their efforts to obtain an equal opportunity were rebuffed by the corporate representative. As the trial judge found, they did not, in any manner, ratify the transaction with Harry Rodd.

Because of the foregoing, we hold that the plaintiff is entitled to relief. Two forms of suitable relief are set out hereinafter. The judge below is to enter an appropriate judgment. The judgment may require Harry Rodd to remit $36,000 with interest at the legal rate from July 15, 1970, to Rodd Electrotype in exchange for forty-five shares of Rodd Electrotype treasury stock. This, in substance, is the specific relief requested in the plaintiff's bill of complaint. Interest is manifestly appropriate. A stockholder, who, in violation of his fiduciary duty to the other stockholders, has obtained assets from his corporation and has had those assets available for his own use, must pay for that use. See Silversmith v. Sydeman, 305 Mass. 65, 74, 25 N.E.2d 215 (1940). Cf. Spiegel v. Beacon Participations, Inc., 297 Mass. 398, 420, 8 N.E.2d 895 (1937). In the alternative, the judgment may require Rodd Electrotype to purchase all of the plaintiff's shares for $36,000 without interest. In the circumstances of this case, we view this as the equal opportunity which the plaintiff should have received. Harry Rodd's retention of thirty-six shares, which were to be sold and given to his children within a year of the Rodd Electrotype purchase, cannot disguise the fact that the corporation acquired one hundred per cent of that portion of his holdings (forty-five shares) which he did not intend his children to own. The plaintiff is entitled to have one hundred per cent of her forty-five shares similarly purchased.[30]

The final decree, in so far as it dismissed the bill as to Harry C. Rodd, Frederick I. Rodd, Charles H. Rodd, Mr. Harold E. Magnuson and Rodd Electrotype Company of New England, Inc., and awarded costs, is reversed. The case is remanded to the Superior Court for entry of judgment in conformity with this opinion.

So ordered.*

WILKINS, Justice (concurring).

I agree with much of what the Chief Justice says in support of granting relief to the plaintiff. However, I do not join in any implication (see, e.g., footnote 18 and the associated text) that the rule concerning a close corporation's purchase of a controlling stockholder's shares applies to all operations of the corporation as they affect minority stockholders. That broader issue, which is apt to arise

---

30. If there has been a significant change in corporate circumstances since this case was argued, this is a matter which can be brought to the attention of the court below and may be considered by the judge in granting appropriate relief in the form of a judgment.

* See also Comolli v. Comolli, 241 Ga. 471, 246 S.E.2d 278 (1978); cf. Schwartz v. Marien, 37 N.Y.2d 487, 335 N.E.2d 334, 373 N.Y.S.2d 122, (1975). For additional cases and materials on the fiduciary obligations of shareholders in close corporations, see Section 7(a), infra. (Footnote by ed.)

in connection with salaries and dividend policy, is not involved in this case.   The analogy to partnerships may not be a complete one.

NOTE

One response to the kinds of problems described in Donahue v. Rodd Electrotype Co. is to plan around them, by making special arrangements designed to suit the needs of the parties.   In a partnership, this would be a relatively simple matter: as regards internal arrangements, partnership law is highly contractual in nature—that is, it gives the parties wide scope to determine the rules by which their relationship will be governed.   In contrast, corporation law has not in the past been as attuned to contractualization, and in the corporate context there has often been serious question whether such arrangements will be deemed valid.   This remains a serious question; but as courts and legislatures have shown themselves increasingly ready to enforce internal arrangements, the close corporation has become increasingly contractual in nature, and eventually close corporation law may become as contractualized as partnership law.

The materials in Sections 2–5, infra, will be concerned to a large extent with the role of *planning* in the close corporation.   Section 6 will then consider the remedies available when planning has been inadequate or the problems are of a kind that resist advance solution.

SECTION 2. SPECIAL VOTING ARRANGEMENTS AT THE SHAREHOLDER LEVEL

(a) VOTING AGREEMENTS

RINGLING BROS.–BARNUM & BAILEY COMBINED SHOWS v. RINGLING

Supreme Court of Delaware, 1947.
29 Del.Ch. 610, 53 A.2d 441.

Suit by Edith Conway Ringling against Ringling Brothers–Barnum & Bailey Circus Combined Shows, Inc., and others to determine the right of individual defendants to hold office as directors or officers of the corporation and to determine the validity of election of directors at the 1946 annual stockholders' meeting.   From a decree for complainant entered in conformity with opinion of the Vice Chancellor, 49 A.2d 603, the defendants appeal. . . .

PEARSON, Judge.

The Court of Chancery was called upon to review an attempted election of directors at the 1946 annual stockholders meeting of the corporate defendant. The pivotal questions concern an agreement between two of the three present stockholders, and particularly the effect of this agreement with relation to the exercise of voting rights by these two stockholders. At the time of the meeting, the corporation had outstanding 1000 shares of capital stock held as follows: 315 by petitioner Edith Conway Ringling; 315 by defendant Aubrey B. Ringling Haley (individually or as executrix and legatee of a deceased husband); and 370 by defendant John Ringling North. The purpose of the meeting was to elect the entire board of seven directors. The shares could be voted cumulatively. Mrs. Ringling asserts that by virtue of the operation of an agreement between her and Mrs. Haley, the latter was bound to vote her shares for an adjournment of the meeting, or in the alternative, for a certain slate of directors. Mrs. Haley contends that she was not so bound for reason that the agreement was invalid, or at least revocable.

The two ladies entered into the agreement in 1941. It makes like provisions concerning stock of the corporate defendant and of another corporation, but in this case, we are concerned solely with the agreement as it affects the voting of stock of the corporate defendant. The agreement recites that each party was the owner "subject only to possible claims of creditors of the estates of Charles Ringling and Richard Ringling, respectively" (deceased husbands of the parties), of 300 shares of the capital stock of the defendant corporation; that in 1938 these shares had been deposited under a voting trust agreement which would terminate in 1947, or earlier, upon the elimination of certain liability of the corporation; that each party also owned 15 shares individually; that the parties had "entered into an agreement in April 1934 providing for joint action by them in matters affecting their ownership of stock and interest in" the corporate defendant; that the parties desired "to continue to act jointly in all matters relating to their stock ownership or interest in" the corporate defendant (and the other corporation). The agreement then provides as follows:

"Now, Therefore, in consideration of the mutual covenants and agreements hereinafter contained the parties hereto agree as follows:

"1. Neither party will sell any shares of stock or any voting trust certificates in either of said corporations to any other person whosoever, without first making a written offer to the other party hereto of all of the shares or voting trust certificates proposed to be sold, for the same price and upon the same terms and conditions as in such proposed sale, and allowing such other party a time of not less than 180 days from the date of such written offer within which to accept same.

"2. In exercising any voting rights to which either party may be entitled by virtue of ownership of stock or voting trust certificates held by them in either of said corporation, each party will consult and confer with the other and the parties will act jointly in exercising such voting rights in accordance with such agreement as they may reach with respect to any matter calling for the exercise of such voting rights.

"3. In the event the parties fail to agree with respect to any matter covered by paragraph 2 above, the question in disagreement shall be submitted for arbitration to Karl D. Loos, of Washington, D.C. as arbitrator and his decision thereon shall be binding upon the parties hereto. Such arbitration shall be exercised to the end of assuring for the respective corporations good management and such participation therein by the members of the Ringling family as the experience, capacity and ability of each may warrant. The parties may at any time by written agreement designate any other individual to act as arbitrator in lieu of said Loos.

"4. Each of the parties hereto will enter into and execute such voting trust agreement or agreements and such other instruments as, from time to time they may deem advisable and as they may be advised by counsel are appropriate to effectuate the purposes and objects of this agreement.

"5. This agreement shall be in effect from the date hereof and shall continue in effect for a period of ten years unless sooner terminated by mutual agreement in writing by the parties hereto.

"6. The agreement of April 1934 is hereby terminated.

"7. This agreement shall be binding upon and inure to the benefit of the heirs, executors, administrators and assigns of the parties hereto respectively."

The Mr. Loos mentioned in the agreement is an attorney and has represented both parties since 1937, and, before and after the voting trust was terminated in late 1942, advised them with respect to the exercise of their voting rights. At the annual meetings in 1943 and the two following years, the parties voted their shares in accordance with mutual understandings arrived at as a result of discussions. In each of these years, they elected five of the seven directors. Mrs. Ringling and Mrs. Haley each had sufficient votes, independently of the other, to elect two of the seven directors. By both voting for an additional candidate, they could be sure of his election regardless of how Mr. North, the remaining stockholder, might vote.[1]

Some weeks before the 1946 meeting, they discussed with Mr. Loos the matter of voting for directors. They were in accord that Mrs. Ringling should cast sufficient votes to elect herself and her son; and that Mrs. Haley should elect herself and her husband; but they

---

1. Each lady was entitled to cast 2205 votes (since each had the cumulative voting rights of 315 shares, and there were 7 vacancies in the directorate). The sum of the votes of both is 4410, which is sufficient to allow 882 votes for each of 5 persons. Mr. North, holding 370 shares, was entitled to cast 2590 votes, which obviously cannot be divided so as to give to more than two candidates as many as 882 votes each. It will be observed that in order for Mrs. Ringling and Mrs. Haley to be sure to elect five directors (regardless of how Mr. North might vote) they must act together in the sense that their combined votes must be divided among five different candidates and at least one of the five must be voted for by both Mrs. Ringling and Mrs. Haley.

did not agree upon a fifth director. The day before the meeting, the discussions were continued, Mrs. Haley being represented by her husband since she could not be present because of illness. In a conversation with Mr. Loos, Mr. Haley indicated that he would make a motion for an adjournment of the meeting for sixty days, in order to give the ladies additional time to come to an agreement about their voting. On the morning of the meeting, however, he stated that because of something Mrs. Ringling had done, he would not consent to a postponement. Mrs. Ringling then made a demand upon Mr. Loos to act under the third paragraph of the agreement "to arbitrate the disagreement" between her and Mrs. Haley in connection with the manner in which the stock of the two ladies should be voted. At the opening of the meeting, Mr. Loos read the written demand and stated that he determined and directed that the stock of both ladies be voted for an adjournment of sixty days. Mrs. Ringling then made a motion for adjournment and voted for it. Mr. Haley, as proxy for his wife, and Mr. North voted against the motion. Mrs. Ringling (herself or through her attorney, it is immaterial which,) objected to the voting of Mrs. Haley's stock in any manner other than in accordance with Mr. Loos' direction. The chairman ruled that the stock could not be voted contrary to such direction, and declared the motion for adjournment had carried. Nevertheless, the meeting proceeded to the election of directors. Mrs. Ringling stated that she would continue in the meeting "but without prejudice to her position with respect to the voting of the stock and the fact that adjournment had not been taken." Mr. Loos directed Mrs. Ringling to cast her votes 882 for Mrs. Ringling, 882 for her son, Robert, and 441 for a Mr. Dunn, who had been a member of the board for several years. She complied. Mr. Loos directed that Mrs. Haley's votes be cast 882 for Mrs. Haley, 882 for Mr. Haley, and 441 for Mr. Dunn. Instead of complying, Mr. Haley attempted to vote his wife's shares 1103 for Mrs. Haley, and 1102 for Mr. Haley. Mr. North voted his shares 864 for a Mr. Woods, 863 for a Mr. Griffin, and 863 for Mr. North. The chairman ruled that the five candidates proposed by Mr. Loos, together with Messrs. Woods and North, were elected. The Haley–North group disputed this ruling insofar as it declared the election of Mr. Dunn; and insisted that Mr. Griffin, instead, had been elected. A directors' meeting followed in which Mrs. Ringling participated after stating that she would do so "without prejudice to her position that the stockholders' meeting had been adjourned and that the directors' meeting was not properly held." Mr. Dunn and Mr. Griffin, although each was challenged by an opposing faction, attempted to join in voting as directors for different slates of officers. Soon after the meeting, Mrs. Ringling instituted this proceeding.

The Vice Chancellor determined that the agreement to vote in accordance with the direction of Mr. Loos was valid as a "stock pooling agreement" with lawful objects and purposes, and that it was not in violation of any public policy of this state. He held that where the arbitrator acts under the agreement and one party refuses to comply with his direction, "the Agreement constitutes the willing party . . . an implied agent possessing the irrevocable proxy of the recalcitrant party for the purpose of casting the particular vote." It was ordered that a new election be held before a master, with the direction that the master should recognize and give effect to the agreement if its terms were properly invoked. [In reaching this result, Vice Chancellor Seitz stated, "Here an implied agency based on an irrevocable proxy is fully justified to implement the Agreement without doing violence to its terms. Moreover, the provisions of the Agreement make it clear that the proxy may be treated as one coupled with an interest so as to render it irrevocable under the circumstances. . . . Obviously, to deny specific performance here would be tantamount to declaring the Agreement invalid. Since petitioner's rights in this respect were properly preserved at the stockholders' meeting, the meeting was a nullity to the extent that it failed to give effect to the provisions of the Agreement here involved. However, I believe it preferable to hold a new election rather than attempt to reconstruct the contested meeting. In this way the parties will be acting with explicit knowledge of their rights."]

Before taking up defendants' objections to the agreement, let us analyze particularly what it attempts to provide with respect to voting, including what functions and powers it attempts to repose in Mr. Loos, the "arbitrator". The agreement recites that the parties desired "to continue to act jointly in all matters relating to their stock ownership or interest in" the corporation. The parties agreed to consult and confer with each other in exercising their voting rights and to act jointly—that is, concertedly; unitedly; towards unified courses of action—in accordance with such agreement as they might reach. Thus, so long as the parties agree for whom or for what their shares shall be voted, the agreement provides no function for the arbitrator. His role is limited to situations where the parties fail to agree upon a course of action. In such cases, the agreement directs that "the question in disagreement shall be submitted for arbitration" to Mr. Loos "as arbitrator and his decision thereon shall be binding upon the parties". These provisions are designed to operate in aid of what appears to be a primary purpose of the parties, "to act jointly" in exercising their voting rights, by providing a means for fixing a course of action whenever they themselves might reach a stalemate.

Should the agreement be interpreted as attempting to empower the arbitrator to carry his directions into effect? Certainly there is no express delegation or grant of power to do so, either by authorizing him to vote the shares or to compel either party to vote them in accordance with his directions. The agreement expresses no other function of the arbitrator than that of deciding questions in disagreement which prevent the effectuation of the purpose "to act jointly". The power to enforce a decision does not seem a necessary or usual incident of such a function. Mr. Loos is not a party to the agreement. It does not contemplate the transfer of any shares or interest in shares to him, or that he should undertake any duties which the parties might compel him to perform. They provided that they might designate any other individual to act instead of Mr. Loos. The agreement does not attempt to make the arbitrator a trustee of an express trust. What the arbitrator is to do is for the benefit of the parties, not for his own benefit. Whether the parties accept or reject his decision is no concern of his, so far as the agreement or the surrounding circumstances reveal. We think the parties sought to bind each other, but to be bound only to each other, and not to empower the arbitrator to enforce decisions he might make.

From this conclusion, it follows necessarily that no decision of the arbitrator could ever be enforced if both parties to the agreement were unwilling that it be enforced, for the obvious reason that there would be no one to enforce it. Under the agreement, something more is required after the arbitrator has given his decision in order that it should become compulsory: at least one of the parties must determine that such decision shall be carried into effect. Thus, any "control" of the voting of the shares, which is reposed in the arbitrator, is substantially limited in action under the agreement in that it is subject to the overriding power of the parties themselves.

The agreement does not describe the undertaking of each party with respect to a decision of the arbitrator other than to provide that it "shall be binding upon the parties". It seems to us that this language, considered with relation to its context and the situations to which it is applicable, means that each party promised the other to exercise her own voting rights in accordance with the arbitrator's decision. The agreement is silent about any exercise of the voting rights of one party by the other. The language with reference to situations where the parties arrive at an understanding as to voting plainly suggests "action" by each, and "exercising" voting rights by each, rather than by one for the other. There is no intimation that this method should be different where the arbitrator's decision is to be carried into effect.

Assuming that a power in each party to exercise the voting rights of the other might be a relatively more effective or convenient means of enforcing a decision of the arbitrator than would be available without the power, this would not justify implying a delegation of the power in the absence of some indication that the parties bargained for that means. The method of voting actually employed by the parties tends to show that they did not construe the agreement as creating powers to vote each other's shares; for at meetings prior to 1946 each party apparently exercised her own voting rights, and at the 1946 meeting, Mrs. Ringling, who wished to enforce the agreement, did not attempt to cast a ballot in exercise of any voting rights of Mrs. Haley. We do not find enough in the agreement or in the circumstances to justify a construction that either party was empowered to exercise voting rights of the other.

[handwritten margin note: No empowerment of parties to exercise voting rights for each other]

Having examined what the parties sought to provide by the agreement, we come now to defendants' contention that the voting provisions are illegal and revocable. They say that the courts of this state have definitely established the doctrine "that there can be no agreement, or any device whatsoever, by which the voting power of stock of a Delaware corporation may be irrevocably separated from the ownership of the stock, except by an agreement which complies with Section 18" of the Corporation Law, Rev.Code 1935, § 2050, and except by a proxy coupled with an interest. . . .*

In our view, neither the cases nor the statute sustain the rule for which the defendants contend. Their sweeping formulation would impugn well-recognized means by which a shareholder may effectively confer his voting rights upon others while retaining various other rights. For example, defendants' rule would apparently not permit holders of voting stock to confer upon stockholders of another class by the device of an amendment of the certificate of incorporation, the exclusive right to vote during periods when dividends are not paid on stock of the latter class. The broad prohibitory meaning which defendants find in Section 18 seems inconsistent with their concession that proxies coupled with an interest may be irrevocable, for the statute contains nothing about such proxies. The statute authorizes, among other things, the deposit or transfer of stock in trust for a specified purpose, namely, "vesting" in the transferee "the right to vote thereon" for a limited period; and prescribes numerous requirements in this connection. Accordingly, it seems reasonable to infer that to establish the relationship and accomplish the purpose which the statute authorizes, its requirements must be complied with.

But the statute does not purport to deal with agreements whereby shareholders attempt to bind each other as to how they shall vote their shares. Various forms of such pooling agreements, as they are sometimes called, have been held valid and have been distinguished from voting trusts. . . . We think the particular agreement before us does not violate Section 18 or constitute an attempted evasion of its requirements, and is not illegal for any other reason.

Generally speaking, a shareholder may exercise wide liberality of judgment in the matter of voting, and it is not objectionable that his motives may be for personal profit, or determined by whims or caprice, so long as he violates no duty owed his fellow shareholders. Heil v. Standard G. & E. Co., 17 Del.Ch. 214, 151 A. 303. The ownership of voting stock imposes no legal duty to vote at all. A group of shareholders may, without impropriety, vote their respective shares so as to obtain advantages of concerted action. They may lawfully contract with each other to vote in the future in such way as they, or a majority of their group, from time to time determine.

Reasonable provisions for cases of failure of the group to reach a determination because of an even division in their ranks seem unobjectionable. The provision here for submission to the arbitrator is plainly designed as a deadlock-breaking measure, and the arbitrator's decision cannot be enforced unless at least one of the parties (entitled to cast one-half of their combined votes) is willing that it be enforced. We find the provision reasonable. It does not appear that the agreement enables the parties to take any unlawful advantage of the

---

* Section 18 was the precursor of Del. Gen.Corp.Law § 218, relating to voting trusts. Proxies coupled with an interest are discussed in the background note following *Ringling*. (Footnote by ed.)

outside shareholder, or of any other person. It offends no rule of law or public policy of this state of which we are aware.

Legal consideration for the promises of each party is supplied by the mutual promises of the other party. The undertaking to vote in accordance with the arbitrator's decision is a valid contract. The good faith of the arbitrator's action has not been challenged and, indeed, the record indicates that no such challenge could be supported.

Accordingly, the failure of Mrs. Haley to exercise her voting rights in accordance with his decision was a breach of her contract. It is no extenuation of the breach that her votes were cast for two of the three candidates directed by the arbitrator. His directions to her were part of a single plan or course of action for the voting of the shares of both parties to the agreement, calculated to utilize an advantage of joint action by them which would bring about the election of an additional director. The actual voting of Mrs. Haley's *no partial* shares frustrates that plan to such an extent that it should not be *performance* treated as a partial performance of her contract.

Throughout their argument, defendants make much of the fact that all votes cast at the meeting were by the registered shareholders. The Court of Chancery may, in a review of an election, reject votes of a registered shareholder where his voting of them is found to be in violation of rights of another person. Compare: In re Giant Portland Cement Co., 26 Del.Ch. 32, 21 A.2d 697; In re Canal Construction Co., 21 Del.Ch. 155, 182 A. 545. It seems to us that upon the application of Mrs. Ringling, the injured party, the votes representing Mrs. Haley's shares should not be counted. Since no infirmity in Mr. North's voting has been demonstrated, his right to recognition of what he did at the meeting should be considered in granting any relief to Mrs. Ringling; for her rights arose under a contract to which Mr. North was not a party.

With this in mind, we have concluded that the election should not be declared invalid, but that effect should be given to a rejection of the votes representing Mrs. Haley's shares. No other relief seems appropriate in this proceeding. Mr. North's vote against the motion for adjournment was sufficient to defeat it. With respect to the election of directors, the return of the inspectors should be corrected to show a rejection of Mrs. Haley's votes, and to declare the election of the six persons for whom Mr. North and Mrs. Ringling voted.

This leaves one vacancy in the directorate. The question of what to do about such a vacancy was not considered by the court below and has not been argued here. For this reason, and because an election of directors at the 1947 annual meeting (which presumably will be held in the near future) may make a determination of the question unimportant, we shall not decide it on this appeal. If a decision of the point appears important to the parties, any of them may apply to raise it in the Court of Chancery, after the mandate of this court is received there.

An order should be entered directing a modification of the order of the Court of Chancery in accordance with this opinion.

NOTE ON VOTING AGREEMENTS AND IRREVOCABLE PROXIES

Contracts among shareholders concerning the manner in which their shares will be voted—usually known as voting or pooling agreements—are of two general types. In one type the parties agree in advance on the exact way in which they will vote their shares during the term of the contract: for example, they may agree to vote for each other as directors. In a second type the parties do not agree in advance on the exact way in which they will vote their shares, but instead agree that during the term of the contract they will vote their shares as a unit, in a way to be decided by agreement, ballot, or other means. In dealing with both types of voting agreement the courts have been confronted with two questions: (i) Are such agreements valid? (ii) Assuming they are valid, how can their effectiveness be assured?

(1) Validity of Voting Agreements. The majority rule—reflected in *Ringling*—is that voting agreements of both types are generally valid. However, a number of cases—few if any of them recent—have held such agreements either invalid or revocable at will.

(a) Some of these cases rested on the theory that such agreements involve violation of a shareholder's duties. For example, in Haldeman v. Haldeman, 176 Ky. 635, 197 S.W. 376 (1917) the court said, "Although a stockholder may vote as he pleases, public policy forbids the enforcement of a contract by which a stockholder undertakes to bargain away his right to vote for directors according to his best judgment, and in the interest of the corporation. He has no right to disable himself by contract from performing this duty." See also Odman v. Oleson, 319 Mass. 24, 64 N.E.2d 439 (1946); Roberts v. Whitson, 188 S.W.2d 875 (Tex.Civ.App.1945). Other cases held that the mutual promises of shareholders in a voting agreement did not in themselves constitute sufficient consideration, or that the particular agreement involved an unreasonable duration. See 1 F.H. O'Neal & R. Thompson, Close Corporations §§ 5.04, 5.09, 5.11 (3d ed. 1987); Bridgers v. Staton, 150 N.C. 216, 63 S.E. 892 (1909); Morel v. Hoge, 130 Ga. 625, 61 S.E. 487 (1908); cf. Berkowitz v. Firestone, 192 So.2d 298 (Fla.Dist.Ct.App.1966).

In many or most of the cases holding voting agreements invalid or revocable (including *Haldeman, Odman,* and *Roberts,* supra), not all the shareholders were parties to the agreement. This element is sometimes stressed by the courts, and may have influenced the decisions even in those cases where it was not stressed. On the other hand, the same element is present in some of the cases (including *Ringling*) which have upheld such agreements. Should it make a difference whether this objection is raised by a shareholder who is a

party to the agreement, on the one hand, or by a nonparty shareholder, on the other?

(b) All courts hold that a voting agreement is invalid if it is based
on a "private benefit"—that is, a side payment—given by one party to
the other in exchange for his vote. A typical case is Palmbaum v.
Magulsky, 217 Mass. 306, 104 N.E. 746 (1914). P and D were
shareholders in American Biscuit Company. P held D's promissory
note, and agreed to surrender the note if D would vote his stock in
favor of a proposal to sell American Biscuit's assets. D voted for the
proposal but P refused to surrender the note, and brought suit upon
it. D set up the agreement as a defense, but the court held the
agreement illegal and therefore unenforceable. "It is the duty of a
stockholder of a corporation, in attendance at meetings of the stockholders, to act fairly and in good faith. He is not justified in entering
into any agreement to vote so as to perpetrate a fraud upon any other
stockholder. The defendant's vote to dispose of all the assets of the
corporation was in consideration of the surrender of the note to him
by the plaintiff. This was illegal and the agreement was void as
against public policy. . . . The contract in the case now before us
operated as a fraud upon [a third shareholder]." [1]

For an analagous statutory rule, see N.Y.Bus.Corp.Law § 609(e).

(c) Even courts that uphold voting agreements usually note that a
different result would follow if oppression or other wrong was
involved. See, e.g., Manson v. Curtis, 223 N.Y. 313, 319, 119 N.E.
559, 561 (1918).

*(2) Enforcement of Voting Agreements, Irrevocable Proxies, or Proxies
Coupled with an Interest.*

(a) *Damages and specific enforcement.* This brings us to the second
question raised by voting agreements—how can their effectiveness be
assured? Despite the fact that damages is normally an inadequate
remedy for breach of a voting agreement, those courts that uphold
such agreements have split on whether they will be specifically
enforced. The trend, however, is strongly in favor of granting this
remedy. See 1 F.H. O'Neal & R. Thompson, Close Corporations
§ 5.37 (3d ed. 1987). For example, in Weil v. Berseth, 154 Conn.

---

1. Accord: Stott v. Stott, 258 Mich. 547,
242 N.W. 747 (1932). See also, e.g., Brady
v. Bean, 221 Ill.App. 279 (1921) (agreement
by C to give S part of the amount C expected to receive as a corporate creditor
after a sale of corporate assets, if S would
withdraw his opposition to the sale);
Dieckmann v. Robyn, 162 Mo.App. 67, 141
S.W. 717 (1911) (agreement by P to pay a
commission to S if S voted to cause the
corporation to purchase P's property).

Although the private-benefit rule normally is not applied to render voting agreements invalid as such, Professor Painter
has observed that "any contract whereby
[a shareholder] agrees to vote in accordance with the wishes of others is bound to
be motivated by factors which, in a sense,

involve a personal benefit. The reasons
for pooling agreements are hardly ever
solely altruistic or confined exclusively to
the good of the corporation. . . ." W.
Painter, Corporate and Tax Aspects of
Closely Held Corporations 138 (2d ed.
1981). See also Note, Shareholder Vote
Buying—A Rebuttable Presumption of Illegality, 1968 Wis.L.Rev. 927.

The rule that a voting agreement based
on a private benefit is invalid is an application of the broader principle, well-established in corporate law, that a shareholder
may not sell his vote. See, e.g., Chew v.
Inverness Management Corp., 352 A.2d 426
(Del.Ch.1976); Macht v. Merchants Mortgage & Credit Co., 22 Del.Ch. 74, 194 A. 19
(1937).

12, 220 A.2d 456 (1966), A, B, C, and D, majority shareholders of Sales Corporation, entered into a voting agreement in 1954 under which they agreed, among other things: (i) to vote for the election of each other as directors; (ii) to vote to amend the by-laws by decreasing the number of directors from five to four; and (iii) not thereafter to vote to amend the new by-laws without the consent of all parties. The agreement was complied with until a shareholders' meeting in 1965, at which B, C, and D voted to adopt a new by-law increasing the number of directors to five, and to elect five directors including A, B, C, D, and B's son. A then filed suit seeking specific enforcement of the voting agreement and restoration of the old by-law. Recognizing that money damages would be an inadequate remedy, the Connecticut court held that A was entitled to an injunction requiring the defendants to repeal the new by-law and re-enact the original bylaw. The court also approved an injunction compelling B's son to resign if the trial court deemed such relief appropriate. See also Galler v. Galler, Section 3, infra; Beresovski v. Warszawski, 28 N.Y.2d 419, 322 N.Y.S.2d 673, 271 N.E.2d 520 (1971). But see Chayes, Madame Wagner and the Close Corporation, 73 Harv.L.Rev. 1532, 1535 (1960);

> The question of the relief to be granted for violation [of agreements among shareholders in the closely held corporation] raises problems more vexing, difficult, and real than ever were to be found on the validity side. What is in issue is the specific enforcement of an ongoing, intimate, personal, consensual relation. This is something the Anglo–American legal system has—wisely it may be supposed—not lightly granted as a matter of course.

(b) Proxies. To the extent the courts are reluctant to grant specific enforcement of voting agreements, the parties may expressly or impliedly substitute a self-executing remedy, such as a proxy. In Smith v. San Francisco & N.P. Ry. Co., 115 Cal. 584, 47 P. 582 (1897) three shareholders agreed to vote their shares together as determined by ballot. The court held that the agreement impliedly gave the two shareholders in the majority on any ballot an irrevocable proxy to vote the shares of the third. In *Ringling,* the Chancellor similarly held that the arbitrator had an implied proxy to vote the parties' shares as he determined, but the Delaware Supreme Court reversed on this issue.[2]

2. Compare Me. § 617:

2. When [a written voting] agreement specifies how the shares shall be voted, or provides a clear formula for ascertaining how the shares shall be voted, in case of a breach or anticipatory breach thereof by one or more parties thereto, the agreement shall, unless it specifically provides otherwise, be deemed to constitute an irrevocable proxy to the parties not in breach to vote all shares subject to the agreement in accordance with the terms of the agreement.

3. When such an agreement provides for a procedure such as the appointment of an arbitrator or umpire in the event of dispute, unless the agreement expressly otherwise provides, it shall be deemed to constitute an irrevocable proxy to such arbitrator or umpire to vote all shares subject to the agreement in accordance with his determination on the matters properly submitted to him under the terms of the agreement.

(c) Power coupled with an interest. Even if a proxy is expressly conferred in connection with a voting agreement, a further problem remains. Classically a proxy has been treated as an agency, in which the shareholder is the principal and the proxyholder is the agent. It is a rule of agency, however, that a principal can terminate an agent's authority at will, even if the termination is in breach of contract (although in such cases the principal may be liable to the agent in damages). There is an exception to this rule in cases where the agent holds a "power coupled with an interest," or, as Restatement (Second) of Agency § 138 calls it, a "power given as security." Generally speaking, this exception is applicable to arrangements in which it is understood that the "agent" or power-holder has an interest in the subject-matter to which the power relates, and is therefore expected not to execute the power solely on the power-giver's behalf—the crux of the normal agency relationship—but on his own behalf as well. Obviously, the safest way to insure that a proxy will be irrevocable is to confer it upon a proxyholder who has an "interest" in the shares to which the proxy relates. Relatively clear examples are cases where the proxyholder is a pledgee of the shares, or has agreed to purchase the shares. See N.Y.Bus.Corp.Law § 609(f)(1), (2).

If the general agency rules are applied to a proxy given pursuant to a voting agreement, the proxy would be revocable notwithstanding the agreement, unless it is deemed to be coupled with an interest. It is often unclear at common law, however, what constitutes a sufficient interest to make a proxy irrevocable. The problem is that where a proxy is given pursuant to a voting agreement, normally the proxyholder is either an arbitrator, who has no proprietary interest in the shares or the corporation, or a shareholder, who has a proprietary interest in the corporation but not in the shares that are the subject-matter of the proxy. In In re Chilson, 19 Del.Ch. 398, 409, 168 A. 82, 86 (1933), the court held that where the proxyholder has "some recognizable property or financial interest in the stock" the proxy would be validly irrevocable. However, the court held, where the proxyholder has only "an interest in the corporation generally," or "an interest in the bare voting power or the results to be accomplished by the use of" the proxy, the proxy would be revocable.[3] On the other hand, in Deibler v. Chas. H. Elliott Co., 368 Pa. 267, 81 A.2d 557 (1951), the Supreme Court of Pennsylvania, construing Delaware law, upheld the irrevocability of a proxy given to secure payment of the purchase price of stock in a Delaware corporation and the seller's continued employment by the corporation.[4] See generally Comment, Irrevocable Proxies, 43 Tex.L.Rev. 733 (1965).

---

3. See also Roberts v. Whitson, 188 S.W.2d 875 (Tex.Civ.App.1945).

4. Compare Breger v. Rusche, 219 Ind. 559, 39 N.E.2d 433 (1942) (agreement among several shareholders giving S a power to sell their stock, together with a proxy stated to be irrevocable, held not to create a power coupled with an interest, so that the proxy was revocable), with Everett Trust & Sav. Bank v. Pacific Waxed Paper Co., 22 Wash.2d 844, 157 P.2d 707 (1945) (agreement between two shareholders owning a majority of corporation's stock, each of whom had a twenty-five year option to buy the other's stock if it was offered for sale, coupled with a proxy in the survivor

(b) LEGISLATIVE STRATEGIES TOWARD THE CLOSE CORPORATION

N.Y. BUS. CORP. LAW §§ 609, 620
[See Statutory Supplement]

DEL. GEN. CORP. LAW §§ 212(c), 218(c), 341–346
[See Statutory Supplement]

CAL. CORP. CODE §§ 158(a), 705(a), 706(a), (d)
[See Statutory Supplement]

REV. MODEL BUS. CORP. ACT §§ 7.22(d), 7.31
[See Statutory Supplement]

MODEL STATUTORY CLOSE CORPORATION SUPPLEMENT §§ 1–3, 10, 20(a)
[See Statutory Supplement]

NOTE ON LEGISLATIVE STRATEGIES TOWARD THE CLOSE CORPORATION

As noted at the outset of this chapter, many of the problems raised by the early close-corporation case law reflects the fact that traditional statutory norms were drafted with publicly held corporations in mind. Accordingly, one of the major responses to these problems has been the enactment of new statutory provisions aimed primarily or exclusively at close corporations. The substantive content of such provisions will be considered throughout this chapter. The purpose of this Note is to lay the groundwork for that consideration by examining several different strategies, and clarifying the applicability of the principal statutes referred to in this chapter. The principal strategies to be examined are those exemplified by the California, Delaware, and New York statutes, and the Model Act. Almost all other close-corporation legislation either derives from or closely parallels one of these statutes.

(1) A Unified Strategy. One legislative strategy is to make no special provision for close corporations as such, but to modify tradi-

stated to be irrevocable, enforced against the deceased's executor). See Note, The Irrevocable Proxy and Voting Control of Small Business Corporations, 98 U.Pa.L. Rev. 401, 407 (1950).

tional statutory norms so that they will meet the needs of close corporations, although applicable to publicly held corporations as well. This kind of "unified" approach, which was exemplified by the Model Act until 1982, has been a very common strategy, although the tide seems to be turning against it.

(2) New York. A second strategy, exemplified by the New York statute, is to follow the unified approach up to a point, but to add one or two important provisions that are applicable only to those corporations with defined shareholding characteristics. Thus while N.Y.Bus. Corp.Law § 620(a) takes a unified approach by authorizing voting agreements in all corporations, N.Y.Bus.Corp.Law § 620(c) takes a definitional approach by authorizing certain kinds of certificate provisions "so long as no shares of the corporation are listed on a national securities exchange or regularly quoted in an over-the-counter market by one or more members of a national or affiliated securities association." [2]

(3) Statutory Close Corporations—Delaware, California, and the Model Act.

(a) Delaware. Like the New York statute, the Delaware statute follows the unified approach up to a point, through various provisions that modify traditional statutory norms so that they will meet the needs of close corporations, although applicable to publicly held corporations as well. Thus, Delaware provides considerable flexibility for close corporations even without special provisions applicable only to a limited class of corporations. The Delaware statute also contains, however, an integrated set of provisions, Subchapter XIV (§§ 341– 356), which are explicitly made applicable *only* to corporations that both qualify for and elect statutory close-corporation status. In effect, therefore, the statute contemplates a special subclass of close corporations, which may be called statutory close corporations. Under Del. Gen.Corp.Law § 342, a corporation can *qualify* for statutory close-corporation status if its certificate provides that:

> (1) All of the corporation's issued stock of all classes, exclusive of treasury shares, shall be represented by certificates and shall be held of record by not more than a specified number of persons, not exceeding 30; and

> (2) All of the issued stock of all classes shall be subject to 1 or more of the restrictions on transfer permitted by § 202 of this title; and

> (3) The corporation shall make no offering of any of its stock of any class which would constitute a "public offering" within the meaning of the United States Securities Act of 1933. . . .

Under § 343, a corporation that qualifies for statutory close-corporation status can *elect* such status by adopting a heading in its certificate

2. For other provisions that authorize certain types of arrangements so long as the corporation's shares are not traded on a securities market, see Mich. § 450.1463; N.C. § 55–73(b); N.J. § 14A:5–21; S.C. § 33–11–220(b), (c).

that states the name of the corporation and the fact that it is a close corporation.[3]

Most of the substantive provisions of Del.Gen.Corp. Law Subchapter XIV are enabling—that is, most of the provisions do not regulate the conduct of the shareholders or managers of such corporations, but simply authorize shareholders in statutory close corporations to enter into arrangements that would otherwise be unenforceable or of doubtful validity. As will be seen below, Subchapter XIV provides enormous flexibility—so much so, that for a well-advised corporation that elects to qualify under this Subchapter, almost everything will turn on the lawyer's drafting, rather than on corporate law. At the same time, the remaining provisions of the Delaware statute are sufficiently flexible so that much the same may be true even for close corporations which do not qualify under Subchapter XIV.[4]

(b) California. The California strategy is comparable to that of Delaware—that is, it involves a combination of (i) unified provisions that are particularly useful for close corporations but are not restricted to such corporations, and (ii) a systematic set of provisions applicable only to statutory close corporations. In contrast to the Delaware legislation, however, California's statutory-close-corporation provisions are scattered through the statute, rather than integrated in a single subchapter. In addition, there are important definitional differences. California does not require the articles of a statutory close corporation to either restrict stock transfers or prohibit public offerings. Instead, the articles need only provide that all of the corporation's issued shares "shall be held of record by not more than a specified number of persons, not exceeding 35"; state that "This corporation is a close corporation"; and include the words "corporation," "incorporated," or "limited" in the corporate name. Cal. §§ 158(a), 202(a).[5] As in Delaware, most of the California statutory close corporation provisions are enabling rather than regulatory.

3. Since the heading must be in the certificate, as a practical matter election of close-corporation status by an about-to-be organized corporation requires unanimous consent of all the organizers. However, where a corporation has already been organized as a nonelecting corporation, § 344 provides that it "may become a close corporation . . . by amending its certificate to conform to §§ 342 and 343 by a two-thirds class vote." Taken by itself, § 344 would therefore enable a two-thirds majority to adopt statutory close-corporation status over the objections of a one-third minority. Under § 342(2), however, a corporation cannot qualify unless all of its issued stock is subject to a transfer restriction authorized by § 202, and under § 202(b), no such restriction will bind securities issued prior to its adoption unless the holders of the securities assent. Arguably, the result is that unless the corporation has already adopted § 202(b) restrictions, a minority shareholder can block election of statutory close-corporation status by refusing to consent to the adoption of such restrictions.

4. Pennsylvania and Kansas have adopted integrated close-corporation statutes that are closely modeled on the Delaware statute. See Kan. §§ 17–7201–7216; Hecker, Close Corporations and the Kansas General Corporations Code of 1972, 22 Kan.L.Rev. 489 (1974); Pa. §§ 1371–86; Zeiter, A Comparison of the Pennsylvania Business Corporation Law and the New Delaware Corporation Law, 74 Dick.L.Rev. 1, 13–15, 64–67 (1969). Illinois has adopted an integrated statute which is generally patterned on the Delaware statute but departs from the latter in several important respects. See Ill. §§ 1201–1216. See also R.I.Gen.Corp.Act § 7–1.1–51.

5. Election of statutory close-corporation status requires a unanimous vote of the outstanding shares.

(c) The Model Statutory Close Corporation Supplement. In 1982, the ABA's Committee on Corporate Laws approved a Model Statutory Close Corporation Supplement ("MSCCS"), thereby reversing the Committee's longstanding posture that a special close corporation statute was unnecessary. The MSCCS is like the Delaware and California statutes in that it is applicable only to statutory close corporations. However, the MSCCS strategy is distinctive in significant respects. To begin with, the MSCCS avoids defining a statutory close corporation in terms of its shareholding or other characteristics. Rather, the MSCCS is applicable to (i) any corporation whose original articles of incorporation contain a statement that the corporation is a statutory close corporation and (ii) any corporation with fifty or less shareholders whose articles are amended by a two-thirds vote to include such a statement. (In the latter case, dissenting shareholders are entitled to elect to be paid the fair value of their shares). Moreover, while Delaware and California simply enable statutory close corporations to adopt reasonable restrictions on the transferability of shares, MSCCS § 11 provides that "[a]n interest in shares of a statutory close corporation may not be voluntarily or involuntarily transferred, by operation of law or otherwise, except to the extent permitted by the articles of incorporation or under section 12." (Section 12 is a first-refusal provision. See Section 5, infra.) Another set of MSCCS provisions, Sections 14–17, set out a standard form for the compulsory purchase of shares after the death of a shareholder, which a statutory close corporation can adopt by specifically so electing in its certificate.

While the MSCCS resembles the Uniform Partnership Act in important respects, it differs in at least one crucial particular. The provisions of the UPA are applicable to any business firm that constitutes a partnership in fact (any "association of two or more persons to carry on as co-owners a business for profit"), whether or not the firm's members denominate or even regard themselves as partners. In contrast, the MSCCS, like the counterpart California and Delaware provisions, is applicable only to those close corporations that specifically elect statutory close corporation treatment.

In considering the statutory provisions referred to throughout this chapter, it is important to keep in mind the following questions: (1) Is the provision applicable to all corporations or only to certain corporations? (2) If it is applicable only to certain corporations, what attributes must a corporation have to qualify under the provision? (3) Is the provision *regulatory* (one that governs corporate and shareholder conduct regardless of the parties' arrangements); *suppletory* (one that governs corporate or shareholder conduct unless the parties specifically make another arrangement); or *enabling* (one that serves principally to validate specific types of arrangements the parties may make)? (4) If the provision is *enabling*, what requirements must be met to adopt the arrangements it validates? (5) If the provision is applicable only to statutory close corporations, does it permit shareholders to accomplish objectives that could not be accomplished under the provisions of the statute applicable to all corporations?

NOTE ON CLOSE CORPORATION STATUTES

Modern statutes governing close corporations mark a considerable advance over close corporation law as it stood thirty or forty years ago. In general, however, the statutes still leave a lot to be desired.

The major problem can be simply stated: Most of the statutes are, for most purposes, applicable only to corporations that opt in, by an explicit election, for special statutory treatment. However, the data convincingly shows that only a tiny fraction of newly formed corporations elect such treatment. See Blunk, Analyzing Texas Articles of Incorporation: Is the Statutory Close Corporation Format Viable, 34 Sw. L.J. 941 (1980); 1 F. H. O'Neal & R. Thompson, O'Neal's Close Corporations § 1.18 (3d ed. 1987). The number of previously existing corporations that make such an election is undoubtedly even smaller. The result is that for many practical purposes, these statutes are much ado about nothing. Most of the modern statutes continue to leave close corporations in the lurch in important ways.

How did we get into such a situation? The legislatures may have adopted elective statutes on the premise that it is impossible to statutorily define the close corporation in a rigorous manner. However, such a definition is unnecessary. What the legislatures could do is draw a line, however arbitrary, based on number of shareholders—say, all corporations with ten shareholders or less—and adopt special provisions that are applicable to all corporations that fall under the line, subject, in most cases, to the corporation's right to opt out. In drawing that line, the legislature would not have to determine that all corporations with more shareholders should not receive special treatment. It would only say, "We know that all corporations that are under the line should receive special treatment; we will leave it to the courts to determine whether special treatment is available for other corporations." (Such an approach is reflected in some statutory provisions. For example, California makes special provision for dissolution in corporations with thirty-five or less shareholders. See Section 6, infra.) Special provisions that were available on an elective basis could stand side-by-side with this kind of legislation. In contrast, under the current regime, in which elective legislation constitutes the predominant statutory response, in most close corporations the shareholders must look to the courts, rather than the legislatures, for realistic rules to govern their enterprise and validate their self-government.

See Bradley, An Analysis of the Model Close Corporation Act and a Proposed Legislative Strategy, 10 J. Corp. Law 817 (1985); Elfin, A Critique of the Proposed Statutory Close Corporation Supplement to the Model Business Corporation Act, 8 J. Corp. Law 439 (1983).

(c) VOTING TRUSTS

DEL. GEN. CORP. LAW § 218

[See Statutory Supplement]

REV. MODEL BUS. CORP. ACT §§ 7.30, 7.31

[See Statutory Supplement]

CAL. CORP. CODE § 706(a)

[See Statutory Supplement]

NOTE ON VOTING TRUSTS

1. The creation of a voting trust normally involves (i) the execution of a written trust agreement between participating shareholders and the voting trustees, and (ii) a transfer to the trustee, for a specified period, of the shareholders' stock certificates and the legal title to their stock. The voting trustee then registers the transfer on the corporation's books, so that during the term of the trust the trustee is the record owner of the shares, entitled to vote in the election of directors and often on other matters as well. Dividends are paid by the corporation to the trustee, but are almost invariably then paid over by the trustee to the beneficial owners. Several statutes, e.g., Mich. § 450.1466, require the trustee to issue certificates of beneficial interest to participating shareholders, and frequently such certificates are issued even where not statutorily required, to facilitate trading in the beneficial interests.

Voting trusts are an effective and a moderately simple way to separate control and beneficial ownership for a limited period of time. The separation is self-executing, because the trustee is the legal owner and is registered as such on the corporation's books. The separation survives transfers by the beneficial owners, since they can transfer only their retained equitable interests (essentially, most ownership rights except the right to vote during the term of the trust). Upon termination of the voting trust, the beneficial owners receive stock certificates which reinstate them as complete owners, registered as such on the corporation's books.

2. The early attitude of the courts toward voting trusts was often highly unfavorable. See, e.g., Shepaug Voting Trust Cases, 60 Conn. 553, 24 A. 32 (1890); Warren v. Pim, 66 N.J.Eq. 353, 375, 59 A. 773, 789 (1904) ("[a]ny arrangement that permanently separates the voting power from stock ownership nullifies, to the extent of the stock involved, the annual submission of the question of the management of

the company to the stockholders"). The majority of courts, however, either declared voting trusts to be valid or held that the plaintiff was not in a position to attack them. See, e.g., Massa v. Stone, 346 Mass. 67, 190 N.E.2d 217 (1963); Carnegie Trust Co. v. Security Life Ins. Co., 111 Va. 1, 68 S.E. 412 (1910).

3. Most states now have statutes that both explicitly validate voting trusts and lay down certain requirements concerning their creation and their content. Among the most common limitations are a maximum time period (usually ten years), and a requirement that the voting-trust agreement be filed with the corporation and open to inspection. Such statutes are normally deemed to preempt the common law rules governing the validity of voting trusts. See, e.g., Abercrombie v. Davies, 36 Del.Ch. 371, 130 A.2d 338 (1957); Smith v. Biggs Boiler Works Co., 32 Del.Ch. 147, 82 A.2d 372 (1951); In re Morse, 247 N.Y. 290, 160 N.E. 374 (1928). The cases are not entirely uniform, however, in dealing with the consequences of failure to comply with the statutory requirements. Some cases have held that such a failure invalidates the voting trust. See, e.g., Abercrombie v. Davies, supra; Smith v. Biggs Boiler Works Co., supra (voting trust held invalid where no provision was made for deposit of stock with trustees); Christopher v. Richardson, 394 Pa. 425, 147 A.2d 375 (1959) (voting trust held invalid where under its terms it might have exceeded statutory ten-year period). Other cases have been considerably more tolerant. For example, in De Marco v. Paramount Ice Corp., 30 Misc.2d 158, 102 N.Y.S.2d 692 (1950), a voting trust was attacked on the ground that a copy of the trust agreement had not been filed in the office of the corporation, as required by the statute. The answer stated that the agreement had been filed after the action was brought. The court held that "the failure to file merely means that the trust agreement is not invalid but merely inoperative to permit the trustees to exercise the voting rights granted thereby until it is so filed." In Matter of Farm Industries, Inc., 41 Del.Ch. 379, 196 A.2d 582 (1963), the parties made an agreement to enter into a voting trust, but neither executed the trust nor filed a copy with the corporation. The court nevertheless specifically enforced the agreement. See also Jackson v. Jackson, 178 Conn. 42, 420 A.2d 893 (1979); Oceanic Exploration Co. v. Grynberg, 428 A.2d 1 (Del.1980).

4. Lack of a proper purpose presumably remains a ground for invalidating a voting trust, even if created under statute. Thus in Grogan v. Grogan, 315 S.W.2d 34 (Tex.Civ.App.1958), writ of error denied 159 Tex. 392, 322 S.W.2d 514 (1959), a voting trust was invalidated where its purpose was to continue the general manager in a "lucrative position" with the corporation and to establish his nephew as his successor. In general, however, "[t]he courts are inclined . . . to uphold any reasonable voting trust agreement for which any plausible reason may be advanced or against which no wrongful purpose may be shown," H. Ballantine, Corporations § 184a (1946).

See also Jackson v. Jackson, 178 Conn. 42, 420 A.2d 893 (1979).

(d) CLASSIFIED STOCK AND WEIGHTED VOTING

DEL. GEN. CORP. LAW § 212

[See Statutory Supplement]

REV. MODEL BUS. CORP. ACT §§ 6.01, 7.21, 8.04

[See Statutory Supplement]

NOTE ON CLASSIFIED STOCK AND WEIGHTED VOTING

Professor O'Neal suggests that "[o]ne of the simplest and most effective ways of assuring that all the participants or that particular minority shareholders will have representation on the board of directors is to set up two or more classes of stock, provide that each class is to vote for and elect a specified number or a stated percentage of the directors, and then issue each class or a majority of shares in each class to a different shareholder or faction of shareholders. . . . Class A common stock might be given power, for instance, to elect three directors and Class B common stock power to elect two." 1 F.H. O'Neal & R. Thompson, O'Neal's Close Corporations § 3.23 (3d ed. 1987). A few statutes validate this technique explicitly (e.g., N.Y. Bus.Corp.Law § 703), and most of the remaining statutes validate it implicitly by providing that a corporation may have one or more classes of stock with such voting powers as shall be stated in the certificate (e.g., Del.Gen.Corp.Law § 151(a)). In its simplest version, the use of classified common does not necessarily involve voting power for any class that is disproportionate to the investment made by that class. Often, however, separate classes carry voting power whose weight differs considerably from the relative investment made by their holders. At the extremes a class of stock may have proprietary rights but no voting power, or voting power but no proprietary rights. The possible utility of nonvoting stock in the close-corporation context has been illustrated as follows by Professor Hecker:

[A] common situation is for parties making unequal capital contributions to desire an equal voice in matters properly the subject of shareholder action. . . . [T]heir needs may be accommodated by use of voting and nonvoting stock. One class of voting stock with relatively few authorized shares and low par value can be allocated equally among the parties. A second class of nonvoting stock, which will represent the bulk of each party's investment, can be allocated among them in accordance with the capital contribution of each. The total of each shareholder's voting and nonvoting stock will then equal the amount of his capital contribution. Thus an arrangement roughly approximating a partnership will be created under which each party will have an equal voice in the election of directors and other shareholder matters but will share in corporate assets in proportion to his capital investment.[1]

SECTION 3. AGREEMENTS CONTROLLING MATTERS WITHIN THE BOARD'S DISCRETION

Voting arrangements of the kind discussed in Section 2, supra, control only those matters that are decided on a shareholder level. Typically, however, the issues that are most important to shareholders in a close corporation are determined on a board level—for example, managerial positions, managerial compensation, and dividends. If the shareholders attempt to also control these matters by agreement, the problem arises whether (or under what conditions) such an agreement is valid, in the face of the normal statutory provision that the business of the corporation shall be managed by or under the direction of the board. That question is addressed by the materials in this section.

McQUADE v. STONEHAM & McGRAW

Court of Appeals of New York, 1934.
263 N.Y. 323, 189 N.E. 234.

Appeal, by permission of Court of Appeals, from judgment of Appellate Division, First Department, unanimously affirming judgment for plaintiff for $42,827.38 and other relief.

POUND, Ch. J. The action is brought to compel specific performance of an agreement between the parties, entered into to secure the control of National Exhibition Company, also called the baseball club (New York Nationals or "Giants"). This was one of Stoneham's enterprises which used the New York Polo Grounds for its home games. McGraw was manager of the Giants. McQuade was, at the time the contract was entered into, a city magistrate. He resigned December 8, 1930.

Defendant Stoneham became the owner of 1,306 shares, or a majority of the stock of National Exhibition Company (there being then 2,500 shares outstanding). Plaintiff and defendant McGraw each purchased seventy shares of his stock. Plaintiff paid Stoneham $50,338.10 for the stock he purchased. As a part of the transaction

---

1. Hecker, Close Corporations and the Kansas General Corporations Code of 1972, 22 Kan.L.Rev. 489, 509 (1974).

the agreement in question was entered into. It was dated May 21, 1919. Some of its pertinent provisions are:

"VIII. The parties hereto will use their best endeavors for the purpose of continuing as directors of said company and as officers thereof the following:

AGREEMENT

"Directors: Charles A. Stoneham, John J. McGraw, Francis X. McQuade, with right to the party of the first part (Stoneham) to name all additional directors as he sees fit.

"Officers: Charles A. Stoneham, president; John J. McGraw, vice-president; Francis X. McQuade, treasurer.

"IX. No salaries are to be paid to any of the above officers or directors, except as follows: President, $45,000; vice-president, $7,500; treasurer, $7,500.

"X. There shall be no change in said salaries, no change in the amount of capital, or the number of shares, no change or amendment of the by-laws of the corporation or any matters regarding the policy of the business of the corporation or any matters which may in anywise affect, endanger or interfere with the rights of minority stockholders, excepting upon the mutual and unanimous consent of all . . . of the parties hereto.

"XIV. This agreement shall continue and remain in force so long as the parties or any of them or the representative of any own the stock referred to in this agreement, to wit, the party of the first part, 1,166 shares, the party of the second part 70 shares and the party of the third part 70 shares, except as may otherwise appear by this agreement. . . ."

In pursuance of this contract Stoneham became president and McGraw vice-president of the corporation. McQuade became treasurer. In June, 1925, his salary was increased to $10,000 a year. He continued to act until May 2, 1928, when Leo J. Bondy was elected to succeed him. The board of directors consisted of seven men. The four outside of the parties hereto were selected by Stoneham and he had complete control over them. At the meeting of May 2, 1928, Stoneham and McGraw refrained from voting, McQuade voted for himself and the other four voted for Bondy. Defendants did not keep their agreement with McQuade to use their best efforts to continue him as treasurer. On the contrary, he was dropped with their entire acquiescence. At the next stockholders' meeting he was dropped as a director, although they might have elected him.

The courts below have refused to order the reinstatement of McQuade, but have given him damages for wrongful discharge, with a right to sue for future damages.

The cause for dropping McQuade was due to the falling out of friends. McQuade and Stoneham had disagreed. The trial court has found in substance that their numerous quarrels and disputes did not affect the orderly and efficient administration of the business of the corporation; that plaintiff was removed because he had antagonized the dominant Stoneham by persisting in challenging his power over the corporate treasury and for no misconduct on his part. The court also finds that plaintiff was removed by Stoneham for protecting the corporation and its minority stockholders. We will assume that Stoneham put him out when he might have retained him, merely in order to get rid of him.

Defendants say that the contract in suit was void because the directors held their office charged with the duty to act for the corporation according to their best judgment and that any contract which compels a director to vote to keep any particular person in office and at a stated salary is illegal. Directors are the exclusive executive representatives of the corporation, charged with administration of its internal affairs and the management and use of its assets. They manage the business of the corporation (Gen.Corp.Law, Cons. Laws, c. 23, sec. 27). "An agreement to continue a man as president is dependent upon his continued loyalty to the interests of the corporation" (Fells v. Katz, 256 N.Y. 67, 72, 175 N.E. 516, 517). So much is undisputed.

Plaintiff contends that the converse of this proposition is true and that an agreement among directors to continue a man as an officer of a corporation is not to be broken so long as such officer is loyal to the interests of the corporation and that, as plaintiff has been found loyal to the corporation, the agreement of defendants is enforceable.

Although it has been held that an agreement among stockholders whereby it is attempted to divest the directors of their power to discharge an unfaithful employee of the corporation is illegal as against public policy (Fells v. Katz, supra), it must be equally true that the stockholders may not, by agreement among themselves, control the directors in the exercise of the judgment vested in them by virtue of their office to elect officers and fix salaries. Their motives may not be questioned so long as their acts are legal. The bad faith or the improper motives of the parties does not change this rule (Manson v. Curtis, 223 N.Y. 313, 324, 119 N.E. 559). Directors may not by agreements entered into by stockholders abrogate their independent judgment (Creed v. Copps, 103 Vt. 164, 71 A.L.R.Ann. 1287).

Stockholders may, of course, combine to elect directors. That rule is well settled. As Holmes, Ch. J., pointedly said (Brightman v. Bates, 175 Mass. 105, 110, 55 N.E. 809, 811): "If stockholders want to make their power felt, they must unite. There is no reason why a majority should not agree to keep together." The power to unite is, however, limited to the election of directors and is not extended to contracts whereby limitations are placed on the power of directors to manage the business of the corporation by the selection of agents at defined salaries.

The minority shareholders whose interests McQuade says he has been punished for protecting, are not, aside from himself, complaining about his discharge. He is not acting for the corporation or for them in this action. It is impossible to see how the corporation has been injured by the substitution of Bondy as treasurer in place of McQuade. As McQuade represents himself in this action and seeks redress for his own wrongs, "we prefer to listen to [the corporation and the minority stockholders] before any decision as to their wrongs" (Faulds v. Yates, 57 Ill. 416).

It is urged that we should pay heed to the morals and manners of the market place to sustain this agreement, and that we should hold that its violation gives rise to a cause of action for damages, rather than base our decision on any outworn notions of public policy. Public policy is a dangerous guide in determining the validity of a contract, and courts should not interfere lightly with the freedom of competent parties to make their own contracts. We do not close our eyes to the fact that such agreements, tacitly or openly arrived at, are not uncommon, especially in close corporations where the stockholders are doing business for convenience under a corporate organization. We know that majority stockholders, united in voting trusts, effectively manage the business of a corporation by choosing trustworthy directors to reflect their policies in the corporate management. Nor are we unmindful that McQuade has, so the court has found, been shabbily treated as a purchaser of stock from Stoneham. We have said: "A trustee is held to something stricter than the morals of the market place" (Meinhard v. Salmon, 249 N.Y. 458, 464, 164 N.E. 545, 546), but Stoneham and McGraw were not trustees for McQuade as an individual. Their duty was to the corporation and its stockholders, to be exercised according to their unrestricted lawful judgment. They were under no legal obligation to deal righteously with McQuade if it was against public policy to do so.

The courts do not enforce mere moral obligations, nor legal ones either, unless someone seeks to establish rights which may be waived by custom and for convenience. We are constrained by authority to hold that a contract is illegal and void so far as it precludes the board of directors, at the risk of incurring legal liability, from changing officers, salaries or policies or retaining individuals in office, except by consent of the contracting parties. On the whole, such a holding is probably preferable to one which would open the courts to pass on the motives of directors in the lawful exercise of their trust. . . .

The judgment of the Appellate Division and that of the Trial Term should be reversed and the complaint dismissed, with costs in all courts.*

[The opinion of Lehman, J., concurring in the result, is omitted.]

———

NOTE ON MANSON v. CURTIS

In an earlier New York case, Manson v. Curtis, 223 N.Y. 313, 119 N.E. 559 (1918), plaintiff and defendant each owned 30 percent

* The court also held that the agreement violated the Inferior Criminal Courts Act, which provided that "[n]o city magistrate shall engage in any other business or profession . . ., but each of said justices and magistrates shall devote his whole time and capacity, so far as the public interest demands, to the duties of his office. . . ." At the date of the agreement McQuade was a city magistrate, and he did not resign his position until after commencement of the action. (Footnote by ed.)

of the corporation's stock. Of the balance, 21 percent was owned by C, who had a contract with plaintiff under which C agreed to acquiesce in and follow business policy laid down by plaintiff, and to offer his shares to plaintiff before selling them to a third party. The other 19 percent was owned by eight other shareholders, whom plaintiff allegedly could control for voting purposes. Plaintiff and defendant then made a contract under which plaintiff allowed defendant to buy C's stock, and thereby become the majority shareholder. Under this contract, defendant agreed to a passive president and directors, none of whom were to interfere for one year with plaintiff's manner of doing business. Defendant broke this part of the contract, and "raided" the corporation until it was bankrupt. In a suit for damages for breach of the contract, held for defendant, on the ground that the contract was illegal because it would have "sterilized the board of directors." The court reasoned that while it was not "illegal or against public policy for . . . stockholders owning the majority of ·stock to unite upon a course of corporate policy or action, or upon the officers whom they will elect," they cannot provide for a passive board of directors.

    . . . In corporate bodies, the powers of the board of directors are, in a very important sense, original and undelegated. The stockholders do not confer, nor can they revoke, those powers. They are derivative only in the sense of being received from the state in the act of incorporation. . . . Clearly the law does not permit the stockholders to create a sterilized board of directors. Corporations are the creatures of the state, and must comply with the exactions and regulations it imposes. . . .

    . . . The rule that all the stockholders by their universal consent may do as they choose with the corporate concerns and assets, provided the interests of creditors are not affected, because they are the complete owners of the corporation, cannot be invoked here. The fact that the plaintiff was able to control for voting purposes the eight minority stockholders, who were not parties to the agreement, if proved, would not make them parties or establish their consent to the agreement. . . .

CLARK v. DODGE

Court of Appeals of New York, 1936.
269 N.Y. 410, 199 N.E. 641.

CROUCH, J. The action is for the specific performance of a contract between the plaintiff Clark and the defendant Dodge, relating to the affairs of the two defendant corporations. To the complaint a joint answer by the three defendants was interposed, consisting of denials and a separate defense and counterclaim. To the separate defense and counterclaim a reply was made. . . . We shall deal . . . with the questions here presented in the light of the facts most favorable to plaintiff appearing in the pleadings only.

Those facts, briefly stated, are as follows: The two corporate defendants are New Jersey corporations manufacturing medicinal preparations by secret formulae. The main office, factory and assets of both corporations are located in the State of New York. In 1921, and at all times since, Clark owned twenty-five per cent and Dodge seventy-five per cent of the stock of each corporation. Dodge took no active part in the business, although he was a director and, through ownership of their qualifying shares, controlled the other directors of both corporations. He was the president of Bell & Company, Inc., and nominally general manager of Hollings–Smith Company, Inc. The plaintiff Clark was a director and held the offices of treasurer and general manager of Bell & Company, Inc., and also had charge of the major portion of the business of Hollings–Smith Company, Inc. The formulae and methods of manufacture of the medicinal preparations were known to him alone.

Under date of February 15, 1921, Dodge and Clark, the sole owners of the stock of both corporations, entered into a written agreement under seal, which after reciting the stock ownership of both parties, the desire of Dodge that Clark should continue in the efficient management and control of the business of Bell & Company, Inc., so long as he should "remain faithful, efficient and competent to so manage and control the said business;" and his further desire that Clark should not be the sole custodian of a specified formula but should share his knowledge thereof and of the method of manufacture with a son of Dodge, provided, in substance, as follows: That Dodge during his lifetime and, after his death, a trustee to be appointed by his will, would so vote his stock and so vote as a director that the plaintiff (a) should continue to be a director of Bell & Company, Inc. and (b) should continue as its general manager so long as he should be "faithful, efficient and competent"; (c) should during his life receive one-fourth of the net income of the corporations either by way of salary or dividends; and (d) that no unreasonable or incommensurate salaries should be paid to other officers or agents which would so reduce the net income as materially to affect Clark's profits. Clark on his part agreed to disclose the specified formula to the son and to instruct him in the details and methods of manufacture; and further, at the end of his life to bequeath his stock—if no issue survived him—to the wife and children of Dodge.

It was further provided that the provisions in regard to the division of net profits and the regulation of salaries should also apply to the Hollings–Smith Company.

The complaint alleges due performance of the contract by Clark and breach thereof by Dodge in that he has failed to use his stock control to continue Clark as a director and as general manager, and has prevented Clark from receiving his proportion of the income, while taking his own, by causing the employment of incompetent persons at excessive salaries, and otherwise.

The relief sought is reinstatement as director and general manager and an accounting by Dodge and by the corporations for waste and for the proportion of net income due plaintiff, with an injunction against further violations.

The only question which need -be discussed is whether the contract is illegal as against public policy within the decision in McQuade v. Stoneham (263 N.Y. 323, 189 N.E. 234), upon the authority of which the complaint was dismissed by the Appellate Division.

"The business of a corporation shall be managed by its board of directors." (General Corporation Law [Cons.Laws, ch. 23], § 27.) That is the statutory norm. Are we committed by the McQuade case to the doctrine that there may be no variation, however slight or innocuous, from that norm, where salaries or policies or the retention of individuals in office are concerned? There is ample authority supporting that doctrine (e.g., West v. Camden, 135 U.S. 507, 10 S.Ct. 838; Jackson v. Hooper, 76 N.J.Eq. 592, 75 A. 568). But cf. Salomon v. Salomon & Co., ([1897] A.C. 22, 44), and something may be said for it, since it furnishes a simple, if arbitrary, test. Apart from its practical administrative convenience, the reasons upon which it is said to rest are more or less nebulous. Public policy, the intention of the Legislature, detriment to the corporation, are phrases which in this connection mean little. Possible harm to bona fide purchasers of stock or to creditors or to stockholding minorities have more substance; but such harms are absent in many instances. If the enforcement of a particular contract damages nobody—not even, in any perceptible degree, the public—one sees no reason for holding it illegal, even though it impinges slightly upon the broad provision of section 27. Damage suffered or threatened is a logical and practical test, and has come to be the one generally adopted by the courts. (See 28 Columbia Law Review 366, 372.)

Where the directors are the sole stockholders, there seems to be no objection to enforcing an agreement among them to vote for certain people as officers. There is no direct decision to that effect in this court, yet there are strong indications that such a rule has long been recognized. The opinion in Manson v. Curtis (223 N.Y. 313, 325, 119 N.E. 559, 562) closed its discussion by saying: "The rule that all the stockholders by their universal consent may do as they choose with the corporate concerns and assets, provided the interests of creditors are not affected, because they are the complete owners of the corporation, cannot be invoked here." That was because all the stockholders were not parties to the agreement there in question. So, where the public was not affected, "the parties in interest, might, by their original agreement of incorporation, limit their respective rights and powers," even where there was a conflicting statutory standard. (Ripin v. U.S. Woven Label Co., 205 N.Y. 442, 448, 98 N.E. 855, 857.) "Such corporations were little more (though not quite the same as) than chartered partnerships." (Id. p. 447.) In Lorillard v. Clyde (86 N.Y. 384) and again in Drucklieb v. Sam H. Harris, Inc. (209 N.Y. 211, 102 N.E. 599), where the questioned agreements were entered into by all the stockholders of small corporations about to be organized, the fact that the agreements conflicted to some extent with the statutory duty of the directors to manage the corporate affairs was thought not to render the agreements illegal as against public policy, though it was said they might not be binding upon the directors of the corporation when organized. (Cf. Lehman, J., dissenting opinion in the McQuade case.) The rule recognized in Manson v. Curtis, and quoted above, was thus stated by Blackmar, J., in Kassel v. Empire Tinware Co. (178 App.Div. 176, 180, 164 N.Y.S. 1033, 1035): "As the parties to the action are the complete owners of the corporation, there is no reason why the exercise of the power and discretion of the directors cannot be controlled by valid agreement between themselves, provided that the interests of creditors are not affected." . . .

[handwritten margin note: Rule of Manson case]

Except for the broad dicta in the McQuade opinion, we think there can be no doubt that the agreement here in question was legal and that the complaint states a cause of action. There was no attempt to sterilize the board of directors, as in the Manson and McQuade cases. The only restrictions on Dodge were (a) that as a stockholder he should vote for Clark as a director—a perfectly legal contract; (b) that as director he should continue Clark as general manager, so long as he proved faithful, efficient and competent—an agreement which could harm nobody; (c) that Clark should always receive as salary or dividends one-fourth of the "net income." For the purposes of this motion, it is only just to construe that phrase as meaning whatever was left for distribution after the directors had in good faith set aside whatever they deemed wise; (d) that no salaries to other officers should be paid, unreasonable in amount or incommensurate with services rendered—a beneficial and not a harmful agreement.

If there was any invasion of the powers of the directorate under that agreement it is so slight as to be negligible; and certainly there is no damage suffered by or threatened to anybody. The broad statements in the McQuade opinion, applicable to the facts there, should be confined to those facts.

[handwritten margin note: McQuade should be confined to its facts.]

The judgment of the Appellate Division should be reversed and the order of the Special Term affirmed, with costs in this court and in the Appellate Division.

CRANE, CH. J., and LEHMAN, O'BRIEN, HUBBS, LOUGHRAN and FINCH, JJ., concur.

Judgment accordingly.*

---

* Accord: Simonson v. Helburn, 198 Misc. 430, 97 N.Y.S.2d 406 (1950). For further history of Clark v. Dodge, see: Clark v. Dodge, 28 N.Y.S.2d 442 (Sup.Ct. 1939), aff'd without opinion on appeal of Dodge, 261 App.Div. 1086, 28 N.Y.S.2d 464 (2nd Dept.1941), aff'd without opinion 287 N.Y. 833, 41 N.E.2d 102 (1942). It is interesting to note that in the end specific performance was never granted. Since Clark did not divulge the formulae to Dodge, Jr., "[t]his conclusion prevents the restoration of Clark to his former position as manager." (28 N.Y.S.2d at 444). (Footnote by ed.)

NOTE ON LONG PARK v. TRENTON–NEW BRUNSWICK THEATRES CO.

In Long Park, Inc. v. Trenton–New Brunswick Theatres Co., 297 N.Y. 174, 77 N.E.2d 633 (1948), Corporations A, B, and C, which owned all the stock in Trenton–New Brunswick Theatres Company, agreed that A would manage the Company for 19 years, with full power to supervise and direct its operations and set business policy. In an action brought by B, the agreement was invalidated. The court held that the arrangement was "clearly in violation of" the statutory norm that "the business of a corporation shall be managed by its board of directors." The court did not purport to find any possible injury to creditors or shareholders, and seemingly considered immaterial the fact that all the shareholders had joined in the agreement. Clark v. Dodge was distinguished as involving only "a slight impingement or innocuous variance from the statutory norm."

Accord: Kennerson v. Burbank Amusement Co., 120 Cal.App.2d 157, 260 P.2d 823 (1953).

GALLER v. GALLER

Supreme Court of Illinois, 1964, reh. denied 1965.
32 Ill.2d 16, 203 N.E.2d 577.

UNDERWOOD, Justice. Plaintiff, Emma Galler, sued in equity for an accounting and for specific performance of an agreement made in July, 1955, between plaintiff and her husband, of one part, and defendants, Isadore A. Galler and his wife, Rose, of the other. Defendants appealed from a decree of the superior court of Cook County granting the relief prayed. The First District Appellate Court reversed the decree and denied specific performance, affirming in part the order for an accounting, and modifying the order awarding master's fees. (45 Ill.App.2d 452, 196 N.E.2d 5.) That decision is appealed here on a certificate of importance.

There is no substantial dispute as to the facts in this case. From 1919 to 1924, Benjamin and Isadore Galler, brothers, were equal partners in the Galler Drug Company, a wholesale drug concern. In 1924 the business was incorporated under the Illinois Business Corporation Act, each owning one half of the outstanding 220 shares of stock. In 1945 each contracted to sell 6 shares to an employee, Rosenberg, at a price of $10,500 for each block of 6 shares, payable within 10 years. They guaranteed to repurchase the shares if Rosenberg's employment were terminated, and further agreed that if they sold their shares, Rosenberg would receive the same price per share as that paid for the brothers' shares. Rosenberg was still indebted for the 12 shares in July, 1955, and continued to make payments on account even after Benjamin Galler died in 1957 and after the institution of this action by Emma Galler in 1959. Rosenberg was not involved in this litigation either as a party or as a witness, and in July of 1961, prior to the time that the master in chancery hearings were concluded, defendants Isadore and Rose Galler purchased the 12 shares from Rosenberg. A supplemental complaint was filed by the plaintiff, Emma Galler, asserting an equitable right to have 6 of the 12 shares transferred to her and offering to pay the defendants one half of the amount that the defendants paid Rosenberg. The parties have stipulated that pending disposition of the instant case, these shares will not be voted or transferred. For approximately one year prior to the entry of the decree by the chancellor in July of 1962, there were no outstanding minority shareholder interests.

In March, 1954, Benjamin and Isadore, on the advice of their accountant, decided to enter into an agreement for the financial protection of their immediate families and to assure their families, after the death of either brother, equal control of the corporation. [The agreement was executed in July 1955, after Benjamin had fallen ill. In September 1956, Emma agreed to permit Isadore's son Aaron to become president for one year and agreed that she would not interfere with the business during that year. In December 1957, Benjamin died.] The evidence is undisputed that defendants had decided prior to Benjamin's death they would not honor the agreement, but never disclosed their intention to plaintiff or her husband. . . .

Shortly after Benjamin's death, Emma went to the office and demanded the terms of the 1955 agreement be carried out. Isadore told her that anything she had to say could be said to Aaron, who then told her that his father would not abide by the agreement. He offered a modification of the agreement by proposing the salary continuation payment but without her becoming a director. When Emma refused to modify the agreement and sought enforcement of its terms, defendants refused and this suit followed.

During the last few years of Benjamin's life both brothers drew an annual salary of $42,000. Aaron, whose salary was $15,000 as manager of the warehouse prior to September, 1956, has since the time that Emma agreed to his acting as president drawn an annual salary of $20,000. In 1957, 1958, and 1959 a $40,000 annual dividend was paid. Plaintiff has received her proportionate share of the dividend.

The July, 1955, agreement in question here, entered into between Benjamin, Emma, Isadore and Rose, recites that Benjamin and Isadore each own 47½% of the issued and outstanding shares of the Galler Drug Company, an Illinois corporation, and that Benjamin and Isadore desired to provide income for the support and maintenance of their immediate families. No reference is made to the shares then being purchased by Rosenberg. The essential features of the contested portions of the agreement are substantially as set forth in the opinion of the Appellate Court: (2) that the bylaws of the corporation will be amended to provide for a board of four directors; that the necessary quorum shall be three directors; and that no directors' meeting shall be held without giving ten days notice to all directors. (3) The shareholders will cast their votes for the above named persons

(Isadore, Rose, Benjamin and Emma) as directors at said special meeting and at any other meeting held for the purpose of electing directors. (4, 5) In the event of the death of either brother his wife shall have the right to nominate a director in place of the decedent. (6) Certain annual dividends will be declared by the corporation. The dividend shall be $50,000 payable out of the accumulated earned surplus in excess of $500,000. If 50% of the annual net profits after taxes exceeds the minimum $50,000 then the directors shall have discretion to declare a dividend up to 50% of the annual net profits. If the net profits are less than $50,000 nevertheless the minimum $50,000 annual dividend shall be declared, providing the $500,000 surplus is maintained. Earned surplus is defined. (9) The certificates evidencing the said shares of Benjamin Galler and Isadore Galler shall bear a legend that the shares are subject to the terms of this agreement. (10) A salary continuation agreement shall be entered into by the corporation which shall authorize the corporation upon the death of Benjamin Galler or Isadore Galler, or both, to pay a sum equal to twice the salary of such officer, payable monthly over a five-year period. Said sum shall be paid to the widow during her widowhood, but should be paid to such widow's children if the widow remarries within the five-year period. (11, 12) The parties to this agreement further agree and hereby grant to the corporation the authority to purchase, in the event of the death of either Benjamin or Isadore, so much of the stock of Galler Drug Company held by the estate as is necessary to provide sufficient funds to pay the federal estate tax, the Illinois inheritance tax and other administrative expenses of the estate. If as a result of such purchase from the estate of the decedent the amount of dividends to be received by the heirs is reduced, the parties shall nevertheless vote for directors so as to give the estate and heirs the same representation as before (2 directors out of 4, even though they own less stock), and also that the corporation pay an additional benefit payment equal to the diminution of the dividends. In the event either Benjamin or Isadore decides to sell his shares he is required to offer them first to the remaining shareholders and then to the corporation at book value, according each six months to accept the offer.

The Appellate Court found the 1955 agreement void because "the undue duration, stated purpose and substantial disregard of the provisions of the Corporation Act outweigh any considerations which might call for divisibility" and held that "the public policy of this state demands voiding this entire agreement".

While the conduct of defendants towards plaintiff was clearly inequitable, the basically controlling factor is the absence of an objecting minority interest, together with the absence of public detriment. . . .

At this juncture it should be emphasized that we deal here with a so-called close corporation. . . . For our purposes, a close corporation is one in which the stock is held in a few hands, or in a few families, and wherein it is not at all, or only rarely, dealt in by buying or selling. (Brooks v. Willcuts, 8th Cir. 1935, 78 F.2d 270, 273.)

Moreover, it should be recognized that shareholder agreements similar to that in question here are often, as a practical consideration, quite necessary for the protection of those financially interested in the close corporation. While the shareholder of a public-issue corporation may readily sell his shares on the open market should management fail to use, in his opinion, sound business judgment, his counterpart of the close corporation often has a large total of his entire capital invested in the business and has no ready market for his shares should he desire to sell. He feels, understandably, that he is more than a mere investor and that his voice should be heard concerning all corporate activity. Without a shareholder agreement, specifically enforceable by the courts, insuring him a modicum of control, a large minority shareholder might find himself at the mercy of an oppressive or unknowledgeable majority. Moreover, as in the case at bar, the shareholders of a close corporation are often also the directors and officers thereof. With substantial shareholding interests abiding in each member of the board of directors, it is often quite impossible to secure, as in the large public-issue corporation, independent board judgment free from personal motivations concerning corporate policy. For these and other reasons too voluminous to enumerate here, often the only sound basis for protection is afforded by a lengthy, detailed shareholder agreement securing the rights and obligations of all concerned. For a discussion of these and other considerations, see Note, "A Plea for Separate Statutory Treatment of the Close Corporation", 33 N.Y.U.L. Rev. 700 (1958).

As the preceding review of the applicable decisions of this court points out, there has been a definite, albeit inarticulate, trend toward eventual judicial treatment of the close corporation as *sui generis*. Several shareholder-director agreements that have technically "violated" the letter of the Business Corporation Act have nevertheless been upheld in the light of the existing practical circumstances, i.e., no apparent public injury, the absence of a complaining minority interest, and no apparent prejudice to creditors. However, we have thus far not attempted to limit these decisions as applicable only to close corporations and have seemingly implied that general considerations regarding judicial supervision of all corporate behavior apply.

The practical result of this series of cases, while liberally giving legal efficacy to particular agreements in special circumstances notwithstanding literal "violations" of statutory corporate law, has been to inject much doubt and uncertainty into the thinking of the bench and corporate bar of Illinois concerning shareholder agreements. See e.g., Cary, "How Illinois Corporations May Enjoy Partnership Advantages: Planning for the Closely Held Firm." 48 N.W.U.L.Rev. 427; Note, "The Validity of Stockholders' Voting Agreements in Illinois," 3 U.Chi.L.Rev. 640.

It is therefore necessary, we feel, to discuss the instant case with the problems peculiar to the close corporation particularly in mind. . . .

This court has recognized, albeit *sub silentio,* the significant conceptual differences between the close corporation and its public-issue counterpart in, among other cases, Kantzler v. Bensinger, 214 Ill. 589, 73 N.E. 874, where an agreement quite similar to the one under attack here was upheld. Where, as in Kantzler and here, no complaining minority interest appears, no fraud or apparent injury to the public or creditors is present, and no clearly prohibitory statutory language is violated, we can see no valid reason for precluding the parties from reaching any arrangements concerning the management of the corporation which are agreeable to all. . . .

Since the question as to the duration of the agreement is a principal source of controversy, we shall consider it first. The parties provided no specific termination date, and while the agreement concludes with a paragraph that its terms "shall be binding upon and shall inure to the benefits of" the legal representatives, heirs and assigns of the parties, this clause is, we believe, intended to be operative only as long as one of the parties is living. It further provides that it shall be so construed as to carry out its purposes, and we believe these must be determined from a consideration of the agreement as a whole. Thus viewed, a fair construction is that its purposes were accomplished at the death of the survivor of the parties. While these life spans are not precisely ascertainable, and the Appellate Court noted Emma Galler's life expectancy at her husband's death was 26.9 years, we are aware of no statutory or public policy provision against stockholders' agreements which would invalidate this agreement on that ground. . . . While defendants argue that the public policy evinced by the legislative restrictions upon the duration of voting trust agreements (Ill.Rev.Stat.1963, chap. 32, par. 157.30a) should be applied here, this agreement is not a voting trust, but as pointed out by the dissenting justice in the Appellate Court, is a straight contractual voting control agreement which does not divorce voting rights from stock ownership. That the policy against agreements in which stock ownership and voting rights are separated, indicated in Luthy v. Ream, 270 Ill. 170, 110 N.E. 373, is inapplicable to voting control agreements was emphasized in Thompson wherein a control agreement was upheld as not attempting to separate ownership and voting power. While limiting voting trusts in 1947 to a maximum duration of 10 years, the legislature has indicated no similar policy regarding straight voting agreements although these have been common since prior to 1870. In view of the history of decisions of this court generally upholding, in the absence of fraud or prejudice to minority interests or public policy, the right of stockholders to agree among themselves as to the manner in which their stock will be voted, we do not regard the period of time within which this agreement may remain effective as rendering the agreement unenforceable.

The clause that provides for the election of certain persons to specified offices for a period of years likewise does not require invalidation. In Kantzler v. Bensinger, 214 Ill. 589, 73 N.E. 874, this court upheld an agreement entered into by all the stockholders providing that certain parties would be elected to the offices of the corporation for a fixed period. In Faulds v. Yates, 57 Ill. 416, we upheld a similar agreement among the majority stockholders of a corporation, notwithstanding the existence of a minority which was not before the court complaining thereof. See also Hornstein, "Judicial Tolerance of the Incorporated Partnership," 18 Law and Contemporary Problems 435 at page 444.

We turn next to a consideration of the effect of the stated purpose of the agreement upon its validity. The pertinent provision is: "The said Benjamin A. Galler and Isadore A. Galler desire to provide income for the support and maintenance of their immediate families." Obviously, there is no evil inherent in a contract entered into for the reason that the persons originating the terms desired to so arrange their property as to provide post-death support for those dependent upon them. Nor does the fact that the subject property is corporate stock alter the situation so long as there exists no detriment to minority stock interests, creditors or other public injury. It is, however, contended by defendants that the methods provided by the agreement for implementation of the stated purpose are, as a whole, violative of the Business Corporation Act (Ill.Rev.Stat.1963, chap. 32, pars. 157.28, 157.30a, 157.33, 157.34, 157.41) to such an extent as to render it void *in toto*.

The terms of the dividend agreement require a minimum annual dividend of $50,000, but this duty is limited by the subsequent provision that it shall be operative only so long as an earned surplus of $500,000 is maintained. It may be noted that in 1958, the year prior to commencement of this litigation, the corporation's net earnings after taxes amounted to $202,759 while its earned surplus was $1,543,270, and this was increased in 1958 to $1,680,079 while earnings were $172,964. The minimum earned surplus requirement is designed for the protection of the corporation and its creditors, and we take no exception to the contractual dividend requirements as thus restricted. Kantzler v. Bensinger, 214 Ill. 589, 73 N.E. 874.

The salary continuation agreement is a common feature, in one form or another, of corporate executive employment. It requires that the widow should receive a total benefit, payable monthly over a five-year period, aggregating twice the amount paid her deceased husband in one year. This requirement was likewise limited for the protection of the corporation by being contingent upon the payments being income tax-deductible by the corporation. The charge made in those cases which have considered the validity of payments to the widow of an officer and shareholder in a corporation is that a gift of its property by a noncharitable corporation is in violation of the rights of its shareholders and *ultra vires*. Since there are no shareholders here other than the parties to the contract, this objection is not here applicable, and its effect, as limited, upon the corporation is not so prejudicial as to require its invalidation.

Having concluded that the agreement, under the circumstances here present, is not vulnerable to the attack made on it, we must consider the accounting feature of this action. The trial court allowed the relief prayed, an action we deem proper except as to the master's fees which were modified by the Appellate Court. Since no question is here raised regarding them, we affirm the action of that court in this respect. The questions as to salary which the Appellate Court correctly held were improperly increased became ones of fact to be determined by the trial court.

We hold defendants must account for all monies received by them from the corporation since September 25, 1956, in excess of that theretofore authorized.

Accordingly, the judgment of the Appellate Court is reversed except insofar as it relates to fees, and is, as to them affirmed. The cause is remanded to the circuit court of Cook County with directions to proceed in accordance herewith.

Affirmed in part and reversed in part, and remanded with directions.

NOTE ON FURTHER PROCEEDINGS IN GALLER v. GALLER

The decree in *Galler* became effective on February 11, 1965. It ordered Isadore and Rose to "account for all monies received by them from the company since September 25, 1956 [up to the time of the decree], in excess of that theretofore authorized," but provided that Isadore and Aaron be allowed "fair compensation . . . for services rendered by them to the corporation during said period." On remand, defendants argued that the salaries of Aaron and Isadore during the relevant period represented the fair market value of their services, and in any event since Isadore's $42,000 salary after Benjamin's death was a continuation of his salary under the agreement, it had been "theretofore authorized" within the meaning of the decree. The Appellate Court rejected both arguments. As to the former issue the court adopted the findings of a master who valued Isadore's services at $10,000/year and Aaron's at $15,000/year. As to whether continuation of Isadore's $42,000 salary was authorized by the agreement, the court said

> . . . Isadore's continued receipt of the same salary upon the death of Benjamin without the *quid pro quo* for his brother's family, is an alteration of the past arrangement, and was without authorization.

Furthermore, the clear import of the 1955 shareholders' agreement is that the partnership-like arrangement was intended to remain after the death of either Benjamin or Isadore. While not specifically addressing itself to salaries, the agreement provides that upon the death of either Benjamin or Isadore, four directors are to be elected; two from Isadore's family and two from Benjamin's family. The officers and their salaries are voted upon by the directors. Dividends are required to be paid provided $500,000 earned surplus is maintained. It may be inferred that this agreement sought to replace a deceased brother's position as an officer with members of his family, thereby permitting them to share equally in the company's earnings, including salaries, a significant means of distributing the corporate profits. This inference is not negated by the fact that no provision in the 1955 agreement requires equality of salaries between the family branches.

For other disputes among the Gallers after the Supreme Court's decree, see Galler v. Galler, 69 Ill.App.2d 397, 217 N.E.2d 111 (1966); Galler v. Galler, 95 Ill.App.2d 340, 238 N.E.2d 274 (1968).*

DEL. GEN. CORP. LAW §§ 102(b)(1), 141(a), 142(b), 350, 351, 354

[See Statutory Supplement]

REV. MODEL BUS. CORP. ACT §§ 2.02(b), 2.06, 8.01(b)

MODEL STAT. CLOSE CORP. SUPP. §§ 20, 21

[See Statutory Supplement]

N.Y. BUS. CORP. LAW § 620

[See Statutory Supplement]

CAL. CORP. CODE §§ 186, 300, 312

[See Statutory Supplement]

NOTE ON ZION v. KURTZ

In Zion v. Kurtz, 50 N.Y.2d 92, 405 N.E.2d 681 (1980) Lombard–Wall Group ("Group") was a Delaware corporation that was not a statutory close corporation. Zion held all of Group's class A stock and Kurtz held all of its class B. Zion, Kurtz, and Group entered into an agreement which provided that without the consent of the holders of class A stock—that is, without the consent of Zion— "the Corporation shall not . . . [e]ngage in any business or activities of any kind directly or indirectly, whether through any Subsidiary or by way of a loan, guarantee or otherwise." Later, two transactions were authorized by Group's board at the instance of Kurtz, over

---

* For another application of the *Galler* decision, see Pohn v. Diversified Industries, Inc., 403 F.Supp. 413 (N.D.Ill.1975).

Zion's objections. Zion brought an action for declaratory and injunctive relief. Held, for Zion.

Clear from [Del. Gen. Corp. Law §§ 141, 350, 351, and 354] is the fact that the public policy of Delaware does not proscribe a provision such as that contained in the shareholders' agreement here in issue even though it takes all management functions away from the directors. Folk, in his work on the Delaware Corporation Law, states concerning section 350 that "Although some decisions outside Delaware have sustained 'reasonable' restrictions upon director discretion contained in stockholder agreements, the theory of § 350 is to declare unequivocally, as a matter of public policy, that stockholder agreements of this character are not invalid" (at p. 518), that section 351 "recognizes a special subclass of close corporations which operate by direct stockholder management" (at p. 520), and with respect to section 354 that it "should be liberally construed to authorize all sorts of internal agreements and arrangements which are not affirmatively improper or, more particularly, injurious to third parties" (at p. 526).

Defendants argue, however, that Group was not incorporated as a close corporation and the stockholders' agreement provision was never incorporated in its certificate. The answer is that any Delaware corporation can elect to become a close corporation by filing an appropriate certificate of amendment (Del.General Corporation Law, § 344) and by such amendment approved by the holders of all of its outstanding stock may include in its certificate provisions restricting directors' authority (*ibid.,* § 351). Here, not only did defendant Kurtz agree in paragraph 8.05(b) of the stockholders' agreement to "without further consideration, do, execute and deliver, or cause to be done, executed and delivered, all such further acts, things and instruments as may be reasonably required more effectively to evidence and give effect to the provisions and the intent and purposes of this Agreement", but [he] executed a consent to the various parts of the transaction under which he was "authorized and empowered to execute and deliver, or cause to be executed and delivered, all such other and further instruments and documents and take, or cause to be taken, all such other and further action as he may deem necessary, appropriate or desirable to implement and give effect to the Stockholders Agreement and the transactions provided for therein." Since there are no intervening rights of third persons, the agreement requires nothing that is not permitted by statute, and all of the stockholders of the corporation assented to it, the certificate of incorporation may be ordered reformed, by requiring Kurtz to file the appropriate amendments, or more directly he may be held estopped to rely upon the absence of those amendments from the corporate charter. . . .

The result thus reached accords with the weight of authority which textwriter F. Hodge O'Neal tells us sustains agreements made by all shareholders dealing with matters normally within the province of the directors (1 Close Corporations § 5.24, p. 83), even though the shareholders could have, but had not, provided similarly by charter or by-law provision sanctioned by statute (*ibid.*, § 5.19, pp. 73–74). Moreover, though we have not yet had occasion to construe subdivision (b) of section 620 of the Business Corporation Law . . . it is worthy of note that in adopting that provision the Legislature had before it the Revisers' Comments that: "Paragraph (b) expands the ruling in *Clark v. Dodge*, 269 N.Y. 410, 199 N.E. 637 [641] (1936), and, to the extent therein provided, overrules *Long Park, Inc. v. Trenton–New Brunswick Theatres Co.*, 297 N.Y. 174, 77 N.E.2d 633 (1948); *Manson v. Curtis*, 223 N.Y. 313, 119 N.E. 559 (1919) and *McQuade v. Stoneham*, 263 N.Y. 323, 189 N.E. 234 (1934)." Thus it is clear that no New York public policy stands in the way of our application of the Delaware statute and decisional law above referred to. . . .

Three judges dissented:

It is beyond dispute that shareholder agreements such as the one relied upon by plaintiff in this case are, as a general rule, void as against public policy. Section 3.01 of the agreement, as interpreted both by plaintiff and by a majority of this court, would have precluded the board of directors of Group from taking any action on behalf of the corporation without first obtaining plaintiff's consent. This contractual provision, if enforced, would effectively shift the authority to manage every aspect of corporate affairs from the board to plaintiff, a minority shareholder who has no fiduciary obligations with respect to either the corporation or its other shareholders. As such, the provision represents a blatant effort to "sterilize" the board of directors in contravention of the statutory and decisional law of both Delaware and New York.

Under the statutes of Delaware, the State in which Group was incorporated, the authority to manage the affairs of a corporation is vested solely in its board of directors (Del.General Corporation Law, § 141, subd. [a]). The same is true under the applicable New York statutes (Business Corporation Law, § 701). Significantly, in both States, the courts have declined to give effect to agreements which purport to vary the statutory rule by transferring effective control of the corporation to a third party other than the board of directors. . . .

True, the common-law rule has been modified somewhat in recent years to account for the business needs of the so-called "close corporation". The courts of our State, for example, have been willing to enforce shareholder agreements where the incursion on the board's authority was insubstantial (*Clark v. Dodge*, 269 N.Y. 410, 199 N.E. 641). . . . Neither the courts of our State nor the courts of

Delaware, however, have gone so far as to hold that an agreement among shareholders such as the agreement in this case, which purported to "sterilize" the board of directors by completely depriving it of its discretionary authority, can be regarded as legal and enforceable. To the contrary, the common-law rule applicable to both closely and publicly held corporations continues to treat agreements to deprive the board of directors of substantial authority as contrary to public policy. . . .

Under Delaware law, as the majority notes, the shareholders of a close corporation are free to enter into private, binding agreements among themselves to restrict the powers of their board of directors (Del.General Corporation Law, § 350). The same appears to be true under the present New York statutes (Business Corporation Law, § 620, subd. [b]). Both the Delaware and the New York statutory schemes, however, contemplate that such variations from the corporate norm will be recorded on the face of the certificate of incorporation (Del.General Corporation Law, § 351; Business Corporation Law, § 620, subd. [b]). New York additionally requires that the existence of a substantial restriction on the powers of the board "shall be noted conspicuously on the face or back of every certificate for shares issued by [the] corporation" (Business Corporation Law, § 620, subd. [g]). Significantly, in both Delaware and New York, a provision in the certificate of incorporation restricting the discretion of the board has the effect of shifting liability for any mismanagement from the directors to the managing shareholders (Del.General Corporation Law, § 351, subds. [2]–[3]; Business Corporation Law, § 620, subd. [f]).

. . . In order to protect potential purchasers of shares and perhaps even potential creditors of the corporation, the Legislatures of Delaware and New York imposed specific strictures upon incorporated businesses managed by shareholders, the most significant of which is the requirement that restrictions on the statutory powers of the board of directors be evidenced in the certificate of incorporation. This requirement is an essential component of the statutory scheme because it ensures that potential purchasers of an interest in the corporation will have at least record notice that the corporation is being managed in an unorthodox fashion. Absent an appropriate notice provision in the certificate, there can be no assurance that an unsuspecting purchaser, not privy to the private shareholder agreement, will not be drawn into an investment that he might otherwise choose to avoid.

Since I regard the statutory requirements discussed above as essentially prophylactic in nature, I cannot subscribe to the notion that the agreement in this case should be enforced merely because there has been no showing that the interests of innocent third parties have actually been impaired. As is apparent from the design of the relevant statutes, the public policies of our own State as well as those of the State of Delaware remain opposed to shareholder agreements to "sterilize" the board of directors unless notice of the agreement is provided in the certificate of incorporation. Where such notice is provided, the public policy objections to the agreement are effectively eliminated and there is no further reason to preclude enforcement (see *Lehrman v. Cohen,* 43 Del.Ch. 222, 235, 222 A.2d 800). On the other hand, where, as here, the shareholders have entered into a private agreement to "sterilize" the board of directors and have failed to comply with the simple statutory prerequisites for "close corporations", the agreement must be deemed void and unenforceable in light of the inherent potential for fraud against the public. Indeed, since it is this very potential for public harm which renders these agreements unlawful, the mere fortuity that no one was actually harmed, if that be the case, cannot be the controlling factor in determining whether the agreement is legally enforceable. For the same reason, the illegality in the instant agreement cannot be cured retroactively, as the majority suggests, by requiring defendants to file the appropriate amendments to the certificate of incorporation. . . .

SECTION 4. SUPERMAJORITY VOTING AND QUORUM REQUIREMENTS AT THE SHAREHOLDER AND BOARD LEVELS

BENINTENDI v. KENTON HOTEL

Court of Appeals of New York, 1945.
294 N.Y. 112, 60 N.E.2d 829.

DESMOND, J. Two men who owned, in inequal amounts, all the stock of a domestic business corporation, made an agreement to vote for, and later did vote for and adopt at a stockholders' meeting, by-laws of the corporation, providing as follows: (1.) That no action should be taken by the stockholders except by unanimous vote of all of them; if, however, thirty days' notice of the meeting had been given, unanimous vote of the stockholders present in person or by proxy should be sufficient; (2.) That the directors of the corporation should be the three persons receiving, at the annual stockholders' meeting, the unanimous vote of all the stockholders; (3.) That no action should be taken by the directors except by unanimous vote of all of them; (4.) That the by-laws should not be amended except by unanimous vote of all the stockholders. The minority stockholder brought this suit to have those by-laws adjudged valid and to enjoin the other stockholder from doing anything inconsistent therewith. Special Term and the Appellate Division held that the two by-laws first above described were invalid and the other two valid. [181 Misc. 897, 45 N.Y.S.2d 705; 268 App.Div. 857, 50 N.Y.S.2d 843]. Both sides have appealed to this court.

In striking down the by-law (No. 2 above) which requires unanimous stock vote for election of directors, Special Term properly relied upon Matter of Boulevard Theatre & Realty Co., 195 App.Div. 518, 186 N.Y.S. 430, affirmed 231 N.Y. 615, 132 N.E. 910. This court wrote no opinion in that case. The Appellate Division had ruled, however, that a provision in the Boulevard Theatre's certificate of incorporation requiring unanimous vote of all stockholders to elect directors, violated <u>section 55 of the Stock Corporation Law,</u> Consol. Laws, c. 59, which says that directors shall be chosen "by a plurality of the votes at such election." We think it unimportant that the condemned provision was found in the certificate of incorporation in the Boulevard Theatre case, and in a by-law in the present case. . . .

The device is intrinsically unlawful because it contravenes an essential part of the <u>State policy,</u> as expressed in the Stock Corporation Law. An agreement by a stockholder to vote for certain persons as directors is not unlawful (Clark v. Dodge, 269 N.Y. 410, 415, 199 N.E. 641) since the directors are still, under such an agreement, elected by a plurality of votes, as the statute mandates. But a requirement, wherever found, that there shall be no election of directors at all unless every single vote be cast for the same nominees, is in direct opposition to the statutory rule—that the receipt of a plurality of the votes entitles a nominee to election.

Although not covered by the Boulevard Theatre case, or any other decision we have found, the by-law (No. 1 above) which requires unanimous action of stockholders to pass any resolution or take any action of any kind, is <u>equally obnoxious to the statutory scheme of stock corporation management.</u> The State, granting to individuals the privilege of limiting their individual liabilities for business debts by forming themselves into an entity separate and distinct from the persons who own it, demands in turn that the entity take a prescribed form and conduct itself, procedurally, according to fixed rules. As Special Term pointed out in this case, the Legislature, for reasons thought by it to be sufficient, has specified the various percentages of stock vote necessary to pass different kinds of resolutions. For instance, sections 36 and 37 of the Stock Corporation Law require an affirmative two-thirds vote for changing the capitalization, while section 102 of the General Corporation Law empowers the holders of a majority of the stock to force the directors to dissolve the corporation, and section 103 of that law gives the same power to holders of half the stock, if there be a deadlock on the question of dissolution. Any corporation may arrive at a condition where dissolution is the right and necessary course. The Legislature has decided that a vote of a majority of the shares, or half of them in case of a deadlock, is sufficient to force a dissolution. Yet under the by-laws of this corporation, the minority stockholder could prevent dissolution until such time as he should decide to vote for it.

Those who own all the stock of a corporation may, so long as they conduct the corporate affairs in accordance with the statutory rules, deal as they will with the corporation's property (always assuming nothing is done prejudicial to creditors' rights). <u>They may, individually, bind themselves in advance to vote in a certain way or for certain persons.</u> But this State has decreed that every stock corporation chartered by it must have a representative government, with <u>voting conducted conformably to the statutes,</u> and the power of decision lodged in certain fractions, always more than half, of the stock. That whole concept is destroyed when the stockholders, by agreement, by-law or certificate of incorporation provision as to unanimous action, give the minority interest an absolute, permanent, all-inclusive power of veto. We do not hold that an arrangement would necessarily be invalid, which, for particular decisions, would require unanimous consent of all stockholders. See for instance, Ripin v. United States Woven Label Co., 205 N.Y. 442, 98 N.E. 855; Tompkins v. Hale, 284 N.Y. 675, 30 N.E.2d 721. In Tompkins v. Hale, supra, the stockholders of a "cooperative apartment house" had agreed in writing that such leases could be canceled and surrendered only if all the stockholder-tenants concurred. That is a far cry from a by-law which prohibits any nonunanimous determination on any corporate question.

The by-law numbered 3 in our list above makes it impossible for the directors to act on any matter except by unanimous vote of all of them. Such a by-law, like the others already discussed herein, is, almost as a matter of law, unworkable and unenforcible for the reason given by the Court of King's Bench in Hascard v. Somany, 1 Freeman 504, in 1693: "primâ facie in all acts done by a corporation, the major number must bind the lesser, or else differences could never be determined."

The directors of a corporation are a select body, chosen by the stockholders. By Section 27 of the General Corporation Law, the board as such is given the power of management of the corporation. At common law only a majority thereof were needed for a quorum and a majority of that quorum could transact business. Ex parte Willcocks, 7 Cow. 402, 17 Am.Dec. 525. Section 27 modifies that common-law rule only to the extent of permitting a corporation to enact a by-law fixing "the number of directors necessary to constitute a quorum at a number less than a majority of the board, but not less than one-third of its number." Every corporation is thus given the privilege of enacting a by-law fixing its own quorum requirement at any fraction not less than one-third, nor more than a majority, of its directors. But the very idea of a "quorum" is that, when that required number of persons goes into session as a body, the votes of a majority thereof are sufficient for binding action. See for example, Harroun v. Brush Electric Light Co., 152 N.Y. 212, 46 N.E. 291, 38 L.R.A. 615, as to a quorum of the Appellate Division. Thus, while by-law No. 3 is not in explicit terms forbidden by Section 27, supra, it seems to flout the plain purpose of the Legislature in passing that statute.

We have not overlooked Section 28 of the General Corporation Law, the first sentence of which is as follows: "Whenever, under the provisions of any corporate law a corporation is authorized to take any action by its directors, action may be taken by the directors, regularly convened as a board, and acting by a majority of a quorum, except when otherwise expressly required by law or the by-laws and any such action shall be executed in behalf of the corporation by such officers as shall be designated by the board." Reading together Sections 27 and

28 and examining their legislative history (see L.1890, Ch. 563; L.1892, Ch. 687; L.1904, Ch. 737), we conclude that there never was a legislative intent so to change the common-law rule as to quorums as to authorize a by-law like the one under scrutiny in this paragraph. A by-law requiring for every action of the board not only a unanimous vote of a quorum of the directors, but of all the directors, sets up a scheme of management utterly inconsistent with Sections 27 and 28.

Before passing to a consideration of the fourth disputed by-law, we comment here on a view expressed in the dissenting opinion herein. The dissenting Judges conclude that, while the two by-laws first herein discussed are invalid as such because violative of statutes, the courts should, nevertheless, enforce as against either stockholder the agreement made by both of them and which finds expression in those by-laws. The substance of that stockholders' agreement was, as the dissenting opinion says, that neither stockholder would vote his stock in opposition to the stock of the other. Each stockholder thus agreed that he would conform his opinion to that of his associate on every occasion, or, absent such accord, that neither would vote at all on any occasion. We are at a loss to understand how any court could entertain a suit, or frame a judgment, to enforce such a compact. . . .

The fourth by-law here in dispute, requiring unanimity of action of all stockholders to amend the by-laws, is not, so far as we can find, specifically or impliedly authorized or forbidden by any statute of this State. Nor do we think it involves any public policy or interest. Every corporation is empowered to make by-laws, General Corporation Law, § 14, subd. 5, and by-laws of some sort or other are usually considered to be essential to the organization of a corporation. But a corporation need not provide any machinery at all for amending its by-laws—and for such an omission it could not be accused of an attempt to escape from the regulatory framework set up by law. . . . [O]nce proper by-laws have been adopted, the matter of amending them is, we think, no concern of the State. We, therefore, see no invalidity in by-law numbered 4 above.

The judgment should be modified in accordance with this opinion, and, as so modified, affirmed, without costs.

CONWAY, Judge (dissenting) . . . [The dissent described the negotiations between Dondero, who owned two-thirds of the shares (part of which were held in his wife's name), and Benintendi, which resulted in an agreement that neither would vote his shares in opposition to the shares of the other.]

. . . The question presented to us is whether the two owners of the entire stock in Kenton Hotel, Inc. (Dondero being the beneficial owner of the stock standing in his wife's name) had the power to amend the by-laws as they did.

The owners of 100% of the stock of a corporation may do with it as they will, even to giving it away, provided the rights of creditors are not involved and the public policy of the State is not offended. . . .

Despite that power of 100% of the stockholders, they may not write into a certificate of incorporation nor adopt in by-laws provisions contrary to applicable statutes. Since corporations are creatures of statute, their charters and by-laws must conform to the will of the creating power. Ripin v. United States Woven Label Co., supra; Matter of Boulevard Theatre & Realty Co., 195 App.Div. 518, 186 N.Y.S. 430, affirmed 231 N.Y. 615, 132 N.E. 910; Lorillard v. Clyde et al., 86 N.Y. 384. For that reason we think that the amendments to article I, section 4, and article II, section 2,* were beyond the power of the stockholders since they contravene General Corporation Law, sections 102 and 103, and Stock Corporation Law, sections 35, subd. c, 36, 55, 86(b), 105, subd. c.

[handwritten: #1 & #2 beyond power of s/h's]

The amendment to article II, section 10, appears to be proper under General Corporation Law, sections 27 and 28.** Those sections are in part as follows and show clearly by the portions we have italicized that the amendment was permissible.

[handwritten: #3 is proper]

"27. Directors; Qualifications; Powers of Majority.

"The business of a corporation shall be managed by its board of directors, all of whom shall be of full age and at least one of whom shall be a citizen of the United States and a resident of this state. *Unless otherwise provided* a majority of the board at a meeting duly assembled shall be necessary to constitute a quorum for the transaction of business and the act of a majority of the directors present at such a meeting shall be the act of the board. The by-laws may fix the number of directors necessary to constitute a quorum at a number less than a majority of the board, but not less than one-third of its number. . . ." (Emphasis supplied.)

"28. Acts of Directors.

"Whenever, under the provisions of any corporate law a corporation is authorized to take any action by its directors, action may be taken by the directors, regularly convened as a board, and acting by a majority of a quorum, *except when otherwise expressly required by law or the by-laws and any such action* shall be executed in behalf of the corporation by such officers as shall be designated by the board. Any business may be transacted by the board at a meeting at which every member of the board is present, though held without notice." (Emphasis supplied.)

The amendment to article VIII, section 1, is not forbidden by any statute.

The question is then presented whether the *agreement* between the parties as to the manner in which they would vote their stock may be specifically enforced through the injunctive process of an equity court *in forbidding a breach of it by Dondero* even though validity may not be accorded to the first two attempted amendments. We think it may.

* These are the by-laws referred to in the majority opinion as by-laws (1) and (2). (Footnote by ed.)   ** This is the by-law referred to in the majority opinion as by-law (3). (Footnote by ed.)

Benintendi and Dondero agreed together as to the manner in which they would vote their respective stock interests. To implement their agreement they chose a method forbidden by statute. The agreement, however, was valid without the method chosen. Both of the parties have lived up to and under that agreement for more than a year. We granted specific performance of an agreement in Clark v. Dodge, supra, to vote for a single-named director—certainly a more drastic limitation upon the power of a stockholder than the limitation here. . . .

There are here no rights of creditors involved. A totality of stockholders may agree among themselves as to how they shall or shall not vote shares of stock owned by them. They may by agreement waive or relinquish as between themselves statutory rights where such waiver or abandonment is not contrary to the public interest. There is here no question of public policy. The State does not need the assistance or leadership of Dondero in vindicating its public policy. . . .

The order should be modified in accordance herewith, with costs to the plaintiffs in the Appellate Division and in this court.

NOTE ON SUPERMAJORITY REQUIREMENTS

1. In accord with *Benintendi* is a Virginia case decided at almost the same time, Kaplan v. Block, 183 Va. 327, 31 S.E.2d 893 (1944). There the bylaws required unanimity for both shareholder and director action, and the charter required that all acts of the board be unanimously ratified by the shareholders. The court invalidated these provisions, stating three reasons: (1) departure from the statutory norm; (2) '[a] private business corporation without a board of directors is an impossible concept''; (3) probability of deadlock. "A recalcitrant director who is also a stockholder may embalm his corporation and hold it helpless. . . . It cannot sue and it cannot defend a suit. It cannot be dissolved, and it must remain forever in a state of suspended animation. A treasurer, who chanced to own a share of stock, might pocket its assets and leave his associates without civil remedy." (This result appears to have been superseded by Virginia §§ 13.1–33, 13.1–39.)

A very different view, however, was taken in Katcher v. Ohsman, 26 N.J.Super. 28, 97 A.2d 180 (1953). K, O, and F each owned one-third of the stock of Crown Fur, a New York corporation, and served as its officers and directors. K claimed that to induce him to buy Crown Fur stock, O and F had represented "that the corporate structure of the company was then such that no binding action could be taken either by the stockholders or directors unless 90% in stock interest voted in favor of such action," and that all future action would be taken in accordance with this representation. Relying on their assurance, K had purchased the stock and was promptly elected a director and officer. For fourteen years all corporate actions were taken by unanimous approval, and any action objected to by a single shareholder was abandoned. Subsequently, however, dissension arose concerning K's investment in a warehouse. Because K was unwilling to share his new investment with O and F, the latter threatened to hold a special directors' meeting to oust him as an officer and director. Contrary to the original representations made by O and F, it appeared that while one Crown Fur by-law required 90 percent shareholder approval for most shareholder actions, other by-laws required only a majority vote for either board action or shareholder removal of a director. K sought a preliminary injunction restraining his ouster, on the basis of the original representations. The court granted the injunction, rejecting the argument that by-laws as represented to K would be invalid:

> . . . Is a by-law requiring a vote from the stockholders greater in interest than 51% or a vote from directors greater than a majority in number of the directors offensive to public policy, since the greater the voting requirement the greater is the likelihood of an impasse or deadlock? That risk, however, is always present even where the provisions call for a mere majority. Many small corporations are formed by two individuals or two separate groups, each of whom seeks protection against being outvoted by the other. In those instances where the stock is equally divided amongst two persons or two groups, a board of directors of an even number of persons is constituted. Therefore a 51% stock vote requirement of such stockholders or a majority vote of such directors actually presents, as a practical matter, a requirement of unanimity.

> Such corporate requirements and effects do not offend the law and there therefore seems to be no reason why stockholders may not provide for *any* minimum vote, either in stock interest amongst the stockholders or in number amongst the directors, even if that minimum translates itself as a practical effect into a requirement of unanimity. In the absence of contrary agreement and provision, the law presumes that stockholders intend to make the rule of the majority controlling, but I know of no valid reason why stockholders are not at liberty to establish for themselves a voting rule or formula which will protect the holder of a single share against the action of all the other shareholders becoming binding or controlling upon him.

2. On grounds not dissimilar to those invoked in *Benintendi*, the courts have sometimes struck down agreements that give a shareholder more voting power than is carried by his shares. For example, in Nickolopoulos v. Sarantis, 102 N.J.Eq. 585, 141 A. 792 (1928), A, B, and C, who wanted to expand their business, asked D to join them in forming a corporation. It was agreed that D would lend the corporation $10,000, would own 25% of the stock, and would have 50 percent of the voting power. The court held the voting-power provision of the agreement unenforceable, on the ground that under the statute shareholders were powerless to alter the voting power of any share except by provisions in the certificate of incorporation. "Hence . . . [the agreement] was in violation of the act, and created

a control of the corporation at variance with that indicated by the charter, by-laws, and stock list. This was a fraud on the corporation and on those dealing with it." See also Piechowski v. Matarese, 54 N.J.Super. 333, 148 A.2d 872 (1959); Christal v. Petry, 275 App. Div. 550, 90 N.Y.S.2d 620, 629 (1st Dept.1949), aff'd mem. 301 N.Y. 562, 93 N.E.2d 450. On the other hand, in Trefethen v. Amazeen, 93 N.H. 110, 36 A.2d 266 (1944), Atlantic Terminal common had 396 shares of common outstanding, of which A and B each owned 50 shares, C owned 270 shares, and 26 shares were owned by others. C wanted to secure additional funds for Atlantic, and to that end A and B each purchased 52 shares of Atlantic preferred, entitling them also to 52 shares of common each. In exchange, C agreed not to vote 92 of his common shares without the consent of A and B so long as either of them owned any Atlantic stock. As a result, even if the other shareholders voted with C he would have no greater voting power than A and B. The court held the agreement enforceable. "A stockholders' agreement reasonably intended to be beneficial to a corporation and injurious to no one save for the contemplated detriment to the contracting parties is valid." See also Sankin v. 5410 Connecticut Avenue Corp., 281 F.Supp. 524 (D.D.C.1968), aff'd 410 F.2d 1060 (D.C.Cir.), cert. denied 396 U.S. 1041, 90 S.Ct. 681, 24 L.Ed.2d 685 (1970) (holding valid an agreement by the holder of two-thirds of a corporation's shares to refrain from voting half his shareholdings so as to give the minority shareholder an equal voice in the corporation's management); E.K. Buck Retail Stores v. Harkert, 157 Neb. 867, 62 N.W.2d 288 (1954).

N.Y. BUS. CORP. LAW §§ 616, 709

[See Statutory Supplement]

NOTE ON NEW YORK'S SUPERMAJORITY PROVISIONS

The predecessor of New York's statutory supermajority provisions was enacted in 1948 for the purpose of offsetting the result in *Benintendi.* However, New York courts continued to apply the principles of *Benintendi* unless the statute was explicitly applicable. Thus in Matter of William Faehndrich, Inc., 2 N.Y.2d 468, 161 N.Y.S.2d 99, 141 N.E.2d 597 (1957), the Court of Appeals held ineffective a bylaw which provided that two-thirds of the stock was necessary for a quorum at special shareholders' meetings, on the ground that the statute only authorized a high-quorum provision in the certificate. Similarly in Model, Roland & Co. v. Industrial Acoustics Co., 16 N.Y.2d 703, 261 N.Y.S.2d 703, 209 N.E.2d 553 (1965), the Court of Appeals struck down a bylaw that required a two-thirds shareholder vote to amend certain bylaws, including a bylaw that fixed the number of directors. "The Business Corporation

Law clearly provides that a simple majority vote of the shareholders is sufficient to amend the bylaws, unless the certificate of incorporation provides otherwise. . . . The two-thirds majority vote provision here involved would have been valid were it placed in the certificate of incorporation, but as a by-law it is invalid." See also Fromkin v. Merrall Realty, Inc., 15 A.D.2d 919, 225 N.Y.S.2d 632 (1962), appeal denied 11 N.Y.2d 647.[1] In Beresovski v. Warszawski, 28 N.Y.2d 419, 271 N.E.2d 520, 322 N.Y.S.2d 673 (1971), the Court of Appeals showed a somewhat more tolerant view. The three shareholders of JPO Corporation had entered into an agreement requiring supermajorities for various actions at the board and shareholder level. Although the supermajority requirements were not put into the certificate, the agreement provided that "[i]n the event any of the provisions of this agreement shall be deemed illegal or against public policy, the validity or legality of any of the other provisions or any part thereof shall not be thereby affected. However, if any illegal provision can be cured by amending the certificate of incorporation, the parties agree to take such action immediately." Thereafter, one of the shareholders made demand for appropriate certificate amendments, but the other refused. The court held that while the contractual provisions requiring supermajorities were unenforceable under *Faehndrich* and *Benintendi,* the promise to amend the certificate could be enforced by specific performance.[2] *Zion v. Kurtz,* supra Section 3, also suggests a much more tolerant view.

DEL. GEN. CORP. LAW §§ 102(b)(4), 141(b), 216

[See Statutory Supplement]

CAL. CORP. CODE §§ 204, 307, 602

[See Statutory Supplement]

REV. MODEL BUS. CORP. ACT §§ 7.27, 8.24

[See Statutory Supplement]

---

1. See also Mook v. Berger, 7 A.D.2d 726, 180 N.Y.S.2d 400 (1958), aff'd per curiam 6 N.Y.2d 833, 188 N.Y.S.2d 219 (principles of *Benintendi* applied to invalidate shareholders' agreement and by-law of a Connecticut corporation).

2. Cf. Shubin v. Surchin, 27 A.D. 452, 280 N.Y.S.2d 55 (1967). A and B, sole shareholders, agreed in writing to vote at shareholders' and directors' meetings so that the board would consist of A and B, both of whom would be necessary to constitute a quorum for the transaction of business at board meetings. It was further provided that the "directors will ratify and adopt this Agreement." The court held,

"[i]t is true . . . that the pertinent provisions of the written agreement have not been incorporated in the certificate of incorporation, which is a prerequisite pursuant to paragraph (b) of section 620 and of section 701 to implement effectively that part of the writing by which the number of directors was reduced to the two shareholders. . . . Minimally, however, triable issues are presented as to . . . whether it was within the intendment of parties thereto that the certificate and bylaws should be suitably amended to implement the provisions of the agreement now permitted by the statute."

SECTION 5. RESTRICTIONS ON THE TRANSFERABILITY OF SHARES

ALLEN v. BILTMORE TISSUE CORP.

New York Court of Appeals, 1957.
2 N.Y.2d 534, 161 N.Y.S.2d 418, 141 N.E.2d 812.

FULD, Judge.

The by-laws of defendant corporation give it an option to purchase, in case of the death of a stockholder, his shares of the corporate stock. The enforcibility of this option is one of the questions for decision.

Biltmore Tissue Corporation was organized under the Stock Corporation Law, Consol.Laws, c. 59, § 1 et seq., in 1932, with an authorized capitalization of 1,000 shares without par value, to manufacture and deal in paper and paper products. The by-laws, adopted by the incorporators-directors, contain provisions limiting the number of shares (originally 5, later 20) available to each stockholder (§ 28) and restricting stock transfers both during the life of the stockholder and in case of his death (§§ 29, 30). Whenever a stockholder desires to sell or transfer his shares, he must, according to one by-law (§ 29), give the corporation or other stockholders "an opportunity to repurchase the stock at the price that was paid for the same to the Corporation at the time the Corporation issued the stock"; if, however, the option is not exercised, "then, after the lapse of sixty days, the stock may be sold by the holder to such person and under such circumstances as he sees fit." The by-law, dealing with the transfer of stock upon the death of a stockholder (§ 30)—the provision with which we are here concerned—is almost identical. It recites that the corporation is to have the right to purchase its late stockholder's shares for the price it originally received for them:

> "Stock Transfer in Case of Death. In case of the death of any stockholder, the Corporation shall have the right to purchase the stock from the legal representative of the deceased for the same price that the Corporation received therefor originally. If the Corporation does not, or cannot, purchase such stock, the Board of Directors shall have the right to empower such of its existing stockholders as it sees fit to make such purchase from such legal representative at the same price. Should the option provided for in this section not be exercised, then, after the lapse of ninety days, the legal representative may dispose of said stock as he sees fit."

Harry Kaplan, a paper jobber, was one of Biltmore's customers and some months after its incorporation purchased 5 shares of stock from the corporation at $5 a share. In 1936, Kaplan received a stock dividend of 5 more shares, and two years later purchased an additional

10 shares for $100. On the face of each of the three certificates, running vertically along the left-hand margin, appeared the legend,

> "Issued subject to restrictions in sections 28, 29, and 30 of the By-laws."

On October 20, 1953, Kaplan wrote to the corporation stating that he was "interested in selling" his 20 shares of stock and requesting that he be given the "price" which the board of directors "will consider, so that I may come to a decision." He died five days later. Some months thereafter, in February, 1954, his son, who was also one of his executors, addressed a letter to Biltmore, inquiring whether it was "still interested in acquiring shares and at what price." By another letter, dated the same day, the attorney for the executors sent to the corporation the three stock certificates, representing the 20 shares, and requested that a new certificate be issued in the name of the estate or the executors. Within 30 days, on March 4, 1954, Biltmore's board of directors voted to exercise its option to purchase the stock, pursuant to section 30 of the by-laws, and about three weeks later the executors' attorney was advised of the corporation's action. He was also informed, that although the by-law provision permitted purchase at "the same price that the company received therefor from the stockholder originally," the corporation had, nevertheless, decided to pay $20 a share, "considerably more than the original purchase price", based on the prices at which it had acquired shares from other stockholders.

Kaplan's executors declined to sell to the corporation, insisting that the stock which had been in the decedent's name be transferred to them. When their demand was refused, they brought this action to compel Biltmore to accept surrender of the decedent's stock certificate and to issue a new certificate for 20 shares to them. They contended . . . that the by-law is void as an unreasonable restraint. The corporation interposed a counterclaim for specific performance based on the exercise of its option to purchase the shares under by-law section 30. The court at Special Term granted judgment to the corporation on its counterclaim and dismissed the complaint. The Appellate Division reversed, rendered judgment directing the transfer of the stock to the plaintiffs and dismissed the defendant's counterclaim upon the ground that the by-law in question is void.

Section 176 of the Personal Property Law, which is identical with section 15 of the Uniform Stock Transfer Act, provides that "there shall be no restriction upon the transfer of shares" represented by a stock certificate "by virtue of any by-law of such corporation, or otherwise, unless the . . . restriction is *stated* upon the certificate." (Emphasis supplied.) In order to comply with this statutory mandate, the corporation printed the words, "Issued subject to restrictions in sections 28, 29, and 30 of the By-laws," on the side of the certificate. . . .

Since . . . the legend on the certificate meets the statute's requirements, we turn to the validity of the by-law restriction.

The validity of qualifications on the ownership of corporate shares through restrictions on the right to transfer has long been a source of confusion in the law. The difficulties arise primarily from the clash between the concept of the shares as "creatures of the company's constitution and therefore . . . essentially contractual choses in action" (Gower, Some Contrasts between British and American Corporation Law, 69 Harv.L.Rev. 1369, 1377) and the concept of the shares as personal property represented so far as possible by the certificate itself and, therefore, subject to the time-honored rule that there be no unreasonable restraint upon alienation. While the courts of this state and of many other jurisdictions, as opposed to those of England and of Massachusetts (Gower, supra, 69 Harv.L.Rev. 1369, 1377–1378; O'Neal, Restrictions on Transfer of Stock in Closely Held Corporations, 65 Harv.L.Rev. 773, 778), have favored the "property" concept (see O'Neal, supra, 65 Harv.L.Rev. 773, 779), the tendency is, as section 176 of the Personal Property Law implies, to sustain a restriction imposed on the transfer of stock if "reasonable" and if the stockholder acquired such stock with requisite notice of the restriction.

The question posed, therefore, is whether the provision, according the corporation a right or first option to purchase the stock at the price which it originally received for it, amounts to an unreasonable restraint. In our judgment, it does not.

The courts have almost uniformly held valid and enforcible the first option provision, in charter or by-law, whereby a shareholder desirous of selling his stock is required to afford the corporation, his fellow stockholders or both an opportunity to buy it before he is free to offer it to outsiders. . . . The courts have often said that this first option provision is "in the nature of a contract" between the corporation and its stockholders and, as such, binding upon them. Hassel v. Pohle, . . . 214 App.Div. 654, 658, 212 N.Y.S.2d 561, 565; see, also, 8 Fletcher, . . . § 4194, p. 736. In Doss v. Yingling, . . . 95 Ind.App. 494, 172 N.E. 801, a leading case on the subject and one frequently cited throughout the country, a by-law provision against transfer by any stockholder—there were three—of any shares until they had first been offered for sale to other stockholders at *book value*, was sustained as reasonable and valid, 95 Ind.App. at page 500, 172 N.E. at page 803: "The weight of authority is to the effect that a corporate by-law which requires the owner of the stock to give the other stockholders of the corporation . . . *an option to purchase the same at an agreed price or the then-existing book value before offering the stock for sale to an outsider, is a valid and reasonable restriction* and binding upon the stockholders." (Emphasis supplied.) And in the Penthouse Properties case, . . . 256 App.Div. 685, 690–691, 11 N.Y.S.2d 417, 422, the court declared that "The general rule that ownership of property cannot exist in one person and the right of alienation in another . . . has in this State been frequently applied to shares of corporate stock . . . and cognizance has been taken of the principle that 'the right of transfer is a right of property, and if another has the arbitrary power to forbid a transfer of property by the owner that amounts to annihilation of property'. . . . But restrictions against the sale of shares of stock, unless other stockholders or the corporation have first been accorded an opportunity to buy, are not repugnant to that principle. . . . The weight of authority elsewhere is to the same effect." [2]

As the cases thus make clear, what the law condemns is, not a *restriction* on transfer, a provision merely postponing sale during the option period, but an effective *prohibition* against transferability itself. Accordingly, if the by-law under consideration were to be construed as rendering the sale of the stock impossible to anyone except to the corporation at whatever price it wished to pay, we would, of course, strike it down as illegal. But that is not the meaning of the provision before us. The corporation had its option only for a 90–day period. If it did not exercise its privilege within that time, the deceased stockholder's legal representative was at liberty to "dispose of said stock as he [saw] fit" (§ 30), and, once so disposed of, it would thereafter be free of the restriction. In a very real sense, therefore, the primary purpose of the by-laws was to enable a particular party, the corporation, to buy the shares, not to prevent the other party, the stockholder, from selling them. (See 3 Simes & Smith on Law of Future Interests [2d ed., 1956], § 1154, p. 61.)

The Appellate Division, however, was impressed with what it deemed the "unreasonableness," that is, "unfairness," of the price specified in the by-law, namely, a price at which the shares had originally been purchased from the corporation. Carried to its logical conclusion, such a rationale would permit, indeed, would encourage, expensive litigation in every case where the price specified in the restriction, or the formula for fixing the price, was other than a recognized and easily ascertainable fair market value. This would destroy part of the social utility of the first option type of restriction which, when imposed, is intended to operate *in futuro* and must, therefore, include some formula for future determination of the option price.

Generally speaking, these restrictions are employed by the so-called "close corporation" as part of the attempt to equate the corporate structure to a partnership by giving the original stockholders a sort of pre-emptive right through which they may if they choose, veto the admission of a new participant. See Bloomingdale v. Bloomingdale, supra, 107 Misc. 646, 651–652, 177 N.Y.S. 873, 875; Model Clothing House v. Dickinson, 146 Minn. 367, 370–371, 178 N.W. 957; see, also, Israels, The Close Corporation and the Law, 33 Corn.L.Q. 488, 492–493. Obviously, the case where there is an easily ascertainable market value for the shares of a closely held corporate enterprise is the exception, not the rule, and, consequently, various methods or formulae for fixing the option price are employed

---

2. The court went further in the Penthouse Properties case than we are called upon to go here; in view of the special purposes of a corporation owning a cooperative apartment house, it sustained a restriction actually requiring the "consent" of the directors to a proposed transfer. 256 App.Div. 685, 689, 11 N.Y.S.2d 416, 420. The present case involves no such "consent" restriction.

in practice—e.g., book or appraisal value, often exclusive of good will, see, e.g., Lawson v. Household Finance Corp., 17 Del.Ch. 343, 152 A. 723, affirming 17 Del.Ch. 1, 147 A. 312; Doss v. Yingling, supra, 95 Ind.App. 494, 172 N.E. 801, or a fixed price, Scruggs v. Cotterill, 67 App.Div. 583, 73 N.Y.S. 882, or the par value of the stock. See, e.g., Boston Safe Dep. & Tr. Co. v. North Attleborough Chapt. of American Red Cross, 330 Mass. 114, 111 N.E.2d 447; Chaffee v. Farmers' Co–Op. Elevator Co., 39 N.D. 585, 590, 168 N.W. 616; O'Neal, supra, 65 Harv.L.Rev. 773, 798 et seq.[3]

In sum, then, the validity of the restriction on transfer does not rest on any abstract notion of intrinsic fairness of price. To be invalid, more than mere disparity between option price and current value of the stock must be shown. See Palmer v. Chamberlin, supra, 191 F.2d 532, 541, 27 A.L.R.2d 416. Since the parties have in effect agreed on a price formula which suited them, and provision is made freeing the stock for outside sale should the corporation not make, or provide for, the purchase, the restriction is reasonable and valid.

The further argument made by the plaintiffs, that the defendant corporation, in any event, waived its right by failing to exercise its option within the prescribed 90 days, cannot avail them. Section 30 of the by-laws provides that the corporation has the right "to purchase the stock from the legal representative of the deceased" and that, if the option is not exercised, "then, after the lapse of ninety days, the legal representative may dispose of said stock as he sees fit." The section is patently deficient in omitting to specify the date upon which the 90-day period is to commence. It cannot mean the date of death (here it was October 25, 1953) or even the date on which the corporation learned of the death (shortly thereafter), for, until letters testamentary or letters of administration are issued, the "legal representative" of the deceased is not ascertainable and there is no one from whom the corporation could purchase the stock. Cf. Motyka v. City of Oswego, 309 N.Y. 881, 131 N.E.2d 291. In the present case, letters testamentary were issued to the plaintiffs on December 17, 1953, but the corporation was not informed of this until February 10, 1954. Consequently, since the corporation's board of directors voted on March 4 to purchase the shares and apprised counsel for the plaintiffs, the legal representatives of the deceased stockholder, of their desire to do so on March 23, the option was clearly exercised within the permitted period.

The judgment of the Appellate Division dismissing the defendant's counterclaim and sustaining the plaintiff's complaint should be reversed, and that of Special Term reinstated, with costs in this court and in the Appellate Division.

CONWAY, C.J., and DESMOND, DYE, FROESSEL, VAN VOORHIS and BURKE, JJ., concur.

---

3.   In the case of no-par shares, it should be noted, the figure usually most comparable to par value is issue price.

Judgment of Appellate Division reversed and that of Special Term reinstated, with costs in this court and in the Appellate Division.

UNIFORM PARTNERSHIP ACT § 18(g)

[See Statutory Supplement]

DEL. GEN. CORP. LAW §§ 202, 342, 347, 349

[See Statutory Supplement]

CAL. CORP. CODE §§ 204(a)(3), (b), 418

[See Statutory Supplement]

REV.MODEL BUS.CORP. ACT § 6.27
MODEL STAT.CLOSE CORP. SUPP. §§ 10–17

[See Statutory Supplement]

GRAY v. HARRIS LAND & CATTLE CO., ___ Mont. ___, 737 P.2d 475 (1987). Harris Land was a close corporation with five shareholders, including Gray. The shareholders had entered into a "Buy-Sell Agreement," which provided that "So long as all of the (five signatory shareholders) are alive, they each shall not encumber or dispose of the stock of the Corporation which he or she now owns without the written consent of the remaining (signatory shareholders) and that of the Corporation." Gray wanted to sell his shares, but the others refused to consent. Mont. Code An. § 35–1–617(2)(c) (essentially comparable to Del. Gen. Corp. Law § 202(c)(3)) provided that "A restriction on the transfer of shares of a corporation is permitted by this section if it . . . requires the corporation or the holder of any class of shares of the corporation to consent to any proposed transfer of the restricted shares. . . ." · Held, the consent restraint in the Agreement was enforceable. The court pointed out that the restraint was not perpetual, because by its terms it lasted only while all five of the signatory shareholders were still living.

JOSEPH E. SEAGRAM & SONS, INC. v. CONOCO, INC., 519 F.Supp. 506 (D.Del.1981). Conoco was a publicly held Delaware corporation. On May 18, 1981, Conoco's board amended its by-laws to limit the percentage of shares that could be held by "alien" companies at any given time, and to provide that a transfer that would result in a higher percentage would be void. After May 18, every stock certificate issued by Conoco, to record a transfer of already-outstanding shares, was imprinted with a legend alerting the holder to the restriction on transfer. Del.Gen.Corp.Law § 202 provided that "No restriction [on the transfer of stock imposed by the certificate of incorporation or by-laws] shall be binding with respect to securities issued prior to the restriction unless the holders of the securities . . . voted in favor of the restriction." Seagram, which qualified as an "alien" under the Conoco by-law, proposed to acquire a substantial amount of Conoco stock through a tender offer, and brought a suit challenging the validity of the restriction on transfer. Conoco argued that stock certificates were "securities," and that the imposition of the restriction on stock certificates issued after the by-law was adopted satisfied section 202, even it the underlying shares represented by the certificate had been issued before the by-law was adopted. Held, for Seagram.

NOTE ON RESTRICTIONS ON THE TRANSFERABILITY OF SHARES

1. Although some of the earlier cases held that all restrictions on the transferability of shares constituted illegal restraints on alienation, the modern cases hold that "reasonable" restrictions are valid and enforceable. Three basic types of restrictions are commonly used in the context of the close corporation: (1) First refusals, which prohibit a sale of stock unless the shares have been first offered to the corporation, the other shareholders, or both, on the terms offered by the third party; (2) First options, which prohibit a transfer of stock unless the shares have been first offered to the corporation, the other shareholders, or both, at a price fixed under the terms of the option; and (3) Consent restraints, which prohibit a transfer of stock without the permission of the corporation's board or shareholders.

Of these three basic types, the *first refusal* is obviously least restrictive in its impact on a shareholder who wants to sell his stock, and such provisions are widely upheld. See, e.g., Groves v. Prickett, 420 F.2d 1119 (9th Cir.1970); Tu–Vu Drive–In Corp. v. Ashkins, 61 Cal.2d 283, 391 P.2d 828, 38 Cal.Rptr. 348 (1964); Hudelson v. Clarks Hill Tel. Co., 139 Ind.App. 507, 218 N.E.2d 154 (1966).

The restrictiveness of a *first option* depends largely on the relationship between the option price and a fair price at the time the option is triggered. As Allen v. Biltmore suggests, the courts have been giving increasing latitude to this type of provision. See, e.g., Lawson v. Household Finance Corp., 17 Del.Ch. 343, 152 A. 723 (1930); In re Mather's Estate, 410 Pa. 361, 189 A.2d 586 (1963), noted, 48 Minn. L.Rev. 808 (1964), 16 Stan.L.Rev. 449 (1964), 49 Va.L.Rev. 1211 (1963) (agreement setting price at $1 per share enforced although actual value was $1,060 per share).

A *consent restraint* is obviously the most restrictive of the three basic types, and at one time such a restraint was almost certain to be deemed invalid. However, some recent statutes specifically contemplate the validity of such restraints (see, e.g., Del. § 202), and the courts have also begun to be more tolerant. Thus in Colbert v.

Hennessey, 351 Mass. 131, 217 N.E.2d 914 (1966), three sharehold-ers owning 55% of Bay State's stock agreed that none would transfer his stock without the others' consent. The court held the agreement valid. "The agreement was a means of securing corporate control of Bay State to those whose enterprise sponsored it and who contributed to the daily operation of the business. This was not a 'palpably unreasonable' purpose." The court cited Holmes's dictum, in Barrett v. King, 181 Mass. 476, 479, 63 N.E. 934, 935 (1902), that "there seems to be no greater objection to retaining the right of choosing one's associates in a corporation than in a firm." See also Irwin v. West End Development Co., 342 F.Supp. 687 (D.Colo.1972); Long-year v. Hardman, 219 Mass. 405, 106 N.E. 1012 (1914); Fayard v. Fayard, 293 So.2d 421, 69 A.L.R.3d 1323 (Miss.1974).

In spite of the increasingly tolerant climate, however, the validity of consent restraints remains uncertain in the absence of statute or authoritative precedent. In Rafe v. Hindin, 29 A.D.2d 481, 288 N.Y.S.2d 662 (1968), P and D each owned 50% of the stock of Bil Cy Realty, which they had organized in 1963. A legend on each stock certificate made the stock nontransferable except to the other shareholder, and written permission from the other shareholder was required to record a transfer of the stock on Bil Cy's books. P brought an action for a judgment that the legend on the certificate was void and the stock was transferable without D's consent. The court so held:

> In New York certificates of stock are regarded as personal property and are subject to the rule that there be no unreasonable restraint on alienation. . . .

> The legend on the stock certificate at bar contains no provi-sion that the individual defendant's consent may not be unreason-ably withheld. Since the individual defendant is thus given the arbitrary power to forbid a transfer of the shares of stock by the plaintiff, the restriction amounts to annihilation of property. The restriction is not only not reasonable, but it is against public policy and, therefore, illegal. It is an unwarrantable and unlawful restraint on the sale of personal property, the sale and interchange of which the law favors, and in restraint of trade.

See also, e.g., Tracey v. Franklin, 31 Del.Ch. 477, 67 A.2d 56 (1949).

2.   The three basic types of restraints discussed above limit the shareholders' power of transfer. Other types of arrangements go further, and give the corporation or the remaining shareholders an option to purchase shares upon the occurrence of designated contin-gencies, even if the shareholder wants to retain the stock. A common example is an arrangement under which the corporation is given an option to repurchase stock that it has issued to an employee, if the employment relationship is terminated. The courts have tended to enforce such arrangements even when the option price is quite low in relation to the value of the stock at the time the buyback right is triggered. See, e.g., St. Louis Union Trust Co. v. Merrill Lynch,

Pierce, Fenner & Smith, Inc., 562 F.2d 1040 (8th Cir.1977), cert. denied 435 U.S. 925, 98 S.Ct. 1490, 55 L.Ed.2d 518 (1978); Howeth v. D.A. Davidson & Co., 163 Mont. 355, 517 P.2d 722 (1973); Georesearch, Inc. v. Morriss, 193 F.Supp. 163 (W.D.La. 1961), aff'd per curiam 298 F.2d 442 (5th Cir.1962). Another example is the buy-sell or survivor-purchase agreement, which provides that on the death or retirement of a shareholder in a close corporation, his estate has an obligation to sell its shares to the corporation or the remaining shareholders at a price fixed under the agreement, and the corporation or the remaining shareholders have an obligation (rather than an option) to purchase the shares. The major purpose of such agreements is to provide liquidity to the seller or his estate. Since the corporation is by hypothesis closely held, any market for the shares is negligible, and in the absence of the agreement the retiring shareholder or his estate might be in a helpless bargaining position if more liquid or higher-yielding assets are needed to meet tax liabilities or other needs. The corporation's obligation is often "funded" in whole or in part by insurance on the shareholders' lives. It is beyond the scope of this Note to treat in detail buy-sell agreements and their insurance and tax implications.[2]

A related type of arrangement is a charter provision making stock redeemable at the corporation's option—that is, empowering the corporation to call the stock for cancellation in exchange for payment of a designated redemption price. While preferred stock is frequently made redeemable, redeemable common is relatively rare, and its legitimacy is frequently unclear. In Starring v. American Hair & Felt Co., 21 Del.Ch. 380, 191 A. 887 (1937), aff'd per curiam 21 Del.Ch. 431, 2 A.2d 249, a majority of the common stock of a corporation engaged in the leather business was held by tanners. Under the certificate, the common stock was redeemable at the board's call, and the tanners moved to redeem the common held by non-tanners. The statute authorized the redemption of "preferred or special shares," but did not explicitly refer to the redemption of common stock. The court held that redeemable common was not statutorily authorized.[3] On the other hand, in Lewis v. H.P. Hood & Sons, Inc., 331 Mass. 670, 121 N.E.2d 850 (1954), noted, 68 Harv.L.Rev. 1240 (1955), a charter provision empowered a unanimous board to call "all or any shares of common stock" at book value. Practically all of the corporation's stock was owned by directors and executives, and when plaintiff retired, the board called his stock for redemption. The statute provided that a corporation could issue "two or more classes of stock with such preferences, voting power, restrictions, and qualifica-

2. Discussion can be found 2 F.H. O'Neal, Close Corporations §§ 7.10, 7.23–29 (2d ed. 1971); A.J. Casner, Estate Planning (5th ed. 1984).

3. In the course of its opinion, the court pointed up, but did not answer, the question whether even if the power to redeem existed, it could be exercised "when the avowed purpose is simply to get rid of certain shareholders of a given class whose presence in the stockholding group is undesirable to the rest. . . ." Cf. Greene v. E.H. Rollins & Sons, 22 Del.Ch. 394, 2 A.2d 249 (1938), noted, 87 U.Pa.L.Rev. 482 (1939), 37 Mich.L.Rev. 1140 (1939), 25 Va.L. Rev. 489 (1939); Grynberg v. Burke, 378 A.2d 139 (Del.Ch.1977).

tions" as might be fixed in the charter, but did not explicitly authorize redemption provisions. The court upheld the call, reasoning in part that since preferred could admittedly be made callable under the statute despite the absence of explicit authority, common stock could be made callable too. Cf. In re West Waterway Lumber Co., 59 Wash.2d 310, 367 P.2d 807 (1962). Query: Would the court in *Lewis* have come to the same decision if the stock were widely held?

Many modern statutes implicitly or explicitly authorize the issuance of redeemable common shares. For example, N.J. § 14A:7–6(1) provides that "[a] corporation may provide in its certificate of incorporation for one or more classes or series of shares which are redeemable . . . at the option of the corporation. . . ." For comparable statutes, see, e.g., Ohio § 1701.23(A); Pa. § 1701. See generally 2 F.H. O'Neal, Close Corporations § 7.11 (2d ed. 1971). Do such statutes authorize the corporation to call shares for no satisfactory reason? For the purpose of benefiting some shareholders at the expense of others?

3. Restrictions on transfer give rise to recurring problems of interpretation—in particular, whether a given type of disposition is within the scope of the restriction. In general, the courts tend to give restrictions on transfer a strict interpretation. For example, unless explicitly otherwise provided, restrictions on transfer are generally interpreted as inapplicable to testamentary transfers, see, e.g., Globe Slicing Machine Co. v. Hasner, 333 F.2d 413 (2d Cir.1964), cert. denied 379 U.S. 969, 85 S.Ct. 666, 13 L.Ed.2d 562; In re Martin's Estate, 15 Ariz.App. 569, 490 P.2d 14 (1971); Vogel v. Melish, 31 Ill.2d 620, 203 N.E.2d 411 (1964); or to transfers by operation of law, see, e.g., Earthman's, Inc. v. Earthman, 526 S.W.2d 192 (Tex. Civ.App.1975) (transfer under a divorce decree); Matter of Trilling & Montague, 140 F.Supp. 260 (E.D.Pa.1956) (transfer in bankruptcy).[4] Transfer restrictions are also normally interpreted as inapplicable to transfers between existing shareholders, see, e.g., Birmingham Artificial Limb Co. v. Allen, 280 Ala. 445, 194 So.2d 848 (1967); Talbott v. Nibert, 167 Kan. 138, 206 P.2d 131 (1949); Remillong v. Schneider, 185 N.W.2d 493 (N.D.1971). This rule of interpretation may result in an uncontemplated shift of control where a transfer between shareholders involves swing shares. Cf. Lank v. Steiner, 43 Del.Ch. 262, 224 A.2d 242 (1966); Talbott v. Nibert, supra.[5]

4. See also Irwin v. West End Development Co., 342 F.Supp. 687 (D.Colo.1972) (restriction held inapplicable to a transfer from a partnership to a partner on dissolution), modified and aff'd on other issues, 481 F.2d 34 (10th Cir.1973), cert. denied 414 U.S. 1158, 94 S.Ct. 915, 39 L.Ed.2d 110 (1974). But see Casady v. Modern Metal Spinning & Mfg. Co., 188 Cal.App.2d 728, 10 Cal.Rptr. 790 (1961) (restriction held applicable to transfer of shares as part of division of community property on divorce).

5. Although there is some uncertainty on the issue, a restriction on transferability is normally interpreted not to prohibit a pledge of the stock unless explicitly so provided. See Crescent City Seltzer & Mineral Water Mfg. Co. v. Deblieux, 40 La.Ann. 155, 3 So. 726 (1888); Good Fellows Associates v. Silverman, 283 Mass. 173, 186 N.E. 48 (1933); Estate Funds, Inc. v. Burton-Fifth Ave. Corp., 111 N.Y.S.2d 596 (Sup.Ct. 1952); 2 F.H. O'Neal, Close Corporations § 7.05a (2d ed. 1971). But cf. Monotype Composition Co. v. Kiernan, 319 Mass. 456, 66 N.E.2d 565 (1946). The pledgee, however, will normally be deemed to hold the shares subject to the restriction. See Good Fellows Associates, Inc. v. Silverman, su-

4. Another kind of problem concerns the pricing clause in first-option, repurchase, or buy-sell arrangements. Where shares are closely held, price cannot realistically be set on the basis of market value, and some alternative pricing provision is therefore required. Even where shares are not closely held, an alternative to market value may be employed for substantive reasons.

(a) One common approach is to use a pricing formula based on book value. Book value, however, may be an unreliable guide to a concern's real worth: it reflects the historical cost of assets rather than their present value, and usually ignores goodwill or going-concern value. Such a formula may therefore be disastrous where goodwill represents the most valuable component of the business—as is typical in non-capital-intensive enterprises, see, e.g., Jones v. Harris, 63 Wash.2d 559, 388 P.2d 539 (1964)—or where there is a significant disparity between historical costs and present values. Thus Marsh notes that "[i]n S.C. Pohlman Co. v. Easterling [211 Cal.App.2d 466, 27 Cal.Rptr. 450 (1962)] the court . . . held that [the accountant who was charged by the agreement with determining book value] had properly omitted . . . the excess of market value of securities over their book value. This decision would seem to be correct in the light of generally accepted accounting principles, and probably the agreement should be interpreted as intending to apply such generally accepted accounting principles in the absence of any indication to the contrary. But it may be questioned whether, if the parties had had their attention called to the matter at the time of the negotiation of the agreement, they would have excluded from the computation of value the excess of the current market value of marketable securities over their original cost." 1 H. Marsh, Marsh's California Corporation Law § 21.19 (2d ed. 1987). See generally 2 F.H. O'Neal, Close Corporations § 7.24 (2d ed. 1971); Stans & Goedert, What is Book Value?, 99 J. Accountancy 38 (1955). Cf. May v. Wilcox Furniture Downtown, Inc., 450 S.W.2d 734 (Tex.Civ.App.1969).

As a general proposition, the courts have tended to hold that a large disparity between book value and real value is not in itself sufficient to avoid the operation of a book-value pricing provision. Thus in Palmer v. Chamberlin, 191 F.2d 532 (5th Cir.1951), the court, quoting New England Trust Co. v. Abbott, 162 Mass. 148, 38 N.E. 432 (1894) stated, " '. . . specific performance of an agreement to convey will not be refused merely because the price is inadequate or excessive. The difference must be so great as to lead to a reasonable conclusion of fraud, mistake, or concealment in the nature of fraud, and to render it plainly inequitable and against conscience that the contract should be enforced.' " See also, e.g., Estate of Brown, 130 Ill.App.2d 514, 264 N.E.2d 287 (1970); Jones v. Harris, 63 Wash.2d 559, 388 P.2d 539 (1964). However, the term "book value" is itself subject to conflicting interpretations. In Aron v. Gillman, 309 N.Y. 157, 128 N.E.2d 284 (1955), which

pra; Estate Funds, Inc. v. Burton–Fifth
Ave. Corp., supra; Monotype Composition
Co. v. Kiernan, supra.

contains a good review of the cases, the court stated, "[t]here appears to be no agreement among the decisions or textbook writers on a complete and authoritative definition of the term 'book value.' At least two principles seem to emerge from the better reasoned authorities: (1) the book entries must be correct and complete, and not made to defeat an outstanding claim, and (2) accepted accounting principles should not be entirely disregarded. . . ." See also, e.g., Schmidt v. Chambers, 265 Md. 9, 288 A.2d 356 (1972); Bank of California v. First Mortgage Co., 6 Wash.App. 718, 495 P.2d 1057 (1972) (accounting method must be uniform). This leaves at least some leeway for interpretation, and in some cases the courts have used this leeway, or contractual ambiguity concerning the precise manner in which book value is to be determined, to permit adjustments to the figures shown on the corporate books. For example in Aron v. Gilman itself, the court substituted a correct inventory figure for a much lower incorrect figure carried on the books as "estimated," and held that accrued-though-not-yet-payable taxes must be deducted from book value, although the books did not reflect such an accrual except by noting that no provision had been made for taxes. Often the cases go considerably further, and appear to be aimed at doing equity under the cover of interpretation. See, e.g., Land & Simmons Co. v. Arcanti, 223 Md. 204, 162 A.2d 478 (1968) (insurance proceeds on shareholder's death included in book value); Chadwick v. Cross, Abbott Co., 124 Vt. 325, 205 A.2d 416 (1964) (straight-line depreciation substituted for accelerated depreciation).

(b) A second common approach is to fix the price on the basis of capitalized earnings. This approach is less likely than a book-value formula to produce an unfair price, but involves a number of drafting or interpretation problems, such as (1) defining earnings, (2) over what period, (3) with or without salaries paid to shareholder-officers, and (4) considering the possible impact of the transferor's withdrawal on the value of the business.

(c) A third common approach is to agree on a dollar price when the provision is adopted, subject to periodic revision at agreed-upon intervals. This approach may lead to trouble when the parties fail to make periodic revision, through carelessness or inability to agree. In Helms v. Duckworth, 249 F.2d 482 (D.C.Cir.1957), Easterday, age 70, and Duckworth, age 37, formed a corporation and agreed that when one died his stock would be sold to the other at $10 a share, which was then a fair price, "provided, however, that such sale and purchase price may, from time to time, be re-determined . . . [annually] by an instrument in writing signed by the parties. . . ." When Easterday died six years later the price had never been adjusted, although the actual value of the stock had risen to $80 a share. Easterday's administratrix brought suit to declare the agreement void, and Duckworth submitted an affidavit in which he stated that it was never his intention to consent to any change in the price provision. The district court granted summary judgment to Duckworth, but the Court of Appeals reversed.

. . . Plainly [the agreement] implied a periodic bargaining or negotiating process in which each party must participate in good faith. . . .

. . . We believe that the holders of closely held stock in a corporation such as shown here bear a fiduciary duty to deal fairly, honestly, and openly with their fellow stockholders and to make disclosure of all essential information.

. . . [T]he very nature of Duckworth's secret intent was such that it had to be kept secret and undisclosed or it would fail of its purpose. . . . [Duckworth's] failure to disclose to his corporate business "partner" his fixed intent never to alter the original price constitutes a flagrant breach of a fiduciary duty. Standing alone this warrants cancellation of the agreement by a court of equity.[6]

(d) A fourth approach is to provide for appraisal at the time the option is triggered. See, e.g., Ginsberg v. Coating Products, Inc., 152 Conn. 592, 210 A.2d 667 (1965); Lawson v. Household Finance Corp., 17 Del.Ch. 343, 152 A. 723 (1930). This approach has the advantage of flexibility, but unless the parties are willing to give the appraisers free rein, it too may involve the use of an agreed-upon standard of valuation that can turn out to have unforeseen and undesired results.

5. Uniform Commercial Code Article 8 is, in effect, a negotiable instrument code dealing with investment securities. Section 8–204(a) provides that "A restriction on transfer of a security imposed by the issuer, even if otherwise lawful, is ineffective against any person without actual knowledge of it unless . . . the security is certificated and the restriction is noted conspicuously thereon . . . ." U.C.C. § 1–201(10) provides that "[a] term or clause is conspicuous when it is so written that a reasonable person against whom it is to operate ought to have noticed it. A printed heading in capitals . . . is conspicuous. Language in the body of a form is 'conspicuous' if it is in larger or other contrasting type or color. . . ."[7] In Ling & Co.

---

6. The court also held that since Duckworth, who drew up the contract, was trained in both business administration and the law, while Easterday did not seek outside counsel, it was apparent that Easterday had relied on Duckworth to formulate the terms of the agreement, and Duckworth therefore had a "special duty . . . [to] reveal any possible conflicts of their respective interests." Cf. Toledo Trust Co. v. Nye, 426 F.Supp. 908 (N.D.Ohio 1977).

Another problem in interpreting first-option provisions based on a predetermined price is whether the price is to be adjusted for dilution where stock dividends have been issued after the price was last fixed. See Meyers v. Southern Nat. Bank, 21 N.C. App. 202, 204 S.E.2d 30 (1974) (no such adjustment required; price was last revised 12 years before option was triggered).

7. U.C.C. § 8–301(1) provides that on delivery of a security the purchaser normally acquires the security free of any adverse claim. Normally, therefore, if a restriction on transfer is not noted conspicuously on the stock certificate, and the transferee has no actual knowledge, he will hold his shares free of the restriction. See, e.g., Norman v. Jerich Corp., 263 Or. 259, 501 P.2d 305 (1972). Cf. Edina State Bank v. Mr. Steak, Inc., 487 F.2d 640 (10th Cir. 1974); Hampton v. Tri–State Finance Corp., 30 Colo.App. 420, 495 P.2d 566 (1972) (charter made Class B nonvoting, but share certificates did not give notice of this fact as required by statute; held, a refusal to enforce the voting restrictions against transferees without notice would be inappropriate, since it would substantially alter the rights of all shareholders and create two classifications of Class B

v. Trinity Sav. & Loan Ass'n, 482 S.W.2d 841 (Tex.1972), noted, 27
Sw.L.J. 96 (1973), the reverse side of a stock certificate contained a
block paragraph of 14 lines in moderately small type referring to
various provisions of the corporation's articles of incorporation, including "the provisions of Article Four . . . which set forth the
designations, preferences, limitations and relative rights of the shares
of each class of capital stock authorized to be issued, which deny pre-
emptive rights, prohibit cumulative voting, [and] restrict the transfer,
sale, assignment, pledge, hypothecation or encumbrance of any of the
shares represented hereby under certain conditions. . . ." The
court held this was insufficient under U.C.C. § 1–201(10). That
section, it concluded, requires "that something must appear on the
face of the certificate to attract the attention of a reasonable person
when he looks at it."

SECTION 6. THE RESOLUTION OF INTRACORPORATE DISPUTES WHERE PLANNING HAS BEEN INADEQUATE OR THE PROBLEMS RESIST ADVANCE SOLUTION

(a) FIDUCIARY OBLIGATIONS OF SHAREHOLDERS IN CLOSE CORPORATIONS: IMPLIED UNDERSTANDINGS

DONAHUE v. RODD ELECTROTYPE CO.

Section 1(b), supra

WILKES v. SPRINGSIDE NURSING HOME, INC.

Supreme Judicial Court of Massachusetts, 1977.
370 Mass. 842, 353 N.E.2d 657.

HENNESSEY, Chief Justice.

[The plaintiff (Wilkes) filed a bill in equity for declaratory
judgment, naming as defendants T. Edward Quinn,[3] Leon L. Riche,
the executors of Lawrence R. Connor, and the Springside Nursing
Home, Inc. Wilkes sought, among other forms of relief, damages in
the amount of the salary he would have received had he continued as
a director and officer of Springside subsequent to March, 1967. The
court referred the suit to a master. The master's report was con-

---

stock; instead, rescission would be granted).

3. T. Edward Quinn died while this action was sub judice. The executrix of his

estate has been substituted as a party-defendant. . . .

firmed, a judgment was entered dismissing Wilkes's action on the merits, and the Massachusetts Supreme Court granted direct appellate review.] On appeal, Wilkes argued in the alternative that (1) he should recover damages for breach of the alleged partnership agreement; and (2) he should recover damages because the defendants, as majority stockholders in Springside, breached their fiduciary duty to him as a minority stockholder by their action in February and March, 1967.

. . . [W]e reverse so much of the judgment as dismisses Wilkes's complaint and order the entry of a judgment substantially granting the relief sought by Wilkes under the second alternative set forth above.

A summary of the pertinent facts as found by the master is set out in the following pages. . . .

In 1951 Wilkes acquired an option to purchase a building and lot located on the corner of Springside Avenue and North Street in Pittsfield, Massachusetts, the building having previously housed the Hillcrest Hospital. Though Wilkes was principally engaged in the roofing and siding business, he had gained a reputation locally for profitable dealings in real estate. Riche, an acquaintance of Wilkes, learned of the option, and interested Quinn (who was known to Wilkes through membership on the draft board in Pittsfield) and Pipkin (an acquaintance of both Wilkes and Riche) in joining Wilkes in his investment. The four men met and decided to participate jointly in the purchase of the building and lot as a real estate investment which, they believed, had good profit potential on resale or rental.

The parties later determined that the property would have its greatest potential for profit if it were operated by them as a nursing home. Wilkes consulted his attorney, who advised him that if the four men were to operate the contemplated nursing home as planned, they would be partners and would be liable for any debts incurred by the partnership and by each other. On the attorney's suggestion, and after consultation among themselves, ownership of the property was vested in Springside, a corporation organized under Massachusetts law.

Each of the four men invested $1,000 and subscribed to ten shares of $100 par value stock in Springside.[6] At the time of incorporation it was understood by all of the parties that each would be a director of Springside and each would participate actively in the management and decision making involved in operating the corporation.[7] It was, further, the understanding and intention of all the

---

6. On May 2, 1955, and again on December 23, 1958, each of the four original investors paid for and was issued additional shares of $100 par value stock, eventually bringing the total number of shares owned by each to 115.

7. Wilkes testified before the master that, when the corporate officers were

elected, all four men "were . . . guaranteed directorships." Riche's understanding of the parties' intentions was that they all wanted to play a part in the management of the corporation and wanted to have some "say" in the risks involved; that, to this end, they all would be directors; and that "unless you [were] a director and of-parties that, corporate resources permitting, each would receive money from the corporation in equal amounts as long as each assumed an active and ongoing responsibility for carrying a portion of the burdens necessary to operate the business. *[handwritten: each received money for active participation]*

The work involved in establishing and operating a nursing home was roughly apportioned, and each of the four men undertook his respective tasks.[8] Initially, Riche was elected president of Springside, Wilkes was elected treasurer, and Quinn was elected clerk.[9] Each of the four was listed in the articles of organization as a director of the corporation.

At some time in 1952, it became apparent that the operational income and cash flow from the business were sufficient to permit the four stockholders to draw money from the corporation on a regular basis. Each of the four original parties initially received $35 a week from the corporation. As time went on the weekly return to each was increased until, in 1955, it totalled $100. *[handwritten: → salary estb.]*

In 1959, after a long illness, Pipkin sold his shares in the corporation to Connor, who was known to Wilkes, Riche and Quinn through past transactions with Springside in his capacity as president of the First Agricultural National Bank of Berkshire County. Connor received a weekly stipend from the corporation equal to that received by Wilkes, Riche and Quinn. He was elected a director of the corporation but never held any other office. He was assigned no specific area of responsibility in the operation of the nursing home but did participate in business discussions and decisions as a director and served additionally as financial adviser to the corporation.

In 1965 the stockholders decided to sell a portion of the corporate property to Quinn who, in addition to being a stockholder in Springside, possessed an interest in another corporation which desired to operate a rest home on the property. Wilkes was successful in prevailing on the other stockholders of Springside to procure a higher sale price for the property than Quinn apparently anticipated paying or desired to pay. After the sale was consummated, the relationship between Quinn and Wilkes began to deteriorate.

The bad blood between Quinn and Wilkes affected the attitudes of both Riche and Connor. As a consequence of the strained relations among the parties, Wilkes, in January of 1967, gave notice of his intention to sell his shares for an amount based on an appraisal of their value. In February of 1967 a directors' meeting was held and the board exercised its right to establish the salaries of its officers and

---

ficer you could not participate in the decisions of [the] enterprise."

  8. Wilkes took charge of the repair, upkeep and maintenance of the physical plant and grounds; Riche assumed supervision over the kitchen facilities and dietary and food aspects of the home; Pipkin was to make himself available if and when medical problems arose; and Quinn dealt with the personnel and administrative aspects of the nursing home, serving informally as a managing director. Quinn further coordinated the activities of the other parties and served as a communication link among them when matters had to be discussed and decisions had to be made without a formal meeting.

  9. Riche held the office of president from 1951 to 1963; Quinn served as president from 1963 on, as clerk from 1951 to 1967, and as treasurer from 1967 on; Wilkes was treasurer from 1951 to 1967.

employees.[10] A schedule of payments was established whereby Quinn was to receive a substantial weekly increase and Riche and Connor were to continue receiving $100 a week. Wilkes, however, was left off the list of those to whom a salary was to be paid. The directors also set the annual meeting of the stockholders for March, 1967.

At the annual meeting in March,[11] Wilkes was not reelected as a director, nor was he reelected as an officer of the corporation. He was further informed that neither his services nor his presence at the nursing home was wanted by his associates.

The meetings of the directors and stockholders in early 1967, the master found, were used as a vehicle to force Wilkes out of active participation in the management and operation of the corporation and to cut off all corporate payments to him. Though the board of directors had the power to dismiss any officers or employees for misconduct or neglect of duties, there was no indication in the minutes of the board of directors' meeting in February, 1967, that the failure to establish a salary for Wilkes was based on either ground. The severance of Wilkes from the payroll resulted not from misconduct or neglect of duties, but because of the personal desire of Quinn, Riche and Connor to prevent him from continuing to receive money from the corporation. Despite a continuing deterioration in his personal relationship with his associates, Wilkes had consistently endeavored to carry on his responsibilities to the corporation in the same satisfactory manner and with the same degree of competence he had previously shown. Wilkes was at all times willing to carry on his responsibilities and participation if permitted so to do and provided that he receive his weekly stipend.

1. We turn to Wilkes's claim for damages based on a breach of the fiduciary duty owed to him by the other participants in this venture. In light of the theory underlying this claim, we do not consider it vital to our approach to this case whether the claim is governed by partnership law or the law applicable to business corporations. This is so because, as all the parties agree, Springside was at all times relevant to this action, a close corporation as we have recently defined such an entity in Donahue v. Rodd Electrotype Co. of New England, Inc.. . . . [where] we held that "stockholders in the close corporation owe one another substantially the same fiduciary duty in the operation of the enterprise that partners owe to one another." . . .

In the *Donahue* case we recognized that one peculiar aspect of close corporations was the opportunity afforded to majority stockhold-

---

10. The by-laws of the corporation provided that the directors, subject to the approval of the stockholders, had the power to fix the salaries of all officers and employees. This power, however, up until February, 1967, had not been exercised formally; all payments made to the four participants in the venture had resulted from the informal but unanimous approval of all the parties concerned.

11. Wilkes was unable to attend the meeting of the board of directors in February or the annual meeting of the stockholders in March, 1967. He was represented, however, at the annual meeting by his attorney, who held his proxy.

ers to oppress, disadvantage or "freeze out" minority stockholders. . . .

. . . One . . . device which has proved to be particularly
effective in accomplishing the purpose of the majority is to deprive
minority stockholders of corporate offices and of employment with the
corporation . . . This "freeze-out" technique has been successful
because courts fairly consistently have been disinclined to interfere in
those facets of internal corporate operations, such as the selection and
retention or dismissal of officers, directors and employees, which
essentially involve management decisions subject to the principle of
majority control. . . .

The denial of employment to the minority at the hands of the
majority is especially pernicious in some instances. A guaranty of
employment with the corporation may have been one of the "basic
reason[s] why a minority owner has invested capital in the firm."
. . . The minority stockholder typically depends on his salary as the
principal return on his investment, since the "earnings of a close
corporation . . . are distributed in major part in salaries, bonuses,
and retirement benefits." 1 F.H. O'Neal, Close Corporations § 1.07
(1971).[13] Other noneconomic interests of the minority stockholder
are likewise injuriously affected by barring him from corporate office.
See F.H. O'Neal, "Squeeze–Outs" of Minority Shareholders 79
(1975). Such action severely restricts his participation in the management of the enterprise, and he is relegated to enjoying those benefits
incident to his status as a stockholder. See Symposium—The Close
Corporation, 52 Nw.U.L.Rev. 345, 386 (1957). In sum, by terminating a minority stockholder's employment or by severing him from a
position as an officer or director, the majority effectively frustrate the
minority stockholder's purposes in entering on the corporate venture
and also deny him an equal return on his investment.

The *Donahue* decision acknowledged, as a "natural outgrowth" of
the case law of this Commonwealth, a strict obligation on the part of
majority stockholders in a close corporation to deal with the minority
with the utmost good faith and loyalty. On its face, this strict standard
is applicable in the instant case. The distinction between the majority
action in *Donahue* and the majority action in this case is more one of
form than of substance. Nevertheless, we are concerned that untempered application of the strict good faith standard enunciated in
Donahue to cases such as the one before us will result in the imposition
of limitations on legitimate action by the controlling group in a close
corporation which will unduly hamper its effectiveness in managing
the corporation in the best interests of all concerned. The majority,
concededly, have certain rights to what has been termed "selfish
ownership" in the corporation which should be balanced against the
concept of their fiduciary obligation to the minority. See Hill, The
Sale of Controlling Shares, 70 Harv.L.Rev. 986, 1013–1015 (1957);

13. We note here that the master found
that Springside never declared or paid a
dividend to its stockholders.

Note, 44 Iowa L.Rev. 734, 740–741 (1959); Symposium—The Close Corporation, 52 Nw.U.L.Rev. 345, 395–396 (1957).

Therefore, when minority stockholders in a close corporation bring suit against the majority alleging a breach of the strict good faith duty owed to them by the majority, we must carefully analyze the action taken by the controlling stockholders in the individual case. It must be asked whether the controlling group can demonstrate a legitimate business purpose for its action. See Bryan v. Brock & Blevins Co., 343 F.Supp. 1062, 1068 (N.D.Ga.1972), aff'd, 490 F.2d 563, 570–571 (5th Cir.1974); Schwartz v. Marien, 37 N.Y.2d 487, 492, 373 N.Y.S.2d 122, 335 N.E.2d 334 (1975). . . . In asking this question, we acknowledge the fact that the controlling group in a close corporation must have some room to maneuver in establishing the business policy of the corporation. It must have a large measure of discretion, for example, in declaring or withholding dividends, deciding whether to merge or consolidate, establishing the salaries of corporate officers, dismissing directors with or without cause, and hiring and firing corporate employees.

When an asserted business purpose for their action is advanced by the majority, however, we think it is open to minority stockholders to demonstrate that the same legitimate objective could have been achieved through an alternative course of action less harmful to the minority's interest. See Schwartz v. Marien, supra. . . . If called on to settle a dispute, our courts must weigh the legitimate business purpose, if any, against the practicability of a less harmful alternative.

Applying this approach to the instant case it is apparent that the majority stockholders in Springside have not shown a legitimate business purpose for severing Wilkes from the payroll of the corporation or for refusing to reëlect him as a salaried officer and director. . . .

It is an inescapable conclusion from all the evidence that the action of the majority stockholders here was a designed "freeze out" for which no legitimate business purpose has been suggested. Furthermore, we may infer that a design to pressure Wilkes into selling his shares to the corporation at a price below their value well may have been at the heart of the majority's plan.[14]

In the context of this case, several factors bear directly on the duty owed to Wilkes by his associates. At a minimum, the duty of utmost good faith and loyalty would demand that the majority consider that their action was in disregard of a long-standing policy of the stockholders that each would be a director of the corporation and that employment with the corporation would go hand in hand with stock ownership; that Wilkes was one of the four originators of the nursing home venture; and that Wilkes, like the others, had invested his capital and time for more than fifteen years with the expectation that he would continue to participate in corporate decisions. Most impor-

---

14. This inference arises from the fact that Connor, acting on behalf of the three controlling stockholders, offered to purchase Wilkes's shares for a price Connor admittedly would not have accepted for his own shares.

tant is the plain fact that the cutting off of Wilkes's salary, together with the fact that the corporation never declared a dividend (see note 13 supra), assured that Wilkes would receive no return at all from the corporation.

2. The question of Wilkes's damages at the hands of the majority has not been thoroughly explored on the record before us. Wilkes, in his original complaint, sought damages in the amount of the $100 a week he believed he was entitled to from the time his salary was terminated up until the time this action was commenced. However, the record shows that, after Wilkes was severed from the corporate payroll, the schedule of salaries and payments made to the other stockholders varied from time to time. In addition, the duties assumed by the other stockholders after Wilkes was deprived of his share of the corporate earnings appear to have changed in significant respects.[15] Any resolution of this question must take into account whether the corporation was dissolved during the pendency of this litigation.

Therefore our order is as follows: So much of the judgment as dismisses Wilkes's complaint and awards costs to the defendants is reversed.[16] The case is remanded . . . for further proceedings concerning the issue of damages. Thereafter a judgment shall be entered declaring that Quinn, Riche and Connor breached their fiduciary duty to Wilkes as a minority stockholder in Springside, and awarding money damages therefor. Wilkes shall be allowed to recover from Riche, the estate of T. Edward Quinn and the estate of Lawrence R. Connor, ratably, according to the inequitable enrichment of each, the salary he would have received had he remained an officer and director of Springside. In considering the issue of damages the judge on remand shall take into account the extent to which any remaining corporate funds of Springside may be diverted to satisfy Wilkes's claim.*

---

15. In fairness to Wilkes, who, as the master found, was at all times ready and willing to work for the corporation, it should be noted that neither the other stockholders nor their representatives may be heard to say that Wilkes's duties were performed by them and that Wilkes's damages should, for that reason, be diminished.

16. We do not disturb the judgment in so far as it dismissed a counterclaim by Springside against Wilkes arising from the payment of money by Quinn to Wilkes after the sale in 1965 of certain property of Springside to a corporation owned at that time by Quinn and his wife. . . .

* For additional cases holding that close corporation shareholders owe each other a fiduciary obligation comparable to that owed by partners, see Comolli v. Comolli, 241 Ga. 471, 246 S.E.2d 278 (1978); Cressy v. Shannon Corp., 378 N.E.2d 941 (Ind.App. 1978). ("While parties incorporate to ob-

tain the benefits of limited liability, perpetual existence . . . or tax considerations . . . they often expect to act and to be treated as partners in their dealings among themselves. . . . [T]he shareholders of such a corporation [owe] to each other a fiduciary duty to deal fairly, honestly and openly. . . . [The evidence in this case shows that the corporation's two shareholders] intended equal ownership and control of the business. The 'partnership' expectation of equality of shareholdings carried with it the duty on the part of each principal to disclose to the other the availability of outstanding shares for sale and to afford the opportunity to share in the purchase of such stock."); Cain v. Cain, 3 Mass.App. 467, 334 N.E.2d 650 (1975) (in applying the principles of Donahue v. Rodd Electrotype Co., court looked to partnership law to assess right of shareholder in close corporation to compete with the cor-

SMITH [1] v. ATLANTIC PROPERTIES, INC. [2]

Appeals Court of Massachusetts, 1981.
12 Mass.App. 201, 422 N.E.2d 798.

FACTS

CUTTER, Justice. In December, 1951, Dr. Louis E. Wolfson agreed to purchase land in Norwood for $350,000, with an initial cash payment of $50,000 and a mortgage note of $300,000 payable in thirty-three months. Dr. Wolfson offered a quarter interest each in the land to Mr. Paul T. Smith, Mr. Abraham Zimble, and William H. Burke. Each paid to Dr. Wolfson $12,500, one quarter of the initial payment. Mr. Smith, an attorney, organized the defendant corporation (Atlantic) in 1951 to operate the real estate. Each of the four subscribers received twenty-five shares of stock. Mr. Smith included, both in the corporation's articles of organization and in its by-laws, a provision reading, "No election, appointment or resolution by the Stockholders and no election, appointment, resolution, purchase, sale, lease, contract, contribution, compensation, proceeding or act by the Board of Directors or by any officer or officers shall be valid or binding upon the corporation until effected, passed, approved or ratified by an affirmative vote of eighty (80%) per cent of the capital stock issued outstanding and entitled to vote." This provision (hereafter referred to as the 80% provision) was included at Dr. Wolfson's request and had the effect of giving to any one of the four original shareholders a veto in corporate decisions.

Super-majority

Atlantic purchased the Norwood land. Some of the land and other assets were sold for about $220,000. Atlantic retained twenty-eight acres on which stood about twenty old brick or wood mill-type structures, which required expensive and constant repairs. After the first year, Atlantic became profitable and showed a profit every year

poration); 68th Street Apts., Inc., v. Lauricella, 142 N.J.Super. 546, 362 A.2d 78 (1976), aff'd per curiam 150 N.J.Super. 47, 374 A.2d 1222; Campbell v. Campbell, 198 Kan. 181, 422 P.2d 932 (1967). See also Note, Corporate Opportunity in the Close Corporation—A Different Result?, 56 Geo. L.J. 381 (1967). Cf. Zidell v. Zidell, Inc., 277 Or. 423, 560 P.2d 1091 (1977). Arnold and Emery Zidell each owned 37½% of four corporations, and Rosenfeld owned the remaining 25%. Emery arranged for the purchase of all of Rosenfeld's shares in one corporation and slightly more than half in the other three, thereby acquiring majority control of all four corporations. In a derivative action brought by Arnold, held, Emery did not violate any duty to the corporations by failing to offer them the opportunity to negotiate for the purchase of Rosenfeld's shares:

The opinion in *Donahue* evidences a concern to provide greater protection for the minority shareholder in a close corporation than had previously been available in the courts. . . . We do not believe, however, that the protective approach taken in that case would require the corporation to tailor its policies to favor a minority shareholder at the expense of the majority. See Wilkes v. Springside Nursing Home, Inc. . . . That, however, is apparently what plaintiff is seeking in the present case. He is asking that the court require these corporations to purchase Rosenfeld's shares in order to prevent, for plaintiff's benefit, a consolidation of control in the hands of Emery Zidell.

(Footnote by ed.)

1. Lillian Zimble, executrix of the will of Abraham Zimble, and Louis Zimble [are also plaintiffs]. William H. Burke was originally a plaintiff. Prior to his death, Atlantic Properties, Inc. purchased Burke's stock in the corporation and it is now held as treasury stock. Mr. Abraham Zimble, while living, sold twelve shares to Louis Zimble.

2. Dr. Louis E. Wolfson [is also a defendant].

prior to 1969, ranging from a low of $7,683 in 1953 to a high of $44,358 in 1954. The mortgage was paid by 1958 and Atlantic has incurred no long-term debt thereafter. Salaries of about $25,000 were paid only in 1959 and 1960. Dividends in the total amount of $10,000 each were paid in 1964 and 1970. By 1961, Atlantic had about $172,000 in retained earnings, more than half in cash.

For various reasons, which need not be stated in detail, disagreements and ill will soon arose between Dr. Wolfson, on the one hand, and the other stockholders as a group.[3] Dr. Wolfson wished to see Atlantic's earnings devoted to repairs and possibly some improvements in its existing buildings and adjacent facilities. The other stockholders desired the declaration of dividends. Dr. Wolfson fairly steadily refused to vote for any dividends. Although it was pointed out to him that failure to declare dividends might result in the imposition by the Internal Revenue Service of a penalty under the Internal Revenue Code, I.R.C. § 531 et seq. (relating to unreasonable accumulation of corporate earnings and profits), Dr. Wolfson persisted in his refusal to declare dividends. The other shareholders did agree over the years to making at least the most urgent repairs to Atlantic's buildings, but did not agree to make all repairs and improvements which were recommended in a 1962 report by an engineering firm retained by Atlantic to make a complete estimate of all repairs and improvements which might be beneficial.

The fears of an Internal Revenue Service assessment of a penalty tax were soon realized. Penalty assessments were made in 1962, 1963, and 1964. These were settled by Dr. Wolfson for $11,767.71 in taxes and interest. Despite this settlement, Dr. Wolfson continued his opposition to declaring dividends. The record does not indicate that he developed any specific and definitive schedule or plan for a series of necessary or desirable repairs and improvements to Atlantic's properties. At least none was proposed which would have had a reasonable chance of satisfying the Internal Revenue Service that expenditures for such repairs and improvements constituted "reasonable needs of the business," I.R.C. § 534(c), a term which includes (see I.R.C. § 537) "the reasonably anticipated needs of the business." Predictably, despite further warnings by Dr. Wolfson's shareholder colleagues, the Internal Revenue Service assessed further penalty taxes for the years 1965, 1966, 1967, and 1968. These taxes were upheld by the United States Tax Court in Atlantic Properties, Inc. v. Commissioner of Int. Rev., 62 T.C. 644 (1974), and on appeal in 519 F.2d 1233 (1st Cir.1975). See the discussion of these opinions in Cathcart, Accumulated Earnings Tax: A Trap for the Wary, 62 A.B.A.J. 1197–1199 (1976). An examination of these decisions makes it apparent that Atlantic has incurred substantial penalty taxes and legal expense largely because of Dr. Wolfson's refusal to vote for the declaration of sufficient dividends to avoid the penalty, a refusal which was (in the

---

3. At least one cause of ill will on Dr. Wolfson's part may have been the refusal of the other shareholders to consent to his transferring his shares in Atlantic to the Louis E. Wolfson Foundation, a charitable foundation created by Dr. Wolfson.

Tax Court and upon appeal) attributed in some measure to a tax avoidance purpose on Dr. Wolfson's part.

On January 30, 1967, the shareholders, other than Dr. Wolfson, initiated this proceeding in the Superior Court, later supplemented to reflect developments after the original complaint. The plaintiffs sought a court determination of the dividends to be paid by Atlantic, the removal of Dr. Wolfson as a director, and an order that Atlantic be reimbursed by him for the penalty taxes assessed against it and related expenses. The case was tried before a justice of the Superior Court (jury waived) in September and October, 1979.

The trial judge made findings (but in more detail) of essentially the facts outlined above and concluded that Dr. "Wolfson's obstinate refusal to vote in favor of . . . dividends was . . . caused more by his dislike for other stockholders and his desire to avoid additional tax payments than . . . by any genuine desire to undertake a program for improving . . . [Atlantic] property." She also determined that Dr. Wolfson was liable to Atlantic for taxes and interest amounting to "$11,767.11 plus interest from the commencement of this action, plus $35,646.14 plus interest from August 11, 1975," the date of the First Circuit decision affirming the second penalty tax assessment. The latter amount includes an attorney's fee of $7,500 in the Federal tax cases. She also ordered the directors of Atlantic to declare "a reasonable dividend at the earliest practical date and reasonable dividends annually thereafter consistent with good business practice." In addition, the trial judge directed that jurisdiction of the case be retained in the Superior Court "for a period of five years to [e]nsure compliance." Judgment was entered pursuant to the trial judge's order. After the entry of judgment, Dr. Wolfson and Atlantic filed a motion for a new trial and to amend the judge's findings. This motion, after hearing, was denied, and Dr. Wolfson and Atlantic claimed an appeal from the judgment and the former from the denial of the motion. The plaintiffs (see note 1, supra) requested payment of their attorneys' fees in this proceeding and filed supporting affidavits. The motion was denied, and the plaintiffs appealed.

1. The trial judge, in deciding that Dr. Wolfson had committed a breach of his fiduciary duty to other stockholders, relied greatly on broad language in Donahue v. Rodd Electrotype Co., 367 Mass. 578, 586–597, 328 N.E.2d 505 (1975). . . . Similar principles were stated in Wilkes v. Springside Nursing Home, Inc., 370 Mass. 842, 848–852, 353 N.E.2d 657 (1976), but with some modifications, mentioned in the margin,[5] of the sweeping language of the *Donahue*

---

5. The court said (at 850–852, 353 N.E.2d 657) that it was "concerned that [the] untempered application of the strict good faith standard . . . will result in the imposition of limitations on legitimate action by the *controlling group* in a close corporation which will unduly hamper its effectiveness. . . . The majority . . . have certain rights to what has been termed 'selfish ownership' in the corporation which should be balanced against the concept of their fiduciary obligation to the minority. . . . [W]hen minority stockholders . . . bring suit . . . alleging a breach of the strict good faith duty . . . we must carefully analyze the action taken by the *controlling stockholders* in the individual case. It must be asked whether the *controlling group* can demonstrate a legitimate business purpose for its action. . . . [T]he *controlling group* in a close corporation must have some room to maneuver in

case. See Jessie v. Boynton, 372 Mass. 293, 304, 361 N.E.2d 1267 (1977); Hallhan v. Haltom Corp., 7 Mass.App. 68, 70–71, 385 N.E.2d 1033 (1979). See also Cain v. Cain, 3 Mass.App. 467, 473–479, 334 N.E.2d 650 (1975).

In the *Donahue* case, 367 Mass. at 593 n. 17, 328 N.E.2d 505, the court recognized that cases may arise in which, in a close corporation, majority stockholders may ask protection from a minority stockholder. Such an instance arises in the present case because Dr. Wolfson has been able to exercise a veto concerning corporate action on dividends by the 80% provision (in Atlantic's articles [of] organization and by-laws) already quoted. The 80% provision may have substantially the effect of reversing the usual roles of the majority and the minority shareholders. The minority, under that provision, becomes an ad hoc controlling interest.[6]

It does not appear to be argued that this 80% provision is not authorized by G.L. c. 156B (inserted by St.1964, c. 723, § 1). See especially § 8(*a*).* See also Seibert v. Milton Bradley Co., 380 Mass. 656, 405 N.E.2d 131 (1980). Chapter 156B was intended to provide desirable flexibility in corporate arrangements.[7] The provision is only one of several methods which have been devised to protect minority shareholders in close corporations from being oppressed by their colleagues and, if the device is used reasonably, there may be no strong public policy considerations against its use. See 1 O'Neal, Close Corporations § 4.21 (2d ed. 1971 & Supp.1980). The textbook just cited contains in §§ 4.01–4.30 a comprehensive discussion of the business considerations (see especially §§ 4.02, 4.03, 4.06, & 4.24) which may recommend use of such a device. See also 2 O'Neal § 8.07 (& Supp.1980 which, at 84–90, discusses the Massachusetts decisions). In the present case, Dr. Wolfson testified that he requested the inclusion of the 80% provision "in case the people [the other shareholders] whom I knew, but not very well, ganged up on me." The possibilities of shareholder disagreement on policy made

establishing the business policy of the corporation. It must have a large measure of discretion, for example, *in declaring or withholding dividends*" (emphasis supplied) and in certain other matters. "When an asserted business purpose . . . is advanced by the majority, however, . . . it is open to minority stockholders to demonstrate that the . . . objective could have been achieved through an alternative course . . . less harmful to the minority's interest."

6. The majority shareholders, in the event of a deadlock, at least may seek dissolution of the corporation if forty percent of the voting power can be mustered, whereas a single stockholder with only twenty-five percent of the stock may not do so. See G.L. c. 156B, § 99(*b*), as amended by St.1969, c. 392, § 23.

* M.G.L.A. c. 156B, § 8(a) provides that "Whenever, with respect to any action to be taken by the stockholders of a corporation, the articles of organization or by-laws require the vote or concurrence of the holders of all of the shares, or of any class or series thereof, or a greater proportion thereof than required by this chapter with respect to such action, the provisions of the articles of organization or by-laws shall control." (Footnote by ed.)

7. See, e.g., Hosmer, New Business Corporation Law, 1964 Ann. Survey of Mass. Law §§ 1.1–1.12: Casey, The New Business Corporation Law, 50 Mass.L.Q. (No. 3) 201 (1965); and Boston Bar Assn., Summary of Principal Changes Made by . . . Chapter 156B (1964), reprinted as an appendix in Mass.Gen.Laws Ann., at 429.

the provision seem a sensible precaution.[8] A question is presented, however, concerning the extent to which such a veto power possessed by a minority stockholder may be exercised as its holder may wish, without a violation of the "fiduciary duty" referred to in the *Donahue* case, 367 Mass. at 593, 328 N.E.2d 505, as modified in the *Wilkes* case. See note 5, supra.

The decided cases in Massachusetts do little to answer this question. The most pertinent guidance is probably found in the *Wilkes* case, 370 Mass. at 849–852, 353 N.E.2d 657, . . . essentially to the effect that in any judicial intervention in such a situation there must be a weighing of the business interests advanced as reasons for their action (a) by the majority or controlling group and (b) by the rival persons or group.[9] It would obviously be appropriate, before a court-ordered solution is sought or imposed, for both sides to attempt to reach a sensible solution of any incipient impasse in the interest of all concerned after consideration of all relevant circumstances. See Helms v. Duckworth, 249 F.2d 482, 485–488 (D.C.Cir.1957).

2. With respect to the past damage to Atlantic caused by Dr. Wolfson's refusal to vote in favor of any dividends, the trial judge was justified in finding that his conduct went beyond what was reasonable. The other stockholders shared to some extent responsibility for what occurred by failing to accept Dr. Wolfson's proposals with much sympathy, but the inaction on dividends seems the principal cause of the tax penalties. Dr. Wolfson had been warned of the dangers of an assessment under the Internal Revenue Code, I.R.C. § 531 et seq. He had refused to vote dividends in any amount adequate to minimize

---

8. Dr. Wolfson himself had discovered the business opportunity which led to the formation of Atlantic, had made the initial $50,000 payment which made possible the Norwood land purchase, and had given the other shareholders an opportunity to share with him in what looked like a probably profitable enterprise. It was reasonably foreseeable that there might be differences of opinion between Dr. Wolfson, a man with substantial income likely to be in a high income tax bracket, and less affluent shareholders on such matters of policy as dividend declarations, salaries, and investment in improvements in the property. The other shareholders, two of whom were attorneys should have known that it was as open to Dr. Wolfson reasonably to exercise the veto provided to him by the 80% provision in favor of a policy of reinvestment of earnings in Atlantic's properties, which would probably avoid taxes and increase the value of the corporate assets, as it was for them (possessed of the same veto) to use reasonably their voting power in favor of a more generous dividend and salary policy.

9. The duties and quasi-fiduciary responsibilities of minority shareholders who find themselves in a position to control corporate action are discussed helpfully in

Hetherington, The Minority's Duty of Loyalty in Close Corporations, 1972 Duke L.J. 921. The author recognizes (at 944) that, in disputes concerning the wisdom of a particular course of corporate action, the majority (or the ad hoc controlling minority) shareholder may be entitled to follow the course he or it thinks best.

The author concludes (at 946) with the general view: "In spite of the . . . imprecision of such criteria for evaluating commercial behavior as good faith, commercial reasonableness, and unconscionability, the courts have moved toward imposing minimum requirements of fair dealing in nonfiduciary business situations. The similarly imprecise concept of fiduciary responsibility, at least as applied to majority shareholders . . . has clearly promoted fair dealing within business enterprises. The majority may not exercise their corporate powers in a manner which is clearly intended to be and is in fact inimical to the corporate interest, or which is intended to deprive the minority of its pro rata share of the present or future gains accruing to the enterprise. A minority shareholder whose conduct is controlling on a particular issue should be bound by no different standard."

that danger and had failed to bring forward, within the relevant taxable years, a convincing, definitive program of appropriate improvements which could withstand scrutiny by the Internal Revenue Service. Whatever may have been the reason for Dr. Wolfson's refusal to declare dividends (and even if in any particular year he may have gained slight, if any, tax advantage from withholding dividends) we think that he recklessly ran serious and unjustified risks of precisely the penalty taxes eventually assessed, risks which were inconsistent with any reasonable interpretation of a duty of "utmost good faith and loyalty." The trial judge (despite the fact that the other shareholders helped to create the voting deadlock and despite the novelty of the situation) was justified in charging Dr. Wolfson with the out-of-pocket expenditure incurred by Atlantic for the penalty taxes and related counsel fees of the tax cases.[10]

3. The trial judge's order to the directors of Atlantic, "to declare a reasonable dividend at the earliest practical date and reasonable dividends annually thereafter," presents difficulties. It may well not be a precise, clear, and unequivocal command which (without further explanation) would justify enforcement by civil contempt proceedings. See United States Time Corp. v. G.E.M. of Boston, Inc., 345 Mass. 279, 282, 186 N.E.2d 920 (1963); United Factory Outlet, Inc. v. Jay's Stores, Inc., 361 Mass. 35, 36–39, 278 N.E.2d 716 (1972). It also fails to order the directors to exercise similar business judgment with respect to Dr. Wolfson's desire to make all appropriate repairs and improvements to Atlantic's factory properties. See the language of the Supreme Judicial Court in the *Wilkes* case, 370 Mass. at 850–852, 353 N.E.2d 657, see note 5, supra.

The somewhat ambiguous injunctive relief is made less significant by the trial judge's reservation of jurisdiction in the Superior Court, a provision which contemplates later judicial supervision. We think that such supervision should be provided now upon an expanded record. The present record does not disclose Atlantic's present financial condition or what, if anything, it has done (since the judgment under review) by way of expenditures for repairs and improvements of its properties and in respect of dividends and salaries. The judgment, of course, necessarily disregards the general judicial reluctance to interfere with a corporation's dividend policy ordinarily based upon the business judgment of its directors. See Crocker v. Waltham Watch Co., 315 Mass. 387, 402, 53 N.E.2d 230 (1944); Donahue v. Rodd Electrotype Co., 367 Mass. at 590, 328 N.E.2d 505, and authorities cited; 1 O'Neal, Close Corporations § 3.63 and 2 O'Neal § 8.08; Forced Dividends, 1 J.Corp.L. 420 (1976).

Although the reservation of jurisdiction is appropriate in this case (see Nassif v. Boston & Maine R.R., 340 Mass. 557, 566–567, 65 N.E.2d 397 [1960]; Department of Pub. Health v. Cumberland

---

10. We do not now suggest that the standard of "utmost good faith and loyalty" may require some relaxation when applied to a minority ad hoc controlling interest, created by some device, similar to the 80% provision, designed in part to protect the selfish interests of a minority shareholder. This seems to us a difficult area of the law best developed on a case by case basis. See note 4, supra.

Cattle Co., 361 Mass. 817, 834, 282 N.E.2d 895 [1972]), its purpose should be stated more affirmatively. Paragraph 2 of the judgment should be revised to provide: (a) a direction that Atlantic's directors prepare promptly financial statements and copies of State and Federal income and excise tax returns for the five most recent calendar or fiscal years, and a balance sheet as of as current a date as is possible; (b) an instruction that they confer with one another with a view to stipulating a general dividend and capital improvements policy for the next ensuing three fiscal years; (c) an order that, if such a stipulation is not filed with the clerk of the Superior Court within sixty days after the receipt of the rescript in the Superior Court, a further hearing shall be held promptly (either before the court or before a special master with substantial experience in business affairs), at which there shall be received in evidence at least the financial statements and tax returns above mentioned, as well as other relevant evidence. Thereafter, the court, after due consideration of the circumstances then existing, may direct the adoption (and carrying out), if it be then deemed appropriate, of a specific dividend and capital improvements policy adequate to minimize the risk of further penalty tax assessments for the then current fiscal year of Atlantic. The court also may reserve jurisdiction to take essentially the same action for each subsequent fiscal year until the parties are able to reach for themselves an agreed program.

4. The plaintiff shareholders requested an allowance for counsel fees incurred by them in accomplishing the recovery by Atlantic from Dr. Wolfson of the amounts to be paid by him. The trial judge did not state her reasons for denying the motion for such fees. Whether to grant such an allowance was within her sound discretion. See Wilson v. Jennings, 344 Mass. 608, 621, 184 N.E.2d 642 (1962), and cases cited; Cain v. Cain, 3 Mass.App. at 479, 334 N.E.2d 650: Nolan, Equitable Remedies § 244, at 366 (1975). We perceive no abuse of discretion. She was entitled to take into account the considerations mentioned in note 8, supra, and that the controversy involved issues of business judgment and somewhat novel legal questions. See note 10, supra. She also properly could give weight to (a) the circumstance that no fraud or diversion of Atlantic's assets was engaged in by Dr. Wolfson, and (b) the portions of the evidence suggesting that the plaintiffs may have been in some measure responsible for the intensity of the bad feeling among the stockholders.

5. The judgment is affirmed so far as it (par. 1) orders payments into Atlantic's treasury by Dr. Wolfson. Paragraph 2 of the judgment is to be modified in a manner consistent with part 3 of this opinion. The trial judge's denial of the plaintiff's motion to be allowed counsel fees is affirmed. Costs of this appeal are to be paid from the assets of Atlantic.

So ordered.

———

(b) DISSOLUTION AT A SHAREHOLDER'S OPTION AND DISSOLUTION FOR DEADLOCK

DEL. GEN. CORP. LAW §§ 273, 355

[See Statutory Supplement]

REV. MODEL BUS. CORP. ACT § 14.30
MODEL STAT. CLOSE CORP. SUPP. §§ 33, 40, 43

[See Statutory Supplement]

N.Y. BUS. CORP. LAW §§ 1002, 1104, 1111

[See Statutory Supplement]

π   Δ
WOLLMAN v. LITTMAN

New York Supreme Court, Appellate Div., First Dept., 1970.
35 A.D.2d 935, 316 N.Y.S.2d 526.

PER CURIAM . . .

The stock of the corporation is held, fifty percent each, by two distinct groups, one of which, the Nierenberg sisters, are plaintiffs, and the other, the Littmans, defendants, each group having equal representation on the board of directors. The corporation's business is the selling of artificial fur fabrics to garment manufacturers. Defendants, the Littmans, allegedly had the idea for the business and developed a market for the fabrics among its manufacturing customers. Plaintiffs are the daughters of Louis Nierenberg, the main stockholder of Louis Nierenberg, Inc., who procures the fabrics and sells them to the corporation. The Littmans, in a separate action in which they are plaintiffs, charge the plaintiffs here (the Nierenberg sisters) and Louis Nierenberg Corporation with seeking to lure away the corporation's customers for Louis Nierenberg Corporation and with doing various acts to affect the corporation's business adversely. The Nierenberg faction countered with this suit, claiming that the bringing of the other action indicates that the corporate management is at such odds among themselves that effective management is impossible. Special Term agreed, but we do not. Irreconcilable differences even among an evenly divided board of directors do not in all cases mandate dissolution. . . . Here, two factors would require further exploration. The first is that the functions of the two disputing interests are distinct, one selling and the other procuring, and each can pursue its own without need for collaboration. The second is that a dissolution which will render nugatory the relief sought in the representative action would actually accomplish the wrongful purpose that defendants (Nierenberg) are charged with in that action. It would not only squeeze the Littmans out of the business but would require the receiver to dispose of the inventory with the Nierenbergs the only interested purchaser financially strong enough to take advantage of the situation. Such a result, if supported by the facts, would be intolerable to a court of equity. A trial of the issues is necessitated. On that trial it has been agreed by both counsel it would be advantageous to have the representative action and the action for dissolution tried together, though not consolidated (for a discussion of the distinction, see the comprehensive opinion in Padilla v. Greyhound Lines, 29 A.D.2d 495, 288 N.Y.S. 641), and it is so directed.

We affirm the appointment of a receiver. His function, however, should be limited to the necessities indicated, namely, to the orderly functioning of the regular course of business of the corporation until the further order of the court.

———

NOTE ON DISSOLUTION FOR DEADLOCK

1. A number of statutes provide for involuntary dissolution on a showing of deadlock. A few of the statutes define deadlock in terms of an "equally divided" board or body of shareholders, see, e.g., Mass. § 50; Cook v. Cook, 270 Mass. 534, 170 N.E. 455 (1930), but most are phrased broadly enough to include deadlock brought about by supermajority or veto arrangements.

2. The deadlock statutes are generally interpreted to make dissolution discretionary even when deadlock as defined in the statute is shown to exist, and the courts have often been reluctant to order the dissolution of a profitable corporation on deadlock grounds. In In re Radom & Neidorff, 307 N.Y. 1, 119 N.E.2d 563 (1954), noted, 68 Harv.L.Rev. 714 (1955), Henry Neidorff and his brother-in-law David Radom were the sole and equal shareholders of Radom & Neidorff, Inc., which was engaged in the business of printing musical compositions. Henry Neidorff died and left his stock to his wife Anna, David's sister. Anna and David were estranged, and five months after Henry Neidorff's death, David brought a proceeding to dissolve the corporation under the predecessor of N.Y. § 1104, supra. David's petition stated that the corporation was successful, but that Anna had refused to co-operate with David as president and had refused to sign his salary checks—leaving him without salary although he had the sole burden of running the business—and that election of any directors had proved impossible because of unresolved disagreements. The Court of Appeals affirmed an order of the Appellate Division denying dissolution, relying in part on N.Y.Gen.Corp.Law § 117, which provided that "If upon the application for the final order [for involuntary dissolution] it shall appear that . . . dissolution will be beneficial to the stockholders or members and not injurious to the public, the court must make a final order dissolving the corporation. . . ."

. . . There is no absolute right to dissolution under such circumstances. Even when majority stockholders file a petition because of internal corporate conflicts, the order is granted only when the competing interests "are so discordant as to prevent efficient management" and the "object of its corporate existence cannot be attained." . . . The prime inquiry is, always, as to necessity for dissolution, that is, whether judicially-imposed death "will be beneficial to the stockholders or members and not injurious to the public," General Corporation Law, § 117. . . . Taking everything in the petition as true, this was not such a case. . . .[1]

In Madame Wagner and The Close Corporation, 73 Harv.L.Rev. 1532, 1546–47 (1960), Professor Chayes commented on this case as follows:

Was [the result] wholly unjustified? In early 1950, Radom offered Mrs. Neidorff $75,000 for her interest in the company. Three years later, accumulated profits (before his salary) were $242,000. This suggests that the shares may have been worth more than $75,000 in 1950. Further, in a court-ordered dissolution, Mrs. Neidorff would have had to content herself with one-half the liquidating value of the corporate assets, $150,000 at the outside. But Radom would have had the going-concern value, since he had the skill and associations to continue to operate the business while his "partner's" widow did not. Surely, when they organized the business the two men did not contemplate this kind of bet on survivorship. . . .

In this view, there is something to be said for denying Radom's petition for dissolution: it is one way to force him to offer his sister a fair price for her interest. More generally, where the company whose demise is sought continues to earn tidily, it is not unlikely that one of the parties (usually the petitioner) will capture the lion's share of the value on liquidation.

Nevertheless, the approach in Radom & Neidorff was criticized in many quarters, and after the decision the New York legislature revised the statute. (See N.Y.Bus.Corp.Law §§ 1102, 1104, 1111, supra.) However, dissolution for deadlock continues to be discretionary, as *Wollman* illustrates.

Although the courts have been reluctant to dissolve profitable corporations, profitability is not an absolute bar to dissolution. In Weiss v. Gordon, 32 A.D.2d 279, 301 N.Y.S.2d 839 (1969), the court stated, "The earlier thinking stressed the distinction between the corporation as an entity and the shareholders, and as long as the former could continue to function profitably the relationship between the shareholders was of no moment (cf. In re Radom & Neidorff, Inc.,

---

1. See also, e.g., Bator v. United Sausage Co., 138 Conn. 18, 81 A.2d 442 (1951); Lush'us Brand Distributors v. Fort Dearborn Lithograph Co., 330 Ill.App. 216, 70 N.E.2d 737 (1947); Gidwitz v. Cohn, 238 Ill. App. 227 (1925); Application of The Hickory House, Inc., 13 Misc.2d 761, 177 N.Y.S.2d 356 (1958); Jackson v. Nicolai-Neppach Co., 219 Or. 560, 348 P.2d 9 (1959).

307 N.Y. 1, 119 N.E.2d 563 (1954)). It is being increasingly realized that the relationship between the stockholders in a close corporation vis-a-vis each other in practice closely approximates the relationship between partners (see Mtr. of Surchin v. Approved Bus. Mach., 55 Misc.2d 888, 890, 286 N.Y.S.2d 580, 583 (1967)). As a consequence, when a point is reached where the shareholders who are actively conducting the business of the corporation cannot agree, it becomes in the best interests of those shareholders to order a dissolution. . . . "[2]

3. Hetherington & Dooley, Illiquidity and Exploitation: A Proposed Statutory Solution to The Remaining Close Corporation Problem, 63 Va.L.Rev. 1, 27 (1977):

In corporate involuntary dissolution cases, the courts appear to assume that a decree will result in the termination of the business. Perceiving a public interest in the continuation of profitable firms, courts understandably grant dissolution reluctantly and only after considering competing interests in preserving the firm. The concern is misplaced. . . . The entry of a decree results in the termination of the business only if both the majority and the minority shareholders desire that result. Each faction has the ability at any stage of the proceeding to insure the continued existence of the firm by buying out, or selling out to, the other faction. The business will cease only if continuing it is not in the interest of any of its shareholders.

The point becomes clearer if one focuses on the motives for bringing a dissolution proceeding. Except for the rare case where the petition is prompted by pique, a shareholder suing for dissolution is trying to accomplish one of three things: (1) to withdraw his investment from the firm; (2) to induce the other shareholders to sell out to him; or (3) to use the threat of dissolution to induce the other shareholders to agree to a change in the balance of power or in the policies of the firm. All of these objectives can be accomplished without dissolution. If the petitioner wants to sell out, he is interested in receiving the highest possible price and is indifferent whether the purchase funds are raised by the other shareholders individually or by a sale of the firm's assets. If the second or third objectives motivate the suit, it is plain that the petitioner does not want dissolution at all. In all three situations, a dissolution petition is a means to another end.

Since the petitioner can always achieve his purposes without dissolution, and since the defendant will always oppose it, the dispute is very likely to be settled without liquidating the firm's assets and terminating its business. The court's decision to grant or to deny dissolution is significant only as it affects the relative

2. See also Application of Pivot Punch & Die Corp., 15 Misc.2d 713, 182 N.Y.S.2d 459 (1959), modified 9 A.D.2d 861, 193 N.Y.S.2d 34; cf. Laskey v. L. & L. Manchester Drive–In, Inc., 216 A.2d 310 (Me.1966); Ellis v. Civic Improvement, Inc., 24 N.C.App. 42, 209 S.E.2d 873 (1974), cert. denied 286 N.C. 413, 211 S.E.2d 794 (1975); Surchin v. Approved Business Machines, 55 Misc.2d 888, 286 N.Y.S.2d 580 (1967).

bargaining strength of the parties; negotiations will go forward in any event. . . .

The authors support their conclusion with empirical data based on 54 involuntary dissolution cases decided between 1960 and 1976. In 36 of these cases, either one party bought out the other or the business was sold to a third party. Only 6 cases resulted in liquidation of the business.

4. The California statute provides for voluntary dissolution by the vote of shareholders holding 50 percent or more of the voting power. In In re Security Finance Co., 49 Cal.2d 370, 317 P.2d 1 (1957), the court stated, "[s]hareholders representing 50 per cent of the voting power do not have an absolute right . . . to dissolve a corporation. . . . [T]he election to dissolve is the election of the corporation, not merely of shareholders representing 50 per cent of the voting power, although it is through their consent that the election is made. There is nothing sacred in the life of a corporation that transcends the interests of its shareholders, but because dissolution falls with such finality on those interests, above all corporate powers it is subject to equitable limitations. The controlling issue, therefore, is whether [the] decision to dissolve the corporation was made in good faith." The facts were that a shareholders' agreement required unanimous consent for all acts of the board and the shareholders. Shareholder R, who was running the business, had sought an increase in salary or in dividends, but the other two shareholders would not agree, nor would they agree to buy his stock or to sell their stock. Under the circumstances the court concluded that R's "purpose in dissolving the corporation was to protect his investment. He did not act in bad faith in doing so, for a shareholder representing the requisite voting power may protect his investment by dissolution . . . when . . . all alternative methods are foreclosed, no advantage is secured over other shareholders, and no rights of third parties will be adversely affected."

5. Some statutes explicitly provide that a shareholders' agreement or the certificate of incorporation can confer upon one or more shareholders the right to dissolve the corporation at will or upon the occurrence of a designated contingency. Some of these statutes are applicable to all corporations. See, e.g., N.J. § 14A:12–5; N.Y.Bus. Corp.Law § 1002, supra. Others are restricted to statutory close corporations, or corporations whose shares are not publicly traded. See, e.g., Del.Gen.Corp.Law § 355; Pa. § 386; S.C. § 33–21–140(a); Tex.art. 12.32(A)(5).

(c) PROVISIONAL DIRECTORS AND CUSTODIANS

DEL. GEN. CORP. LAW §§ 226, 352, 353

[See Statutory Supplement]

CAL. CORP. CODE §§ 308, 1802

[See Statutory Supplement]

MODEL STAT. CLOSE CORP. SUPP. §§ 40, 41

[See Statutory Supplement]

(d) DISSOLUTION AND OTHER REMEDIES FOR UNFAIR CONDUCT

REV. MODEL BUS. CORP. ACT § 14.30
MODEL STAT. CLOSE CORP. SUPP. §§ 40–43

[See Statutory Supplement]

CAL. CORP. CODE §§ 1800, 1804, 2000

[See Statutory Supplement]

N.Y. BUS. CORP. LAW §§ 1104–a, 1111

[See Statutory Supplement]

MATTER OF KEMP & BEATLEY, INC.

Court of Appeals of New York, 1984.
64 N.Y.2d 63, 484 N.Y.S.2d 799, 473 N.E.2d 1173.

COOKE, Chief Judge.

When the majority shareholders of a close corporation award *de facto* dividends to all shareholders except a class of minority shareholders, such a policy may constitute "oppressive actions" and serve as a basis for an order made pursuant to section 1104–a of the Business Corporation Law dissolving the corporation. In the instant matter, there is sufficient evidence to support the lower courts' conclusion that the majority shareholders had altered a long-standing policy to distribute corporate earnings on the basis of stock ownership, as against petitioners only. Moreover, the courts did not abuse their discretion by concluding that dissolution was the only means by which petitioners could gain a fair return on their investment.

I

The business concern of Kemp & Beatley, incorporated under the laws of New York, designs and manufactures table linens and sundry tabletop items. The company's stock consists of 1,500 outstanding shares held by eight shareholders. Petitioner Dissin had been employed by the company for 42 years when, in June 1979, he resigned. Prior to resignation, Dissin served as vice-president and a director of Kemp & Beatley. Over the course of his employment, Dissin had acquired stock in the company and currently owns 200 shares.

Petitioner Gardstein, like Dissin, had been a long-time employee of the company. Hired in 1944, Gardstein was for the next 35 years involved in various aspects of the business including material procurement, product design, and plant management. His employment was terminated by the company in December 1980. He currently owns 105 shares of Kemp & Beatley stock.

Apparent unhappiness surrounded petitioners' leaving the employ of the company. Of particular concern was that they no longer received any distribution of the company's earnings. Petitioners considered themselves to be "frozen out" of the company; whereas it had been their experience when with the company to receive a distribution of the company's earnings according to their stockholdings, in the form of either dividends or extra compensation, that distribution was no longer forthcoming.

Gardstein and Dissin, together holding 20.33% of the company's outstanding stock, commenced the instant proceeding in June 1981, seeking dissolution of Kemp & Beatley pursuant to section 1104-a of the Business Corporation Law. Their petition alleged "fraudulent and oppressive" conduct by the company's board of directors such as to render petitioners' stock "a virtually worthless asset." Supreme Court referred the matter for a hearing, which was held in March 1982.

Upon considering the testimony of petitioners and the principals of Kemp & Beatley, the referee concluded that "the corporate management has by its policies effectively rendered petitioners' shares worthless, and . . . . the only way petitioners can expect any return is by dissolution". Petitioners were found to have invested capital in the company expecting, among other things, to receive dividends or "bonuses" based upon their stock holdings. Also found was the company's "established buyout policy" by which it would purchase the stock of employee shareholders upon their leaving its employ.

The involuntary-dissolution statute (Business Corporation Law, § 1104-a) permits dissolution when a corporation's controlling faction is found guilty of "oppressive action" toward the complaining shareholders. The referee considered oppression to arise when "those in control" of the corporation "have acted in such a manner as to defeat those expectations of the minority stockholders which formed the basis of [their] participation in the venture." The expectations of petitioners that they would not be arbitrarily excluded from gaining a return on their investment and that their stock would be purchased by the corporation upon termination of employment, were deemed defeated by prevailing corporate policies. Dissolution was recommended in the referee's report, subject to giving respondent corporation an opportunity to purchase petitioners' stock.

Supreme Court confirmed the referee's report. It, too, concluded that due to the corporation's new dividend policy petitioners had been prevented from receiving any return on their investments. Liquidation of the corporate assets was found the only means by which petitioners would receive a fair return. The court considered judicial dissolution of a corporation to be "a serious and severe remedy." Consequently, the order of dissolution was conditioned upon the corporation's being permitted to purchase petitioners' stock. The Appellate Division affirmed, without opinion. 99 A.D.2d 445, 471 N.Y.S.2d 245.

At issue in this appeal is the scope of section 1104–a of the Business Corporation Law. Specifically, this court must determine whether the provision for involuntary dissolution when the "directors or those in control of the corporation have been guilty of . . . oppressive actions toward the complaining shareholders" was properly applied in the circumstances of this case. We hold that it was, and therefore affirm.

II

Judicially ordered dissolution of a corporation at the behest of minority interests is a remedy of relatively recent vintage in New York. Historically, this State's courts were considered divested of equity jurisdiction to order dissolution, as statutory prescriptions were deemed exclusive (see Hitch v. Hawley, 132 N.Y. 212, 217, 30 N.E. 401). Statutes permitting judicial dissolution of corporations either limited the types of corporations under their purview (see L.1817, ch. 146, §§ 1–4; see, also, Matter of Niagara Ins. Co., 1 Paige Ch. 258) or restricted the parties who could petition for dissolution to the Attorney–General, or the directors, trustees, or majority shareholders of the corporation (see Hitch v. Hawley, 132 N.Y., at pp. 218–219, 30 N.E. 401, supra; see, generally, Business Corporation Law, §§ 1101–1104).

Minority shareholders were granted standing in the absence of statutory authority to seek dissolution of corporations when controlling shareholders engaged in certain egregious conduct (see Leibert v. Clapp, 13 N.Y.2d 313, 247 N.Y.S.2d 102, 196 N.E.2d 540; Fontheim v. Walker, 282 App.Div. 373, 122 N.Y.S.2d 642, affd. no opn. 306 N.Y. 926, 119 N.E.2d 605). Predicated on the majority shareholders' fiduciary obligation to treat all shareholders fairly and equally, to preserve corporate assets, and to fulfill their responsibilities of corporate management with "scrupulous good faith," the courts' equitable power can be invoked when "it appears that the directors and majority shareholders 'have so palpably breached the fiduciary duty they owe to the minority shareholders that they are disqualified from exercising the exclusive discretion and the dissolution power given to them by statute.'" (Leibert v. Clapp, 13 N.Y.2d, at p. 317, 247 N.Y.S.2d 102, 196 N.E.2d 540, supra, quoting Hoffman, New Horizons for the Close Corporation, 28 Brooklyn L.Rev. 1, 14.) True to the ancient principle that equity jurisdiction will not lie when there exists a remedy at law (see Brady v. McCosker, 1 N.Y. 214, 217), the courts have not entertained a minority's petition in equity when their rights and interests could be adequately protected in a legal action, such as by a shareholder's derivative suit (see Matter of Nelkin v. H.J.R. Realty Corp., 25 N.Y.2d 543, 550, 307 N.Y.S.2d 454, 255 N.E.2d 713; cf. Leibert v. Clapp, 13 N.Y.2d, at p. 317, 247 N.Y.S.2d 102, 196 N.E.2d 540, supra).

Supplementing this principle of judicially ordered equitable dissolution of a corporation, the Legislature has shown a special solicitude toward the rights of minority shareholders of closely held corporations by enacting section 1104–a of the Business Corporation Law. That statute provides a mechanism for the holders of at least 20% of the outstanding shares of a corporation whose stock is not traded on a securities market to petition for its dissolution "under special circumstances" (see Business Corporation Law, § 1104–a, subd. [a]). The circumstances that give rise to dissolution fall into two general classifications: mistreatment of complaining shareholders (subd. [a], par. [1]), or misappropriation of corporate assets (subd. [a], par. [2]) by controlling shareholders, directors or officers.

Section 1104–a (subd. [a], par. [1]) describes three types of proscribed activity: "illegal", "fraudulent", and "oppressive" conduct. The first two terms are familiar words that are commonly understood at law. The last, however, does not enjoy the same certainty gained through long usage. As no definition is provided by the statute, it falls upon the courts to provide guidance (see Goncalves v. Regent Int. Hotels, 58 N.Y.2d 206, 218, 460 N.Y.S.2d 750, 447 N.E.2d 693).

The statutory concept of "oppressive actions" can, perhaps, best be understood by examining the characteristics of close corporations and the Legislature's general purpose in creating this involuntary-dissolution statute. It is widely understood that, in addition to supplying capital to a contemplated or ongoing enterprise and expecting a fair and equal return, parties comprising the ownership of a close corporation may expect to be actively involved in its management and operation. . . . The small ownership cluster seeks to "contribute their capital, skills, experience and labor" toward the corporate enterprise. . . .

As a leading commentator in the field has observed: "Unlike the typical shareholder in a publicly held corporation, who may be simply an investor or a speculator and cares nothing for the responsibilities of management, the shareholder in a close corporation is a co-owner of the business and wants the privileges and powers that go with ownership. His participation in that particular corporation is often his principal or sole source of income. As a matter of fact, providing employment for himself may have been the principal reason why he participated in organizing the corporation. He may or may not anticipate an ultimate profit from the sale of his interest, but he normally draws very little from the corporation as dividends. In his capacity as an officer or employee of the corporation, he looks to his salary for the principal return on his capital investment, because earnings of a close corporation, as is well known, are distributed in major part in salaries, bonuses and retirement benefits." (O'Neal, Close Corporations [2d ed.], § 1.07, at pp. 21–22 [n. omitted].)

Shareholders enjoy flexibility in memorializing these expectations through agreements setting forth each party's rights and obligations in corporate governance (see, generally, Kessler, Shareholder–Managed Close Corporation Under the New York Business Corporation Law, 43 Fordham L.Rev. 197; Davidian, op. cit., 56 St. John's L.Rev. 24, 29–30, and nn. 21–22). In the absence of such an agreement, however, ultimate decision-making power respecting corporate policy will be reposed in the holders of a majority interest in the corporation (see, e.g., Business Corporation Law, §§ 614, 708). A wielding of this power by any group controlling a corporation may serve to destroy a stockholder's vital interests and expectations.

As the stock of closely held corporations generally is not readily salable, a minority shareholder at odds with management policies may be without either a voice in protecting his or her interests or any reasonable means of withdrawing his or her investment. This predicament may fairly be considered the legislative concern underlying the provision at issue in this case; inclusion of the criteria that the corporation's stock not be traded on securities markets and that the complaining shareholder be subject to oppressive actions supports this conclusion.

Defining oppressive conduct as distinct from illegality in the present context has been considered in other forums. The question has been resolved by considering oppressive actions to refer to conduct that substantially defeats the "reasonable expectations" held by minority shareholders in committing their capital to the particular enterprise (see, e.g., Mardikos v. Arger, 116 Misc.2d 1028, 457 N.Y.S.2d 371; Matter of Barry One Hour Photo Process, 111 Misc. 2d 559, 444 N.Y.S.2d 540 . . . . This concept is consistent with the apparent purpose underlying the provision under review. A shareholder who reasonably expected that ownership in the corporation would entitle him or her to a job, a share of corporate earnings, a place in corporate management, or some other form of security, would be oppressed in a very real sense when others in the corporation seek to defeat those expectations and there exists no effective means of salvaging the investment.

Given the nature of close corporations and the remedial purpose of the statute, this court holds that utilizing a complaining shareholder's "reasonable expectations" as a means of identifying and measuring conduct alleged to be oppressive is appropriate. A court considering a petition alleging oppressive conduct must investigate what the majority shareholders knew, or should have known, to be the petitioner's expectations in entering the particular enterprise. Majority conduct should not be deemed oppressive simply because the petitioner's subjective hopes and desires in joining the venture are not fulfilled. Disappointment alone should not necessarily be equated with oppression.

Rather, oppression should be deemed to arise only when the majority conduct substantially defeats expectations that, objectively viewed, were both reasonable under the circumstances and were central to the petitioner's decision to join the venture. It would be inappropriate, however, for us in this case to delineate the contours of the courts' consideration in determining whether directors have been guilty of oppressive conduct. As in other areas of the law, much will depend on the circumstances in the individual case.

The appropriateness of an order of dissolution is in every case vested in the sound discretion of the court considering the application (see Business Corporation Law, § 1111, subd. [a]). Under the terms of this statute, courts are instructed to consider both whether "liquidation of the corporation is the only feasible means" to protect the complaining shareholder's expectation of a fair return on his or her investment and whether dissolution "is reasonably necessary" to protect "the rights or interests of any substantial number of shareholders" not limited to those complaining (Business Corporation Law, § 1104-a, subd. [b], pars. [1], [2]). Implicit in this direction is that once oppressive conduct is found, consideration must be given to the totality of circumstances surrounding the current state of corporate affairs and relations to determine whether some remedy short of or other than dissolution, constitutes a feasible means of satisfying both the petitioner's expectations and the rights and interests of any other substantial group of shareholders (see, also, Business Corporation Law, § 1111, subd. [b], par. [1]).

By invoking the statute, a petitioner has manifested his or her belief that dissolution may be the only appropriate remedy. Assuming the petitioner has set forth a prima facie case of oppressive conduct, it should be incumbent upon the parties seeking to forestall dissolution to demonstrate to the court the existence of an adequate, alternative remedy (cf. Baker v. Commercial Body Bldrs., 264 Or. 614, 507 P.2d 387, supra; White v. Perkins, 213 Va. 129, 189 S.E.2d 315). A court has broad latitude in fashioning alternative relief, but when fulfillment of the oppressed petitioner's expectations by these means is doubtful, such as when there has been a complete deterioration of relations between the parties, a court should not hesitate to order dissolution. Every order of dissolution, however, must be conditioned upon permitting any shareholder of the corporation to elect to purchase the complaining shareholder's stock at fair value (see Business Corporation Law, § 1118).

One further observation is in order. The purpose of this involuntary dissolution statute is to provide protection to the minority shareholder whose reasonable expectations in undertaking the venture have been frustrated and who has no adequate means of recovering his or her investment. It would be contrary to this remedial purpose to permit its use by minority shareholders as merely a coercive tool (see Davidian, op. cit., 56 St. John's L.Rev. 24, 59–60, and nn. 159–160). Therefore, the minority shareholder whose own acts, made in bad faith and undertaken with a view toward forcing an involuntary dissolution, give rise to the complained-of oppression should be given no quarter in the statutory protection (cf. Mardikos v. Arger, 116 Misc.2d 1028, 1032, 457 N.Y.S.2d 371, supra).

III

There was sufficient evidence presented at the hearing to support the conclusion that Kemp & Beatley had a long-standing policy of awarding *de facto* dividends based on stock ownership in the form of "extra compensation bonuses." Petitioners, both of whom had extensive experience in the management of the company, testified to this effect. Moreover, both related that receipt of this compensation, whether as true dividends or disguised as "extra compensation", was a known incident to ownership of the company's stock understood by all of the company's principals. Finally, there was uncontroverted proof that this policy was changed either shortly before or shortly after petitioners' employment ended. Extra compensation was still awarded by the company. The only difference was that stock ownership was no longer a basis for the payments; it was asserted that the basis became services rendered to the corporation. It was not unreasonable for the fact finder to have determined that this change in policy amounted to nothing less than an attempt to exclude petitioners from gaining any return on their investment through the mere recharacterization of distributions of corporate income. Under the circumstances of this case, there was no error in determining that this conduct constituted oppressive action within the meaning of section 1104–a of the Business Corporation Law.[2]

Nor may it be said that Supreme Court abused its discretion in ordering Kemp & Beatley's dissolution, subject to an opportunity for a buy-out of petitioners' shares. After the referee had found that the

---

2. Respondent is correct in arguing that there is no basis in the record for the referee's conclusion that the corporation had an established policy to buy-out the shares of employees when they left the company. Although the record reflects that petitioners intended to offer proof on this issue, the referee erroneously concluded that the issue was beyond the scope of the reference. He considered such evidence only as "background." In light of this limitation of the issues under consideration, which neither side objected to, the referee could not then properly ground his decision on a failure by respondent to abide by any buy-out policy. The referee's reliance on this ground is irrelevant for the purposes of this appeal, however, as Supreme Court's confirmation of the report was based solely on the principal ground for the finding of oppression, the company's failure to award dividends.

controlling faction of the company was, in effect, attempting to "squeeze-out" petitioners by offering them no return on their investment and increasing other executive compensation, respondents, in opposing the report's confirmation, attempted only to controvert the factual basis of the report. They suggested no feasible, alternative remedy to the forced dissolution. In light of an apparent deterioration in relations between petitioners and the governing shareholders of Kemp & Beatley, it was not unreasonable for the court to have determined that a forced buy-out of petitioners' shares or liquidation of the corporation's assets was the only means by which petitioners could be guaranteed a fair return on their investments.

Accordingly, the order of the Appellate Division should be modified, with costs to petitioners-respondents, by affirming the substantive determination of that court but extending the time for exercising the option to purchase petitioners-respondents' shares to 30 days following this court's determination.

JASEN, JONES, WACHTLER, MEYER and SIMONS, JJ., concur.

KAYE, J., taking no part.

Order modified, with costs to petitioners-respondents, in accordance with the opinion herein and, as so modified, affirmed.

———

MEISELMAN v. MEISELMAN, 309 N.C. 279, 307 S.E.2d 551 (1983). "Professor O'Neal, perhaps the foremost authority on close corporations, points out that many close corporations are companies based on personal relationships that give rise to certain 'reasonable expectations' on the part of those acquiring an interest in the close corporation. Those 'reasonable expectations' include, for example, the parties' expectation that they will participate in the management of the business or be employed by the company. O'Neal, *Close Corporations: Existing Legislation and Recommended Reform,* 33 Bus. Law 873, 885 (1978). . . .

"Thus, when personal relations among the participants in a close corporation break down, the 'reasonable expectations' the participants had, for example, an expectation that their employment would be secure, or that they would enjoy meaningful participation in the management of the business—become difficult if not impossible to fulfill. In other words, when the personal relationships among the participants break down, the majority shareholder, because of his greater voting power, is in a position to terminate the minority shareholder's employment and to exclude him from participation in management decisions.

"Some may argue that the minority shareholder should have bargained for greater protection before agreeing to accept his minority shareholder position in a close corporation. However, the practical realities of this particular business situation oftentimes do not allow for such negotiations. . . .

"Apparently in response to these commentators' uniform calls for reform in this area of corporate law, many state legislatures have enacted statutes giving the tribunals in their states the power to grant relief to minority shareholders under more liberal circumstances. . . .

"In helping to establish this growing trend toward enactment of more liberal grounds under which dissolution will be granted to a complaining shareholder, the legislature in this State enacted in 1955 N.C.G.S. § 55–125(a)(4), the statute granting superior court judges the 'power to liquidate the assets and business of a corporation in an action by a shareholder when it is established' that '[l]iquidation is reasonably necessary for the protection of the rights or interests of the complaining shareholder.' . . .

"[B]efore it can be determined whether, in any given case, it has been 'established' that liquidation is 'reasonably necessary' to protect the complaining shareholder's 'rights or interest,' the particular 'rights or interests' of the complaining shareholder must be articulated. This is so because N.C.G.S. § 55–125(a)(4) refers to the 'rights or interests' of '*the complaining shareholder*'; the statute does not refer to the 'rights or interests' of shareholders generally. . . . [W]e hold that a complaining shareholder's 'rights or interests' in a close corporation include the 'reasonable expectations' the complaining shareholder has in the corporation. These 'reasonable expectations' are to be ascertained by examining the entire history of the participants' relationship. That history will include the 'reasonable expectations' created at the inception of the participants' relationship; those 'reasonable expectations' as altered over time; and the 'reasonable expectations' which develop as the participants engage in a course of dealing in conducting the affairs of the corporation. The interests and views of the other participants must be considered in determining 'reasonable expectations.' The key is '*reasonable*.' In order for plaintiff's expectations to be reasonable, they must be known to or assumed by the other shareholders and concurred in by them. Privately held expectations which are not made known to the other participants are not 'reasonable.' Only expectations embodied in understandings, express or implied, among the participants should be recognized by the court. . . .

"Defendants argue, however, that . . . [a shareholder] is only entitled to relief if his traditional shareholder rights have been infringed. They contend that those traditional shareholder rights include the right to notice of stockholders' meetings, the right to vote cumulatively, the right of access to the corporate offices and to corporate financial information, and the right to compel the payment of dividends. . . .

"While it may be true that a shareholder in, for example, a publicly held corporation may have 'rights or interests' defined as defendants argue, a shareholder's rights in a closely held corporation may not necessarily be so narrowly defined. . . ."

———

NOTE ON THE DUTY OF CARE AND THE DUTY OF LOYALTY IN THE CLOSELY HELD CORPORATION

Two major legal bulwarks for minority shareholders in publicly held corporations are the duty of care and the duty of loyalty imposed by law on corporate directors and officers. These duties are extremely complex in their details, and are the subject of Chapters VII–IX. To oversimplify somewhat, the duty of care renders a director or officer liable for certain types of managerial negligence, and the duty of loyalty renders a director or officer liable for unfair self-interested transactions with the corporation. However, under the business judgment rule, a decision by an officer or director will not subject him to liability for violation of the duty of care, even if the decision is unreasonable, if it was taken in good faith, there was no self-interest, the director or officer properly informed himself before making the decision, and the decision was not so unreasonable as to be irrational. Under the duty of loyalty, a self-interested transaction will not subject a director or officer to liability if he made full disclosure and the transaction was objectively fair.

The duties of care and loyalty protect minority shareholders in closely held as well as publicly held corporations, but in the closely held context they are often an insufficient protection. For example, the discharge of a minority shareholder from corporate office might qualify for protection under the business judgment rule. A purchase of stock from majority shareholders might not violate the duty of loyalty if the price paid for the stock was fair. The real vice of such actions lies in the fact that they treat shareholders unequally, defeat legitimate expectations of a sort found in closely but not publicly held corporations, or both. Accordingly, the "reasonable expectations" analysis that is made explicit in cases like Meiselman v. Meiselman, that is implicit in cases like Donahue v. Rodd, and that in part underlies the concept of dissolution for oppression, fills a major gap in corporate law. It would be a mistake, however, to believe that analysis based on expectations can be separated from the concept of fairness. One way in which a court determines that reasonable expectations have been defeated by majority shareholders is by asking itself what similarly situated shareholders would have probably expected. Often the only way to answer that question is to ask what similarly situated shareholders would have regarded as fair.

QUESTION

Hetherington & Dooley, Illiquidity and Exploitation: A Proposed Statutory Solution to the Remaining Close Corporation Problem, 63 Va.L.Rev. 1, at 1–3, 6 (1977) propose that the corporate statutes should give every minority shareholder in a close corporation a continuing and unconditional right to demand that the corporation or the remaining shareholders purchase his shares at a price determined by agreement or appraisal. If the defendants refused to purchase at that price, the firm would be dissolved. The theory behind this proposal is that "no other form of business organization subjects an owner to the dual hazards of a complete loss of liquidity and an indefinite exclusion from sharing in the profitability of the firm. . . . [T]he problem of exploitation is uniquely related to illiquidity and, for that reason, it is resistant to solution by ex ante contractual arrangements or by ex post judicial relief for breach of fiduciary duty." Do you agree with the proposal?

NOTE ON INVOLUNTARY DISSOLUTION FOR OPPRESSION

1. In Baker v. Commercial Body Builders, Inc., 264 Or. 614, 507 P.2d 387 (1973), where the relevant statute authorized dissolution for "illegal, oppressive or fraudulent" conduct, the court adopted a view somewhat different from that expressed in *Meiselman* and *Kemp & Beatley*:

> While general definitions of "oppressive" conduct are of little value for application in a specific case, perhaps the most widely quoted definitions are that "oppressive conduct" for the purposes of such a statute is:
>
> " 'burdensome, harsh and wrongful conduct; a lack of probity and fair dealing in the affairs of a company to the prejudice of some of its members; or a visual departure from the standards of fair dealing, and a violation of fair play on which every shareholder who entrusts his money to a company is entitled to rely.' " [9]
>
> We agree, however, that the question of what is "oppressive" conduct by those in control of a "close" corporation as its majority stockholders is closely related to what we agree to be the fiduciary duty of a good faith and fair dealing owed by them to its minority stockholders.
>
> Thus, an abuse of corporate position for private gain at the expense of the stockholders is "oppressive" conduct. Or the plundering of a "close" corporation by the siphoning off of profits by excessive salaries or bonus payments and the operation of the business for the sole benefit of the majority of the stockholders, to the detriment of the minority stockholders, would constitute such "oppressive" conduct as to authorize a dissolution of the corporation under the terms of ORS 57.595.
>
> On the other hand, it has been said that a single act in breach of such a fiduciary duty may not constitute such "oppressive"

---

9. Comment, 1965 Duke L.J. 128, 134, quoting from Scottish Co-op. Wholesale Soc'y, Ltd. v. Meyer, [1958] 3 All E.R. 66, 71, 86 (HL) and Elder v. Elder & Watson, Ltd., [1952] Sess.Cas. 49, 55. Both of these cases involve construction of an English statute which is similar to ORS 57.595, and authorizes dissolution if "the affairs of the company are being conducted in a manner oppressive to some part of the members." The [British] Companies Act of 1948, 11 & 12 Geo. 6, c. 38 § 210. [Footnote by the Court.]

conduct as to authorize the dissolution of a corporation unless extremely serious in nature and that even a continuing course of "oppressive" conduct may not be sufficient for that purpose unless it appears that, as a result, there has been a disproportionate loss to the minority or that those in control of the corporation are so incorrigible that they can no longer be trusted to manage it fairly in the interests of its stockholders.

See also Compton v. Paul K. Harding Realty Co., 6 Ill.App.3d 488, 285 N.E.2d 574 (1972) ("arbitrary, overbearing and heavy-handed course of conduct" held to justify finding of oppression); Central Standard Life Ins. Co. v. Davis, 10 Ill.2d 566, 573–74, 141 N.E.2d 45, 50 (1957). Cases like *Baker* focus on the conduct of those in control. Cases like *Meiselman* and *Kemp & Beatley* focus on the effect of that conduct on those not in control. See Hillman, The Dissatisfied Participant in the Solvent Business Venture, 67 Minn.L.Rev. 1 (1982).

2. As in the deadlock and dissension cases, the courts have often been reluctant to order involuntary dissolution of profitable corporations under oppression statutes. Thus in Baker v. Commercial Body Builders the appellate court agreed with the trial court's decision finding that the defendants' conduct had been oppressive, but nevertheless declined to order dissolution. See also Polikoff v. Dole & Clark Bldg. Corp., 37 Ill.App.2d 29, 184 N.E.2d 792 (1962); Fix v. Fix Material Co., 538 S.W.2d 351 (Mo.App.1976); Gonseth v. K & K Oil Co., 439 S.W.2d 18, 27 (Mo.App.1969). But see Gidwitz v. Lanzit Corrugated Box Co., 20 Ill.2d 208, 170 N.E.2d 131 (1960); cf. Stumpf v. C.E. Stumpf & Sons, Inc., 47 Cal.App.3d 230, 120 Cal. Rptr. 671 (1975). The possibility of ordering a mandatory buy-out should make the courts more liberal in ordering dissolution.

3. According to Professor O'Neal, "[t]he general rule has been laid down in many decisions that aside from statute, courts do not have power to wind up a solvent corporation or appoint a receiver for the liquidation of its affairs. . . . Most of the modern courts, however, recognize a number of exceptions to the general rule . . . [including fraud, abuse, or oppression by those in control, deadlock, and incapacitating dissension]. . . . Modern courts recognize so many exceptions to the general rule . . . and the exceptions are applied so frequently, that the exceptions seem to have eaten up the rule. No longer is the question whether the courts have jurisdiction or power to appoint a receiver to wind up a corporation or even dissolve it in the sense of terminating its legal existence. The real question is whether a court will exercise its power in the particular case before it." 2 F.H. O'Neal, Close Corporations § 9.27 (2d ed. 1971).

Chapter VII

THE DUTY OF CARE AND THE DUTY TO ACT LAWFULLY

SECTION 1.   THE DUTY OF CARE

BATES v. DRESSER

Supreme Court of the United States, 1920.
251 U.S. 524, 40 S.Ct. 247, 64 L.Ed. 388.

Mr. Justice HOLMES delivered the opinion of the court.

This is a bill in equity brought by the receiver of a national bank to charge its former president and directors with the loss of a great part of its assets through the thefts of an employee of the bank while they were in power. The case was sent to a master who found for the defendants; but the District Court entered a decree against all of them. 229 Fed.Rep. 772. The Circuit Court of Appeals reversed this decree, dismissed the bill as against all except the administrator of Edwin Dresser, the president, cut down the amount with which he was charged and refused to add interest from the date of the decree of the District Court. 250 Fed.Rep. 525. 162 C.C.A. 541. Dresser's administrator and the receiver both appeal, the latter contending that the decree of the District Court should be affirmed with interest and costs.

The bank was a little bank at Cambridge with a capital of $100,000 and average deposits of somewhere about $300,000. It had a cashier, a bookkeeper, a teller and a messenger. Before and during the time of the losses Dresser was its president and executive officer, a large stockholder, with an inactive deposit of from $35,000 to $50,000. From July, 1903, to the end, Frank L. Earl was cashier. Coleman, who made the trouble, entered the service of the bank as messenger in September, 1903. In January, 1904, he was promoted to be bookkeeper, being then not quite eighteen but having studied bookkeeping. In the previous August an auditor employed on the retirement of a cashier had reported that the daily balance book was very much behind, that it was impossible to prove the deposits, and that a competent bookkeeper should be employed upon the work immediately. Coleman kept the deposit ledger and this was the work that fell into his hands. There was no cage in the bank, and in 1904 and 1905 there were some small shortages in the accounts of three successive tellers that were not accounted for, and the last of them, Cutting, was asked by Dresser to resign on that ground. Before doing so he told Dresser that someone had taken the money and that

342

if he might be allowed to stay he would set a trap and catch the man, but Dresser did not care to do that and thought that there was nothing wrong. From Cutting's resignation on October 7, 1905, Coleman acted as paying and receiving teller, in addition to his other duty, until November, 1907. During this time there were no shortages disclosed in the teller's accounts. In May, 1906, Coleman took $2,000 cash from the vaults of the bank, but restored it the next morning. In November of the same year he began the thefts that come into question here. Perhaps in the beginning he took the money directly. But as he ceased to have charge of the cash in November, 1907, he invented another way. Having a small account at the bank, he would draw checks for the amount he wanted, exchange checks with a Boston broker, get cash for the broker's check, and, when his own check came to the bank through the clearing house, would abstract it from the envelope, enter the others on his book and conceal the difference by a charge to some other account or a false addition in the column of drafts or deposits in the depositors' ledger. He handed to the cashier only the slip from the clearing house that showed the totals. The cashier paid whatever appeared to be due and thus Coleman's checks were honored. So far as Coleman thought it necessary, in view of the absolute trust in him on the part of all concerned, he took care that his balances should agree with those in the cashier's book.

By May 1, 1907, Coleman had abstracted $17,000, concealing the fact by false additions in the column of total checks, and false balances in the deposit ledger. Then for the moment a safer concealment was effected by charging the whole to Dresser's account. Coleman adopted this method when a bank examiner was expected. Of course when the fraud was disguised by overcharging a depositor it could not be discovered except by calling in the pass-books, or taking all the deposit slips and comparing them with the depositors' ledger in detail. By November, 1907, the amount taken by Coleman was $30,100, and the charge on Dresser's account was $20,000. In 1908 the sum was raised from $33,000 to $49,671. In 1909 Coleman's activity began to increase. In January he took $6,829.26; in March, $10,833.73; in June, his previous stealings amounting to $83,390.94, he took $5,152.06; in July, $18,050; in August, $6,250; in September, $17,350; in October, $47,277.08; in November, $51,847; in December, $46,956.44; in January, 1910, $27,395.53; in February, $6,473.97; making a total of $310,143.02, when the bank closed on February 21, 1910. As a result of this the amount of the monthly deposits seemed to decline noticeably and the directors considered the matter in September, 1909, but concluded that the falling off was due in part to the springing up of rivals, whose deposits were increasing, but was parallel to a similar decrease in New York. An examination by a bank examiner in December, 1909, disclosed nothing wrong to him.

In this connection it should be mentioned that in the previous semi-annual examinations by national bank examiners nothing was discovered pointing to malfeasance. The cashier was honest and everybody believed that they could rely upon him, although in fact he relied too much upon Coleman, who also was unsuspected by all. If Earl had opened the envelopes from the clearing house, and had seen the checks, or had examined the deposit ledger with any care he would have found out what was going on. The scrutiny of anyone accustomed to such details would have discovered the false additions and other indicia of fraud that were on the face of the book. But it may be doubted whether anything less than a continuous pursuit of the figures through pages would have done so except by a lucky chance.

The question of the liability of the directors in this case is the question whether they neglected their duty by accepting the cashier's statement of liabilities and failing to inspect the depositors' ledger. The statements of assets always were correct. A by-law that had been allowed to become obsolete or nearly so is invoked as establishing their own standard of conduct. By that a committee was to be appointed every six months "to examine into the affairs of the bank, to count its cash, and compare its assets and liabilities with the balances on the general ledger, for the purpose of ascertaining whether or not the books are correctly kept, and the condition of the bank is in a sound and solvent condition." Of course liabilities as well as assets must be known to know the condition and, as this case shows, peculations may be concealed as well by a false understatement of liabilities as by a false show of assets. But the former is not the direction in which fraud would have been looked for, especially on the part of one who at the time of his principal abstractions was not in contact with the funds. A debtor hardly expects to have his liability understated. Some animals must have given at least one exhibition of dangerous propensities before the owner can be held. This fraud was a novelty in the way of swindling a bank so far as the knowledge of any experience had reached Cambridge before 1910. We are not prepared to reverse the finding of the master and the Circuit Court of Appeals that the directors should not be held answerable for taking the cashier's statement of liabilities to be as correct as the statement of assets always was. If he had not been negligent without their knowledge it would have been. Their confidence seemed warranted by the semi-annual examinations by the government examiner and they were encouraged in their belief that all was well by the president, whose responsibility, as executive officer; interest, as large stockholder and depositor; and knowledge, from long daily presence in the bank, were greater than theirs. They were not bound by virtue of the office gratuitously assumed by them to call in the pass-books and compare them with the ledger, and until the event showed the possibility they hardly could have seen that their failure to look at the ledger opened a way to fraud. See *Briggs v. Spaulding,* 141 U.S. 132; *Warner v. Penoyer,* 91 Fed.Rep. 587. We are not laying down general principles, however, but confine our decision to the circumstances of the particular case.*

* Compare the opinion in the same case in the District Court, 229 F. 772, 796 (1915): "The directors knew that the national bank examiners examined the bank

The position of the president is different. Practically he was the master of the situation. He was daily at the bank for hours, he had the deposit ledger in his hands at times and might have had it at any time. He had had hints and warnings in addition to those that we have mentioned, warnings that should not be magnified unduly, but still that taken with the auditor's report of 1903, the unexplained shortages, the suggestion of the teller, Cutting, in 1905, and the final seeming rapid decline in deposits, would have induced scrutiny but for an invincible repose upon the *status quo.* In 1908 one Fillmore learned that a package containing $150 left with the bank for safe keeping was not to be found, told Dresser of the loss, wrote to him that he could but conclude that the package had been destroyed or removed by someone connected with the bank, and in later conversation said that it was evident that there was a thief in the bank. He added that he would advise the president to look after Coleman, that he believed he was living at a pretty fast pace, and that he had pretty good authority for thinking that he was supporting a woman. In the same year or the year before, Coleman, whose pay was never more than twelve dollars a week, set up an automobile, as was known to Dresser and commented on unfavorably, to him. There was also some evidence of notice to Dresser that Coleman was dealing in copper stocks. In 1909 came the great and inadequately explained seeming shrinkage in the deposits. No doubt plausible explanations of his conduct came from Coleman and the notice as to speculations may have been slight, but taking the whole story of the relations of the parties, we are not ready to say that the two courts below erred in finding that Dresser had been put upon his guard. However little the warnings may have pointed to the specific facts, had they been accepted they would have led to an examination of the depositors' ledger, a discovery of past and a prevention of future thefts.

We do not perceive any ground for applying to this case the limitations of liability *ex contractu* adverted to in *Globe Refining Co. v. Landa Cotton Oil Co.,* 190 U.S. 540. In accepting the presidency Dresser must be taken to have contemplated responsibility for losses to the bank, whatever they were, if chargeable to his fault. Those that happened were chargeable to his fault, after he had warnings that should have led to steps that would have made fraud impossible, even

twice a year. They knew that only one examiner at a time made the examination, and Mr. Edwin Dresser knew that the time allotted to the examination of the depositors' ledger was very brief. The other directors had no knowledge of the time allotted to the depositors' ledger, but in a general way knew that the time consumed in making the entire examination was but a portion of a day. Mr. Edwin Dresser, Sumner Dresser, and Mr. Gale must have known that the examination made by the bank examiner was not the equivalent of an audit, for they were directors in 1903 when they caused an audit to be made, and that it took from 12 to 14 days for two men to make it, and, while the directors, as a board, were not aware of the warnings regarding Mr. Coleman, which were brought to the attention of Mr. Edwin Dresser and Mr. Barber, and their knowledge that examinations were made by national bank examiners may have been a sufficient justification for their not causing an audit to be made, it was not a justification for their failure to perform their duty to examine the bank twice a year before declaring dividends. And it would seem very doubtful whether it should be regarded as a justification for their failure to cause an audit to be made in September, 1909, when they were aware the shrinkage in their deposits was abnormal." (Footnote by ed.)

though the precise form that the fraud would take hardly could have been foreseen. We accept with hesitation the date of December 1, 1908, as the beginning of Dresser's liability. . . .

> *Decree modified by charging the estate of Dresser with interest from February 1, 1916, to June 1, 1918, upon the sum found to be due, and affirmed.*

Mr. Justice McKENNA and Mr. Justice PITNEY dissent, upon the ground that not only the administrator of the president of the bank but the other directors ought to be held liable to the extent to which they were held by the District Court, 229 Fed.Rep. 772.

Mr. Justice VAN DEVANTER and Mr. Justice BRANDEIS took no part in the decision.

REV. MODEL BUS. CORP. ACT § 8.30

§ 8.30. General Standards for Directors

(a) A director shall discharge his duties as a director, including his duties as a member of a committee:

   (1) in good faith;

   (2) with the care an ordinarily prudent person in a like position would exercise under similar circumstances; and

   (3) in a manner he reasonably believes to be in the best interests of the corporation.

(b) In discharging his duties a director is entitled to rely on information, opinions, reports, or statements, including financial statements and other financial data, if prepared or presented by:

   (1) one or more officers or employees of the corporation whom the director reasonably believes to be reliable and competent in the matters presented;

   (2) legal counsel, public accountants, or other persons as to matters the director reasonably believes are within the person's professional or expert competence; or

   (3) a committee of the board of directors of which he is not a member if the director reasonably believes the committee merits confidence.

(c) A director is not acting in good faith if he has knowledge concerning the matter in question that makes reliance otherwise permitted by subsection (b) unwarranted.

(d) A director is not liable for any action taken as a director, or any failure to take any action, if he performed the duties of his office in compliance with this section.

CAL. CORP. CODE § 309(a)

A director shall perform the duties of a director, including duties as a member of any committee of the board upon which the director may serve, in good faith, in a manner such director believes to be in the best interests of the corporation and with such care, including reasonable inquiry, as an ordinarily prudent person in a like position would use under similar circumstances. . . .

NEW JERSEY STAT. ANN. § 14A:6–14

Directors and members of any committee designated by the board shall discharge their duties in good faith and with that degree of diligence, care and skill which ordinarily prudent men would exercise under similar circumstances in like positions. . . .

NEW YORK BUS. CORP. LAW § 717

A director shall perform his duties as a director, including his duties as a member of any committee of the board upon which he may serve, in good faith and with that degree of care which an ordinarily prudent person in a like position would use under similar circumstances. . . . *

NOTE ON STATUTORY FORMULATIONS OF THE DUTY OF CARE

1. Twenty-two states have enacted statutory due-care provisions comparable to those of the RMBCA, California, New Jersey, and New York. See ALI, Principles of Corporate Governance § 4.01, Reporters' Note 1, at 29 (Tent. Draft No. 4, 1985). A few of these statutes use a phrase like "[with that care which] ordinarily prudent men would exercise under similar circumstances in their personal affairs." In Selheimer v. Manganese Corp. of America, 423 Pa. 563, 224 A.2d 634 (1966), the court held, perhaps questionably, that the phrase "in their personal affairs" imposed a higher standard of care than the more usual phrase, "in a like position."

2. About half the statutes refer to officers as well as directors. It is not clear why the remaining statutes omit officers. Is the implication that officers owe a different level of care than directors? If not, why leave officers out of the statute? If so, just what level of care do officers owe? Is that level to be determined as a matter of corporation law or under general principles of agency law? On the latter question, see Restatement, Agency, Second § 379: "Unless otherwise agreed, a paid agent is subject to a duty to the principal to

---

* The California, New Jersey, and New York statutes all go on to cover the issue of reliance in a manner comparable to the Revised Model Business Corporation Act.

act with standard care and with the skill which is standard in the locality for the kind of work which he is employed to perform and, in addition, to exercise any special skill that he has."

KAMIN v. AMERICAN EXPRESS CO.

Supreme Court, Special Term, N.Y. County, Part 1, 1976.
86 Misc.2d 809, 383 N.Y.S.2d 807, aff'd on opinion below 54 A.D.2d 654, 387
N.Y.S.2d 993 (1st Dept.1976).

EDWARD J. GREENFIELD, Justice:

In this stockholders' derivative action, the individual defendants, who are the directors of the American Express Company, move for an order dismissing the complaint for failure to state a cause of action pursuant to CPLR 3211(a)(7), and alternatively, for summary judgment pursuant to CPLR 3211(c).

The complaint is brought derivatively by two minority stockholders of the American Express Company, asking for a declaration that a certain dividend in kind is a waste of corporate assets, directing the defendants not to proceed with the distribution, or, in the alternative, for monetary damages. The motion to dismiss the complaint requires the Court to presuppose the truth of the allegations. It is the defendants' contention that, conceding everything in the complaint, no viable cause of action is made out.

After establishing the identity of the parties, the complaint alleges that in 1972 American Express acquired for investment 1,954,418 shares of common stock of Donaldson, Lufken and Jenrette, Inc. (hereafter DLJ), a publicly traded corporation, at a cost of $29.9 million. It is further alleged that the current market value of those shares is approximately $4.0 million. On July 28, 1975, it is alleged, the Board of Directors of American Express declared a special dividend to all stockholders of record pursuant to which the shares of DLJ would be distributed in kind. Plaintiffs contend further that if American Express were to sell the DLJ shares on the market, it would sustain a capital loss of $25 million, which could be offset against taxable capital gains on other investments. Such a sale, they allege, would result in tax savings to the company of approximately $8 million, which would not be available in the case of the distribution of DLJ shares to stockholders. It is alleged that on October 8, 1975 and October 16, 1975, plaintiffs demanded that the directors rescind the previously declared dividend in DLJ shares and take steps to preserve the capital loss which would result from selling the shares. This demand was rejected by the Board of Directors on October 17, 1975.

It is apparent that all the previously-mentioned allegations of the complaint go to the question of the exercise by the Board of Directors of business judgment in deciding how to deal with the DLJ shares. The crucial allegation which must be scrutinized to determine the legal sufficiency of the complaint is paragraph 19, which alleges:

Complaint

"19. All of the defendant Directors engaged in or acquiesced in or negligently permitted the declaration and payment of the Dividend in violation of the fiduciary duty owed by them to Amex to care for and preserve Amex's assets in the same manner as a man of average prudence would care for his own property."

Plaintiffs never moved for temporary injunctive relief, and did nothing to bar the actual distribution of the DLJ shares. The dividend was in fact paid on October 31, 1975. Accordingly, that portion of the complaint seeking a direction not to distribute the shares is deemed to be moot, and the Court will deal only with the request for declaratory judgment or for damages.

Examination of the complaint reveals that there is no claim of fraud or self-dealing, and no contention that there was any bad faith or oppressive conduct. The law is quite clear as to what is necessary to ground a claim for actionable wrongdoing.

"In actions by stockholders, which assail the acts of their directors or trustees, courts will not interfere unless the powers have been illegally or unconscientiously executed; or unless it be made to appear that the acts were fraudulent or collusive, and destructive of the rights of the stockholders. Mere errors of judgment are not sufficient as grounds for equity interference, for the powers of those entrusted with corporate management are largely discretionary." Leslie v. Lorillard, 110 N.Y. 519, 532, 18 N.E. 363, 365. . . .

More specifically, the question of whether or not a dividend is to be declared or a distribution of some kind should be made is exclusively a matter of business judgment for the Board of Directors.

". . . Courts will not interfere with such discretion unless it be first made to appear that the directors have acted or are about to act in bad faith and for a dishonest purpose. It is for the directors to say, acting in good faith of course, when and to what extent dividends shall be declared . . . The statute confers upon the directors this power, and the minority stockholders are not in a position to question this right, so long as the directors are acting in good faith . . ."

Thus, a complaint must be dismissed if all that is presented is a decision to pay dividends rather than pursuing some other course of conduct. Weinberger v. Quinn, 264 App.Div. 405, 35 N.Y.S.2d 567, affd. 290 N.Y. 635, 49 N.E.2d 131. A complaint which alleges merely that some course of action other than that pursued by the Board of Directors would have been more advantageous gives rise to no cognizable cause of action. Courts have more than enough to do in adjudicating legal rights and devising remedies for wrongs. The directors' room rather than the courtroom is the appropriate forum for thrashing out purely business questions which will have an impact on profits, market prices, competitive situations, or tax advantages. As stated by Cardozo, J., when sitting at Special Term, the substitution of someone else's business judgment for that of the directors "is no business for any court to follow." Holmes v. St. Joseph Lead Co., 84

Misc. 278, 283, 147 N.Y.S. 104, 107, quoting from Gamble v. Queens County Water Co., 123 N.Y. 91, 99, 25 N.E. 201, 208.

It is not enough to allege, as plaintiffs do here, that the directors made an imprudent decision, which did not capitalize on the possibility of using a potential capital loss to offset capital gains. More than imprudence or mistaken judgment must be shown.

> "Questions of policy of management, expediency of contracts or action, adequacy of consideration, lawful appropriation of corporate funds to advance corporate interests, are left solely to their honest and unselfish decision, for their powers therein are without limitation and free from restraint, and the exercise of them for the common and general interests of the corporation may not be questioned, although the results show that what they did was unwise or inexpedient." Pollitz v. Wabash Railroad Co., 207 N.Y. 113, 124, 100 N.E. 721, 724.

Section 720 of the Business Corporation Law permits an action against directors for "the neglect of, or failure to perform, or other violations of his duties in the management and disposition of corporate assets committed to his charge." This does not mean that a director is chargeable with ordinary negligence for having made an improper decision, or having acted imprudently. The "neglect" referred to in the statute is neglect of duties (i.e., malfeasance or nonfeasance) and not misjudgment. To allege that a director "negligently permitted the declaration and payment" of a dividend without alleging fraud, dishonesty or nonfeasance, is to state merely that a decision was taken with which one disagrees.

Nor does this appear to be a case in which a potentially valid cause of action is inartfully stated. . . . The affidavits of the defendants and the exhibits annexed thereto demonstrate that the objections raised by the plaintiffs to the proposed dividend action were carefully considered and unanimously rejected by the Board at a special meeting called precisely for that purpose at the plaintiffs' request. The minutes of the special meeting indicate that the defendants were fully aware that a sale rather than a distribution of the DLJ shares might result in the realization of a substantial income tax saving. Nevertheless, they concluded that there were countervailing considerations primarily with respect to the adverse effect such a sale, realizing a loss of $25 million, would have on the net income figures in the American Express financial statement. Such a reduction of net income would have a serious effect on the market value of the publicly traded American Express stock. This was not a situation in which the defendant directors totally overlooked facts called to their attention. They gave them consideration, and attempted to view the total picture in arriving at their decision. While plaintiffs contend that according to their accounting consultants the loss on the DLJ stock would still have to be charged against current earnings even if the stock were distributed, the defendants' accounting experts assert that the loss would be a charge against earnings only in the event of a sale, whereas in the event of distribution of the stock as a dividend, the proper accounting treatment would be to charge the loss only against surplus. While the chief accountant for the SEC raised some question as to the appropriate accounting treatment of this transaction, there was no basis for any action to be taken by the SEC with respect to the American Express financial statement.

The only hint of self-interest which is raised, not in the complaint but in the papers on the motion, is that four of the twenty directors were officers and employees of American Express and members of its Executive Incentive Compensation Plan. Hence, it is suggested, by virtue of the action taken earnings may have been overstated and their compensation affected thereby. Such a claim is highly speculative and standing alone can hardly be regarded as sufficient to support an inference of self-dealing. There is no claim or showing that the four company directors dominated and controlled the sixteen outside members of the Board. Certainly, every action taken by the Board has some impact on earnings and may therefore affect the compensation of those whose earnings are keyed to profits. That does not disqualify the inside directors, nor does it put every policy adopted by the Board in question. All directors have an obligation, using sound business judgment, to maximize income for the benefit of all persons having a stake in the welfare of the corporate entity. See, Amdur v. Meyer, 15 A.D.2d 425, 224 N.Y.S.2d 440, appeal dismissed 14 N.Y.2d 541, 248 N.Y.S.2d 639, 198 N.E.2d 30. What we have here as revealed both by the complaint and by the affidavits and exhibits, is that a disagreement exists between two minority stockholders and a unanimous Board of Directors as to the best way to handle a loss already incurred on an investment. The directors are entitled to exercise their honest business judgment on the information before them, and to act within their corporate powers. That they may be mistaken, that other courses of action might have differing consequences, or that their action might benefit some shareholders more than others presents no basis for the superimposition of judicial judgment, so long as it appears that the directors have been acting in good faith. The question of to what extent a dividend shall be declared and the manner in which it shall be paid is ordinarily subject only to the qualification that the dividend be paid out of surplus (Business Corporation Law Section 510, subd. b). The Court will not interfere unless a clear case is made out of fraud, oppression, arbitrary action, or breach of trust.

Courts should not shrink from the responsibility of dismissing complaints or granting summary judgment when no legal wrongdoing is set forth. . . .

In this case it clearly appears that the plaintiffs have failed as a matter of law to make out an actionable claim. Accordingly, the motion by the defendants for summary judgment and dismissal of the complaint is granted.

AMERICAN LAW INSTITUTE, PRINCIPLES OF CORPORATE GOVERNANCE § 4.01

Tent.Draft No. 4, 1985.

§ 4.01. Duty of Care of Directors and Officers; the Business Judgment Rule

(a) A director or officer has a duty to his corporation to perform his functions in good faith, in a manner that he reasonably believes to be in the best interests of the corporation, and with the care that an ordinarily prudent person would reasonably be expected to exercise in a like position and under similar circumstances.

(1) This duty includes the obligation to make, or cause to be made, an inquiry when, but only when, the circumstances would alert a reasonable director or officer to the need therefor. The extent of such inquiry shall be such as the director or officer reasonably believes to be necessary.

(2) In performing any of his functions (including his oversight functions), a director or officer is entitled to rely on materials and persons in accordance with §§ 4.02–.03.

(b) Except as otherwise provided by statute or by a standard of the corporation * . . . and subject to the board's ultimate responsibility for oversight, in performing its functions (including oversight functions), the board may delegate, formally or informally by course of conduct, any function (including the function of identifying matters requiring the attention of the board) to committees of the board or to directors, officers, employees, experts, or other persons; a director may rely on such committees and persons in fulfilling his duty under this Section with respect to any delegated function if his reliance is in accordance with §§ 4.02–.03.

(c) A director or officer who makes a business judgment in good faith fulfills his duty under this Section if:

(1) he is not interested **, in the subject of his business judgment;

---

* Under § 1.30, the term "standard of the corporation" means a valid certificate or by-law provision, or board or shareholder resolution, regulating corporate governance. (Footnote by ed.)

** Section 1.18 defines the term "interested" as follows:

(a) A director . . . or officer . . . is "interested" in a transaction if:

(1) The director or officer is a party to the transaction, or

(2) The director or officer or an associate . . . of the director or officer has a pecuniary interest in the transaction, or the director or officer has a financial or familial relationship with,

or is subject to a controlling influence by, a party to the transaction, that in each instance is sufficiently substantial that it would reasonably be expected to affect the director's or officer's judgment with respect to the transaction in a manner adverse to the corporation.

(b) A shareholder is interested in a transaction if either the shareholder or, to his knowledge, an associate of the shareholder is a party to the transaction or the shareholder is also an interested director with respect to the same transaction.

(Footnote by ed.)

(2) he is informed with respect to the subject of his business judgment to the extent he reasonably believes to be appropriate under the circumstances; and

(3) he rationally believes that his business judgment is in the best interests of the corporation.

[(d) A person challenging the conduct of a director or officer under this Section has the burden of proving a breach of duty of care (and the inapplicability of the provisions as to the fulfillment of duty under Subsection (b) or (c)), and the burden of proving that the breach was the legal cause of damage suffered by the corporation.]

Comment to § 4.01(a) . . .

Illustrations . . .

6. C, who is rich and charming, has been a director of Y Corporation for several years. His only significant contribution to Y has been his willingness to entertain important customers. C says that he does not have the capacity to oversee Y's business and he has made no attempt to oversee it. Y Corporation has gone into bankruptcy because of mismanagement. C, as a result of his failure to oversee the conduct of Y's business, has committed a breach of his duty of care. The fact that C may not have the capacity of an "ordinarily prudent person" is no defense. He will be held to an objective standard. . . .

f. Subjective aspects of the duty of care standard. The terms "good faith," "reasonably believes," and "like position," in § 4.01(a), recognize that in determining whether reasonable care has been exercised, the special skills, background, or expertise of a director or officer are properly accorded weight. Special skills (e.g., in engineering, accounting, or law) may, for example, alert a director to a significant corporate problem before other directors would recognize it. Such a director, being obliged to act in the best interests of the corporation, cannot reasonably ignore this knowledge. The *Corporate Director's Guidebook* (p. 1601) "recognizes that the special background and qualifications of a particular director . . . may place greater responsibility on that director."

Comment to § 4.01(a)(1)–(a)(2) . . .

Illustrations:

1. Last year X Corporation, which had annual sales of $900,000,000 and a wide distribution system for its consumer products, was fined $1 million for horizontal price-fixing, a criminal violation of the Sherman Act. It also had to settle a number of civil antitrust actions by paying an aggregate of $16.8 million. The directors of X Corporation have never been concerned with the existence of an antitrust compliance program, and X Corporation still has no company statement on antitrust policy and no compliance program. A new horizontal price-fixing violation has just occurred. It is clear, however, that the directors of X Corporation had no knowledge of the new antitrust

violation. The directors of X Corporation may well have violated their duty of care. The recent antitrust violations, the size of X Corporation, and its wide distribution system should have made compliance with the antitrust laws a particularly prominent concern. Unless other facts were present, such as the delegation of antitrust law compliance functions to the general counsel and proper reliance on him in accordance with § 4.01(b), the failure of the directors of X Corporation to be reasonably concerned with the existence of an antitrust compliance program would constitute a breach of the directors' duty of care.

2. The facts being otherwise as stated in Illustration 1, after the $1 million fine was paid, X Corporation did in fact install an antitrust compliance program which required X's local staff attorneys to refer all antitrust questions—and report all suspicious circumstances—to a designated staff attorney at company headquarters. An attorney in one regional office has, however, failed to report questionable conduct that may constitute a *per se* antitrust violation. X's directors cannot be subjected to liability for an isolated breakdown in the compliance program. No violation of § 4.01(a) has occurred.

Comment to § 4.01(c) . . .

f. The "rationally believes" requirement. If the requirements of "good faith" and § 4.01(c)(1)–(c)(2) are met, § 4.01(c)(3) will protect a director or officer from liability for a business judgment if he "rationally believes that his business judgment is in the best interests of the corporation." Like the term "reasonably believes," the term "rationally believes" has both an objective and a subjective content. A director or officer must actually believe that his business judgment is in the best interests of the corporation and that belief must be rational. This "rationally believes" test is the basis of the legal insulation provided by Subsection (c)'s formulation of the business judgment rule. See, e.g., Panter v. Marshall Field & Co., 646 F.2d 271, 293 (7th Cir.1981) (courts will not disturb a business judgment if "any rational business purpose can be attributed" to a director's decision); Sinclair Oil Corp. v. Levien, 280 A.2d 717, 720 (Del.Sup. Ct.1971) ("rational business purpose" test).

There have been varying approaches taken in the cases and by commentators as to the proper standard for judicial review of business judgments. Some courts have stated that a director's or officer's business judgment must be "reasonable" to be upheld. See, e.g., Meyers v. Moody, 693 F.2d 1196, 1211 (5th Cir.1982); McDonnell v. American Leduc Petroleums, Ltd., 491 F.2d 380, 384 (2d Cir. 1974) (the Court, applying California law, concluded that the "business judgment rule protects only reasonable acts of a director or officer"). Similarly, the *Corporate Director's Guidebook* (p. 1604) speaks of the business judgment rule applying only to a director who acts "with a reasonable basis for believing that the action was in the lawful and legitimate furtherance of the corporation's purposes."

Other courts (in a few cases, usually involving the termination of derivative suits) have wholly omitted reference to "rationally believes" or "reasonableness" in setting forth their business judgment criteria, and have simply said that a director's or officer's judgment would be upheld if made with disinterest, in an informed manner, and in good faith. Both a "reasonableness" test and the "good faith alone" approach have been rejected in § 4.01(c).

Sound public policy dictates that directors and officers be given greater protection than courts and commentators using a "reasonableness" test would afford. Indeed, some courts and commentators, even when using a "reasonableness" test, have expressly indicated that they do not intend that business judgments be given the rigorous review that the word "reasonable" may be read to imply. In Cramer v. General Tel. & Electronics Corp., 582 F.2d 259, 275 (3d Cir. 1978), cert. denied, 439 U.S. 1129 (1979), for example, the Court used the word reasonable, but concluded that directors' judgments must be "so unwise or unreasonable as to fall outside the permissible bounds of the directors' sound discretion" before the business judgment rule would become inapplicable. See *Corporate Director's Guidebook* (p. 1604).

The "rationally believes" standard set forth in § 4.01(c)(3) is intended to afford directors and officers wide latitude when making business decisions that meet the other prerequisites of Subsection (c). The approach taken in Subsection (c)(3) is consistent with the large majority of business judgment cases and with sound public policy. Many courts have used words like "reckless disregard" or "recklessness" to convey a similar sense of the wide latitude that directors or officers should be afforded. See Reporter's Note 4 to § 4.01(c). Prior to the Delaware Supreme Court's recent decision in Smith v. Van Gorkom, 488 A.2d 858 (Del.Supr.1985), which used a "gross negligence" test, Delaware case law was summarized as follows:

"[A] court will interfere with the discretion vested in the board of directors upon a finding that the judgment of the directors was arbitrary, resulted from a reckless disregard of the corporation's and its stockholders' best interests, or is simply so removed from the realm of reason that it cannot be sustained." Arsht & Hinsey, Codified Standard—Same Harbor But Charted Channel: A Response, 35 Bus.Law. ix, xxii (1980).

On the other hand, courts that have articulated only a "good faith" test provide too much legal insulation for directors and officers. There is no reason to insulate an objectively irrational business decision—one so removed from the realm of reason that it should not be sustained—solely on the basis that it was made in subjective good faith. The weight of authority and wise public policy favor barring from § 4.01(c)'s safe harbor directors and officers who do not believe, or do not *rationally* believe, that their business judgments are in the best interests of the corporation. See Reporter's Note hereto.

Under § 4.01, directors and officers have continuing obligations to act in the best interests of the corporation and to use reasonable care. Thus, if circumstances change so that a decision that was once a proper business judgment would, if made again in the current context, lack a rational belief, then the protection of the business judgment rule would not be available to a repetition of the same decision. Similarly, if circumstances change and a director or officer knows, or should know, of these changed circumstances and if he is still in a position to change or modify a prior decision, then the protection of the business judgment rule would not be available if he makes a judgment not to change course and this judgment is improper under the "rationally believes" test. . . .

MANNING, THE BUSINESS JUDGMENT RULE AND THE DIRECTOR'S DUTY OF ATTENTION: TIME FOR REALITY

39 Bus.Law. 1477, 1481, 1483–85, 1486, 1489–91 (1984).

. . . In the real world, what do . . . ["outside"] directors— "good" directors—actually do in the discharge of their responsibilities? What is generally expected of them in the market place? . . .

DECISIONAL PROCESS

To judge by their statements, many lawyers without personal boardroom experience have a total misconception of the decisional process as it actually functions in the boardroom. The lawyer's professional experience in courts, legislatures, and semi-political bodies tends to lead him to assume that all decisional process is inevitably made up of a series of discrete, separate issues presented one at a time, debated by both or all sides, and voted on. In fact boards of directors typically do not operate that way at all, except, perhaps, in conditions of internal warfare or mortal crisis. Actions are usually by consensus. If a significant sentiment of disagreement is sensed by the chairman, the matter is usually put over for later action, and sources of compromise and persuasion are pursued in the interim. Advice from individual directors is most often volunteered to, or solicited by, the CEO informally on a one-on-one basis, rather than pursued in group debate at a board meeting.

CHARACTER OF THE AGENDA

A transcript of a typical board meeting will reflect four kinds of items on the agenda. Fully three quarters of the board's time will be devoted to reports by the management and board committees, routine housekeeping resolutions passed unanimously with little or no discussion, and information responding to specific questions that had earlier been put to the management by directors about a wide range of topics sometimes accompanied by suggestions from the board members, usually procedural in character. Perhaps the remaining one quarter of the meeting time will be addressed to a decision, typically unanimous, on one or two specific different business items, such as the sale of a subsidiary or the establishment of a compensation plan. If, as is the average, a board meets eight times a year, the arithmetic would indicate that a full year of the board's work would contain only ten or fifteen discrete transactional decisions of the type that are generally assumed to make up the main work of the board; and of those discrete transactional matters, many will be neither very important nor controversial, such as a decision to terminate a long-standing banking relationship in favor of a new one that provides better service. . . .

Contrariwise, some issues that have little economic significance may, because of their delicacy, consume great amounts of the board's time—such as the awkward matter of imposing mandatory retirement on the aging founder, builder, and principal owner of the company.

AGENDA–SETTING—INITIATIVES BY THE BOARD

Agenda-setting and the scope of board initiative together comprise the single most important, and least understood, aspect of the board's work life.

With the two very important exceptions noted below, the question of what the board will discuss and act on is typically determined by the management or by the corporation's automatic built-in secular equivalent of an ecclesiastical calendar, that is, shareholders' meeting date, fiscal year, cycle of audit committee meetings, and similar matters. The board can, and a good board will, from time to time suggest topics for exploration or discussion, or request the management to report in the near future on this or that matter of interest to the board. The board can press management to get on with a necessary undertaking or desired program, such as the establishment of a job classification system, and to report back to the board about the action taken. But the board itself has little capacity to generate significant proposals, other than generalized suggestions looking toward the establishment of procedures or systems. Almost all of what a board does is made up of matters that are brought to it; matters generated by the board itself are very rare. Typically, boards cannot take, and are not expected to take, initiatives.

There are two major exceptions to this generalization about agenda-setting. Both are of extreme importance, and both are fully understood by normal, healthily functioning boards and managements.

First, no board can deny the existence of a built-in paramount responsibility with regard to what may be called the organic or structural integrity of the company. This organic integrity is essentially made up of two elements. A company must have a *functioning management* in place and operating at all times. A board can itself see that this is done. And a company must have an *internal information system* in place that is generally suitable for an enterprise of the company's character to keep the management informed about what is going on and particularly to provide the accounting data on which to base financial statements. The board cannot design, install, operate, or monitor the operation of such systems; but the board can press for the installation and call for periodic assurances that they are in place. As to these two organic elements of the enterprise, the directors may not wait for the management to bring issues to their attention. The responsibility of the board in these two key regards is inherent and ongoing; it is up to the board to take the initiative to keep itself informed about them and to take such periodic action as its business judgment dictates.

Second, no director or group of directors may choose to ignore credible signals of serious trouble in the company. If a director is informed through a credible source that there is reason to believe that the chief financial officer is a compulsive gambler, the director must take an initiative; he may not sit back and wait for the management to bring the matter to the board's attention. There will usually be a wide range of possible actions which a director could reasonably take to pursue such a matter and thereby fulfill his obligation as a director; but he cannot simply do nothing. Execution of this responsibility of a director will be episodic and, typically, infrequent, but the responsibility itself is ongoing and present every day. . . .

JUDGMENT . . .

. . . [A]part from organic structural decisions discussed earlier, judgments of boards of directors are mainly in the nature of decisions whether to hurl a veto.

A chief executive who generally enjoys the confidence of his board will usually be able to carry any proposal he makes if he does his homework, prepares his supporting arguments, is backed up by his other officers, and—of key importance—personally throws his full weight behind the proposal. Courts and the public must understand that quite commonly a director will go along with a business proposal that he does not really like. He may well think, and will sometimes say aloud in the board meeting, "I do not like this proposal. It seems risky and I believe other uses for the same resources would be more promising. But I may be wrong; I respect the contrary views of my colleagues; and I have to accord great weight to the CEO's strong support for this project. *After all, he is the one who will have the primary responsibility for seeing to it that it works out successfully.* So I will not vote no." When that happens, everyone in the corporate world knows the meaning of the italicized words. The director is saying that he will go along this time, but the CEO is on notice that if he proves to be wrong and the project fails, he may well have lost that director's confidence. . . .

AMERICAN LAW INSTITUTE, PRINCIPLES OF CORPORATE GOVERNANCE §§ 3.01–3.02

See Chapter IV, Section 3, supra.

AMERICAN LAW INSTITUTE, PRINCIPLES OF CORPORATE GOVERNANCE §§ 4.02, 4.03
Tent.Draft No. 4, 1985.

§ 4.02 Reliance on Directors, Officers, Employees, Experts, and Other Persons

In performing his duty and functions, a director or officer who acts in good faith, and reasonably believes that his reliance is warranted, is entitled to rely on information, opinions, reports, statements (including financial statements and other financial data), and decisions, judgments, or performance (including decisions, judgments, or performance within the scope of § 4.01(b)), in each case prepared, presented, made, or performed by:

(a) One or more directors, officers, or employees of the corporation, or of a business organization . . . under joint control or common control . . ., whom the director or officer reasonably believes merit confidence; or

(b) Legal counsel, public accountants, engineers, or other persons whom the director or officer reasonably believes merit confidence.

Comment. . . .

The fact that a director or officer is "entitled to rely" may not provide a complete defense. For example, . . . proper reliance on the auditing reports presented by the accounting firm might provide strong evidence that a director had not failed in his oversight obligations, but other relevant evidence might be produced pointing in the opposite direction (e.g., evidence that a tip from a reliable source to the director, indicating that the corporation's financial records were being manipulated, had not been followed up). See, e.g., Hawes & Sherrard, Reliance on Advice of Counsel as a Defense in Corporate and Securities Cases, 62 Va. L.Rev. 1, 7–8 (1976) ("reliance is recognized only as a factor or circumstance tending to show the defendant's good faith or exercise of due care; it is not in itself a complete and absolute defense"); Longstreth, Reliance on Advice of Counsel as a Defense to Securities Law Violations, 37 Bus.Law. 1185, 1187 (1982).

§ 4.03. Reliance on a Committee of the Board

In performing his duty and functions, a director who acts in good faith, and reasonably believes that his reliance is warranted, is entitled to rely on:

(a) The decisions, judgments, or performance . . . of a duly authorized committee of the board upon which the director does not serve, with respect to matters properly delegated to that committee, provided that the director reasonably believes the committee merits confidence.

(b) Information, opinions, reports, or statements (including financial statements and other financial data), in each case prepared or presented by a duly authorized committee of the board upon which the director does not serve, provided that the director reasonably believes the committee merits confidence.

NOTE ON CAUSATION

Cases in the duty-of-care area sometimes raise difficult causation issues. Two of these issues often arise together: (1) Where the violation of the duty of care consists of an omission, would the loss have occurred even if the defendant had not violated his duty? (2) If the whole board (or a majority of the directors) violates the duty of care, can an individual director be excused on the ground that the result would have been the same even if he had acted differently?

These issues were addressed in the well-known case of Barnes v. Andrews, 298 Fed. 614 (S.D.N.Y.1924), decided by Judge Learned Hand, sitting as a trial judge. Liberty Starters Corporation was organized in 1918 to manufacture starters for Ford motors and airplanes. Andrews became a director in October 1919, and served until he resigned in June 1920. During Andrews's incumbency there had been only two board meetings, one of which he could not attend. Andrews was the largest shareholder and a friend of Liberty's president, Maynard, who had induced him to become a director. Andrews's only attention to Liberty's affairs consisted of talks with Maynard as they met from time to time. In 1921, Liberty went into receivership as a result of mismanagement.

Judge Hand began by holding that Andrews had violated his duty of care:

> . . . While directors are collectively the managers of the company, they are not expected to interfere individually in the actual conduct of its affairs. To do so would disturb the authority of the officers and destroy their individual responsibility, without which no proper discipline is possible. To them must be left the initiative and the immediate direction of the business; the directors can act individually only by counsel and advice to them. Yet they have an individual duty to keep themselves informed in some detail, and it is this duty which the defendant in my judgment failed adequately to perform.
>
> All he did was talk with Maynard as they met, while commuting from Flushing, or at their homes. That, indeed, might be enough, because Andrews had no reason to suspect Maynard's candor, nor has any reason to question it been yet disclosed. But it is plain that he did not press him for details, as he should. It is not enough to content oneself with general answers that the business looks promising and that all seems prosperous. Andrews was bound, certainly as

the months wore on, to inform himself of what was going on with some particularity, and, if he had done so, he would have learned that there were delays in getting into production which were putting the enterprise in most serious peril. It is entirely clear . . . that he had made no effort to keep advised of the actual conduct of the corporate affairs, but had allowed himself to be carried along as a figurehead, in complete reliance upon Maynard. In spite of his own substantial investment in the company, which I must assume was as dear to him as it would be to other men, his position required of him more than this. Having accepted a post of confidence, he was charged with an active duty to learn whether the company was moving to production, and why it was not, and to consider, as best he might, what could be done to avoid the conflicts among the personnel, or their incompetence, which was slowly bleeding it to death.

Id. at 615–16.

Hand went on to hold, however, that the plaintiff also had to prove that Liberty's losses would not have occurred if Andrews had properly performed his duties, and that no such showing had been made.

> . . . This cause of action rests upon a tort, as much though it be a tort of omission as though it had rested upon a positive act. The plaintiff must accept the burden of showing that the performance of the defendant's duties would have avoided loss, and what loss it would have avoided. . . .

> When the corporate funds have been illegally lent, it is a fair inference that a protest would have stopped the loan, and that the director's neglect caused the loss. But when a business fails from general mismanagement, business incapacity, or bad judgment, how is it possible to say that a single director could have made the company successful, or how much in dollars he could have saved? Before this cause can go to a master, the plaintiff must show that, had Andrews done his full duty, he could have made the company prosper, or at least could have broken its fall. He must show what sum he could have saved the company. Neither of these has he made any effort to do.

> The defendant is not subject to the burden of proving that the loss would have happened, whether he had done his duty or not. If he were, it would come to this: That, if a director were once shown slack in his duties, he would stand charged prima facie with the difference between the corporate treasury as it was, and as it would be, judged by a hypothetical standard of success. How could such a standard be determined? How could any one guess how far a director's skill and judgment would have prevailed upon his fellows, and what would have been the ultimate fate of the

business, if they had? How is it possible to set any measure of liability, or to tell what he would have contributed to the event? Men's fortunes may not be subjected to such uncertain and speculative conjectures. It is hard to see how there can be any remedy, except one can put one's finger on a definite loss and say with reasonable assurance that protest would have deterred, or counsel persuaded, the managers who caused it. No men of sense would take the office, if the law imposed upon them a guaranty of the general success of their companies as a penalty for any negligence.

It is, indeed, hard to determine just what went wrong in the management of this company. Any conclusion is little better than a guess. Still some discussion of the facts is necessary, and I shall discuss them. The claim that there were too many general employees turned out to be true, but, so far as I can see, only because of the delay in turning out the finished product. Had the factory gone into production in the spring of 1920, I cannot say, and the plaintiff cannot prove, that the selling department would have been prematurely or extravagantly organized. The expense of the stock sales was apparently not undue, and in any event Andrews was helpless to prevent it, because he found the contract an existing obligation of the company. So far as I can judge, the company had a fair chance of life, if the factory could have begun to turn out starters at the time expected. Whether this was the fault of Delano [an engineer], as I suspect, is now too uncertain to say. It seems to me to make no difference in the result whether Delano, through inattention, or through sickness, or through contempt for Taylor [the factory manager], or for all these reasons, did not send along [certain items called "Van Dycks,"] or whether Taylor should have got along with them, or should have shown more initiative and competence than he did. Between them the production lagged, until it was too late to resuscitate the dying company; its funds had oozed out in fixed payments, till there was nothing left with which to continue the business.

Suppose I charge Andrews with a complete knowledge of all that we have now learned. What action should he have taken, and how can I say that it would have stopped the losses? The plaintiff gives no definite answer to that question. Certainly he had no right to interject himself personally into the tangle; that was for Maynard to unravel. He would scarcely have helped to a solution by adding another cook to the broth. What suggestion could he have made to Maynard, or to his colleagues? The trouble arose either from an indifferent engineer, on whom the company was entirely dependent, or from an incompetent factory manager, who should have been discharged, or because the executives were themselves inefficient. Is Andrews to be charged for not insisting upon Taylor's discharge, or for not suggesting it? Suppose he did suggest it; have I the slightest reason for saying that the directors would have discharged him? Or, had they discharged him, is it certain that a substitute employed in medias res would have speeded up production? Was there not as . . . [fair a] chance that Delano and Taylor might be brought to an accommodation as there was in putting in a green man at that juncture? How can I, sitting here, lay it down that Andrews' intervention would have brought order out of this chaos, or how can I measure in dollars the losses he would have saved? Or am I to hold Andrews because he did not move to discharge Maynard? How can I know that a better man was available? It is easy to say that he should have done something, but that will not serve to harness upon him the whole loss, nor is it the equivalent of saying that, had he acted, the company would now flourish.

Id. at 616–18.

Some passages in Barnes v. Andrews may be read to suggest that a director will not be liable for a loss that would have been prevented by an attentive board unless it is shown that if the director had been attentive, his colleagues would have followed his lead. Such a suggestion would be out of keeping with general legal rules on the responsibility of joint actors, and hard to accept as a matter of either fairness or policy. Given Hand's analysis of the facts, however, Barnes v. Andrews can be read to stand for the more modest proposition that an inattentive director will not be liable for a corporate loss if full attentiveness by all the directors would not have saved the situation, simply because in that case the inattentiveness will not have been a cause-in-fact of the loss.

That is the position taken in § 7.16 of the ALI's Principles of Corporate Governance. Under this Section, if the board as a whole has violated its duty of care, by either commission or omission, each director will be liable for any loss of which the board's failure is the cause-in-fact and the legal (or proximate) cause:

> An omission that constitutes a breach of the [duties of care or loyalty] . . . is the legal cause of loss incurred by the corporation . . . if the plaintiff proves that . . . the performance of the duty would have been a substantial factor in averting the loss. . . . If such an omission is on the part of two or more defendants, each is jointly and severally liable.

The Comment to § 7.16 elaborates this position as follows:

> When multiple corporate officials fail to perform a duty whose omission is a legal cause of the loss, a problem of concurrent causation arises. Potentially, each defendant might claim that his conduct was less causally significant than that of others. To prevent each member of the collective body from evading liability by pointing to the concurrent omissions of others, the last

sentence of § 7.16(b) specifies that each shall be jointly and severally liable. This is consistent with the general approach of the law of torts to problems of concurrent causation. See Restatement, Second, Torts § 886A. . . .

See also Francis v. United Jersey Bank, 87 N.J. 15, 432 A.2d 814 (1981).

NOTE ON GRAHAM v. ALLIS–CHALMERS MFG. CO.

In Graham v. Allis–Chalmers Manufacturing Co., 41 Del. Ch. 78, 188 A.2d 125 (1963), Allis–Chalmers and four employees had pleaded guilty to indictments based on price-fixing and other violations of federal antitrust laws. FTC consent decrees, entered some twenty years earlier against Allis and nine other companies, had enjoined Allis from making agreements to fix uniform prices on products similar to those involved in the indictments. The plaintiff brought a derivative action against Allis's directors and the four employees for damages to Allis resulting from the conduct that was the subject of the indictments. Plaintiff claimed that the directors were liable under various theories, one of which was that the board should have taken action to learn about and prevent antitrust violations. Allis's operations were extensive and complex, and decentralized management was encouraged. The board formulated general policy, but did not deal with the details of corporate affairs. Held, for the directors:

> The duties of the Allis-Chalmers Directors were fixed by the nature of the enterprise which employed in excess of 30,000 persons, and extended over a large geographical area. By force of necessity, the company's Directors could not know personally all the company's employees. The very magnitude of the enterprise required them to confine their control to the broad policy decisions. That they did this is clear from the record. At the meetings of the Board in which all Directors participated, these questions were considered and decided on the basis of summaries, reports and corporate records. These they were entitled to rely on, not only, we think, under general principles of the common law, but by reason of 8 Del. C. § 141(f) as well, which in terms fully protects a director who relies on such in the performance of his duties.

Id. at 85, 188 A.2d at 130.

Allis–Chalmers, although perhaps correctly decided on its facts (at least as concerns the outside directors) seems to envision a passive role for the board that would not be consistent with the modern view of the board's monitoring obligation. As stated in the Comment to § 4.01 of the ALI's Principles of Corporate Governance (Tent. Draft No. 4, 1985):

> The *Allis–Chalmers* case was decided over twenty years ago and a basic theme of the commentaries in Part IV has been that the "obligation" component of duty of care provisions is a

flexible and dynamic concept. Today, an ordinarily prudent person serving as the director of a corporation of any significant scale or complexity should recognize the need to be reasonably concerned with the existence and effectiveness of programs or procedures (which may involve appropriate delegations in accordance with § 4.01(b)) to assist the board in its oversight role.

In contrast to the passive implications of the *Allis–Chalmers* reasoning (e.g., "no duty . . . to install and operate a corporate system . . . to ferret out wrongdoing"), the *Corporate Director's Guidebook* (p. 1610) states:

> "The corporate director should be concerned that the corporation has programs looking toward compliance with applicable laws and regulations, both foreign and domestic, that it circulates (as appropriate) policy statements to this effect to its employees, and that it maintains procedures for monitoring such compliance."

A comparable view is expressed in Veasey & Manning, Codified Standard—Safe Harbor or Uncharted Reef?, 35 Bus.Law. 919 (1980):

> . . . [A] final "core function" of the board identified by the Business Roundtable (compliance with the law) was discussed by the Roundtable in the following terms:

> > Some recent lapses in corporate behavior have emphasized the need for policies and implementing procedures on corporate law compliance. These policies should be designed to promote such compliance on a sustained and systematic basis by all levels of operating management.

> > Certain requirements are of major importance from both business and public points of view. Examples of these are antitrust compliance. . . . It is appropriate in these cases for the board to assure itself that there are policy directives and compliance procedures designed to prevent breaches of the law.

> . . . [A] comparison of the results of *Graham* and . . . [The position reflected in the Business Roundtable Statement] exposes not a philosophical difference between Delaware courts and the Business Roundtable; rather, it shows a natural development in the role of an "ordinarily prudent director" since 1963, the year in which *Graham* was decided.

SMITH v. VAN GORKOM

Supreme Court of Delaware, 1985.
488 A.2d 858.

Before HERRMANN, C.J., and McNEILLY, HORSEY, MOORE and CHRISTIE, JJ., constituting the Court en banc.

HORSEY, Justice (for the majority):

This appeal from the Court of Chancery involves a class action brought by shareholders of the defendant Trans Union Corporation ("Trans Union" or "the Company"), originally seeking rescission of a cash-out merger of Trans Union into the defendant New T Company ("New T"), a wholly-owned subsidiary of the defendant, Marmon Group, Inc. ("Marmon"). Alternate relief in the form of damages is sought against the defendant members of the Board of Directors of Trans Union, New T, and Jay A. Pritzker and Robert A. Pritzker, owners of Marmon.[1]

Following trial, the former Chancellor granted judgment for the defendant directors by unreported letter opinion dated July 6, 1982.[2] Judgment was based on two findings: (1) that the Board of Directors had acted in an informed manner so as to be entitled to protection of the business judgment rule in approving the cash-out merger; and (2) that the shareholder vote approving the merger should not be set aside because the stockholders had been "fairly informed" by the Board of Directors before voting thereon. The plaintiffs appeal.

Speaking for the majority of the Court, we conclude that both rulings of the Court of Chancery are clearly erroneous. Therefore, we reverse and direct that judgment be entered in favor of the plaintiffs and against the defendant directors for the fair value of the plaintiffs' stockholdings in Trans Union, in accordance with Weinberger v. UOP, Inc., Del.Supr., 457 A.2d 701 (1983).

HOLDING We hold: (1) that the Board's decision, reached September 20, 1980, to approve the proposed cash-out merger was not the product of an informed business judgment; (2) that the Board's subsequent efforts to amend the Merger Agreement and take other curative action were ineffectual, both legally and factually; and (3) that the Board did not deal with complete candor with the stockholders by failing to disclose all material facts, which they knew or should have known, before securing the stockholders' approval of the merger.

I.

The nature of this case requires a detailed factual statement. The following facts are essentially uncontradicted. . . .

1. The plaintiff, Alden Smith, originally sought to enjoin the merger; but, following extensive discovery, the Trial Court denied the plaintiff's motion for preliminary injunction by unreported letter opinion dated February 3, 1981. On February 10, 1981, the proposed merger was approved by Trans Union's stockholders at a special meeting and the merger became effective on that date. Thereafter, John W. Gosselin was permitted to intervene as an additional plaintiff; and Smith and Gosselin were certified as representing a class consisting of all persons, other than defendants, who held shares of Trans Union common stock on all relevant dates. At the time of the merger, Smith owned 54,000 shares of Trans Union stock, Gosselin owned 23,600 shares, and members of Gosselin's family owned 20,000 shares.

2. Following trial, and before decision by the Trial Court, the parties stipulated to the dismissal, with prejudice, of the Messrs. Pritzker as parties defendant. However, all references to defendants hereinafter are to the defendant directors of Trans Union, unless otherwise noted.

Trans Union was a publicly-traded, diversified holding company, the principal earnings of which were generated by its railcar leasing business. During the period here involved, the Company had a cash flow of hundreds of millions of dollars annually. However, the Company had difficulty in generating sufficient taxable income to offset increasingly large investment tax credits (ITCs). . . .

B.

[Jerome Van Gorkom, Trans Union's Chairman and Chief Executive Officer, met with senior management on August 27, 1980, to discuss Trans Union's difficulty in producing sufficient taxable income to offset its increasing investment-tax credits and accelerated-depreciation deductions.] Donald Romans, Chief Financial Officer of Trans Union, stated that his department had done a "very brief bit of work on the possibility of a leveraged buy-out." . . . The work consisted of a "preliminary study" of the cash which could be generated by the Company if it participated in a leveraged buy-out. As Romans stated, this analysis "was very first and rough cut at seeing whether a cash flow would support what might be considered a high price for this type of transaction."

On September 5, at another Senior Management meeting which Van Gorkom attended, Romans again brought up the idea of a leveraged buy-out as a "possible strategic alternative" to the Company's acquisition program. Romans and Bruce S. Chelberg, President and Chief Operating Officer of Trans Union, had been working on the matter in preparation for the meeting. According to Romans: They did not "come up" with a price for the Company. They merely "ran the numbers" at $50 a share and at $60 a share with the "rough form" of their cash figures at the time. Their "figures indicated that $50 would be very easy to do but $60 would be very difficult to do under those figures." This work did not purport to establish a fair price for either the Company or 100% of the stock. It was intended to determine the cash flow needed to service the debt that would "probably" be incurred in a leveraged buy-out, based on "rough calculations" without "any benefit of experts to identify what the limits were to that, and so forth." These computations were not considered extensive and no conclusion was reached.

At this meeting, Van Gorkom stated that he would be willing to take $55 per share for his own 75,000 shares. He vetoed the suggestion of a leveraged buy-out by Management, however, as involving a potential conflict of interest for Management. Van Gorkom, a certified public accountant and lawyer, had been an officer of Trans Union for 24 years, its Chief Executive Officer for more than 17 years, and Chairman of its Board for 2 years. It is noteworthy in this connection that he was then approaching 65 years of age and mandatory retirement.

For several days following the September 5 meeting, Van Gorkom pondered the idea of a sale. . . .

Van Gorkom decided to meet with Jay A. Pritzker, a well-known corporate takeover specialist and a social acquaintance. However, rather than approaching Pritzker simply to determine his interest in acquiring Trans Union, Van Gorkom assembled a proposed per share price for sale of the Company and a financing structure by which to accomplish the sale. Van Gorkom did so without consulting either his Board or any members of Senior Management except one: Carl Peterson, Trans Union's Controller. Telling Peterson that he wanted no other person on his staff to know what he was doing, but without telling him why, Van Gorkom directed Peterson to calculate the feasibility of a leveraged buy-out at an assumed price per share of $55. Apart from the Company's historic stock market price,[5] and Van Gorkom's long association with Trans Union, the record is devoid of any competent evidence that $55 represented the per share intrinsic value of the Company. . . .

Van Gorkom arranged a meeting with Pritzker at the latter's home on Saturday, September 13, 1980. Van Gorkom prefaced his presentation by stating to Pritzker: "Now as far as you are concerned, I can, I think, show how you can pay a substantial premium over the present stock price and pay off most of the loan in the first five years. . . . If you could pay $55 for this Company, here is a way in which I think it can be financed."

Van Gorkom then reviewed with Pritzker his calculations based upon his proposed price of $55 per share. Although Pritzker mentioned $50 as a more attractive figure, no other price was mentioned. However, Van Gorkom stated that to be sure that $55 was the best price obtainable, Trans Union should be free to accept any better offer. Pritzker demurred, stating that his organization would serve as a "stalking horse" for an "auction contest" only if Trans Union would permit Pritzker to buy 1,750,000 shares of Trans Union stock at market price which Pritzker could then sell to any higher bidder. After further discussion on this point, Pritzker told Van Gorkom that he would give him a more definite reaction soon.

On Monday, September 15, Pritzker advised Van Gorkom that he was interested in the $55 cash-out merger proposal and requested more information on Trans Union. . . .

On Thursday, September 18, Van Gorkom met again with Pritzker. At that time, Van Gorkom knew that Pritzker intended to make a cash-out merger offer at Van Gorkom's proposed $55 per share. Pritzker instructed his attorney, a merger and acquisition specialist, to begin drafting merger documents. There was no further discussion of the $55 price. However, the number of shares of Trans Union's treasury stock to be offered to Pritzker was negotiated down to one million shares; the price was set at $38—75 cents above the per share price at the close of the market on September 19. At this point,

5. The common stock of Trans Union was traded on the New York Stock Exchange. Over the five year period from 1975 through 1979, Trans Union's stock had traded within a range of a high of $39½ and a low of $24¼. Its high and low range for 1980 through September 19 (the last trading day before announcement of the merger) was $38¼–$29½.

Pritzker insisted that the Trans Union Board act on his merger proposal within the next three days, stating to Van Gorkom: "We have to have a decision by no later than Sunday [evening, September 21] before the opening of the English stock exchange on Monday morning." Pritzker's lawyer was then instructed to draft the merger documents, to be reviewed by Van Gorkom's lawyer, "sometimes with discussion and sometimes not, in the haste to get it finished."

On Friday, September 19, Van Gorkom, Chelberg, and Pritzker consulted with Trans Union's lead bank regarding the financing of Pritzker's purchase of Trans Union. The bank indicated that it could form a syndicate of banks that would finance the transaction. On the same day, Van Gorkom retained James Brennan, Esquire, to advise Trans Union on the legal aspects of the merger. Van Gorkom did not consult with William Browder, a Vice–President and director of Trans Union and former head of its legal department, or with William Moore, then the head of Trans Union's legal staff.

On Friday, September 19, Van Gorkom called a special meeting of the Trans Union Board for noon the following day. He also called a meeting of the Company's Senior Management to convene at 11:00 a.m., prior to the meeting of the Board. No one, except Chelberg and Peterson, was told the purpose of the meetings. Van Gorkom did not invite Trans Union's investment banker, Salomon Brothers or its Chicago-based partner, to attend.

Of those present at the Senior Management meeting on September 20, only Chelberg and Peterson had prior knowledge of Pritzker's offer. Van Gorkom disclosed the offer and described its terms, but he furnished no copies of the proposed Merger Agreement. Romans announced that his department had done a second study which showed that, for a leveraged buy-out, the price range for Trans Union stock was between $55 and $65 per share. Van Gorkom neither saw the study nor asked Romans to make it available for the Board meeting.

Senior Management's reaction to the Pritzker proposal was completely negative. No member of Management, except Chelberg and Peterson, supported the proposal. Romans objected to the price as being too low [6]. . . .

Ten directors served on the Trans Union Board, five inside (defendants Bonser, O'Boyle, Browder, Chelberg, and Van Gorkom) and five outside (defendants Wallis, Johnson, Lanterman, Morgan and Reneker). All directors were present at the meeting, except O'Boyle who was ill. Of the outside directors, four were corporate chief executive officers and one was the former Dean of the University of Chicago Business School. None was an investment banker or trained financial analyst. All members of the Board were well informed about the Company and its operations as a going concern. They were

6. Van Gorkom asked Romans to express his opinion as to the $55 price. Romans stated that he "thought the price was too low in relation to what he could derive for the company in a cash sale, particularly one which enabled us to realize the values of certain subsidiaries and independent entities."

familiar with the current financial condition of the Company, as well as operating and earnings projections reported in the recent Five Year Forecast. The Board generally received regular and detailed reports and was kept abreast of the accumulated investment tax credit and accelerated depreciation problem.

Van Gorkom began the Special Meeting of the Board with a twenty-minute oral presentation. Copies of the proposed Merger Agreement were delivered too late for study before or during the meeting.[7] He reviewed the Company's ITC and depreciation problems and the efforts theretofore made to solve them. He discussed his initial meeting with Pritzker and his motivation in arranging that meeting. Van Gorkom did not disclose to the Board, however, the methodology by which he alone had arrived at the $55 figure, or the fact that he first proposed the $55 price in his negotiations with Pritzker.

Van Gorkom outlined the terms of the Pritzker offer as follows: Pritzker would pay $55 in cash for all outstanding shares of Trans Union stock upon completion of which Trans Union would be merged into New T Company, a subsidiary wholly-owned by Pritzker and formed to implement the merger; for a period of 90 days, Trans Union could receive, but could not actively solicit, competing offers; the offer had to be acted on by the next evening, Sunday, September 21; Trans Union could only furnish to competing bidders published information, and not proprietary information; the offer was subject to Pritzker obtaining the necessary financing by October 10, 1980; if the financing contingency were met or waived by Pritzker, Trans Union was required to sell to Pritzker one million newly-issued shares of Trans Union at $38 per share.

Van Gorkom took the position that putting Trans Union "up for auction" through a 90–day market test would validate a decision by the Board that $55 was a fair price. He told the Board that the "free market will have an opportunity to judge whether $55 is a fair price." Van Gorkom framed the decision before the Board not as whether $55 per share was the highest price that could be obtained, but as whether the $55 price was a fair price that the stockholders should be given the opportunity to accept or reject.[8]

Attorney Brennan advised the members of the Board that they might be sued if they failed to accept the offer and that a fairness opinion was not required as a matter of law.

Romans attended the meeting as chief financial officer of the Company. He told the Board that he had not been involved in the negotiations with Pritzker and knew nothing about the merger propo-

---

7. The record is not clear as to the terms of the Merger Agreement. The Agreement, as originally presented to the Board on September 20, was never produced by defendants despite demands by the plaintiffs. Nor is it clear that the directors were given an opportunity to study the Merger Agreement before voting on it. All that can be said is that Brennan had the Agreement before him during the meeting.

8. In Van Gorkom's words: The "real decision" is whether to "let the stockholders decide it" which is "all you are being asked to decide today."

sal until the morning of the meeting; that his studies did not indicate either a fair price for the stock or a valuation of the Company; that he did not see his role as directly addressing the fairness issue; and that he and his people "were trying to search for ways to justify a price in connection with such a [leveraged buy-out] transaction, rather than to say what the shares are worth." Romans testified:

> I told the Board that the study ran the numbers at 50 and 60, and then the subsequent study at 55 and 65, and that was not the same thing as saying that I have a valuation of the company at X dollars. But it was a way—a first step towards reaching that conclusion.

Romans told the Board that, in his opinion, $55 was "in the range of a fair price," but "at the beginning of the range." . . .

The Board meeting of September 20 lasted about two hours. Based solely upon Van Gorkom's oral presentation, Chelberg's supporting representations, Romans' oral statement, Brennan's legal advice, and their knowledge of the market history of the Company's stock, the directors approved the proposed Merger Agreement. However, the Board later claimed to have attached two conditions to its acceptance: (1) that Trans Union reserved the right to accept any better offer that was made during the market test period; and (2) that Trans Union could share its proprietary information with any other potential bidders. While the Board now claims to have reserved the right to accept any better offer received after the announcement of the Pritzker agreement (even though the minutes of the meeting do not reflect this), it is undisputed that the Board did not reserve the right to actively solicit alternate offers.

The Merger Agreement was executed by Van Gorkom during the evening of September 20 at a formal social event that he hosted for the opening of the Chicago Lyric Opera. Neither he nor any other director read the agreement prior to its signing and delivery to Pritzker.

* * *

On Monday, September 22, the Company issued a press release announcing that Trans Union had entered into a "definitive" Merger Agreement with an affiliate of the Marmon Group, Inc., a Pritzker holding company. Within 10 days of the public announcement, dissent among Senior Management over the merger had become widespread. Faced with threatened resignations of key officers, Van Gorkom met with Pritzker who agreed to several modifications of the Agreement. Pritzker was willing to do so provided that Van Gorkom could persuade the dissidents to remain on the Company payroll for at least six months after consummation of the merger.

Van Gorkom reconvened the Board on October 8 and secured the directors' approval of the proposed amendments—sight unseen. The Board also authorized the employment of Salomon Brothers, its investment banker, to solicit other offers for Trans Union during the proposed "market test" period.

The next day, October 9, Trans Union issued a press release announcing: (1) that Pritzker had obtained "the financing commitments necessary to consummate" the merger with Trans Union; (2) that Pritzker had acquired one million shares of Trans Union common stock at $38 per share; (3) that Trans Union was now permitted to actively seek other offers and had retained Salomon Brothers for that purpose; and (4) that if a more favorable offer were not received before February 1, 1981, Trans Union's shareholders would thereafter meet to vote on the Pritzker proposal.

It was not until the following day, October 10, that the actual amendments to the Merger Agreement were prepared by Pritzker and delivered to Van Gorkom for execution. As will be seen, the amendments were considerably at variance with Van Gorkom's representations of the amendments to the Board on October 8; and the amendments placed serious constraints on Trans Union's ability to negotiate a better deal and withdraw from the Pritzker agreement. Nevertheless, Van Gorkom proceeded to execute what became the October 10 amendments to the Merger Agreement without conferring further with the Board members and apparently without comprehending the actual implications of the amendments.

* * *

Salomon Brothers' efforts over a three-month period from October 21 to January 21 produced only one serious suitor for Trans Union—General Electric Credit Corporation ("GE Credit"), a subsidiary of the General Electric Company. However, GE Credit was unwilling to make an offer for Trans Union unless Trans Union first rescinded its Merger Agreement with Pritzker. When Pritzker refused, GE Credit terminated further discussions with Trans Union in early January.

In the meantime, in early December, the investment firm Kohlberg, Kravis, Roberts & Co. ("KKR"), the only other concern to make a firm offer for Trans Union, withdrew its offer under circumstances hereinafter detailed.

On December 19, this litigation was commenced and, within four weeks, the plaintiffs had deposed eight of the ten directors of Trans Union, including Van Gorkom, Chelberg and Romans, its Chief Financial Officer. On January 21, Management's Proxy Statement for the February 10 shareholder meeting was mailed to Trans Union's stockholders. On January 26, Trans Union's Board met and, after a lengthy meeting, voted to proceed with the Pritzker merger. The Board also approved for mailing, "on or about January 27," a Supplement to its Proxy Statement. The Supplement purportedly set forth all information relevant to the Pritzker Merger Agreement, which had not been divulged in the first Proxy Statement.

* * *

On February 10, the stockholders of Trans Union approved the Pritzker merger proposal. Of the outstanding shares, 69.9% were voted in favor of the merger; 7.25% were voted against the merger; and 22.85% were not voted.

II.

We turn to the issue of the application of the business judgment rule to the September 20 meeting of the Board.

The Court of Chancery concluded from the evidence that the Board of Directors' approval of the Pritzker merger proposal fell within the protection of the business judgment rule. The Court found that the Board had given sufficient time and attention to the transaction, since the directors had considered the Pritzker proposal on three different occasions, on September 20, and on October 8, 1980 and finally on January 26, 1981. On that basis, the Court reasoned that the Board had acquired, over the four-month period, sufficient information to reach an informed business judgment on the cash-out merger proposal. The Court ruled:

> . . . that given the market value of Trans Union's stock, the business acumen of the members of the board of Trans Union, the substantial premium over market offered by the Pritzkers and the ultimate effect on the merger price provided by the prospect of other bids for the stock in question, that the board of directors of Trans Union did not act recklessly or improvidently in determining on a course of action which they believed to be in the best interest of the stockholders of Trans Union.

The Court of Chancery made but one finding; i.e., that the Board's conduct over the entire period from September 20 through January 26, 1981 was not reckless or improvident, but informed. This ultimate conclusion was premised upon three subordinate findings, one explicit and two implied. The Court's explicit finding was that Trans Union's Board was "free to turn down the Pritzker proposal" not only on September 20 but also on October 8, 1980 and on January 26, 1981. The Court's implied, subordinate findings were: (1) that no legally binding agreement was reached by the parties until January 26; and (2) that if a higher offer were to be forthcoming, the market test would have produced it, and Trans Union would have been contractually free to accept such higher offer. However, the Court offered no factual basis or legal support for any of these findings; and the record compels contrary conclusions. . . .

Under Delaware law, the business judgment rule is the offspring of the fundamental principle, codified in 8 Del.C. § 141(a), that the business and affairs of a Delaware corporation are managed by or under its board of directors. . . . The rule itself "is a presumption that in making a business decision, the directors of a corporation acted on an informed basis, in good faith and in the honest belief that the action taken was in the best interests of the company." . . . [Aronson v. Lewis, 473 A.2d 805, 812 (Del.1984)]. Thus, the party attacking a board decision as uninformed must rebut the presumption that its business judgment was an informed one. Id.

The determination of whether a business judgment is an informed one turns on whether the directors have informed themselves "prior to making a business decision, of all material information reasonably available to them." Id.

Under the business judgment rule there is no protection for directors who have made "an unintelligent or unadvised judgment." Mitchell v. Highland–Western Glass, Del.Ch., 167 A. 831, 833 (1933). A director's duty to inform himself in preparation for a decision derives from the fiduciary capacity in which he serves the corporation and its stockholders. Lutz v. Boas, Del.Ch., 171 A.2d 381 (1961). See Weinberger v. UOP, Inc., supra; Guth v. Loft, supra. . . . [F]ulfillment of the fiduciary function requires more than the mere absence of bad faith or fraud. Representation of the financial interests of others imposes on a director an affirmative duty to protect those interests and to proceed with a critical eye in assessing information of the type and under the circumstances present here. . . .

The standard of care applicable to a director's duty of care has also been recently restated by this Court. In Aronson, supra, we stated:

> While the Delaware cases use a variety of terms to describe the applicable standard of care, our analysis satisfies us that under the business judgment rule director liability is predicated upon concepts of gross negligence. (footnote omitted)

473 A.2d at 812.

We again confirm that view. We think the concept of gross negligence is also the proper standard for determining whether a business judgment reached by a board of directors was an informed one.[13]

In the specific context of a proposed merger of domestic corporations, a director has a duty under 8 Del.C. 251(b),[14] along with his fellow directors, to act in an informed and deliberate manner in determining whether to approve an agreement of merger before submitting the proposal to the stockholders. Certainly in the merger context, a director may not abdicate that duty by leaving to the shareholders alone the decision to approve or disapprove the agreement. See Beard v. Elster, Del.Supr., 160 A.2d 731, 737 (1960). Only an agreement of merger satisfying the requirements of 8 Del.C.

---

13. Compare Mitchell v. Highland–Western Glass, supra, where the Court posed the question as whether the board acted "so far without information that they can be said to have passed an unintelligent and unadvised judgment." 167 A. at 833. Compare also Gimbel v. Signal Companies, Inc., 316 A.2d 599, aff'd per curiam Del. Supr., 316 A.2d 619 (1974), where the Chancellor, after expressly reiterating the *Highland–Western Glass* standard, framed the question, "Or to put the question in its legal context, did the Signal directors act without the bounds of reason and recklessly in approving the price offer of Burmah?" Id.

14. 8 Del.C. § 251(b) provides in pertinent part:

(b) The board of directors of each corporation which desires to merge or consolidate *shall adopt a resolution approving an agreement of merger* or consolidation. . . . Any of the terms of the agreement of merger or consolidation may be made dependent upon facts ascertainable outside of such agreement, provided that the manner in which such facts shall operate upon the terms of the agreement is clearly and expressly set forth in the agreement of merger or consolidation. (underlining added [by the court] for emphasis)

§ 251(b) may be submitted to the shareholders under § 251(c). See generally Aronson v. Lewis, supra at 811–13; see also Pogostin v. Rice, supra.

It is against those standards that the conduct of the directors of Trans Union must be tested, as a matter of law and as a matter of fact, regarding their exercise of an informed business judgment in voting to approve the Pritzker merger proposal.

III.

The defendants argue that the determination of whether their decision to accept $55 per share for Trans Union represented an informed business judgment requires consideration, not only of that which they knew and learned on September 20, but also of that which they subsequently learned and did over the following four-month period before the shareholders met to vote on the proposal in February, 1981. The defendants thereby seek to reduce the significance of their action on September 20 and to widen the time frame for determining whether their decision to accept the Pritzker proposal was an informed one. Thus, the defendants contend that what the directors did and learned subsequent to September 20 and through January 26, 1981, was properly taken into account by the Trial Court in determining whether the Board's judgment was an informed one. We disagree with this *post hoc* approach.

The issue of whether the directors reached an informed decision to "sell" the Company on September 20, 1980 must be determined only upon the basis of the information then reasonably available to the directors and relevant to their decision to accept the Pritzker merger proposal. This is not to say that the directors were precluded from altering their original plan of action, had they done so in an informed manner. What we do say is that the question of whether the directors reached an informed business judgment in agreeing to sell the Company, pursuant to the terms of the September 20 Agreement presents, in reality, two questions: (A) whether the directors reached an informed business judgment on September 20, 1980; and (B) if they did not, whether the directors' actions taken subsequent to September 20 were adequate to cure any infirmity in their action taken on September 20. We first consider the directors' September 20 action in terms of their reaching an informed business judgment.

–A–

On the record before us, we must conclude that the Board of Directors did not reach an informed business judgment on September 20, 1980 in voting to "sell" the Company for $55 per share pursuant to the Pritzker cash-out merger proposal. Our reasons, in summary, are as follows:

The directors (1) did not adequately inform themselves as to Van Gorkom's role in forcing the "sale" of the Company and in establishing the per share purchase price; (2) were uninformed as to the intrinsic value of the Company; and (3) given these circumstances, at a minimum, were grossly negligent in approving the "sale" of the Company upon two hours' consideration, without prior notice, and without the exigency of a crisis or emergency.

As has been noted, the Board based its September 20 decision to approve the cash-out merger primarily on Van Gorkom's representations. None of the directors, other than Van Gorkom and Chelberg, had any prior knowledge that the purpose of the meeting was to propose a cash-out merger of Trans Union. . . .

Without any documents before them concerning the proposed transaction, the members of the Board were required to rely entirely upon Van Gorkom's 20–minute oral presentation of the proposal. No written summary of the terms of the merger was presented; the directors were given no documentation to support the adequacy of $55 price per share for sale of the Company; and the Board had before it nothing more than Van Gorkom's statement of his understanding of the substance of an agreement which he admittedly had never read, nor which any member of the Board had ever seen.

Under 8 Del.C. § 141(e), "directors are fully protected in relying in good faith on reports made by officers." Michelson v. Duncan, Del.Ch., 386 A.2d 1144, 1156 (1978); aff'd in part and rev'd in part on other grounds, Del.Supr., 407 A.2d 211 (1979). See also Graham v. Allis–Chalmers Mfg. Co., Del.Supr., 188 A.2d 125, 130 (1963); Prince v. Bensinger, Del.Ch., 244 A.2d 89, 94 (1968). The term "report" has been liberally construed to include reports of informal personal investigations by corporate officers, Cheff v. Mathes, Del.Supr., 199 A.2d 548, 556 (1964). However, there is no evidence that any "report," as defined under § 141(e), concerning the Pritzker proposal, was presented to the Board on September 20. Van Gorkom's oral presentation of his understanding of the terms of the proposed Merger Agreement, which he had not seen, and Romans' brief oral statement of his preliminary study regarding the feasibility of a leveraged buy-out of Trans Union do not qualify as § 141(e) "reports" for these reasons: The former lacked substance because Van Gorkom was basically uninformed as to the essential provisions of the very document about which he was talking. Romans' statement was irrelevant to the issues before the Board since it did not purport to be a valuation study. At a minimum for a report to enjoy the status conferred by § 141(e), it must be pertinent to the subject matter upon which a board is called to act, and otherwise be entitled to good faith, not blind, reliance. Considering all of the surrounding circumstances—hastily calling the meeting without prior notice of its subject matter, the proposed sale of the Company without any prior consideration of the issue or necessity therefor, the urgent time constraints imposed by Pritzker, and the total absence of any documentation whatsoever—the directors were duty bound to make reasonable inquiry of Van Gorkom and Romans, and if they had done so, the inadequacy of that upon which they now claim to have relied would have been apparent.

The defendants rely on the following factors to sustain the Trial Court's finding that the Board's decision was an informed one: (1) the magnitude of the premium or spread between the $55 Pritzker offering price and Trans Union's current market price of $38 per share; (2) the amendment of the Agreement as submitted on September 20 to permit the Board to accept any better offer during the "market test" period; (3) the collective experience and expertise of the Board's "inside" and "outside" directors; and (4) their reliance on Brennan's legal advice that the directors might be sued if they rejected the Pritzker proposal. We discuss each of these grounds *seriatim:*

(1)

A substantial premium may provide one reason to recommend a merger, but in the absence of other sound valuation information, the fact of a premium alone does not provide an adequate basis upon which to assess the fairness of an offering price. Here, the judgment reached as to the adequacy of the premium was based on a comparison between the historically depressed Trans Union market price and the amount of the Pritzker offer. Using market price as a basis for concluding that the premium adequately reflected the true value of the Company was a clearly faulty, indeed fallacious, premise. . . .

The record is clear that before September 20, Van Gorkom and other members of Trans Union's Board knew that the market had consistently undervalued the worth of Trans Union's stock. . . .

The parties do not dispute that a publicly-traded stock price is solely a measure of the value of a minority position and, thus, market price represents only the value of a single share. Nevertheless, on September 20, the Board assessed the adequacy of the premium over market, offered by Pritzker, solely by comparing it with Trans Union's current and historical stock price. . . .

Indeed, as of September 20, the Board had no other information on which to base a determination of the intrinsic value of Trans Union as a going concern. As of September 20, the Board had made no evaluation of the Company designed to value the entire enterprise, nor had the Board ever previously considered selling the Company or consenting to a buy-out merger. Thus, the adequacy of a premium is indeterminate unless it is assessed in terms of other competent and sound valuation information that reflects the value of the particular business.

Despite the foregoing facts and circumstances, there was no call by the Board, either on September 20 or thereafter, for any valuation study or documentation of the $55 price per share as a measure of the fair value of the Company in a cash-out context. It is undisputed that the major asset of Trans Union was its cash flow. Yet, at no time did the Board call for a valuation study taking into account that highly significant element of the Company's assets.

We do not imply that an outside valuation study is essential to support an informed business judgment; nor do we state that fairness opinions by independent investment bankers are required as a matter of law. Often insiders familiar with the business of a going concern are in a better position than are outsiders to gather relevant information; and under appropriate circumstances, such directors may be fully protected in relying in good faith upon the valuation reports of their management. See 8 Del.C. § 141(e). . . .

Here, the record establishes that the Board did not request its Chief Financial Officer, Romans, to make any valuation study or review of the proposal to determine the adequacy of $55 per share for sale of the Company. On the record before us: The Board rested on Romans' elicited response that the $55 figure was within a "fair price range" within the context of a leveraged buy-out. No director sought any further information from Romans. No director asked him why he put $55 at the bottom of his range. No director asked Romans for any details as to his study, the reason why it had been undertaken or its depth. No director asked to see the study; and no director asked Romans whether Trans Union's finance department could do a fairness study within the remaining 36–hour period available under the Pritzker offer.

Had the Board, or any member, made an inquiry of Romans, he presumably would have responded as he testified: that his calculations were rough and preliminary; and, that the study was not designed to determine the fair value of the Company, but rather to assess the feasibility of a leveraged buy-out financed by the Company's projected cash flow, making certain assumptions as to the purchaser's borrowing needs. Romans would have presumably also informed the Board of his view, and the widespread view of Senior Management, that the timing of the offer was wrong and the offer inadequate.

The record also establishes that the Board accepted without scrutiny Van Gorkom's representation as to the fairness of the $55 price per share for sale of the Company—a subject that the Board had never previously considered. The Board thereby failed to discover that Van Gorkom had suggested the $55 price to Pritzker and, most crucially, that Van Gorkom had arrived at the $55 figure based on calculations designed solely to determine the feasibility of a leveraged buy-out. No questions were raised either as to the tax implications of a cash-out merger or how the price for the one million share option granted Pritzker was calculated.

We do not say that the Board of Directors was not entitled to give some credence to Van Gorkom's representation that $55 was an adequate or fair price. Under § 141(e), the directors were entitled to rely upon their chairman's opinion of value and adequacy, provided that such opinion was reached on a sound basis. Here, the issue is whether the directors informed themselves as to all information that was reasonably available to them. Had they done so, they would have learned of the source and derivation of the $55 price and could not reasonably have relied thereupon in good faith.

None of the directors, Management or outside, were investment bankers or financial analysts. Yet the Board did not consider recessing the meeting until a later hour that day (or requesting an extension of Pritzker's Sunday evening deadline) to give it time to elicit more information as to the sufficiency of the offer, either from inside Management (in particular Romans) or from Trans Union's own investment banker, Salomon Brothers, whose Chicago specialist in merger and acquisitions was known to the Board and familiar with Trans Union's affairs.

Thus, the record compels the conclusion that on September 20 the Board lacked valuation information adequate to reach an informed business judgment as to the fairness of $55 per share for sale of the Company.

(2)

This brings us to the post-September 20 "market test" upon which the defendants ultimately rely to confirm the reasonableness of their September 20 decision to accept the Pritzker proposal. In this connection, the directors present a two-part argument: (a) that by making a "market test" of Pritzker's $55 per share offer a condition of their September 20 decision to accept his offer, they cannot be found to have acted impulsively or in an uninformed manner on September 20; and (b) that the adequacy of the $17 premium for sale of the Company was conclusively established over the following 90 to 120 days by the most reliable evidence available—the marketplace. Thus, the defendants impliedly contend that the "market test" eliminated the need for the Board to perform any other form of fairness test either on September 20, or thereafter.

Again, the facts of record do not support the defendants' argument. There is no evidence: (a) that the Merger Agreement was effectively amended to give the Board freedom to put Trans Union up for auction sale to the highest bidder; or (b) that a public auction was in fact permitted to occur. The minutes of the Board meeting make no reference to any of this. Indeed, the record compels the conclusion that the directors had no rational basis for expecting that a market test was attainable, given the terms of the Agreement as executed during the evening of September 20. We rely upon the following facts which are essentially uncontradicted:

The Merger Agreement, specifically identified as that originally presented to the Board on September 20, has never been produced by the defendants, notwithstanding the plaintiffs' several demands for production before as well as during trial. No acceptable explanation of this failure to produce documents has been given to either the Trial Court or this Court. . . .

Van Gorkom states that the Agreement as submitted incorporated the ingredients for a market test by authorizing Trans Union to receive competing offers over the next 90-day period. However, he concedes that the Agreement barred Trans Union from actively soliciting such offers and from furnishing to interested parties any information about the Company other than that already in the public domain. Whether the original Agreement of September 20 went so

far as to authorize Trans Union to receive competitive proposals is
arguable. The defendants' unexplained failure to produce and identify the original Merger Agreement permits the logical inference that
the instrument would not support their assertions in this regard. . . .

The defendant directors assert that they "insisted" upon including
two amendments to the Agreement, thereby permitting a market test:
(1) to give Trans Union the right to accept a better offer; and (2) to
reserve to Trans Union the right to distribute proprietary information
on the Company to alternative bidders. Yet, the defendants concede
that they did not seek to amend the Agreement to permit Trans Union
to solicit competing offers.

Several of Trans Union's outside directors resolutely maintained
that the Agreement as submitted was approved on the understanding
that, "if we got a better deal, we had a right to take it." Director
Johnson so testified; but he then added, "And if they didn't put that
in the agreement, then the management did not carry out the conclusion of the Board. And I just don't know whether they did or not."
The only clause in the Agreement as finally executed to which the
defendants can point as "keeping the door open" is the following
underlined statement found in subparagraph (a) of section 2.03 of the
Merger Agreement as executed:

> The Board of Directors shall recommend to the stockholders of
> Trans Union that they approve and adopt the Merger Agreement
> ("the stockholders' approval") and to use its best efforts to obtain
> the requisite votes therefor. *GL acknowledges that Trans Union
> directors may have a competing fiduciary obligation to the shareholders
> under certain circumstances.*

Clearly, this language on its face cannot be construed as incorporating
either of the two "conditions" described above: either the right to
accept a better offer or the right to distribute proprietary information
to third parties. . . . No reference to either of the so-called
"conditions" or of Trans Union's reserved right to test the market
appears in any notes of the Board meeting or in the Board Resolution
accepting the Pritzker offer or in the Minutes of the meeting itself.
That evening, in the midst of a formal party which he hosted for the
opening of the Chicago Lyric Opera, Van Gorkom executed the
Merger Agreement without he or any other member of the Board
having read the instruments.

The defendants attempt to downplay the significance of the
prohibition against Trans Union's actively soliciting competing offers
by arguing that the directors "understood that the entire financial
community would know that Trans Union was for sale upon the
announcement of the Pritzker offer, and anyone desiring to make a
better offer was free to do so." Yet, the press release issued on
September 22, with the authorization of the Board, stated that Trans
Union had entered into "definitive agreements" with the Pritzkers;
and the press release did not even disclose Trans Union's limited right
to receive and accept higher offers. Accompanying this press release

was a further public announcement that Pritzker had been granted an option to purchase at any time one million shares of Trans Union's capital stock at 75 cents above the then-current price per share.

Thus, notwithstanding what several of the outside directors later claimed to have "thought" occurred at the meeting, the record compels the conclusion that Trans Union's Board had no rational basis to conclude on September 20 or in the days immediately following, that the Board's acceptance of Pritzker's offer was conditioned on (1) a "market test" of the offer; and (2) the Board's right to withdraw from the Pritzker Agreement and accept any higher offer received before the shareholder meeting.

(3)

The directors' unfounded reliance on both the premium and the market test as the basis for accepting the Pritzker proposal undermines the defendants' remaining contention that the Board's collective experience and sophistication was a sufficient basis for finding that it reached its September 20 decision with informed, reasonable deliberation.[21] Compare Gimbel v. Signal Companies, Inc., Del.Ch., 316 A.2d 599 (1974), aff'd per curiam, Del.Supr., 316 A.2d 619 (1974). There, the Court of Chancery preliminary enjoined a board's sale of stock of its wholly-owned subsidiary for an alleged grossly inadequate price. It did so based on a finding that the business judgment rule had been pierced for failure of management to give its board "the opportunity to make a reasonable and reasoned decision." 316 A.2d at 615. The Court there reached this result notwithstanding the board's sophistication and experience; the company's need of immediate cash; and the board's need to act promptly due to the impact of an energy crisis on the value of the underlying assets being sold—all of its subsidiary's oil and gas interests. The Court found those factors denoting competence to be outweighed by evidence of gross negligence; that management in effect sprang the deal on the board by negotiating the asset sale without informing the board; that the buyer intended to "force a quick decision" by the board; that the board meeting was called on only one-and-a-half days' notice; that its outside directors were not notified of the meeting's purpose; that during a meeting spanning "a couple of hours" a sale of assets worth $480 million was approved; and that the Board failed to obtain a *current* appraisal of its oil and gas interests. The analogy of *Signal* to the case at bar is significant.

21. Trans Union's five "inside" directors had backgrounds in law and accounting, 116 years of collective employment by the Company and 68 years of combined experience on its Board. Trans Union's five "outside" directors included four chief executives of major corporations and an economist who was a former dean of a major school of business and chancellor of a university. The "outside" directors had 78 years of combined experience as chief executive officers of major corporations and 50 years of cumulative experience as directors of Trans Union. Thus, defendants argue that the Board was eminently qualified to reach an informed judgment on the proposed "sale" of Trans Union notwithstanding their lack of any advance notice of the proposal, the shortness of their deliberation, and their determination not to consult with their investment banker or to obtain a fairness opinion.

(4)

* * *

We conclude that Trans Union's Board was grossly negligent in that it failed to act with informed reasonable deliberation in agreeing to the Pritzker merger proposal on September 20; and we further conclude that the Trial Court erred as a matter of law in failing to address that question before determining whether the directors' later conduct was sufficient to cure its initial error. . . .

–B–

We now examine the Board's post-September 20 conduct for the purpose of determining first, whether it was informed and not grossly negligent; and second, if informed, whether it was sufficient to legally rectify and cure the Board's derelictions of September 20.[23]

(1)

First, as to the Board meeting of October 8. . . .

The public announcement of the Pritzker merger resulted in an "en masse" revolt of Trans Union's Senior Management. The head of Trans Union's tank car operations (its most profitable division) informed Van Gorkom that unless the merger were called off, fifteen key personnel would resign.

Instead of reconvening the Board, Van Gorkom again privately met with Pritzker, informed him of the developments, and sought his advice. Pritzker then made the following suggestions for overcoming Management's dissatisfaction: (1) that the Agreement be amended to permit Trans Union to solicit, as well as receive, higher offers; and (2) that the shareholder meeting be postponed from early January to February 10, 1981. In return, Pritzker asked Van Gorkom to obtain a commitment from Senior Management to remain at Trans Union for at least six months after the merger was consummated.

Van Gorkom then advised Senior Management that the Agreement would be amended to give Trans Union the right to solicit competing offers through January, 1981, if they would agree to remain with Trans Union. Senior Management was temporarily mollified; and Van Gorkom then called a special meeting of Trans Union's Board for October 8.

Thus, the primary purpose of the October 8 Board meeting was to amend the Merger Agreement, in a manner agreeable to Pritzker, to permit Trans Union to conduct a "market test."[24] Van Gorkom

---

23. As will be seen, we do not reach the second question.

24. As previously noted, the Board mistakenly thought that it had amended the September 20 draft agreement to include a market test.

A secondary purpose of the October 8 meeting was to obtain the Board's approval for Trans Union to employ its investment advisor, Salomon Brothers, for the limited purpose of assisting Management in the solicitation of other offers. Neither Management nor the Board then or thereafter requested Salomon Brothers to submit its opinion as to the fairness of Pritzker's $55

understood that the proposed amendments were intended to give the Company an unfettered "right to openly solicit offers down through January 31." Van Gorkom presumably so represented the amendments to Trans Union's Board members on October 8. In a brief session, the directors approved Van Gorkom's oral presentation of the substance of the proposed amendments, the terms of which were not reduced to writing until October 10. But rather than waiting to review the amendments, the Board again approved them sight unseen and adjourned, giving Van Gorkom authority to execute the papers when he received them.[25] . . .

The next day, October 9, and before the Agreement was amended, Pritzker moved swiftly to off-set the proposed market test amendment. First, Pritzker informed Trans Union that he had completed arrangements for financing its acquisition and that the parties were thereby mutually bound to a firm purchase and sale arrangement. Second, Pritzker announced the exercise of his option to purchase one million shares of Trans Union's treasury stock at $38 per share—75 cents above the current market price. Trans Union's Management responded the same day by issuing a press release announcing: (1) that all financing arrangements for Pritzker's acquisition of Trans Union had been completed; and (2) Pritzker's purchase of one million shares of Trans Union's treasury stock at $38 per share.

The next day, October 10, Pritzker delivered to Trans Union the proposed amendments to the September 20 Merger Agreement. Van Gorkom promptly proceeded to countersign all the instruments on behalf of Trans Union without reviewing the instruments to determine if they were consistent with the authority previously granted him by the Board. The amending documents were apparently not approved by Trans Union's Board until a much later date, December 2. The record does not affirmatively establish that Trans Union's directors ever read the October 10 amendments.[26]

The October 10 amendments to the Merger Agreement did authorize Trans Union to solicit competing offers, but the amendments had more far-reaching effects. The most significant change was in the definition of the third-party "offer" available to Trans Union as a possible basis for withdrawal from its Merger Agreement with Pritzker. Under the October 10 amendments, a better *offer* was no longer sufficient to permit Trans Union's withdrawal. Trans Union was now permitted to terminate the Pritzker Agreement and abandon the merger only if, prior to February 10, 1981, Trans Union had either consummated a merger (or sale of assets) with a third party or

cash-out merger proposal or to value Trans Union as an entity. . . .

25. We do not suggest that a board must read *in haec verba* every contract or legal document which it approves, but if it is to successfully absolve itself from charges of the type made here, there must be some credible contemporary evidence demonstrating that the directors knew what they were doing, and ensured that

their purported action was given effect. That is the consistent failure which cast this Board upon its unredeemable course.

26. There is no evidence of record that Trans Union's directors ever raised any objections, procedural or substantive, to the October 10 amendments or that any of them, including Van Gorkom, understood the opposite result of their intended effect—until it was too late.

had entered into a "definitive" merger agreement more favorable than Pritzker's and for a greater consideration—subject only to stockholder approval. Further, the "extension" of the market test period to February 10, 1981 was circumscribed by other amendments which required Trans Union to file its preliminary proxy statement on the Pritzker merger proposal by December 5, 1980 and use its best efforts to mail the statement to its shareholders by January 5, 1981. Thus, the market test period was effectively reduced, not extended. . . .

In our view, the record compels the conclusion that the directors' conduct on October 8 exhibited the same deficiencies as did their conduct on September 20. The Board permitted its Merger Agreement with Pritzker to be amended in a manner it had neither authorized nor intended. . . .

We conclude that the Board acted in a grossly negligent manner on October 8; and that Van Gorkom's representations on which the Board based its actions do not constitute "reports" under § 141(e) on which the directors could reasonably have relied. Further, the amended Merger Agreement imposed on Trans Union's acceptance of a third party offer conditions more onerous than those imposed on Trans Union's acceptance of Pritzker's offer on September 20. After October 10, Trans Union could accept from a third party a better offer only if it were incorporated in a definitive agreement between the parties, and not conditioned on financing or on any other contingency.

The October 9 press release, coupled with the October 10 amendments, had the clear effect of locking Trans Union's Board into the Pritzker Agreement. Pritzker had thereby foreclosed Trans Union's Board from negotiating any better "definitive" agreement over the remaining eight weeks before Trans Union was required to clear the Proxy Statement submitting the Pritzker proposal to its shareholders.

(2)

Next, as to the "curative" effects of the Board's post-September 20 conduct, we review in more detail the reaction of Van Gorkom to the KKR proposal and the results of the Board-sponsored "market test."

The KKR proposal was the first and only offer received subsequent to the Pritzker Merger Agreement. The offer resulted primarily from the efforts of Romans and other senior officers to propose an alternative to Pritzker's acquisition of Trans Union. In late September, Romans' group contacted KKR about the possibility of a leveraged buy-out by all members of Management, except Van Gorkom. By early October, Henry R. Kravis of KKR gave Romans written notice of KKR's "interest in making an offer to purchase 100%" of Trans Union's common stock.

Thereafter, and until early December, Romans' group worked with KKR to develop a proposal. It did so with Van Gorkom's knowledge and apparently grudging consent. On December 2, Kravis and Romans hand-delivered to Van Gorkom a formal letter-offer to purchase all of Trans Union's assets and to assume all of its liabilities for an aggregate cash consideration equivalent to $60 per share. The offer was contingent upon completing equity and bank financing of $650 million, which Kravis represented as 80% complete. . . .

Van Gorkom's reaction to the KKR proposal was completely negative; he did not view the offer as being firm because of its financing condition. It was pointed out, to no avail, that Pritzker's offer had not only been similarly conditioned, but accepted on an expedited basis. Van Gorkom refused Kravis' request that Trans Union issue a press release announcing KKR's offer, on the ground that it might "chill" any other offer.[27] . . .

Within a matter of hours and shortly before the scheduled Board meeting, Kravis withdrew his letter-offer. He gave as his reason a sudden decision by the Chief Officer of Trans Union's rail car leasing operation to withdraw from the KKR purchasing group. Van Gorkom had spoken to that officer about his participation in the KKR proposal immediately after his meeting with Romans and Kravis. However, Van Gorkom denied any responsibility for the officer's change of mind. . . .

GE Credit Corporation's interest in Trans Union did not develop until November; and it made no written proposal until mid-January. Even then, its proposal was not in the form of an offer. Had there been time to do so, GE Credit was prepared to offer between $2 and $5 per share above the $55 per share price which Pritzker offered. But GE Credit needed an additional 60 to 90 days; and it was unwilling to make a formal offer without a concession from Pritzker extending the February 10 "deadline" for Trans Union's stockholder meeting. As previously stated, Pritzker refused to grant such extension. . . .

* * *

In the absence of any explicit finding by the Trial Court as to the reasonableness of Trans Union's directors' reliance on a market test and its feasibility, we may make our own findings based on the record. Our review of the record compels a finding that confirmation of the appropriateness of the Pritzker offer by an unfettered or free market test was virtually meaningless in the face of the terms and time limitations of Trans Union's Merger Agreement with Pritzker as amended October 10, 1980.

. . . Under [Del.] § 251(b), the Board had but two options: (1) to proceed with the merger and the stockholder meeting, with the Board's recommendation of approval; *or* (2) to rescind its agreement with Pritzker, withdraw its approval of the merger, and notify its stockholders that the proposed shareholder meeting was cancelled.

---

27. This was inconsistent with Van Gorkom's espousal of the September 22 press release following Trans Union's acceptance of Pritzker's proposal. Van Gorkom had then justified a press release as encouraging rather than chilling later offers.

There is no evidence that the Board gave any consideration to these, its only legally viable alternative courses of action. . . .

* * *

. . . [W]e hold that the defendants' post-September conduct did not cure the deficiencies of their September 20 conduct; and that, accordingly, the Trial Court erred in according to the defendants the benefits of the business judgment rule. . . .

V.

The defendants ultimately rely on the stockholder vote of February 10 for exoneration. The defendants contend that the stockholders' "overwhelming" vote approving the Pritzker Merger Agreement had the legal effect of curing any failure of the Board to reach an informed business judgment in its approval of the merger. . . .

[The court rejected this defense on the ground that Trans Union's stockholders were not fully informed of all facts material to their vote on the Pritzker Merger, and that the Trial Court's ruling to the contrary was clearly erroneous.] . . .

VI.

. . . We hold, therefore, that the Trial Court committed reversible error in applying the business judgment rule in favor of the director defendants in this case.

On remand, the Court of Chancery shall conduct an evidentiary hearing to determine the fair value of the shares represented by the plaintiffs' class, based on the intrinsic value of Trans Union on September 20, 1980. Such valuation shall be made in accordance with Weinberger v. UOP, Inc., supra. . . . Thereafter, an award of damages may be entered to the extent that the fair value of Trans Union exceeds $55 per share.

* * *

Reversed and Remanded for proceedings consistent herewith.

McNEILLY, Justice, dissenting . . .

Following the October 8 board meeting of Trans Union, the investment banking firm of Salomon Brothers was retained by the corporation to search for better offers than that of the Pritzkers, Salomon Brothers being charged with the responsibility of doing "whatever possible to see if there is a superior bid in the marketplace over a bid that is on the table for Trans Union". In undertaking such project, it was agreed that Salomon Brothers would be paid the amount of $500,000 to cover its expenses as well as a fee equal to ³⁄₈ths of 1% of the aggregate fair market value of the consideration to be received by the company in the case of a merger or the like, which meant that in the event Salomon Brothers should find a buyer willing to pay a price of $56.00 a share instead of $55.00, such firm would receive a fee of roughly $2,650,000 plus disbursements.

As the first step in proceeding to carry out its commitment, Salomon Brothers had a brochure prepared, which set forth Trans

Union's financial history, described the company's business in detail and set forth Trans Union's operating and financial projections. Salomon Brothers also prepared a list of over 150 companies which it believed might be suitable merger partners, and while four of such companies, namely, General Electric, Borg–Warner, Bendix, and Genstar, Ltd. showed some interest in such a merger, none made a firm proposal to Trans Union and only General Electric showed a sustained interest. As matters transpired, no firm offer which bettered the Pritzker offer of $55 per share was ever made. . . .

I have no quarrel with the majority's analysis of the business judgment rule. It is the application of that rule to these facts which is wrong. An overview of the entire record, rather than the limited view of bits and pieces which the majority has exploded like popcorn, convinces me that the directors made an informed business judgment which was buttressed by their test of the market.

At the time of the September 20 meeting the 10 members of Trans Union's Board of Directors were highly qualified and well informed about the affairs and prospects of Trans Union. These directors were acutely aware of the historical problems facing Trans Union which were caused by the tax laws. They had discussed these problems *ad nauseam.* In fact, within two months of the September 20 meeting the board had reviewed and discussed an outside study of the company done by The Boston Consulting Group and an internal five year forecast prepared by management. At the September 20 meeting Van Gorkom presented the Pritzker offer, and the board then heard from James Brennan, the company's counsel in this matter, who discussed the legal documents. Following this, the Board directed that certain changes be made in the merger documents. These changes made it clear that the Board was free to accept a better offer than Pritzker's if one was made. The above facts reveal that the Board did not act in a grossly negligent manner in informing themselves of the relevant and available facts before passing on the merger. To the contrary, this record reveals that the directors acted with the utmost care in informing themselves of the relevant and available facts before passing on the merger. . . .

CHRISTIE, Justice, dissenting:

I respectfully dissent.

Considering the standard and scope of our review under Levitt v. Bouvier, Del.Supr., 287 A.2d 671, 673 (1972), I believe that the record taken as a whole supports a conclusion that the actions of the defendants are protected by the business judgment rule. Aronson v. Lewis, Del.Supr., 473 A.2d 805, 812 (1984); Pogostin v. Rice, Del. Supr., 480 A.2d 619, 627 (1984). . . .

It is reported that after the decision of the Delaware Supreme Court, an agreement was reached to settle *Van Gorkom* by the payment of $23.5 million to the plaintiff class. Of that amount, $10 million, the policy limit, was provided by Trans Union's directors' and officers' liability-insurance carrier. Nearly all of the $13.5 million balance was paid by the Pritzker group on behalf of the Trans Union defendant directors, although the Pritzker group was not a defendant. See Manning, Reflections and Practical Tips on Life in the Boardroom After *Van Gorkom,* 41 Bus.Law. 1 (1985).

NOTE ON SUBSTANCE AND PROCESS IN THE DUTY OF CARE

In many areas of law, a distinction is drawn between substance and process. The duty of care may be understood in that way too. In effect, the business judgment rule gives wide latitude to a substantive decision of a director or senior executive if, but only if, he has followed a process that is reasonable, in terms of due preparation, in arriving at that decision. The process elements of the duty of care, involving such matters as preparing to make a decision, general monitoring, and following up suspicious circumstances, are governed by a standard of reasonability, while the substantive element, involving review of management decisions, is governed by the much looser standard of rationality.

VIRGINIA CORPORATIONS CODE § 13.1–690

§ 13.1–690   General standards of conduct for director.

A.   A director shall discharge his duties as a director, including his duties as a member of a committee, in accordance with his good faith business judgment of the best interests of the corporation.

OHIO GEN. CORP. LAW § 1701.59

§ 1701.59   Authority of directors; bylaws. . . .

(B) A director shall perform his duties as a director, including his duties as a member of any committee of the directors upon which he may serve, in good faith, in a manner he reasonably believes to be in or not opposed to the best interests of the corporation, and with the care that an ordinarily prudent person in a like position would use under similar circumstances. . . .

(C) For purposes of division (B) of this section: (1) A director shall not be found to have violated his duties under division (B) of this section unless it is proved by clear and convincing evidence that the director has not acted in good faith, in a manner he reasonably believes to be in or not opposed to the best interests of the corporation, or with the care that an ordinarily prudent person in a like position would use under similar circumstances. . . .

(D) A director shall be liable in damages for any action he takes or fails to take as a director only if it is proved by clear and convincing evidence in a court of competent jurisdiction that his action or failure to act involved an act or omission undertaken with deliberate intent to cause injury to the corporation or undertaken with reckless disregard for the best interests of the corporation. . . .

DEL. GEN. CORP. LAW § 102(b)(7)

(b) [T]he certificate of incorporation may . . . contain any or all of the following matters. . . .

(7) A provision eliminating or limiting the personal liability of a director to the corporation or its stockholders for monetary damages for breach of fiduciary duty as a director, provided that such provision shall not eliminate or limit the liability of a director (i) for any breach of the director's duty of loyalty to the corporation or its stockholders, (ii) for acts or omissions not in good faith or which involve intentional misconduct or a knowing violation of law, (iii) under section 174 of this Title [Liability of Directors for Unlawful Payment of Dividend or Unlawful Stock Purchase or Redemption], or (iv) for any transaction from which the director derived an improper personal benefit. No such provision shall eliminate or limit the liability of a director for any act or omission occurring prior to the date when such provision becomes effective. . . .

NOTE ON SPECIAL CIVIL LIABILITIES OF DIRECTORS AND OFFICERS

In addition to the general obligation to exercise due care, a variety of special civil liabilities are imposed upon directors and officers by corporate and noncorporate statutes. For example:

1. The corporate statutes often impose special obligations on directors, apart from the general obligation to use care. Most prominently, the corporate statutes typically make directors liable for the payment of improper dividends. See, Chapter XII, Section 1(i), infra.

2. The securities acts impose a variety of obligations on directors. For example, a director is liable for untrue statements or the omission of material facts in a registration statement, unless he exercised due diligence, or for causing the corporation to sell or offer to sell a security that has not been properly registered. 15 U.S.C.A. §§ 77k, 77*l*.

3. Some noncorporate statutes impose a duty of care on directors and officers that is comparable to that imposed by the common law or the corporate statutes. The purpose of such a statute may be to add to the class of beneficiaries of the director's duty of care, to add to the class of persons authorized to enforce that duty, to confer jurisdiction on the federal courts, or simply to focus the directors' attention on the relevant subject matter. For example, Employee Retirement

Securities Act (ERISA) § 404, 129 U.S.C.A. § 1104, requires a fiduciary of a pension plan to discharge his duties to plan participants and beneficiaries with the care that "a prudent man acting in a like capacity and familiar with such matters" would exercise in a similar enterprise with similar aims under the prevailing circumstances. Section 502(a), 29 U.S.C.A. § 1132(a), permits the Secretary of Labor, plan participants, beneficiaries, and co-fiduciaries to sue for damages for breach of duties under the Act. Section 502k, 29 U.S.C.A. § 1132(k), confers jurisdiction on the federal courts in such suits.

4. Some statutes impose special duties on the directors of specific types of corporations. For example, 12 U.S.C.A. § 93(a) provides that directors are personally liable for "knowing" violations of certain provisions of the National Bank Act, such as exceeding the lending limits set forth in 12 U.S.C.A. § 84.

From the perspective of a director who is concerned with personal liability, special statutory liabilities may be much more serious concerns than traditional duty-of-care liability. A recent survey of claims under directors' and officers' liability insurance policies found that only half the claims involving nonfinancial corporations were based on a breach of the duties owed to shareholders. 1987 Wyatt Directors and Officers and Fiduciary Liability Survey.

SECTION 2. THE DUTY TO ACT LAWFULLY

MILLER v. AMERICAN TELEPHONE & TELEGRAPH CO.

United States Court of Appeals, Third Circuit, 1974.
507 F.2d 759.

Before SEITZ, Chief Judge, GIBBONS and GARTH, Circuit Judges.

SEITZ, Chief Judge.

Plaintiffs, stockholders in American Telephone and Telegraph Company ("AT & T"), brought a stockholders' derivative action in the Eastern District of Pennsylvania against AT & T and all but one of its directors. The suit centered upon the failure of AT & T to collect an outstanding debt of some $1.5 million owed to the company by the Democratic National Committee ("DNC") for communications services provided by AT & T during the 1968 Democratic national convention. Federal diversity jurisdiction was invoked under 28 U.S.C. § 1332.

Plaintiffs' complaint alleged that "neither the officers or directors of AT & T have taken any action to recover the amount owed" from on or about August 20, 1968, when the debt was incurred, until May 31, 1972, the date plaintiffs' amended complaint was filed. The

failure to collect was alleged to have involved a breach of the
defendant directors' duty to exercise diligence in handling the affairs
of the corporation, to have resulted in affording a preference to the
DNC in collection procedures in violation of § 202(a) of the Communications Act of 1934, 47 U.S.C. § 202(a) (1970), and to have
amounted to AT & T's making a "contribution" to the DNC in
violation of a federal prohibition on corporate campaign spending, 18
U.S.C. § 610 (1970).

Plaintiffs sought permanent relief in the form of an injunction
requiring AT & T to collect the debt, an injunction against providing
further services to the DNC until the debt was paid in full, and a
surcharge for the benefit of the corporation against the defendant
directors in the amount of the debt plus interest from the due date. A
request for a preliminary injunction against the provision of services to
the 1972 Democratic convention was denied by the district court after
an evidentiary hearing.

On motion of the defendants, the district court dismissed the
complaint for failure to state a claim upon which relief could be
granted. 364 F.Supp. 648 (E.D.Pa.1973). The court stated that
collection procedures were properly within the discretion of the
directors whose determination would not be overturned by the court
in the absence of an allegation that the conduct of the directors was
"plainly illegal, unreasonable, or in breach of a fiduciary duty. . . ." *Id.* at 651. Plaintiffs appeal from dismissal of their
complaint.

In viewing the motion to dismiss, we must consider all facts
alleged in the complaint and every inference fairly deductible therefrom in the light most favorable to the plaintiffs. A complaint should
not be dismissed unless it appears that the plaintiffs would not be
entitled to relief under any facts which they might prove in support of
their claim. Judging plaintiffs' complaint by these standards, we feel
that it does state a claim upon which relief can be granted for breach
of fiduciary duty arising from the alleged violation of 18 U.S.C.
§ 610.

I.

The pertinent law on the question of the defendant directors'
fiduciary duties in this diversity action is that of New York, the state
of AT & T's incorporation. *See* Perlman v. Feldmann, 219 F.2d 173,
175 (2d Cir.), cert. denied, 349 U.S. 952, 75 S.Ct. 880, 99 L.Ed.
1277 (1955); Kroese v. General Castings Corporation, 179 F.2d 760,
765 (3d Cir.), cert. denied, 339 U.S. 983, 70 S.Ct. 1026, 94 L.Ed.
1386 (1950); Restatement (Second) of Conflicts § 309 (1971). The
sound business judgment rule, the basis of the district court's dismissal
of plaintiffs' complaint, expresses the unanimous decision of American
courts to eschew intervention in corporate decision-making if the
judgment of directors and officers is uninfluenced by personal considerations and is exercised in good faith. Pollitz v. Wabash Railroad
Co., 207 N.Y. 113, 100 N.E. 721 (1912); Bayer v. Beran, 49

N.Y.S.2d 2, 4–7 (Sup.Ct.1944); 3 Fletcher, Private Corporations § 1039 (perm. ed. rev. vol. 1965). Underlying the rule is the assumption that reasonable diligence has been used in reaching the decision which the rule is invoked to justify. Casey v. Woodruff, 49 N.Y.S.2d 625, 643 (Sup.Ct.1944).

Had plaintiffs' complaint alleged only failure to pursue a corporate claim, application of the sound business judgment rule would support the district court's ruling that a shareholder could not attack the directors' decision. *See* United Copper Securities Co. v. Amalgamated Copper Co., 244 U.S. 261, 37 S.Ct. 509, 61 L.Ed. 1119 (1917); Clifford v. Metropolitan Life Insurance Co., 264 App.Div. 168, 34 N.Y.S.2d 693 (2d Dept.1942); 13 Fletcher, Private Corporations § 5822 (perm. ed. rev. vol. 1970). Where, however, the decision not to collect a debt owed the corporation is itself alleged to have been an illegal act, different rules apply. When New York law regarding such acts by directors is considered in conjunction with the underlying purposes of the particular statute involved here, we are convinced that the business judgment rule cannot insulate the defendant directors from liability if they did in fact breach 18 U.S.C. § 610, as plaintiffs have charged.

Roth v. Robertson, 64 Misc. 343, 118 N.Y.S. 351 (Sup.Ct. 1909), illustrates the proposition that even though committed to benefit the corporation, illegal acts may amount to a breach of fiduciary duty in New York. In *Roth*, the managing director of an amusement park company had allegedly used corporate funds to purchase the silence of persons who threatened to complain about unlawful Sunday operation of the park. Recovery from the defendant director was sustained on the ground that the money was an illegal payment:

> For reasons of public policy, we are clearly of the opinion that payments of corporate funds for such purposes as those disclosed in this case must be condemned, and officers of a corporation making them held to a strict accountability, and be compelled to refund the amounts so wasted for the benefit of stockholders. . . . To hold any other rule would be establishing a dangerous precedent, tacitly countenancing the wasting of corporate funds for purposes of corrupting public morals. *Id.* at 346, 118 N.Y.S. at 353.

The plaintiffs' complaint in the instant case alleges a similar "waste" of $1.5 million through an illegal campaign contribution.

Abrams v. Allen, 297 N.Y. 52, 74 N.E.2d 305 (1947), reflects an affirmation by the New York Court of Appeals of the principle of *Roth* that directors must be restrained from engaging in activities which are against public policy. In *Abrams* the court held that a cause of action was stated by an allegation in a derivative complaint that the directors of Remington Rand, Inc., had relocated corporate plants and curtailed production solely for the purpose of intimidating and punishing employees for their involvement in a labor dispute. The Court of Appeals acknowledged that, "depending on the circumstances," proof of the allegations in the complaint might sustain recovery, *inter alia,* under the rule that directors are liable for corporate loss caused by the commission of an "unlawful or immoral act." *Id.* at 55, 74 N.E.2d at 306. In support of its holding, the court noted that the closing of factories for the purpose alleged was opposed to the public policy of the state and nation as embodied in the New York Labor Law and the National Labor Relations Act. *Id.* at 56, 74 N.E.2d at 307.[3]

The alleged violation of the federal prohibition against corporate political contributions not only involves the corporation in criminal activity but similarly contravenes a policy of Congress clearly enunciated in 18 U.S.C. § 610.[4] That statute and its predecessor reflect congressional efforts: (1) to destroy the influence of corporations over elections through financial contributions and (2) to check the practice of using corporate funds to benefit political parties without the consent of the stockholders. United States v. CIO, 335 U.S. 106, 113, 68 S.Ct. 1349, 92 L.Ed. 1849 (1948).

The fact that shareholders are within the class for whose protection the statute was enacted gives force to the argument that the alleged breach of that statute should give rise to a cause of action in those shareholders to force the return to the corporation of illegally contributed funds. Since political contributions by corporations can be checked and shareholder control over the political use of general corporate funds effectuated only if directors are restrained from causing the corporation to violate the statute, such a violation seems a particularly appropriate basis for finding breach of the defendant directors' fiduciary duty to the corporation. Under such circumstances, the directors cannot be insulated from liability on the ground that the contribution was made in the exercise of sound business judgment.

Since plaintiffs have alleged actual damage to the corporation from the transaction in the form of the loss of a $1.5 million increment to AT & T's treasury,[5] we conclude that the complaint does state a claim upon which relief can be granted sufficient to withstand a motion to dismiss.[6]

3. That violation of a federal statute is the basis of the breach of fiduciary duty and that therefore the court is required to interpret the federal statute has not deterred New York courts from entertaining such suits against directors. *See* Knopfler v. Bohen, 15 A.D.2d 922, 225 N.Y.S.2d 609 (2d Dept.1962); *cf.* Simon v. Socony Vacuum Oil Co., 179 Misc. 202, 38 N.Y.S.2d 270 (Sup.Ct.1942).

4. We note that prior to June 1, 1974, corporate political contributions made "directly or indirectly" violated New York law. Law of July 20, 1965, ch. 1031, § 43, [1965] N.Y.Laws 1783 (repealed 1974). Furthermore, apart from the statutory prohibition, political donations by corporations were apparently ultra vires acts in New York. *See* People ex rel. Perkins v. Moss, 187 N.Y. 410, 80 N.E. 383 (1907).

Corporations or organizations financially supported by corporations doing business in the state are now permitted to make contributions up to $5,000 per year. N.Y. Election Law § 480 (McKinney's Consol. Laws, c. 17, Supp.1974).

5. Under New York law, allegation of breach even of a federal statute is apparently insufficient to state a cause of action unless the breach caused independent damage to the corporation. *See* Diamond v. Davis, 263 App.Div. 68, 31 N.Y.S.2d 582 (1st Dept.1941); Borden v. Cohen, 231 N.Y.S.2d 902 (Sup.Ct.1962). *But see* Runcie v. Bankers Trust Co., 6 N.Y.S.2d 623 (Sup.Ct.1938).

6. We express no opinion today on the question of whether plaintiffs' complaint may also state a cause of action for breach

II.

We have accepted plaintiffs' allegation of a violation of 18 U.S.C. § 610 as a shorthand designation of the elements necessary to establish a breach of that statute. This is consonant with the federal practice of notice pleading. *See* Conley v. Gibson, 355 U.S. 41, 47–48, 78 S.Ct. 99, 2 L.Ed.2d 80 (1957); Fed.R.Civ.P. 8(f). That such a designation is sufficient for pleading purposes does not, however, relieve plaintiffs of their ultimate obligation to prove the elements of the statutory violation as part of their proof of breach of fiduciary duty. At the appropriate time, plaintiffs will be required to produce evidence sufficient to establish three distinct elements comprising a violation of 18 U.S.C. § 610: that AT & T (1) made a contribution of money or anything of value to the DNC (2) in connection with a federal election (3) for the purpose of influencing the outcome of that election. *See* United States v. Boyle, 157 U.S.App.D.C. 166, 482 F.2d 755, cert. denied, 414 U.S. 1076, 94 S.Ct. 593, 38 L.Ed.2d 483 (1973); United States v. Lewis Food Co., Inc., 366 F.2d 710 (9th Cir. 1966). The first two of these elements are obvious from the face of the statute; the third was supplied by legislative history prior to being made explicit by 1972 amendments to definitions applicable to § 610.[7]

A "Contribution" to the DNC

In proving a contribution to the DNC, plaintiffs will be required to establish that AT & T did in fact make a gift to the DNC of the value of the communications services provided to the 1968 Democratic convention. Such a gift could be shown, for example, by demonstrating that the services were provided with no intention to collect for them. Likewise, plaintiffs could meet their burden in this respect by proving that although a valid debt was created at the time the services were rendered, that debt was discharged formally or informally by the defendants or is no longer legally collectible as a result of the defendants' failure to sue upon it within the appropriate period of limitation.[8] In any event, as a threshold matter, plaintiffs will be required to show that actions of the defendants have resulted in the

of fiduciary duty arising from the alleged violation of 47 U.S.C. § 202(a).

  7. *See* United States v. UAW, 352 U.S. 567, 589, 77 S.Ct. 529, 1 L.Ed.2d 563 (1957), where, after examining the legislative history and chronological development of federal prohibitions on campaign contributions by corporations and labor organizations, the Supreme Court stated: "The evil at which Congress has struck in § 313 [now 18 U.S.C. § 610] is the use of corporation or union funds to influence the public at large to vote for a particular candidate or a particular party."

As amended by the Federal Election Campaign Act of 1971 (effective April 7,

1972), the definition of "contribution" for purposes of 18 U.S.C. § 610 is a gift of money or anything of value "made for the purpose of influencing the nomination for election, or election" of any person to federal office or for influencing the outcome of a primary or national nominating convention. 18 U.S.C. § 591 (1970), as amended (Supp. II 1972).

  8. *See* 47 U.S.C. § 415(a) (1970) which requires communications carriers to commence actions for recovery of charges within one year from the time the cause of action accrues.

surrender of a valid claim of $1.5 million for services rendered to the DNC.

In Connection With a Federal Election

Plaintiffs must also establish that the contribution was in connection with a federal election. Obviously, the communications services were provided in connection with the 1968 election. If, however, a valid debt was created at that time and the alleged gift was made at some later time when the debt was forgiven or became legally uncollectible, the contribution may have been made in connection with a subsequent federal election. Plaintiffs did not allege the date of the contribution in their complaint, but their burden on remand will include establishing a nexus between the alleged gift and a federal election.

For the Purpose of Influencing an Election

Finally, plaintiffs must also convince the fact finder that the gift, whenever made, was made for the purpose of aiding one candidate or party in a federal election. Proof of non-collection of a debt owed by the DNC will be insufficient to establish the statutory violation upon which the defendants' breach of fiduciary duty is predicated; plaintiffs must shoulder the burden of proving an impermissible motivation underlying the alleged inaction. In the absence of direct proof of a partisan purpose on the part of the defendants, plaintiffs may produce evidence sufficient to justify the inference that the only discernible reason for the failure to pursue the debtor was a desire to assist the Democratic Party in achieving success in a federal election. At a minimum, plaintiffs must establish that legitimate business justifications did not underlie the alleged inaction of the defendant directors. The possibility of the existence of such reasonable business motives illustrates the need for proof of more than mere non-collection even of the debt of a political party in order to establish a breach of 18 U.S.C. § 610.[9]

III.

In addition to advancing claims of breach of fiduciary duty by the defendants, plaintiffs have urged in this court that we "imply" a direct federal cause of action in their favor against the defendant directors for the alleged violations of 18 U.S.C. § 610 and 47 U.S.C. § 202(a). A federal law count was nowhere included in the plaintiffs' complaint and there is no indication in the record that this question was ever presented to the district court. After remand of this case, plaintiffs will have an opportunity to move to amend their complaint pursuant

---

9. Compiling an unsecured debt of this magnitude is no longer possible under new regulations of the Federal Communications Commission adopted May 5, 1972. The FCC regulations, 47 C.F.R. § 64.801–804 (1973), permit the granting of unsecured credit to political candidates but require termination of services if charges remain unpaid for 15 days and the debtor does not pay within 7 days after notice given "forthwith" upon expiration of the 15 day period. Common carriers are explicitly required to act to collect the unpaid balance prior to the running of the one year statute of limitations found in 47 U.S.C. § 415(a) (1970).

to Rule 15, Fed.R.Civ.P., and the district court will act upon any such motion within the discretion afforded under that rule.

The order of the district court will be reversed and the case remanded for further proceedings consistent with this opinion.

AMERICAN LAW INSTITUTE, PRINCIPLES OF CORPORATE GOVERNANCE §§ 4.01(a), Comment d, 7.16(c)

Tent. Draft No. 4, 1985, Tent. Draft No. 8, 1988.

[§ 4.01(a), Comment d.]

d.   The Relationship between § 4.01 and § 2.01.   Section 2.01 sets forth principles with respect to "The Objective and Conduct of the Business Corporation." *   Sections 3.01 and 3.02 call for officers and directors to act consistently with § 2.01.** . . .

The concept of profit maximization is . . . qualified by the provision in § 2.01(a) that obliges the corporation "to the same extent as a natural person, to act within the boundaries set by law." . . . [A] director or officer violates his duty to perform his functions in good faith if he knowingly causes his corporation to disobey the law. . . . In Abrams v. Allen, 297 N.Y. 52, 55–56, 74 N.E.2d 305, 306 (1947), for example, the Court of Appeals held that a derivative cause of action was stated by an allegation that directors were wrongfully attempting to intimidate and punish corporate employees, by causing the dismantling and removal of corporate plants and equipment, and that this constituted "using the corporation's property for the doing of an unlawful or immoral act." See Wilshire Oil Co. v. Riffle, 409 F.2d 1277, 1283–86 (10th Cir.1969) ("fiduciary duty" owed to the corporation by employees whose antitrust violations subjected the corporation to civil and criminal liability); DiTomasso v. Loverro, 250 A.D. 206, 209, 293 N.Y.S. 912, 916–17, aff'd mem., 276 N.Y. 551, 12 N.E.2d 570 (1937) (injunction granted and directors liable for damages, in derivative action, "where they knew, or should have known, the contract" was in restraint of trade).

. . . See Arsht, The Business Judgment Rule Revisited, 8 Hofstra L.Rev. 93, 129–30 (1979) ("Bad faith may preclude the application of the business judgment defense where directors knowingly violate a statute or comparable expression of public policy, even if such a violation is undertaken in the corporation's best interests").

§ 7.16.   Damages Resulting from a Breach of Duty: General Rules . . .

(c) A plaintiff bears the burden of proving causation and the amount of any losses incurred by the corporation or the shareholders

---

* Section 2.01 is set out in Chapter III, Section 5, supra.   ** Sections 3.01–3.02 are set out in Chapter IV, Section 3, supra.

as the result of a defendant's violation of [§ 4.01],[†] but a defendant is entitled to offset against such liability any gains to the corporation that the defendant can establish arose out of the same transaction. . . .

Comment. . . .

e. The "net loss" rule. Section 7.16(c) places the burden on the plaintiff to prove both causation and the amount of the loss, but allows the defendant to offset the damages if he can show a gain to the corporation arising out of the same transaction. This latter provision has special significance in cases involving an illegal act undertaken to benefit the corporation that resulted in a fine or other loss. . . .

[A] recurring problem in this area arises when a series of unlawful transactions is involved: for example, consider the case of five illegal loans, only one of which resulted in a loss. Here, the "same transaction" test in § 7.16(c) should deny the defendant the ability to mitigate his liability by offsetting gains on unrelated transactions. Only if the five loans were part of the "same transaction" can the gains on one be offset against the losses on the other.

† Section 4.01 is set out in Section 1, supra.

Chapter VIII

THE DUTY OF LOYALTY

SECTION 1. SELF–INTERESTED TRANSACTIONS

MARSH, ARE DIRECTORS TRUSTEES?—CONFLICTS OF INTEREST AND CORPORATE MORALITY
22 Bus.Law. 35, 36–43 (1966).

a. *Prohibition.*

In 1880 it could have been stated with confidence that in the United States the general rule was that any contract between a director and his corporation was voidable at the instance of the corporation or its shareholders, without regard to the fairness or unfairness of the transaction. This rule was stated in powerful terms by a number of highly regarded courts and judges in cases which arose generally out of the railroad frauds of the 1860's and 1870's.

In *Wardell v. Union Pacific R.R. Co.*[4] Mr. Justice Field stated that:

> It is among the rudiments of the law that the same person cannot act for himself and at the same time, with respect to the same matter, as agent for another, whose interests are conflicting. . . . The two positions impose different obligations, and their union would at once raise a conflict between interest and duty; and 'Constituted as humanity is, in the majority of cases duty would be overborne in the struggle.' . . . Hence, all arrangements by directors of a railroad company, to secure an undue advantage to themselves at its expense, by the formation of a new company as an auxiliary to the original one, with an understanding that they or some of them shall take stock in it, and then, that valuable contracts shall be given to it, in the profits of which they, as stockholders in the new company, are to share, are so many unlawful devices to enrich themselves to the detriment of the stockholders and creditors of the original company, and will be condemned whenever properly brought before the courts for consideration.[5]

Under this rule it mattered not the slightest that there was a majority of so-called disinterested directors who approved the contract. The courts stated that the corporation was entitled to the unprejudiced judgment and advice of all of its directors and therefore it did no good to say that the interested director did not participate in

---

4. 103 U.S. 651 (1880).   5. 103 U.S. at 658.

the making of the contract on behalf of the corporation. ". . . the very words in which he asserts his right declare his wrong; he ought to have participated. . . ."[6] Furthermore, the courts said that it was impossible to measure the influence which one director might have over his associates, even though ostensibly abstaining from participation in the discussion or vote. ". . . a corporation, in order to defeat a contract entered into by directors, in which one or more of them had a private interest, is not bound to show that the influence of the director or directors having the private interest determined the action of the board. The law cannot accurately measure the influence of a trustee with his associates, nor will it enter into the inquiry. . . ."[7]

Perhaps the strongest reason for this inflexibility of the law was given by the Maryland Supreme Court which stated that, when a contract is made with even one of the directors, "the remaining directors are placed in the embarrassing and invidious position of having to pass upon, scrutinize and check the transactions and accounts of one of their *own body, with* whom they are associated on terms of equality in the general management of all the affairs of the corporation."[8] Or, as Justice Davies of the New York Supreme Court expressed the same thought: "The moment the directors permit one or more of their number to deal with the property of the stockholders, they surrender their own independence and self control."[9]

This rule applied not only to individual contracts with directors, but also to the situation of interlocking directorates where even a minority of the boards were common to the two contracting corporations. Not only that, it was also applied to the situation where one corporation owned a majority of the stock of another and appointed its directors, even though they might not be the same men as sat on the board of the parent corporation. . . .

This principle, absolutely inhibiting contracts between a corporation and its directors or any of them, appeared to be impregnable in 1880. It was stated in ringing terms by virtually every decided case, with arguments which seemed irrefutable, and it was sanctioned by age. As Justice Davies stated:

> To hold otherwise, would be to overturn principles of equity which have been regarded as well settled since the days of Lord Keeper Bridgman, in the 22nd of Charles second, to the present time—principles enunciated and enforced by Hardwicke, Thurlow, Loughborough, Eldon, Cranworth, Story and Kent, and which the highest courts in our country have declared to be founded on immutable truth and justice, and to stand upon our

6. Stewart v. Lehigh Valley R. R. Co., 38 N.J.Law 505, at 523 (Ct. Err. & App. 1875).

7. Munson v. Syracuse, G. & C. Ry. Co., 103 N.Y. 58, at 74, 8 N.E. 355, at 358 (1886).

8. Cumberland Coal and Iron Co. v. Parish, 42 Md. 598, at 606 (1875).

9. Cumberland Coal and Iron Co. v. Sherman, 30 Barb. 553, at 573 (N.Y.Sup.Ct. 1859).

great moral obligation to refrain from placing ourselves in relations which excite a conflict between self interest and integrity.
Thirty years later this principle was dead.

b. *Approval by a disinterested majority of the board.*

It could have been stated with reasonable confidence in 1910 that
the general rule was that a contract between a director and his
corporation was valid if it was approved by a disinterested majority of
his fellow directors and was not found to be unfair or fraudulent by
the court if challenged; but that a contract in which a majority of the
board was interested was voidable at the instance of the corporation or
its shareholders without regard to any question of fairness.

One searches in vain in the decided cases for a reasoned defense
of this change in legal philosophy, or for the slightest attempt to refute
the powerful arguments which had been made in support of the
previous rule. Did the courts discover in the last quarter of the
Nineteenth Century that greed was no longer a factor in human
conduct? If so, they did not share the basis of this discovery with the
public; nor did they humbly admit their error when confronted with
the next wave of corporate frauds arising out of the era of the
formation of the "trusts" during the 1890's and early 1900's. . . .

The only explanation which seems to have been given for this
change in position was the technical one that a trustee, while forbidden to deal with himself in connection with the trust property, could
deal directly with the cestui que trust if he made full disclosure and
took no unfair advantage; and that the case of a director who
abstained from representing the corporation but dealt in his personal
capacity with a majority of disinterested directors was properly analo-
gized to a trustee dealing with the cestui que trust. As the Texas
court said: [19]

> . . . we think it is not true that one who holds the position
> of director is incapable, under all circumstances, of divesting
> himself of his representative character in a particular transaction,
> and dealing with the corporation through others competent to
> represent it, as other trustees may deal directly with the benefi-
> ciaries. . . . [T]he company is represented by those who
> alone can act for it, and, if they are disinterested, he can, we
> think, deal with them as any other trustee can deal with the cestui
> que trust, if he makes a full disclosure of all facts known to him
> about the subject, takes no advantage of his position, deals
> honestly and openly, and concludes a contract fair and beneficial
> to the company.

But in no case is there any discussion or attempted refutation of
the reasons previously given by the courts as to why it is impossible, in
such a situation, for any director to be disinterested. Some courts
seem simply to admit that the practice has grown too widespread for
them to cope with. In *South Side Trust Co. v. Washington Tin Plate Co.*

19. Tennison v. Patton, 95 Tex. 284, at
292–93, 67 S.W. 92, at 95 (1902).

the Supreme Court of Pennsylvania said:[20] "The interests of corporations are sometimes so interwoven that it is desirable to have joint representatives in their respective managements, and at any rate it is a not uncommon and [therefore?] not unlawful practice." . . .

Under the rule that a disinterested majority of the directors must approve a transaction with one of their number, the question arose whether this meant a disinterested quorum (i.e., normally a majority of the whole board) or merely a disinterested majority of a quorum, so that the interested director or directors could be counted to make up the quorum. Virtually all of the cases held that the interested director could not be counted for quorum purposes. As the California court said, the interested director for this purpose was "as much a stranger to the board as if he had never been elected a director. . . ."[28]

c. *Judicial review of the fairness of the transaction.*

By 1960 it could be said with some assurance that the general rule was that no transaction of a corporation with any or all of its directors was automatically voidable at the suit of a shareholder, whether there was a disinterested majority of the board or not; but that the courts would review such a contract and subject it to rigid and careful scrutiny, and would invalidate the contract if it was found to be unfair to the corporation. . . .

LEWIS v. S.L. & E., INC.

United States Court of Appeals, Second Circuit, 1980.
629 F.2d 764.

Before TIMBERS and KEARSE, Circuit Judges, and LASKER, District Judge.

KEARSE, Circuit Judge:

This case arises out of an intra-family dispute over the management of two closely-held affiliated corporations. Plaintiff Donald E. Lewis ("Donald"), a shareholder of S.L. & E., Inc. ("SLE"), appeals from judgments entered against him in the United States District Court for the Western District of New York, Harold P. Burke, *Judge,* after a bench trial of his derivative claim against directors of SLE, and of a claim asserted against him by the other corporation, Lewis General Tires, Inc. ("LGT"), which intervened in the suit. The defendants Alan E. Lewis ("Alan"), Leon E. Lewis, Jr. ("Leon, Jr."), and Richard E. Lewis ("Richard"), are the brothers of Donald; they were, at pertinent times herein, directors of SLE and officers, directors and shareholders of LGT. Donald charged that his brothers had wasted the assets of SLE by causing SLE to lease business premises to LGT from 1966 to 1972 at an unreasonably low rental. LGT was permitted to intervene in the action, and filed a complaint seeking

20. 252 Pa. 237 at 241, 97 A. 450 at 451 (1916).

28. Curtis v. Salmon River Hydraulic Gold-Mining & Dutch Co., . . . 10 Cal. at 349, 62 P. at 554.

specific performance of an agreement by Donald to sell his SLE stock to LGT in 1972. The district court held that Donald had failed to prove waste by the defendant directors, and entered judgment in their favor. The court also awarded attorneys' fees to the defendant directors and to SLE, and granted LGT specific performance of Donald's agreement to sell his SLE stock.

On appeal, Donald argues that the district court improperly allocated to him the burden of proving his claims of waste, and that since defendants failed to prove that the transactions in question were fair and reasonable, he was entitled to judgment. Donald also argues that the awards of attorneys' fees were improper. We agree with each of these contentions, and therefore reverse and remand.

I

For many years Leon Lewis, Sr., the father of Donald and the defendant directors, was the principal shareholder of SLE and LGT. LGT, formed in 1933, operated a tire dealership in Rochester, New York. SLE, formed in 1943, owned the land and complex of buildings at 260 East Avenue in Rochester. This property was SLE's only significant asset. Prior to 1956 LGT occupied SLE's premises without benefit of a lease; the rent paid was initially $200 per month, and had increased over the years to $800 per month by 1956, when additional parcels were added. On February 28, 1956, SLE granted LGT a 10–year lease on the newly expanded property ("the Property"), for a rent of $1200 per month, or $14,400 per year. Under the terms of the lease, SLE was responsible for payment of real estate taxes on the Property, while all other current expenses were to be borne by the tenant, LGT.[1]

In 1962, Leon Lewis, Sr., transferred his SLE stock, 90 shares in all, to his six children (defendants Richard, Alan and Leon, Jr., plaintiff Donald, and two daughters, Margaret and Carol), giving 15 shares to each.[2] At that time Richard, Alan and Leon, Jr., were already shareholders, officers and directors of LGT. Contemporaneously with their receipt of SLE stock, all six of the children entered into a "shareholders' agreement" with LGT, under which each child who was not a shareholder of LGT on June 1, 1972 would be required to sell his or her SLE shares to LGT, within 30 days of that date, at a price equal to the book value of the SLE stock as of June 1, 1972.[3]

LGT's lease on the SLE property expired on February 28, 1966. At that time the directors of SLE were Richard, Alan, Leon, Jr., Leon,

---

1. It appears that SLE was also responsible for payments due on a mortgage on the Property. In addition, LGT charged SLE for the costs of certain capital improvements, such as the major structural repairs to the principal building's facade, carried out in 1969.

2. SLE had 150 shares outstanding, and each child thus received a ten percent in-

terest. At the same time LGT purchased the remaining 60 outstanding shares from the elder Lewis's business partner, Henry Etsberger.

3. The agreement specified procedures by which the book value, and hence the price of the shares, would be determined.

Sr., and Henry Etsberger; these five were also the directors of LGT. In 1966 Alan owned 44% of LGT, Richard owned 30%, Leon, Jr., owned 19%, and Leon, Sr., owned 7%. From 1967 to 1972 Richard owned 61% of LGT and Leon, Jr., owned the remaining 39%. When the lease expired in 1966, no new lease was entered into. LGT nonetheless continued to occupy the property and to pay SLE at the old rate, $14,400 per year. According to the defendants' testimony at trial, there was never any thought or discussion among the SLE directors of entering into a new lease or of increasing the rent. Richard testified: "We never gave consideration to a new lease." From all that appears, the defendant directors viewed SLE as existing purely for the benefit of LGT. Richard testified, for example, that although real estate taxes rose sharply during the period 1966–1971, from approximately $7,800 to more than $11,000, to be paid by SLE out of its constant $14,400 rental income, raising the rent was never mentioned. He testified that SLE was "only a shell to protect the operating company [LGT]." When this suit was commenced there had not been a formal meeting of either the shareholders or the directors of SLE since 1962. Richard, Alan and Leon, Jr., had largely ignored SLE's separate corporate existence [4] and disregarded the fact that SLE had shareholders who were not shareholders of LGT and who therefore could not profit from actions that used SLE solely for the benefit of LGT.

Neither Donald nor his sisters ever owned LGT stock. As the June 1972 date approached for the required sale of their SLE stock to LGT, Donald apparently came to believe that SLE's book value was lower than it should have been. He sought SLE financial information from Richard, who had been president of SLE since 1967.[5] Richard refused to provide information. Donald therefore refused to sell his SLE shares in 1972,[6] and commenced this shareholders' derivative action in the district court in August 1973, basing jurisdiction on diversity of citizenship.[7] The sole claim raised in the complaint was that the defendant directors[8] had wasted the assets of SLE by "grossly

4. For example, Richard's testimony includes the following statements:

Q Mr. Lewis, you have always looked at these two corporations as being one and the same, haven't you, Lewis General Tires and S.L. & E.?

A Yes.

* * *

I never really got into S.L. & E. at all. (Tr. 6/21/78, at 972–73.)

* * *

I don't think I ever looked at an operating statement of S.L. & E. seriously. (Id. at 991.)

* * *

I had very little to do with S.L. & E. (Tr. 7/28/78, at 80.)

Alan testified that at no time after 1964 did he participate in any discussions of any increase in rent for SLE. (Id. at 160, 164.)

And Leon, Jr., testified, "I didn't have anything to do with running S.L. & E. . . . ." (Id. at 230.)

5. It does not appear that SLE paid salaries to any of its officers or directors.

6. Donald's sisters Carol and Margaret sold their SLE shares to LGT in 1972 and 1973 respectively. Alan, who had sold his LGT stock in 1967, sold his SLE stock to LGT in 1972.

7. When suit was commenced, plaintiff was a citizen of Ohio, Alan was a citizen of Florida and all of the other individual defendants were citizens of New York. SLE is a New York corporation and has its principal place of business in New York.

8. Leon E. Lewis, Sr., also was originally named as a defendant in this action. When he died in 1975 his executor was substituted as a defendant; subsequently the parties stipulated to dismissal of the

undercharging" LGT for the latter's occupancy and use of the Property. Although the complaint charged such mismanagement for the period 1962 to 1973, plaintiff subsequently limited this claim to the period between February 28, 1966, the date on which the lease expired,[9] and June 1, 1972, the date contractually set for valuation of the SLE shares which plaintiff had agreed to sell to LGT. LGT intervened and demanded specific performance of Donald's agreement to sell his SLE stock. Donald did not contest his ultimate obligation to sell, but took the position that since the book value of the shares would be increased if he prevailed on his derivative claim, specific performance should be granted only after adjudication of that claim.

There ensued an eight-day bench trial, at which plaintiff sought to prove, by the testimony of several expert witnesses, that the fair rental value of the Property was greater than the $14,400 per year that SLE had been paid by LGT. Defendants sought to show that the rental paid was reasonable, by offering evidence concerning the financial straits of LGT, the cost to LGT of operating the Property, the general economic decline of the East Avenue neighborhood, and rentals paid on two other properties in that neighborhood. LGT presented expert testimony that the value of plaintiff's stock as of June 1972, assuming a successful defense of the derivative claims, was $15,650.

The district court subsequently filed lengthy and detailed findings of fact and conclusions of law. Many of the court's findings went to the validity and probative value of the testimony given by plaintiff's expert witnesses, and the court ultimately declined to credit that testimony. On this basis, the court held that Donald had failed to establish the rental value of the Property during the period at issue, and that defendants were therefore entitled to judgment on the derivative claims. Implicit in the district court's ruling, granting judgment for defendants upon plaintiff's failure to prove waste, was a determination that plaintiff bore the burden of proof on that issue. The court also ruled that LGT was entitled to specific performance of Donald's agreement to sell his SLE stock, and that Donald was not entitled to recover attorneys' fees from SLE, but that SLE and the individual defendants were entitled to attorneys' fees from Donald. This appeal followed.

II

Turning first to the question of burden of proof, we conclude that the district court erred in placing upon plaintiff the burden of proving waste. Because the directors of SLE were also officers, directors and/or shareholders of LGT, the burden was on the defendant directors to demonstrate that the transactions between SLE and LGT were fair and reasonable. New York Business Corporation Law ("BCL") § 713(b)

executor. Etsberger died in about 1969, and his estate was not named as a defendant.

9. Donald was not a shareholder of SLE in 1956 when the lease was entered into

and hence had no standing to challenge its terms. BCL § 626(b); *Bernstein v. Polo Fashions, Inc.*, 55 A.D.2d 530, 389 N.Y.S.2d 368 (1st Dep't 1976).

(McKinney Supp.1979) (eff. September 1, 1971); BCL § 713(a)(3) (McKinney 1963) (repealed as of September 1, 1971); *see Cohen v. Ayers,* 596 F.2d 733, 739–40 (7th Cir.1979) (construing current BCL § 713); *Remillard Brick Co. v. Remillard–Dandini Co.,* 109 Cal.App.2d 405, 241 P.2d 66, 75 (1952) (construing California Corporations Code § 820, upon which the prior BCL § 713 was patterned).

Under normal circumstances the directors of a corporation may determine, in the exercise of their business judgment, what contracts the corporation will enter into and what consideration is adequate, without review of the merits of their decisions by the courts. The business judgment rule places a heavy burden on shareholders who would attack corporate transactions. *Galef v. Alexander,* 615 F.2d 51, 57–58 (2d Cir.1980); *Auerbach v. Bennett,* 47 N.Y.2d 619, 629, 419 N.Y.S.2d 920, 926, 393 N.E.2d 994, 1000 (1979); 3A Fletcher, *Cyclopedia of the Law of Private Corporations* § 1039 (perm. ed. 1975). But the business judgment rule presupposes that the directors have no conflict of interest. When a shareholder attacks a transaction in which the directors have an interest other than as directors of the corporation, the directors may not escape review of the merits of the transaction. At common law such a transaction was voidable unless shown by its proponent to be fair, and reasonable to the corporation.[11] BCL § 713, in both its current and its prior versions, carries forward this common law principle, and provides special rules for scrutiny of a transaction between the corporation and an entity in which its directors are directors or officers or have a substantial financial interest.

The current version of § 713,[12] which became effective on September 1, 1971, and governs at least so much of the dealing

11. *E.g., Geddes v. Anaconda Copper Co.,* 254 U.S. 590, 599 (1921); *Sage v. Culver,* 147 N.Y. 241, 41 N.E. 513 (1895); *Kaminsky v. Kahn,* 23 App.Div.2d 231, 240, 259 N.Y.S.2d 716, 725 (1st Dep't 1965); *Tomarkin v. Vitron Research Corp.,* 12 App.Div.2d 496, 206 N.Y.S.2d 869 (2d Dep't 1960). *See also* 3 Fletcher, *supra* § 921.

12. BCL § 713 (McKinney Supp.1979) provides in pertinent part:

(a) No contract or other transaction between a corporation and one or more of its directors, or between a corporation and any other corporation, firm, association or other entity in which one or more of its directors are directors or officers, or have a substantial financial interest, shall be either void or voidable for this reason alone or by reason alone that such director or directors are present at the meeting of the board, or of a committee thereof, which approves such contract or transaction, or that his or their votes are counted for such purpose:

(1) If the material facts as to such director's interest in such contract or transaction and as to any such common directorship, officership or financial interest are disclosed in good faith or

known to the board or committee, and the board or committee approves such contract or transaction by a vote sufficient for such purpose without counting the vote of such interested director or, if the votes of the disinterested directors are insufficient to constitute an act of the board as defined in section 708 (Action by the board), by unanimous vote of the disinterested directors; or

(2) If the material facts as to such director's interest in such contract or transaction and as to any such common directorship, officership or financial interest are disclosed in good faith or known to the shareholders entitled to vote thereon, and such contract or transaction is approved by vote of such shareholders.

(b) If such good faith disclosure of the material facts as to the director's interest in the contract or transaction and as to any such common directorship, officership or financial interest is made to the directors or shareholders, or known to the board or committee or shareholders approving such contract or transaction, as provided in paragraph (a), the contract or transaction may not be avoided

between SLE and LGT as occurred after that date, expressly provides that a contract between a corporation and an entity in which its directors are interested may be set aside unless the proponent of the contract "shall establish affirmatively that the contract or transaction was fair and reasonable as to the corporation at the time it was approved by the board. . . ." § 713(b). Thus when the transaction is challenged in a derivative action against the interested directors, they have the burden of proving that the transaction was fair and reasonable to the corporation. *Cohen v. Ayers, supra.*

The same was true under the predecessor to § 713(b), former § 713(a)(3), which was in effect prior to September 1, 1971.[13] Section 713(a)(3) was not explicit as to the burden of proof, but simply stated that a transaction with interested directors would not be voidable "If the contract or transaction is fair and reasonable as to the corporation at the time it is approved by the board. . . ." The consensus among the commentators was that § 713(a)(3) carried forward the common law rule, which placed the burden of proof as to fairness on the interested directors. *E.g.,* Hoffman, The Status of Shareholders and Directors Under New York's Business Corporation Law: A Comparative View, 11 Buff.L.Rev. 496, 566 (1962); Note, "Interested Director's" Contracts—Section 713 of the New York Business Corporation Law and the "Fairness" Test, 41 Fordham L.Rev. 639, 648–49 (1973); *see also* Note, The Status of the Fairness Test Under Section 713 of the New York Business Corporation Law, 76 Colum.L.Rev. 1156, 1167–74 (1976) (discussing legislative history). We agree with this construction. *Cf. Remillard Brick Co. v. Remillard–Dandini Co., supra* (burden of proof allocated to interested directors under California Corporations Code § 820, upon which § 713(a)(3) was modeled).

by the corporation for the reasons set forth in paragraph (a). If there was no such disclosure or knowledge, or if the vote of such interested director was necessary for the approval of such contract or transaction at a meeting of the board or committee at which it was approved, the corporation may avoid the contract or transaction unless the party or parties thereto shall establish affirmatively that the contract or transaction was fair and reasonable as to the corporation at the time it was approved by the board, a committee or the shareholders.

13. BCL § 713 (McKinney 1963) (repealed) provided in pertinent part:

(a) No contract or other transaction between a corporation and one or more of its directors, or between a corporation and any other corporation, firm, association or other entity in which one or more of its directors are directors or officers, or are financially interested, shall be either void or voidable for this reason alone or by reason alone that such direc-

tor or directors are present at the meeting of the board, or of a committee thereof, which approves such contract or transaction, or that his or their votes are counted for such purpose:

(1) If the fact of such common directorship, officership or financial interest is disclosed or known to the board or committee, and the board or committee approves such contract or transaction by a vote sufficient for such purpose without counting the vote or votes of such interested director or directors;

(2) If such common directorship, officership or financial interest is disclosed or known to the shareholders entitled to vote thereon, and such contract or transaction is approved by vote of the shareholders; or

(3) If the contract or transaction is fair and reasonable as to the corporation at the time it is approved by the board, a committee or the shareholders.

During the entire period 1966–1972, Richard, Alan and Leon, Jr., were directors of both SLE and LGT;[14] there were no SLE directors who were not also directors of LGT. Richard, Alan and Leon, Jr., were all shareholders of LGT in 1966, and from 1967 to 1972 Richard and Leon, Jr., were the sole shareholders of LGT. Under BCL § 713, therefore, Richard, Alan and Leon, Jr., had the burden of proving that $14,400 was a fair and reasonable annual rent for the SLE property for the period February 28, 1966 through June 1, 1972.

Our review of the record convinces us that defendants failed to carry their burden. At trial, there was no direct testimony as to what would have been a fair rental during the relevant period, i.e., 1966 to 1972, and the evidence that was introduced fell far short of establishing that $14,400 was a fair annual rental value for those years.

Quite clearly Richard, Alan and Leon, Jr., had made no effort to determine contemporaneously what rental would be fair during the years 1966–1972. Their view was that the rent should simply cover expenses and that SLE existed for the benefit of LGT.[15] During this period no appraisals were made; no attempts were made to sell or rent the Property; no thought whatever was given to whether $14,400 was a fair and reasonable rent even when real estate taxes had risen to consume nearly all of that amount.

Defendants offered instead evidence of rents paid on other properties. Among their best evidence was the expert testimony of Harvey Rosenbloom, a real estate appraiser. Rosenbloom testified that two other East Avenue buildings, which the district court found to be comparable to the 260 East Avenue premises, were leased at lower per-square-foot rentals than was paid by LGT to SLE. However, as to one of these properties, Rosenbloom testified only to rent paid in 1973 and 1974, and did not consider the 1966–1972 period. As to the other property, Rosenbloom described a fifteen year lease that was entered into in 1961. This testimony, while perhaps not wholly irrelevant to the issues in this suit, fell far short of demonstrating what rental the Property could have fetched in 1966, or in any other of the relevant years. Indeed, Rosenbloom himself testified that rental value could well be different for each year of the period. Thus, rentals that Rosenbloom testified were agreed to in 1961 or 1973 might well have been unfair in 1966 or 1967. This evidence thus could not support a finding that defendants acted fairly in maintaining an annual rental of $14,400 during the years from 1966 to 1972.[16]

14. Alan ceased to be a director in November 1972; Leon, Jr., ceased to be a director in 1977. Richard remains a director.

15. *See* footnote 4 *supra,* and accompanying text.

16. Defendant Richard E. Lewis testified that defendants tried, without success, to sell the Property in 1975, listing it with a realtor for $200,000. In addition he testified that an effort was made to rent the Property in 1973, and that only one offer, for $700 per month, was forthcoming. Since these efforts were made in 1973 and 1975, this evidence, like the evidence as to rentals of other property, was too remote in time to establish a fair rental value, especially as to the earlier years of the 1966–1972 period.

Defendants also produced considerable evidence that over the relevant period, the East End neighborhood had been on an economic decline; that businesses had been leaving the area; that urban renewal projects and increased crime had depressed property values there; and that the area had, in general, become a less desirable place to do business. There was also evidence of specific developments that had an adverse effect on the Property: for example, the street running along one side of the Property was made a one-way street, thus limiting customers' access to LGT's premises. The district court credited all of this testimony, and it is fair to say that defendants proved that there was a general downward trend in the value of the Property. However, as noted above, defendants did not establish what was a fair rental value for the Property in 1966. Absent such a point of reference, a general downward trend in value is of no assistance in determining whether the rental actually paid was fair and reasonable during the ensuing years.

Moreover, working in reverse, some of defendants' own evidence as to the value of the Property at the end of the relevant period suggested that $14,400 was less than a fair rental in 1966, and that the figure of $38,099, estimated by plaintiff's expert, was perhaps not far off the mark.[17] First, there was a variety of evidence suggesting that in 1972 the Property was worth more than $200,000. An appraisal by defense witness Harold Grunert in 1972 set the fair market value of the Property as of June 30, 1972, at $220,000. In 1972 Leon, Jr., had offered personally to buy the Property for $200,000, an offer which Richard had rejected.[18] And in 1971, Richard had informed Donald that evaluations by another appraiser, Harold Galloway, had set the value of the Property at $200,000 and $236,000. Second, defendants' expert witness Rosenbloom, asked what he would consider a fair rent for the property, given Grunert's 1972 valuation of $220,000, stated that ten percent of the value would be inadequate and that fifteen to seventeen percent would be closer to adequate. Fifteen percent of $220,000 would have yielded a rent of $33,000 on the basis of the 1972 valuation. Grunert's own expert testimony was entirely consistent with this. While he had made no estimate as to the fair rental value of the property for 1966–1972, he opined that a fair rental as of June 30, 1972, would be $20–21,000 with the tenant paying all expenses including real estate taxes. According to Richard, SLE's real estate taxes in 1972 were about $12,000. Thus Grunert's testimony, too, suggests about $33,000 as the fair rental value in 1972. Finally, consistent with their view of the general downward economic trend, Richard and Alan conceded that, whatever the Property was worth in 1972, it was worth more in 1966.[19] Thus the evidence presented by defendants, far from carrying their burden of showing that $14,400 was a fair and reasonable annual rental in

17. Plaintiff's expert made his evaluation as of February 1973. He did not make any evaluation for the period 1966–1972.

18. Leon, Jr., had just been fired from LGT by Richard.

19. Leon, Jr., did not know whether value had decreased from 1966 to 1972, but did not believe it had risen.

1966–1972, suggested that the fair rental value of the Property throughout that period exceeded $33,000 per year.

The defendants argued, however, that LGT could not have afforded to pay SLE rent higher than $14,400. They produced evidence designed to show that LGT had made little profit; that this low profitability was due to the expenses of maintenance and upkeep of the 260 East Avenue property; and that LGT therefore would not have been able to pay a higher rent to SLE. The district court credited this evidence, finding that LGT had "experienced a number of years of very severe losses," that during the period from 1962–1973, LGT's overall profit was only $53,876, and that payment of rent at the rate of $39,099 per year during this period could have led to the "demise" of LGT. These findings have only a distorted relationship to this lawsuit.

The period in issue here is 1966–1972. The only "severe" losses shown, totaling nearly $83,000, occurred in 1963 and 1973. Their inclusion in the computation of what LGT could afford to pay in 1966–1972 was patently unfair. In fact LGT's only unprofitable year during the period in issue was 1969 when its loss was small: $1,168. LGT's after-tax profits in 1966–1972 in fact totaled $102,963, or an average of $14,709 per year. Thus, even on paper, LGT could have "afforded" to double its rent payments to SLE during the period in question.

Moreover, the proposition that LGT could not afford to pay as rent more than what its own books showed as profits ignores the fact that LGT was owned and managed by members of the Lewis family, some of whom were also employees of that corporation. It is entirely possible that these family members granted to themselves unusually high salaries or other perquisites, thus reducing LGT's paper profits. For example, in 1966 Richard's salary was approximately $21,000; Leon, Jr.'s compensation was $3,000 salary plus commissions. In 1967, LGT acquired all of Alan's LGT stock; and Richard and Leon, Jr., acquired all of the LGT stock of their father, agreeing to pay the purchase price over a ten-year period. Richard and Leon, Jr., thus became LGT's only shareholders, and their LGT salaries were immediately increased by a total of $23,000 per year (Richard's salary went from $21,000 to $36,000; Leon, Jr.'s went from $3,000 to $11,000), to cover the cost of the LGT stock they had just acquired.[20] Defendants bore the burden of proof on the question of a fair and reasonable rental; if they would rely on the proposition that LGT was unable to pay more, it was incumbent on them to demonstrate the fairness of the management and the reasonableness of the conduct of LGT's affairs. It does not appear that they made any effort to do so.

Finally, even if we were to assume that LGT's financial records provided a fair basis for evaluating the SLE–LGT transactions, defendants would not have carried their burden of proof. Defendants did

20. Richard had no doubt he could have paid for his newly acquired shares without the increase in his LGT salary. Leon, Jr., apparently lacked other resources from which to pay for the LGT stock (at least after he was fired from LGT in 1972).

not demonstrate that SLE could not have found some other tenant, stronger financially than LGT, which would have been willing and able to pay a higher rental. Even given the general downward trend of the East Avenue neighborhood, it is entirely possible that at least during the early years of the 1966–1972 period, such a tenant might have been secured. No effort was made during that period to rent to anyone other than LGT.

We conclude, therefore, that defendants failed to prove that the rental paid by LGT to SLE for the years 1966–1972 was fair and reasonable. Thus, Donald is not required to sell his SLE shares to LGT without such upward adjustment in the June 1, 1972, book value of SLE as may be necessary to reflect the amount by which the fair rental value of the Property exceeded $14,400 in any of the years 1966–1972. . . .

* * *

We remand to the district court (a) for the entry of judgment in favor of SLE against Richard, Alan and Leon, Jr., jointly and severally, in such amount as the district court shall determine to be equal to the amounts by which the annual fair rental value of the Property exceeded $14,400 in the period February 28, 1966–June 1, 1972, (b) for an accounting as to the value of Donald's SLE shares as of June 1, 1972, in light of such judgment, (c) for an order, following such accounting, of specific performance of the shareholders' agreement, and (d) for such other proceedings as are not inconsistent with this opinion.

ANDERSON, CONFLICTS OF INTEREST: EFFICIENCY, FAIRNESS AND CORPORATE STRUCTURE

25 U.C.L.A.L.Rev. 738, 759–61 (1975).

In most contractual exchanges, each party knows what his own best interests are. In a fiduciary relationship, the client or beneficiary depends on the fiduciary to an unusual degree to determine for the client what his best interests are. Given this disparity of expertise, it would be extremely difficult and costly for the client to draft a detailed contract defining the duties of the fiduciary. . . .

Fiduciary duties economize on transaction costs by simply obliging the fiduciary to act in the best interests of his client or beneficiary and to refrain from self-interested behavior not specifically allowed by the employment contract. They codify the reasonable expectations of the client, by obliging the fiduciary to do what the client would tell him to do if the client had the same expertise as the fiduciary. They are thus more efficient than detailed contracts or detailed regulation since they restrict the fiduciary's opportunity to cheat without the costly drafting of elaborate rules while leaving him free to use his special skills in the client's interest.

As in the case of contract and warranty law, fiduciary duties are waivable when they perform only an efficiency function. Where bargaining power is roughly equal, specific fiduciary duties can be waived by the parties on the basis of full disclosure to and consent by the client. Because informational disparities so often mean that bargaining power is unequal, however, all fiduciaries have an unwaivable obligation of fairness toward the other party. Moreover, when fiduciary duties are waived, the waiver may be closely scrutinized to make sure it is valid. The ease with which fiduciary duties can be waived will be a function of the likelihood of unfairness; the greater the inequality in bargaining power, the greater the difficulty of waiver.

Fiduciary duties alone are not an adequate safeguard of fairness, since violations of fiduciary duty are frequently very difficult to detect. Special conflict of interest rules therefore apply to fiduciaries in situations in which the likelihood of cheating is regarded as particularly great. All such special rules are designed to protect the process of fiduciary decisionmaking from being affected by self-interest, since it is so difficult to detect the impact of self-interest by evaluating the decision itself.

———

EASTERBROOK & FISCHEL, CORPORATE CONTROL TRANSACTIONS

91 Yale L.J. 698, 700–03 (1982).

Corporate directors and other managers are said to be fiduciaries, who must behave in certain upright ways toward the beneficiaries of fiduciary duties. Yet, as Justice Frankfurter put it, "to say that a man is a fiduciary only begins analysis; it gives direction to further inquiry. To whom is he a fiduciary? What obligations does he owe as a fiduciary?" In this section we provide a framework for analyzing the meaning and scope of the duty owed by corporate managers.

Fiduciary principles govern agency relationships. An agency relationship is an agreement in which one or more persons (the principal) delegates authority to another person (the agent) to perform some service on the principal's behalf. The entire corporate structure is a web of agency relationships. Investors delegate authority to directors, who subdelegate to upper managers, and so on. Delegation of authority enables skilled managers to run enterprises even though they lack personal wealth, and it enables wealthy people to invest even though they lack managerial skills. It reduces the risks that investors must incur, because it enables them to spread investments among many enterprises. Delegation also helps managers to pool enough capital to take advantage of available economies of scale in production, to reduce the costs of bargaining and contracting, and to obtain the benefits of productive information that must be used in secret or not at all.

Delegation—including the "separation of ownership and control"—exists because both principal and agent share in the benefits of agency relationships. Nonetheless, the interests of agents may diverge from the interests of principals after the delegation has occurred. Directors and other managers often hold only a small stake in the firm and thus capture only a small part of the gains from their efforts; correspondingly, they suffer through the stock market only a small part of the losses they create. The smaller the managers' share in the enterprise, the more the managers' interest diverge from the interests of the principals. This phenomenon exists in any agency relationship. For example, a real estate agent on a five percent commission will not undertake even $10 worth of effort to improve the realized price by $100, because the agent reaps only $5 of this sum. The $10 effort, however, would be highly advantageous to the principal.

This divergence of interests between principals and agents may be controlled by the operation of the employment market. An unfaithful or indolent agent may be penalized by a lower salary, and a diligent agent may be rewarded by a bonus for good performance. In addition, the threat of sales of corporate control induces managers to perform well in order to keep their positions. Finally, competition in product markets helps to control agents' conduct, because a poorly-managed firm cannot survive in competition with a well-managed firm (other things being equal).

Although these market mechanisms automatically reduce the divergence of interests between agents and principals, they do not eliminate the costs of the agency relationship. They do not work without extensive, and costly, monitoring, so that principals and others know how well the agents perform. And the mechanisms may be inadequate to deal with one-time defalcations, when the agent concludes that the opportunities of the moment exceed any subsequent penalties in the employment market.

Investors might try to deal with these problems by hiring full-time monitors to look over the shoulders of managers, but this is costly and does not deal with the question, "Who monitors the monitors?" Full-time monitors become managers themselves, in all but name, and monitors who do not work full time lack both the incentive to watch carefully and the information to determine how well others are performing their tasks.

The fiduciary principle is an alternative to direct monitoring. It replaces prior supervision with deterrence, much as the criminal law uses penalties for bank robbery rather than pat-down searches of everyone entering banks. Acting as a standard-form penalty clause in every agency contract, the elastic contours of the fiduciary principle reflect the difficulty that contracting parties have in anticipating when and how their interests may diverge.

Socially optimal fiduciary rules approximate the bargain that investors and agents would strike if they were able to dicker at no cost. Such rules preserve the gains resulting from the delegation of authority and the division of labor while limiting the ability of agents to further their own interests at the expense of investors. The existence of such "off-the-rack" rules reduces the costs of transacting and of enforcing restrictions on the agent's powers. It also reduces the risk that managers will manipulate the articles of incorporation to their advantage once they assume control.

Fiduciary principles contain anti-theft directives, constraints on conflict of interest, and other restrictions on the ability of managers to line their own pockets at the expense of shareholders. But these principles have limits that reflect the distinction between managerial practices that harm investors' interests and practices that simultaneously benefit managers and investors. For example, managers of a corporation are free to funnel business to another corporation in which they have an interest if the transaction is approved by disinterested directors or is "fair" (advantageous) to the firm.

Because the fiduciary principle is fundamentally a standard term in a contract to which investors are parties, it makes little sense to say that managers may, consistent with the fiduciary principle, sacrifice the interests of investors to other ends, so long as investors are not hurt "too much." Presumably "too much" in this context means "by so much that investors start contracting around the rule." Such re-contracting may be exceedingly costly, however, because once a firm has been established shareholders have no practical way of revising the articles on their own to overcome intervening legal surprises. To use the fiduciary principle for any purpose other than maximizing the welfare of investors subverts its function by turning the high costs of direct monitoring—the reason fiduciary principles are needed—into a shield that prevents investors from controlling their agents' conduct.

NOTE ON REMEDIES FOR VIOLATION OF THE DUTY OF LOYALTY

The traditional remedies for violation of the duty of loyalty are restitutionary in nature. For example, if a director has engaged in improper self-dealing with the corporation, normally the remedy is rescission—or, if rescission is not feasible, an accounting for the difference between the contract price and a fair price. Similarly, if an officer has improperly appropriated a corporate opportunity (see Section 4, infra), normally the remedy is to impose a constructive trust in the corporation's favor, conditioned on reimbursement by the corporation of the officer's outlay in acquiring the opportunity.

The result of this restitutionary theory of remedies is that as a practical matter, the legal sanctions for violation of the duty of loyalty are much less severe than the legal sanctions for violation of the duty of care. If D, a director or officer, violates his duty of care, he must pay damages although he made no gain from his wrongful action. This leaves D much worse off than he was before the wrong. In contrast, if D violates his duty of fair dealing, under a restitutionary remedy he need only return a gain to which he was not entitled in the first place. This simply places D where he was before the wrong.

Indeed, putting aside important nonlegal remedies such as discharge and negative publicity, if D is totally immoral, he would conclude that under a strictly restitutionary regime it normally paid to engage in a course of wrongful self-interested transactions. Some of the transactions may remain undiscovered. Where D's wrongdoing is discovered, he will only be required to surrender his wrongful gains. Where D's wrongdoing is not discovered, he will retain his wrongful gains. If D engages in enough transactions, he will come out ahead.

In some cases, however, the remedies for violation of the duty of loyalty may make the director or officer worse off than he was before the wrong. For example:

(i) Where the director or officer sells property to the corporation at an unfairly high price, and the value of the property later drops below its fair value at the time of the transaction, rescission may leave him worse off than if he had sold the property to a third party. For example, suppose that in 1985, D sells property to his corporation, without full disclosure, at $110,000, when it had a fair value of $100,000. In 1986, the corporation discovers the wrong and rescinds. Meanwhile, the market has fallen and the property is only worth $70,000. If D had sold the property to a third party to whom he owed no duty of disclosure, the third party would (let us assume) not be able to rescind. Thus D is $30,000 worse off than if he had not engaged in wrongful self-dealing. A comparable result may obtain where D buys property from the corporation, the market rises, and the corporation rescinds.

(ii) A director or officer who violates the duty of fair dealing may be required to repay the corporation any salary he earned during the relevant period in addition to making restitution of his wrongful gain. This remedy was granted, for example, in American Timber & Trading Co. v. Niedermeyer, 276 Or. 1135, 558 P.2d 1211 (1976), a case in which the fiduciary had depleted the corporation's assets by a series of unfair deals. The court there said:

> The remedy of restoration of compensation is an equitable principle and its applicability is dependent upon the individual facts of each case. *See, e.g., Lawson v. Baltimore Paint & Chem. Corp.,* 347 F Supp 967 (D Md 1972); *Lydia E. Pinkham Med. Co. v. Gove,* 303 Mass 1, 20 NE2d 482 (1939); 5 Fletcher, supra § 2145 at 635 (rev ed 1967). The general rule, however, is that a corporate officer who engages in activities which constitute either a breach of his duty of loyalty or a wilful breach of his contract of employment is not entitled to any compensation for services rendered during that period of time even though part of those services may have been properly performed. . . .

Id. at 1155–56, 558 P.2d 1223.

(iii) Courts have sometimes awarded punitive damages against directors or officers who have breached their duty of loyalty. See, e.g., Rowen v. Le Mars Mutual Insurance Co. of Iowa, 282 N.W.2d 639, 662 (Iowa 1979).

(iv) ALI, Principles of Corporate Governance § 7.16(d) (Tent. Draft No. 6, 1986) provides that a director or officer who violates the duty of fair dealing should normally be required to pay the counsel fees and other expenses incurred by the corporation in establishing the violation:

> (d) The losses legally caused by a knowing violation of [the duty of loyalty] . . . include the costs and expense to which the corporation was subjected as a result of the violation, including the counsel fees and expenses of a successful plaintiff in a derivative action, except to the extent the court determines that inclusion of some or all of such costs and expenses would be inequitable under the circumstances.

(v) The categories described in (i)—(iv) are illustrative, not exhaustive. In considering the remaining cases in this Chapter, you should be alert to remedies in general, and in particular to whether the remedy granted in a given case is more than restitutionary.

TALBOT v. JAMES
Supreme Court of South Carolina, 1972.
259 S.C. 73, 190 S.E.2d 759.

MOSS, Chief Justice:

This equitable action was brought by C.N. Talbot and Lula E. Talbot, appellants herein, against W.A. James, individually, and as President of Chicora Apartments, Inc., and Chicora Apartments, Inc., respondents herein, for an accounting. In the complaint it is alleged that W.A. James, as an officer and director of the Corporation, violated his fiduciary relationship to the Corporation and the appellants as stockholders thereof, by diverting specific funds to himself. *Complaint*

The respondents, by answer, denied the allegations of the complaint and alleged that W.A. James had received no funds from the Corporation except for the sums paid for the erection of Chicora Apartments, pursuant to a contract between Chicora Apartments, Inc., and the said W.A. James. *Answer*

The case was referred to the Master in Equity for Horry County, who after taking the testimony, filed a report in which he found that W.A. James was not entitled to general overhead expense and profits *P.C,* arising out of the construction contract with Chicora Apartments, Inc., and recommended judgment in favor of Chicora Apartments, Inc., against him in the amount of $25,025.31.

The respondents timely appealed from the recommendations contained in the Report of the Master. The appeal was heard by the Honorable Dan F. Laney, Jr., presiding judge, and he issued his order reversing the findings of the Master and ordered judgment in favor of the respondents. This appeal followed.

1. This being an equity case and the Master and the Circuit Judge having disagreed and made contrary findings on the material issues in the case, this Court has jurisdiction to consider the evidence and make findings in accordance with our view of the preponderance or greater weight of the evidence. *Gantt v. Van Der Hoek*, 251 S.C. 307, 162 S.E. (2d) 267.

Lula E. Talbot owned a tract of land fronting on U.S. Highway 17, in Myrtle Beach, South Carolina. The title thereto was conveyed to her by her husband, C.N. Talbot. The appellants were approached by W.A. James with a proposal that the tract of land be used for the erection thereon of an apartment complex. After preliminary talks and negotiations, the parties on January 12, 1963, entered into a written agreement thereabout. Basically, the parties agreed to form a Corporation to construct and operate an apartment complex. Lula E. Talbot was to convey to said Corporation the tract of land owned by her and W.A. James agreed, as set forth in paragraph 5, of said contract,

"To promote the project aforementioned and shall be responsible for the planning, architectural work, construction, landscaping, legal fees, and loan processing of the entire project, same to contain at least fifty (50) one, two and three room air conditioned apartments for customer as approved by FHA appraisers."

It was further agreed that upon the formation of the Corporation that the appellants were to receive 50% of the stock of the Corporation in consideration for their transfer of the land to it. This was to be the absolute limit of the contribution of the appellants. W.A. James was to receive 50% of the stock of the Corporation in consideration of his efforts on its behalf.

It appears, that after the aforementioned contract was entered into, that W.A. James obtained the services of an architectural firm on a contingency basis and preliminary plans and sketches of the proposed apartment complex were made by such firm. James was also successful in obtaining commitments from the Federal Housing Administration and from an acceptable mortgagee with regard to financing. These commitments having been obtained, a corporation was formed to be known as Chicora Apartments, Inc., and a charter was duly issued by the Secretary of State on November 5, 1963.

Pursuant to the terms of the agreement dated January 12, 1963, 20 shares of no par value capital stock were issued, with W.A. James receiving 10 shares, C.N. Talbot one share and Lula E. Talbot 9 shares. At an organizational meeting of the corporation W.A. James was elected president, his wife, B.N. James, was elected secretary, C.N. Talbot was elected vice president, and Lula E. Talbot was elected treasurer. W.A. James and C.N. Talbot were elected as directors of the Corporation.

At a meeting of the Board of Directors held on November 5, 1963, a resolution was adopted accepting the offer of Lula E. Talbot to transfer the tract of land in question to Chicora Apartments, Inc., in exchange for 10 shares of the no par value capital stock thereof. In the said resolution, it was declared that the said property, to be so transferred, was of a value of $44,000.00. At the same meeting, a resolution was adopted accepting the offer of W.A. James to transfer to Chicora Apartments, Inc., in exchange for 10 shares of the no par value stock thereof, at a valuation of $44,000.00 the following:

"1. FHA Commitment issued pursuant to Title 2, Section 207 of the National Housing Act, whereby the FHA agrees to insure a mortgage loan in the amount of $850,700.00, on a parcel of land in Myrtle Beach, South Carolina, more particularly described in Schedule 'A' hereto attached, provided 66 apartment units are constructed thereon in accordance with plans and specifications as prepared by Lyles, Bissett, Carlisle & Wolff, Architects–Engineers, of Columbia, South Carolina.

"2. Commitment from United Mortgagee Servicing Corp. agreeing to make a mortgage loan on said property in the amount of $850,700.00 and also commitment from said mortgagee to make an interim construction loan in an identical amount.

"3. Certain contracts and agreements which W.A. James over the past two years have worked out and developed in connection with the architectural and construction services required for said project.

"4. The use of the finances and credit of W.A. James during the past two years (and including the construction period) in order to make it possible to proceed with the project."

The day following the election of the officers and the issuance of the capital stock, the Board of Directors of Chicora Apartments, Inc., met in Columbia, South Carolina, and passed a resolution authorizing the Corporation to borrow from United Mortgagee Servicing Corporation of Norfolk, Virginia, the sum of $850,700.00, upon the terms stated, said loan to be insured with the Federal Housing Administration. It was further resolved:

"That the President of the corporation, W.A. James, be authorized, empowered and directed to make, execute and deliver such documents and instruments as are required by the F.H.A. and the lender, in order to close the loan transaction; said documents including but not limited to, note, mortgage, Building Loan Agreement, Construction Contract, Architect's Agreement, Mortgagor's Certificate, Regulatory Agreement, Mortgagor's Oath and Agreement and Certificate."

The record shows that on November 6, 1963, James Construction Company entered into a construction contract with Chicora Apartments, Inc. This contract was executed by W.A. James, as president, and attested by B.N. James, secretary, on behalf of Chicora Apartments, Inc., and by W.A. James, sole proprietor, for James Construction Company. The contract sum was to be the actual cost of construction plus a fee equal to $20,000.00 but in no event was the contract price, including the fee, to exceed $736,000.00. Attached to the contract was a "Trade Payment Breakdown" which made an allowance for overhead expenses in the amount of $31,589.00, but, this said sum was to be paid by means other than cash. The aforementioned loan was obtained and the apartment complex was constructed. All funds from the mortgage loan were received and disbursed by W.A. James and the renting of the apartments was begun, such being conducted by a resident manager, who was an employee of the Corporation.

It appears, that in 1968, an accountant, who was employed by the corporation, advised James and C.N. Talbot that it was in financial straits. It was at this time that the appellants questioned the disbursement of the mortgage funds by W.A. James. Their demands to examine the corporate records were refused by James. Thereafter, an order was obtained from the Honorable James B. Morrison, Resident Judge of the Fifteenth Judicial Circuit, making available the corporate records to the appellants. This action was thereafter instituted.

The record in this case clearly shows that W.A. James personally received or there was paid for his benefit the sum of $25,025.31 from the proceeds of the mortgage loan. He received this directly or by payments of his own personal debts by the corporation. He contends that he was entitled to these funds and more under the construction contract which he had with Chicora Apartments, Inc. This raises the question of whether James, who was a stockholder, officer, and director of Chicora Apartments, Inc., could enter into a contract with himself as an individual and made a profit therefrom for himself.

The Master found that Chicora Apartments, Inc., through W.A. James as president thereof, entered into a contract with himself, as sole proprietor of James Construction Company, without disclosing his identity of interest to the other officers or stockholders of the corporation, and that such contract has not been acquiesced in or ratified by the other director, officers or stockholders. He further found that the initial agreement between the parties required W.A. James to perform the same duties that he later contracted with the corporation to perform and for which he now seeks to justify the payment to him from the mortgage funds of the corporation. It was also found that according to the initial agreement these services were to be performed and, in consideration of such performance, James was to receive one-half of the shares of the capital stock of Chicora Apartments, Inc. The trial judge, upon exceptions to the Master's Report, made contrary findings of fact and reversed the Master and entered judgment in favor of the respondents.

The first question for determination is whether the fiduciary relationship existing between W.A. James as a stockholder, officer and director of Chicora Apartments, Inc., prevented him from contracting with the said corporation for his profit without first having disclosed the terms of the contract to the disinterested officers and directors of the corporation.

2. The officers and directors of the corporation stand in a fiduciary relationship to the individual stockholders and in every instance must make a full disclosure of all relevant facts when entering into a contract with said corporation. *Jacobson v. Yaschik*, 249 S.C. 577, 155 S.E. (2d) 601. The object of this rule is to prevent

directors from secretly using their fiduciary positions to their own advantage and to the detriment of the corporation and of the stockholders.

3. The cases of *Peurifoy v. Loyal,* 154 S.C. 267, 151 S.E. 579, and *Fidelity Fire Ins. Co. v. Harby,* 156 S.C. 238, 153 S.E. 141, firmly establish the ineligibility of a director to participate in corporate action with respect to a transaction in which he has an interest adverse to the corporation. He may not even be counted to make a quorum at a meeting where the matter is acted upon, which is the general rule.

The case of *Gilbert v. McLeod Infirmary,* 219 S.C. 174, 64 S.E. (2d) 524, contains a good statement of the law relating to personal dealings of an officer or director with his corporation or its property. We quote the following from this case:

"From the extensive review of the authorities there is extracted the rule that when a director, in selling corporate property to himself, represents or joins in the representation of the corporation, the transaction is voidable at the option of the corporation, or others suing in its behalf, merely upon proof of the fact stated; but when the purchasing director abstains from participation in behalf of the corporation and it is properly represented by others who are personally disinterested, the transaction will stand under attack if the director made full disclosure, paid full value, and the corporation has not been imposed upon; and the burden is upon the director to establish these requisites by evidence."

We quote again from the *Gilbert* case the following:

"A director or officer of a corporation is not absolutely precluded by his official position from dealing or entering into a contract with the corporation, nor is such a transaction void *per se.* While it is true, on the one hand, that where the directors or officers of a corporation deal with themselves as individuals, the transactions are subject to the closest scrutiny, under the most searching light of truth, and must be characterized by absolute good faith, it is also true, on the other hand, that where persons holding positions of trust and confidence in a corporation deal with the corporation, which is also represented by others, in entire good faith, fairness, and honesty, such transactions are not invalid and will be upheld. It would also seem that the mere fact that a director with whom the contract was made voted at the directors' meeting authorizing the same would not necessarily invalidate the contract, where the disinterested directors, who themselves constituted a quorum, were unanimous in the action." 13 Am.Jur. 958, sec. 1005.

4. We point out that in the *Gilbert* case a director of a corporation was purchasing from it corporate property. The rationale of the rule stated in *Gilbert* is applicable to the situation where a director is entering into a contract individually with the corporation.

We examined the evidence in this case in the light of the foregoing rules. The testimony of C.N. Talbot is that he discussed with James as to who was going to construct the Chicora Apartments and was told that Dargan Construction Company was going to take the

contract. He further testified that during the period of construction
he saw Dargan Construction Company signs on the premises and also
trucks bearing its name. This witness further testified that James
never discussed with him or his wife the matter of his constructing the
apartments. Talbot denied that he knew that James was to be the
contractor.

James testified that he explained to C.N. Talbot that the only
possible way that the apartments could be built without putting in
money was that he be the building contractor. James further testified
that the only way the project could survive and the only way that
"we" could get the builder's equity was that he should be the builder.
He says that everybody understood that because his attorney had
explained it at a meeting of the directors.

5, 6. Assuming that James revealed to Talbot that he was to be
the building contractor for the Chicora Apartments complex, his
testimony does not show that he disclosed his entitlement to a fee of
$20,000.00 and an allowance for overhead expenses in the amount of
$31,589.00. It is thus apparent that he did not make a full disclosure
of the profits or monetary benefits that he was to receive under the
terms of the contract. It was his duty to make such full disclosure and
the burden of proof was upon him to show that such had been done.

We have carefully examined the minutes of the several meetings
of the stockholders and directors of the corporation. We find from
such examination that they reflect each and every detail and transaction looking toward the construction of the apartment complex but
nowhere in said minutes is there any mention that James was to be the
building contractor. The minutes reflect that there was a meeting of
the directors of the corporation on November 6, 1963, and a resolution adopted at such meeting authorizing the borrowing of the sum of
$850,700.00 from the United Mortgagee Servicing Corporation, and
authorizing James, as president, to make, execute and deliver such
documents and instruments as were required by the FHA and the
lender. If James was to be the building contractor and such was
discussed at this meeting, as he contends, the minutes should have
reflected such, particularly in view of the fact that the building
contract was being awarded to him when he was a director and
president of the corporation. There is no explanation of why such a
resolution or authorization was not considered or passed at this
meeting of the Board of Directors.

7. The record shows that the appellants were stockholders and
officers of the corporation. As such, they were entitled to inspect the
books of the corporation at any and all times. Section 12–263 of the
Code. When they demanded their right to exercise this privilege,
such was refused by James and they only obtained the right to inspect
the records and books of the corporation by an order of the court.
James' only explanation was that the Talbots were not entitled to see
the books. It is inferable from this action on the part of James that he
did not want the appellants to discover how the funds of the corpora-

tion had been disbursed and see that he had received benefit in such disbursement.

8. It appears that at the meeting of the directors of the corporation held on November 6, 1963, W.A. James, as president, was authorized to execute and deliver several documents including a "construction contract." The respondents argue that this gave W.A. James the authority to make the construction contract here involved. It is true that he was authorized to sign a "construction contract" on behalf of the corporation but such resolution did not authorize him to sign one on behalf of the corporation in favor of himself individually.

9. The respondents contend and place great emphasis on the fact that the construction contract was approved by the Federal Housing Administration and the fees provided therein were allowed by it. This has no relevancy to the issue here.

10. Considering the entire record in this case, it is our conclusion that W.A. James, as president of Chicora Apartments, Inc., entered into a contract with himself as sole proprietor of James Construction Company without making full disclosure of his identity of interest to the other officers and stockholders of the corporation. In this conclusion, we agree with the findings of the Master. It follows that the Chicora Apartments, Inc., is entitled to judgment against the said W.A. James in the amount of $25,025.31, this being the amount of the corporate funds received by or paid in behalf of W.A. James.

Holding

The Master found that under the language in paragraph 5 of the pre-incorporation agreement, hereinbefore quoted, that W.A. James was to be responsible for overseeing, supervising and generally managing all aspects of the construction of the apartment complex. He found that W.A. James, as sole proprietor of James Construction Company, performed the contract obligations and for such he received one-half of the shares of the capital stock of Chicora Apartments, Inc. The trial judge reversed this finding of the Master. The appellants allege error.

11. James testified that he was the general contractor for the construction of the apartment complex. He testified further that the apartment complex was constructed by some eighteen to twenty subcontractors with whom he negotiated contracts. The record reveals that the only service that James rendered in connection with the construction of the apartment complex was supervisory. These duties were those contemplated by the pre-incorporation agreement of the parties. He was compensated for these services when he received one-half of the capital stock in the corporation. He was not entitled to any other compensation for the services rendered. We think the trial judge was in error in not so holding.

not entitled to extra compensat

The order of the trial judge is reversed and this case remanded to the Court of Common Pleas for Horry County for an appropriate order to effectuate the views herein expressed.

Reversed and remanded.

LEWIS and LITTLEJOHN, JJ., concur.

BUSSEY and BRAILSFORD, JJ., dissent.

BUSSEY, Justice (dissenting):

While admittedly there is some evidence tending to support the findings of fact by the master, adopted in the majority opinion, I have concluded after considerable study of the record and exhibits that the clear weight of the evidence preponderates in favor of the findings of fact by the circuit judge rather than those of the master. Being of this view, I am compelled to dissent.

The apartment complex was completed in July 1964, whereupon the plaintiff, C.N. Talbot, with the help of a resident manager, selected by him but approved by James, took charge of the management and operation of the apartment complex, all receipts being deposited by Talbot and all checks being written by Talbot. In 1968, after Talbot and his manager had been in charge of the apartment complex for nearly four years, the corporation was virtually insolvent and the recommendation of Talbot's auditor was that the project be surrendered to FHA as a failure. To this James did not agree; instead he took charge of the operation of the apartment complex himself for the corporation, and a little more than a year later the corporation had seventeen to eighteen thousand dollars in the bank with all current bills paid.

Talbot was obviously chagrined at this course of events and it was not until after he was ousted from management that he actively asserted any claim on behalf of the corporation against James. While he denied knowing that James Construction Company was the general contractor on the project, by his own testimony about January or February 1965 he knew that a check for more than fifteen thousand dollars had been drawn on the construction account for the benefit of James. There is no suggestion that he then made any issue thereabout; instead, he waited until nearly four years later and until after he had been ousted from the active management of the operation. . . .

The resolution of the Board of Directors at the meeting on November 5, 1963, unanimously confirmed by the meeting of the stockholders on the same date, as evidenced by their written signatures, clearly shows that all parties agreed that James' efforts over a two year period and the contracts and commitments thereby produced plus the continued use of the finances and credit of James during the actual construction period represented a value of $44,000, which was accepted in full payment for James' ten shares of stock. According to the literal terms of this resolution, nothing remained to be done by James to fully earn his ten shares except allow the use of his credit throughout the construction period. As president of the corporation, he would have been expected to at least reasonably supervise the construction of the project in the interest of the corporation, whether or not required to do so by either the resolution of November 5 or the pre-incorporation agreement between the parties. The general supervisory duties of a corporation president or a pre-incorporation promoter are a far cry from the arduous, time consuming and expensive duties of a general contractor.

Supervising a general contractor is one thing; while acting as a general contractor, engaging, supervising, and following up eighteen or twenty subcontractors is an entirely different thing. There is uncontradicted evidence of voluminous paper work, record keeping, reports, etc., on the part of James and his personnel in the performance of the general construction contract. The record leaves no doubt whatever, to my mind, that James Construction Company performed services to the corporation subsequent to November 5, 1963 far over and above the service contemplated by either the aforesaid resolution or the pre-incorporation agreement.

As mentioned in the majority opinion, the "Trade Payment Breakdown" attached to the approved FHA construction contract made an allowance for overhead expenses in the amount of $31,589, payable by means other than cash. Apparently from the evidence, this amount, otherwise drawable, as overhead by James, was to form a part of the equity of the corporation required for the FHA loan and, of course, not actually received by James. Aside, however, from this item, the record reflects that where, as here, there was an identity of interest between the contractor and the sponsor, FHA, within certain limitations, permitted the contractor to include in his certification of the actual cost of a project a reasonable allocation of his general overhead expense, *i.e.*, the proportion of his actual general overhead expense attributable to the particular contract job.

In his cost certification to FHA James showed the entire overhead of James Construction Company during the period that the apartment project was under construction, and represented that 88.98% thereof, or $22,817.34, was attributable to the construction of Chicora Apartments. Of this amount, FHA allowed only $21,231.90 (3% of other costs) as a portion of the actual cost of Chicora Apartments. James' figures as to his overhead and the portion thereof attributable to the construction of Chicora Apartments may or may not have been accurate, but he was not even cross-examined thereabout. Assuming the accuracy of his figures it follows that his net profit from this general construction contract was the sum of $25,025.31 less $22,817.34 overhead, or $2,207.97. Even Talbot had to frankly admit that he did not know of any loss suffered by the Talbots or the corporation as a result of the general contract being let to James. He tacitly, if not expressly, conceded that Dargan, or any other reputable contractor, would have cost the corporation some twenty-five or thirty thousand dollars more. . . .

For the foregoing reasons, I would affirm the judgment of the lower court, but at the very least, if the corporation is to recover at all from James, its recovery should be limited to any profit actually received, as opposed to his overhead expense. If the judgment below be not affirmed, the cause should be remanded for the purpose of determining the amount of actual overhead which James should equitably be allowed to retain.

BRAILSFORD, J., concurs.

ALI, PRINCIPLES OF CORPORATE GOVERNANCE
§§ 1.09, 1.20, 5.02
Tent. Draft No. 5, 1986.

§ 1.09 Disclosure

(a) *Disclosure Concerning a Conflict of Interest.* A director . . ., senior executive . . ., or dominating shareholder . . . makes "disclosure concerning a conflict of interest" if he discloses to the corporate decisionmaker . . . who authorizes or ratifies the transaction in question the material facts . . . known to him concerning his conflict of interest, or if, at the time the transaction is approved, the corporate decisionmaker knows of those facts.

(b) *Disclosure Concerning a Transaction.* A director . . ., senior executive . . ., or dominating shareholder . . . makes "disclosure concerning a transaction" if he discloses to the corporate decisionmaker . . . who approves the transaction in question the material facts . . . known to him concerning the transaction, or if, at the time the transaction is approved, the corporate decisionmaker knows of those facts. . . .

§ 1.20 Material Fact

A fact is "material" if there is a substantial likelihood that a reasonable person would consider it important under the circumstances in determining his course of action.

§ 5.02 Transactions with the Corporation

(a) *General Rule.* A director . . . or senior executive . . . who enters into a transaction with the corporation (other than a transaction involving the payment of compensation) fulfills his duty of loyalty to the corporation with respect to the transaction if:

    (1) disclosure concerning the conflict of interest . . . and the transaction . . . is made to the corporate decisionmaker . . . who authorizes or ratifies the transaction; and

    (2)(A) the transaction is fair to the corporation when entered into; or

        (B) the transaction is authorized, following such disclosure, by disinterested directors [§ 1.10],* and could reasona-

---

* Section 1.18 defines the term "interested" as follows:

(a) A director . . . or officer . . . is "interested" in a transaction if:

    (1) The director or officer is a party to the transaction, or

    (2) The director or officer or an associate . . . of the director or officer has a pecuniary interest in the transaction, or the director or officer has a financial or familial relationship with, or is subject to a controlling influence by, a party to the transaction, that in each instance is sufficiently substantial that it would reasonably be expected to affect the director's or officer's judgment with respect to the transaction in a manner adverse to the corporation.

(b) A shareholder is interested in a transaction if either the shareholder or, to his knowledge, an associate of the shareholder is a party to the transaction or the shareholder is also an interested director with respect to the same transaction.

Under § 1.10:

bly be believed to be fair to the corporation at the time of
such authorization; or

    (C) the transaction is authorized or ratified, following
such disclosure, by disinterested shareholders . . ., and
does not constitute a waste of corporate assets . . . at the
time of the shareholder action.

    (b) *Burden of Proof; Ratification of Defective Disclosure.* A party
who challenges a transaction between a director or senior executive
and the corporation has the burden of proof, except that the director
or the senior executive has the burden of proving that the transaction
is fair to the corporation if the transaction was not authorized by
disinterested directors, or authorized or ratified by disinterested shareholders, following disclosure concerning the conflict of interest and
the transaction. The disclosure requirements of § 5.02(a)(1) will be
deemed to be satisfied if at any time (but no later than a reasonable
time after suit is filed challenging the transaction) the transaction is
ratified, following such disclosure, by the board, the shareholders, or
the corporate decisionmaker who initially approved the transaction or
his successor.

Comment to § 5.02(a)(1):

    A director or senior executive may not deal with the corporation
as a stranger at arm's length. Even where his conflict of interest is
made known, he has a relation of "trust and confidence" with the
corporation, so as to require disclosure of "material matters," rather
than the relationship of a stranger to the corporation with a much
more limited duty of disclosure. Compare Restatement, Second,
Torts § 551(2)(a) with Restatement, Second, Torts § 551(2)
(e). . . .

    Section 1.09 sets forth the required elements of disclosure and
§ 1.20 sets forth the definition of material facts which are required to
be disclosed. Under § 5.02, a director or senior executive who fails
to make required disclosure has failed to fulfill his duty of loyalty,
even if the terms of the transaction are fair. A contract price might be
fair in the sense that it corresponds to market price, and yet the
corporation might have refused to make the contract if a given
material fact had been disclosed. See, e.g., Illustrations 2 and 4.
Furthermore, . . . fairness is often a range, rather than a point, and
disclosure of a material fact might have induced the corporation to
bargain the price down lower in the range. . . .

    Illustrations. . . .

    2. X Corporation is seeking a new headquarters building.
D, a vice president of X Corporation, owns all the stock of R
Corporation, which owns an office building. D causes a real
estate agent to offer R Corporation's building to X Corporation,

A provision that gives a specified effect to action by disinterested directors requires the affirmative votes of a majority, but not less than two, of the directors on the board or an appropriate committee who are not interested [§ 1.18] in the transaction in question.

but does not disclose his ownership of R Corporation. X Corporation's board of directors agrees to purchase the building for a fair price. Two weeks later, X Corporation learns of D's interest in R Corporation. D has not fulfilled his duty to the corporation under §§ 5.02(a)(1) and 5.07 (Conduct on Behalf of Associates of Directors or Senior Executives).

3. The facts being otherwise as stated in Illustration 2, X Corporation's board ratifies the acquisition after it learns of D's interest in R Corporation. X Corporation cannot thereafter seek rescission of the transaction with R Corporation.

4. The facts being otherwise as stated in Illustration 2, D discloses to X Corporation, prior to the acquisition, his interest in R Corporation. D fails to disclose, however, that he has information, not publicly available, that the State Highway Department has formally decided to run a highway through the property on which R Corporation's building stands, and to condemn the building under its power of eminent domain. The price paid by X Corporation is fair, even taking the proposed condemnation into account, since the condemnation award is likely to equal or exceed the price. Two weeks after the acquisition, X Corporation learns of the Highway Department's decision. D has not fulfilled his duty to the corporation under § 5.02(a)(1).

5. The facts being otherwise as stated in Illustration 4, X Corporation's board ratifies the acquisition after it learns of the Highway Department's decision. X Corporation cannot thereafter seek rescission of the transaction with R Corporation.

Comment to § 5.02(a)(2)(B):

Under § 5.02(a)(2)(B), if a transaction has been authorized in advance by disinterested directors, the burden of proof will be on the party challenging the transaction. Furthermore, the required level of proof of unfairness will be much higher than it would be in the absence of such authorization, although the party challenging the transaction would not have to show lack of rationality, as in the case of business judgment review under § 4.01(c). A person attacking a transaction approved by disinterested directors must clearly demonstrate that the transaction is outside of the range of reasonableness, so that the transaction could not reasonably be believed to be fair. The test of fairness as so formulated is intended to give substantial deference to the judgment of disinterested directors, while recognizing that the presence of close relationships among directors, particularly in smaller corporations, may sometimes interfere with the ability of directors to deal with a colleague with the degree of wariness that is employed in arm's-length transactions. The test of fairness as so formulated is intended to set forth an objective standard. . . .

Illustrations:

6. Corporation C is engaged in commercial agriculture. C's board consists of L, its president, and N, O, and P, who own other types of agricultural businesses. C is potentially in the

market for a new headquarters building. L recently inherited a commercial building that is somewhat rundown and only partially rented. Although L has no experience in real estate, he is convinced that with a $1 million renovation the building will be worth $9 million. L offered the building to a number of sophisticated buyers, whose bids ranged between $3 and 5 million. Subsequently, L listed the building with a commercial real estate broker for six months at a price of $7.5 million, but received no offers. L then offered the building to C's board for $7.5 million, making full disclosure, but arguing that this was a bargain price. N, O, and P, who are disinterested within the meaning of § 1.10, consulted a real estate expert, who advised that the building might conceivably be worth $7.5 million, but this was an extremely high price, and he would not pay it. The board nevertheless accepted L's offer. N, O, and P did not act irrationally, since real estate cannot be precisely valued, and the value that will be added to a building by renovation is always somewhat problematic. However, the $7.5 million price could not reasonably be regarded as fair, considering that the building had been extensively marketed to sophisticated real estate investors who were aware of the possibility of renovation; that none of these investors was willing to pay more than $5 million; and that N, O, and P were not themselves experts in real estate. The transaction fails to meet the standard of § 5.02(a)(2)(B), and an action may be brought against L to rescind the transaction. However, N, O, and P are protected from liability as individuals since they meet the standard of the business judgment rule [§ 4.01(c)].

7. A, the chief executive officer of X Corporation, a real property development corporation, enters into a contract to sell a parcel of undeveloped real property to X Corporation for $500,000. The board of directors of X Corporation (consisting of A and two other directors who are not officers or employees of X Corporation) authorizes the transaction, with A not participating in the voting, relying on an appraisal of $500,000 supplied by an employee of X Corporation to support the fairness of the purchase price. The directors had also been supplied with an appraisal of an independent appraiser showing the property to have a fair value of $150,000. The transaction may be set aside, since the board could not properly rely on the appraisal of an employee of A (whose job security was subject to A's control) rather than on an independent appraiser, and therefore could not reasonably have believed the transaction to be fair, particularly in light of the value assigned to the property by an independent appraiser. If the transaction had been with an unrelated third party rather than A, the directors would not be required to utilize an independent appraiser, since no special procedures would have been required to protect X Corporation.

SECTION 2. STATUTORY APPROACHES

DEL. GEN. CORP. LAW § 144

[See Statutory Supplement]

REV. MODEL BUS. CORP. ACT § 8.31

[See Statutory Supplement]

SCOTT v. MULTI–AMP CORP.

United States District Court, D. New Jersey, 1974.
386 F.Supp. 44.

LACEY, District Judge:

INTRODUCTORY STATEMENT

This matter is before the court on the parties' cross motions for interim injunctive and other relief, as hereinafter detailed. . . .

RELIEF SOUGHT

In their complaint, plaintiffs, who sue in their own right and derivatively, Fed.R.Civ.P. 23.1; N.J.S.A. 14A:3–6, in the right of Multi–Amp Corporation (M–A), defendant herein, seek preliminary and permanent injunctive relief which would enjoin the defendants Lerner, Saltzman, Redlhammer and Esquivel from utilizing as soliciting material management's Proxy Statement dated August 16, 1974, . . . from committing any violations of the Exchange Act, and from implementing or consummating the proposed sale of assets, by M–A to the defendant MUL Company (MUL), which is at the core of this proceeding. . . .

THE PARTIES

Plaintiffs = S/H's of M-A

Plaintiffs Scott and Puttkammer are stockholders of defendant M–A, a New Jersey corporation, with its principal place of business in Texas, which, with its subsidiaries, is engaged in various aspects of the electrical testing industry.

Defendants = S/H's of MUL

MUL is a recently organized Delaware corporation, the stock of which is entirely owned by defendants Lerner, Saltzman, Redlhammer and Esquivel, formed by them to acquire M–A's assets. Lerner (M–A's Board Chairman and Chief Executive Officer) and Saltzman each own beneficially 81,798 shares (8.99%) of M–A's common stock (totalling in excess of 900,000 shares), acquired on April 15, 1970, and registered in the name of L & S, a partnership owned fifty-percent by Lerner, with the other fifty-percent owned by Saltzman and a corporation (Lodar, Inc.) he controls. Redlhammer (M–A's President) and Esquivel (M–A's Vice President for Finance) own respectively 28,471 (3.13%) and 196 (.02%) shares of M–A common stock, and are, with Lerner and Saltzman, directors of M–A, as is Baker (who was elected on July 10, 1974). Berick is also an M–A director and a partner in the Cleveland, Ohio law firm of Burke, Hahn & Berick, which has served as M–A's general counsel; he owns 500 shares (.05%) of M–A's common stock. Other M–A directors were, until recently, Glenn Golenberg, whose place was taken by Baker, and James Hellmuth, an outside director whose principal occupation is as a vice president of Bankers Trust Company. Their resignations were filed and accepted on July 10 and August 1, 1974, respectively.

DISCUSSION

Generally, plaintiffs charge that at a time prior to July 26, 1974, defendants Lerner, Saltzman, Redlhammer and Esquivel, in addition to violating certain securities laws, conspired to acquire M–A's assets "at a grossly inadequate price [$5,494,965 or $6.04 per share of M–A stock] and to liquidate . . . [M–A], to the detriment of the stockholders . . . and, pursuant to said conspiracy, formed defendant MUL for the purpose of acquiring the assets of Multi–Amp." Complaint, para. 11. More specifically, plaintiffs charge defendants have acted illegally in the particulars hereinafter set forth.

[The discussion of plaintiff's securities law claims is omitted.]

Plaintiffs' State–Created Claims

Pendent to plaintiffs' Exchange Act claims are their claims that the Lerner group, as directors and controlling stockholders, have violated their fiduciary obligations to M–A and its other stockholders by entering into a contract with MUL for the sale of M–A's assets for an inadequate and inequitable price. . . .

As plaintiffs concede, and defendants proclaim, the principle of a century ago that any contract between a director and his corporation was voidable at the instance of the corporation or its shareholders, without regard to the fairness of the transaction, has been supplanted widely, and in New Jersey by N.J.S.A. 14A:6–8, which in pertinent part provides:

> *Effect Of Common Directorships And Directors' Personal Interest.*—
> (1) No contract or other transaction between a corporation and one or more of its directors . . . or . . . any . . . corporation . . . in which one or more of its directors are directors or are otherwise interested, shall be void or voidable solely by reason of such common directorship or interest, or solely because such director or directors are present at the meeting of the board or a committee thereof which authorizes or approves the contract

or transaction, or solely because his or their votes are counted for such purpose, if

(a) the contract or other transaction is fair and reasonable as to the corporation at the time it is authorized, approved or ratified; or

(b) the fact of the common directorship or interest is disclosed or known to the board or committee and the board or committee authorizes, approves, or ratifies the contract or transaction by unanimous written consent, provided at least one director so consenting is disinterested, or by affirmative vote of a majority of the disinterested directors, even though the disinterested directors be less than a quorum; or

(c) the fact of the common directorship or interest is disclosed or known to the shareholders, and they authorize, approve or ratify the contract or transaction.

While no New Jersey decision has as yet addressed the subject, it is this court's view that, notwithstanding the use of "or" to connect the subdivisions of the statute, the preferable construction is to require that a particular transaction pass muster under each subdivision. Israels, The Corporate Triangle—Some Corporate Aspects of the New Jersey, New York and Delaware Statutes, 23 Rutgers L.Rev. 615, 627 (1969); *and see,* Remillard Brick Co. v. Remillard–Dandini Co., 109 Cal.App.2d 405, 241 P.2d 66 (1952), applying a similar construction to § 820 of the California Corporations Code, from which 14A:6–8 was derived. As the California court states, the requirements of the fiduciary obligation of a director are not lessened because he may disclose to his co-directors his interest in a transaction with the corporation. *See also* Kennerson v. Burbank Amusement Co., 120 Cal.App.2d 157, 260 P.2d 823 (1953). . . .

The parties disagree over whether the aforesaid statutory revision operates to relieve a director of the burden of proving the fairness of contracts between his corporation and himself. Manifestly it does not. This court, like the California courts in *Remillard* and *Kennerson,* perceives nothing in the revised enactment to suggest that the legislature intended it to alter the traditional doctrine that a fiduciary who engages in self-dealing must endure the burden of proving that a challenged transaction is fair and equitable. Thus the Commissioners' Notes accompanying the statute are enlightening:

Subsections 14A:6–8(1) and 14A:6–8(2) of this section have been adapted from section 820 of the California Act and have no counterpart in Title 14. Substantially similar provisions are contained in the New York and Delaware Acts. The rule presently in effect in New Jersey is that any contract or other transaction between a corporation and one or more of its directors is voidable at the election of the corporation unless the party seeking to enforce the contract or transaction demonstrates by *clear and convincing proof* that it is honest, fair and reasonable. Abeles v. Adams Engineering Co. Inc., 35 N.J. 411, 428–429, 173 A.2d 246 (1961). The Commission believed that this rule operates harshly in many cases, and that the rule stated in this section would eliminate the inequities and uncertainties caused by the present rule, *leaving undisturbed the power of the courts to deal with such matters under general equitable principles.* (emphasis supplied)

The change worked by the statute, then, does not relieve the directors of the burden, as fiduciaries, of proving the fairness of the transaction. It simply sets a less stringent standard for the requisite proof, substituting the "preponderance of the evidence" test for the "clear and convincing" requirement. No other conclusion can be reasonably drawn from the [italicized] portion of the aforesaid commentary.

Now to be considered is whether the defendants have sufficiently demonstrated, at this stage of the case, the fairness of the challenged transaction, and their compliance with the other provisions of 14A:8-6.

On the issue of fairness, it is noted that the amount per share a shareholder will receive ($6.04) is 31% over the closing market price of 4⅝ on July 26, 1974; and is in excess of the per share book value as at April 30, 1974 ($5.64) and the per share net tangible asset figure ($5.22) as at the same date. Moreover, since commencement of suit, defendants, as has been recounted earlier, have obtained an independent appraisal which styles as fair the price set for M–A's assets.

Plaintiffs oppose this evidence with none of their own. Their flimsy reference to M–A's proposed transaction with Research–Cottrell is unpersuasive. These discussions were terminated, not only because the Research–Cottrell shares had greatly diminished in value, but because they gave every indication of continuing their plunge—which is exactly what occurred. Accordingly, the court finds at this time that defendants have made a prima facie showing of the fairness of the challenged transaction.

At oral argument plaintiffs' counsel, in recognition of the weakness of his position on the issue of fairness, suggested that, if management wins the election, he be allowed a brief period thereafter to obtain "fairness" proof before the M–A/MUL sale's culmination. This court cannot put itself into the position of favoring one side or the other in this case. Thus it will not order defendants at this time to defer consummation of the transaction for any period after the meeting, should defendants prevail in the voting.

As to the other provisions of 14A:6-8, when the M–A Board voted on August 15, 1974 to approve the challenged transaction, there was disclosure of the interest in MUL of the Lerner group, there was "unanimous written consent", and among those consenting were Baker and Berick, who, so far as the record presently stands, were and are "disinterested directors" under N.J.S.A. 14A:6–8(b). Furthermore, "the fact of the common directorship or interest" [N.J.S.A. 14A:6–8(c)] is being disclosed in the Proxy Statement; the shareholders will be thus advised.

Under all the circumstances, therefore, plaintiffs are not entitled to interim relief on their state-based claims. . . .

***

NOTE ON DUTY–OF–LOYALTY STATUTES

Thirty-eight corporation statutes have provisions relating to self-interested contracts. Many of these statutes are comparable to New Jersey § 14A:6–8, the statute involved in *Scott v. Multi–Amp.* The general structure of these statutes is fairly uniform, but they vary in important respects. Some explicitly require disclosure concerning the conflict of interest and the transaction; others explicitly require disclosure of only the conflict of interest. A few explicitly require some form of fairness test even if disinterested directors have approved the transaction; most do not. Cases like *Scott* suggest that despite such textual variations, the results under the statutes are likely to be similar; the courts are unlikely to uphold a self-interested transaction if there has not been full disclosure concerning the transaction or if the transaction is evidently unfair.

The position of the Delaware court is unclear. In Fliegler v. Lawrence, 361 A.2d 218 (Del.1976), a shareholder in Agau Mines, Inc. brought a derivative action attacking a self-interested transaction that had been ratified by Agau's shareholders. The court said:

> The purported ratification by the Agau shareholders would not affect the burden of proof in this case because the majority of shares voted in favor of exercising the option were cast by defendants in their capacity as Agau shareholders. Only about one-third of the "disinterested" shareholders voted, and we cannot assume that such non-voting shareholders either approved or disapproved. Under these circumstances, we cannot say that "the entire atmosphere has been freshened" and that departure from the objective fairness test is permissible. . . .

> Nor do we believe the Legislature intended a contrary policy and rule to prevail by enacting 8 Del.C. § 144. . . .

> Defendants argue that the transaction here in question is protected by § 144(a)(2) which, they contend, does not require that ratifying shareholders be "disinterested" or "independent"; nor, they argue, is there warrant for reading such a requirement into the statute. See Folk, *The Delaware General Corporation Law—A Commentary and Analysis* (1972), pp. 85–86. We do not read the statute as providing the broad immunity for which defendants contend. It merely removes an "interested director" cloud when its terms are met and provides against invalidation of an agreement "solely" because such a director or officer is involved. Nothing in the statute sanctions unfairness to Agau or removes the transaction from judicial scrutiny.

It is sometimes assumed that the self-interests option transaction that was at issue in *Fliegler* was not approved by a majority of the disinterested shareholders who voted on it, and that *Fliegler* therefore should be construed to apply only to the question whether approval by interested shareholders satisfies § 144(a)(2). The language in *Fliegler,* however, is much broader, and in fact the option may well have been approved by a majority of the voting disinterested shareholders. The only facts stated in the opinion that bear on this question are that (i) only about one-third of the disinterested shareholders voted, and (ii) of the shares voted in favor of the option, a majority were cast by defendants. It would be consistent with those facts that, of the disinterested shareholders who voted on the option, a majority approved. That approval would satisfy § 144(a)(2), because that provision does not require that the disinterested shareholders voting on a transaction constitute a quorum.

In Marciano v. Nakash, 535 A.2d 400 (Del.1987), the court upheld, as fair, a self-interested transaction that had not been approved by either disinterested directors or disinterested shareholders. In the course of its opinion, the court seemed to reiterate *Fliegler*:

> . . . This Court in Fliegler v. Lawrence, Del.Supr., 361 A.2d 218 (1976), a post-section 144 decision, refused to view section 144 as either completely preemptive of the common law duty of director fidelity or as constituting a grant of broad immunity. As we stated in *Fliegler*: "It merely removes an 'interested director' cloud when its terms are met and provides against invalidation of an agreement solely because such a director or officer is involved." Id. at 222. In *Fliegler* this Court applied a two-tiered analysis; application of section 144 coupled with an intrinsic fairness test. . . .

> . . . Just as the statute cannot "sanction unfairness" neither can it invalidate fairness if, upon judicial review, the transaction withstands close scrutiny of its intrinsic elements.

However, the court, in dictum, added the following in a footnote:

> Although in this case none of the curative steps afforded under section 144(a) were available because of the director-shareholder deadlock, a non-disclosing director seeking to remove the cloud of interestedness would appear to have the same burden under section 144(a)(3), as under prior case law, of proving the intrinsic fairness of a questioned transaction which had been approved or ratified by the directors or shareholders. Folk, The Delaware General Corp. Law: A Commentary and Analysis, 86 (1972). On the other hand, approval by fully-informed disinterested directors under section 144(a)(1), or disinterested stockholders under section 144(a)(2), permits invocation of the business judgment rule and limits judicial review to issues of gift or waste with the burden of proof upon the party attacking the transaction.

SECTION 3. COMPENSATION AND THE DOCTRINE OF WASTE

DEL. GEN. CORP. LAW §§ 141(h), 157

[See Statutory Supplement]

REV. MODEL BUS. CORP. ACT §§ 6.24, 8.11

[See Statutory Supplement]

NOTE ON THE AMERICAN TOBACCO LITIGATION *

In 1911, the Supreme Court held that The American Tobacco Company was a monopoly in violation of the Sherman Antitrust Act. United States v. American Tobacco Co., 221 U.S. 106, 31 S.Ct. 632, 55 L.Ed. 663 (1911). As a result, American Tobacco was broken up into a number of new companies, one of which retained the American Tobacco name. In 1912, the shareholders of the new American Tobacco Company adopted the following by-law, Article XII:

> Section 1. As soon as practicable after the end of the year 1912 and of each year of the Company's operations thereafter, the Treasurer of the Company shall ascertain the net profits, as hereinafter defined, earned by the Company during such year, and if such net profits exceed the sum of $8,222,245.82, which is the estimated amount of such net profits earned during the year 1910 by the businesses that now belong to the Company, the Treasurer shall pay an amount equal in the aggregate to ten per cent of such excess to the President and five Vice–Presidents of the Company in the following proportions, to wit: One-fourth thereof, or $2\frac{1}{2}$ per cent of such amount, to the President; one-fifth of the remainder thereof or $1\frac{1}{2}$ per cent of such amount, to each of the five Vice–Presidents as salary for the year, in addition to the fiscal salary of each of said officers. . . .

* Except as otherwise indicated, the facts in this Note are drawn from Rogers v. Hill, 289 U.S. 582, 53 S.Ct. 731, 77 L.Ed. 1385 (1933), *reversing,* 60 F.2d 109 (1932); Heller v. Boylan, 29 N.Y.S.2d 653 (1941), aff'd without opinion 263 A.D. 815, 32 N.Y.S.2d 131; Rogers v. Guaranty Trust Co. of New York, 288 U.S. 123, 53 S.Ct. 295, 77 L.Ed. 652 (1933); Rogers v. Hill, 34 F.Supp. 358 (S.D.N.Y.1940); J. Baker, Directors and Their Functions (1945); and 2 G. Washington & V. Rothschild, Compensating the Corporate Executive, 880–89 (3d ed. 1962).

Section 5. This By–Law may be modified or repealed only by the action of the stockholders of the Company and not by the directors.

Rogers v. Hill, 289 U.S. 582, 584 n. 1, 53 S.Ct. 731, 732 n. 1, 77 L.Ed. 1385 (1933).

By the late 1920's, the compensation of American Tobacco's top executives had reached great heights. For example, George W. Hill, American Tobacco's second president, received the following salary, "cash credits," and By-law XII bonuses in 1929 and 1930:

Year	Salary	Special Cash Credits	Bonus Under By–Law XII
1929	144,500	$136,507.71	447,870.30
1930	168,000	273,470.76	842,507.72

Hill received amounts in 1931 and 1932 comparable to his 1930 compensation. He also received certain very large stock allotments; his 1931 allotment alone was worth $1,169,280, and was in addition to all other compensation. American Tobacco's vice-presidents received lesser but nevertheless extremely large amounts during this period. For example, two vice-presidents each received bonuses of more than $400,000 in 1930, 1931, and 1932.

Shareholders filed several suits attacking these compensation arrangements. One of these suits, Rogers v. Hill, claimed that By-law XII was invalid, and that, even if valid, the amounts paid under it were unreasonably large. The Second Circuit dismissed Rogers' complaint 2–1, with a ringing dissent by Judge Swan. 60 F.2d 109 (2d Cir.1932). The majority opinion was written by Judge Manton. On appeal, the Supreme Court reversed. It held that the by-law was valid when adopted, but that

the payments under the by-law have by reason of increase of profits become so large as to warrant investigation in equity in the interest of the company. Much weight is to be given to the action of the stockholders, and the by-law is supported by the presumption of regularity and continuity. But the rule prescribed by it cannot, against the protest of a shareholder, be used to justify payments of sums as salaries so large as in substance and effect to amount to spoliation or waste of corporate property. The dissenting opinion of Judge Swan [below] indicates the applicable rule: "If a bonus payment has no relation to the value of services for which it is given, it is in reality a gift in part and the majority stockholders have no power to give away corporate property against the protest of the minority." 60 F. (2d) 109, 113. The facts alleged by plaintiff are sufficient to require that the district court, upon a consideration of all the relevant facts brought forward by the parties, determine whether and to what extent payments to the individual defendants under the by-law constitute misuse and waste of the money of the corporation.

289 U.S. at 591–92, 53 S.Ct. at 735. (It was later learned that Judge Manton, who wrote the Second Circuit's majority opinion in Rogers v. Hill, had been paid $250,000 by American Tobacco's lawyer. Manton was convicted and the lawyer was disbarred.)

Following Rogers' victory in the Supreme Court, negotiations eventuated in a settlement in 1933. Under the settlement, no past compensation was repaid, but the point at which By-law XII compensation began was increased to $15,500,000, and once profits reached $32,500,000 the percentage was scaled down in increments from 10% to 5%. Managers also surrendered certain stock allotments that had been challenged by Rogers in a companion suit.

In Heller v. Boylan, 29 N.Y.S.2d 653 (1941), aff'd without opinion, 263 A.D. 815, 32 N.Y.S.2d 131, another American Tobacco shareholder brought suit, attacking both the adequacy of the settlement in Rogers v. Hill and the executive compensation paid during 1928–1939. The court held that the bonuses had been incorrectly calculated in certain important respects, but otherwise declined to set them aside:

> Assuming, arguendo, that the compensation should be revised, what yardstick is to be employed? Who or what is to supply the measuring-rod? The conscience of equity? Equity is but another name for human being temporarily judicially robed. He is not omnipotent or omniscient. Can equity be so arrogant as to hold that it knows more about managing this corporation than its stockholders?

> Yes, the Court possesses the *power* to prune these payments, but openness forces the confession that the pruning would be synthetic and artificial rather than analytic or scientific. Whether or not it would be fair and just, is highly dubious. Yet, merely because the problem is perplexing is no reason for eschewing it. It is not timidity, however, which perturbs me. It is finding a rational or just gauge for revising these figures were I inclined to do so. No blueprints are furnished. The elements to be weighed are incalculable; the imponderables, manifold. To act out of whimsy or caprice or arbitrariness would be more than inexact—it would be the precise antithesis of justice; it would be a farce.

> If comparisons are to be made, with whose compensation are they to be made—executives? Those connected with the motion picture industry? Radio artists? Justices of the Supreme Court of the United States? The President of the United States? . . .

> On this branch of the case, I find for the defendants. Yet it does not follow that I affirmatively approve these huge payments. It means that I cannot by any reliable standard find them to be waste or spoliation; it means that I find no valid ground for disapproving what the great majority of stockholders have approved. In the circumstances, if a ceil-

ing for these bonuses is to be erected, the stockholders who built and are responsible for the present structure must be the architects.

29 N.Y.S.2d at 679–80.

AMERICAN LAW INSTITUTE, PRINCIPLES OF CORPORATE GOVERNANCE § 5.03

(Tent. Draft No. 5, 1986).

§ 5.03 Compensation of Directors and Senior Executives:

(a) *General Rule:* A director . . . or senior executive . . . who receives compensation from the corporation for services in that capacity fulfills his duty of loyalty to the corporation with respect to the compensation if:

(1) disclosure concerning the transaction . . . is made to the corporate decisionmaker . . . who authorizes or ratifies the compensation; and

(2)(A) the compensation is fair to the corporation when approved; or

(B) the compensation is authorized, following disclosure concerning the transaction, by disinterested directors . . ., in a manner that satisfies the standards of the business judgment rule [§ 4.01(c)]; or

(C) the compensation is authorized or ratified, following such disclosure, by disinterested shareholders . . ., and does not constitute a waste of corporate assets . . . at the time of the shareholder action.

(b) *Burden of Proof; Ratification of Defective Disclosure.* A party who challenges a transaction involving the payment of compensation to a director or senior executive has the burden of proof, except that the director or the senior executive has the burden of proving that the transaction is fair to the corporation if the transaction was not authorized by disinterested directors, or authorized or ratified by disinterested shareholders, following such disclosure. The disclosure requirements of § 5.03(a)(1) will be deemed to be satisfied if at any time (but no later than a reasonable time after suit is filed challenging the transaction) the transaction is ratified, following such disclosure, by the board, the shareholders, or the corporate decisionmaker who initially approved the transaction or his successor.

SUBCOMMITTEE ON EXECUTIVE COMPENSATION OF THE ABA SECTION ON CORPORATION, BANKING AND BUSINESS LAW, EXECUTIVE COMPENSATION: A 1987 ROAD MAP FOR THE CORPORATE ADVISOR

43 Bus.Law. 185, 259–264, 266–270, 274–75, 278, 290, 301–302, 312–314, 318, 323–324 (1987).

CHAPTER 2: PERFORMANCE–RELATED INCENTIVE PROGRAMS

I. SHORT–TERM INCENTIVE PLANS: ANNUAL BONUS PLANS

An executive bonus or incentive compensation plan is one of the most significant executive compensation programs an employer can have. Basically, it is a short-term incentive plan designed to stimulate individuals who contribute to the successful operation of the business. A participant in an executive bonus plan is eligible to receive an award which is tied directly to the employer's success during its fiscal year. . . .

All executive bonus plans have similar purposes and goals. First, they try to stimulate behavior that will lead to the attainment of the employer's goals. For example, the corporation that wants to increase its earnings per share for one year will gear its executive bonus plan so that participants will be paid a bonus only if that earnings per share goal is met.

Second, an employer will want to extend its executive bonus plan only to those executives whose duties and responsibilities give them the opportunity to make a material and substantial impact on the achievement of goals. . . .

In most cases the limit of eligibility is somewhat arbitrary, but is typically based on one or more of the following criteria:

    (i) Salary level (such as "all employees who earn $30,000 per year or more");

    (ii) Salary grade (such as "all employees who are a compensation grade 12 or higher");

    (iii) Organizational level (such as "all employees who are in the two top levels directly below the president"); or

    (iv) Combination approach (such as "all employees in the two top levels directly below the president who are also in compensation grade 12 or higher"). . . .

Obviously, the money needed to fund an executive bonus plan must come from somewhere. But the "where" is one of the variables at the very heart of the plan. An employer's determination of where the money will come from is in essence a determination of what it wants to motivate.

For example, it is unquestionable that companies are in business to make profits. Thus, one of the goals of an executive bonus plan is to maximize profits. However, the inquiry does not end here. The term "profits" has to be defined for purposes of the plan. "Profits" can be defined as net income before extraordinary items, or net income after extraordinary items. Furthermore, profits can be defined as profits *before or after* provision for income taxes. "In past years the majority of executive bonus plans were predicated on pre-tax profits, but today the majority of new plans seems to be based on after-tax profits." Stockholders are evidently happier knowing that executives are not getting their annual bonus until corporate taxes have been paid.

But profits alone may not be sufficient for purposes of determining what to motivate. An increasingly popular measurement for the plan fund is "return on investment" ("ROI").

Briefly stated, ROI is equal to profits divided by investment. It is a measurement of how much profit is gained per dollar of investment contributed. For executive bonus plan purposes, ROI can be stated in four possible ways: (i) earnings per share, i.e., profits divided by the number of shares outstanding; (ii) return on stockholders' equity, i.e., profits divided by the sum of capital stock, capital surplus, and retained earnings; (iii) return on capital employed in the business, i.e., the sum of profits and amounts charged against profits for interest on long-term debt, divided by the sum of stockholders' equity and long-term debt; or (iv) return on assets, i.e., the sum of profits and amounts charged against profits for interest on all debts, divided by total assets.

The great bulk of employers that use the ROI measures for determining a plan fund use either return on stockholders' equity or return on capital employed.

Most employers use a mathematical formula to determine how much money will go into the executive bonus plan fund each year. One common formula is simply to state that the fund will be a certain percentage of profits.

Another common formula uses a built-in threshold above which profits must rise before a bonus fund can be established. This built-in threshold is sometimes referred to as a "deductible," and many plans have it. A deductible prevents executives from taking the first slice from the profits pie. Rather, they must wait until an additional goal is met. For example, if the formula is "two percent of after-tax profits in excess of three-percent return on stockholders' equity," it is not sufficient that after-tax profits reach a certain level. There must also be a three-percent return on stockholders' equity before there is any money to pay for bonuses. . . .

II. LONG–TERM INCENTIVE PLANS: PERFORMANCE UNIT AND PERFORMANCE SHARE PLANS . . .

A substantial number of publicly-held companies have adopted performance unit or performance share plans. Awards under these plans are usually contingent upon the attainment of corporate performance goals measured over a period of years, as contrasted with executive bonus plans which use annual goals. Furthermore, a performance unit plan is contractual in nature, with awards payable when and measured by the degree to which the prescribed goals are attained, whereas an executive bonus plan may provide for awards in the discretion of a committee or officer on the basis of individual accomplishment. Typically, a performance unit plan provides for payment to participants to the extent that average annual compound growth in earnings per share of common stock of the corporation during a three- to five-year period equals or exceeds pre-established objectives. Other performance measures also can be used.

A performance unit plan is based on the contingent credit of a unit or units, each valued at a designated dollar amount. A performance share plan is based on the contingent credit of units whose value is measured by that of the corporate stock. Accordingly, the amount paid by a performance share plan depends not only on the degree to which the specified performance goals are achieved, but also on the value of the stock. In both cases, upon attainment of the goals specified, the award is paid in either cash or by the delivery of shares of stock. Because there is no material difference between the two plans, this discussion will be confined to performance unit plans except as otherwise stated.

A performance unit plan generally is viewed as a long-term compensation device comparable to a stock option or other stock plan. Many corporations award their executives performance units and stock options, providing opportunities to benefit from internal corporate performance and appreciation in the market value of the stock. . . .

Goals as Basis of Awards. As previously stated, the goals for a performance unit plan are usually based on a substantial increase in primary earnings per share of common stock of the employer averaged over the performance period. This increase in primary earnings is compared to the same financial measures during a base period preceding commencement of the performance period. Other goals, such as an increase in return on stockholder equity or growth of market share, may be used. . . .

Unit Valuations. For the purposes of judging performance against the performance targets, the value of each unit must be established at the commencement of the performance period. The following is an example of a typical unit value design:

EPS Growth Rate	Unit Value
4.5%	$50
7.0%	$100
9.5%	$150

If earnings per share grow at a rate of less than 4.5%, the units have no value. Intermediate unit values are computed on a pro rata basis. . . .

CHAPTER 3: STOCK–RELATED LONG–TERM INCENTIVE PROGRAMS

I. NON–QUALIFIED (NONSTATUTORY) STOCK OPTIONS . . .

As used in the context of an executive compensation program, the term "non-qualified stock option" means a right granted to one or more employees or executives by a corporation (or by a parent or subsidiary corporation) to acquire shares of the corporation's stock (or stock of a parent or subsidiary). Non-qualified stock options derive their name from the fact that neither the options nor the shares issued upon exercise of the options satisfy the criteria of, or "qualify" for, the special, and heretofore generally favorable, income tax treatment provided under the Code for incentive stock options (formerly "statutory" or "qualified" options). Since non-qualified stock options are neither afforded special tax treatment under nor defined in the Code, by way of contrast to the old statutory stock options, such options are also sometimes referred to as "nonstatutory options."

Stock options often constitute an important part of the compensation and incentive program of a corporation. They may be offered pursuant to a plan applicable to one or more executives, or they may represent part of the premium offered to attract new executives or retain the services of valued existing executives. By obtaining the right to acquire an equity interest in the corporation, whether at a discount or at market value, the executive acquires a stake in the long-term growth of the corporation, benefits from the capital appreciation of the corporation's stock, and therefore presumably will work diligently for the success of the venture. However, there is little empirical evidence to prove that corporate performance can be improved by granting stock options. . . .

Neither grant nor vesting of a non-qualified stock option would ordinarily result in recognition of taxable income. First, the grant of an option does not constitute a transfer of the underlying stock. Second, the option itself is not treated as "property" for federal income tax purposes unless the option has a readily ascertainable fair market value. According to the regulations, an option has a readily ascertainable fair market value where either: (i) the option itself is actively traded on an established market, or (ii) if not so traded, the option is transferable, immediately exercisable in full, and subject to no restrictions which would affect the fair market value of the option, and the option privilege has a readily ascertainable fair market value. . . .

At the time of exercise of a non-qualified stock option, if the stock received on exercise is not restricted, the executive will recognize income immediately. . . .

II. INCENTIVE STOCK OPTIONS

One of the most significant developments in the area of executive compensation prior to the passage of the 1986 Tax Act was the reinstatement by the Economic Recovery Tax Act of 1981 ("ERTA") of a special class of statutory stock options known as "incentive stock options." Incentive stock options provided several advantages for executives over nonstatutory stock options and were generally well received by major employers. However, although the 1986 Tax Act included certain changes to the Code which are favorable to incentive stock options, the loss of favorable long-term capital gains treatment has eliminated the most important benefit of incentive stock options for executives, and . . . leaves tax deferral as the only major benefit for executives to derive from incentive stock options. . . .

If the requirements for incentive stock option treatment are satisfied, the executive is not subject to federal income tax either at the time of grant of the option or at the time of its exercise. However, upon exercise of the option, the spread between the fair market value of the stock at the time of exercise and the option price is an item of tax preference subject to the possible application of the twenty-one-percent alternative minimum tax. Upon disposition of stock acquired pursuant to an incentive stock option, the executive will be taxed at long-term capital gains rates, provided certain holding period requirements are satisfied. Since under current law, effective in 1988, capital gains will be taxed at the same marginal rates as ordinary income, the major benefit of incentive stock options to the executive is deferral of the imposition of tax on the option gain until disposition of the stock. . . .

III. STOCK APPRECIATION RIGHTS

A stock appreciation right is the right to be paid an amount equal to the increase in value or spread between the value (or a fraction of the value) of a share of employer stock on the date the SAR is granted and the value (or a fraction of the value) of the share on the date the SAR is exercised. SARs are distinguishable from "phantom stock" . . . units (discussed in the next section) because SARs are usually granted in tandem or in conjunction with another right, usually a stock option, and SARs generally do not include (as phantom stock often does) a right to receive the value of dividends payable on the underlying stock while the SAR is outstanding. . . .

IV. PHANTOM STOCK . . .

The term "phantom stock" can be used to describe any form of long-term executive incentive arrangement using units that are equivalent to, but are not, actual shares of employer stock. Thus, a phantom stock plan might provide outright grants of phantom "shares" or options based on phantom stock.

Under a phantom stock arrangement, the value of a unit of phantom stock typically equals the appreciation in the market value of the underlying stock between the date the unit is acquired by the executive and its settlement date. . . .

SECTION 4. THE CORPORATE OPPORTUNITY DOCTRINE

KLINICKI v. LUNDGREN

Supreme Court of Oregon, In Banc, 1985.
298 Or. 662, 695 P.2d 906.

JONES, Justice.

The factual and legal background of this complicated litigation was succinctly set forth by Chief Judge Joseph in the Court of Appeals opinion as follows:

"In January, 1977, plaintiff Klinicki conceived the idea of *FACTS* engaging in the air transportation business in Berlin, West Germany. He discussed the idea with his friend, defendant Lundgren. At that time, both men were furloughed Pan American pilots stationed in West Germany. They decided to enter the air transportation business, planning to begin operations with an air taxi service and later to expand into other service, such as regularly scheduled flights or charter flights. In April, 1977, they incorporated Berlinair, Inc., as a closely held Oregon corporation. Plaintiff was a vice-president and a director. Lundgren was the corporation's president and a director. Each man owned 33 percent of the company stock. Lelco, Inc., a corporation owned by Lundgren and members of his family, owned 33 percent of the stock. The corporation's attorney owned the remaining one percent of the stock. Berlinair obtained the necessary governmental licenses, purchased an aircraft and in November, 1977, began passenger service.

"As president, Lundgren was responsible, in part, for developing and promoting Berlinair's transportation business. Plaintiff was in charge of operations and maintenance. In November, 1977, plaintiff and Lundgren, as representatives of Berlinair, met with representatives of the Berliner Flug Ring (BFR), a consortium of Berlin travel agents that contracts for charter flights to take sallow German tourists to sunnier climes. The BFR contract was considered a lucrative business opportunity by those familiar with the air transportation business, and plaintiff and defendant had contemplated pursuing the contract when they formed Berlinair. After the initial meeting, all subsequent contacts with BFR were made by Lundgren or other Berlinair employes acting under his directions.

"During the early stages of negotiations, Lundgren believed that Berlinair could not obtain the contract because BFR was then satisfied with its carrier. In early June, 1978, however, Lundgren learned that there was a good chance that the BFR contract might be available. He informed a BFR representative that he would make a proposal on behalf of a new company. On July 7, 1978, he incorporated Air Berlin Charter Company (ABC) and was its sole owner. On August 20, 1978, ABC presented BFR with a contract proposal, and after a series of discussions it was awarded the contract on September 1, 1978. Lundgren effectively concealed from plaintiff his negotiations with BFR and his diversion of the BFR contract to ABC, even though he used Berlinair working time, staff, money and facilities.

"Plaintiff, as a minority stockholder in Berlinair, brought a derivative action against ABC for usurping a corporate opportunity of Berlinair. He also brought an individual claim against Lundgren for compensatory and punitive damages based on breach of fiduciary duty.[1]

"The trial court found that ABC, acting through Lundgren, had wrongfully diverted the BFR contract, which was a corporate opportunity of Berlinair. The court imposed a constructive trust on ABC in favor of Berlinair, ordered an accounting by ABC and enjoined ABC from transferring its assets. The trial court also found that Lundgren, as an officer and director of Berlinair, had breached his fiduciary duties of good faith, fair dealing and full disclosure owed to plaintiff individually and to Berlinair. The court did not award plaintiff any actual damages on the breach of fiduciary duty claim. All the issues were tried to the court, except that a jury was empaneled to try the punitive damages issue. It returned a verdict in favor of plaintiff and assessed punitive damages against Lundgren in the amount of $750,000. Lundgren then moved to dismiss plaintiff's claim for punitive damages. The court granted the motion to dismiss and, *sua sponte*, entered judgment in favor of Lundgren notwithstanding the verdict on the punitive damages claim." Klinicki v. Lundgren, 67 Or.App. 160, 162–63, 678 P.2d 1250, 1251–52 (1984) (footnote omitted).

1. The named plaintiff in the complaint is F.R. Klinicki. The named defendants are Kim Lundgren, Berlinair, Inc., an Oregon corporation, and Air Berlin Charter Company, an Oregon corporation. The complaint set forth four causes of suit summarized as follows:

(A) The first cause of suit was brought by plaintiff as a derivative stockholders suit in his own behalf and on behalf of all other stockholders of Berlinair, Inc. "and in the right of Berlinair, Inc. and for its benefit" seeking a constructive trust against Lundgren and ABC jointly and severally, an accounting by all defendants and an injunction and attorney fees.

(B) The second cause of suit involves a personal claim by Klinicki requesting the court to require Lundgren to purchase the stock of plaintiff in Berlinair after the BFR corporate opportunity held by ABC is restored to Berlinair, Inc.

(C) The third cause of suit—Count I—is an individual claim of Klinicki for an accounting from Lundgren and ABC.

(D) The third cause of suit—Count II—is plaintiff's individual claim for unjust enrichment against Lundgren.

(E) The third cause of suit—Count III—is a personal claim by plaintiff against Lundgren for breach of implied covenant of good faith and fair dealing to plaintiff. For the third cause of suit plaintiff sought a constructive trust and accounting decree against Lundgren and ABC covering any "monies, funds, assets, facilities and properties received and acquired as a result of Lundgren's breach of fiduciary duty."

(F) The fourth cause of action is an individual suit by Klinicki solely against Lundgren for breach of fiduciary duty seeking general damages of $50,000 and $1 million in punitive damages.

ABC appealed to the Court of Appeals contending that it did not usurp a corporate opportunity of Berlinair. . . .

ABC petitions for review to this court contending that the concealment and diversion of the BFR contract was not a usurpation of a corporate opportunity, because Berlinair did not have the financial ability to undertake that contract. ABC argues that proof of financial ability is a necessary part of a corporate opportunity case and that plaintiff had the burden of proof on that issue and did not carry that burden.

There is no dispute that the corporate opportunity doctrine precludes corporate fiduciaries from diverting to themselves business opportunities in which the corporation has an expectancy, property interest or right, or which in fairness should otherwise belong to the corporation. See Henn & Alexander, Laws of Corporations 632–37, § 237 (3rd ed. 1983). The doctrine follows from a corporate fiduciary's duty of undivided loyalty to the corporation.[2] ABC agrees that, unless Berlinair's financial inability to undertake the contract makes a difference, the BFR contract was a corporate opportunity of Berlinair.[3]

We first address the issue, resolved by the Court of Appeals in Berlinair's favor, of the relevance of a corporation's financial ability to undertake a business opportunity to proving a diversion of corporate opportunity claim. This is an issue of first impression in Oregon.

The Court of Appeals held that a corporation's financial ability to undertake a business opportunity is not a factor in determining the existence of a corporate opportunity unless the defendant demonstrates that the corporation is technically or de facto insolvent. Without defining these terms, the Court of Appeals specifically placed the burden of proof as to this issue on the fiduciary by saying: "To avoid liability for usurping a corporate opportunity on the basis that the corporation was insolvent, the fiduciary must prove insolvency." 67 Or.App. at 165, 678 P.2d at 1254. The Court of Appeals then concluded "that ABC usurped a corporate opportunity belonging to Berlinair when, acting through Lundgren, the BFR contract was

---

2. " '. . . [Officers and directors] must devote themselves to the corporate affairs with a view to promote the common interests and not their own, and they cannot, either directly or indirectly, utilize their position to obtain any personal profit or advantage other than that enjoyed also by their fellow shareholders [citations omitted]. In short, there is demanded of the officer or director of a corporation that he furnish to it his undivided loyalty; if there is presented to him a business opportunity which is within the scope of its own activities and of present or potential advantage to it, the law will not permit him to seize the opportunity for himself; if he does so, the corporation may elect to claim all of the benefits of the transaction. Nor is it material that his dealings may not have caused a loss or been harmful to the corpo- ration; the test of his liability is whether he has unjustly gained enrichment. Bailey v. Jacobs, 325 Pa. 187, 194, 189 A. 320, 324 [(1937)].' . . . see generally Fletcher, Cyclopedia Corporations § 861.1 (rev. ed. 1965); . . . Note, 'Corporate Opportunity', 74 Harv.L.Rev. 765 (1961)." Seaboard Industries, Inc. v. Monaco, 442 Pa. 256, 261–62, 276 A.2d 305, 309 (1971). . . .

3. ABC asserts in its brief that the single issue in the corporate opportunity portion of this appeal is the financial ability of Berlinair to undertake the BFR contract. It makes no point of the fact that the trial court found Kim Lundgren usurped the corporate opportunity for himself, yet ABC was controlled and owned by Kim Lundgren, his father, Leonard Lundgren, and their attorney.

diverted" because nothing in Lundgren's testimony or otherwise in the record suggested that Berlinair was insolvent or was no longer a viable corporate entity. 67 Or.App. at 166, 678 P.2d at 1254. Accordingly, the Court of Appeals held that the constructive trust, injunction, duty to account and other relief granted by the trial court against ABC were appropriate remedies. . . .

Before proceeding further our initial task must be to define what is meant by "corporate opportunity," and to determine when, if ever, a corporate fiduciary may take personal advantage of such an opportunity. Our resolution of this case will be limited to announcing a rule to be applied when allegations of usurpation of a corporate opportunity are made against a director of a close corporation. The determination of a rule to apply to similar situations arising between a director and a publicly held corporation presents problems and concepts which may not necessarily require us to apply an identical rule in that similar but distinguishable context.

As we mentioned at the outset, this issue is a matter of first impression in this state. While courts universally stress the high standard of fiduciary duty owed by directors and officers to their corporation, there are distinct schools of thought on the circumstances in which business opportunities may be taken for personal advantage. One group of jurisdictions severely restricts the corporate official's freedom to take advantage of opportunities by saying that the ability to undertake the opportunity is irrelevant and usurpation is essentially prohibited; other jurisdictions use a test which gives relatively wide latitude to the corporate official on the theory that financial ability to undertake a corporate opportunity is a prerequisite to the existence of a corporate opportunity.

A rigid rule was applied in Irving Trust Co. v. Deutsch, 73 F.2d 121 (2nd Cir.1934). In that case a syndicate made up of directors of Acoustic Products Co. purchased for themselves from another corporation the rights to manufacture under certain radio patents which were concededly essential to Acoustic. They justified this on the ground that Acoustic was not financially able to purchase the patents on which the defendants later made very substantial profits. The court refused to inquire whether the conclusion of financial inability was justified. Referring to the facts which raised a question whether Acoustic actually did lack the funds or credit necessary to make the acquisition, the court said:

> ". . . Nevertheless, they [the facts in the case concerning whether Acoustic lacked funds to carry out the contract] tend to show the wisdom of a rigid rule forbidding directors of a solvent corporation to take over for their own profit a corporate contract on the plea of the corporation's financial inability to perform. If the directors are uncertain whether the corporation can make the necessary outlays, they need not embark it upon the venture; if they do, they may not substitute themselves for the corporation any place along the line and divert possible benefits into their own pockets. . . ." 73 F.2d at 124.

An oft-cited Harvard Law Review note discussed executive appropria-tion of corporate opportunities and the *Irving Trust* case as follows:

"Where an opportunity is within the corporation's line of business, the executive seems normally required to offer it for consideration by the board of directors and to await rejection— should it be forthcoming—before seizing it himself. There are, however, some exceptions to this disclosure requirement, all of which rest immediately on the proposition that the circumstances clearly evidence corporate inability . . . to seize the opportuni-ty. . . . [An] exception to the requirement of tender arises where the corporation is insolvent and nearly defunct. [Jasper v. Appalachian Gas Co., 152 Ky. 68, 153 S.W. 50 (1913).] The problem with this exception is the difficulty of its extension to cases where the corporation is in serious financial difficulty or lacks liquid assets but may still be a going concern. [In Hannerty v. Standard Theatre Co., 109 Mo. 297, 19 S.W. 82 (1891), a finding of absence of corporate opportunity was based on the financial inability of the corporation. But see Irving Trust Co. v. Deutsch, 73 F.2d 121 (2d Cir.1934), and Electronic Dev. Co. v. Robson, 148 Neb. 526, 28 N.W.2d 130 (1947), where mere financial inability was held inadequate to exonerate an executive who appropriated an opportunity.] In neither case will it ordina-rily be entirely clear that, given knowledge of the opportunity, the corporation will be unable to secure needed financing with reasonable rapidity. The very existence of a prospective profitmaking venture may generate additional financial backing and may convince creditors to be less importunate in their demands. Every major executive, including the one who has discovered the opportunity, would seem obligated to make a genuine effort to enable the corporation to secure the anticipated profit. . . .

"Fearing that anything less than a prophylactic rule would discourage executives from expending their full efforts to obtain financing for the corporation, at least one court has articulated the rule that the executive is precluded from appropriating the oppor-tunity where the corporation is allegedly unable to obtain the required funds. [Citing Irving Trust Co. v. Deutsch, supra.] . . ." Note, Corporate Opportunity, 74 (Vol. I) Harv.L.Rev. 765, 772–73 (1961) (brackets contain text of footnotes; other footnotes omitted). . . .

Representing a more relaxed view of a corporate official's respon-sibility, in Guth v. Loft, Inc., 23 Del.Ch. 255, 272–73, 5 A.2d 503, 511 (1939), the Supreme Court of Delaware said:

". . . [I]f there is presented to a corporate officer or director a business opportunity *which the corporation is financially able to undertake*, is, from its nature, in the line of the corporation's business and is of practical advantage to it, is one in which the corporation has an interest or a reasonable expectancy, and, by embracing the opportunity, the self-interest of the officer or director will be brought into conflict with that of his corporation, the law will not permit him to seize the opportunity for himself. . . ." (Emphasis added.)

The language in *Guth* implies that financial ability to undertake a corporate opportunity is not only relevant, but perhaps a condition precedent to the existence of a corporate opportunity. But the language in *Guth* was dictum because that famous case, involving the creation of the Pepsi–Cola enterprise, did not involve the issue of financial ability to undertake the opportunity. The court may have thought that a lack of funds short of insolvency was relevant because it discussed Guth's defense in this area, finding that "Loft's net asset position at that time was amply sufficient to finance the enterprise." [6] But other language in *Guth* raises the question whether the terms "ability to undertake" and "ability to take advantage of" have broader concerns than mere financial capacity or incapacity:

". . . Where a corporation is engaged in a certain business, and an opportunity is presented to it embracing an activity as to which it has *fundamental knowledge, practical experience and ability to pursue, which, logically and naturally is adaptable to its business having regard for its financial position, and is one that is consonant with its reasonable needs and aspirations for expansion,* it may be properly said that the opportunity is in the line of the corporation's business." 23 Del.Ch. at 279, 5 A.2d at 514 (emphasis added).

On the other end of the legal spectrum from Irving Trust Co. v. Deutsch, supra, are two Minnesota cases: Miller v. Miller, 301 Minn. 207, 222 N.W.2d 71, 77 A.L.R.3d 941 (1974), and A.C. Petters v. St. Cloud Enterprises, Inc., 301 Minn. 261, 222 N.W.2d 83 (1974). In *Miller,* the Minnesota Supreme Court stated a two-step test to be applied in corporate opportunity cases. The first step, the "line of business" part of the test, was described as follows:

". . . The threshold question to be answered is whether a business opportunity presented is also a 'corporate' opportunity, i.e., whether the business opportunity is of sufficient importance and is so closely related to the existing or prospective activity of the corporation as to warrant judicial sanctions against its personal

---

6. In Guth v. Loft, Inc., 23 Del.Ch. 255, 270, 5 A.2d 503, 510 (1939), the court held that determination of the issue of breach of duty should be made from a consideration of all the circumstances of the transactions, noting the accepted rule that corporate officers and directors are not permitted to use their position of trust and confidence to further their private interests:

". . . The standard of loyalty is measured by no fixed scale.

"If an officer or director of a corporation, in violation of his duty as such, acquires gain or advantage for himself, the law charges the interest so acquired with a trust for the benefit of the corporation, at its election, while it denies to the betrayer all benefit and profit. The rule, inveterate and uncompromising in its rigidity, does not rest upon the narrow ground of injury or damage to the corporation resulting from a betrayal of confidence, but upon a broader foundation of a wise public policy that, for the purpose of removing all temptation, extinguishes all possibility of profit flowing from a breach of the confidence imposed by the fiduciary relation. Given the relation between the parties, a certain result follows; and a constructive trust is the remedial device through which precedence of self is compelled to give way to the stern demands of loyalty. [Citations omitted.]"

acquisition by a managing officer or director of the corporation. This question, necessarily one of fact, can best be resolved, we believe, by resort to a flexible application of the 'line of business' test set forth in Guth v. Loft, Inc., supra. The inquiry of the factfinder should be directed to all facts and circumstances relevant to the question, the most significant being: Whether the business opportunity presented is one in which the complaining corporation has an interest or an expectancy growing out of an existing contractual right; the relationship of the opportunity to the corporation's business purposes and current activities—whether essential, necessary, or merely desirable to its reasonable needs and aspirations—; whether within or without its corporate powers, the opportunity embraces areas adaptable to its business and into which the corporation might easily, naturally, or logically expand; the competitive nature of the opportunity—whether prospectively harmful or unfair—; *whether the corporation, by reason of insolvency or lack of resources, has the financial ability to acquire the opportunity;* and whether the opportunity includes activities as to which the corporation has a fundamental knowledge, practical experience, facilities, equipment, personnel, and the ability to pursue. The fact that the opportunity is not within the scope of the corporation's powers, while a factor to be considered, should not be determinative, especially where the corporate fiduciary dominates the board of directors or is the majority shareholder." 301 Minn. at 224–25, 222 N.W.2d at 81 (emphasis added).*

* The Court in Miller v. Miller went on to delineate the second step in its two-step test as follows:

Absent any evidence of fraud or a breach of fiduciary duty, if it is determined that a business opportunity is not a corporate opportunity, the corporate officer should not be held liable for its acquisition. If, however, the opportunity is found to be a corporate one, liability should not be imposed upon the acquiring officer if the evidence establishes that his acquisition did not violate his fiduciary duties of loyalty, good faith, and fair dealing toward the corporation. Thus the second step in the two-step process leading to the determination of the ultimate question of liability involves close scrutiny of the equitable considerations existing prior to, at the time of, and following the officer's acquisition. Resolution will necessarily depend upon a consideration of all the facts and circumstances of each case considered in the light of those factors which control the decision that the opportunity was in fact a corporate opportunity. Significant factors which should be considered are the nature of the officer's relationship to the management and control of the corporation; whether the opportunity was presented to him in his official or individual capacity; his prior disclosure of the opportunity to the board of directors or shareholders and their response; whether or not he used or exploited corporate facilities, assets, or personnel in acquiring the opportunity; whether his acquisition harmed or benefited the corporation; and all other facts and circumstances bearing on the officer's good faith and whether he exercised the diligence, devotion, care, and fairness toward the corporation which ordinarily prudent men would exercise under similar circumstances in like positions. . . .

We are not to be understood, by adopting this two-step process, as suggesting that a finding of bad faith is essential to impose liability upon the acquiring officer. Nor, conversely, that good faith alone, apart from the officer's fiduciary duty requiring loyalty and fair dealing toward the corporation, will absolve him from liability. And it must be acknowledged, in adopting corporate opportunity doctrine expanded beyond the narrow preexisting property interest or expectancy standard, that there can be cases where the officer's personal seizure of an opportunity so clearly essential to the continuance of a corporation or so intimately related to its activities as to amount to a direct interference with its existing activities would negate any at-

In other words, the court found that financial ability is a prerequisite to establishing a corporate opportunity. The court went on to hold that, where the facts were in dispute, the burden of proof on the financial issue rests upon the "party attacking the acquisition":

"If the facts are undisputed that the business opportunity presented bears no logical or reasonable relation to the existing or prospective business activities of the corporation *or that it lacks either the financial or fundamental practical or technical ability to pursue it*, then such opportunity would have to be found to be noncorporate as a matter of law. If the facts are disputed or reasonable minds functioning judicially could disagree as to whether the opportunity is closely associated with the existing or prospective activities of the corporation or its financial or technical ability to pursue it, *the question is one of fact with the burden of proof resting upon the party attacking the acquisition.*" 301 Minn. at 225, 222 N.W.2d at 81 (emphasis added).

The companion case of A.C. Petters v. St. Cloud Enterprises, Inc., supra, applied the rule of Miller v. Miller, supra. See also Ellzey v. Fyr–Pruf, Inc. 376 So.2d 1328 (Miss.1979).

Counsel for defendant, relying on *Miller,* contends there is no corporate opportunity if there is no capacity to take advantage of the corporate opportunity. We reject this argument. By the same token, we reject plaintiff's contention, relying on *Irving Trust,* that financial ability is totally irrelevant in an unlawful taking of a corporate opportunity. . . .

On April 13, 1984, the American Law Institute published its "Tentative Draft No. 3" concerning "Principles of Corporate Governance: Analysis and Recommendations." The draft, of course, does not represent the position of the ALI, but it does contain definitions and rules which we find helpful in resolving the main issue in this case. Section 5.12 of the draft, which contains the proposed general rule and definition, reads as follows:

"(a) *General Rule:*

"A director or principal senior executive may not take a corporate opportunity for himself or an associate unless:

(1) The corporate opportunity has first been offered to the corporation, and disclosure has been made to the corporate decisionmaker of all material facts known to the director or principal senior executive concerning his conflict of interest and the corporate opportunity (unless the corporate decisionmaker is otherwise aware of such material facts); and

(2) The corporate opportunity has been rejected by the corporation in a manner that meets one of the following standards:

(A) In the case of a rejection of a corporate opportunity that was authorized by disinterested directors following such disclo-

tempt by the officer to prove his good faith, loyalty, and fair dealing.   301 Minn. at 225–27; 222 N.W.2d at 81–82.

sure, the directors who authorized the rejection acted in a manner that meets the standards of the business judgment rule set forth in § 4.01(d);[8]

(B) In the case of a rejection that was authorized or ratified by disinterested shareholders following such disclosure, the rejection was not equivalent to a waste of corporate assets; and

(C) In the case of a rejection that was not authorized or ratified in the manner contemplated in § 5.12(a)(2)(A) or (B) or permitted by the terms of a [validly adopted] standard of the corporation . . ., the taking of the opportunity was fair to the corporation.

"(b) *Definition of a Corporate Opportunity:*

"A corporate opportunity means any opportunity to engage in a business activity (including acquisition or use of any contract right or other tangible or intangible property) that:

(1) In the case of a principal senior executive or any director, is an opportunity that is communicated or otherwise made available to him either:

(A) in connection with the performance of his obligations as a principal senior executive or director or under circumstances that should reasonably lead him to believe that the person offering the opportunity expects him to offer it to the corporation, or

(B) through the use of corporate information or property, if the resulting opportunity is one that the principal senior executive or director should reasonably be expected to believe would be of interest to the corporation; or

(2) In the case of a principal senior executive or a director who is a full-time employee of the corporation, is an opportunity that he knows or reasonably should know is closely related to the business in which the corporation is engaged or may reasonably be expected to engage." (Bracketed section references omitted.) *

Section 5.12 presents an approach very similar to that suggested by Chief Judge Joseph in the Court of Appeals decision rendered in this case. Section 5.12 generally would require an opportunity that could be advantageous to the corporation to be offered to the corporation by a director or principal senior executive before he takes it for himself. Section 5.12 declines to adopt the rigid rule expressed

---

8. Section 4.01 provides in pertinent part:

"A director has a duty to his corporation to perform his functions in good faith, in a manner that he reasonably believes to be in the best interests of the corporation * * * and with the care that an ordinarily prudent person would reasonably be expected to exercise in a like profession and under similar circumstances."

See, Devlin v. Moore, 64 Or. 433, 462, 130 P. 35, 45 (1913).

* Section 5.12 of ALI, Principles of Corporate Governance has been renumbered § 5.05 and somewhat revised, but is substantially equivalent to the provision quoted in *Klinicki*. See ALI, Principles of Corporate Governance § 5.05 (Tent.Draft No. 5, 1986). (Footnote by ed.)

in Irving Trust Co. v. Deutsch, supra, which precludes a person subject to the duty of loyalty from pursuing a rejected opportunity. The proposed rule permits a director or principal senior executive to deal with his corporation so long as he deals fairly with full disclosure and bears the burden of proving fairness unless the corporate opportunity was rejected by disinterested directors or shareholders.

The comment to Section 5.12(a) reads:

"Section 5.12(a) sets forth the general rule requiring a director or principal senior executive to first offer an opportunity to the corporation before taking it for himself. If the opportunity is not offered to the corporation, the director or principal senior executive will have violated § 5.12(a).

"Section 5.12(a) contemplates that a corporate opportunity will be promptly offered to the corporation, and that the corporation will promptly accept or reject the opportunity. Failure to accept the opportunity promptly will be considered tantamount to a rejection. . . ."

and that

". . . Rejection in the context of § 5.12(a)(2) may be based on one or more of a number of factors, such as lack of interest of the corporation in the opportunity, *its financial inability to acquire the opportunity,* legal restrictions on its ability to accept the opportunity, or unwillingness of a third party to deal with the corporation. . . ." (Emphasis added.)

The comment to Section 5.12(b) reads:

"Section 5.12(b) defines a corporate opportunity broadly as including any proposed acquisition of contract rights or other tangible or intangible property which falls into one of the categories set forth in §§ 5.12(b)(1) or 5.12(b)(2). . . ."

Section 5.12(c) would allocate the burden of proof in corporate opportunity cases as follows:

"(c) *Burden of Proof:*

"In any proceeding in which there is a challenge under § 5.12(a), the challenging party has the burden of proof, except if the rejection of a corporate opportunity was not authorized or ratified in the manner contemplated in § 5.12(a)(2)(A) or (B) or permitted by the terms of a [validly adopted] standard of the corporation . . ., the director or principal senior executive has the burden of proving that his taking of the opportunity was fair to the corporation. . . . *If the challenging party satisfies the burden of proving that a corporate opportunity was taken without being offered to the corporation, the challenging party will prevail."* (Emphasis added.)

The comment to Section 5.12(c) reads in part:

"The burden of coming forward with evidence and the ultimate burden of proof will be upon the person attacking a director's or principal senior executive's conduct to prove that (1) the director or principal senior executive acquired a corporate opportunity . . .. The complainant will also have the burden of proof with respect to all other aspects of the transaction, including lack of disclosure to the corporate decisionmaker and establishing that the requisite number of directors or shareholders who approved or ratified the transaction were not disinterested. *However, if disinterested directors or shareholders have not approved or ratified the rejection of the opportunity, the director or principal senior executive will have the burden of proving that his taking of the opportunity was fair and that the rejection of the opportunity was fair to the corporation at the time of the rejection. . . ."* (Emphasis added.)

Whether the rejection was fair or not includes consideration of whether the corporation was financially or otherwise incapacitated from undertaking the corporate opportunity. We agree with the proposed ALI Principles of Corporate Governance, supra, as to the following rules for application in close corporation corporate opportunity cases.

Where a director or principal senior executive of a close corporation wishes to take personal advantage of a "corporate opportunity," as defined by the proposed rule, the director or principal senior executive must comply strictly with the following procedure:

(1) the director or principal senior executive must promptly offer the opportunity and disclose all material facts known regarding the opportunity to the disinterested directors [10] or, if there is no disinterested director, to the disinterested shareholders.[11] If the director or

---

10. The term "disinterested director" is not specifically defined in the tentative proposal for ALI's "Principles of Corporate Governance and Structure" (1984). Instead, an "interested director" is defined in Section 1.15(1) of the ALI's Principles of Corporate Governance and Structure (Tent.Draft No. 2 1984):

"(1) a director or officer is 'interested' in a transaction if:

(a) the director or officer is a party to the transaction, or

(b) the director or officer or an associate of the director or officer has a pecuniary interest in the transaction, or the director or officer has a financial or familial relationship to a party to the transaction, that is sufficiently substantial that it would reasonably be expected to affect the director's or officer's judgment with respect to the transaction in a manner adverse to the corporation." (Bracketed section references omitted.)

Section 5.04 of Tentative Draft No. 3 provides:

"A provision that gives a specified effect to action by disinterested directors requires the affirmative votes of a majority of the directors on the board or an appropriate committee who are not in-

terested [§ 1.15] in the transaction in question."

Thus we define a "disinterested director" as any director other than one "interested" as defined by Section 1.15(1).

11. The term "disinterested shareholder" is not specifically defined in the ALI tentative drafts. Section 1.09 reads:

"[This definition will be written in connection with Part V. On what constitutes a majority of disinterested shareholders, see [§ 1.27(2)].]"

However, no definition of "disinterested shareholder" was written in Part V. Our definition of "disinterested shareholder" is derived from Section 1.15 of the ALI's Second Tentative Draft, supra. Subsection (2) of Section 1.15 provides:

"A shareholder is interested in a transaction if either the shareholder or, to his knowledge, an associate of the shareholder, is a party to the transaction."

Section 5.05 of the Third Tentative Draft, supra, provides:

"A provision that gives a specified effect to action by disinterested shareholders requires approval of the proposal by a majority of the votes cast by sharehold-

principal senior executive learns of other material facts after such disclosure, the director or principal senior executive must disclose these additional facts in a like manner before personally taking the opportunity.

(2) The director or principal senior executive may take advantage of the corporate opportunity only after full disclosure and only if the opportunity is rejected by a majority of the disinterested directors or, if there are no disinterested directors, by a majority of the disinterested shareholders.[12] If, after full disclosure, the disinterested directors or shareholders unreasonably fail to reject the offer,[13] the interested director or principal senior executive may proceed to take the opportunity if he can prove the taking was otherwise "fair" to the corporation. Full disclosure to the appropriate corporate body is, however, an absolute condition precedent to the validity of any forthcoming rejection as well as to the availability to the director or principal senior executive of the defense of fairness.

(3) An appropriation of a corporate opportunity may be ratified by rejection of the opportunity by a majority of disinterested directors or a majority of disinterested shareholders, after full disclosure subject to the same rules as set out above for prior offer, disclosure and rejection. Where a director or principal senior executive of a close corporation appropriates a corporate opportunity without first fully disclosing the opportunity and offering it to the corporation, absent ratification, that director or principal senior executive holds the opportunity in trust for the corporation.

Applying these rules to the facts in this case, we conclude:

(1) Lundgren, as director and principal executive officer of Berlinair, owed a fiduciary duty to Berlinair.

(2) The BFR contract was a "corporate opportunity" of Berlinair.

(3) Lundgren formed ABC for the purpose of usurping the opportunity presented to Berlinair by the BFR contract.

(4) Lundgren did not offer Berlinair the BFR contract.

(5) Lundgren did not attempt to obtain the consent of Berlinair to his taking of the BFR corporate opportunity.

(6) Lundgren did not fully disclose to Berlinair his intent to appropriate the opportunity for himself and ABC.

ers who are not interested [§ 1.15] in the transaction in question."

Thus, we define a "disinterested shareholder" as one who is not a party nor an associate of a party to the transaction in question.

12. A simple majority of disinterested directors or shareholders is sufficient to authorize or ratify an appropriation of a corporate opportunity by a director or principal executive officer.

13. A valid acceptance of the offer by the disinterested directors or shareholders would bar the fiduciary from appropriating the opportunity. An acceptance of the offer by the disinterested directors which failed to meet the standards of the business judgment rule, or an acceptance by the disinterested shareholders which was the equivalent of a waste of corporate assets would have the same effect as an unreasonable failure to reject. The corporate fiduciary could appropriate the opportunity only upon a showing that the taking was fair to the corporation. See ALI, Principles of Corporate Governance and Structure § 5.12(a)(2) (Tent.Draft No. 3 1984).

(7) Berlinair never rejected the opportunity presented by the BFR contract.

(8) Berlinair never ratified the appropriation of the BFR contract.

(9) Lundgren, acting for ABC, misappropriated the BFR contract.

Because of the above, the defendant may not now contend that Berlinair did not have the financial ability to successfully pursue the BFR contract. As stated in proposed Section 5.12(c) of the Principles of Corporate Governance, supra, "If the challenging party satisfies the burden of proving that a corporate opportunity was taken without being offered to the corporation, the challenging party will prevail."

This specific conclusion is also backed by what some might call a legal platitude and others might call a legal classic. When placing special burdens on those in positions of trust, it is worthwhile to recall the well-known admonition of Chief Justice Cardozo speaking for the New York Court of Appeals:

> "Joint adventurers, like copartners, owe to one another, while the enterprise continues, the duty of the finest loyalty. Many forms of conduct permissible in a workaday world for those acting at arm's length, are forbidden to those bound by fiduciary ties. A trustee is held to something stricter than the morals of the market place. Not honesty alone, but the punctilio of an honor the most sensitive, is then the standard of behavior. As to this there has developed a tradition that is unbending and inveterate. Uncompromising rigidity has been the attitude of courts of equity when petitioned to undermine the rule of undivided loyalty by the 'disintegrating erosion' of particular exceptions. . . . Only thus has the level of conduct for fiduciaries been kept at a level higher than that trodden by the crowd. It will not consciously be lowered by any judgment of this court." Meinhard v. Salmon, 249 N.Y. 458, 463–64, 164 N.E. 545, 546 (1928). . . .

The Court of Appeals is affirmed.

NOTE ON THE CORPORATE OPPORTUNITY DOCTRINE

A variety of tests have been utilized to determine whether a director or officer has wrongfully appropriated a corporate opportunity.

Under one test, often associated with Lagarde v. Anniston Lime & Stone Co., 126 Ala. 496, 502, 28 So. 199, 201 (1900), the corporate opportunity doctrine applies only when the director or officer has acquired property in which "the corporation has an interest already existing or in which it has an expectancy growing out of an existing right," or his "interference will in some degree balk the corporation in effecting the purposes of its creation."

The application of the first branch of the *Lagarde* test is uncertain, because the terms "interest" and "expectancy" have no fixed meaning in this context. See, e.g., Abbott Redmont Thinlite Corp. v. Redmont, 475 F.2d 85, 88–89 (2d Cir.1973). In *Lagarde* itself, the court held that real estate in which the corporation was a tenant constituted a corporate expectancy, but real estate in which the corporation owned an undivided one-third interest did not.

The application of the second branch of the *Lagarde* test is also uncertain. Presumably, it would cover cases in which the corporation's need for the property is very substantial. See, e.g., Harmony Way Bridge Co. v. Leathers, 353 Ill. 378, 187 N.E. 432 (1933) (a director purchased a right of way that was needed as an approach to his corporation's bridge); News–Journal Corp. v. Gore, 147 Fla. 217, 2 So.2d 741 (1941) (a director purchased a tract of land that the corporation leased for its building, and immediately increased the rent).

Insofar as the meaning of the *Lagarde* test can be determined, it is unduly narrow. Even the Alabama Supreme Court may now be seeking more leeway, by broadening the second branch:

> The last restriction in *Lagarde,* that which prohibits "balking the corporate purpose," is really quite broad in its formulation, although the case has often been described as restrictive. . . . We think that *Lagarde* when properly read enforces responsibilities for the corporate officer or director comparable to those outlined in *Guth v. Loft, Inc.,* 23 Del.Ch. 255, 5 A.2d 503 (1939), where the Delaware Supreme Court employed the doctrine of corporate opportunity and observed that it
>
> > ". . . demands of a corporate officer or director, peremptorily and inexorably, the most scrupulous observance of his duty, not only affirmatively to protect the interests of the corporation committed to his charge, but also to refrain from doing anything that would work injury to the corporation, or to deprive it of profit or advantage which his skill and ability might properly bring to it, or to enable it to make in the reasonable and lawful exercise of its powers. . . .

Morad v. Coupounas, 361 So.2d 6, 8–9 (Ala.1978).

A second test is whether the opportunity was in the corporation's "line of business." This test was adopted in the leading case of Guth v. Loft, Inc., 23 Del.Ch. 255, 5 A.2d 503 (1939), relied on in *Morad.* Guth was the president and chief executive of Loft, Inc., which was engaged in the manufacture and sale of beverages. Guth became dissatisfied with Loft's existing business arrangements with Coca–Cola Company. National Pepsi–Cola Company was then bankrupt, and Guth and an associate organized Pepsi–Cola Company to acquire National's secret formula and trademark. The opportunity came to Guth as a result of his connection with Loft. Guth used Loft's funds and facilities to acquire and develop Pepsi–Cola Company's business, and Loft purchased large quantities of Pepsi–Cola. Partly by these means, and partly by his own efforts, Pepsi–Cola's shares became very valuable. The court required Guth to transfer those shares to Loft.

> Where a corporation is engaged in a certain business, and an opportunity is presented to it embracing an activity as to which it has fundamental knowledge, practical experience and ability to pursue, which, logically and naturally, is adaptable to its business having regard for its financial position, and is one that is consonant with its reasonable needs and aspirations for expansion, it may be properly said that the opportunity is in the line of the corporation's business.

Id. at 279, 5 A.2d at 514. The opinion clearly implied that Guth would have been liable even if he had not used Loft funds and facilities, because Pepsi–Cola was so closely related to Loft's existing business.

Delaware also appears to place weight on how the opportunity comes to the corporate director or officer. If the offer is made to the director or officer as an agent of the corporation, the "line of business" test is employed. If the opportunity is offered to the director or officer as an individual, however, liability will apparently arise only if the opportunity is "essential" to the corporation, or is subject to an "interest or expectancy" of the corporation, or if the director or officer uses corporate resources to exploit the opportunity. Kaplan v. Fenton, 278 A.2d 834, 836 (Del.1971). See Carrad, The Corporate Opportunity Doctrine in Delaware: A Guide to Corporate Planning and Anticipatory Defensive Measures, 2 Del.J.Corp.L. 1, 5 (1977).

A third test is the "fairness" test. A typical example is Durfee v. Durfee & Canning, Inc., 323 Mass. 187, 199, 80 N.E.2d 522, 529 (1948), in which the court approved a statement in H. Ballantine, Corporations 204–05 (rev. ed.1946) that "the true basis of the doctrine should not be found in any 'expectancy' or property interest concept, but in the unfairness on the particular facts of a fiduciary taking advantage of an opportunity when the interests of the corporation justly call for protection. This calls for the application of ethical standards of what is fair and equitable to particular sets of facts."

Still another test, calling for a two-step line-of-business and fairness analysis, was adopted in Miller v. Miller, 301 Minn. 207, 222 N.W.2d 71 (1974). This test is discussed in Klinicki v. Lundgren, below, which reflects yet another approach.

JOHNSTON v. GREENE, 35 Del.Ch. 479, 121 A.2d 919 (1956). Odlum, a prominent financier and an officer and director of numerous corporations, owned 11% of the stock of Atlas, which in turn owned 18% of the stock of Airfleets, Inc. Odlum was also president of Airfleets, serving without compensation. Airfleets was in a highly liquid state, with $3.5 million in cash and marketable securities. Odlum was offered, in his individual capacity, a chance to acquire the stock of Nutt–Shel Corporation, which manufactured aircraft parts, and also several patents pertaining to Nutt–Shel's business. There was some suggestion that it would be advisable for the stock and patents to be held separately to satisfy the contracting requirements of the federal government, an important customer of Nutt–Shel. Odlum offered Airfleets the opportunity to buy the stock, but purchased the patents for his friends, associates, and himself. The court held that Odlum had not acted improperly, on the ground that the offer came to him as an individual, the patents were not essential to the maintenance of Airfleets' business, and Airfleets had no real interest or expectancy in the opportunity. Although a corporation that has liquid funds has a "general interest in investing" them, it does not follow that it "has a specific interest attaching in equity to any and every business opportunity that may come to any of its directors in his individual capacity." Id. at 488, 121 A.2d at 924.

The court also asked, to which of the several corporations of which Odlum was a director would he owe the duty to pass on the opportunity, and why to Airfleets specifically? Did the court mean, by this question, that a person who is an officer and director of several corporations owes a duty to none as regards what would otherwise be corporate opportunities? [1]

SECTION 5.   SALE OF CONTROL

ZETLIN v. HANSON HOLDINGS, INC.

New York Court of Appeals, 1979.
48 N.Y.2d 684, 421 N.Y.S.2d 877, 397 N.E.2d 387.

MEMORANDUM.

The order of the Appellate Division should be affirmed, with costs.

Plaintiff Zetlin owned approximately 2% of the outstanding shares of Gable Industries, Inc., with defendants Hanson Holdings, Inc., and Sylvestri, together with members of the Sylvestri family, owning 44.4% of Gable's shares. The defendants sold their interests to Flintkote Co. for a premium price of $15 per share, at a time when Gable stock was selling on the open market for $7.38 per share. It is undisputed that the 44.4% acquired by Flintkote represented effective control of Gable.

---

1. Cf. Burg v. Horn, 380 F.2d 897 (2d Cir.1967): "It has been urged that the reasoning of Johnston v. Greene is fallacious because the fact that a director may be under fiduciary obligations to more than one corporation should lead a court to find and enforce the strongest obligation, not to allow the director to disregard them all. . . . This criticism seems to us to miss the point . . . that a person's involvement in more than one venture of the same kind may negate the obligation which might otherwise be implied to offer similar opportunities to any one of them, absent some contrary understanding."

Recognizing that those who invest the capital necessary to acquire a dominant position in the ownership of a corporation have the right of controlling that corporation, it has long been settled law that, absent looting of corporate assets, conversion of a corporate opportunity, fraud or other acts of bad faith, a controlling stockholder is free to sell, and a purchaser is free to buy, that controlling interest at a premium price (see *Barnes v Brown*, 80 NY 527; *Levy v American Beverage Corp.*, 265 App Div 208; *Essex Universal Corp. v Yates*, 305 F2d 572).

Certainly, minority shareholders are entitled to protection against such abuse by controlling shareholders. They are not entitled, however, to inhibit the legitimate interests of the other stockholders. It is for this reason that control shares usually command a premium price. The premium is the added amount an investor is willing to pay for the privilege of directly influencing the corporation's affairs.

In this action plaintiff Zetlin contends that minority stockholders are entitled to an opportunity to share equally in any premium paid for a controlling interest in the corporation. This rule would profoundly affect the manner in which controlling stock interests are now transferred. It would require, essentially, that a controlling interest be transferred only by means of an offer to all stockholders, i.e., a tender offer. This would be contrary to existing law and if so radical a change is to be effected it would best be done by the Legislature.

Chief Judge COOKE and Judges JASEN, GABRIELLI, JONES, WACHTLER, FUCHSBERG and MEYER concur in memorandum.

Order affirmed.

ANDREWS, THE STOCKHOLDER'S RIGHT TO EQUAL OPPORTUNITY IN THE SALE OF SHARES
78 Harv.L.Rev. 505, 515–22 (1965).

The rule to be considered can be stated thus: whenever a controlling stockholder sells his shares, every other holder of shares (of the same class) is entitled to have an equal opportunity to sell his shares, or a prorata part of them, on substantially the same terms. Or in terms of the correlative duty: before a controlling stockholder may sell his shares to an outsider he must assure his fellow stockholders an equal opportunity to sell their shares, or as high a proportion of theirs as he ultimately sells of his own. There are qualifications in the application of the rule, to which I will return; but for purposes of argument we can begin with this broad statement of it. . . .

[*Practical reasons for the proposed rule*] (a).—There is a substantial danger that following a transfer of controlling shares corporate affairs may be conducted in a manner detrimental to the interests of the stockholders who have not had an opportunity to sell their shares. The corporation may be looted; it may just be badly run. Or the sale of controlling shares may operate to destroy a favorable opportunity for corporate action. . . .

The equal opportunity rule does not deal directly with the problem of mismanagement, which may occur even after a transfer of control complying with the rule; but enforcement of the rule will remove much of the incentive a purchaser can offer a controlling stockholder to sell on profitable terms. Indeed, in the case of a purchasing looter there is nothing in it for the purchaser unless he can buy less than all the shares; there is no profit in stealing from a solvent corporation if the thief owns all the stock. But the controlling stockholder will be loath to sell only part of his shares (except at a price that compensates him for all of his shares) if he expects the purchaser to destroy the value of what he keeps. The rule forces the controlling stockholder to share equally with his fellow stockholders both the benefits of the price he receives for the shares he sells and the business risks incident to the shares he retains. This will tend strongly to discourage a sale of controlling shares when the risk of looting, or other harm to the corporation, is apparent; and it will provide the seller with a direct incentive to investigate and evaluate with care when the risks are not apparent, since his own financial interest continues to be at stake. . . .

Of course a transfer of control may have advantageous effects for a corporation and its stockholders—and these may be just as subtle as any adverse effects. Many sales of controlling shares come about because the selling stockholders are not doing as well with a business as a purchaser believes he can do; and the belief is often right. Often the sellers are members of a family that has simply run out of managerial talent or interest.

If the rule of equal opportunity would prevent sales in this sort of situation, that would be a high price to pay for the prevention of harm in other cases. . . . For my own part I do not believe the rule of equal opportunity would have much tendency to discourage beneficial transactions. After all, if the purchaser is optimistic—and can convince his bankers to share his optimism—he should be willing to buy out everyone. If the seller is optimistic about the consequences of the transfer, he should be willing to retain some of his shares. If minority stockholders are optimistic, they should be willing to hold their shares. If the financial community is optimistic (in the case of a publicly held corporation), the market itself should offer the minority stockholders a chance to sell at a price that satisfies the rule. Thus, on the face of it the rule would only operate to prevent a sale when all four of these— the seller, the purchaser, the minority stockholders, and the financial community—take a pessimistic view of the transfer. . . .

(*b*). . . . [A] purchaser attains control of the corporation's business and assets equally whether he purchases all the shares or a smaller controlling block. When a purchaser buys less than all the shares, he is acquiring a business worth more than what he pays in cash, and is financing the difference by leaving the minority shares outstanding. We think of mortgage debts that way; if a person buys property subject to a mortgage and leaves the mortgage outstanding, we recognize that the mortgage provides financing for the purchaser because it has the same effect, substantially, as a new loan with the proceeds of which the purchaser might have paid full value for the property. But stock provides financing just as much as a mortgage does. A purchaser who buys only part of the stock of an enterprise might have accomplished much the same net result by purchasing all the assets in the name of a newly organized corporation in which he takes only a part of the stock. The other stockholders in the new corporation would then be viewed as providing equity financing for the acquisition. The chief difference then between a sale of assets, or of all the stock, and a sale of a controlling block of shares only, is that in the latter case the purchaser has had his acquisition partially financed, perhaps unwillingly, by the stockholders from whom he does not buy. That is no reason to give the minority stockholders less protection than if the purchaser gave them an opportunity to sell, even at a lower price. . . .

(*c*).—A somewhat broader way of putting the argument is even simpler: each stockholder is entitled to share proportionately in the profits of the enterprise; from the stockholder's point of view a sale of stock is one very important way of realizing a profit on his investment; profits from stock sales ought to be regarded as profits of the enterprise subject to equal sharing among stockholders just as much as profits realized through corporate action.

A minority stockholder must invest largely on the strength of the expectation that decisions will tend to be made for his benefit because of the general identity of interest between him and those in control. This identity of interest is qualified when controlling stockholders have an opportunity to profit by entering into dealings with their corporation; this is permitted because such transactions may be mutually profitable, and there is no way to enforce equality of interest beyond allowing judicial scrutiny of such transactions for fairness. It would be impossible to insist, for example, that a publicly held corporation offer all its stockholders a proportionate opportunity to serve in an executive capacity. But when an opportunity arises for profit by selling shares, there is no such simple practical reason why it cannot be made equally available to all stockholders. . . .

JAVARAS, EQUAL OPPORTUNITY IN THE SALE OF CONTROLLING SHARES: A REPLY TO PROFESSOR ANDREWS

32 U.Chi.L.Rev. 420, 425–27 (1965).

I believe that the gravest defect in Professor Andrews' theory is a grievous underassessment of the costs of a preventive rule in restraining beneficial transactions. Such restraint would operate on the purchaser by imposing higher required investment—the price of all the shares of the corporation rather than only those owned by the controlling shareholder. Professor Andrews minimizes the effects of this factor on two grounds. First, the controlling shareholder under the rule of equal opportunity, when confronted with a purchaser who wants the controlling shares and no more, may be induced to retain some of his shares and share the sale ratably with the non-controlling shareholders. Admittedly, this requires faith in the management of the purchaser. Second, a beneficial purchaser should be willing to buy all the shares because, after all, the non-controlling shares have the same investment value as the controlling shares. All the purchaser would have to do, therefore, if he did not have the capital is to borrow it. If he could not, that would be a reflection either of superior knowledge in the financial community or dislocations in the capital market.

It is doubtful whether sufficient controlling sellers can be induced to retain their shares so as to eliminate the higher capital requirement. First, . . . sales of securities are not dictated merely by an appraisal of investment value. Many sellers simply want immediate cash. Second, a controlling seller may not wish to hold, say twenty-five per cent as compared to his prior fifty per cent, because of the possibility of his views differing from those of the controlling purchaser in the future. This reticence would partly stem from . . . the controlling sellers assessment of the change in risks when he is deprived of control. The loss of control would subject him to the risk of poor management, which might dictate a lesser investment in this corporation on the principle of risk diversification.

Likewise the purchaser himself might be unwilling that the seller retain some of his shares, particularly where working control (less than fifty per cent) is the subject of the offer. He might well be reluctant to have a large block of stock outstanding whose owners, under conditions of dissension, could mobilize the other shareholders and displace his control of the board of directors.

In effect then, the rule of equal treatment would impose higher capital requirements on beneficial purchasers in a substantial number of transactions. Professor Andrews inappropriately assumes, however, that the purchasers should be willing to meet these higher costs because the investment value of the additional shares is the same. He errs in that his reasoning is incomplete. It is true that the investment value is the same. But even if the capital market did function perfectly and the purchaser could arrange the financing, a rational businessman might not want to buy all the shares at a premium price justified by the investment potential. It might be sensible to decline to buy more than the bare amount necessary for control on the principles of diversification of risk and of opportunity. This might render the equal treatment rule ineffectual as a means of automatically distinguishing "good" and "bad" purchasers. I would think that the number of prospective beneficial purchasers prevented because of a desire to diversify will be much larger than those simply unable to raise the capital. Until empirical evidence is adduced to the contrary, I am predisposed to consider this cost of restraining beneficial transactions substantial when compared with the cases of detriment with which the present law is incompetent to deal. . . .

EASTERBROOK & FISCHEL, CORPORATE CONTROL TRANSACTIONS

91 Yale L.J. 698, 705–10 (1982).

It should be clear that managers do not always maximize the wealth of investors. . . . Because managers have only a small stake in the fortunes of the firm, [the costs of principal-agency relationships] may be quite high. Managers may not work as hard as they would if they could claim a higher share of the proceeds—they may consume excessive perquisites, and they may select inferior projects for the firm without bearing the consequences of their action. Corporate control transactions can reduce agency costs if better managers obtain control of the firm's assets or if they alter the incentive structure facing existing managers. . . .

The sale of a control bloc of stock, for example, allows the buyer to install his own management team, producing the same gains available from a tender offer for a majority of shares but at lower cost to the buyer. Because such a buyer believes he can manage the assets of a firm more profitably, he is willing to pay a premium over the market price to acquire control. The premium will be some percentage of the anticipated increase in value once the transfer of control is effectuated. If there were no anticipated increase in value, it would be irrational for the buyer to pay the premium. There is a strong presumption, therefore, that free transferability of corporate control, like any other type of voluntary exchange, moves assets to higher valued uses. . . .

A sharing requirement . . . may make an otherwise profitable transaction unattractive to the prospective seller of control. To illustrate, suppose that the owner of a control bloc of shares finds that his perquisites or the other amenities of his position are worth $10. A prospective acquiror of control concludes that, by eliminating these perquisites and other amenities, he could produce a gain of $15. The shareholders in the company benefit if the acquiror pays a premium of $11 to the owner of the controlling bloc, ousts the current managers, and makes the contemplated improvements. The net gains of $4 inure to each investor according to his holdings, and although the acquiror obtains the largest portion because he holds the largest bloc, no one is left out. If the owner of the control bloc must share the $11 premium with all of the existing shareholders, however, the deal collapses. The owner will not part with his bloc for less than a $10 premium. A sharing requirement would make the deal unprofitable to him, and the other investors would lose the prospective gain from the installation of better managers.

HAMILTON, PRIVATE SALE OF CONTROL TRANSACTIONS: WHERE WE STAND TODAY

36 Case–Western Res.L.Rev. 248, 256–59 (1985).

There are several problems [with the Easterbrook & Fischel analysis]. . . . The hypothetical the authors create assumes the correctness of their thesis. The assumption that the purchasers of control will reduce the "perquisites or the other amenities" enjoyed as a result of the seller's position by $10, thereby producing a corporate gain of $15, illustrates that situations may exist in which unequal division is necessary for the realization of societally desirable transactions. It does not, however, bear directly on Easterbrook and Fischel's basic thesis. One can equally plausibly assume that the buyer feels that he can enjoy the same "perquisites or the other amenities" as the seller enjoyed, and even increase them to, for instance, $14. On this assumption, the minority shareholders are clearly worse off as a result of the sale, and both the purchaser and seller of the control shares are benefiting at the minority shareholders' expense.

The critical question is: Which assumption is more realistic? I suspect, from personal experience, that losses occur from the change of managements, particularly in smaller unlisted companies, in a large number of cases; quite possibly more often than net gains. . . .

NOTE ON THE DUTY OF INQUIRY IN A SALE OF CONTROL

There are several well-established exceptions to the rule reflected in Zetlin v. Hanson Holdings, Inc., supra. One of the most important exceptions is that it is wrongful for a controlling shareholder to transfer control under circumstances that put him on notice that the buyer is likely to loot the corporation. See, e.g., Gerdes v. Reynolds, 28 N.Y.S.2d 622 (Sup.Ct.1941). Suppose that B offers to purchase S's controlling shares in C corporation; S, who has not investigated B, knows of no facts to indicate that B is likely to loot C; but an investigation would have disclosed such facts. S sells, and B loots. Is S liable? In Levy v. American Beverage Corp., 265 A.D. 208, 218–19, 38 N.Y.S.2d 517, 526–27 (1942), the court said:

> [T]o say . . . that the failure to investigate the moral character, or financial ability of the purchaser of one's stock is an actionable wrong, is to place an unwarranted burden upon the ownership of stock. Knowledge that the purchasers were about to loot the corporate treasury, or were persons who had previously engaged in such practices would be one thing. Concluding on the basis of mere lack of knowledge concerning the business integrity of the purchaser that the seller assumes the risk that the buyer has an intention to loot the company would be quite another. The law does not require one to act on the assumption that a person with

whom a business transaction, even of large amount, is had, will commit a fraudulent or criminal act if given the opportunity to do so. Quite the contrary may be assumed, in the absence of actual notice.

Similarly, in Swinney v. Keebler Co., 480 F.2d 573 (4th Cir.1973), the Fourth Circuit said that the plaintiff's right to recover in a looting case depended on whether the controlling shareholder "had sufficient knowledge to foresee the likelihood of fraud so as to give rise to a duty to conduct a further investigation and to satisfy itself, by the test of a reasonable man, that no fraud was intended or likely to result." Id. at 578. This view was reaffirmed by the Fourth Circuit in Clagett v. Hutchison, 583 F.2d 1259 (4th Cir.1978).

These cases suggest that in the hypothetical, S would have no liability. This conclusion, however, is doubtful. The language in the cases considerably overshoots the facts. In none of the cases was it shown that an investigation would have put the sellers on notice that the buyer would be likely to loot. Indeed, in *Swinney* and *Clagett* it's not clear that the original buyers did loot. In both cases, the damage appears to have been done by persons to whom the buyers resold. (In *Clagett*, the plaintiff joined the reselling buyers as original defendants, but that action effectively became moot when the plaintiff dropped his charges that the ultimate buyer had mismanaged the corporation.)

In today's era of readily available information, it is doubtful that a responsible seller would hand over control of a corporation to a buyer without any knowledge of the buyer whatsoever. A seller who did so, when even a cursory check would have revealed facts that would have put him on notice, should and probably would be held to have violated his duty to the noncontrolling shareholders.

Displaced Company Level Oportunity theory

PERLMAN v. FELDMANN

United States Court of Appeals, Second Circuit, 1955.
219 F.2d 173, cert. denied 349 U.S. 952, 75 S.Ct. 880, 99 L.Ed. 1277 (1955).

CLARK, Chief Judge. This is a derivative action brought by minority stockholders of Newport Steel Corporation to compel accounting for, and restitution of, allegedly illegal gains which accrued to defendants as a result of the sale in August, 1950, of their controlling interest in the corporation. The principal defendant, C. Russell Feldmann, who represented and acted for the others, members of his family,[1] was at that time not only the dominant stockholder, but also the chairman of the board of directors and the president of the corporation. Newport, an Indiana corporation, operated mills for the

---

1. The stock was not held personally by Feldmann in his own name, but was held by the members of his family and by personal corporations. The aggregate of stock thus [held] amounted to 33% of the outstanding Newport stock and gave working control to the holder. The actual sale included 55,552 additional shares held by friends and associates of Feldmann, so that a total of 37% of the Newport stock was transferred.

production of steel sheets for sale to manufacturers of steel products, first at Newport, Kentucky, and later also at other places in Kentucky and Ohio. The buyers, a syndicate organized as Wilport Company, a Delaware corporation, consisted of end-users of steel who were interested in securing a source of supply in a market becoming ever tighter in the Korean War. Plaintiffs contend that the consideration paid for the stock included compensation for the sale of a corporate asset, a power held in trust for the corporation by Feldmann as its fiduciary. This power was the ability to control the allocation of the corporate product in a time of short supply, through control of the board of directors; and it was effectively transferred in this sale by having Feldmann procure the resignation of his own board and the election of Wilport's nominees immediately upon consummation of the sale.

The present action represents the consolidation of three pending stockholders' actions in which yet another stockholder has been permitted to intervene. Jurisdiction below was based upon the diverse citizenship of the parties. Plaintiffs argue here, as they did in the court below, that in the situation here disclosed the vendors must account to the nonparticipating minority stockholders for that share of their profit which is attributable to the sale of the corporate power. Judge Hincks denied the validity of the premise, holding that the rights involved in the sale were only those normally incident to the possession of a controlling block of shares, with which a dominant stockholder, in the absence of fraud or foreseeable looting, was entitled to deal according to his own best interests. Furthermore, he held that plaintiffs had failed to satisfy their burden of proving that the sales price was not a fair price for the stock per se. Plaintiffs appeal from these rulings of law which resulted in the dismissal of their complaint.

The essential <u>facts</u> found by the trial judge are not in dispute. Newport was a relative newcomer in the steel industry with predominantly old installations which were in the process of being supplemented by more modern facilities. Except in times of extreme shortage Newport was not in a position to compete profitably with other steel mills for customers not in its immediate geographical area. Wilport, the purchasing syndicate, consisted of geographically remote end-users of steel who were interested in buying more steel from Newport than they had been able to obtain during recent periods of tight supply. The price of $20 per share was found by Judge Hincks to be a fair one for a control block of stock, although the over-the-counter market price had not exceeded $12 and the book value per share was $17.03. But this finding was limited by Judge Hincks' statement that "[w]hat value the block would have had if shorn of its appurtenant power to control distribution of the corporate product, the evidence does not show." It was also conditioned by his earlier ruling that the burden was on plaintiffs to prove a lesser value for the stock.

Both as director and as dominant stockholder, Feldmann stood in a fiduciary relationship to the corporation and to the minority stockholders as beneficiaries thereof. Pepper v. Litton, 308 U.S. 295, 60 S.Ct. 238, 84 L.Ed. 281; Southern Pac. Co. v. Bogert, 250 U.S. 483,

39 S.Ct. 533, 63 L.Ed. 1099. His fiduciary obligation must in the first instance be measured by the law of Indiana, the state of incorporation of Newport. Rogers v. Guaranty Trust Co. of New York, 288 U.S. 123, 136, 53 S.Ct. 295, 77 L.Ed. 652; Mayflower Hotel Stockholders Protective Committee v. Mayflower Hotel Corp., 89 U.S.App.D.C. 171, 193 F.2d 666, 668. Although there is no Indiana case directly in point, the most closely analogous one emphasizes the close scrutiny to which Indiana subjects the conduct of fiduciaries when personal benefit may stand in the way of fulfillment of trust obligations. In Schemmel v. Hill, 91 Ind.App. 373, 169 N.E. 678, 682, 683, McMahan, J., said: "Directors of a business corporation act in a strictly fiduciary capacity. Their office is a trust. Stratis v. Andreson, 1926, 254 Mass. 536, 150 N.E. 832, 44 A.L.R. 567; Hill v. Nisbet, 1885, 100 Ind. 341, 353. When a director deals with his corporation, his acts will be closely scrutinized. Bossert v. Geis, 1914, 57 Ind.App. 384, 107 N.E. 95. Directors of a corporation are its agents, and they are governed by the rules of law applicable to other agents, and, as between themselves and their principal, the rules relating to honesty and fair dealing in the management of the affairs of their principal are applicable. They must not, in any degree, allow their official conduct to be swayed by their private interest, which must yield to official duty. Leader Publishing Co. v. Grant Trust Co., 1915, 182 Ind. 651, 108 N.E. 121. In a transaction between a director and his corporation, where he acts for himself and his principal at the same time in a matter connected with the relation between them, it is presumed, where he is thus potentially on both sides of the contract, that self-interest will overcome his fidelity to his principal, to his own benefit and to his principal's hurt." And the judge added: "Absolute and most scrupulous good faith is the very essence of a director's obligation to his corporation. The first principal duty arising from his official relation is to act in all things of trust wholly for the benefit of his corporation."

In Indiana, then, as elsewhere, the responsibility of the fiduciary is not limited to a proper regard for the tangible balance sheet assets of the corporation, but includes the dedication of his uncorrupted business judgment for the sole benefit of the corporation, in any dealings which may adversely affect it. . . . Although the Indiana case is particularly relevant to Feldmann as a director, the same rule should apply to his fiduciary duties as majority stockholder, for in that capacity he chooses and controls the directors, and thus is held to have assumed their liability. Pepper v. Litton, supra, 308 U.S. 295, 60 S.Ct. 238. This, therefore, is the standard to which Feldmann was by law required to conform in his activities here under scrutiny.

It is true, as defendants have been at pains to point out, that this is not the ordinary case of breach of fiduciary duty. We have here no fraud, no misuse of confidential information, no outright looting of a helpless corporation. But on the other hand, we do not find compliance with that high standard which we have just stated and which we and other courts have come to expect and demand of corporate fiduciaries. In the often-quoted words of Judge Cardozo: "Many forms of conduct permissible in a workaday world for those acting at arm's length, are forbidden to those bound by fiduciary ties. A trustee is held to something stricter than the morals of the market place. Not honesty alone, but the punctilio of an honor the most sensitive, is then the standard of behavior. As to this there has developed a tradition that is unbending and inveterate. Uncompromising rigidity has been the attitude of courts of equity when petitioned to undermine the rule of undivided loyalty by the 'disintegrating erosion' of particular exceptions." Meinhard v. Salmon, supra, 249 N.Y. 458, 464, 164 N.E. 545, 546, 62 A.L.R. 1. The actions of defendants in siphoning off for personal gain corporate advantages to be derived from a favorable market situation do not betoken the necessary undivided loyalty owed by the fiduciary to his principal.

The corporate opportunities of whose misappropriation the minority stockholders complain need not have been an absolute certainty in order to support this action against Feldmann. If there was possibility of corporate gain, they are entitled to recover. In Young v. Higbee Co., supra, 324 U.S. 204, 65 S.Ct. 594, two stockholders appealing the confirmation of a plan of bankruptcy reorganization were held liable for profits received for the sale of their stock pending determination of the validity of the appeal. They were held accountable for the excess of the price of their stock over its normal price, even though there was no indication that the appeal could have succeeded on substantive grounds. And in Irving Trust Co. v. Deutsch, supra, 2 Cir., 73 F.2d 121, 124, an accounting was required of corporate directors who bought stock for themselves for corporate use, even though there was an affirmative showing that the corporation did not have the finances itself to acquire the stock. Judge Swan speaking for the court pointed out that "The defendants' argument, contrary to Wing v. Dillingham [5 Cir., 239 F. 54], that the equitable rule that fiduciaries should not be permitted to assume a position in which their individual interests might be in conflict with those of the corporation can have no application where the corporation is unable to undertake the venture, is not convincing. If directors are permitted to justify their conduct on such a theory, there will be a temptation to refrain from exerting their strongest efforts on behalf of the corporation since, if it does not meet the obligations, an opportunity of profit will be open to them personally."

This rationale is equally appropriate to a consideration of the benefits which Newport might have derived from the steel shortage. In the past Newport had used and profited by its market leverage by operation of what the industry had come to call the "Feldmann Plan." This consisted of securing interest-free advances from prospective purchasers of steel in return for firm commitments to them from future production. The funds thus acquired were used to finance improvements in existing plants and to acquire new installations. In the summer of 1950 Newport had been negotiating for cold-rolling facilities which it needed for a more fully integrated operation and a more marketable product, and Feldmann plan funds might well have been used toward this end.

Further, as plaintiffs alternatively suggest, Newport might have used the period of short supply to build up patronage in the geographical area in which it could compete profitably even when steel was more abundant. Either of these opportunities was Newport's, to be used to its advantage only. Only if defendants had been able to negate completely any possibility of gain by Newport could they have prevailed. It is true that a trial court finding states: "Whether or not, in August, 1950, Newport's position was such that it could have entered into 'Feldmann Plan' type transactions to procure funds and financing for the further expansion and integration of its steel facilities and whether such expansion would have been desirable for Newport, the evidence does not show." This, however, cannot avail the defendants, who—contrary to the ruling below—had the burden of proof on this issue, since fiduciaries always have the burden of proof in establishing the fairness of their dealings with trust property. . . .

Defendants seek to categorize the corporate opportunities which might have accrued to Newport as too unethical to warrant further consideration. It is true that reputable steel producers were not participating in the gray market brought about by the Korean War and were refraining from advancing their prices, although to do so would not have been illegal. But Feldmann plan transactions were not considered within this self-imposed interdiction; the trial court found that around the time of the Feldmann sale Jones & Laughlin Steel Corporation, Republic Steel Company, and Pittsburgh Steel Corporation were all participating in such arrangements. In any event, it ill becomes the defendants to disparage as unethical the market advantages from which they themselves reaped rich benefits.

We do not mean to suggest that a majority stockholder cannot dispose of his controlling block of stock to outsiders without having to account to his corporation for profits or even never do this with impunity when the buyer is an interested customer, actual or potential, for the corporation's product. But when the sale necessarily results in a sacrifice of this element of corporate good will and consequent unusual profit to the fiduciary who has caused the sacrifice, he should account for his gains. So in a time of market shortage, where a call on a corporation's product commands an unusually large premium, in one form or another, we think it sound law that a fiduciary may not appropriate to himself the value of this premium. Such personal gain at the expense of his coventurers seems particularly reprehensible when made by the trusted president and director of his company. In this case the violation of duty seems to be all the clearer because of this triple role in which Feldmann appears, though we are unwilling to say, and are not to be understood as saying, that we should accept a lesser obligation for any one of his roles alone.

Hence to the extent that the price received by Feldmann and his codefendants included such a bonus, he is accountable to the minority stockholders who sue here. Restatement, Restitution §§ 190, 197 (1937); Seagrave Corp. v. Mount, supra, 6 Cir., 212 F.2d 389. And plaintiffs, as they contend, are entitled to a recovery in their own right, instead of in right of the corporation (as in the usual derivative actions), since neither Wilport nor their successors in interest should share in any judgment which may be rendered. See Southern Pacific Co. v. Bogert, 250 U.S. 483, 39 S.Ct. 533, 63 L.Ed. 1099. Defendants cannot well object to this form of recovery, since the only alternative, recovery for the corporation as a whole, would subject them to a greater total liability.

The case will therefore be remanded to the district court for a determination of the question expressly left open below, namely, the value of defendants' stock without the appurtenant control over the corporation's output of steel. We reiterate that on this issue, as on all others relating to a breach of fiduciary duty, the burden of proof must rest on the defendants. Bigelow v. RKO Radio Pictures, 327 U.S. 251, 265–266, 66 S.Ct. 574, 90 L.Ed. 652; Package Closure Corp. v. Sealright Co., 2 Cir., 141 F.2d 972, 979. Judgment should go to these plaintiffs and those whom they represent for any premium value so shown to the extent of their respective stock interests.

The judgment is therefore reversed and the action remanded for further proceedings pursuant to this opinion.

SWAN, Circuit Judge (dissenting). . . .

The power to control the management of a corporation, that is, to elect directors to manage its affairs, is an inseparable incident to the ownership of a majority of its stock, or sometimes, as in the present instance, to the ownership of enough shares, less than a majority, to control an election. Concededly a majority or dominant shareholder is ordinarily privileged to sell his stock at the best price obtainable from the purchaser. In so doing he acts on his own behalf, not as an agent of the corporation. If he knows or has reason to believe that the purchaser intends to exercise to the detriment of the corporation the power of management acquired by the purchase, such knowledge or reasonable suspicion will terminate the dominant shareholder's privilege to sell and will create a duty not to transfer the power of management to such purchaser. The duty seems to me to resemble the obligation which everyone is under not to assist another to commit a tort rather than the obligation of a fiduciary. But whatever the nature of the duty, a violation of it will subject the violator to liability for damages sustained by the corporation. Judge Hincks found that Feldmann had no reason to think that Wilport would use the power of management it would acquire by the purchase to injure Newport, and that there was no proof that it ever was so used. Feldmann did know, it is true, that the reason Wilport wanted the stock was to put in a board of directors who would be likely to permit Wilport's members to purchase more of Newport's steel than they might otherwise be able to get. But there is nothing illegal in a dominant shareholder purchasing from his own corporation at the same prices it offers to other customers. That is what the members of Wilport did, and there is no proof that Newport suffered any detriment therefrom.

My brothers say that "the consideration paid for the stock included compensation for the sale of a corporate asset", which they describe as "the ability to control the allocation of the corporate product in a time of short supply, through control of the board of directors; and it was effectively transferred in this sale by having Feldmann procure the resignation of his own board and the election of Wilport's nominees immediately upon consummation of the sale." The implications of this are not clear to me. If it means that when market conditions are such as to induce users of a corporation's product to wish to buy a controlling block of stock in order to be able to purchase part of the corporation's output at the same mill list prices as are offered to other customers, the dominant stockholder is under a fiduciary duty not to sell his stock, I cannot agree. For reasons already stated, in my opinion Feldmann was not proved to be under any fiduciary duty as a stockholder not to sell the stock he controlled.

Feldmann was also a director of Newport. Perhaps the quoted statement means that as a director he violated his fiduciary duty in voting to elect Wilport's nominees to fill the vacancies created by the resignations of the former directors of Newport. As a director Feldmann was under a fiduciary duty to use an honest judgment in acting on the corporation's behalf. A director is privileged to resign, but so long as he remains a director he must be faithful to his fiduciary duties and must not make a personal gain from performing them. Consequently, if the price paid for Feldmann's stock included a payment for voting to elect the new directors, he must account to the corporation for such payment, even though he honestly believed that the men he voted to elect were well qualified to serve as directors. He can not take pay for performing his fiduciary duty. There is no suggestion that he did do so, unless the price paid for his stock was more than its value. So it seems to me that decision must turn on whether finding 120 and conclusion 5 of the district judge are supportable on the evidence. They are set out in the margin.[1]

Judge Hincks went into the matter of valuation of the stock with his customary care and thoroughness. He made no error of law in applying the principles relating to valuation of stock. Concededly a controlling block of stock has greater sale value than a small lot. While the spread between $10 per share for small lots and $20 per share for the controlling block seems rather extraordinarily wide, the $20 valuation was supported by the expert testimony of Dr. Badger, whom the district judge said he could not find to be wrong. I see no justification for upsetting the valuation as clearly erroneous. Nor can I agree with my brothers that the $20 valuation "was limited" by the last sentence in finding 120. The controlling block could not by any possibility be shorn of its appurtenant power to elect directors and through them to control distribution of the corporate product. It is

---

1. "120. The 398,927 shares of Newport stock sold to Wilport as of August 31, 1950, had a fair value as a control block of $20 per share. What value the block would have had if shorn of its appurtenant power to control distribution of the corporate product, the evidence does not show."

"5. Even if Feldmann's conduct in cooperating to accomplish a transfer of control to Wilport immediately upon the sale constituted a breach of a fiduciary duty to Newport, no part of the moneys received by the defendants in connection with the sale constituted profits for which they were accountable to Newport."

this "appurtenant power" which gives a controlling block its value as such block. What evidence could be adduced to show the value of the block "if shorn" of such appurtenant power, I cannot conceive, for it cannot be shorn of it. . . .

I would affirm the judgment on appeal.

NOTE ON PERLMAN v. FELDMANN

1. Upon remand, the district court determined the enterprise value of the corporation, based upon its book value and earnings potential, to be $15,825,777, or $14.67 per share. This made the premium $5.33 a share, or $2,126,280. The complaining stockholders, owning sixty-three percent of the stock, were therefore entitled to judgment of $1,339,769, with interest of 6 percent from the sale date, plus costs. Perlman v. Feldmann, 154 F.Supp. 436 (D.Conn.1957) (see opinion for valuation methods).

2. Would the court's decision be strengthened by the additional finding with respect to the same transaction, as follows:

"During this period [June to August, 1950] Follansbee Steel Corporation and Newport were negotiating for a merger of the two corporations, which merger, on the terms offered by Follansbee, would have been highly profitable to all the stockholders of Newport. However, in August of 1950, Feldmann, acting in his official capacity as president of Newport, rejected the Follansbee offer, and on August 3 1950, sold his stock to the defendant Wilport Company at a price of approximately $22. per share which was twice the then market value of the stock."

This finding appears in Birnbaum v. Newport Steel Corp., 193 F.2d 461, 462 (2d Cir. 1952), cert. denied, 343 U.S. 956, 72 S.Ct. 1051, 96 L.Ed. 1356.

NOTE ON THE THEORY OF CORPORATE ACTION

If a prospective purchaser, P, wants to acquire complete control of the assets and business of a corporation, C, he has a choice of several means to do so: (1) He can try to acquire all of C's shares, and his first step would naturally be to approach those who hold the majority or at least large blocks of the shares, without which his efforts will fail. (2) He can try to induce holders of sufficient shares to make the requisite majority needed to vote for a merger with or a sale of all assets to a corporation he controls.

If P takes the first course, he deals with C's present holders individually. Each holder seems free to make his own terms of sale, and controlling shares may bring a better price than shares that do not give control. If P takes the second course, he is looking towards corporate action by C. If C's assets are sold, the consideration will pass into C's treasury. Usually the corporation will then be liquidated, and the net proceeds will be distributed pro rata to all C shares, so that each old C shareholder will receive the same amount per share. If C merges, the plan of conversion of C's shares for shares of the surviving corporation will normally provide for equal treatment of all shares of the same class. It may therefore be to the advantage of those who hold the majority, or at least large blocks, of shares of a corporation to have a purchaser like P take the first course.

If P originally proposes to take the second course, but is persuaded to take the first course, and the majority shareholders of C realize more per share for their holdings than the minority, the latter may assert that the difference in technique between the first and second courses of action is immaterial. This is the theory of "corporate action." It has been successfully employed in several cases where the buyer began on the second course and the controlling shareholders switched him to the first. See Commonwealth Title Ins. & Trust Co. v. Seltzer, 227 Pa. 410, 76 A. 77 (1910); Dunnett v. Arn, 71 F.2d 912 (10th Cir.1934); Roby v. Dunnett, 88 F.2d 68 (10th Cir.1937), cert. denied 301 U.S. 706, 57 S.Ct. 940, 81 L.Ed. 1360; American Trust Co. v. California Western States Life Ins. Co., 15 Cal.2d 42, 98 P.2d 497 (1940).

The problem with the theory of corporate action is that a controlling shareholder cannot be compelled to sell his shares at a price he does not accept. A knowledgeable seller therefore can avoid the application of the theory by simply voting down an offer to the corporation, and waiting for an offer to buy his shares.

ESSEX UNIVERSAL CORP. v. YATES

United States Court of Appeals, Second Circuit, 1962.
305 F.2d 572.

Before LUMBARD, Chief Judge, and CLARK and FRIENDLY, Circuit Judges.

LUMBARD, Chief Judge.

This appeal from the district court's summary judgment in favor of the defendant raises the question whether a contract for the sale of 28.3 per cent of the stock of a corporation is, under New York law, invalid as against public policy solely because it includes a clause giving the purchaser an option to require a majority of the existing directors to replace themselves, by a process of seriatim resignation, with a majority designated by the purchaser. Despite the disagreement evidenced by the diversity of our opinions, my brethren and I agree that such a provision does not on its face render the contract illegal and unenforceable, and thus that it was improper to grant summary judgment. Judge Friendly would reject the defense of illegality without further inquiry concerning the provision itself (as distinguished from any contention that control could not be safely transferred to the particular purchaser). Judge Clark and I are agreed that on remand, which must be had in any event to consider other defenses raised by the pleadings, further factual issues may be raised by the parties upon which the legality of the clause in question will depend; we disagree, however, on the nature of those factual issues, as our separate opinions reveal. Accordingly, the grant of summary judgment is reversed and the case is remanded for trial of the question of the legality of the contested provision and such further proceedings as may be proper on the other issues raised by the pleadings.

Since we are in agreement on certain preliminary questions, this opinion constitutes the opinion of the court up to the point where it is indicated that it thenceforth states only my individual views.

The defendant Herbert J. Yates, a resident of California, was president and chairman of the board of directors of Republic Pictures Corporation, a New York corporation which at the time relevant to this suit had 2,004,190 shares of common stock outstanding. Republic's stock was listed and traded on the New York Stock Exchange. In August 1957, Essex Universal Corporation, a Delaware corporation owning stock in various diversified businesses, learned of the possibility of purchasing from Yates an interest in Republic. Negotiations proceeded rapidly, and on August 28 Yates and Joseph Harris, the president of Essex, signed a contract in which Essex agreed to buy, and Yates agreed "to sell or cause to be sold" at least 500,000 and not more than 600,000 shares of Republic stock. The price was set at eight dollars a share, roughly two dollars above the then market price on the Exchange. Three dollars per share was to be paid at the closing on September 18, 1957 and the remainder in twenty-four equal monthly payments beginning January 31, 1958. The shares were to be transferred on the closing date, but Yates was to retain the certificates, endorsed in blank by Essex, as security for full payment. In addition to other provisions not relevant to the present motion, the contract contained the following paragraph:

"6. Resignations.

Upon and as a condition to the closing of this transaction if requested by Buyer at least ten (10) days prior to the date of the closing:

(a) Seller will deliver to Buyer the resignations of the majority of the directors of Republic.

(b) Seller will cause a special meeting of the board of directors of Republic to be held, legally convened pursuant to law and the by-laws of Republic, and simultaneously with the acceptance of the directors' resignations set forth in paragraph 6(a) immediately preceding will cause nominees of Buyer to be elected directors of Republic in place of the resigned directors."

Before the date of the closing, as provided in the contract, Yates notified Essex that he would deliver 566,223 shares, or 28.3 per cent of the Republic stock then outstanding, and Essex formally requested Yates to arrange for the replacement of a majority of Republic's directors with Essex nominees pursuant to paragraph 6 of the contract. This was to be accomplished by having eight of the fourteen directors resign seriatim, each in turn being replaced by an Essex nominee elected by the others; such a procedure was *in form* permissible under the charter and by-laws of Republic, which empowered the board to choose the successor of any of its members who might resign.

On September 18, the parties met as arranged for the closing at Republic's office in New York City. Essex tendered bank drafts and cashier's checks totalling $1,698,690, which was the 37½ per cent of the total price of $4,529,784 due at this time. The drafts and checks were payable to one Benjamin C. Cohen, who was Essex' banker and had arranged for the borrowing of the necessary funds. Although Cohen was prepared to endorse these to Yates, Yates upon advice of his lawyer rejected the tender as "unsatisfactory" and said, according to his deposition testimony, "Well, there can be no deal. We can't close it."

Essex began this action in the New York Supreme Court, and it was removed to the district court on account of diversity of citizenship. Essex seeks damages of $2,700,000, claiming that at the time of the aborted closing the stock was in actuality worth more than $12.75 a share.[1] Yates' answer raised a number of defenses, but the motion for summary judgment now before us was made and decided only on the theory that the provision in the contract for immediate transfer of control of the board of directors was illegal *per se* and tainted the entire contract. We have no doubt, and the parties agree, that New York law governs.

Appellant's contention that the provision for transfer of director control is separable from the rest of the contract can quickly be rejected. . . .

. . . [W]e hold the provision regarding directors inseparable from the sale of shares, and proceed to a consideration of its legality.

Up to this point my brethren and I are in agreement. The following analysis is my own, except insofar as the separate opinions of Judges Clark and Friendly may indicate agreement.

It is established beyond question under New York law that it is illegal to sell corporate office or management control by itself (that is, accompanied by no stock or insufficient stock to carry voting control). . . . The rationale of the rule is undisputable: persons enjoying management control hold it on behalf of the corporation's stockholders, and therefore may not regard it as their own personal property to dispose of as they wish.[3] Any other rule would violate the most fundamental principle of corporate democracy, that management must represent and be chosen by, or at least with the consent of, those who own the corporation.

Essex was, however, contracting with Yates for the purchase of a very substantial percentage of Republic stock. If, by virtue of the

1. In 1959, while this action was pending, the stock was sold to another party for ten dollars a share.

3. The cases have made no distinction between contracts by directors or officers to resign and contracts by persons who in actuality control the actions of officers or directors to procure their resignations, and of course none should exist.

voting power carried by this stock, it could have elected a majority of the board of directors, then the contract was not a simple agreement for the sale of office to one having no ownership interest in the corporation, and the question of its legality would require further analysis. Such stock voting control would incontestably belong to the owner of a majority of the voting stock, and it is commonly known that equivalent power usually accrues to the owner of 28.3% of the stock. For the purpose of this analysis, I shall assume that Essex was contracting to acquire a majority of the Republic stock, deferring consideration of the situation where, as here, only 28.3% is to be acquired.

Republic's board of directors at the time of the aborted closing had fourteen members divided into three classes, each class being "as nearly as may be" of the same size. Directors were elected for terms of three years, one class being elected at each annual shareholder meeting on the first Tuesday in April. Thus, absent the immediate replacement of directors provided for in this contract, Essex as the hypothetical new majority shareholder of the corporation could not have obtained managing control in the form of a majority of the board in the normal course of events until April 1959, some eighteen months after the sale of the stock. The first question before us then is whether an agreement to accelerate the transfer of management control, in a manner legal in form under the corporation's charter and by-laws, violates the public policy of New York.

There is no question of the right of a controlling shareholder under New York law normally to derive a premium from the sale of a controlling block of stock. In other words, there was no impropriety *per se* in the fact that Yates was to receive more per share than the generally prevailing market price for Republic stock. Levy v. American Beverage Corp., 265 App.Div. 208, 218, 38 N.Y.S.2d 517, 526 (1st Dept.1942); Stanton v. Schenck, 140 Misc. 621, 251 N.Y.S. 221 (N.Y.County Sup.Ct.1931); see Hill, supra, 70 Harv.L.Rev. at 991–92.

The next question is whether it is legal to give and receive payment for the immediate transfer of management control to one who has achieved majority share control but would not otherwise be able to convert that share control into operating control for some time. I think that it is.

Of course under some circumstances controlling shareholders transferring immediate control may be compelled to account to the corporation for that part of the consideration received by them which exceeds the fair value of the block of stock sold, as well as for the injury which they may cause to the corporation. In Gerdes v. Reynolds, 28 N.Y.S.2d 622 (N.Y.County Sup.Ct.1941), the purchasers of control of an investment company proceeded immediately to loot the corporation of its assets, and the court required the sellers to account on the theory that the circumstances of the sale put them on notice of the buyers' evil intentions. The court found the price paid grossly in excess of the calculable fair value of a controlling interest in the corporation, and found the differential to be payment for the immediate control which, foreseeably, the buyers used to the detriment of the corporation and its other shareholders. . . .

In Perlman v. Feldmann, 219 F.2d 173, 50 A.L.R.2d 1134 (2 Cir.), cert. denied, 349 U.S. 952, 75 S.Ct. 880, 99 L.Ed. 1277 (1955), this court, in a decision based only nominally on Indiana law, went beyond this rule to hold liable controlling shareholders who similarly sold immediate control even in the absence of illegitimate activity on the part of the purchasers. Our theory was basically that the controlling shareholders in selling control to a potential customer had appropriated to their personal benefit a corporate asset: the premium which the company's product could command in a time of market shortage. Porter v. Healy, 244 Pa. 427, 91 A. 428 (1914), may similarly be explained as "condemning . . . a personal profit derived by the insiders in a liquidation situation involving in substance the sale of the corporation's assets. . . ." Hill, supra, 70 Harv.L. Rev. at 1000–01.

A fair generalization from these cases may be that a holder of corporate control will not, as a fiduciary, be permitted to profit from facilitating actions on the part of the purchasers of control which are detrimental to the interests of the corporation or the remaining shareholders. There is, however, no suggestion that the transfer of control over Republic to Essex carried any such threat to the interests of the corporation or its other shareholders.

Our examination of the New York cases discussed thus far gives us no reason to regard as impaired the holding of the early case of Barnes v. Brown, 80 N.Y. 527 (1880), that a bargain for the sale of a majority stock interest is not made illegal by a plan for immediate transfer of management control by a program like that provided for in the Essex–Yates contract. Judge Earl wrote:

> "[The seller] had the right to sell out all his stock and interest in the corporation, . . . and when he ceased to have any interest in the corporation, it was certainly legitimate and right that he should cease to control it . . . It was simply the mode of transferring the control of the corporation to those who by the policy of the law ought to have it, and I am unable to see how any policy of the law was violated, or in what way, upon the evidence, any wrong was thereby done to anyone." 80 N.Y. at 537.

To be sure, in Barnes v. Brown no term of the contract of sale *required* the seller to effectuate the immediate replacement of directors, as did paragraph 6 of the Essex–Yates contract, but Judge Earl stated that "I shall assume that it was the understanding and a part of the scheme that he should do so." 80 N.Y. at 536. . . .

The easy and immediate transfer of corporate control to new interests is ordinarily beneficial to the economy and it seems inevitable that such transactions would be discouraged if the purchaser of a majority stock interest were required to wait some period before his purchase of control could become effective. Conversely it would greatly hamper the efforts of any existing majority group to dispose of its interest if it could not assure the purchaser of immediate control over corporation operations. I can see no reason why a purchaser of majority control should not ordinarily be permitted to make his control effective from the moment of the transfer of stock.

Thus if Essex had been contracting to purchase a majority of the stock of Republic, it would have been entirely proper for the contract to contain the provision for immediate replacement of directors. Although in the case at bar only 28.3 per cent of the stock was involved, it is commonly known that a person or group owning so large a percentage of the voting stock of a corporation which, like Republic, has at least the 1,500 shareholders normally requisite to listing on the New York Stock Exchange, is almost certain to have share control as a practical matter. If Essex was contracting to acquire what in reality would be equivalent to ownership of a majority of stock, i.e., if it would as a practical certainty have been guaranteed of the stock voting power to choose a majority of the directors of Republic in due course, there is no reason why the contract should not similarly be legal.[6] Whether Essex was thus to acquire the equivalent of majority stock control would, if the issue is properly raised by the defendants, be a factual issue to be determined by the district court on remand.

Because 28.3 per cent of the voting stock of a publicly owned corporation is usually tantamount to majority control, I would place the burden of proof on this issue on Yates as the party attacking the legality of the transaction. Thus, unless on remand Yates chooses to raise the question whether the block of stock in question carried the equivalent of majority control, it is my view that the trial court should regard the contract as legal and proceed to consider the other issues raised by the pleadings. If Yates chooses to raise the issue, it will, on my view, be necessary for him to prove the existence of circumstances which would have prevented Essex from electing a majority of the Republic board of directors in due course. It will not be enough for Yates to raise merely hypothetical possibilities of opposition by the other Republic shareholders to Essex' assumption of management control. Rather, it will be necessary for him to show that, assuming neutrality on the part of the retiring management, there was at the time some concretely foreseeable reason why Essex' wishes would not have prevailed in shareholder voting held in due course. In other words, I would require him to show that there was at the time of the contract some other organized block of stock of sufficient size to outvote the block Essex was buying, or else some circumstance making it likely that enough of the holders of the remaining Republic stock would band together to keep Essex from control.

6. The fact that under the Essex-Yates contract only 37½% of the price of the stock was to be paid at the closing and the balance was not to be fully paid for twenty-eight months is irrelevant to this case. There is no indication that Essex did not have sound financial backing sufficient to discharge properly the obligation which had been incurred.

Reversed and remanded for further proceedings not inconsistent with the judgment of this court.

CLARK, Circuit Judge (concurring in the result).

Since Barnes v. Brown, 80 N.Y. 527, teaches us that not all contracts like the one before us are necessarily illegal, summary judgment seems definitely improper and the action should be remanded for trial. But particularly in view of our lack of knowledge of corporate realities and the current standards of business morality, I should prefer to avoid too precise instructions to the district court in the hope that if the action again comes before us the record will be generally more instructive on this important issue than it now is. . . .

. . . I am constrained to point out that I do not believe a district court determination as to whether or not "working control" was transferred to the vendee can or should affect the outcome of this case. The contract provides for transfer of 28.3 per cent of the outstanding stock and effective control of the board of directors, and there is no evidence at this stage that the vendor's power to transfer control of the board was to be secured unlawfully, as, for example, by bribe or duress. Surely in the normal course of events a management which has behind it 28.3 per cent of the stock has working control, absent perhaps a pitched proxy battle which might unseat it. But the court cannot foresee such an unlikely event or predict its outcome; thus it is difficult to see what further evidence on the question of control could be adduced. My conclusion that there is no reason to declare this contract illegal on its face would remain unaffected by any hypothetical findings on "control." It seems that we are all agreed on the need of a remand for trial, though we disagree as to the scope of such remand. Since our decision returns the case to the jurisdiction of the trial court, with nothing settled beyond that, the trial judge will have to decide initially at least how extensive that trial is to be. For my part I believe it incumbent on the judge to explore all issues which the pleadings may eventually raise.

FRIENDLY, Circuit Judge (concurring). . . .

I have no doubt that many contracts, drawn by competent and responsible counsel, for the purchase of blocks of stock from interests thought to "control" a corporation although owning less than a majority, have contained provisions like paragraph 6 of the contract *sub judice.* However, developments over the past decades seem to me to show that such a clause violates basic principles of corporate democracy. To be sure, stockholders who have allowed a set of directors to be placed in office, whether by their vote or their failure to vote, must recognize that death, incapacity or other hazard may prevent a director from serving a full term, and that they will have no voice as to his immediate successor. But the stockholders are entitled to expect that, in that event, the remaining directors will fill the vacancy in the exercise of their fiduciary responsibility. A mass seriatim resignation directed by a selling stockholder, and the filling of vacancies by his henchmen at the dictation of a purchaser and without any consideration of the character of the latter's nominees, are beyond what the stockholders contemplated or should have been expected to contemplate. This seems to me a wrong to the corporation and the other stockholders which the law ought not countenance, whether the selling stockholder has received a premium or not. . . . To hold the seller for delinquencies of the new directors only if he knew the purchaser was an intending looter is not a sufficient sanction. The difficulties of proof are formidable even if receipt of too high a premium creates a presumption of such knowledge, and, all too often, the doors are locked only after the horses have been stolen. Stronger medicines are needed—refusal to enforce a contract with such a clause, even though this confers an unwarranted benefit on a defaulter, and continuing responsibility of the former directors for negligence of the new ones until an election has been held. Such prophylactics are not contraindicated, as Judge Lumbard suggests, by the conceded desirability of preventing the dead hand of a former "controlling" group from continuing to dominate the board after a sale, or of protecting a would-be purchaser from finding himself without a majority of the board after he has spent his money. A special meeting of stockholders to replace a board may always be called, and there could be no objection to making the closing of a purchase contingent on the results of such an election. I perceive some of the difficulties of mechanics such a procedure presents, but I have enough confidence in the ingenuity of the corporate bar to believe these would be surmounted.

Hence, I am inclined to think that if I were sitting on the New York Court of Appeals, I would hold a provision like Paragraph 6 violative of public policy save when it was entirely plain that a new election would be a mere formality—i.e., when the seller owned more than 50% of the stock. . . .

As a judge of this Court, my task is the more modest one of predicting how the judges of the New York Court of Appeals would rule, and I must make this prediction on the basis of legal materials rather than of personal acquaintance or hunch. . . . and I can find nothing . . . to indicate that New York would not apply Barnes v. Brown to a case where a stockholder with much less than a majority conditioned a sale on his causing the resignation of a majority of the directors and the election of the purchaser's nominees.

Chief Judge Lumbard's proposal goes part of the way toward meeting the policy problem I have suggested. Doubtless proceeding from what, as it seems to me, is the only justification in principle for permitting even a majority stockholder to condition a sale on delivery of control of the board—namely that in such a case a vote of the stockholders would be a useless formality, he sets the allowable bounds at the line where there is "a practical certainty" that the buyer would be able to elect his nominees and, in this case, puts the burden of disproving that on the person claiming illegality.

Attractive as the proposal is in some respects, I find difficulties with it. One is that I discern no sufficient intimation of the distinction in the New York cases, or even in the writers, who either would go further in voiding such a clause, see Berle, "Control" in Corporate Law, 58 Colum.L.Rev. 1212, 1224 (1958); Leech, Transactions in Corporate Control, 104 U.Pa.L.Rev. 725, 809 (1956) [proposing legislation], or believe the courts have not yet gone that far, see Baker & Cary, Corporations: Cases and Materials (3d ed. unabr. 1959) 590. To strike down such a condition only in cases falling short of the suggested line accomplishes little to prevent what I consider the evil; in most instances a seller will not enter into a contract conditioned on his "delivering" a majority of the directors unless he has good reason to think he can do that. When an issue does arise, the "practical certainty" test is difficult to apply. The existence of such certainty will depend not merely on the proportion of the stock held by the seller but on many other factors—whether the other stock is widely or closely held, how much of it is in "street names," what success the corporation has experienced, how far its dividend policies have satisfied its stockholders, the identity of the purchasers, the presence or absence of cumulative voting, and many others. Often, unless the seller has nearly 50% of the stock, whether he has "working control" can be determined only by an election; groups who thought they had such control have experienced unpleasant surprises in recent years. Judge Lumbard correctly recognizes that, from a policy standpoint, the pertinent question must be the buyer's prospects of election, not the seller's—yet this inevitably requires the court to canvass the likely reaction of stockholders to a group of whom they know nothing and seems rather hard to reconcile with a position that it is "right" to insert such a condition if a seller has a larger proportion of the stock and "wrong" if he has a smaller. At the very least the problems and uncertainties arising from the proposed line of demarcation are great enough, and its advantages small enough, that in my view a Federal court would do better simply to overrule the defense here, thereby accomplishing what is obviously the "just" result in this particular case, and leave the development of doctrine in this area to the State, which has primary concern for it.

I would reverse the grant of summary judgment and remand for consideration of defenses other than a claim that the inclusion of paragraph 6 *ex mero motu* renders the contract void.

NOTE ON ESSEX UNIVERSAL CORP. v. YATES

It is not at all clear that 28.3% will necessarily carry control of a publicly held corporation in and of itself, that is, unless coupled with control of the board. Consider Brannigan, Florida Businessman Seeks to Steer Bank Toward Sale, Wall Street Journal, Sept. 2, 1987, at 27, col. 1: "[Hugh F. Culverhouse] has launched a tender offer for 10% of Florida Commercial Banks Inc's shares, . . . He already holds . . . 39.9% of the bank's shares. Since 1984, Mr. Culverhouse has struggled unsuccessfully to win a seat on the company's board or to acquire control of the concern. As of earlier this year, 28.4% of the company's shares were controlled by a well-entrenched group of officers and directors that has opposed him. . . ."

SECURITIES EXCHANGE ACT RULE 14f–1

[See Statutory Supplement]

SECTION 6. DUTIES OF CONTROLLING SHAREHOLDERS

SINCLAIR OIL CORPORATION v. LEVIEN
Supreme Court of Delaware, 1971.
280 A.2d 717.

WOLCOTT, Chief Justice. This is an appeal by the defendant, Sinclair Oil Corporation (hereafter Sinclair), from an order of the Court of Chancery, 261 A.2d 911, in a derivative action requiring Sinclair to account for damages sustained by its subsidiary, Sinclair Venezuelan Oil Company (hereinafter Sinven), organized by Sinclair for the purpose of operating in Venezuela, as a result of dividends paid by Sinven, the denial to Sinven of industrial development, and a breach of contract between Sinclair's wholly-owned subsidiary, Sinclair International Oil Company, and Sinven.

Sinclair, operating primarily as a holding company, is in the business of exploring for oil and of producing and marketing crude oil and oil products. At all times relevant to this litigation, it owned about 97% of Sinven's stock. The plaintiff owns about 3000 of 120,000 publicly held shares of Sinven. Sinven, incorporated in 1922, has been engaged in petroleum operations primarily in Venezuela and since 1959 has operated exclusively in Venezuela.

Sinclair nominates all members of Sinven's board of directors. The Chancellor found as a fact that the directors were not independent of Sinclair. Almost without exception, they were officers, directors, or employees of corporations in the Sinclair complex. By reason of Sinclair's domination, it is clear that Sinclair owed Sinven a fiduciary duty. Getty Oil Company v. Skelly Oil Co., 267 A.2d 883 (Del.Supr.1970); Cottrell v. Pawcatuck Co., 35 Del.Ch. 309, 116 A.2d 787 (1955). Sinclair concedes this.

The Chancellor held that because of Sinclair's fiduciary duty and its control over Sinven, its relationship with Sinven must meet the test of intrinsic fairness. The standard of intrinsic fairness involves both a high degree of fairness and a shift in the burden of proof. Under this standard the burden is on Sinclair to prove, subject to careful judicial scrutiny, that its transactions with Sinven were objectively fair. Guth v. Loft, Inc., 23 Del.Ch. 255, 5 A.2d 503 (1939); Sterling v.

Mayflower Hotel Corp., 33 Del.Ch. 293, 93 A.2d 107, 38 A.L.R.2d 425 (Del.Supr.1952); Getty Oil Co. v. Skelly Oil Co., supra.

Sinclair argues that the transactions between it and Sinven should be tested, not by the test of intrinsic fairness with the accompanying shift of the burden of proof, but by the business judgment rule under which a court will not interfere with the judgment of a board of directors unless there is a showing of gross and palpable overreaching. Meyerson v. El Paso Natural Gas Co., 246 A.2d 789 (Del.Ch.1967). A board of directors enjoys a presumption of sound business judgment, and its decisions will not be disturbed if they can be attributed to any rational business purpose. A court under such circumstances will not substitute its own notions of what is or is not sound business judgment.

We think, however, that Sinclair's argument in this respect is misconceived. When the situation involves a parent and a subsidiary, with the parent controlling the transaction and fixing the terms, the test of intrinsic fairness, with its resulting shifting of the burden of proof, is applied. Sterling v. Mayflower Hotel Corp., supra; David J. Greene & Co. v. Dunhill International, Inc., 249 A.2d 427 (Del.Ch. 1968); Bastian v. Bourns, Inc., 256 A.2d 680 (Del.Ch.1969) aff'd. Per Curiam (unreported) (Del.Supr.1970). The basic situation for the application of the rule is the one in which the parent has received a benefit to the exclusion and at the expense of the subsidiary.

Recently, this court dealt with the question of fairness in parent-subsidiary dealings in Getty Oil Co. v. Skelly Oil Co., supra. In that case, both parent and subsidiary were in the business of refining and marketing crude oil and crude oil products. The Oil Import Board ruled that the subsidiary, because it was controlled by the parent, was no longer entitled to a separate allocation of imported crude oil. The subsidiary then contended that it had a right to share the quota of crude oil allotted to the parent. We ruled that the business judgment standard should be applied to determine this contention. Although the subsidiary suffered a loss through the administration of the oil import quotas, the parent gained nothing. The parent's quota was derived solely from its own past use. The past use of the subsidiary did not cause an increase in the parent's quota. Nor did the parent usurp a quota of the subsidiary. Since the parent received nothing from the subsidiary to the exclusion of the minority stockholders of the subsidiary, there was no self-dealing. Therefore, the business judgment standard was properly applied.

A parent does indeed owe a fiduciary duty to its subsidiary when there are parent-subsidiary dealings. However, this alone will not evoke the intrinsic fairness standard. This standard will be applied only when the fiduciary duty is accompanied by self-dealing—the situation when a parent is on both sides of a transaction with its subsidiary. Self-dealing occurs when the parent, by virtue of its domination of the subsidiary causes the subsidiary to act in such a way that the parent receives something from the subsidiary to the exclusion of, and detriment to, the minority stockholders of the subsidiary.

We turn now to the facts. The plaintiff argues that, from 1960 through 1966, Sinclair caused Sinven to pay out such excessive dividends that the industrial development of Sinven was effectively prevented, and it became in reality a corporation in dissolution.

From 1960 through 1966, Sinven paid out $108,000,000 in dividends ($38,000,000 in excess of Sinven's earnings during the same period). The Chancellor held that Sinclair caused these dividends to be paid during a period when it had a need for large amounts of cash. Although the dividends paid exceeded earnings, the plaintiff concedes that the payments were made in compliance with 8 Del.C. § 170, authorizing payment of dividends out of surplus or net profits. However, the plaintiff attacks these dividends on the ground that they resulted from an improper motive—Sinclair's need for cash. The Chancellor, applying the intrinsic fairness standard, held that Sinclair did not sustain its burden of proving that these dividends were intrinsically fair to the minority stockholders of Sinven.

Since it is admitted that the dividends were paid in strict compliance with 8 Del.C. § 170, the alleged excessiveness of the payments alone would not state a cause of action. Nevertheless, compliance with the applicable statute may not, under all circumstances, justify all dividend payments. If a plaintiff can meet his burden of proving that a dividend cannot be grounded on any reasonable business objective, then the courts can and will interfere with the board's decision to pay the dividend.

Sinclair contends that it is improper to apply the intrinsic fairness standard to dividend payments even when the board which voted for the dividends is completely dominated. In support of this contention, Sinclair relies heavily on American District Telegraph Co. [ADT] v. Grinnell Corp., (N.Y.Sup.Ct.1969) aff'd. 33 A.D.2d 769, 306 N.Y.S. 2d 209 (1969). Plaintiffs were minority stockholders of ADT, a subsidiary of Grinnell. The plaintiffs alleged that Grinnell, realizing that it would soon have to sell its ADT stock because of a pending anti-trust action, caused ADT to pay excessive dividends. Because the dividend payments conformed with applicable statutory law, and the plaintiffs could not prove an abuse of discretion, the court ruled that the complaint did not state a cause of action. Other decisions seem to support Sinclair's contention. In Metropolitan Casualty Ins. Co. v. First State Bank of Temple, 54 S.W.2d 358 (Tex.Civ.App.1932), rev'd. on other grounds, 79 S.W.2d 835 (Sup.Ct.1935), the court held that a majority of interested directors does not void a declaration of dividends because all directors, by necessity, are interested in and benefited by a dividend declaration. See, also, Schwartz v. Kahn, 183 Misc. 252, 50 N.Y.S.2d 931 (1944); Weinberger v. Quinn, 264 A.D. 405, 35 N.Y.S.2d 567 (1942).

We do not accept the argument that the intrinsic fairness test can never be applied to a dividend declaration by a dominated board, although a dividend declaration by a dominated board will not inevitably demand the application of the intrinsic fairness standard. Moskowitz v. Bantrell, 41 Del.Ch. 177, 190 A.2d 749 (Del.Supr.

1963). If such a dividend is in essence self-dealing by the parent, then the intrinsic fairness standard is the proper standard. For example, suppose a parent dominates a subsidiary and its board of directors. The subsidiary has outstanding two classes of stock, X and Y. Class X is owned by the parent and Class Y is owned by minority stockholders of the subsidiary. If the subsidiary, at the direction of the parent, declares a dividend on its Class X stock only, this might well be self-dealing by the parent. It would be receiving something from the subsidiary to the exclusion of and detrimental to its minority stockholders. This self-dealing, coupled with the parent's fiduciary duty, would make intrinsic fairness the proper standard by which to evaluate the dividend payments.

Consequently it must be determined whether the dividend payments by Sinven were, in essence, self-dealing by Sinclair. The dividends resulted in great sums of money being transferred from Sinven to Sinclair. However, a proportionate share of this money was received by the minority shareholders of Sinven. Sinclair received nothing from Sinven to the exclusion of its minority stockholders. As such, these dividends were not self-dealing. We hold therefore that the Chancellor erred in applying the intrinsic fairness test as to these dividend payments. The business judgment standard should have been applied.

We conclude that the facts demonstrate that the dividend payments complied with the business judgment standard and with 8 Del. C. § 170. The motives for causing the declaration of dividends are immaterial unless the plaintiff can show that the dividend payments resulted from improper motives and amounted to waste. The plaintiff contends only that the dividend payments drained Sinven of cash to such an extent that it was prevented from expanding.

The plaintiff proved no business opportunities which came to Sinven independently and which Sinclair either took to itself or denied to Sinven. As a matter of fact, with two minor exceptions which resulted in losses, all of Sinven's operations have been conducted in Venezuela, and Sinclair had a policy of exploiting its oil properties located in different countries by subsidiaries located in the particular countries.

From 1960 to 1966 Sinclair purchased or developed oil fields in Alaska, Canada, Paraguay, and other places around the world. The plaintiff contends that these were all opportunities which could have been taken by Sinven. The Chancellor concluded that Sinclair had not proved that its denial of expansion opportunities to Sinven was intrinsically fair. He based this conclusion on the following findings of fact. Sinclair made no real effort to expand Sinven. The excessive dividends paid by Sinven resulted in so great a cash drain as to effectively deny to Sinven any ability to expand. During this same period Sinclair actively pursued a company-wide policy of developing through its subsidiaries new sources of revenue, but Sinven was not permitted to participate and was confined in its activities to Venezuela.

However, the plaintiff could point to no opportunities which came to Sinven. Therefore, Sinclair usurped no business opportunity belonging to Sinven. Since Sinclair received nothing from Sinven to the exclusion of and detriment to Sinven's minority stockholders, there was no self-dealing. Therefore, business judgment is the proper standard by which to evaluate Sinclair's expansion policies.

Since there is no proof of self-dealing on the part of Sinclair, it follows that the expansion policy of Sinclair and the methods used to achieve the desired result must, as far as Sinclair's treatment of Sinven is concerned, be tested by the standards of the business judgment rule. Accordingly, Sinclair's decision absent fraud or gross overreaching, to achieve expansion through the medium of its subsidiaries, other than Sinven, must be upheld.

Even if Sinclair was wrong in developing these opportunities as it did, the question arises, with which subsidiaries should these opportunities have been shared? No evidence indicates a unique need or ability of Sinven to develop these opportunities. The decision of which subsidiaries would be used to implement Sinclair's expansion policy was one of business judgment with which a court will not interfere absent a showing of gross and palpable overreaching. Meyerson v. El Paso Natural Gas Co., 246 A.2d 789 (Del.Ch.1967). No such showing has been made here.

Next, Sinclair argues that the Chancellor committed error when he held it liable to Sinven for breach of contract.

In 1961 Sinclair created Sinclair International Oil Company (hereafter International), a wholly owned subsidiary used for the purpose of coordinating all of Sinclair's foreign operations. All crude purchases by Sinclair were made thereafter through International.

On September 28, 1961, Sinclair caused Sinven to contract with International whereby Sinven agreed to sell all of its crude oil and refined products to International at specified prices. The contract provided for minimum and maximum quantities and prices. The plaintiff contends that Sinclair caused this contract to be breached in two respects. Although the contract called for payment on receipt, International's payments lagged as much as 30 days after receipt. Also, the contract required International to purchase at least a fixed minimum amount of crude and refined products from Sinven. International did not comply with this requirement.

Clearly, Sinclair's act of contracting with its dominated subsidiary was self-dealing. Under the contract Sinclair received the products produced by Sinven, and of course the minority shareholders of Sinven were not able to share in the receipt of these products. If the contract was breached, then Sinclair received these products to the detriment of Sinven's minority shareholders. We agree with the Chancellor's finding that the contract was breached by Sinclair, both as to the time of payments and the amounts purchased.

Although a parent need not bind itself by a contract with its dominated subsidiary, Sinclair chose to operate in this manner. As

Sinclair has received the benefits of this contract, so must it comply with the contractual duties.

Under the intrinsic fairness standard, Sinclair must prove that its causing Sinven not to enforce the contract was intrinsically fair to the minority shareholders of Sinven. Sinclair has failed to meet this burden. Late payments were clearly breaches for which Sinven should have sought and received adequate damages. As to the quantities purchased, Sinclair argues that it purchased all the products produced by Sinven. This, however, does not satisfy the standard of intrinsic fairness. Sinclair has failed to prove that Sinven could not possibly have produced or some way have obtained the contract minimums. As such, Sinclair must account on this claim.

Finally, Sinclair argues that the Chancellor committed error in refusing to allow it a credit or setoff of all benefits provided by it to Sinven with respect to all the alleged damages. The Chancellor held that setoff should be allowed on specific transactions, e.g., benefits to Sinven under the contract with International, but denied an overall setoff against all damages claimed. We agree with the Chancellor, although the point may well be moot in view of our holding that Sinclair is not required to account for the alleged excessiveness of the dividend payments.

We will therefore reverse that part of the Chancellor's order that requires Sinclair to account to Sinven for damages sustained as a result of dividends paid between 1960 and 1966, and by reason of the denial to Sinven of expansion during that period. We will affirm the remaining portion of that order and remand the cause for further proceedings.

NOTE ON INDEPENDENT NEGOTIATING STRUCTURES

Under Delaware law, "[t]he requirement of fairness is unflinching in its demand that where [a controlling shareholder] stands on both sides of a transaction, he has the burden of establishing its entire fairness, sufficient to pass the test of careful scrutiny by the courts." See, e.g., Rosenblatt v. Getty Oil Co., 493 A.2d 929 (Del.1985); Weinberger v. UOP, Inc., Del.Supr., 457 A.2d 701, 710 (1983); Sterling v. Mayflower Hotel Corp., Del.Supr., 93 A.2d 107, 110 (1952). However, the Delaware courts have also taken the position that if the controlled corporation creates an independent negotiating committee of outside directors to bargain at arm's length on its behalf, "[t]his is of considerable importance when addressing ultimate questions of fairness, since it may give rise to the proposition that the directors' actions are more appropriately measured by business judgment standards." Rosenblatt v. Getty Oil Co., supra, at 937–38. See also Weinberger v. UOP, supra, at 709 n. 7; Rabkin v. Phillip A. Hunt Chemical Corp., 498 A.2d 1099, 1106 n. 7 (1985).

NOTE ON THE DUTY OF COMPLETE CANDOR

In a series of cases, the Delaware court has held that a controlling shareholder has a duty of "complete candor" when dealing with the minority. Lynch v. Vickers Energy Corp., 383 A.2d 278 (Del.1977) involved a tender offer by Vickers, the majority shareholder of TransOcean stock, for the 46% of TransOcean stock held by the public. The trial court held that in preparing the offering circular through which the tender offer was made, Vickers owed a fiduciary duty that required "complete candor" in disclosing fully "all of the facts and circumstances surrounding" the tender offer. The Delaware Supreme Court agreed with that rule, but reversed because the trial court had not applied the rule with sufficient vigor:

> . . . [A]t the time of the offer, defendants were in possession of [an] estimate, prepared by Forrest Harrell, a petroleum engineer and a vice-president of TransOcean, fixing the net asset value [of TransOcean] at $250.8 million, which computes to approximately $20 per share, and from which one could conclude that the value could be as high as $300 million. Both of these estimates were . . . substantially higher than the minimum amount stated in the tender offer.

> The Trial Court closely examined the Harrell report and concluded that nondisclosure thereof was not fatal; the Court reasoned that [the language used in the offering circular] ". . . furnished the TransOcean stockholders with adequate facts on which to make an educated choice . . . ."

> * * *

> This approach to the controversy was, in our view, mistaken in two respects: First, to reach such a conclusion it was necessary for the Court to weigh the merits of the Harrell report and, in the context of this case, that was error. The Court's function was not to go through Harrell's estimates of oil reserves and recoveries, for example, and make its own judgment about whether these should be "substantially discounted," nor should it have substituted its judgment for Harrell's about the rate which the Federal Power Commission would approve for a sale of natural gas. The stockholders and not the Court should have been permitted to make such qualitative judgments.

> The Court's duty was to examine what information defendants had and to measure it against what they gave to the minority stockholders, in a context in which "complete candor" is required. In other words, the limited function of the Court was to determine whether defendants had disclosed all information in their possession germane to the transaction in issue. And by "germane" we mean, for present purposes, information such as a reasonable shareholder would consider important in deciding whether to sell or retain stock. . . .

A second reason why we think that the Court of Chancery was mistaken in applying the law was that it incorrectly substituted a "disclosure of adequate facts" standard . . . for the correct standard, which requires disclosure of *all* germane facts. Completeness, not adequacy, is both the norm and the mandate under present circumstances.

The duty of complete candor was reaffirmed in Weinberger v. UOP, Inc., 457 A.2d 701, 710–11 (Del.1983), and Rosenblatt v. Getty Oil Co., 493 A.2d 929 (Del.1985), both of which involved mergers. *Rosenblatt* also refined the contours of the duty, by substituting the term "material facts" for the term "germane facts," and explicitly adopting the test of materiality set out in TSC Industries, Inc. v. Northway, Inc., supra, Chapter V, Section 4.

JONES v. H. F. AHMANSON & CO.

Supreme Court of California, 1969.
1 Cal.3d 93, 81 Cal.Rptr. 592, 460 P.2d 464.

TRAYNOR, C.J.—June K. Jones, the owner of 25 shares of the capital stock of United Savings and Loan Association of California brings this action on behalf of herself individually and of all similarly situated minority stockholders of the Association. The defendants are United Financial Corporation of California, fifteen individuals, and four corporations, all of whom are present or former stockholders or officers of the Association. Plaintiff seeks damages and other relief for losses allegedly suffered by the minority stockholders of the Association because of claimed breaches of fiduciary responsibility by defendants in the creation and operation of United Financial, a Delaware holding company that owns 87 percent of the outstanding Association stock.

Plaintiff appeals from the judgment entered for defendants after an order sustaining defendants' general and special demurrers to her third amended complaint without leave to amend. Defendants have filed a protective cross-appeal. We have concluded that the allegations of the complaint and certain stipulated facts sufficiently state a cause of action and that the judgment must therefore be reversed.

The following facts appear from the allegations of the complaint and stipulation.

United Savings and Loan Association of California is a California chartered savings and loan association that first issued stock on April 5, 1956. Theretofore it had been owned by its depositors, who, with borrowing members, elected the board of directors. No one depositor had sufficient voting power to control the Association.

The Association issued 6,568 shares of stock on April 5, 1956. No additional stock has been issued. Of these shares, 987 (14.8 percent) were purchased by depositors pursuant to warrants issued in proportion to the amount of their deposits. Plaintiff was among these purchasers. The shares allocated to unexercised warrants were sold to the then chairman of the board of directors who later resold them to defendants and others. The stockholders have the right to elect a majority of the directors of the Association.

The Association has retained the major part of its earnings in tax-free reserves with the result that the book value of the outstanding shares has increased substantially.[2] The shares were not actively traded. This inactivity is attributed to the high book value, the closely held nature of the Association,[3] and the failure of the management to provide investment information and assistance to shareholders, brokers, or the public. Transactions in the stock that did occur were primarily among existing stockholders. Fourteen of the nineteen defendants comprised 95 percent of the market for Association shares prior to 1959.

In 1958 investor interest in shares of savings and loan associations and holding companies increased. Savings and loan stocks that were publicly marketed enjoyed a steady increase in market price thereafter until June 1962, but the stock of United Savings and Loan Association was not among them. Defendants determined to create a mechanism by which they could participate in the profit taking by attracting investor interest in the Association. They did not, however, undertake to render the Association shares more readily marketable. Instead, the United Financial Corporation of California was incorporated in Delaware by all of the other defendants except defendant Thatcher on May 8, 1959. On May 14, 1959, pursuant to a prior agreement, certain Association stockholders who among them owned a majority of the Association stock exchanged their shares for those of United Financial, receiving a "derived block" of 250 United Financial shares for each Association share.[4]

After the exchange, United Financial held 85 percent of the outstanding Association stock. More than 85 percent of United Financial's consolidated earnings[5] and book value of its shares reflected its ownership of this Association stock. The former majority stockholders of the Association had become the majority shareholders of United Financial and continued to control the Association through the holding company. They did not offer the minority stockholders of the Association an opportunity to exchange their shares.

The first public offering of United Financial stock was made in June 1960. To attract investor interest, 60,000 units were offered, each of which comprised two shares of United Financial stock and one $100, 5 percent interest-bearing, subordinated, convertible debenture bond. The offering provided that of the $7,200,000 return from the

---

2. Between 1959 and 1966 the book value of each share increased from $1,131 to $4,143.70.

3. H.F. Ahmanson & Co. acquired a majority of the shares in May 1958. On May 14, 1959, the company owned 4,171 of the outstanding shares.

4. The number of shares in these derived blocks of United Financial stock was later modified by pro-rata surrenders and stock dividends in a series of transactions not pertinent here.

5. The balance reflected United Financial's ownership of three insurance agencies and stock in a fourth.

sale of these units, $6,200,000 would be distributed immediately as a return of capital to the original shareholders of United Financial, *i.e.*, the former majority stockholders of the Association.[6]   To obtain a permit from the California Corporations Commissioner for the sale, United Financial represented that the financial reserve requirement for debenture repayment established by Commissioner's Rules 480 subdivision (a) and 486 would be met by causing the Association to liquidate or encumber its income producing assets for cash that the Association would then distribute to United Financial to service and retire the bonds.

In the Securities and Exchange Commission prospectus accompanying this first public offering, United Financial acknowledged that its prior earnings were not sufficient to service the debentures and noted that United Financial's direct earnings would have to be augmented by dividends from the Association.

A public offering of 50,000 additional shares by United Financial with a secondary offering of 600,000 shares of the derived stock by the original investors was made in February 1961 for a total price of $15,275,000.   The defendants sold 568,190 shares of derived stock in this secondary offering.   An underwriting syndicate of 70 brokerage firms participated.   The resulting nationwide publicity stimulated trading in the stock until, in mid–1961, an average of 708.5 derived blocks were traded each month.   Sales of Association shares decreased during this period from a rate of 170 shares per year before the formation of United Financial to half that number.   United Financial acquired 90 percent of the Association shares that were sold.

Shortly after the first public offering of United Financial shares, defendants caused United Financial to offer to purchase up to 350 shares of Association stock for $1,100 per share.   The book value of each of these shares was $1,411.57, and earnings were $301.15 per share.   The derived blocks of United Financial shares then commanded an aggregate price of $3,700 per block exclusive of the $927.50 return of capital.   United Financial acquired an additional 130 shares of Association stock as a result of this offer.

In 1959 and 1960 extra dividends of $75 and $57 per share had been paid by the Association, but in December 1960, after the foregoing offer had been made, defendants caused the Association's president to notify each minority stockholder by letter that no dividends other than the regular $4 per share annual dividend would be paid in the near future.   The Association president, defendant M.D. Jameson, was then a director of both the Association and United Financial.

Defendants then proposed an exchange of United Financial shares for Association stock.   Under this proposal each minority stockholder would have received approximately 51 United Financial shares of a total value of $2,400 for each Association share.   When the applica-

---

6. This distribution was equivalent to a $927.50 return of capital on each derived block of shares.

tion for a permit was filed with the California Corporations Commissioner on August 28, 1961, the value of the derived blocks of United Financial shares received by defendants in the initial exchange had risen to approximately $8,800.[9] The book value of the Association stock was in excess of $1,700 per share, and the shares were earning at an annual rate of $615 per share. Each block of 51 United Financial shares had a book value of only $210 and earnings of $134 per year, 85 percent of which reflected Association earnings. At the hearings held on the application by the Commissioner, representatives of United Financial justified the higher valuation of United Financial shares on the ground that they were highly marketable, whereas Association stock was unmarketable and poor collateral for loans. Plaintiff and other minority stockholders objected to the proposed exchange, contending that the plan was not fair, just, and equitable. Defendants then asked the Commissioner to abandon the application without ruling on it.

Plaintiff contends that in following this course of conduct defendants breached the fiduciary duty owed by majority or controlling shareholders to minority shareholders. She alleges that they used their control of the Association for their own advantage to the detriment of the minority when they created United Financial, made a public market for its shares that rendered Association stock unmarketable except to United Financial, and then refused either to purchase plaintiff's Association stock at a fair price or exchange the stock on the same basis afforded to the majority. She further alleges that they also created a conflict of interest that might have been avoided had they offered all Association stockholders the opportunity to participate in the initial exchange of shares. Finally, plaintiff contends that the defendants' acts constituted a restraint of trade in violation of common law and statutory antitrust laws.

I

Plaintiff's Capacity to Sue

We are faced at the outset with defendants' contention that if a cause of action is stated, it is derivative in nature since any injury suffered is common to all minority stockholders of the Association. Therefore, defendants urge, plaintiff may not sue in an individual capacity or on behalf of a class made up of stockholders excluded from the United Financial exchange, and in any case may not maintain a derivative action without complying with Financial Code section 7616.[10] . . .

9. The derived block sold for as much as $13,127.41 during 1960–1961. On January 30, 1962, the date upon which plaintiff commenced this action, the mean value was $9,116.08.

10. Section 7616 provides: "No action may be instituted or maintained in the right of any savings and loan association . . . by a stockholder of any association, unless . . . [the banking] commissioner shall have determined, after a hearing upon at least 20 days' written notice to such association and each of its directors, that such action (a) is proposed in good faith and (b) there is reasonable possibility that the prosecution of such action will benefit the association and its stockholders. . . ."

It is clear from the stipulated facts and plaintiff's allegations that she does not seek to recover on behalf of the corporation for injury done to the corporation by defendants. Although she does allege that the value of her stock has been diminished by defendants' actions, she does not contend that the diminished value reflects an injury to the corporation and resultant depreciation in the value of the stock. Thus the gravamen of her cause of action is injury to herself and the other minority stockholders [and her action is individual rather than derivative]. . . .

II

Majority Shareholders' Fiduciary Responsibility

Defendants take the position that as shareholders they owe no fiduciary obligation to other shareholders, absent reliance on inside information, use of corporate assets, or fraud. This view has long been repudiated in California. The Courts of Appeal have often recognized that majority shareholders, either singly or acting in concert to accomplish a joint purpose, have a fiduciary responsibility to the minority and to the corporation to use their ability to control the corporation in a fair, just, and equitable manner. Majority shareholders may not use their power to control corporate activities to benefit themselves alone or in a manner detrimental to the minority. Any use to which they put the corporation or their power to control the corporation must benefit all shareholders proportionately and must not conflict with the proper conduct of the corporation's business. (*Brown v. Halbert,* 271 Cal.App.2d 252 [76 Cal.Rptr. 781]; *Burt v. Irvine Co.,* 237 Cal.App.2d 828 [47 Cal.Rptr. 392]; *Efron v. Kalmanovitz,* 226 Cal.App.2d 546 [38 Cal.Rptr. 148]; *Remillard Brick Co. v. Remillard–Dandini Co.,* 109 Cal.App.2d 405 [241 P.2d 66].)

The extensive reach of the duty of controlling shareholders and directors to the corporation and its other shareholders was described by the Court of Appeal in *Remillard Brick Co. v. Remillard–Dandini Co., supra,* 109 Cal.App.2d 405, where, quoting from the opinion of the United States Supreme Court in *Pepper v. Litton,* 308 U.S. 295 [84 L.Ed. 281, 60 S.Ct. 238], the court held: " 'A director is a fiduciary . . . So is a dominant or controlling stockholder or group of stockholders . . . Their powers are powers of trust . . . Their dealings with the corporation are subjected to rigorous scrutiny and where any of their contracts or engagements with the corporation is challenged the burden is on the director or stockholder not only to prove the good faith of the transaction but also to show its inherent fairness from the viewpoint of the corporation and those interested therein . . .' " . . .

. . . The rule that has developed in California is a comprehensive rule of "inherent fairness from the viewpoint of the corporation and those interested therein." (*Remillard Brick Co. v. Remillard–Dandini Co., supra,* 109 Cal.App.2d 405, 420. See also, *In re Security Finance Co., supra,* 49 Cal.2d 370; *Brown v. Halbert, supra,* 271 Cal. App.2d 252; *Burt v. Irvine Co., supra,* 237 Cal.App.2d 828; *Efron v.*

Kalmanovitz, supra, 226 Cal.App.2d 546.) The rule applies alike to officers, directors, and controlling shareholders in the exercise of powers that are theirs by virtue of their position and to transactions wherein controlling shareholders seek to gain an advantage in the sale or transfer or use of their controlling block of shares. . . .

The increasingly complex transactions of the business and financial communities demonstrate the inadequacy of the traditional theories of fiduciary obligation as tests of majority shareholder responsibility to the minority. These theories have failed to afford adequate protection to minority shareholders and particularly to those in closely held corporations whose disadvantageous and often precarious position renders them particularly vulnerable to the vagaries of the majority. Although courts have recognized the potential for abuse or unfair advantage when a controlling shareholder sells his shares at a premium over investment value (*Perlman v. Feldmann,* 219 F.2d 173 [50 A.L.R.2d 1134] [premium paid for control over allocation of production in time of shortage]; *Gerdes v. Reynolds,* 28 N.Y.S.2d 622 [sale of control to looters or incompetents]; *Porter v. Healy,* 244 Pa. 427 [91 A. 428]; *Brown v. Halbert, supra,* 271 Cal.App.2d 252 [sale of only controlling shareholder's shares to purchaser offering to buy assets of corporation or all shares]) or in a controlling shareholder's use of control to avoid equitable distribution of corporate assets (*Zahn v. Transamerica Corp.* (3rd Cir.1946) 162 F.2d 36 [172 A.L.R. 495] [use of control to cause subsidiary to redeem stock prior to liquidation and distribution of assets]), no comprehensive rule has emerged in other jurisdictions. Nor have most commentators approached the problem from a perspective other than that of the advantage gained in the sale of control. Some have suggested that the price paid for control shares over their investment value be treated as an asset belonging to the corporation itself (Berle and Means, The Modern Corporation and Private Property (1932) p. 243), or as an asset that should be shared proportionately with all shareholders through a general offer (Jennings, *Trading in Corporate Control* (1956) 44 Cal.L. Rev. 1, 39), and another contends that the sale of control at a premium is always evil (Bayne, *The Sale-of-Control Premium: the Intrinsic Illegitimacy* (1969) 47 Texas L.Rev. 215).

The additional potential for injury to minority shareholders from majority dealings in its control power apart from sale has not gone unrecognized, however. The ramifications of defendants' actions here are not unlike those described by Professor Gower as occurring when control of one corporation is acquired by another through purchase of less than all of the shares of the latter: "The [acquired] company's existence is not affected, nor need its constitution be altered; all that occurs is that its shareholders change. From the legal viewpoint this methodological distinction is formidable, but commercially the two things may be almost identical. If . . . a controlling interest is acquired, the [acquired] company . . . will become a subsidiary of the acquiring company . . . and cease, in fact though not in law, to be an independent entity.

"This may produce the situation in which a small number of dissentient members are left as a minority in a company intended to be operated as a member of a group. As such, their position is likely to be unhappy, for the parent company will wish to operate the subsidiary for the benefit of the group as a whole and not necessarily for the benefit of that particular subsidiary." (Gower, The Principles of Modern Company Law (2d ed. 1957) p. 561.) Professor Eisenberg notes that as the purchasing corporation's proportionate interest in the acquired corporation approaches 100 percent, the market for the latter's stock disappears, a problem that is aggravated if the acquiring corporation for its own business purposes reduces or eliminates dividends. (Eisenberg, *The Legal Role of Shareholders and Management in Modern Corporate Decision–Making* (1969) 57 Cal.L.Rev. 1, 132. See also, O'Neal and Derwin, Expulsion or Oppression of Business Associates (1961) *passim;* Leech, *Transactions in Corporate Control* (1956) 104 U.Pa.L.Rev. 725, 728; Comment, *The Fiduciary Relation of the Dominant Shareholder to the Minority Shareholders* (1958) 9 Hastings L.J. 306, 314.) The case before us, in which no sale or transfer of actual control is directly involved, demonstrates that the injury anticipated by these authors can be inflicted with impunity under the traditional rules and supports our conclusion that the comprehensive rule of good faith and inherent fairness to the minority in any transaction where control of the corporation is material properly governs controlling shareholders in this state.

We turn now to defendants' conduct to ascertain whether this test is met.

III

Formation of United Financial and Marketing its Shares

Defendants created United Financial during a period of unusual investor interest in the stock of savings and loan associations. They then owned a majority of the outstanding stock of the Association. This stock was not readily marketable owing to a high book value, lack of investor information and facilities, and the closely held nature of the Association. The management of the Association had made no effort to create a market for the stock or to split the shares and reduce their market price to a more attractive level. Two courses were available to defendants in their effort to exploit the bull market in savings and loan stock. Both were made possible by defendants' status as controlling stockholders. The first was either to cause the Association to effect a stock split (Corp. Code, § 1507) and create a market for the Association stock or to create a holding company for Association shares and permit all stockholders to exchange their shares before offering holding company shares to the public. All stockholders would have benefited alike had this been done, but in realizing their gain on the sale of their stock the majority stockholders would of necessity have had to relinquish some of their control shares. Because a public market would have been created, however, the minority stockholders would have been able to extricate themselves without sacrificing their investment had they elected not to remain with the new management.

The second course was that taken by defendants. A new corporation was formed whose major asset was to be the control block of Association stock owned by defendants, but from which minority shareholders were to be excluded. The unmarketable Association stock held by the majority was transferred to the newly formed corporation at an exchange rate equivalent to a 250 for 1 stock split. The new corporation thereupon set out to create a market for its own shares. Association stock constituted 85 percent of the holding company's assets and produced an equivalent proportion of its income. The same individuals controlled both corporations. It appears therefrom that the market created by defendants for United Financial shares was a market that would have been available for Association stock had defendants taken the first course of action.[13]

After United Financial shares became available to the public it became a virtual certainty that no equivalent market could or would be created for Association stock. United Financial had become the controlling stockholder and neither it nor the other defendants would benefit from public trading in Association stock in competition with

---

13. The situation of minority stockholders and the difficulties they faced in attempting to market their savings and loan stock were described in The Savings and Loan Industry in California, a report prepared by the Stanford Research Institute for the California Savings and Loan Commissioner, and published by the Commissioner in 1960. The attractiveness of the holding company as a device to enhance liquidity was recognized: "The majority and minority stockholders in the original associations often found that they had difficulties in selling their shares at a price approximating their book value. Their main difficulties arose from the fact that book values and prices of shares often ran into many thousands of dollars, a price not generally suitable for wide public sale. These shares were usually owned by a relatively small number of stockholders. When one of them, or his heirs, wished to sell his shares, he had to negotiate with a buyer in this small group or attempt to find an outside purchaser. Minority stockholders had a special problem, because they could not sell control with their stock.

"The holding company was regarded by many stockholders as an attractive device to solve the problem of the marketability of their shares. Through this method, the control of one, two, or several associations could be consolidated and offered to the investing public in a single large stock issue at relatively low prices, either over the counter or through a stock exchange. The wide public ownership of holding company shares would thus provide a more active market and more protection against

large capital losses in the event the original owners or their heirs wished to sell their holding company stock.

" * * *

"Large capital gains on the sale of holding company stock to the public have been an important incentive and consequence of this form of organization. The issuance of holding company stock to the general public usually found an enthusiastic demand which made it possible to sell the stock for as much as two to three times book value. In many but not all cases the majority stockholders in the original associations have offered less than 50 percent of the holding company's stock to the public, thus retaining control of the association and the holding companies." (The Savings and Loan Industry in California (1960) pp. VI–6–VI–7.) Although defendants suggest that their transfer of the insurance businesses and the later acquisition of another savings and loan association by United Financial were necessary to the creation of a market for United Financial shares and that no market could be created for the shares of a single savings and loan association, the study does not support their claim. Whether defendants could have created a market for a holding company that controlled a single association or reasonably believed that they could not, goes to their good faith and to the existence of a proper business purpose for electing the course that they chose to follow. At the trial of the cause defendants can introduce evidence relevant to the necessity for inclusion of other businesses.

United Financial shares. Investors afforded an opportunity to acquire United Financial shares would not be likely to choose the less marketable and expensive Association stock in preference. Thus defendants chose a course of action in which they used their control of the Association to obtain an advantage not made available to all stockholders. They did so without regard to the resulting detriment to the minority stockholders and in the absence of any compelling business purpose. Such conduct is not consistent with their duty of good faith and inherent fairness to the minority stockholders. Had defendants afforded the minority an opportunity to exchange their stock on the same basis or offered to purchase them at a price arrived at by independent appraisal, their burden of establishing good faith and inherent fairness would have been much less. At the trial they may present evidence tending to show such good faith or compelling business purpose that would render their action fair under the circumstances. On appeal from the judgment of dismissal after the defendants' demurrer was sustained we decide only that the complaint states a cause of action entitling plaintiff to relief.

Defendants gained an additional advantage for themselves through their use of control of the Association when they pledged that control over the Association's assets and earnings to secure the holding company's debt, a debt that had been incurred for their own benefit. In so doing the defendants breached their fiduciary obligation to the minority once again and caused United Financial and its controlling shareholders to become inextricably wedded to a conflict of interest between the minority stockholders of each corporation. Alternatives were available to them that would have benefited all stockholders proportionately. . . .

In so holding we do not suggest that the duties of corporate fiduciaries include in all cases an obligation to make a market for and to facilitate public trading in the stock of the corporation. But when, as here, no market exists, the controlling shareholders may not use their power to control the corporation for the purpose of promoting a marketing scheme that benefits themselves alone to the detriment of the minority. Nor do we suggest that a control block of shares may not be sold or transferred to a holding company. We decide only that the circumstances of any transfer of controlling shares will be subject to judicial scrutiny when it appears that the controlling shareholders may have breached their fiduciary obligation to the corporation or the remaining shareholders.

IV

Damages . . .

If, after the trial of the cause, plaintiff has established facts in conformity with the allegations of the complaint and stipulation, then upon tender of her Association stock to defendants she will be entitled to receive at her election either the appraised value of her shares on the date of the exchange, May 14, 1959, with interest at 7 percent a year from the date of this action, or a sum equivalent to the fair market value of a "derived block" of United Financial stock on the date of this action with interest thereon from that date, and the sum of $927.50 (the return of capital paid to the original United Financial shareholders) with interest thereon from the date United Financial first made such payments to its original shareholders, for each share tendered. The appraised or fair market value shall be reduced, however, by the amount by which dividends paid on Association shares during the period from May 14, 1959, to the present exceeds the dividends paid on a corresponding block of United Financial shares during the same period. . . .

The judgment appealed from by plaintiff is reversed. The trial court is directed to overrule the demurrer in conformity with this opinion. Defendants' appeal is dismissed.

Peters, J., Tobriner, J., Burke, J., Sullivan, J., and Coughlin, J. pro tem., concurred.

. . . McComb, J., was of the opinion that the petition should be granted.

———

Chapter IX

INSIDER TRADING

SECTION 1. THE COMMON LAW

GOODWIN v. AGASSIZ

Massachusetts Supreme Judicial Court, 1933.
283 Mass. 358, 186 N.E. 659.

BILL IN EQUITY, filed in the Supreme Judicial Court for the county of Suffolk on September 17, 1928, described in the opinion. . . .

RUGG, C.J. A stockholder in a corporation seeks in this suit relief for losses suffered by him in selling shares of stock in Cliff Mining Company by way of accounting, rescission of sales, or redelivery of shares. The named defendants are MacNaughton, a resident of Michigan not served or appearing, and Agassiz, a resident of this Commonwealth, the active party defendant.

The trial judge made findings of fact, rulings, and an order dismissing the bill. There is no report of the evidence. The case must be considered on the footing that the findings are true. The facts thus displayed are these: The defendants, in May, 1926, purchased through brokers on the Boston stock exchange seven hundred shares of stock of the Cliff Mining Company which up to that time the plaintiff had owned. Agassiz was president and director and MacNaughton a director and general manager of the company. They had certain knowledge, material as to the value of the stock, which the plaintiff did not have. The plaintiff contends that such purchase in all the circumstances without disclosure to him of that knowledge was a wrong against him. That knowledge was that an experienced geologist had formulated in writing in March, 1926, a theory as to the possible existence of copper deposits under conditions prevailing in the region where the property of the company was located. That region was known as the mineral belt in northern Michigan, where are located mines of several copper mining companies. Another such company, of which the defendants were officers, had made extensive geological surveys of its lands. In consequence of recommendations resulting from that survey, exploration was started on property of the Cliff Mining Company in 1925. That exploration was ended in May, 1926, because completed unsuccessfully, and the equipment was removed. The defendants discussed the geologist's theory shortly after it was formulated. Both felt that the theory had value and should be tested, but they agreed that, before starting to test it, options should be obtained by another copper company of which they were officers on land adjacent to or nearby in the copper belt, that if the geologist's theory were known to the owners of such other land there might be difficulty in securing options, and that that theory should not be communicated to any one unless it became absolutely necessary. Thereafter, options were secured which, if taken up, would involve a large expenditure by the other company. The defendants both thought, also, that, if there was any merit in the geologist's theory, the price of Cliff Mining Company stock in the market would go up. Its stock was quoted and bought and sold on the Boston stock exchange. Pursuant to agreement, they bought many shares of that stock through agents on joint account. The plaintiff first learned of the closing of exploratory operations on property of the Cliff Mining Company from an article in a paper on May 15, 1926, and immediately sold his shares of stock through brokers. It does not appear that the defendants were in any way responsible for the publication of that article. The plaintiff did not know that the purchase was made for the defendants and they did not know that his stock was being bought for them. There was no communication between them touching the subject. The plaintiff would not have sold his stock if he had known of the geologist's theory. The finding is express that the defendants were not guilty of fraud, that they committed no breach of duty owed by them to the Cliff Mining Company, and that that company was not harmed by the nondisclosure of the geologist's theory, or by their purchases of its stock, or by shutting down the exploratory operations.

The contention of the plaintiff is that the purchase of his stock in the company by the defendants without disclosing to him as a stockholder their knowledge of the geologist's theory, their belief that the theory had value, the keeping secret the existence of the theory, discontinuance by the defendants of exploratory operations begun in 1925 on property of the Cliff Mining Company and their plan ultimately to test the value of the theory, constitute actionable wrong for which he as stockholder can recover.

The trial judge ruled that conditions may exist which would make it the duty of an officer of a corporation purchasing its stock from a stockholder to inform him as to knowledge possessed by the buyer and not by the seller, but found, on all the circumstances developed by the trial and set out at some length by him in his decision, that there was no fiduciary relation requiring such disclosure by the defendants to the plaintiff before buying his stock in the manner in which they did.

The question presented is whether the decree dismissing the bill rightly was entered on the facts found.

The directors of a commercial corporation stand in a relation of trust to the corporation and are bound to exercise the strictest good faith in respect to its property and business. *Elliott v. Baker,* 194 Mass. 518, 523. *Beaudette v. Graham,* 267 Mass. 7. *L.E. Fosgate Co. v. Boston Market Terminal Co.,* 275 Mass. 99, 107. The contention that directors also occupy the position of trustee toward individual stockholders in the corporation is plainly contrary to repeated decisions of this court and cannot be supported. In *Smith v. Hurd,* 12 Met. 371, 384, it was said by Chief Justice Shaw: "There is no legal privity, relation, or immediate connexion, between the holders of shares in a bank, in their individual capacity, on the one side, and the directors of the bank on the other. The directors are not the bailees, the factors, agents or trustees of such individual stockholders." In *Stewart v. Joyce,* 201 Mass. 301, 311, 312, and *Lee v. Fisk,* 222 Mass. 424, 426, the same principle was reiterated. In *Blabon v. Hay,* 269 Mass. 401, 407, occurs this language with reference to sale of stock in a corporation by a stockholder to two of its directors: "The fact that the defendants were directors created no fiduciary relation between them and the plaintiff in the matter of the sale of his stock."

The principle thus established is supported by an imposing weight of authority in other jurisdictions. *Steinfeld v. Nielsen,* 15 Ariz. 424. *Bawden v. Taylor,* 254 Ill. 464. *Tippecanoe County Commissioners v. Reynolds,* 44 Ind. 509. *Waller v. Hodge,* 214 Ky. 705. *Buckley v. Buckley,* 230 Mich. 504. *Dutton v. Barnes,* 162 Minn. 430. *Crowell v. Jackson,* 24 Vroom, 656. *Carpenter v. Danforth,* 52 Barb.S.C. 581. *Shaw v. Cole Manuf. Co.,* 132 Tenn. 210. *White v. Texas Co.,* 59 Utah, 180, 188. *Percival v. Wright,* [1902] 2 Ch.D. 421. *Tackey v. McBain,* [1912] A.C. 186. A rule holding that directors are trustees for individual stockholders with respect to their stock prevails in comparatively few States; but in view of our own adjudications it is not necessary to review decisions to that effect. See, for example, *Oliver v. Oliver,* 118 Ga. 362; *Dawson v. National Life Ins. Co. of America,* 176 Iowa, 362; *Stewart v. Harris,* 69 Kans. 498. See, also, for collection of authorities, 14A C.J. § 1896; 27 Yale L.J. 731; 32 Yale L.J. 637.

While the general principle is as stated, circumstances may exist requiring that transactions between a director and a stockholder as to stock in the corporation be set aside. The knowledge naturally in the possession of a director as to the condition of a corporation places upon him a peculiar obligation to observe every requirement of fair dealing when directly buying or selling its stock. Mere silence does not usually amount to a breach of duty, but parties may stand in such relation to each other that an equitable responsibility arises to communicate facts. *Wellington v. Rugg,* 243 Mass. 30, 35. Purchases and sales of stock dealt in on the stock exchange are commonly impersonal affairs. An honest director would be in a difficult situation if he could neither buy nor sell on the stock exchange shares of stock in his corporation without first seeking out the other actual ultimate party to the transaction and disclosing to him everything which a court or jury might later find that he then knew affecting the real or speculative value of such shares. Business of that nature is a matter to be governed by practical rules. Fiduciary obligations of directors ought not to be made so onerous that men of experience and ability will be deterred from accepting such office. Law in its sanctions is not coextensive with morality. It cannot undertake to put all parties to every contract on an equality as to knowledge, experience, skill and shrewdness. It cannot undertake to relieve against hard bargains made between competent parties without fraud. On the other hand, directors cannot rightly be allowed to indulge with impunity in practices which do violence to prevailing standards of upright business men. Therefore, where a director personally seeks a stockholder for the purpose of buying his shares without making disclosure of material facts within his peculiar knowledge and not within reach of the stockholder, the transaction will be closely scrutinized and relief may be granted in appropriate instances. *Strong v. Repide,* 213 U.S. 419. *Allen v. Hyatt,* 30 T.L.R. 444. *Gammon v. Dain,* 238 Mich. 30. *George v. Ford,* 36 App.D.C. 315. See, also, *Old Dominion Copper Mining & Smelting Co. v. Bigelow,* 203 Mass. 159, 194–195. The applicable legal principles "have almost always been the fundamental ethical rules of right and wrong." *Robinson v. Mollett,* L.R. 7 H.L. 802, 817.

The precise question to be decided in the case at bar is whether on the facts found the defendants as directors had a right to buy stock of the plaintiff, a stockholder. Every element of actual fraud or misdoing by the defendants is negatived by the findings. Fraud cannot be presumed; it must be proved. *Brown v. Little, Brown & Co. (Inc.)* 269 Mass. 102, 117. The facts found afford no ground for inferring fraud or conspiracy. The only knowledge possessed by the defendants not open to the plaintiff was the existence of a theory formulated in a thesis by a geologist as to the possible existence of copper deposits where certain geological conditions existed common to the property of the Cliff Mining Company and that of other mining companies in its neighborhood. This thesis did not express an opinion that copper deposits would be found at any particular spot or on property of any specified owner. Whether that theory was sound or fallacious, no one knew, and so far as appears has never been demonstrated. The defendants made no representations to anybody about the theory. No facts found placed upon them any obligation to disclose the theory. A few days after the thesis expounding the theory was brought to the attention of the defendants, the annual report by the directors of the Cliff Mining Company for the calendar year 1925, signed by Agassiz for the directors, was issued. It did not cover the time when the theory was formulated. The report described the status of the operations under the exploration which had been begun in 1925. At the annual meeting of the stockholders of the company held early in April, 1926, no reference was made to the theory. It was then at most a hope, possibly an expectation. It had not passed the nebulous stage. No disclosure was made of it. The Cliff Mining Company was not harmed by the nondisclosure. There would have been no advantage to it, so far as appears, from a disclosure. The disclosure would have been detrimental to the interests of another mining corporation in which the defendants were directors. In the circumstances there was no duty on the part of the defendants to set forth to the stockholders at the annual meeting their faith, aspirations and plans for the future. Events as they developed might render advisable radical changes in such views. Disclosure of the theory, if it ultimately was proved to be erroneous or without foundation in fact, might involve the defendants in litigation with those who might act on the hypothesis that it was correct. The stock of the Cliff Mining Company was bought and sold on the stock exchange. The identity of buyers and seller of the stock in question in fact was not known to the parties and perhaps could not readily have been ascertained. The defendants caused the shares to be bought through brokers on the stock exchange. They said nothing to anybody as to the reasons actuating them. The plaintiff was no novice. He was a member of the Boston stock exchange and had kept a record of sales of Cliff Mining Company stock. He acted upon his own judgment in selling his stock. He made no inquiries of the defendants or of other officers of the company. The result is that the plaintiff cannot prevail.

Decree dismissing bill affirmed with costs.

NOTE ON THE DUTIES OF DIRECTORS AND OFFICERS UNDER THE COMMON LAW WHEN TRADING IN THEIR CORPORATION'S STOCK

1. The rule adopted in *Goodwin v. Agassiz* was the majority rule under the common law. Although the transactions in *Goodwin v. Agassiz* occurred in an impersonal market, there are cases in which the rule was applied to face-to-face transactions. See, e.g., Lank v. Steiner, 43 Del.Ch. 262, 224 A.2d 242 (1966); Gladstone v. Murray Co., 314 Mass. 584, 50 N.E.2d 958 (1943). However, there was a minority rule, sometimes known as the Kansas rule, which required full disclosure by a director or officer, at least in face-to-face transactions. For example, in Hotchkiss v. Fischer, 136 Kan. 530, 16 P.2d 531 (1932), appeal after remand 139 Kan. 333, 31 P.2d 37 (1934), Hotchkiss, a widow in need of money, was a shareholder in Elmhurst Corporation. Hotchkiss came to Elmhurst's offices in advance of the corporation's annual meeting to ascertain whether a dividend would be declared. She had two interviews with Fischer, Elmhurst's president, who said he could not inform her whether a dividend would be declared until he conferred with directors coming from New York. Fischer showed Hotchkiss the year-end financial statements and explained the items on the statements, but painted a somewhat dark picture, saying finally, "[w]hat you regard your stock to be worth . . . is a matter you have to determine yourself." 136 Kan. at 533, 16 P.2d at 532. In fact, the condition of the corporation was much better than the financial statements suggested. Hotchkiss sold her stock to Fischer for $1.25 per share. Three days later, the directors declared a dividend of $1.00 per share. In a suit for damages, the court held for Hotchkiss. The court likened a director's duty to that of a trustee, and said that a director is under a duty to deal fairly with the shareholder and "communicate . . . all material facts in connection with the transaction which the [director] knows or should know." 136 Kan. at 537, 16 P.2d at 534. See also, e.g., Jacobson v. Yaschik, 249 S.C. 577, 155 S.E.2d 601 (1967).

2. The majority rule itself was subject to several very important exceptions. First, the rule did not apply when a director engaged in fraud. Under the common law, fraud occurs not only when a speaker knowingly makes a false statement, but also when he knowingly tells a half-truth. "A representation stating the truth so far as it goes but which the maker knows or believes to be materially misleading because of his failure to state additional or qualifying matter is a fraudulent misrepresentation. . . . Thus, a statement that contains only favorable matters and omits all references to unfavorable matters is as much a false representation as if all the facts stated were untrue." Restatement (Second) of Torts § 529 and Comment a (1976).

It is also fraudulent at common law to take affirmative steps to prevent the truth from being discovered. "One party to a transaction who by concealment or other action intentionally prevents the other from acquiring material information is subject to the same liability to the other, for pecuniary loss as though he had stated the nonexistence of the matter that the other was thus prevented from discovering. . . . Even a false denial of knowledge or information by one party to a transaction, who is in possession of the facts, may subject him to liability as fully as if he had expressly misstated the facts, if its effect upon the plaintiff is to lead him to believe that the facts do not exist or cannot be discovered." Id. § 550 and Comment b.

Perhaps the most important exception to the majority rule was the "special facts" exception, adopted in Strong v. Repide 213 U.S. 419, 29 S.Ct. 521, 53 L.Ed. 853 (1909) and later in many other cases. Repide was a director, the administrator general, and owner of nearly three-fourths of the shares of Philippine Sugar. Philippine Sugar owned certain lands in the Philippines that the United States government wished to buy. The corporation was without funds, and the value of its shares was wholly dependent on making an advantageous sale of its properties to the government. Repide was in charge of the negotiations with the government, which dragged on for months, primarily because Repide was holding out for a higher price. Strong, who owned shares in Philippine Sugar, had given a power of attorney to sell her shares to Jones, who had an office next door to that of Repide. While negotiations with the government were pending, Repide, knowing that a sale to the government was probable, used an intermediary to employ a broker to purchase Strong's shares from Jones. Jones was given no information as to the state of the negotiations with the government, and neither Strong nor Jones knew that Repide was the purchaser. The price paid to Strong was about one-tenth what the shares became worth less than three months later, when the sale of the corporation's property to the government was consummated.

The Supreme Court affirmed an award of damages to Strong, on the ground that even if a director has no general duty to disclose facts known to him before he purchases shares, "there are cases where, by reason of the special facts, such duty exists." Id. at 431, 29 S.Ct. at 525. Jones sold Strong's shares because the corporation was paying no dividends and the negotiations with the government had gone on for so long that he thought that there was no prospect that a sale of the corporation's property would be made in the near term. Repide was not only a director but, by reason of his ownership of three-fourths of the shares, his position as administrator general, and the acquiescence of the other shareholders, was in full charge of the negotiations and was able to come to an agreement with the government if and when he chose to do so. He concealed his identity as a purchaser and dealt in a roundabout fashion with Jones. In view of all these facts, "the law would indeed be impotent if the sale could not be set aside or [Repide] cast in damages for his fraud." Id. at 433, 29 S.Ct. at 526.

3. Since there was no meaningful way to differentiate those cases that involved "special facts" from those that didn't, the special-facts exception either ate up the majority rule or made the rule impossible to administer in a consistent fashion. At bottom, the exception was inconsistent with the majority rule, and was employed by the courts as a mechanism to escape from that rule while purporting to follow it.

The common law rule atrophied after the 1940's, due to the development of Rule 10b–5 under the Securities Exchange Act, which came to occupy most of the field. It is conceivable that if Rule 10b–5 had not been adopted, and the common law concerning the obligations of directors and officers in the purchase and sale of stock had continued to develop, the minority rule would eventually have become the majority rule. In general, the common law of fraud has evolved in the direction of requiring greater disclosure. For example, Restatement (Second) of Contracts § 161 (1979) provides that a "person's nondisclosure of a fact known to him is equivalent to an assertion that the fact does not exist . . . where the other person is entitled to know the fact because of a relation of trust and confidence between them."

SECTION 2. SECURITIES EXCHANGE ACT § 10(b) and RULE 10b–5

SECURITIES EXCHANGE ACT § 10(b)

Sec. 10. It shall be unlawful for any person, directly or indirectly, by the use of any means or instrumentality of interstate commerce or of the mails, or of any facility of any national securities exchange

. . .

(b) To use or employ, in connection with the purchase or sale of any security registered on a national securities exchange or any security not so registered, any manipulative or deceptive device or contrivance in contravention of such rules and regulations as the Commission may prescribe as necessary or appropriate in the public interest or for the protection of investors.

SECURITIES EXCHANGE ACT RULE 10b–5

It shall be unlawful for any person, directly or indirectly, by the use of any means or instrumentality of interstate commerce, or of the mails, or of any facility of any national securities exchange,

(1) to employ any device, scheme, or artifice to defraud,

(2) to make any untrue statement of a material fact or to omit to state a material fact necessary in order to make the statements made, in the light of the circumstances under which they were made, not misleading, or

(3) to engage in any act, practice, or course of business which operates or would operate as a fraud or deceit upon any person,

in connection with the purchase or sale of any security.

IN THE MATTER OF CADY, ROBERTS & CO., 40 S.E.C. 907, 911–12 (1961). "[Rule 10b–5 applies] to securities transactions by 'any person.' Misrepresentations will lie within [its] ambit, no matter who the speaker may be. An affirmative duty to disclose material information has been traditionally imposed on corporate 'insiders,' particularly officers, directors, or controlling stockholders. We, and the courts have consistently held that insiders must disclose material facts which are known to them by virtue of their position but which are not known to persons with whom they deal and which, if known, would affect their investment judgment. Failure to make disclosure in these circumstances constitutes a violation of the anti-fraud provisions. If, on the other hand, disclosure prior to effecting a purchase or sale would be improper or unrealistic under the circumstances, we believe the alternative is to forego the transaction. . . .

We have already noted that the anti-fraud provisions are phrased in terms of 'any person' and that a special obligation has been traditionally required of corporate insiders, e.g., officers, directors and controlling stockholders. These three groups, however, do not exhaust the classes of persons upon whom there is such an obligation. Analytically, the obligation rests on two principal elements; first, the existence of a relationship giving access, directly or indirectly, to information intended to be available only for a corporate purpose and not for the personal benefit of anyone, and second, the inherent unfairness involved where a party takes advantage of such information knowing it is unavailable to those with whom he is dealing. In considering these elements under the broad language of the anti-fraud provisions we are not to be circumscribed by fine distinctions and rigid classifications. Thus our task here is to identify those persons who are in a special relationship with a company and privy to its internal affairs, and thereby suffer correlative duties in trading in its securities. Intimacy demands restraint lest the uninformed be exploited."

SECURITIES AND EXCHANGE COMMISSION v. TEXAS GULF SULPHUR CO.

United States Court of Appeals, Second Circuit, 1968.
401 F.2d 833 (en banc), cert. denied 394 U.S. 976, 89 S.Ct. 1454, 22 L.Ed.2d 756
(1969).

[This was an action brought by the S.E.C. against Texas Gulf Sulphur, (TGS), based on the issuance of a misleading press release, and against certain officers and employees of TGS based on their trading and tipping. The case grew out of an important mineral discovery by TGS. Four of the individual defendants were members of the geological exploration group that made the discovery: Mollison, a vice-president and mining engineer who headed the exploration group; Holyk, TGS' chief geologist; Clayton, an electrical engineer and geophysicist, and Darke, a geologist. The other individual defendants included Stephens, who was TGS's President; Fogarty, its Executive Vice–President; Kline, its Vice–President and General Counsel; and Coates, a director.

[Those portions of the opinion dealing with the liability of TGS for the misleading press release, and the liability of individual defendants for tipping, have been omitted, because the discussion of those issues has been largely superseded by later Supreme Court cases, set out below.]

This action derives from the exploratory activities of TGS begun in 1957 on the Canadian Shield in eastern Canada. In March of 1959, aerial geophysical surveys were conducted over more than 15,000 square miles of this area by a group led by defendant Mollison, a mining engineer and a Vice President of TGS. The group included defendant Holyk, TGS's chief geologist, defendant Clayton, an electrical engineer and geophysicist, and defendant Darke, a geologist. These operations resulted in the detection of numerous anomalies, i.e., extraordinary variations in the conductivity of rocks, one of which was on the Kidd 55 segment of land located near Timmins, Ontario.

On October 29 and 30, 1963, Clayton conducted a ground geophysical survey on the northeast portion of the Kidd 55 segment which confirmed the presence of an anomaly and indicated the necessity of diamond core drilling for further evaluation. Drilling of the initial hole, K–55–1, at the strongest part of the anomaly was commenced on November 8 and terminated on November 12 at a depth of 655 feet. Visual estimates by Holyk of the core of K–55–1 indicated an average copper content of 1.15% and an average zinc content of 8.64% over a length of 599 feet. This visual estimate convinced TGS that it was desirable to acquire the remainder of the Kidd 55 segment, and in order to facilitate this acquisition TGS President Stephens instructed the exploration group to keep the results of K–55–1 confidential and undisclosed even as to other officers, directors, and employees of TGS. The hole was concealed and a barren core was intentionally drilled off the anomaly. Meanwhile, the core of K–55–1 had been shipped to Utah for chemical assay which, when received in early December, revealed an average mineral content of 1.18% copper, 8.26% zinc, and 3.94% ounces of silver per ton over a length of 602 feet. These results were so remarkable that neither Clayton, an experienced geophysicist, nor four other TGS expert witnesses, had ever seen or heard of a comparable initial exploratory drill hole in a base metal deposit. So, the trial court concluded, "There is no doubt that the drill core of K–55–1 was unusually good and that it excited the interest and speculation of those who knew about it." Id. at 282. By March 27, 1964, TGS decided that the land acquisition program had advanced to such a point that the company might well resume drilling, and drilling was resumed on March 31.

During this period, from November 12, 1963 when K–55–1 was completed, to March 31, 1964 when drilling was resumed, certain of the individual defendants . . . and persons . . . said to have received 'tips' from them, purchased TGS stock or calls thereon. Prior to these transactions these persons had owned 1135 shares of TGS stock and possessed no calls; thereafter they owned a total of 8235 shares and possessed 12,300 calls.

On February 20, 1964, also during this period, TGS issued stock options to 26 of its officers and employees whose salaries exceeded a specified amount, five of whom were the individual defendants Stephens, Fogarty, Mollison, Holyk, and Kline. Of these, only Kline was unaware of the detailed results of K–55–1, but he, too, knew that a hole containing favorable bodies of copper and zinc ore had been drilled in Timmins. At this time, neither the TGS Stock Option Committee nor its Board of Directors had been informed of the results of K–55–1, presumably because of the pending land acquisition program which required confidentiality. All of the foregoing defendants accepted the options granted them.

When drilling was resumed on March 31, hole K–55–3 was commenced 510 feet west of K–55–1 and was drilled easterly at a 45° angle so as to cross K–55–1 in a vertical plane. Daily progress reports of the drilling of this hole K–55–3 and of all subsequently drilled holes were sent to defendants Stephens and Fogarty (President and Executive Vice President of TGS) by Holyk and Mollison. Visual estimates of K–55–3 revealed an average mineral content of 1.12% copper and 7.93% zinc over 641 of the hole's 876–foot length. On April 7, drilling of a third hole, K–55–4, 200 feet south of and parallel to K–55–1 and westerly at a 45° angle, was commenced and mineralization was encountered over 366 of its 579–foot length. Visual estimates indicated an average content of 1.14% copper and 8.24% zinc. Like K–55–1, both K–55–3 and K–55–4 established substantial copper mineralization on the eastern edge of the anomaly. On the basis of these findings relative to the foregoing drilling results, the trial court concluded that the vertical plane created by the intersection of K–55–1 and K–55–3, which measured at least 350 feet wide by 500 feet deep extended southward 200 feet to its intersection with K–55–4, and that "There was real evidence that a body of commercially mineable ore might exist." Id. at 281–82.

On April 8 TGS began with a second drill rig to drill another hole, K–55–6, 300 feet easterly of K–55–1. This hole was drilled westerly at an angle of 60° and was intended to explore mineralization beneath K–55–1. While no visual estimates of its core were immediately available, it was readily apparent by the evening of April 10 that substantial copper mineralization had been encountered over the last 127 feet of the hole's 569–foot length. On April 10, a third drill rig commenced drilling yet another hole, K–55–5, 200 feet north of K–55–1, parallel to the prior holes, and slanted westerly at a 45° angle. By the evening of April 10 in this hole, too, substantial copper mineralization had been encountered over the last 42 feet of its 97–foot length.

Meanwhile, rumors that a major ore strike was in the making had been circulating throughout Canada. On the morning of Saturday, April 11, Stephens at his home in Greenwich, Conn. read in the New York Herald Tribune and in the New York Times unauthorized reports of the TGS drilling which seemed to infer a rich strike from the fact that the drill cores had been flown to the United States for chemical assay. Stephens immediately contacted Fogarty at his home in Rye, N.Y., who in turn telephoned and later that day visited Mollison at Mollison's home in Greenwich to obtain a current report and evaluation of the drilling progress.[7] The following morning, Sunday, Fogarty again telephoned Mollison, inquiring whether Mollison had any further information and told him to return to Timmins with Holyk, the TGS Chief Geologist, as soon as possible "to move things along." With the aid of one Carroll, a public relations consultant, Fogarty drafted a press release designed to quell the rumors, which release, after having been channeled through Stephens and Huntington, a TGS attorney, was issued at 3:00 P.M. on Sunday, April 12, and which appeared in the morning newspapers of general circulation on Monday, April 13. It read in pertinent part as follows:

> New York, April 12—The following statement was made today by Dr. Charles F. Fogarty, executive vice president of Texas Gulf Sulphur Company, in regard to the company's drilling operations near Timmins, Ontario, Canada. Dr. Fogarty said:
>
> > "During the past few days, the exploration activities of Texas Gulf Sulphur in the area of Timmins, Ontario, have been widely reported in the press, coupled with rumors of a substantial copper discovery there. These reports exaggerate the scale of opera-

---

7. Mollison had returned to the United States for the weekend. Friday morning, April 10, he had been on the Kidd tract "and had been advised by defendant Holyk as to the drilling results to 7:00 p.m. on April 10. At that time drill holes K–55–1, K–55–3 and K–55–4 had been completed; drilling of K–55–5 had started on Section 2200 S and had been drilled to 97 feet, encountering mineralization on the last 42 feet; and drilling of K–55–6 had been started on Section 2400 S and had been drilled to 569 feet, encountering mineralization over the last 127 feet." Id. at 294.

tions, and mention plans and statistics of size and grade of ore that are without factual basis and have evidently originated by speculation of people not connected with TGS.

"The facts are as follows. TGS has been exploring in the Timmins area for six years as part of its overall search in Canada and elsewhere for various minerals—lead, copper, zinc, etc. During the course of this work, in Timmins as well as in Eastern Canada, TGS has conducted exploration entirely on its own, without the participation by others. Numerous prospects have been investigated by geophysical means and a large number of selected ones have been core-drilled. These cores are sent to the United States for assay and detailed examination as a matter of routine and on advice of expert Canadian legal counsel. No inferences as to grade can be drawn from this procedure.

"Most of the areas drilled in Eastern Canada have revealed either barren pyrite or graphite without value; a few have resulted in discoveries of small or marginal sulphide ore bodies.

"Recent drilling on one property near Timmins has led to preliminary indications that more drilling would be required for proper evaluation of this prospect. The drilling done to date has not been conclusive, but the statements made by many outside quarters are unreliable and include information and figures that are not available to TGS.

"The work done to date has not been sufficient to reach definite conclusions and any statement as to size and grade of ore would be premature and possibly misleading. When we have progressed to the point where reasonable and logical conclusions can be made, TGS will issue a definite statement to its stockholders and to the public in order to clarify the Timmins project."

* * *

The release purported to give the Timmins drilling results as of the release date, April 12. From Mollison Fogarty had been told of the developments through 7:00 P.M. on April 10, and of the remarkable discoveries made up to that time, detailed supra, which discoveries, according to the calculations of the experts who testified for the SEC at the hearing, demonstrated that TGS had already discovered 6.2 to 8.3 million tons of proven ore having gross assay values from $26 to $29 per ton. TGS experts, on the other hand, denied at the hearing that proven or probable ore could have been calculated on April 11 or 12 because there was then no assurance of continuity in the mineralized zone.

The evidence as to the effect of this release on the investing public was equivocal and less than abundant. On April 13 the New York Herald Tribune in an article head-noted "Copper Rumor Deflated" quoted from the TGS release of April 12 and backtracked from its original April 11 report of a major strike but nevertheless inferred from the TGS release that "recent mineral exploratory activity near Timmins, Ontario, has provided preliminary favorable results, sufficient at least to require a step-up in drilling operations." Some witnesses who testified at the hearing stated that they found the release encouraging. On the other hand, a Canadian mining security specialist, Roche, stated that "earlier in the week [before April 16] we had a Dow Jones saying that they [TGS] didn't have anything basically" and a TGS stock specialist for the Midwest Stock Exchange became concerned about his long position in the stock after reading the release. The trial court stated only that "While, in retrospect, the press release may appear gloomy or incomplete, this does not make it misleading or deceptive on the basis of the facts then known." Id. at 296.

Meanwhile, drilling operations continued. . . .

While drilling activity ensued to completion, TGC officials were taking steps toward ultimate disclosure of the discovery. On April 13, a previously-invited reporter for The Northern Miner, a Canadian mining industry journal, visited the drillsite, interviewed Mollison, Holyk and Darke, and prepared an article which confirmed a 10 million ton ore strike. This report, after having been submitted to Mollison and returned to the reporter unamended on April 15, was published in the April 16 issue. A statement relative to the extent of the discovery, in substantial part drafted by Mollison, was given to the Ontario Minister of Mines for release to the Canadian media. Mollison and Holyk expected it to be released over the airways at 11 P.M. on April 15th, but, for undisclosed reasons, it was not released until 9:40 A.M. on the 16th. An official detailed statement, announcing a strike of at least 25 million tons of ore, based on the drilling data set forth above, was read to representatives of American financial media from 10:00 A.M. to 10:10 or 10:15 A.M. on April 16, and appeared over Merrill Lynch's private wire at 10:29 A.M. and, somewhat later than expected, over the Dow Jones ticker tape at 10:54 A.M.

Between the time the first press release was issued on April 12 and the dissemination of the TGS official announcement on the morning of April 16, the only defendants before us on appeal who engaged in market activity were Clayton and Crawford and TGS director Coates. Clayton ordered 200 shares of TGS stock through his Canadian broker on April 15 and the order was executed that day over the Midwest Stock Exchange. Crawford ordered 300 shares at midnight on the 15th and another 300 shares at 8:30 A.M. the next day, and these orders were executed over the Midwest Exchange in Chicago at its opening on April 16. Coates left the TGS press conference and called his broker son-in-law Haemisegger shortly before 10:20 A.M. on the 16th and ordered 2,000 shares of TGS for family trust accounts of which Coates was a trustee but not a beneficiary; Haemisegger executed this order over the New York and Midwest Exchanges, and he and his customers purchased 1500 additional shares.

During the period of drilling in Timmins, the market price of TGS stock fluctuated but steadily gained overall. On Friday, November 8, when the drilling began, the stock closed at 17⅜; on Friday, November 15, after K-55-1 had been completed, it closed at 18. After a slight decline to 16⅜ by Friday, November 22, the price rose to 20⅞ by December 13, when the chemical assay results of K-55-1 were received, and closed at a high of 24⅛ on February 21, the day after the stock options had been issued. It had reached a price of 26 by March 31, after the land acquisition program had been completed and drilling had been resumed, and continued to ascend to 30⅛ by the close of trading on April 10, at which time the drilling progress up to then was evaluated for the April 12th press release. On April 13, the day on which the April 12 release was disseminated, TGS opened at 30⅛, rose immediately to a high of 32 and gradually tapered off to close at 30⅞. It closed at 30¼ the next day, and at 29⅜ on April 15. On April 16, the day of the official announcement of the Timmins discovery, the price climbed to a high of 37 and closed at 36⅜. By May 15, TGS stock was selling at 58¼. . . .*

---

* The purchases by the parties during this period were:

Purchase Date	Purchaser	Shares Number	Price	Calls Number	Price
Hole K–55–1 Completed November 12, 1963					
1963					
Nov. 12	Fogarty	300	17¾–18		
15	Clayton	200	17¾		
15	Fogarty	700	17⅝–17⅞		
15	Mollison	100	17⅞		
19	Fogarty	500	18⅛		
26	Fogarty	200	17¾		
29	Holyk (Mrs.)	50	18		
Chemical Assays of Drill Core of K–55–1 Received December 9–13, 1963					
Dec. 10	Holyk (Mrs.)	100	20⅜		
12	Holyk (or wife)			200	21
13	Mollison	100	21⅛		
30	Fogarty	200	22		
31	Fogarty	100	23¼		
1964					
Jan. 6	Holyk (or wife)			100	23⅝
8	Murray			400	23¼
24	Holyk (or wife)			200	22¼–23⅜
Feb. 10	Fogarty	300	22⅛–22¼		
20	Darke	300	24⅛		
24	Clayton	400	23⅞		
24	Holyk (or wife)			200	24⅛
26	Holyk (or wife)			200	23⅜
26	Huntington	50	23¼		
27	Darke (Moran as nominee)			1000	22⅝–22¾
Mar. 2	Holyk (Mrs.)	200	22⅜		
3	Clayton	100	22¼		
16	Huntington			100	22⅜
16	Holyk (or wife)			300	23¼
17	Holyk (Mrs.)	100	23⅞		
23	Darke			1000	24¾
26	Clayton	200	25		
Land Acquisition Completed March 27, 1964					
Mar. 30	Darke			1000	25½
30	Holyk (Mrs.)	100	25⅞		
Core Drilling of Kidd Segment Resumed March 31, 1964					
April 1	Clayton	60	26½		
1	Fogarty	400	26½		
2	Clayton	100	26⅞		
6	Fogarty	400	28⅛–28⅞		
8	Mollison (Mrs.)	100	28⅛		

I. THE INDIVIDUAL DEFENDANTS

A. *Introductory*

. . . Whether predicated on traditional fiduciary concepts, see, e.g., Hotchkiss v. Fisher, 136 Kan. 530, 16 P.2d 531 (Kan.1932), or on the "special facts" doctrine, see, e.g., Strong v. Repide, 213 U.S. 419, 29 S.Ct. 521, 53 L.Ed. 853 (1909), . . . Rule [10b–5] is based in policy on the justifiable expectation of the securities marketplace that all investors trading on impersonal exchanges have relatively equal access to material information, see Cary, Insider Trading in Stocks, 21 Bus.Law. 1009, 1010 (1966), Fleischer, Securities Trading and Corporation Information Practices: The Implications of the Texas Gulf Sulphur Proceeding, 51 Va.L.Rev. 1271, 1278–80 (1965). The essence of the Rule is that anyone who, trading for his own account in the securities of a corporation has "access, directly or indirectly, to information intended to be available only for a corporate purpose and not for the personal benefit of anyone" may not take "advantage of such information knowing it is unavailable to those with whom he is dealing," i.e., the investing public. Matter of Cady, Roberts & Co., 40 SEC 907, 912 (1961). Insiders, as directors or management officers are, of course, by this Rule, precluded from so unfairly dealing, but the Rule is also applicable to one possessing the information who may not be strictly termed an "insider" within the meaning of Sec. 16(b) of the Act. Cady, Roberts, supra. Thus, anyone in possession of material inside information must either disclose it to the investing public, or, if he is disabled from disclosing it in order to protect a corporate confidence, or he chooses not to do so, must abstain from trading in or recommending the securities concerned while such inside information remains undisclosed. So, it is here no justification for insider activity that disclosure was forbidden by the legitimate corporate objective of acquiring options to purchase the land surrounding the exploration site; if the information was, as the SEC contends, material,[9] its possessors should have kept out of the market until disclosure was accomplished. Cady, Roberts, supra at 911.

Purchase Date	Purchaser	Shares Number	Price	Calls Number	Price
First Press Release Issued April 12, 1964					
April 15	Clayton	200	29⅜		
16	Crawford (and wife)	600	30⅛–30¼		

Second Press Release Issued 10:00–10:10 or 10:15 A.M., April 16, 1964 . . .

1963

April 16	(app. 10:20 A.M.)				
	Coates (for family trusts)	2000	31–31⅝		

[Footnote by the court; relocated by the editor.]

9. Congress intended by the Exchange Act to eliminate the idea that the use of inside information for personal advantage was a normal emolument of corporate office. See Sections 2 and 16 of the Act; H.R.Rep. No. 1383, 73rd Cong., 2d Sess. 13 (1934); S.Rep. No. 792, 73rd Cong., 2d Sess. 9 (1934); S.E.C., Tenth Annual Report 50 (1944). See Cady, Roberts, supra at 912.

B. *Material Inside Information*

An insider is not, of course, always foreclosed from investing in his own company merely because he may be more familiar with company operations than are outside investors. An insider's duty to disclose information or his duty to abstain from dealing in his company's securities arises only in "those situations which are essentially extraordinary in nature and which are reasonably certain to have a substantial effect on the market price of the security if [the extraordinary situation is] disclosed." Fleischer, Securities Trading and Corporate Information Practices: The Implications of the Texas Gulf Sulphur Proceeding, 51 Va.L.Rev. 1271, 1289.

Nor is an insider obligated to confer upon outside investors the benefit of his superior financial or other expert analysis by disclosing his educated guesses or predictions. 3 Loss, op. cit. supra at 1463. The only regulatory objective is that access to material information be enjoyed equally, but this objective requires nothing more than the disclosure of basic facts so that outsiders may draw upon their own evaluative expertise in reaching their own investment decisions with knowledge equal to that of the insiders.

This is not to suggest, however, as did the trial court, that "the test of materiality must necessarily be a conservative one, particularly since many actions under Section 10(b) are brought on the basis of hindsight," 258 F.Supp. 262 at 280, in the sense that the materiality of facts is to be assessed solely by measuring the effect the knowledge of the facts would have upon prudent or conservative investors. As we stated in List v. Fashion Park, Inc., 340 F.2d 457, 462, "The basic test of materiality . . . is whether a *reasonable* man would attach importance . . . in determining his choice of action in the transaction in question. Restatement, Torts § 538(2)(a); accord Prosser, Torts 554–55; I Harper & James, Torts 565–66." (Emphasis supplied.) . . . [M]aterial facts include not only information disclosing the earnings and distributions of a company but also those facts which affect the probable future of the company and those which may affect the desire of investors to buy, sell, or hold the company's securities.

In each case, then, whether facts are material within Rule 10b–5 when the facts relate to a particular event and are undisclosed by those persons who are knowledgeable thereof will depend at any given time upon a balancing of both the indicated probability that the event will occur and the anticipated magnitude of the event in light of the totality of the company activity. Here, notwithstanding the trial court's conclusion that the results of the first drill core, K–55–1, were "too 'remote' . . . to have had any significant impact on the market, i.e., to be deemed material," [11] 258 F.Supp. at 283, knowledge of the

---

11. We are not, of course, bound by the trial court's determination as to materiality unless we find it "clearly erroneous" for that standard of appellate review is applicable only to issues of basic fact and not to issues of ultimate fact. See Baranow v. Gibraltar Factors Corp., 366 F.2d 584, 587 (2 Cir.1966); Mamiye Bros. v. Barber S.S. Lines, Inc., 360 F.2d 774, 776–778 (2 Cir.), cert. denied, 385 U.S. 835, 87 S.Ct. 80, 17 L.Ed.2d 70 (1966); see also SEC v. R.A.

possibility, which surely was more than marginal, of the existence of a mine of the vast magnitude indicated by the remarkably rich drill core located rather close to the surface (suggesting mineability by the less expensive openpit method) within the confines of a large anomaly (suggesting an extensive region of mineralization) might well have affected the price of TGS stock and would certainly have been an important fact to a reasonable, if speculative, investor in deciding whether he should buy, sell, or hold. After all, this first drill core was "unusually good and . . . excited the interest and speculation of those who knew about it." 258 F.Supp. at 282.

. . . Our survey of the facts found below conclusively establishes that knowledge of the results of the discovery hole, K–55–1, would have been important to a reasonable investor and might have affected the price of the stock.[12] On April 16, The Northern Miner, a trade publication in wide circulation among mining stock specialists, called K–55–1, the discovery hole, "one of the most impressive drill holes completed in modern times." Roche, a Canadian broker whose firm specialized in mining securities, characterized the importance to investors of the results of K–55–1. He stated that the completion of "the first drill hole" with "a 600 foot drill core is very very significant . . . anything over 200 feet is considered very significant and 600 feet is just beyond your wildest imagination." He added, however, that it "is a natural thing to buy more stock once they give you the first drill hole." Additional testimony revealed that the prices of stocks of other companies, albeit less diversified, smaller firms, had increased substantially solely on the basis of the discovery of good anomalies or even because of the proximity of their lands to the situs of a potentially major strike.

Finally, a major factor in determining whether the K–55–1 discovery was a material fact is the importance attached to the drilling results by those who knew about it. In view of other unrelated recent developments favorably affecting TGS, participation by an informed person in a regular stock-purchase program, or even sporadic trading by an informed person, might lend only nominal support to the inference of the materiality of the K–55–1 discovery; nevertheless, the timing by those who knew of it of their stock purchases and their purchases of *short-term* calls—purchases in some cases by individuals who had never before purchased calls or even TGS stock—virtually compels the inference that the insiders were influenced by the drilling results. This insider trading activity, which surely constitutes highly

Holman & Co., 366 F.2d 456, 457–458 (2 Cir.1966) (by implication).

12. We do not suggest that material facts must be disclosed immediately; the timing of disclosure is a matter for the business judgment of the corporate officers entrusted with the management of the corporation within the affirmative disclosure requirements promulgated by the exchanges and by the SEC. Here, a valuable corporate purpose was served by delaying the publication of the K–55–1 discovery.

We do intend to convey, however, that where a corporate purpose is thus served by withholding the news of a material fact, those persons who are thus quite properly true to their corporate trust must not during the period of non-disclosure deal personally in the corporation's securities or give to outsiders confidential information not generally available to all the corporations' stockholders and to the public at large.

pertinent evidence and the only truly objective evidence of the materiality of the K–55–1 discovery, was apparently disregarded by the court below in favor of the testimony of defendants' expert witnesses, all of whom "agreed that one drill core does not establish an ore body, much less a mine," 258 F.Supp. at 282–283. Significantly, however, the court below, while relying upon what these defense experts said the defendant insiders *ought* to have thought about the worth to TGS of the K–55–1 discovery, and finding that from November 12, 1963 to April 6, 1964 Fogarty, Murray, Holyk and Darke spent more than $100,000 in purchasing TGS stock and calls on that stock, made no finding that the insiders were motivated by any factor other than the extraordinary K–55–1 discovery when they bought their stock and their calls. No reason appears why outside investors, perhaps better acquainted with speculative modes of investment and with, in many cases, perhaps more capital at their disposal for intelligent speculation, would have been less influenced, and would not have been similarly motivated to invest if they had known what the insider investors knew about the K–55–1 discovery.

Our decision to expand the limited protection afforded outside investors by the trial court's narrow definition of materiality is not at all shaken by fears that the elimination of insider trading benefits will deplete the ranks of capable corporate managers by taking away an incentive to accept such employment. Such benefits, in essence, are forms of secret corporate compensation, see Cary, Corporate Standards and Legal Rules, 50 Calif.L.Rev. 408, 409–10 (1962), derived at the expense of the uninformed investing public and not at the expense of the corporation which receives the sole benefit from insider incentives. Moreover, adequate incentives for corporate officers may be provided by properly administered stock options and employee purchase plans of which there are many in existence. In any event, the normal motivation induced by stock ownership, i.e., the identification of an individual with corporate progress, is ill-promoted by condoning the sort of speculative insider activity which occurred here; for example, some of the corporation's stock was sold at market in order to purchase short-term calls upon that stock, calls which would never be exercised to increase a stockholder equity in TGS unless the market price of that stock rose sharply.

The core of Rule 10b–5 is the implementation of the Congressional purpose that all investors should have equal access to the rewards of participation in securities transactions. It was the intent of Congress that all members of the investing public should be subject to identical market risks,—which market risks include, of course the risk that one's evaluative capacity or one's capital available to put at risk may exceed another's capacity or capital. The insiders here were not trading on an equal footing with the outside investors. They alone were in a position to evaluate the probability and magnitude of what seemed from the outset to be a major ore strike; they alone could invest safely, secure in the expectation that the price of TGS stock would rise substantially in the event such a major strike should materialize, but would decline little, if at all, in the event of failure, for the public, ignorant at the outset of the favorable probabilities would likewise be unaware of the unproductive exploration, and the additional exploration costs would not significantly affect TGS market prices. Such inequities based upon unequal access to knowledge should not be shrugged off as inevitable in our way of life, or, in view of the congressional concern in the area, remain uncorrected.

We hold, therefore, that all transactions in TGS stock or calls by individuals apprised of the drilling results [14] of K–55–1 were made in violation of Rule 10b–5.[15] Inasmuch as the visual evaluation of that drill core (a generally reliable estimate though less accurate than a chemical assay) constituted material information, those advised of the results of the visual evaluation as well as those informed of the chemical assay traded in violation of law. The geologist Darke possessed undisclosed material information and traded in TGS securities. Therefore we reverse the dismissal of the action as to him and his personal transactions. . . .

With reference to Huntington, the trial court found that he "had no detailed knowledge as to the work" on the Kidd–55 segment, 258 F.Supp. 281. Nevertheless, the evidence shows that he knew about and participated in TGS's land acquisition program which followed the receipt of the K–55–1 drilling results, and that on February 26, 1964 he purchased 50 shares of TGS stock. Later, on March 16, he helped prepare a letter for Dr. Holyk's signature in which TGS made a substantial offer for lands near K–55–1, and on the same day he, who had never before purchased calls on any stock, purchased a call on 100 shares of TGS stock. We are satisfied that these purchases in February and March, coupled with his readily inferable and probably reliable, understanding of the highly favorable nature of preliminary operations on the Kidd segment, demonstrate that Huntington possessed material inside information such as to make his purchase violative of the Rule and the Act.

C.   *When May Insiders Act?*

Appellant Crawford, who ordered [17] the purchase of TGS stock shortly before the TGS April 16 official announcement, and defendant

---

14. The trial court found that defendant Murray "had no detailed knowledge as to the work" on the Kidd–55 segment. There is no evidence in the record suggesting that Murray purchased his stock on January 8, 1964, on the basis of material undisclosed information, and the disposition below is undisturbed as to him.

15. Even if insiders were in fact ignorant of the broad scope of the Rule and acted pursuant to a mistaken belief as to the applicable law such an ignorance does not insulate them from the consequences of their acts. Tager v. SEC, 344 F.2d 5, 8 (2 Cir.1965).

17. The effective protection of the public from insider exploitation of advance notice of material information requires that the time that an insider places an order, rather than the time of its ultimate execution, be determinative for Rule 10b–5 purposes. Otherwise, insiders would be able to "beat the news," cf. Fleischer, supra, 51 Va.L.Rev. at 1291, by requesting in advance that their orders be executed immediately after the dissemination of a major news release but before outsiders could act on the release. Thus it is immaterial whether Crawford's orders were executed before or after the announcement was made in Canada (9:40 A.M., April 16) or in the United States (10:00 A.M.) or whether Coates's order was executed before or after the news appeared over the Merrill Lynch (10:29 A.M.) or Dow Jones (10:54 A.M.) wires.

Coates, who placed orders with and communicated the news to his broker immediately after the official announcement was read at the TGS-called press conference, concede that they were in possession of material information. They contend, however, that their purchases were not proscribed purchases for the news had already been effectively disclosed. We disagree.

Crawford telephoned his orders to his Chicago broker about midnight on April 15 and again at 8:30 in the morning of the 16th, with instructions to buy at the opening of the Midwest Stock Exchange that morning. The trial court's finding that "he sought to, and did, 'beat the news,' " 258 F.Supp. at 287, is well documented by the record. The rumors of a major ore strike which had been circulated in Canada and, to a lesser extent, in New York, had been disclaimed by the TGS press release of April 12, which significantly promised the public an official detailed announcement when possibilities had ripened into actualities. The abbreviated announcement to the Canadian press at 9:40 A.M. on the 16th by the Ontario Minister of Mines and the report carried by The Northern Miner, parts of which had sporadically reached New York on the morning of the 16th through reports from Canadian affiliates to a few New York investment firms, are assuredly not the equivalent of the official 10–15 minute announcement which was not released to the American financial press until after 10:00 A.M. Crawford's orders had been placed before that. Before insiders may act upon material information, such information must have been effectively disclosed in a manner sufficient to insure its availability to the investing public. Particularly here, where a formal announcement to the entire financial news media had been promised in a prior official release known to the media, all insider activity must await dissemination of the promised official announcement.

Coates was absolved by the court below because his telephone order was placed shortly before 10:20 A.M. on April 16, which was after the announcement had been made even though the news could not be considered already a matter of public information. 258 F.Supp. at 288. This result seems to have been predicated upon a misinterpretation of dicta in *Cady, Roberts,* where the SEC instructed insiders to "keep out of the market until the established procedures for public release of the information are *carried out* instead of hastening to execute transactions in advance of, and in frustration of, the objectives of the release," 40 SEC at 915 (emphasis supplied). The reading of a news release, which prompted Coates into action, is merely the first step in the process of dissemination required for compliance with the regulatory objective of providing all investors with an equal opportunity to make informed investment judgments. Assuming that the contents of the official release could instantaneously be acted upon,[18] at the minimum Coates should have waited until the

---

18. Although the only insider who acted after the news appeared over the Dow Jones broad tape is not an appellant and therefore we need not discuss the necessity of considering the advisability of a "reasonable waiting period" during which outsiders may absorb and evaluate disclosures, we note in passing that, where the news is

news could reasonably have been expected to appear over the media of widest circulation, the Dow Jones broad tape, rather than hastening to insure an advantage to himself and his broker son-in-law.[19]   . . .

E. *May Insiders Accept Stock Options Without Disclosing Material Information to the Issuer?*

On February 20, 1964, defendants Stephens, Fogarty, Mollison, Holyk and Kline accepted stock options issued to them and a number of other top officers of TGS, although not one of them had informed the Stock Option Committee of the Board of Directors or the Board of the results of K–55–1, which information we have held was then material. The SEC sought rescission of these options. The trial court, in addition to finding the knowledge of the results of the K–55 discovery to be immaterial, held that Kline had no detailed knowledge of the drilling progress and that Holyk and Mollison could reasonably assume that their superiors, Stephens and Fogarty, who were directors of the corporation, would report the results if that was advisable; indeed all employees had been instructed not to divulge this information pending completion of the land acquisition program, 258 F.Supp. at 291. Therefore, the court below concluded that only directors Stephens and Fogarty, of the top management, would have violated the Rule by accepting stock options without disclosure, but it also found that they had not acted improperly as the information in their possession was not material. 258 F.Supp. at 292. In view of our conclusion as to materiality we hold that Stephens and Fogarty violated the Rule by accepting them. However, as they have surrendered the options and the corporation has canceled them, supra at 292, n. 17, we find it unnecessary to order that the injunctions prayed for be actually issued. We point out, nevertheless, that the surrender of these options after the SEC commenced the case is not a satisfaction of the SEC claim, and a determination as to whether the issuance of injunctions against Stephens and Fogarty is advisable in order to prevent or deter future violations of regulatory provisions is remanded for the exercise of discretion by the trial court.

Contrary to the belief of the trial court that Kline had no duty to disclose his knowledge of the Kidd project before accepting the stock option offered him, we believe that he, a vice president, who had

of a sort which is not readily translatable into investment action, insiders may not take advantage of their advance opportunity to evaluate the information by acting immediately upon dissemination. In any event, the permissible timing of insider transactions after disclosures of various sorts is one of the many areas of expertise for appropriate exercise of the SEC's rule-making power, which we hope will be utilized in the future to provide some predictability of certainty for the business community.

19. The record reveals that news usually appears on the Dow Jones broad tape 2–

3 minutes after the reporter completes dictation. Here, assuming that the Dow Jones reporter left the press conference as early as possible, 10:10 A.M., the 10–15 minute release (which took at least that long to dictate) could not have appeared on the wire before 10:22, and for other reasons unknown to us did not appear until 10:54. Indeed, even the abbreviated version of the release reported by Merrill Lynch over its private wire did not appear until 10:29. Coates, however, placed his call no later than 10:20.

become the general counsel of TGS in January 1964, but who had been secretary of the corporation since January 1961, and was present in that capacity when the options were granted, and who was in charge of the mechanics of issuance and acceptance of the options, was a member of top management and under a duty before accepting his option to disclose any material information he may have possessed, and, as he did not disclose such information to the Option Committee we direct rescission of the option he received.[24] As to Holyk and Mollison, the SEC has not appealed the holding below that they, not being then members of top management (although Mollison was a vice president) had no duty to disclose their knowledge of the drilling before accepting their options. Therefore, the issue of whether, by accepting, they violated the Act, is not before us, and the holding below is undisturbed. . . .

FRIENDLY, Circuit Judge (concurring):

Agreeing with the result reached by the majority and with most of Judge Waterman's searching opinion, I take a rather different approach to two facets of the case.

I.

The first is a situation that will not often arise, involving as it does the acceptance of stock options during a period when inside information likely to produce a rapid and substantial increase in the price of the stock was known to some of the grantees but unknown to those in charge of the granting. I suppose it would be clear, under Ruckle v. Roto American Corp., 339 F.2d 24 (2 Cir.1964), that if a corporate officer having such knowledge persuaded an unknowing board of directors to grant him an option at a price approximating the current market, the option would be rescindable in an action under Rule 10b–5. It would seem, by the same token, that if, to make the pill easier to swallow, he urged the directors to include others lacking the knowledge he possessed, he would be liable for all the resulting damage.

---

24. The options granted on February 20, 1964 to Mollison, Holyk, and Kline were ratified by the Texas Gulf directors on July 15, 1965 after there had been, of course, a full disclosure and after this action had been commenced. However, the ratification is irrelevant here, for we would hold with the district court that a member of top management, as was Kline, is required, before accepting a stock option, to disclose material inside information which, if disclosed, might affect the price of the stock during the period when the accepted option could be exercised. Kline had known since November 1962 that K-55-1 had been drilled, that the drilling had intersected a sulphide body containing copper and zinc, and that TGS desired to acquire adjacent property.

Of course, if any of the five knowledgeable defendants had rejected his option there might well have been speculation as

to the reason for the rejection. Therefore, in a case where disclosure to the grantors of an option would seriously jeopardize corporate security, it could well be desirable, in order to protect a corporation from selling securities to insiders who are in a position to appreciate their true worth at a price which may not accurately reflect the true value of the securities and at the same time to preserve when necessary the secrecy of corporate activity, not to require that an insider possessed of undisclosed material information reject the offer of a stock option, but only to require that he abstain from exercising it until such time as there shall have been a full disclosure and, after the full disclosure, a ratification such as was voted here. However, as this suggestion was not presented to us, we do not consider it or make any determination with reference to it.

The novel problem in the instant case is to define the responsibility of officers when a directors' committee administering a stock option plan proposes of its own initiative to make options available to them and others at a time when they know that the option price, geared to the market value of the stock, did not reflect a substantial increment likely to be realized in short order and was therefore unfair to the corporation.

A rule requiring a minor officer to reject an option so tendered would not comport with the realities either of human nature or of corporate life. If the SEC had appealed the ruling dismissing this portion of the complaint as to Holyk and Mollison, I would have upheld the dismissal quite apart from the special circumstance that a refusal on their part could well have broken the wall of secrecy it was important for TGS to preserve. Whatever they knew or didn't know about Timmins, they were entitled to believe their superiors had reported the facts to the Option Committee unless they had information to the contrary. Stephens, Fogarty and Kline stand on an altogether different basis; as senior officers they had an obligation to inform the Committee that this was not the right time to grant options at 95% of the current price. Silence, when there is a duty to speak, can itself be a fraud. I am unimpressed with the argument that Stephens, Fogarty and Kline could not perform this duty on the peculiar facts of this case, because of the corporate need for secrecy during the land acquisition program. Non-management directors would not normally challenge a recommendation for postponement of an option plan from the President, the Executive Vice President, and the Vice President and General Counsel. Moreover, it should be possible for officers to communicate with directors, of all people, without fearing a breach of confidence. Hence, as one of the foregoing hypotheticals suggests, I am not at all sure that a company in the position of TGS might not have a claim against top officers who breached their duty of disclosure for the entire damage suffered as a result of the untimely issuance of options, rather than merely one for rescission of the options issued to them.[2] Since that issue is not before us, I merely make the reservation of my position clear. . . .

[The opinions of Judges Kaufman and Anderson (concurring), Judge Hays (concurring in part and dissenting in part), and Judges Moore and Lumbard (dissenting) are omitted.]

---

2. Though the Board of Directors of TGS ratified the issuance of the options after the Timmins discovery had been fully publicized, it obviously was of the belief that Kline had committed no serious wrong in remaining silent. Throughout this litigation TGS has supported the legality of the actions of all the defendants—the company's counsel having represented, among others, Stephens, Fogarty and Kline. Consequently, I agree with the majority in giving the Board's action no weight here. If a fraud of this kind may ever be cured by ratification, compare Continental Securities Co. v. Belmont, 206 N.Y. 7, 99 N.E. 138, 51 L.R.A., N.S., 112 (1912), with Claman v. Robertson, 164 Ohio St. 61, 128 N.E.2d 429 (1955); cf. Wilko v. Swan, 346 U.S. 427, 74 S.Ct. 182, 98 L.Ed. 168 (1953), that cannot be done without an appreciation of the illegality of the conduct proposed to be excused, cf. United Hotels Co. v. Mealey, 147 F.2d 816, 819 (2 Cir. 1945).

REYNOLDS v. TEXAS GULF SULPHUR CO., 309 F.Supp. 548, 559–60 (D.Utah 1970), aff'd in part, rev'd in part sub nom. Mitchell v. Texas Gulf Sulphur Co., 446 F.2d 90 (10th Cir.1971). "From the record the court concludes that the press release dated April 12, 1964, was inaccurate, misleading and deceptive with respect to material matters disclosed by the company's drilling near Timmins. The authors of the release knew from visual and chemical analyses that the first core disclosed the presence of copper and zinc mineralization of ore-grade; that the second test hole (K–55–3) virtually eliminated any chance that the initial test hole had been drilled 'down-dip'; that cores from drill holes located 200 feet south and 200 feet north of the initial test hole contained similar mineralization; and that still another drill hole core had disclosed similar mineralization at greater depths than were reached by the other drill holes.

"The release painted a bleak and gloomy picture—most of the areas drilled in Eastern Canada revealed either barren pyrite or graphite without value; a few resulted in discoveries of small or marginal sulphide ore bodies, etc. Not a word, however, about the results of any of the drilling near Timmins, except that it had led to 'preliminary indications' that more drilling would be necessary for a proper evaluation. The drilling 'to date had not been conclusive' and has not been 'sufficient to reach definite conclusions' and 'any' statement 'as to size and grade of ore would be premature and possibly misleading.' But a newspaper reporter's finding, made on the same day the press release was printed, that the drillings indicated more than 10,000,000 tons of ore, and the same reporter's statement that one hole averaged in excess of 1% copper and 8% zinc, went unchallenged when submitted to vice president Richard D. Mollison who released the article on April 15th for publication. Obviously, the reporter was quoting figures given to him by officials of the company, and given to him on April 13th. It may very well have been that the company officials when they prepared the release dated April 12, were trying to hold the big news until just before, or on the day of, the stockholders annual meeting which was held on April 23rd."

SEC v. TEXAS GULF SULPHUR CO., 446 F.2d 1301, 1307–08 (2d Cir.1971). [On remand, the] district court required Holyk, Huntington, Clayton, and Darke to pay to TGS the profits they had derived (and, in Darke's case, also the profits which his tippees had derived) from their TGS stock between their respective purchase dates and April 17, 1964, when the ore strike was fully known to the public. The payments are to be held in escrow in an interest-bearing account for a period of five years, subject to disposition in such manner as the court might direct upon application by the SEC or other interested person, or on the court's own motion. At the end of five years any money remaining undisposed of would become the property of TGS. To protect the appellants against double liability, any private judgments against these appellants arising out of the events of this case are to be paid from this fund. . . .

"Appellants, of course, contend that the required restitution is . . . a penalty assessment. . . . [However, restitution] of the profits on these transactions merely deprives the appellants of the gains of their wrongful conduct. . . .

"Finally, appellants contend that the order is punitive because it contains no element of compensation to those who have been damaged. However, as the New York Court of Appeals in Diamond v. Oreamuno, 24 N.Y.2d 494, 499, 301 N.Y.S.2d 78, 81–82, 248 N.E.2d 910, 912–913 (1969), recognized, a corporate enterprise may well suffer harm 'when officers and directors abuse their position to obtain personal profits' since 'the effect may be to cast a cloud on the corporation's name, injure stockholder relations and undermine public regard for the corporation's securities.' Although the sellers of TGS stock who sold before April 17, 1964, may have a higher equity than TGS to recover from appellants the wrongful profits appellants obtained, this fact does not preclude conditional compensation to TGS."

NOTE ON PROCEDURAL ASPECTS OF ACTIONS UNDER RULE 10b–5

In addition to affording greater substantive rights than the majority common law rule, Rule 10b–5 affords some significant procedural advantages.

1. Many plaintiffs prefer federal courts to state courts. In the absence of Rule 10b–5, a plaintiff in a securities transaction could get into federal court only if there was complete diversity. Under section 27 of the Securities Exchange Act, however, the federal courts have "exclusive jurisdiction of violations of this chapter or the rules and regulations thereunder, and of all suits in equity and actions at law brought to enforce any liability or duty created by this chapter or the rules and regulations thereunder."

2. A plaintiff prefers to bring suit in the state where he resides. Normally, however, a court sitting outside the state where the defendant resides can acquire jurisdiction over him only if he appears or is personally served in the forum state, or he can be reached under a long-arm statute. A plaintiff also prefers to sue multiple defendants in one action. If the defendants live in different states, however, that is often impossible unless a long-arm statute applies. Both kinds of problems may be solved by section 27. Under that section, actions to enforce any liability created by the Securities Exchange Act or the rules thereunder may be brought in any district "wherein the defendant is found or is an inhabitant or transacts business," or "wherein any act or transactions constituting the violation occurred." It is not necessary, to lay venue under the latter clause, to show that the entire transaction occurred within the district. "[T]elephone calls from the forum district, transmissions of written confirmations, [and] mailings designed to lull the victim into inaction all have been held sufficient to support venue." Lowenfels, Rule 10b–5 and the Stockholder's Derivative Action, 18 Vand.L.Rev. 893, 899 (1965). Once venue is

founded under section 27, process can be served upon a defendant in the district of which he is an inhabitant, or "wherever the defendant may be found," inside or outside the state in which suit is brought.[1] In short, Rule 10b–5 gives a plaintiff the power to gather multiple defendants residing in different states into a single action,[2] and, if a significant part of the transaction occurred in the plaintiff's district, gives him the power to bring the action in that district.

3. In a derivative action—that is, an action brought by a plaintiff-shareholder in the name and right of his corporation—the plaintiff may obtain an additional advantage under Rule 10b–5. A procedural obstacle to derivative actions in some states, known as security for expenses (see Chapter X), is inapplicable to federal-law claims, such as those under Rule 10b–5.

AMERICAN BAR ASSOCIATION, COMMITTEE ON FEDERAL REGULATION OF SECURITIES, REPORT OF THE TASK FORCE ON REGULATION OF INSIDER TRADING, PART I: REGULATION UNDER THE ANTIFRAUD PROVISIONS OF THE SECURITIES EXCHANGE ACT OF 1934

41 Bus.Law. 223 (1985).

THE POLICY BASIS FOR INSIDER TRADING REGULATION

The task force first considered whether, in today's market and legal environment, a sound policy basis remains for prohibiting the use of nonpublic information by one trader to gain advantage over others. . . .

In today's securities markets, where vast amounts of information are quickly available about corporate issuers (at least widely followed ones) and electronic communication is instantaneous, some respected scholars have argued that the markets themselves provide an adequate corrective for temporary informational advantage by promptly reporting the trading that occurs. They argue that the economic incentive of allowing a trader to use nonpublic information is of social value because it encourages and rewards analytic research and initiative. But other scholars see valid policy bases for continued regulation of unfair informational advantage even in today's impersonal, high-speed

---

1. See § 27. This is subject to 28 U.S. C.A. § 1404(a), which provides that: "For the convenience of parties and witnesses, in the interest of justice, a district court may transfer any civil action to any other district or division where it might have been brought."

2. State-law claims may be joined with Rule 10–5 claims, even in the absence of diversity, under the pendent jurisdiction doctrine. Under this doctrine, "original federal jurisdiction resting on the basis of a plaintiff's federal claim extends to any nonfederal claim which the plaintiff may have against the same defendant, so long as the nonfederal claim bears the requisite relationship to the federal claim." Lowenfels, Pendent Jurisdiction and the Federal Securities Acts, 67 Colum.L.Rev. 474 (1967). The prevailing test for pendent jurisdiction requires that the state and federal claims derive from "a common nucleus of operative fact." See United Mine Workers v. Gibbs, 383 U.S. 715 (1966).

securities markets. The task force has considered these policy arguments and is persuaded that there are still valid and persuasive reasons for continuing insider trading regulation.

In our society, we traditionally abhor those who refuse to play by the rules, that is, the cheaters and the sneaks. A spitball pitcher, or a card shark with an ace up his sleeve, may win the game but not our respect. And if we know such a person is in the game, chances are we won't play. These commonsense observations suggest that two of the traditional bases for prohibitions against insider trading are still sound: the "fair play" and "integrity of the markets" arguments. The first relies on the basic policy that cheating is wrong and on the traditional sympathy for the victim of the cheat. The second rests on the oft-repeated argument that people will not entrust their resources to a marketplace they don't believe is fair, any more than a card player will put his chips on the table in a poker game that may be fixed. Although the task force knows of no empirical research that directly demonstrates that concerns about integrity affect market activity, both authoritative commentators [8] and common sense tell us that if investors do not anticipate fair treatment, they will avoid investing in securities. As a result, capital formation through securities offerings will become less attractive and more difficult. . . .

Several other forceful policy arguments favor insider trading prohibitions. When the nonpublic information originates within the corporation—as in the case of a new product discovery or an unannounced earnings increase or decrease—the information itself is corporate property until publicly released. Those who "take" it for their own advantage rather than the corporate good may be sued for their "misappropriation" of it.

If there were no penalty for personal use of such nonpublic information to gain a market profit, then officers, employees, and even directors of a corporation might keep such information to themselves for a time and trade upon it, rather than act in the corporate interest by promptly communicating the information through appropriate corporate channels. The flow of information from its corporate source to officers, directors, and other decision makers and to the investing public could thus be impeded by the incentive to delay long enough to speculate on a stock market profit. Some have argued that such profits are an appropriate reward for corporate entrepreneurs. The task force disagrees. Unbridled insider trading would distort the intended impact of corporate compensation programs approved by directors and shareholders and based on business performance. Both the beneficiaries and the amount of benefit would be unpredictable and not subject to corporate control; the random rewards would be unrelated to overall corporate performance or to specific compensation objectives.

8. *See, e.g.,* comments of Arthur Levitt, Jr., Chairman of the American Stock Exchange, *quoted in* Business Week, April 29, 1985, at 79 ("If the investor thinks he's not getting a fair share, he's not going to invest and that is going to hurt capital formation in the long run").

These corporate structure arguments certainly provide support for prohibiting trading on nonpublic, *inside* information, that is, information originating from within the corporation. But these arguments provide less support for prohibiting trading on *market* information, that is, information that comes from outside the issuer but may affect the value of its securities, such as advance news of an impending tender offer, a favorable newspaper article, or an announcement of a major governmental decision.

We continue to believe, however, that a "disclose or abstain" rule should be applied even when only *market* information is involved. The traditional fairness and market integrity bases for regulating insider trading are still important to uphold when market information is involved. Moreover, one can posit that, if those having material, nonpublic market information could trade on it without fear of liability, the incentive to promptly move such information into the marketplace would be greatly reduced. Rather, those "in the know" would keep secret, and accumulate or liquidate a position on the basis of, the information for as long as possible to maximize their gain or minimize their loss. The task force believes the result of such behavior would be a less informed (not to mention less attractive) marketplace. The task force believes that fairness, information efficiency, and market integrity are served by laws that discourage retaining material market information for personal advantage.

Although it has been argued that insider trading activity affects the market quickly, so that the economic value of the undisclosed information is reflected in market prices even before the information is announced, at a minimum this involves some fundamental, and potentially costly, unfairness to the uninformed traders on the other side of the initial trades by the insiders and their tippees.

In the judgment of the task force, these policy bases provide persuasive support for prohibitions against trading on the basis of material, nonpublic "inside information." They also support extending the prohibitions beyond corporate insiders to others who may, through improper means, obtain or abuse selective access to either material "inside information" or material "market information."

In a federal system like ours, another question should be considered: to what extent are the above policies the concern of federal as opposed to state law? If insider trading prohibitions are to be imposed because of a concern for market integrity and market information efficiency, the interests would clearly be federal since the securities markets are an integral part of interstate commerce. Although the corporate structure and the misappropriation of business property are not traditional areas of federal interest, because the securities markets are national—even international—in scope, the task force believes that exclusive reliance on state regulation would be both impractical and unwise. Federal standards are required.

———

NOTE ON BLUE CHIP STAMPS v. MANOR DRUG STORES, ERNST & ERNST v. HOCHFELDER, AND SANTA FE INDUSTRIES, INC. v. GREEN

It was early established that private actions could be brought under Rule 10b–5. Although *Texas Gulf Sulphur* was a government action, it helped give impetus to an explosion of private actions. Three important Supreme Court cases decided between 1975 and 1977 placed important limits on actions under Rule 10b–5, but by and large the law that emerged from these cases was more important in setting outer boundaries on Rule 10b–5 than in curbing the Rule's central vitality.

In the first of these cases, Blue Chip Stamps v. Manor Drug Stores, 421 U.S. 723, 95 S.Ct. 1917, 44 L.Ed.2d 539 (1975), the plaintiff alleged that defendants' misrepresentations had caused him to refrain from purchasing stock, to his loss. The Court rejected this claim, approving a rule (previously adopted by several Court of Appeal cases) that only a person who had actually bought or sold securities—only a buyer or a seller—could bring a private action under Rule 10b–5.

In the second case, Ernst & Ernst v. Hochfelder, 425 U.S. 185, 96 S.Ct. 1375, 47 L.Ed.2d 668 (1976), the Court held that scienter was a necessary element of a Rule 10b–5 damage action, so that conduct by a defendant that was deceptive merely as a result of the defendant's negligence did not give rise to damages liability under the Rule. (The opinion in *Ernst & Ernst* left open whether scienter also had to be established in an injunctive action under Rule 10b–5. The Court resolved that point four years later by holding that scienter was a necessary element of an injunctive action as well. Aaron v. SEC, 446 U.S. 680, 100 S.Ct. 1945, 64 L.Ed.2d 611 (1980). *Ernst & Ernst* also left open whether recklessness was sufficient to satisfy the scienter requirement. Subsequent decisions by the Courts of Appeals have unanimously held that recklessness satisfies the scienter requirement. See, e.g., Rolf v. Blyth, Eastman Dillon & Co., Inc., 570 F.2d 38, 44–47 (2d Cir.1978), cert. denied, 439 U.S. 1039, 99 S.Ct. 642, 58 L.Ed.2d 698 (1978).)

In the third case, Santa Fe Industries, Inc. v. Green, 430 U.S. 462, 97 S.Ct. 1292, 51 L.Ed.2d 480 (1977), minority shareholders who were being involuntarily cashed out through a short-form merger alleged that the price to be paid for their shares was unfairly low. However, the underlying facts concerning the value of the minority's shares had been disclosed to the minority shareholders, and under state law any minority shareholder could have turned down the merger price, and chosen instead to be paid the fair value of his shares as determined by a court. The Supreme Court rejected the plaintiffs' claim, adopting the rule that Rule 10b–5 requires deception or manipulation, so that conduct that is fully disclosed at the time it occurs will not give rise to a Rule 10b–5 action.

Although the language of the majority opinion in *Santa Fe* indicated a reluctance to extend Rule 10b–5 into the province of state law regarding corporate mismanagement, the full import of the language is not clear. It seems clear that if D, a director of Corporation C, persuades C's board, by fraud, to sell him stock, C can sue D under Rule 10b–5 even though it can also sue D for breach of fiduciary duty. Similarly, if C's board doesn't sue D, a shareholder could sue D under Rule 10b–5 in a derivative action. Suppose that a controlling shareholder causes a corporation to issue stock to him at an unfair price with the approval of a majority of the directors, when material facts are not disclosed to the minority shareholders. In Schoenbaum v. Firstbrook, 405 F.2d 215 (2d Cir.1968) (en banc), cert. denied, 395 U.S. 906, 89 S.Ct. 1747, 23 L.Ed.2d 219 (1969), decided before *Santa Fe,* Aquitaine was a majority shareholder of Banff Oil Ltd. and had appointed three of its eight directors. It was alleged that Aquitaine used its controlling influence to cause Banff to sell Banff shares to Aquitaine for wholly inadequate consideration. The Second Circuit held that a minority shareholder in Banff could bring a derivative action on Banff's behalf under Rule 10b–5:

> . . . [I]t is alleged that Aquitaine exercised a controlling influence over the issuance to it of treasury stock of Banff for a wholly inadequate consideration. If it is established that the transaction took place as alleged, it constituted a violation of Rule 10b–5, subdivision (3), because Aquitaine engaged in an "act, practice or course of business which operates or would operate as a fraud or deceit upon any person, in connection with the purchase or sale of any security." Moreover, Aquitaine and the directors of Banff were guilty of deceiving the stockholders of Banff (other than Aquitaine).

Id. at 219–20.

In Goldberg v. Meridor, 567 F.2d 209 (2d Cir.1977), cert. denied 434 U.S. 1069, 98 S.Ct. 1249, 55 L.Ed.2d 771 (1978), decided shortly after *Santa Fe,* UGO Corporation was controlled by Maritimecor, which in turn was controlled by Maritime Fruit. A UGO shareholder alleged that Maritimecor, Maritime Fruit, and directors of the various companies, had caused UGO to acquire Maritimecor's assets in exchange for UGO stock, and that the agreement "was fraudulent and unfair in that the assets of Maritimecor were overpriced." Id. at 211. Press releases that described the agreement failed to disclose certain material facts concerning the value of Maritimecor's assets. The Second Circuit, in an opinion by Judge Friendly, held that *Schoenbaum* had survived *Santa Fe.* A derivative action could be brought under Rule 10b–5 on the basis of an unfair transaction between a corporation and a fiduciary or a controlling shareholder if the transaction involved stock, and material facts concerning the transaction had not been disclosed to all shareholders:

> *Schoenbaum* . . . can rest solidly on the now widely recognized ground that there is deception of the corporation (in effect, of its minority shareholders) when the corporation is

influenced by its controlling shareholder to engage in a transaction adverse to the corporation's interests (in effect, the minority shareholders' interests) and there is nondisclosure or misleading disclosures as to the material facts of the transaction. . . . The Supreme Court noted in [Green v. Santa Fe Industries, Inc.] that the court of appeals "did not disturb the District Court's conclusion that the complaint did not allege a material misrepresentation or nondisclosure with respect to the value of the stock" of Kirby; the Court's quarrel was with this court's holding that "neither misrepresentation nor nondisclosure was a necessary element of a Rule 10b–5 action," . . . and that a breach of fiduciary duty would alone suffice. . . . It was because "the complaint failed to allege a material misrepresentation or material failure to disclose" that the Court found "inapposite the cases [including *Schoenbaum*] relied upon by respondents and the court below, in which the breaches of fiduciary duty held violative of Rule 10b–5 included some element of deception". . . .

Here the complaint alleged "deceit . . . upon UGO's minority shareholders". . . . The nub of the matter is that the conduct attacked in *Green* did not violate the " 'fundamental purpose' of the Act as implementing a 'philosophy of full disclosure' ", . . . [T]he conduct here attacked does. . . .

Id. at 217–18.

Goldberg v. Meridor has been widely followed. See Kas v. Financial General Bankshares, Inc., 796 F.2d 508, 512 (D.C.Cir. 1986); Madison Consultants v. FDIC, 710 F.2d 57, 63 (2d Cir.1983); IIT v. Cornfeld, 619 F.2d 909, 922–23 (2d Cir.1980); Healey v. Catalyst Recovery, 616 F.2d 641, 645–47 (3d Cir.1980); Alabama Farm Bureau Mutual Casualty Co. v. American Fidelity Life Insurance Co., 606 F.2d 602, 613–14 (5th Cir.1979), cert. denied 449 U.S. 820, 101 S.Ct. 77, 66 L.Ed.2d 22 (1980); Kidwell ex rel. Penfold v. Meikle, 597 F.2d 1273, 1291–92 (9th Cir.1979); see also Wright v. Heizer Corp., 560 F.2d 236, 249–51 (7th Cir.1977), cert. denied 434 U.S. 1066, 98 S.Ct. 1243, 55 L.Ed.2d 767 (1978).

————

NOTE ON REMEDIES IN PRIVATE ACTIONS UNDER RULE 10b–5 WHERE THE PLAINTIFFS TRADED ON AN OPEN MARKET

The measurement of damages under Rule 10b–5 can raise a number of complex issues. Perhaps the most difficult problems occur when the plaintiff did not trade face-to-face with the defendant, but instead bought or sold publicly held stock on an anonymous open market, like the New York Stock Exchange. If the defendant has made a public misrepresentation that had the foreseeable effect of causing members of the public to buy or sell the stock, it has been generally accepted in the case-law that he would be liable for all the resulting damages. See, e.g., Mitchell v. Texas Gulf Sulphur Co.; Lipton v. Documation, Inc., 734 F.2d 740 (11th Cir.1984), cert. denied 469 U.S. 1132, 105 S.Ct. 814, 83 L.Ed.2d 807 (1985); Blackie v. Barrack, 524 F.2d 891 (9th Cir.1975), cert. denied 429 U.S. 816, 97 S.Ct. 57, 50 L.Ed.2d 75 (1976).

The case is much more difficult when the defendant has not made a misrepresentation, but rather has traded on the basis of inside information without having made a required disclosure; and it is particularly difficult where the defendant is liable only as a tipper or tippee. In Shapiro v. Merrill Lynch, Pierce, Fenner & Smith, Inc., 495 F.2d 228 (2d Cir.1974), Merrill Lynch had been engaged as the prospective managing underwriter of a proposed offering of Douglas Aircraft securities. On June 7, 1966, Douglas released a statement to the effect that it had earned 85 cents per share for the first five months of its 1966 fiscal year. During the period June 17 through June 22, however, Merrill Lynch was advised by Douglas that it would report substantially lower earnings for the first six months of its 1966 fiscal year, and now expected little or no profit for the full year. During the period June 20 through June 24, Merrill Lynch disclosed this confidential information to certain of its customers, most of whom were institutional investors. These customers then sold more than 165,000 shares of Douglas common on the New York Stock Exchange, accounting for approximately half of all Douglas shares sold during the period June 20 through June 23. Officials of Merrill Lynch, and the firm itself, received substantial direct and indirect commissions from these sales. Beginning about June 22 or 23, the market price of Douglas common took a sudden drop. On June 23 and 24, plaintiffs purchased Douglas shares without knowledge of the adverse earnings information. After disclosure, plaintiffs brought suit, on behalf of themselves and all other similarly situated persons who purchased Douglas stock during the period June 21 through June 24, against Merrill Lynch and the Merrill Lynch officers and employees who were involved (as "tippers"), and the selling institutional shareholders (as "tippees").

Defendants argued that even if they did violate Rule 10b–5, their conduct did not cause damage to plaintiffs, since defendants' sales were unrelated to plaintiffs' purchases, and plaintiffs would have purchased Douglas stock regardless of defendants' actions. The Second Circuit rejected this argument:

> The short, and we believe conclusive, answer to defendants' assertion that their conduct did not "cause" damage to plaintiffs is the "causation in fact" holding by the Supreme Court in Affiliated Ute Citizens v. United States, 406 U.S. 128, 153–54 (1972). . . . [The opinion then quoted from *Affiliated Ute,* as follows:
>
>> Under the circumstances of this case, involving primarily a failure to disclose, positive proof of reliance is not a prerequisite to recovery. *All that is necessary is that the*

facts withheld be material in the sense that a reasonable investor might have considered them important in the making of this definition. [Mills v. Electric Auto–Lite. . . .] . . . This obligation to disclose and this withholding of a material fact establish the requisite element of causation in fact." (Emphasis added by Second Circuit).]

As applied to the instant case, this holding in *Affiliated Ute* surely warrants our conclusion that the requisite element of causation in fact has been established by the admitted withholding by defendants of material inside information which they were under an obligation to disclose, such information being clearly material in the sense that plaintiffs as reasonable investors might have considered it important in making their decision to purchase Douglas stock.

Defendants argue that the *Affiliated Ute* rule of causation in fact should be confined to the facts of that case which involved face-to-face transactions. We disagree. That rule is dependent not upon the character of the transaction—face-to-face versus national securities exchange—but rather upon whether the defendant is obligated to disclose the inside information. Here, as we have held above, defendants were under a duty to the investing public, including plaintiffs, not to trade in or to recommend trading in Douglas stock without publicly disclosing the revised earnings information which was in their possession. They breached that duty. Causation in fact therefore has been established.

Having said this, however, the Second Circuit suggested that under the circumstances, the trial court might properly limit the damages that the defendants would be required to pay:

[Q]uestions bearing upon the appropriate form of relief which must await trial include the extent of the selling defendants' trading in Douglas stock, whether such trading effectively impaired the integrity of the market, what compensation if any was paid by the selling defendants to Merrill Lynch for the inside information, what profits or other benefits were realized by defendants, what expenses were incurred and what losses were sustained by plaintiffs, and what should be the difference, if any, in the extent of liability imposed on the individual defendants and the selling defendants, respectively. Moreover, we do not foreclose the possibility that an analysis by the district court of the nature and character of the Rule 10b–5 violations committed may require limiting the extent of liability imposed on either class of defendants.

In Fridrich v. Bradford, 542 F.2d 307 (6th Cir.1976), cert. denied 429 U.S. 1053, 97 S.Ct. 767, 50 L.Ed.2d 679 (1977), Bradford was the son of a principal stockholder of Old Line Life Insurance Company. Acting on a tip from his father about an impending merger, Bradford purchased 1225 shares of Old Line stock on April 27, 1972. The prospective merger was publicly announced in June 29. Bradford sold the shares in late July, making a profit of $13,000. After an investigation by the SEC, Bradford entered into a consent decree with the Commission under which he disgorged that profit. Certain persons who had sold Old Line stock during the period of nondisclosure brought suit. The trial court awarded the plaintiffs damages of $361,186.75 under the modified out-of-pocket measure. According to the opinion on appeal, "if all those who sold their shares of Old Line stock on [the three days in June when plaintiffs sold] had joined in the instant lawsuit, [Bradford's] potential liability in damages would have totalled approximately $800,000. If a class action had been brought which included all investors who sold Old Line stock between April 21 and June 29, 1972, the damages could have totalled approximately $3,700,000." Id. at 321 n. 29. The Sixth Circuit, disagreeing with the principles adopted in Shapiro v. Merrill Lynch, held that the defendant's conduct had caused no injury to the plaintiffs:

> The flaw in [Shapiro's] logic . . . is that it assumes the very injury which it then declares compensable. It does so by presupposing that the duty to disclose is absolute, and that the plaintiff is injured when the information is denied him. The duty to disclose, however, is not an absolute one, but an alternative one, that of either disclosing or abstaining from trading. We conceive it to be the act of trading which essentially constitutes the violation of Rule 10b–5, for it is this which brings the illicit benefit to the insider, and it is this conduct which impairs the integrity of the market and which is the target of the rule. If the insider does not trade, he has an absolute right to keep material information secret. SEC v. Texas Gulf Sulphur Co., supra, at 848. Investors must be prepared to accept the risk of trading in an open market without complete or always accurate information. Defendants' trading did not alter plaintiffs' expectations when they sold their stock, and in no way influenced plaintiffs' trading decision.

Id. at 318.

This reasoning is very questionable. Once the defendant traded, he took on an obligation to simultaneously disclose. Had he not violated this obligation, the plaintiffs would not have sold at the then-market price. Therefore, the causation requirement was satisfied. By way of analogy, suppose that L accepts a paying job as a lifeguard at a secluded ocean beach. No one else applied for the job. S decides to go swimming at this beach, not knowing there is supposed to be a lifeguard there. L negligently leaves his post before S arrives. S drowns. S's next-of-kin sue L, and prove that S would have been saved if L had been at his post. L argues that he didn't cause S's death: when S decided to go swimming he didn't know there was supposed to be a lifeguard at the beach, and since no one else wanted the job, S was no worse off with L away than he would have been if L had never become a lifeguard. Presumably, the court would decline to hold that L was not the cause of S's death on the ground that a swimmer "must be prepared to accept the risk" of swimming, and that L's absence "did not alter [S's] expectations . . . and in no way influenced [S's] . . . decision." See Restatement (Second) of Torts § 323.

However, that a defendant's wrongful nondisclosure makes him liable to those who have traded in an open market does not necessarily mean that the defendant should be liable for all of the loss in value incurred by such traders prior to disclosure. There is a problem of scale here between the degree of the defendant's wrong and the scope of the traders' losses. Sometimes it is appropriate to limit damages in the interest of justice. See, e.g., Restatement (Second) of Contracts § 351(3) (1979); ALI, Principles of Corporate Governance § 7.17 (Tent.Draft No. 6, 1986). This seems to be such a case. That possibility, which was suggested in Shapiro v. Merrill Lynch, was later made explicit in another Second Circuit decision, Elkind v. Liggett & Myers, Inc., 635 F.2d 156, 170–73 (2d Cir.1980):

> Within the flexible framework authorized [by *Shapiro*] for determining what amounts should be recoverable by the uninformed trader from the tipper and tippee trader, several measures are possible. First, there is the traditional out-of-pocket measure used by the district court in this case. For several reasons this measure appears to be inappropriate. In the first place . . . it is directed toward compensating a person for losses directly traceable to the defendant's fraud upon him. No such fraud or inducement may be attributed to a tipper or tippee trading on an impersonal market. . . .

> An equally compelling reason for rejecting the theory is its potential for imposition of Draconian, exorbitant damages, out of all proportion to the wrong committed, lining the pockets of all interim investors and their counsel at the expense of innocent corporate stockholders. Logic would compel application of the theory to a case where a tippee sells only 10 shares of a heavily traded stock (e.g., IBM), which then drops substantially when the tipped information is publicly disclosed. To hold the tipper and tippee liable for the losses suffered by every open market buyer of the stock as a result of the later decline in value of the stock after the news became public would be grossly unfair. . . .

> [An] alternative is (1) to allow any uninformed investor, where a reasonable investor would either have delayed his purchase or not purchased at all if he had had the benefit of the tipped information, to recover any post-purchase decline in market value of his shares up to a reasonable time after he learns of the tipped information or after there is a public disclosure of it but (2) limit his recovery to the amount gained by the tippee as a result of his selling at the earlier date rather than delaying his sale until the parties could trade on an equal informational basis. Under this measure if the

tippee sold 5,000 shares at $50 per share on the basis of inside information and the stock thereafter declined to $40 per share within a reasonable time after public disclosure, an uninformed purchaser, buying shares during the interim (e.g., at $45 per share) would recover the difference between his purchase price and the amount at which he could have sold the shares on an equal informational basis (i.e., the market price within a reasonable time after public disclosure of the tip), subject to a limit of $50,000, which is the amount gained by the tippee as a result of his trading on the inside information rather than on an equal basis. Should the intervening buyers, because of the volume and price of their purchases, claim more than the tippee's gain, their recovery (limited to that gain) would be shared *pro rata.*

This . . . alternative, which may be described as the disgorgement measure . . . offers several advantages. To the extent that it makes the tipper and tippees liable up to the amount gained by their misconduct, it should deter tipping of inside information and tippee-trading. On the other hand, by limiting the total recovery to the tippee's gain, the measure bars windfall recoveries of exorbitant amounts bearing no relation to the seriousness of the misconduct. It also avoids the extraordinary difficulties faced in trying to prove traditional out-of-pocket damages based on the true "value" of the shares purchased or damages claimed by reason of market erosion attributable to tippee trading. A plaintiff would simply be required to prove (1) the time, amount, and price per share of his purchase, (2) that a reasonable investor would not have paid as high a price or made the purchase at all if he had had the information in the tippee's possession, and (3) the price to which the security had declined by the time he learned the tipped information or at a reasonable time after it became public, whichever event first occurred. He would then have a claim and, up to the limits of the tippee's gain, could recover the decline in market value of his shares before the information became public or known to him. In most cases the damages recoverable under the disgorgement measure would be roughly commensurate to the actual harm caused by the tippee's wrongful conduct. In a case where the tippee sold only a few shares, for instance, the likelihood of his conduct causing any substantial injury to intervening investors buying without benefit of his confidential information would be small. If, on the other hand, the tippee sold large amounts of stock, realizing substantial profits, the likelihood of injury to intervening uninformed purchasers would be greater and the amount of potential recovery thereby proportionately enlarged. . . .

In the present case the sole Rule 10b–5 violation was the tippee-trading of 1,800 Liggett shares on the afternoon of July 17, 1972. Since the actual preliminary Liggett earnings were released publicly at 2:15 P.M. on July 18 and were effectively disseminated in a Wall Street Journal article published on the morning of July 19, the only outside purchasers who might conceivably have been damaged by the insider-trading were those who bought Liggett shares between the afternoon of July 17 and the opening of the market on July 19. Thereafter all purchasers bought on an equal information footing, and any outside purchaser who bought on July 17 and 18 was able to decide within a reasonable time after the July 18–19 publicity whether to hold or sell his shares in the light of the publicly-released news regarding Liggett's less favorable earnings.

The market price of Liggett stock opened on July 17, 1972, at $55⅝, and remained at substantially the same price on that date, closing at $55¼. By the close of the market on July 18 the price declined to $52½ per share. Applying the disgorgement measure, any member of the plaintiff class who bought Liggett shares during the period from the afternoon of July 17 to the close of the market on July 18 and met the reasonable investor requirement would be entitled to claim a *pro rata* portion of the tippee's gain, based on the difference between their purchase price and the price to which the market price declined within a reasonable time after the morning of July 19. By the close of the market on July 19 the market price had declined to $46⅜ per share. The total recovery thus would be limited to the gain realized by the tippee from the inside information, i.e., 1,800 shares multiplied by approximately $9.35 per share.[29]

Both *Shapiro* and *Elkind* arose in a tipper/tippee/nondisclosure context. There is no indication that either court intended the same kinds of limits to be set in cases involving a public misrepresentation that was made with knowing or reckless intent and had the foreseeable effect of causing members of the public to buy or sell stock.

INSIDER TRADING SANCTIONS ACT OF 1984—AMENDMENTS TO SECURITIES EXCHANGE ACT § 21

(2)(A) Whenever it shall appear to the Commission that any person has violated any provision of this chapter or the rules or

---

29. Since, . . . the tipped information was not as adverse as the bad news ultimately disclosed, the defendants could plausibly argue that the tippee's gain (and therefore the limit of plaintiffs' recovery) should be only the difference between the price at which he sold and the hypothetical price to which the stock would have declined if the tip had been disclosed. While that approach would make sense if a tippee were held liable for the out-of-pocket losses of all plaintiffs, we think that when only a disgorgement measure of damages is used, a tippee who trades is liable for the entire difference between the price at which he sold and the price the stock reached after the tip became known. By trading on tipped information, the tippee takes the risk that by the time the tip is disclosed the market price may reflect disclosure of information more adverse than the tip and other adverse market conditions.

regulations thereunder by purchasing or selling a security while in possession of material nonpublic information in a transaction (i) on or through the facilities of a national securities exchange or from or through a broker or dealer, and (ii) which is not part of a public offering by an issuer of securities other than standardized options, the Commission may bring an action in a United States district court to seek, and the court shall have jurisdiction to impose, a civil penalty to be paid by such person, or any person aiding and abetting the violation of such person. The amount of such penalty shall be determined by the court in light of the facts and circumstances, but shall not exceed three times the profit gained or loss avoided as a result of such unlawful purchase or sale, and shall be payable into the Treasury of the United States. . . . The actions authorized by this paragraph may be brought in addition to any other actions that the Commission or the Attorney General are entitled to bring. . . . The Commission, by rule or regulation, may exempt from the provisions of this paragraph any class of persons or transactions.

(B) No person shall be subject to a sanction under subparagraph (A) of this paragraph solely because that person aided and abetted a transaction covered by such subparagraph in a manner other than by communicating material nonpublic information. . . .

(C) For purposes of this paragraph "profit gained" or "loss avoided" is the difference between the purchase or sale price of the security and the value of that security as measured by the trading price of the security a reasonable period after public dissemination of the nonpublic information. . . .

————

BASIC, INC. v. LEVINSON

United States Supreme Court, 1988.
—— U.S. ——, 108 S.Ct. 978, 99 L.Ed.2d 194.

Justice BLACKMUN delivered the opinion of the Court.

This case requires us to apply the materiality requirement of § 10(b) of the Securities Exchange Act of 1934, 48 Stat. 881, as amended, 15 U.S.C. § 78a *et seq.* (1934 Act), and the Securities and Exchange Commission's Rule 10b–5, promulgated thereunder, see 17 CFR § 240.10b–5 (1987), in the context of preliminary corporate merger discussions. We must also determine whether a person who traded a corporation's shares on a securities exchange after the issuance of a materially misleading statement by the corporation may invoke a rebuttable presumption that, in trading, he relied on the integrity of the price set by the market.

I

Prior to December 20, 1978, Basic Incorporated was a publicly traded company primarily engaged in the business of manufacturing chemical refractories for the steel industry. As early as 1965 or 1966, Combustion Engineering, Inc., a company producing mostly alumina-based refractories, expressed some interest in acquiring Basic, but was deterred from pursuing this inclination seriously because of antitrust concerns it then entertained. See App. 81–83. In 1976, however, regulatory action opened the way to a renewal of Combustion's interest.[1] The "Strategic Plan," dated October 25, 1976, for Combustion's Industrial Products Group included the objective: "Acquire Basic Inc. $30 million." App. 337.

Beginning in September 1976, Combustion representatives had meetings and telephone conversations with Basic officers and directors, including petitioners here,[2] concerning the possibility of a merger.[3] During 1977 and 1978, Basic made three public statements denying that it was engaged in merger negotiations.[4] On December 18, 1978, Basic asked the New York Stock Exchange to suspend trading in its shares and issued a release stating that it had been "approached" by another company concerning a merger. Id., at 413. On December 19, Basic's board endorsed Combustion's offer of $46 per share for its common stock, id., at 335, 414–416, and on the following day publicly announced its approval of Combustion's tender offer for all outstanding shares.

Respondents are former Basic shareholders who sold their stock after Basic's first public statement of October 21, 1977, and before the suspension of trading in December 1978. Respondents brought a class action against Basic and its directors, asserting that the defendants issued three false or misleading public statements and thereby were in

1. In what are known as the *Kaiser-Lavino* proceedings, the Federal Trade Commission took the position in 1976 that basic or chemical refractories were in a market separate from nonbasic or acidic or alumina refractories; this would remove the antitrust barrier to a merger between Basic and Combustion's refractories subsidiary. On October 12, 1978, the Initial Decision of the Administrative Law Judge confirmed that position. See *In re Kaiser Aluminum & Chemical Corp.*, 93 F.T.C. 764, 771, 809–810 (1979). See also the opinion of the Court of Appeals in this case, 786 F.2d 741, 745 (CA6 1986).

2. In addition to Basic itself, petitioners are individuals who had been members of its board of directors prior to 1979; Anthony M. Caito, Samuel Eells, Jr., John A. Gelbach, Harley C. Lee, Max Muller, H. Chapman Rose, Edmund Q. Sylvester, and John C. Wilson, Jr. Another former director, Mathew J. Ludwig, was a party to the proceedings below but died on July 17, 1986, and is not a petitioner here. See Brief for Petitioners ii.

3. In light of our disposition of this case, any further characterization of these discussions must await application, on remand, of the materiality standard adopted today.

4. On October 21, 1977, after heavy trading and a new high in Basic stock, the

following news item appeared in the Cleveland Plain Dealer:

"[Basic] President Max Muller said the company knew no reason for the stock's activity and that no negotiations were under way with any company for a merger. He said Flintkote recently denied Wall Street rumors that it would make a tender offer of $25 a share for control of the Cleveland-based maker of refractories for the steel industry." App. 363.

On September 25, 1978, in reply to an inquiry from the New York Stock Exchange, Basic issued a release concerning increased activity in its stock and stated that

"management is unaware of any present or pending company development that would result in the abnormally heavy trading activity and price fluctuation in company shares that have been experienced in the past few days." Id., at 401.

On November 6, 1978, Basic issued to its shareholders a "Nine Months Report 1978." This Report stated:

"With regard to the stock market activity in the Company's shares we remain unaware of any present or pending developments which would account for the high volume of trading and price fluctuations in recent months." Id., at 403.

violation of § 10(b) of the 1934 Act and of Rule 10b–5. Respondents alleged that they were injured by selling Basic shares at artificially depressed prices in a market affected by petitioners' misleading statements and in reliance thereon.

The District Court adopted a presumption of reliance by members of the plaintiff class upon petitioners' public statements that enabled the court to conclude that common questions of fact or law predominated over particular questions pertaining to individual plaintiffs. See Fed.Rule Civ.Proc. 23(b)(3). The District Court therefore certified respondents' class.[5] On the merits, however, the District Court granted summary judgment for the defendants. It held that, as a matter of law, any misstatements were immaterial: there were no negotiations ongoing at the time of the first statement, and although negotiations were taking place when the second and third statements were issued, those negotiations were not "destined, with reasonable certainty, to become a merger agreement in principle." App. to Pet. for Cert. 103a.

The United States Court of Appeals for the Sixth Circuit affirmed the class certification, but reversed the District Court's summary judgment, and remanded the case. 786 F.2d 741 (1986). The court reasoned that while petitioners were under no general duty to disclose their discussions with Combustion, any statement the company voluntarily released could not be " 'so incomplete as to mislead.' " *Id.,* at 746, quoting *SEC v. Texas Gulf Sulphur Co.,* 401 F.2d 833, 862 (CA2 1968) (en banc), cert. denied *sub nom. Coates v. SEC,* 394 U.S. 976 (1969). In the Court of Appeals' view, Basic's statements that no negotiations were taking place, and that it knew of no corporate developments to account for the heavy trading activity, were misleading. With respect to materiality, the court rejected the argument that preliminary merger discussions are immaterial as a matter of law, and held that "once a statement is made denying the existence of any discussions, even discussions that might not have been material in absence of the denial are material because they make the statement made untrue." 786 F.2d, at 749.

The Court of Appeals joined a number of other circuits in accepting the "fraud-on-the-market theory" to create a rebuttable presumption that respondents relied on petitioners' material misrepresentations, noting that without the presumption it would be impractical to certify a class under Fed.Rule Civ.Proc. 23(b)(3). See 786 F.2d, at 750–751.

5. Respondents initially sought to represent all those who sold Basic shares between October 1, 1976, and December 20, 1978. See Amended Complaint in No. C79–1220 (ND Ohio) ¶ 5. The District Court, however, recognized a class period extending only from October 21, 1977, the date of the first public statement, rather than from the date negotiations allegedly commenced. In its certification decision, as subsequently amended, the District Court also excluded from the class those who had purchased Basic shares after the October 1977 statement but sold them before the September 1978 statement, App. to Pet. for Cert. 123a–124a, and those who sold their shares after the close of the market on Friday, December 15, 1978. *Id.,* at 137a.

We granted certiorari, 484 U.S. ___ (1987), to resolve the split, see Part III, *infra*, among the Courts of Appeals as to the standard of materiality applicable to preliminary merger discussions, and to determine whether the courts below properly applied a presumption of reliance in certifying the class, rather than requiring each class member to show direct reliance on Basic's statements.

II

The 1934 Act was designed to protect investors against manipulation of stock prices. See S.Rep.No. 792, 73d Cong., 2d Sess., 1–5 (1934). Underlying the adoption of extensive disclosure requirements was a legislative philosophy: "There cannot be honest markets without honest publicity. Manipulation and dishonest practices of the market place thrive upon mystery and secrecy." H.R.Rep. No. 1383, 73d Cong., 2d Sess., 11 (1934). This Court "repeatedly has described the 'fundamental purpose' of the Act as implementing a 'philosophy of full disclosure.'" *Santa Fe Industries, Inc. v. Green*, 430 U.S. 462, 477–478 (1977), quoting *SEC v. Capital Gains Research Bureau, Inc.*, 375 U.S. 180, 186 (1963).

Pursuant to its authority under § 10(b) of the 1934 Act, 15 U.S.C. § 78j, the Securities and Exchange Commission promulgated Rule 10b–5. Judicial interpretation and application, legislative acquiescence, and the passage of time have removed any doubt that a private cause of action exists for a violation of § 10(b) and Rule 10b–5, and constitutes an essential tool for enforcement of the 1934 Act's requirements. See, *e. g.*, *Ernst & Ernst v. Hochfelder*, 425 U.S. 185, 196 (1976); *Blue Chip Stamps v. Manor Drug Stores*, 421 U.S. 723, 730 (1975).

The Court previously has addressed various positive and common-law requirements for a violation of § 10(b) or of Rule 10b–5. See, *e. g.*, *Santa Fe Industries, Inc. v. Green, supra* ("manipulative or deceptive" requirement of the statute); *Blue Chip Stamps v. Manor Drug Stores, supra* ("in connection with the purchase or sale" requirement of the Rule); *Dirks v. SEC*, 463 U.S. 646 (1983) (duty to disclose); *Chiarella v. United States*, 445 U.S. 222 (1980) (same); *Ernst & Ernst v. Hochfelder, supra* (scienter). See also *Carpenter v. United States*, ___ U.S. ___ (1987) (confidentiality). The Court also explicitly has defined a standard of materiality under the securities laws, see *TSC Industries, Inc. v. Northway, Inc.*, 426 U.S. 438 (1976), concluding in the proxy-solicitation context that "[a]n omitted fact is material if there is a substantial likelihood that a reasonable shareholder would consider it important in deciding how to vote." *Id.*, at 449. Acknowledging that certain information concerning corporate developments could well be of "dubious significance," *id.*, at 448, the Court was careful not to set too low a standard of materiality; it was concerned that a minimal standard might bring an overabundance of information within its reach, and lead management "simply to bury the shareholders in an avalanche of trivial information—a result that is hardly conducive to informed decisionmaking." *Id.*, at 448–449. It further explained that to fulfill the materiality requirement "there must be a substantial likelihood that the disclosure of the omitted fact would have been viewed by the reasonable investor as having significantly altered the 'total mix' of information made available." *Id.*, at 449. We now expressly adopt the *TSC Industries* standard of materiality for the § 10(b) and Rule 10b–5 context.

III

The application of this materiality standard to preliminary merger discussions is not self-evident. Where the impact of the corporate development on the target's fortune is certain and clear, the *TSC Industries* materiality definition admits straightforward application. Where, on the other hand, the event is contingent or speculative in nature, it is difficult to ascertain whether the "reasonable investor" would have considered the omitted information significant at the time. Merger negotiations, because of the ever-present possibility that the contemplated transaction will not be effectuated, fall into the latter category.[9]

A

Petitioners urge upon us a Third Circuit test for resolving this difficulty.[10] See Brief for Petitioners 20–22. Under this approach, preliminary merger discussions do not become material until "agreement-in-principle" as to the price and structure of the transaction has been reached between the would-be merger partners. See *Greenfield v. Heublein, Inc.,* 742 F.2d 751, 757 (CA3 1984), cert. denied, 469 U.S. 1215 (1985). By definition, then, information concerning any negotiations not yet at the agreement-in-principle stage could be withheld or even misrepresented without a violation of Rule 10b–5.

Three rationales have been offered in support of the "agreement-in-principle" test. The first derives from the concern expressed in *TSC Industries* that an investor not be overwhelmed by excessively detailed and trivial information, and focuses on the substantial risk that preliminary merger discussions may collapse: because such discussions are inherently tentative, disclosure of their existence itself could

9. We do not address here any other kinds of contingent or speculative information, such as earnings forecasts or projections. See generally Hiler, The SEC and the Courts' Approach to Disclosure of Earnings Projections, Asset Appraisals, and Other Soft Information: Old Problems, Changing Views, 46 Md.L.Rev. 1114 (1987).

10. See *Staffin v. Greenberg,* 672 F.2d 1196, 1207 (CA3 1982) (defining duty to disclose existence of ongoing merger negotiations as triggered when agreement-in-principle is reached); *Greenfield v. Heublein, Inc.,* 742 F.2d 751 (CA3 1984) (applying agreement-in-principle test to materiality inquiry), cert. denied, 469 U.S. 1215 (1985). Citing *Staffin,* the United States Court of Appeals for the Second Circuit has

rejected a claim that defendant was under an obligation to disclose various events related to merger negotiations. *Reiss v. Pan American World Airways, Inc.,* 711 F.2d 11, 13–14 (CA2 1983). The Seventh Circuit recently endorsed the agreement-in-principle test of materiality. See *Flamm v. Eberstadt,* 814 F.2d 1169, 1174–1179 (CA7) (describing agreement-in-principle as an agreement on price and structure), cert. denied, ___ U.S. ___ (1987). In some of these cases it is unclear whether the court based its decision on a finding that no duty arose to reveal the existence of negotiations, or whether it concluded that the negotiations were immaterial under an interpretation of the opinion in *TSC Industries, Inc. v. Northway, Inc., supra.*

mislead investors and foster false optimism. See *Greenfield v. Heublein, Inc.,* 742 F.2d, at 756; *Reiss v. Pan American World Airways, Inc.,* 711 F.2d 11, 14 (CA2 1983). The other two justifications for the agreement-in-principle standard are based on management concerns: because the requirement of "agreement-in-principle" limits the scope of disclosure obligations, it helps preserve the confidentiality of merger discussions where earlier disclosure might prejudice the negotiations; and the test also provides a usable, bright-line rule for determining when disclosure must be made. See *Greenfield v. Heublein, Inc.,* 742 F.2d, at 757; *Flamm v. Eberstadt,* 814 F.2d 1169, 1176–1178 (CA7), cert. denied, ___ U.S. ___ (1987).

None of these policy-based rationales, however, purports to explain why drawing the line at agreement-in-principle reflects the significance of the information upon the investor's decision. The first rationale, and the only one connected to the concerns expressed in *TSC Industries,* stands soundly rejected, even by a Court of Appeals that otherwise has accepted the wisdom of the agreement-in-principle test. "It assumes that investors are nitwits, unable to appreciate— even when told—that mergers are risky propositions up until the closing." *Flamm v. Eberstadt,* 814 F.2d, at 1175. Disclosure, and not paternalistic withholding of accurate information, is the policy chosen and expressed by Congress. We have recognized time and again, a "fundamental purpose" of the various securities acts, "was to substitute a philosophy of full disclosure for the philosophy of *caveat emptor* and thus to achieve a high standard of business ethics in the securities industry." *SEC v. Capital Gains Research Bureau, Inc.,* 375 U.S. 180, 186 (1963). Accord, *Affiliated Ute Citizens v. United States,* 406 U.S. 128, 151 (1972); *Santa Fe Industries, Inc. v. Green,* 430 U.S. 462, 477 (1977). The role of the materiality requirement is not to "attribute to investors a child-like simplicity, an inability to grasp the probabilistic significance of negotiations," *Flamm v. Eberstadt,* 814 F.2d, at 1175, but to filter out essentially useless information that a reasonable investor would not consider significant, even as part of a larger "mix" of factors to consider in making his investment decision. *TSC Industries, Inc. v. Northway, Inc.,* 426 U.S., at 448–449.

The second rationale, the importance of secrecy during the early stages of merger discussions, also seems irrelevant to an assessment whether their existence is significant to the trading decision of a reasonable investor. To avoid a "bidding war" over its target, an acquiring firm often will insist that negotiations remain confidential, see, *e. g., In re Carnation Co.,* Exchange Act Release No. 22214, 33 SEC Docket 1025 (1985), and at least one Court of Appeals has stated that "silence pending settlement of the price and structure of a deal is beneficial to most investors, most of the time." *Flamm v. Eberstadt,* 814 F.2d, at 1177.[11]

11. Reasoning backwards from a goal of economic efficiency, that Court of Appeals stated: "Rule 10b–5 is about *fraud,* after all, and it is not fraudulent to conduct business in a way that makes investors better off . . . ." *Flamm v. Eberstadt,* 814 F.2d, at 1177.

We need not ascertain, however, whether secrecy necessarily maximizes shareholder wealth—although we note that the proposition is at least disputed as a matter of theory and empirical research—for this case does not concern the *timing* of a disclosure; it concerns only its accuracy and completeness.[13] We face here the narrow question whether information concerning the existence and status of preliminary merger discussions is significant to the reasonable investor's trading decision. Arguments based on the premise that some disclosure would be "premature" in a sense are more properly considered under the rubric of an issuer's duty to disclose. The "secrecy" rationale is simply inapposite to the definition of materiality.

The final justification offered in support of the agreement-in-principle test seems to be directed solely at the comfort of corporate managers. A bright-line rule indeed is easier to follow than a standard that requires the exercise of judgment in the light of all the circumstances. But ease of application alone is not an excuse for ignoring the purposes of the securities acts and Congress' policy decisions. Any approach that designates a single fact or occurrence as always determinative of an inherently fact-specific finding such as materiality, must necessarily be over- or underinclusive. In *TSC Industries* this Court explained: "The determination [of materiality] requires delicate assessments of the inferences a 'reasonable shareholder' would draw from a given set of facts and the significance of those inferences to him. . . ." 426 U.S., at 450. After much study, the Advisory Committee on Corporate Disclosure cautioned the SEC against administratively confining materiality to a rigid formula.[14] Courts also would do well to heed this advice.

We therefore find no valid justification for artificially excluding from the definition of materiality information concerning merger discussions, which would otherwise be considered significant to the trading decision of a reasonable investor, merely because agreement-in-principle as to price and structure has not yet been reached by the parties or their representatives.

B

The Sixth Circuit explicitly rejected the agreement-in-principle test, as we do today, but in its place adopted a rule that, if taken literally, would be equally insensitive, in our view, to the distinction

---

13. See *SEC v. Texas Gulf Sulphur Co.,* 401 F.2d 833, 862 (CA2 1968) (en banc) ("Rule 10b–5 is violated whenever assertions are made, as here, in a manner reasonably calculated to influence the investing public . . . if such assertions are false or misleading or are so incomplete as to mislead. . . ."), cert. denied *sub nom. Coates v. SEC,* 394 U.S. 976 (1969).

14. "Although the Committee believes that ideally it would be desirable to have absolute certainty in the application of the materiality concept, it is its view that such

a goal is illusory and unrealistic. The materiality concept is judgmental in nature and it is not possible to translate this into a numerical formula. The Committee's advice to the [SEC] is to avoid this quest for certainty and to continue consideration of materiality on a case-by-case basis as problems are identified."

Report of the Advisory Committee on Corporate Disclosure to the Securities and Exchange Commission 327 (House Committee on Interstate and Foreign Commerce, 95th Cong., 1st Sess.) (Comm. Print) (1977).

between materiality and the other elements of an action under Rule 10b–5:

> "When a company whose stock is publicly traded makes a statement, as Basic did, that 'no negotiations' are underway, and that the corporation knows of 'no reason for the stock's activity,' and that 'management is unaware of any present or pending corporate development that would result in the abnormally heavy trading activity,' information concerning ongoing acquisition discussions becomes material *by virtue of the statement denying their existence.*

> *   *   *

> In analyzing whether information regarding merger discussions is material such that it must be affirmatively disclosed to avoid a violation of Rule 10b–5, the discussions and their progress are the primary considerations. However, once a statement is made denying the existence of any discussions, even discussions that might not have been material in absence of the denial are material because they make the statement made untrue." 786 F.2d, at 748–749 (emphasis in original).[15]

This approach, however, fails to recognize that, in order to prevail on a Rule 10b–5 claim, a plaintiff must show that the statements were *misleading* as to a *material* fact. It is not enough that a statement is false or incomplete, if the misrepresented fact is otherwise insignificant.

C

Even before this Court's decision in *TSC Industries*, the Second Circuit had explained the role of the materiality requirement of Rule 10b–5, with respect to contingent or speculative information or events, in a manner that gave that term meaning that is independent of the other provisions of the Rule. Under such circumstances, materiality "will depend at any given time upon a balancing of both the indicated probability that the event will occur and the anticipated magnitude of the event in light of the totality of the company activity." *SEC v. Texas Gulf Sulphur Co.*, 401 F.2d, at 849. Interestingly, neither the Third Circuit decision adopting the agreement-in-principle test nor petitioners here take issue with this general standard. Rather, they suggest that with respect to preliminary merger discussions, there are good reasons to draw a line at agreement on price and structure.

In a subsequent decision, the late Judge Friendly, writing for a Second Circuit panel, applied the *Texas Gulf Sulphur* probability/ magnitude approach in the specific context of preliminary merger

---

15. Subsequently, the Sixth Circuit denied a petition for rehearing en banc in this case. App. to Pet. for Cert. 144a. Concurring separately, Judge Wellford, one of the original panel members, then explained that he did not read the panel's opinion to create a "conclusive presumption of materiality for any undisclosed information claimed to render inaccurate statements denying the existence of alleged preliminary merger discussions." *Id.*, at 145a. In his view, the decision merely reversed the District Court's judgment, which had been based on the agreement-in-principle standard. *Ibid.*

negotiations. After acknowledging that materiality is something to be determined on the basis of the particular facts of each case, he stated:

> "Since a merger in which it is bought out is the most important event that can occur in a small corporation's life, to wit, its death, we think that inside information, as regards a merger of this sort, can become material at an earlier stage than would be the case as regards lesser transactions—and this even though the mortality rate of mergers in such formative stages is doubtless high."

SEC v. Geon Industries, Inc., 531 F.2d 39, 47–48 (CA2 1976). We agree with that analysis.

Whether merger discussions in any particular case are material therefore depends on the facts. Generally, in order to assess the probability that the event will occur, a factfinder will need to look to indicia of interest in the transaction at the highest corporate levels. Without attempting to catalog all such possible factors, we note by way of example that board resolutions, instructions to investment bankers, and actual negotiations between principals or their intermediaries may serve as indicia of interest. To assess the magnitude of the transaction to the issuer of the securities allegedly manipulated, a factfinder will need to consider such facts as the size of the two corporate entities and of the potential premiums over market value. No particular event or factor short of closing the transaction need be either necessary or sufficient by itself to render merger discussions material.[17]

As we clarify today, materiality depends on the significance the reasonable investor would place on the withheld or misrepresented information. The fact-specific inquiry we endorse here is consistent with the approach a number of courts have taken in assessing the materiality of merger negotiations.[19] Because the standard of materi-

---

17. To be actionable, of course, a statement must also be misleading. Silence, absent a duty to disclose, is not misleading under Rule 10b–5. "No comment" statements are generally the functional equivalent of silence. See *In re Carnation Co., supra.* See also New York Stock Exchange Listed Company Manual § 202.01, reprinted in 3 CCH Fed. Sec. L. Rep. ¶23,515 (premature public announcement may properly be delayed for valid business purpose and where adequate security can be maintained); American Stock Exchange Company Guide §§ 401–405, reprinted in 3 CCH Fed. Sec. L. Rep. ¶¶ 23,124A–23,124E (similar provisions).

It has been suggested that given current market practices, a "no comment" statement is tantamount to an admission that merger discussions are underway. See *Flamm v. Eberstadt*, 814 F.2d, at 1178. That may well hold true to the extent that issuers adopt a policy of truthfully denying merger rumors when no discussions are underway, and of issuing "no comment" statements when they are in the midst of

negotiations. There are, of course, other statement policies firms could adopt; we need not now advise issuers as to what kind of practice to follow, within the range permitted by law. Perhaps more importantly, we think that creating an exception to a regulatory scheme founded on a prodisclosure legislative philosophy, because complying with the regulation might be "bad for business," is a role for Congress, not this Court. See also *id.*, at 1182 (opinion concurring in the judgment and concurring in part).

19. See, *e. g., SEC v. Shapiro*, 494 F.2d 1301, 1306–1307 (CA2 1974) (in light of projected very substantial increase in earnings per share, negotiations material, although merger still less than probable); *Holmes v. Bateson*, 583 F.2d 542, 558 (CA1 1978) (merger negotiations material although they had not yet reached point of discussing terms); *SEC v. Gaspar*, CCH Fed. Sec. L. Rep. (1984–1985 Transfer Binder) ¶92,004, pp. 90,977–90,978 (SDNY 1985) (merger negotiations material although they did not proceed to actual tender offer);

ality we have adopted differs from that used by both courts below, we remand the case for reconsideration of the question whether a grant of summary judgment is appropriate on this record.[20]

IV

A

We turn to the question of reliance and the fraud-on-the-market theory. Succinctly put:

> "The fraud on the market theory is based on the hypothesis that, in an open and developed securities market, the price of a company's stock is determined by the available material information regarding the company and its business. . . . Misleading statements will therefore defraud purchasers of stock even if the purchasers do not directly rely on the misstatements. . . . The causal connection between the defendants' fraud and the plaintiffs' purchase of stock in such a case is no less significant than in a case of direct reliance on misrepresentations." *Peil v. Speiser*, 806 F.2d 1154, 1160–61 (CA3 1986).

Out task, of course, is not to assess the general validity of the theory, but to consider whether it was proper for the courts below to apply a rebuttable presumption of reliance, supported in part by the fraud-on-the-market theory.

This case required resolution of several common questions of law and fact concerning the falsity or misleading nature of the three public statements made by Basic, the presence or absence of scienter, and the materiality of the misrepresentations, if any. In their amended complaint, the named plaintiffs alleged that in reliance on Basic's statements they sold their shares of Basic stock in the depressed market created by petitioners. See Amended Complaint in No. C79–1220 (ND Ohio) ¶¶27, 29, 35, 40; see also *id.*, at ¶33 (alleging effect on market price of Basic's statements). Requiring proof of individualized reliance from each member of the proposed plaintiff class effectively would have prevented respondents from proceeding with a class

---

Dungan v. Colt Industries, Inc., 532 F.Supp. 832, 837 (ND Ill. 1982) (fact that defendants were seriously exploring the sale of their company was material); *American General Ins. Co. v. Equitable General Corp.*, 493 F.Supp. 721, 744–745 (ED Va. 1980) (merger negotiations material four months before agreement-in-principle reached). Cf. *Susquehanna Corp. v. Pan American Sulphur Co.*, 423 F.2d 1075, 1084–1085 (CA5 1970) (holding immaterial "unilateral offer to negotiate" never acknowledged by target and repudiated two days later); *Berman v. Gerber Products Co.*, 454 F.Supp. 1310, 1316, 1318 (WD Mich. 1978) (mere "overtures" immaterial).

20. The Sixth Circuit rejected the District Court's narrow reading of Basic's "no developments" statement, see n. 4, *supra*,

which focused on whether petitioners *knew* of any reason for the activity in Basic stock, that is, whether petitioners were aware of leaks concerning ongoing discussions. 786 F.2d, at 747. See also Comment, Disclosure of Preliminary Merger Negotiations Under Rule 10b–5, 62 Wash. L. Rev. 81, 82–84 (1987) (noting prevalence of leaks and studies demonstrating that substantial trading activity immediately preceding merger announcements is the "rule, not the exception"). We accept the Court of Appeals' reading of the statement as the more natural one, emphasizing management's knowledge of *developments* (as opposed to leaks) that would explain unusual trading activity. See *id.*, at 92–93; see also *SEC v. Texas Gulf Sulphur Co.*, 401 F.2d, at 862–863.

action, since individual issues then would have overwhelmed the common ones. The District Court found that the presumption of reliance created by the fraud-on-the-market theory provided "a practical resolution to the problem of balancing the substantive requirement of proof of reliance in securities cases against the procedural requisites of [Fed. Rule Civ. Proc.] 23." The District Court thus concluded that with reference to each public statement and its impact upon the open market for Basic shares, common questions predominated over individual questions, as required by Fed. Rule Civ. Proc. 23(a)(2) and (b)(3).

Petitioners and their *amici* complain that the fraud-on-the-market theory effectively eliminates the requirement that a plaintiff asserting a claim under Rule 10b–5 prove reliance. They note that reliance is and long has been an element of common-law fraud, see *e. g.*, Restatement (Second) of Torts § 525 (1977); Prosser and Keeton on The Law of Torts § 108 (5th ed. 1984), and argue that because the analogous express right of action includes a reliance requirement, see, *e. g.*, § 18(a) of the 1934 Act, as amended, 15 U.S.C. § 78r(a), so too must an action implied under § 10(b).

We agree that reliance is an element of a Rule 10b–5 cause of action. See *Ernst & Ernst v. Hochfelder*, 425 U.S., at 206 (quoting Senate Report). Reliance provides the requisite causal connection between a defendant's misrepresentation and a plaintiff's injury. See, *e. g.*, *Wilson v. Comtech Telecommunications Corp.*, 648 F.2d 88, 92 (CA2 1981); *List v. Fashion Park, Inc.*, 340 F.2d 457, 462 (CA2), cert. denied *sub nom. List v. Lerner*, 382 U.S. 811 (1965). There is, however, more than one way to demonstrate the causal connection. Indeed, we previously have dispensed with a requirement of positive proof of reliance, where a duty to disclose material information had been breached, concluding that the necessary nexus between the plaintiffs' injury and the defendant's wrongful conduct had been established. See *Affiliated Ute Citizens v. United States*, 406 U.S., at 153–154. Similarly, we did not require proof that material omissions or misstatements in a proxy statement decisively affected voting, because the proxy solicitation itself, rather than the defect in the solicitation materials, served as an essential link in the transaction. See *Mills v. Electric Auto-Lite Co.*, 396 U.S. 375, 384–385 (1970).

The modern securities markets, literally involving millions of shares changing hands daily, differ from the face-to-face transactions contemplated by early fraud cases,[21] and our understanding of Rule 10b–5's reliance requirement must encompass these differences.[22]

21. Prosser and Keeton on The Law of Torts 726 (5th ed. 1984) ("The reasons for the separate development of [the tort action for misrepresentation and nondisclosure], and for its peculiar limitations, are in part historical, and in part connected with the fact that in the great majority of the cases which have come before the courts the misrepresentations have been made in the course of a bargaining transaction between the parties. Consequently the action has been colored to a considerable extent by the ethics of bargaining between distrustful adversaries") (footnote omitted).

22. Actions under Rule 10b–5 are distinct from common-law deceit and misrepresentation claims, see *Blue Chip Stamps v. Manor Drug Stores*, 421 U.S. 723, 744–745 (1975), and are in part designed to add to the protections provided investors by the

"In face-to-face transactions, the inquiry into an investor's reliance upon information is into the subjective pricing of that information by that investor. With the presence of a market, the market is interposed between seller and buyer and, ideally, transmits information to the investor in the processed form of a market price. Thus the market is performing a substantial part of the valuation process performed by the investor in a face-to-face transaction. The market is acting as the unpaid agent of the investor, informing him that given all the information available to it, the value of the stock is worth the market price." *In re LTV Securities Litigation*, 88 F.R.D. 134, 143 (ND Tex. 1980).

Accord, *e. g., Peil v. Speiser*, 806 F.2d, at 1161 ("In an open and developed market, the dissemination of material misrepresentations or withholding of material information typically affects the price of the stock, and purchasers generally rely on the price of the stock as a reflection of its value"); *Blackie v. Barrack*, 524 F.2d 891, 908 (CA9 1975) ("the same causal nexus can be adequately established indirectly, by proof of materiality coupled with the common sense that a stock purchaser does not ordinarily seek to purchase a loss in the form of artificially inflated stock"), cert. denied, 429 U.S. 816 (1976).

B

Presumptions typically serve to assist courts in managing circumstances in which direct proof, for one reason or another, is rendered difficult. See, *e. g.*, D. Louisell & C. Mueller, Federal Evidence 541–542 (1977). The courts below accepted a presumption, created by the fraud-on-the-market theory and subject to rebuttal by petitioners, that persons who had traded Basic shares had done so in reliance on the integrity of the price set by the market, but because of petitioners' material misrepresentations that price had been fraudulently depressed. Requiring a plaintiff to show a speculative state of facts, *i. e.*, how he would have acted if omitted material information had been disclosed, see *Affiliated Ute Citizens v. United States*, 406 U.S., at 153–154, or if the misrepresentation had not been made, see *Sharp v. Coopers & Lybrand*, 649 F.2d 175, 188 (CA3 1981), cert. denied, 455 U.S. 938 (1982), would place an unnecessarily unrealistic evidentiary burden on the Rule 10b–5 plaintiff who has traded on an impersonal market. Cf. *Mills v. Electric Auto-Lite Co.*, 396 U.S., at 385.

Arising out of considerations of fairness, public policy, and probability, as well as judicial economy, presumptions are also useful devices for allocating the burdens of proof between parties. See E. Cleary, McCormick on Evidence 968–969 (3rd ed. 1984); see also Fed. Rule Evid. 301 and notes. The presumption of reliance employed in this case is consistent with, and, by facilitating Rule 10b–5 litigation, supports, the congressional policy embodied in the 1934 Act. In drafting that Act, Congress expressly relied on the premise that securities markets are affected by information, and enacted legisla-

common law, see *Herman & MacLean v. Huddleston*, 459 U.S. 375, 388–389 (1983).

tion to facilitate an investor's reliance on the integrity of those markets:

> "No investor, no speculator, can safely buy and sell securities upon the exchanges without having an intelligent basis for forming his judgment as to the value of the securities he buys or sells. The idea of a free and open public market is built upon the theory that competing judgments of buyers and sellers as to the fair price of a security brings [*sic*] about a situation where the market price reflects as nearly as possible a just price. Just as artificial manipulation tends to upset the true function of an open market, so the hiding and secreting of important information obstructs the operation of the markets as indices of real value." H.R. Rep. No. 1383, *supra*, at 11.

See *Lipton v. Documation, Inc.*, 734 F.2d 740, 748 (CA11 1984), cert. denied, 469 U.S. 1132 (1985).

The presumption is also supported by common sense and probability. Recent empirical studies have tended to confirm Congress' premise that the market price of shares traded on well-developed markets reflects all publicly available information, and, hence, any material misrepresentations.[24] It has been noted that "it is hard to imagine that there ever is a buyer or seller who does not rely on market integrity. Who would knowingly roll the dice in a crooked crap game?" *Schlanger* v. *Four–Phase Systems Inc.*, 555 F.Supp. 535, 538 (SDNY 1982). Indeed, nearly every court that has considered the proposition has concluded that where materially misleading statements have been disseminated into an impersonal, well-developed market for securities, the reliance of individual plaintiffs on the integrity of the market price may be presumed. Commentators generally have applauded the adoption of one variation or another of the fraud-on-the-market theory. An investor who buys or sells stock at the price set by the market does so in reliance on the integrity of that price. Because most publicly available information is reflected in market price, an investor's reliance on any public material misrepresentations, therefore, may be presumed for purposes of a Rule 10b–5 action.

C

The Court of Appeals found that petitioners "made public, material misrepresentations and [respondents] sold Basic stock in an impersonal, efficient market. Thus the class, as defined by the district

24. See *In re LTV Securities Litigation*, 88 F.R.D. 134, 144 (ND Tex.1980) (citing studies); Fischel, Use of Modern Finance Theory in Securities Fraud Cases Involving Actively Traded Securities, 38 Bus.Law. 1, 4, n. 9 (1982) (citing literature on efficient-capital-market theory); Dennis, Materiality and the Efficient Capital Market Model: A Recipe for the Total Mix, 25 Wm. & Mary L.Rev. 373, 374–381, and n. 1 (1984). We need not determine by adjudication what economists and social scientists have debated through the use of sophisticated statistical analysis and the application of economic theory. For purposes of accepting the presumption of reliance in this case, we need only believe that market professionals generally consider most publicly announced material statements about companies, thereby affecting stock market prices.

court, has established the threshold facts for proving their loss." 786 F.2d, at 751.[27]   The court acknowledged that petitioners may rebut proof of the elements giving rise to the presumption, or show that the misrepresentation in fact did not lead to a distortion of price or that an individual plaintiff traded or would have traded despite his knowing the statement was false. *Id.*, at 750, n. 6.

Any showing that severs the link between the alleged misrepresentation and either the price received (or paid) by the plaintiff, or his decision to trade at a fair market price, will be sufficient to rebut the presumption of reliance.   For example, if petitioners could show that the "market makers" were privy to the truth about the merger discussions here with Combustion, and thus that the market price would not have been affected by their misrepresentations, the causal connection could be broken: the basis for finding that the fraud had been transmitted through market price would be gone.[28]   Similarly, if, despite petitioners' allegedly fraudulent attempt to manipulate market price, news of the merger discussions credibly entered the market and dissipated the effects of the misstatements, those who traded Basic shares after the corrective statements would have no direct or indirect connection with the fraud.[29]   Petitioners also could rebut the presumption of reliance as to plaintiffs who would have divested themselves of their Basic shares without relying on the integrity of the market.   For example, a plaintiff who believed that Basic's statements were false and that Basic was indeed engaged in merger discussions, and who consequently believed that Basic stock was artificially underpriced, but sold his shares nevertheless because of other unrelated concerns, *e.g.*, potential antitrust problems, or political pressures to divest from shares of certain businesses, could not be said to have relied on the integrity of a price he knew had been manipulated.

27. The Court of Appeals held that in order to invoke the presumption, a plaintiff must allege and prove: (1) that the defendant made public misrepresentations; (2) that the misrepresentations were material; (3) that the shares were traded on an efficient market; (4) that the misrepresentations would induce a reasonable, relying investor to misjudge the value of the shares; and (5) that the plaintiff traded the shares between the time the misrepresentations were made and the time the truth was revealed. See 786 F.2d, at 750.

Given today's decision regarding the definition of materiality as to preliminary merger discussions, elements (2) and (4) may collapse into one.

28. By accepting this rebuttable presumption, we do not intend conclusively to adopt any particular theory of how quickly and completely publicly available information is reflected in market price. Furthermore, our decision today is not to be interpreted as addressing the proper measure of damages in litigation of this kind.

29. We note there may be a certain incongruity between the assumption that Basic shares are traded on a well-developed, efficient, and information-hungry market, and the allegation that such a market could remain misinformed, and its valuation of Basic shares depressed, for 14 months, on the basis of the three public statements.   Proof of that sort is a matter for trial, throughout which the District Court retains the authority to amend the certification order as may be appropriate. See Fed.Rule Civ.Proc. 23(c)(1) and (c)(4). See 7B C. Wright, A. Miller & M. Kane, Federal Practice and Procedure 128–132 (1986).   Thus, we see no need to engage in the kind of factual analysis the dissent suggests that manifests the "oddities" of applying a rebuttable presumption of reliance in this case. . . .

V

In summary:

1. We specifically adopt, for the § 10(b) and Rule 10b–5 context, the standard of materiality set forth in *TSC Industries, Inc. v. Northway, Inc.*, 426 U.S., at 449.

2. We reject "agreement-in-principle as to price and structure" as the bright-line rule for materiality.

3. We also reject the proposition that "information becomes material by virtue of a public statement denying it."

4. Materiality in the merger context depends on the probability that the transaction will be consummated, and its significance to the issuer of the securities. Materiality depends on the facts and thus is to be determined on a case-by-case basis.

5. It is not inappropriate to apply a presumption of reliance supported by the fraud-on-the-market theory.

6. That presumption, however, is rebuttable.

7. The District Court's certification of the class here was appropriate when made but is subject on remand to such adjustment, if any, as developing circumstances demand.

The judgment of the Court of Appeals is vacated and the case is remanded to that court for further proceedings consistent with this opinion.

It is so ordered.

The Chief Justice, Justice SCALIA, and Justice KENNEDY took no part in the consideration or decision of this case.

Justice WHITE, with whom Justice O'CONNOR joins, concurring in part and dissenting in part.

I join Parts I–III of the Court's opinion, as I agree that the standard of materiality we set forth in *TSC Industies, Inc. v. Northway, Inc.*, 426 U.S. 438, 449 (1976), should be applied to actions under § 10(b) and Rule 10b–5. But I dissent from the remainder of the Court's holding because I do not agree that the "fraud-on-the-market" theory should be applied in this case. . . .

. . . [W]hile the economists' theories which underpin the fraud-on-the-market presumption may have the appeal of mathematical exactitude and scientific certainty, they are—in the end—nothing more than theories which may or may not prove accurate upon further consideration. Even the most earnest advocates of economic analysis of the law recognize this. See, *e.g.*, Easterbrook, Afterword: Knowledge and Answers, 85 Colum.L.Rev. 1117, 1118 (1985). Thus, while the majority states that, for purposes of reaching its result it need only make modest assumptions about the way in which "market professionals generally" do their jobs, and how the conduct of market professionals affects stock prices, . . . I doubt that we are in much of a position to assess which theories aptly describe the functioning of the securities industry.

Consequently, I cannot join the Court in its effort to reconfigure the securities laws, based on recent economic theories, to better fit what it perceives to be the new realities of financial markets. I would leave this task to others more equipped for the job than we. . . .

At the bottom of the Court's conclusion that the fraud-on-the-market theory sustains a presumption of reliance is the assumption that individuals rely "on the integrity of the market price" when buying or selling stock in "impersonal, well-developed market[s] for securities." *Ante*, at 21–22. Even if I was prepared to accept (as a matter of common sense or general understanding) the assumption that most persons buying or selling stock do so in response to the market price, the fraud-on-the-market theory goes further. For in adopting a "presumption of reliance," the Court *also* assumes that buyers and sellers rely—not just on the market price—but on the *"integrity"* of that price. It is this aspect of the fraud-on-the-market hypothesis which most mystifies me.

To define the term "integrity of the market price," the majority quotes approvingly from cases which suggest that investors are entitled to " 'rely on the price of a stock as a reflection of its value.' " But the meaning of this phrase eludes me, for it implicitly suggests that stocks have some "true value" that is measurable by a standard other than their market price. While the Scholastics of Medieval times professed a means to make such a valuation of a commodity's "worth," I doubt that the federal courts of our day are similarly equipped.

Even if securities had some "value"—knowable and distinct from the market price of a stock—investors do not always share the Court's presumption that a stock's price is a "reflection of [this] value." Indeed, "many investors purchase or sell stock because they believe the price *inaccurately* reflects the corporation's worth." See Black, Fraud on the Market: A Criticism of Dispensing with Reliance Requirements in Certain Open Market Transactions, 62 N.C.L.Rev. 435, 455 (1984) (emphasis added). If investors really believed that stock prices reflected a stock's "value," many sellers would never sell, and many buyers never buy (given the time and cost associated with executing a stock transaction). As we recognized just a few years ago: "[I]nvestors act on inevitably incomplete or inaccurate information, [consequently] there are always winners and losers; but those who have 'lost' have not necessarily been defrauded." *Dirks* v. *SEC*, 463 U.S. 646, 667, n. 27 (1983). Yet today, the Court allows investors to recover who can show little more than that they sold stock at a lower price than what might have been.

I do not propose that the law retreat from the many protections that § 10(b) and Rule 10b–5, as interpreted in our prior cases, provide to investors. But any extension of these laws, to approach something closer to an investor insurance scheme, should come from Congress, and not from the courts. . . .

———

GORDON & KORNHAUSER, EFFICIENT MARKETS, COSTLY INFORMATION, AND SECURITIES RESEARCH

60 N.Y.U.L.Rev. 761 (1985).

Particular conceptions of the function and operation of securities markets underlie every regulatory scheme for those markets. Formulation of intelligent policy requires an understanding of these conceptions. In this Part, we outline some fundamental elements of the view of securities markets embedded in the efficient market hypothesis.

Before we begin, however, we offer two parallel distinctions: between "real" and "financial" assets and between "allocative" and "speculative" efficiency, on which much of our discussion of the efficient market hypothesis turns. A real capital asset is the actual physical good, while a financial asset represents a claim on the income generated from the physical good (or perhaps some other ownership right). Thus, an equity share in Company A represents a bundle of claims on the revenues generated by the physical goods (and employees) that constitute the real assets called Company A.

The distinction between allocative and speculative efficiency depends on a distinction between (real) investment (i.e., the creation of physical goods) and (financial) savings (i.e., the deferral of consumption from one period to the next). In an allocatively efficient market, investment decisions are made optimally; in a speculatively efficient market, savings decisions are made optimally. The subsequent discussion will clarify and elaborate the role of these two distinctions.

A. *Ideal Capital Markets in Simple Worlds*

Capital markets serve two functions. First, individuals may want to shift consumption from one period to another. If A's income or anticipated expenses vary, she may wish to save during periods of plenty and to "dissave" (spend her savings) or borrow in periods of income shortfall. Capital markets facilitate individual planning of consumption over time in light of anticipated resources. Second, capital markets provide and allocate investment funds. Investment funds are used to produce "new capital," production facilities that will provide goods and services to be consumed in future periods. These two functions are linked because the consumption that individuals defer today releases resources to be invested in new capital that will produce the goods to be consumed tomorrow. To make a "good" *savings* decision, an individual must know how much consumption she will get tomorrow for the consumption she gives up today. That is, she must know the *financial* returns of any security she purchases—namely, the payout of dividends or interest and capital gain or loss. To make a "good" *investment* decision, the investor must know how much value the new capital will produce in the future. That is, she must know the real returns of the (real) investment—namely, gross revenues less costs of production. We shall call a capital market that induces "good" savings decisions "speculatively efficient" and one that induces "good" (real) investment decisions, "allocatively efficient." A speculatively efficient market need not be allocatively efficient.

Capital markets guide investment and saving decisions through prices. In raising money for new capital expenditures, investors consider the price they can charge in the sale of financial assets. In deciding how much consumption to defer, savers consider the security's financial returns given the security's price. Any claim that capital markets work well, therefore, reduces to a claim about the "accuracy" of the prices prevailing on the capital market. The efficient market hypothesis makes a strong claim about the accuracy of prices on well-developed capital markets such as the New York Stock Exchange or the market for government bonds. To evaluate this claim we must understand what it means for prices to be "accurate."

To begin, let us identify accurate prices for a capital market in a world much simpler than the one in which the New York Stock Exchange operates. The hallmark of this simpler world is certainty. Let us assume that securities are identified by the date of maturity and the (invariable) (financial) returns on that date. Certainty suggests that each trader knows the returns from owning any security. Prices should accurately reflect the relative returns of securities. Thus, if two securities, X and Y, mature on the same date and offer the same returns, their prices should be identical. Similarly, if X and Y have the same maturity date but X offers higher returns than Y, the price of X should be higher than the price of Y. In fact, prices in this perfect market would equalize the financial returns available from purchasing different securities.

Notice why accurate capital market prices are desirable in this certain world. Suppose some security was "undervalued." That would mean that its price was lower than warranted by its returns. On the maturity date a purchaser of the security would be pleasantly surprised; she would receive more than the price entitled her to expect. At the date of purchase, however, those who judged returns only by market prices would thus have been less willing to purchase the undervalued security than was warranted by the promised returns. In fact, a purchaser who judged her savings opportunities only by market prices would have underestimated the amount of future consumption available to her from saving. Consequently she would save too little. The analysis reverses itself in the case of "overvalued" securities; the individual would save more than was warranted by the actual returns received. If prices were accurate, however, the market would be speculatively efficient and savers would make appropriate decisions about the proportion of their current incomes they wished to save.

Allocative efficiency in this certain world depends upon the connection between financial returns and real returns. For example, assume that two firms each desire to issue securities to finance a new plant. The plant that will generate more profits per invested dollar is the more desirable real investment and should attract funds first. In a perfectly certain world, the most productive real investments would receive funds first because financial returns would always correspond to real returns. Therefore the capital market would be both speculatively and allocatively efficient. Outside of this certain world, however, financial returns of securities may not be accurate measures of the real returns of the issuer's investment in new capital. Thus, a capital market might accurately reflect financial returns but not accurately reflect real returns. It would then be speculatively efficient, but not allocatively efficient.

Let us now turn to the decidedly uncertain world of the New York Stock Exchange. Traders on the Exchange do not know with certainty the financial returns of securities. They must predict future prices, dividends, and interest to estimate the returns they will receive. On the basis of these estimated returns they will decide how much to save. If all traders held the same beliefs about returns, future prices could be extended with little difficulty from a certain world to an uncertain one. Accurate prices would reflect the shared belief of each person about the financial returns of securities. If some price did not reflect this shared belief, the security would be under- or overvalued and traders would either bid up its price (because they thought it offered higher returns) or bid down its price (because they thought it offered lower returns). This process would result in speculatively efficient markets. A similar logic underlies the desirability of allocatively efficient markets when investors share beliefs about prospective (real) returns.

The complexity of the analysis increases if we allow participants to have divergent beliefs about real or financial returns. If investors' beliefs about returns differ, different individuals would rank potential investment opportunities in different orders. Consequently, traders estimate future prices differently, and accurate prices become difficult to identify. Ideally, we want the capital market to perform as it did under certainty where stocks are "properly" valued. Security prices therefore should reflect, in some sense, our "best estimate" of the returns of each security. This best estimate would result in allocatively, as well as speculatively, efficient capital markets if the financial returns of securities were also accurate measures of the real returns of the issuer.

B. *The Efficient Market Hypothesis*

The efficient market hypothesis defines the best estimate of the financial returns of each security. Thus, a good estimate should take into account all available information about future prices. Prices are "efficient" in two senses: (1) the current price of a security best predicts its future price and (2) the prevailing price immediately assimilates new information provided to the market. As a consequence, no trader can earn (financial) arbitrage profits in an efficient market because no one can identify (except by chance) securities which are under- or overvalued.

The efficient market hypothesis thus posits that the mechanism that sets prices in securities markets possesses a startling property. The mechanism of price formation somehow captures information about and predicts the future payout of a security (dividends, interest, and capital gain or loss) as well as about the investor who happens to know, with concrete particularity, all of this relevant information. Thus the efficient market hypothesis embraces two different kinds of claims: that all relevant information will be available to the market and that the market rapidly, if not instantaneously, digests all information as it becomes available. . . .

It is not difficult to specify conditions under which capital markets will inevitably be speculatively efficient: no transaction costs in trading securities, costless access by all market participants to all available information, and agreement by market participants as to implications of such information for the current price and distributions of future price of each security (i.e., homogenous expectations). Prices that prevail under these conditions by definition "fully reflect" all available information. The efficient market hypothesis, however, purports to make a strong statement where some of these conditions are not present. It states that despite transaction costs, the lack of universal access to available information, and differing assessments of information, prevailing prices fully reflect available information. . . .

R. BREALY & S. MYERS, PRINCIPLES OF CORPORATE FINANCE
270–271 (3d ed. 1988).

Three Forms of the Efficient-Market Theory

Harry Roberts has defined three levels of market efficiency. The first is the case in which prices reflect all the information contained in the record of past prices. Roberts called this a *weak* form of efficiency. The random-walk research shows that the market is at *least* efficient in this weak sense.

The second level of efficiency is the case in which prices reflect not only past prices but all other published information. Roberts called this a *semistrong* form of efficiency. Researchers have tested this by looking at specific items of news such as announcements of earnings and dividends, forecasts of company earnings, changes in accounting practices, and mergers. Most of this information was rapidly and acurately impounded in the price of the stock.

Finally, Harry Roberts envisaged a *strong* form of efficiency in which prices reflect not just public information but *all* the information that can be acquired by painstaking fundamental analysis of the company and the economy. In such a case, the stock market would be like our ideal auction house: prices would *always* be fair and *no* investor would be able to make consistently superior forecasts of stock prices. Most tests of this view have involved an analysis of the performance of professionally managed portfolios. These studies have concluded that, after taking account of differences in risk, no group of institutions has been able to outperform the market consistently and that even the differences between the performance of individual funds are no greater than you would expect from chance.

Although few simple economic ideas are as well supported by the evidence as the efficient-market theory, it would be wrong to pretend that there are no puzzles or apparent exceptions. For instance, New York Stock Exchange specialists seem to have made consistently superior profits; so do company managers when they deal in their own company's stock. These are two cases that don't seem to square well with the strong form of the efficient-market theory. . . .

The efficient-market hypothesis is frequently misinterpreted. One common error is to think that it implies perfect forecasting ability. In fact it implies only that prices reflect all available information. In the same vein, some have suggested that prices cannot represent fair value because they go up and down. The answer, however, is that they would not represent fair value *unless* they went up and down. It is because the future is so uncertain and people are so often surprised that prices fluctuate. (Of course, when we look *back*, nothing seems quite so surprising: It is easy to convince ourselves that we really knew all along how prices were going to change.) A rather different temptation is to believe that the inability of institutions to achieve superior portfolio performance is an indication that their portfolio managers are incompetent. This is incorrect. Market efficiency exists only because competition is keen and portfolio managers are doing their job. . . .

The weak form of the efficient-market hypothesis states that the sequence of past price changes contains no information about future changes. Economists express the same idea more concisely when they say that the market has no memory. Sometimes financial managers *seem* to act as if this were not the case. For example, they are often reluctant to issue stock after a fall in price. They are inclined to wait for a rebound. Similarly, managers favor equity rather than debt financing after an abnormal price rise. The idea is to "catch the market while it is high." But we know that the market has no memory and the cycles that financial managers seem to rely on do not exist. . . .

In an efficient market you can trust prices. They impound all available information about the value of each security.

This means that in an efficient market there is no way for most investors to achieve consistently superior rates of return. To do so, you not only need to know more than *anyone* else; you need to know more than *everyone* else. This message is important for the financial manager who is responsible for the firm's exchange rate policy or for its purchases and sales of debt. If you operate on the basis that you are smarter than others at predicting currency changes or interest rate moves, you will trade a consistent financial policy for an elusive will-ó -the wisp.

The company's assets may also be directly affected by management's faith in its investment skills. For example, one company will often purchase another simply because its management thinks that the stock is undervalued. On approximately half the occasions the stock of the acquired firm really will be undervalued. But on the other half it will be overvalued. On average the value will be correct, so that the acquiring company is playing a fair game except for the costs of the acquisition.

NOTE ON THE OBLIGATIONS OF A NONTRADING CORPORATION UNDER RULE 10b–5

Most private actions under Rule 10b–5 are brought against persons who have traded or tipped, or have aided or abetted trading or tipping. As *Basic, Inc.* shows, an action can also be brought on the basis of a statement or omission that influences trading but is made by a person who did not himself trade, tip, aid, or abet:

> [I]t seems clear . . . that Congress when it used the phrase "in connection with the purchase or sale of any security" intended only that the device employed, whatever it might be, be of a sort that would cause reasonable investors to rely thereon, and, in connection therewith, so relying, cause them to purchase or sell a corporation's securities. There is no indication that Congress intended that the corporations or persons responsible for the issuance of a misleading statement would not violate the section unless they engaged in related securities transactions or otherwise acted with wrongful motives; indeed, the obvious purposes of the Act to protect the investing public and to secure fair dealing in the securities markets would be seriously undermined by applying such a gloss onto the legislative language. . . . The mere fact that an insider did not engage in securities transactions does not negate the possibility of wrongful purpose; perhaps the market did not react to the misleading statement as much as was anticipated or perhaps the wrongful purpose was something other than the desire to buy at a low price or sell at a high price.

SEC v. Texas Gulf Sulphur Co., 401 F.2d 833, 860 (2d Cir.1968), cert. denied 394 U.S. 976, 89 S.Ct. 1454, 22 L.Ed.2d 756 (1969).

Accordingly, a corporation that makes misstatements may be liable under Rule 10b–5 even if it does not trade.

However, the imposition of Rule 10b–5 liability on a nontrading corporation on the basis of *nondisclosure* is unlikely. In *Texas Gulf Sulphur Co., supra,* the court stated that "the timing of the disclosure [of material facts] is a matter for the business judgment of the corporate officers entrusted with the management of the corporation within the affirmative disclosure requirements promulgated by the exchanges and by the SEC." Id. at 850 n. 12. This is still the general rule. See Staffin v. Greenberg, 672 F.2d 1196, 1204 (3d Cir. 1982); Financial Industrial Fund, Inc. v. McDonnell Douglas Corp., 474 F.2d 514, 518 (10th Cir.1973), cert. denied 414 U.S. 874, 94 S.Ct. 155, 38 L.Ed.2d 114; Electronic Specialty Co. v. International Controls Corp., 409 F.2d 937, 949 (2d Cir.1969). There are, however, several potential exceptions to this rule:

(i) It is sometimes suggested, in dictum or by inference, that nondisclosure by a corporation may violate Rule 10b–5 if no valid corporate purpose requires nondisclosure. It is not easy to see why this should be so, and no corporation seems to have been held liable under this theory.

(ii) A corporation may so involve itself in the preparation of statements about the corporation by outsiders—such as analysts' reports or earnings projections—that it assumes a duty to correct material errors in those statements. Such a duty "may occur when officials of the company have, by their activity, made an implied representation that the information they have reviewed is true or at least in accordance with the company's views." Elkind v. Liggett & Myers, Inc., 635 F.2d 156, 163 (2d Cir.1980).

(iii) If a corporation voluntarily makes a public statement that is correct when issued, but has become materially misleading in light of subsequent events, it may have a duty to correct the statement. Greenfield v. Heublein, Inc., 742 F.2d 751, 758 (3d Cir.1984), cert. denied 469 U.S. 1215, 105 S.Ct. 1189, 84 L.Ed.2d 336 (1985); Sharp v. Coopers & Lybrand, 83 F.R.D. 343, 346–47 (E.D.Pa.1979), aff'd 649 F.2d 175 (3d Cir.1981), cert. denied 455 U.S. 938, 102 S.Ct. 1427, 71 L.Ed.2d 648 (1982).

(iv) A corporation may be under a duty to correct erroneous rumors resulting from leaks by the corporation or its agents. See State Teachers Retirement Board v. Fluor Corp., 654 F.2d 843, 850 (2d Cir.1981) (dictum).

CAVEAT: This Note concerns only Rule 10b–5. Wholly apart from Rule 10b–5, corporations are obliged to disclose certain material information under federal and state laws and Stock Exchange rules. See Chapter V, Section 2, supra.

NOTE ON RELIANCE

1.   It was early established that the plaintiff in a Rule 10b–5 case must prove that the Rule 10b–5 violation caused him a loss. At first, this seemed to require the plaintiff to prove that he relied on the defendant's wrongful statement or omission. Later, however, the requirement of reliance broke down, or at least became transformed. The reasons for the transformation differed somewhat as to (i) omissions and (ii) affirmative misstatements.

The problem as to omissions is that reliance on an omission is an illogical concept. We can say that *A* acted—bought or sold—at a given price in reliance on what *B* told him, but we can't say *A* acted—

bought or sold at a given price—in reliance on what *B* didn't tell him. What we can say in the latter case is that a *reasonable investor* who knew the omitted fact *probably* would or would not have bought or sold at the given price. In *Basic*, the Supreme Court held that the standard of *materiality* is satisfied by a showing of " 'a reasonable likelihood that the disclosure of the omitted fact would have been viewed by the reasonable investor as having significantly altered the "total mix" of information made available' " (quoting TSC Industries, Inc. v. Northway). This standard is so close to what must be shown to prove causation in an omissions case that for all intents and purposes, causation in such a case collapses into materiality. In Affiliated Ute Citizens of Utah v. United States, 406 U.S. 128, 92 S.Ct. 1456, 31 L.Ed.2d 741 (1972), a bank purchased stock from a group of unsophisticated investors without disclosing that the stock was selling at a higher price on a secondary market made by the bank. The Tenth Circuit denied recovery because the record failed to show that the plaintiffs relied on any misstatements made by the bank. The Supreme Court reversed:

> Under the circumstances of this case, involving primarily a failure to disclose, positive proof of reliance is not a prerequisite to recovery. All that is necessary is that the facts withheld be material in the sense that a reasonable investor might have considered them important in the making of this decision.

406 U.S. at 153–54.

2. On its face, *Ute* seemed to eliminate any requirement of reliance in a case of nondisclosure. In general, however, the cases have held that *Ute* "merely established a presumption that made it possible for the plaintiffs to meet their burden." Shores v. Sklar, 647 F.2d 462, 468 (5th Cir.1981) (en banc), cert. denied 459 U.S. 1102, 63 S.Ct. 722, 74 L.Ed.2d 949 (1983). The defendant can rebut this presumption "by showing that the . . . plaintiff would have have followed the same course of conduct even with full and honest disclosure, [so that] the defendant's action (or lack thereof) cannot be said to have caused plaintiff's loss." Id. The defendant might carry this burden by showing, for example, that the plaintiff learned the omitted fact from an independent source before making his investment decision, so that the decision could not have been caused by the defendant's nondisclosure. Although the cases continue to use the language of "reliance" in the omissions context, the real question is causation. When the question is properly framed, in causation terms, once the plaintiff has shown that defendant omitted to disclose a material fact he was obliged to disclose, the burden is on the defendant to prove that the plaintiff would have made the same investment decision even if disclosure had been made.

3. Fridrich v. Bradford, 542 F.2d 307, 318–20 (6th Cir.1976), cert. denied, 429 U.S. 1053, 97 S.Ct. 767, 50 L.Ed.2d 769 (1977), and Cavalier Carpets, Inc. v. Caylor, 746 F.2d 749 (11th Cir.1984) held that *Affiliated Ute* didn't apply unless the relationship of the

plaintiff and the defendant preceded the omission. Since the concept of reliance in an omissions case is illogical, it's hard to find the logic in *Cavalier* and *Fridrich*. (The real problem in *Fridrich* was not reliance, but whether, as a matter of policy, an omission in an open-market case should result in damages enormously larger than the defendants' benefit. See Note on Remedies in Private Actions Under Rule 105–5, supra.)

4. Unlike the case of an omission, in the case of a face-to-face misrepresentation, reliance is a meaningful concept. For example, the defendant might be able to show that the plaintiff did not rely on a representation because he knew from other sources that the misrepresentation was false. In face-to-face misrepresentation cases, therefore, reliance continues to be an element of plaintiff's case. However, although a lack of reliance in such cases is possible, it is extremely unlikely. People who trade soon after material misrepresentations have been made to them will have almost always have relied on the misrepresentations. Accordingly, once the plaintiff shows that a material misrepresentation was made to him, and that he traded soon thereafter, as a practical matter reliance will normally be presumed, and the burden will shift to the defendant to show that the plaintiff did not rely on the misrepresentation. In the end, therefore, the misrepresentation case is similar to the omission case—that is, once the plaintiff makes a showing of materiality, the burden shifts to the defendant to show that reliance did not occur.

CHIARELLA v. UNITED STATES

United States Supreme Court, 1980.
445 U.S. 222, 100 S.Ct. 1108, 63 L.Ed.2d 348.

Mr. Justice POWELL, delivered the opinion of the Court.

The question in this case is whether a person who learns from the confidential documents of one corporation that it is planning an attempt to secure control of a second corporation violates § 10(b) of the Securities Exchange Act of 1934 if he fails to disclose the impending takeover before trading in the target company's securities.

I

Petitioner is a printer by trade. In 1975 and 1976, he worked as a "markup man" in the New York composing room of Pandick Press, a financial printer. Among documents that petitioner handled were five announcements of corporate takeover bids. When these documents were delivered to the printer, the identities of the acquiring and target corporations were concealed by blank spaces or false names. The true names were sent to the printer on the night of the final printing.

The petitioner, however, was able to deduce the names of the target companies before the final printing from other information contained in the documents. Without disclosing his knowledge, petitioner purchased stock in the target companies and sold the shares immediately after the takeover attempts were made public. By this method, petitioner realized a gain of slightly more than $30,000 in the course of 14 months. Subsequently, the Securities and Exchange Commission (Commission or SEC) began an investigation of his trading activities. In May 1977, petitioner entered into a consent decree with the Commission in which he agreed to return his profits to the sellers of the shares. On the same day, he was discharged by Pandick Press.

In January 1978, petitioner was indicted on 17 counts of violating § 10(b) of the Securities Exchange Act of 1934 (1934 Act) and SEC Rule 10b–5. After petitioner unsuccessfully moved to dismiss the indictment, he was brought to trial and convicted on all counts.

The Court of Appeals for the Second Circuit affirmed petitioner's conviction. 588 F.2d 1358 (1978). We granted certiorari, 441 U.S. 942 (1979), and we now reverse.

II . . .

This case concerns the legal effect of the petitioner's silence. The District Court's charge permitted the jury to convict the petitioner if it found that he willfully failed to inform sellers of target company securities that he knew of a forthcoming takeover bid that would make their shares more valuable. In order to decide whether silence in such circumstances violates § 10(b), it is necessary to review the language and legislative history of that statute as well as its interpretation by the Commission and the federal courts.

Although the starting point of our inquiry is the language of the statute, *Ernst & Ernst v. Hochfelder,* 425 U.S. 185, 197 (1976), § 10(b) does not state whether silence may constitute a manipulative or deceptive device. Section 10(b) was designed as a catchall clause to prevent fraudulent practices. 425 U.S., at 202, 206. But neither the legislative history nor the statute itself affords specific guidance for the resolution of this case. When Rule 10b–5 was promulgated in 1942, the SEC did not discuss the possibility that failure to provide information might run afoul of § 10(b).

The SEC took an important step in the development of § 10(b) when it held that a broker-dealer and his firm violated that section by selling securities on the basis of undisclosed information obtained from a director of the issuer corporation who was also a registered representative of the brokerage firm. In *Cady, Roberts & Co.,* 40 S.E.C. 907 (1961), the Commission decided that a corporate insider must abstain from trading in the shares of his corporation unless he has first disclosed all material inside information known to him. The obligation to disclose or abstain derives from

> "[a]n affirmative duty to disclose material information[, which] has been traditionally imposed on corporate 'insiders,' particularly officers, directors, or controlling stockholders. We, and the courts have consistently held that insiders must disclose material facts which are known to them by virtue of their position but

which are not known to persons with whom they deal and which, if known, would affect their investment judgment." *Id.,* at 911.

The Commission emphasized that the duty arose from (i) the existence of a relationship affording access to inside information intended to be available only for a corporate purpose, and (ii) the unfairness of allowing a corporate insider to take advantage of that information by trading without disclosure. *Id.,* at 912, and n. 15.[8]

That the relationship between a corporate insider and the stockholders of his corporation gives rise to a disclosure obligation is not a novel twist of the law. At common law, misrepresentation made for the purpose of inducing reliance upon the false statement is fraudulent. But one who fails to disclose material information prior to the consummation of a transaction commits fraud only when he is under a duty to do so. And the duty to disclose arises when one party has information "that the other [party] is entitled to know because of a fiduciary or other similar relation of trust and confidence between them."[9] In its *Cady, Roberts* decision, the Commission recognized a relationship of trust and confidence between the shareholders of a corporation and those insiders who have obtained confidential information by reason of their position with that corporation.[10] This relationship gives rise to a duty to disclose because of the "necessity of preventing a corporate insider from . . . tak[ing] unfair advantage of the uninformed minority stockholders." *Speed v. Transamerica Corp.,* 99 F.Supp. 808, 829 (Del.1951).

The federal courts have found violations of § 10(b) where corporate insiders used undisclosed information for their own benefit. *E.g., SEC v. Texas Gulf Sulphur Co.,* 401 F.2d 833 (CA2 1968), cert. denied, 404 U.S. 1005 (1971). The cases also have emphasized, in accordance with the common-law rule, that "[t]he party charged with failing to disclose market information must be under a duty to disclose it." *Frigitemp Corp. v. Financial Dynamics Fund, Inc.,* 524 F.2d 275, 282 (CA2 1975). Accordingly, a purchaser of stock who has no duty to a prospective seller because he is neither an insider nor a fiduciary has been held to have no obligation to reveal material facts. See

---

8. In *Cady, Roberts,* the broker-dealer was liable under § 10(b) because it received nonpublic information from a corporate insider of the issuer. Since the insider could not use the information, neither could the partners in the brokerage firm with which he was associated. The transaction in *Cady, Roberts* involved sale of stock to persons who previously may not have been shareholders in the corporation. 40 S.E.C., at 913, and n. 21. The Commission embraced the reasoning of Judge Learned Hand that "the director or officer assumed a fiduciary relation to the buyer by the very sale; for it would be a sorry distinction to allow him to use the advantage of his position to induce the buyer into the position of a beneficiary although he was forbidden to do so once the buyer had become one." *Id.,* at 914, n. 23, quoting

Gratz v. Claughton, 187 F.2d 46, 49 (CA2), cert. denied, 341 U.S. 920 (1951).

9. Restatement (Second) of Torts § 551(2)(a) (1976). See James & Gray, Misrepresentation—Part II, 37 Md.L.Rev. 488, 523–527 (1978). As regards securities transactions, the American Law Institute recognizes that "silence when there is a duty to . . . speak may be a fraudulent act." ALI, Federal Securities Code § 262(b) (Prop.Off.Draft 1978).

10. See 3 W. Fletcher, Cyclopedia of the Law of Private Corporations § 838 (rev. 1975); 3A *id.,* §§ 1168.2, 1171, 1174; 3 L. Loss, Securities Regulation 1446–1448 (2d ed. 1961); 6 *id.,* at 3557–3558 (1969 Supp.). See also *Brophy v. Cities Service Co.,* 31 Del.Ch. 241, 70 A.2d 5 (1949). . . .

General Time Corp. v. Talley Industries, Inc., 403 F.2d 159, 164 (CA2 1968), cert. denied, 393 U.S. 1026 (1969). . . .

Thus, administrative and judicial interpretations have established that silence in connection with the purchase or sale of securities may operate as a fraud actionable under § 10(b) despite the absence of statutory language or legislative history specifically addressing the legality of nondisclosure. But such liability is premised upon a duty to disclose arising from a relationship of trust and confidence between parties to a transaction. Application of a duty to disclose prior to trading guarantees that corporate insiders, who have an obligation to place the shareholder's welfare before their own, will not benefit personally through fraudulent use of material, nonpublic information.[12]

III

In this case, the petitioner was convicted of violating § 10(b) although he was not a corporate insider and he received no confidential information from the target company. Moreover, the "market information" upon which he relied did not concern the earning power or operations of the target company, but only the plans of the acquiring company. Petitioner's use of that information was not a fraud under § 10(b) unless he was subject to an affirmative duty to disclose it before trading. In this case, the jury instructions failed to specify any such duty. In effect, the trial court instructed the jury that petitioner owed a duty to everyone; to all sellers, indeed, to the market as a whole. The jury simply was told to decide whether petitioner used material, nonpublic information at a time when "he knew other people trading in the securities market did not have access to the same information." Record 677.

The Court of Appeals affirmed the conviction by holding that "[*a*]*nyone*—corporate insider or not—who regularly receives material nonpublic information may not use that information to trade in securities without incurring an affirmative duty to disclose." 588 F.2d, at 1365 (emphasis in original). Although the court said that its test would include only persons who regularly receive material, nonpublic information, *id.,* at 1366, its rationale for that limitation is unrelated to the existence of a duty to disclose.[14] The Court of

---

12. "Tippees" of corporate insiders have been held liable under § 10(b) because they have a duty not to profit from the use of inside information that they know is confidential and know or should know came from a corporate insider, *Shapiro v. Merrill Lynch, Pierce, Fenner & Smith, Inc.,* 495 F.2d 228, 237–238 (CA2 1974). The tippee's obligation has been viewed as arising from his role as a participant after the fact in the insider's breach of a fiduciary duty. . . .

14. The Court of Appeals said that its "regular access to market information" test would create a workable rule embrac-

ing "those who occupy . . . strategic places in the market mechanism." 588 F.2d, at 1365. These considerations are insufficient to support a duty to disclose. A duty arises from the relationship between parties, see nn. 9 and 10, *supra,* and accompanying text, and not merely from one's ability to acquire information because of his position in the market.

The Court of Appeals also suggested that the acquiring corporation itself would not be a "market insider" because a tender offeror creates, rather than receives, information and takes a substantial economic risk that its offer will be unsuccessful. 588

Appeals, like the trial court, failed to identify a relationship between petitioner and the sellers that could give rise to a duty. Its decision thus rested solely upon its belief that the federal securities laws have "created a system providing equal access to information necessary for reasoned and intelligent investment decisions." *Id.,* at 1362. The use by anyone of material information not generally available is fraudulent, this theory suggests, because such information gives certain buyers or sellers an unfair advantage over less informed buyers and sellers.

This reasoning suffers from two defects. First, not every instance of financial unfairness constitutes fraudulent activity under § 10(b). See *Santa Fe Industries, Inc. v. Green,* 430 U.S. 462, 474–477 (1977). Second, the element required to make silence fraudulent—a duty to disclose—is absent in this case. No duty could arise from petitioner's relationship with the sellers of the target company's securities, for petitioner had no prior dealings with them. He was not their agent, he was not a fiduciary, he was not a person in whom the sellers had placed their trust and confidence. He was, in fact, a complete stranger who dealt with the sellers only through impersonal market transactions.

We cannot affirm petitioner's conviction without recognizing a general duty between all participants in market transactions to forgo actions based on material, nonpublic information. Formulation of such a broad duty, which departs radically from the established doctrine that duty arises from a specific relationship between two parties, see n. 9, *supra,* should not be undertaken absent some explicit evidence of congressional intent.

As we have seen, no such evidence emerges from the language or legislative history of § 10(b). Moreover, neither the Congress nor the Commission ever has adopted a parity-of-information rule. Instead the problems caused by misuse of market information have been addressed by detailed and sophisticated regulation that recognizes when use of market information may not harm operation of the securities markets. For example, the Williams Act [15] limits but does not completely prohibit a tender offeror's purchases of target corporation stock before public announcement of the offer. Congress' careful action in this and other areas contrasts, and is in some tension, with the broad rule of liability we are asked to adopt in this case.

F.2d at 1366–1367. Again, the Court of Appeals departed from the analysis appropriate to recognition of a duty. The Court of Appeals for the Second Circuit previously held, in a manner consistent with our analysis here, that a tender offeror does not violate § 10(b) when it makes preannouncement purchases precisely because there is no relationship between the offeror and the seller:

"We know of no rule of law . . . that a purchaser of stock, who was not an 'insider' and had no fiduciary relation to a prospective seller, had any obligation to reveal circumstances that might raise a seller's demands and thus abort the sale." *General Time Corp. v. Talley Industries, Inc.,* 403 F.2d 159, 164 (1968), cert. denied, 393 U.S. 1026 (1969).

15. Title 15 U.S.C. § 78m(d)(1) (1976 ed., Supp. II) permits a tender offeror to purchase 5% of the target company's stock prior to disclosure of its plan for acquisition.

Indeed, the theory upon which the petitioner was convicted is at odds with the Commission's view of § 10(b) as applied to activity that has the same effect on sellers as the petitioner's purchases. "Warehousing" takes place when a corporation gives advance notice of its intention to launch a tender offer to institutional investors who then are able to purchase stock in the target company before the tender offer is made public and the price of shares rises. In this case, as in warehousing, a buyer of securities purchases stock in a target corporation on the basis of market information which is unknown to the seller. In both of these situations, the seller's behavior presumably would be altered if he had the nonpublic information. Significantly, however, the Commission has acted to bar warehousing under its authority to regulate tender offers after recognizing that action under § 10(b) would rest on a "somewhat different theory" than that previously used to regulate insider trading as fraudulent activity.

We see no basis for applying such a new and different theory of liability in this case. As we have emphasized before, the 1934 Act cannot be read " 'more broadly than its language and the statutory scheme reasonably permit.' " *Touche Ross & Co. v. Redington,* 442 U.S. 560, 578 (1979), quoting *SEC v. Sloan,* 436 U.S. 103, 116 (1978). Section 10(b) is aptly described as a catchall provision, but what it catches must be fraud. When an allegation of fraud is based upon nondisclosure, there can be no fraud absent a duty to speak. We hold that a duty to disclose under § 10(b) does not arise from the mere possession of nonpublic market information. The contrary result is without support in the legislative history of § 10(b) and would be inconsistent with the careful plan that Congress has enacted for regulation of the securities markets. Cf. *Santa Fe Industries, Inc. v. Green,* 430 U.S., at 479.[20]

IV

In its brief to this Court, the United States offers an alternative theory to support petitioner's conviction. It argues that petitioner breached a duty to the acquiring corporation when he acted upon information that he obtained by virtue of his position as an employee of a printer employed by the corporation. The breach of this duty is said to support a conviction under § 10(b) for fraud perpetrated upon both the acquiring corporation and the sellers.

We need not decide whether this theory has merit for it was not submitted to the jury. . . .

The jury instructions demonstrate that petitioner was convicted merely because of his failure to disclose material, nonpublic information to sellers from whom he bought the stock of target corporations. The jury was not instructed on the nature or elements of a duty owed by petitioner to anyone other than the sellers. Because we cannot

---

20. . . . It is worth noting that this is apparently the first case in which criminal liability has been imposed upon a purchaser for § 10(b) nondisclosure. Petitioner was sentenced to a year in prison, suspended except for one month, and a 5–year term of probation. 588 F.2d, at 1373, 1378 (Meskill, J., dissenting).

affirm a criminal conviction on the basis of a theory not presented to the jury, *Rewis v. United States,* 401 U.S. 808, 814 (1971), see *Dunn v. United States,* 442 U.S. 100, 106 (1979), we will not speculate upon whether such a duty exists, whether it has been breached, or whether such a breach constitutes a violation of § 10(b).

The judgment of the Court of Appeals is

Reversed.

Mr. Justice STEVENS, concurring.

Before liability, civil or criminal, may be imposed for a Rule 10b–5 violation, it is necessary to identify the duty that the defendant has breached. Arguably, when petitioner bought securities in the open market, he violated (a) a duty to disclose owed to the sellers from whom he purchased target company stock and (b) a duty of silence owed to the acquiring companies. I agree with the Court's determination that petitioner owed no duty of disclosure to the sellers, that his conviction rested on the erroneous premise that he did owe them such a duty, and that the judgment of the Court of Appeals must therefore be reversed.

The Court correctly does not address the second question: whether the petitioner's breach of his duty of silence—a duty he unquestionably owed to his employer and to his employer's customers—could give rise to criminal liability under Rule 10b–5. Respectable arguments could be made in support of either position. On the one hand, if we assume that petitioner breached a duty to the acquiring companies that had entrusted confidential information to his employers, a legitimate argument could be made that his actions constituted "a fraud or a deceit" upon those companies "in connection with the purchase or sale of any security." On the other hand, inasmuch as those companies would not be able to recover damages from petitioner for violating Rule 10b–5 because they were neither purchasers nor sellers of target company securities, see *Blue Chip Stamps v. Manor Drug Stores,* 421 U.S. 723, it could also be argued that no actionable violation of Rule 10b–5 had occurred. I think the Court wisely leaves the resolution of this issue for another day.

I write simply to emphasize the fact that we have not necessarily placed any stamp of approval on what this petitioner did, nor have we held that similar actions must be considered lawful in the future. Rather, we have merely held that petitioner's criminal conviction cannot rest on the theory that he breached a duty he did not owe.

I join the Court's opinion.

Mr. Justice BRENNAN, concurring in the judgment.

The Court holds, correctly in my view, that "a duty to disclose under § 10(b) does not arise from the mere possession of nonpublic market information." . . . Prior to so holding, however, it suggests that no violation of § 10(b) could be made out absent a breach of some duty arising out of a fiduciary relationship between buyer and seller. I cannot subscribe to that suggestion. On the contrary, it seems to me that Part I of THE CHIEF JUSTICE's dissent . . .

correctly states the applicable substantive law—a person violates § 10(b) whenever he improperly obtains or converts to his own benefit nonpublic information which he then uses in connection with the purchase or sale of securities.

While I agree with Part I of THE CHIEF JUSTICE's dissent, I am unable to agree with Part II. Rather, I concur in the judgment of the majority because I think it clear that the legal theory sketched by THE CHIEF JUSTICE is not the one presented to the jury. As I read them, the instructions in effect permitted the jurors to return a verdict of guilty merely upon a finding of failure to disclose material, nonpublic information in connection with the purchase of stock. I can find no instruction suggesting that one element of the offense was the improper conversion or misappropriation of that nonpublic information. . . .

Mr. Chief Justice BURGER, dissenting.

I believe that the jury instructions in this case properly charged a violation of § 10(b) and Rule 10b–5, and I would affirm the conviction.

I

As a general rule, neither party to an arm's-length business transaction has an obligation to disclose information to the other unless the parties stand in some confidential or fiduciary relation. See W. Prosser, Law of Torts § 106 (2d ed. 1955). This rule permits a businessman to capitalize on his experience and skill in securing and evaluating relevant information; it provides incentive for hard work, careful analysis, and astute forecasting. But the policies that underlie the rule also should limit its scope. In particular, the rule should give way when an informational advantage is obtained, not by superior experience, foresight, or industry, but by some unlawful means. One commentator has written:

> "[T]he way in which the buyer acquires the information which he conceals from the vendor should be a material circumstance. The information might have been acquired as the result of his bringing to bear a superior knowledge, intelligence, skill or technical judgment; it might have been acquired by mere chance; or it might have been acquired by means of some tortious action on his part. . . . *Any time information is acquired by an illegal act it would seem that there should be a duty to disclose that information.*"
> Keeton, Fraud—Concealment and Non–Disclosure, 15 Texas L.Rev. 1, 25–26 (1936) (emphasis added).

I would read § 10(b) and Rule 10b–5 to encompass and build on this principle: to mean that a person who has misappropriated nonpublic information has an absolute duty to disclose that information or to refrain from trading.

The language of § 10(b) and of Rule 10b–5 plainly supports such a reading. By their terms, these provisions reach *any* person engaged in *any* fraudulent scheme. This broad language negates the suggestion that congressional concern was limited to trading by "corporate insiders" or to deceptive practices related to "corporate information." [1] Just as surely Congress cannot have intended one standard of fair dealing for "white collar" insiders and another for the "blue collar" level. The very language of § 10(b) and Rule 10b–5 "by repeated use of the word 'any' [was] obviously meant to be inclusive." *Affiliated Ute Citizens v. United States*, 406 U.S. 128, 151 (1972).

The history of the statute and of the Rule also supports this reading. The antifraud provisions were designed in large measure "to assure that dealing in securities is fair and without undue preferences or advantages among investors." H.R.Conf.Rep. No. 94–229, p. 91 (1975). These provisions prohibit "those manipulative and deceptive practices which have been demonstrated to fulfill no useful function." S.Rep. No. 792, 73d Cong., 2d Sess., 6 (1934). An investor who purchases securities on the basis of misappropriated nonpublic information possesses just such an "undue" trading advantage; his conduct quite clearly serves no useful function except his own enrichment at the expense of others.

This interpretation of § 10(b) and Rule 10b–5 is in no sense novel. It follows naturally from legal principles enunciated by the Securities and Exchange Commission in its seminal *Cady, Roberts* decision. 40 S.E.C. 907 (1961). There, the Commission relied upon two factors to impose a duty to disclose on corporate insiders: (1) ". . . access . . . to information intended to be available only for a corporate purpose *and not for the personal benefit of anyone*" (emphasis added); and (2) the unfairness inherent in trading on such information when it is inaccessible to those with whom one is dealing. Both of these factors are present whenever a party gains an informational advantage by unlawful means. Indeed, in *In re Blyth & Co.*, 43 S.E.C. 1037 (1969), the Commission applied its *Cady, Roberts* decision in just such a context. In that case a broker-dealer had traded in Government securities on the basis of confidential Treasury Department information which it received from a Federal Reserve Bank employee. The Commission ruled that the trading was "improper use of inside information" in violation of § 10(b) and Rule 10b–5. 43 S.E.C., at 1040. It did not hesitate to extend *Cady, Roberts* to reach a "tippee" of a Government insider.

Finally, it bears emphasis that this reading of § 10b and Rule 10b–5 would not threaten legitimate business practices. So read, the antifraud provisions would not impose a duty on a tender offeror to disclose its acquisition plans during the period in which it "tests the water" prior to purchasing a full 5% of the target company's stock. Nor would it proscribe "warehousing." See generally SEC, Institu-

---

1. Academic writing in recent years has distinguished between "corporate information"—information which comes from within the corporation and reflects on expected earnings or assets—and "market information." See, *e.g.*, Fleischer, Mundheim, & Murphy, An Initial Inquiry into the Responsibility to Disclose Market Information, 121 U.Pa.L.Rev. 798, 799 (1973). It is clear that § 10(b) and Rule 10b–5 by their terms and by their history make no such distinction. See Brudney, Insiders, Outsiders, and Informational Advantages Under the Federal Securities Laws, 93 Harv.L.Rev. 322, 329–333 (1979).

tional Investor Study Report, H.R.Doc. No. 92-64, pt. 4, p. 2273 (1971). Likewise, market specialists would not be subject to a disclose-or-refrain requirement in the performance of their everyday market functions. In each of these instances, trading is accomplished on the basis of material, nonpublic information, but the information has not been unlawfully converted for personal gain.

II

The Court's opinion, as I read it, leaves open the question whether § 10(b) and Rule 10b-5 prohibit trading on misappropriated nonpublic information.[4] Instead, the Court apparently concludes that this theory of the case was not submitted to the jury. In the Court's view, the instructions given the jury were premised on the erroneous notion that the mere failure to disclose nonpublic information, however acquired, is a deceptive practice. . . .

The Court's reading of the District Court's charge is unduly restrictive. Fairly read as a whole and in the context of the trial, the instructions required the jury to find that Chiarella obtained his trading advantage by misappropriating the property of his employer's customers. . . .

In sum, the evidence shows beyond all doubt that Chiarella, working literally in the shadows of the warning signs in the printshop, misappropriated—stole to put it bluntly—valuable nonpublic information entrusted to him in the utmost confidence. He then exploited his ill-gotten informational advantage by purchasing securities in the market. In my view, such conduct plainly violates § 10(b) and Rule 10b-5. Accordingly, I would affirm the judgment of the Court of Appeals.

Mr. Justice BLACKMUN, with whom Mr. Justice MARSHALL joins, dissenting.

Although I agree with much of what is said in Part I of the dissenting opinion of THE CHIEF JUSTICE, . . . I write separately because, in my view, it is unnecessary to rest petitioner's conviction on a "misappropriation" theory. The fact that petitioner Chiarella purloined, or, to use THE CHIEF JUSTICE's word, . . . "stole," information concerning pending tender offers certainly is the most dramatic evidence that petitioner was guilty of fraud. He has conceded that he knew it was wrong, and he and his co-workers in the printshop were specifically warned by their employer that actions of this kind were improper and forbidden. But I also would find petitioner's conduct fraudulent within the meaning of § 10(b) of the Securities Exchange Act of 1934, 15 U.S.C. § 78j(b), and the Securities and Exchange Commission's Rule 10b-5, 17 CFR § 240.10b-5

4. There is some language in the Court's opinion to suggest that only "a relationship between petitioner and the sellers . . . could give rise to a duty [to disclose]." . . . The Court's holding, however, is much more limited, namely, that mere possession of material, nonpublic information is insufficient to create a duty to disclose or to refrain from trading. . . . Accordingly, it is my understanding that the Court has not rejected the view, advanced above, that an absolute duty to disclose or refrain arises from the very act of misappropriating nonpublic information.

(1979), even if he had obtained the blessing of his employer's principals before embarking on his profiteering scheme. Indeed, I think petitioner's brand of manipulative trading, with or without such approval, lies close to the heart of what the securities laws are intended to prohibit.

The Court continues to pursue a course, charted in certain recent decisions, designed to transform § 10(b) from an intentionally elastic "catchall" provision to one that catches relatively little of the misbehavior that all too often makes investment in securities a needlessly risky business for the uninitiated investor. See, *e.g., Ernst & Ernst v. Hochfelder,* 425 U.S. 185 (1976); *Blue Chip Stamps v. Manor Drug Stores,* 421 U.S. 723 (1975). Such confinement in this case is now achieved by imposition of a requirement of a "special relationship" akin to fiduciary duty before the statute gives rise to a duty to disclose or to abstain from trading upon material, nonpublic information.[1] The Court admits that this conclusion finds no mandate in the language of the statute or its legislative history. . . . Yet the Court fails even to attempt a justification of its ruling in terms of the purposes of the securities laws, or to square that ruling with the longstanding but now much abused principle that the federal securities laws are to be construed flexibly rather than with narrow technicality. . . .

I, of course, agree with the Court that a relationship of trust can establish a duty to disclose under § 10(b) and Rule 10b–5. But I do not agree that a failure to disclose violates the Rule only when the responsibilities of a relationship of that kind have been breached. As applied to this case, the Court's approach unduly minimizes the importance of petitioner's *access* to confidential information that the honest investor, no matter how diligently he tried, could not legally obtain. In doing so, it further advances an interpretation of § 10(b) and Rule 10b–5 that stops short of their full implications. Although the Court draws support for its position from certain precedent, I find its decision neither fully consistent with developments in the common law of fraud, nor fully in step with administrative and judicial application of Rule 10b–5 to "insider" trading. . . .

By its narrow construction of § 10(b) and Rule 10b–5, the Court places the federal securities laws in the rearguard of this movement, a position opposite to the expectations of Congress at the time the securities laws were enacted. Cf. H.R.Rep. No. 1383, 73d Cong., 2d Sess., 5 (1934). I cannot agree that the statute and Rule are so limited. The Court has observed that the securities laws were not intended to replicate the law of fiduciary relations. *Santa Fe Industries, Inc. v. Green,* 430 U.S. 462, 474–476 (1977). Rather, their purpose is to ensure the fair and honest functioning of impersonal national securities markets where common-law protections have proved inade-

---

1. The Court fails to specify whether the obligations of a special relationship must fall directly upon the person engaging in an allegedly fraudulent transaction, or whether the derivative obligations of "tippees," that lower courts long have recognized, are encompassed by its rule. See *ante* . . . n. 12; cf. *Foremost–McKesson, Inc. v. Provident Securities Co.,* 423 U.S. 232, 255, n. 29 (1976).

quate. Cf. *United States v. Naftalin,* 441 U.S. 768, 775 (1979). As Congress itself has recognized, it is integral to this purpose "to assure that dealing in securities is fair and without undue preferences or advantages among investors." H.R.Conf.Rep. No. 94–229, p. 91 (1975). . . .

. . . I would hold that persons having access to confidential material information that is not legally available to others generally are prohibited by Rule 10b–5 from engaging in schemes to exploit their structural informational advantage through trading in affected securities. To hold otherwise, it seems to me, is to tolerate a wide range of manipulative and deceitful behavior. See *Blyth & Co.,* 43 S.E.C. 1037 (1969); *Herbert L. Honohan,* 13 S.E.C. 754 (1943); see generally Brudney, Insiders, Outsiders, and Informational Advantages under the Federal Securities Laws, 93 Harv.L.Rev. 322 (1979).

Whatever the outer limits of the Rule, petitioner Chiarella's case fits neatly near the center of its analytical framework. He occupied a relationship to the takeover companies giving him intimate access to concededly material information that was sedulously guarded from public access. The information, in the words of *Cady, Roberts & Co.,* 40 S.E.C., at 912, was "intended to be available only for a corporate purpose and not for the personal benefit of anyone." Petitioner, moreover, knew that the information was unavailable to those with whom he dealt. And he took full, virtually riskless advantage of this artificial information gap by selling the stocks shortly after each takeover bid was announced. By any reasonable definition, his trading was "inherent[ly] unfai[r]." *Ibid.* This misuse of confidential information was clearly placed before the jury. Petitioner's conviction, therefore, should be upheld, and I dissent from the Court's upsetting that conviction.

SECURITIES EXCHANGE ACT § 14(e) and RULE 14(e)(3)

[See Statutory Supplement]

DIRKS v. SECURITIES AND EXCHANGE COMMISSION

Supreme Court of the United States, 1983.
463 U.S. 646, 103 S.Ct. 3255, 77 L.Ed.2d 911.

Justice POWELL delivered the opinion of the Court.

Petitioner Raymond Dirks received material nonpublic information from "insiders" of a corporation with which he had no connection. He disclosed this information to investors who relied on it in trading in the shares of the corporation. The question is whether Dirks violated the antifraud provisions of the federal securities laws by this disclosure.

I

In 1973, Dirks was an officer of a New York broker-dealer firm who specialized in providing investment analysis of insurance company securities to institutional investors.[1] On March 6, Dirks received information from Ronald Secrist, a former officer of Equity Funding of America. Secrist alleged that the assets of Equity Funding, a diversified corporation primarily engaged in selling life insurance and mutual funds, were vastly overstated as the result of fraudulent corporate practices. Secrist also stated that various regulatory agencies had failed to act on similar charges made by Equity Funding employees. He urged Dirks to verify the fraud and disclose it publicly.

Dirks decided to investigate the allegations. He visited Equity Funding's headquarters in Los Angeles and interviewed several officers and employees of the corporation. The senior management denied any wrongdoing, but certain corporation employees corroborated the charges of fraud. Neither Dirks nor his firm owned or traded any Equity Funding stock, but throughout his investigation he openly discussed the information he had obtained with a number of clients and investors. Some of these persons sold their holdings of Equity Funding securities, including five investment advisers who liquidated holdings of more than $16 million.[2]

While Dirks was in Los Angeles, he was in touch regularly with William Blundell, the Wall Street Journal's Los Angeles bureau chief. Dirks urged Blundell to write a story on the fraud allegations. Blundell did not believe, however, that such a massive fraud could go undetected and declined to write the story. He feared that publishing such damaging hearsay might be libelous.

During the two-week period in which Dirks pursued his investigation and spread word of Secrist's charges, the price of Equity Funding stock fell from $26 per share to less than $15 per share. This led the New York Stock Exchange to halt trading on March 27. Shortly thereafter California insurance authorities impounded Equity Funding's records and uncovered evidence of the fraud. Only then did the Securities and Exchange Commission (SEC) file a complaint against Equity Funding[3] and only then, on April 2, did the Wall Street

---

1. The facts stated here are taken from more detailed statements set forth by the Administrative Law Judge, App. 176–180, 225–247; the opinion of the Securities and Exchange Commission, 21 S.E.C. Docket 1401, 1402–1406 (1981); and the opinion of Judge Wright in the Court of Appeals, 220 U.S.App.D.C. 309 314–318, 681 F.2d 824, 829–833 (1982).

2. Dirks received from his firm a salary plus a commission for securities transactions above a certain amount that his clients directed through his firm. See 21 S.E.C. Docket, at 1402, n. 3. But "[i]t is not clear how many of those with whom Dirks

spoke promised to direct some brokerage business through [Dirks' firm] to compensate Dirks, or how many actually did so." 220 U.S.App.D.C., at 316, 681 F.2d, at 831. The Boston Company Institutional Investors, Inc., promised Dirks about $25,000 in commissions, but it is unclear whether Boston actually generated any brokerage business for his firm. See App. 199, 204–205; 21 S.E.C. Docket, at 1404, n. 10; 220 U.S. App.D.C., at 316, n. 5, 681 F.2d, at 831, n. 5.

3. As early as 1971, the SEC had received allegations of fraudulent accounting practices at Equity Funding. Moreover, on

Journal publish a front-page story based largely on information assembled by Dirks. Equity Funding immediately went into receivership.[4]

The SEC began an investigation into Dirks' role in the exposure of the fraud. After a hearing by an administrative law judge, the SEC found that Dirks had aided and abetted violations of § 17(a) of the Securities Act of 1933, 15 U.S.C. § 77q(a), § 10(b) of the Securities Exchange Act of 1934, 15 U.S.C. § 78j(b), and SEC Rule 10b–5, 17 CFR § 240.10b–5 (1982), by repeating the allegations of fraud to members of the investment community who later sold their Equity Funding stock. The SEC concluded: "Where 'tippees'—regardless of their motivation or occupation—come into possession of material 'information that they know is confidential and know or should know came from a corporate insider,' they must either publicly disclose that information or refrain from trading." 21 S.E.C. Docket 1401, 1407 (1981) (footnote omitted) (quoting Chiarella v. United States, 445 U.S. 222, 230 n. 12, 100 S.Ct. 1108, 1115 n. 12, 63 L.Ed.2d 348 (1980)). Recognizing, however, that Dirks "played an important role in bringing [Equity Funding's] massive fraud to light," 21 S.E.C. Docket, at 1412,[8] the SEC only censured him.[9]

Dirks sought review in the Court of Appeals for the District of Columbia Circuit. The court entered judgment against Dirks "for the reasons stated by the Commission in its opinion." App. to Pet. for Cert. C–2. Judge Wright, a member of the panel, subsequently issued an opinion. Judge Robb concurred in the result and Judge Tamm dissented; neither filed a separate opinion. Judge Wright believed that "the obligations of corporate fiduciaries pass to all those to whom they disclose their information before it has been disseminated to the public at large." 220 U.S.App.D.C. 309, 324, 681 F.2d 824, 839 (1982). Alternatively, Judge Wright concluded that, as an employee of a broker-dealer, Dirks had violated "obligations to the SEC and to the public completely independent of any obligations he acquired" as a result of receiving the information. Id., at 325, 681 F.2d, at 840.

March 9, 1973, an official of the California Insurance Department informed the SEC's regional office in Los Angeles of Secrist's charges of fraud. Dirks himself voluntarily presented his information at the SEC's regional office beginning on March 27.

4. A federal grand jury in Los Angeles subsequently returned a 105–count indictment against 22 persons, including many of Equity Funding's officers and directors. All defendants were found guilty of one or more counts, either by a plea of guilty or a conviction after trial. See Brief for Petitioner 15; App. 149–153.

8. Justice Blackmun's dissenting opinion minimizes the role Dirks played in making public the Equity Funding fraud. . . . The dissent would rewrite the history of Dirks' extensive investigative efforts. See, e.g., 21 S.E.C., at 1412 ("It is clear that Dirks played an important

role in bringing [Equity Funding's] massive fraud to light, and it is also true that he reported the fraud allegation to [Equity Funding's] auditors and sought to have the information published in the Wall Street Journal."); 681 F.2d, at 829 (Wright, J.) ("Largely thanks to Dirks one of the most infamous frauds in recent memory was uncovered and exposed, while the record shows that the SEC repeatedly missed opportunities to investigate Equity Funding.").

9. Section 15 of the Securities Exchange Act, 15 U.S.C. § 78*o* (b)(4)(E), provides that the SEC may impose certain sanctions, including censure, on any person associated with a registered broker-dealer who has "willfully aided [or] abetted" any violation of the federal securities laws. See 15 U.S.C. § 78ff(a) (providing criminal penalties).

In view of the importance to the SEC and to the securities industry of the question presented by this case, we granted a writ of certiorari. 459 U.S. 1014, 103 S.Ct. 371, 74 L.Ed.2d 506 (1982). We now reverse.

II

In the seminal case of In re Cady, Roberts & Co., 40 S.E.C. 907 (1961), the SEC recognized that the common law in some jurisdictions imposes on "corporate 'insiders,' particularly officers, directors, or controlling stockholders" an "affirmative duty of disclosure . . . when dealing in securities." Id., at 911, and n. 13.[10] The SEC found that not only did breach of this common-law duty also establish the elements of a Rule 10b–5 violation,[11] but that individuals other than corporate insiders could be obligated either to disclose material nonpublic information [12] before trading or to abstain from trading altogether. Id., at 912. In *Chiarella,* we accepted the two elements set out in *Cady, Roberts* for establishing a Rule 10b–5 violation: "(i) the existence of a relationship affording access to inside information intended to be available only for a corporate purpose, and (ii) the unfairness of allowing a corporate insider to take advantage of that information by trading without disclosure." 445 U.S., at 227, 100 S.Ct. at 1114. In examining whether Chiarella had an obligation to disclose or abstain, the Court found that there is no general duty to disclose before trading on material nonpublic information,[13] and held that "a duty to disclose under § 10(b) does not arise from the mere possession of nonpublic market information." Id., at 235, 100 S.Ct., at 1118. Such a duty arises rather from the existence of a fiduciary relationship. See id., at 227–235, 100 S.Ct., at 1114–1118.

Not "all breaches of fiduciary duty in connection with a securities transaction," however, come within the ambit of Rule 10b–5. Santa

10. The duty that insiders owe to the corporation's shareholders not to trade on inside information differs from the common-law duty that officers and directors also have to the corporation itself not to mismanage corporate assets, of which confidential information is one. See 3 Fletcher Cyclopedia of the Laws of Private Corporations §§ 848, 900 (1975 ed. and Supp. 1982); 3A Fletcher §§ 1168.1, 1168.2. In holding that breaches of this duty to shareholders violated the Securities Exchange Act, the *Cady, Roberts* Commission recognized, and we agree, that "[a] significant purpose of the Exchange Act was to eliminate the idea that use of inside information for personal advantage was a normal emolument of corporate office." See 40 S.E.C., at 912, n. 15.

11. Rule 10b–5 is generally the most inclusive of the three provisions on which the SEC rested its decision in this case, and we will refer to it when we note the statutory basis for the SEC's inside-trading rules.

12. The SEC views the disclosure duty as requiring more than disclosure to purchasers or sellers: "Proper and adequate disclosure of significant corporate developments can only be effected by a public release through the appropriate public media, designed to achieve a broad dissemination to the investing public generally and without favoring any special person or group." In re Faberge, Inc., 45 S.E.C. 249, 256 (1973).

13. See 445 U.S., at 233, 100 S.Ct., at 1117; id., at 237, 100 S.Ct., at 1119 (Stevens, J., concurring); id., at 238–239, 100 S.Ct., at 1119–1120 (Brennan, J., concurring in the judgment); id., at 239–240, 100 S.Ct., at 1120 (Burger, C.J., dissenting). Cf. id., at 252, n. 2, 100 S.Ct., at 1126, n. 2 (Blackmun, J., dissenting) (recognizing that there is no obligation to disclose material nonpublic information obtained through the exercise of "diligence or acumen" and "honest means," as opposed to "stealth").

Fe Industries, Inc. v. Green, 430 U.S. 462, 472, 97 S.Ct. 1292, 1300, 51 L.Ed.2d 480 (1977). There must also be "manipulation or deception." Id., at 473, 97 S.Ct., at 1300. In an inside-trading case this fraud derives from the "inherent unfairness involved where one takes advantage" of "information intended to be available only for a corporate purpose and not for the personal benefit of anyone." In re Merrill Lynch, Pierce, Fenner & Smith, Inc., 43 S.E.C. 933, 936 (1968). Thus, an insider will be liable under Rule 10b-5 for inside trading only where he fails to disclose material nonpublic information before trading on it and thus makes "secret profits." *Cady, Roberts,* 40 S.E.C., at 916, n. 31.

III

We were explicit in *Chiarella* in saying that there can be no duty to disclose where the person who has traded on inside information "was not [the corporation's] agent, . . . was not a fiduciary, [or] was not a person in whom the sellers [of the securities] had placed their trust and confidence." 445 U.S., at 232, 100 S.Ct., at 1116. Not to require such a fiduciary relationship, we recognized, would "depar[t] radically from the established doctrine that duty arises from a specific relationship between two parties" and would amount to "recognizing a general duty between all participants in market transactions to forgo actions based on material, nonpublic information." Id., at 232, 233, 100 S.Ct., at 1116, 1117. This requirement of a specific relationship between the shareholders and the individual trading on inside information has created analytical difficulties for the SEC and courts in policing tippees who trade on inside information. Unlike insiders who have independent fiduciary duties to both the corporation and its shareholders, the typical tippee has no such relationships.[14] In view of this absence, it has been unclear how a tippee acquires the *Cady, Roberts* duty to refrain from trading on inside information.

A

The SEC's position, as stated in its opinion in this case, is that a tippee "inherits" the *Cady, Roberts* obligation to shareholders whenever he receives inside information from an insider:

14. Under certain circumstances, such as where corporate information is revealed legitimately to an underwriter, accountant, lawyer, or consultant working for the corporation, these outsiders may become fiduciaries of the shareholders. The basis for recognizing this fiduciary duty is not simply that such persons acquired nonpublic corporate information, but rather that they have entered into a special confidential relationship in the conduct of the business of the enterprise and are given access to information solely for corporate purposes. See SEC v. Monarch Fund, 608 F.2d 938, 942 (CA2 1979); In re Investors Management Co., 44 S.E.C. 633, 645 (1971); In re Van Alystne, Noel & Co., 43 S.E.C. 1080, 1084–1085 (1969); In re Merrill Lynch, Pierce, Fenner & Smith, Inc., 43 S.E.C. 933, 937 (1968); Cady, Roberts, 40 S.E.C., at 912. When such a person breaches his fiduciary relationship, he may be treated more properly as a tipper than a tippee. See Shapiro v. Merrill Lynch, Pierce, Fenner & Smith, Inc., 495 F.2d 228, 237 (CA2 1974) (investment banker had access to material information when working on a proposed public offering for the corporation). For such a duty to be imposed, however, the corporation must expect the outsider to keep the disclosed nonpublic information confidential, and the relationship at least must imply such a duty.

"In tipping potential traders, Dirks breached a duty which he had assumed as a result of knowingly receiving confidential information from [Equity Funding] insiders. Tippees such as Dirks who receive non-public material information from insiders become 'subject to the same duty as [the] insiders.' Shapiro v. Merrill Lynch, Pierce, Fenner & Smith, Inc. [495 F.2d 228, 237 (CA2 1974) (quoting Ross v. Licht, 263 F.Supp. 395, 410 (SDNY 1967))]. Such a tippee breaches the fiduciary duty which he assumes from the insider when the tippee knowingly transmits the information to someone who will probably trade on the basis thereof. . . . Presumably, Dirks' informants were entitled to disclose the [Equity Funding] fraud in order to bring it to light and its perpetrators to justice. However, Dirks—standing in their shoes—committed a breach of the fiduciary duty which he had assumed in dealing with them, when he passed the information on to traders." 21 S.E.C. Docket, at 1410, n. 42.

This view differs little from the view that we rejected as inconsistent with congressional intent in *Chiarella.* In that case, the Court of Appeals agreed with the SEC and affirmed Chiarella's conviction, holding that " '[*a*]*nyone* —corporate insider or not—who regularly receives material nonpublic information may not use that information to trade in securities without incurring an affirmative duty to disclose.' " United States v. Chiarella, 588 F.2d 1358, 1365 (CA2 1978) (emphasis in original). Here, the SEC maintains that anyone who knowingly receives nonpublic material information from an insider has a fiduciary duty to disclose before trading.[15]

In effect, the SEC's theory of tippee liability in both cases appears rooted in the idea that the antifraud provisions required equal information among all traders. This conflicts with the principle set forth in *Chiarella* that only some persons, under some circumstances, will be barred from trading while in possession of material nonpublic information.[16] Judge Wright correctly read our opinion in *Chiarella* as repudiating any notion that all traders must enjoy equal information

---

15. Apparently, the SEC believes this case differs from *Chiarella* in that Dirks' receipt of inside information from Secrist, an insider, carried Secrist's duties with it, while Chiarella received the information without the direct involvement of an insider and thus inherited no duty to disclose or abstain. The SEC fails to explain, however, why the receipt of nonpublic information from an insider automatically carries with it the fiduciary duty of the insider. As we emphasized in *Chiarella,* mere possession of nonpublic information does not give rise to a duty to disclose or abstain; only a specific relationship does that. And we do not believe that the mere receipt of information from an insider creates such a special relationship between the tippee and the corporation's shareholders.

Apparently recognizing the weakness of its argument in light of *Chiarella,* the SEC attempts to distinguish that case factually as involving not "inside" information, but rather "market" information, i.e., "information generated within the company relating to its assets or earnings." Brief for Respondent 23. This Court drew no such distinction in *Chiarella* and, as The Chief Justice noted, "[i]t is clear that § 10(b) and Rule 10b–5 by their terms and by their history make no such distinction." 445 U.S., at 241, n. 1 (dissenting opinion). See ALI Fed.Sec. Code § 1603, Comment (2)(j) (Proposed Official Draft 1978).

16. In *Chiarella,* we noted that formulation of an absolute equal information rule "should not be undertaken absent some explicit evidence of congressional intent." 445 U.S., at 233, 100 S.Ct., at 1117. . . .

before trading: "[T]he 'information' theory is rejected. Because the disclose-or-refrain duty is extraordinary, it attaches only when a party has legal obligations other than a mere duty to comply with the general antifraud proscriptions in the federal securities laws." 220 U.S.App.D.C., at 322, 681 F.2d at 837. See *Chiarella,* 445 U.S., at 235, n. 20, 100 S.Ct., at 1118, n. 20. We reaffirm today that "[a] duty [to disclose] arises from the relationship between parties . . . and not merely from one's ability to acquire information because of his position in the market." 445 U.S., at 232–233, n. 14, 100 S.Ct., at 1116–1117, n. 14.

Imposing a duty to disclose or abstain solely because a person knowingly receives material nonpublic information from an insider and trades on it could have an inhibiting influence on the role of market analysts, which the SEC itself recognizes is necessary to the preservation of a healthy market.[17] It is commonplace for analysts to "ferret out and analyze information," 21 S.E.C., at 1406,[18] and this often is done by meeting with and questioning corporate officers and others who are insiders. And information that the analysts obtain normally may be the basis for judgments as to the market worth of a corporation's securities. The analyst's judgment in this respect is made available in market letters or otherwise to clients of the firm. It is the nature of this type of information, and indeed of the markets themselves, that such information cannot be made simultaneously available to all of the corporation's stockholders or the public generally.

B

The conclusion that recipients of inside information do not invariably acquire a duty to disclose or abstain does not mean that such

17. The SEC expressly recognized that "[t]he value to the entire market of [analysts'] efforts cannot be gainsaid; market efficiency in pricing is significantly enhanced by [their] initiatives to ferret out and analyze information, and thus the analyst's work redounds to the benefit of all investors." 21 S.E.C., at 1406. The SEC asserts that analysts remain free to obtain from management corporate information for purposes of "filling in the 'interstices in analysis'. . . ." Brief for Respondent 42 (quoting *Investors Management Co.,* 44 S.E.C., at 646). But this rule is inherently imprecise, and imprecision prevents parties from ordering their actions in accord with legal requirements. Unless the parties have some guidance as to where the line is between permissible and impermissible disclosures and uses, neither corporate insiders nor analysts can be sure when the line is crossed. Cf. Adler v. Klawans, 267 F.2d 840, 845 (CA2 1959) (Burger, J., sitting by designation.)

18. On its facts, this case is the unusual one. Dirks is an analyst in a broker-dealer firm, and he did interview management in the course of his investigation. He uncovered, however, startling information that required no analysis or exercise of judgment as to its market relevance. Nonetheless, the principle at issue here extends beyond these facts. The SEC's rule—applicable without regard to any breach by an insider—could have serious ramifications on reporting by analysts of investment views.

Despite the unusualness of Dirks' "find," the central role that he played in uncovering the fraud at Equity Funding, and that analysts in general can play in revealing information that corporations may have reason to withhold from the public, is an important one. Dirks' careful investigation brought to light a massive fraud at the corporation. And until the Equity Funding fraud was exposed, the information in the trading market was grossly inaccurate. But for Dirks' efforts, the fraud might well have gone undetected longer. See n. 8, supra.

tippees always are free to trade on the information. The need for a ban on some tippee trading is clear. Not only are insiders forbidden by their fiduciary relationship from personally using undisclosed corporate information to their advantage, but they may not give such information to an outsider for the same improper purpose of exploiting the information for their personal gain. See 15 U.S.C. § 78t(b) (making it unlawful to do indirectly "by means of any other person" any act made unlawful by the federal securities laws). Similarly, the transactions of those who knowingly participate with the fiduciary in such a breach are "as forbidden" as transactions "on behalf of the trustee himself." Mosser v. Darrow, 341 U.S. 267, 272, 71 S.Ct. 680, 683, 95 L.Ed. 927 (1951). See Jackson v. Smith, 254 U.S. 586, 589, 41 S.Ct. 200, 202, 65 L.Ed. 418 (1921); Jackson v. Ludeling, 88 U.S. 616, 631–632, 22 L.Ed. 492 (1874). As the Court explained in *Mosser,* a contrary rule "would open up opportunities for devious dealings in the name of the others that the trustee could not conduct in his own." 341 U.S., at 271, 71 S.Ct., at 682. See SEC v. Texas Gulf Sulphur Co., 446 F.2d 1301, 1308 (CA2), cert. denied, 404 U.S. 1005, 92 S.Ct. 561, 30 L.Ed.2d 558 (1971). Thus, the tippee's duty to disclose or abstain is derivative from that of the insider's duty. See Tr. of Oral Arg. 38. Cf. *Chiarella,* 445 U.S., at 246, n. 1, 100 S.Ct., at 1122, n. 1 (Blackmun, J., dissenting). As we noted in *Chiarella,* "[t]he tippee's obligation has been viewed as arising from his role as a participant after the fact in the insider's breach of a fiduciary duty." 445 U.S., at 230, n. 12, 100 S.Ct., at 1115, n. 12.

Thus, some tippees must assume an insider's duty to the shareholders not because they receive inside information, but rather because it has been made available to them *improperly.*[19] And for Rule 10b–5 purposes, the insider's disclosure is improper only where it would violate his *Cady, Roberts* duty. Thus, a tippee assumes a fiduciary duty to the shareholders of a corporation not to trade on material nonpublic information only when the insider has breached his fiduciary duty to the shareholders by disclosing the information to the tippee and the tippee knows or should know that there has been a breach.[20] As Commissioner Smith perceptively observed in *Investors*

19. The SEC itself has recognized that tippee liability properly is imposed only in circumstances where the tippee knows, or has reason to know, that the insider has disclosed improperly inside corporate information. In *Investors Management Co.,* supra, the SEC stated that one element of tippee liability is that the tippee knew or had reason to know "that [the information] was non-public and had been obtained *improperly* by selective revelation or otherwise." 44 S.E.C., at 641 (emphasis added). Commissioner Smith read this test to mean that a tippee can be held liable only if he received information in breach of an insider's duty not to disclose it. Id., at 650 (concurring in the result).

20. Professor Loss has linked tippee liability to the concept in the law of restitu-

tion that " '[w]here a fiduciary in violation of his duty to the beneficiary communicates confidential information to a third person, the third person, if he had notice of the violation of duty, holds upon a constructive trust for the beneficiary any profit which he makes through the use of such information.' " 3 L. Loss, Securities Regulation 1451 (2d ed.1961) (quoting Restatement of Restitution § 201(2) (1937)). Other authorities likewise have expressed the view that tippee liability exists only where there has been a breach of trust by an insider of which the tippee had knowledge. See, e.g., Ross v. Licht, 263 F.Supp. 395, 410 (SDNY 1967); A. Jacobs, The Impact of Rule 10b–5, § 167, at 7–4 (1975) ("[T]he better view is that a tipper must know or have reason to know the information is

Management Co.: "[T]ippee responsibility must be related back to insider responsibility by a necessary finding that the tippee knew the information was given to him in breach of a duty by a person having a special relationship to the issuer not to disclose the information. . . ." 44 S.E.C., at 651 (concurring in the result). Tipping thus properly is viewed only as a means of indirectly violating the *Cady, Roberts* disclose-or-abstain rule.[21]

C

In determining whether a tippee is under an obligation to disclose or abstain, it thus is necessary to determine whether the insider's "tip" constituted a breach of the insider's fiduciary duty. All disclosures of confidential corporate information are not inconsistent with the duty insiders owe to shareholders. In contrast to the extraordinary facts of this case, the more typical situation in which there will be a question whether disclosure violates the insider's *Cady, Roberts* duty is when insiders disclose information to analysts. See n. 16, supra. In some situations, the insider will act consistently with his fiduciary duty to shareholders, and yet release of the information may affect the market. For example, it may not be clear—either to the corporate insider or to the recipient analyst—whether the information will be viewed as material nonpublic information. Corporate officials may mistakenly think the information already has been disclosed or that it is not material enough to affect the market. Whether disclosure is a breach of duty therefore depends in large part on the purpose of the disclosure. This standard was identified by the SEC itself in *Cady, Roberts* : a purpose of the securities laws was to eliminate "use of inside information for personal advantage." 40 S.E.C., at 912, n. 15. See n. 10, supra. Thus, the test is whether the insider personally will benefit, directly or indirectly, from his disclosure. Absent some personal gain, there has been no breach of duty to stockholders. And absent a breach by the insider, there is no derivative breach.[22] As

nonpublic and was improperly obtained."); Fleischer, Mundheim & Murphy, An Initial Inquiry Into the Responsibility to Disclose Market Information, 121 U.Pa.L.Rev. 798, 818, n. 76 (1973) ("The extension of rule 10b–5 restrictions to tippees of corporate insiders can best be justified on the theory that they are participating in the insider's breach of his fiduciary duty."). Cf. Restatement (Second) of Agency § 312, comment c (1958) ("A person who, with notice that an agent is thereby violating his duty to his principal, receives confidential information from the agent, may be [deemed] . . . a constructive trustee.").

21. We do not suggest that knowingly trading on inside information is ever "socially desirable or even that it is devoid of moral considerations." Dooley, Enforcement of Insider Trading Restrictions, 66 Va.L.Rev. 1, 55 (1980). Nor do we imply an absence of responsibility to disclose promptly indications of illegal actions by a

corporation to the proper authorities—typically the SEC and exchange authorities in cases involving securities. Depending on the circumstances, and even where permitted by law, one's trading of material nonpublic information is behavior that may fall below ethical standards of conduct. But in a statutory area of the law such as securities regulation, where legal principles of general application must be applied, there may be "significant distinctions between actual legal obligations and ethical ideals." SEC, Report of the Special Study of Securities Markets, H.R.Doc. No. 95, 88th Cong., 1st Sess., pt. 1, pp. 237–238 (1963). . . .

22. An example of a case turning on the court's determination that the disclosure did not impose any fiduciary duties on the recipient of the inside information is Walton v. Morgan Stanley & Co., 623 F.2d 796 (CA2 1980). There, the defendant investment banking firm, representing one of

Commissioner Smith stated in *Investors Management Co.* "It is important in this type of case to focus on policing insiders and what they do . . . rather than on policing information *per se* and its possession. . . ." 44 S.E.C., at 648 (concurring in the result).

The SEC argues that, if inside-trading liability does not exist when the information is transmitted for a proper purpose but is used for trading, it would be a rare situation when the parties could not fabricate some ostensibly legitimate business justification for transmitting the information. We think the SEC is unduly concerned. In determining whether the insider's purpose in making a particular disclosure is fraudulent, the SEC and the courts are not required to read the parties' minds. Scienter in some cases is relevant in determining whether the tipper has violated his *Cady, Roberts* duty.[23] But to determine whether the disclosure itself "deceive[s], manipulate[s], or defraud[s]" shareholders, Aaron v. SEC, 446 U.S. 680, 686, 100 S.Ct. 1945, 1950, 64 L.Ed.2d 611 (1980), the initial inquiry is whether there has been a breach of duty by the insider. This requires courts to focus on objective criteria, i.e., whether the insider receives a direct or indirect personal benefit from the disclosure, such as a pecuniary gain or a reputational benefit that will translate into future earnings. Cf. 40 S.E.C., at 912, n. 15; Brudney, Insiders, Outsiders, and Informational Advantages Under the Federal Securities Laws, 93 Harv.L.Rev. 324, 348 (1979) ("The theory . . . is that the insider, by giving the information out selectively, is in effect selling the information to its recipient for cash, reciprocal information, or other things of value for himself . . ."). There are objective facts and circumstances that often justify such an inference. For example, there may be a relationship between the insider and the recipient that suggests a *quid pro quo* from the latter, or an intention to benefit the particular recipient. The elements of fiduciary duty and exploitation of nonpublic information also exist when an insider makes a gift of confidential information to a trading relative or friend. The tip and

its own corporate clients, investigated another corporation that was a possible target of a takeover bid by its client. In the course of negotiations the investment banking firm was given, on a confidential basis, unpublished material information. Subsequently, after the proposed takeover was abandoned, the firm was charged with relying on the information when it traded in the target corporation's stock. For purposes of the decision, it was assumed that the firm knew the information was confidential, but that it had been received in arm's-length negotiations. See id., at 798. In the absence of any fiduciary relationship, the Court of Appeals found no basis for imposing tippee liability on the investment firm. See id., at 799.

23. *Scienter*—"a mental state embracing intent to deceive, manipulate, or defraud," Ernst & Ernst v. Hochfelder, 425 U.S. 185, 193, n. 12, 96 S.Ct. 1375, 1380, n. 12, 47 L.Ed.2d 668 (1976)—is an independent element of a Rule 10b–5 violation. See Aaron v. SEC, 446 U.S. 680, 695, 100 S.Ct. 1945, 1954, 64 L.Ed.2d 611 (1980). Contrary to the dissent's suggestion, see post, at . . . n. 10, motivation is not irrelevant to the issue of *scienter*. It is not enough that an insider's conduct results in harm to investors; rather, a violation may be found only where there is "intentional or willful conduct designed to deceive or defraud investors by controlling or artificially affecting the price of securities." *Ernst & Ernst v. Hochfelder,* supra, at 199, 100 S.Ct., at 1383. The issue in this case, however, is not whether Secrist or Dirks acted with *scienter,* but rather whether there was any deceptive or fraudulent conduct at all, i.e., whether Secrist's disclosure constituted a breach of his fiduciary duty and thereby caused injury to shareholders. See n. 27, infra. Only if there was such a breach did Dirks, a tippee, acquire a fiduciary duty to disclose or abstain.

trade resemble trading by the insider himself followed by a gift of the profits to the recipient.

Determining whether an insider personally benefits from a particular disclosure, a question of fact, will not always be easy for courts. But it is essential, we think, to have a guiding principle for those whose daily activities must be limited and instructed by the SEC's inside-trading rules, and we believe that there must be a breach of the insider's fiduciary duty before the tippee inherits the duty to disclose or abstain. In contrast, the rule adopted by the SEC in this case would have no limiting principle.[24]

IV

Under the inside-trading and tipping rules set forth above, we find that there was no actionable violation by Dirks.[25] It is undisputed that Dirks himself was a stranger to Equity Funding, with no pre-existing fiduciary duty to its shareholders. He took no action, directly or indirectly, that induced the shareholders or officers of Equity Funding to repose trust or confidence in him. There was no expectation by Dirks' sources that he would keep their information in confidence. Nor did Dirks misappropriate or illegally obtain the information about Equity Funding. Unless the insiders breached their *Cady, Roberts* duty to shareholders in disclosing the nonpublic information to Dirks, he breached no duty when he passed it on to investors as well as to the Wall Street Journal.

It is clear that neither Secrist nor the other Equity Funding employees violated their *Cady, Roberts* duty to the corporation's shareholders by providing information to Dirks.[27] The tippers received no

24. Without legal limitations, market participants are forced to rely on the reasonableness of the SEC's litigation strategy, but that can be hazardous, as the facts of this case make plain. Following the SEC's filing of the *Texas Gulf Sulphur* action, Commissioner (and later Chairman) Budge spoke of the various implications of applying Rule 10b–5 in inside-trading cases:

"Turning to the realm of possible defendants in the present and potential civil actions, the Commission certainly does not contemplate suing every person who may have come across inside information. In the Texas Gulf action neither tippees nor persons in the vast rank and file of employees have been named as defendants. In my view, the Commission in future cases normally should not join rank and file employees or persons outside the company *such as an analyst or reporter* who learns of inside information." Speech of Hamer Budge to the New York Regional Group of the American Society of Corporate Secretaries, Inc. (Nov. 18, 1965) (emphasis added), reprinted in Budge, The Texas Gulf Sulphur Case—What It Is and What It

Isn't, Corp. Secretary No. 127, at 6 (Dec. 17, 1965).

25. Dirks contends that he was not a "tippee" because the information he received constituted unverified allegations of fraud that were denied by management and were not "material facts" under the securities laws that required disclosure before trading. He also argues that the information he received was not truly "inside" information, i.e., intended for a confidential corporate purpose, but was merely evidence of a crime. The Solicitor General agrees. See Brief for United States as *Amicus Curiae* 22. We need not decide, however, whether the information constituted "material facts," or whether information concerning corporate crime is properly characterized as "inside information." For purposes of deciding this case, we assume the correctness of the SEC's findings, accepted by the Court of Appeals, that petitioner was a tippee of material inside information.

27. In this Court, the SEC appears to contend that an insider invariably violates a fiduciary duty to the corporation's shareholders by transmitting nonpublic corpo-

monetary or personal benefit for revealing Equity Funding's secrets, nor was their purpose to make a gift of valuable information to Dirks. As the facts of this case clearly indicate, the tippers were motivated by a desire to expose the fraud. . . . In the absence of a breach of duty to shareholders by the insiders, there was no derivative breach by Dirks. See n. 20, supra. Dirks therefore could not have been "a participant after the fact in [an] insider's breach of a fiduciary duty." *Chiarella,* 445 U.S., at 230, n. 12, 100 S.Ct., at 1115, n. 12.

V

We conclude that Dirks, in the circumstances of this case, had no duty to abstain from use of the inside information that he obtained. The judgment of the Court of Appeals therefore is reversed.

Justice BLACKMUN, with whom Justice BRENNAN and Justice MARSHALL join, dissenting.

The Court today takes still another step to limit the protections provided investors by § 10(b) of the Securities Exchange Act of 1934. . . . The device employed in this case engrafts a special motivational requirement on the fiduciary duty doctrine. This innovation excuses a knowing and intentional violation of an insider's duty to shareholders if the insider does not act from a motive of personal gain. Even on the extraordinary facts of this case, such an innovation is not justified.

I

As the Court recognizes, . . . the facts here are unusual. After a meeting with Ronald Secrist, a former Equity Funding employee, on March 7, 1973, App. 226, petitioner Raymond Dirks found himself in possession of material nonpublic information of massive fraud within

rate information to an outsider when he has reason to believe that the outsider may use it to the disadvantage of the shareholders. "Thus, regardless of any ultimate motive to bring to public attention the derelictions at Equity Funding, Secrist breached his duty to Equity Funding shareholders." Brief for Respondent 31. This perceived "duty" differs markedly from the one that the SEC identified in *Cady, Roberts* and that has been the basis for federal tippee-trading rules to date. In fact, the SEC did not charge Secrist with any wrongdoing, and we do not understand the SEC to have relied on any theory of a breach of duty by Secrist in finding that Dirks breached his duty to Equity Funding's shareholders. . . .

Moreover, to constitute a violation of Rule 10b–5, there must be fraud. See Ernst & Ernst v. Hochfelder, 425 U.S. 185, 199, 96 S.Ct. 1375, 1383, 47 L.Ed.2d 668 (1976) (statutory words "manipulative," "device," and "contrivance . . . connot[e] intentional or willful conduct designed to *deceive or defraud* investors by controlling or artificially affecting the price of securities") (emphasis added). There is no evidence that Secrist's disclosure was intended to or did in fact "deceive or defraud" anyone. Secrist certainly intended to convey relevant information that management was unlawfully concealing, and—so far as the record shows—he believed that persuading Dirks to investigate was the best way to disclose the fraud. Other efforts had proved fruitless. Under any objective standard, Secrist received no direct or indirect personal benefit from the disclosure.

. . . [T]here is little legal significance to the dissent's argument that Secrist and Dirks created new "victims" by disclosing the information to persons who traded. In fact, they prevented the fraud from continuing and victimizing many more investors.

the company.[2] In the Court's words, "[h]e uncovered . . . startling information that required no analysis or exercise of judgment as to its market relevance." . . . In disclosing that information to Dirks, Secrist intended that Dirks would disseminate the information to his clients, those clients would unload their Equity Funding securities on the market, and the price would fall precipitously, thereby triggering a reaction from the authorities. App. 16, 25, 27.

Dirks complied with his informant's wishes. Instead of reporting that information to the Securities and Exchange Commission (SEC or Commission) or to other regulatory agencies, Dirks began to disseminate the information to his clients and undertook his own investigation.[3] One of his first steps was to direct his associates at Delafield Childs to draw up a list of Delafield clients holding Equity Funding securities. On March 12, eight days before Dirks flew to Los Angeles to investigate Secrist's story, he reported the full allegations to Boston Company Institutional Investors, Inc., which on March 15 and 16 sold approximately $1.2 million of Equity securities.[4] See id., at 199. As he gathered more information, he selectively disclosed it to his clients. To those holding Equity Funding securities he gave the "hard" story—all the allegations; others received the "soft" story—a recitation of vague factors that might reflect adversely on Equity Funding's management. See id., at 211, n. 24.

Dirks' attempts to disseminate the information to nonclients were feeble, at best. On March 12, he left a message for Herbert Lawson, the San Francisco bureau chief of The Wall Street Journal. Not until March 19 and 20 did he call Lawson again, and outline the situation. William Blundell, a Journal investigative reporter based in Los Angeles, got in touch with Dirks about his March 20 telephone call. On March 21, Dirks met with Blundell in Los Angeles. Blundell began his own investigation, relying in part on Dirks' contacts, and on March 23 telephoned Stanley Sporkin, the SEC's Deputy Director of Enforce-

2. Unknown to Dirks, Secrist also told his story to New York insurance regulators the same day. App. 23. They immediately assured themselves that Equity Funding's New York subsidiary had sufficient assets to cover its outstanding policies and then passed on the information to California regulators who in turn informed Illinois regulators. Illinois investigators, later joined by California officials, conducted a surprise audit of Equity Funding's Illinois subsidiary, id., at 87–88, to find $22 million of the subsidiary's assets missing. On March 30, these authorities seized control of the Illinois subsidiary. Id., at 271.

3. In the same administrative proceeding at issue here, the Administrative Law Judge (ALJ) found that Dirks' clients—five institutional investment advisors—violated § 17(a) of the Securities Act of 1933, 15 U.S.C. § 77q(a), § 10(b) of the Securities Exchange Act of 1934, 15 U.S.C. § 78j(b), and Rule 10b–5, 17 CFR § 240.10b–5, by trading on Dirks' tips. App. 297. All the

clients were censured, except Dreyfus Corporation. The ALJ found that Dreyfus had made significant efforts to disclose the information to Goldman, Sachs, the purchaser of its securities. App. 299, 301. None of Dirks' clients appealed these determinations. App. to Pet. for Cert. B–2, n. 1.

4. The Court's implicit suggestion that Dirks did not gain by this selective dissemination of advice, ante, at . . . n. 2, is inaccurate. The ALJ found that because of Dirks' information, Boston Company Institutional Investors, Inc., directed business to Delafield Childs that generated approximately $25,000 in commissions. App. 199, 204–205. While it is true that the exact economic benefit gained by Delafield Childs due to Dirks' activities is unknowable because of the structure of compensation in the securities market, there can be no doubt that Delafield and Dirks gained both monetary rewards and enhanced reputations for "looking after" their clients.

ment. On March 26, the next business day, Sporkin and his staff interviewed Blundell and asked to see Dirks the following morning. Trading was halted by the New York Stock Exchange at about the same time Dirks was talking to Los Angeles SEC personnel. The next day, March 28, the SEC suspended trading in Equity Funding securities. By that time, Dirks' clients had unloaded close to $15 million of Equity Funding stock and the price had plummeted from $26 to $15. The effect of Dirks' selective dissemination of Secrist's information was that Dirks' clients were able to shift the losses that were inevitable due to the Equity Funding fraud from themselves to uninformed market participants.

II

A

No one questions that Secrist himself could not trade on his inside information to the disadvantage of uninformed shareholders and purchasers of Equity Funding securities. See Brief for United States as *Amicus Curiae* 19, n. 12. Unlike the printer in *Chiarella,* Secrist stood in a fiduciary relationship with these shareholders. As the Court states . . . corporate insiders have an affirmative duty of disclosure when trading with shareholders of the corporation. See *Chiarella,* 445 U.S., at 227, 100 S.Ct. at 1114. This duty extends as well to purchasers of the corporation's securities. Id., at 227, n. 8, 100 S.Ct., at 1114, n. 8, citing Gratz v. Claughton, 187 F.2d 46, 49 (CA2), cert. denied, 341 U.S. 920, 71 S.Ct. 741, 95 L.Ed. 1353 (1951).

The Court also acknowledges that Secrist could not do by proxy what he was prohibited from doing personally. . . . Mosser v. Darrow, 341 U.S. 267, 272, 71 S.Ct. 680, 685, 95 L.Ed. 927 (1951). But this is precisely what Secrist did. Secrist used Dirks to disseminate information to Dirks' clients, who in turn dumped stock on unknowing purchasers. Secrist thus intended Dirks to injure the purchasers of Equity Funding securities to whom Secrist had a duty to disclose. Accepting the Court's view of tippee liability,[5] it appears that Dirks' knowledge of this breach makes him liable as a participant in the breach after the fact. . . .; *Chiarella,* 445 U.S., at 230, n. 12, 100 S.Ct., at 1115, n. 12.

B

The Court holds, however, that Dirks is not liable because Secrist did not violate his duty; according to the Court, this is so because Secrist did not have the improper purpose of personal gain. . . . In so doing, the Court imposes a new, subjective limitation on the

5. I interpret the Court's opinion to impose liability on tippees like Dirks when the tippee knows or has reason to know that the information is material and non-public and was obtained through a breach of duty by selective revelation or otherwise. See In re Investors Management Co., 44 S.E.C. 633, 641 (1971).

scope of the duty owed by insiders to shareholders. The novelty of this limitation is reflected in the Court's lack of support for it.[6]

The insider's duty is owed directly to the corporation's shareholders. See Langevoort, Insider Trading and the Fiduciary Principle: A Post-*Chiarella* Restatement, 70 Calif.L.Rev. 1, 5 (1982); 3A W. Fletcher, Private Corporations § 1168.2, pp. 288–289 (1975). As *Chiarella* recognized, it is based on the relationship of trust and confidence between the insider and the shareholder. 445 U.S., at 228. That relationship assures the shareholder that the insider may not take actions that will harm him unfairly. The affirmative duty of disclosure protects against this injury. . . .

C

The fact that the insider himself does not benefit from the breach does not eradicate the shareholder's injury. Cf. Restatement (Second) of Trusts § 205, Comments c and d (1959) (trustee liable for acts causing diminution of value of trust); 3 A. Scott on Trusts § 205, p. 1665 (1967) (trustee liable for any losses to trust caused by his breach). It makes no difference to the shareholder whether the corporate insider gained or intended to gain personally from the transaction; the shareholder still has lost because of the insider's misuse of nonpublic information. The duty is addressed not to the insider's motives,[10] but to his actions and their consequences on the shareholder. Personal gain is not an element of the breach of this duty.[11] . . .

---

6. The Court cites only a footnote in a SEC decision and Professor Brudney to support its rule. . . . The footnote, however, merely identifies one result the securities laws are intended to prevent. It does not define the nature of the duty itself. See n. 9, infra. Professor Brudney's quoted statement appears in the context of his assertion that the duty of insiders to disclose prior to trading with shareholders is in large part a mechanism to correct the information available to noninsiders. Professor Brudney simply recognizes that the most common motive for breaching this duty is personal gain; he does not state, however, that the duty prevents only personal aggrandizement. Insiders, Outsiders, and Informational Advantages Under the Federal Securities Laws, 93 Harv.L. Rev. 322, 345–348 (1979). Surely, the Court does not now adopt Professor Brudney's access-to-information theory, a close cousin to the equality-of-information theory it accuses the SEC of harboring. . . .

10. Of course, an insider is not liable in a Rule 10b–5 administrative action unless he has the requisite scienter. Aaron v. SEC, 446 U.S. 680, 691, 100 S.Ct. 1945, 1952, 64 L.Ed.2d 611 (1980). He must know or intend that his conduct violates his duty. Secrist obviously knew and intended that Dirks would cause trading on

the inside information and that Equity Funding shareholders would be harmed. The scienter requirement addresses the intent necessary to support liability; it does not address the motives behind the intent.

11. The Court seems concerned that this case bears on insiders' contacts with analysts for valid corporate reasons. . . . It also fears that insiders may not be able to determine whether the information transmitted is material or nonpublic. . . . When the disclosure is to an investment banker or some other adviser, however, there is normally no breach because the insider does not have scienter: he does not intend that the inside information be used for trading purposes to the disadvantage of shareholders. Moreover, if the insider in good faith does not believe that the information is material or nonpublic, he also lacks the necessary scienter. Ernst & Ernst v. Hochfelder, 425 U.S. 185, 197, 96 S.Ct. 1375, 1382–1383, 47 L.Ed.2d 668 (1976). In fact, the scienter requirement functions in part to protect good faith errors of this type. Id., at 211, n. 31, 96 S.Ct., at 1389, n. 31. . . .

The situation here, of course, is radically different. . . . Secrist divulged the information for the precise purpose of causing Dirks' clients to trade on it. I fail to

Although Secrist's general motive to expose the Equity Funding fraud was laudable, the means he chose were not. Moreover, even assuming that Dirks played a substantial role in exposing the fraud,[15] he and his clients should not profit from the information they obtained from Secrist. . . .

IV

In my view, Secrist violated his duty to Equity Funding shareholders by transmitting material nonpublic information to Dirks with the intention that Dirks would cause his clients to trade on that information. Dirks, therefore, was under a duty to make the information publicly available or to refrain from actions that he knew would lead to trading. Because Dirks caused his clients to trade, he violated § 10(b) and Rule 10b–5. Any other result is a disservice to this country's attempt to provide fair and efficient capital markets. I dissent.

NOTE ON UNITED STATES v. NEWMAN, MOSS v. MORGAN STANLEY, SEC v. MATERIA, AND CARPENTER v. UNITED STATES

In United States v. Newman, 664 F.2d 12 (2d Cir.1981), aff'd after remand 722 F.2d 729 (2d Cir.1983) (unpublished order), cert. denied, 464 U.S. 863, 104 S.Ct. 193, 78 L.Ed.2d 170, Warner–Lambert Co. retained Morgan Stanley, an investment-banking firm, to assess the desirability of making a tender offer for Deseret Pharmaceutical Co. Courtois, who was then employed in Morgan Stanley's mergers-and-acquisitions department, learned of Warner's plan, passed along the information to Adrian Antoniu, an employee of another investment banker, and urged Antoniu to purchase Deseret stock. Antoniu in turn informed Newman, a stockbroker. Newman, acting pursuant to an agreement with Courtois and Antoniu, purchased 11,700 shares of Deseret stock at approximately $28.

On December 1, 1976, the New York Stock Exchange halted trading in Deseret stock pending announcement of the tender offer. Trading remained suspended until December 7, when Warner publicly announced a tender offer for Deseret stock at $38. Newman, Courtois, and Antoniu tendered their shares and reaped a substantial profit. The Second Circuit applied the misappropriation theory and held that Newman (the only one of the three who was then within the jurisdiction of the district court) had criminally violated Rule 10b–5, if the Government's allegations were true.[1]

---

understand how imposing liability on Dirks will affect legitimate insider-analyst contacts.

15. The Court uncritically accepts Dirks' own view of his role in uncovering the Equity Funding fraud. . . . It ignores the fact that Secrist gave the same information at the same time to state insurance regulators, who proceeded to expose massive fraud in a major Equity Funding subsidiary. The fraud surfaced before Dirks ever spoke to the SEC.

1. Courtois and Antoniu were eventually sentenced. What Happened to 50 People Involved in Insider–Trading Cases, Wall St. J., November 18, 1987, p. 27, col. 3.

In Moss v. Morgan Stanley Inc., 719 F.2d 5 (2d Cir.1983), cert. denied, 465 U.S. 1025, 104 S.Ct. 1280, 79 L.Ed.2d 684 (1984), Moss, who had sold Deseret stock the day before trading was suspended, brought a private damages action against Newman, Courtois, Antoniu, and Morgan Stanley. The Second Circuit held that although Newman's trading was criminal, it did not give rise to a private action:

> In *Newman* we held that Courtois' and Antoniu's securities transactions constituted a breach of their fiduciary duty of confidentiality and loyalty to their employers (Morgan Stanley and Kuhn Loeb & Co., respectively) and thereby provided the basis for *criminal* prosecution under section 10(b) and rule 10b–5. . . . Nothing in our opinion in *Newman* suggests that an employee's duty to "abstain or disclose" with respect to his employer should be stretched to encompass an employee's "duty of disclosure" to the general public.

Id. at 13. (Emphasis in original.)

In SEC v. Materia, 745 F.2d 197 (2d Cir.1984), cert. denied, 471 U.S. 1053, 105 S.Ct. 2112, 85 L.Ed.2d 477 (1985), Materia, like Chiarella, was employed by a financial printer and utilized confidential information obtained in that capacity to trade in the stock of target corporations. The Second Circuit upheld a conviction and fine. "[The Supreme Court in *Chiarella*] did not . . . disavow the misappropriation theory. . . . We announced [in *Newman*], and reiterate now, that one who misappropriates nonpublic information in breach of a fiduciary duty and trades on that information to his own advantage violates section 10(b) and Rule 10b–5." 745 F.2d at 203.

In Carpenter v. United States, ___ U.S. ___, 108 S.Ct. 316, 98 L.Ed.2d 275 (1987), Winans, a reporter for the Wall Street Journal, was responsible for a column called *Heard on the Street*, which provided positive or negative information about selected stocks and took a point of view on whether to buy or sell the stocks. The column was influential: positive information and advice about a stock tended to cause a rise in its price; negative information and advice tended to cause a decline. Winans used his knowledge of the contents of impending columns to participate in a scheme with Felis and Carpenter. Under the scheme, the parties used their prepublication information to trade in stocks that were about to be featured in the column. In so doing, Winans acted in violation of the Wall Street Journal's written policy. The Second Circuit applied the misappropriation theory to uphold criminal convictions of Winans, Felis, and Carpenter under Rule 10b–5, and also held that their use of the prepublication information violated the federal Wire Fraud Act. The Supreme Court affirmed the Rule 10b–5 conviction, without opinion, by an equally divided Court. The Wire Fraud conviction was affirmed unanimously:

> Petitioners assert that their activities were not a scheme to defraud the Journal within the meaning of the mail and wire

fraud statutes;[6] and that in any event, they did not obtain any "money or property" from the Journal, which is a necessary element of the crime under our decision last Term in *McNally v. United States,* 483 U.S. ___ (1987). We are unpersuaded by either submission and address the latter first.

We held in *McNally* that the mail fraud statute does not reach "schemes to defraud citizens of their intangible rights to honest and impartial government," . . . and that the statute is "limited in scope to the protection of property rights." . . . Petitioners argue that the Journal's interest in prepublication confidentiality for the "Heard" columns is no more than an intangible consideration outside the reach of § 1341; nor does that law, it is urged, protect against mere injury to reputation. This is not a case like *McNally,* however. The Journal, as Winans' employer, was defrauded of much more than its contractual right to his honest and faithful service, an interest too ethereal in itself to fall within the protection of the mail fraud statute, which "had its origin in the desire to protect individual property rights." *McNally, supra,* . . .. Here, the object of the scheme was to take the Journal's confidential business information—the publication schedule and contents of the "Heard" column—and its intangible nature does not make it any less "property" protected by the mail and wire fraud statutes. *McNally* did not limit the scope of § 1341 to tangible as distinguished from intangible property rights.

Both courts below expressly referred to the Journal's interest in the confidentiality of the contents and timing of the "Heard" column as a property right, 791 F.2d, at 1034–1035; 612 F.Supp., at 846, and we agree with that conclusion. Confidential business information has long been recognized as property. See *Ruckelshaus v. Monsanto Co.,* 467 U.S. 986, 1001–1004 (1984); *Dirks v. SEC,* 463 U.S. 646, 653, n. 10 (1983); *Board of Trade of Chicago v. Christie Grain & Stock Co.,* 198 U.S. 236, 250–251 (1905); cf. 5 U.S.C. § 552(b)(4). "Confidential information acquired or compiled by a corporation in the course and conduct of its business is a species of property to which the corporation has the exclusive right and benefit, and which a court of equity will protect through the injunctive process or other appropriate remedy." 3 W. Fletcher, Cyclopedia of Law of Private Corporations § 857.1, p. 260 (rev. ed. 1986) (footnote omitted). The Journal had a property right in keeping confidential and making exclusive use, prior to publication, of the schedule and contents of the "Heard" columns. *Christie Grain, supra.* . . .

We cannot accept petitioners' further argument that Winans' conduct in revealing prepublication information was no more than a violation of workplace rules and did not amount to fraudulent activity that is proscribed by the mail fraud statute. Sections 1341 and 1343 reach any scheme to deprive another of

---

6. The mail and wire fraud statutes share the same language in relevant part, and accordingly we apply the same analysis to both sets of offenses here.

money or property by means of false or fraudulent pretenses, representations, or promises. As we observed last Term in *McNally,* the words "to defraud" in the mail fraud statute have the "common understanding" of " 'wronging one in his property rights by dishonest methods or schemes,' and 'usually signify the deprivation of something of value by trick, deceit, chicane or overreaching.' " 483 U.S., at ___ (quoting *Hammerschmidt v. United States,* 265 U.S. 182, 188 (1924)). The concept of "fraud" includes the act of embezzlement, which is " 'the fraudulent appropriation to one's own use of the money or goods entrusted to one's care by another.' " *Grin v. Shine,* 187 U.S. 181, 189 (1902).

The District Court found that Winans' undertaking at the Journal was not to reveal prepublication information about his column, a promise that became a sham when in violation of his duty he passed along to his co-conspirators confidential information belonging to the Journal, pursuant to an ongoing scheme to share profits from trading in anticipation of the "Heard" column's impact on the stock market. In *Snepp v. United States,* 444 U.S. 507, 515, n. 11 (1980) (*per curiam*), although a decision grounded in the provisions of a written trust agreement prohibiting the unapproved use of confidential government information, we noted the similar prohibitions of the common law, that "even in the absence of a written contract, an employee has a fiduciary obligation to protect confidential information obtained during the course of his employment." As the New York courts have recognized, "It is well established, as a general proposition, that a person who acquires special knowledge or information by virtue of a confidential or fiduciary relationship with another is not free to exploit that knowledge or information for his own personal benefit but must account to his principal for any profits derived therefrom." *Diamond v. Oreamuno,* 24 N.Y.2d 494, 497, 248 N.E.2d 910, 912 (1969); see also Restatement (Second) of Agency §§ 388, Comment *c,* 396(c) (1958).

We have little trouble in holding that the conspiracy here to trade on the Journal's confidential information is not outside the reach of the mail and wire fraud statutes, provided the other elements of the offenses are satisfied. The Journal's business information that it intended to be kept confidential was its property; the declaration to that effect in the employee manual merely removed any doubts on that score and made the finding of specific intent to defraud that much easier. Winans continued in the employ of the Journal, appropriating its confidential business information for his own use, all the while pretending to perform his duty of safeguarding it. In fact, he told his editors twice about leaks of confidential information not related to the stock-trading scheme, 612 F.Supp., at 831, demonstrating both his knowledge that the Journal viewed information concerning the "Heard" column as confidential and his deceit as he played the role of a loyal employee. Furthermore, the District Court's conclusion that each of the petitioners acted with the required specific intent to defraud is strongly supported by the evidence. *Id.,* at 847–850.

Lastly, we reject the submission that using the wires and the mail to print and send the Journal to its customers did not satisfy the requirement that those mediums be used to execute the scheme at issue. The courts below were quite right in observing that circulation of the "Heard" column was not only anticipated but an essential part of the scheme. Had the column not been made available to Journal customers, there would have been no effect on stock prices and no likelihood of profiting from the information leaked by Winans.

SECTION 3. LIABILITY FOR SHORT-SWING TRADING UNDER § 16(b) OF THE SECURITIES EXCHANGE ACT

SECURITIES EXCHANGE ACT § 16

Sec. 16. (a) Every person who is directly or indirectly the beneficial owner of more than 10 per centum of any class of any equity security (other than an exempted security) which is registered pursuant to section 12 of this title, or who is a director or an officer of the issuer of such security, shall file, at the time of the registration of such security on a national securities exchange or by the effective date of a registration statement filed pursuant to section 12(g) of this title, or within ten days after he becomes such beneficial owner, director, or officer, a statement with the Commission (and, if such security is registered on a national securities exchange, also with the exchange) of the amount of all equity securities of such issuer of which he is the beneficial owner, and within ten days after the close of each calendar month thereafter, if there has been a change in such ownership during such month, shall file with the Commission (and if such security is registered on a national securities exchange, shall also file with the exchange), a statement indicating his ownership at the close of the calendar month and such changes in his ownership as have occurred during such calendar month.

(b) For the purpose of preventing the unfair use of information which may have been obtained by such beneficial owner, director, or officer by reason of his relationship to the issuer, any profit realized by him from any purchase and sale, or any sale and purchase, of any equity security of such issuer (other than an exempted security) within any period of less than six months, unless such security was acquired in good faith in connection with a debt previously contracted, shall inure to and be recoverable by the issuer, irrespective of any intention on the part of such beneficial owner, director, or officer in entering into such transaction of holding the security purchased or of not repurchasing the security sold for a period exceeding six months. Suit to recover such profit may be instituted at law or in equity in any court of competent jurisdiction by the issuer, or by the owner of any security of the issuer in the name and in behalf of the issuer if the issuer shall fail or refuse to bring such suit within sixty days after request or shall fail diligently to prosecute the same thereafter; but no such suit shall be brought more than two years after the date such profit was realized. This subsection shall not be construed to cover any transaction where such beneficial owner was not such both at the time of the purchase and sale, or the sale and purchase, of the security involved, or any transaction or transactions which the Commission by rules and regulations may exempt as not comprehended within the purpose of this subsection.

SECURITIES EXCHANGE ACT RULES 3a–11–1, 3b–2; FORM 3; FORM 4

[See Statutory Supplement]

FELDMAN & TEBERG, BENEFICIAL OWNERSHIP UNDER SECTION 16 OF THE SECURITIES EXCHANGE ACT OF 1934, 17 Western Res.L.Rev. 1054, 1063–65 (1966).

"The juxtaposition of section 16(a) and 16(b), plus the fact that both operate with respect to the same persons, has led many to erroneously conclude that section 16(a) was enacted only to reveal transactions within the scope of section 16(b). That section 16(a) is not confined to transactions within the scope of section 16(b) is clear not only from the fact that section 16(a) pre-existed section 16(b) [as a matter of legislative history], but also from the different language of the two subsections. For while section 16(b) speaks of purchases and sales within six months of each other, section 16(a) speaks of changes in beneficial ownership, a much broader concept. . . .

"Since the terms of section 16(a) require insiders to disclose any changes in their beneficial ownership of securities, it provides a means for bringing to light possible violations of . . . Rule 10b–5, as well as a 'purchase and sale' within the scope of section 16(b). However, two other functions of the section 16(a) reports are equally important to the efficacious operations of the Exchange Act's scheme to banish investors' ignorance and upgrade the ethics of corporate managers. Its second function is to reveal information which may be used in evaluating the securities of the issuer. This is a pure disclosure device in which the conclusions to be drawn from the reports and the weight to be attached thereto are left to the judgment of the individual investor. The information contained in the reports may be used (1) as a guide to the insiders' current confidence or lack thereof in the company's fortunes or (2) to detect an evolving change in control in the company. Undoubtedly this investment information function of the section largely explains why the Commission's monthly summary of transactions reported under section 16(a) has become a perennial best seller. Finally, section 16(a) is itself a deterrent to the misuse of inside information through the publicity which attaches to the reports, apart from any other statutory prohibition or liability. This is a standard by-product or goal of any disclosure provision, since presumably people are likely to refrain from improper acts, or acts which may appear improper, if they know such acts will be exposed to public scrutiny."

REPORT OF THE TASK FORCE ON REGULATION OF INSIDER TRADING, PART II: REFORM OF SECTION 16

42 Bus.Law. 1087, 1091–92 (1987).

In recent years, a number of commentators have suggested that section 16(b) causes more harm than good and that it should be repealed. It has been argued that section 16(b) is ineffectual in preventing insider trading and does not even address all of the ways in which insider trades can be perpetrated, while it imposes punitive liability on the innocent, the naive, and the unaware corporate officers who unwittingly sell in violation of, for example, the labyrinthine restrictions of rule 16b–3. These commentators raise the question: Given the development of the insider trading doctrine under rule 10b–5, the substantial limitations of section 16(b) in preventing insider trading, and the hardships that it imposes, is the statute needed?

The task force believes that it is. Section 16(b) has a different legislative focus than the prohibition of trading on inside information. Indeed, it is the only provision of the 1934 Act that specifically regulates insider trading. It is aimed at three specific types of insider trading abuses, only one of which involves abuse of inside information.

First, section 16(b) was intended to remove the temptation for corporation executives to profit from short-term stock price fluctuations at the expense of the long-term financial health of their companies. It prevents insiders from being obsessed with trading in their companies' securities to the detriment of their managerial and fiduciary responsibilities. In this regard, based on the testimony of insider abuses presented at the hearings, it was Congress's judgment that short-swing trading by corporate executives is not good for their companies or the American capital markets.

Second, the section was intended to penalize the unfair use of inside information by insiders. This includes both trading on inside information in violation of rule 10b–5 and the use of "softer" information of the type that insiders often have but that members of the investing public do not: the ability to make better informed guesses as to the success of new products, the likely results of negotiations, and the real risks of contingencies and other uncertainties, the underlying facts of which have been publicly disclosed.

Third, section 16(b) was designed to eliminate the temptation for insiders to manipulate corporate events so as to maximize their own short-term trading profits. Before the enactment of section 16(b), insiders had been able to make quick profits from short-term price swings by such practices as the announcement of generous (but imprudent) dividend programs followed by postinsider trading dividend reductions. Thus, the section provides a minimum standard of fiduciary conduct for corporate insiders.

The task force thus concludes that section 16 remains a useful tool for preventing speculative abuses by insiders and for focusing their attention on their fiduciary duty and on long-term corporate health, rather than on short-term trading profits.

GRATZ v. CLAUGHTON

United States Court of Appeals, Second Circuit, 1951.
187 F.2d 46, cert. denied 341 U.S. 920, 71 S.Ct. 741, 95 L.Ed. 1353 (1951).

Before L. HAND, Chief Judge, and SWAN and AUGUSTUS N. HAND, Circuit Judges.

L. HAND, Chief Judge.

This is an appeal by the defendant, Claughton, from a judgment against him, entered upon the report of a master, in an action by a shareholder of the Missouri–Kansas–Texas Railroad Company under § 16(b) of the Securities Exchange Act of 1934. . . . The court first granted a summary judgment as to all the issues except the amount of the profits made by the defendant, which it referred to a master, on whose report it entered final judgment. The defendant does not dispute the propriety of a summary disposition of all the issues except that referred, but he does dispute the propriety of the judgment in law. First, he argues that the venue was wrong because he was domiciled in Florida, and the summons was served upon him in that state. Second, he disputes the rule adopted by the master in computing his profits. Third, he challenges the constitutionality of the statute which imposes the liability, and of the provisions for venue. We shall take up the first and third in sequence, reserving the second for the last.

[The court held that venue was proper.] . . .

The challenge to the constitutionality of § 16(b) we have answered twice before. For many years a grave omission in our corporation law had been its indifference to dealings of directors or other corporate officers in the shares of their companies. When they bought shares, they came literally within the conventional prohibitions of the law of trusts; yet the decisions were strangely slack in so deciding. When they sold shares, it could indeed be argued that they were not dealing with a beneficiary, but with one whom his purchase made a beneficiary. That should not, however, have obscured the fact that the director or officer assumed a fiduciary relation to the buyer by the very sale; for it would be a sorry distinction to allow him to use the advantage of his position to induce the buyer into the position of a beneficiary, although he was forbidden to do so, once the buyer had become one. Certainly this is true, when the buyer knows he is buying of a director or officer, for he expects to become the seller's *cestui que* trust. If the buyer does not know, he is entitled to assume that if his seller in fact is already a director or officer, he will remain so after the sale. Nor was it necessary to confine this disability to directors or other officers of the corporation. The reason for the doctrine was that a director or officer may have information not accessible to a shareholder, actual or prospective, and that advantage is not confined to them. We take judicial notice that an effective control over the affairs of a corporation often does not require anything approaching a majority of the shares; and this is particularly true in the case of those corporations whose shares are dealt in upon national exchanges. Nor is it common for the control so obtained to be in the hands of one individual; more often a number share it, who are all in a position to gain a more intimate acquaintance with the enterprise and its prospects than the shareholders at large. It is of course true that the ownership of ten per cent of the shares does not always put the owner among those who do control; but neither Congress, nor any other legislature, is obliged to limit the means which it chooses so exactly to its ends that the correspondence is exact. If only those persons were liable, who could be proved to have a bargaining advantage, the execution of the statute would be so encumbered as to defeat its whole purpose. We do not mean that the interest, of which a statute deprives an individual, may never be so vital that he must not be given a trial of his personal guilt; but that is not so when all that is at stake is a director's, officer's or "beneficial owner's" privilege to add to, or subtract from, his holdings for a period of six months. In such situations it is well settled that a statute may provide any means which can reasonably be thought necessary to deal with the evil, even though they may cover instances where it is not present. . . .

There remains the question of the computation of profits, which we dealt with in Smolowe v. Delendo Corporation. . . .[8] Section 16(b) declares that "any profit realized . . . from any purchase and sale, or any sale and purchase . . . within any period of less than six months . . . shall inure to and be recoverable by the issuer": the corporation. It is plain that this presupposes some matching of (1) purchases against sales, or of (2) sales against purchases, and that there must therefore be some principle upon which both the minuend—the sale price—and the subtrahend—the purchase price—can be determined. At first blush it might seem that the statute limited the recovery to profits derived from transactions in the same shares; as, for example, that a dealer's profit upon the sale of any given number of shares was to be measured by subtracting what he paid for those shares from what he got upon a sale of the same certificate. Howev-

---

8. 2 Cir., 136 F.2d 231, 148 A.L.R. 300.

er, as we observed in Smolowe v. Delendo Corporation, supra, that would allow an easy avoidance of the statute; in order to speculate freely an officer, director, or "beneficial owner" need only hold a substantial block of shares for more than six months. If, for example, on January 1st, he had 10,000 shares which he had bought before October 1st, he could buy 1,000 shares on February 1st and sell 1,000 shares at a profit on April 1st, making delivery out of certificates from the 10,000 shares purchased before October 1st. After the two transactions his position would be what it had been on January 1st save that in two months he had made a profitable turn in 1,000 shares—exactly the evil against which the statute is directed. Moreover, there is an added reason for this interpretation, if one be needed. In the case of a sale followed by a purchase it is impossible to identify any purchase with any previous sale; one would have to confine such transactions to the practically non-existent occasions when the proceeds of the sale were used to purchase. Thus it appears, regardless of anything said during the passage of the bill through Congress and of the different forms it took, that the Act does not demand—that the same shares should be sold which were bought. This accords with the fungible nature of shares of stock. Indeed, if we translate the transaction into sales and purchases, or purchases and sales, of gallons of oil in a single tank, or of bushels of wheat in a single bin, it at once appears that the ascertainment of the particular shares bought or sold must be wholly irrelevant.

Although for these reasons it appears that the transactions—sales and purchases, or purchases and sales—are not to be matched by identifying the shares dealt in, we are no nearer than before to finding an answer as to how transactions shall be matched; all that so far appeared, is that the matching is to be between contracts of sale and contracts of purchase, or vice versa. On the other hand it is manifest that the intent of the fiduciary cannot be the test; first, because he generally has no ascertainable intent; and second, because that would open the door even more widely to the evil in question. The statute does not allow the fiduciary to minimize his profits, any more than to set off his losses against them. We can therefore find no principle by which to select any two transactions which are to be matched; and, so far as we can see, we are forced to one of two alternatives: to match any given sale taken as minuend, against any given purchase, taken as subtrahend, in such a way as to reduce profits to their lowest possible amount, or in such a way as to increase them to the greatest possible amount. The master adopted the second course, following what he supposed to be the doctrine of Smolowe v. Delendo Corporation, supra. We think that he was right for the following reasons.

The question is in substance the same as when a trustee's account is to be surcharged, for, as we have said, the statute makes the fiduciary a constructive trustee for any profits he may make. It is true that on the beneficiary in an accounting rests the burden of proof of a surcharge,[9] although the fiduciary has the burden of establishing any

9. Ewen v. Peoria & Eastern Ry., D.C., 78 F.Supp. 312, 334.

credits.[10]   Since the plaintiff was seeking to surcharge the defendant we will therefore assume that it rested upon her to show how the transactions are to be matched; and, that, if there were nothing more, since she cannot do so, she must be content to have them matched in the way that shows the least profit.   Obviously that cannot be the right answer, for the reasons we have given; and perhaps the fact that it cannot be, is reason enough for adopting the alternative.   But there is another ground for reaching the same result.   As we have said, the statute makes all such dealings unlawful, and makes the fiduciary accountable to the corporation.   Although it is impossible in the case at bar to compute the defendant's profits, except that they must fall between two limits—the minimum and the maximum—the cause of this uncertainty is the number of transactions within six months: that is, the number of defendant's derelictions.   The situation falls within the doctrine which has been law since the days of the "Chimney Sweeper's Jewel Case," [11] that when damages are at some unascertainable amount below an upper limit and when the uncertainty arises from the defendant's wrong, the upper limit will be taken as the proper amount.[12]

This results in looking for six months both before and after any sale, and not for three months only, as the defendant insists.   If one is seeking an equation of purchase and sale, one may take any sale as the minuend and look back for six months for a purchase at less price to match against it.   On the other hand, if one is looking for an equation of sale and purchase, one may take the same sale and look forward for six months for any purchase at a lower price.   Although obviously no transaction can figure in more than one equation, with that exception we can see no escape from what we have just said.   It is true that this means that no director, officer, or "beneficial owner" may safely buy and sell, or sell and buy, shares of stock in the company except at intervals of six months.   Whether that is too drastic a means of meeting the evil, we have not to decide; it is enough that we can find no other way to administer the statute.   Therefore, not only will we follow Smolowe v. Delendo Corporation, supra, as a precedent; but as *res integra* and after independent analysis we reassert its doctrine.   The defendant concedes that, except for carrying the transactions backward and forward for six months, instead of for three, the master followed the rule laid down in that decision; and the plaintiff has not appealed, so that she is not entitled to any more than she has recovered.   On this account we have not examined the master's computations in detail and are not to be understood to have passed

10. Wootton Land and Fuel Co. v. Ownbey, 8 Cir., 265 F. 91.

11. Armory v. Delamirie, 1722, 1 Strange 505.

12. Eastman Kodak Co. v. Southern Photo Co., 273 U.S. 359, 379, 47 S.Ct. 400, 71 L.Ed. 684; Schnell v. The Vallescura, 293 U.S. 296, 307, 55 S.Ct. 194, 79 L.Ed. 373; Story Parchment Co. v. Paterson Parchment Paper Co., 282 U.S. 565, 563–565, 51 S.Ct. 248, 75 L.Ed. 544; Bigelow v. R.K.O. Radio Pictures, Inc., 327 U.S. 251, 264, 265, 66 S.Ct. 574, 90 L.Ed. 652; Great Southern Gas & Oil Co. v. Logan Natural Gas & Fuel Co., 6 Cir., 155 F. 114; Package Closure Corp. v. Seal–Right Co., Inc., 2 Cir., 141 F.2d 972, 979; President & Directors of Manhattan Co. v. Kelby, 2 Cir., 147 F.2d 465, 476.

upon them. The crushing liabilities which § 16(b) may impose are apparent from this action in which the judgment was for over $300,000; it should certainly serve as a warning, and may prove a deterrent.*

Judgment affirmed.

––––––––––

NOTE ON THE COMPUTATION OF PROFITS UNDER § 16(b)

1. In Smolowe v. Delendo Corporation, 136 F.2d 231 (2d Cir. 1943), cert. denied, 320 U.S. 751, 64 S.Ct. 56, 88 L.Ed. 446, which was cited and relied upon in Gratz v. Claughton, the court considered and rejected several formulas for computing profits under § 16(b) other than those analyzed in *Gratz:*

> Once the principle of [measuring damages based on the identification of the stock certificates involved] is rejected, its corollary, the first-in, first-out rule, is left at loose ends. . . . Its rationalization is the same as that for the identification rule, for which it operates as a presumptive principle; and it has no other support. If we reject one, we reject the other and for like reasons. Its application would render the large stockholder with a backlog of stock not immediately devoted to trading immune from the Act. Further, we should note that it does not fit the broad statutory language; a purchase followed immediately by a sale, albeit a transaction within the exact statutory language, would often be held immune from the statutory penalty because the purchase would be deemed by arbitrary rule to have been made at an earlier date; while a sale followed by purchase would never even be within the terms of the rule. . . .
>
> Another possibility might be the striking of an average purchase price and an average sale price during the period, and using these as bases of computation. What this rule would do in concrete effect is to allow as offsets all losses made by such trading. This in effect the district court first planned to do. . . . But it corrected this in its supplemental opinion, properly pointing out that the statute provided for the recovery of "any" profit realized and obviously precluded a setting off of losses. Even had the statutory language been more uncertain, this rule seems one not to be favored in the light of the statutory purpose. Compared to other possible rules, it tends to stimulate more active trading by reducing the chance of penalty. . . . Its application to a case where trading continued more than six months might be most uncertain, depending upon how the beginning of each six months' period was ascertained. It is not a clear-cut

––––––––––

* In Adler v. Klawans, 267 F.2d 840, 848 (2d Cir.1959), it is reported that "during the pertinent periods, [Gratz] suffered a net loss of $400,000 on trading in the stock for which he was charged under section 16(b)." (Footnote by ed.)

taking of "any profit" for the corporation, and we agree with the district court in rejecting it.

Id. at 238–39.

2. The formula adopted in *Smolowe* and *Gratz* has been generally approved by the courts. It is often referred to the "lowest purchase price, highest sale price" method. See, e.g., Whittaker v. Whittaker Corp., 639 F.2d 516, 530 (9th Cir.1981). Here are three illustrations of this method:

(i) D is a director of C Corporation, whose stock is traded on a national securities exchange. On January 2, D purchases 1,000 shares of C at $10. On April 1, D sells 1,000 shares at $15. This is a short-swing "purchase and sale," and D is liable under § 16(b) for his profit of $5,000.

(ii) On January 2, D purchases 1,000 shares of C at $10. On August 1, D sells 1,000 shares at $15. On November 1, D purchases 1,000 shares at $10. D has no liability on the basis of the January–August swing, because the two ends of the swing did not occur within six months. However, the August and November transactions constitute a short-swing "sale and purchase," and D would be liable under § 16(b) for a profit of $5,000 on these two transactions. Why has D made a $5,000 "profit"? Because after D's November 1 purchase, his position in C Corporation's stock is exactly as it was just before August 1 (that is, he owns 1,000 C shares) but he has also added $5,000 cash to his bank account. D may have accomplished this result by using inside information. The sale at $15 may have been made on the basis of undisclosed bad news. The purchase at $10 may have been made on the basis of undisclosed good news.

(iii) D engages in the following pattern of activity:

Date	Action	Amount	Price
2/1	Purchase	1,000	$30
3/1	Sale	1,000	$25
4/1	Purchase	1,000	$20
5/1	Sale	1,000	$15

Under the *Smolowe/Gratz* formula, D has a profit of $5,000, because the purchase at $20 on 4/1 can be matched with the sale at $25 on 3/1. At first glance, this looks counterintuitive: it seems that D has a $10,000 loss in his total trading, not a $5,000 profit. But it may be that except for inside information, D would not have sold on 3/1, and instead would have ridden the C stock all the way down from $30 to $15, for a loss of $15,000. Accordingly, there is a possibility (which is all that § 16(b) requires) that D has profited by $5,000 by holding his loss to $10,000 through the use of inside information.[1]

---

1. For a hypothetical in which a finding of profits under the *Smolowe/Gratz* formula does seem counterintuitive, see Lowenfels, Section 16(b): A New Trend in Regulating Insider Trading, 54 Cornell L.Rev. 45, 46–47 n. 6 (1968).

NOTE ON INSIDER STATUS AT ONLY ONE END
OF A SWING

Suppose a person has insider status under § 16(b) when he makes a sale, but not when he makes a matching short-swing purchase, or when he makes a purchase, but not when he makes a matching short-swing sale. The last sentence of § 16(b) sets out an exemptive provision under which "[T]his subsection shall not be construed to cover any transaction where [a 10%] beneficial owner was not such both at the time of the purchase and sale, or the sale and purchase, of the security involved." In Foremost–McKesson, Inc. v. Provident Securities Co., 423 U.S. 232, 96 S.Ct. 508, 46 L.Ed.2d 464 (1976) the Supreme Court held, largely on the basis of this exemptive provision and the legislative history, that in the case of a purchase-sale sequence a 10% beneficial owner is not liable unless he was a 10% owner *before* he made the purchase in question. To put this differently, the purchase that first lifts a beneficial owner above 10% cannot be matched with a subsequent sale under § 16(b). (The *Foremost* opinion did not cover a sale-repurchase sequence by a person who was a 10% owner before the sale, and left considerable room for arguing that this sequence should result in liability under § 16(b).)

On the other hand, the clear implication of the exemptive clause is that § 16(b) does apply to a short-swing transaction by a director or officer even where the director or officer "was not such both at the time of purchase and sale, or sale and purchase." In Feder v. Martin Marietta Corp., 406 F.2d 260 (2d Cir.1969), cert. denied 396 U.S. 1036, 90 S.Ct. 678, 24 L.Ed.2d 681 (1970), the court held that a director or officer who purchases, resigns, and then sells within six months of the purchase, is liable under § 16(b). In Adler v. Klawans, 267 F.2d 840 (2d Cir.1959), the court held that a person who purchases, becomes a director or officer, and then sells within six months of the purchase is liable under § 16(b).[1] However, no liability will be imposed if both ends of a swing occur after the

---

1. In Allis–Chalmers Mfg. Co. v. Gulf & Western Indus., Inc., 527 F.2d 335 (7th Cir. 1975), cert. denied, 423 U.S. 1078 (1976), the Seventh Circuit adopted the theory that § 16(b) should be interpreted to cover only cases in which there was a capacity for using inside information at both ends of a short swing. Under this theory, § 16(b) would apply to a director or officer who purchased, resigned, and sold, as in Feder v. Martin Marietta Corp., but would not apply to a person who purchased, became a director or officer, and sold, as in Adler v. Klawans, because the person would not have had access to inside information at the time of the purchase. See Hecker, Section 16(b) of the Securities Exchange Act: An Analysis of the Time When Insider Status is Required, 24 Kan.L.Rev. 255 (1976). In footnote 16 to its opinion in *Foremost–McKesson,* the Court stated:

"Shortly before this case was argued the Court of Appeals for the Seventh Circuit reached the same conclusion on somewhat difference analysis. *Allis–Chalmers Mfg. Co. . . . .* The court apparently would have reached its result even in the absence of the exemptive provision, reasoning that § 16(b) covers no transactions by any § 16(b) insiders who were not insiders before their initial transaction. . . . Since we rely on the exemptive provision, we intimate no view on the proper analysis of a case where a director or officer makes an initial transaction before obtaining insider status. See, *e.g.,* Adler v. Klawans, 267 F.2d 840 (CA2 1959). Nor do we have occasion here to assess the approach taken by the Court of Appeals for the Seventh Circuit to the exemptive provision. . . ."

director or officer resigns. Lewis v. Mellon Bank, N.A., 513 F.2d 921 (3d Cir.1975); Lewis v. Varnes, 505 F.2d 785 (2d Cir.1974).

NOTE ON THE INTERPRETATION OF § 16(b)

Until the early 1960's the predominant theory of interpreting § 16(b) was that it should be construed to cover all transactions within its literal reach. "[T]he statute. . . . was intended to be thoroughgoing, to squeeze all possible profits out of stock transactions, and thus to establish a standard so high as to prevent any conflict between the selfish interest of [an insider] and the faithful performance of his duty." Smolowe v. Delendo Corp., 136 F.2d 231, 239 (2d Cir.), cert. denied, 320 U.S. 751 (1943). This theory of interpreting § 16(b) was known as the "objective" approach. Beginning in the mid–1960's, § 16(b) came to be perceived by some as a harsh statute because it operates without regard to fault. A different theory of interpretation then set in, known as the "pragmatic" approach. Under this approach, in borderline or "unorthodox" cases the question is whether the transaction is of a type that carries a potential for insider abuse. See Whittaker v. Whittaker Corp., 639 F.2d 516, 522 (9th Cir.), cert. denied, 454 U.S. 1031 (1981); Lowenfels, Section 16(b): A New Trend in Regulating Insider Trading, 54 Cornell Law Review 45 (1968).

> However, the pragmatic approach has not ousted the objective view. Rather, the pragmatic approach is used to determine the boundaries of the statute's definitional scope in borderline situations, especially unorthodox transactions. . . . For a garden-variety transaction which cannot be regarded as unorthodox, the pragmatic approach is not applicable. . . . In such cases, if the situation is within the requirements established by Congress for § 16, then the mechanical, "objective," operation of the statute imposes liability.

Whittaker v. Whittaker Corp., supra, at 522.

As the matter stands today, therefore, in "garden variety" transactions (most prominently, cash purchase and sales) the objective approach is applied, and liability is imposed if the transaction is within the literal reach of § 16(b). In "unorthodox" transactions (such as mergers) the pragmatic approach is applied, and liability is imposed only if the transaction is of a type that has a potential for insider abuse. It is important to emphasize that even in the case of unorthodox transactions, the issue should not be whether the particular transaction actually gave rise to abuse, but whether the transaction was of a type that could give rise to abuse. Although the polar cases on the garden-variety/unorthodox spectrum are relatively well delineated, the courts have not evolved clear rules on how to categorize cases in the middle of the spectrum.

NOTE ON ATTRIBUTION AND DEPUTIZATION UNDER § 16(b)

1. Problems of attribution may arise under § 16(b) either when an insider trades on behalf of another person (using the term "person" broadly, to include a business enterprise), or when a person who has some relationship to the insider trades on his own behalf. Although one may fall within the reporting requirements of § 16(a) without being subject to the liability rules of § 16(b), the SEC's views on attribution under § 16(a) are instructive for attribution under § 16(b) as well. These views are to be found in SEC releases, in the instructions to Forms 3 and 4, and in the rules promulgated under § 16(a). Only a portion of this material will be considered in this Note.

Perhaps the most general SEC statement on attribution is found in Exchange Act Release No. 7824 (1966), which states that in determining beneficial ownership under Section 16(a):

> Generally a person is regarded as the beneficial owner of securities held in the name of his or her spouse and their minor children. Absent special circumstances such relationship ordinarily results in such person obtaining benefits substantially equivalent to ownership, e.g., application of the income derived from such securities to maintain a common home, to meet expenses which such person otherwise would meet from other sources, or the ability to exercise a controlling influence over the purchase, sale, or voting of such securities. Accordingly, a person ordinarily should include in his reports filed pursuant to section 16(a) securities held in the name of spouse or minor children as being beneficially owned by him.
>
> A person also may be regarded as the beneficial owner of securities held in the name of another person, if by reason of any contract, understanding, relationship, agreement, or other arrangement, he obtains therefrom benefits substantially equivalent to those of ownership. Accordingly, where such benefits are present such securities should be reported as being beneficially owned by the reporting person. Moreover, the fact that the person is a relative or relative of a spouse and sharing the same home as the reporting person may in itself indicate that the reporting person would obtain benefits substantially equivalent to those of ownership from securities held in the name of such relative. Thus, absent countervailing facts, it is expected that securities held by relatives who share the same home as the reporting person will be reported as being beneficially owned by such person.

Instruction 11 to Forms 3 and 4 states that:

> A person may also be the indirect beneficial owner of securities held in the name of a partnership, corporation, trust or other entity if such person, or a spouse or relative of

such person, individually or collectively, may exercise a controlling influence over the purchase, sale or voting of such securities.

Instruction 10 to Form 4 states that:

In the case of securities indirectly owned beneficially through a spouse, relative or other natural person, or through a partnership, corporation, trust or other entity, the entire amount of securities involved in the transaction or owned by such natural person, partnership, corporation, trust or other entity shall be stated. The person whose ownership is reported may, if he so desires, also indicate in a footnote or other appropriate manner, the extent of his interest in the holdings of the partnership, corporation, trust or other entity through which securities are beneficially owned.

Under Rule 16a–8(a):

Beneficial ownership of a security for the purpose of section 16(a) shall include . . . [t]he ownership of securities as a trustee where either the trustee or members of his immediately family have a vested interest in the income or corpus of the trust.

See generally Feldman & Teberg, Beneficial Ownership Under Section 16 of the Securities Exchange Act of 1934, 17 West.Reserve L.Rev. 1054 (1966).

2. In Whiting v. Dow Chemical Co., 523 F.2d 680 (2d Cir. 1975) Helen Dow Whiting sold 29,770 shares of Dow stock for $1.6 million during September and November 1973, at an average price of $55–$56. In December 1973, her husband, a director of Dow, exercised an option to purchase 21,420 Dow shares for $520,000 at an average price of just over $24. Mr. Whiting exercised the option with funds he borrowed from his wife, and which were part of the proceeds of her sales of Dow stock in the preceding two months. Mrs. Whiting was a granddaughter of the founder of Dow. She had acquired substantial amounts of stock over the years by gift and inheritance, and these assets were segregated from those of Mr. Whiting. However, the resources of both husband and wife were significantly directed toward their common prosperity. Mr. Whiting contributed virtually his entire salary toward family expenses, but Mrs. Whiting was primarily responsible for the Whiting's considerable living costs. The Whitings' separate accounts were managed by the same financial advisors, and Mrs. Whitings' sales of the Dow stock were made pursuant to a long-term investment plan arranged by the Whitings and their joint financial advisor. Mrs. Whiting upon occasion consulted her husband concerning the desirability of certain investments in areas of his expertise, but Mr. Whiting did not communicate with his wife concerning Dow's affairs. The Second Circuit held Mr. Whiting liable under § 16(b):

. . . For purposes of the family unit, shares to which legal title is held by one spouse may be said to be "beneficially owned" by the other, the insider, if the ordinary rewards of ownership are used for their joint benefit. . . .

Turning to the specific facts, while there was no exclusive "control" by appellant over his wife's separate investments generally, there was sufficient evidence to establish that the questioned transactions were part of a common plan, jointly managed by husband and wife.

If, then, appellant is "the beneficial owner" of his wife's securities of the issuer for § 16(b) purposes, how does one interpret the statutory language of § 16(b) "any profit realized by *him*" (emphasis added).

If we hold that he is a "beneficial owner" he must be chargeable with all the profits or none, in the absence of a way to measure benefit. . . . It is fiction, of course, to say that he will get all the profit for himself, but here the prophylaxis comes in. The whole profit is "his" profit, "realized by him" because the shares are "his" by the statutory "beneficial owner" concept as applied, and because he is a person in a position to obtain inside information.

See also Whittaker v. Whittaker Corp., 639 F.2d 516 (9th Cir.), cert. denied, 454 U.S. 1031 (1981); but see CBI Industries, Inc. v. Horton, 682 F.2d 643 (7th Cir.1982).

3. Closely related to the theory of attribution under § 16(b) is the theory of deputization. In Blau v. Lehman, 368 U.S. 403, 82 S.Ct. 451, 7 L.Ed.2d 403 (1962), the Supreme Court held that one enterprise, A, could be a "director" of second enterprise, B, within the meaning of § 16(b), if a director of B acts as A's deputy. Here Thomas, a partner in Lehman Brothers, (Enterprise A), sat on the board of Tide Water (Enterprise B), and Lehman profited from short-swing trading in Tide Water stock. The Court said:

> No doubt Lehman Brothers, though a partnership, could for purposes of § 16 be a "director" of Tide Water and function through a deputy, since § 3(a)(9) of the Act provides that "'person' means . . . partnership" and § 3(a)(7) that "'director' means any director of a corporation or any person performing similar functions with respect to any organization, whether incorporated or unincorporated." Consequently, Lehman Brothers would be a "director" of Tide Water, if as petitioner's complaint charged Lehman actually functioned as a director through Thomas, who had been deputized by Lehman to perform a director's duties not for himself but for Lehman.

Id. at 409. However, the courts below had made findings that the Supreme Court believed precluded the conclusion that deputization had actually occurred, and Lehman Brothers was therefore not held liable. (Thomas was held liable below for his pro rata share of the short-swing profits made by Lehman, and this aspect of the case was not appealed.)

Deputization was found to be present in Feder v. Martin Marietta Corp., 406 F.2d 260 (2d Cir.1969), cert. denied, 396 U.S. 1036, 90 S.Ct. 678, 24 L.Ed.2d 681 (1970). Bunker, the president of Martin Marietta (Enterprise A), had become a director of Sperry (Enterprise B), in which Martin Marietta held substantial stock. Bunker was ultimately responsible for the total operation of Martin Marietta, and personally approved all the firm's financial investments—in particular, its purchase of the Sperry stock. Bunker's control over Martin Marietta, coupled with his membership on Sperry's Board, placed him in a position in which he could acquire inside information concerning Sperry and could utilize such information for Martin. Further, Bunker admitted discussing Sperry's affairs with two officials at Martin Marietta and participating in sessions when Martin Marietta's investment in Sperry was reviewed, and Bunker's ultimate letter of resignation to Martin Marietta's president stated that "When I became a member of the [Sperry] board . . . it appeared to your associates that the Martin Marietta ownership of a substantial number of shares of Sperry Rand should have representation on your Board." On these facts, the Second Circuit concluded that "The control possessed by Bunker, his letter of resignation, the approval by the Martin Board of Bunker's directorship with Sperry and the functional similarity between Bunker's acts as a Sperry director and the acts of Martin's representatives on other boards . . . are all definite and concrete indicatives that Bunker, in fact, was a Martin deputy." Martin Marietta was therefore held liable, as a director, for its short-swing profits in Sperry stock.

SECTION 4. THE COMMON LAW REVISITED

DIAMOND v. OREAMUNO

New York Court of Appeals, 1969.
24 N.Y.2d 494, 301 N.Y.S.2d 78, 248 N.E.2d 910.

Chief Judge FULD. Upon this appeal from an order denying a motion to dismiss the complaint as insufficient on its face, the question presented—one of first impression in this court—is whether officers and directors may be held accountable to their corporation for gains realized by them from transactions in the company's stock as a result of their use of material inside information.

The complaint was filed by a shareholder of Management Assistance, Inc. (MAI) asserting a derivative action against a number of its officers and directors to compel an accounting for profits allegedly acquired as a result of a breach of fiduciary duty. It charges that two of the defendants—Oreamuno, chairman of the board of directors, and Gonzalez, its president—had used inside information, acquired by them solely by virtue of their positions, in order to reap large personal profits from the sale of MAI shares and that these profits rightfully belong to the corporation. Other officers and directors were joined as defendants on the ground that they acquiesced in or ratified the assertedly wrongful transactions.

MAI is in the business of financing computer installations through sale and lease back arrangements with various commercial and industrial users. Under its lease provisions, MAI was required to maintain and repair the computers but, at the time of this suit, it lacked the capacity to perform this function itself and was forced to engage the manufacturer of the computers, International Business Machines (IBM), to service the machines. As a result of a sharp increase by IBM of its charges for such service, MAI's expenses for August of 1966 rose considerably and its net earnings declined from $262,253 in July to $66,233 in August, a decrease of about 75%. This information, although earlier known to the defendants, was not made public until October of 1966. Prior to the release of the information, however, Oreamuno and Gonzalez sold off a total of 56,500 shares of their MAI stock at the then current market price of $28 a share.

After the information concerning the drop in earnings was made available to the public, the value of a share of MAI stock immediately fell from the $28 realized by the defendants to $11. Thus, the plaintiff alleges, by taking advantage of their privileged position and their access to confidential information, Oreamuno and Gonzalez were able to realize $800,000 more for their securities than they would have had this inside information not been available to them. Stating that the defendants were "forbidden to use [such] information . . . for their own personal profit or gain", the plaintiff brought this derivative action seeking to have the defendants account to the corporation for this difference. A motion by the defendants to dismiss the complaint—pursuant to CPLR 3211 (subd. [a], par. 7)— for failure to state a cause of action was granted by the court at Special Term. The Appellate Division, with one dissent, modified Special Term's order by reinstating the complaint as to the defendants Oreamuno and Gonzalez. The appeal is before us on a certified question.

In reaching a decision in this case, we are, of course, passing only upon the sufficiency of the complaint and we necessarily accept the charges contained in that pleading as true.

It is well established, as a general proposition, that a person who acquires special knowledge or information by virtue of a confidential or fiduciary relationship with another is not free to exploit that knowledge or information for his own personal benefit but must account to his principal for any profits derived therefrom. (See, e.g., *Byrne v. Barrett,* 268 N.Y. 199.) This, in turn, is merely a corollary of the broader principle, inherent in the nature of the fiduciary relationship, that prohibits a trustee or agent from extracting secret profits from his position of trust.

In support of their claim that the complaint fails to state a cause of action, the defendants take the position that, although it is admittedly wrong for an officer or director to use his position to obtain trading profits for himself in the stock of his corporation, the action ascribed to them did not injure or damage MAI in any way. Accordingly, the defendants continue, the corporation should not be permitted to recover the proceeds. They acknowledge that, by virtue of the exclusive access which officers and directors have to inside information, they possess an unfair advantage over other shareholders and, particularly, the persons who had purchased the stock from them but, they contend, the corporation itself was unaffected and, for that reason, a derivative action is an inappropriate remedy.

It is true that the complaint before us does not contain any allegation of damages to the corporation but this has never been considered to be an essential requirement for a cause of action founded on a breach of fiduciary duty. (See, e.g., *Matter of People [Bond & Mtge. Guar. Co.]*, 303 N.Y. 423, 431; *Wendt v. Fischer*, 243 N.Y. 439, 443; *Dutton v. Willner*, 52 N.Y. 312, 319.) This is because the function of such an action, unlike an ordinary tort or contract case, is not merely to *compensate* the plaintiff for wrongs committed by the defendant but, as this court declared many years ago (*Dutton v. Willner*, 52 N.Y. 312, 319, *supra*), "to *prevent* them, by removing from agents and trustees all inducement to attempt dealing for their own benefit in matters which they have undertaken for others, or to which their agency or trust relates." (Emphasis supplied.)

Just as a trustee has no right to retain for himself the profits yielded by property placed in his possession but must account to his beneficiaries, a corporate fiduciary, who is entrusted with potentially valuable information, may not appropriate that asset for his own use even though, in so doing, he causes no injury to the corporation. The primary concern, in a case such as this, is not to determine whether the corporation has been damaged but to decide, as between the corporation and the defendants, who has a higher claim to the proceeds derived from the exploitation of the information. In our opinion, there can be no justification for permitting officers and directors, such as the defendants, to retain for themselves profits which, it is alleged, they derived solely from exploiting information gained by virtue of their inside position as corporate officials.

In addition, it is pertinent to observe that, despite the lack of any specific allegation of damage, it may well be inferred that the defendants' actions might have caused some harm to the enterprise. Although the corporation may have little concern with the day-to-day transactions in its shares, it has a great interest in maintaining a reputation of integrity, an image of probity, for its management and in insuring the continued public acceptance and marketability of its stock. When officers and directors abuse their position in order to gain personal profits, the effect may be to cast a cloud on the corporation's name, injure stockholder relations and undermine public regard for the corporation's securities. As Presiding Justice BOTEIN aptly put it, in the course of his opinion for the Appellate Division, "[t]he prestige and good will of a corporation, so vital to its prosperity, may be undermined by the revelation that its chief officers had been making personal profits out of corporate events which they had not disclosed to the community of stockholders." (29 A D 2d, at p. 287.)

The defendants maintain that extending the prohibition against personal exploitation of a fiduciary relationship to officers and directors of a corporation will discourage such officials from maintaining a stake in the success of the corporate venture through share ownership, which, they urge, is an important incentive to proper performance of their duties. There is, however, a considerable difference between corporate officers who assume the same risks and obtain the same benefits as other shareholders and those who use their privileged position to gain special advantages not available to others. The sale of shares by the defendants for the reasons charged was not merely a wise investment decision which any prudent investor might have made. Rather, they were assertedly able in this case to profit solely because they had information which was not available to any one else—including the other shareholders whose interests they, as corporate fiduciaries, were bound to protect.

Although no appellate court in this State has had occasion to pass upon the precise question before us, the concept underlying the present cause of action is hardly a new one. (See, e.g., Securities Exchange Act of 1934 [48 U.S.Stat. 881], § 16[b]; U.S.Code, tit. 15, § 78p, subd. [b]; *Brophy v. Cities Serv. Co.,* 31 Del.Ch. 241; Restatement, 2d, Agency, § 388, comment *c*; Israels, A New Look at Corporate Directorship, 24 Business Lawyer 727, 732 *et seq.;* Note, 54 Cornell L.Rev. 306, 309–312.) Under Federal law (Securities Exchange Act of 1934, § 16[b]), for example, it is conclusively presumed that, when a director, officer or 10% shareholder buys and sells securities of his corporation within a six-month period, he is trading on inside information. The remedy which the Federal statute provides in that situation is precisely the same as that sought in the present case under State law, namely, an action brought by the corporation or on its behalf to recover all profits derived from the transactions.

In providing this remedy, Congress accomplished a dual purpose. It not only provided for an efficient and effective method of accomplishing its primary goal—the protection of the investing public from unfair treatment at the hands of corporate insiders—but extended to the corporation the right to secure for itself benefits derived by those insiders from their exploitation of their privileged position. The United States Court of Appeals for the Second Circuit has stated the policy behind section 16(b) in the following terms (*Adler v. Klawans,* 267 F.2d 840, 844):

> "The undoubted congressional intent in the enactment of § 16(b) was to discourage what was reasonably thought to be a widespread abuse of a fiduciary relationship—specifically to discourage if not prevent three classes of persons from making private and gainful use of information acquired by them by virtue of their official relationship to a corporation."

Although the provisions of section 16(b) may not apply to all cases of trading on inside information, it demonstrates that a derivative action can be an effective method for dealing with such abuses which may be used to accomplish a similar purpose in cases not specifically covered by the statute. In *Brophy v. Cities Serv. Co.* (31 Del.Ch. 241, *supra*), for example, the Chancery Court of Delaware allowed a similar remedy in a situation not covered by the Federal legislation. One of the defendants in that case was an employee who had acquired inside information that the corporate plaintiff was about to enter the market and purchase its own shares. On the basis of this confidential information, the employee, who was not an officer and, hence, not liable under Federal law, bought a large block of shares and, after the corporation's purchases had caused the price to rise, resold them at a profit. The court sustained the complaint in a derivative action brought for an accounting, stating that "[p]ublic policy will not permit an employee occupying a position of trust and confidence toward his employer to abuse that relation to his own profit, regardless of whether his employer suffers a loss" (31 Del.Ch., at p. 246). And a similar view has been expressed in the Restatement, 2d, Agency (§ 388, comment *c*):

> "*c. Use of confidential information.* An agent who acquires confidential information in the course of his employment or in violation of his duties has a duty . . . to account for any profits made by the use of such information, although this does not harm the principal. . . . So, if [a corporate officer] has 'inside' information that the corporation is about to purchase or sell securities, or to declare or to pass a dividend, profits made by him in stock transactions undertaken because of his knowledge are held in constructive trust for the principal."

In the present case, the defendants may be able to avoid liability to the corporation under section 16(b) of the Federal law since they had held the MAI shares for more than six months prior to the sales. Nevertheless, the alleged use of the inside information to dispose of their stock at a price considerably higher than its known value constituted the same sort of "abuse of a fiduciary relationship" as is condemned by the Federal law. Sitting as we are in this case as a court of equity, we should not hesitate to permit an action to prevent any unjust enrichment realized by the defendants from their allegedly wrongful act.

The defendants recognize that the conduct charged against them directly contravened the policy embodied in the Securities Exchange Act but, they maintain, the Federal legislation constitutes a comprehensive and carefully wrought plan for dealing with the abuse of inside information and that allowing a derivative action to be maintained under State law would interfere with the Federal scheme. Moreover, they urge, the existence of dual Federal and State remedies for the same act would create the possibility of double liability.

Individ. investors sold to a they sold the corp

An examination of the Federal regulatory scheme refutes the contention that it was designed to establish any particular remedy as exclusive. In addition to the specific provisions of section 16(b), the Securities and Exchange Act contains a general anti-fraud provision in section 10(b), (U.S.Code, tit. 15, § 78j, subd. [b]) which, as implemented by rule 10b–5 (Code of Fed.Reg., tit. 17, § 240.10b–5) under that section, renders it unlawful to engage in a variety of acts considered to be fraudulent. In interpreting this rule, the Securities and Exchange Commission and the Federal courts have extended the common-law definition of fraud to include not only affirmative misrepresentations, relied upon by the purchaser or seller, but also a failure to disclose material information which might have affected the transaction. (See, e.g., *Securities & Exch. Comm. v. Texas Gulf Sulphur Co.*, 401 F.2d 833, 847–848; *Myzel v. Fields*, 386 F.2d 718, 733–735.)

Accepting the truth of the complaint's allegations, there is no question but that the defendants were guilty of withholding material information from the purchasers of the shares and, indeed, the defendants acknowledge that the facts asserted constitute a violation of rule 10b–5. The remedies which the Federal law provides for such violation, however, are rather limited. An action could be brought, in an exceptional case, by the SEC for injunctive relief. This, in fact, is what happened in the *Texas Gulf Sulphur* case (401 F.2d 833, *supra*). The purpose of such an action, however, would appear to be more to establish a principle than to provide a regular method of enforcement. A class action under the Federal rule might be a more effective remedy but the mechanics of such an action have, as far as we have been able to ascertain, not yet been worked out by the Federal courts and several questions relating thereto have never been resolved. These include the definition of the class entitled to bring such an action, the measure of damages, the administration of the fund which would be recovered and its distribution to the members of the class. (See Note, 54 Cornell L.Rev. 306, 309, *supra*.) Of course, any individual purchaser, who could prove his own injury as a result of a rule 10b–5 violation can bring an action for rescission but we have not been referred to a single case in which such an action has been successfully prosecuted where the public sale of securities is involved. The reason for this is that sales of securities, whether through a stock exchange or over-the-counter, are characteristically anonymous transactions, usually handled through brokers, and the matching of the ultimate buyer with the ultimate seller presents virtually insurmountable obstacles. Thus, unless a section 16(b) violation is also present, the Federal law does not yet provide a really effective remedy.

In view of the practical difficulties inherent in an action under the Federal law, the desirability of creating an effective common-law remedy is manifest. "Dishonest directors should not find absolution from retributive justice", Ballantine observed in his work on Corporations ([rev. ed., 1946], p. 216), "by concealing their identity from their victims under the mask of the stock exchange." There is ample room in a situation such as is here presented for a "private Attorney General" to come forward and enforce proper behavior on the part of corporate officials through the medium of the derivative action brought in the name of the corporation. (See, e.g., *Associated Ind. v. Ickes,* 134 F.2d 694, 704; *Cherner v. Transitron Electronic Corp.,* 201 F.Supp. 934, 936.) Only by sanctioning such a cause of action will there be any effective method to prevent the type of abuse of corporate office complained of in this case.

There is nothing in the Federal law which indicates that it was intended to limit the power of the States to fashion additional remedies to effectuate similar purposes. Although the impact of Federal securities regulation has on occasion been said to have created a "Federal corporation law," in fact, its effect on the duties and obligations of directors and officers and their relation to the corporation and its shareholders is only occasional and peripheral. The primary source of the law in this area ever remains that of the State which created the corporation. Indeed, Congress expressly provided against any implication that it intended to pre-empt the field by declaring, in section 28(a) of the Securities Exchange Act of 1934 (48 U.S.Code 903), that "[t]he rights and remedies provided by this title shall be in addition to any and all other rights and remedies that may exist at law or in equity".

Nor should we be deterred, in formulating a State remedy, by the defendants' claim of possible double liability. Certainly, as already indicated, if the sales in question were publicly made, the likelihood that a suit will be brought by purchasers of the shares is quite remote. But, even if it were not, the mere possibility of such a suit is not a defense nor does it render the complaint insufficient. It is not unusual for an action to be brought to recover a fund which may be subject to a superior claim by a third party. If that be the situation, a defendant should not be permitted to retain the fund for his own use on the chance that such a party may eventually appear. A defendant's course, if he wishes to protect himself against double liability, is to interplead any and all possible claimants and bind them to the judgment (CPLR 1006, subd. [b]).

In any event, though, no suggestion has been made either in brief or on oral argument that any purchaser has come forward with a claim against the defendants or even that anyone is in a position to advance such a claim.[1] As we have stated, the defendants' assertion that such a party may come forward at some future date is not a basis for permitting them to retain for their own benefit the fruits of their allegedly wrongful acts. For all that appears, the present derivative action is the only effective remedy now available against the abuse by these defendants of their privileged position.

As we have previously indicated, what we have written must be read in the light of the charges contained in the complaint, and it must be borne in mind that "it will be incumbent upon the plaintiff, if he is

---

1. In the absence of any such appearance by adverse claimants, we need not now decide whether the corporation's recovery would be affected by any amounts which might have to be refunded by the defendant to the injured purchasers.

to succeed, to prove upon the trial the truth and correctness of his allegations." (*Walkovszky v. Carlton,* 23 N Y 2d 714, 715.)

The order appealed from should be affirmed, with costs, and the question certified answered in the affirmative.

Judges BURKE, SCILEPPI, BERGAN, KEATING, BREITEL and JASEN concur.

Order affirmed, etc.

Accord: Brophy v. Cities Service Co., 31 Del.Ch. 241, 70 A.2d 5 (1949). See also Carpenter v. United States, ___ U.S. ___, 108 S.Ct. 316, 98 L.Ed.2d 275 (1987), supra p. 881; Thomas v. Roblin Indus., Inc., 520 F.2d 1393, 1397 (3d Cir.1975); In re ORFA Securities Litigation, 654 F.Supp. 1449 (D.N.J.1987). Contra: Freeman v. Decio, 584 F.2d 186 (7th Cir.1978); Schein v. Chasen, 313 So.2d 739 (Fla.1975).

Chapter X

SHAREHOLDER SUITS

SECTION 1. INTRODUCTION

BACKGROUND NOTE

If the duties of care and loyalty that managers owe to their corporations could be enforced only in suits by the corporation, many wrongs done by managers would never be remedied. Where a majority of the corporation's shareholders benefit by the managers' breach of duty, they will normally continue to elect either the same managers or others who can be relied on not to institute litigation designed to remedy the wrong. Even where a majority of the shareholders do not benefit by the managers' wrongdoing, in publicly held corporations the difficulty of organizing the shareholders to oust the wrongdoers from office, and elect new directors who will bring suit against their predecessors, is often insuperable. To overcome these obstacles and hold wrongdoing managers and controlling shareholders to account, the law permits shareholders to bring suit on the corporation's behalf.

In Ross v. Bernhard, 396 U.S. 531, 534–35, 90 S.Ct. 733, 735–6, 24 L.Ed.2d 729 (1970), the Supreme Court sketched the background and nature of such suits in the following terms:

> The common law refused . . . to permit stockholders to call corporate managers to account in actions at law. The possibilities for abuse, thus presented, were not ignored by corporate officers and directors. Early in the 19th century, equity provided relief both in this country and in England. Without detailing these developments, it suffices to say that the remedy in this country, first dealt with by this Court in Dodge v. Woolsey, 18 How. 331 (1856), provided redress not only against faithless officers and directors but also against third parties who had damaged or threatened the corporate properties and whom the corporation through its managers refused to pursue. The remedy made available in equity was the derivative suit, viewed in this country as a suit to enforce a *corporate* cause of action against officers, directors, and third parties. As elaborated in the cases, one precondition for the suit was a valid claim on which the corporation could have sued; another was that the corporation itself had refused to proceed after suitable demand, unless excused by extraordinary conditions. Thus the dual nature of the stockholder's action: first, the plaintiff's right to sue on behalf of

the corporation and, second, the merits of the corporation's claim itself.

This type of suit is commonly known as a derivative action, since the shareholder's right to bring the suit derives from the corporation.

Two features of the derivative action warrant highlighting at the outset. First is the extraordinary procedural complexity inherent in such actions—complexity involving, for example, proper parties and their alignment, jurisdiction, demand on the board, demand on the shareholders, right to sue, intervention, settlement, and dismissal. Second is the difficult problem of social policy raised by such actions, particularly in the publicly held corporation. Through the derivative action, a shareholder with a tiny investment can force an expenditure by the corporation of a large amount of funds and executive time. The question is whether the overall benefits of such actions justify their overall costs, which are, in effect, borne involuntarily by the non-complaining shareholders.

Many or most of the issues to be considered in this chapter, although couched in technical terms, reflect an underlying tension between a concern that managers be held accountable for their wrongdoing, on the one hand, and a concern with the strike-suit potential of derivative actions, on the other. Emphasis on the former element leads to liberality in permitting derivative actions; emphasis on the latter leads to rules that restrict their maintenance. In weighing these concerns, it should be borne in mind that the derivative action and the disclosure requirements of the securities acts constitute the two major legal bulwarks against managerial self-dealing. The strike suit, in contrast, may very well be no more than an over-the-hill dragon, puffed into life to frighten the courts away from deciding substantive issues. In considering the various rules taken up in this chapter, it is therefore critical to evaluate the extent to which each rule cuts into the effectiveness of the derivative action, and whether the benefits of the rule justify that cost.

It should also be kept in mind, while considering the problems raised in this chapter, that significant substantive consequences often turn on the success of a motion to dismiss a derivative action on procedural grounds. If the plaintiff can survive such a motion, the facts that he already knows together with the material that he can develop through discovery will often lead to a quick and substantial settlement. If the defendant can get the case dismissed on procedural grounds, however, no other plaintiff may come forward—either because no other shareholder who would bring suit knows all the relevant facts, or because the statute of limitations has run. For practical purposes, then, many derivative actions will be won or lost on the basis of procedural motions that do not go to the merits of the case.

———

AMERICAN LAW INSTITUTE, PRINCIPLES OF CORPORATE GOVERNANCE, INTRODUCTION TO PART VI, REPORTER'S NOTE

Tent.Draft No. 8, 1988.

. . . 2. *The competing rationales of the derivative action.* As with other forms of tort actions, the derivative action's principal goals are deterrence and compensation. In addition, the action may at times provide the necessary opportunity for judicial law-making, both in updating the common law and in filling the inevitable gaps left by legislation. In this respect, the action has an educational and social-izing function, because in its absence considerable doubt might remain over what were the duties of corporate officers and directors in a given context. One of the most difficult policy questions concerning the derivative action is the appropriate balance to be struck among these competing rationales, because the end purposes of deterrence and compensation can frequently conflict. . . .

3. *Economic analysis of the derivative action.* A central concept in modern institutional economics is that of "agency cost," which refers to the costs that shareholders must incur to hold their management accountable. See, e.g., Jensen & Meckling, Theory of the Firm: Managerial Behavior, Agency Costs and Ownership Structure, 3 J.Fin. Econ. 305 (1970). Given the separation of management from owner-ship in public corporations, this concept assumes that the self-regard-ing manager may sometimes find it both possible and profitable to divert income or assets from the corporation to himself. In response, shareholders can seek to limit these opportunities by a variety of means, including monitoring and incentive compensation. In princi-ple, the stock market will also penalize the manager to a limited degree by discounting the value of the corporation's stock (which he also presumably holds), at least if it believes repetition of the miscon-duct is likely. Yet, none of these techniques is costless. Monitoring in particular is cost-efficient only up to the point that additional expenditures spent on monitoring avert a greater discounted loss in the future. Further expenditures on loss prevention would not be rational if the cost of detection or enforcement will exceed the additional loss prevented. As a result, there is a minimum level of exposure to losses caused by managerial misbehavior that rational shareholders must accept; this level is called the firm's "agency cost." Of course, no single firm's "agency cost" can be specified with any precision, but it is exactly this uncertainty that compounds the prob-lem. Because only imperfect information is available to the stock market about the agency cost associated with any given firm, an efficient market can be expected to discount the value of each firm by an average agency cost factor. See Ackerlof, The Market for "Lem-ons": Quality Uncertainty and the Market Mechanism, 84 Q.J. of Econ. 488 (1970). That is, because shareholders cannot reliably differentiate among firms in terms of the relative likelihood that their managements will misbehave in the future, shareholders will to a

degree treat both "good" and "bad" firms alike. In turn, this average discount implies that even the shares of corporations whose managements have not misbehaved will be discounted, and some shareholders may suffer to the extent that their corporation's stock is excessively discounted because the average agency cost exceeds the "true" agency cost applicable to their corporation.

The most important claim that can therefore be made for the derivative action is that it can reduce average agency costs. Both because the plaintiff's attorney is typically a specialist in such litigation and because shareholder coordination is not necessary in the case of the derivative action, it seems reasonable to believe that the availability of this action economizes on costs that otherwise would be necessarily incurred if shareholders were required to take collective action. For example, the costs incurred when a plaintiff's attorney obtains an injunction are likely to be far less than those that stockholders would have to incur to organize a proxy fight or that a hostile bidder would face in determining whether to make an unsolicited tender offer. Also, because the plaintiff's attorney is only compensated to the extent he is successful, the cost of wasted efforts is not directly borne by shareholders. In this light, the derivative action has been viewed as an efficient solution to the intractable organizational problem that would otherwise arise were it necessary to allocate the costs of opposing management proportionately among all shareholders.

The law applicable to derivative actions has long specified that the plaintiff's attorneys' fees are to be paid by the corporation. In practical effect, this rule creates a mechanism that taxes these legal costs proportionately among all shareholders, thereby ensuring that no shareholder is able to "free ride" on the efforts of another. See Scott, Corporation Law and the American Law Institute Corporate Governance Project, 35 Stan.L.Rev. 927, 940 (1980). Thus, the derivative action may represent the cost-effective means of deterring opportunistic behavior by agents, particularly in the case of non-recurring "one shot" transactions that the market cannot be expected to discipline effectively. See Cox, Compensation, Deterrence and the Market as Boundaries for Derivative Suit Procedures, 52 Geo.Wash.L.Rev. 745 (1984). Finally, because most shareholders hold a portfolio of securities, the fact that the costs in an individual derivative action may exceed the recovery to the corporation is not necessarily adverse to their interests, if there is a generic benefit to their broader interests as diversified shareholders in the form of enhanced deterrence against unfair self-dealing. These considerations in turn suggest that if meritorious derivative actions seeking to enforce legal rules that protect all shareholders could be easily terminated simply by showing that they would not yield a positive net recovery, average agency costs might rise, even though the individual corporation avoided a financial loss as a result of the termination.

AMERICAN LAW INSTITUTE, PRINCIPLES OF CORPORATE GOVERNANCE §§ 7.04, 7.05

Tent.Draft No. 8, 1988.

§ 7.04 Pleading and Procedure in Derivative Actions

The procedural rules applicable to a derivative action should require that:

(a) Each party's attorney of record in a derivative action sign every pleading, motion, and other paper filed on behalf of the party, and that such signature constitutes the attorney's certification that (1) to the best of the attorney's knowledge, information, and belief, formed after reasonable inquiry, the pleading, motion, or other paper is well grounded in fact and is warranted by existing law or by a good faith argument for the extension, modification, or reversal of existing law, and (2) the pleading, motion, or other paper is not interposed for any improper purpose, such as to harass or to cause unnecessary delay or needless increase in the cost of litigation.

(b) Allegations of fraud, bias, or control be pleaded with particularity.

§ 7.05 Judicial Control over Derivative Actions

The court having jurisdiction over a derivative action may:

(a) award applicable costs, including reasonable attorney's fees and expenses, against a party, or a party's counsel, in the following circumstances:

(1) at any time, if the court finds that any specific cause of action was asserted, or any motion, defense, pleading, request for discovery, or other action was made, in bad faith or without reasonable cause; or

(2) upon final judgment, if the court finds, in light of all the evidence, and considering both the state and trend of the substantive law, that the action taken as a whole was brought in bad faith or without reasonable cause or was defended in bad faith or in an unreasonable manner . . .

NOTE ON WHO CAN BRING A DERIVATIVE ACTION

1. It is generally agreed that the plaintiff in a derivative action must be a shareholder at the time the action is begun,[1] and must remain a shareholder during the pendency of the action.[2] What constitutes shareholdership for derivative-action purposes? In a few

---

1. See deHaas v. Empire Petroleum Co., 435 F.2d 1223 (10th Cir.1970); Werfel v. Kramarsky, 61 F.R.D. 674 (S.D.N.Y.1974); Vista Fund v. Garis, 277 N.W.2d 19 (Minn. 1979).

2. See Schilling v. Belcher, 582 F.2d 995 (5th Cir.1978); Tryforos v. Icarian Develop. Co., 518 F.2d 1258 (7th Cir.1975), cert. denied 423 U.S. 1091, 96 S.Ct. 887, 47 L.Ed.2d 103 (1976).

states, a statute or rule speaks to the issue directly. For example, N.Y.Bus.Corp. Law § 626(a) provides that the plaintiff in a derivative suit must be "a holder of shares or of voting trust certificates . . . or of a beneficial interest in such shares or certificates."

Where the statute is silent, courts normally define shareholdership in a very expansive manner. First, record ownership is generally not required; an unregistered shareholder will qualify. Rosenthal v. Burry Biscuit Corp., 30 Del.Ch. 299, 60 A.2d 106 (Ch.1948), noted in 17 U.Chi.L.Rev. 194 (1949); H.F.G. Co. v. Pioneer Pub. Co., 162 F.2d 536 (7th Cir.1947); Gallup v. Caldwell, 120 F.2d 90 (3d Cir. 1941). Second, legal ownership is not required—equitable ownership suffices. The latter category has been held to include, among others, an owner of stock held by a broker in a margin account in the broker's street name, a pledgee, the beneficiary of a trust, a legatee, a surviving widow with a community interest in stock held in her husband's name, and a person who has contracted to purchase stock.

It is also established that in an appropriate case a shareholder in a parent corporation can bring a derivative action on behalf of a subsidiary, despite the fact that he is not a shareholder in the subsidiary. See Painter, Double Derivative Suits and Other Remedies With Regard to Damaged Subsidiaries, 36 Ind.L.J. 143, 147–49 (1961); Note, Suits by a Shareholder in a Parent Corporation to Redress Injuries to the Subsidiary, 64 Harv.L.Rev. 1313 (1951).

2. An implication from the rule that the plaintiff in a derivative action must be a shareholder at the time he brings suit is that a creditor (including a bondholder) ordinarily has no right to bring a derivative action. Dodge v. First Wisconsin Trust Co., 394 F.Supp. 1124 (E.D.Wis.1975); Brooks v. Weiser, 57 F.R.D. 491 (S.D.N.Y. 1972); Dorfman v. Chemical Bank, 56 F.R.D. 363 (S.D.N.Y.1972).[3] Compare Hoff v. Sprayregan, 52 F.R.D. 243 (S.D.N.Y.1971) (holder of a convertible bond is a shareholder for derivative-action purposes)

3. This is the thrust of the modern cases, although the rule is not entirely clear, particularly when the older cases are taken into account. See Comment, 34 Mich.L.Rev. 521 (1936); Note, 82 U.Pa.L. Rev. 364, 369–71 (1934). Furthermore, some statutes allow derivative actions by creditors in certain cases, see, e.g., Wis. § 286.32, and some modern cases have either allowed a derivative action by a creditor without discussion, see Devereux v. Berger, 264 Md. 20, 284 A.2d 605 (1971), or have indicated in dicta that such an action would be allowed, see Capitol Wine & Spirits v. Pokrass, 277 A.D. 184, 98 N.Y.S.2d 291 (1950), aff'd 302 N.Y. 734, 98 N.E.2d 704 (1951).

Furthermore, a creditor who cannot bring a derivative action may nevertheless be able to bring a direct suit against an officer or director through some other mechanism. For example, a statute may permit direct suit by a creditor against an

officer or director in certain defined cases, such as misappropriation of corporate assets. If a corporation is insolvent, its receiver or trustee-in-bankruptcy can pursue a corporate cause of action against officers or directors on the creditors' behalf. (Such a suit is not derivative, since the receiver or trustee is vested with power to manage the corporation's affairs. However, where the receiver or trustee fails to bring such a suit a creditor may be able to bring it on the corporation's behalf if he is given permission to do so by a court with jurisdiction over the insolvent corporation's affairs.) See generally Note, Creditors' Derivative Suits on Behalf of Solvent Corporations, 88 Yale L.J. 1299 (1979).

If the corporation is in receivership, a shareholder may also need permission of the supervising court to bring suit. See Fields v. Fidelity General Ins. Co., 454 F.2d 682, 685 (7th Cir.1971).

with Harff v. Kerkorian, 324 A.2d 215 (Del.Ch.1974), aff'd in pertinent part 347 A.2d 133 (Del.1975) (contra).

3. Occasionally a statute gives an officer or director the right to bring a derivative action. See N.Y. Bus. Corp. Law § 720(b).

SECTION 2. THE NATURE OF THE DERIVATIVE SUIT

EISENBERG v. FLYING TIGER LINE, INC.

United States Circuit Court of Appeals, Second Circuit, 1971.
451 F.2d 267.

IRVING R. KAUFMAN, Circuit Judge:

Max Eisenberg, a resident of New York, "as stockholder of The Flying Tiger Line, Inc. [Flying Tiger], on behalf of himself and all other stockholders of said corporation similarly situated" commenced this action in the Supreme Court of the State of New York to enjoin the effectuation of a plan of reorganization and merger. Flying Tiger, a Delaware corporation with its principal place of business in California, removed the action to the District Court for the Eastern District of New York.

Flying Tiger pleaded several affirmative defenses and moved for an order to require Eisenberg to comply with New York Business Corporation Law § 627 (McKinney's Consol. Laws, c. 4, 1963), which requires a plaintiff suing derivatively on behalf of a corporation to post security for the corporation's costs. Judge Travia granted the motion without opinion and afforded Eisenberg thirty days to post security in the sum of $35,000. Eisenberg did not comply, his action was dismissed and he appeals. We find Eisenberg's cause of action to be personal and not derivative within the meaning of § 627. We therefore reverse the dismissal.

In this action, Eisenberg is seeking to overturn a reorganization and merger which Flying Tiger effected in 1969. He charges that a series of corporate maneuvers were intended to dilute his voting rights. In order to achieve this end, he alleges, Flying Tiger in July 1969 organized a wholly owned Delaware subsidiary, the Flying Tiger Corporation ("FTC"). In August, FTC in turn organized a wholly owned subsidiary, FTL Air Freight Corporation ("FTL"). The three Delaware corporations then entered into a plan of reorganization, subject to stockholder approval, by which Flying Tiger merged into FTL and only FTL survived. A proxy statement dated August 11 was sent to stockholders, who approved the plan by the necessary two-thirds vote at the stockholders' meeting held on September 15.

Upon consummation of this merger Flying Tiger ceased as the operating company, FTL took over operations and Flying Tiger shares were converted into an identical number of FTC shares. Thereafter,

FTL changed its name to "Flying Tiger Line, Inc.," for the obvious purpose of continuing without disruption the business previously conducted by Flying Tiger. The approximately 4,500,000 shares of the company traded on the New York and Pacific Coast stock exchanges are now those of the holding company, FTC, rather than those of the operating company, Flying Tiger. The effect of the merger is that business operations are now confined to a wholly owned subsidiary of a holding company whose stockholders are the former stockholders of Flying Tiger.

It is of passing interest that Eisenberg contends that the end result of this complex plan was to deprive minority stockholders of any vote or any influence over the affairs of the newly spawned company. Flying Tiger insists the plan was devised to bring about diversification without interference from the Civil Aeronautics Board, which closely regulates air carriers, and to better use available tax benefits. Even if any of these motives prove to be relevant, the alleged illegality is not relevant to the questions before this court. We are called on to decide, assuming Eisenberg's complaint is sufficient on its face, only whether he should have been required to post security for costs as a condition to prosecuting his action.

To resolve this question we look first to Cohen v. Beneficial Industrial Loan Corp., 337 U.S. 541, 62 S.Ct. 1221, 93 L.Ed. 1528 (1949), which instructs that a federal court with diversity jurisdiction must apply a state statute providing security for costs if the state court would require the security in similar circumstances. *Cohen* teaches that the applicability of costs security statutes cannot be determined upon a simplistic determination whether substantive or procedural law will govern. Justice Jackson, writing for the Court concluded that Erie RR. Co. v. Tompkins, 304 U.S. 64, 58 S.Ct. 817, 82 L.Ed. 1188 (1938), compelled the utilization of such statutes in federal courts. But, this Court still must determine whether to apply the New York costs security statute, Business Corporation Law § 627, or, as Eisenberg contends, Delaware law, which has no such requirement. New York clearly has indicated that § 627 will be applied in its courts whether or not New York substantive law controls the merits of the case. Business Corporation Law § 1319(a)(3) expressly enables foreign corporations doing business in New York to invoke § 627 against resident plaintiffs. See also, Gilbert v. Case, 3 A.D.2d 930, 163 N.Y.S.2d 179, 181 (App.Div.2d Dept.), rearg. and app. denied, 164 N.Y.S.2d 995, motion dismissed, 3 N.Y.2d 876, 166 N.Y.S.2d 498, (1957) (General Corporation Law § 61–a, predecessor of § 627, "may be invoked by a foreign corporation provided that it is doing business here and thus subjects itself to the jurisdiction of the courts of this State"). Since New York courts would invoke its own law on security for costs rather than Delaware's, we are required to do the same. See Klaxon Co. v. Stentor Elec. Mfg. Co., 313 U.S. 487, 61 S.Ct. 1020, 85 L.Ed. 1477 (1941).

Eisenberg argues, however, that New York courts would refuse to invoke § 627 in the instant case because the section applies exclusively to derivative actions specified in Business Corporation Law

§ 626.   He urges that his class action is representative and not derivative.

We are told that if the gravamen of the complaint is injury to the corporation the suit is derivative, but "if the injury is one to the plaintiff as a stockholder and to him individually and not to the corporation," the suit is individual in nature and may take the form of a representative class action.   13 Fletcher, Private Corporation § 5911 (1970 Rev.Vol.).   This generalization is of little use in our case which is one of those "borderline cases which are more or less troublesome to classify."   Id.   The essence of Eisenberg's claimed injury is that the reorganization has deprived him and fellow stockholders of their right to vote on the operating company affairs and that this right in no sense ever belonged to Flying Tiger itself.   This right, he says, belonged to the stockholders *per se.*   Flying Tiger notes, however, that the stockholders were harmed, if at all, only because their company was dissolved, and their vote can be restored only if that company is revived.   It insists, therefore, that stockholders are affected only secondarily or derivatively because we must first breathe life back into their dissolved corporation before the stockholders can be helped.

Despite a leading New York case which would seem at first glance to support Flying Tiger's position, we find that its contention misses the mark by a wide margin in its failure to distinguish between derivative and non-derivative class actions.   In Gordon v. Elliman, 306 N.Y. 456, 119 N.E.2d 331 (1954), by a vote of 4 to 3, the Court of Appeals took an expansive view of the coverage of § 627's predecessor, General Corporation Law § 61–b.   The majority held that an action to compel the payment of a dividend was derivative in nature and security for costs could be required.   The test formulated by the majority was "whether the object of the lawsuit is to recover upon a chose in action belonging directly to the stockholders, or whether it is to compel the performance of corporate acts which good faith requires the directors to take in order to perform a duty which they owe to the corporation, and through it, to its stockholders."   306 N.Y. at 459, 119 N.E.2d at 334.   Pursuant to this test it is argued that, if Flying Tiger's directors had a duty not to merge the corporation that duty was owed to the corporation and only derivatively to its stockholders.   Both the 4–1 Appellate Division and the 4–3 Court of Appeals opinions evoked the quick and unanimous condemnation of commentators.   Moreover, this test, "which appears to sweep away the distinction between a representative and a derivative action," in effect classifying all stockholder class actions as derivative, has been limited strictly to its facts by lower New York courts.[5]   Lazar v. Knolls Cooperative Section No. 2, Inc., 205 Misc. 748, 130 N.Y.S.2d 407, 410 (Sup.Ct.1954).   See also, Lehrman v. Godchaux Sugars, Inc., 207 Misc. 314, 138 N.Y.S. 163 (Sup.Ct.1955); (action to enjoin a

---

5.   In his dissenting opinion, Judge Fuld noted "[i]n a very real sense, all suits against corporations * * * involve the actions of the directors or of officers re- sponsible to the directors" so the majority's test would do away with representative class actions altogether.   306 N.Y. at 470, 119 N.E.2d at 340.

recapitalization); Davidson v. Rabinowitz, 140 N.Y.S.2d 875 (Sup. Ct.1955) (Botein, J.) (action to force dissolution). In *Lazar,* a stockholder sought to force directors to call a stockholders' meeting. The court stated security for costs could not be required where a plaintiff

> "does not challenge acts of the management on behalf of the corporation. He challenges the right of the present management to exclude him and other stockholders from proper participation in the affairs of the corporation. He claims that the defendants are interfering with the plaintiff's rights and privleges as stock-holders."

130 N.Y.S. at 410, 205 Misc. at 752. In substance, this is . . . similar to what Eisenberg challenges here.

The legislature also was concerned with the sweeping breadth of *Gordon.* In the recodification of corporate statutes completed in 1963, it added three words to the definition of derivative suits contained in § 626. Suits are now derivative only if brought in the right of a corporation to procure a judgment "in its favor." This was to "forestall any such pronouncement in the future as that made by the Court of Appeals in Gordon v. Elliman." Hornstein, "Analysis of Business Corporation Law," 6 McKinney's Consolidated Laws of New York Ann. 483 (1963).

Other New York cases which have distinguished between derivative and representative actions are of some interest. In Horwitz v. Balaban, 112 F.Supp. 99 (S.D.N.Y.1949), a stockholder sought to restrain the exercise of conversion rights that the corporation had granted to its president. The court found the action representative and refused to require security, setting forth the test as "[w]here the corporation has no right of action by reason of the transaction complained of, the suit is representative, not derivative." Id. at 101. Similarly, actions to compel the dissolution of a corporation have been held representative, since the corporation could not possibly benefit therefrom. Fontheim v. Walker, 141 N.Y.S.2d 62 (Sup.Ct.1955); Davidson v. Rabinowitz, supra. Lennan v. Blakely, 80 N.Y.S.2d 288 (Sup.Ct.1948), teaches that an action by preferred stockholders against directors is not derivative. And Lehrman v. Godchaux Sugars, Inc., supra, discloses that an action by a stockholder complaining that a proposed recapitalization would unfairly benefit holders of another class of stock was representative. These cases and *Lazar,* supra, are totally consistent with the postulates of the leading treatises. See, e.g., 13 W. Fletcher, Private Corporation § 5915 (Rev.Vol.1970); 3B J. Moore, Federal Practice ¶ 23.1.16[1] (2d ed. 1969). Professor Moore instructs that "where a shareholder sues on behalf of himself and all others similarly situated to * * * enjoin a proposed merger or consolidation * * * he is not enforcing a derivative right; he is, by an appropriate type of class suit enforcing a right common to all the shareholders which runs against the corporation."

Eisenberg's position is even stronger than it would be in the ordinary merger case. In routine merger circumstances the stockholders retain a voice in the operation of the company, albeit a corporation other than their original choice. Here, however, the reorganization deprived him and other minority stockholders of any voice in the affairs of their previously existing operating company.

It is thus clear to us that *Gordon* is factually distinguishable from the instant case. Moreover, a close analysis of other New York cases, the amendment to § 626 and the major treatises, lead us to conclude that *Gordon* has lost its viability as stating a broad principle of law. . . .

Furthermore, we view as an objective of a requirement for security for costs the prevention of strike suits and collusive settlements. Where directors are sued for mismanagement, the risk of personal monetary liability is a strong motive for bringing the suit and inducing settlement. Here, no monetary damages are sought, and no individuals will be liable.

Perhaps the strongest string in Eisenberg's bow is one he helped to fashion when he made an investment some forty years ago in Central Zone Property Corp. In 1952 that New York corporation obtained stockholder approval to transfer its assets to a new Delaware corporation in return for the new company's stock. The stock was to be held by trustees in a voting trust, and the former stockholders received voting trust certificates. Eisenberg complained that this effectively deprived him of a voice in the operation of his company which would be run in the future by the trustees of the voting trust. The Court of Appeals agreed that New York law did not permit such a reorganization. Eisenberg v. Central Zone Property Corp., 203 Misc. 59, 116 N.Y.S.2d 154, aff'd, 306 N.Y. 58, 115 N.E.2d 652 (1953). Although we have emphasized that we do not reach the merits of Eisenberg's present complaint, it is of some interest that security for costs was neither sought nor was it discussed in the *Central Zone* opinions. . . . It was clear to all that the allegations of the complaint, quite similar in character to the instant one, stated a representative cause of action. We cannot conceive that the question of security for costs was not considered by the able counsel for the corporation or by the court, particularly since *Gordon* had been decided in the Appellate Division less than one year before the *Central Zone* decision in the Court of Appeals and extensive commentaries had already appeared. We believe Eisenberg's action should not have been dismissed for failure to post security pursuant to § 627.

Reversed.

NOTE ON THE DISTINCTION BETWEEN DERIVATIVE AND DIRECT ACTIONS

1. Two kinds of reasons are commonly advanced for distinguishing between a *derivative* action, which is brought on the corporation's behalf against either corporate fiduciaries or third persons, and a *direct* action, which is brought on a shareholder's own behalf against either

corporate fiduciaries or the corporation itself. The first kind of reason is theoretical: Since a corporation is a legal person separate from its shareholders, an injury to the corporation is not an injury to its shareholders. This proposition is somewhat dubious, since every injury to a corporation must also have an impact, however slight, on the shareholders as well. The second kind of reason is pragmatic: "(1) To avoid a multiplicity of suits by each injured shareholder, (2) to protect the corporate creditors, and (3) to protect all the stockholders since a corporate recovery benefits all equally." Watson v. Button, 235 F.2d 235, 237 (9th Cir.1956).

2. Some principles concerning the distinction between derivative and direct actions are relatively well-established. At one end of the spectrum, a wrongful act that depletes or destroys corporate assets, and affects the shareholder only by reducing the value of his stock, gives rise only to an action on the corporation's behalf. At the other end, a wrongful act that does not deplete or divert corporate assets, and interferes with rights that are traditionally viewed as either incident to the ownership of stock or inhering in the shares themselves (such as voting or pre-emptive rights), gives rise only to a direct action by the injured shareholders. Thus in Reifsnyder v. Pittsburgh Outdoor Advertising Co., 405 Pa. 142, 173 A.2d 319 (1961), Reifsnyder had brought suit attacking a transaction in which Pittsburgh Outdoor Advertising, acting pursuant to a shareholder resolution, had purchased all the Pittsburgh stock owned by General (Pittsburgh's largest shareholder), and had increased its indebtedness to finance the purchase. Reifsnyder's theories were that (i) the transaction was accomplished only by the vote of General, acting in its shareholder capacity, and General's shares were not entitled to vote on the resolution because of its self-interest; and (ii) the price paid by Pittsburgh for General's shares was excessive. The court held the suit was direct, not derivative. If the complaint had been limited to the excessive-price theory, the court said, the action may have been deemed derivative. However, the gravamen of the complaint concerned the right of a majority shareholder to vote on a resolution in which it had a personal pecuniary interest, and this theory gave rise to a direct action. "If it should become a rule of law that a shareholder cannot vote on matters in which he has an interest, an aggrieved shareholder would necessarily be permitted to bring an action to enjoin the voting of 'interested' shares or to require the corporate officers to rescind action taken in reliance upon the votes of such shares. The aggrieved shareholder in those instances would, in essence, be preventing the dilution of his own votes by challenging and disqualifying improper votes. The right to vote is basic and fundamental to most shares of stock and is independent of any right that the corporate entity possesses and the shareholder could enforce and protect such rights by bringing a direct action." [1]

1. In Knapp v. Bankers Securities Corp., 230 F.2d 717, 721 (3d Cir.1956), the Third Circuit held that as a matter of Pennsylvania law "[t]he right to dividends is an incident of the ownership of stock," so that a suit to compel the declaration of dividends lies as a direct action. The New York Court of Appeals had earlier reached a different result in Gordon v. Elliman, 306 N.Y. 456, 119 N.E.2d 331 (1954), but as the

3. Many kinds of cases fall between the two ends of the spectrum described in the preceding paragraph. In some of these cases, the rules are relatively clear; in others, rules are just beginning to emerge. For example, it is relatively clear that a direct action will lie based on the issuance of stock for the wrongful purpose of perpetuating or shifting control (e.g., Sheppard v. Wilcox, 210 Cal.App.2d 53, 26 Cal.Rptr. 412 (1962)), or to enjoin a threatened ultra vires act (e.g., Alexander v. Atlanta & West Point R.R., 113 Ga. 193, 38 S.E. 772 (1901)). A rule permitting a direct action seems to be emerging in suits based on wrongs by controlling against noncontrolling shareholders (e.g., Jones v. H.F. Ahmanson & Co., Chapter VIII, Section 6, supra. Suits to enjoin improperly authorized corporate actions are also commonly treated as direct actions, either implicitly (that is, without discussion of the issue), or explicitly, but the authorities are in conflict on this type of case. See G. Hornstein, 2 Corporation Law and Practice § 627 (1959).

4. In many cases a wrongful act both depletes corporate assets *and* interferes with rights traditionally viewed as inhering in shares. The general principle governing such cases is that a direct action is not precluded simply because the same facts could also give rise to a derivative action. A recent illustration is Snyder v. Epstein, 290 F.Supp. 652, 655 (E.D.Wis.1968), where the court held that "[t]he sale of a corporate office gives rise to a cause of action for breach . . . of the fiduciary duties owed to both the corporation and the stockholders." Similarly, in Bennett v. Breuil Petroleum Corp., 34 Del.Ch. 6, 99 A.2d 236 (Ch.1953), the plaintiff claimed that the controlling shareholders had caused the corporation to issue stock for an improper purpose (impairing his interest and forcing him out on management's terms), and at a grossly inadequate consideration. The court held that the first claim stated a direct and the second a derivative cause of action.[2]

Another important kind of case in which suit may be either direct or derivative is that involving proxy-rule violations. Insofar as such a violation interferes with the individual shareholder's voting right, suit can be regarded as direct; insofar as it involves a breach of management's fiduciary obligations, suit can be regarded as derivative. See Borak v. J.I. Case Co., 317 F.2d 838 (7th Cir.1963).

---

opinion in *Flying Tiger* points out, that decision was widely criticized and the rule it handed down was eventually reversed by the New York legislature. See also Bokat v. Getty Oil Co., 262 A.2d 246 (Del.1970).

2. See also, e.g., Buschmann v. Professional Men's Ass'n, 405 F.2d 659 (7th Cir. 1969). In General Rubber Co. v. Benedict, 215 N.Y. 18, 109 N.E. 96 (1915), a parent corporation sued one of its directors for acquiescing in the looting of a subsidiary, thereby injuring the parent by reducing the value of its shares in the subsidiary. The court held that the complaint stated a good cause of action. In answer to the argument that recovery would subject the defendant to double liability, the court said: (1) the subsidiary might not have a cause of action, since the defendant was not its director and would be liable to it only if he participated in—rather than merely failed to prevent—the wrong; and (2) the possibility that the subsidiary had an enforceable cause of action should be taken into consideration in determining the extent to which the value of the parent's shares had been depreciated. Cf. In re Auditore's Will, 249 N.Y.S. 335, 164 N.E. 242 (1928).

AMERICAN LAW INSTITUTE, PRINCIPLES OF CORPORATE GOVERNANCE § 7.01

Tent. Draft No. 8, 1988.

§ 7.01   Direct and Derivative Actions Distinguished

* * *

(d) If a corporation is closely held, the court may in its discretion treat an action raising derivative claims as a direct action, exempt it from those restrictions and defenses applicable only to derivative actions, and direct an individual recovery, if it finds that to do so will not (i) unfairly expose the corporation or the defendants to a multiplicity of actions, (ii) materially prejudice the interests of creditors in the corporation, or (iii) interfere with a fair distribution of the recovery among all interested persons.

SECTION 3.   INDIVIDUAL RECOVERY IN DERIVATIVE ACTIONS

KEENAN v. ESHLEMAN

Supreme Court of Delaware, 1938.
23 Del.Ch. 234, 2 A.2d 904, 120 A.L.R. 227.

[H.A. Stone & Company, a corporation (hereafter referred to as Stone) was organized in 1915 for the purpose of financing small companies in need of financial assistance. Its plan was to sell on behalf of any company which it had accepted as a client, an issue of the latter's preferred shares, Stone receiving in payment for its services a majority of the common shares. Stone organized and owned all the shares of General Stabilizing & Guaranty Fund, Inc. (hereafter referred to as General) which, although having no assets, made a practice of undertaking to guarantee the payment of dividends on the preferred shares of the client companies of Stone. Sanitary Company of America (hereafter referred to as Sanitary) was one of these client companies and was engaged in the manufacture of sewer pipe and plumbing supplies.

[In 1923 Stone and General failed and their assets, which consisted of shares of the common stock of Sanitary and other companies and of waterfront land in Mobile, Alabama, were taken over by a shareholders' committee. In 1924 these assets were transferred to Consolidated Management Association (hereafter referred to as Consolidated) which was organized for the purpose of attempting to salvage something for the shareholders of Stone. All the shares of Consolidated were issued to defendants Keenan and Brewer as voting trustees, voting trust certificates being issued to the old shareholders of Stone. As a result Keenan and Brewer controlled Consolidated as voting trustees and controlled Sanitary by reason of the fact that Consolidated owned a majority of the voting shares of Sanitary.

[From 1924 to 1933 defendants Keenan, Marvin, and Brewer were, respectively, the president, vice president, and secretary and treasurer of Consolidated, and were officers and majority directors of Sanitary.

[By resolution of the directors of Sanitary adopted November 15, 1924, that company agreed to pay $300 a month for management services to be rendered it by Consolidated, the total amount paid by Sanitary to Consolidated pursuant to this resolution being $28,800. This amount was substantially identical with the amount paid by Consolidated to Keenan, Brewer and Marvin, who were its only officers and employees, with the exception of a part-time stenographer. During the same period Sanitary paid Keenan and Brewer substantial salaries and bonuses.

[Minority shareholders of Sanitary brought a bill for an accounting claiming that in effect Sanitary paid Keenan and Brewer a double compensation for the same services and that Marvin participated in the wrong. After the suit had been pending for nearly three years, the majority shareholders of Sanitary voted to ratify and confirm the action of the directors and officers of that company with respect to the matters complained of in this suit.

[The court, after holding that the conduct of the defendants "constituted fraud on the corporation and that it was not in the power of the majority of the stockholders to deprive the minority of their right to insist upon a rectification," considered the question whether only those shareholders who had not ratified the defendants' acts should share in the recovery.]

LAYTON, C.J. . . . Finally the appellants contend that the recovery decreed by the Court below should have been limited to those stockholders who had not acquiesced in, ratified, approved and confirmed the wrongful acts complained of. The question was first suggested by the Chancellor in his opinion reported in 21 Del.Ch. 259, 187 A. 25: whether ratification by a majority of the stockholders, while not sufficient to bar a remedy to the minority, may yet be shown for the purpose of confining the relief of the decree to the dissentients only. In his opinion reported in 22 Del.Ch. 82, 194 A. 40, the question was posed as follows [page 42]: "should the defendants pay to the corporation the full amount of restitution, or should they only pay to the complainants individually the pro rata amount of the recoverable sum which the proportion of their shares bears to the total number of shares outstanding?" He observed that the bill was filed on behalf of the corporation; that the relief sought was in redress of a wrong to the corporation; and that if the recoverable amount should be reduced to a sum sufficient to recompense only the dissentient stockholders and should be decreed to be paid to those of them asserting their claim, the suit would be transformed by the decree to one seeking an individual redress from one asserting a corporate claim; that the only theory upon which this case could be justified was that as the corporation's claim against the officers was a part of its assets, and that as the assets were derivatively the property of the stockholders, it must follow that if the complainants and others in like situations should be paid this aliquot part of the recovery, they would be fully compensated; that this view treats the recovery as an asset available for dividends immediately to be distributed; and that as some of the stockholders had by their votes waived their rights to their share of the dividends, payment should be decreed only to the dissenting stockholders. After reviewing the cases, the court below disapproved entirely of the theory of such decree in the circumstances presented, and ordered restitution in full to be made to the corporation. The appellants assign this as error, and urge that, within the principles of remedial equity, adequate redress of the wrong would be accomplished by a decree awarding to the dissentients an aliquot part of the recovery; and they offer certain authorities in support of their contention. In Bailey v. Jacobs, 325 Pa. 187, 189 A. 320, it appears that the bill of complaint was filed by the complainants to compel the defendant, as President of a corporation, to account to the complainants as shareholders, for profits made through his personal use of corporate assets. The court observed that while the bill asserted a cause of action which was essentially derivative from the company itself, yet that distribution of the amount recoverable could be properly made directly to the plaintiffs, and that it was not necessary that the money be paid into the treasury of the company and then redistributed, since shareholders other than the plaintiff had presumably either assented to the defendant's acts or waived their rights in the present proceeding by failure to join therein. A distinguishing feature of this case, however, is that the corporations involved had liquidated their assets, and existed, as the court stated, "merely as legal entities." . . .

. . . Matthews v. Headley Chocolate Co., 130 Md. 523, 100 A. 645, arose upon an exceptional state of facts. The bill was filed by the company itself to recover from Matthews and others exorbitant salaries. The defendants, officers of the company, owned seventy-five per cent. of the company's stock. They sold to new interests a majority of the stock, presumably 351 shares at an assured price of $35,100.00. The bill was brought to recover from the former officers exorbitant salaries which they had caused to be voted to themselves. It was found that the purchasers of the stock had got exactly what they had bargained for and had not been imposed upon by Matthews. While the bill was brought by the company, the court found that it could be maintained for the benefit of minority stockholders, but that recovery should be limited "to the extent of the proportions of the sum recovered due such minority stockholders, if any, as are not barred by laches, limitations or acquiescence . . . and anything recovered should be directed to be paid to them by the corporation." [Page 651.] The court was impressed with the fact that if the former officers should be required to pay to the corporation the entire amount of the recoverable claim, the purchaser's share of the recovery would exceed by $11,000 the amount they paid for their stock. Brown v. DeYoung, supra, was greatly relied upon, the court either not knowing or ignoring, the fact that the Illinois Court in Voorhees v. Mason et al., supra, declined to follow it. Whatever view may be taken of the case its factual situation is so different as to make it inapplicable as an authority here.

The question is whether ratification of fraudulent acts by a majority of the stockholders enures to the benefit of the defendants to the extent that the decree against them should be in such amount as to redress the wrong suffered by the dissenting stockholders by causing to be paid to them a dividend of the recoverable amount measured by their stock holdings. The answer must be in the negative. In the first place, it does not appear that the financial position of the company was such as to permit the disbursement of the recoverable amount as a dividend. The misappropriations were a fraud on Sanitary, acts which the directors could not have authorized, and which the stockholders could not ratify. To allow the defendants to retain a part of the misappropriations in proportion to the stock interest of the ratifying stockholders would be to permit ratification of illegal acts to that extent. In the circumstances it was ultra vires the corporation, its directors and stockholders, to make donations of corporate assets. In effect, to allow the defendants to retain a part of their unlawful gains would constitute a gift. The action here was a derivative one, brought on behalf of the corporation, and the complaint and the defenses are to be considered as though the corporation itself were suing the defendants. If such were the action, releases to the individual defendants by one or more stockholders would be without legal effect, and in a derivative suit, such as this, releases, ratifications or waivers are equally ineffective. To permit the recovery to be diminished by an amount in proportion to the stock holdings of the ratifying stockholders would tend to encourage fraud; the effect would be to transform, by molding the decree, a derivative action into one for the benefit of the individual; and would not accord with the theory of the complaint, the prayer for relief, or the inherent nature of the wrong sought to be redressed. It would tend to weaken, if not to destroy, the efficacy of a stockholder's action to correct a corporate wrong; and would compel the complaining stockholder to accept that for which he had not sued.

It is true that the benefit of an action brought by a corporation, or a derivative action on its behalf, necessarily results to all of the shareholders equally, even when some of them have been wrongdoers, or have by acquiescence, or ratification, forfeited their equitable claims to redress; but the best method to work out the rights of the parties in a case of this kind is to preserve the fiction of corporate entity. If the misappropriation is to be regarded as a fund for a dividend in which the dissenting stockholders are to share, the result is a subterfuge, and in most cases, violative of equity. It is an old saying that one should be just before being generous, and this common sense truth is especially applicable to stockholders who, for one reason or another, are willing to condone a wrong done to their corporation and themselves. They cannot be generous with the corporation's money.

They, of course, may be as generous as they please when the money has become their own.

While there may be exceptional cases, as for example, Bailey v. Jacobs, supra, and Matthews v. Headley Chocolate Co., supra, where remedial equity is satisfied by allowing a recovery in an amount sufficient to satisfy non-assenting stockholders measured by their stock holdings, we are of opinion that, generally, where the action is a derivative one, brought for the benefit of a going corporation, equitable principles demand that the theory of the action be recognized and that the whole recoverable amount be decreed to be paid to the corporation, notwithstanding releases, ratifications or waivers after the event. . . .

The decree of the Court below entered on July 14, 1937, is sustained.

PERLMAN v. FELDMANN
United States Court of Appeals, Second Circuit, 1955.
219 F.2d 173.

Chapter VIII, Section 5, supra.

NOTE ON INDIVIDUAL RECOVERY IN DERIVATIVE ACTIONS

1. It is frequently said that pro rata recovery may be decreed to prevent the wrongdoers from sharing in the recovery. See, e.g., Atkinson v. Marquart, 112 Ariz. 304, 541 P.2d 556 (1975). However, in most derivative actions the defendants own stock in the corporation, and this in itself seldom leads to pro rata recovery. Nor should it, in the typical case. For example, suppose D, the owner of forty percent of Blue Corporation, is found liable in a derivative suit in the amount of $1 million. If corporate recovery is decreed, D must pay Blue $1 million. Since D "shares" in the recovery, his net output is only $600,000 (assuming that he can recover the balance through a dividend or appreciation in the value of his stock). But if pro rata recovery is decreed, D's output will also be $600,000. Indeed, for reasons of liquidity D may very well prefer the pro rata alternative. The fact that D "shares" in a corporate recovery is therefore not sufficient in itself to justify pro rata relief.

2. Similarly, it is sometimes said that pro rata recovery is appropriate where the wrongdoers are still in control of the corporation, and therefore would control any corporate recovery. See Backus v. Finkelstein, 23 F.2d 357, 366 (D.C.Minn.1927); Note, 69 Harv.L.Rev. 1314, at 1314–16 (1956). However, derivative actions in situations where the wrongdoers still control the corporation are legion, and pro rata recovery will normally not be decreed on this ground alone.

3. Notwithstanding some of the language in Keenan v. Eshleman, the cases suggest that pro rata relief will be decreed where the great bulk of the corporation's shares are held by persons who could not themselves have brought suit because they are subject to a personal defense. For example, in Young v. Columbia Oil Co., 110 W.Va. 364, 158 S.E. 678 (1931), pro rata recovery was decreed where thirteen of sixteen shareholders were barred by laches or acquiescence, and the remaining three shareholders owned only 145 of the corporation's 5000 outstanding shares. In Joyce v. Congdon, 114 Wash. 239, 195 P. 29 (1921), pro rata recovery was decreed where 423 out of the corporation's 429 shares were owned by either the wrongdoers, persons alleged by the plaintiff to be in collusion with the wrongdoers, or persons who had acquired their stock from the wrongdoers. In Chounis v. Laing, 125 W.Va. 275, 23 S.E.2d 628 (1942), more than ninety-five percent of the shareholders had either ratified or participated in the defendant's wrongful actions. The court held that the ratification was not effective as against innocent minority shareholders, but decreed pro rata relief, excluding all those shareholders who had either participated or ratified. See also, e.g., May v. Midwest Refining Co., 121 F.2d 431 (1st Cir.1941), cert. denied 314 U.S. 668, 62 S.Ct. 129, 86 L.Ed. 534, noted, 30 Calif.L.Rev. 338 (1942).

4. Still another type of case in which pro rata recovery may be decreed is that in which Corporation A, against whom a wrong was committed, is merged into Corporation B, and some or all of B's shareholders are barred from bringing a derivative suit—for example, because they had all participated in the wrong. In Gabhart v. Gabhart, 267 Ind. 370, 370 N.E.2d 345 (1977) the court said that in such cases, "[s]ince no wrong should be without a remedy a Court of Equity may grant relief, pro-rata, to a former shareholder of a merged corporation, whose equity was adversely affected by the fraudulent act of an officer or director and whose means of redress otherwise would be cut off by the merger, if there is no shareholder of the surviving corporation eligible to maintain a derivative action for such wrong and said shareholder had no prior opportunity for redress by derivative action against either the merged or the surviving corporation." Cf. Bokat v. Getty Oil Co., 262 A.2d 246 (Del.1970).

SECTION 4. THE RIGHT TO TRIAL BY JURY IN DERIVATIVE ACTIONS

NOTE ON THE RIGHT TO TRIAL BY JURY IN DERIVATIVE ACTIONS

Since a derivative action has traditionally been conceived of as an equitable remedy, until recently it did not carry the right to a trial by jury. In 1970, however, the Supreme Court held in Ross v. Bernhard, 396 U.S. 531, 90 S.Ct. 733, 24 L.Ed.2d 729 that in a derivative action brought in federal court, under the Seventh Amendment, the parties have a right to a jury where the action would be triable to a jury if it had been brought by the corporation itself rather than by a shareholder.

The Seventh Amendment applies only to federal proceedings, and the extent to which state courts will follow Ross v. Bernhard remains to be seen. Compare Rankin v. Frebank Co., 47 Cal.App.3d 75, 121 Cal.Rptr. 348 (1975) (under the California Constitution there is no right to a jury in derivative actions), and Pelfrey v. Bank of Greer, 270 S.C. 691, 244 S.E.2d 315 (1978) (same result under South Carolina statute) with Finance, Investment & Rediscount Co. v. Wells, 409 So.2d 1341 (Ala.1981) (there is a right to a jury trial under Alabama law), and Fedoryszyn v. Weiss, 62 Misc.2d 889, 310 N.Y.S.2d 55 (1970) (same under New York law). See generally D. DeMott, Shareholder Derivative Actions § 4.18 (1987).

SECTION 5.   THE CONTEMPORANEOUS–OWNERSHIP RULE

FED. RULES OF CIVIL PROC., RULE 23.1

[See Statutory Supplement]

REV. MODEL BUS. CORP. ACT § 7.40

[See Statutory Supplement]

N.Y. BUS. CORP. LAW § 626

[See Statutory Supplement]

BANGOR PUNTA OPERATIONS, INC. v. BANGOR & AROOSTOOK R.R.

Supreme Court of the United States, 1974.
417 U.S. 703, 94 S.Ct. 2578, 41 L.Ed.2d 418.

Mr. Justice POWELL delivered the opinion of the Court. . . .

I

[Prior to October 1964, Bangor & Aroostook Corporation ("B & A") held 98.3% of the stock of the Bangor & Aroostook Railroad Company ("BAR"), a Maine corporation. In October 1964, B & A sold its BAR stock to Bangor Punta, a Delaware corporation. Bangor Punta held the stock for five years, and then sold it in October 1969 to Amoskeag Co. for $5 million. Amoskeag later acquired additional shares which gave it ownership of more than 99% (but less than 100%) of BAR.] *

In 1971, BAR . . . filed the present action against Bangor Punta . . . in the United States District Court for the District of Maine. The complaint specified 13 counts of alleged mismanagement, misappropriation, and waste of BAR's corporate assets occurring during the period from 1960 through 1967 when B & A and then Bangor Punta controlled BAR.[1] Damages were sought in the amount of $7,000,000 for violations of both federal and state laws. The federal statutes and regulations alleged to have been violated included § 10 of the Clayton Act, 15 U.S.C.A. § 20; § 10(b) of the Securities Exchange Act of 1934, 15 U.S.C.A. § 78j(b); and Rule 10b–5 . . . . The state claims were grounded on § 104 of the Maine Public Utilities Act, Maine Rev.Stat.Ann., Tit. 35, § 104 (1965), and the common law of Maine.

The complaint focused on four intercompany transactions which allegedly resulted in injury to BAR. Counts I and II averred that B & A, and later Bangor Punta, overcharged BAR for various legal, accounting, printing, and other services. Counts III, IV, V, and VI averred that B & A improperly acquired the stock of the St. Croix Paper Co. which BAR owned through its subsidiary. Counts VII, VIII, IX, and X charged that B & A and Bangor Punta improperly caused BAR to declare special dividends to its stockholders, including B & A and Bangor Punta, and also caused BAR's subsidiary to borrow in order to pay regular dividends. Counts XI, XII, and XIII charged that B & A improperly caused BAR to excuse payment by B & A and Bangor Punta of the interest due on a loan made by BAR to B & A. In sum, the complaint alleged that during the period of their control of BAR, Bangor Punta, and its predecessor in interest B & A, "exploited it solely for their own purposes" and "calculatedly drained the resources of BAR in violation of law for their own benefit."

The District Court granted petitioners' motion for summary judgment and dismissed the action. 353 F.Supp. 724 (1972). The court first observed that although the suit purported to be a primary action brought in the name of the corporation, the real party in interest and hence the actual beneficiary of any recovery, was Amoskeag, the present owner of more than 99% of the outstanding stock of BAR. The court then noted that Amoskeag had acquired all of its BAR stock long after the alleged wrongs occurred and that Amoskeag did not contend that it had not received full value for its purchase

---

* In the interests of clarity, the statement of facts eliminates subsidiaries that do not figure in the opinion. (Footnote by ed.)

1. Several of the alleged acts of corporate mismanagement occurred between 1960 and 1964 when B & A . . . was in control of the railroad. Liability for these acts was nevertheless sought to be imposed on Bangor Punta, even though it had no interest in either BAR or B & A during this period. The apparent basis for liability was the 1964 purchase agreement between B & A and Bangor Punta. The complaint in the instant case alleged that under the agreement Bangor Punta, through its subsidiary, assumed "all . . . debts, obligations, contracts and liabilities" of B & A.

price, or that the purchase transaction was tainted by fraud or deceit. Thus, any recovery on Amoskeag's part would constitute a windfall because it had sustained no injury.   With this in mind, the court then addressed the claims based on federal law and determined that Amoskeag would have been barred from maintaining a shareholder derivative action because of its failure to satisfy the "contemporaneous ownership" requirement of Fed.Rule Civ.Proc. 23.1(1).[3]   Finding that equitable principles prevented the use of the corporate fiction to evade the proscription of Rule 23.1, the court concluded that Amoskeag's efforts to recover under the Securities Exchange Act and the Clayton Act must fail.   Turning to the claims based on state law, the court recognized that the applicability of Rule 23.1(1) has been questioned where federal jurisdiction is based on diversity of citizenship.[4]   The court found it unnecessary to resolve this issue, however, since its examination of state law indicated that Maine probably followed the "prevailing rule" requiring contemporaneous ownership in order to maintain a shareholder derivative action.   Thus, whether the federal rule or state substantive law applied, the present action could not be maintained.

The United States Court of Appeals for the First Circuit reversed. . . .

We granted petitioners' application for certiorari.   414 U.S. 1127 (1974).   We now reverse.

II

A

We first turn to the question whether respondent corporations * may maintain the present action under § 10 of the Clayton Act, 15 U.S.C.A. § 20, and § 10(b) of the Securities Exchange Act of 1934, 15 U.S.C.A. § 78j(b), and Rule 10b–5, 17 CFR § 240.10b–5.   The resolution of this issue depends upon the applicability of the settled principle of equity that a shareholder may not complain of acts of corporate mismanagement if he acquired his shares from those who participated or acquiesced in the allegedly wrongful transactions.   See, e.g., Bloodworth v. Bloodworth, 225 Ga. 379, 387, 169 S.E.2d 150,

3. Rule 23.1(1), which specifies the requirements applicable to shareholder derivative actions, states that the complaint shall aver that "the plaintiff was a shareholder or member at the time of the transaction of which he complains. . . ." This provision is known as the "contemporaneous ownership" requirement. See 3B J. Moore, Federal Practice ¶ 23.1 et seq. (2d ed. 1974).

4. The "contemporaneous ownership" requirement in shareholder derivative actions was first announced in Hawes v. Oakland, 104 U.S. 450 (1882), and soon thereafter adopted as Equity Rule 97. This provision was later incorporated in Equity Rule 27 and finally in the present Rule

23.1. After the decision in Erie R. Co. v. Tompkins, 304 U.S. 64 (1938), the question arose whether the contemporaneous-ownership requirement was one of procedure or substantive law. If the requirement were substantive, then under the regime of *Erie* it could not be validly applied in federal diversity cases where state law permitted a noncontemporaneous shareholder to maintain a derivative action. See 3B J. Moore, Federal Practice ¶¶ 23.1.01–23.1.15[2] (2d ed. 1974). Although most cases treat the requirement as one of procedure, this Court has never resolved the issue. Ibid.

* The respondents were BAR and a wholly owned subsidiary. (Footnote by ed.)

156–157 (1969). . . .[5] This principle has been invoked with special force where a shareholder purchases all or substantially all the shares of a corporation from a vendor at a fair price, and then seeks to have the corporation recover against that vendor for prior corporate mismanagement. See, e.g., Matthews v. Headley Chocolate Co., 130 Md. 523, 532–535, 100 A. 645, 650–651 (1917); Home Fire Insurance Co. v. Barber, 67 Neb. 644, 661–662, 93 N.W. 1024, 1030–1031 (1903). See also Amen v. Black, 234 F.2d 12, 23 (CA10 1956). The equitable considerations precluding recovery in such cases were explicated long ago by Dean (then Commissioner) Roscoe Pound in Home Fire Insurance Co. v. Barber, supra. Dean Pound, writing for the Supreme Court of Nebraska, observed that the shareholders of the plaintiff corporation in that case had sustained no injury since they had acquired their shares from the alleged wrongdoers after the disputed transactions occurred and had received full value for their purchase price. Thus, any recovery on their part would constitute a windfall, for it would enable them to obtain funds to which they had no just title or claim. Moreover, it would in effect allow the shareholders to recoup a large part of the price they agreed to pay for their shares, notwithstanding the fact that they received all they had bargained for. Finally, it would permit the shareholders to reap a profit from wrongs done to others, thus encouraging further such speculation. Dean Pound stated that these consequences rendered any recovery highly inequitable and mandated dismissal of the suit.

The considerations supporting the *Home Fire* principle are especially pertinent in the present case. As the District Court pointed out, Amoskeag, the present owner of more than 99% of the BAR shares, would be the principal beneficiary of any recovery obtained by BAR. Amoskeag, however, acquired 98.3% of the outstanding shares of BAR from petitioner Bangor Punta in 1969, well after the alleged wrongs were said to have occurred. Amoskeag does not contend that the purchase transaction was tainted by fraud or deceit, or that it received less than full value for its money. Indeed, it does not assert that it has sustained any injury at all. Nor does it appear that the alleged acts of prior mismanagement have had any continuing effect on the corporations involved or the value of their shares.[6] Nevertheless, by causing the present action to be brought in the name of respondent corporations, Amoskeag seeks to recover indirectly an amount equal to the $5,000,000 it paid for its stock, plus an additional $2,000,000. All this would be in the form of damages for wrongs petitioner Bangor Punta is said to have inflicted, not upon Amoskeag, but upon respondent corporations during the period in which Bangor

---

5. This principle obtains in the great majority of jurisdictions. See, e.g., Russell v. Louis Melind Co., 331 Ill.App. 182, 72 N.E.2d 869 (1947).

6. In *Home Fire*, Dean Pound suggested that equitable principles might not prevent recovery where the effects of the wrongful acts continued and resulted in injury to present shareholders. 67 Neb. 644, 662, 93 N.W. 1024, 1031. In their complaint in the instant case, respondents alleged that "[t]he injury to BAR is a continuing one surviving the aforesaid sale [from petitioner BPO] to Amoskeag." The District Court noted that respondents alleged no facts to support this contention and therefore found any such exception inapplicable. 353 F.Supp. 724, 727 n. 1 (1972). Respondents apparently did not renew this contention on appeal.

Punta owned 98.3% of the BAR shares. In other words, Amoskeag seeks to recover for wrongs Bangor Punta did to *itself* as owner of the railroad.[7] At the same time it reaps this windfall, Amoskeag desires to retain all its BAR stock. Under *Home Fire,* it is evident that Amoskeag would have no standing in equity to maintain the present action.[8]

We are met with the argument, however, that since the present action is brought in the name of respondent corporations, we may not look behind the corporate entity to the true substance of the claims and the actual beneficiaries. The established law is to the contrary. Although a corporation and its shareholders are deemed separate entities for most purposes, the corporate form may be disregarded in the interests of justice where it is used to defeat an overriding public policy. New Colonial Ice Co. v. Helvering, 292 U.S. 435, 442 (1934); Chicago, M. & St. P.R. Co. v. Minneapolis Civic Assn., 247 U.S. 490, 501 (1918). In such cases, courts of equity, piercing all fictions and disguises, will deal with the substance of the action and not blindly adhere to the corporate form. Thus, where equity would preclude the shareholders from maintaining an action in their own right, the corporation would also be precluded. Amen v. Black, supra; Capitol Wine & Spirit Corp. v. Pokrass, 277 App.Div. 184, 98 N.Y.S.2d 291 (1950), aff'd, 302 N.Y. 734, 98 N.E.2d 704 (1951); Matthews v. Headley Chocolate Co., supra; Home Fire Insurance Co. v. Barber, supra. It follows that Amoskeag, the principal beneficiary of any recovery and itself estopped from complaining of petitioners' alleged wrongs, cannot avoid the command of equity through the guise of proceeding in the name of respondent corporations which it owns and controls.

B

Respondents fare no better in their efforts to maintain the present actions under state law, specifically § 104 of the Maine Public Utilities Act, Maine Rev.Stat.Ann., Tit. 35, § 104 (1965), and the common law of Maine. In Forbes v. Wells Beach Casino, Inc., 307 A.2d 210, 223 n. 10 (1973), the Maine Supreme Judicial Court recently declared that it had long accepted the equitable principle that a "stockholder has no standing if either he or his vendor participated or

---

7. Similarly, as to the period before October 1964, Amoskeag seeks to recover for wrongs B & A and its shareholders did to *themselves* as owners of the railroad.

8. Conceding the lack of equity in any recovery by Amoskeag, the dissent argues that the present action can nevertheless be maintained because there are 20 minority shareholders, holding less than 1% of the BAR stock, who owned their shares "during the period from 1960 through 1967 when the transactions underlying the railroad's complaint took place, and who still owned that stock in 1971 when the complaint was filed." . . . The dissent would conclude that the existence of these innocent minority shareholders entitled BAR,

and hence Amoskeag, to recover the entire $7,000,000 amount of alleged damages.

Aside from the illogic of such an approach, the dissent's position is at war with the precedents, for the *Home Fire* principle has long been applied to preclude full recovery by a corporation even where there are innocent minority shareholders who acquired their shares prior to the alleged wrongs. See cases cited at n. 5, supra, and accompanying text. The dissent also mistakes the factual posture of this case, since the respondent corporations did not institute this action for the benefit of the minority shareholders. See discussion at n. 15, infra.

acquiesced in the wrong. . . ." See Hyams v. Old Dominion Co., 113 Me. 294, 302, 93 A. 747, 750 (1959).[9] . . .

III

In reaching the contrary conclusion, the Court of Appeals stated that it could not accept the proposition that Amoskeag would be the "sole beneficiary" of any recovery by BAR. 482 F.2d, at 868. The court noted that in view of the railroad's status as a "quasi-public" corporation and the essential nature of the services it provides, the public had an identifiable interest in BAR's financial health. Thus, any recovery by BAR would accrue to the benefit of the public through the improvement in BAR's economic position and the quality of its services. The court thought that this factor rendered any windfall to Amoskeag irrelevant.

At the outset, we note that the Court of Appeals' assumption that any recovery would necessarily benefit the public is unwarranted. As that court explicitly recognized, any recovery by BAR could be diverted to its shareholders, namely Amoskeag, rather than re-invested in the railroad for the benefit of the public. . . .

The Court of Appeals' position also appears to overlook the fact that Amoskeag, the actual beneficiary of any recovery through its ownership of more than 99% of the BAR shares, would be unjustly enriched since it has sustained no injury. . . .

The Court of Appeals further stated that it was important to insure that petitioners would not be immune from liability for their wrongful conduct and noted that BAR's recovery would provide a needed deterrent to mismanagement of railroads. Our difficulty with this argument is that it proves too much. If deterrence were the only objective, then in logic any plaintiff willing to file a complaint would suffice. No injury or violation of a legal duty to the particular plaintiff would have to be alleged. The only prerequisite would be that the plaintiff agree to accept the recovery, lest the supposed wrongdoer be allowed to escape a reckoning. Suffice it to say that we have been referred to no authority which would support so novel a result, and we decline to adopt it.

We therefore conclude that respondent corporations may not maintain the present action.[15] The judgment of the Court of Appeals is reversed.

---

9. In addition, the new Maine Business Corporation Act adopts the contemporaneous-ownership requirement for shareholder derivative actions. See Maine Rev.Stat. Ann., Tit. 13–A, § 627.1.A (1974). This provision apparently became effective two days after the present action was filed. As the District Court noted, it is an open question whether Maine in fact had a contemporaneous-ownership requirement prior to that time. 353 F.Supp., at 727. See R. Field, V. McKusick & L. Wroth, Maine Civil Practice § 23.2, p. 393 (2d ed. 1970). In the absence of any indication that Maine would not have followed the "prevailing view," the District Court determined that the contemporaneous-ownership requirement of Fed.Rule Civ.Proc. 23.1 applied.

15. Our decision rests on the conclusion that equitable principles preclude recovery by Amoskeag, the present owner of more than 99% of the BAR shares. The record does not reveal whether the minority shareholders who hold the remaining fraction of 1% of the BAR shares stand in the same position as Amoskeag. Some courts

Mr. Justice MARSHALL, with whom Mr. Justice DOUGLAS, Mr. Justice BRENNAN, and Mr. Justice WHITE join, dissenting. . . .

The majority places primary reliance on Dean Pound's decision in Home Fire Insurance Co. v. Barber, supra. In that case, *all* of the shares of the plaintiff corporation had been acquired from the alleged wrongdoers after the transactions giving rise to the causes of action stated in the complaint. Since none of the corporation's shareholders held stock at the time of the alleged wrongful transactions, none had been injured thereby. Dean Pound therefore held that equity barred the corporation from pursuing a claim where none of its shareholders could complain of injury.

Dean Pound thought it clear, however, that the opposite result would obtain if *any* of the present shareholders

> "are entitled to complain of the acts of the defendant and of his past management of the company; for if any of them are so entitled, there can be no doubt of the right and duty of the corporation to maintain this suit. It would be maintainable in such a case even though the wrongdoers continued to be stockholders and would share in the proceeds." 67 Neb., at 655, 93 N.W., at 1028.

Cf. Capitol Wine & Spirit Corp. v. Pokrass, 277 App.Div. 184, 186, 98 N.Y.S.2d 291, 293 (1950), aff'd, 302 N.Y. 734, 98 N.E.2d 704 (1951).

The rationale for the distinction drawn by Dean Pound is simple enough. The sole shareholder who defrauds or mismanages his own corporation hurts only himself. For the corporation to sue him for his wrongs is simply to take money out of his right pocket and put it in his left. It is therefore appropriate for equity to intervene to pierce the corporate veil. But where there are minority shareholders, misappropriation and conversion of corporate assets injure their interests as well as the interest of the majority shareholder. The law imposes upon the directors of a corporation a fiduciary obligation to all of the corporation's shareholders, and part of that obligation is to use due care to ensure that the corporation seek redress where a majority

have adopted the concept of a pro-rata recovery where there are innocent minority shareholders. Under this procedure, damages are distributed to the minority shareholders individually on a proportional basis, even though the action is brought in the name of the corporation to enforce primary rights. See, e.g., Matthews v. Headley Chocolate Co., 130 Md. 523, 536–540, 100 A. 645, 650–652 (1917). In the present case, respondents have expressly disavowed any intent to obtain a pro-rata recovery on behalf of the 1% minority shareholders of BAR. We therefore do not reach the question whether such recovery would be appropriate.

The dissent asserts that the alleged acts of corporate mismanagement have placed BAR "close to the brink of bankruptcy" and that the present action is maintained for the benefit of BAR's creditors. . . . With all respect, it appears that the dissent has sought to redraft respondents' complaint. As the District Court noted, respondents have not brought this action on behalf of any creditors. 353 F.Supp., at 726. Indeed, they have never so contended. Moreover, respondents have conceded that the financial health of the railroad is excellent. Tr. of Oral Arg. 18.

shareholder has drained the corporation's resources for his own benefit and to the detriment of minority shareholders.[1] . . .

See also Courtland Manor, Inc. v. Leeds, 347 A.2d 144 (Del.Ch. 1975); cf. American Timber & Trading Co. v. Niedermeyer, 276 Or. 1135, 558 P.2d 1211 (1976).

NOTE

The Pennsylvania statute provides that a plaintiff who would be entitled to maintain a derivative action except for the fact that he is not a contemporaneous shareholder "may, nevertheless, in the discretion of the court, be allowed to maintain such suit on preliminary showing to the court . . . that there is a strong prima facie case in favor of the claim asserted on behalf of the corporation and that without such suit serious injustice will result." Pa. § 1516(A).*

NOTE ON THE CONTEMPORANEOUS–OWNERSHIP RULE

1. At common law, the cases were divided on whether a shareholder was barred from bringing a derivative action if he was not a "contemporaneous shareholder"—that is, if he did not hold his shares when the wrong occurred. 2 Model Bus.Corp.Act Ann. § 49, ¶ 4.11 (1971). Today, however, most jurisdictions have adopted some version of the contemporaneous-ownership rule by either case-law, statute, or court rule. 13 W. Fletcher, Cyclopedia of the Law of Private Corporations § 5981 (1984 rev. vol.).[1] The rule is subject to several important exceptions:

(a) *Devolution by Operation of Law.* A non-contemporaneous shareholder is normally allowed to bring a derivative action if his shares devolved upon him "by operation of law"—for example, by inheritance. (This exception is sometimes made applicable only where the shares have devolved from a person who was a shareholder at the time of the wrong.) See Note, 54 B.U.L.Rev. 355 (1974).

(b) *Continuing–Wrong Theory.* Under the continuing-wrong theory, a plaintiff can bring an action to challenge a wrong that began before he acquired his shares, but continued thereafter. In principle

---

1. See generally 3 W. Fletcher, Cyclopedia Corporations § 1012 (1965). Indeed, the failure to exercise reasonable care to seek redress for wrongs done the corporation might well subject the directors to personal liability. See, e.g., Briggs v. Spaulding, 141 U.S. 132 (1891); Kavanaugh v. Commonwealth Trust Co. of New York, 223 N.Y. 103, 119 N.E. 237 (1918).

* For a comparable provision, see Cal. Corp.Code § 800(b)(1).

1. Under a separate rule, the plaintiff must be a shareholder at the time the action is brought. See Note on Who Can Bring a Derivative Action, Section 1, supra. The two rules are bridged by a third rule requiring that the plaintiff's ownership between the time of the wrong and the time of the suit must be uninterrupted. Vista Fund v. Garis, 277 N.W.2d 19 (Minn. 1979); Gresov v. Shattuck Denn Mining Corp., 40 Misc.2d 569, 243 N.Y.S.2d 760 (1963).

this may not seem to be an exception at all, since the plaintiff is only complaining about what happened after he became a shareholder. In practice, however, it is often difficult to distinguish between a wrongful continuing course of conduct, on the one hand, and the continued effect of a completed wrongful transaction, on the other. Therefore, while the continuing-wrong exception is widely accepted in principle, in practice there is considerable divergence in the way it is applied, and different cases often seem to come out differently on virtually the same facts. For example, in Maclary v. Pleasant Hills, Inc., 35 Del. Ch. 39, 109 A.2d 830 (Ch.1954), the plaintiff was allowed to sue under the continuing-wrong theory where he had purchased his stock after an allegedly wrongful resolution authorizing the issuance of stock certificates, but before the certificates were actually issued. In contrast, in Elster v. American Airlines, Inc., 34 Del.Ch. 94, 100 A.2d 219 (Ch.1953), the continuing-wrong theory was deemed inapplicable where the plaintiff had purchased after the corporation had allegedly issued stock options for no consideration, but before the options were exercised. Similarly, in Forbes v. Wells Beach Casino, Inc., 307 A.2d 210 (Me.1973), the plaintiff was allowed to sue under the continuing-wrong theory where he had purchased his stock after a fiduciary had wrongfully taken possession of corporate property, but while the fiduciary continued to hold it. In contrast, in Weinhaus v. Gale, 237 F.2d 197 (7th Cir.1956), the continuing-wrong theory was deemed inapplicable where plaintiff had purchased after stock had been sold by a subsidiary to its parent at a price alleged to be unfairly low, but before the parent had resold the stock. In Palmer v. Morris, 316 F.2d 649 (5th Cir.1963), the plaintiff was allowed to sue under the continuing-wrong theory where he had purchased his stock after an allegedly wrongful deal was made, but while payments under the deal continued. In contrast, in Chaft v. Kass, 19 A.D.2d 610, 241 N.Y.S.2d 284 (1963), the theory was deemed inapplicable where plaintiff purchased his stock after the corporation had entered into an allegedly invalid contract, but while payments under the contract were still being made.

Several statutes provide that the plaintiff must allege that he was a shareholder at the time of the transaction "or any part thereof." E.g., Cal. § 800(b)(1); Wis. § 180.405. Where there is a close question whether the continuing-wrong theory applies to a given case, such a statute might tip the scale in the plaintiff's favor.

———

SECTION 6. DEMAND ON THE BOARD AND TERMINATION OF DERIVATIVE ACTIONS ON THE RECOMMENDATION OF THE BOARD OR A COMMITTEE

NOTE ON DEMAND ON THE BOARD

All states require a shareholder to make a demand on the board to bring suit on a corporate cause of action before the shareholder brings a derivative suit, unless demand is excused. It has not always been clear, however, (i) when demand is excused, and (ii) what is the consequence if demand is required, made, and rejected. Broadly speaking, there are three possible standards that might govern the effect of a rejection of demand.

First, a rejection might be given no substantive weight. The theory here would be that the reason for allowing derivative actions is that if a shareholder is not allowed to sue a director or officer derivatively, the duties of care and loyalty might come to little or nothing, because the board will often be disinclined to sue a colleague. Given that reason, demand is required because, but only because, the board should be given a chance to sue (or take other remedial action) if it is willing to do so. If, however, the demand is rejected, the way is then cleared for the shareholder to bring suit.

Second, rejection of a demand, where demand is required, might be treated like an ordinary business decision of the board dealing with third parties, so that a rejection precludes a derivative action if the board has satisfied the standards of the business judgment rule.

Third, rejection of a demand might be given effect if but only if it satisfies some sort of reasonability test.

Variations and permutations on these standards can be (and have been) constructed.

There is a close relationship between the issue, what effect should be given to a rejection of demand, and the issue, when should demand be excused. If the board's rejection is tested only under the business judgment rule, it has very serious consequences. Accordingly, it is to be expected that under such a regime the courts will formulate a relatively broad test for when demand should be excused. In particular, under such a regime it is to be expected that demand would be excused whenever there is more than a minimal possibility that a majority of the board is not disinterested and independent. If, on the other hand, rejection has no substantive effect, or is reviewed under a standard more demanding than the business judgment rule, it is to be expected that the courts will formulate a relatively narrow rule for when demand should be excused.

The material in the balance of this Section will concern the effect of a board or committee recommendation to terminate a derivative action; the effect of a rejection of demand; the relationship between the requirement of demand and the effect to be given to a board or committee recommendation; and the question when demand is required. Because the rule governing excuse may depend partly on the rule governing the effect of rejection, the latter question will be addressed first.

AUERBACH v. BENNETT

Court of Appeals of New York, 1979.
47 N.Y.2d 619, 419 N.Y.S.2d 920, 393 N.E.2d 994.

JONES, Judge.

While the substantive aspects of a decision to terminate a shareholders' derivative action against defendant corporate directors made by a committee of disinterested directors appointed by the corporation's board of directors are beyond judicial inquiry under the business judgment doctrine, the court may inquire as to the disinterested independence of the members of that committee and as to the appropriateness and sufficiency of the investigative procedures chosen and pursued by the committee. In this instance, however, no basis is shown to warrant either inquiry by the court. Accordingly we hold that it was error to reverse the lower court's dismissal of the shareholders' derivative action.

In the summer of 1975 the management of General Telephone & Electronics Corporation, in response to reports that numerous other multinational companies had made questionable payments to public officials or political parties in foreign countries, directed that an internal preliminary investigation be made to ascertain whether that corporation had engaged in similar transactions. On the basis of the report of this survey, received in October, 1975, management brought the issue to the attention of the corporation's board of directors. At a meeting held on November 6 of that year the board referred the matter to the board's audit committee. The audit committee retained as its special counsel the Washington, D.C., law firm of Wilmer, Cutler & Pickering which had not previously acted as counsel to the corporation. With the assistance of such special counsel and Arthur Andersen & Co., the corporation's outside auditors, the audit committee engaged in an investigation into the corporation's worldwide operations, focusing on whether, in the period January 1, 1971 to December 31, 1975, corporate funds had been (1) paid directly or indirectly to any political party or person or to any officer, employee, shareholder or director of any governmental or private customer, or (2) used to reimburse any officer of the corporation or other person for such payments.

On March 4, 1976 the audit committee released its report which was filed with the Securities and Exchange Commission and disclosed to the corporation's shareholders in a proxy statement prior to the annual meeting of shareholders held in April, 1976. The audit committee reported that it had found evidence that in the period from 1971 to 1975 the corporation or its subsidiaries had made payments abroad and in the United States constituting bribes and kickbacks in amounts perhaps totaling more than 11 million dollars and that some of the individual defendant directors had been personally involved in certain of the transactions.

Almost immediately Auerbach, a shareholder in the corporation, instituted the present shareholders' derivative action on behalf of the corporation against the corporation's directors, Arthur Andersen & Co. and the corporation. The complaint alleged that in connection with the transactions reported by the audit committee defendants, present and former members of the corporation's board of directors and Arthur Andersen & Co., are liable to the corporation for breach of their duties to the corporation and should be made to account for payments made in those transactions.

On April 21, 1976 the board of directors of the corporation adopted a resolution creating a special litigation committee "for the purpose of establishing a point of contact between the Board of Directors and the Corporation's General Counsel concerning the position to be taken by the Corporation in certain litigation involving shareholder derivative claims on behalf of the Corporation against certain of its directors and officers" and authorizing that committee "to take such steps from time to time as it deems necessary to pursue its objectives including the retention of special outside counsel." The special committee comprised three disinterested directors who had joined the board after the challenged transactions had occurred. The board subsequently additionally vested in the committee "all of the authority of the Board of Directors to determine, on behalf of the Board, the position that the Corporation shall take with respect to the derivative claims alleged on its behalf" in the present and similar shareholder derivative actions.

The special litigation committee reported under date of November 22, 1976. It found that defendant Arthur Andersen & Co. had conducted its examination of the corporation's affairs in accordance with generally accepted auditing standards and in good faith and concluded that no proper interest of the corporation or its shareholders would be served by the continued assertion of a claim against it. The committee also concluded that none of the individual defendants had violated the New York State statutory standard of care, that none had profited personally or gained in any way, that the claims asserted in the present action are without merit, that if the action were allowed to proceed the time and talents of the corporation's senior management would be wasted on lengthy pretrial and trial proceedings, that litigation costs would be inordinately high in view of the unlikelihood of success, and that the continuing publicity could be damaging to the corporation's business. The committee determined that it would not be in the best interests of the corporation for the present derivative action to proceed, and, exercising the authority delegated to it, directed the corporation's general counsel to take that position in the present litigation as well as in pending comparable shareholders' derivative actions.

On December 17, 1976 the corporation and the four individual defendants who had been served moved for an order pursuant to CPLR 3211 (subd. [a], pars. [3], [7]) dismissing the complaint or in the alternative for an order pursuant to CPLR 3211 (subd. [c]) for summary judgment. On January 7, 1977 Arthur Andersen & Co. made a similar motion. On May 13, 1977 Supreme Court, Special Term, granted the motions of all defendants and dismissed the complaint on the merits. . . .

As all parties and both courts below recognize, the disposition of this case on the merits turns on the proper application of the business judgment doctrine, in particular to the decision of a specially appointed committee of disinterested directors acting on behalf of the board to terminate a shareholders' derivative action. That doctrine bars judicial inquiry into actions of corporate directors taken in good faith and in the exercise of honest judgment in the lawful and legitimate furtherance of corporate purposes. "Questions of policy of management, expediency of contracts or action, adequacy of consideration, lawful appropriation of corporate funds to advance corporate interests, are left solely to their honest and unselfish decision, for their powers therein are without limitation and free from restraint, and the exercise of them for the common and general interests of the corporation may not be questioned, although the results show that what they did was unwise or inexpedient." (Pollitz v. Wabash, R.R. Co., 207 N.Y. 113, 124, 100 N.E. 721, 724.)

In this instance our inquiry, to the limited extent to which it may be pursued, has a two-tiered aspect. The complaint initially asserted liability on the part of defendants based on the payments made to foreign governmental customers and privately owned customers, some unspecified portions of which were allegedly passed on to officials of the customers, i.e., the focus was on first-tier bribes and kickbacks. Then subsequent to the service of the complaint there came the report of a special litigation committee, particularly appointed by the corporation's board of directors to consider the merits of the present and similar shareholders' derivative actions, and its determination that it would not be in the best interests of the corporation to press claims against defendants based on their possible first-tier liability. The motions for summary judgment were predicated principally on the report and determination of the special litigation committee and on the contention that this second-tier corporate action insulated the first-tier transactions from judicial inquiry and was itself subject to the shelter of the business judgment doctrine. The disposition at Special Term was predicated on this analysis; its decision focused on the actions of the special litigation committee, and the motions for summary judgment were granted on the ground that the business judgment doctrine precluded the courts from going back of the decision of the special litigation committee on behalf of the corporation not to pursue the claims alleged in the complaint. Similarly the reversal at the Appellate Division was based on that court's perception of the proper application of the business judgment rule to the actions and determination of the special litigation committee. We proceed on the same analysis, concluding, however, on the record before us, at variance with the Appellate Division, that the determination of the special litigation committee forecloses further judicial inquiry in this case.

It appears to us that the business judgment doctrine, at least in part, is grounded in the prudent recognition that courts are ill equipped and infrequently called on to evaluate what are and must be essentially business judgments. The authority and responsibilities vested in corporate directors both by statute and decisional law proceed on the assumption that inescapably there can be no available objective standard by which the correctness of every corporate decision may be measured, by the courts or otherwise. Even if that were not the case, by definition the responsibility for business judgments must rest with the corporate directors; their individual capabilities and experience peculiarly qualify them for the discharge of that responsibility. Thus, absent evidence of bad faith or fraud (of which there is none here) the courts must and properly should respect their determinations.

Derivative claims against corporate directors belong to the corporation itself. As with other questions of corporate policy and management, the decision whether and to what extent to explore and prosecute such claims lies within the judgment and control of the corporation's board of directors. Necessarily such decision must be predicated on the weighing and balancing of a variety of disparate considerations to reach a considered conclusion as to what course of action or inaction is best calculated to protect and advance the interests of the corporation. This is the essence of the responsibility and role of the board of directors, and courts may not intrude to interfere.

In the present case we confront a special instance of the application of the business judgment rule and inquire whether it applies in its full vigor to shield from judicial scrutiny the decision of a three-person minority committee of the board acting on behalf of the full board not to prosecute a shareholder's derivative action. The record in this case reveals that the board is a 15–member board, and that the derivative suit was brought against four of the directors. Nothing suggests that any of the other directors participated in any of the challenged first-tier transactions. Indeed the report of the audit committee on which the complaint is based specifically found that no other directors had any prior knowledge of or were in any way involved in any of these transactions. Other directors had, however, been members of the board in the period during which the transactions occurred. Each of the three director members of the special litigation committee joined the board thereafter.

The business judgment rule does not foreclose inquiry by the courts into the disinterested independence of those members of the board chosen by it to make the corporate decision on its behalf—here the members of the special litigation committee. Indeed the rule shields the deliberations and conclusions of the chosen representatives of the board only if they possess a disinterested independence and do not stand in a dual relation which prevents an unprejudicial exercise of judgment. (Cf. Koral v. Savory, Inc., 276 N.Y. 215, 11 N.E.2d 883.)

We examine then the proof submitted by defendants. It is not disputed that the members of the special litigation committee were not members of the corporation's board of directors at the time of the first-tier transactions in question. Howard Blauvelt, chairman of the board of Continental Oil Company, had been elected to the corporation's board of directors on October 9, 1975. Dr. John T. Dunlop, Lamont University professor at the Graduate School of Business Administration of Harvard University had been elected to the board on April 21, 1976. James R. Barker, chairman of the board and chief executive officer of Moore McCormack Resources, Inc., was added as the third member of the committee when he was elected to the board on July 19, 1976. None of the three had had any prior affiliation with the corporation. Notwithstanding the vigorous and imaginative hypothesizing and innuendo of counsel there is nothing in this record to raise a triable issue of fact as to the independence and disinterested status of these three directors.

The contention of Wallenstein that any committee authorized by the board of which defendant directors were members must be held to be legally infirm and may not be delegated power to terminate a derivative action must be rejected. In the very nature of the corporate organization it was only the existing board of directors which had authority on behalf of the corporation to direct the investigation and to assure the cooperation of corporate employees, and it is only that same board by its own action—or as here pursuant to authority duly delegated by it—which had authority to decide whether to prosecute the claims against defendant directors. The board in this instance, with slight adaptation, followed prudent practice in observing the general policy that when individual members of a board of directors prove to have personal interests which may conflict with the interests of the corporation, such interested directors must be excluded while the remaining members of the board proceed to consideration and action. (Cf. Business Corporation Law, § 713, which contemplates such situations and provides that the interested directors may nonetheless be included in the quorum count.) Courts have consistently held that the business judgment rule applies where some directors are charged with wrongdoing, so long as the remaining directors making the decision are disinterested and independent. (Swanson v. Traer, 249 F.2d 854, 858–859; Gall v. Exxon Corp., 418 F.Supp. 508, supplemented 75 Civ. 3582 [U.S.Dist.Ct., S.D.N.Y., Jan. 17, 1977]; Issner v. Aldrich, 254 F.Supp. 696, 701–702; Republic Nat. Life Ins.

Co. v. Beasley, 73 F.R.D. 658, 668–669; Gilbert v. Curtiss–Wright Corp., 179 Misc. 641, 645, 38 N.Y.S.2d 548, 552.)

To accept the assertions of the intervenor and to disqualify the entire board would be to render the corporation powerless to make an effective business judgment with respect to prosecution of the derivative action. The possible risk of hesitancy on the part of the members of any committee, even if composed of outside, independent, disinterested directors, to investigate the activities of fellow members of the board where personal liability is at stake is an inherent, inescapable, given aspect of the corporation's predicament. To assign responsibility of the dimension here involved to individuals wholly separate and apart from the board of directors would, except in the most extraordinary circumstances, itself be an act of default and breach of the nondelegable fiduciary duty owed by the members of the board to the corporation and to its shareholders, employees and creditors. For the courts to preside over such determinations would similarly work an ouster of the board's fundamental responsibility and authority for corporate management.

We turn then to the action of the special litigation committee itself which comprised two components. First, there was the selection of procedures appropriate to the pursuit of its charge, and second, there was the ultimate substantive decision; predicated on the procedures chosen and the data produced thereby, not to pursue the claims advanced in the shareholders' derivative actions. The latter, substantive decision falls squarely within the embrace of the business judgment doctrine, involving as it did the weighing and balancing of legal, ethical, commercial, promotional, public relations, fiscal and other factors familiar to the resolution of many if not most corporate problems. To this extent the conclusion reached by the special litigation committee is outside the scope of our review. Thus, the courts cannot inquire as to which factors were considered by that committee or the relative weight accorded them in reaching that substantive decision—"the reasons for the payments, the advantages or disadvantages accruing to the corporation by reason of the transactions, the extent of the participation or profit by the respondent directors and the loss, if any, of public confidence in the corporation which might be incurred" (64 A.D.2d, at p. 107, 408 N.Y.S.2d at pp. 87–88). Inquiry into such matters would go to the very core of the business judgment made by the committee. To permit judicial probing of such issues would be to emasculate the business judgment doctrine as applied to the actions and determinations of the special litigation committee. Its substantive evaluation of the problems posed and its judgment in their resolution are beyond our reach.

As to the other component of the committee's activities, however, the situation is different, and here we agree with the Appellate Division. As to the methodologies and procedures best suited to the conduct of an investigation of facts and the determination of legal liability, the courts are well equipped by long and continuing experience and practice to make determinations. In fact they are better qualified in this regard than are corporate directors in general. Nor do the determinations to be made in the adoption of procedures partake of the nuances or special perceptions or comprehensions of business judgment or corporate activities or interests. The question is solely how appropriately to set about to gather the pertinent data.

While the court may properly inquire as to the adequacy and appropriateness of the committee's investigative procedures and methodologies, it may not under the guise of consideration of such factors trespass in the domain of business judgment. At the same time those responsible for the procedures by which the business judgment is reached may reasonably be required to show that they have pursued their chosen investigative methods in good faith. What evidentiary proof may be required to this end will, of course, depend on the nature of the particular investigation, and the proper reach of disclosure at the instance of the shareholders will in turn relate inversely to the showing made by the corporate representatives themselves. The latter may be expected to show that the areas and subjects to be examined are reasonably complete and that there has been a good-faith pursuit of inquiry into such areas and subjects. What has been uncovered and the relative weight accorded in evaluating and balancing the several factors and considerations are beyond the scope of judicial concern. Proof, however, that the investigation has been so restricted in scope, so shallow in execution, or otherwise so *pro forma* or halfhearted as to constitute a pretext or sham, consistent with the principles underlying the application of the business judgment doctrine, would raise questions of good faith or conceivably fraud which would never be shielded by that doctrine.

In addition to the issue of the disinterested independence of the special litigation committee, addressed above, the disposition of the present appeal turns, then, on whether on defendants' motions for summary judgment predicated on the investigation and determination of the special litigation committee, Wallenstein by tender of evidentiary proof in admissible form has shown facts sufficient to require a trial of any material issue of fact as to the adequacy or appropriateness of the *modus operandi* of that committee or has demonstrated acceptable excuse for failure to make such tender. (Friends of Animals v. Associated Fur Mfrs., 46 N.Y.2d 1065, 416 N.Y.S.2d 790, 390 N.E. 2d 298; CPLR 3212, subd. [b].) We conclude that the requisite showing has not been made on this record.

At the outset we observe that Wallenstein, the intervenor, must accept the record in the state in which he finds it at the time he was granted leave to intervene in the Appellate Division. No application for intervention was made prior thereto, nor did the application when made seek any relief other than the right to appeal from the order of Special Term. (Cf. Matter of Martin v. Ronan, 47 N.Y.2d 486, 419 N.Y.S.2d 42, 392 N.E.2d 1226). Thus, because plaintiff Auerbach had submitted none, the record in this case is devoid of any affidavits or documentary evidence in opposition to the motions for summary judgment.

On the submissions made by defendants in support of their motions, we do not find either insufficiency or infirmity as to the procedures and methodologies chosen and pursued by the special litigation committee. That committee promptly engaged eminent special counsel to guide its deliberations and to advise it. The committee reviewed the prior work of the audit committee, testing its completeness, accuracy and thoroughness by interviewing representatives of Wilmer, Cutler & Pickering, reviewing transcripts of the testimony of 10 corporate officers and employees before the Securities and Exchange Commission, and studying documents collected by and work papers of the Washington law firm. Individual interviews were conducted with the directors found to have participated in any way in the questioned payments, and with representatives of Arthur Andersen & Co. Questionnaires were sent to and answered by each of the corporation's nonmanagement directors. At the conclusion of its investigation the special litigation committee sought and obtained pertinent legal advice from its special counsel. The selection of appropriate investigative methods must always turn on the nature and characteristics of the particular subject being investigated, but we find nothing in this record that requires a trial of any material issue of fact concerning the sufficiency or appropriateness of the procedures chosen by this special litigation committee. Nor is there anything in this record to raise a triable issue of fact as to the good-faith pursuit of its examination by that committee.

Finally, there should be a word as to the contention advanced by the intervenor that summary judgment should at least be withheld until there has been opportunity for disclosure. We note preliminarily as a matter of procedure that there was no application at Special Term for any such relief nor is there in the record any opposing affidavit from which it appears that essential facts may exist which could be obtained by disclosure (CPLR 3212, subd. [f]). It is also significant that neither in his brief nor on oral argument did Wallenstein identify any particulars as to which he desires discovery relating to the disinterestedness of the members of the special litigation committee or to the procedures followed by that committee. To speculate that something might be caught on a fishing expedition provides no basis to postpone decision on the summary judgment motions under the authority of CPLR 3212 (subd. [f]). The disclosure proposed and described by Wallenstein on oral argument would go only to particulars as to the results of the committee's investigation and work, the factors bearing on its substantive decision not to prosecute the derivative actions and the factual aspects of the underlying first-tier activities of defendants—all matters falling within the ambit of the business judgment doctrine and thus excluded from judicial scrutiny.

For the reasons stated the order of the Appellate Division should be modified, with costs to defendants, by reversing so much thereof as reversed the order of Supreme Court, and, as so modified, affirmed.

COOKE, Chief Judge (dissenting).

There should be an affirmance for the reasons set forth in the excellent analysis of Mr. Justice James D. Hopkins who wrote for a unanimous Appellate Division. In response to the majority opinion, a few remarks are added.

True, the "business judgment rule" is potentially applicable in these circumstances. But this case differs markedly from the typical situation in which that rule would be invoked. Here, the alleged wrongdoers are directors of the corporation. Of course, it would be most inappropriate to allow these interested directors to vote to preclude a shareholder's suit and thereby insulate themselves from liability (see Koral v. Savory, Inc., 276 N.Y. 215, 217–218, 11 N.E.2d 883, 885; see, also, United Copper Co. v. Amalgamated Copper Co., 244 U.S. 261, 263, 37 S.Ct. 509, 61 L.Ed. 1119). Hence, the lawsuit should be terminated only if a sufficient number of disinterested directors (cf. Business Corporation Law, § 713; Rapoport v. Schneider, 29 N.Y.2d 396, 402, 328 N.Y.S.2d 431, 436, 278 N.E.2d 642, 645), in this case the special litigation committee, rendered a good faith, " 'unprejudiced exercise of judgment' ", determining that maintenance of the action would not be in the best interests of the corporation (see Koral v. Savory, Inc., supra, 276 N.Y. at p. 217, 11 N.E.2d at p. 885).

Since the continuation of the suit is dependent, in large measure, upon the motives and actions of the defendants and the special litigation committee, and since knowledge of these matters "is peculiarly in the possession of the defendants themselves", summary judgment should not be granted prior to disclosure proceedings (Terranova v. Emil, 20 N.Y.2d 493, 496–497, 285 N.Y.S.2d 51, 54, 231 N.E.2d 753, 755). That the intervenor has not proposed potentially fruitful areas for disclosure should not, contrary to the majority holding, be determinative (see Udoff v. Zipf, 44 N.Y.2d 117, 122, 404 N.Y.S.2d 332, 334, 375 N.E.2d 392, 394). It is precisely because certain defendants and the members of the committee are possessed of exclusive knowledge of the facts that the intervenor is now unable to suggest the possible avenues which might successfully be pursued upon pretrial disclosure. And it is for this reason that we have formulated a rule precluding a grant of summary judgment where the case is likely to turn on "knowledge in the possession of the" moving party (e.g., Udoff v. Zipf, 44 N.Y.2d 117, 122, 404 N.Y.S.2d 332, 334, 375 N.E.2d 392, 394, supra; Terranova v. Emil, supra, 20 N.Y.2d at p. 497, 285 N.Y.S.2d at p. 53, 231 N.E.2d 753, 755; 4 Weinstein–Korn–Miller, N.Y.Civ.Prac., par. 3212.18). No reason can be discerned for denying application of that rule at this early stage in these obvious circumstances. The result of the majority ruling is to place the intervenor in a classic "Catch–22" situation, denying him disclosure because he has not come forward with facts—facts which by their very nature are discernible only after disclosure.

In sum, to deny the intervenor an opportunity for pretrial disclosure is to mistakenly group this case with the typical case involving the business judgment rule. Since the business judgment rule is only conditionally applicable here, and since certain defendants as well as the members of the special litigation committee have the sole knowledge of the facts upon which its applicability turns, summary judgment should be withheld pending disclosure proceedings. The result reached by the majority not only effectively dilutes the substantive rule of law at issue, but may also render corporate directors largely unaccountable to the shareholders whose business they are elected to govern.

JASEN, WACHTLER, FUCHSBERG and MEYER, JJ., concur with JONES, J.

COOKE, C.J., dissents and votes to affirm in a separate opinion.

GABRIELLI, J., taking no part.

Order modified, with costs to defendants, in accordance with the opinion herein and, as so modified, affirmed. Question certified answered in the negative.

ZAPATA CORP. v. MALDONADO

Supreme Court of Delaware, 1981.
430 A.2d 779.

Before DUFFY, QUILLEN and HORSEY, JJ.

QUILLEN, Justice. This is an interlocutory appeal from an order entered on April 9, 1980, by the Court of Chancery denying appellant-defendant Zapata Corporation's (Zapata) alternative motions to dismiss the complaint or for summary judgment. The issue to be addressed has reached this Court by way of a rather convoluted path.

In June, 1975, William Maldonado, a stockholder of Zapata, instituted a derivative action in the Court of Chancery on behalf of Zapata against ten officers and/or directors of Zapata, alleging, essentially, breaches of fiduciary duty. Maldonado did not first demand that the board bring this action, stating instead such demand's futility because all directors were named as defendants and allegedly participated in the acts specified.[1] In June, 1977, Maldonado commenced an action in the United States District Court for the Southern District of New York against the same defendants, save one, alleging federal security law violations as well as the same common law claims made previously in the Court of Chancery.

By June, 1979, four of the defendant-directors were no longer on the board, and the remaining directors appointed two new outside directors to the board. The board then created an "Independent Investigation Committee" (Committee), composed solely of the two new directors, to investigate Maldonado's actions . . . and to deter-

---

1. Court of Chancery Rule 23.1 states in part: "The complaint shall also allege with particularity the efforts, if any, made by the plaintiff to obtain the action he desires from the directors or comparable authority and the reasons for his failure to obtain the action or for not making the effort."

mine whether the corporation should continue any or all of the litigation. The Committee's determination was stated to be "final, . . . not . . . subject to review by the Board of Directors and . . . in all respects . . . binding upon the Corporation."

Following an investigation, the Committee concluded, in September, 1979, that each action should "be dismissed forthwith as their continued maintenance is inimical to the Company's best interests. . . ." Consequently, Zapata moved for dismissal or summary judgment. . . .

On March 18, 1980, the Court of Chancery, in a reported opinion, the basis for the order of April 9, 1980, denied Zapata's motions, holding that Delaware law does not sanction this means of dismissal. More specifically, it held that the "business judgment" rule is not a grant of authority to dismiss derivative actions and that a stockholder has an individual right to maintain derivative actions in certain instances. Maldonado v. Flynn, Del.Ch., 413 A.2d 1251 (1980) (herein *Maldonado*). Pursuant to the provisions of Supreme Court Rule 42, Zapata filed an interlocutory appeal with this Court shortly thereafter. . . .

. . . As the Vice Chancellor noted, 413 A.2d at 1257, "it is the law of the State of incorporation which determines whether the directors have this power of dismissal, Burks v. Lasker, 441 U.S. 471, 99 S.Ct. 1831, 60 L.Ed.2d 404 (1979)". We limit our review in this interlocutory appeal to whether the Committee has the power to cause the present action to be dismissed.

We begin with an examination of the carefully considered opinion of the Vice Chancellor which states, in part, that the "business judgment" rule does not confer power "to a corporate board of directors to terminate a derivative suit", 413 A.2d at 1257. His conclusion is particularly pertinent because several federal courts, applying Delaware law, have held that the business judgment rule enables boards (or their committees) to terminate derivative suits, decisions now in conflict with the holding below.

As the term is most commonly used, and given the disposition below, we can understand the Vice Chancellor's comment that "the business judgment rule is irrelevant to the question of whether the Committee has the authority to compel the dismissal of this suit." 413 A.2d at 1257. Corporations, existing because of legislative grace, possess authority as granted by the legislature. Directors of Delaware corporations derive their managerial decision making power, which encompasses decisions whether to initiate, or refrain from entering, litigation, from 8 Del.C. § 141(a). This statute is the fount of directorial powers. The "business judgment" rule is a judicial creation that presumes propriety, under certain circumstances, in a board's decision. Viewed defensively, it does not create authority. In this sense the "business judgment" rule is not relevant in corporate decision making until after a decision is made. It is generally used as a defense to an attack on the decision's soundness. The board's managerial decision making power, however, comes from § 141(a).

The judicial creation and legislative grant are related because the "business judgment" rule evolved to give recognition and deference to directors' business expertise when exercising their managerial power under § 141(a).

In the case before us, although the corporation's decision to move to dismiss or for summary judgment was, literally, a decision resulting from an exercise of the directors' (as delegated to the Committee) business judgment, the question of "business judgment", in a defensive sense, would not become relevant until and unless the decision to seek termination of the derivative lawsuit was attacked as improper. . . . This question was not reached by the Vice Chancellor because he determined that the stockholder had an individual right to maintain this derivative action. . . .

Thus, the focus in this case is on the power to speak for the corporation as to whether the lawsuit should be continued or terminated. As we see it, this issue in the current appellate posture of this case has three aspects: the conclusions of the Court below concerning the continuing right of a stockholder to maintain a derivative action; the corporate power under Delaware law of an authorized board committee to cause dismissal of litigation instituted for the benefit of the corporation; and the role of the Court of Chancery in resolving conflicts between the stockholder and the committee.

Accordingly, we turn first to the Court of Chancery's conclusions concerning the right of a plaintiff stockholder in a derivative action. We find that its determination that a stockholder, once demand is made and refused, possesses an independent, individual right to continue a derivative suit for breaches of fiduciary duty over objection by the corporation, *Maldonado,* 413 A.2d at 1262–63, as an absolute rule, is erroneous. . . .

. . . McKee v. Rogers, Del.Ch., 156 A. 191 (1931), stated "as a general rule" that "a stockholder cannot be permitted . . . to invade the discretionary field committed to the judgment of the directors and sue in the corporation's behalf when the managing body refuses. This rule is a well settled one." 156 A. at 193.

The *McKee* rule, of course, should not be read so broadly that the board's refusal will be determinative in every instance. Board members, owing a well-established fiduciary duty to the corporation, will not be allowed to cause a derivative suit to be dismissed when it would be a breach of their fiduciary duty. Generally disputes pertaining to control of the suit arise in two contexts.

Consistent with the purpose of requiring a demand, a board decision to cause a derivative suit to be dismissed as detrimental to the company, after demand has been made and refused, will be respected unless it was wrongful.[10] . . . A claim of a wrongful decision not to

10. In other words, when stockholders, after making demand and having their suit rejected, attack the board's decision as improper, the board's decision falls under the "business judgment" rule and will be respected if the requirements of the rule are met. . . . That situation should be distinguished from the instant case, where demand was not made, and the *power* of the board to seek a dismissal, due to disqualification, presents a threshold issue. . . .

sue is thus the first exception and the first context of dispute. Absent a wrongful refusal, the stockholder in such a situation simply lacks legal managerial power. . . .

But it cannot be implied that, absent a wrongful board refusal, a stockholder can never have an individual right to initiate an action. For, as is stated in *McKee,* a "well settled" exception exists to the general rule.

"[A] stockholder may sue in equity in his derivative right to assert a cause of action in behalf of the corporation, *without prior demand* upon the directors to sue, when it is apparent that a demand would be futile, that the officers are under an influence that sterilizes discretion and could not be proper persons to conduct the litigation."

156 A. at 193 (emphasis added). This exception, the second context for dispute, is consistent with the Court of Chancery's statement below, that "[t]he stockholders' individual right to bring the action does not ripen, however, . . . unless he can show a demand to be futile." *Maldonado,* 413 A.2d at 1262.[11]

These comments in *McKee* and in the opinion below make obvious sense. A demand, when required and refused (if not wrongful), terminates a stockholder's legal ability to initiate a derivative action. But where demand is properly excused, the stockholder does possess the ability to initiate the action on his corporation's behalf.

These conclusions, however, do not determine the question before us. Rather, they merely bring us to the question to be decided. It is here that we part company with the Court below. Derivative suits enforce corporate rights and any recovery obtained goes to the corporation. . . . We see no inherent reason why the "two phases" of a derivative suit, the stockholder's suit to compel the corporation to sue and the corporation's suit, . . . should automatically result in the placement in the hands of the litigating stockholder [of] sole control of the corporate right throughout the litigation. To the contrary, it seems to us that such an inflexible rule would recognize the interest of one person or group to the exclusion of all others within the corporate entity. Thus, we reject the view of the Vice Chancellor as to the first aspect of the issue on appeal.

The question to be decided becomes: When, if at all, should an authorized board committee be permitted to cause litigation, properly initiated by a derivative stockholder in his own right, to be dismissed? As noted above, a board has the power to choose not to pursue litigation when demand is made upon it, so long as the decision is not wrongful. If the board determines that a suit would be detrimental to the company, the board's determination prevails. Even when demand is excusable, circumstances may arise when continuation of the litigation would not be in the corporation's best interests. Our inquiry is whether, under such circumstances, there is a permissible procedure

11. These statements are consistent with Rule 23.1's "reasons for . . . failure" to make demand. . . .

under § 141(a) by which a corporation can rid itself of detrimental litigation. If there is not, a single stockholder in an extreme case might control the destiny of the entire corporation. This concern was bluntly expressed by the Ninth Circuit in Lewis v. Anderson, 9th Cir., 615 F.2d 778, 783 (1979), cert. denied, 449 U.S. 869, 101 S.Ct. 206, 66 L.Ed.2d 89 (1980): "To allow one shareholder to incapacitate an entire board of directors merely by leveling charges against them gives too much leverage to dissident shareholders." But, when examining the means, including the committee mechanism examined in this case, potentials for abuse must be recognized. This takes us to the second and third aspects of the issue on appeal.

Before we pass to equitable considerations as to the mechanism at issue here, it must be clear that an independent committee possesses the corporate power to seek the termination of a derivative suit. Section 141(c) allows a board to delegate all of its authority to a committee. Accordingly, a committee with properly delegated authority would have the power to move for dismissal or summary judgment if the entire board did.

Even though demand was not made in this case and the initial decision of whether to litigate was not placed before the board, Zapata's board, it seems to us, retained all of its corporate power concerning litigation decisions. If Maldonado had made demand on the board in this case, it could have refused to bring suit. Maldonado could then have asserted that the decision not to sue was wrongful and, if correct, would have been allowed to maintain the suit. The board, however, never would have lost its statutory managerial authority. The demand requirement itself evidences that the managerial power is retained by the board. When a derivative plaintiff is allowed to bring suit after a wrongful refusal, the board's authority to choose whether to pursue the litigation is not challenged although its conclusion—reached through the exercise of that authority—is not respected since it is wrongful. Similarly, Rule 23.1, by excusing demand in certain instances, does not strip the board of its corporate power. It merely saves the plaintiff the expense and delay of making a futile demand resulting in a probable tainted exercise of that authority in a refusal by the board or in giving control of litigation to the opposing side. But the board entity remains empowered under § 141(a) to make decisions regarding corporate litigation. The problem is one of member disqualification, not the absence of power in the board.

The corporate power inquiry then focuses on whether the board, tainted by the self-interest of a majority of its members, can legally delegate its authority to a committee of two disinterested directors. We find our statute clearly requires an affirmative answer to this question. As has been noted, under an express provision of the statute, § 141(c), a committee can exercise all of the authority of the board to the extent provided in the resolution of the board. Moreover, at least by analogy to our statutory section on interested directors, 8 Del.C. § 141, it seems clear that the Delaware statute is designed to permit disinterested directors to act for the board.[14] Compare Puma v. Marriott, Del.Ch., 283 A.2d 693, 695–96 (1971).

We do not think that the interest taint of the board majority is per se a legal bar to the delegation of the board's power to an independent committee composed of disinterested board members. The committee can properly act for the corporation to move to dismiss derivative litigation that is believed to be detrimental to the corporation's best interest.

Our focus now switches to the Court of Chancery which is faced with a stockholder assertion that a derivative suit, properly instituted, should continue for the benefit of the corporation and a corporate assertion, properly made by a board committee acting with board authority, that the same derivative suit should be dismissed as inimical to the best interests of the corporation.

At the risk of stating the obvious, the problem is relatively simple. If, on the one hand, corporations can consistently wrest bona fide derivative actions away from well-meaning derivative plaintiffs through the use of the committee mechanism, the derivative suit will lose much, if not all, of its generally-recognized effectiveness as an intra-corporate means of policing boards of directors. See Dent, supra note 5, 75 Nw.U.L.Rev. at 96 & n. 3, 144 & n. 241. If, on the other hand, corporations are unable to rid themselves of meritless or harmful litigation and strike suits, the derivative action, created to benefit the corporation, will produce the opposite, unintended result. For a discussion of strike suits, see Dent, supra, 75 Nw.U.L.Rev. at 137. See also Cramer v. General Telephone & Electronics Corp., 3d Cir., 582 F.2d 259, 275 (1978), cert. denied, 439 U.S. 1129, 99 S.Ct. 1048, 59 L.Ed.2d 90 (1979). It thus appears desirable to us to find a balancing point where bona fide stockholder power to bring corporation causes of action cannot be unfairly trampled on by the board of directors, but the corporation can rid itself of detrimental litigation.

As we noted, the question has been treated by other courts as one of the "business judgment" of the board committee. If a "committee, composed of independent and disinterested directors, conducted a proper review of the matters before it, considered a variety of factors and reached, in good faith, a business judgment that [the] action was not in the best interest of [the corporation]", the action must be dismissed. See, e.g., Maldonado v. Flynn, . . . 485 F.Supp. at 282, 286. The issues become solely independence, good faith, and reasonable investigation. The ultimate conclusion of the committee, under that view, is not subject to judicial review.

We are not satisfied, however, that acceptance of the "business judgment" rationale at this stage of derivative litigation is a proper balancing point. While we admit an analogy with a normal case respecting board judgment, it seems to us that there is sufficient risk in the realities of a situation like the one presented in this case to justify caution beyond adherence to the theory of business judgment.

---

14. [The court quoted Del. § 144.]

The context here is a suit against directors where demand on the board is excused. We think some tribute must be paid to the fact that the lawsuit was properly initiated. It is not a board refusal case. Moreover, this complaint was filed in June of 1975 and, while the parties undoubtedly would take differing views on the degree of litigation activity, we have to be concerned about the creation of an "Independent Investigation Committee" four years later, after the election of two new outside directors. Situations could develop where such motions could be filed after years of vigorous litigation for reasons unconnected with the merits of the lawsuit.

Moreover, notwithstanding our conviction that Delaware law entrusts the corporate power to a properly authorized committee, we must be mindful that directors are passing judgment on fellow directors in the same corporation and fellow directors, in this instance, who designated them to serve both as directors and committee members. The question naturally arises whether a "there but for the grace of God go I" empathy might not play a role. And the further question arises whether inquiry as to independence, good faith and reasonable investigation is sufficient safeguard against abuse, perhaps subconscious abuse.

There is another line of exploration besides the factual context of this litigation which we find helpful. The nature of this motion finds no ready pigeonhole, as perhaps illustrated by its being set forth in the alternative. It is perhaps best considered as a hybrid summary judgment motion for dismissal because the stockholder plaintiff's standing to maintain the suit has been lost. But it does not fit neatly into a category described in Rule 12(b) of the Court of Chancery Rules nor does it correspond directly with Rule 56 since the question of genuine issues of fact on the merits of the stockholder's claim are not reached.

It seems to us that there are two other procedural analogies that are helpful in addition to reference to Rules 12 and 56. There is some analogy to a settlement in that there is a request to terminate litigation without a judicial determination of the merits. See Perrine v. Pennroad Corp., Del.Super., 47 A.2d 479, 487 (1946). "In determining whether or not to approve a proposed settlement of a derivative stockholders' action [when directors are on both sides of the transaction], the Court of Chancery is called upon to exercise its own business judgment." Neponsit Investment Co. v. Abramson, Del.Super., 405 A.2d 97, 100 (1979) and cases therein cited. In this case, the litigating stockholder plaintiff facing dismissal of a lawsuit properly commenced ought, in our judgment, to have sufficient status for strict Court review.

Finally, if the committee is in effect given status to speak for the corporation as the plaintiff in interest, then it seems to us there is an analogy to Court of Chancery Rule 41(a)(2) where the plaintiff seeks a dismissal after an answer. Certainly, the position of record of the litigating stockholder is adverse to the position advocated by the corporation in the motion to dismiss. Accordingly, there is perhaps some wisdom to be gained by the direction in Rule 41(a)(2) that "an action shall not be dismissed at the plaintiff's instance save upon order of the Court and upon such terms and conditions as the Court deems proper."

Whether the Court of Chancery will be persuaded by the exercise of a committee power resulting in a summary motion for dismissal of a derivative action, where a demand has not been initially made, should rest, in our judgment, in the independent discretion of the Court of Chancery. We thus steer a middle course between those cases which yield to the independent business judgment of a board committee and this case as determined below which would yield to unbridled plaintiff stockholder control. In pursuit of the course, we recognize that "[t]he final substantive judgment whether a particular lawsuit should be maintained requires a balance of many factors—ethical, commercial, promotional, public relations, employee relations, fiscal as well as legal." Maldonado v. Flynn, supra, 485 F.Supp. at 285. But we are content that such factors are not "beyond the judicial reach" of the Court of Chancery which regularly and competently deals with fiduciary relationships, disposition of trust property, approval of settlements and scores of similar problems. We recognize the danger of judicial overreaching but the alternatives seem to us to be outweighed by the fresh view of a judicial outsider. Moreover, if we failed to balance all the interests involved, we would in the name of practicality and judicial economy foreclose a judicial decision on the merits. At this point, we are not convinced that is necessary or desirable.

After an objective and thorough investigation of a derivative suit, an independent committee may cause its corporation to file a pretrial motion to dismiss in the Court of Chancery. The basis of the motion is the best interests of the corporation, as determined by the committee. The motion should include a thorough written record of the investigation and its findings and recommendations. Under appropriate court supervision, akin to proceedings on summary judgment, each side should have an opportunity to make a record on the motion. As to the limited issues presented by the motion noted below, the moving party should be prepared to meet the normal burden under Rule 56 that there is no genuine issue as to any material fact and that the moving party is entitled to dismiss as a matter of law.[15] The Court should apply a two-step test to the motion.

First, the Court should inquire into the independence and good faith of the committee and the bases supporting its conclusions. Limited discovery may be ordered to facilitate such inquiries. The corporation should have the burden of proving independence, good faith and a reasonable investigation, rather than presuming independence, good faith and reasonableness.[17] If the Court determines that

---

15. We do not foreclose a discretionary trial of factual issues but that issue is not presented in this appeal. See Lewis v. Anderson, supra, 615 F.2d at 780. Nor do we foreclose the possibility that other motions may proceed or be joined with such a pretrial summary judgment motion to dis-miss, e.g., a partial motion for summary judgment on the merits.

17. Compare Auerbach v. Bennett, 47 N.Y.2d 619, 419 N.Y.S.2d 920, 928–29, 393 N.E.2d 994 (1979). Our approach here is analogous to and consistent with the Dela-

the committee is not independent or has not shown reasonable bases for its conclusions, or, if the Court is not satisfied for other reasons relating to the process, including but not limited to the good faith of the committee, the Court shall deny the corporation's motion. If, however, the Court is satisfied under Rule 56 standards that the committee was independent and showed reasonable bases for good faith findings and recommendations, the Court may proceed, in its discretion, to the next step.

The second step provides, we believe, the essential key in striking the balance between legitimate corporate claims as expressed in a derivative stockholder suit and a corporation's best interests as expressed by an independent investigating committee. The Court should determine, applying its own independent business judgment, whether the motion should be granted.[18] This means, of course, that instances could arise where a committee can establish its independence and sound bases for its good faith decisions and still have the corporation's motion denied. The second step is intended to thwart instances where corporate actions meet the criteria of step one, but the result does not appear to satisfy its spirit, or where corporate actions would simply prematurely terminate a stockholder grievance deserving of further consideration in the corporation's interest. The Court of Chancery of course must carefully consider and weigh how compelling the corporate interest in dismissal is when faced with a non-frivolous lawsuit. The Court of Chancery should, when appropriate, give special consideration to matters of law and public policy in addition to the corporation's best interests.

If the Court's independent business judgment is satisfied, the Court may proceed to grant the motion, subject, of course, to any equitable terms or conditions the Court finds necessary or desirable.

The interlocutory order of the Court of Chancery is reversed and the cause is remanded for further proceedings consistent with this opinion.

ALFORD v. SHAW, 320 N.C. 465, 358 S.E.2d 323 (1987). "The recent trend among courts which have been faced with the choice of applying an *Auerbach*-type rule of judicial deference or a *Zapata*-type rule of judicial scrutiny has been to require judicial inquiry on the merits of the special litigation committee's report. . . .

". . . We interpret the trend away from *Auerbach* among other jurisdictions as an indication of growing concern about the deficiencies inherent in a rule giving great deference to the decisions of a corporate committee whose institutional symbiosis with the corpora-

---

ware approach to "interested director" transactions, where the directors, once the transaction is attacked, have the burden of establishing its "intrinsic fairness" to a court's careful scrutiny. See, e.g., Sterling v. Mayflower Hotel Corp., Del.Supr., 93 A.2d 107 (1952).

18. This step shares some of the same spirit and philosophy of the statement by the Vice Chancellor: "Under our system of law, courts and not litigants should decide the merits of litigation." 413 A.2d at 1263.

tion necessarily affects its ability to render a decision that fairly considers the interest of plaintiffs forced to bring suit on behalf of the corporation. *See generally* Cox & Munsinger, *Bias in the Boardroom: Psychological Foundations and Legal Implications of Corporate Cohesion,* 48 Law and Contemporary Problems, Summer 1985 at 83 (1985). Such concerns are legitimate ones and, upon further reflection, we find that they must be resolved not by slavish adherence to the business judgment rule, but by careful interpretation of the provisions of our own Business Corporation Act. . . .

"[A] policy of protecting minority shareholders is manifested by section 55–55(c), which states that a shareholder's derivative action

> shall not be discontinued, dismissed, compromised or settled without the approval of the court. If the court shall determine that the interest of the shareholders or any class or classes thereof, or of the creditors of the corporation, will be substantially affected by such discontinuance, dismissal, compromise or settlement, the court, in its discretion, may direct that notice, by publication or otherwise, shall be given to such shareholders or creditors whose interests it determines will be so affected. . . .

"Although the recommendation of the special litigation committee is not binding on the court, in making this determination the court may choose to rely on such recommendation. To rely blindly on the report of a corporation-appointed committee which assembled such materials on behalf of the corporation is to abdicate the judicial duty to consider the interests of shareholders imposed by the statute. . . .

"The *Zapata* Court limited its two-step judicial inquiry to cases in which demand upon the corporation was futile and therefore excused. However, we find no justification for such limitation in our statutes. The language of section 55–55(c) is inclusive and draws no distinctions between demand-excused and other types of cases. *Cf.* ALI Principles of Corporate Governance: Analysis and Recommendations § 7.08 & Reporter's Notes 2 & 4 at 135–139 (Council Draft No. 6, Oct. 10, 1986) (issue of demand of minimal importance in determining scope of review; demand-excused/demand-required distinction not determinative). Thus, court approval is required for disposition of *all* derivative suits, even where the directors are not charged with fraud or self-dealing, or where the plaintiff and the board agree to discontinue, dismiss, compromise, or settle the lawsuit."

ARONSON v. LEWIS, 473 A.2d 805 (1984). "The gap in our law, which we address today, arises from this Court's decision in Zapata Corp. v. Maldonado. There, the Court defined the limits of a board's managerial power granted by Section 141(a) and restricted application of the business judgment rule in a factual context similar to this action. . . .

ISSUE

"After *Zapata* numerous derivative suits were filed without prior demand upon boards of directors. The complaints in such actions all alleged that demand was excused because of board interest, approval or acquiescence in the wrongdoing. In any event, the *Zapata* demand-excused/demand-refused bifurcation, has left a crucial issue unanswered: when is demand futile and, therefore, excused?

"Delaware courts have addressed the issue of demand futility on several earlier occasions. . . . The rule emerging from these decisions is that where officers and directors are under an influence which sterilizes their discretion, they cannot be considered proper persons to conduct litigation on behalf of the corporation. Thus, demand would be futile. See e.g., McKee v. Rogers, Del.Ch., 156 A. 191, 192 (1931) (holding that where a defendant controlled the board of directors, '[i]t is manifest then that there can be no expectation that the corporation would sue him, and if it did, it can hardly be said that the prosecution of the suit would be entrusted to proper hands'). . . .

"However, those cases cannot be taken to mean that any board approval of a challenged transaction automatically connotes 'hostile interest' and 'guilty participation' by directors, or some other form of sterilizing influence upon them. Were that so, the demand requirements of our law would be meaningless, leaving the clear mandate of Chancery Rule 23.1 devoid of its purpose and substance. . . .

Test for Demand Excused

"Our view is that in determining demand futility the Court of Chancery in the proper exercise of its discretion must decide whether, under the particularized facts alleged, a reasonable doubt is created that: (1) the directors are disinterested and independent and (2) the challenged transaction was otherwise the product of a valid exercise of business judgment. Hence, the Court of Chancery must make two inquiries, one into the independence and disinterestedness of the directors and the other into the substantive nature of the challenged transaction and the board's approval thereof. As to the latter inquiry the court does not assume that the transaction is a wrong to the corporation requiring corrective steps by the board. Rather, the alleged wrong is substantively reviewed against the factual background alleged in the complaint. As to the former inquiry, directorial independence and disinterestedness, the court reviews the factual allegations to decide whether they raise a reasonable doubt, as a threshold matter, that the protections of the business judgment rule are available to the board. Certainly, if this is an 'interested' director transaction, such that the business judgment rule is inapplicable to the board majority approving the transaction, then the inquiry ceases. In that event futility of demand has been established by any objective or subjective standard.[8] See, e.g., Bergstein v. Texas Internat'l Co., Del.

---

8. We recognize that drawing the line at a majority of the board may be an arguably arbitrary dividing point. Critics will charge that we are ignoring the structural bias common to corporate boards throughout America, as well as the other unseen socialization processes cutting against independent discussion and decisionmaking in the boardroom. The difficulty with structural bias in a demand futile case is simply one of establishing it in the complaint for purposes of Rule 23.1. We are satisfied that discretionary review by the Court of Chancery of complaints

Ch., 453 A.2d 467, 471 (1982) (because five of nine directors approved stock appreciation rights plan likely to benefit them, board was interested for demand purposes and demand held futile). This includes situations involving self-dealing directors. . . .

"However, the mere threat of personal liability for approving a questioned transaction, standing alone, is insufficient to challenge either the independence or disinterestedness of directors, although in rare cases a transaction may be so egregious on its face that board approval cannot meet the test of business judgment, and a substantial likelihood of director liability therefore exists. . . . In sum the entire review is factual in nature. The Court of Chancery in the exercise of its sound discretion must be satisfied that a plaintiff has alleged facts with particularity which, taken as true, support a reasonable doubt that the challenged transaction was the product of a valid exercise of business judgment. Only in that context is demand excused."

GROBOW v. PEROT

Supreme Court of Delaware, 1988.
539 A.2d 180

In these consolidated shareholder derivative suits, plaintiffs-shareholders appeal the Court of Chancery's dismissal of their suits for failure of plaintiffs to make presuit demand under Court of Chancery Rule 23.1. The Court of Chancery held that plaintiffs' complaints as amended failed to allege particularized facts which, if taken as true, would excuse demand under the demand futility test of *Aronson v. Lewis*, Del.Supr., 473 A.2d 805 (1984). The Court interpreted *Aronson*'s "reasonable doubt" standard for establishing demand futility as requiring plaintiffs to plead particularized facts sufficient to sustain "a judicial finding" either of director interest or lack of director independence, or whether the directors exercised proper business judgment in approving the challenged transaction—placing the transaction beyond the protection of the business judgment rule. *Grobow v. Perot*, Del.Ch., 526 A.2d 914, 921 (1987). We find the Vice Chancellor to have erred in formulating an excessive criterion for satisfying *Aronson*'s reasonable doubt test. Moreover, the Vice Chancellor erred in his statement that fairness is a "pivotal" question under an *Aronson* analysis. *See* 526 A.2d at 927. Unless the presumption of the business judgment rule is overcome by the pleadings, questions of fairness play no part in the analysis. *Aronson*, 473 A.2d at 812. However, applying the correct standard, we conclude that the complaints (singly or collectively) fail to state facts which, if taken as true, would create a reasonable doubt either of director disinterest or independence, or that the transaction was other than the product of

alleging specific facts pointing to bias on a particular board will be sufficient for determining demand futility.

the Board's valid exercise of business judgment. Therefore, we affirm the decision below, finding the Court's error to have been harmless.

I

The well-pleaded facts of these proceedings come principally from the complaints, as amended, and are fully set forth in the Court of Chancery Opinion. *See Grobow*, 526 A.2d 918–20. They will thus be repeated here in summary fashion and only as necessary.

A.

In 1984, General Motors Corporation ("GM") acquired 100 percent of Electronic Data Systems' ("EDS") stock. Under the terms of the merger, H. Ross Perot, founder, chairman and largest stockholder of EDS, exchanged his EDS stock for GM Class E stock and contingent notes. Perot became GM's largest shareholder, holding 0.8 percent of GM voting stock. Perot was also elected to GM's Board of Directors (the "Board") while remaining chairman of EDS.

The merger proved mutually beneficial to both corporations and was largely a success. However, management differences developed between Perot and the other officers and directors of GM's Board over the way GM was running EDS, and Perot became increasingly vocal in his criticism of GM management. By mid-1986, Perot announced to GM that he could no longer be a "company man." Perot demanded that GM allow him to run EDS as he saw fit or that GM buy him out. Perot then began publicly criticizing GM management with such statements as: "Until you nuke the old GM system, you'll never tap the full potential of your people"; and "GM cannot become a world-class and cost-competitive company simply by throwing technology and money at its problems." Thereafter, GM and American Telephone and Telegraph entered into exploratory negotiations for AT&T's purchase of EDS from GM allegedly as a means of GM's eliminating Perot. However, their negotiations did not proceed beyond the preliminary stage.

By late fall of 1986, Perot, anxious, for tax reasons, for a definitive decision before year-end, offered to sell his entire interest in GM. GM responded with a purchase proposal. Perot replied, suggesting additional terms, which Perot characterized as "a giant premium." When a definitive agreement was reached, the Board designated a three-member Special Review Committee ("SRC"), chaired by one of the Board's outside directors to review its terms.[1] The SRC met on November 30, 1986 to consider the repurchase proposal and unanimously recommended that GM's Board approve its terms. The following day, December 1, 1986, the GM Board of Directors met and approved the repurchase agreement.

---

1. The complaints fail to state whether the other two directors on the SRC were inside or outside directors. Since plaintiffs do not allege that they were members of management, we will presume that they were outside directors. For purposes of this case, we define "outside" directors to mean nonemployee, nonmanagement directors.

Under the terms of the repurchase, GM acquired all of Perot's GM Class E stock and contingent notes and those of his close EDS associates for nearly $745,000,000.[2] GM also received certain commitments, termed "covenants," from Perot. In addition to resigning immediately from GM's Board and as Chairman of EDS, Perot further agreed: (1) to stop criticizing GM management, in default of which Perot agreed to pay GM damages in a liquidated sum of up to $7.5 million;[3] (2) not to purchase GM stock or engage in a proxy contest against the Board for five years; and (3) not to compete with EDS for three years or recruit EDS executives for eighteen months.

At all relevant times, a majority of the GM Board of Directors consisted of outside directors. The exact number and composition of the GM Board at the time is not clear. However, from the limited record, it appears that the Board was comprised of twenty-six directors (excluding Perot), of whom eighteen were outside directors.

The GM repurchase came at a time when GM was experiencing financial difficulty and was engaged in cost cutting. Public reaction to the announcement ranged from mixed to adverse. The repurchase was sharply criticized by industry analysts and by members within GM's management ranks as well. The criticism focused on two features of the repurchase: (1) the size of the premium over the then market price of GM Class E stock;[4] and (2) the hush mail provision.

B.

Plaintiffs filed separate derivative actions (later consolidated) against GM, EDS, GM's directors, H. Ross Perot, and three of Perot's EDS associates. The suits collectively allege: (i) that the GM director defendants breached their fiduciary duties to GM and EDS by paying a grossly excessive price for the repurchase of Perot's and the EDS associates' Class E stock of GM; (ii) that the repurchase included a unique hush mail feature to buy not only Perot's resignation, but his silence, and that such a condition lacked any valid business purpose and was a waste of GM assets; and (iii) that the repurchase was entrenchment motivated and was carried out principally to save GM's Board from further public embarrassment by Perot. The complaints

2. "Of the aggregate cost of $742.8 million, $396 million ($33 per share) was attributed to the Class E stock, $282 million ($23.50 per share) was attributed to the contingent notes, and $64.8 million ($5.40 per share) was attributed to 'Special Interest' federal tax compensation under the terms of the contingent notes." *Grobow*, 526 A.2d at 919 n.6.

3. This commitment by Perot would later be characterized as the "hush mail" feature of the agreement. The colloquial term is not defined in the pleadings but is assumed by this Court to combine the terms "green mail" and "hush money" to connote a variation on an unlawful and secret payment to assure silence. Here, the commitment is cast in the form of an explicit liquidated damage clause for future breach of contract. *See infra* section III B.

4. Plaintiffs allege that the total repurchase price per share . . . was double the market price of the GM Class E stock on the last day of trading before consummation of the repurchase . . . . However, the extent of premium over market cannot be mathematically calculated with any precision without disregarding the value of the contingent notes. The total repurchase price per share includes not only the price paid for the Class E stock, but also the price paid for the contingent notes and the value of the special interest federal tax compensation. *See infra* note 7.

charge the individual defendants with acting out of self-interest and with breaching their duties of loyalty and due care to GM and EDS.

All defendants moved to dismiss the suits for plaintiffs' failure to comply with Court of Chancery Rule 23.1, as construed and applied under *Aronson*—that is, either to make presuit demand on GM's Board or to plead particularized facts demonstrating that demand was excused as futile.[5] Plaintiffs responded that the complaints state a case for demand excusal. They contended that the complaints detail factual allegations that create a reasonable doubt that GM's Board was disinterested or independent, or that the transaction was the product of a valid exercise of business judgment. Defendants dispute the sufficiency of the allegations that GM Board approval of the stock repurchase of dissident Perot was the result of the Board's failure to act in good faith and in the exercise of due care.

As noted the Court of Chancery, finding to the contrary, ruled that plaintiffs had failed to establish demand futility by satisfying *Aronson*'s demand futility test. Plaintiffs seek reversal for error of law and abuse of discretion. Reversible legal error is said to have resulted from the Trial Court's erroneous application of *Aronson* to require a derivative complaint to state particularized facts sufficient to sustain a "judicial finding" of demand excusal. Additionally, plaintiffs argue that the Court abused its discretion in finding the well-pleaded allegations of the complaints not to establish demand excusal under Rule 23.1.

II

We first note this Court's standard of review of the Court of Chancery's ruling that plaintiffs have failed to plead a demand-futility case consistent with *Aronson*. Assuming no rule of law is implicated, a decision on a Rule 23.1 motion based on failure to make presuit demand involves essentially a discretionary ruling on a predominantly factual issue. *Aronson*, 473 A.2d at 814–15. Therefore, this Court will disturb the Court of Chancery's Rule 23.1 ruling only on a showing of abuse of discretion, assuming no legal error led to an erroneous holding. *Id.* (the Court's determination of a Rule 23.1 motion is discretionary); *see also Pogostin v. Rice*, Del.Supr., 480 A.2d 619, 624 (1984) (the Court of Chancery, exercising its sound discretion, must determine whether demand is excused under either prong of *Aronson*).

However, before applying our standard of review, we briefly revisit the underlying requirements of a well-pleaded derivative complaint to withstand a Rule 23.1 motion to dismiss for failure to make

---

5. Rule 23.1 provides, in pertinent part:

In a derivative action brought by 1 or more shareholders or members to enforce a right of a corporation or of an unincorporated association, the corporation or association having failed to enforce a right which may properly be asserted by it, the complaint . . . shall also allege with particularity the efforts, if any, made by the plaintiff to obtain the action he desires from the directors or comparable authority and the reasons for his failure to obtain the action or for not making the effort. The action shall not be dismissed or compromised without the approval of the Court.. . . .

presuit demand upon a board in accordance with *Aronson* and *Pogostin*. Our standard or test for determining whether a derivative complaint states a demand futility claim under Rule 23.1 is: whether taking the well-pleaded facts as true, the allegations raise a reasonable doubt as to (i) director disinterest or independence or (ii) whether the directors exercised proper business judgment in approving the challenged transaction. *Aronson*, 473 A.2d at 814, and *Pogostin*, 480 A.2d at 624.

Thus, the ultimate question before us is the same as was presented in *Aronson*: whether the complaints, as amended, allege facts with particularity "which create a reasonable doubt that the directors' action was entitled to the protection of the business judgment rule." *Aronson*, 473 A.2d at 808. That is so because "demand futility [in the context of director-approved transactions] is inextricably bound to issues of business judgment" by the power conferred on a board of directors under 8 *Del.C.* § 141(a). *Id.* at 812. Necessarily, this involves an objective analysis of the facts.

Addressing plaintiffs' claim of legal error, we find the Vice Chancellor's use of a "judicial finding" criterion for judging a derivative claim for demand excusal to be erroneous, but not reversible error. First, the Court's "judicial finding" criterion would impose a more stringent standard for demand futility than is warranted under *Aronson*. The test for demand futility should be whether the well-pleaded facts of the particular complaint support a reasonable doubt of business judgment protection, not whether the facts support a judicial finding that the directors' actions are not protected by the business judgment rule. *See Aronson*, 473 A.2d at 815.

Second, given the highly factual nature of the inquiry presented to the Trial Court by a Rule 23.1 defense, we conclude that it would be neither practicable nor wise to attempt to forumlate a criterion of general application for determining reasonable doubt. The facts necessary to support a finding of reasonable doubt either of director disinterest or independence, or whether proper business judgment was exercised in the transaction will vary with each case. Reasonable doubt must be decided by the trial court on a case-by-case basis employing an objective analysis. Were we to adopt a standard criterion for resolving a motion to dismiss based on Rule 23.1, the test for demand excusal would, in all likelihood, become rote and inelastic.

Finally, since a Rule 23.1 motion normally precedes rather than follows discovery, a plaintiff may be able in one case and without formal discovery to plead facts sufficient to raise a reasonable doubt of business judgment protection, but be unable in another case without such discovery to plead facts sufficient to support a judicial finding of the lack of business judgment protection. On the other hand, if a derivative complaint alleges facts which would support a judicial finding of a lack of business judgment protection, then such facts would more than satisfy *Aronson*'s reasonable doubt standard.

Therefore, we decline to approve the use of a "judicial finding" standard as the minimum criterion below which presuit demand will not be excused. We think it sufficient simply to say that the Court of

Chancery must weight the presumption of the business judgment rule that attaches to a board of directors' decision against the well-pleaded facts alleged in a plaintiff's demand-futility complaint. In that respect, the suggestion in the Trial Court's Opinion that a transaction is first analyzed from the standpoint of fairness is erroneous. *See* 526 A.2d at 927. Fairness becomes an issue only if the presumption of the business judgment rule is defeated. *Aronson*, 473 A.2d at 812–817.

III

Although the Vice Chancellor's use of a "judicial finding" criterion and fairness analysis were erroneous, the errors do not require reversal if we, under our review of the pleadings and applying the proper standard of reasonable doubt, conclude that a claim of demand futility has not been pleaded. Thus, we turn to the underlying issue— whether plaintiffs' complaints as amended state a case for demand excusal sufficient to withstand defendant's Rule 23.1 motions to dismiss. The answer to the question requires relating the business judgment rule to the issue of demand excusal.

As previously noted, the business judgment rule is but a presumption that directors making a business decision, not involving self-interest, act on an informed basis, in good faith and in the honest belief that their actions are in the corporation's best interest. *See Aronson*, 473 A.2d at 812. Thus, good faith and the absence of self-dealing are threshold requirements for invoking the rule. *Id.; cf. Unocal Corp. v. Mesa Petroleum Co.*, Del.Supr., 493 A.2d 946 (1985). Assuming the presumptions of director good faith and lack of self-dealing are not rebutted by well-pleaded facts, a shareholder derivative complainant must then allege further facts with particularity which, "taken as true, support a reasonable doubt that the challenged transaction was [in fact] the product of a valid exercise of business judgment." *Aronson*, 473 A.2d at 815; *see also Pogostin*, 480 A.2d at 624–25. The complaints as amended do not even purport to plead a claim of fraud, bad faith, or self-dealing in the usual sense of personal profit or betterment. *See, e.g. Sinclair Oil Corp. v. Levien*, Del.Supr., 280 A.2d 717, 720 (1971). Therefore, we must presume that the GM directors reached their repurchase decision in good faith. *See Allaun v. Consolidated Oil Co.*, Del.Ch., 147 A. 257, 261 (1929).

The burden then clearly falls upon plaintiffs claiming demand futility to plead particularized facts sufficient to rebut the presumption that the GM Board exercised sound business judgment "in the honest belief that the action taken was in the best interest of the company." *Aronson*, 473 A.2d at 812 (citations omitted); *cf. Puma v. Marriott*, Del.Ch., 283 A.2d 693, 695 (1971). Moreover, upon a motion to dismiss, only well-pleaded allegations of fact must be accepted as true; conclusionary allegations of fact or law not supported by allegations of specific fact may not be taken as true.[6] A trial court need not blindly

---

6. Even under the less stringent standard of a Chancery Court Rule 12(b)(6) motion to dismiss, all facts of the pleadings and reasonable inferences to be drawn therefrom are accepted as true, but neither inferences nor conclusions of fact unsupported by allegations of specific facts upon which the inferences or conclusions rest

accept as true all allegations, nor must it draw all inferences from them in plaintiffs' favor unless they are reasonable inferences. Thus, for plaintiffs to meet the *Aronson* reasonable doubt standard, we must examine the complaints, as amended, to determine whether their well-pleaded facts raise a reasonable doubt sufficient to rebut the presumption that the business judgment rule attaches to the repurchase transaction. This brings us to the application of the two-pronged demand futility test of *Aronson*.

A. *Disinterest and Independence*

In order to satisfy *Aronson*'s first prong involving director disinterest, *see Aronson*, 473 A.2d at 812, plaintiffs must plead particularized facts demonstrating either a financial interest or entrenchment on the part of the GM directors. Plaintiffs plead no facts demonstrating a financial interest on the part of GM's directors. The only averment permitting such an inference is the allegation that all GM's directors are paid for their services as directors. However, such allegations, without more, do not establish any financial interest. *See, e.g., In re E.F. Hutton Banking Practices Litigation*, S.D.N.Y., 634 F.Supp. 265, 271 (1986) (construing Delaware law); *Moran v. Household Internat'l, Inc.*, Del.Ch., 490 A.2d 1059, 1074–75, *aff'd*, Del.Supr., 500 A.2d 1346 (1985).

Having failed to plead financial interest with any particularity, plaintiffs' complaints must raise a reasonable doubt of director disinterest based on entrenchment. Plaintiffs attempt to do so mainly through reliance on *Unocal Corp. v. Mesa Petroleum Co.*, Del.Supr., 493 A.2d 946 (1985); *Unocal*, however, is distinguishable. The enhanced duty of care that the *Unocal* directors were found to be under was triggered by a struggle for corporate control and the inherent presumption of director self-interest associated with such a contest. *See id.* at 954–55. Here there was no outside threat to corporate policy of GM sufficient to raise a *Unocal* issue of whether the directors' response was reasonable to the threat posed. *Id.* at 955.

Plaintiffs also do not plead any facts tending to show that the GM directors' positions were actually threatened by Perot, who owned only 0.8 percent of GM's voting stock, nor do plaintiffs allege that the repurchase was motivated and reasonably related to the directors' retention of their positions on the Board. *See Cheff v. Mathes*, Del.Supr., 199 A.2d 548, 554 (1964). Plaintiffs merely argue that Perot's public criticism of GM management could cause the directors embarrassment sufficient to lead to their removal from office. Such allegations are tenuous at best and are too speculative to raise a reasonable doubt of director disinterest. Speculation on motives for undertaking corporate action are wholly insufficient to establish a case of demand excusal. *Cf. Sinclair Oil Corp.*, 280 A.2d at 722. Therefore, we agree with the Vice Chancellor that plaintiffs' entrenchment theory is based largely on supposition rather than fact.

are accepted as true. *See, e.g., Weinberger v. UOP, Inc.*, Del.Ch., 409 A.2d 1262, 1264 (1979); *Cohen v. Mayor of Wilmington*, Del.Ch., 99 A.2d 393, 395 (1953).

Plaintiffs' remaining allegations bearing on the issue of entrenchment are: the rushed nature of the transaction during a period of GM financial difficulty; the giant premium paid;[7] and the criticism (after the fact) of the repurchase by industry analysts and top GM management. Plaintiffs argue that these allegations are sufficient to raise a reasonable doubt of director disinterest. We cannot agree. Not one of the asserted grounds would support a reasonable belief of entrenchment based on director self-interest. The relevance of these averments goes largely to the issue of due care, next discussed. Such allegations are patently insufficient to raise a reasonable doubt as to the ability of the GM Board to act with disinterest. Thus, we find plaintiffs' entrenchment claim to be essentially conclusory and lacking in factual support sufficient to establish excusal based on director interest.

To otherwise qualify for demand excusal under *Aronson*'s first prong, a derivative complaint must raise a reasonable doubt of director independence. This would require plaintiffs to allege with particularity that the GM directors were dominated or otherwise controlled by an individual or entity interested in the transaction. *Aronson*, 473 A.2d 815–16. Such allegations are not to be found within plaintiffs' complaints. Thus, the plaintiffs cannot satisfy *Aronson*'s first prong for excusal based on lack of director independence.

B. *Director Due Care*

Having concluded that plaintiffs have failed to plead a claim of financial interest or entrenchment sufficient to excuse presuit demand, we examine the complaints as amended to determine whether they raise a reasonable doubt that the directors exercised proper business judgment in the transaction. By proper business judgment we mean both substantive due care (purchase terms), *see Saxe v. Brady*, Del.Ch., 184 A.2d 602, 610 (1962), and procedural due care (an informed decision), *see Smith v. Van Gorkom*, Del.Supr., 488 A.2d 858, 872–73 (1985).

With regard to the nature of the transactions and the terms of repurchase, especially price, plaintiffs allege that the premium paid Perot constituted a *prima facie* waste of GM's assets. Plaintiffs argue that the transaction, on its face, was "so egregious as to be afforded no presumption of business judgment protection." In rejecting this contention, the Vice Chancellor reasoned that, apart from the hush-mail provision, the transaction must be viewed as any other repurchase

---

7. The formula plaintiffs use to establish the existence of a "giant premium" is ambiguous, making the allegation conclusory. The total repurchase price includes not only the price paid for the class E stock, but also the price paid for the contingent notes and the value of the tax compensation. Ambiguity is caused when these items are factored in, especially the contingent note discounts. For example, in their complaints, plaintiffs appear to discount the contingent notes by $16.20, reflecting present value ($62.50–$46.30). The GM directors, however, discount the notes by $6.00. This disparity appears to be due to plaintiffs' use of a base figure of $46.30, which is $16.20 less than that used by the defendants. The plaintiffs fail to explain this disparity with particularity, thus failing to satisfy their burden under *Aronson*.

by a corporation, at a premium over market, of its own stock held by a single dissident shareholder or shareholder group at odds with management, [which] have repeatedly been upheld as valid exercises of business judgment. *See Polk v. Good*, Del.Supr., 507 A.2d 531 (1986); *Cheff v. Mathes*, Del.Supr., 199 A.2d 548 (1964); *Edelman v. Phillips Petroleum Co.*, Del.Ch., Civil Action No. 7899, Walsh, V.C. (February 12, 1985); *Lewis v. Daum*, Del.Ch., Civil Action No. 6733, Brown, C. (May 24, 1984); *Kaplan v. Goldsamt*, Del.Ch., 380 A.2d 556 (1977); *Kors v. Carey*, Del.Ch., 158 A.2d 136 (1960).

Grobow, 526 A.2d at 927. We agree with this analysis.

The law of Delaware is well established that, in the absence of evidence of fraud or unfairness, a corporation's repurchase of its capital stock at a premium over market from a dissident shareholder is entitled to the protection of the business judgment rule. (See *Polk*, 507 A.2d at 536–37, for this Court's most recent statement of this principle.) We have already determined that plaintiffs have not stated a claim of financial interest or entrenchment as the compelling motive for the repurchase, and it is equally clear that the complaints as amended do not allege a claim of fraud. They allege, at most, a claim of waste based on the assertion that GM's Board paid such a premium for the Perot holdings as to shock the conscience of the ordinary person.

Thus, the issue becomes whether the complaints state a claim of waste of assets, i.e., whether "what the corporation has received is so inadequate in value that no person of ordinary, sound business judgment would deem it worth that which the corporation has paid." *Saxe*, 184 A.2d at 610. By way of reinforcing their claim of waste, plaintiffs seize upon the hush-mail feature of the repurchase as being the motivating reason for the "giant premium" approved by the GM Board. Plaintiffs then argue that buying the silence of a dissident within management constitutes an invalid business purpose. Ergo, plaintiffs argue that a claim of waste of corporate assets evidencing lack of director due care has been well pleaded.

The Vice Chancellor was not persuaded by this reasoning to reach such a conclusion and neither are we. Plaintiffs' assertions by way of argument go well beyond their factual allegations, and it is the latter which are controlling. Plaintiffs' complaints as amended fail to plead with particularity any facts supporting a conclusion that the primary or motivating purpose of the Board's payment of a "giant premuim" for the Perot holdings was to buy Perot's silence rather than simply to buy him out and remove him from GM's management team. To the contrary, plaintiffs themselves state in their complaints as amended several legitimate business purposes for the GM Board's decision to sever its relationship with Perot: (1) the Board's determination that it would be in GM's best interest to retain control over its wholly-owned subsidiary, EDS; and (2) the decision to rid itself of the principal cause of the growing internal policy dispute over EDS' management and direction.

The defendant directors also defend the liquidated damage clause in the repurchase agreement as serving a legitimate purpose of protecting GM's contractual rights by, in effect, providing a forfeiture clause should Perot breach that portion of his agreement. Defendants argue that such a damage clause is not unusual and, indeed, would be expected to be found in contractual commitments of this nature. Such a clause strengthens the likelihood of compliance and, in the event of breach, puts an agreed dollar value on the breach, intended to avoid disagreement (or litigation) over the loss and measure of damages attributable to the breach. A failure to anticipate a breach and to stipulate the monetary consequences to GM might well be considered a costly oversight. *See* E. Farnsworth, *Contracts* § 12.18, at 896 (1982).

In addition to regaining control over the management affairs of EDS, GM also secured, through the complex repurchase agreement, significant covenants from Perot, of which the hush-mail provision was but one of many features and multiple considerations of the repurchase. Quite aside from whatever consideration could be attributed to buying Perot's silence, GM's Board received for the $742.8 million paid: all the class E stock and contingent notes of Perot and his fellow EDS directors; Perot's covenant not to compete or hire EDS employees; his promise not to purchase GM stock or engage in proxy contests; Perot's agreement to stay out of and away from GM's and EDS' affairs, plus the liquidated damages provision should Perot breach his no-criticism covenant.

Plaintiffs' effort to quantify the size of the premium paid by GM is flawed, as we have already noted, by their inability to place a dollar value on the various promises made by Perot, particularly his covenant not to compete with EDS or to attempt to hire away EDS employees. (*See supra* notes 2, 4, and 7.) Thus, viewing the transaction in its entirety, we must agree with the Court of Chancery that plaintiffs have failed to plead with particularity facts sufficient to create a reasonable doubt that the substantive terms of the repurchase fall within the protection of the business judgment rule. *See Polk*, 507 A.2d at 536–37.

Finally, we turn to the other aspect of director due care, whether plaintiffs have pleaded facts which would support a reasonable belief that the GM Board acted with gross negligence, i.e., that it was uninformed in critical respects in negotiating the terms of the repurchase. *See Smith v. Van Gorkom*, Del.Supr., 488 A.2d 858, 873 (1985). On this remaining issue, plaintiffs assert that GM's Board failed to exercise due care and to reach an informed business judgment due to the absence of arms-length negotiations between the Board and Perot and the absence of "appropriate board deliberation."

Approval of a transaction by a majority of independent, disinterested directors almost always bolsters a presumption that the business judgment rule attaches to transactions approved by a board of directors that are later attacked on grounds of lack of due care. In such cases, a heavy burden falls on a plaintiff to avoid presuit demand. *Cf.*

Polk, 507 A.2d at 537 (1986); *Unocal*, 493 A.2d at 955 (1985). This principle of law clearly applies in this case.

To support their allegation of lack of procedural due care, plaintiffs point principally to the lack of negotiations between Perot and GM and the speed with which the Perot repurchase was submitted to and approved by GM's Board of Directors. However, we find plaintiffs' complaints as amended (a) to contradict these assertions and (b) otherwise to be lacking in averments essential to raise a reasonable doubt that the GM Board failed to exercise due care.

The complaints implicitly concede that the repurchase agreement was the subject of "give and take" negotiations and was conducted at arms length. Plaintiffs also expressly concede that the Board did not "supinely accede to all of Perot's demands" because all of his demands were not included in the final agreement. *See Grobow*, 526 A.2d at 919 n.5 and 926. Furthermore, plaintiffs recount that the repurchase proposal was first submitted to a Special Review Committee, consisting (presumably) of three outside directors and thereafter to the full Board. The complaints as amended, however, contain no allegations raising directly or by inference a reasonable doubt either that the Committee served a purposeful role in the review of the repurchase proposal or that the full Board reached an informed decision. On the contrary, it is clear from the record before us that the GM directors had been living with the internal dispute for months and had been considering a buy-out of Perot's interests for a number of weeks.

Viewing plaintiffs' assertions of lack of director due care against the well-pleaded facts, we conclude that the complaints as amended lack essential requirements for stating a claim of waste premised on failure of the directors to exercise due care. *See Smith v. Van Gorkom*, 488 A.2d at 873; *Kaplan v. Centex Corp.*, Del.Ch., 284 A.2d 119, 124 (1971). By way of illustration, plaintiffs do not allege that the Committee failed to: (i) give thorough and diligent consideration to all relevant facts; (ii) review carefully the negotiations leading to the proposed agreement; (iii) consult with and consider the views of investment bankers, accountants, and counsel; or (iv) report its findings and analysis to the full Board. With respect to Board deliberation, plaintiffs do not allege that the Board failed to: (i) inform themselves of available critical information before approving the transaction; (ii) consider expert opinion; (iii) provide all Board members with adequate and timely notice of the repurchase before the full Board meeting and of its purpose; or (iv) inquire adequately into the reasons for or terms of repurchase (though plaintiffs allege the Board did not ask Perot himself questions). Finally, it should be emphasized that plaintiffs do not allege that the GM directors, and in particular its outside directors, were dominated or controlled by GM's management or other Board members or by any other party. *Aronson*, 473 A.2d 815, 816. Thus, we find plaintiffs' assertion that the GM Board failed to exercise due care to be insufficient to avoid presuit demand because such assertion is not to be found in well-pleaded supporting allegations of the complaints.

IV. *Conclusion*

Apart from whether the Board of Directors may be subject to criticism for the premium paid Perot and his associates for the repurchase of their entire interest in GM, on the present record the repurchase of dissident Perot's interests can only be viewed legally as representing an exercise of business judgment by the General Motors Board with which a court may not interfere. Only through a considerable stretch of the imagination could one reasonably believe this Board of Directors to be "interested" in a self-dealing sense in Perot's ouster from GM's management. We view a board of directors with a majority of outside directors, such as this Board, as being in the nature of overseers of management. So viewed, the Board's exercise of judgment in resolving an internal rift in management of serious proportions and at the highest executive level should be accorded the protection of the business judgment rule absent well-pleaded averments implicating financial self-interest, entrenchment, or lack of due care. These complaints fall far short of stating a claim for demand excusal.

Notwithstanding the Vice Chancellor's misstatement of the test for determining when demand on a board of directors will be considered excused as futile, we reach the same result. We hold that the complaints as amended fail to allege facts sufficient to create a reasonable doubt that the GM Board-approved repurchase transaction is not within the protection of the business judgment rule; thus, the plaintiffs have failed to establish the futility of demand required under *Aronson* and *Pogostin* for casting reasonable doubt thereon. The Trial Court, therefore, correctly dismissed the suits under Del.Ch.Ct.R. 23.1 for failure of plaintiffs to make presuit demand upon the GM Board.[8]

Affirmed.

NOTE ON KAPLAN v. WYATT

In Kaplan v. Wyatt, 499 A.2d 1184 (Del.1985), the Delaware Supreme Court put still another gloss on *Zapata*. There the trial court had dismissed a derivative action on the basis of a litigation committee report. The trial court reviewed the independence of the committee and the conduct of the investigation, but did not formally proceed to the "second step" of *Zapata,* as set out at the end of that opinion. In *Zapata,* the Delaware court had said that the second step was discretionary. In *Kaplan,* the court held that it meant what it had said:

----

8. Plaintiffs request of this Court leave to amend once again their complaints if we affirm the judgment of the Court of Chancery. Under Court of Chancery Rule 15, a leave to amend is freely granted when justice so requires. However, such a ruling is always a discretionary matter with the trial judge, reviewable on appeal solely for abuse of discretion. *Bokat v. Getty Oil Co.,* Del.Supr., 262 A.2d 246, 251 (1970). Since plaintiffs did not file motions to amend in the Chancery Court, no motions are now before this Court. *See* Supr.Ct.R. 8. Plaintiffs' request for leave to amend is, therefore, denied.

Kaplan contends that even if the Court of chancery found that Coastal's Committee satisfied the first step of *Zapata,* the Court erred in not proceeding to the discretionary second step of the analysis. This step "is intended to thwart instances where corporate actions meet the criterion of step one, but the result does not appear to satisfy its spirit, or where the corporate actions would simply prematurely terminate a stockholder grievance deserving of further consideration in the corporation's interest." 430 A.2d at 789. Kaplan contends that his suit is one that this step is meant to preserve.

Proceeding to the second step of the *Zapata* analysis is wholly within the discretion of the court, and the Court of Chancery did not abuse its discretion when it declined to proceed to this step. Dismissing Kaplan's suit does not disturb the spirit of *Zapata.* The Committee's report supports the finding that further litigation would not be in the best interest of Coastal. The corporation's resources would be misspent in litigation based on the allegations in Kaplan's complaint. Therefore, the Court of Chancery properly applied the *Zapata* guidelines, and its decision to dismiss the suit was correct.

It is difficult to fit *Kaplan* together with *Zapata.* Although the court in *Zapata* said that the second step was discretionary, it also said that the second step "provides . . . the *essential* key in striking the balance between legitimate corporate claims as expressed in a derivative stockholder suit and a corporation's best interests as expressed by an independent investigating committee." (Emphasis added.)

It is also difficult to assess the significance of *Kaplan.* Even under the first step, as formulated in *Zapata,* the court must inquire into the bases supporting the committee's conclusions. If, as a result of that inquiry, "the Court determines either that the committee . . . has not shown reasonable bases for its conclusions, or . . . the Court is not satisfied for other reasons relating to the process, including but not limited to the good faith of the committee, the Court shall deny the corporation's motion." Thus the distinction between the first and second steps is not entirely clear. While the trial court in *Kaplan* did not proceed to the second step as a formal matter, it nevertheless considered with care the report of the litigation committee and the justifications advanced in that report, as did the Supreme Court. Furthermore, the committee had caused the defendant to return $195,000 to the corporation, based on overpayments and billing errors the committee unearthed, and the plaintiff apparently could come up with no information in support of the charges in its complaint.

———

AMERICAN LAW INSTITUTE, PRINCIPLES OF CORPORATE GOVERNANCE §§ 7.08, 7.10

Tentative Draft No. 8, 1988.

§ 7.08. Termination of Actions Against Directors, Senior Executives, Controlling Persons, or Associates Based on Action Taken by the Board or a Committee

The court should dismiss a derivative action against a defendant who is a director . . ., a senior executive . . ., a person having control . . . over the corporation, or an associate . . . of any such person, if the court determines in response to a motion made on behalf of the corporation by its board of directors, or a properly delegated committee thereof, that the conditions set forth below in subparagraphs (a), (b) and (d) have been satisfied:

(a) The procedures specified in § 7.10 for the conduct of an internal evaluation of the action were substantially complied with (either in response to a demand or following commencement of the action), or any material departures therefrom were justified under the circumstances;

(b) Based on adequately supported findings that the court deems to warrant reliance, the board of directors or committee reasonably concluded (either in response to a demand or following commencement of the action) that one of the following standards, or a combination of the considerations specified in any of them, justified rejection of demand or dismissal of the action as contrary to the corporation's best interests:

(1) The likelihood of a judgment in favor of the plaintiff is remote; or

(2) The expected recovery (or other potential relief) from the defendant does not clearly exceed the corporation's probable out-of-pocket costs if the action were to continue against that defendant; or

(3) Before the commencement of the action, the corporation had itself undertaken appropriate corrective or disciplinary action with respect to the subject matter of the action; or

(4) The balance of corporate interests warrants dismissal of the action, regardless of its merits;

(c) In evaluating whether the board's or committee's findings warrant reliance and the reasonableness of the board's or committee's conclusions, the court (i) may consider any relevant information introduced by any party, including information as to material developments occurring subsequent to the time of demand or the board's or committee's report; (ii) should independently review any findings of the board or committee as to the lawfulness of a defendant's conduct, unless immaterial, and any relevant legal matters; and (iii) where the conduct of the defendant is alleged to have violated a duty set forth in Part IV (Duty of Care), but did not involve a knowing and culpable violation of law, should accept any findings and conclusions as to business matters, unless the plaintiff establishes that such findings and conclusions are so clearly unreasonable as to fall outside the bounds of the directors' discretion;

(d) Dismissal of the action would not permit a defendant, or an associate . . . thereof to retain a significant improper benefit where:

(1) the defendant, either alone or collectively with others who are also found to have received a significant improper benefit arising out of the same transaction, possesses control . . . over the corporation; or

(2) such benefit was obtained:

(A) as the result of a knowing and material misrepresentation or omission or other fraudulent act; or

(B) without authorization of such benefit by disinterested directors . . . or authorization or ratification by disinterested shareholders . . ., in breach of § 5.02 ("Transactions with the Corporation") or § 5.04 ("Use of Corporate Information, Non-Public Information Concerning the Corporation, or Corporate Property").

§ 7.10. Board Procedures for Termination of Derivative Actions

A determination by the corporation that a derivative action is adverse to its interests may be relied upon by the court as a basis for dismissing an action . . . if:

(a) The determination was based upon an adequate inquiry, conducted by the board or a committee of two or more directors, none of whose members was interested . . . with respect to the action and who as a group were capable of objective judgment under the circumstances;

(b) The board or committee was assisted by a counsel of its choice, capable of objective judgment under the circumstances, and such other agents as it deemed necessary; and

(c) The board or committee prepared and submitted to the court a written report meeting the standards specified in § 7.08(b).

SECTION 7. DEMAND ON THE SHAREHOLDERS

BACKGROUND NOTE ON DEMAND ON SHAREHOLDERS

1. The rules governing demand on the shareholders vary widely, both from state to state and among federal courts. Under the law of some jurisdictions demand on shareholders is not required at all. For example, the California and New York statutory counterparts to FRCP 23.1—Cal. § 800(b) and N.Y. § 626—omit any reference to demand on the shareholders, and it is clear that this omission was deliberate. See Syracuse Television, Inc. v. Channel 9, Syracuse, Inc., 51 Misc.2d 188, 273 N.Y.S.2d 16 (1966). In the majority of jurisdictions, demand on the shareholders is required unless excused, but, as Mayer v. Adams indicates, there is considerable divergence concerning what constitutes an acceptable excuse.

2. Of those jurisdictions that normally require demand:

(a) All agree that demand is excused when the alleged wrongdoers hold a majority of the stock. See, e.g., Heilbrunn v. Hanover Equities Corp., 259 F.Supp. 936 (S.D.N.Y.1966). Most would probably come to the same result where the wrongdoers hold a controlling but less-than-majority interest. See Gottesman v. General Motors Corp., 268 F.2d 194 (2d Cir.1959). But see Levitan v. Stout, 97 F.Supp. 105 (W.D.Ky.1951).

(b) All would probably agree that demand is also excused when it is futile for other reasons (although there might be considerable divergence as to whether a given state of facts constitutes futility). See, e.g., Pioche Mines Consolidated, Inc. v. Dolman, 333 F.2d 257, 264–65 (9th Cir.1964), cert. denied 380 U.S. 956, 85 S.Ct. 1081, 13 L.Ed.2d 972 (1965) (demand excused where only one shareholders' meeting had been held for many years, and management had ignored earlier demands that such meetings be held).

(c) The cases are split on whether demand is excused because the corporation has a large number of shareholders, compare Weiss v. Sunasco Inc., 316 F.Supp. 1197 (E.D.Pa.1970) (demand excused), with Quirke v. St. Louis–San Francisco Ry., 277 F.2d 705 (8th Cir. 1960), cert. denied 363 U.S. 845, 80 S.Ct. 1615, 4 L.Ed.2d 1728 (contra); or because management has refused to supply plaintiff with a shareholders' list, compare Escoett v. Aldecress Country Club, 16 N.J. 438, 109 A.2d 277 (1954) (demand excused), with Bell v. Arnold, 175 Colo. 277, 487 P.2d 545 (1971) (plaintiffs alleged that the corporation had 26,000 shareholders, but this allegation was apparently made as part of the argument that access to the shareholder list had been unreasonably restricted. The court stated, "[s]ince the number of shareholders . . . was not pled as an excuse, nor was it accompanied by any allegation regarding unreasonable costs of making the demand, we do not, on this writ of error, determine whether 26,000 shareholders did, or did not, formulate a valid basis for an excuse in making demand on them'').

(d) The cases are also split on whether demand is excused where the alleged wrong could not be ratified. The majority rule, reflected in Mayer v. Adams, 37 Del.Ch. 298, 141 A.2d 458 (1958), is that nonratifiability excuses demand. However, there is a very strong minority view. For example, in Bell v. Arnold, supra, the court stated:

> One reason set forth in the complaint for not making a demand on the shareholders is that they could not ratify the alleged wrongs because of the illegal nature of the wrongs. We hold this is not an acceptable reason or a valid excuse for not making a demand on the shareholders here. The purpose of making demand on the shareholders is to inform them of the alleged nonratifiable wrongs; to seek their participation in available courses of action, such as, the removal of the involved directors and the election of new directors who will seek the redress required in the circumstances; or to secure shareholder approval of an action for damages to the corporation caused by the alleged wrongdoing directors.

See also Claman v. Robertson, 164 Ohio St. 61, 128 N.E.2d 429 (1955).

As a practical matter, precisely how does a shareholder in a publicly held corporation go about making a demand on the shareholders where such a demand is required? By a shareholder proposal under the Proxy Rules? If so, must the shareholder wait until the next annual meeting? What if the corporation is publicly held, but not registered under the 1934 Act?

3. Cases like Bell v. Arnold and Claman v. Robertson point up the difference between the question whether a plaintiff must make a demand on shareholders and the question whether shareholder ratification has a substantive effect. A further distinction is drawn by some courts (most notably Massachusetts) which hold that the shareholders have power to preclude suit even where they do not have power to ratify. The leading case is S. Solomont & Sons Trust v. New England Theatres Operating Corp., 326 Mass. 99, 111–12, 93 N.E.2d 241, 247–48 (1950):

> Much of the plaintiffs' argument is devoted to limitations upon the power of the stockholders to ratify wrongs to a corporation. . . . We shall not rest our decision upon any power to ratify. The question whether it is good judgment to sue is quite apart from the question of ratification. This is a distinction of substance and not of form. . . .
>
> . . . It is not always best to insist upon all one's rights; and a corporation, acting by its directors or by vote of its members, may properly refuse to bring a suit which one of its stockholders believes should be prosecuted. In such a case the will of the majority must control. It is only when the action of a corporation

in refusing to proceed at the request of a stockholder is fraudulent as against him, or in disregard of his rights, that he can maintain a suit in his own name in the corporate right. . . .[1]

Construing Massachusetts law, Judge Wyzanski concluded in Pomerantz v. Clark, 101 F.Supp. 341, 344 (D.Mass.1951), that "The fundamental basis of the [Massachusetts] rule is the . . . view that neither an individual member nor a court is usually best fitted to determine whether it is to the interest of a corporation publicly to enforce corporate claims even if those claims are founded on plainly unlawful conduct participated in by corporate officers or directors." Although the company there involved was John Hancock Mutual Life Insurance Company, a mutual with millions of policy holders, hardly any of whom either attended meetings or even signed proxies, the court did not feel warranted in creating an exception to the "stiff" Massachusetts rule.

SECTION 8.   PLAINTIFF'S COUNSEL FEES

BOSCH v. MEEKER COOPERATIVE LIGHT & POWER ASS'N

Supreme Court of Minnesota, 1960.
257 Minn. 362, 101 N.W.2d 423.

MURPHY, Justice.   This is an appeal from an order of the district court denying the plaintiff's application for allowance of attorneys' fees.   The issue grows out of Bosch v. Meeker Co-op. Light & Power Ass'n, 253 Minn. 77, 91 N.W.2d 148, which was a derivative action prosecuted by a stockholder against certain directors and counsel of the defendant corporation.   The action resulted in a determination that a purported election of directors and a proposed amendment to the corporate bylaws was illegal.   The prevailing plaintiff-stockholder now seeks reimbursement from the corporation for his litigation expenses including attorneys' fees.   The lower court was of the view that since the plaintiff's action did not result in pecuniary benefits to the corporation or its stockholders no recovery may be allowed.

The trial court relied upon authorities to the effect that a corporation is not liable for a stockholder's expenses in prosecuting a suit in regard to corporate affairs which does not result in pecuniary benefit to the corporation.   The authority most often quoted in support of this proposition is Burley Tobacco Co. v. Vest, 165 Ky. 762, 178 S.W. 1102.

1.   Compare Note, Demand on Directors and Shareholders as a Prerequisite to a Derivative Suit, 73 Harv.L.Rev. 746, at 747 (1960): "[Where] there is skepticism concerning the utility of the remedy and fear of its abuse, the demands [upon directors and shareholders] are insisted upon in a broader class of cases.   The difficulty with this latter approach is that it subordinates the basic purpose of the derivative suit to the policy of curbing its abuses."

1. We have approved the common-law rule that, where an action brought by a stockholder on behalf of himself and other stockholders, or of the corporation involving the internal affairs of the corporation, results in a pecuniary benefit to the corporation, attorneys' fees and other expenses incurred by the stockholder in the prosecution of the action are chargeable to the corporation. Eriksson v. Boyum, 150 Minn. 192, 184 N.W. 961; In re Dissolution of E.C. Warner Co., 232 Minn. 207, 45 N.W.2d 388.

2-3. Both parties rely on the latter authority. That case, however, involved the question whether the reasonable costs and expenses incurred by a corporate director in defending an action brought against him charging him with dereliction of duty could be paid out of corporate funds. We there came to the conclusion that a judicially vindicated corporate officer is entitled to such reimbursement. This is on the theory that to hold otherwise would be to discourage responsible men from accepting corporate offices, and (232 Minn. 214, 45 N.W.2d 393) "this right of reimbursement has its foundation in the maintenance of a sound public policy favorable to the development of sound corporate management as a prerequisite for responsible corporate action." We took the view that the vindication of the integrity of corporate management "is in a certain general sense" beneficial to the corporation from the standpoint of preserving the confidence of its creditors and of its prospective investors. We think there is merit to the plaintiff's argument that the same public-policy reasons favor his position. He argues that certain ultra vires acts of the directors of the defendant were prevented and, although none of the property rights of the corporation were protected, the action served "as a deterrent to irresponsible leadership" which resulted in a sufficiently substantial benefit to the corporation to justify an award of attorneys' fees. The plaintiff's argument presents a novel question under Minnesota law and one on which there is apparently little clear-cut authority throughout the nation.

It should be conceded that where a corporation stands to suffer loss if some action is not taken to protect its interests and those in authority fail or refuse to act a stockholder may proceed on behalf of the corporation without incurring personal expense. Since the corporation is the beneficiary of the recovery of funds or of the corrective benefit of the action, it should stand the expense of it. It should further be conceded that there may be stockholder's actions which do not result in the creation of cash funds or in the protection or conservation of corporate assets, but which nevertheless result in a correction or straightening out of corporate affairs, so as to provide a substantial benefit which will warrant recovery of costs and attorneys' fees. Annotations, 152 A.L.R. 921 and 39 A.L.R.2d 587.

In Schechtman v. Wolfson, 2 Cir., 244 F.2d 537, 540, Chief Judge Clark stated:

". . . The modern equity practice is to allow counsel fees to successful prosecutors of derivative suits although no judgment has been obtained if they show substantial benefit to the corporation through their efforts, . . . [citations]. Nor is it necessary that a cash fund be produced. . . . [citations.] But there should be some check on derivative actions lest they be purely strike suits of great nuisance and no affirmative good, and hence it is ruled generally that *the benefit to the corporation and the general body of shareholders must be substantial.*" (Italics supplied.)

It should be recognized that to grant an award of fees and expenditures against a corporation in every instance where the officers of the corporation act outside of their corporate powers would be to invite and encourage certain actions intended not to redress real wrongs but to realize upon their nuisance value. Nevertheless, it would be unrealistic to deny that derivative suits instituted in good faith to correct or prevent misconduct of corporate officers and directors may be of substantial benefit. Commitment by officers of a corporation to ultra vires acts, contracts, or obligations may entail hazards to the corporation, its stockholders, and creditors. Actions to prevent such acts may maintain the health of the corporation and raise the standards of "fiduciary relationships and of other economic behavior." Hornstein, Legal Therapeutics: The "Salvage" Factor in Counsel Fee Awards, 69 Harv.L.Rev. 658, 663. In the face of unwise, arbitrary, or unreasonable ultra vires acts or conduct of corporate officers which would be harmful to the interests of the corporation, a stockholder should be permitted to prosecute a suit to redress a wrong or prevent a threatened wrong to his corporation even though such action might not result in "pecuniary benefit." To assure the stockholder that he will not be required personally to pay the entire costs of suit in the event he prevails is not too much of an inducement for him to take the initiative to challenge questionable act. Hornstein, The Counsel Fee in Stockholder's Derivative Suits, 39 Col.L.Rev. 784, 791. Such actions may have a wholesome effect on the corporate management in keeping it within the limits of its legal responsibility and at the same time act as a deterrent to arbitrary, unreasonable, and harmful managerial conduct. Where an action by a stockholder results in a substantial benefit to a corporation he should recover his costs and expenses. As to what is a "substantial benefit" is for the trial court to determine in the light of the facts and circumstances of the particular case. Without attempting in any way to define the term or circumscribe its application, we would say that a substantial benefit must be something more than technical in its consequence and be one that accomplishes a result which corrects or prevents an abuse which would be prejudicial to the rights and interests of the corporation or affect the enjoyment or protection of an essential right to the stockholder's interest.

4. We have examined the findings of fact, conclusions of law, and memorandum filed by the trial court in the original action. While the findings characterize certain acts of the managing officers of the corporation as being "unreasonable and arbitrary," they do not cover the issue as to whether or not the judgment results in a substantial benefit to the corporation or its stockholders. We are

accordingly remanding the case to the trial court for further findings on that issue.

If it is found that the corporation and its stockholders did in fact receive a substantial benefit as a result of such action, the trial court is to be guided by In re Dissolution of E.C. Warner Co., 232 Minn. 207, 45 N.W.2d 388, where it was held that the reasonable amount to be allowed for expenses and attorneys' fees rests in the sound discretion of the trial court.

5.   The defendant has also contended that, irrespective of the "substantial benefit to the corporation" issue, the plaintiff must bear his own attorneys' fees for the reason that the action involved the enforcement of a personal rather than a corporate right. We are of the view that recovery does not depend on whether this is a derivative or representative action. Once it is established that the shareholder's action has in fact substantially benefited the corporation, it necessarily follows that he is entitled to recovery. Holthusen v. Edward G. Budd Mfg. Co., D.C.E.D.Pa., 55 F.Supp. 945.

Reversed and remanded.

QUESTION

Is the result in *Bosch* inconsistent with the usual American rule that the losing party in a lawsuit does not have to pay the winner's expenses?

BACKGROUND NOTE ON THE AWARD OF COUNSEL FEES TO SUCCESSFUL DERIVATIVE-ACTION PLAINTIFFS

1.   As indicated in the Introduction to this chapter, the derivative action constitutes a major legal bulwark against managerial self-dealing. As a practical matter this means that the rules governing plaintiffs' legal fees are critical to the operation of the corporate system: Since very few shareholders would pay an attorney's fee out of their own pocket to finance a suit that is brought on the corporation's behalf and normally holds only a slight and indirect benefit for the plaintiff, very few derivative actions would be brought if the law did not allow the plaintiff's attorney to be compensated by a contingent fee payable out of the corporate recovery.

2.   As a conceptual matter, the award of counsel fees to successful plaintiffs in derivative actions has been justified by several overlapping theories, none of which is unique to derivative actions. The most important of these is the "common fund" theory, under which a plaintiff who has successfully established a fund under the control of the court, from which many besides himself will benefit, may recover his counsel fees out of that fund. As stated in the seminal case of Trustees v. Greenough, 105 U.S. (15 Otto) 527, 532, 26 L.Ed. 1157

(1882), to deny an allowance for fees in such circumstances "would not only be unjust to [plaintiff], but . . . would give to the other parties entitled to participate in the benefits of the fund an unfair advantage." This theory was later elaborated, under the heading of the "substantial benefit" (or common-benefit) theory, to cover cases where the plaintiff had not brought a fund into the court's control but had established a right to a fund from which others would benefit. See Sprague v. Ticonic Nat. Bank, 307 U.S. 161, 59 S.Ct. 777, 83 L.Ed. 1184 (1939). Eventually the substantial benefit theory was extended to cover cases involving the establishment of nonpecuniary benefits.

Another basic theory is the "private attorney-general" doctrine—that plaintiff's counsel fees should be awarded in appropriate cases to encourage the initiation of private actions that vindicate important legal policies.[1] In the corporate area this doctrine is important chiefly as a reinforcement to the common-fund or common-benefit theory, particularly where the benefit is not pecuniary. For example, in Mills v. Electric Auto–Lite Co., 396 U.S. 375, 90 S.Ct. 616, 24 L.Ed.2d 593 (1970), plaintiffs, who were former Auto–Lite shareholders, alleged that defendants had violated the Proxy Rules in connection with a merger of Auto–Lite into Mergenthaler. The Court held that plaintiffs were entitled to summary judgment on the merits. It then went on to award interim counsel fees, although it recognized that if on remand the merger were found to be fair, there might be no feasible way to remedy the violation, and therefore no economically measurable benefit to either Auto–Lite or its shareholders. The opinion began by attempting to bring the case within the common benefit rule: "In many suits under § 14(a) . . . it may be impossible to assign monetary value to the benefit. Nevertheless, the stress placed by Congress on the importance of fair and informed corporate suffrage leads to the conclusion that, in vindicating the statutory policy, petitioners have rendered a substantial service to the corporation and its shareholders." However, the Court then seemed to shift rationales by stressing that the action conferred a benefit on a subsector of the public, that is, shareholders as a class.

In Alyeska Pipeline Service Co. v. Wilderness Society, 421 U.S. 240, 95 S.Ct. 1612, 44 L.Ed.2d 141 (1975), the Supreme Court held that in the absence of statutory authorization, attorney's fees may not be awarded on the private-attorney-general theory in suits brought under federal statutes. While the opinion left the common-fund theory (and its derivative, the common-benefit theory) undisturbed, and cited *Sprague* and *Mills* with approval, it is open to question whether the Court would again go as far as it did in *Mills* in determining what constitutes a benefit for these purposes.

3. How does a court go about determining the amount of plaintiff's counsel fees? A widely accepted list of the criteria to be

---

1. See Newman v. Piggy Park Enterprises, Inc., 390 U.S. 400, 402, 88 S.Ct. 964, 966, 19 L.Ed.2d 1263 (1968).

considered is set out in Angoff v. Goldfine, 270 F.2d 185, 189 (1st Cir.1959):

> [T]he amount recovered for the corporation; the time fairly required to be spent on the case; the skill required and employed on the case with reference to the intricacy, novelty and complexity of issues; the difficulty encountered in unearthing the facts and the skill and resourcefulness of opposing counsel; the prevailing rate of compensation for those with the skill, experience and standing of the attorneys, accountants or others involved; the contingent nature of the fees, with the accompanying risk of wasting hours of work, overhead and expenses (for it is clearly established that compensation is awarded only in the event of success); and the benefits accruing to the public from such suits as this.

Traditionally, the most important of these elements was the first—the amount recovered by the corporation—and as a practical matter the courts tended to calculate counsel fees in derivative actions as a percentage of that amount.[2]　Although the percentage varied from case to case, awards calculated on this basis tended to run around 20–35% of the recovery when the recovery was less than $1 million, and 15–25% when it was more.　Since recoveries in derivative actions are often very large, the dollar amounts produced by these percentages could be extremely substantial.　Fees of several hundred thousand dollars were common, and fees in excess of $2 million were not unknown.　In the *Equity Funding* litigation, which produced a settlement pool of $60 million, attorneys' fees were awarded in the amount of approximately $6.5 million.　In re Equity Funding Corp. of America, 438 F.Supp. 1303 (C.D.Cal.1977).　(*Equity Funding* was a class rather than a derivative action, but the principles governing attorneys' fees in the two types of action are closely comparable.)

4.　The 1973 revision of the Federal Judicial Manual for Complex Litigation stated that "the reasonableness of the fee arrived at [in class actions] should not rest primarily on the selection of a percentage of the total recovery," and suggested instead emphasizing "the time and labor required and the effect of the allowance on the public interest and the reputation of the courts." Id. at § 1.47.　This approach was adopted by the Third Circuit in the leading case of Lindy Bros. Builders, Inc. v. American Radiator & Standard Sanitary Corp., 487 F.2d 161 (3d Cir.1973), a class action under the antitrust laws.　Under *Lindy,* the value of the lawyer's time is made the dominant factor:

> . . . To this end the first inquiry of the court should be into the hours spent by the attorneys. . . .

2.　"[These cases] find their true analogue in salvage causes on a pure salvage basis of no cure no pay. . . .　[B]enefits conferred in the light of the efforts required are the real basis of the salvage awards, as they should be in causes like these."　Murphy v. North American Light & Power Co., 33 F.Supp. 567, 570–571 (S.D. N.Y.1940).

> After determining . . . the services performed by the attorneys, the district court must attempt to value those services. . . .
>
> The value of an attorney's time generally is reflected in his normal billing rate. A logical beginning in valuing an attorney's services is to fix a reasonable hourly rate for his time—taking account of the attorney's legal reputation and status (partner, associate). . . .
>
> While the amount thus found to constitute reasonable compensation should be the lodestar of the court's fee determination, there are at least two other factors that must be taken into account in computing the value of attorneys' services. The first of these is the contingent nature of success. . . .
>
> The second additional factor the district court must consider is the extent, if any, to which the quality of an attorney's work mandates increasing or decreasing the amount to which the court has found the attorney reasonably entitled.[3]

Under this approach, the benefit produced is important chiefly insofar as it bears on the quality of the lawyer's work, as where "a particularly resourceful attorney . . . secures a substantial benefit for his clients with a minimum of time invested. . . ."[4]

In 1974 the Second Circuit fell into line with *Lindy* in Detroit v. Grinnell Corp., 495 F.2d 448 (2d Cir.1974).[5]

There is considerable variation in the percentages applied to basic hourly rates, under *Lindy* and *Grinnell,* to adjust for contingency and quality factors. Increases of 50 or 100% are common, but much higher and much lower increases can also be found. An empirical study suggests that fees awarded under the *Lindy/Grinnell* approach have tended to be somewhat lower than fees calculated chiefly on the basis of benefit produced. Mowrey, Attorney Fees in Class Action and Derivative Suits, 3 J.Corp.Law 267 (1978).

Since a derivative action is in effect a special type of class action, the emphasis placed on lawyer's time by cases like *Lindy* and *Grinnell* has come to figure in derivative actions.[6] The technique is particularly well suited for cases involving nonpecuniary benefits, since it allows the court to finesse the problems involved in measuring such benefits.

In Sugarland Industries, Inc. v. Thomas, 420 A.2d 142 (Del. 1980), the Delaware Supreme Court declined to limit attorneys' fee

---

3. 487 F.2d at 167–69.

4. Lindy Bros. Builders, Inc. v. American Radiator & Standard Sanitary Corp., 540 F.2d 102, 118 (3d Cir.1976) (Lindy II). Under another new line of cases, stemming from Johnson v. Georgia Highway Express, Inc., 488 F.2d 714 (5th Cir.1974)—which in turn reflects the guidelines set out in the ABA's Code of Professional Responsibility—the lawyer's time is also deemed paramount, but the factor of benefit produced is given independent significance.

5. In adopting this standard, the court stated, "For the sake of their own integrity, the integrity of the legal profession, and the integrity of Rule 23, it is important that the courts should avoid awarding 'windfall fees' and that they should likewise avoid every appearance of having done so."

6. See, e.g., Wolf v. Frank, 555 F.2d 1213 (5th Cir.1977); Republic National Life Ins. Co. v. Beasley, 73 F.R.D. 658 (S.D.N.Y. 1977).

awards to hourly compensation under the lodestar approach. In approving an award based largely on a percentage-of-benefit approach, the court said:

> As to the amount of the fee, Sugarland observes that there is no real dispute between the parties as to the "elements of the Delaware standard" governing fees. It argues that the "results achieved" by counsel plus the following factors stated by the Chancellor are pertinent:
>
>> ". . . the amount of time and effort applied to a case by counsel for plaintiff, the relative complexities of the litigation, the skills applied to their resolution by counsel, as well as any contingency factor and the standing and ability of petitioning counsel are, of course, considered in the award of fees in an appropriate case. . . .
>
> Under *Lindy I,* the Court's analysis must begin with a calculation of the number of hours to be credited to the attorney seeking compensation. The total hours multiplied by the approved hourly rate is the "lodestar" in the Third Circuit's formulation. It has, indeed, been said that the time approach is virtually the sole consideration in making a fee ruling under *Lindy I.* Be that as it may, we conclude that our Chancery Judges should not be obliged to make the kind of elaborate analyses called for by the several opinions in *Lindy I* and *Lindy II.* To put it another way, while *Lindy's* careful craftsmanship has much to commend it, we are not persuaded that our case law governing fee applications is an inadequate criterion for a fair judgment in this case, nor that new guidelines are needed for the Court of Chancery.

5. While *success* is a prerequisite to an award of counsel fees, a *judgment* is not. Counsel fees may be awarded even if a case is settled, or a unilateral act by the defendant renders moot the plaintiff's demand or complaint. In the latter case, the plaintiff must show that his course of action was a significant cause of the defendant's act. Normally, however, the plaintiff is allowed to prove causation indirectly by showing that his claim or demand was meritorious. It has been said that "[a] claim is meritorious within the meaning of the rule if it can withstand a motion to dismiss on the pleadings [and] if, at the same time, the plaintiff possesses knowledge of provable facts which hold out some reasonable likelihood of ultimate success. It is not necessary that factually there be absolute assurance of ultimate success, but only that there be some reasonable hope." Chrysler Corp. v. Dann, 43 Del.Ch. 252, 256–57, 223 A.2d 384, 387 (1966). A few cases suggest that meritoriousness is the only relevant issue in such cases. The rule that seems to be emerging, however, is that the plaintiff has the burden of showing meritoriousness, and once that showing is made the burden shifts to defendants to show that their actions did not result from plaintiff's course of action.[7]

---

7. See Wechsler v. Southeastern Properties, Inc., 506 F.2d 631 (2d Cir.1974); McDonnell Douglas Corp. v. Palley, 310 A.2d 635 (Del.1973); Baron v. Allied Art-

SECTION 9. SECURITY FOR EXPENSES

N.Y. BUS. CORP. LAW § 627

[See Statutory Supplement]

CAL. CORP. CODE § 800(c)–(f)

[See Statutory Supplement]

SECURITIES ACT § 11(e)

[See Statutory Supplement]

BACKGROUND NOTE ON SECURITY–FOR–EXPENSES STATUTES

1. Security-for-expenses statutes must be considered against the background of the general American rule that the losing party in a lawsuit does not have to pay the winner's expenses, except for "taxable costs," such as clerk's, witness, docket, and transcript fees. Security-for-expenses statutes are normally not interpreted to impose *individual* liability on the plaintiff for expenses—that is, liability beyond the amount of his bond.

2. A shareholder who wants to bring a derivative action in a state that has a security-for-expenses statute is under heavy pressure to find some way to bring suit without posting security. Since the statutes are normally interpreted to be inapplicable to direct (as opposed to derivative) actions, one alternative is to frame the suit as a direct action. A second alternative is to bring the action under some provision of federal law, such as the Proxy Rules or Rule 10b–5.[1]

Even where these alternatives are infeasible, two judicial practices tend to soften the impact of the security-for-expenses statutes. The first practice is to stay the effectiveness of an order to post security so that the plaintiff can find intervenors to help qualify under an exemption based on the percentage or dollar value of complaining shares. See Baker v. MacFadden Publications, 300 N.Y. 325, 90 N.E.2d 876 (1950).

A second judicial practice, which builds on the first, is to order a corporation that moves for the posting of security to produce a

---

ists Pictures Corp., 395 A.2d 375 (Del.Ch. 1978); cf. Kahan v. Rosenstiel, 424 F.2d 161 (3d Cir.1970), cert. denied 398 U.S. 950, 90 S.Ct. 1870, 26 L.Ed.2d 290; Academic Computing Systems, Inc. v. Yarmuth, 71 F.R.D. 198 (S.D.N.Y.1976).

1. The security-for-expenses requirement may also be avoided in certain types of cases by petitioning for dissolution or the appointment of a receiver. See Leibert v. Clapp, 13 N.Y.2d 313, 247 N.Y.S.2d 102 (1963); Chapter V, Section 7, supra.

shareholders' list, so that during the period of the stay the plaintiff can solicit other shareholders to join the action. A study based on interviews with knowledgeable plaintiffs' and defense attorneys in New York concluded that the courts have been extremely permissive in granting these motions. The study continues:

> [Thus if] the motion for security for expenses were to be made, it is likely that the plaintiff would request and obtain a 60-day stay and access to the corporate stocklist. By granting the plaintiff access to the list, defendants have hurt themselves in several ways. The motion involves additional expense in corporate time and effort in furnishing a stockholders' list to the plaintiff. Moreover, circularization by the plaintiff apprises stockholders and the press that a lawsuit involving management is pending. "Most if not all directors don't like to have their deeds or misdeeds advertised. They are sensitive to public opinion, particularly when a proxy fight is involved or imminent." Further, the plaintiffs' counsel now has a list of potential plaintiffs which may be used against the corporation in future litigation. Finally, there is a risk that a motion for security may cause the plaintiff to discontinue the original action and start another in a sister-state having no security-for-expenses statute. . . .

As a result, it is not uncommon for defendants in New York cases to refrain from moving for security. Note, Security for Expenses in Shareholders' Derivative Suits: 23 Years' Experience, 4 Colum.J.L. & Soc.Prob. 50, 62–65 (1968).

SECTION 10. INDEMNIFICATION AND INSURANCE

TOMASH v. MIDWEST TECHNICAL DEVELOPMENT CORP.

Supreme Court of Minnesota, 1968.
281 Minn. 21, 160 N.W.2d 273.

KNUTSON, Chief Justice. This is an appeal from an order denying plaintiffs' post-trial alternative motion for amended findings or for a new trial.

Defendant Midwest Technical Development Corporation (hereinafter referred to as Midwest) was incorporated under Minnesota law in October 1958. Its primary purpose is to provide venture capital by investing in securities of companies operating in the technological field which are thought to have a good chance for growth. In November 1958 it was registered as a closed-end investment company under the Investment Company Act of 1940, 54 Stat. 789, 15 U.S. C.A. § 80a–1, et seq.

Plaintiff Willis K. Drake was a charter stockholder and director of Midwest. Plaintiff Erwin Tomash joined the board within a month of its incorporation and became a shareholder shortly thereafter. Both men remained directors until early 1962.

During their tenure as directors, plaintiffs made personal investments in some of the stocks held in Midwest portfolios. To briefly recite a few, within a year of the time that Midwest purchased stock and a $75,000 debenture from Electro–Logic Corporation, a company then in its formative stage, plaintiffs, together with other Midwest directors, bought shares in the same company. Subsequently Midwest loaned Electro–Logic $35,000 and guaranteed its notes for another $50,000. In May 1960, Midwest authorized investment of $60,000 in the common stock and $100,000 in a convertible note of Electro–Nuclear Systems Corporation. It purchased this stock on June 16 and the note on August 4, 1960. Meanwhile, from June to September plaintiffs, again with other Midwest directors, personally purchased $70,000 worth of Electro–Nuclear stock. Most of the directors sold their Electro–Nuclear stock in 1960 and early 1961, for an aggregate profit of $144,000. As of May 1, 1962, Midwest still held its stock in this corporation. Plaintiffs and other directors of Midwest acquired stock in Telex, Inc., in 1959, prior to the acquisition of stock by Midwest. Subsequently many of the individuals' shares were sold, plaintiff Drake making a profit of $245,026.50, and plaintiff Tomash, $108,096.95. During the time the stock was sold, Midwest retained most of its Telex shares, although it did dispose of a few shares.

These are only a few examples of the actions of plaintiffs in dealing in portfolio stocks held by Midwest. There was no attempt to conceal the directors' dealings in portfolio assets and the attorney for Midwest knew the directors were dealing in these portfolio stocks and advised them that what they were doing was not a violation of the Investment Company Act of 1940.

In 1959 Midwest's board of directors adopted a statement of policy reading:

> "Any Director who influences the market price or value of a security held by, or under consideration for purchase by the Corporation by his own act of selling, buying, offering to sell, offering to buy, or by any equivalent act shall be requested to immediately resign from the Board of Directors. In particular, no Officer or Director should purchase any securities under discussion where there is a limited market until such time as the requirements of the corporation have been fully satisfied. The facts of any such instance shall be reviewed and judged by a quorum of the Board of Directors at the request of any officer of the Corporation."

When Midwest registered securities for a public issue in 1960, the attorney for Midwest disclosed the directors' holdings to the Securities and Exchange Commission (hereinafter called SEC), and that information appeared on the prospectus offering the stock for sale. However, plaintiffs failed to secure the approval of SEC to deal in the portfolio stocks held by Midwest, and in 1962 SEC brought an action against plaintiffs, charging them with "gross abuse of trust and gross misconduct because they had placed themselves in positions of conflicting interests whereby they made decisions 'with other than disinterested motives'" and also with a violation of § 17(d) of the Investment Company Act and Rule 17d–1 issued pursuant to it. Section 17(d) makes it unlawful for any affiliated person of a registered investment company to participate in any arrangement or joint enterprise with that company unless such participation has been approved by SEC.

This action came on for trial in Federal court before the Honorable Gunnar H. Nordbye. He issued a memorandum decision on July 5, 1963, in which he found that the evidence did not sustain a finding that the directors had been guilty of gross misconduct or gross abuse of trust, but, after noting that their practice had placed them in a "continual danger of conflict of interests," he held that they had violated § 17(d) of the Investment Company Act of 1940. In his final decree, issued December 13, 1963, Judge Nordbye enjoined them from engaging in a joint enterprise or arrangement with Midwest unless they received prior approval from SEC.

While it is true that the injunction granted by Judge Nordbye did not apply to the plaintiffs in this case, that was due to the fact that both had, by that time, ceased to be directors of the company.

The present action was brought by plaintiffs to recover indemnity for their expenses incurred in defending the action brought by SEC. At a meeting held on April 13, 1964, the board of directors referred the matter to the law firm of Best, Flanagan, Lewis, Simonet and Bellows for an opinion, and it advised that plaintiffs were not entitled to indemnification as a matter of right. The board of directors thereafter denied plaintiffs indemnification and this suit was brought on the ground that the board had acted arbitrarily and capriciously and that plaintiffs were entitled to indemnification as a matter of right.

Plaintiffs rely mainly on the case of In re Dissolution of E.C. Warner Co., 232 Minn. 207, 45 N.W.2d 388. There a stockholder objected to an order entered in voluntary dissolution proceedings directing the receiver of the corporation to pay attorneys' fees incurred by a director in defending a derivative suit brought by a minority stockholder. We held that where a derivative suit is brought by a minority stockholder against the officers or directors of a corporation they are entitled to indemnification of their defense expenses if they are vindicated in that action. The facts in the Warner case and those now before us are clearly distinguishable. In the first place, the action in which the expenses were incurred was a derivative suit by a minority stockholder against the corporation as nominal defendant and one A.E. Wilson, who was president and treasurer of the corporation as well as a director. Warner v. E.C. Warner Co., 226 Minn. 565, 33 N.W.2d 721. The derivative action had been brought for the benefit of the corporation and, even though the corporation was named as a party-defendant, we held in the later action (232 Minn. 210, 45 N.W.2d 391) that "such action by a minority stockholder is essentially for the benefit of the corporation, and in that beneficiary sense the corporation, although standing as a neutral *pendente lite,* is the true plaintiff," citing Meyers v. Smith, 190 Minn. 157, 251 N.W. 20, and other authorities. Furthermore, Wilson was completely vindicated in the derivative suit. Warner v. E.C. Warner Co. supra. The basis for the holding in the later case that he was entitled to indemnification is summed up in these words (232 Minn. 215, 45 N.W.2d 393):

> ". . . [I]rrespective of any showing of direct or tangible benefit to the corporation, a corporate director, *after he has been vindicated on the merits* in a shareholder's derivative suit charging him with dereliction of duty, is entitled to be repaid his reasonable expenses out of corporate funds. Undoubtedly a vindication of the integrity of the corporate management is in a certain general sense beneficial to the corporation from the standpoint of preserving the confidence of its creditors and of its prospective investors, as well as in the maintenance of the morale of its employes and stockholders, but such a general benefit is not the foundation of the right of recovery. A general benefit of this nature is but an incident of sound corporate management."

In the case now before us it cannot be said that the officers and directors were completely vindicated by the decision of the Federal court referred to above. While Judge Nordbye did hold that the proof was insufficient to find the directors guilty of gross abuse of trust, he granted injunctive relief to restrain them from some of the alleged violations of the Investment Company Act. Among other things he said:

> ". . . [A]djudication of gross abuse of trust must be based upon evidence that a director is so untrustworthy that he should not be permitted to act in that capacity for any other company. The Court would not be justified in painting these directors with a broad brush of malfeasance and stigmatize them with a finding of gross misconduct and gross abuse of trust. In the launching of new electronic companies in 1960 and 1961, some of these directors, if not all, may have failed to recognize their inherent responsibilities as directors of an investment company, and therefore unwittingly placed themselves in situations which should have had approval of the Commission."

In the case of McMenomy v. Ryden, 276 Minn. 55, 148 N.W.2d 804, we held that the decision of the Federal court was not res judicata so as to bar a stockholder's action against the officers of Midwest for violation of their duties as corporate officers under the tests for determining the officers' liability applied in the state court. We held that the parties were not the same, nor were the tests for determining liability the same in the two actions.

Originally Midwest had adopted a bylaw relating to directors or officers which apparently made indemnification mandatory. Upon demand of SEC this bylaw was amended by substitution of the word "may" for "shall" and as so amended reads in part:

"Indemnification of Directors and Officers and Members of Advisory Board

"Each director, officer and member of the Board of Advisors, whether or not then in office (and his heirs, executors, and administrators) may be indemnified by the Corporation against reasonable costs and expenses incurred by him in connection with any action, suit or proceeding to which he may be made a party by reason of his being or having been a director, officer or member of the Advisory Board of the corporation, except in relation to any actions, suits, or proceedings in which he has been adjudged liable because of willful misfeasance, bad faith, gross negligence or reckless disregard of the duties involved in the conduct of his office. In the absence of an adjudication which expressly absolves the director, officer or member of the Advisory Board of liability to the Corporation or its stockholders for willful misfeasance, bad faith, gross negligence and reckless disregard of the duties involved in the conduct of his office, or, in the event of a settlement, each director, officer and member of the Advisory Board (and his heirs, executors, and administrators) may be indemnified by the Corporation against payments made, including reasonable costs and expenses, provided that such indemnity shall be conditional upon the prior determination by a resolution of two-thirds of those members of the Board of Directors of the Corporation who are not involved in the action, suit or proceeding that the director, officer or member of the Advisory Board has no liability by reason of willful misfeasance, bad faith, gross negligence or reckless disregard of the duties involved in the conduct of his office, and provided further that if a majority of the members of the Board of Directors of the Corporation are involved in the action, suit or proceeding, such determination shall have been made by a written opinion of independent counsel."

Significantly, the legislature, after In re Dissolution of E.C. Warner Co., supra, was decided, enacted L.1951, c. 98, § 2, now Minn.St. 301.09(7), which provides that every corporation shall have power:

"To indemnify each director or officer or former director or officer against all expenses, including attorneys' fees, but excluding amounts paid pursuant to a judgment or settlement agreement, reasonably incurred by him in connection with or arising out of any action, suit or proceeding to which he is a party, by reason of being or having been a director or officer of the corporation, except with respect to matters as to which he shall be finally adjudged in such action, suit or proceeding to be liable for negligence or misconduct in the performance of his duties. Such indemnification shall not be exclusive of any other rights to which he may be entitled under any bylaw, agreement, vote of stock-holders or otherwise."

Even assuming that the bylaw of the corporation is consistent with the statute, it is obvious that both speak in terms permissive rather than mandatory. Inasmuch as Warner does not compel indemnification under the circumstances of this case, and the bylaw and statute permit but do not require indemnification, there is no absolute right to it here, and the action of the board of directors under the circumstances of this case in denying indemnification was clearly justified.

It should be noted that the Warner case, as well as the corporate bylaw and the statute, speak in terms of indemnification to one who defends himself as a director or officer of the corporation. That is not true of the SEC case. There, the officers and directors were defending themselves from alleged violations of the Investment Company Act, from which they personally profited. The two are not the same.

The trial court, in addition to finding that the directors were not absolved or vindicated of all the charges brought in the action by SEC, found that the actions of these directors were negligent and amounted to misconduct in the performance of their duties as directors. That finding was unnecessary to the result reached and we do not pass upon it here. It is enough to hold that, inasmuch as the directors were not vindicated of all misconduct by the decision of the Federal court, the board of directors was not required to grant indemnification even if In re Dissolution of E.C. Warner Co. supra, still controls in the area covered by the facts of that case after the passage of § 301.09(7). Thus, the decision of the trial court must be affirmed.

Affirmed.

DEL. GEN. CORP. LAW § 145

[See Statutory Supplement]

REV. MODEL BUS. CORP. ACT §§ 8.50–8.58

[See Statutory Supplement]

N.Y. BUS. CORP. LAW §§ 721–726

[See Statutory Supplement]

QUESTIONS

(1) In what cases is an officer or director entitled to indemnification as of right under the Model Act? Under the New York statute? Under the Delaware statute?

(2) Are there any cases where the corporation can indemnify an adjudged wrongdoer under the New York statute? Under the Delaware statute? Under the Model Act?

(3) Suppose an officer or director settles a derivative action against him. Under what conditions and to what extent can he be indemnified under the New York statute? Under the Delaware statute? Under the Model Act?

BACKGROUND NOTE ON INDEMNIFICATION

1. The right of a director or officer to indemnification under the common law was not completely clear. New York Dock Co. v. McCollom, 173 Misc. 106, 16 N.Y.S.2d 844 (1939), decided prior to the enactment of the New York indemnification statute, held that directors who had successfully defended themselves in a derivative suit were not entitled to reimbursement of their counsel fees, absent a showing that the corporation had benefited. Later decisions in other jurisdictions, however, upheld the common law right of a vindicated director to recover the expenses of his defense without any showing of a specific benefit. In re E.C. Warner Co., 232 Minn. 207, 45 N.W. 2d 388 (1950); Solimine v. Hollander, 129 N.J.Eq. 264, 19 A.2d 344 (Ch.1941). The policy reasons why the corporation should indemnify a director, as set forth in *Solimine,* are (1) to encourage innocent directors to resist unjust charges and provide them an opportunity to hire competent counsel; (2) to induce "responsible business men to accept the post of directors": and (3) "to discourage in large measure stockholders' litigation of the strike variety." Id. at 272, 19 A.2d at 348.

2. Today virtually every state has an indemnification statute, but the statutes vary widely in detail.[1] Some apply only to the indemnification of officers and directors, while others also apply to the indemnification of employees and agents. Some are exclusive—that is, they prohibit any provision for indemnification that is not consistent with the statute—while others are non-exclusive. In corporations governed by a nonexclusive statute, charter and by-law provisions affording indemnification in situations well beyond the boundaries explicitly authorized by statute are not uncommon. However, the permissible scope of such provisions is unclear, and some cases have either ignored such provisions altogether, or given them an extremely restrictive interpretation. See, e.g., SEC v. Continental Growth Fund, Inc., [1964–'66 Transfer Binder] CCH Fed.Sec.L.Rep. ¶ 91,437 (S.D. N.Y.1964); Essential Enterprises Corp. v. Dorsey Corp., 40 Del.Ch. 343, 182 A.2d 647 (Ch.1962).

3. Most modern indemnification statutes provide for indemnification as of right when the director or officer has been successful.

---

1. In Gross v. Texas Plastics, Inc., 344 F.Supp. 564 (D.N.J.1972), the court held that under accepted conflicts principles indemnification is governed by the law of the state of incorporation, not the law of the forum state. For a statutory treatment of this issue, see N.Y.Law § 726(d).

However, what constitutes "success" for these purposes varies widely. Under Rev.Model Bus.Corp. Act § 8.54, the director must be "wholly successful, on the merits or otherwise." Under Del.Gen.Corp.Law § 145(c) and N.Y.Bus.Corp.Law § 722(a), the officer or director must be "successful, on the merits or otherwise." Under Cal.Corp. Code § 317(d), the officer or director must be "successful on the merits." Each of these phrases is subject to considerable interpretation. See, e.g., Wisener v. Air Express Int'l Corp., 583 F.2d 579 (2d Cir.1978) (where a third-party claim against an officer is terminated without any payment, the officer is "successful, on the merits or otherwise" under the Illinois statute); Dornan v. Humphrey, 278 App.Div. 1010, 1011, 106 N.Y.S.2d 142, 144 (1951), modified 279 App.Div. 1040, 112 N.Y.S.2d 585 (1952) (where a complaint is dismissed under the statute of limitations, the defendants are "successful" under the predecessor of N.Y. § 724); American Nat. Bank & Trust Co. v. Schigur, 83 Cal.App.3d 790, 148 Cal.Rptr. 116 (1978). Suppose that a four-count indictment is issued against a director, one count is dismissed by the court, the jury is unable to reach a verdict, the director enters a plea on count 2, and in exchange counts 3 and 4 are dropped. In Merritt–Chapman & Scott v. Wolfson, 321 A.2d 138 (Del.Super.1974), it was held in such a case that the director was "successful" on counts 3 and 4 within the meaning of the Delaware statute. According to the Official Comment to section 8.54 of the Model Act, which adopts the "wholly successful, on the merits or otherwise" standard, "[t]he word 'wholly' is added to avoid the argument accepted in Merritt–Chapman & Scott Corp. v. Wolfson, 321 A.2d 138 (Del.1974), that a defendant may be entitled to partial mandatory indemnification if he succeeded by plea bargaining or otherwise to obtain the dismissal of some but not all counts of an indictment. A defendant is 'wholly successful' only if the entire proceeding is disposed of on a basis which involves a finding of nonliability. However, the language in earlier versions of the Model Act and in many other state statutes that the basis of success may be 'on the merits or otherwise' is retained. While this standard may result in an occasional defendant becoming entitled to indemnification because of procedural defenses not related to merits—e.g., the statute of limitations or disqualification of the plaintiff, it is unreasonable to require a defendant with a valid procedural defense to undergo a possibly prolonged and expensive trial on the merits in order to establish eligibility for mandatory indemnification."

4.   Many of the modern indemnification statutes permit a corporation to indemnify an officer or director for fines and judgments levied against him because he has violated some rule of civil or criminal law other than the rules governing his obligations to the corporation itself. The theory of these provisions is that indemnification may be appropriate where the officer or director incurred the liability in a good faith attempt to further the corporation's interests. These provisions raise an obvious issue of policy, however, since the prospect of indemnification may diminish the fear of liability that normally provides one of the major incentives for obedience to law.

As a result, corporate interests and social interests may cut in two very different directions.

CHUBB GROUP EXECUTIVE LIABILITY AND INDEMNIFICATION POLICY

* * *

INSURING CLAUSES

In consideration of payment of the required premium and subject to the declarations, the limitations, conditions, provisions and other terms of this policy, the Company agrees as follows:

EXECUTIVE LIABILITY COVERAGE—INSURING CLAUSE 1

1.1 The Company shall pay on behalf of each of the **Insured Persons** all **Loss** for which the **Insured Person** is not indemnified by the **Insured Organization** and which the **Insured Person** becomes legally obligated to pay on account of any claim first made against him, individually or otherwise, during the **Policy Period** or, if exercised, during the Extended Reporting Period for a **Wrongful Act** committed, attempted, or allegedly committed or attempted, by the **Insured Person**(s) before or during the **Policy Period**.

EXECUTIVE INDEMNIFICATION COVERAGE— INSURING CLAUSE 2

1.2 The Company shall pay on behalf of the **Insured Organization** all **Loss** for which the **Insured Organization** grants indemnification to each **Insured Person**, as permitted or required by law, which the **Insured Person** has become legally obligated to pay on account of any claim first made against him, individually or otherwise, during the **Policy Period** or, if exercised, during the Extended Reporting Period for a **Wrongful Act** committed, attempted, or allegedly committed or attempted, by such **Insured Person**(s) before or during the **Policy Period**. . . .

EXCLUSIONS

3.1 The Company shall not be liable under this policy to make any payment for **Loss** in connection with any claim(s) made against any **Insured Person**(s):

(a) arising from any circumstance if written notice of such circumstance has been given under any policy, the term of which has expired prior to or upon the inception of this policy, and if such prior policy affords coverage (or would afford such coverage except for the exhaustion of its limits of liability) for such **Loss**, in whole or in part, as a result of such notice;

(b) based upon an actual or alleged violation of the responsibilities, obligations or duties imposed upon fiduciaries by the Employee Retirement Income Security Act of 1974 and amendments thereto or similar provisions of any federal, state or local statutory law or common law;

(c) for bodily injury, sickness, disease or death of any person, or for damage to or destruction of any tangible property including loss of use thereof; or

(d) for seepage, pollution or contamination and based upon or attributable to violation or alleged violation of any federal, state, municipal or other governmental statute, regulation or ordinance prohibiting or providing for the control or regulation of emissions or effluents of any kind into the atmosphere or any body of land, water, waterway or watercourse or arising from any action or proceeding brought for enforcement purposes by any public official, agency, commission, board or pollution control administration pursuant to any such statutes, regulations or ordinances or arising from any claims alleging seepage, pollution or contamination based upon common law nuisance or trespass.

3.2 The Company shall not be liable under Insuring Clause 1 to make any payment for **Loss** in connection with any claim(s) made against any of the **Insured Person(s)**:

(a) for libel or slander;

(b) for the return by any such **Insured Person** of any remuneration paid in fact to him without the previous approval of the stockholders of the **Insured Organization** if it shall be determined by a judgment or other final adjudication that such remuneration is in violation of law or if such remuneration is to be repaid to the **Insured Organization** under a settlement agreement;

(c) for an accounting of profits made from the purchase or sale by such **Insured Person** of securities of the **Insured Organization** within the meaning of Section 16(b) of the Securities Exchange Act of 1934 and amendments thereto or similar provisions of any federal, state or local statutory law or common law;

(d) brought about or contributed to by the dishonesty of such **Insured Person** if a judgment or other final adjudication adverse to such **Insured Person** establishes that acts of active and deliberate dishonesty were committed or attempted by such **Insured Person** with actual dishonest purpose and intent and were material to the cause of action so adjudicated; or

(e) based upon or attributable to such **Insured Person** having gained any personal profit or advantage to which he was not legally entitled regardless of whether or not (1) a judgment or other final adjudication adverse to such **Insured Person** establishes that such **Insured Person** in fact gained such personal profit or other advantage to which he was not entitled, or (2) the **Insured Person** has entered into a settlement agreement to repay such unentitled personal profit or advantage to the **Insured Organization**.

3.3 With respect to the exclusions in section 3, no fact pertaining to or knowledge possessed by any **Insured Person(s)** shall be imputed to any other **Insured Person(s)** for the purpose of determining the availability of coverage for, or with respect to claims made against, any **Insured Person(s)**.

REPORTING AND NOTICE

4.1 The **Insureds** shall, as a condition precedent to exercising their rights under this policy, give to the Company written notice as soon as practicable of any claim made against any of them for an identifiable **Wrongful Act** and shall give the Company such information and cooperation as it may reasonably require, including but not limited to, the nature of the **Wrongful Act**, the alleged injury, the names of claimants, and the manner in which the **Insured** first became aware of the claim.

4.2 If during the **Policy Period** or Extended Reporting Period (if exercised), any **Insured** becomes aware of circumstances which could give rise to a claim and written notice of such circumstance(s) is given to the Company as outlined in paragraph 4.1, then any claims subsequently arising from such circumstances shall be considered to have been reported during the **Policy Period** or the Extended Reporting Period in which the circumstances were reported. . . .

LIMIT OF LIABILITY, DEDUCTIBLE AND COINSURANCE

5.1 For the purposes of this policy, all **Loss** arising out of all interrelated **Wrongful Acts** of any **Insured Person(s)** shall be deemed one **Loss**, and such **Loss** shall be deemed to have originated in the earliest **Policy Year** in which a claim is made against any **Insured Person** alleging any such **Wrongful Acts**.

5.2 The total limit of the Company's liability to pay any **Loss** hereunder, whether covered under Insuring Clause 1 or Insuring Clause 2 or both, shall not exceed the amount(s) set forth in item 3 of the declarations page.

5.3 The Company's liability hereunder shall apply only to that part of each **Loss** which is excess of the deductible amount specified in item 5 of the declarations, and such deductible amount shall be borne by the **Insureds** uninsured and at their own risk.

5.4 The deductible amount applicable to each **Loss** under Insuring Clause 1 shall be the amount set forth in item 5(a) of the declarations for each of the **Insured Persons** against whom claim is made, but not more than the amount set forth in item 5(b) of the declarations for all such **Insured Persons**. The deductible amount applicable to each **Loss** under Insuring Clause 2 shall be the amount set forth in item 5(c) of the declarations.

5.5 If a single **Loss** is covered in part under Insuring Clause 1 and in part under Insuring Clause 2, the maximum deductible amount applicable to such **Loss** shall be the amount set forth in item 5(c) of the declarations.

5.6 With respect to all **Loss** (excess of applicable deductible amounts) originating in any one **Policy Year**, the **Insureds** shall bear uninsured and at their own risk that percent of all such **Loss** specified as the Coinsurance Percent in item 4 of the declarations, and the Company's liability hereunder shall apply only to the remaining percent of all such **Loss**. . . .

DEFINITIONS

9.1 When used in this policy:

Defense Costs means that part of **Loss** consisting of costs, charges and expenses (other than regular or overtime wages, salaries or fees of the directors, officers or employees of the **Insured Organization**) incurred in defending, investigating or monitoring legal actions, claims, or proceedings and appeals therefrom and the cost of appeal, attachment or similar bonds.

Insured(s) means the **Insured Organization** and/or any **Insured Person(s)**.

Insured Capacity(ies) means the position or capacity designated in item 7 of the declarations held by any **Insured Person**.

Insured Organization means, collectively, those organizations designated in item 6 of the declarations.

Insured Person(s) means any of those persons designated in item 7 of the declarations.

Loss means the total amount which any **Insured Person(s)** becomes legally obligated to pay on account of each claim and for all claims in each **Policy Year** made against them for **Wrongful Acts** for which coverage applies, including, but not limited to, damages, judgments, settlements, costs and **Defense Costs**. **Loss** does not include fines or penalties imposed by law or matters uninsurable under the law pursuant to which this policy is construed.

Outside Directorship means the executive position held by an **Insured Person** at the specific request of the **Insured Organization** in any corporation, joint venture, partnership, trust or other enterprise which is not included in the definition of **Insured Organization**.

Parent Organization means the organization designated in item 1 of the declarations.

Policy Period means the period from the inception of this policy until its termination, in accordance with paragraph 8.7.

Policy Year means the period of one year following the inception of this policy or any anniversary, or, if the time between inception or any anniversary and the termination of the policy is less than one year, the lesser period. If the Extended Reporting Period is exercised, then it shall be part of the last **Policy Year** and not an additional period.

Subsidiary(ies) means any organization controlled by any entity included in the **Insured Organization** through ownership of more than 50 percent of the outstanding voting stock.

Wrongful Act means any error, misstatement, misleading statement, act, omission, neglect, or breach of duty committed, attempted, or allegedly committed or attempted, by any **Insured Person,** individually or otherwise, in his **Insured Capacity,** or any matter claimed against him solely by reason of his serving in such **Insured Capacity.** All such causally connected errors, statements, acts, omissions, neglects or breaches of duty or other such matters committed or attempted by, allegedly committed or attempted by, or claimed against one or more of the **Insured Persons** shall be deemed interrelated **Wrongful Acts.**

QUESTIONS

1.   To what extent does the Chubb form insure directors and officers against liabilities that cannot be indemnified under the Model Act? Under the Delaware statute? Under the New York statute? To what extent does it insure directors and officers against liabilities that are indemnifiable under those statutes in the discretion of the board or the shareholders, but not as a matter of right?

2.   If a director settles a claim against him based on self-dealing, does the Chubb form cover his expenses?

3.   To what extent, if any, does the Chubb form cover liability based on violations of Rule 10b–5?

BACKGROUND NOTE ON DIRECTORS' AND OFFICERS' LIABILITY INSURANCE

1.   Within the last thirty years, D & O insurance has become a pervasive institution, particularly among large corporations. The Wyatt Survey reported that such insurance was carried by 82% of all survey participants, 94% of participants with assets of $1 billion or more, and 97% of participants listed on the New York Stock Exchange. The Wyatt Company, Directors and Officers & Fiduciary Liability Survey 80, 87 (1987) at 51–54. At least as regards large publicly held corporations, it appears that a majority of claims against directors and officers occur in situations where a D & O policy is in

force, and most of these claims are covered by the policy. Id. at 17.[1] Given the prevalence of D & O insurance, it has become impossible to fully analyze the operational meaning of the duty of care without analyzing the scope and impact of such insurance. As a practical matter, the question "Am I insured?" is likely to be at least as important to the director as the question "How shall I vote?" See generally Conard, A Behavioral Analysis of Directors' Liability for Negligence, 1972 Duke L.J. 895.

2. At one time it was quite common practice for corporations to require the directors and officers to pay part of the premium for D & O liability insurance—usually 10%. However, very few insured corporations follow this practice today. The result is that the corporation pays out money to protect the director or officer against liabilities that the corporation could not legally indemnify. See Bishop, Sitting Ducks and Decoy Ducks, 77 Yale L.J. 1078, 1090–91 (1968).

SECTION 11. SETTLEMENT OF DERIVATIVE SUITS

CLARKE v. GREENBERG
Court of Appeals of New York, 1947.
296 N.Y. 146, 71 N.E.2d 443.

DYE, Judge. The challenge to the within complaint, for failure to state a cause of action, raises the question of whether a plaintiff in a stockholder's derivative action may be required to account to the corporation for moneys received in private settlement for discontinuance of the action.

The complaint alleges that the defendants commenced a stockholder's derivative action in behalf of the Associated Gas & Electric Company (called AGECO) entitled "Greenberg v. Mange et al." in which it was alleged that the defendants, as officers and directors, had so mismanaged its affairs that the company and its stockholders were damaged and prayed that an accounting be had, and that the court "impress a trust in favor of the Company (AGECO) upon all secret profits and gains obtained by any of the defendant directors," etc. No individual relief was asked except reimbursement for expenses. Later and before trial, a stipulation was made settling and discontinuing the action without notice to other stockholders and without approval of the court, by the terms of which Greenberg executed releases in his individual and representative capacity and transferred and delivered his stock, having a market value of $51.88, to the defendant directors and defendants herein received from them the sum of $9,000.

---

1. About 60% of the claims made against directors and officers are made by third parties—such as employees, customers, government agencies, and prior owners of acquired companies—rather than by shareholders. Id. at 28.

The complaint in this action alleges that the defendants received the money "to the use of, and in trust for AGECO"; that they had failed to account to it or its trustee, the plaintiff herein, and had accordingly unjustly enriched themselves in the sum of $8,948.12 which, in equity, should be paid over to the plaintiff, and prayed judgment accordingly.

The Appellate Division unanimously affirmed the dismissal of the complaint by the Special Term which relied upon Manufacturers Mutual Fire Ins. Co. of Rhode Island v. Hopson, 176 Misc. 220, 25 N.Y.S.2d 502, affirmed 262 App.Div. 731, 29 N.Y.S.2d 139, affirmed 288 N.Y. 668, 43 N.E.2d 71 in which we refused to set aside a stipulation settling a stockholder's derivative suit and revive the action. That case was limited to the right to discontinue and it did not consider whether the moneys received in settlement were impressed with a trust in favor of the corporation for which an accounting should be made.

The very nature of the derivative suit by a stockholder-plaintiff suing in the corporation's behalf suggests the application of the fiduciary principle to the proceeds realized from such litigation whether received by way of judgment, by settlement with approval of the court, which presupposes stockholders' approval, or by private settlement and discontinuance of the action at any stage of the proceeding. Such action, we have held, belongs primarily to the corporation, the real party in interest . . . and a judgment so obtained, as well as the proceeds of a settlement with court approval belongs to it and not the individual stockholder plaintiffs. . . . While the stockholder-plaintiff, with such others as join with him, controls the course of the litigation at all stages of the proceeding before final judgment, he does not bind the nonparticipating stockholders by his action, or deprive them of their own right of action against the unfaithful directors, nor is he subject to their interference. . . . When, however, success crowns his effort, the amount received is in behalf and for the account of the corporation. This is so because the action belongs primarily to it. The manner and method by which such success is accomplished whether by way of judgment, settlement with court approval or by stipulation of the parties, makes no substantial difference in the interest of the corporation upon distribution of the proceeds. Requiring an accounting for moneys received in a private settlement introduces no new element. It simply amounts to a logical application of a fundamental principle inherent in the representative relation. When one assumes to act for another, regardless of the manner or method used in accomplishing a successful termination, he should willingly account for his stewardship. The plaintiff-stockholder, in good conscience, should not be allowed to retain the proceeds of a derivative suit discontinued by stipulation, to his individual use, in opposition to the corporation, any more than the proceeds of a judgment or a settlement with court approval.

The complaint, we believe, states a cause of action.

The judgments should be reversed and the motion to dismiss the complaint denied, with costs in all courts.

LOUGHRAN, C.J., and LEWIS, CONWAY, DESMOND, THACHER, and FULD, JJ., concur.

Judgments reversed, etc.*

BACKGROUND NOTE ON THE PROBLEM OF ILLICIT SETTLEMENTS

1. In Manufacturer's Mutual Fire Ins. Co. v. Hopson, cited in Clarke v. Greenberg, shareholders of Associated Gas & Electric had brought a derivative action against AG & E directors for mismanagement and waste. Thereafter the plaintiffs had agreed to discontinue the action in exchange for a payment made to them in their individual capacities. (The payment took the form of a purchase of the plaintiffs' AG & E stock for seven times its market value.) On petition by other shareholders and AG & E's trustee in bankruptcy, the court refused to set aside the discontinuance:

> If this were a case of first impression, my conclusion might be otherwise. But this court is bound by a line of cases in New York, to the effect that a minority stockholder may discontinue his action at any time before another stockholder has intervened or judgment has been entered. The exclusive control of the action belongs to him and he can settle his individual damages, leaving other shareholders to seek their remedy in a new action.

176 Misc. at 223, 25 N.Y.S.2d at 505. While not all courts took the position reflected in *Manufacturer's Mutual*, that position was the majority rule at common law:

> . . . From the early days of the class suit, it had been widely accepted doctrine that a . . . derivative plaintiff . . . was the *dominus litis;* since he bore all the expenses of the action, he could dismiss or compromise it at pleasure and on any terms he saw fit. . . .

The prevailing state of the law plainly invited abuse. Most stockholders' suits involve corporate or class claims of considerable magnitude. The temptation for the defendants to buy off the plaintiff by a relatively modest private settlement was therefore great. Many stockholders' actions of doubtful merit were brought simply to secure private settlements for the plaintiff and his lawyer. Private settlements also were employed to stifle meritorious suits brought initially in good faith. In derivative suits, the corporation, frequently controlled by the alleged wrong-

---

* Cf. Young v. Higbee Co., 324 U.S. 204, 65 S.Ct. 594, 89 L.Ed. 800 (1945). In Certain-Teed Products Corporation v. Topping, 171 F.2d 241 (2d Cir.1948) a shareholder-plaintiff in a derivative suit consented to the entry of a summary judgment in favor of the individual defendant on payment of $5,000 to the plaintiff's attorney. Plaintiff was held liable to the corporation for the $5,000 less such amount as the district court might allow as a reasonable attorney's fee. (Footnote by eds.)

doers or their allies, could not be expected to resist the sacrifice of claims which it had been unwilling to assert by direct action. Even without a private settlement, complaining stockholders often dropped their suits simply to avoid further expense and trouble. By the time the class suit was dismissed, the statute of limitations or laches often barred other stockholders from bringing actions of their own; advantages already gained in the litigation were lost. The termination of the action without notice to the class also served to conceal whatever wrongs had been done, so that uninformed class members were unable to safeguard their rights. The stockholder's suit was in danger of becoming a tool for defeating the class rights it was intended to protect.

Haudek, The Settlement and Dismissal of Stockholders' Actions—Part I, 22 Sw.L.J. 767, 768–70 (1968).

2.   The problems described by Haudek led to the adoption, in many though not all jurisdictions, of rules like Fed.R.Civ.P. 23.1, which provides that a derivative action "shall not be dismissed or compromised without the approval of the court, and notice of the proposed dismissal or compromise shall be given to shareholders or members in such manner as the court directs." [1] (Fed.R.Civ.P. 23.1 is quoted in full at Section 1(a), supra. For a comparable state rule, see N.Y. § 626(d), also set out in Section 1(a).) These rules, in turn, raise new problems of administration and interpretation, which will be considered in the remainder of this section.

LEWIS v. NEWMAN

United States District Court, Southern Dist. of New York, 1973.
59 F.R.D. 525.

Edward WEINFELD, District Judge.[*]

This is a motion pursuant to Rule 23.1 of the Federal Rules of Civil Procedure for approval of a settlement agreement in a derivative action brought on behalf of Howard Stores Corporation against present and former directors of the corporation and the executors of the estate of a former employee. The Court ordered that a hearing be held on April 9, 1973, upon appropriate notice to each Howard stockholder of record. On the return date only proponents of the settlement appeared; no stockholder appeared in opposition. Plaintiff's counsel seeks an award of $27,500 for legal services rendered and for expenses, reference to which was made in the notice sent to stockholders and which, to the extent it is granted, is payable by Howard.

The complaint charges the defendants with violations of the Securities Exchange Act of 1934, section 10(b), and Rule 10b–5

1. Settlements are often submitted for judicial approval even in jurisdictions that do not have such rules, either because the jurisdiction does not follow the theory of *Manufacturer's Mutual* or because the defendants want to secure the res judicata effect that follows from judicial approval.

* Internal captions omitted. (Footnote by ed.)

promulgated thereunder. In substance, it alleges that defendant directors Samuel O. Newman and J. Moe Newman (the Newmans), prior to May 29, 1969, were obligated under an agreement with Jacob Hausman, the former employee, to purchase from him 31,250 shares of Howard stock; that thereafter the Newmans, whose shareholdings gave them practical voting control of the corporate affairs and domination of the Board of Directors, to evade this obligation caused Howard to acquire the Hausman stock at a cost of $32 per share, or $1,000,000, payable over a five-year period; that the price was substantially higher than the true value of those shares; that there was no business justification for such purchase; that the market price of the stock was about to decline; that in furtherance of their plan to foist their obligation upon Howard, the Newmans, aided and abetted by other director defendants and Hausman, concealed the foregoing as well as other facts from some of Howard's directors in inducing the Board to approve and authorize the purchase of the Hausman shares. The complaint further alleges that Howard suffered a loss of $750,000 because of the subsequent decline in the market price of the shares and a decree is sought ordering the defendants to account to Howard for its losses and for related relief.

All the defendants deny the material allegations of the complaint and the charges of wrongdoing, and assert affirmative defenses, including that the transaction was a matter of business judgment and when entered into was fair and advantageous to the corporation.

Plaintiff propounded interrogatories to all the individual defendants and made requests for document production to them and to Howard, and appropriate responses were made. Plaintiff also deposed defendants Arthur Singer and David Shivitz, references to which is made hereafter. The parties also engaged in several pretrial conferences under the supervision of a magistrate. This Court is satisfied that sufficient discovery has been conducted for both the parties and the Court to evaluate the relative strengths and weaknesses of plaintiff's claims and the defenses thereto.

The proposed compromise provides that the director defendants are to pay Howard $45,000, and the Hausman executors will consent to a $65,000 reduction in the balance due on the purchase of Hausman's shares. If the settlement is approved, all claims asserted or based upon allegations in the complaint will be dismissed with prejudice.

The Court's function on this motion is not to try out or attempt to decide the merits of the action. Rather, the Court's responsibility is to reach "an intelligent and objective opinion of the probabilities of ultimate success should the claim be litigated" and to "form an educated estimate of the complexity, expense and likely duration of such litigation . . . and all other factors relevant to a full and fair assessment of the wisdom of the proposed compromise." The test is often more concisely phrased—is the settlement "fair, reasonable, and adequate."

It must be recognized that stockholder litigation is notably difficult and notoriously uncertain. This case is no exception. It is easy enough to draft a complaint, alleging a cause of action under section 10(b), but it is quite another matter to establish free wheeling charges of fraud or manipulative conduct. Here plaintiff's counsel is forced to concede that as the discovery process went forward the prospects of success upon a trial diminished. Answers to interrogatories failed to reveal any meaningful evidence that the Newmans had advance knowledge of the forthcoming decline in the value of Howard's stock or that the final quarter of 1969 would prove to be disastrous for the corporation. A key issue in the case is whether the directors had exercised a prudent business judgment. The burden is upon the plaintiff to establish that a number of directors had been overreached by the Newmans and others allegedly acting in concert with them. The evidence discovered by the plaintiff was that no fact was concealed from any director, that each was fully informed and aware of all relevant facts. The directors maintained that it was their judgment that the acquisition of the Hausman stock would be beneficial to the corporation; they believed the stock was being offered at a relatively low price; [12] that the purchase would increase the per share earnings of the remaining outstanding shares and provide treasury stock for use in stock option plans or for stock dividends. [13]

Plaintiff's counsel recognized that the answers of the directors to the interrogatories undermined the theory of the charges set forth in the complaint. He thereupon decided to take the oral depositions of the two "independent" directors, defendants Arthur Singer and David Shivitz, who are lawyers. Their testimony dimmed rather than enhanced the prospect of success—indeed plaintiff's counsel was forced to concede that the deposition testimony "cast further doubt on the provability of plaintiff's charges." The depositions confirmed that the acquisition of the shares was viewed as beneficial to Howard; in addition, both directors urged the Newmans not to buy the shares, since they regarded it as a corporate opportunity. The strength of the defense led plaintiff's counsel to explore the prospect of settlement, with the result that an accord was reached. The defense, while vigorously continuing to deny plaintiff's charges, felt that a settlement was justified in an effort to avoid further expense.

The settlement in effect will reduce the purchase price of the shares acquired by the corporation by $110,000, less the allowance to be made to plaintiff's counsel and less such other expenses the corporation may incur in connection with this suit. Viewed as against the initial recovery sought, admittedly the amount is slight; but the real gain of the corporation is the termination of an expensive and time-consuming litigation. Taking into account all the circumstances

12. The contract price was $32 per share; on the over-the-counter market, on the date of the agreement, Howard stock was quoted at 35¼ bid, 36 asked.

13. It should be noted that permission to effect the purchase was granted by sev-

eral banks which had entered into a revolving credit agreement with the corporation.

of the case, particularly the unlikelihood that plaintiff will prevail upon the basis of the evidence disclosed under the discovery procedure, the settlement falls within that "range of reasonableness" which warrants its approval, and it is hereby approved.

We next consider the application made by plaintiff's counsel for an award of $27,500 in fees and expenses. The criteria to be considered in passing upon the requested allowance are well known and need not be repeated in extenso here. A prime factor is the benefit to the corporation on whose behalf the action is brought. In end result the amount of recovery may be said to be minimal. Indeed, in the light of the requested allowance it may be observed that the principal beneficiary is the attorney representing the plaintiff and not the corporation. As noted, the gross settlement is $110,000. Legal and other expenses already incurred and likely to be incurred by Howard in this action total $4,500; in addition, it may incur expenses for indemnification of directors for the uninsured portion of their reasonable expenses in connection with the defense of this action under the corporation's by-laws and sections 721–727 of the New York Business Corporation Law, which expenses it is estimated will not exceed $24,000, or a total of $28,500. If the $27,500 requested by plaintiff's counsel is allowed, a grand total of $56,000 must be deducted from the $110,000, resulting in a reduction in cost of the shares which are the subject matter of this litigation by $54,000. And against this slight dollar gain, there should fairly be considered the loss imposed upon the corporation when its various employees were diverted from their normal corporate activities and instead required to devote time and attention to the litigation in assembling and furnishing information and documents.

Taking into account the alleged benefit to the corporation, as well as other significant factors, the Court allows the sum of $15,000.

Judgment may be entered in accordance with the foregoing.

———

DESIMONE v. INDUSTRIAL BIO–TEST LABORATORIES, INC., 83 F.R.D. 615 (S.D.N.Y.1979). "The court will approve a proposed settlement of a class action if the proposal is fair, reasonable and adequate. This determination requires three levels of analysis. First, the proponents have the burden of proving that (1) the settlement is not collusive but was reached after arm's length negotiation; (2) the proponents are counsel experienced in similar cases; (3) there has been sufficient discovery to enable counsel to act intelligently and (4) the number of objectants or their relative interest is small. If the proponents establish these propositions, the burden of attacking the settlement then shifts to the objectants, if any. Finally, the court must approve the settlement only after finding it to be reasonable in light of the plaintiffs' ultimate probability of success in the lawsuit. . . .

"In determining reasonableness, the courts in this circuit have not applied any single, inflexible test. Instead, they have considered the amount of the settlement in light of all the circumstances, including such factors as: (1) the best possible recovery; (2) the likely recovery if the claims were fully litigated; (3) the complexity, expense and probable duration of continued litigation; (4) the risk of establishing liability; (5) the risk of establishing damages; (6) the risk of maintaining the class action throughout trial; (7) the reaction of the class to the settlement; (8) the stage of the proceedings and (9) the ability of the defendants to withstand a greater judgment.". . .

BACKGROUND NOTE ON JUDICIAL APPROVAL OF SETTLEMENTS

1. The mechanics of obtaining judicial approval of a settlement agreement are described in Haudek, The Settlement and Dismissal of Stockholders' Action—Part II: The Settlement, 23 Sw.L.J. 765 (1969). Generally speaking, the courts tend to rely heavily on affidavits, documents, depositions, and answers to interrogatories.

2. Once notice of settlement has been given, shareholders who object to the proposed settlement can enter the case. The objector becomes, in effect, a party to the settlement proceedings (although not to the underlying action). He therefore has a right to cross-examine the proponent's witnesses, to obtain a reasonable adjournment of the settlement hearing, and to appeal approval of the settlement, and he may also be given discovery rights. See Wolf v. Nazareth Enterprises, 303 F.2d 152, 154–55 (2d Cir.1962); Haudek, 23 Sw.L.J., supra, at 803–06. Moreover, if he succeeds in improving the settlement, he— or more accurately his lawyer—is entitled to counsel fees. White v. Auerbach, 500 F.2d 822 (2d Cir.1974), noted, 1 J.Corp.Law 194 (1975). Not infrequently the efforts of objectors result in a significant improvement of the settlement. In a well-known episode involving the Alleghany Corporation, a settlement involving a cash payment of $700,000 was increased under objection to $1,000,000, and under continued objection was further increased to $3 million. See Alleghany Corp. v. Kirby, 333 F.2d 327 (2d Cir.1964), aff'd in banc by an equally divided court 340 F.2d 311 (2d Cir.1965), cert. dismissed 384 U.S. 28, 86 S.Ct. 1250, 16 L.Ed.2d 335 (1966).

3. As a practical matter, the engine that normally drives a derivative action involving a publicly held corporation is not the plaintiff, but the plaintiff's attorney. The plaintiff typically makes little or no investment in the action and stands to gain very little benefit. His attorney, on the other hand, makes a very substantial investment (in the form of his time and disbursements) and stands to reap a very substantial benefit (in the form of a fee). This raises the unwholesome possibility that the defendants may be able to make an improper settlement by giving their acquiescence to an inflated fee in exchange for acquiescence by plaintiff's counsel to an inadequate corporate recovery.[1]

---

1. Cf. Fistel v. Christman, 133 F.Supp. 300 (S.D.N.Y.1955) (plaintiff's attorney agreed to dismiss a § 16(b) action on condition that the defendant pay him $2,500 for

SECTION 12. THE ROLE OF CORPORATE COUNSEL

NOTE ON THE ROLE OF CORPORATE COUNSEL

1. In the leading case of Garner v. Wolfinbarger, 430 F.2d 1093 (5th Cir.1970), cert. denied 401 U.S. 974, 91 S.Ct. 1191, 28 L.Ed.2d 323 (1971), the court held that in derivative actions, the attorney-client privilege is not automatically available for communications between the corporation and its attorney, since "the client asserting the privilege is an entity which in the performance of its functions acts wholly or partly in the interests of others . . . some of [whom] seek access to the subject matter of the communications." The court concluded:

> In summary, we say this. The attorney-client privilege still has viability for the corporate client. The corporation is not barred from asserting it merely because those demanding information enjoy the status of stockholders. But where the corporation is in suit against its stockholders on charges of acting inimically to stockholder interests, protection of those interests as well as those of the corporation and of the public require that the availability of the privilege be subject to the right of the stockholders to show cause why it should not be invoked in the particular instance. . . .

> There are many indicia that may contribute to a decision of presence or absence of good cause, among them the number of shareholders and the percentage of stock they represent; the bona fides of the shareholders; the nature of the shareholders' claim and whether it is obviously colorable; the apparent necessity or desirability of the shareholders having the information and the availability of it from other sources; whether, if the shareholders' claim is of wrongful action by the corporation, it is of action criminal, or illegal but not criminal, or of doubtful legality; whether the communication related to past or to prospective actions; whether the communication is of advice concerning the litigation itself; the extent to which the communication is identified versus the extent to which the shareholders are blindly fishing; the risk of revelation of trade secrets or other information in whose confidentiality the corporation has an interest for independent reasons. The court can freely use *in camera* inspection or oral examination and freely avail itself of protective orders, a familiar device to preserve confidentiality in trade secret

legal services); Jamison v. Butcher & Sherrerd, 68 F.R.D. 479 (E.D.Pa.1975) (proposed settlement of class action involved no benefit to the class but called for payment by defendants of a $50,000 attorneys' fee);

Norman v. McKee, 290 F.Supp. 29 (N.D. Cal.1968), aff'd 431 F.2d 769 (9th Cir.1970) (similar to Jamison); Rosenfeld, An Empirical Test of Class–Action Settlement, 5 J.Leg.Studies 113 (1976).

and other cases where the impact of revelation may be as great as in revealing a communication with counsel.

On remand, the district court held that the lawyer-client privilege was inapplicable under the standards *Garner* set out. Garner v. Wolfinbarger, 56 F.R.D. 499 (S.D.Ala.1972).

2. In derivative suits, the plaintiffs sue on behalf of the corporation, naming the corporation itself as a nominal defendant. The actual defendants, also named, are generally individual directors and officers. May corporate counsel represent both the corporation and the individual defendants? In Cannon v. U.S. Acoustics, 398 F.Supp. 209 (N.D. Ill.1975), aff'd in part 532 F.2d 118 (7th Cir.1976), the court ruled that the same firm could not represent the corporate and individual defendants even though counsel believed in good faith that no conflict would result. The court held that even when the corporate defendant is inactive, the inherent conflict in representing the alleged wrongdoers and the ultimate beneficiaries, and the danger that confidences of one client might be compromised in the representation of the other, require separate counsel. *Cannon* is in line with recent federal decisions in this area, Murphy v. Washington American League Base Ball Club, Inc., 324 F.2d 394 (D.C.Cir.1963); Lewis v. Shaffer Stores Co., 218 F.Supp. 238 (S.D.N.Y.1963), although the older cases are to the contrary. See, e.g., Otis & Co. v. Penn R. Co., 57 F.Supp. 680 (F.D.Pa.1944), aff'd 155 F.2d 522 (3d Cir.1946) (per curiam).

How should new counsel be selected and for whom? In *Cannon* the plaintiffs asked the court to appoint counsel for the corporation, since the individual defendants still sat on the board of directors. However, the court allowed the corporation to select new counsel. See also Lewis v. Shaffer Stores, supra. Which is the better procedure? And should the individual defendants be required to select new counsel, rather than the corporation?

3. In In re International Systems & Controls Corp. Securities Litigation, 693 F.2d 1235 (5th Cir.1982), the Court held that the good cause standard of *Garner* is inapplicable to material covered by the workproduct immunity, that is, material prepared in anticipation of litigation (as opposed to the advice of counsel in the course of business decisionmaking). Workproduct, it said, is covered by the substantial need/undue hardship test of FRCP Rule 26(b)(3).

4. In Upjohn Co. v. United States, 449 U.S. 383, 101 S.Ct. 677, 66 L.Ed.2d 584 (1981), Upjohn's independent accountant discovered that an Upjohn subsidiary had made improper payments to secure foreign government business. After consultation among Upjohn's general counsel, outside counsel, and chairman of the board, it was decided that the company would conduct an internal investigation of "questionable payments." As part of this investigation the attorneys prepared a letter containing a questionnaire which was sent to "All Foreign General and Area Managers" over the chairman's signature. Subsequently, the Internal Revenue Service issued a summons demanding production of certain records, including the questionnaires. (Note, therefore, that this case involved a suit by a third

party, not a shareholder's action.) The Supreme Court held that the questionnaires were protected from disclosure by the attorney-client privilege. Chief Justice Burger, concurring, stated:

. . . Because of the great importance of the issue, in my view the Court should make clear now that, as a general rule, a communication is privileged at least when, as here, an employee or former employee speaks at the direction of the management with an attorney regarding conduct or proposed conduct within the scope of employment. The attorney must be one authorized by the management to inquire into the subject and must be seeking information to assist counsel in performing any of the following functions: (a) evaluating whether the employee's conduct has bound or would bind the corporation; (b) assessing the legal consequences, if any, of that conduct; or (c) formulating appropriate legal responses to actions that have been or may be taken by others with regard to that conduct. . . . Other communications between employees and corporate counsel may indeed be privileged . . . but the need for certainty does not compel us now to prescribe all the details of the privilege in this case.

ABA MODEL RULES OF PROFESSIONAL CONDUCT, RULE 1.13

Rule 1.13   Organization as the Client

[As Proposed by the ABA's Commission on Evaluation of Professional Standards]

(a) A lawyer employed or retained to represent an organization represents the organization as distinct from its directors, officers, employees, members, shareholders or other constituents.

(b) If a lawyer for an organization knows that an officer, employee or other person associated with the organization is engaged in action, intends to act or refuses to act in a manner related to the representation that is a violation of a legal obligation to the organization, or a violation of law which reasonably might be imputed to the organization, and is likely to result in substantial injury to the organization, the lawyer shall proceed as is reasonably necessary in the best interest of the organization. In determining how to proceed, the lawyer shall give due consideration to the seriousness of the violation and its consequences, the scope and nature of the lawyer's representation, the responsibility in the organization and the apparent motivation of the person involved, the policies of the organization concerning such matters and any other relevant considerations. Any measures taken shall be designed to minimize disruption of the organization and the risk of revealing information relating to the representation to persons outside the organization. Such measures may include among others:

(1) asking reconsideration of the matter;

(2) advising that a separate legal opinion on the matter be sought for presentation to appropriate authority in the organization; and

(3) referring the matter to higher authority in the organization, including, if warranted by the seriousness of the matter, referral to the highest authority that can act on behalf of the organization as determined by applicable law.

(c) When the organization's highest authority insists upon action, or refuses to take action, that is clearly a violation of a legal obligation to the organization, or a violation of law which reasonably might be imputed to the organization, and is likely to result in substantial injury to the organization, the lawyer may take further remedial action that the lawyer reasonably believes to be in the best interest of the organization. Such action may include revealing information otherwise protected by Rule 1.6 [Confidentiality of Information] only if the lawyer reasonably believes that:

(1) the highest authority in the organization has acted to further the personal or financial interests of members of that authority which are in conflict with the interests of the organization; and

(2) revealing the information is necessary in the best interest of the organization.

(d) In dealing with an organization's directors, officers, employees, members, shareholders or other constituents, a lawyer shall explain the identity of the client when the lawyer believes that such explanation is necessary to avoid misunderstandings on their part.

(e) A lawyer representing an organization may also represent any of its directors, officers, employees, members, shareholders or other constituents, subject to the provisions of Rule 1.7 [Conflict of Interest: General Rule]. If the organization's consent to the dual representation is required by Rule 1.7, the consent shall be given by an appropriate official of the organization other than the individual who is to be represented or by the shareholders.

[As Adopted]

(a) A lawyer employed or retained by an organization represents the organization, through its constituents.

(b) (no change)

(c) If, despite the lawyer's efforts in accordance with paragraph (b), the highest authority that can act on behalf of the organization insists upon action, or a refusal to act, that is clearly a violation of law and is likely to result in substantial injury to the organization, the lawyer may resign. . . .

(d) In dealing with an organization's directors, officers, employees, members, shareholders or other constituents, a lawyer shall explain the identity of the client when it is apparent that the organization's interests are adverse to those of the constituents with whom the lawyer is dealing.

(e) (no change)

COMMENT . . . .

In an extreme case, it may be reasonably necessary for the lawyer to refer the matter to the organization's highest authority. Ordinarily, that is the board of directors or similar governing body. However, applicable law may prescribe that under certain conditions highest authority reposes elsewhere; for example, in the independent directors of a corporation. . . .

Chapter XI

STRUCTURAL CHANGES: COMBINATIONS, TENDER OFFERS, AND RECAPITALIZATIONS

SECTION 1. CORPORATE COMBINATIONS

(a) INTRODUCTION; MOTIVES FOR BUSINESS COMBINATIONS

1. The combination of two corporations presents in a single transaction basic questions of business policy, finance, accounting, corporate law, taxation, and, at times, antitrust law. The prototypical corporate combination is a transaction that may be referred to as a "classical merger." Although "merger" is often used by nonlawyers to describe any form of combination, to a lawyer it normally means a combination involving the fusion of two constituent corporations, pursuant to a formal agreement executed with reference to specific statutory merger provisions, under which the stock of one corporation (the transferor) is converted into stock of the other (the survivor). The survivor then succeeds to the transferor's assets and liabilities by operation of law. At one time the classical merger probably was the dominant mode of corporate combination, but in present times its scope has been significantly reduced. Broadly speaking, the upstart modes of combination that have shouldered this form aside fall into four categories: cash-for-assets, cash-for-stock, stock-for-assets, and stock-for-stock.

In a *cash-for-assets* combination, Corporation A purchases substantially all of the assets of Corporation B for cash or equivalent.

In a *cash-for-stock* combination, Corporation A purchases (at least) a majority of the stock of Corporation B for cash or equivalent.

In a *stock-for-assets* combination, Corporation A issues shares of its own stock to Corporation B in exchange for substantially all of B's assets. Often, in such a combination, A agrees to assume B's liabilities. In some cases, however, A may assume B's liabilities on only a selective basis. (Indeed, one reason for using this mode in preference to a classical merger may be A's desire to avoid assuming all of B's liabilities.) Usually, B agrees that it will dissolve and distribute its stock in A to its own shareholders. (The major reason for this is that A does not want a large block of its stock concentrated in a single holder.) Frequently it is also agreed or understood that some or all of B's officers and directors will join A's management.

713

In a *stock-for-stock* combination, Corporation A issues shares of its own stock directly to the shareholders of Corporation B in exchange for an amount of B stock—normally at least a majority—sufficient to carry control. By virtue of such a combination the shareholder groups of the two corporations are combined to a substantial extent, and B becomes a subsidiary of A. Frequently B is then liquidated or merged into A, but whether or not this occurs, B's assets will be under A's control. Such a combination does not require approval by B's management (since corporate action by B is not required). Often, however, the terms of the exchange of stock are worked out beforehand by the managements of both corporations, and often too it is agreed or understood that some or all of B's management will stay on with B in its new role as a subsidiary, or will join Corporation A itself.

2. The corporate-law problems raised by combinations can be very difficult, in part because the transactions can be fairly complex. To facilitate analysis, the material on combinations will progress from the simpler modes and problems to the more complex, in the following order: cash-for-assets combinations; dissenters' appraisal rights; statutory mergers (including short-form and small-scale mergers); tax, accounting, and financial aspects of combinations; stock-for-assets and stock-for-stock combinations; triangular mergers; issues of fairness, including freeze-outs and going private; and takeover contests.

———

(b) SALE OF SUBSTANTIALLY ALL ASSETS

———

DEL. GEN. CORP. LAW § 271

[See Statutory Supplement]

———

REV. MODEL BUS. CORP. ACT §§ 12.01, 12.02, 13.02

[See Statutory Supplement]

———

KATZ v. BREGMAN

Court of Chancery of Delaware, 1981.
431 A.2d 1274, appeal ref'd sub nom. Plant Indus., Inc. v. Katz, 435 A.2d 1044
(Del.1981).

MARVEL, Chancellor:

The complaint herein seeks the entry of an order preliminarily enjoining the proposed sale of the Canadian assets of Plant Industries, Inc. to Vulcan Industrial Packaging, Ltd., the plaintiff Hyman Katz allegedly being the owner of approximately 170,000 shares of common stock of the defendant Plant Industries, Inc., on whose behalf he has brought this action, suing not only for his own benefit as a stockholder but for the alleged benefit of all other record owners of common stock of the defendant Plant Industries, Inc. . . . . Significantly, at common law, a sale of all or substantially all of the assets of a corporation required the unanimous vote of the stockholders, Folk, The Delaware General Corporation Law, p. 400.

The complaint alleges that during the last six months of 1980 the board of directors of Plant Industries, Inc., under the guidance of the individual defendant Robert B. Bregman, the present chief executive officer of such corporation, embarked on a course of action which resulted in the disposal of several unprofitable subsidiaries of the corporate defendant located in the United States, namely Louisiana Foliage Inc., a horticultural business, Sunaid Food Products, Inc., a Florida packaging business, and Plant Industries (Texas), Inc., a business concerned with the manufacture of woven synthetic cloth. As a result of these sales Plant Industries, Inc. by the end of 1980 had disposed of a significant part of its unprofitable assets.

According to the complaint, Mr. Bregman thereupon proceeded on a course of action designed to dispose of a subsidiary of the corporate defendant known as Plant National (Quebec) Ltd., a business which constitutes Plant Industries, Inc.'s entire business operation in Canada and has allegedly constituted Plant's only income producing facility during the past four years. The professed principal purpose of such proposed sale is to raise needed cash and thus improve Plant's balance sheets. And while interest in purchasing the corporate defendant's Canadian plant was thereafter evinced not only by Vulcan Industrial Packaging, Ltd. but also by Universal Drum Reconditioning Co., which latter corporation originally undertook to match or approximate and recently to top Vulcan's bid, a formal contract was entered into between Plant Industries, Inc. and Vulcan on April 2, 1981 for the purchase and sale of Plant National (Quebec) despite the constantly increasing bids for the same property being made by Universal. One reason advanced by Plant's management for declining to negotiate with Universal is that a firm undertaking having been entered into with Vulcan that the board of directors of Plant may not legally or ethically negotiate with Universal. But see *Thomas v. Kempner,* C.A. 4138, March 22, 1973.

In seeking injunctive relief, as prayed for, plaintiff relies on two principles, one that found in 8 Del.C. § 271 to the effect that a decision of a Delaware corporation to sell ". . . all or substantially all of its property and assets . . ." requires not only the approval of such corporation's board of directors but also a resolution adopted by a majority of the outstanding stockholders of the corporation entitled to vote thereon at a meeting duly called upon at least twenty days' notice.

Support for the other principle relied on by plaintiff for the relief sought, namely an alleged breach of fiduciary duty on the part of the board of directors of Plant Industries, Inc. is allegedly found in such board's studied refusal to consider a potentially higher bid for the assets in question which is being advanced by Universal, *Thomas v. Kempner,* supra.

Turning to the possible application of 8 Del.C. § 271 to the proposed sale of substantial corporate assets of National to Vulcan, it is stated in *Gimbel v. Signal Companies, Inc.,* Del.Ch., 316 A.2d 599 (1974) as follows:

> "If the sale is of assets quantitatively vital to the operation of the corporation and is out of the ordinary [course] and substantially affects the existence and purpose of the corporation then it is beyond the power of the Board of Directors."

According to Plant's 1980 10K form, it appears that at the end of 1980, Plant's Canadian operations represented 51% of Plant's remaining assets. Defendants also concede that National represents 44.9% of Plant's sales' revenues and 52.4% of its pretax net operating income. Furthermore, such report by Plant discloses, in rough figures, that while National made a profit in 1978 of $2,900,000, the profit from the United States businesses in that year was only $770,000. In 1979, the Canadian business profit was $3,500,000 while the loss of the United States businesses was $344,000. Furthermore, in 1980, while the Canadian business profit was $5,300,000, the corporate loss in the United States was $4,500,000. And while these figures may be somewhat distorted by the allocation of overhead expenses and taxes, they are significant. In any event, defendants concede that ". . . National accounted for 34.9% of Plant's pretax income in 1976, 36.9% in 1977, 42% in 1978, 51% in 1979 and 52.4% in 1980."

While in the case of *Philadelphia National Bank v. B.S.F. Co.,* Del. Ch., 199 A.2d 557 (1969), rev'd on other grounds, Del.Supr., 204 A.2d 746 (1964), the question of whether or not there had been a proposed sale of substantially all corporate assets was tested by provisions of an indenture agreement covering subordinated debentures, the result was the same as if the provisions of 8 Del.C. § 271 had been applicable, the trial Court stating:

> "While no pertinent Pennsylvania case is cited, the critical factor in determining the character of a sale of assets is generally considered not the amount of property sold but whether the sale is in fact an unusual transaction or one made in the regular course of business of the seller * * *".

Furthermore, in the case of *Wingate v. Bercut* (C.A.9) 146 F.2d 725 (1945), in which the Court declined to apply the provisions of 8 Del.C. § 271, it was noted that the transfer of shares of stock there involved, being a dealing in securities, constituted an ordinary business transaction.

In the case at bar, I am first of all satisfied that historically the principal business of Plant Industries, Inc. has not been to buy and sell industrial facilities but rather to manufacture steel drums for use in bulk shipping as well as for the storage of petroleum products, chemicals, food, paint, adhesives and cleaning agents, a business which has been profitably performed by National of Quebec. Furthermore, the proposal, after the sale of National, to embark on the manufacture of plastic drums represents a radical departure from Plant's historically successful line of business, namely steel drums. I therefore conclude that the proposed sale of Plant's Canadian operations, which constitute over 51% of Plant's total assets and in which are generated approximately 45% of Plant's 1980 net sales, would, if consummated, constitute a sale of substantially all of Plant's assets. By way of contrast, the proposed sale of Signal Oil in *Gimbel v. Signal Companies, Inc.,* supra, represented only about 26% of the total assets of Signal Companies, Inc. And while Signal Oil represented 41% of Signal Companies, Inc. total net worth, it generated only about 15% of Signal Companies, Inc. revenue and earnings.

I conclude that because the proposed sale of Plant National (Quebec) Ltd. would, if consummated, constitute a sale of substantially all of the assets of Plant Industries, Inc., as presently constituted, that an injunction should issue preventing the consummation of such sale at least until it has been approved by a majority of the outstanding stockholders of Plant Industries, Inc., entitled to vote at a meeting duly called on at least twenty days' notice. Compare *Robinson v. Pittsburg Oil Refining Company,* Del.Ch., 126 A. 46 (1933).

In light of this conclusion it will be unnecessary to consider whether or not the sale here under attack, as proposed to be made, is for such an inadequate consideration, viewed in light of the competing bid of Universal, as to constitute a breach of trust on the part of the directors of Plant Industries, Inc., *Robinson v. Pittsburg Oil Refining Company,* supra.

Being persuaded for the reasons stated that plaintiff has demonstrated a reasonable probability of ultimate success on final hearing in the absence of stockholder approval of the proposed sale of the corporate assets here in issue to Vulcan, a preliminary injunction against the consummation of such transaction, at least until stockholder approval is obtained, will be granted.

On notice, an appropriate form of order in conformity with the above may be submitted.

NOTE

It is generally accepted that at common law a sale of substantially all assets required unanimous shareholder approval, on the theory that it breached an implied contract among the shareholders to further the corporate enterprise. See, e.g., Note, Interplay of Rights of Stockholders Dissenting from Sale of Corporate Assets, 58 Colum.L.Rev. 251, 251–252 (1958); Comment, Disposition of Corporate Assets, 43 N.C.L.Rev. 957, 958–59 (1965); Fontaine v. Brown County Motors Co., 251 Wis. 433, 437, 29 N.W.2d 744, 746–47 (1947). The sale-of-substantially-all assets provisions were enacted against this backdrop. It has been held that a sale of substantially all assets in the ordinary course of business does not require shareholder approval. See Jeppi v. Brockman Holding Co., 34 Cal.2d 11, 206 P.2d 847 (1949); Comment, Disposition of Corporate Assets, supra, at 960.

The theory is that since such a sale does not prevent furtherance of the corporate enterprise it would not have required unanimous shareholder approval at common law, and the sale-of-substantially-all-assets statutes were not intended to change that result.

(c) THE APPRAISAL REMEDY

DEL. GEN. CORP. LAW § 262

[See Statutory Supplement]

REV. MODEL BUS. CORP. ACT §§ 13.01–13.03, 13.20–13.28, 13.30–13.31

[See Statutory Supplement]

PIEMONTE v. NEW BOSTON GARDEN CORP.[1]

Supreme Judicial Court of Massachusetts, 1979.
377 Mass. 719, 387 N.E.2d 1145.

WILKINS, Justice.

The plaintiffs were stockholders in Boston Garden Arena Corporation (Garden Arena), a Massachusetts corporation whose stockholders voted on July 19, 1973, to merge with the defendant corporation in circumstances which entitled each plaintiff to "demand payment for his stock from the resulting or surviving corporation and an appraisal in accordance with the provisions of [G.L. c. 156B, §§ 86–98]." G.L. c. 156B, § 85, as amended by St.1969, c. 392, § 22. The plaintiffs commenced this action under G.L. c. 156B, § 90, seeking a judicial determination of the "fair value" of their shares "as of the day preceding the date of the vote approving the proposed corporate action."[2] G.L. c. 156B, § 92, inserted by St.1964, c. 723, § 1. Each party has appealed from a judgment determining the fair value of the plaintiffs' stock. We granted the defendant's application for direct appellate review.

On July 18, 1973, Garden Arena owned all the stock in a subsidiary corporation that owned both a franchise in the National Hockey League (NHL), known as the Boston Bruins, and a corporation that held a franchise in the American Hockey League (AHL),

---

1. The fifteen plaintiffs collectively owned 6,289 shares in Garden Arena Corporation, representing approximately 2.8% of its 224,892 shares of outstanding stock.

2. The plaintiffs took all the necessary, preliminary steps to preserve their rights. Each plaintiff objected in writing to the proposed merger; none of their shares was voted in favor of the proposed corporate action (see G.L. c. 156B, § 86); each plaintiff seasonably demanded in writing payment from the defendant for the fair value of his stock (see G.L. c. 156B, § 89); and no agreement as to that fair value was reached within thirty days of the demand (see G.L. c. 156B, § 90).

known as the Boston Braves. Garden Arena also owned and operated Boston Garden Sports Arena (Boston Garden), an indoor auditorium with facilities for the exhibition of sporting and other entertainment events, and a corporation that operated the food and beverage concession at the Boston Garden. A considerable volume of documentary material was introduced in evidence concerning the value of the stock of Garden Arena on July 18, 1973, the day before Garden Arena's stockholders approved the merger. Each side presented expert testimony. The judge gave consideration to the market value of the Garden Arena stock, to the value of its stock based on its earnings, and to the net asset value of Garden Arena's assets. Weighting these factors, the judge arrived at a total, per share value of $75.27.[3]

In this appeal, the parties raise objections to certain of the judge's conclusions. We will expand on the facts as necessary when we consider each issue. We conclude that the judge followed acceptable procedures in valuing the Garden Arena stock; that his determinations were generally within the range of discretion accorded a fact finder; but that, in three instances, the judge's treatment of the evidence was or may have been in error and, accordingly, the case should be remanded to him for further consideration of those three points.

General Principles of Law

The statutory provisions applicable to this case were enacted in 1964 as part of the Massachusetts Business Corporation Law. St. 1964, c. 723, § 1. The appraisal provisions (G.L. c. 156B, §§ 86–98) were based on a similar, but not identical, Delaware statute (Del. Code tit. 8, § 262). See Notes by Boston Bar Committee—1964, M.G.L.A. c. 156B, §§ 86–92, 94–97 (West). In these circumstances, consideration of the Delaware law, including judicial decisions, is appropriate, but in no sense should we feel compelled to adhere without question to that law, which has been in the process of development since our enactment of G.L. c. 156B in 1964. We do not perceive a legislative intent to adopt judicial determinations of Delaware law made prior to the enactment of G.L. c. 156B and certainly no such intent as to judicial interpretations made since that date.[4]

The Delaware courts have adopted a general approach to the appraisal of stock which a Massachusetts judge might appropriately follow, as did the judge in this case. The Delaware procedure, known as the "Delaware block approach," calls for a determination of the market value, the earnings value, and the net asset value of the

---

3. The judge determined the market value, earnings value, and net asset value of the stock and then weighted these values as follows:

	Value		Weight		Result
Market Value:	$ 26.50	×	10%	=	$ 2.65
Earnings Value:	$ 52.60	×	40%	=	$21.04
Net Asset Value:	$103.16	×	50%	=	$51.58
			Total Value Per Share:		$75.27

4. This is not a case in which the statute of another jurisdiction was subsequently enacted here. . . . The Massachusetts appraisal provisions differ somewhat from the Delaware appraisal provisions. Compare G.L. c. 156B, §§ 86–98, with Del. Code tit. 8, § 262.

stock, followed by the assignment of a percentage weight to each of the elements of value. See generally, Note, Valuation of Dissenters' Stock under Appraisal Statutes, 79 Harv.L.Rev. 1453, 1456–1471 (1966).

There have been no appellate decisions in this State concerning the appraisal of stock since the present appraisal statute was enacted, and there were few under the previously applicable, somewhat similar, statute.[5] See Martignette v. Sagamore Mfg. Co., 340 Mass. 136, 163 N.E.2d 9 (1959); Cole v. Wells, 224 Mass. 504, 113 N.E. 189 (1916). In the *Martignette* case, the court held that, even where stock had an established market, market price was not determinative and that "it is for the appraisers in the particular case to determine the weight of the relevant factors." Martignette v. Sagamore Mfg. Co., supra, 340 Mass. at 142, 163 N.E.2d at 13. If the corporation is solvent or has significant earnings prospects, "the earnings and worth of the corporation as a going concern are important." Id. at 142–143, 163 N.E.2d at 13 (overruling in this respect Cole v. Wells, supra, 224 Mass. at 513, 113 N.E. 189, which had held that the value of a dissenting stockholder's shares should be ascertained "as if liquidation had been voted"). We perceive no legislative intention to overrule these cases by the enactment of the new appraisal provisions in 1964.

With these considerations in mind, we turn to the specific issues that have been argued on appeal, considering, in order, the judge's determination of market value, earnings value and net asset value of the stock; his decision concerning the weighting of these components; the defendant's objection to the consideration of certain evidence; and, finally, the judge's decision on the rate of interest to be allowed to the plaintiffs.

Market Value

The judge was acting within reasonable limits when he determined that the market value of Garden Arena stock on July 18, 1973, was $26.50 a share. Each party challenges this determination. The plaintiffs' contention is that market value should be disregarded because it was not ascertainable due to the limited trading in Garden Arena stock.[6] The defendant argues that the judge was obliged to reconstruct market value based on comparable companies, and, in doing so, should have arrived at a market value of $22 a share.

Market value may be a significant factor, even the dominant factor, in determining the "fair value" of shares of a particular corporation under G.L. c. 156B, § 92. Shares regularly traded on a recognized stock exchange are particularly susceptible to valuation on the basis of their market price, although even in such cases the market

---

5. Under the previously applicable statute, a panel of three appraisers (rather than a judge) valued the stock. See G.L. c. 156, § 46.

6. This argument also bears on the relative weight to be assigned to market value as against net asset value and earnings value, a subject we shall consider subsequently.

value may well not be conclusive. See Martignette v. Sagamore Mfg. Co., 340 Mass. 136, 141–142, 163 N.E.2d 9 (1959). On the other hand, where there is no established market for a particular stock, actual market value cannot be used. In such cases, a judge might undertake to "reconstruct" market value, but he is not obliged to do so.[7] Indeed, the process of the reconstruction of market value may actually be no more than a variation on the valuation of corporate assets and corporate earnings.

In this case, Garden Arena stock was traded on the Boston Stock Exchange, but rarely. Approximately ninety per cent of the company's stock was held by the controlling interests and not traded. Between January 1, 1968, and December 4, 1972, 16,741 shares were traded. During this period, an annual average of approximately 1.5% of the outstanding stock changed hands. In 1972, 4,372 shares were traded at prices ranging from $20.50 a share to $29 a share. The public announcement of the proposed merger was made on December 7, 1972. The last prior sale of 200 shares on December 4, 1972, was made at $26.50 a share. The judge accepted that sale price as the market price to be used in his determination of value.

The judge concluded that the volume of trading was sufficient to permit a determination of market value and expressed a preference for the actual sale price over any reconstruction of a market value, which he concluded would place "undue reliance on corporations, factors, and circumstances not applicable to Garden Arena stock." The decision to consider market value and the market value selected were within the judge's discretion.

Valuation Based on Earnings

The judge determined that the average per share earnings of Garden Arena for the five-fiscal-year period which ended June 30, 1973, was $5.26. To this amount he applied a factor, or multiplier, of 10 to arrive at $52.60 as the per share value based on earnings.

Each party objects to certain aspects of this process. We reject the plaintiffs' argument that the judge could not properly use any value based on earnings, and also reject the parties' various challenges to the judge's method of determining value based on earnings.

Delaware case law, which, as we have said, we regard as instructive but not binding, has established a method of computing value based on corporate earnings. The appraiser generally starts by computing the average earnings of the corporation for the past five years.[8] Universal City Studios, Inc. v. Francis I. duPont & Co., 334 A.2d 216, 218 (Del.1975); Application of Del. Racing Ass'n, 213 A.2d 203, 212 (Del.1965). Extraordinary gains and losses are excluded from

7. The Delaware cases require the reconstruction of market value only when the actual market value cannot be determined and a hypothetical market value can be reconstructed. Compare Application of Del. Racing Ass'n, 213 A.2d 203, 211–212 (Del.1965), with Universal City Studios, Inc. v. Francis I. duPont & Co., 334 A.2d 216, 222 (Del.1975).

8. A 1976 amendment to the Delaware statute requires the court to appraise the stock rather than appoint an appraiser. 60 Del.Laws, c. 371, Del.Code tit. 8, § 262(f).

the average earnings calculation. Gibbons v. Schenley Indus., Inc., 339 A.2d 460, 468–470 (Del.Ch.1975); Felder v. Anderson, Clayton & Co., 39 Del.Ch. 76, 86–87, 159 A.2d 278 (1960). The appraiser then selects a multiplier (to be applied to the average earnings) which reflects the prospective financial condition of the corporation and the risk factor inherent in the corporation and the industry. Universal City Studios, Inc. v. Francis I. duPont & Co., supra. In selecting a multiplier, the appraiser generally looks to other comparable corporations. Universal City Studios, Inc. v. Francis I. duPont & Co., supra at 219–221 (averaging price-earnings ratios of nine other motion picture companies as of date of merger); Gibbons v. Schenley Indus., Inc., supra at 471 (using Standard & Poor's Distiller's Index as of date of merger); Felder v. Anderson, Clayton & Co., supra, 39 Del.Ch. at 87, 159 A.2d 278 (averaging price-earnings ratios of representative stocks over previous five-year period because of recent boom in industry). The appraiser's choice of a multiplier is largely discretionary and will be upheld if it is "within the range of reason." Universal City Studios, Inc. v. Francis I. duPont & Co., supra at 219 (approving multiplier of 16.1); Application of Del. Racing Ass'n, supra at 213 (approving multiplier of 10); Swanton v. State Guar. Corp., 42 Del. Ch. 477, 483, 215 A.2d 242 (1965) (approving multiplier of 14).[9]

The judge chose not to place "singular reliance on comparative data preferring to choose a multiplier based on the specific situation and prospects of the Garden Arena." He weighed the favorable financial prospects of the Bruins: the popularity and success of the team, the relatively low average age of its players, the popularity of Bobby Orr and Phil Esposito, the high attendance record at home games (each home team retained all gate receipts), and the advantageous radio and television contracts. On the other hand, he recognized certain risks, the negative prospects: the existence of the World Hockey Association with its potential, favorable impact on players' bargaining positions, and legal threats to the players' reserve clause. He concluded that a multiplier of 10 was appropriate. There was ample evidentiary support for his conclusion. He might have looked to and relied on price-earnings ratios of other corporations, but he was not obliged to.

The judge did not have to consider the dividend record of Garden Arena, as the defendant urges. Dividends tend to reflect the same factors as earnings and, therefore, need not be valued separately. See Felder v. Anderson, Clayton & Co., 39 Del.Ch. 76, 88–89, 159 A.2d 278 (1960). And since dividend policy is usually reflected in market value, the use of market value as a factor in the valuation process permitted the low and sporadic dividend rate to be given some weight in the process. Beyond that, the value of the plaintiffs'

---

9. Although Delaware courts have relied on, and continue to rely on, Professor Dewing's capitalization chart (see 1 A.S. Dewing, The Financial Policy of Corporations 390–391 [5th ed. 1953]), they have recognized that it is somewhat outdated and no longer the "be-all and end-all" on the subject of earnings value. See Universal City Studios, Inc. v. Francis I. duPont & Co., supra at 219; Swanton v. State Guar. Corp., 42 Del.Ch. 477, 483–484, 215 A.2d 242 (1965).

stock should not be depreciated because the controlling interests often chose to declare low dividends or none at all.

The judge did not abuse his discretion in including expansion income (payments from teams newly admitted to the NHL) received during two of the five recent fiscal years.   His conclusion was well within the guidelines of decided cases.   See Gibbons v. Schenley Indus., Inc., 339 A.2d 460, 470 (Del.Ch.1975) (gain from sale of real estate not extraordinary where corporation often sold such assets); Felder v. Anderson, Clayton & Co., 39 Del.Ch. 76, 86–87, 159 A.2d 278 (1960) (loss attributable to a drought not extraordinary).   The Bruins first received expansion income ($2,000,000) during the fiscal year which ended on June 30, 1967, a year not included in the five-year average.   The franchise received almost $1,000,000 more in 1970 and approximately $860,000 in 1972.   This 1970 and 1972 income was reflected in the computation of earnings.   Expansion income did not have to be treated as extraordinary income.   The judge concluded that it did not distort "an accurate projection of the earnings value of Garden Arena" and noted, as of July 18, 1973, an NHL expansion plan for the admission of two more teams in 1974–1975 and for expansion thereafter.

Valuation Based on Net Asset Value

The judge determined total net asset value by first valuing the net assets of Garden Arena apart from the Bruins franchise and the concession operations at Boston Garden.   He selected $9,400,000 (the June 30, 1973, book value of Garden Arena) as representing that net asset value.   Then, he added his valuations of the Bruins franchise ($9,600,000) and the concession operation ($4,200,000) to arrive at a total asset value of $23,200,000, or $103.16 a share.[10]

The parties raise various objections to these determinations.   The defendant argues that the judge included certain items twice in his valuation of the net assets of Garden Arena and that he should have given no separate value to the concession operation.   The plaintiff argues that the judge undervalued both the Boston Garden and the value of the Bruins franchise.

The defendant objects to the judge's refusal to deduct $1,116,000 from the $9,400,000 that represented the net asset value of Garden Arena (exclusive of the net asset value of the Bruins franchise and the concession operation).   The defendant's expert testified that the $9,400,000 figure included $1,116,000 attributable to the goodwill of the Bruins, net player investment, and the value of the AHL franchise.   The judge recognized that the items included in the $1,116,000 should not be valued twice and seemingly agreed that they would be more appropriately included in the value of the Bruins franchise than in the $9,400,000.   He was not plainly wrong, however, in declining to deduct them from the $9,400,000, because, as is fully warranted from the testimony of the defendant's expert, the

---

10. $23,200,000 ÷ 224,892 (the number of outstanding shares).

judge concluded that the defendant's expert did not include these items in his determination of the value of the Bruins franchise.[11] The defendant's expert, whose determination the judge accepted, arrived at his value of the Bruins franchise by adding certain items to the cost of a new NHL franchise, but none of those items included goodwill, net player investment, or the value of an AHL franchise. Acceptance of the defendant's argument would have resulted in these items being entirely omitted from the net asset valuation of Garden Arena.[12]

The plaintiffs object that the judge did not explicitly determine the value of the Boston Garden and implicitly undervalued it. Garden Arena had purchased the Boston Garden on May 25, 1973, for $4,000,000, and accounted for it on the June 30, 1973, balance sheet as a $4,000,000 asset with a corresponding mortgage liability of $3,437,065. Prior to the purchase, Garden Arena had held a long-term lease which was unfavorable to the owner of the Boston Garden.[13] The existence of the lease would tend to depress the purchase price.

The judge stated that the $9,400,000 book value *"includes* a reasonable value for Boston Garden"* (emphasis supplied). He did not indicate whether, if he had meant to value the Boston Garden at its purchase price (with an adjustment for the mortgage liabilities), he had considered the effect the lease would have had on that price. While we recognize that the fact-finding role of the judge permits him to reject the opinions of the various experts,[14] we conclude, in the absence of an explanation of his reasons, that it is possible that the judge did not give adequate consideration to the value of the Garden property. The judge should consider this subject further on remand.

A major area of dispute was the value of the Bruins franchise. The judge rejected the value advanced by the plaintiffs' expert ($18,000,000), stating that "[a]lthough the defendant's figure of [$9,600,000] seems somewhat low in comparison with the cost of expansion team franchises, *the Court is constrained* to accept defendant's value as it is the more creditable and legally appropriate expert opinion in the record" (emphasis supplied). Although the choice of the word "constrained" may have been inadvertent, it connotes a sense of obligation. As the trier of fact, the judge was not bound to

---

11. The defendant makes no special argument concerning the judge's failure to deduct certain relatively minor, intangible assets, including merger costs.

12. One of the points on which we will remand this case is the valuation of the Bruins franchise. Since, as discussed below, the judge need not have felt constrained to accept the defendant's expert's opinion on this issue, on remand he will be free to determine the value of the franchise based on such evidence as he chooses to accept. Assignment of a different value to the franchise may require an adjustment in the net asset value of Garden Arena if the franchise value determined by

the judge includes some or all of the items supposedly included in the $1,116,000.

13. The lease, which ran until June 1, 1986, contained a fixed maximum rent and an obligation on the lessee to pay only two-thirds of any increase in local real estate taxes. In a period of inflation and rising local real estate taxes, the value of the lease to the lessor was decreasing annually.

14. The lowest value expressed by any expert for the plaintiffs was $8,250,000 (exclusive of mortgage liabilities), based on depreciated reproduction cost. The defendant offered no testimony concerning the value of the property on July 18, 1973.

accept the valuation of either one expert or the other. He was entitled to reach his own conclusion as to value. . . .

Because the judge may have felt bound to accept the value placed on the Bruins franchise by the defendant's expert, we shall remand this case for him to arrive at his own determination of the value of the Bruins franchise. He would be warranted in arriving at the same valuation as that advanced on behalf of the defendant, but he is not obliged to do so.

The defendant argues that, in arriving at the value of the assets of Garden Arena, the judge improperly placed a separate value on the right to operate concessions at the Boston Garden. We agree with the judge. The fact that earnings from concessions were included in the computation of earnings value, one component in the formula, does not mean that the value of the concessions should have been excluded from the computation of net asset value, another such component.

The value of the concession operation was not reflected in the value of the real estate. Real estate may be valued on the basis of rental income, but it is not valued on the basis of the profitability of business operations within the premises. . . . Moreover, it is manifest that the value of the concession operation was not included in the value placed on the Boston Garden. The record indicates that Garden Arena already owned the concession rights when it purchased the Boston Garden. The conclusion that the value of the concession operation was not reflected in the value of the Boston Garden is particularly warranted because the determined value of the right to operate the concessions ($4,200,000) was higher than the May 25, 1973, purchase price ($4,000,000) of the Boston Garden.

We do conclude, however, that the judge may have felt unnecessarily bound to accept the plaintiffs' evidence of the value of the concession operation. He stated that "since the defendant did not submit evidence on this issue, the Court will accept plaintiffs' expert appraisal of the value of the concession operation." Although the judge did not express the view that he was "constrained" to accept the plaintiffs' valuation, as he did concerning the defendant's valuation of the Bruins franchise, he may have misconstrued his authority on this issue. The judge was not obliged to accept the plaintiffs' evidence at face value merely because no other evidence was offered. . . .

On remand, the judge should reconsider his determination of the value of the concession operation and exercise his own judgment concerning the bases for the conclusion arrived at by the plaintiffs' expert. However, the evidence did warrant the value selected by the judge, and no reduction in that value is required on this record.

Weighting of Valuations

The judge weighted the three valuations as follows:

Market Value	—	10%
Earnings Value	—	40%
Net Asset Value	—	50%

We accept these allocations as reasonable and within the range of the judge's discretion.

Any determination of the weight to be given the various elements involved in the valuation of a stock must be based on the circumstances. Heller v. Munsingwear, Inc., 33 Del.Ch. 593, 598, 98 A.2d 774 (1953). The decision to weight market value at only 10% was appropriate, considering the thin trading in the stock of Garden Arena. The decision to attribute 50% weight to net asset value was reasonably founded. The judge concluded that, because of tax reasons, the value of a sports franchise, unlike many corporate activities, depends more on its assets than on its earnings; that Garden Arena had been largely a family corporation in which earnings were of little significance; that Garden Arena had approximately $5,000,000 in excess liquid assets; and that the Garden property was a substantial real estate holding in an excellent location.

The judge might have reached different conclusions on this record. He was not obliged, however, to reconstruct market value and, as the defendant urges, attribute 50% weight to it. Nor was he obliged, as the plaintiffs argue, to consider only net asset value. See Martignette v. Sagamore Mfg. Co., 340 Mass. 136, 142, 163 N.E.2d 9 (1959). Market value and earnings value properly could be considered in these circumstances.

Although we would have found no fault with a determination to give even greater weight to the price per share based on the net asset value of Garden Arena, the judge was acting within an acceptable range of discretion in selecting the weights he gave to the various factors.

Evidentiary Objections

The defendant objects to the introduction and consideration of evidence of events arising after the statutory valuation date. The judge carefully noted his statutory obligation to value the shares "as of the day preceding the date of the vote approving the proposed corporate action" and "exclusive of any element of value arising from the expectation or accomplishment of the proposed corporate action." G.L. c. 156B, § 92. . . . Even more significant is the plain fact that there is no showing that the judge relied on any evidence of events occurring after July 18, 1973, or on any expert opinion that was based on any such events.

Interest Allowance

The defendant objects to the judge's determination to award interest at 8% per annum. It does not object to the judge's decision to award interest, a matter within his discretion (see G.L. c. 156B, §§ 92 and 95), nor to his decision to compound interest annually. . . . [T]he judge reasonably could have concluded that 8% per annum reflected "the rate of interest at which a prudent investor could have invested money." Universal City Studios, Inc. v. Francis I. duPont & Co., 334 A.2d 216, 222 (Del.1975). . . .

Conclusion

We have concluded that the judge's method of valuing the Garden Arena stock was essentially correct. In this opinion, we have indicated, however, that the case should be remanded to him for clarification and further consideration on the record of three matters: his valuation of the Boston Garden, the Bruins franchise, and the concession operation.

So ordered.

————

M. EISENBERG, THE STRUCTURE OF THE CORPORATION
77–82 (1976).

§ 7.2 The Place of Appraisal Rights in Closely Held Corporations

To understand the real utility—and perhaps the real origin—of the appraisal right, we must return once more to the partnership form. It will be recalled that absent contrary agreement, decisions on matters outside the scope of the partnership business can be made only by unanimous consent, new partners cannot be admitted without unanimous consent, and partnerships are normally short-lived and easy to dissolve. These various partnership incidents, although apparently disparate, are actually complementary. The veto power of each partner in matters outside the scope of the partnership business seriously restricts his copartners' freedom of action to make changes in the business that seem to them desirable and even necessary to meet changing conditions. This restriction might be intolerable except for the fact that each partner has agreed to the identity of his fellow veto-bearers, and that the timespan of such a veto is ordinarily short, since the remaining partners can either dissolve the partnership or await the end of its term and then reconstitute the enterprise along the desired lines.

But neither of the conditions making a veto tolerable in the partnership is normally present in the corporation: absent contrary agreement, the identity of fellow shareholders is not within a shareholder's control, and the duration of the enterprise is normally perpetual. Given those elements it is predictable that corporate law would permit a majority, or at least a high majority, to make structural changes even over the objection of minority shareholders. But just as a veto power might be intolerable in a corporation, so might be an unrestricted power in the majority to make structural changes, unless some method was provided whereby minority shareholders would not be locked into the restructured enterprise over their objections. The minority, in other words, should have the right to say to the majority, "We recognize your right to restructure the enterprise, provided you are willing to buy us out at a fair price if we object, so that we are not forced to participate in an enterprise other than the one contemplated at the outset of our mutual association." Seen from this perspective, the appraisal right is a mechanism admirably suited to reconcile, in the corporate context, the need to give the majority the right to make drastic changes in the enterprise to meet new conditions as they arise, with the need to protect the minority against being involuntarily dragged along into a drastically restructured enterprise in which it has no confidence. . . .

§ 7.3   The Place of Appraisal Rights in Publicly Held Corporations

In contrast [to the shareholder in a close corporation], a shareholder in a publicly held corporation normally can withdraw by selling his shares on the market. . . .   Is the appraisal right therefore unnecessary in the case of publicly held corporations?

. . . While it is true that many shareholders in publicly-held corporations are [oriented to the market rather than to the enterprise,] many others are likely to own an amount of stock sufficient to orient their expectations around the long-term prospects of the enterprise rather than around a market which tends to fluctuate severely over any given short-run period.   It may be questioned whether such shareholders should be remitted to the market to find relief from structural changes to which they object . . . .   To give a random illustration, [the following table] . . . shows the highs and lows for the first ten common stocks, alphabetically, on the New York Stock Exchange, in 1973. . . .

Corporation	High	Low
Abbt Lb	$61\frac{1}{4}$	$30\frac{1}{2}$
ACF In	$61\frac{1}{4}$	$28\frac{3}{4}$
Acme Clev	$14\frac{5}{8}$	7
Adm Dg	$5\frac{5}{8}$	$1\frac{3}{8}$
Adm E	$13\frac{1}{4}$	$7\frac{3}{8}$
Ad Mill	$5\frac{1}{4}$	$1\frac{3}{4}$
Addres	$11\frac{3}{4}$	3
Adv Inv.	$11\frac{7}{8}$	$6\frac{1}{2}$
Aetna Lf.	31	$15\frac{1}{8}$
Aquirre Co.	$9\frac{1}{8}$	$4\frac{3}{8}$

When fluctuations like these occur within a twelve-month . . . period, it seems arbitrary, to say the least, to remit an enterprise-oriented shareholder to the market for relief.

Furthermore, . . . remitting a dissenting shareholder to the market will fail to adequately protect him where (1) his block is so large that the mere act of selling the block will depress the market—and . . . large blocks are common even in stocks listed on the New York Stock Exchange; (2) the very effect of the structural change is to depress the market price of the stock because the change is an ill-considered one; or (3) so many shareholders want to opt out that the market is flooded with sell orders.

———

CAL. CORP. CODE § 1300

[See Statutory Supplement]

———

BACKGROUND NOTE ON APPRAISAL RIGHTS

1. Traditionally, virtually all corporate statutes have granted appraisal rights to the shareholders of both constituents to a statutory merger, although many statutes now carve out some important exceptions, discussed below and in Section (d), infra. Most statutes also grant appraisal rights to the shareholders of the transferor in a sale of substantially all assets. Some recent statutes grant appraisal rights to shareholders of the survivor in certain stock-for-assets or stock-for-stock combinations and case-law has often reached the same result even without a statute. See Section (f), infra. A few statutes provide for appraisal rights in the case of certain certificate amendments. For example, under the New York statute and the Model Act, a certificate amendment gives rise to appraisal rights if it adversely affects the shareholder's interest by altering or abolishing a preference or a preemptive right, excluding or limiting a voting right, or creating, altering, or abolishing a redemption or sinking-fund provision. N.Y. Bus.Corp.Law § 806(b)(6); Rev.Model Bus.Corp. Act § 13.02(a) (4).

2. A number of states have statutes which generally deny appraisal rights, in any kind of transaction, with respect to stock that is publicly traded in a defined manner. Almost all of these statutes are applicable to stock that is listed on a "national" securities exchange, although some, such as the California statute, adopt slightly different formulas. A majority of these statutes are also applicable to stock which is held by at least 2000 shareholders. See Note, A Reconsideration of the Stock Market Exception to the Dissenting Shareholder's Right of Appraisal, 74 Mich.L.Rev. 1023 (1976). In 1978, the ABA's Corporation Law Committee eliminated from the Model Act a stock-market exception which had been inserted nine years earlier.

> The . . . exception for shares listed on stock exchanges has been eliminated in the light of facts which have become more visible since the stock market exception was added to the Model Act in 1969. The 1970s have demonstrated again the possibility of a demoralized market in which fair prices are not available, and in which many companies publicly offer to buy their own shares because the market grossly undervalues them. Under these circumstances, access to market value is not a reasonable alternative for a dissenting shareholder. Moreover, a shareholder may be disqualified by state or federal securities laws from using the market because his shares are "restricted," because he is an

"insider" who has acquired shares within six months, or because he possesses "inside information." Even if the dissenter is free to use the market, he may find it impractical to do so because his holdings are large and the market is thin. In any event, the market cannot reflect the value of the shares "excluding any appreciation or depreciation in anticipation" of the corporate change which gives rise to the dissenters' rights.

Rev.Model Bus.Corp. Act § 13.02, Annotation (1978).

R. BREALY & S. MYERS

PRINCIPLES OF CORPORATE FINANCE

12–14, 22 (3d ed. 1988)

INTRODUCTION TO PRESENT VALUE . . .

Suppose your apartment house burns down, leaving you with a vacant lot worth $50,000 and a check for $200,000 from the fire insurance company. You consider rebuilding, but your real estate adviser suggests putting up an office building instead. The construction cost would be $300,000, and there would also be the cost of the land, which might otherwise be sold for $50,000. On the other hand, your adviser foresees a shortage of office space and predicts that a year from now the new building would fetch $400,000 if you sold it. Thus you would be investing $350,000 now in the expectation of realizing $400,000 a year hence. You should go ahead if the **present value** of the expected $400,000 payoff is greater than the investment of $350,000. Therefore, you need to ask yourself, "What is the value today of $400,000 1 year from now, and is that present value greater than $350,000?"

The present value of $400,000 1 year from now must be less than $400,00. After all, *a dollar today is worth more than a dollar tomorrow*, because the dollar today can be invested to start earning interest immediately. This is the first basic principle of finance.

Thus, the present value of a delayed payoff may be found by multiplying the payoff by a **discount factor** which is less than 1. (If the discount factor were more than 1, a dollar today would be worth *less* than a dollar tommorrow.) If C_1 denotes the expected payoff at time period 1 (1 year hence), then

$$\text{Present value (PV)} = \text{discount factor} \times C_1$$

This discount factor is expressed as the reciprocal of 1 plus a *rate of return:*

$$\text{Discount factor} = \frac{1}{1 + r}$$

The rate of return r is the reward that investors demand for accepting delayed payment.

Let us consider the real estate investment, assuming for the moment that the $400,000 payoff is a sure thing. The office building is not the only way to obtain $400,000 a year from now. You could invest in United States government securities maturing in a year. Suppose these securities yield 7 percent interest. How much would you have to invest in them in order to receive $400,000 at the end of the year? That's easy: you would have to invest $400,000/1.07, which is $373,832. Therefore, at an interest rate of 7 percent, the present value of $400,000 1 year from now is $373,832.

Let's assume that, as soon as you've committed the land and begun construction on the building, you decide to sell your project. How much could you sell it for? That's another easy question. Since the property produces $400,000, investors would be willing to pay $373,832 for it. That's what it would cost them to get a $400,000 payoff from investing in government securities. Of course you could always sell your property for less, but why sell for less than the market will bear? The $373,832 present value is the only feasible price that satisfies both buyer and seller. Therefore, the present value of the property is also its market price.

To calculate present value, we discount expected future payoffs by the rate of return offered by comparable investment alternatives. This rate of return is often referred to as the **discount rate, hurdle rate,** or **opportunity cost of capital.** It is called the *opportunity cost* because it is the return forgone by investing in the project rather than investing in securities. In our example the opportunity cost was 7 percent. Present value was obtained by dividing $400,000 by 1.07:

$$\text{PV} = \text{discount factor} \times C_1 = \frac{1}{1 + r} \times C_1 = \frac{400{,}000}{1.07} = \$373{,}832$$

The building is worth $373,832, but this does not mean that you are $373,832 better off. You committed $350,000, and therefore your **net present value** is $23,832. Net present value (**NPV**) is found by subtracting the required investment:

$$\text{NPV} = \text{PV} - \text{required investment} = 373{,}832 - 350{,}000 = \$23{,}832$$

In other words, your office development is worth more than it costs— it makes a *net* contribution to value. The formula for calculating NPV can be written as

$$\text{NPV} = C_0 + \frac{C_1}{1 + r}$$

remembering that C_0, the cash flow at time period 0 (that is, today) will usually be a negative number. In other words, C_0 is an investment and therefore a cash *outflow*. In our example, $C_0 = -\$350,000$.

We made one unrealistic assumption in our discussion of the office development: Your real estate adviser cannot be *certain* about future values of office buildings. The $400,000 figure represents the best *forecast*, but it is not a sure thing.

Therefore, our conclusion about how much investors would pay for the building is wrong. Since they could achieve $400,000 with certainty by buying $373,832 worth of United States government securities, they would not buy your building for that amount. You would have to cut your asking price to attract investors' interest.

Here we can invoke a second basic financial principle: *A safe dollar is worth more that a risky one.* Most investors avoid risk when they can do so without sacrificing return. However, the concepts of present value and the opportunity cost of capital still make sense for risky investments. It is still proper to discount the payoff by the rate of return offered by a comparable investment. But we have to think of *expected* payoffs and the *expected* rates of return on other investments.

Not all investments are equally risky. The office development is riskier than a government security but is probably less risky than drilling a wildcat oil well. Suppose you believe the project is as risky as investment in the stock market and that you forecast a 12 percent rate of return for stock market investments. Then 12 percent becomes the appropriate opportunity cost of capital. That is what you are giving up by not investing in comparable securities. You can now recompute NPV:

$$PV = \frac{400,000}{1.12} = \$357,143$$

$$NPV = PV - 350,000 = \$7143$$

If other investors agree with your forecast of a $400,000 payoff and with your assessment of a 12 percent opportunity cost of capital, then your property ought to be worth $357,143 once construction is under way. If you tried to sell it for more than that, there would be no takers, because the property would then offer an expected rate of return lower than the 12 percent available in the stock market. The office building still makes a net contribution to value, but it is much smaller than our earlier calculations indicated.

In Chapter 1 we said that the financial manager must be concerned with time and uncertainty and their effects on value. This is clearly so in our example. The $400,000 payoff would be worth exactly that if it could be realized instantaneously. If the office building is as risk-free as government securities, the 1-year delay reduces value to $373,382. If the office building is as risky as investment in the stock market, then uncertainty reduces value by a further $16,689 to $357,143. . . .

We have decided that construction of the office building is a smart thing to do, since it is worth more than it costs—it has a positive net present value. To calculate how much it is worth, we worked out how much one would have to pay to achieve the same income by investing directly in securities. The project's present value is equal to its future income discounted at the rate of return offered by these securities.

We can reexpress our criterion by saying that our property venture is worth undertaking because the return exceeds the cost of capital. The return on the capital invested is simply the profit as a proportion of the initial outlay:

$$\text{Return} = \frac{\text{profit}}{\text{investment}} = \frac{400,000 - 350,000}{350,000} = 14\%$$

The cost of capital invested is once again just the return forgone by *not* investing in securities. In our present case, if the office building is about as risky as investing in the stock market, the return forgone is 12 percent. Since the 14 percent return on the office building exceeds the 12 percent cost, we should start digging the foundations of the building.

Here then we have two equivalent decision rules for capital investment.

1. *Net present value rule.* Accept investments that have positive net present values.

2. *Rate-of-return rule.* Accept investments that offer rates of return in excess of their opportunity costs of capital. . . .

A FUNDAMENTAL RESULT

The present value rule really dates back to the work of the great American economist Irving Fisher, in 1930. What was so exciting about Fisher's analysis was his discovery that the capital investment criterion has nothing to do with the individual's preferences for current versus future consumption. The prodigal and the miser are unanimous in the amount that they want to invest in real assets. Because they have the same investment criterion, they can cooperate in the same enterprise and can safely delegate the operation of that enterprise to a professional manager. Managers do not need to know anything about the personal tastes of their shareholders and should not consult their own tastes. Their task is to maximize net present value. If they succeed, they can rest assured that they have acted in the best interests of their shareholders.

Our justification of the net present value rule has been restricted to two periods and to certain cash flows. However, the rule also makes sense for cases in which the cash flows extend beyond the next period. The argument goes like this:

1. A financial manager should act in the interest of the firm's stockholders.

2. Each stockholder wants three things:

   (*a*) To be as rich as possible, that is, to maximize current wealth

   (*b*) To transform that wealth into whatever time pattern of consumption he or she most desires

   (*c*) To choose the risk characteristics of that consumption plan

3. But stockholders do not need the financial manager's help to reach the best time pattern of consumption. They can do that on their own, providing they have free access to compe-

tive capital markets. They can also choose the risk characteristics of their consumption plan by investing in more or less
risky securities.

4. How then can the financial manager help the firm's stockholders? By increasing the market value of each stockholder's stake in the firm. The way to do that is to seize all
investment opportunities that have a positive net present
value.

This gives us the fundamental condition for the successful operation of a capitalist economy. Separation of ownership and management is a practical necessity for large organizations. Many corporations have hundreds of thousands of shareholders, no two with the
same tastes, wealth, or personal opportunities. There is no way for all
the firm's owners to be actively involved in management: It would be
like running New York City through a series of town meetings for all
its citizens. Therefore, authority has to be delegated. The remarkable thing is that managers of firms can all be given one simple
instruction: Maximize net present value.

NOTE ON WEINBERGER v. UOP

In Weinberger v. UOP, 457 A.2d 701 (1983), the Delaware
Supreme Court overturned the traditional Delaware block method of
valuation:

> Turning to the matter of price, plaintiff also challenges its
> fairness. His evidence was that on the date the merger was
> approved the stock was worth at least $26 per share. In support,
> he offered the testimony of a chartered investment analyst who
> used two basic approaches to valuation: a comparative analysis of
> the premium paid over market in ten other tender offer-merger
> combinations, and a discounted cash flow analysis.
>
> In this breach of fiduciary duty case, the Chancellor per-
> ceived that the approach to valuation was the same as that in an
> appraisal proceeding. Consistent with precedent, he rejected
> plaintiff's method of proof and accepted defendants' evidence of
> value as being in accord with practice under prior case law. This
> means that the so-called "Delaware block" or weighted average
> method was employed wherein the elements of value, i.e., assets,
> market price, earnings, etc., were assigned a particular weight and
> the resulting amounts added to determine the value per share.
> This procedure has been in use for decades. See In re General
> Realty & Utilities Corp., Del.Ch., 52 A.2d 6, 14–15 (1947).
> However, to the extent it excludes other generally accepted
> techniques used in the financial community and the courts, it is
> now clearly outmoded. It is time we recognize this in appraisal
> and other stock valuation proceedings and bring our law current
> on the subject.

While the Chancellor rejected plaintiff's discounted cash flow method of valuing UOP's stock, as not corresponding with "either logic or the existing law" (426 A.2d at 1360), it is significant that this was essentially the focus, i.e., earnings potential of UOP, of Messrs. Arledge and Chitiea in their evaluation of the merger. Accordingly, the standard "Delaware block" or weighted average method of valuation, formerly employed in appraisal and other stock valuation cases, shall no longer exclusively control such proceedings. We believe that a more liberal approach must include proof of value by any techniques or methods which are generally considered acceptable in the financial community and otherwise admissible in court, subject only to our interpretation of 8 Del.C. § 262(h), infra. . . . . This will obviate the very structured and mechanistic procedure that has heretofore governed such matters. See Jacques Coe & Co. v. Minneapolis–Moline Co., Del.Ch., 75 A.2d 244, 247 (1950); Tri–Continental Corp. v. Battye, Del.Ch., 66 A.2d 910, 917–18 (1949); In re General Realty and Utilities Corp., supra.

. . . This [approach] is not only in accord with the realities of present day affairs, but it is thoroughly consonant with the purpose and intent of our statutory law. Under 8 Del.C. § 262(h), the Court of Chancery:

> shall appraise the shares, determining their *fair* value exclusive of any element of value arising from the accomplishment or expectation of the merger, together with a fair rate of interest, if any, to be paid upon the amount determined to be the *fair* value. In determining such *fair* value, the Court shall take into account *all relevant factors* . . . (Emphasis added)

See also Bell v. Kirby Lumber Corp., Del.Supr., 413 A.2d 137, 150–51 (1980) (Quillen, J., concurring).

It is significant that section 262 now mandates the determination of "fair" value based upon "all relevant factors". Only the speculative elements of value that may arise from the "accomplishment or expectation" of the merger are excluded. We take this to be a very narrow exception to the appraisal process, designed to eliminate use of *pro forma* data and projections of a speculative variety relating to the completion of a merger. But elements of future value, including the nature of the enterprise, which are known or susceptible of proof as of the date of the merger and not the product of speculation, may be considered. When the trial court deems it appropriate, fair value also includes any damages, resulting from the taking, which the stockholders sustain as a class. If that was not the case, then the obligation to consider "all relevant factors" in the valuation process would be eroded.

NEW YORK BUS. CORP. LAW § 623(h)(4)

[See Statutory Supplement]

LEADER v. HYCOR, INC., 395 Mass. 215, 479 N.E.2d 173 (1985). "Because the issue of the continuing validity of the 'Delaware block method' of stock valuation is likely to arise on remand, we express our opinion on this matter. We do not agree that the 'Delaware block method' for valuing closely held stock, as set forth in our decision in *Piemonte v. New Boston Garden Corp.,* 377 Mass. 719, 387 N.E.2d 1145 (1979), is outmoded. Citing *Weinberger v. UOP, Inc.,* 457 A.2d 701 (Del.1983), the plaintiffs contend that the Delaware Supreme Court has rejected this valuation method. The *Weinberger* court stated that this method is outmoded 'to the extent it excludes other generally accepted techniques used in the financial community and the courts' and that it would no longer '*exclusively* control such proceedings' (emphasis added). *Weinberger, supra* at 712–713. We need not accept judicial interpretations of Delaware law made subsequent to our Legislature's adoption of c. 156B. *Id.* at 723. In any event, we have never held that the Delaware block method is the only approach that a judge may employ in valuing stock. In *Piemonte,* we stated that a judge 'might appropriately follow' this general approach. *Id.* at 723–724."

(d) STATUTORY MERGERS

---

(1) Classical Mergers

DEL. GEN. CORP. LAW §§ 251(a)–(e), 259–61

[See Statutory Supplement]

REV. MODEL BUS. CORP. ACT §§ 11.01, 11.03, 11.05, 11.06

[See Statutory Supplement]

NOTE ON STATUTORY MERGERS

1. Del.Gen.Corp.Law §§ 251(a)–(e), 259–61 and Rev. Model Bus.Corp.Act §§ 11.01, 11.03, 11.05, 11.06 authorize a type of transaction commonly referred to as a statutory merger. While details vary from state to state, generally the first formal step in such a merger, after negotiations have been completed, is a preliminary agreement (often embodied in a "letter of intent") signed by repre-

sentatives of the constituent companies. If the merger is approved by the board and shareholders of each constituent, articles of merger are then filed with the secretary of state, and securities of the surviving corporation are exchanged for those of the disappearing or transferor corporation, which is fused into the transferee, and loses its identity. In general, no instruments of conveyance, such as deeds or bills of sale, are necessary to pass title from the transferor to the survivor: by operation of law the survivor has all the rights, privileges, franchises, and assets of the constituents, and assumes all of their liabilities.

2. In most merger agreements, authority is given to both boards to abandon the merger at any time up to the effective date, upon the occurrence of certain defined conditions—for example, if any material litigation or governmental proceeding is instituted against a constituent, or if a constituent suffers substantial loss as a result of catastrophe, or any material adverse change in its condition, or the merger "would be impracticable because of the number of stockholders who assert the right to have their stock appraised and to receive payment."

3. A statutory consolidation is identical to a statutory merger except for the fact that in a merger one constituent fuses into another, while in a consolidation the constituents fuse to form a new corporation. Because the consolidation technique is seldom employed, and when employed is treated almost identically to a merger, no separate consideration will be given in this Chapter to statutory consolidations.

4. At one time, virtually all statutory mergers required approval by a majority or two-thirds vote of the outstanding shares of each constituent and also triggered appraisal rights for the shareholders of each constituent. Many statutes now carve out exceptions to these requirements in the case of "short-form" and "small-scale" mergers. These types of merger will be considered in the next two sections.

———

(2) Small–Scale Mergers

———

DEL. GEN. CORP. LAW § 251(f)

[See Statutory Supplement]

———

REV. MODEL BUS. CORP. ACT § 11.03(g)

[See Statutory Supplement]

———

E. Folk, R. Ward & E. Welch, FOLK ON THE DELAWARE GENERAL CORPORATION LAW § 251.2.1.1

2d ed. 1988.

1. [The requirement of Del. § 251(f) that the survivor's certificate of incorporation not be amended] is designed to assure that the merger technique cannot be used to deprive stockholders of the voting rights that they would enjoy if the certificate were being amended under section 242. . . .

2. The theory underlying the second condition—the 20 percent limitation on increasing the number of common shares—is that a merger which involves less than 20 percent of the survivor's shares is not such a major change as to require a stockholder vote, and is really no more than an enlargement of the business that could be achieved by other means without triggering voting rights. For instance, a corporation purchasing assets need not secure approval of its stockholders to issue already authorized shares to the seller. Nor would voting rights exist if a corporation offered its own authorized shares in exchange for the shares of another corporation and thereby gained control, or if the corporation were to sell its authorized shares for cash and then use the proceeds of the sale to purchase assets. When business needs demand that the acquisition take the form of a merger rather than a purchase of assets or shares, the premise of the statute is that the merger should not require a stockholder vote when other procedures with nearly identical economic consequences do not require a stockholder vote. Stated otherwise, [§ 251(f)] puts mergers more on a parity with acquisition of assets or shares so far as the legal requirements are concerned.

———

(3) Short–Form Mergers

———

DEL. GEN. CORP. LAW § 253

[See Statutory Supplement]

———

REV. MODEL BUS. CORP. ACT § 11.04

[See Statutory Supplement]

———

NOTE ON SHORT–FORM MERGERS

Most of the major corporate statutes now include provisions authorizing the so-called short-form merger, under which certain parent-subsidiary mergers can be effected simply by vote of the parent's board—that is, without a vote of the parent's or the subsidiary's shareholders, without appraisal rights in the parent's shareholders, and frequently without a vote of the subsidiary's board. Most of the early short-form statutes were applicable only to mergers involving a parent and its 100–percent–owned subsidiary, and were probably conceived as procedural in nature, designed to simplify the mechanics of mergers. Today, however, the reach of short-form merger provisions has been substantively extended in two important ways. First, many such provisions are now applicable to mergers between parents and less–than–100–percent–owned subsidiaries—typically, although not invariably, the floor is set at 90 percent. Second, it has been held that the purpose of these statutes is to provide the parent corporation with a means of eliminating the minority shareholder's interest in the enterprise by issuing cash rather than stock to the minority.[1] To the extent this view is followed, these statutory provisions operate as *cash-out* rather than *merger* statutes. Furthermore, they are cash-out statutes that run in one direction only: the parent can force the minority to sell at any time, but the minority cannot force the parent to buy.

(e) TAX AND ACCOUNTING ASPECTS OF CORPORATE COMBINATIONS

NOTE ON TAX AND ACCOUNTING TREATMENTS

1. *Tax Treatment.* Much is made of taxation as a principal motive for corporate combinations, but this factor, while significant, can be exaggerated. Whatever its role as a motive, taxation is often critical in determining *how* a combination will be effected. The principal issue is whether the combination will be tax-free—which means, essentially, that taxes on the transferor's gain will be postponed, that the basis in the stock or property received will remain the same, and that past operating losses of both companies can be carried over to apply against future earnings. See IRC §§ 354(a)(1), 358, 361(a), 381, 382.

In general, the Code provides three basic routes by which a tax-free combination—or, in tax parlance, a "reorganization"—can be achieved. These routes are popularly known as Type A, B, and C reorganizations, and are the tax counterparts of statutory mergers, stock-for-stock combinations, and stock-for-assets combinations, respectively.

(a) A "Type A" reorganization—covered by IRC § 368(a)(1)(A)—is defined as a statutory merger or consolidation.

(b) A "Type B" reorganization—covered by § 368(a)(1)(B)—is defined as the acquisition by one corporation, in exchange solely for all or part of its voting stock (or the voting stock of a parent

---

1. See Joseph v. Wallace–Murray Corp., 354 Mass. 477, 238 N.E.2d 360 (1968); Willcox v. Stern, 18 N.Y.2d 195, 273 N.Y.S.2d 38, 219 N.E.2d 401 (1966); Beloff v. Consolidated Edison Co., 300 N.Y. 11, 87 N.E.2d 561 (1949).

corporation) of stock of another corporation, if the acquiring corporation has control of the acquired corporation immediately after the acquisition. Control is defined by § 368(c) as the ownership of stock possessing at least 80 percent of total combined voting power, plus at least 80 percent of the total number of shares of all other classes of stock.

(c) A "Type C" reorganization—covered by § 368(a)(1)(C)—is defined as the acquisition by one corporation, in exchange for all or part of its voting stock (or the voting stock of a parent corporation), of substantially all the properties of another corporation.

In a Type B reorganization the consideration given by the acquiring corporation must consist solely of voting stock. In a Type C reorganization the consideration must consist primarily of voting stock, but the use of money or other property is permitted if at least 80 percent of the fair market value of all the property of the transferor corporation is acquired for voting stock.[1] Section 368(a)(1)(A), which covers Type A reorganizations, does not explicitly restrict the consideration issued by the survivor to voting stock, or indeed to stock. Thus the survivor in a statutory merger can use consideration other than voting stock—including bonds, nonvoting stock, short-term notes, and cash. However, if property other than "stock or securities" is permissibly issued to the transferor or its shareholders under a Type A or Type C reorganization, gain will be recognized in an amount not exceeding the value of this property or "boot." IRC § 356. Furthermore, under the "continuity of interest" doctrine, in a statutory merger the transferor's shareholders must receive a significant equity interest in the survivor if the merger is to qualify as a tax-free reorganization. See Treas.Reg. § 1.368–1(b), (c). In Helvering v. Minnesota Tea Co., 296 U.S. 378, 56 S.Ct. 269, 80 L.Ed. 284 (1935), the Supreme Court held that under this doctrine the equity issued to the transferor must represent a "substantial part of the value of the [transferred assets]" and that 56 percent was sufficient under this standard. See also May B. Kass, 60 T.C. 218 (1973) (16 percent insufficient); Yoc Heating Corp., 61 T.C. 168 (1973) (15 percent insufficient).

2. *Accounting Aspects.* Although in theory accounting statements should simply report the results of business decisions, in practice business decisions are frequently controlled by the manner in which they will be accounted for. This is nowhere more true than in the area of business combinations.

There are two basic methods of accounting for business combinations—purchase, and pooling of interests. Under the *purchase* method, a combination is accounted for as an acquisition by one corporation (herein called A) of another (herein called B). Accordingly, A records B's assets at A's cost—i.e., the price A paid to effect the combination. If that price exceeds the fair value of B's tangible

---

1. IRC § 368(a)(2)(B). The survivor's assumption of the transferor's liabilities is not treated as money paid for the transfer-or's property unless the survivor uses consideration other than voting stock. Id.

assets, the excess is recorded as "goodwill." Under the *pooling of interests* method, a combination is accounted for as a uniting of ownership interests. Accordingly, A records B's assets at B's costs, and the assets, liabilities, and equity accounts of A and B are then carried forward at their combined historical or book values.

The two methods can be illustrated by the following example. Suppose A engages in a combination with B involving the issuance by A of $4000 in A common stock (with a par value of $400), in exchange for all of B's assets and the assumption by A of B's liabilities of $1000, i.e., a total price of $5000. A's business has a fair market value of $7000. B's business, if sold as a going concern, has a fair market value of $5000, and its physical assets have a fair market value of $3800 ($3300 plant and $500 inventory). The results under the pooling and purchase methods are as follows:

	A's Pre-Combination Balance Sheet	B's Pre-Combination Balance Sheet	A's Post-Combination Balance Sheet Under Pooling Accounting	A's Post-Combination Balance Sheet Under Purchase Accounting
Plant	$800	$2,000	$2,800	$4,100
Inventory	$200	$ 500	$ 700	$ 700
Goodwill	—	—	—	$1,200
Liabilities	$ 0	$1,000	$1,000	$1,000
Stated Capital	$500	$ 700	$ 900 (1)	$ 900 (1)
Capital Surplus	$300	$ 0	$ 600 (2)	$3,900 (4)
Earned Surplus	$200	$ 800	$1,000 (3)	$ 200 (5)

Notes: (1) Under either purchase or pooling accounting, A adds to its stated capital the par value of the shares it issues to effect the combination.

(2) Under pooling accounting, A adds to its capital surplus the amount of B's equity ($1500), minus the increases in A's stated capital ($400) and earned surplus ($800).

(3) Under pooling accounting, A adds to its earned surplus the amount of B's earned surplus.

(4) Under purchase accounting, A adds to its capital surplus the value of the consideration received for its stock ($4000), minus the amount of that consideration allocated to stated capital ($400).

(5) Under purchase accounting, A's earned surplus is not increased by B's, since the transaction is treated as if A was acquiring assets, rather than combining.

(f) THE STOCK MODES AND THE DE FACTO MERGER THEORY

We now pass to a consideration of two newer modes of corporate combination—stock-for-assets and stock-for-stock. (For a description of these modes, see Section 1(a).) Several statutes have come directly to grips with these modes (see Section (f)(2), infra), but traditional corporate statutes still fail to deal with them explicitly. In cases decided under the traditional statutes, there has been a sharp division as to exactly which statutory provisions are applicable. A stock-for-assets combination, for example, might be viewed as either (1) a merger, or (2) a purchase and sale of the tranferor's assets, effected through the issuance of stock by the survivor. The rights of shareholders will often differ sharply according to which view is taken. For a *merger,* the traditional statutes usually require approval by a majority or two-thirds of the outstanding voting shares of each constituent, and normally give appraisal rights to shareholders of both constituents. For a *sale of substantially all assets,* the traditional statutes speak only to the rights of the transferor's shareholders (except insofar as they confer on the board the power to issue authorized but unissued stock, or the power to determine the consideration for which stock can be issued). While the traditional statutes normally do require approval by the transferor's shareholders, they do not invariably confer appraisal rights even on those shareholders. Critical shareholder rights may therefore depend on precisely how a corporate combination is viewed. In fact, the desire to accomplish a corporate combination without giving shareholders voting or appraisal rights, or at least holding such rights to a minimum, has probably been a major impetus behind the rise of the stock modes.

(1) Stock–for–Assets Combinations

HARITON v. ARCO ELECTRONICS, INC.
Supreme Court of Delaware, 1963.
41 Del.Ch. 74, 188 A.2d 123.

SOUTHERLAND, Chief Justice: This case involves a sale of assets under § 271 of the corporation law, 8 Del.C. It presents for decision the question presented, but not decided, in Heilbrunn v. Sun Chemical Corporation, 38 Del.Ch. 321, 150 A.2d 755. It may be stated as follows:

A sale of assets is effected under § 271 in consideration of shares of stock of the purchasing corporation. The agreement of sale embodies also a plan to dissolve the selling corporation and distribute the shares so received to the stockholders of the seller, so as to accomplish the same result as would be accomplished by a merger of the seller into the purchaser. Is the sale legal?

The facts are these:

The defendant Arco and Loral Electronics Corporation, a New York corporation, are both engaged, in somewhat different forms, in the electronic equipment business. In the summer of 1961 they negotiated for an amalgamation of the companies. As of October 27,

1961, they entered into a "Reorganization Agreement and Plan." The provisions of this Plan pertinent here are in substance as follows:

　　1.　Arco agrees to sell all its assets to Loral in consideration (*inter alia*) of the issuance to it of 283,000 shares of Loral.

　　2.　Arco agrees to call a stockholders meeting for the purpose of approving the Plan and the voluntary dissolution.

　　3.　Arco agrees to distribute to its stockholders all the Loral shares received by it as a part of the complete liquidation of Arco.*

At the Arco meeting all the stockholders voting (about 80%) approved the Plan. It was thereafter consummated.

Plaintiff, a stockholder who did not vote at the meeting, sued to enjoin the consummation of the Plan on the grounds (1) that it was illegal, and (2) that it was unfair. The second ground was abandoned. Affidavits and documentary evidence were filed, and defendant moved for summary judgment and dismissal of the complaint. The Vice Chancellor granted the motion and plaintiff appeals.

The question before us we have stated above. Plaintiff's argument that the sale is illegal runs as follows:

The several steps taken here accomplish the same result as a merger of Arco into Loral. In a "true" sale of assets, the stockholder of the seller retains the right to elect whether the selling company shall continue as a holding company. Moreover, the stockholder of the selling company is forced to accept an investment in a new enterprise without the right of appraisal granted under the merger statute. § 271 cannot therefore be legally combined with a dissolution proceeding under § 275 and a consequent distribution of the purchaser's stock. Such a proceeding is a misuse of the power granted under § 271, and a *de facto* merger results.

The foregoing is a brief summary of plaintiff's contention.

Plaintiff's contention that this sale has achieved the same result as a merger is plainly correct. The same contention was made to us in Heilbrunn v. Sun Chemical Corporation, 38 Del.Ch. 321, 150 A.2d 755. Accepting it as correct, we noted that this result is made possible by the overlapping scope of the merger statute and section 271, mentioned in Sterling v. Mayflower Hotel Corporation, 33 Del. Ch. 293, 93 A.2d 107, 38 A.L.R.2d 425. We also adverted to the increased use, in connection with corporate reorganization plans, of § 271 instead of the merger statute. Further, we observed that no Delaware case has held such procedure to be improper, and that two cases appear to assume its legality. Finch v. Warrior Cement Corporation, 16 Del.Ch. 44, 141 A. 54, and Argenbright v. Phoenix Finance Co., 21 Del.Ch. 288, 187 A. 124. But we were not required in the *Heilbrunn* case to decide the point.

* According to the Vice Chancellor's opinion below, 40 Del.Ch. 326, 182 A.2d 22 (1962), the agreement also provided that Loral would assume and pay all of Arco's debts and liabilities, and that after the closing date Arco would not engage in any business or activity except as might be required to complete the liquidation and dissolution of Arco. (Footnote by ed.)

We now hold that the reorganization here accomplished through § 271 and a mandatory plan of dissolution and distribution is legal. This is so because the sale-of-assets statute and the merger statute are independent of each other. They are, so to speak, of equal dignity, and the framers of a reorganization plan may resort to either type of corporate mechanics to achieve the desired end. This is not an anomalous result in our corporation law. As the Vice Chancellor pointed out, the elimination of accrued dividends, though forbidden under a charter amendment (Keller v. Wilson & Co., 21 Del.Ch. 391, 190 A. 115) may be accomplished by a merger. Federal United Corporation v. Havender, 24 Del.Ch. 318, 11 A.2d 331.

In Langfelder v. Universal Laboratories, D.C., 68 F.Supp. 209, Judge Leahy commented upon "the general theory of the Delaware Corporation Law that action taken pursuant to the authority of the various sections of that law constitute acts of independent legal significance and their validity is not dependent on other sections of the Act." 68 F.Supp. 211, footnote.

In support of his contentions of a *de facto* merger plaintiff cites Finch v. Warrior Cement Corporation, 16 Del.Ch. 44, 141 A. 54, and Drug Inc. v. Hunt, 5 W.W.Harr. 339, 35 Del. 339, 168 A. 87. They are patently inapplicable. Each involved a disregard of the statutory provisions governing sales of assets. Here it is admitted that the provisions of the statute were fully complied with.

Plaintiff concedes, as we read his brief, that if the several steps taken in this case had been taken separately they would have been legal. That is, he concedes that a sale of assets, followed by a separate proceeding to dissolve and distribute, would be legal, even though the same result would follow. This concession exposes the weakness of his contention. To attempt to make any such distinction between sales under § 271 would be to create uncertainty in the law and invite litigation.

We are in accord with the Vice Chancellor's ruling, and the judgment below is affirmed.

NOTE ON HEILBRUNN v. SUN CHEM. CORP.

In *Hariton,* suit was brought by a shareholder of the *transferor* in a stock-for-assets combination. In the earlier case of Heilbrunn v. Sun Chem. Corp., 38 Del.Ch. 321, 150 A.2d 755 (1959), referred to in the *Hariton* opinion, suit was brought by the shareholders of Sun, the *survivor* in a stock-for-assets combination between Sun and Ansbacher. Plaintiff claimed that the transaction was a merger, and therefore gave rise to appraisal rights. The court rejected this claim:

> The argument that the result of this transaction is substantially the same as the result that would have followed a merger may be readily accepted. As plaintiffs correctly say, the Ansbacher enterprise is continued in altered form as a part of Sun. This is ordinarily a typical characteristic of a merger. . . . Moreover

the plan of reorganization *requires* the dissolution of Ansbacher and the distribution to its stockholders of the Sun stock received by it for the assets. As a part of the plan, the Ansbacher stockholders are compelled to receive Sun stock. From the viewpoint of Ansbacher, the result is the same as if Ansbacher had formally merged into Sun.

This result is made possible, of course, by the overlapping scope of the merger statute and the statute authorizing the sale of all the corporate assets. . . .

Our Court of Chancery has said that the appraisal right is given to the stockholder in compensation for his former right at common law to prevent a merger. . . . By the use of the sale-of-assets method of reorganization, it is contended, he has been unjustly deprived of this right.

. . . [W]e do not reach this question, because we fail to see how any injury has been inflicted upon the Sun stockholders. Their corporation has simply acquired property and paid for it in shares of stock. The business of Sun will go on as before, with additional assets. The Sun stockholder is not forced to accept stock in another corporation. Nor has the reorganization changed the essential nature of the enterprise of the purchasing corporation. . . .

FARRIS v. GLEN ALDEN CORP.

Supreme Court of Pennsylvania, 1958.
393 Pa. 427, 143 A.2d 25.

COHEN, Justice. We are required to determine on this appeal whether, as a result of a "Reorganization Agreement" executed by the officers of Glen Alden Corporation and List Industries Corporation, and approved by the shareholders of the former company, the rights and remedies of a dissenting shareholder accrue to the plaintiff.

Glen Alden is a Pennsylvania corporation engaged principally in the mining of anthracite coal and lately in the manufacture of air conditioning units and fire-fighting equipment. In recent years the company's operating revenue has declined substantially, and in fact, its coal operations have resulted in tax loss carryovers of approximately $14,000,000. In October 1957, List, a Delaware holding company owning interests in motion picture theaters, textile companies and real estate, and to a lesser extent, in oil and gas operations, warehouses and aluminum piston manufacturing, purchased through a wholly owned subsidiary 38.5% of Glen Alden's outstanding stock.[1] This acquisition enabled List to place three of its directors on the Glen Alden board.

1. Of the purchase price of $8,719,109,
$5,000,000 was borrowed.

On March 20, 1958, the two corporations entered into a "reorganization agreement," subject to stockholder approval, which contemplated the following actions:

1. Glen Alden is to acquire all of the assets of List, excepting a small amount of cash reserved for the payment of List's expenses in connection with the transaction. These assets include over $8,000,000 in cash held chiefly in the treasuries of List's wholly owned subsidiaries.

2. In consideration of the transfer, Glen Alden is to issue 3,621,703 shares of stock to List. List in turn is to distribute the stock to its shareholders at a ratio of five shares of Glen Alden stock for each six shares of List stock. In order to accomplish the necessary distribution, Glen Alden is to increase the authorized number of its shares of capital stock from 2,500,000 shares to 7,500,000 shares without according preemptive rights to the present shareholders upon the issuance of any such shares.

3. Further, Glen Alden is to assume all of List's liabilities including a $5,000,000 note incurred by List in order to purchase Glen Alden stock in 1957, outstanding stock options, incentive stock options plans, and pension obligations.

4. Glen Alden is to change its corporate name from Glen Alden Corporation to List Alden Corporation.

5. The present directors of both corporations are to become directors of List Alden.

6. List is to be dissolved and List Alden is to then carry on the operations of both former corporations.

Two days after the agreement was executed notice of the annual meeting of Glen Alden to be held on April 11, 1958, was mailed to the shareholders together with a proxy statement analyzing the reorganization agreement and recommending its approval as well as approval of certain amendments to Glen Alden's articles of incorporation and bylaws necessary to implement the agreement. At this meeting the holders of a majority of the outstanding shares, (not including those owned by List), voted in favor of a resolution approving the reorganization agreement.

On the day of the shareholders' meeting, plaintiff, a shareholder of Glen Alden, filed a complaint in equity against the corporation and its officers seeking to enjoin them temporarily until final hearing, and perpetually thereafter, from executing and carrying out the agreement.[2]

The gravamen of the complaint was that the notice of the annual shareholders' meeting did not conform to the requirements of the Business Corporation Law, 15 P.S. § 2852–1 et seq., in three respects: (1) It did not give notice to the shareholders that the true

2. The plaintiff also sought to enjoin the shareholders of Glen Alden from approving the reorganization agreement and from adopting amendments to Glen Alden's articles of incorporation, certificate of incorporation and bylaws in implementation of the agreement. However, apparently because of the shortness of time, this prayer was refused by the court.

intent and purpose of the meeting was to effect a merger or consolidation of Glen Alden and List; (2) It failed to give notice to the shareholders of their right to dissent to the plan of merger or consolidation and claim fair value for their shares, and (3) It did not contain copies of the text of certain sections of the Business Corporation Law as required.[3]

By reason of these omissions, plaintiff contended that the approval of the reorganization agreement by the shareholders at the annual meeting was invalid and unless the carrying out of the plan were enjoined, he would suffer irreparable loss by being deprived of substantial property rights.[4]

The defendants answered admitting the material allegations of fact in the complaint but denying that they gave rise to a cause of action because the transaction complained of was a purchase of corporate assets as to which shareholders had no rights of dissent or appraisal. For these reasons the defendants then moved for judgment on the pleadings.[5]

The court below concluded that the reorganization agreement entered into between the two corporations was a plan for a *de facto* merger, and that therefore the failure of the notice of the annual meeting to conform to the pertinent requirements of the merger provisions of the Business Corporation Law rendered the notice defective and all proceedings in furtherance of the agreement void. Wherefore, the court entered a final decree denying defendants' motion for judgment on the pleadings, entering judgment upon plaintiff's complaint and granting the injunctive relief therein sought. This appeal followed.

When use of the corporate form of business organization first became widespread, it was relatively easy for courts to define a "merger" or a "sale of assets" and to label a particular transaction as one or the other. See, e.g., 15 Fletcher, Corporations §§ 7040–7045 (rev. vol. 1938); In re Buist's Estate, 1929, 297 Pa. 537, 541, 147 A. 606; Koehler v. St. Mary's Brewing Co., 1910, 228 Pa. 648, 653–654, 77 A. 1016. But prompted by the desire to avoid the impact of adverse, and to obtain the benefits of favorable, government regulations, particularly federal tax laws, new accounting and legal tech-

3. The proxy statement included the following declaration: "Appraisal Rights.

"In the opinion of counsel, the shareholders of neither Glen Alden nor List Industries will have any rights of appraisal or similar rights of dissenters with respect to any matter to be acted upon at their respective meetings."

4. The complaint also set forth that the exchange of shares of Glen Alden's stock for those of List would constitute a violation of the pre-emptive rights of Glen Alden shareholders as established by the law of Pennsylvania at the time of Glen Alden's incorporation in 1917. The defendants answered that under both statute and prior common law no pre-emptive rights existed with respect to stock issued in exchange for property.

5. Counsel for the defendants concedes that if the corporation is required to pay the dissenting shareholders the appraised fair value of their shares, the resultant drain of cash would prevent Glen Alden from carrying out the agreement. On the other hand, plaintiff contends that if the shareholders had been told of their rights as dissenters, rather than specifically advised that they had no such rights, the resolution approving the reorganization agreement would have been defeated.

niques were developed by lawyers and accountants which interwove the elements characteristic of each, thereby creating hybrid forms of corporate amalgamation. Thus, it is no longer helpful to consider an individual transaction in the abstract and solely by reference to the various elements therein determine whether it is a "merger" or a "sale". Instead, to determine properly the nature of a corporate transaction, we must refer not only to all the provisions of the agreement, but also to the consequences of the transaction and to the purposes of the provisions of the corporation law said to be applicable. We shall apply this principle to the instant case.

Section 908, subd. A of the Pennsylvania Business Corporation Law provides: "If any shareholder of a domestic corporation which becomes a party to a plan of merger or consolidation shall object to such plan of merger or consolidation . . . such shareholder shall be entitled to . . . [the fair value of his shares upon surrender of the share certificate or certificates representing his shares]." Act of May 5, 1933, P.L. 364, as amended, 15 P.S. § 2852–908, subd. A.[6]

This provision had its origin in the early decision of this Court in Lauman v. Lebanon Valley R.R. Co., 1858, 30 Pa. 42. There a shareholder who objected to the consolidation of his company with another was held to have a right in the absence of statute to treat the consolidation as a dissolution of his company and to receive the value of his shares upon their surrender.

The rationale of the Lauman case, and of the present section of the Business Corporation Law based thereon, is that when a corporation combines with another so as to lose its essential nature and alter the original fundamental relationships of the shareholders among themselves and to the corporation, a shareholder who does not wish to continue his membership therein may treat his membership in the original corporation as terminated and have the value of his shares paid to him. See Lauman v. Lebanon Valley R.R. Co., supra, 30 Pa. at pages 46–47. See also Bloch v. Baldwin Locomotive Works, C.P. Del.1950, 75 Pa.Dist. & Co.R. 24, 35–38.

Does the combination outlined in the present "reorganization" agreement so fundamentally change the corporate character of Glen Alden and the interest of the plaintiff as a shareholder therein, that to refuse him the rights and remedies of a dissenting shareholder would in reality force him to give up his stock in one corporation and against his will accept shares in another? If so, the combination is a merger within the meaning of section 908, subd. A of the corporation law. See Bloch v. Baldwin Locomotive Works, supra. Cf. Marks v. Autocar Co., D.C.E.D.Pa.1954, 153 F.Supp. 768. See also Troupiansky v. Henry Disston & Sons, D.C.E.D.Pa.1957, 151 F.Supp. 609.

---

6. Furthermore, section 902, subd. B provides that notice of the proposed merger and of the right to dissent thereto must be given the shareholders. "There shall be included in, or enclosed with . . . notice [of meeting of shareholders to vote on plan of merger] a copy or a summary of the plan of merger or plan of consolidation, as the case may be, and . . . a copy of subsection A of section 908 and of subsections B, C and D of section 515 of this act." Act of May 5, 1933, P.L. 364, § 902, subd. B, as amended, 15 P.S. § 2852–902, subd. B.

If the reorganization agreement were consummated plaintiff would find that the "List Alden" resulting from the amalgamation would be quite a different corporation than the "Glen Alden" in which he is now a shareholder. Instead of continuing primarily as a coal mining company, Glen Alden would be transformed, after amendment of its articles of incorporation, into a diversified holding company whose interests would range from motion picture theaters to textile companies. Plaintiff would find himself a member of a company with assets of $169,000,000 and a long-term debt of $38,000,000 in lieu of a company one-half that size and with but one-seventh the long-term debt.

While the administration of the operations, and properties of Glen Alden as well as List would be in the hands of management common to both companies, since all executives of List would be retained in List Alden, the control of Glen Alden would pass to the directors of List; for List would hold eleven of the seventeen directorships on the new board of directors.

As an aftermath of the transaction plaintiff's proportionate interest in Glen Alden would have been reduced to only two-fifths of what it presently is because of the issuance of an additional 3,621,703 shares to List which would not be subject to pre-emptive rights. In fact, ownership of Glen Alden would pass to the stockholders of List who would hold 76.5% of the outstanding shares as compared with but 23.5% retained by the present Glen Alden shareholders.

Perhaps the most important consequence to the plaintiff, if he were denied the right to have his shares redeemed at their fair value, would be the serious financial loss suffered upon consummation of the agreement. While the present book value of his stock is $38 a share after combination it would be worth only $21 a share. In contrast, the shareholders of List who presently hold stock with a total book value of $33,000,000 or $7.50 a share, would receive stock with a book value of $76,000,000 or $21 a share.

Under these circumstances it may well be said that if the proposed combination is allowed to take place without right of dissent, plaintiff would have his stock in Glen Alden taken away from him and the stock of a new company thrust upon him in its place. He would be projected against his will into a new enterprise under terms not of his own choosing. It was to protect dissident shareholders against just such a result that this Court one hundred years ago in the Lauman case, and the legislature thereafter in section 908, subd. A, granted the right of dissent. And it is to accord that protection to the plaintiff that we conclude that the combination proposed in the case at hand is a merger within the intendment of section 908, subd. A.

Nevertheless, defendants contend that the 1957 amendments to sections 311 and 908 of the corporation law preclude us from reaching this result and require the entry of judgment in their favor. Subsection F of section 311 dealing with the voluntary transfer of corporate assets provides: "The shareholders of a business corporation which acquires by sale, lease or exchange all or substantially all of the property of another corporation by the issuance of stock, securities or otherwise shall not be entitled to the rights and remedies of dissenting shareholders. . . ." Act of July 11, 1957, P.L. 711, § 1, 15 P.S. § 2852–311, subd. F.

And the amendment to section 908 reads as follows: "The right of dissenting shareholders . . . shall not apply to the purchase by a corporation of assets whether or not the consideration therefor be money or property, real or personal, including shares or bonds or other evidences of indebtedness of such corporation. The shareholders of such corporation shall have no right to dissent from any such purchase." Act of July 11, 1957, P.L. 711, § 1, 15 P.S. § 2852–908, subd. C.

Defendants view these amendments as abridging the right of shareholders to dissent to a transaction between two corporations which involves a transfer of assets for a consideration even though the transfer has all the legal incidents of a merger. They claim that only if the merger is accomplished in accordance with the prescribed statutory procedure does the right of dissent accrue. In support of this position they cite to us the comment on the amendments by the Committee on Corporation Law of the Pennsylvania Bar Association, the committee which originally drafted these provisions. The comment states that the provisions were intended to overrule cases which granted shareholders the right to dissent to a sale of assets when accompanied by the legal incidents of a merger. See 61 Ann.Rep.Pa.Bar Ass'n. 277, 284 (1957).[7] Whatever may have been the intent of the *committee,* there is no evidence to indicate that the *legislature* intended the 1957 amendments to have the effect contended for. But furthermore, the language of these two provisions does not support the opinion of the committee and is inept to achieve any such purpose. The amendments of 1957 do not provide that a transaction between two corporations which has the effect of a merger but which includes a transfer of assets for consideration is to be exempt from the protective provisions of sections 908, subd. A and 515. They provide only that the shareholders of a corporation which acquires the property or purchases the assets of another corporation, *without more,* are not entitled to the right to dissent from the transaction. So, as in the

---

7. "The amendment to Section 311 expressly provides that a sale, lease or exchange of substantially all corporate assets in connection with its liquidation or dissolution is subject to the provisions of Article XI of the Act, and that no consent or authorization of shareholders other than what is required by Article XI is necessary. The recent decision in Marks v. Autocar Co., D.C.E.D.Pa., Civil Action No. 16075 [153 F.Supp. 768] is to the contrary. This amendment, together with the proposed amendment to Section 1104 expressly permitting the directors in liquidating the corporation to sell only such assets as may be required to pay its debts and distribute any assets remaining among shareholders (Section 1108, [subd.] B now so provides in the case of receivers) have the effect of overruling Marks v. Autocar Co. case which permits a shareholder dissenting from such a sale to obtain the fair value of his shares. The Marks case relies substantially on Bloch v. Baldwin Locomotive Works, 75 [Pa.] Dist. & Co. R. 24, also believed to be an undesirable decision. That case permitted a holder of stock in a corporation which *purchased* for stock all the assets of another corporation to obtain the fair value of his shares. That case is also in effect overruled by the new Sections 311 [subd.] F and 908 [subd.] C." 61 Ann.Rep. Pa.Bar Ass'n. 277, 284 (1957).

present case, when as part of a transaction between two corporations, one corporation dissolves, its liabilities are assumed by the survivor, its executives and directors take over the management and control of the survivor, and, as consideration for the transfer, its stockholders acquire a majority of the shares of stock of the survivor, then the transaction is no longer simply a purchase of assets or acquisition of property to which sections 311, subd. F and 908, subd. C apply, but a merger governed by section 908, subd. A of the corporation law. To divest shareholders of their right of dissent under such circumstances would require express language which is absent from the 1957 amendments.

Even were we to assume that the combination provided for in the reorganization agreement is a "sale of assets" to which section 908, subd. A does not apply, it would avail the defendants nothing; we will not blind our eyes to the realities of the transaction. Despite the designation of the parties and the form employed, Glen Alden does not in fact acquire List, rather, List acquires Glen Alden, cf. Metropolitan Edison Co. v. Commissioner, 3 Cir., 1938, 98 F.2d 807, affirmed sub nom., Helvering v. Metropolitan Edison Co., 1939, 306 U.S. 522, 59 S.Ct. 634, 83 L.Ed. 957, and under section 311, subd. D [8] the right of dissent would remain with the shareholders of Glen Alden.

We hold that the combination contemplated by the reorganization agreement, although consummated by contract rather than in accordance with the statutory procedure, is a merger within the protective purview of sections 908, subd. A and 515 of the corporation law. The shareholders of Glen Alden should have been notified accordingly and advised of their statutory rights of dissent and appraisal. The failure of the corporate officers to take these steps renders the stockholder approval of the agreement at the 1958 shareholders' meeting invalid. The lower court did not err in enjoining the officers and directors of Glen Alden from carrying out this agreement.[9]

Decree affirmed at appellants' costs.**

---

8. "If any shareholder of a business corporation which sells, leases or exchanges all or substantially all of its property and assets otherwise than (1) in the usual and regular course of its business, (2) for the purpose of relocating its business, or (3) in connection with its dissolution and liquidation, shall object to such sale, lease or exchange and comply with the provisions of section 515 of this act, such shareholder shall be entitled to the rights and remedies of dissenting shareholders as therein provided." Act of July 11, 1957, P.L. 711, 15 P.S. § 2852–311, subd. D.

9. Because of our disposition of this appeal, it is unnecessary for us to consider whether the plaintiff had any pre-emptive rights in the proposed issuance of newly authorized shares as payment for the transfer of assets from List, or whether amended sections 908, subd. C and 311, subd. F of the corporation law may consti-

tutionally be applied to the present transaction to divest the plaintiff of his dissenter's rights.

** Pa. §§ 311(F) and 908(B)—numbered §§ 1311(F) and 1908(B) in the annotated statutes—were subsequently amended, and now read as follows:

§ 1311. Voluntary Transfer of Corporate Assets

* * *

F. The shareholders of a business corporation which acquires by purchase, lease or exchange all or substantially all of the property of another corporation by the issuance of shares, evidences of indebtedness or otherwise, with or without assuming the liabilities of such other corporation, shall be entitled to the rights and remedies of dissenting shareholders provided in . . . this act, if any, if, but only if, such acquisition shall have been

NOTE ON FARRIS

It is clear that a major reason for structuring the transaction in *Farris* as a stock-for-assets combination, rather than as a classical merger, was to avoid conferring appraisal rights on the Glen Alden shareholders. (In many cases, the stock-for-assets form is used to deny voting rights to the survivor's shareholders, but this may not have been significant in *Farris* itself.) Given the stock-for-assets mode, why did the parties use the upside-down format, in which the smaller corporation "purchased" the larger corporation's assets? Again, one reason had to do with appraisal rights. List was a Delaware corporation, and under Delaware law in a purchase and sale of assets neither the purchaser's nor the seller's shareholders had appraisal rights. Under Pennsylvania law, however, the seller's shareholders clearly had appraisal rights, while the purchaser's did not—or so counsel thought. Therefore, by making List the seller and Glen Alden the purchaser, the parties hoped to avoid appraisal rights for the shareholders of either corporation. A second reason for the upside-down format may have been a desire to keep alive Glen Alden's tax loss carryover. While the rules governing the survival of such carryovers were complex, in general survival was more likely if the entity of the carryover corporation was left intact. A third reason is given in the Supplemental Brief for Appellee: "In answer to the question of Mr. Justice Bell as to why List did not purchase the assets of Glen Alden, Mr. Littleton answered that the one percent Pennsylvania realty tax on the transfer of [the huge coal-mining] holdings of Glen Alden would make such a sale prohibitive." Following the decision in Farris v. Glen Alden, the two corporations were combined pursuant to a statutory merger. Probably for the reasons just given, Glen Alden was the surviving corporation. The List shareholders received one Glen Alden share for each List share, and the Glen Alden shareholders ended up with five Glen Alden shares for each four they had previously held. New York Times, March 7, 1959; Moody's Industrial Manual 954 (1972).

---

accomplished by the issuance of voting shares of such corporation to be outstanding immediately after the acquisition sufficient to elect a majority of the directors of the corporation.

§ 1908. **Rights of Dissenting Shareholders**

* * *

B. Where a corporation acquires assets by purchase, lease or exchange, by the issuance of shares, evidences of indebtedness or otherwise, with or without assuming liabilities other than by the procedure for merger or consolidation prescribed in this Article IX, the rights, if any, of dissenting shareholders shall be governed by section [1311] and not by this section.

(Footnote by ed.)

(2) Codified Treatment

NEW YORK STOCK EXCHANGE, LISTED COMPANY MANUAL § 312.00

Shareholder approval is a prerequisite to listing securities to be issued [by a company listed on the Exchange] in connection with the following: . . .

3. The acquisition, direct or indirect, of a business, a company, tangible or intangible assets or property or securities representing any such interests . . .

(b) Where the present or potential issuance of common stock or securities convertible into common stock [by the listed company, to effect the acquisition] could result in an increase in outstanding common shares of 18½ or more; or

(c) Where the present or potential issuance of common stock and any other consideration has a combined fair value of 18½% or more of the market value of the outstanding common shares. . . .

The minimum vote that will constitute stockholder approval for these purposes is defined as "approval by a majority of votes cast . . . on the particular matter, provided that the total vote cast on the proposal represents over 50% in interest of all securities entitled to vote on the proposal."

(The American Stock Exchange has a comparable rule. See CCH, American Stock Exchange Guide 8938. See generally M. Eisenberg, The Structure of the Corporation 234–36, 249–50 (1976).)

CAL. CORP. CODE §§ 152, 160, 168, 181, 187, 194.5, 1001, 1101, 1200, 1201, 1300

[See Statutory Supplement]

(g) TRIANGULAR MERGERS AND SHARE EXCHANGES

TERRY v. PENN CENTRAL CORP.

United States Court of Appeals, Third Circuit, 1981.
668 F.2d 188.

Before ADAMS, MARIS and HIGGINBOTHAM, Circuit Judges. . . .

ADAMS, Circuit Judge.

The Penn Central Corporation ("Penn Central"), an appellee in this case, has sought to acquire Colt Industries Inc. ("Colt"), also an appellee, by merging Colt with PCC Holdings, Inc. ("Holdings"), a wholly-owned subsidiary of Penn Central. Howard L. Terry and W.H. Hunt, the appellants, are shareholders of Penn Central who objected to the transaction. In a diversity action before the United States District Court for the Eastern District of Pennsylvania, appellants sought injunctive and declaratory relief to enforce voting and dissenters' rights to which appellants asserted they were entitled. Appellants further sought to enjoin Holdings from proceeding with the proposed merger, and in particular moved to enjoin a vote on the transaction, scheduled for October 29, 1981, by the shareholders of Penn Central. In an opinion issued on October 22, 1981, Judge Pollak denied appellants' requests. Appellants thereupon filed an appeal in this Court, and then petitioned for a temporary injunction against the proposed shareholder vote until the appeal on the merits of the district court order could be heard. On October 27, following oral argument, we entered an order denying the petition for temporary injunction, stating that appellants had failed to demonstrate a sufficient likelihood of prevailing on the merits. C.A. No. 81–3955. The shareholders of Penn Central voted, as scheduled, on October 29. Pursuant to an expedited hearing schedule, the appeal from the district court's denial of injunctive and declaratory relief was submitted to this Court following oral argument on November 5.

After argument on appeal, the shareholders disapproved of the merger, and the corporations thereafter publicly announced their abandonment of this particular merger. Penn Central, however, has not abandoned its proposed series of acquisitions, of which the Colt acquisition was merely one instance.

I.

Penn Central is the successor to the Penn Central Transportation Corporation, which underwent a reorganization under the bankruptcy laws that was completed in 1978. No longer involved in the railroading business, Penn Central, since 1978, has had the advantage, for tax purposes, of a large loss carry-forward. In order to put that loss carry-forward to its best use, Penn Central has embarked on a program of acquiring corporations whose profits could be sheltered. To this end Penn Central created Holdings, a wholly-owned subsidiary which was to acquire the businesses that Penn Central desired. The first acquisition under the plan was Marathon Manufacturing Company ("Marathon"), in 1979. In the Marathon acquisition, a class of preferred Penn Central stock was created, and 30 million shares of "First Series Preference Stock" was issued to the owners of Marathon stock. Appellants were shareholders of Marathon who thereby obtained shares of this First Series Preference Stock. Terry was promptly elected to the Penn Central board of directors.

In 1981, Penn Central decided upon another acquisition: Colt. The management and directors of Colt and Penn Central agreed upon a merger of Colt into Holdings, compensated for by issuance of a second series of Penn Central preference stock to Colt shareholders. Terry opposed the merger at the directors' meeting, and sought to preclude the consummation of the transaction.

. . . [A]ppellants argue that under Pennsylvania's corporate law, they are entitled to dissent and appraisal rights if the merger is adopted over their opposition.[2] . . .

Because Colt and Penn Central have now announced their abandonment of the proposed merger, the request for injunctive relief considered by the district court is now conceded by all parties to be moot. However, the appellants' request for declaratory relief, which the appellants now contend is moot as well, involves legal questions that go to Penn Central's plan of acquisitions, rather than to the Colt transaction alone, and these questions appear likely to recur in future disputes between the parties here. . . . In a case such as this, a voluntary termination by the parties of the specific activity challenged in the lawsuit—here, the proposed treatment of the dissenting preferred shareholders in the Colt–Holdings plan—does not render the action moot because there is "a reasonable likelihood that the parties or those in privity with them will be involved in a suit on the same issues in the future." American Bible Society v. Blount, 446 F.2d 588, 595 (3d Cir.1971). . . .

III.

Terry and Hunt contend that under Pennsylvania law they are entitled to dissent and appraisal rights if a merger is approved by the Penn Central shareholders. As the district court concluded, this assertion is unsupported by Pennsylvania statute or caselaw. Sitting as a court in diversity, we are not at liberty to diverge from the outcome that the Pennsylvania legislature and the Pennsylvania courts pre-

---

2. In addition, appellants claim a right under Pennsylvania law to require approval of an absolute majority vote of the shares outstanding on the proposed merger, relying on § 902(B), of the Pennsylvania Business Corporation Law (PBCL), 15 P.S. § 1902(B) (Purdon Supp.1981–82). For the reasons discussed in Part III of this opinion, we conclude that Penn Central is not a "party" to the merger, within the technical meaning of the term under that section and the related Section 908 of the PBCL, 15 P.S. § 1908 (Purdon Supp.1981–82). Accordingly, section 902 does not apply to the Penn Central vote on the merger.

scribe. Briefly, appellants' argument is that the proposed merger between Holdings and Colt constitutes a *de facto* merger between Colt and Penn Central, and that the Penn Central shareholders are therefore entitled to the protections for dissenting shareholders that Pennsylvania corporate law provides for shareholders of parties to a merger. Although this reasoning, with its emphasis on the substance of the transaction rather than its formal trappings, may be attractive as a matter of policy, see, e.g., Note, Three–Party Mergers: The Fourth Form of Corporate Acquisition, 57 Va.L.Rev. 1242 (1971), it contravenes the language employed by the Pennsylvania legislature in setting out the rights of shareholders.

Section 908 of the Pennsylvania Business Corporation Law (PBCL), 15 P.S. § 1908, provides that shareholders of corporations that are parties to a plan of merger are entitled to dissent and appraisal rights, but adds that for an acquisition other than such a merger, the only rights are those provided for in Section 311 of the PBCL, 15 P.S. § 1311 (Purdon 1967 & Supp.1981–82). Section 311, in turn, provides for dissent and appraisal rights only when an acquisition has been accomplished by "the issuance of voting shares of such corporation to be outstanding immediately after the acquisition sufficient to elect a majority of the directors of the corporation." In this case the shares of Penn Central stock to be issued in the Colt transaction do not exceed the number of shares already existing, and thus the transaction is not covered by Section 311. Any statutory dissent and appraisal rights for Penn Central shareholders are therefore contingent upon Penn Central's status as a party to the merger within the meaning of Section 908. And as the district court points out, the PBCL describes the parties to a merger as those entities that are *actually* combined into a single corporation. Section 907, 15 P.S. § 1907 (Purdon Supp.1981–82), states that:

> Upon the merger or consolidation becoming effective, the several corporations parties to the plan of merger or consolidation shall be a single corporation which, in the case of a merger, shall be that corporation designated in the plan of merger as the surviving corporation. . . .

At the consummation of the proposed merger plan here, both Holdings and Penn Central would survive as separate entities, and it would therefore appear that Penn Central is not a party within the meaning of . . . Section 907. We can discern no reason to infer that the legislature intended the word "party" to have different meanings in Sections 907 and 908, and accordingly conclude that Penn Central is not a party to the merger.

Appellants argue that Penn Central is nevertheless brought into the amalgamation by the *de facto* merger doctrine as set out in Pennsylvania law in Farris v. Glen Alden Corp., 393 Pa. 427, 143 A.2d 25 (1958). *Farris* was the penultimate step in a *pas de deux* involving the Pennsylvania courts and the Pennsylvania legislature regarding the proper treatment for transactions that reached the same practical result as a merger but avoided the legal form of merger and the concomitant legal obligations. In the 1950s the Pennsylvania courts advanced the doctrine that a transaction having the effect of an amalgamation would be treated as a *de facto* merger. See, e.g., Bloch v. The Baldwin Locomotive Works, 75 Pa.D. & C. 24 (1950). The legislature responded with efforts to constrict the *de facto* merger doctrine. *Farris,* addressing those efforts, held that the doctrine still covered a reorganization agreement that had the effect of merging a large corporation into a smaller corporation. In a 1959 response to *Farris,* the legislature made explicit its objection to earlier cases that found certain transactions to be *de facto* mergers. The legislature enacted a law, modifying *inter alia* Sections 311 and 908, entitled in part:

> An Act . . . changing the law as to . . . the acquisition or transfer of corporate assets, the rights of dissenting shareholders, . . . abolishing the doctrine of de facto mergers or consolidation and reversing the rules laid down in *Bloch v. Baldwin Locomotive Works,* 75 D. & C. 24, and *Marks v. The Autocar Co.,* 153 F.Supp. 768,. . . .

Act of November 10, 1959 (P.L. 1406, No. 502).

Following this explicit statement, the *de facto* merger doctrine has rarely been invoked by the Pennsylvania courts. Only once has the Pennsylvania Supreme Court made reference to it, in In re Jones & Laughlin Steel Corp., 488 Pa. 524, 412 A.2d 1099 (1980). Even there, the Court's reference was oblique. It merely cited *Farris* for the proposition that shareholders have the right to enjoin "proposed unfair or fraudulent corporate actions." 488 Pa. at 533, 412 A.2d at 1104. This Court, sitting in diversity in Knapp v. North American Rockwell Corp., 506 F.2d 361 (3d Cir.1974), cert. denied, 421 U.S. 965, 95 S.Ct. 1955, 44 L.Ed.2d 452 (1975), made reference to the *de facto* merger doctrine to hold that a transaction structured as a sale of assets could nevertheless be deemed a merger for purposes of requiring the merging corporation to assume the acquired corporation's liability for damages to a worker who was injured by a faulty piece of equipment manufactured by the acquired company. Perhaps the broadest application of the doctrine was made in In re Penn Central Securities Litigation, 367 F.Supp. 1158 (E.D.Pa.1973), in which the district court held that the doctrine provided the plaintiffs in that case with standing for a 10b–5 lawsuit alleging *fraud* and also gave rise to dissent and appraisal rights in a triangular merger situation.[6]

None of these cases persuades us that a Pennsylvania court would apply the *de facto* merger doctrine to the situation before us. Al-

---

6. Two other cases in the Eastern District of Pennsylvania have also discussed *Farris* and de facto mergers, each case holding that the transaction before the court did not constitute a *de facto* merger. In Dower v. Mosser Industries, Inc., 488 F.Supp. 1328, 1341 (E.D.Pa.1980), aff'd, 648 F.2d 183 (1981), the district court distinguished *Farris* because the transaction in *Dower,* unlike that in *Farris,* was not fraudulent in any way. In Lopata v. Bemis Co., 383 F.Supp. 342 (E.D.Pa.1974), vacated on other grounds, 517 F.2d 1398 (1975), the district court found *Farris* inapplicable because in *Lopata,* unlike *Farris,* there was no "basic fundamental change in the relationship of the stockholders to their respective corporations." 383 F.Supp. at 345.

though *Jones & Laughlin Steel* suggests that dissent and appraisal rights might be available if fraud or fundamental unfairness were shown, we are not faced with such a situation. No allegation of fraud has been advanced, and the only allegation of fundamental unfairness is that the appellants will, if the merger is consummated, be forced into what they consider a poor investment on the part of Penn Central without the opportunity to receive an appraised value for their stock. Even if appellants' evaluation of the merits of the proposed merger is accurate, poor business judgment on the part of management would not be enough to constitute unfairness cognizable by a court. And the denial of appraisal rights to dissenters cannot constitute fundamental unfairness, or the *de facto* merger doctrine would apply in every instance in which dissenters' rights were sought and the 1959 amendments by the legislature would be rendered nugatory.[7]

The two federal cases invoking the doctrine, *Knapp* and *Penn Central Securities,* are not persuasive as to the applicability of the *de facto* merger to the present situation. *Knapp* was not concerned with the rights of shareholders as the Pennsylvania legislature was in 1959. Although *Penn Central Securities* did hold, in part, that the triangular merger there constituted a *de facto* merger, it is clear from the briefs submitted to the district court in that case that the court was not made aware of the post-*Farris* 1959 amendments or the legislative statement of intent to limit the *de facto* merger doctrine.

In the absence of any explicit guidance to the contrary by the Pennsylvania courts, we conclude that the language of the legislature in 1959 precludes a decision that the transaction in this case constitutes a *de facto* merger sufficient to entitle Penn Central shareholders to dissent and appraisal rights. We therefore hold that appellants do not possess such rights if a transaction such as the one involved here is consummated. . . .

———

REV. MODEL BUS. CORP. ACT §§ 11.02, 11.03, 11.05, 11.06

[See Statutory Supplement]

———

NOTE ON TRIANGULAR MERGERS AND SHARE EXCHANGES

1. *Triangular Mergers.* As the previous section suggests, in many cases a statutory merger would be the preferred form of combination except for a particular disadvantage of that mode which looms large in a given transaction. A number of states have therefore amended their

———

7. A different result might be reached if here, as in *Farris,* the acquiring corporation were significantly smaller than the acquired corporation such that the acquisition greatly transformed the nature of the successor corporation. But in this situation we do not have such a case; after the merger Penn Central would remain a major, diversified corporation, and would continue on the course of acquiring other corporations.

statutory merger provisions to allow new forms of combination, known as "triangular mergers" and "reverse triangular mergers," which carry the advantages of a statutory merger without some of the disadvantages.

A conventional or foreward triangular merger works this way: Assume that Corporations S and T want to engage in a merger in which S will be the survivor and T's shareholders will end up with 100,000 shares of S. In a normal merger this would be accomplished by having S issue 100,000 shares to T's shareholders. In a conventional triangular merger, however, S instead begins by creating a new subsidiary, S/Sub, and then transfers 100,000 shares of its own stock to S/Sub in exchange for all of S/Sub's stock. S/Sub and T then engage in a statutory merger, but instead of issuing its *own* stock to T's shareholders, S/Sub issues its 100,000 shares of S stock. The net result is that T's business is owned by S's wholly owned subsidiary (rather than by S itself, as in a normal merger), and T's shareholders own 100,000 shares of S stock. By use of this technique, S may therefore achieve the advantages of a statutory merger while insulating itself from direct responsibility for T's liabilities.[1]

Such a transaction would probably not have been permissible under the traditional statutory merger provisions, because those provisions usually contemplated that the surviving corporation would issue its *own* shares or securities. In the last 10 or 15 years, however, the merger statutes of most leading corporate jurisdictions have been amended to permit the survivor to issue shares or securities of *any* corporation. (See, e.g., Del. § 251(b)(4).) In tandem with this development, the Internal Revenue Code was amended by adding § 368(a)(2)(D), which permits a conventional triangular merger to qualify as a tax-free A reorganization, if (i) substantially all of T's properties are acquired by S/Sub; (ii) the merger would have qualified as an A reorganization if T had merged directly into S; and (iii) no stock of S/Sub is used in the transaction.

A *reverse* triangular merger proceeds like a conventional triangular merger, except that instead of merging T into S/Sub, S/Sub is merged into T. The merger agreement provides that all previously outstanding T shares are automatically converted into the 100,000 shares of S held by S/Sub, and that all shares in S/Sub (which are held by S) are automatically converted into shares in T. When all the shooting is over, therefore, S/Sub will have disappeared, T will be a wholly owned subsidiary of S, and T's shareholders will own 100,000 shares of S stock. By use of this technique S may therefore achieve the advantages of a statutory merger while preserving T's legal status, which could be important where T has valuable rights under contracts, leases, licenses, or franchises. Under IRC § 368(a)(2)(E), a reverse triangular merger will qualify as a tax-free A reorganization, if (i) T ends up with substantially all of the properties of both S/Sub and T, and (ii) S voting stock is exchanged for at least 80% of T's voting and

---

1. However, a court might impose these liabilities on S under the de facto merger doctrine, on the theory that in effect S itself is a constituent to the merger.

nonvoting stock. (The balance of T's stock can be acquired for other types of consideration.)

An important problem raised by triangular mergers is that they may allow subversion of shareholder voting and appraisal rights, since it can be argued that voting and appraisal rights on the survivor's side are vested in S (as the sole shareholder of S/Sub) rather than in S's shareholders. Ideally this problem should be dealt with by statute. For example, under Cal. §§ 1200(d), 1201, a merger reorganization must be approved by the shareholders of a corporation which is "in control of any constituent . . . corporation . . . and whose equity securities are issued or transferred in the reorganization." Even where a statute does not deal with the problem explicitly, it can be argued that a triangular merger triggers voting and appraisal rights in S's shareholders on the theory that S should be deemed a constituent to the merger, or alternatively that such a result is necessary to prevent subversion of the merger statutes. See generally M. Eisenberg, The Structure of the Corporation 275–315 (1976). This argument was rejected in Terry v. Penn Central Corp., supra, but that case was at least partly controlled by the unusual Pennsylvania legislative history.

2. *Share Exchanges.* The newest mode of combination, inspired by the triangular merger, is known as the share exchange. This mode is similar to a stock-for-stock combination, in that the survivor issues stock in exchange for stock of the acquired corporation. However, in a stock-for-stock combination each shareholder of the acquired corporation makes an individual decision whether or not to sell his stock, and there is no formal action by the acquired corporation itself. In contrast, in a share exchange the shareholders of the acquired corporation vote on whether to engage in the exchange. If the proposed transaction is approved by a majority of that corporation's outstanding shares, *all of the shares* must be surrendered—including those of nonconsenting shareholders (unless they exercise appraisal rights). So far, only a few statutes have authorized share exchanges for ordinary business corporations.

(h) SUBSTANTIVE FAIRNESS; EXCLUSIVITY OF THE APPRAISAL REMEDY

-----

(1) Substantive Fairness

A corporate combination may raise two kinds of fairness issues. First is the problem of substantive fairness, or fairness in exchange—that is, whether the package of rights each shareholder ends up with is the fair equivalent of the package of rights he had before the combination occurred. Second is the problem whether, assuming the test of substantive fairness is met, controlling shareholders can utilize a corporate combination as a vehicle for eliminating minority shareholders. The first issue will be considered in this section; the latter in Section 1(i), infra.

———

STERLING v. MAYFLOWER HOTEL CORP.

Supreme Court of Delaware, 1952.
33 Del.Ch. 293, 93 A.2d 107, 38 A.L.R.2d 425.

SOUTHERLAND, Chief Justice. The principal question presented is whether the terms of a proposed merger of Mayflower Hotel Corporation (herein "Mayflower") into its parent corporation, Hilton Hotels Corporation (herein "Hilton"), are fair to the minority stockholders of Mayflower.

The essential facts are these:

Mayflower and Hilton are both Delaware corporations. Mayflower's sole business is the ownership and operation of the Mayflower Hotel in Washington, D.C. It has outstanding 389,738 shares of common stock of $1 par value. Hilton and its subsidiary corporations are engaged in the business of owning, leasing, operating and managing hotel properties in many of the large centers of population in the country. Hilton has outstanding, in addition to an issue of Convertible Preference stock, 1,592,878 shares of common stock of $5 par value.

On December 18, 1946, Hilton acquired a majority of the outstanding shares of Mayflower. Thereafter it continued to make purchases of Mayflower stock. On or about February 4, 1952, it purchased 21,409 shares at a price of $19.10 a share, and on that date made an offer to all other minority stockholders to buy their shares at the same price. As of March 25, 1952, Hilton owned 321,883 shares, or nearly five-sixths of the outstanding stock.

From the time of the acquisition by Hilton of a majority interest in Mayflower, Hilton's management had contemplated a merger of Mayflower with Hilton. Soon after such acquisition, however, litigation ensued in the District of Columbia between Hilton and certain minority stockholders of Mayflower, not terminated until late in the year 1951. In the early part of 1950 the Mayflower directors discussed the question of ascertaining a fair basis of exchange of Mayflower stock for Hilton stock. All of the Mayflower directors (nine in number) were nominees of Hilton, and it was the view of the board (as well as of the Hilton board) that an independent study should be made by competent and disinterested financial analysts for the purpose of evolving a fair plan of exchange. Three of the members of the board (Messrs. Fleming, Folger and Baxter) had been directors before the acquisition by Hilton of its interest in Mayflower, and appear to have had little or no interest in Hilton. Messrs. Fleming and Folger were of opinion that although the study should be made no definite action should be taken upon the plan thereby to be developed until the Washington litigation should be finally terminated. The other directors deferred to this view.

In the early part of 1950 Standard Research Consultants, Inc., a subsidiary of Standard & Poor, was retained to make the study, and Mr. John G. Haslam, its Vice President, undertook the work. Later he submitted a study which determined a fair basis of exchange of Hilton stock for Mayflower stock to be three-fourths of a share of Hilton for one share of Mayflower. No action was taken on the basis of this study.

The Washington litigation having been finally terminated, Mr. Haslam on January 7, 1952, was again retained to continue and bring up to date his prior study and to develop a fair plan of exchange. Thereafter he submitted his final study (hereinafter referred to as "the Haslam report"), which embodies his conclusion that a fair rate of exchange would be share for share. A plan for a merger upon this basis was approved by the boards of directors of both corporations. The directors—at least the Mayflower directors—appear to have relied largely on the Haslam report to justify their action. A formal agreement of merger was entered into on March 14, 1952, providing for the merger of Mayflower (the constituent corporation) into Hilton (the surviving corporation), as authorized by the provisions of Section 59 of the General Corporation Law, Rev.Code of Del.1935, par. 2091, as amended. Each outstanding share of Mayflower is converted into one share of Hilton. A separate agreement between Hilton and Mayflower provides that for a limited period Hilton will pay $19.10 a share for any Mayflower stock tendered to it by any minority stockholder. At stockholders' meetings held in April the requisite approval of the merger was obtained. At the Mayflower meeting 329,106 shares were voted in favor; 4,645 against. Holders of 35,191 shares of Mayflower who objected to the merger did not vote. The Hilton stockholders voted overwhelmingly to approve the merger.

On April 7, 1952, plaintiffs below (herein "plaintiffs"), holders of 32,295 shares of Mayflower stock, filed their complaint in the court below, seeking injunctive relief against the consummation of the merger, on the ground that the terms of the merger are grossly unfair to the minority stockholders of Mayflower, and that the Mayflower directors entered into the merger agreement in bad faith.

The Chancellor, having issued a temporary restraining order against the consummation of the merger, heard the case on a motion for a preliminary injunction. A large number of affidavits were filed and voluminous depositions were taken. The Chancellor found no fraud or bad faith in the case and concluded that the plan was fair to the minority. He also determined that a quorum of Mayflower directors was present at the board meeting of March 6 when the merger was approved. See 89 A.2d 862. On June 18 he denied injunctive relief, and plaintiffs thereafter appealed.

Plaintiffs' principal contention here, as in the court below, is that the terms of the merger are unfair to Mayflower's minority stockholders. Plaintiffs invoke the settled rule of law that Hilton as majority stockholder of Mayflower and the Hilton directors as its nominees occupy, in relation to the minority, a fiduciary position in dealing with

Mayflower's property. Since they stand on both sides of the transaction, they bear the burden of establishing its entire fairness, and it must pass the test of careful scrutiny by the courts. Keenan v. Eshleman, 23 Del.Ch. 234, 2 A.2d 904, 120 A.L.R. 227; Gottlieb v. Heyden Chemical Corp., Del.Ch., 90 A.2d 660. Defendants agree that their acts must meet this test. We therefore inquire whether the facts sustain the conversion ratio of share for share which forms the basis of the merger agreement.

As the Chancellor observed, the Haslam report forms the principal justification for the terms of the merger. We accordingly examine it.

The report is an elaborate study of some forty pages (including charts) with a long appendix containing analyses of pertinent financial data. The principles upon which it is based are set forth in the Chancellor's opinion. See 89 A.2d page 867. Implicit in the report is the assumption that the legal principles governing the transaction require a comparison of the value of the stock of Hilton with the stock of Mayflower. Since the report is the basis of the conversion terms of the merger agreement, it is in effect directed to a determination of the question whether, upon the conversion of Mayflower stock into Hilton stock, the Mayflower minority stockholder will receive the substantial equivalent in value of the shares he held before the merger. Thus a comparison is required of factors entering into the ascertainment of the values of both stocks. In Haslam's opinion the problem reduces to "a comparison of the operating trends of each of the corporations and of the investment characteristics of the two stock issues." A summary of some of the more important comparisons developed in the report is set forth in the margin.[1] On the basis of these comparisons, as well as upon consideration of the past history and future prospects of the two corporations, Haslam concludes that the financial record of Hilton has been substantially superior to that of Mayflower, and that purely upon a statistical basis it could be argued that Hilton should not offer better than three-fourths of a share of

1. Comparisons drawn from Haslam report:

Average Earnings Per Share

	Hilton	Mayflower
1947–1951 Average:		
Before income taxes and extraordinary items	4.31	2.17
After " " " " "	2.79	1.17
1951 to Nov. 30:		
Before income taxes and extraordinary items	4.22	3.14
After " " " " "	2.37	1.15

Dividends Per Share

	Hilton	Mayflower
1947–1951 Average	1.07	.34
1951	1.20	.40

Book Value Per Share

		Hilton	Mayflower
Nov. 30, 1951	Per books	18.26	14.38
	Adjusted	18.42	13.98

Market Value Per Share

	Hilton	Mayflower
1950 Average	12.88	11.25
1951 Average	15.46	15.56
Approximate current price [at date of study]	14.75	16.25

Hilton for one share of Mayflower. Nevertheless it is his opinion that, because of the problems incident to Hilton's control of Mayflower and the advantages incident to complete ownership, a share-for-share exchange will be fair and reasonable to all concerned.

An affidavit of J. Sellers Bancroft, Vice President in charge of Trust Department investments of Wilmington Trust Company, sets forth in his conclusion, reached after a review of Mr. Haslam's study and an examination of pertinent financial data, that a share-for-share exchange is unquestionably fair.

The Haslam report contains no finding of net asset value—a factor nevertheless proper to be considered. Plaintiffs submitted affidavits containing an appraisal of the Mayflower Hotel (including land) and an estimate of reproduction cost (less depreciation) of the hotel proper. These affidavits indicate a value of upwards of $10,000,000. If plaintiffs' figure of a minimum value of $10,500,000 [2] be accepted (it was accepted by the Chancellor), a share of Mayflower stock would have a liquidating or net asset value of about $27 a share. Defendants submitted an affidavit of J.B. Herndon, Jr., Vice President and Treasurer of Hilton, to the effect that two of the hotel properties of Hilton (the Conrad Hilton and the Palmer House in Chicago), which are carried on the books at $26,800,000, have a value of at least $60,000,000. Mr. Hilton gave some testimony to the same effect. If the indicated increase of $33,200,000 be accepted, there is added to Hilton's per share book value about $20, making an asset value of about $38 a share. Haslam submitted a comparison of "indicated values" of the hotel properties, arrived at by assuming rates of capitalization of earnings derived from plaintiffs' appraisal of the Mayflower Hotel and applying such rates to the Hilton earnings, and, by two different methods, arrived at figures of $30.56 and $40.82 as "indicated" net asset values of a share of Hilton stock. Plaintiffs submitted no evidence of value of the Hilton Hotel properties.

Now, it will be noted that all of the comparisons above set forth except that of market value are in favor of Hilton. As for the market value of Mayflower stock, it appears to be conceded by all parties to be fictitious, that is, higher than would be justified in a free and normal market uninfluenced by Hilton's desire to acquire it and its policy of continued buying. At all events, that is the natural inference from the evidence. If we lay aside market value, and also disregard the comparison of book values—a factor, as the Chancellor said, of little relevancy in this case—we find three comparisons of various degrees of importance—earnings, dividends and net asset value—all in favor of Hilton.

If, therefore, we should accept the findings in the Haslam report and the principles on which it is based, and also accept the evidence

---

2. Arrived at by adding to the appraised value $500,000 in liquid assets.

bearing on comparative net asset value of Mayflower and Hilton stock, we should have to conclude that a share of Hilton stock has a value at least equal to a share of Mayflower stock, and that no unfair treatment of the Mayflower minority stockholders has been shown.

But we are confronted at the outset with the contention of the plaintiffs, basic to their case, that the Haslam report and the comparisons of value therein developed are wholly irrelevant to the issues before us. This contention, urged with much vigor—and repetition—is that the transaction here assailed is in substance a sale of assets by a fiduciary to himself. That the transaction is cast in the form of a merger, they say, is of no consequence; it is in effect a sale, and the only relevant comparison to be made is the comparison of the value of the transferred assets—worth $10,500,000—with the value of the consideration—389,738 shares of Hilton stock of a market value of $5,846,700; a disparity so shocking as to stamp the transaction as a fraud upon the Mayflower minority stockholders.

If plaintiffs' contention should be accepted it would follow that upon every merger of a subsidiary into its parent corporation that involves a conversion of the subsidiary's shares into shares of the parent, the *market* value of the parent stock issued to the stockholders of the subsidiary must equal the *liquidating* value of the subsidiary's stock. On its face this proposition is unsound, since it attempts to equate two different standards of value. In the case of many industrial corporations, and also in the instant case, there is a substantial gap between the market value and the liquidating value of the stock; and to apply to the merger of such corporations the proposition advanced by plaintiffs would be to bestow upon the stockholder of the subsidiary something which he did not have before the merger and could not obtain—the liquidating value of his stock. See Porges v. Vadsco Sales Corp., 27 Del.Ch. 127, 32 A.2d 148.

What is the reasoning by which plaintiffs would lead us to sanction such a result? . . .

. . . [P]laintiffs say in effect: A merger is essentially a sale of assets; this transaction is a sale of assets by a fiduciary (Hilton) to itself for shares of stock worth shockingly less than the assets sold; therefore the transaction is a fraud. So runs the syllogism.

A manifest fallacy, we think, lurks in the basic premise of this reasoning. A merger may be said to "involve" a sale of assets, in the sense that the title to the assets is by operation of law transferred from the constituent corporation to the surviving corporation; but it is not the same thing. . . .

A merger ordinarily contemplates the continuance of the enterprise and of the stockholder's investment therein, though in altered form; a sale of all assets (the type of sale referred to in the Cole case) ordinarily contemplates the liquidation of the enterprise. In the first case the stockholder of the merged corporation is entitled to receive directly securities substantially equal in value to those he held before the merger; in the latter case he receives nothing directly, but his corporation is entitled to receive the value of the assets sold. The scope of the applicable sections of our General Corporation Law (Section 59, relating to mergers and consolidations, and Section 65, relating to sales of all the corporate assets) may to some extent overlap; but this is not to say that the two procedures differ only in form. They are, in general, distinct and designed for different ends.

The instant case supplies an apt illustration. The Mayflower assets are not to be liquidated; the property is not for sale. Its directors and stockholders have determined, not that the venture should be terminated, but that it should be integrated completely with the Hilton enterprise. Having made this decision they had the right to avail themselves of the means which the law provides for just such a purpose, subject always to their imperative duty to accord to the minority fair and equitable terms of conversion. . . .

Plaintiffs' attempt to push to extremes the analogy drawn from a sale of assets leads them to a wholly untenable position, viz., that upon a merger a stockholder of a subsidiary is entitled to receive securities equal in value to the liquidating value of his stock. As we have already indicated, this proposition is unsound. Speaking generally, a merger effects an exchange of shares of stock in a going concern for shares in another going concern. In determining the fairness of the exchange liquidating value is not the sole test of the value of either. . . .

In the instant case the Chancellor held that in a case of merger "all relevant value factors must be considered in arriving at a fair value for comparison purposes." 89 A.2d 866.

For the reasons above given, we find no error in this ruling. . . .

Hilton's Offer to Buy Mayflower Stock at $19.10 a Share

The facts with respect to this offer are set forth above. The price derives from a purchase by Hilton in February, 1952, of 21,409 shares of Mayflower stock at $19.10 a share from a group headed by John E. Meyers, one of the interveners in the Washington litigation. A similar offer is now made to the remaining minority stockholders in connection with but not technically as a part of the plan of merger.

Upon these facts plaintiffs build an argument that the price thus voluntarily paid by Hilton, and still offered for Mayflower shares, shows the unfairness of converting one share of Mayflower into one share of Hilton. This argument assumes that the price in Hilton's offer is better evidence of value than the prices of the over-the-counter market and the values indicated by the Haslam report. This does not follow; on the contrary, the true inference would seem to be that, for whatever reason, Hilton paid for a large block of shares somewhat higher than real value. Messrs. Baxter and Fleming, two of the directors who had served under the prior management, are of the opinion that Mayflower stock is not worth $19.10 a share. After the Meyers purchase, Hilton may have determined to continue the offer to others in order to avoid any charge of having accorded the Meyers group special treatment. But Hilton's reasons for doing so are not here important; it is enough to say, as the Chancellor said, that the minority stockholders of Mayflower suffer no harm from the offer and have no ground of complaint.

Conclusion

We have considered all of plaintiffs' objections to the fairness of the proposed merger, and find ourselves in accord with the Chancellor's conclusion that no fraud or unfairness has been shown. . . .

The order of the Court of Chancery of New Castle County dated June 18, 1952, is affirmed; and the cause is remanded to that court for further proceedings in conformity with this opinion.

-----

(2) Exclusivity of the Appraisal Remedy

REV. MODEL BUS. CORP. ACT § 13.02(b)

[See Statutory Supplement]

NOTE ON EXCLUSIVITY OF THE APPRAISAL REMEDY

The question frequently arises whether the appraisal right is intended by the legislature as an exclusive remedy, so that the availability of appraisal precludes shareholders from seeking equitable relief such as injunction or rescission. This question does not always admit of a hard-and-fast answer.

1. In some cases the issue is specifically addressed by language in the appraisal statute itself. However, such language is not always read literally. For example, an exclusivity provision in former Mich. § 450.44(2) was interpreted as applicable only to transactions undertaken in good faith. Weckler v. Valley City Mill. Co., 93 F.Supp. 444 (W.D.Mich.1950), aff'd per curiam, 188 F.2d 367 (6th Cir.1951).[1] See also Miller v. Steinbach, 268 F.Supp. 255 (S.D.N.Y.1967). But see In re Jones & Laughlin Steel Corp., 263 Pa.Super. 378, 398 A.2d 186 (1979).

2. At least in the absence of explicit statutory language, it is clear that the availability of appraisal rights normally does not preclude an attack based on any of the following grounds:

> (a) That the transaction is illegal under corporation law in that it is not authorized by the statute. See, e.g., Eisenberg v. Central Zone Property Corp., 306 N.Y. 58, 115 N.E.2d 652 (1953).

-----

1. The present Michigan statute, Mich. Comp.Laws § 450.1771, resembles the Model Act.

(b) That the transaction is illegal under corporation law in that the procedural steps required to authorize the transaction were not properly taken. See, e.g., Starrett Corp. v. Fifth Ave. & Twenty–Ninth St. Corp., 1 F.Supp. 868, 878 (S.D.N.Y.1932) (lack of adequate notice to shareholders); Johnson v. Spartanburg County Fair Ass'n, 210 S.C. 56, 41 S.E.2d 599 (1947) (required number of votes not validly cast).

(c) That shareholder approval of the transaction was improperly obtained, as through fraudulent misrepresentation or violation of the Proxy Rules. See Victor Broadcasting Co. v. Mahurin, 236 Ark. 196, 365 S.W.2d 265 (1963).[2]

At least in the past, it has also been clear that the availability of appraisal rights normally *does* preclude a shareholder from seeking to recover the money value of his shares under a nonstatutory remedy in connection with transactions for which appraisal rights are given. See, e.g., Walter J. Schloss Associates v. Arkwin Industries, Inc., 61 N.Y.2d 700, 472 N.Y.S.2d 605, 460 N.E.2d 1090 (1984), reversing, 90 A.D.2d 149, 455 N.Y.S.2d 844 (1982); Adams v. United States Distributing Corp., 184 Va. 134, 34 S.E.2d 244 (1945).

Beyond this, the matter is less clear.[3] A few cases have suggested or implied that even in the absence of explicit statutory language, the availability of appraisal rights precludes an attack based on any ground other than illegality or fraudulent misrepresentation. See, e.g., Blumenthal v. Roosevelt Hotel, Inc., 202 Misc. 988, 115 N.Y.S.2d 52 (1952); Blumner v. Federated Department Stores, 99 N.Y.S.2d 691 (1950).[4] The general rule, however, is that the mere availability of appraisal rights does not preclude shareholders from seeking injunctive relief or rescission for fraud, using that term in the broad sense to include unfair self-dealing by fiduciaries.[5] The net result is that, in the

2. See also Golden v. Oahe Enterprises, Inc., 240 N.W.2d 102 (S.D.1976) (appraisal not exclusive remedy where defendants prevented plaintiff from complying with the statutory procedure to exercise that right).

It is also well established that the existence of appraisal rights does not preclude relief under Rule 10b–5. See Swanson v. American Consumer Industries, Inc., 415 F.2d 1326 (7th Cir.1969); Vine v. Beneficial Finance Co., 374 F.2d 627 (2d Cir.1967), cert. denied 389 U.S. 970, 88 S.Ct. 463, 19 L.Ed.2d 460 (1967); Miller v. Steinbach, 268 F.Supp. 255 (S.D.N.Y.1967).

3. Cf. Vorenberg, Exclusiveness of the Dissenting Stockholder's Appraisal Right, 77 Harv.L.Rev. 1189, 1213 (1964): "[A] complaint can fairly be made as to the futility of a labored attempt to gauge the exact weight which courts give to the availability of appraisal in the complex process of evaluating a business transaction. . . . [I]f an examination of the statutes and the few relevant cases shows anything, it is the absence of clear lines on the basis of which

to guide thinking and planning of this question."

4. The New York cases, such as *Blumenthal* and *Blumner,* that took this position, seem to have been overturned by N.Y. § 633(k), adopted in 1963. See Willcox v. Stern, 18 N.Y.2d 195, 273 N.Y.S.2d 38, 219 N.E.2d 401 (1966); Yoss v. Sacks, 26 A.D.2d 671, 272 N.Y.S.2d 387 (1966); Clark v. Pattern Analysis & Recognition Corp., 87 Misc.2d 385, 384 N.Y.S.2d 660 (1976). But see Sandfield v. Goldstein, 33 A.D.2d 376, 308 N.Y.S.2d 25 (1970); Note, Delaware Reexamines its Merger Laws: New Protection for Minority Shareholders?, 6 Hofstra L.Rev. 973, 990–994 (1978); cf. Tanzer Economic Assocs., Inc. v. Masoneilan Int'l, Inc., N.Y.L.J., May 26, 1977, at 7, col. 15 (N.Y.Sup.Ct. May 25, 1977); Cross v. Communications Channels, Inc., N.Y.L.J., July 6, 1977, at 6, col. 3 (N.Y.Sup.Ct. July 5, 1977).

5. See, e.g., Robb v. Eastgate Hotel, Inc., 347 Ill.App. 261, 106 N.E.2d 848 (1952); Opelka v. Quincy Memorial Bridge Co., 335 Ill.App. 402, 82 N.E.2d 184 (1948);

absence of explicit statutory language, the availability of appraisal rights may preclude a shareholder from attacking an *arm's-length* transaction on the ground of unfairness, but will usually not insulate *self-interested* transactions from an attack on that ground—although in the latter case it may lead the court to impose a somewhat less rigorous standard of fairness than would otherwise prevail. See Vorenberg, Exclusiveness of the Dissenting Stockholder's Appraisal Right, 77 Harv.L.Rev. 1189, 1214–15 (1964).

CAL. CORP. CODE § 1312

[See Statutory Supplement]

(i) FREEZEOUTS

NOTE ON FREEZEOUT TECHNIQUES

A freezeout is a corporate transaction whose principal purpose is to reconstitute the corporation's ownership by involuntarily eliminating the equity interest of minority shareholders.[1] Until twenty or twenty-five years ago, freezeouts tended to take one of three forms, all of which met with only indifferent success at the hands of the courts.

1. *Dissolution Freezeouts.* Assume that S (who may be an individual, a group, or a corporation) owns 70% of C Corporation, and wishes to eliminate C's minority shareholders. In a dissolution freezeout, S causes C to dissolve under a plan of dissolution which provides that C's productive assets will be distributed to S (or to an entity S controls), while cash or notes will be distributed to C's minority shareholders. This technique has been held illegal in a number of cases, most of which stress that such a plan of dissolution violates a corporate norm of equal treatment among all shareholders of the same class. See Mason v. Pewabic Mining Co., 133 U.S. 50, 10 S.Ct. 224, 33 L.Ed. 524 (1890); Kellogg v. Georgia–Pacific Paper Corp., 227 F.Supp. 719 (W.D.Ark.1964); Zimmerman v. Tide Water Associated Oil Co., 61 Cal.App.2d 585, 143 P.2d 409 (1943); In re San Joaquin Light & Power Co., 52 Cal.App.2d 814, 127 P.2d 29 (1942); In re Paine, 200 Mich. 58, 166 N.W. 1036 (1918).[2]

2. *Sale-of-Assets Freezeouts.* In a sale-of-assets freezeout, C's controlling shareholder, S, organizes a new corporation, T, all of whose stock S owns. S then causes C to sell its assets to T for cash or notes.

Gabhart v. Gabhart, 267 Ind. 370, 370 N.E. 2d 345 (1977); Pupecki v. James Madison & Co., 376 Mass. 212, 382 N.E.2d 1030 (1978).

1. In some cases controlling shareholders have adopted a corporate policy (such as cutting dividends) which puts pressure on minority shareholders to sell their shares, but does not in itself terminate the minority's interest. Such a technique is sometimes referred to as a "squeezeout."

2. Cf. Kirtz v. Grossman, 463 S.W.2d 541 (Mo.App.1971); Kavanaugh v. Kavanaugh Knitting Co., 226 N.Y. 185, 123 N.E. 148 (1919). But see Rossing v. State Bank, 181 Iowa 1013, 165 N.W. 254 (1917).

Result: S owns C's business through T, while the equity interest of C's minority shareholders in C's business is involuntarily terminated. (C is then normally dissolved, although a freezeout will be effected even without dissolution.) Such a procedure was disapproved in Cathedral Estates, Inc. v. Taft Realty Corp., 157 F.Supp. 895, 897 (D.Conn. 1954), aff'd 251 F.2d 340 (2d Cir.1957); Cardiff v. Johnson, 126 Wash. 454, 218 P. 269 (1923); and Theis v. Spokane Falls Gaslight Co., 34 Wash. 23, 74 P. 1004 (1904).[3]

3. *Debt or redeemable-preferred mergers.* A debt or redeemable-preferred merger begins, like a sale-of-assets freezeout, with the organization by S of a new corporation, T. S then causes C to merge with T, but instead of issuing common stock, T issues either short-term debentures or redeemable preferred stock. Accordingly, the interest of C's minority shareholders in T either terminates automatically after a period of years (in the case of debentures) or is terminable at T's election (in the case of redeemable preferred).

Modern freezeouts commonly employ still a fourth technique. Many states have amended their regular merger statutes to allow the survivor in a regular merger to issue cash as well as stock or securities. This opened the door to the possibility of cash mergers, which resemble debt or redeemable stock mergers except that the survivor issues cash rather than stock or securities. Under this technique, the freezeout possibilities of the short-form merger are extended to cases where the parent does not own the percentage of stock requisite for a short-form merger.

A recurrent issue in the freezeout area is whether such transactions are permissible if effected with no business purpose other than to increase the controlling shareholders' portion of the pie.

WEINBERGER v. UOP, INC.

Supreme Court of Delaware, 1983.
457 A.2d 701.

Before HERRMANN, C.J., McNEILLY, QUILLEN, HORSEY and MOORE, JJ., constituting the Court en Banc.

MOORE, Justice:

This post-trial appeal was reheard en banc from a decision of the Court of Chancery. It was brought by the class action plaintiff below, a former shareholder of UOP, Inc., who challenged the elimination of UOP's minority shareholders by a cash-out merger between UOP and

3. Cf. Efron v. Kalmanovitz, 226 Cal. App.2d 546, 38 Cal.Rptr. 148 (1964); Eisenberg v. Central Zone Property Corp., 306 N.Y. 58, 115 N.E.2d 652 (1953). But see Alcott v. Hyman, 42 Del.Ch. 233, 208 A.2d 501 (1965); Abelow v. Midstates Oil Corp., 41 Del.Ch. 145, 189 A.2d 675 (1963). In Blumenthal v. Roosevelt Hotel, Inc., 202 Misc.2d 988, 115 N.Y.S.2d 52 (1952), a lower New York court held that the availability of appraisal rights precluded an attack by minority shareholders on a sale-of-assets freezeout. The status of that holding seems questionable in light of the subsequent amendment of the New York statute dealing with exclusivity. See N.Y. § 623(k), and Note on Exclusivity of the Appraisal Remedy, Section 1(j)(2), supra.

its majority owner, The Signal Companies, Inc.[2] Originally, the defendants in this action were Signal, UOP, certain officers and directors of those companies, and UOP's investment banker, Lehman Brothers Kuhn Loeb, Inc.[3] The present Chancellor held that the terms of the merger were fair to the plaintiff and the other minority shareholders of UOP. Accordingly, he entered judgment in favor of the defendants.

Numerous points were raised by the parties, but we address only the following questions presented by the trial court's opinion:

(1) The plaintiff's duty to plead sufficient facts demonstrating the unfairness of the challenged merger;

(2) The burden of proof upon the parties where the merger has been approved by the purportedly informed vote of a majority of the minority shareholders;

(3) The fairness of the merger in terms of adequacy of the defendants' disclosures to the minority shareholders;

(4) The fairness of the merger in terms of adequacy of the price paid for the minority shares and the remedy appropriate to that issue; and

(5) The continued force and effect of Singer v. Magnavox Co., Del.Supr., 380 A.2d 969, 980 (1977), and its progeny.

In ruling for the defendants, the Chancellor re-stated his earlier conclusion that the plaintiff in a suit challenging a cash-out merger must allege specific acts of fraud, misrepresentation, or other items of misconduct to demonstrate the unfairness of the merger terms to the minority.[4] We approve this rule and affirm it.

The Chancellor also held that even though the ultimate burden of proof is on the majority shareholder to show by a preponderance of the evidence that the transaction is fair, it is first the burden of the plaintiff attacking the merger to demonstrate some basis for invoking the fairness obligation. We agree with that principle. However, where corporate action has been approved by an informed vote of a majority of the minority shareholders, we conclude that the burden entirely shifts to the plaintiff to show that the transaction was unfair to the minority. See, e.g., Michelson v. Duncan, Del.Supr., 407 A.2d 211, 224 (1979). But in all this, the burden clearly remains on those relying on the vote to show that they completely disclosed all material facts relevant to the transaction.

Here, the record does not support a conclusion that the minority stockholder vote was an informed one. Material information, necessary to acquaint those shareholders with the bargaining positions of Signal and UOP, was withheld under circumstances amounting to a breach of fiduciary duty. We therefore conclude that this merger

---

2. For the opinion of the trial court see Weinberger v. UOP, Inc., Del.Ch., 426 A.2d 1333 (1981).

3. Shortly before the last oral argument, the plaintiff dismissed Lehman Brothers from the action. Thus, we do not deal with the issues raised by the plaintiff's claims against this defendant.

4. In a pre-trial ruling the Chancellor ordered the complaint dismissed for failure to state a cause of action. See Weinberger v. UOP, Inc., Del.Ch., 409 A.2d 1262 (1979).

does not meet the test of fairness, at least as we address that concept, and no burden thus shifted to the plaintiff by reason of the minority shareholder vote. Accordingly, we reverse and remand for further proceedings consistent herewith.

In considering the nature of the remedy available under our law to minority shareholders in a cash-out merger, we believe that it is, and hereafter should be, an appraisal under 8 Del.C. § 262 as hereinafter construed. We therefore overrule Lynch v. Vickers Energy Corp., Del.Supr., 429 A.2d 497 (1981) (*Lynch II*) to the extent that it purports to limit a stockholder's monetary relief to a specific damage formula. See *Lynch II*, 429 A.2d at 507–08 (McNeilly & Quillen, JJ., dissenting). But to give full effect to section 262 within the framework of the General Corporation Law we adopt a more liberal, less rigid and stylized, approach to the valuation process than has heretofore been permitted by our courts. While the present state of these proceedings does not admit the plaintiff to the appraisal remedy per se, the practical effect of the remedy we do grant him will be co-extensive with the liberalized valuation and appraisal methods we herein approve for cases coming after this decision.

Our treatment of these matters has necessarily led us to a reconsideration of the business purpose rule announced in the trilogy of Singer v. Magnavox Co., supra; Tanzer v. International General Industries, Inc., Del.Supr., 379 A.2d 1121 (1977); and Roland International Corp. v. Najjar, Del.Supr., 407 A.2d 1032 (1979). For the reasons hereafter set forth we consider that the business purpose requirement of these cases is no longer the law of Delaware.

I.

The facts found by the trial court, pertinent to the issues before us, are supported by the record, and we draw from them as set out in the Chancellor's opinion.[5]

Signal is a diversified, technically based company operating through various subsidiaries. Its stock is publicly traded on the New York, Philadelphia and Pacific Stock Exchanges. UOP, formerly known as Universal Oil Products Company, was a diversified industrial company engaged in various lines of business, including petroleum and petro-chemical services and related products, construction, fabricated metal products, transportation equipment products, chemicals and plastics, and other products and services including land development, lumber products and waste disposal. Its stock was publicly held and listed on the New York Stock Exchange.

In 1974 Signal sold one of its wholly-owned subsidiaries for $420,000,000 in cash. See Gimbel v. Signal Companies, Inc., Del. Ch., 316 A.2d 599, aff'd, Del.Supr., 316 A.2d 619 (1974). While looking to invest this cash surplus, Signal became interested in UOP as a possible acquisition. Friendly negotiations ensued, and Signal proposed to acquire a controlling interest in UOP at a price of $19 per

5. Weinberger v. UOP, Inc., Del.Ch., 426 A.2d 1333, 1335–40 (1981).

share. UOP's representatives sought $25 per share. In the arm's length bargaining that followed, an understanding was reached whereby Signal agreed to purchase from UOP 1,500,000 shares of UOP's authorized but unissued stock at $21 per share.

This purchase was contingent upon Signal making a successful cash tender offer for 4,300,000 publicly held shares of UOP, also at a price of $21 per share. This combined method of acquisition permitted Signal to acquire 5,800,000 shares of stock, representing 50.5% of UOP's outstanding shares. The UOP board of directors advised the company's shareholders that it had no objection to Signal's tender offer at that price. Immediately before the announcement of the tender offer, UOP's common stock had been trading on the New York Stock Exchange at a fraction under $14 per share.

The negotiations between Signal and UOP occurred during April 1975, and the resulting tender offer was greatly oversubscribed. However, Signal limited its total purchase of the tendered shares so that, when coupled with the stock bought from UOP, it had achieved its goal of becoming a 50.5% shareholder of UOP.

Although UOP's board consisted of thirteen directors, Signal nominated and elected only six. Of these, five were either directors or employees of Signal. The sixth, a partner in the banking firm of Lazard Freres & Co., had been one of Signal's representatives in the negotiations and bargaining with UOP concerning the tender offer and purchase price of the UOP shares.

However, the president and chief executive officer of UOP retired during 1975, and Signal caused him to be replaced by James V. Crawford, a long-time employee and senior executive vice president of one of Signal's wholly-owned subsidiaries. Crawford succeeded his predecessor on UOP's board of directors and also was made a director of Signal.

By the end of 1977 Signal basically was unsuccessful in finding other suitable investment candidates for its excess cash, and by February 1978 considered that it had no other realistic acquisitions available to it on a friendly basis. Once again its attention turned to UOP.

The trial court found that at the instigation of certain Signal management personnel, including William W. Walkup, its board chairman, and Forrest N. Shumway, its president, a feasibility study was made concerning the possible acquisition of the balance of UOP's outstanding shares. This study was performed by two Signal officers, Charles S. Arledge, vice president (director of planning), and Andrew J. Chitiea, senior vice president (chief financial officer). Messrs. Walkup, Shumway, Arledge and Chitiea were all directors of UOP in addition to their membership on the Signal board.

Arledge and Chitiea concluded that it would be a good investment for Signal to acquire the remaining 49.5% of UOP shares at any price up to $24 each. Their report was discussed between Walkup and Shumway who, along with Arledge, Chitiea and Brewster L. Arms, internal counsel for Signal, constituted Signal's senior management. In particular, they talked about the proper price to be paid if the acquisition was pursued, purportedly keeping in mind that as UOP's majority shareholder, Signal owed a fiduciary responsibility to both its own stockholders as well as to UOP's minority. It was ultimately agreed that a meeting of Signal's Executive Committee would be called to propose that Signal acquire the remaining outstanding stock of UOP through a cash-out merger in the range of $20 to $21 per share.

The Executive Committee meeting was set for February 28, 1978. As a courtesy, UOP's President, Crawford, was invited to attend, although he was not a member of Signal's executive committee. On his arrival, and prior to the meeting, Crawford was asked to meet privately with Walkup and Shumway. He was then told of Signal's plan to acquire full ownership of UOP and was asked for his reaction to the proposed price range of $20 to $21 per share. Crawford said he thought such a price would be "generous", and that it was certainly one which should be submitted to UOP's minority shareholders for their ultimate consideration. He stated, however, that Signal's 100% ownership could cause internal problems at UOP. He believed that employees would have to be given some assurance of their future place in a fully-owned Signal subsidiary. Otherwise, he feared the departure of essential personnel. Also, many of UOP's key employees had stock option incentive programs which would be wiped out by a merger. Crawford therefore urged that some adjustment would have to be made, such as providing a comparable incentive in Signals' shares, if after the merger he was to maintain his quality of personnel and efficiency at UOP.

Thus, Crawford voiced no objection to the $20 to $21 price range, nor did he suggest that Signal should consider paying more than $21 per share for the minority interests. Later, at the Executive Committee meeting the same factors were discussed, with Crawford repeating the position he earlier took with Walkup and Shumway. Also considered was the 1975 tender offer and the fact that it had been greatly oversubscribed at $21 per share. For many reasons, Signal's management concluded that the acquisition of UOP's minority shares provided the solution to a number of its business problems.

Thus, it was the consensus that a price of $20 to $21 per share would be fair to both Signal and the minority shareholders of UOP. Signal's executive committee authorized its management "to negotiate" with UOP "for a cash acquisition of the minority ownership in UOP, Inc., with the intention of presenting a proposal to [Signal's] board of directors . . . on March 6, 1978". Immediately after this February 28, 1978 meeting, Signal issued a press release stating:

> The Signal Companies, Inc. and UOP, Inc. are conducting negotiations for the acquisition for cash by Signal of the 49.5 per cent of UOP which it does not presently own, announced Forrest N. Shumway, president and chief executive officer of Signal, and James V. Crawford, UOP president.
>
> Price and other terms of the proposed transaction have not yet been finalized and would be subject to approval of the boards

of directors of Signal and UOP, scheduled to meet early next week, the stockholders of UOP and certain federal agencies.

The announcement also referred to the fact that the closing price of UOP's common stock on that day was $14.50 per share.

Two days later, on March 2, 1978, Signal issued a second press release stating that its management would recommend a price in the range of $20 to $21 per share for UOP's 49.5% minority interest. This announcement referred to Signal's earlier statement that "negotiations" were being conducted for the acquisition of the minority shares.

Between Tuesday, February 28, 1978 and Monday, March 6, 1978, a total of four business days, Crawford spoke by telephone with all of UOP's non-Signal, i.e., outside, directors. Also during that period, Crawford retained Lehman Brothers to render a fairness opinion as to the price offered the minority for its stock. He gave two reasons for this choice. First, the time schedule between the announcement and the board meetings was short (by then only three business days) and since Lehman Brothers had been acting as UOP's investment banker for many years, Crawford felt that it would be in the best position to respond on such brief notice. Second, James W. Glanville, a long-time director of UOP and a partner in Lehman Brothers, had acted as a financial advisor to UOP for many years. Crawford believed that Glanville's familiarity with UOP, as a member of its board, would also be of assistance in enabling Lehman Brothers to render a fairness opinion within the existing time contraints.

Crawford telephoned Glanville, who gave his assurance that Lehman Brothers had no conflicts that would prevent it from accepting the task. Glanville's immediate personal reaction was that a price of $20 to $21 would certainly be fair, since it represented almost a 50% premium over UOP's market price. Glanville sought a $250,000 fee for Lehman Brothers' services, but Crawford thought this too much. After further discussions Glanville finally agreed that Lehman Brothers would render its fairness opinion for $150,000.

During this period Crawford also had several telephone contacts with Signal officals. In only one of them, however, was the price of the shares discussed. In a conversation with Walkup, Crawford advised that as a result of his communications with UOP's non-Signal directors, it was his feeling that the price would have to be the top of the proposed range, or $21 per share, if the approval of UOP's outside directors was to be obtained. But again, he did not seek any price higher than $21.

Glanville assembled a three-man Lehman Brothers team to do the work on the fairness opinion. These persons examined relevant documents and information concerning UOP, including its annual reports and its Securities and Exchange Commission filings from 1973 through 1976, as well as its audited financial statements for 1977, its interim reports to shareholders, and its recent and historical market prices and trading volumes. In addition, on Friday, March, 3, 1978, two members of the Lehman Brothers team flew to UOP's headquarters in Des Plaines, Illinois, to perform a "due diligence" visit, during the course of which they interviewed Crawford as well as UOP's general counsel, its chief financial officer, and other key executives and personnel.

As a result, the Lehman Brothers team concluded that "the price of either $20 or $21 would be a fair price for the remaining shares of UOP". They telephoned this impression to Glanville, who was spending the weekend in Vermont.

On Monday morning, March 6, 1978, Glanville and the senior member of the Lehman Brothers team flew to Des Plaines to attend the scheduled UOP directors meeting. Glanville looked over the assembled information during the flight. The two had with them the draft of a "fairness opinion letter" in which the price had been left blank. Either during or immediately prior to the directors' meeting, the two-page "fairness opinion letter" was typed in final form and the price of $21 per share was inserted.

On March 6, 1978, both the Signal and UOP boards were convened to consider the proposed merger. Telephone communications were maintained between the two meetings. Walkup, Signal's board chairman, and also a UOP director, attended UOP's meeting with Crawford in order to present Signal's position and answer any questions that UOP's non-Signal directors might have. Arledge and Chitiea, along with Signal's other designees on UOP's board, participated by conference telephone. All of UOP's outside directors attended the meeting either in person or by conference telephone.

First, Signal's board unanimously adopted a resolution authorizing Signal to propose to UOP a cash merger of $21 per share as outlined in a certain merger agreement and other supporting documents. This proposal required that the merger be approved by a majority of UOP's outstanding minority shares voting at the stockholders meeting at which the merger would be considered, and that the minority shares voting in favor of the merger, when coupled with Signal's 50.5% interest would have to comprise at least two-thirds of all UOP shares. Otherwise the proposed merger would be deemed disapproved.

UOP's board then considered the proposal. Copies of the agreement were delivered to the directors in attendance, and other copies had been forwarded earlier to the directors participating by telephone. They also had before them UOP financial data for 1974–1977, UOP's most recent financial statements, market price information, and budget projections for 1978. In addition they had Lehman Brothers' hurriedly prepared fairness opinion letter finding the price of $21 to be fair. Glanville, the Lehman Brothers partner, and UOP director, commented on the information that had gone into preparation of the letter.

Signal also suggests that the Arledge–Chitiea feasibility study, indicating that a price of up to $24 per share would be a "good investment" for Signal, was discussed at the UOP directors' meeting. The Chancellor made no such finding, and our independent review of the record, detailed infra, satisfies us by a preponderance of the evidence that there was no discussion of this document at UOP's board meeting. Furthermore, it is clear beyond peradventure that nothing in that report was ever disclosed to UOP's minority shareholders prior to their approval of the merger.

After consideration of Signal's proposal, Walkup and Crawford left the meeting to permit a free and uninhibited exchange between UOP's non-Signal directors. Upon their return a resolution to accept Signal's offer was then proposed and adopted. While Signal's men on UOP's board participated in various aspects of the meeting they abstained from voting. However, the minutes show that each of them "if voting would have voted yes".

On March 7, 1978, UOP sent a letter to its shareholders advising them of the action taken by UOP's board with respect to Signal's offer. This document pointed out, among other things, that on February 28, 1978 "both companies had announced negotiations were being conducted."

Despite the swift board action of the two companies, the merger was not submitted to UOP's shareholders until their annual meeting on May 26, 1978. In the notice of that meeting and proxy statement sent to shareholders in May, UOP's management and board urged that the merger be approved. The proxy statement also advised:

The price was determined after *discussions* between James V. Crawford, a director of Signal and Chief Executive Officer of UOP, and officers of Signal which took place during meetings on February 28, 1978, and in the course of several subsequent telephone conversations. (Emphasis added.)

In the original draft of the proxy statement the word "negotiations" had been used rather than "discussions". However, when the Securities and Exchange Commission sought details of the "negotiations" as part of its review of these materials, the term was deleted and the word "discussions" was substituted. The proxy statement indicated that the vote of UOP's board in approving the merger had been unanimous. It also advised the shareholders that Lehman Brothers had given its opinion that the merger price of $21 per share was fair to UOP's minority. However, it did not disclose the hurried method by which this conclusion was reached.

As of the record date for UOP's annual meeting, there were 11,488,302 shares of UOP common stock outstanding, 5,688,302 of which were owned by the minority. At the meeting only 56%, or 3,208,652, of the minority shares were voted. Of these, 2,953,812, or 51.9% of the total minority, voted for the merger, and 254,840 voted against it. When Signal's stock was added to the minority shares voting in favor, a total of 76.2% of UOP's outstanding shares approved the merger while only 2.2% opposed it.

By its terms the merger became effective on May 26, 1978, and each share of UOP's stock held by the minority was automatically converted into a right to receive $21 cash.

II.

A.

A primary issue mandating reversal is the preparation by two UOP directors, Arledge and Chitiea, of their feasibility study for the exclusive use and benefit of Signal. This document was of obvious significance to both Signal and UOP. Using UOP data, it described the advantages to Signal of ousting the minority at a price range of $21–$24 per share. Mr. Arledge, one of the authors, outlined the benefits to Signal: [6]

Purpose of the Merger

(1) Provides an outstanding investment opportunity for Signal—(Better than any recent acquisition we have seen.)

(2) Increases Signal's earnings.

(3) Facilitates the flow of resources between Signal and its subsidiaries—(Big factor—works both ways.)

(4) Provides cost savings potential for Signal and UOP.

(5) Improves the percentage of Signal's 'operating earnings' as opposed to 'holding company earnings'.

(6) Simplifies the understanding of Signal.

(7) Facilitates technological exchange among Signal's subsidiaries.

(8) Eliminates potential conflicts of interest.

Having written those words, solely for the use of Signal, it is clear from the record that neither Arledge nor Chitiea shared this report with their fellow directors of UOP. We are satisfied that no one else did either. This conduct hardly meets the fiduciary standards applicable to such a transaction. While Mr. Walkup, Signal's chairman of the board and a UOP director, attended the March 6, 1978 UOP board meeting and testified at trial that he had discussed the Arledge–Chitiea report with the UOP directors at this meeting, the record does not support this assertion. Perhaps it is the result of some confusion on Mr. Walkup's part. In any event Mr. Shumway, Signal's president, testified that he made sure the Signal outside directors had this report prior to the March 6, 1978 Signal board meeting, but he did not testify that the Arledge–Chitiea report was also sent to UOP's outside directors.

Mr. Crawford, UOP's president, could not recall that any documents, other than a draft of the merger agreement, were sent to UOP's directors before the March 6, 1978 UOP meeting. Mr. Chitiea, an author of the report, testified that it was made available to Signal's directors, but to his knowledge it was not circulated to the outside directors of UOP. He specifically testified that he "didn't

---

6. The parentheses indicate certain handwritten comments of Mr. Arledge.

share" that information with the outside directors of UOP with whom he served.

None of UOP's outside directors who testified stated that they had seen this document. The minutes of the UOP board meeting do not identify the Arledge–Chitiea report as having been delivered to UOP's outside directors. This is particularly significant since the minutes describe in considerable detail the materials that actually were distributed. While these minutes recite Mr. Walkup's presentation of the Signal offer, they do not mention the Arledge–Chitiea report or any disclosure that Signal considered a price of up to $24 to be a good investment. If Mr. Walkup had in fact provided such important information to UOP's outside directors, it is logical to assume that these carefully drafted minutes would disclose it. The post-trial briefs of Signal and UOP contain a thorough description of the documents purportedly available to their boards at the March 6, 1978, meetings. Although the Arledge–Chitiea report is specifically identified as being available to the Signal directors, there is no mention of it being among the documents submitted to the UOP board. Even when queried at a prior oral argument before this Court, counsel for Signal did not claim that the Arledge–Chitiea report had been disclosed to UOP's outside directors. Instead, he chose to belittle its contents. This was the same approach taken before us at the last oral argument.

Actually, it appears that a three-page summary of figures was given to all UOP directors. Its first page is identical to one page of the Arledge–Chitiea report, but this dealt with nothing more than a justification of the $21 price. Significantly, the contents of this three-page summary are what the minutes reflect Mr. Walkup told the UOP board. However, nothing contained in either the minutes or this three-page summary reflects Signal's study regarding the $24 price.

The Arledge–Chitiea report speaks for itself in supporting the Chancellor's finding that a price of up to $24 was a "good investment" for Signal. It shows that a return on the investment at $21 would be 15.7% versus 15.5% at $24 per share. This was a difference of only two-tenths of one percent, while it meant over $17,000,000 to the minority. Under such circumstances, paying UOP's minority shareholders $24 would have had relatively little long-term effect on Signal, and the Chancellor's findings concerning the benefit to Signal, even at a price of $24, were obviously correct. Levitt v. Bouvier, Del.Supr., 287 A.2d 671, 673 (1972).

Certainly, this was a matter of material significance to UOP and its shareholders. Since the study was prepared by two UOP directors, using UOP information for the exclusive benefit of Signal, and nothing whatever was done to disclose it to the outside UOP directors or the minority shareholders, a question of breach of fiduciary duty arises. This problem occurs because there were common Signal–UOP directors participating, at least to some extent, in the UOP board's decision-making processes without full disclosure of the conflicts they faced.[7]

---

7. Although perfection is not possible, or expected, the result here could have been entirely different if UOP had appointed an independent negotiating com-

B.

In assessing this situation, the Court of Chancery was required to: examine what information defendants had and to measure it against what they gave to the minority stockholders, in a context in which "complete candor" is required. In other words, the limited function of the Court was to determine whether defendants had disclosed all information in their possession germane to the transaction in issue. And by "germane" we mean, for present purposes, information such as a reasonable shareholder would consider important in deciding whether to sell or retain stock.

* * *

. . . Completeness, not adequacy, is both the norm and the mandate under present circumstances.

Lynch v. Vickers Energy Corp., Del.Supr., 383 A.2d 278, 281 (1977) (*Lynch I*). This is merely stating in another way the long-existing principle of Delaware law that these Signal designated directors on UOP's board still owed UOP and its shareholders an uncompromising duty of loyalty. The classic language of Guth v. Loft, Inc., Del.Supr., 5 A.2d 503, 510 (1939), requires no embellishment:

A public policy, existing through the years, and derived from a profound knowledge of human characteristics and motives, has established a rule that demands of a corporate officer or director, peremptorily and inexorably, the most scrupulous observance of his duty, not only affirmatively to protect the interests of the corporation committed to his charge, but also to refrain from doing anything that would work injury to the corporation, or to deprive it of profit or advantage which his skill and ability might properly bring to it, or to enable it to make in the reasonable and lawful exercise of its powers. The rule that requires an undivided and unselfish loyalty to the corporation demands that there shall be no conflict between duty and self-interest.

Given the absence of any attempt to structure this transaction on an arm's length basis, Signal cannot escape the effects of the conflicts it faced, particularly when its designees on UOP's board did not totally abstain from participation in the matter. There is no "safe harbor" for such divided loyalties in Delaware. When directors of a Delaware corporation are on both sides of a transaction, they are required to demonstrate their utmost good faith and the most scrupulous inherent fairness of the bargain. Gottlieb v. Heyden Chemical Corp., Del.

mittee of its outside directors to deal with Signal at arm's length. See, e.g., Harriman v. E.I. duPont de Nemours & Co., 411 F.Supp. 133 (D.Del.1975). Since fairness in this context can be equated to conduct by a theoretical, wholly independent, board of directors acting upon the matter before them, it is unfortunate that this course apparently was neither considered nor pursued. Johnston v. Greene, Del.Supr., 121 A.2d 919, 925 (1956). Particularly in a parent-subsidiary context, a showing that the action taken was as though each of the contending parties had in fact exerted its bargaining power against the other at arm's length is strong evidence that the transaction meets the test of fairness. Getty Oil Co. v. Skelly Oil Co., Del.Supr., 267 A.2d 883, 886 (1970); Puma v. Marriott, Del.Ch., 283 A.2d 693, 696 (1971).

Supr., 91 A.2d 57, 57–58 (1952). The requirement of fairness is unflinching in its demand that where one stands on both sides of a transaction, he has the burden of establishing its entire fairness, sufficient to pass the test of careful scrutiny by the courts. Sterling v. Mayflower Hotel Corp., Del.Supr., 93 A.2d 107, 110 (1952); Bastian v. Bourns, Inc., Del.Ch., 256 A.2d 680, 681 (1969), aff'd, Del. Supr., 278 A.2d 467 (1970); David J. Greene & Co. v. Dunhill International Inc., Del.Ch., 249 A.2d 427, 431 (1968).

There is no dilution of this obligation where one holds dual or multiple directorships, as in a parent-subsidiary context. Levien v. Sinclair Oil Corp., Del.Ch., 261 A.2d 911, 915 (1969). Thus, individuals who act in a dual capacity as directors of two corporations, one of whom is parent and the other subsidiary, owe the same duty of good management to both corporations, and in the absence of an independent negotiating structure (see note 7, supra), or the directors' total abstention from any participation in the matter, this duty is to be exercised in light of what is best for both companies. Warshaw v. Calhoun, Del.Supr., 221 A.2d 487, 492 (1966). The record demonstrates that Signal has not met this obligation.

C.

The concept of fairness has two basic aspects: fair dealing and fair price. The former embraces questions of when the transaction was timed, how it was initiated, structured, negotiated, disclosed to the directors, and how the approvals of the directors and the stockholders were obtained. The latter aspect of fairness relates to the economic and financial considerations of the proposed merger, including all relevant factors: assets, market value, earnings, future prospects, and any other elements that affect the intrinsic or inherent value of a company's stock. Moore, The "Interested" Director or Officer Transaction, 4 Del.J.Corp.L. 674, 676 (1979); Nathan & Shapiro, Legal Standard of Fairness of Merger Terms Under Delaware Law, 2 Del.J. Corp.L. 44, 46–47 (1977). See Tri–Continental Corp. v. Battye, Del. Supr., 74 A.2d 71, 72 (1950); 8 Del.C. § 262(h). However, the test for fairness is not a bifurcated one as between fair dealing and price. All aspects of the issue must be examined as a whole since the question is one of entire fairness. However, in a non-fraudulent transaction we recognize that price may be the preponderant consideration outweighing other features of the merger. Here, we address the two basic aspects of fairness separately because we find reversible error as to both.

D.

Part of fair dealing is the obvious duty of candor required by *Lynch I,* supra. Moreover, one possessing superior knowledge may not mislead any stockholder by use of corporate information to which the latter is not privy. Lank v. Steiner, Del.Supr., 224 A.2d 242, 244 (1966). Delaware has long imposed this duty even upon persons who are not corporate officers or directors, but who nonetheless are privy to matters of interest or significance to their company. Brophy v. Cities Service Co., Del.Ch., 70 A.2d 5, 7 (1949). With the well-established Delaware law on the subject, and the Court of Chancery's findings of fact here, it is inevitable that the obvious conflicts posed by Arledge and Chitiea's preparation of their "feasibility study", derived from UOP information, for the sole use and benefit of Signal, cannot pass muster.

The Arledge–Chitiea report is but one aspect of the element of fair dealing. How did this merger evolve? It is clear that it was entirely initiated by Signal. The serious time constraints under which the principals acted were all set by Signal. It had not found a suitable outlet for its excess cash and considered UOP a desirable investment, particularly since it was now in a position to acquire the whole company for itself. For whatever reasons, and they were only Signal's, the entire transaction was presented to and approved by UOP's board within four business days. Standing alone, this is not necessarily indicative of any lack of fairness by a majority shareholder. It was what occurred, or more properly, what did not occur, during this brief period that makes the time constraints imposed by Signal relevant to the issue of fairness.

The structure of the transaction, again, was Signal's doing. So far as negotiations were concerned, it is clear that they were modest at best. Crawford, Signal's man at UOP, never really talked price with Signal, except to accede to its management's statements on the subject, and to convey to Signal the UOP outside directors' view that as between the $20–$21 range under consideration, it would have to be $21. The latter is not a surprising outcome, but hardly arm's length negotiations. Only the protection of benefits for UOP's key employees and the issue of Lehman Brothers' fee approached any concept of bargaining.

As we have noted, the matter of disclosure to the UOP directors was wholly flawed by the conflicts of interest raised by the Arledge–Chitiea report. All of those conflicts were resolved by Signal in its own favor without divulging any aspect of them to UOP.

This cannot but undermine a conclusion that this merger meets any reasonable test of fairness. The outside UOP directors lacked one material piece of information generated by two of their colleagues, but shared only with Signal. True, the UOP board had the Lehman Brothers' fairness opinion, but that firm has been blamed by the plaintiff for the hurried task it performed, when more properly the responsibility for this lies with Signal. There was no disclosure of the circumstances surrounding the rather cursory preparation of the Lehman Brothers' fairness opinion. Instead, the impression was given UOP's minority that a careful study had been made, when in fact speed was the hallmark, and Mr. Glanville, Lehman's partner in charge of the matter, and also a UOP director, having spent the weekend in Vermont, brought a draft of the "fairness opinion letter" to the UOP directors' meeting on March 6, 1978 with the price left blank. We can only conclude from the record that the rush imposed on Lehman Brothers by Signal's timetable contributed to the difficulties under which this investment banking firm attempted to perform its responsibilities. Yet, none of this was disclosed to UOP's minority.

Finally, the minority stockholders were denied the critical information that Signal considered a price of $24 to be a good investment. Since this would have meant over $17,000,000 more to the minority, we cannot conclude that the shareholder vote was an informed one. Under the circumstances, an approval by a majority of the minority was meaningless. *Lynch I,* 383 A.2d at 279, 281; *Cahall v. Lofland,* Del.Ch., 114 A. 224 (1921).

Given these particulars and the Delaware law on the subject, the record does not establish that this transaction satisfies any reasonable concept of fair dealing, and the Chancellor's findings in that regard must be reversed.

E.

Turning to the matter of price, plaintiff also challenges its fairness. His evidence was that on the date the merger was approved the stock was worth at least $26 per share. In support, he offered the testimony of a chartered investment analyst who used two basic approaches to valuation: a comparative analysis of the premium paid over market in ten other tender offer-merger combinations, and a discounted cash flow analysis.

In this breach of fiduciary duty case, the Chancellor perceived that the approach to valuation was the same as that in an appraisal proceeding. Consistent with precedent, he rejected plaintiff's method of proof and accepted defendants' evidence of value as being in accord with practice under prior case law. This means that the so-called "Delaware block" or weighted average method was employed wherein the elements of value, i.e., assets, market price, earnings, etc., were assigned a particular weight and the resulting amounts added to determine the value per share.

[The court held that the use of this valuation technique was in error. See pp. 1115–1116, supra.]

Although the Chancellor received the plaintiff's evidence, his opinion indicates that the use of it was precluded because of past Delaware practice. While we do not suggest a monetary result one way or the other, we do think the plaintiff's evidence should be part of the factual mix and weighed as such. Until the $21 price is measured on remand by the valuation standards mandated by Delaware law, there can be no finding at the present stage of these proceedings that the price is fair. Given the lack of any candid disclosure of the material facts surrounding establishment of the $21 price, the majority of the minority vote, approving the merger, is meaningless.

The plaintiff has not sought an appraisal, but rescissory damages of the type contemplated by Lynch v. Vickers Energy Corp., Del. Supr., 429 A.2d 497, 505–06 (1981) (*Lynch II*). In view of the approach to valuation that we announce today, we see no basis in our law for *Lynch II* 's exclusive monetary formula for relief. On remand the plaintiff will be permitted to test the fairness of the $21 price by the standards we herein establish, in conformity with the principle applicable to an appraisal—that fair value be determined by taking "into account all relevant factors" [see 8 Del.C. § 262(h), supra]. In our view this includes the elements of rescissory damages if the Chancellor considers them susceptible of proof and a remedy appropriate to all the issues of fairness before him. To the extent that *Lynch II,* 429 A.2d at 505–06, purports to limit the Chancellor's discretion to a single remedial formula for monetary damages in a cash-out merger, it is overruled.

While a plaintiff's monetary remedy ordinarily should be confined to the more liberalized appraisal proceeding herein established, we do not intend any limitation on the historic powers of the Chancellor to grant such other relief as the facts of a particular case may dictate. The appraisal remedy we approve may not be adequate in certain cases, particularly where fraud, misrepresentation, self-dealing, deliberate waste of corporate assets, or gross and palpable overreaching are involved. Cole v. National Cash Credit Association, Del.Ch., 156 A. 183, 187 (1931). Under such circumstances, the Chancellor's powers are complete to fashion any form of equitable and monetary relief as may be appropriate, including rescissory damages. Since it is apparent that this long completed transaction is too involved to undo, and in view of the Chancellor's discretion, the award, if any, should be in the form of monetary damages based upon entire fairness standards, i.e., fair dealing and fair price.

Obviously, there are other litigants, like the plaintiff, who abjured an appraisal and whose rights to challenge the element of fair value must be preserved.[8] Accordingly, the quasi-appraisal remedy we grant the plaintiff here will apply only to: (1) this case; (2) any case now pending on appeal to this Court; (3) any case now pending in the Court of Chancery which has not yet been appealed but which may be eligible for direct appeal to this Court; (4) any case challenging a cash-out merger, the effective date of which is on or before February 1, 1983; and (5) any proposed merger to be presented at a shareholders' meeting, the notification of which is mailed to the stockholders on or before February 23, 1983. Thereafter, the provisions of 8 Del.C. § 262, as herein construed, respecting the scope of an appraisal and the means for perfecting the same, shall govern the financial remedy available to minority shareholders in a cash-out merger. Thus, we return to the well established principles of Stauffer v. Standard Brands, Inc., Del.Supr., 187 A.2d 78 (1962) and David J. Greene & Co. v. Schenley Industries, Inc., Del.Ch., 281 A.2d 30 (1971), mandating a stockholder's recourse to the basic remedy of an appraisal.

---

8. Under 8 Del.C. § 262(a), (d) & (e), a stockholder is required to act within certain time periods to perfect the right to an appraisal.

III.

Finally, we address the matter of business purpose. The defendants contend that the purpose of this merger was not a proper subject of inquiry by the trial court. The plaintiff says that no valid purpose existed—the entire transaction was a mere subterfuge designed to eliminate the minority. The Chancellor ruled otherwise, but in so doing he clearly circumscribed the thrust and effect of *Singer.* Weinberger v. UOP, 426 A.2d at 1342–43, 1348–50. This has led to the thoroughly sound observation that the business purpose test "may be . . . virtually interpreted out of existence, as it was in *Weinberger* ".[9]

The requirement of a business purpose is new to our law of mergers and was a departure from prior case law. See Stauffer v. Standard Brands, Inc., supra; David J. Greene & Co. v. Schenley Industries, Inc., supra.

In view of the fairness test which has long been applicable to parent-subsidiary mergers, Sterling v. Mayflower Hotel Corp., Del. Supr., 93 A.2d 107, 109–10 (1952), the expanded appraisal remedy now available to shareholders, and the broad discretion of the Chancellor to fashion such relief as the facts of a given case may dictate we do not believe that any additional meaningful protection is afforded minority shareholders by the business purpose requirement of the trilogy of *Singer, Tanzer,*[10] *Najjar,*[11] and their progeny. Accordingly, such requirement shall no longer be of any force or effect.

The judgment of the Court of Chancery, finding both the circumstances of the merger and the price paid the minority shareholders to be fair, is reversed. The matter is remanded for further proceedings consistent herewith. Upon remand the plaintiff's post-trial motion to enlarge the class should be granted.

* * *

Reversed and Remanded.

RABKIN v. PHILIP A. HUNT CHEMICAL CORP., 498 A.2d 1099 (Del.1985). "The issue we address is whether the trial court erred, as a matter of law, in dismissing these claims on the ground that absent deception the plaintiffs' sole remedy under *Weinberger* is an appraisal. . . .

"The Court of Chancery seems to have limited its focus to our statement in *Weinberger* that:

[T]he provisions of 8 Del.C. § 262, as herein construed, respecting the scope of an appraisal and the means for perfecting the same, shall govern the financial remedy available to minority shareholders in a cash-out merger. Thus, we return to the well

---

9. Weiss, The Law of Take Out Mergers: A Historical Perspective, 56 N.Y.U.L. Rev. 624, 671, n. 300 (1981).

10. Tanzer v. International General Industries, Inc., Del.Supr., 379 A.2d 1121, 1124–25 (1977).

11. Roland International Corp. v. Najjar, Del.Supr., 407 A.2d 1032, 1036 (1979).

established principles of Stauffer v. Standard Brands, Inc., Del. Supr., 187 A.2d 78 (1962) and David J. Greene & Co. v. Schenley Industries, Inc., Del.Ch., 281 A.2d 30 (1971), mandating a stockholder's recourse to the basic remedy of an appraisal.

Weinberger, 457 A.2d at 715. However, *Weinberger* makes clear that appraisal is not necessarily a stockholder's sole remedy. We specifically noted that:

> [W]hile a plaintiff's monetary remedy ordinarily should be confined to the more liberalized appraisal proceeding herein established, we do not intend any limitation on the historic powers of the Chancellor to grant such other relief as the facts of a particular case may dictate. The appraisal remedy we approve may not be adequate in certain cases, particularly where fraud, misrepresentation, self-dealing, deliberate waste of corporate assets, or gross and palpable overreaching are involved. Cole v. National Cash Credit Association, Del.Ch., 156 A. 183, 187 (1931).

Id. at 714.

"Thus, the trial court's narrow interpretation of *Weinberger* would render meaningless our extensive discussion of fair dealing found in that opinion. In *Weinberger* we defined fair dealing as embracing 'questions of when the transaction was timed, how it was initiated, structured, negotiated, disclosed to the directors, and how the approvals of the directors and the stockholders were obtained.' 457 A.2d at 711. While this duty of fairness certainly incorporates the principle that a cash-out merger must be free of fraud or misrepresentation, *Weinberger's* mandate of fair dealing does not turn solely on issues of deception. We particularly noted broader concerns respecting the matter of procedural fairness. *Weinberger,* 457 A.2d at 711, 714. Thus, while 'in a non-fraudulent transaction . . . price *may* be the preponderant consideration,' id. at 711 (emphasis added), it is not necessarily so.

"Although the Vice Chancellor correctly understood *Weinberger* as limiting collateral attacks on cash-out mergers, her analysis narrowed the procedural protections which we still intended *Weinberger* to guarantee. Here, plaintiffs are not arguing questions of valuation which are the traditional subjects of an appraisal. . . .

"While a plaintiff's mere allegation of 'unfair dealing', without more, cannot survive a motion to dismiss, averments containing 'specific acts of fraud, misrepresentation, or other items of misconduct' must be carefully examined in accord with our views expressed both here and in *Weinberger.* . . .

". . . [T]he defendants are charged with bad faith which goes beyond issues of 'mere inadequacy of price.' Cole v. National Cash Credit Association, Del.Ch., 156 A. 183, 187–88 (1931). In *Weinberger* we specifically relied upon this aspect of *Cole* in acknowledging the imperfections of an appraisal where circumstances of this sort are present. See 457 A.2d at 714.

"Necessarily, this will require the Court of Chancery to closely focus upon *Weinberger's* mandate of entire fairness based on a careful analysis of both the fair price and fair dealing aspects of a transaction. See 457 A.2d at 711, 714. We recognize that this can present certain practical problems, since stockholders may invariably claim that the price being offered is the result of unfair dealings. However, we think that plaintiffs will be tempered in this approach by the prospect that an ultimate judgment in defendants' favor may have cost plaintiffs their unperfected appraisal rights. Moreover, our courts are not without a degree of sophistication in such matters. A balance must be struck between sustaining complaints averring faithless acts, which taken as true would constitute breaches of fiduciary duties that are reasonably related to and have a substantial impact upon the price offered, and properly dismissing those allegations questioning judgmental factors of valuation. Cole v. National Cash Credit Association, 156 A. at 187–88. Otherwise, we face the anomalous result that stockholders who are eliminated without appraisal rights can bring class actions, while in other cases a squeezed-out minority is limited to an appraisal, provided there was no deception, regardless of the degree of procedural unfairness employed to take their shares. Without that balance, *Weinberger's* concern for entire fairness loses all force."

———

COGGINS v. NEW ENGLAND PATRIOTS FOOTBALL CLUB, INC., 397 Mass. 525, 492 N.E.2d 1112 (1986). "Unlike the Delaware court . . . we believe that the "business-purpose" test is an additional useful means under our statutes and case law for examining a transaction in which a controlling stockholder eliminates the minority interest in a corporation. . . . This concept of fair dealing is not limited to close corporations but applies to judicial review of cash freeze-out mergers. . . .

"The defendants argue that judicial review of a merger cannot be invoked by disgruntled stockholders, absent illegal or fraudulent conduct. They rely on G.L. c. 156B, § 98 (1984 ed.).[12] In the defendants' view, 'the Superior Court's finding of liability was premised solely on the claimed inadequacy of the offering price.' Any dispute over offering price, they urge, must be resolved solely through the statutory remedy of appraisal. . . .

"We have held in regard to so called 'close corporations' that the statute does not divest the courts of their equitable jurisdiction to assure that the conduct of controlling stockholders does not violate the fiduciary principles governing the relationship between majority and minority stockholders. *Pupecki v. James Madison Corp.,* 376 Mass. 212, 216–217, 382 N.E.2d 1030 (1978) (when controlling stockholder fails to assure that corporation receives adequate consideration for its

12. "The enforcement by a stockholder of his right to receive payment for his shares in the manner provided in this chapter shall be an exclusive remedy except that this chapter shall not exclude the right of such stockholder to bring or maintain an appropriate proceeding to obtain relief on the ground that such corporate action will be or is illegal or fraudulent as to him." G.L. c. 156B, § 98.

assets, transaction is illegal or fraudulent, and G.L. c. 156B, § 98, does not foreclose review). 'Where the director's duty of loyalty to the corporation is in conflict with his self-interest the court will vigorously scrutinize the situation.' *American Discount Corp. v. Kaitz,* 348 Mass. 706, 711, 206 N.E.2d 156 (1965). The court is justified in exercising its equitable power when a violation of fiduciary duty is claimed.

"The dangers of self-dealing and abuse of fiduciary duty are greatest in freeze-out situations like the Patriots merger, where a controlling stockholder and corporate director chooses to eliminate public ownership. It is in these cases that a judge should examine with closest scrutiny the motives and the behavior of the controlling stockholder. A showing of compliance with statutory procedures is an insufficient substitute for the inquiry of the courts when a minority stockholder claims that the corporate action 'will be or is illegal or fraudulent as to him.' G.L. c. 156B, § 98. *Leader v. Hycor, Inc.,* 395 Mass. 215, 221, 479 N.E.2d 173 (1985) (judicial review may be had of claims of breach of fiduciary duty and unfairness).

"Judicial scrutiny should begin with recognition of the basic principle that the duty of a corporate director must be to further the legitimate goals of the corporation. The result of a freeze-out merger is the elimination of public ownership in the corporation. The controlling faction increases its equity from a majority to 100%, using corporate processes and corporate assets. The corporate directors who benefit from this transfer of ownership must demonstrate how the legitimate goals of the corporation are furthered. A director of a corporation violates his fiduciary duty when he uses the corporation for his or his family's personal benefit in a manner detrimental to the corporation. *Widett & Widett v. Snyder,* 392 Mass. 778, 785–786, 467 N.E.2d 1312 (1984). See *Buckman v. Elm Hill Realty Co. of Peabody,* 312 Mass. 10, 15, 42 N.E.2d 814 (1942). Because the danger of abuse of fiduciary duty is especially great in a freeze-out merger, the court must be satisfied that the freeze-out was for the advancement of a legitimate corporate purpose. If satisfied that elimination of public ownership is in furtherance of a business purpose, the court should then proceed to determine if the transaction was fair by examining the totality of the circumstances. . . . .''

ALPERT v. 28 WILLIAMS ST. CORP., 63 N.Y.2d 557, 483 N.Y.S.2d 667, 473 N.E.2d 19 (1984). "In the context of a freeze-out merger, variant treatment of the minority shareholders—i.e., causing their removal—will be justified when related to the advancement of a general corporate interest. The benefit need not be great, but it must be for the corporation. For example, if the sole purpose of the merger is reduction of the number of profit sharers—in contrast to increasing the corporation's capital or profits, or improving its management structure—there will exist no 'independent corporate interest' (see Schwartz v. Marien, 37 N.Y.2d 487, 492, 373 N.Y.S.2d 122, 335 N.E.2d 334, supra). All of these purposes ultimately seek to increase the individual wealth of the remaining shareholders. What distinguishes a proper corporate purpose from an improper one is that, with the former, removal of the minority shareholders furthers the objective of conferring some general gain upon the corporation. Only then will the fiduciary duty of good and prudent management of the corporation serve to override the concurrent duty to treat all shareholders fairly (see Klurfeld v. Equity Enterprises, 79 A.D.2d 124, 136, 436 N.Y.S.2d 303, supra). We further note that a finding that there was an independent corporate purpose for the action taken by the majority will not be defeated merely by the fact that the corporate objective could have been accomplished in another way, or by the fact that the action chosen was not the best way to achieve the bona fide business objective."

CAL. CORP. CODE §§ 1001, 1101, 1101.1, 1312

[See Statutory Supplement]

CAL. CORP. CODE § 407

[See Statutory Supplement]

(j) Going Private

"Going private" involves the conversion of a corporation that is publicly held into one that is privately held—or, more particularly, the conversion of a corporation whose stock is registered under the 1934 Act, and listed on a Stock Exchange or actively traded over the counter, into one whose stock is unregistered, unlisted, and traded thinly if at all. While going private is often accomplished through a freezeout, the two categories are not entirely coextensive: going private, unlike freezeouts, does not necessarily involve *legal* compulsion, since it may be accomplished through purchase of the minority's shares. On the other hand, as the following material shows, such purchases, while apparently involving voluntary action on the minority's part, may in fact involve very little meaningful choice, and are often accomplished in part by the implicit or explicit threat that those who do not sell voluntarily will be made to sell involuntarily through use of a cashout merger or other freezeout device.

ADDRESS BY A.A. SOMMER, JR., COMMISSIONER, SECURITIES AND EXCHANGE COMMISSION, CCH, FED'L SEC.L.REP. [1974–'75 TRANSFER BINDER] ¶ 80,010

During the sixties and early seventies innumerable companies "went public," that is, publicly offered their securities. . . . All of these companies invited the public to share in their fortunes. . . .

What is happening now is this: as market prices of stock have plummeted, often to levels below book value, many companies have commenced the process of going private. . . .

The simplest way is an offer to pay the shareholders who accept a stipulated price, usually something in excess of the market price. This seems simple enough: the shareholder can take the offer or leave it, he is under no compulsion, and in fact, the offer may be a significant favor to him, since it may be the highest price he will see for some time. But even this simple approach has within it, in my estimation, troublesome elements. Usually, because of the necessities of full disclosure in our corporate life—largely policed and demanded by the SEC—the document which communicates the tender offer tells the awful truth. First, if significant numbers of shareholders respond to the tender, the shareholder who considers staying aboard faces significant losses. If the number of shareholders drops under 300 he will lose the network of federal protections built over a period of forty years for his benefit: no assurance of comprehensive disclosure, only limited protections against insider chicanery and so on. If he chooses to stay aboard he may find the liquidity of his investment—the ability to sell readily at a price reasonably proximate to the last sale—reduced, perhaps completely destroyed. Further, if management buys or otherwise acquires or has the power to bring it about, it may "merge out" the remaining minority and compel them in effect to sell their investments. Under the laws of the states in which most public corporations are incorporated, so-called cash mergers are allowed, that is, the shareholders of a company being acquired by another, instead of receiving stock of the acquiring company (the pattern of the typical merger) can be compelled to take cash in the amount determined by the merger agreement. . . .

Faced with the prospect of a force-out merger, or a market reduced to glacial activity and the liquidity of the Mojave Desert, and deprived of most of the benefits of the federal securities laws, how real is the choice of the shareholder confronting the offer of management to acquire his shares, usually not with their own resources, but with the corporation's resources that really belong to him and his fellow shareholders? In short, he usually decides he damn well better take the money and run. . . .

Is all this ethical? I would say to you there is at the minimum deep doubt of that. The spectacle of entrepreneurs inviting the public in when they can command high prices for their stock, and then squeezing them out with little or no practical choice in the matter at substantially reduced prices is hardly one to warm the soul of Thomas Aquinas or Aristotle. The corporation, and often the controlling interests, have been enriched with the proceeds of the public offerings of the past; with those proceeds the corporation grew and prospered, then, with the power deriving from their managerial positions and shareholdings, the insiders take over the whole corporation for themselves.

In one recent instance public offerings netted $696,000 for the corporation, over $12,500,000 for the offering shareholders. The corporation has now proposed to acquire all the stock held by minority shareholders for $11.00 per share. If all of the minority shareholders tender, they would receive $3.00 in cash and $8.00 in ten year subordinated debentures (which the company believes will sell at a substantial discount) for shares which were originally offered at $17.50 a share and three years ago at $21.75 a share; the dominant shareholder would go from a 7% interest to 43%, with over 3.7 million dollars (less taxes) provided by the public now safely locked up for her benefit. On a pro forma basis, had all public shares been repurchased on the basis proposed at the beginning of 1973, the corporate profits attributable to her interest would have risen from $236,000 to $1,107,000 in 1973—over 400%—and from $167,000 to $688,000 for the first ten months of 1974—again over 400%—and without a single dime of additional investment by her!

I would suggest there is something wrong with that. . . .

SECURITIES EXCHANGE ACT RULE 13e–3 AND SCHEDULE 13e–3

[See Statutory Supplement]

SECTION 2.   TENDER OFFERS

SECURITIES EXCHANGE ACT §§ 13(d), (e), 14(d), (e)

SECURITIES EXCHANGE ACT RULES 13d–3, 13d–5, 13e–1, 13e–4, 14d–1 to 14d–4, 14d–6 to 14d–10, 14e–1 to 14e–3

[See Statutory Supplement]

NOTE ON TERMINOLOGY

The legal profession has developed a rich terminology in connection with tender offers. The terms are too numerous and change too quickly to permit a comprehensive glossary, and some of the terms are fairly well defined in the cases that follow. This Note defines a few of the more important terms that are not defined in those cases.

Raider. The term *raider* refers to a person (normally, although not necessarily, a corporation) that makes a tender offer. The term is invidious; a more accurate term is *bidder.*

Target. The corporation whose shares the bidder seeks to acquire is referred to as the *target.*

White knight. Often the management of a target realizes that it will be taken over, but prefers a takeover by someone (sometimes, anyone) other than the original bidder. The management therefore solicits competing tender offers from other corporations. These more friendly corporations are known as *white knights.*

Lock-up. A *lock-up* is a device that is designed to protect one bidder (normally, a friendly bidder) against competition by other bidders (deemed less friendly). The favored bidder is given an option to acquire selected assets or a given amount of shares of the target at a favorable price under designated conditions. These conditions usually involve either defeat of the favored bidder's attempt to acquire the corporation, or the occurrence of events that would make that defeat likely.

Crown jewels. To defeat or discourage a takeover bid by a disfavored bidder, the target's management may sell or (more usually) give to a white knight a lock-up option that covers the target's most desirable business or, at least, the business most coveted by the disfavored bidder—its *crown jewels.*

Standstill. A target may seek an accomodation with a shareholder who has acquired a significant amount of stock, under which the shareholder agrees to limit his stock purchases—hence, *standstill.* In the typical standstill agreement, the shareholder makes one or more commitments: (i) it will not increase its shareholdings above designated limits for a specified period of time; (ii) it will not sell its shares without giving the corporation a right of first refusal; (iii) it will not engage in a proxy contest; and (iv) it will vote its stock in a designated manner in the election of directors, and perhaps on other issues. In return, the corporation typically agrees to give the shareholder board representation, to register the shareholder's stock under the Securities Act on demand, and not to oppose the shareholder's acquisition of stock up to the specified limit. See ALI, Principles of Corporate Governance, Council Draft No. 11, Section 6.01, Reporters' Note (1988).

No-shop clauses. A board of a corporation that enters into an agreement for a merger or other corporate combination (whether with a white knight or otherwise) may agree that it will recommend the combination to the shareholders, that it will not shop around for a more attractive deal, or both. The courts have divided on the question whether such provisions are unenforceable on the ground that they conflict with the director's fiduciary obligation to maximize the shareholders' best interests. Compare Jewel Companies, Inc. v. Pay Less Drug Stores Northwest, Inc., 741 F.2d 1555 (9th Cir. 1984) (no-shop clause enforceable) with Great Western Producers Co-Operative v. Great Western United Corporation, 200 Colo. 180, 613 P.2d 873 (1980) (agreement to recommend transaction to the shareholders not effectively enforceable).

Fair-price provisions. A fair-price provision requires that a supermajority (usually eighty percent) of the voting power of a corporation must approve any merger or similar combination with an acquiror who owns a specified interest in the corporation (usually twenty percent of the voting power). The supermajority vote is not required under certain conditions—most notably, if the transaction is approved by a majority of those directors who are not affiliated with the acquiror and were directors at the time the acquiror reached the specified level of ownership of the company, or if certain minimum-price criteria and procedural requirements are satisfied. A fair-price provision discourages purchasers whose objective is to seek control of a corporation at a relatively cheap price, and discourages accumulations of large blocks, since it reduces the options an acquiror has once it reaches the specified level of shares. M. Lipton & E. Steinberger, Takeovers & Freezeouts § 6.03[2] (1987).

Leveraged buyout. A leveraged buyout is a combination of a management buyout and a high degree of leverage. A *management buyout* (MBO) is the acquisition for cash or non-convertible senior securities of the business of a public corporation, by a newly organized corporation in which members of the former management of the public corporation will have a significant equity interest, pursuant to a merger or other form of combination. See Lowenstein, Management Buyouts, 85 Colum.L.Rev. 730, 732 (1985). *Leverage* involves the use of debt to increase the return on equity. The extent of leverage is measured by the ratio of (i) debt to (ii) debt plus equity. The higher the ratio, the greater the leverage (or, to put it differently, the more highly leveraged the corporation is). A *leveraged buyout* (LBO) is an MBO that is highly leveraged—that is, in which the newly organized acquiring corporation has a very high amount of debt in relation to its equity. Characteristically, an LBO is arranged by a firm that specializes in such transactions, can find investors (or will itself invest) along with senior management in the new firm's securities, and can arrange for (or help arrange for) placement of the massive amount of debt that the new corporation must issue to finance the acquisition of the old corporation's business.

Junk bonds. A *junk bond* is a bond that has an unusually high risk of default (and is therefore below investment grade), but, correspondingly, carries an unusually high yield. (The theory is that by diversification—that is, by holding a portfolio of junk bonds—investors in junk bonds can insulate themselves from catastrophic loss if any one bond issue goes under.) Because an LBO is so highly leveraged, much or most of the debt issued to finance an LBO usually consists of junk bonds.

UNOCAL CORP. v. MESA PETROLEUM CO.

Supreme Court of Delaware, 1985.
493 A.2d 946.

Before McNEILLY and MOORE, JJ., and TAYLOR, Judge
(Sitting by designation pursuant to Del.Const., Art. 4, § 12.)

MOORE, Justice.

We confront an issue of first impression in Delaware—the validity of a corporation's self-tender for its own shares which excludes from participation a stockholder making a hostile tender offer for the company's stock.

The Court of Chancery granted a preliminary injunction to the plaintiffs, Mesa Petroleum Co., Mesa Asset Co., Mesa Partners II, and Mesa Eastern, Inc. (collectively "Mesa")[1], enjoining an exchange offer of the defendant, Unocal Corporation (Unocal) for its own stock. The trial court concluded that a selective exchange offer, excluding Mesa, was legally impermissible. We cannot agree with such a blanket rule. The factual findings of the Vice Chancellor, fully supported by the record, establish that Unocal's board, consisting of a majority of independent directors, acted in good faith, and after reasonable investigation found that Mesa's tender offer was both inadequate and coercive. Under the circumstances the board had both the power and duty to oppose a bid it perceived to be harmful to the corporate enterprise. On this record we are satisfied that the device Unocal adopted is reasonable in relation to the threat posed, and that the board acted in the proper exercise of sound business judgment. We will not substitute our views for those of the board if the latter's decision can be "attributed to any rational business purpose." Sinclair Oil Corp. v. Levien, Del.Supr., 280 A.2d 717, 720 (1971). Accordingly, we reverse the decision of the Court of Chancery and order the preliminary injunction vacated.[2]

I.

The factual background of this matter bears a significant relationship to its ultimate outcome.

On April 8, 1985, Mesa, the owner of approximately 13% of Unocal's stock, commenced a two-tier "front loaded" cash tender offer for 64 million shares, or approximately 37%, of Unocal's outstanding stock at a price of $54 per share. The "back-end" was designed to eliminate the remaining publicly held shares by an exchange of securities purportedly worth $54 per share. However, pursuant to an order entered by the United States District Court for the Central District of California on April 26, 1985, Mesa issued a

---

1. T. Boone Pickens, Jr., is President and Chairman of the Board of Mesa Petroleum and President of Mesa Asset and controls the related Mesa entities.

2. This appeal was heard on an expedited basis in light of the pending Mesa tender offer and Unocal exchange offer. We announced our decision to reverse in an oral ruling in open court on May 17, 1985 with the further statement that this opinion would follow shortly thereafter. See infra n. 5.

supplemental proxy statement to Unocal's stockholders disclosing that the securities offered in the second-step merger would be highly subordinated, and that Unocal's capitalization would differ significantly from its present structure. Unocal has rather aptly termed such securities "junk bonds".[3]

Unocal's board consists of eight independent outside directors and six insiders. It met on April 13, 1985, to consider the Mesa tender offer. Thirteen directors were present, and the meeting lasted nine and one-half hours. The directors were given no agenda or written materials prior to the session. However, detailed presentations were made by legal counsel regarding the board's obligations under both Delaware corporate law and the federal securities laws. The board then received a presentation from Peter Sachs on behalf of Goldman Sachs & Co. (Goldman Sachs) and Dillon, Read & Co. (Dillon Read) discussing the bases for their opinions that the Mesa proposal was wholly inadequate. Mr. Sachs opined that the minimum cash value that could be expected from a sale or orderly liquidation for 100% of Unocal's stock was in excess of $60 per share. In making his presentation, Mr. Sachs showed slides outlining the valuation techniques used by the financial advisors, and others, depicting recent business combinations in the oil and gas industry. The Court of Chancery found that the Sachs presentation was designed to apprise the directors of the scope of the analyses performed rather than the facts and numbers used in reaching the conclusion that Mesa's tender offer price was inadequate.

Mr. Sachs also presented various defensive strategies available to the board if it concluded that Mesa's two-step tender offer was inadequate and should be opposed. One of the devices outlined was a self-tender by Unocal for its own stock with a reasonable price range of $70 to $75 per share. The cost of such a proposal would cause the company to incur $6.1–6.5 billion of additional debt, and a presentation was made informing the board of Unocal's ability to handle it. The directors were told that the primary effect of this obligation

---

3. Mesa's May 3, 1985 supplement to its proxy statement states:

(i) following the Offer, the Purchasers would seek to effect a merger of Unocal and Mesa Eastern or an affiliate of Mesa Eastern (the "Merger") in which the remaining Shares would be acquired for a combination of subordinated debt securities and preferred stock; (ii) the securities to be received by Unocal shareholders in the Merger would be subordinated to $2,400 million of debt securities of Mesa Eastern, indebtedness incurred to refinance up to $1,000 million of bank debt which was incurred by affiliates of Mesa Partners II to purchase Shares and to pay related interest and expenses and all then-existing debt of Unocal; (iii) the corporation surviving the Merger would be responsible for the payment of all securities of Mesa Eastern (including any such securities issued pursuant to the Merger) and the indebtedness referred to in item (ii) above, and such securities and indebtedness would be repaid out of funds generated by the operations of Unocal; (iv) the indebtedness incurred in the Offer and the Merger would result in Unocal being much more highly leveraged, and the capitalization of the corporation surviving the Merger would differ significantly from that of Unocal at present; and (v) in their analyses of cash flows provided by operations of Unocal which would be available to service and repay securities and other obligations of the corporation surviving the Merger, the Purchasers assumed that the capital expenditures and expenditures for exploration of such corporation would be significantly reduced.

would be to reduce exploratory drilling, but that the company would nonetheless remain a viable entity.

The eight outside directors, comprising a clear majority of the thirteen members present, then met separately with Unocal's financial advisors and attorneys. Thereafter, they unanimously agreed to advise the board that it should reject Mesa's tender offer as inadequate, and that Unocal should pursue a self-tender to provide the stockholders with a fairly priced alternative to the Mesa proposal. The board then reconvened and unanimously adopted a resolution rejecting as grossly inadequate Mesa's tender offer. Despite the nine and one-half hour length of the meeting, no formal decision was made on the proposed defensive self-tender.

On April 15, the board met again with four of the directors present by telephone and one member still absent.[4] This session lasted two hours. Unocal's Vice President of Finance and its Assistant General Counsel made a detailed presentation of the proposed terms of the exchange offer. A price range between $70 and $80 per share was considered, and ultimately the directors agreed upon $72. The board was also advised about the debt securities that would be issued, and the necessity of placing restrictive covenants upon certain corporate activities until the obligations were paid. The board's decisions were made in reliance on the advice of its investment bankers, including the terms and conditions upon which the securities were to be issued. Based upon this advice, and the board's own deliberations, the directors unanimously approved the exchange offer. Their resolution provided that if Mesa acquired 64 million shares of Unocal stock through its own offer (the Mesa Purchase Condition), Unocal would buy the remaining 49% outstanding for an exchange of debt securities having an aggregate par value of $72 per share. The board resolution also stated that the offer would be subject to other conditions that had been described to the board at the meeting, or which were deemed necessary by Unocal's officers, including the exclusion of Mesa from the proposal (the Mesa exclusion). Any such conditions were required to be in accordance with the "purport and intent" of the offer.

Unocal's exchange offer was commenced on April 17, 1985, and Mesa promptly challenged it by filing this suit in the Court of Chancery. On April 22, the Unocal board met again and was advised by Goldman Sachs and Dillon Read to waive the Mesa Purchase Condition as to 50 million shares. This recommendation was in response to a perceived concern of the shareholders that, if shares were tendered to Unocal, no shares would be purchased by either offeror. The directors were also advised that they should tender their own Unocal stock into the exchange offer as a mark of their confidence in it.

---

4. Under Delaware law directors may participate in a board meeting by telephone. . . .

Another focus of the board was the Mesa exclusion. Legal counsel advised that under Delaware law Mesa could only be excluded for what the directors reasonably believed to be a valid corporate purpose. The directors' discussion centered on the objective of adequately compensating shareholders at the "back-end" of Mesa's proposal, which the latter would finance with "junk bonds". To include Mesa would defeat that goal, because under the proration aspect of the exchange offer (49%) every Mesa share accepted by Unocal would displace one held by another stockholder. Further, if Mesa were permitted to tender to Unocal, the latter would in effect be financing Mesa's own inadequate proposal.

On April 24, 1985 Unocal issued a supplement to the exchange offer describing the partial waiver of the Mesa Purchase Condition. On May 1, 1985, in another supplement, Unocal extended the withdrawal, proration and expiration dates of its exchange offer to May 17, 1985.

Meanwhile, on April 22, 1985, Mesa amended its complaint in this action to challenge the Mesa exclusion. A preliminary injunction hearing was scheduled for May 8, 1985. However, on April 23, 1985, Mesa moved for a temporary restraining order in response to Unocal's announcement that it was partially waiving the Mesa Purchase Condition. After expedited briefing, the Court of Chancery heard Mesa's motion on April 26.

On April 29, 1985, the Vice Chancellor temporarily restrained Unocal from proceeding with the exchange offer unless it included Mesa. The trial court recognized that directors could oppose, and attempt to defeat, a hostile takeover which they considered adverse to the best interests of the corporation. However, the Vice Chancellor decided that in a selective purchase of the company's stock, the corporation bears the burden of showing: (1) a valid corporate purpose, and (2) that the transaction was fair to all of the stockholders, including those excluded.

Unocal immediately sought certification of an interlocutory appeal to this Court pursuant to Supreme Court Rule 42(b). On May 1, 1985, the Vice Chancellor declined to certify the appeal on the grounds that the decision granting a temporary restraining order did not decide a legal issue of first impression, and was not a matter to which the decisions of the Court of Chancery were in conflict.

However, in an Order dated May 2, 1985, this Court ruled that the Chancery decision was clearly determinative of substantive rights of the parties, and in fact decided the main question of law before the Vice Chancellor, which was indeed a question of first impression. We therefore concluded that the temporary restraining order was an appealable decision. However, because the Court of Chancery was scheduled to hold a preliminary injunction hearing on May 8 at which there would be an enlarged record on the various issues, action on the interlocutory appeal was deferred pending an outcome of those proceedings.

In deferring action on the interlocutory appeal, we noted that on the record before us we could not determine whether the parties had articulated certain issues which the Vice Chancellor should have an opportunity to consider in the first instance. These included the following:

a) Does the directors' duty of care to the corporation extend to protecting the corporate enterprise in good faith from perceived depredations of others, including persons who may own stock in the company?

b) Have one or more of the plaintiffs, their affiliates, or persons acting in concert with them, either in dealing with Unocal or others, demonstrated a pattern of conduct sufficient to justify a reasonable inference by defendants that a principle objective of the plaintiffs is to achieve selective treatment for themselves by the repurchase of their Unocal shares at a substantial premium?

c) If so, may the directors of Unocal in the proper exercise of business judgment employ the exchange offer to protect the corporation and its shareholders from such tactics? See Pogostin v. Rice, Del.Supr., 480 A.2d 619 (1984).

d) If it is determined that the purpose of the exchange offer was not illegal as a matter of law, have the directors of Unocal carried their burden of showing that they acted in good faith? See Martin v. American Potash & Chemical Corp., 33 Del.Ch. 234, 92 A.2d 295 at 302.

After the May 8 hearing the Vice Chancellor issued an unreported opinion on May 13, 1985 granting Mesa a preliminary injunction. Specifically, the trial court noted that "[t]he parties basically agree that the directors' duty of care extends to protecting the corporation from perceived harm whether it be from third parties or shareholders." The trial court also concluded in response to the second inquiry in the Supreme Court's May 2 order, that "[a]lthough the facts, . . . do not appear to be sufficient to prove that Mesa's principle objective is to be bought off at a substantial premium, they do justify a reasonable inference to the same effect."

As to the third and fourth questions posed by this Court, the Vice Chancellor stated that they "appear to raise the more fundamental issue of whether directors owe fiduciary duties to shareholders who they perceive to be acting contrary to the best interests of the corporation as a whole." While determining that the directors' decision to oppose Mesa's tender offer was made in a good faith belief that the Mesa proposal was inadequate, the court stated that the business judgment rule does not apply to a selective exchange offer such as this.

On May 13, 1985 the Court of Chancery certified this interlocutory appeal to us as a question of first impression, and we accepted it on May 14. The entire matter was scheduled on an expedited basis.[5]

---

5. Such expedition was required by the fact that if Unocal's exchange offer was permitted to proceed, the proration date for the shares entitled to be exchanged was May 17, 1985, while Mesa's tender offer expired on May 23. After acceptance of

II.

The issues we address involve these fundamental questions: Did the Unocal board have the power and duty to oppose a takeover threat it reasonably perceived to be harmful to the corporate enterprise, and if so, is its action here entitled to the protection of the business judgment rule?

Mesa contends that the discriminatory exchange offer violates the fiduciary duties Unocal owes it. Mesa argues that because of the Mesa exclusion the business judgment rule is inapplicable, because the directors by tendering their own shares will derive a financial benefit that is not available to *all* Unocal stockholders. Thus, it is Mesa's ultimate contention that Unocal cannot establish that the exchange offer is fair to *all* shareholders, and argues that the Court of Chancery was correct in concluding that Unocal was unable to meet this burden.

Unocal answers that it does not owe a duty of "fairness" to Mesa, given the facts here. Specifically, Unocal contends that its board of directors reasonably and in good faith concluded that Mesa's $54 two-tier tender offer was coercive and inadequate, and that Mesa sought selective treatment for itself. Furthermore, Unocal argues that the board's approval of the exchange offer was made in good faith, on an informed basis, and in the exercise of due care. Under these circumstances, Unocal contends that its directors properly employed this device to protect the company and its stockholders from Mesa's harmful tactics.

III.

We begin with the basic issue of the power of a board of directors of a Delaware corporation to adopt a defensive measure of this type. Absent such authority, all other questions are moot. Neither issues of fairness nor business judgment are pertinent without the basic underpinning of a board's legal power to act.

The board has a large reservoir of authority upon which to draw. Its duties and responsibilities proceed from the inherent powers conferred by 8 Del.C. § 141(a), respecting management of the corporation's "business and affairs". Additionally, the powers here being exercised derive from 8 Del.C. § 160(a), conferring broad authority upon a corporation to deal in its own stock. From this it is now well established that in the acquisition of its shares a Delaware corporation may deal selectively with its stockholders, provided the directors have not acted out of a sole or primary purpose to entrench themselves in office. Cheff v. Mathes, Del.Supr., 199 A.2d 548, 554 (1964); Bennett v. Propp, Del.Supr., 187 A.2d 405, 408 (1962); Martin v. American Potash & Chemical Corporation, Del.Supr., 92 A.2d 295, 302 (1952); Kaplan v. Goldsamt, Del.Ch., 380 A.2d 556,

this appeal on May 14, we received excellent briefs from the parties, heard argument on May 16 and announced our oral ruling in open court at 9:00 a.m. on May 17. *See supra* n. 2.

568–569 (1977); Kors v. Carey, Del.Ch., 158 A.2d 136, 140–141 (1960).

Finally, the board's power to act derives from its fundamental duty and obligation to protect the corporate enterprise, which includes stockholders, from harm reasonably perceived, irrespective of its source. See e.g. Panter v. Marshall Field & Co., 646 F.2d 271, 297 (7th Cir.1981); Crouse–Hinds Co. v. Internorth, Inc., 634 F.2d 690, 704 (2d Cir.1980); Heit v. Baird, 567 F.2d 1157, 1161 (1st Cir. 1977); Cheff v. Mathes, 199 A.2d at 556; Martin v. American Potash & Chemical Corp., 92 A.2d at 302; Kaplan v. Goldsamt, 380 A.2d at 568–69; Kors v. Carey, 158 A.2d at 141; Northwest Industries, Inc. v. B.F. Goodrich Co., 301 F.Supp. 706, 712 (M.D.Ill.1969). Thus, we are satisfied that in the broad context of corporate governance, including issues of fundamental corporate change, a board of directors is not a passive instrumentality.[8]

Given the foregoing principles, we turn to the standards by which director action is to be measured. In Pogostin v. Rice, Del.Supr., 480 A.2d 619 (1984), we held that the business judgment rule, including the standards by which director conduct is judged, is applicable in the context of a takeover. Id. at 627. The business judgment rule is a "presumption that in making a business decision the directors of a corporation acted on an informed basis, in good faith and in the honest belief that the action taken was in the best interests of the company." Aronson v. Lewis, Del.Supr., 473 A.2d 805, 812 (1984) (citations omitted). A hallmark of the business judgment rule is that a court will not substitute its judgment for that of the board if the latter's decision can be "attributed to any rational business purpose." Sinclair Oil Corp. v. Levien, Del.Supr., 280 A.2d 717, 720 (1971).

When a board addresses a pending takeover bid it has an obligation to determine whether the offer is in the best interests of the corporation and its shareholders. In that respect a board's duty is no different from any other responsibility it shoulders, and its decision should be no less entitled to the respect they otherwise would be accorded in the realm of business judgment.[9] See also Johnson v. Trueblood, 629 F.2d 287, 292–293 (3d Cir.1980). There are, however, certain caveats to a proper exercise of this function. Because of the omnipresent specter that a board may be acting primarily in its own interests, rather than those of the corporation and its

8. Even in the traditional areas of fundamental corporate change, i.e., charter, amendments [8 Del.C. § 242(b)], mergers [8 Del.C. §§ 251(b), 252(c), 253(a), and 254(d)], sale of assets [8 Del.C. § 271(a)], and dissolution [8 Del.C. § 275(a)], director action is a prerequisite to the ultimate disposition of such matters. See also, Smith v. Van Gorkom, Del.Supr., 488 A.2d 858, 888 (1985).

9. This is a subject of intense debate among practicing members of the bar and legal scholars. Excellent examples of these contending views are: Block & Mill-

er, The Responsibilities and Obligations of Corporate Directors in Take-over Contests, 11 Sec.Reg.L.J. 44 (1983); Easterbrook & Fischel, Takeover Bids, Defensive Tactics, and Shareholders' Welfare, 36 Bus.Law. 1733 (1981); Easterbrook & Fischel, The Proper Role of a Target's Management In Responding to a Tender Offer, 94 Harv.L. Rev. 1161 (1981). Herzel, Schmidt & Davis, Why Corporate Directors Have a Right To Resist Tender Offers, 3 Corp.L.Rev. 107 (1980); Lipton, Takeover Bids in the Target's Boardroom, 35 Bus.Law. 101 (1979).

shareholders, there is an enhanced duty which calls for judicial examination at the threshold before the protections of the business judgment rule may be conferred.

This Court has long recognized that:

We must bear in mind the inherent danger in the purchase of shares with corporate funds to remove a threat to corporate policy when a threat to control is involved. The directors are of necessity confronted with a conflict of interest, and an objective decision is difficult.

Bennett v. Propp, Del.Supr., 187 A.2d 405, 409 (1962). In the face of this inherent conflict directors must show that they had reasonable grounds for believing that a danger to corporate policy and effectiveness existed because of another person's stock ownership. Cheff v. Mathes, 199 A.2d at 554–55. However, they satisfy that burden "by showing good faith and reasonable investigation. . . ." *Id.* at 555. Furthermore, such proof is materially enhanced, as here, by the approval of a board comprised of a majority of outside independent directors who have acted in accordance with the foregoing standards. See Aronson v. Lewis, 473 A.2d at 812, 815; Puma v. Marriott, Del. Ch., 283 A.2d 693, 695 (1971); Panter v. Marshall Field & Co., 646 F.2d 271, 295 (7th Cir.1981).

IV.

A.

In the board's exercise of corporate power to forestall a takeover bid our analysis begins with the basic principle that corporate directors have a fiduciary duty to act in the best interests of the corporation's stockholders. Guth v. Loft, Inc., Del.Supr., 5 A.2d 503, 510 (1939). As we have noted, their duty of care extends to protecting the corporation and its owners from perceived harm whether a threat originates from third parties or other shareholders.[10] But such powers are not absolute. A corporation does not have unbridled discretion to defeat any perceived threat by any Draconian means available.

The restriction placed upon a selective stock repurchase is that the directors may not have acted solely or primarily out of a desire to perpetuate themselves in office. See Cheff v. Mathes, 199 A.2d at 556; Kors v. Carey, 158 A.2d at 140. Of course, to this is added the further caveat that inequitable action may not be taken under the guise of law. Schnell v. Chris–Craft Industries, Inc., Del.Supr. 285 A.2d 437, 439 (1971). The standard of proof established in Cheff v. Mathes . . . is designed to ensure that a defensive measure to thwart or impede a takeover is indeed motivated by a good faith concern for the welfare of the corporation and its stockholders, which in all circumstances must be free of any fraud or other misconduct. Cheff

---

10. It has been suggested that a board's response to a takeover threat should be a passive one. Easterbrook & Fischel, supra, 36 Bus.Law. at 1750. However, that clearly is not the law of Delaware, and as the proponents of this rule of passivity readily concede, it has not been adopted either by courts or state legislatures. Easterbrook & Fischel, supra, 94 Harv.L.Rev. at 1194.

v. Mathes, 199 A.2d at 554–55. However, this does not end the inquiry.

B.

A further aspect is the element of balance. If a defensive measure is to come within the ambit of the business judgment rule, it must be reasonable in relation to the threat posed. This entails an analysis by the directors of the nature of the takeover bid and its effect on the corporate enterprise. Examples of such concerns may include: inadequacy of the price offered, nature and timing of the offer, questions of illegality, the impact on "constituencies" other than shareholders (i.e., creditors, customers, employees, and perhaps even the community generally), the risk of nonconsummation, and the quality of securities being offered in the exchange. See Lipton and Brownstein, Takeover Responses and Directors' Responsibilities: An Update, p. 7, ABA National Institute on the Dynamics of Corporate Control (December 8, 1983). While not a controlling factor, it also seems to us that a board may reasonably consider the basic stockholder interests at stake, including those of short term speculators, whose actions may have fueled the coercive aspect of the offer at the expense of the long term investor.[11] Here, the threat posed was viewed by the Unocal board as a grossly inadequate two-tier coercive tender offer coupled with the threat of greenmail.

Specifically, the Unocal directors had concluded that the value of Unocal was substantially above the $54 per share offered in cash at the front end. Furthermore, they determined that the subordinated securities to be exchanged in Mesa's announced squeeze out of the remaining shareholders in the "back-end" merger were "junk bonds" worth far less than $54. It is now well recognized that such offers are a classic coercive measure designed to stampede shareholders into tendering at the first tier, even if the price is inadequate, out of fear of what they will receive at the back end of the transaction. Wholly beyond the coercive aspect of an inadequate two-tier tender offer, the threat was posed by a corporate raider with a national reputation as a "greenmailer".[13]

11. There has been much debate respecting such stockholder interests. One rather impressive study indicates that the stock of over 50 percent of target companies, who resisted hostile takeovers, later traded at higher market prices than the rejected offer price, or were acquired after the tender offer was defeated by another company at a price higher than the offer price. See Lipton, supra 35 Bus.Law. at 106–109, 132–133. Moreover, an update by Kidder Peabody & Company of this study, involving the stock prices of target companies that have defeated hostile tender offers during the period from 1973 to 1982 demonstrates that in a majority of cases the target's shareholders benefited from the defeat. The stock of 81% of the targets studied has, since the tender offer, sold at prices higher than the tender offer price. When adjusted for the time value of money, the figure is 64%. See Lipton & Brownstein, supra ABA Institute at 10. The thesis being that this strongly supports application of the business judgment rule in response to takeover threats. There is, however, a rather vehement contrary view. See Easterbrook & Fischel, supra 36 Bus.Law. at 1739–1745.

13. The term "greenmail" refers to the practice of buying out a takeover bidder's stock at a premium that is not available to other shareholders in order to prevent the takeover. The Chancery Court noted that "Mesa has made tremendous profits from its takeover activities although in the past few years it has not been successful in

In adopting the selective exchange offer, the board stated that its objective was either to defeat the inadequate Mesa offer or, should the offer still succeed, provide the 49% of its stockholders, who would otherwise be forced to accept "junk bonds", with $72 worth of senior debt. We find that both purposes are valid.

However, such efforts would have been thwarted by Mesa's participation in the exchange offer. First, if Mesa could tender its shares, Unocal would effectively be subsidizing the former's continuing effort to buy Unocal stock at $54 per share. Second, Mesa could not, by definition, fit within the class of shareholders being protected from its own coercive and inadequate tender offer.

Thus, we are satisfied that the selective exchange offer is reasonably related to the threats posed. It is consistent with the principle that "the minority stockholder shall receive the substantial equivalent in value of what he had before." Sterling v. Mayflower Hotel Corp., Del.Supr., 93 A.2d 107, 114 (1952). See also Rosenblatt v. Getty Oil Co., Del.Supr., 493 A.2d 929, 940 (1985). This concept of fairness, while stated in the merger context, is also relevant in the area of tender offer law. Thus, the board's decision to offer what it determined to be the fair value of the corporation to the 49% of its shareholders, who would otherwise be forced to accept highly subordinated "junk bonds", is reasonable and consistent with the directors' duty to ensure that the minority stockholders receive equal value for their shares.

V.

Mesa contends that it is unlawful, and the trial court agreed, for a corporation to discriminate in this fashion against one shareholder. It argues correctly that no case has ever sanctioned a device that precludes a raider from sharing in a benefit available to all other stockholders. However, as we have noted earlier, the principle of selective stock repurchases by a Delaware corporation is neither unknown nor unauthorized. Cheff v. Mathes, 199 A.2d at 554; Bennett v. Propp, 187 A.2d at 408; Martin v. American Potash & Chemical Corporation, 92 A.2d at 302; Kaplan v. Goldsamt, 380 A.2d 568–569; Kors v. Carey, 158 A.2d at 140–141; 8 Del.C. § 160. The only difference is that heretofore the approved transaction was the payment of "greenmail" to a raider or dissident posing a threat to the corporate enterprise. All other stockholders were denied such favored treatment, and given Mesa's past history of greenmail, its claims here are rather ironic.

However, our corporate law is not static. It must grow and develop in response to, indeed in anticipation of, evolving concepts and needs. Merely because the General Corporation Law is silent as to a specific matter does not mean that it is prohibited. See Provi-

acquiring any of the target companies on an unfriendly basis." Moreover, the trial court specifically found that the actions of the Unocal board were taken in good faith to eliminate both the inadequacies of the tender offer and to forestall the payment of "greenmail".

dence and Worcester Co. v. Baker, Del.Supr., 378 A.2d 121, 123–124 (1977). In the days when *Cheff, Bennett, Martin* and *Kors* were decided, the tender offer, while not an unknown device, was virtually unused, and little was known of such methods as two-tier "front-end" loaded offers with their coercive effects. Then, the favored attack of a raider was stock acquisition followed by a proxy contest. Various defensive tactics, which provided no benefit whatever to the raider, evolved. Thus, the use of corporate funds by management to counter a proxy battle was approved. Hall v. Trans–Lux Daylight Picture Screen Corp., Del.Supr., 171 A. 226 (1934); Hibbert v. Hollywood Park, Inc., Del.Supr., 457 A.2d 339 (1983). Litigation, supported by corporate funds, aimed at the raider has long been a popular device.

More recently, as the sophistication of both raiders and targets has developed, a host of other defensive measures to counter such ever mounting threats has evolved and received judicial sanction. These include defensive charter amendments and other devices bearing some rather exotic, but apt, names: Crown Jewel, White Knight, Pac Man, and Golden Parachute. Each has highly selective features, the object of which is to deter or defeat the raider.

Thus, while the exchange offer is a form of selective treatment, given the nature of the threat posed here the response is neither unlawful nor unreasonable. If the board of directors is disinterested, has acted in good faith and with due care, its decision in the absence of an abuse of discretion will be upheld as a proper exercise of business judgment.

To this Mesa responds that the board is not disinterested, because the directors are receiving a benefit from the tender of their own shares, which because of the Mesa exclusion, does not devolve upon *all* stockholders equally. See Aronson v. Lewis, Del.Supr., 473 A.2d 805, 812 (1984). However, Mesa concedes that if the exclusion is valid, then the directors and all other stockholders share the same benefit. The answer of course is that the exclusion is valid, and the directors' participation in the exchange offer does not rise to the level of a disqualifying interest. The excellent discussion in Johnson v. Trueblood, 629 F.2d at 292–293, of the use of the business judgment rule in takeover contests also seems pertinent here.

Nor does this become an "interested" director transaction merely because certain board members are large stockholders. As this Court has previously noted, that fact alone does not create a disqualifying "personal pecuniary interest" to defeat the operation of the business judgment rule. Cheff v. Mathes, 199 A.2d at 554.

Mesa also argues that the exclusion permits the directors to abdicate the fiduciary duties they owe it. However, that is not so. The board continues to owe Mesa the duties of due care and loyalty. But in the face of the destructive threat Mesa's tender offer was perceived to pose, the board had a supervening duty to protect the corporate enterprise, which includes the other shareholders, from threatened harm.

Mesa contends that the basis of this action is punitive, and solely in response to the exercise of its rights of corporate democracy.[14] Nothing precludes Mesa, as a stockholder, from acting in its own self-interest. See e.g., DuPont v. DuPont, 251 Fed. 937 (D.Del.1918), aff'd 256 Fed. 129 (3d Cir.1918); Ringling Bros.-Barnum & Bailey Combined Shows, Inc. v. Ringling, Del.Supr., 53 A.2d 441, 447 (1947); Heil v. Standard Gas & Electric Co., Del.Ch., 151 A. 303, 304 (1930). But see, Allied Chemical & Dye Corp. v. Steel & Tube Co. of America, Del.Ch., 120 A. 486, 491 (1923) (majority shareholder owes a fiduciary duty to the minority shareholders). However, Mesa, while pursuing its own interests, has acted in a manner which a board consisting of a majority of independent directors has reasonably determined to be contrary to the best interests of Unocal and its other shareholders. In this situation, there is no support in Delaware law for the proposition that, when responding to a perceived harm, a corporation must guarantee a benefit to a stockholder who is deliberately provoking the danger being addressed. There is no obligation of self-sacrifice by a corporation and its shareholders in the face of such a challenge.

Here, the Court of Chancery specifically found that the "directors' decision [to oppose the Mesa tender offer] was made in the good faith belief that the Mesa tender offer is inadequate." Given our standard of review under Levitt v. Bouvier, Del.Supr., 287 A.2d 671, 673 (1972), and Application of Delaware Racing Association, Del. Supr., 213 A.2d 203, 207 (1965), we are satisfied that Unocal's board has met its burden of proof. Cheff v. Mathes, 199 A.2d at 555.

VI.

In conclusion, there was directorial power to oppose the Mesa tender offer, and to undertake a selective stock exchange made in good faith and upon a reasonable investigation pursuant to a clear duty to protect the corporate enterprise. Further, the selective stock repurchase plan chosen by Unocal is reasonable in relation to the threat that the board rationally and reasonably believed was posed by Mesa's inadequate and coercive two-tier tender offer. Under those circumstances the board's action is entitled to be measured by the standards of the business judgment rule. Thus, unless it is shown by a preponderance of the evidence that the directors' decisions were primarily based on perpetuating themselves in office, or some other breach of fiduciary duty such as fraud, overreaching, lack of good faith, or being uninformed, a Court will not substitute its judgment for that of the board.

---

14. This seems to be the underlying basis of the trial court's principal reliance on the unreported Chancery decision of Fisher v. Moltz, Del.Ch. No. 6068 (1979), published in 5 Del.J.Corp.L. 530 (1980). However, the facts in *Fisher* are thoroughly distinguishable. There, a corporation offered to repurchase the shares of its former employees, except those of the plaintiffs, merely because the latter were then engaged in lawful competition with the company. No threat to the enterprise was posed, and at best it can be said that the exclusion was motivated by pique instead of a rational corporate purpose.

In this case that protection is not lost merely because Unocal's directors have tendered their shares in the exchange offer. Given the validity of the Mesa exclusion, they are receiving a benefit shared generally by all other stockholders except Mesa. In this circumstance the test of Aronson v. Lewis, 473 A.2d at 812, is satisfied. See also Cheff v. Mathes, 199 A.2d at 554. If the stockholders are displeased with the action of their elected representatives, the powers of corporate democracy are at their disposal to turn the board out. Aronson v. Lewis, Del.Supr., 473 A.2d 805, 811 (1984). See also 8 Del.C. §§ 141(k) and 211(b).

With the Court of Chancery's findings that the exchange offer was based on the board's good faith belief that the Mesa offer was inadequate, that the board's action was informed and taken with due care, that Mesa's prior activities justify a reasonable inference that its principle objective was greenmail, and implicitly, that the substance of the offer itself was reasonable and fair to the corporation and its stockholders if Mesa were included, we cannot say that the Unocal directors have acted in such a manner as to have passed an "unintelligent and unadvised judgment". Mitchell v. Highland–Western Glass Co., Del.Ch., 167 A. 831, 833 (1933). The decision of the Court of Chancery is therefore REVERSED, and the preliminary injunction is VACATED.

MORAN v. HOUSEHOLD INTERNATIONAL, INC.

Supreme Court of Delaware, 1985.
500 A.2d 1346.

Before CHRISTIE, Chief Justice, and McNEILLY and MOORE, JJ.

McNEILLY, Justice:

This case presents to this Court for review the most recent defensive mechanism in the arsenal of corporate takeover weaponry—the Preferred Share Purchase Rights Plan ("Rights Plan" or "Plan"). The validity of this mechanism has attracted national attention. *Amici curiae* briefs have been filed in support of appellants by the Security and Exchange Commission ("SEC")[1] and the Investment Company Institute. An *amicus curiae* brief has been filed in support of appellees ("Household") by the United Food and Commercial Workers International Union.

In a detailed opinion, the Court of Chancery upheld the Rights Plan as a legitimate exercise of business judgment by Household. Moran v. Household International, Inc., Del.Ch., 490 A.2d 1059 (1985). We agree, and therefore, affirm the judgment below.

---

1. The SEC split 3–2 on whether to intervene in this case. The two dissenting Commissioners have publicly disagreed with the other three as to the merits of the Rights Plan. 17 Securities Regulation Law Report 400; The Wall Street Journal, March 20, 1985, at 6.

I

The facts giving rise to this case have been carefully delineated in the Court of Chancery's opinion. Id. at 1064–69. A review of the basic facts is necessary for a complete understanding of the issues.

On August 14, 1984, the Board of Directors of Household International, Inc. adopted the Rights Plan by a fourteen to two vote.[2] The intricacies of the Rights Plan are contained in a 48–page document entitled "Rights Agreement". Basically, the Plan provides that Household common stockholders are entitled to the issuance of one Right per common share under certain triggering conditions. There are two triggering events that can activate the Rights. The first is the announcement of a tender offer for 30 percent of Household's shares ("30% trigger") and the second is the acquisition of 20 percent of Household's shares by any single entity or group ("20% trigger").

If an announcement of a tender offer for 30 percent of Household's shares is made, the Rights are issued and are immediately exercisable to purchase $1/100$ share of new preferred stock for $100 and are redeemable by the Board for $.50 per Right. If 20 percent of Household's shares are acquired by anyone, the Rights are issued and become non-redeemable and are exercisable to purchase $1/100$ of a share of preferred. If a Right is not exercised for preferred, and thereafter, a merger or consolidation occurs, the Rights holder can exercise each Right to purchase $200 of the common stock of the tender offeror for $100. This "flip-over" provision of the Rights Plan is at the heart of this controversy.

Household is a diversified holding company with its principal subsidiaries engaged in financial services, transportation and merchandising. HFC, National Car Rental and Vons Grocery are three of its wholly-owned entities.

Household did not adopt its Rights Plan during a battle with a corporate raider, but as a preventive mechanism to ward off future advances. The Vice–Chancellor found that as early as February 1984, Household's management became concerned about the company's vulnerability as a takeover target and began considering amending its charter to render a takeover more difficult. After considering the matter, Household decided not to pursue a fair price amendment.[3]

In the meantime, appellant Moran, one of Household's own Directors and also Chairman of the Dyson–Kissner–Moran Corporation, ("D–K–M") which is the largest single stockholder of Household, began discussions concerning a possible leveraged buy-out of Household by D–K–M. D–K–M's financial studies showed that

---

2. Household's Board has ten outside directors and six who are members of management. Messrs. Moran (appellant) and Whitehead voted against the Plan. The record reflects that Whitehead voted against the Plan not on its substance but because he thought it was novel and would bring unwanted publicity to Household.

3. A fair price amendment to a corporate charter generally requires supermajority approval for certain business combinations and sets minimum price criteria for mergers. *Moran*, 490 A.2d at 1064, n. 1.

Household's stock was significantly undervalued in relation to the company's break-up value. It is uncontradicted that Moran's suggestion of a leveraged buy-out never progressed beyond the discussion stage.

Concerned about Household's vulnerability to a raider in light of the current takeover climate, Household secured the services of Wachtell, Lipton, Rosen and Katz ("Wachtell, Lipton") and Goldman, Sachs & Co. ("Goldman, Sachs") to formulate a takeover policy for recommendation to the Household Board at its August 14 meeting. After a July 31 meeting with a Household Board member and a pre-meeting distribution of material on the potential takeover problem and the proposed Rights Plan, the Board met on August 14, 1984.

Representatives of Wachtell, Lipton and Goldman, Sachs attended the August 14 meeting. The minutes reflect that Mr. Lipton explained to the Board that his recommendation of the Plan was based on his understanding that the Board was concerned about the increasing frequency of "bust-up" [4] takeovers, the increasing takeover activity in the financial service industry, such as Leucadia's attempt to take over Arco, and the possible adverse effect this type of activity could have on employees and others concerned with and vital to the continuing successful operation of Household even in the absence of any actual bust-up takeover attempt. Against this factual background, the Plan was approved.

Thereafter, Moran and the company of which he is Chairman, D–K–M, filed this suit. On the eve of trial, Gretl Golter, the holder of 500 shares of Household, was permitted to intervene as an additional plaintiff. The trial was held, and the Court of Chancery ruled in favor of Household.[5] Appellants now appeal from that ruling to this Court.

II

The primary issue here is the applicability of the business judgment rule as the standard by which the adoption of the Rights Plan should be reviewed. Much of this issue has been decided by our recent decision in Unocal Corp. v. Mesa Petroleum Co., Del.Supr., 493 A.2d 946 (1985). In *Unocal*, we applied the business judgment rule to analyze Unocal's discriminatory self-tender. We explained:

> When a board addresses a pending takeover bid it has an obligation to determine whether the offer is in the best interests of the corporation and its shareholders. In that respect a board's duty is no different from any other responsibility it shoulders, and its decisions should be no less entitled to the respect they otherwise would be accorded in the realm of business judgment.

Id. at 954 (citation and footnote omitted).

Other jurisdictions have also applied the business judgment rule to actions by which target companies have sought to forestall takeover

---

4. "Bust-up" takeover generally refers to a situation in which one seeks to finance an acquisition by selling off pieces of the acquired company.

5. The Vice–Chancellor did rule in favor of appellants on Household's counterclaim, but that ruling is not at issue in this appeal.

activity they considered undesirable. See Gearhart Industries, Inc. v. Smith International, 5th Cir., 741 F.2d 707 (1984) (sale of discounted subordinate debentures containing springing warrants); Treco, Inc. v. Land of Lincoln Savings and Loan, 7th Cir., 749 F.2d 374 (1984) (amendment to by-laws); Panter v. Marshall Field, 7th Cir., 646 F.2d 271 (1981) (acquisitions to create antitrust problems); Johnson v. Trueblood, 3d Cir., 629 F.2d 287 (1980), cert. denied, 450 U.S. 999, 101 S.Ct. 1704, 68 L.Ed.2d 200 (1981) (refusal to tender); Crouse-hinds Co. v. InterNorth, Inc., 2d Cir., 634 F.2d 690 (1980) (sale of stock to favored party); Treadway v. Cane Corp., 2d Cir., 638 F.2d 357 (1980) (sale to White Knight), Enterra Corp. v. SGS Associates, E.D.Pa., 600 F.Supp. 678 (1985) (standstill agreement); Buffalo Forge Co. v. Ogden Corp., W.D.N.Y., 555 F.Supp. 892, aff'd, (2d Cir.) 717 F.2d 757, cert. denied, 464 U.S. 1018, 104 S.Ct. 550, 78 L.Ed.2d 724 (1983) (sale of treasury shares and grant of stock option to White Knight); Whittaker Corp. v. Edgar, N.D.Ill., 535 F.Supp. 933 (1982) (disposal of valuable assets); Martin Marietta Corp. v. Bendix Corp., D.Md., 549 F.Supp. 623 (1982) (Pac–Man defense).[6]

This case is distinguishable from the ones cited, since here we have a defensive mechanism adopted to ward off possible future advances and not a mechanism adopted in reaction to a specific threat. This distinguishing factor does not result in the Directors losing the protection of the business judgment rule. To the contrary, pre-planning, for the contingency of a hostile takeover might reduce the risk that, under the pressure of a takeover bid, management will fail to exercise reasonable judgment. Therefore, in reviewing a pre-planned defensive mechanism it seems even more appropriate to apply the business judgment rule. See Warner Communications v. Murdoch, D.Del., 581 F.Supp. 1482, 1491 (1984).

Of course, the business judgment rule can only sustain corporate decision making or transactions that are within the power or authority of the Board. Therefore, before the business judgment rule can be applied it must be determined whether the Directors were authorized to adopt the Rights Plan.

III

Appellants vehemently contend that the Board of Directors was unauthorized to adopt the Rights Plan. First, appellants contend that no provision of the Delaware General Corporation Law authorizes the issuance of such Rights. Secondly, appellants, along with the SEC, contend that the Board is unauthorized to usurp stockholders' rights to receive hostile tender offers. Third, appellants and the SEC also contend that the Board is unauthorized to fundamentally restrict stockholders' rights to conduct a proxy contest. We address each of these contentions in turn.

---

6. The "Pac–Man" defense is generally a target company countering an unwanted tender offer by making its own tender offer for stock of the would-be acquirer. Block & Miller, The Responsibilities and Obligations of Corporate Directors in Takeover Contests, 11 Sec.Reg.L.J. 44, 64 (1983).

A.

While appellants contend that no provision of the Delaware General Corporation Law authorizes the Rights Plan, Household contends that the Rights Plan was issued pursuant to 8 Del.C. §§ 151(g) and 157. It explains that the Rights are authorized by § 157[7] and the issue of preferred stock underlying the Rights is authorized by § 151.[8] Appellants respond by making several attacks upon the authority to issue the Rights pursuant to § 157.

Appellants begin by contending that § 157 cannot authorize the Rights Plan since § 157 has never served the purpose of authorizing a takeover defense. Appellants contend that § 157 is a corporate financing statute, and that nothing in its legislative history suggests a purpose that has anything to do with corporate control or a takeover defense. Appellants are unable to demonstrate that the legislature, in its adoption of § 157, meant to limit the applicability of § 157 to only the issuance of Rights for the purposes of corporate financing. Without such affirmative evidence, we decline to impose such a limitation upon the section that the legislature has not. Compare Providence & Worchester Co. v. Baker, Del.Supr., 378 A.2d 121, 124 (1977) (refusal to read a bar to protective voting provisions into 8 Del.C. § 212(a)).

As we noted in *Unocal:*

> [O]ur corporate law is not static. It must grow and develop in response to, indeed in anticipation of, evolving concepts and needs. Merely because the General Corporation Law is silent as to a specific matter does not mean that it is prohibited.

493 A.2d at 957. See also Cheff v. Mathes, Del.Supr., 199 A.2d 548 (1964).

Secondly, appellants contend that § 157 does not authorize the issuance of sham rights such as the Rights Plan. They contend that the Rights were designed never to be exercised, and that the Plan has no economic value. In addition, they contend the preferred stock

---

7. The power to issue rights to purchase shares is conferred by 8 Del.C. § 157 which provides in relevant part:

> Subject to any provisions in the certificate of incorporation, every corporation may create and issue, whether or not in connection with the issue and sale of any shares of stock or other securities of the corporation, rights or options entitling the holders thereof to purchase from the corporation any shares of its capital stock of any class or classes, such rights or options to be evidenced by or in such instrument or instruments as shall be approved by the board of directors.

8. 8 Del.C. § 151(g) provides in relevant part:

> When any corporation desires to issue any shares of stock of any class or of any series of any class of which the voting powers, designations, preferences and relative, participating, optional or other rights, if any, or the qualifications, limitations or restrictions thereof, if any, shall not have been set forth in the certificate of incorporation or in any amendment thereto but shall be provided for in a resolution or resolutions adopted by the board of directors pursuant to authority expressly vested in it by the provisions of the certificate of incorporation or any amendment thereto, a certificate setting forth a copy of such resolution or resolutions and the number of shares of stock of such class or series shall be executed, acknowledged, filed, recorded, and shall become effective, in accordance with § 103 of this title.

made subject to the Rights is also illusory, citing Telvest, Inc. v. Olson, Del.Ch., C.A. No. 5798, Brown, V.C. (March 8, 1979).

Appellants' sham contention fails in both regards. As to the Rights, they can and will be exercised upon the happening of a triggering mechanism, as we have observed during the current struggle of Sir James Goldsmith to take control of Crown Zellerbach. See Wall Street Journal, July 26, 1985, at 3, 12. As to the preferred shares, we agree with the Court of Chancery that they are distinguishable from sham securities invalidated in *Telvest,* supra. The Household preferred, issuable upon the happening of a triggering event, have superior dividend and liquidation rights.

Third, appellants contend that § 157 authorizes the issuance of Rights "entitling holders thereof to purchase from the corporation any shares of *its* capital stock of any class . . ." (emphasis added). Therefore, their contention continues, the plain language of the statute does not authorize Household to issue rights to purchase another's capital stock upon a merger of consolidation.

Household contends, *inter alia,* that the Rights Plan is analogous to "anti-destruction" or "anti-dilution" provisions which are customary features of a wide variety of corporate securities. While appellants seem to concede that "anti-destruction" provisions are valid under Delaware corporate law, they seek to distinguish the Rights Plan as not being incidental, as are most "anti-destruction" provisions, to a corporation's statutory power to finance itself. We find no merit to such a distinction. We have already rejected appellants' similar contention that § 157 could only be used for financing purposes. We also reject that distinction here.

"Anti-destruction" clauses generally ensure holders of certain securities of the protection of their right of conversion in the event of a merger by giving them the right to convert their securities into whatever securities are to replace the stock of their company. See Broad v. Rockwell International Corp., 5th Cir., 642 F.2d 929, 946, cert. denied, 454 U.S. 965, 102 S.Ct. 506, 70 L.Ed.2d 380 (1981); Wood v. Coastal States Gas Corp., Del.Supr., 401 A.2d 932, 937–39 (1979); B.S.F. Co. v. Philadelphia National Bank, Del.Supr., 204 A.2d 746, 750–51 (1964). The fact that the rights here have as their purpose the prevention of coercive two-tier tender offers does not invalidate them. . . .

Having concluded that sufficient authority for the Rights Plan exists in 8 Del.C. § 157, we note the inherent powers of the Board conferred by 8 Del.C. § 141(a), concerning the management of the corporation's "business and *affairs*" (emphasis added), also provides the Board additional authority upon which to enact the Rights Plan. *Unocal,* 493 A.2d at 953.

B.

Appellants contend that the Board is unauthorized to usurp stockholders' rights to receive tender offers by changing Household's fundamental structure. We conclude that the Rights Plan does not prevent stockholders from receiving tender offers, and that the change of Household's structure was less than that which results from the implementation of other defensive mechanisms upheld by various courts.

Appellants' contention that stockholders will lose their right to receive and accept tender offers seems to be premised upon an understanding of the Rights Plan which is illustrated by the SEC *amicus* brief which states: "The Chancery Court's decision seriously understates the impact of this plan. In fact, as we discuss below, the Rights Plan will deter not only two-tier offers, but virtually all hostile tender offers."

The fallacy of that contention is apparent when we look at the recent takeover of Crown Zellerbach, which has a similar Rights Plan, by Sir James Goldsmith. Wall Street Journal, July 26, 1985, at 3, 12. The evidence at trial also evidenced many methods around the Plan ranging from tendering with a condition that the Board redeem the Rights, tendering with a high minimum condition of shares and Rights, tendering and soliciting consents to remove the Board and redeem the Rights, to acquiring 50% of the shares and causing Household to self-tender for the Rights. One could also form a group of up to 19.9% and solicit proxies for consents to remove the Board and redeem the Rights. These are but a few of the methods by which Household can still be acquired by a hostile tender offer.

In addition, the Rights Plan is not absolute. When the Household Board of Directors is faced with a tender offer and a request to redeem the Rights, they will not be able to arbitrarily reject the offer. They will be held to the same fiduciary standards any other board of directors would be held to in deciding to adopt a defensive mechanism, the same standard as they were held to in originally approving the Rights Plan. See *Unocal*, 493 A.2d at 954–55, 958.

In addition, appellants contend that the deterence of tender offers will be accomplished by what they label "a fundamental transfer of power from the stockholders to the directors." They contend that this transfer of power, in itself, is unauthorized.

The Rights Plan will result in no more of a structural change than any other defensive mechanism adopted by a board of directors. The Rights Plan does not destroy the assets of the corporation. The implementation of the Plan neither results in any outflow of money from the corporation nor impairs its financial flexibility. It does not dilute earnings per share and does not have any adverse tax consequences for the corporation or its stockholders. The Plan has not adversely affected the market price of Household's stock.

Comparing the Rights Plan with other defensive mechanisms, it does less harm to the value structure of the corporation than do the other mechanisms. Other mechanisms result in increased debt of the corporation. See Whittaker Corp. v. Edgar, supra (sale of "prize asset"), Cheff v. Mathes, supra, (paying greenmail to eliminate a threat), Unocal Corp. v. Mesa Petroleum Co., supra, (discriminatory self-tender).

There is little change in the governance structure as a result of the adoption of the Rights Plan. The Board does not now have unfettered discretion in refusing to redeem the Rights. The Board has no more discretion in refusing to redeem the Rights than it does in enacting any defensive mechanism.

The contention that the Rights Plan alters the structure more than do other defensive mechanisms because it is so effective as to make the corporation completely safe from hostile tender offers is likewise without merit. As explained above, there are numerous methods to successfully launch a hostile tender offer.

C.

Appellant's third contention is that the Board was unauthorized to fundamentally restrict stockholders' rights to conduct a proxy contest. Appellants contend that the "20% trigger" effectively prevents any stockholder from first acquiring 20% or more shares before conducting a proxy contest and further, it prevents stockholders from banding together into a group to solicit proxies if, collectively, they own 20% or more of the stock.[12] In addition, at trial, appellants contended that read literally, the Rights Agreement triggers the Rights upon the mere acquisition of the right to vote 20% or more of the shares through a proxy solicitation, and thereby precludes any proxy contest from being waged.[13]

Appellants seem to have conceded this last contention in light of Household's response that the receipt of a proxy does not make the recipient the "beneficial owner" of the shares involved which would trigger the Rights. In essence, the Rights Agreement provides that the Rights are triggered when someone becomes the "beneficial owner" of 20% or more of Household stock. Although a literal reading of the Rights Agreement definition of "beneficial owner" would seem to include those shares which one has the right to vote, it has long been recognized that the relationship between grantor and recipient of a proxy is one of agency, and the agency is revocable by the grantor at any time. Henn, Corporations § 196, at 518. Therefore, the holder of a proxy is not the "beneficial owner" of the stock. As a result, the mere acquisition of the right to vote 20% of the shares does not trigger the Rights.

The issue, then, is whether the restriction upon individuals or groups from first acquiring 20% of shares before waging a proxy contest fundamentally restricts stockholders' right to conduct a proxy contest. Regarding this issue the Court of Chancery found:

> Thus, while the Rights Plan does deter the formation of proxy efforts of a certain magnitude, it does not limit the voting power of individual shares. On the evidence presented it is

---

12. Appellants explain that the acquisition of 20% of the shares trigger the Rights, making them non-redeemable, and thereby would prevent even a future friendly offer for the ten-year life of the Rights.

13. The SEC still contends that the mere acquisition of the right to vote 20% of the shares through a proxy solicitation triggers the rights. We do not interpret the Rights Agreement in that manner.

highly conjectural to assume that a particular effort to assert shareholder views in the election of directors or revisions of corporate policy will be frustrated by the proxy feature of the Plan. Household's witnesses, Troubh and Higgins described recent corporate takeover battles in which insurgents holding less than 10% stock ownership were able to secure corporate control through a proxy contest or the threat of one.

Moran, 490 A.2d at 1080.

We conclude that there was sufficient evidence at trial to support the Vice–Chancellor's finding that the effect upon proxy contests will be minimal. Evidence at trial established that many proxy contests are won with an insurgent ownership of less than 20%, and that very large holdings are no guarantee of success. There was also testimony that the key variable in proxy contest success is the merit of an insurgent's issues, not the size of his holdings.

IV

Having concluded that the adoption of the Rights Plan was within the authority of the Directors, we now look to whether the Directors have met their burden under the business judgment rule.

The business judgment rule is a "presumption that in making a business decision the directors of a corporation acted on an informed basis, in good faith and in the honest belief that the action taken was in the best interests of the company." Aronson v. Lewis, Del.Supr., 473 A.2d 805, 812 (1984) (citations omitted). Notwithstanding, in *Unocal* we held that when the business judgment rule applies to adoption of a defensive mechanism, the initial burden will lie with the directors. The "directors must show that they had reasonable grounds for believing that a danger to corporate policy and effectiveness existed. . . . [T]hey satisfy that burden 'by showing good faith and reasonable investigation. . . .'" *Unocal,* 493 A.2d at 955 (citing Cheff v. Mathes, 199 A.2d at 554–55). In addition, the directors must show that the defensive mechanism was "reasonable in relation to the threat posed." *Unocal,* 493 A.2d at 955. Moreover, that proof is materially enhanced, as we noted in *Unocal,* where, as here, a majority of the board favoring the proposal consisted of outside independent directors who have acted in accordance with the foregoing standards. *Unocal,* 493 A.2d at 955; *Aronson,* 473 A.2d at 815. Then, the burden shifts back to the plaintiffs who have the ultimate burden of persuasion to show a breach of the directors' fiduciary duties. *Unocal,* 493 A.2d at 958.

There are no allegations here of any bad faith on the part of the Directors' action in the adoption of the Rights Plan. There is no allegation that the Directors' action was taken for entrenchment purposes. Household has adequately demonstrated, as explained above, that the adoption of the Rights Plan was in reaction to what it perceived to be the threat in the market place of coercive two-tier tender offers. Appellants do contend, however, that the Board did not exercise informed business judgment in its adoption of the Plan.

Appellants contend that the Household Board was uninformed since they were, *inter alia,* told the Plan would not inhibit a proxy contest, were not told the plan would preclude all hostile acquisitions of Household, and were told that Delaware counsel opined that the plan was within the business judgment of the Board.

As to the first two contentions, as we explained above, the Rights Plan will not have a severe impact upon proxy contests and it will not preclude all hostile acquisitions of Household. Therefore, the Directors were not misinformed or uninformed on these facts.

Appellants contend the Delaware counsel did not express an opinion on the flip-over provision of the Rights, rather only that the Rights would constitute validly issued and outstanding rights to subscribe to the preferred stock of the company.

To determine whether a business judgment reached by a board of directors was an informed one, we determine whether the directors were grossly negligent. Smith v. Van Gorkom, Del.Supr., 488 A.2d 858, 873 (1985). Upon a review of this record, we conclude the Directors were not grossly negligent. The information supplied to the Board on August 14 provided the essentials of the Plan. The Directors were given beforehand a notebook which included a three-page summary of the Plan along with articles on the current takeover environment. The extended discussion between the Board and representatives of Wachtell, Lipton and Goldman, Sachs before approval of the Plan reflected a full and candid evaluation of the Plan. Moran's expression of his views at the meeting served to place before the Board a knowledgeable critique of the Plan. The factual happenings here are clearly distinguishable from the actions of the directors of Trans Union Corporation who displayed gross negligence in approving a cash-out merger. Id.

In addition, to meet their burden, the Directors must show that the defensive mechanism was "reasonable in relation to the threat posed". The record reflects a concern on the part of the Directors over the increasing frequency in the financial services industry of "boot-strap" and "bust-up" takeovers. The Directors were also concerned that such takeovers may take the form of two-tier offers.[14] In addition, on August 14, the Household Board was aware of Moran's overture on behalf of D–K–M. In sum, the Directors reasonably believed Household was vulnerable to coercive acquisition techniques and adopted a reasonable defensive mechanism to protect itself.

V

In conclusion, the Household Directors receive the benefit of the business judgment rule in their adoption of the Rights Plan.

The Directors adopted the Plan pursuant to statutory authority in 8 Del.C. §§ 141, 151, 157. We reject appellants' contentions that

---

14. We have discussed the coercive nature of two-tier tender offers in *Unocal,* 493 A.2d at 956, n. 12. We explained in *Unocal* that a discriminatory self-tender was reasonably related to the threat of two-tier tender offers and possible green-mail.

the Rights Plan strips stockholders of their rights to receive tender offers, and that the Rights Plan fundamentally restricts proxy contests.

The Directors adopted the Plan in the good faith belief that it was necessary to protect Household from coercive acquisition techniques. The Board was informed as to the details of the Plan. In addition, Household has demonstrated that the Plan is reasonable in relation to the threat posed. Appellants, on the other hand, have failed to convince us that the Directors breached any fiduciary duty in their adoption of the Rights Plan.

While we conclude for present purposes that the Household Directors are protected by the business judgment rule, that does not end the matter. The ultimate response to an actual takeover bid must be judged by the Directors' actions at that time, and nothing we say here relieves them of their basic fundamental duties to the corporation and its stockholders. *Unocal,* 493 A.2d at 954–55, 958; Smith v. Van Gorkom, 488 A.2d at 872–73; *Aronson,* 473 A.2d at 812–13; Pogostin v. Rice, Del.Supr., 480 A.2d 619, 627 (1984). Their use of the Plan will be evaluated when and if the issue arises.

* * *

AFFIRMED.

REVLON, INC. v. MacANDREWS & FORBES HOLDINGS, INC.

Supreme Court of Delaware, 1986.
506 A.2d 173.

In this battle for corporate control of Revlon, Inc. (Revlon), the Court of Chancery enjoined certain transactions designed to thwart the efforts of Pantry Pride, Inc. (Pantry Pride) to acquire Revlon.[1] The defendants are Revlon, its board of directors, and Forstmann Little & Co. and the latter's affiliated limited partnership (collectively, Forstmann). The injunction barred consummation of an option granted Forstmann to purchase certain Revlon assets (the lock-up option), a promise by Revlon to deal exclusively with Forstmann in the face of a takeover (the no-shop provision), and the payment of a $25 million cancellation fee to Forstmann if the transaction was aborted. The Court of Chancery found that the Revlon directors had breached their duty of care by entering into the foregoing transactions and effectively ending an active auction for the company. The trial court ruled that such arrangements are not illegal *per se* under Delaware law, but that their use under the circumstances here was impermissible. We agree. See MacAndrews & Forbes Holdings, Inc. v. Revlon, Inc., Del.Ch., 501 A.2d 1239 (1985). Thus, we granted this expedited interlocutory appeal to consider for the first time the validity of such defensive measures in the face of an active bidding contest for corporate

---

1. The nominal plaintiff, MacAndrews & Forbes Holdings, Inc., is the controlling stockholder of Pantry Pride. For all practical purposes their interests in this litigation are virtually identical, and we hereafter will refer to Pantry Pride as the plaintiff.

control.[2] Additionally, we address for the first time the extent to which a corporation may consider the impact of a takeover threat on constituencies other than shareholders. See Unocal Corp. v. Mesa Petroleum Co., 493 A.2d 946, 955 (1985).

In our view, lock-ups and related agreements are permitted under Delaware law where their adoption is untainted by director interest or other breaches of fiduciary duty. The actions taken by the Revlon directors, however, did not meet this standard. Moreover, while concern for various corporate constituencies is proper when addressing a takeover threat, that principle is limited by the requirement that there be some rationally related benefit accruing to the stockholders. We find no such benefit here.

Thus, under all the circumstances we must agree with the Court of Chancery that the enjoined Revlon defensive measures were inconsistent with the directors' duties to the stockholders. Accordingly, we affirm.

I.

The somewhat complex maneuvers of the parties necessitate a rather detailed examination of the facts. The prelude to this controversy began in June 1985, when Ronald O. Perelman, chairman of the board and chief executive officer of Pantry Pride, met with his counterpart at Revlon, Michel C. Bergerac, to discuss a friendly acquisition of Revlon by Pantry Pride. Perelman suggested a price in the range of $40–50 per share, but the meeting ended with Bergerac dismissing those figures as considerably below Revlon's intrinsic value. All subsequent Pantry Pride overtures were rebuffed, perhaps in part based on Mr. Bergerac's strong personal antipathy to Mr. Perelman.

Thus, on August 14, Pantry Pride's board authorized Perelman to acquire Revlon, either through negotiation in the $42–$43 per share range, or by making a hostile tender offer at $45. Perelman then met with Bergerac and outlined Pantry Pride's alternate approaches. Bergerac remained adamantly opposed to such schemes and conditioned any further discussions of the matter on Pantry Pride executing a standstill agreement prohibiting it from acquiring Revlon without the latter's prior approval.

On August 19, the Revlon board met specially to consider the impending threat of a hostile bid by Pantry Pride.[3] At the meeting,

---

2. This appeal was heard on an expedited basis in light of the pending Pantry Pride offer and the Revlon–Forstmann transactions. We accepted the appeal on Friday, October 25, 1985, received the parties' opening briefs on October 28, their reply briefs on October 29, and heard argument on Thursday, October 31. We announced our decision to affirm in an oral ruling in open court at 9:00 a.m. on Friday, November 1, with the proviso that this more detailed written opinion would follow in due course.

3. There were 14 directors on the Revlon board. Six of them held senior management positions with the company, and two others held significant blocks of its stock. Four of the remaining six directors were associated at some point with entities that had various business relationships with Revlon. On the basis of this limited record, however, we cannot conclude that this board is entitled to certain presumptions that generally attach to the decisions of a board whose majority consists of truly outside independent directors. See Polk v.

Lazard Freres, Revlon's investment banker, advised the directors that $45 per share was a grossly inadequate price for the company. Felix Rohatyn and William Loomis of Lazard Freres explained to the board that Pantry Pride's financial strategy for acquiring Revlon would be through "junk bond" financing followed by a break-up of Revlon and the disposition of its assets. With proper timing, according to the experts, such transactions could produce a return to Pantry Pride of $60 to $70 per share, while a sale of the company as a whole would be in the "mid 50" dollar range. Martin Lipton, special counsel for Revlon, recommended two defensive measures: first, that the company repurchase up to 5 million of its nearly 30 million outstanding shares; and second, that it adopt a Note Purchase Rights Plan. Under this plan, each Revlon shareholder would receive as a dividend one Note Purchase Right (the Rights) for each share of common stock, with the Rights entitling the holder to exchange one common share for a $65 principal Revlon note at 12% interest with a one-year maturity. The Rights would become effective whenever anyone acquired beneficial ownership of 20% or more of Revlon's shares, unless the purchaser acquired all the company's stock for cash at $65 or more per share. In addition, the Rights would not be available to the acquiror, and prior to the 20% triggering event the Revlon board could redeem the rights for 10 cents each. Both proposals were unanimously adopted.

Pantry Pride made its first hostile move on August 23, with a cash tender offer for any and all shares of Revlon at $47.50 per common share and $26.67 per preferred share, subject to (1) Pantry Pride's obtaining financing for the purchase, and (2) the Rights being redeemed, rescinded or voided.

The Revlon board met again on August 26. The directors advised the stockholders to reject the offer. Further defensive measures also were planned. On August 29, Revlon commenced its own offer for up to 10 million shares, exchanging for each share of common stock tendered one Senior Subordinated Note (the Notes) of $47.50 principal at 11.75% interest, due 1995, and one-tenth of a share of $9.00 Cumulative Convertible Exchangeable Preferred Stock valued at $100 per share. Lazard Freres opined that the notes would trade at their face value on a fully distributed basis.[4] Revlon stockholders tendered 87 percent of the outstanding shares (approximately 33 million), and the company accepted the full 10 million shares on a pro rata basis. The new Notes contained convenants which limited Revlon's ability to incur additional debt, sell assets, or pay dividends

Good & Texaco, Del.Supr., __ A.2d __, __ (1986); Moran v. Household International, Inc., Del.Supr., 500 A.2d 1346, 1356 (1985); Unocal Corp. v. Mesa Petroleum Co., Del.Supr., 493 A.2d 946, 955 (1985); Aronson v. Lewis, Del.Supr., 473 A.2d 805, 812, 815 (1984); Puma v. Marriott, Del.Ch., 283 A.2d 693, 695 (1971).

4. Like bonds, the Notes actually were issued in denominations of $1,000 and integral multiples thereof. A separate certificate was issued in a total principal amount equal to the remaining sum to which a stockholder was entitled. Likewise, in the esoteric parlance of bond dealers, a Note trading at par ($1,000) would be quoted on the market at 100.

unless otherwise approved by the "independent" (non-management) members of the board.

At this point, both the Rights and the Note covenants stymied Pantry Pride's attempted takeover. The next move came on September 16, when Pantry Pride announced a new tender offer at $42 per share, conditioned upon receiving at least 90% of the outstanding stock. Pantry Pride also indicated that it would consider buying less than 90% , and at an increased price, if Revlon removed the impeding Rights. While this offer was lower on its face than the earlier $47.50 proposal, Revlon's investment banker, Lazard Freres, described the two bids as essentially equal in view of the completed exchange offer.

The Revlon board held a regularly scheduled meeting on September 24. The directors rejected the latest Pantry Pride offer and authorized management to negotiate with other parties interested in acquiring Revlon. Pantry Pride remained determined in its efforts and continued to make cash bids for the company, offering $50 per share on September 27, and raising its bid to $53 on October 1, and then to $56.25 on October 7.

In the meantime, Revlon's negotiations with Forstmann and the investment group Adler & Shaykin had produced results. The Revlon directors met on October 3, to consider Pantry Pride's $53 bid and to examine possible alternatives to the offer. Both Forstmann and Adler & Shaykin made certain proposals to the board. As a result, the directors unanimously agreed to a leveraged buyout by Forstmann. The terms of this accord were as follows: each stockholder would get $56 cash per share; management would purchase stock in the new company by the exercise of their Revlon "golden parachutes";[5] Forstmann would assume Revlon's $475 million debt incurred by the issuance of the Notes; and Revlon would redeem the Rights and waive the Notes covenants for Forstmann or in connection with any other offer superior to Forstmann's. The board did not actually remove the covenants at the October 3, meeting, because Forstmann then lacked a firm commitment on its financing, but accepted the Forstmann capital structure, and indicated that the outside directors would waive the covenants in due course. Part of Forstmann's plan was to sell Revlon's Norcliff Thayer and Reheis divisions to American Home Products for $335 million. Before the merger, Revlon was to sell its cosmetics and fragrance division to Adler & Shaykin for $905 million. These transactions would facilitate the purchase by Forstmann or any other acquiror of Revlon.

When the merger, and thus the waiver of the Notes covenants, was announced, the market value of these securities began to fall. The Notes, which originally traded near par, around 100, dropped to 87.50 by October 8. One director later reported (at the October 12 meeting) a "deluge" of telephone calls from irate noteholders, and on

5. In the takeover context "golden parachutes" generally are understood to be termination agreements providing substan- tial bonuses and other benefits for managers and certain directors upon a change in control of a company.

October 10 the Wall Street Journal reported threats of litigation by these creditors.

Pantry Pride countered with a new proposal on October 7, raising its $53 offer to $56.25, subject to nullification of the Rights, a waiver of the Notes covenants, and the election of three Pantry Pride directors to the Revlon board. On October 9, representatives of Pantry Pride, Forstmann and Revlon conferred in an attempt to negotiate the fate of Revlon, but could not reach agreement. At this meeting Pantry Pride announced that it would engage in fractional bidding and top any Forstmann offer by a slightly higher one. It is also significant that Forstmann, to Pantry Pride's exclusion, had been made privy to certain Revlon financial data. Thus, the parties were not negotiating on equal terms.

Again privately armed with Revlon data, Forstmann met on October 11 with Revlon's special counsel and investment banker. On October 12, Forstmann made a new $57.25 per share offer, based on several conditions.[6] The principal demand was a lock-up option to purchase Revlon's Vision Care and National Health Laboratories divisions for $525 million, some $100–$175 million below the value ascribed to them by Lazard Freres, if another acquiror got 40% of Revlon's shares. Revlon also was required to accept a no-shop provision. The Rights and Notes covenants had to be removed as in the October 3 agreement. There would be a $25 million cancellation fee to be placed in escrow, and released to Forstmann if the new agreement terminated or if another acquiror got more than 19.9% of Revlon's stock. Finally, there would be no participation by Revlon management in the merger. In return, Forstmann agreed to support the par value of the Notes, which had faltered in the market, by an exchange of new notes. Forstmann also demanded immediate acceptance of its offer, or it would be withdrawn. The board unanimously approved Forstmann's proposal because: (1) it was for a higher price than the Pantry Pride bid, (2) it protected the noteholders, and (3) Forstmann's financing was firmly in place.[7] The board further agreed to redeem the rights and waive the covenants on the preferred stock in response to any offer above $57 cash per share. The covenants were waived, contingent upon receipt of an investment banking opinion that the Notes would trade near par value once the offer was consummated.

Pantry Pride, which had initially sought injunctive relief from the Rights plan on August 22, filed an amended complaint on October 14

6. Forstmann's $57.25 offer ostensibly is worth $1 more than Pantry Pride's $56.25 bid. However, the Pantry Pride offer was immediate, while the Forstmann proposal must be discounted for the time value of money because of the delay in approving the merger and consummating the transaction. The exact difference between the two bids was an unsettled point of contention even at oral argument.

7. Actually, at this time about $400 million of Forstmann's funding was still subject to two investment banks using their "best effort" to organize a syndicate to provide the balance. Pantry Pride's entire financing was not firmly committed at this point either, although Pantry Pride represented in an October 11 letter to Lazard Freres that its investment banker, Drexel Burnham Lambert, was highly confident of its ability to raise the balance of $350 million. Drexel Burnham had a firm commitment for this sum by October 18.

challenging the lock-up, the cancellation fee, and the exercise of the Rights and the Notes covenants. Pantry Pride also sought a temporary restraining order to prevent Revlon from placing any assets in escrow or transferring them to Forstmann. Moreover, on October 22, Pantry Pride again raised its bid, with a cash offer of $58 per share conditioned upon nullification of the Rights, waiver of the covenants, and an injunction of the Forstmann lock-up.

On October 15, the Court of Chancery prohibited the further transfer of assets, and eight days later enjoined the lock-up, no-shop, and cancellation fee provisions of the agreement. The trial court concluded that the Revlon directors had breached their duty of loyalty by making concessions to Forstmann, out of concern for their liability to the noteholders, rather than maximizing the sale price of the company for the stockholders' benefit. MacAndrews & Forbes Holdings, Inc. v. Revlon, Inc., 501 A.2d at 1249–50.

II.

To obtain a preliminary injunction, a plaintiff must demonstrate both a reasonable probability of success on the merits and some irreparable harm which will occur absent the injunction. Gimbel v. Signal Companies, Del.Ch., 316 A.2d 599, 602 (1974), aff'd, Del. Supr., 316 A.2d 619 (1974). Additionally, the Court shall balance the conveniences of and possible injuries to the parties. Id.

A.

We turn first to Pantry Pride's probability of success on the merits. The ultimate responsibility for managing the business and affairs of a corporation falls on its board of directors. 8 Del.C. § 141(a). In discharging this function the directors owe fiduciary duties of care and loyalty to the corporation and its shareholders. Guth v. Loft, Inc., 23 Del.Supr. 255, 5 A.2d 503, 510 (1939); Aronson v. Lewis, Del.Supr., 473 A.2d 805, 811 (1984). These principles apply with equal force when a board approves a corporate merger pursuant to 8 Del.C. § 251(b); [9] Smith v. Van Gorkom, Del. Supr., 488 A.2d 858, 873 (1985); and of course they are the bedrock of our law regarding corporate takeover issues. Pogostin v. Rice, Del.Supr., 480 A.2d 619, 624 (1984); Unocal Corp. v. Mesa Petroleum Co., Del.Supr., 493 A.2d 946, 953, 955 (1985); Moran v. Household International, Inc., Del.Supr., 500 A.2d 1346, 1350 (1985). While the business judgment rule may be applicable to the actions of corporate directors responding to takeover threats, the principles upon which it is founded—care, loyalty and independence—must first be satisfied.[10] Aronson v. Lewis, 473 A.2d at 812.

---

9. The statute provides in pertinent part:

(b) The board of directors of each corporation which desires to merge or consolidate shall adopt a resolution approving an agreement of merger or consolidation. 8 Del.C. § 251(b).

10. One eminent corporate commentator has drawn a distinction between the business judgment rule, which insulates directors and management from personal liability for their business decisions, and the business judgment doctrine, which protects the decision itself from attack. The principles upon which the rule and doctrine op-

If the business judgment rule applies, there is a "presumption that in making a business decision the directors of a corporation acted on an informed basis, in good faith and in the honest belief that the action taken was in the best interests of the company." Aronson v. Lewis, 473 A.2d at 812. However, when a board implements anti-takeover measures there arises "the omnipresent specter that a board may be acting primarily in its own interests, rather than those of the corporation and its shareholders . . ." Unocal Corp. v. Mesa Petroleum Co., 493 A.2d at 954. This potential for conflict places upon the directors the burden of proving that they had reasonable grounds for believing there was a danger to corporate policy and effectiveness, a burden satisfied by a showing of good faith and reasonable investigation. Id. at 955. In addition, the directors must analyze the nature of the takeover and its effect on the corporation in order to ensure balance—that the responsive action taken is reasonable in relation to the threat posed. Id.

B.

The first relevant defensive measure adopted by the Revlon board was the Rights Plan, which would be considered a "poison pill" in the current language of corporate takeovers—a plan by which shareholders receive the right to be bought out by the corporation at a substantial premium on the occurrence of a stated triggering event. See generally Moran v. Household International, Inc., Del.Supr., 500 A.2d 1346 (1985). By 8 Del.C. §§ 141 and 157,[11] the board clearly had the power to adopt the measure. Moran v. Household International, Inc., 500 A.2d at 1351. Thus, the focus becomes one of reasonableness and purpose.

The Revlon board approved the Rights Plan in the face of an impending hostile takeover bid by Pantry Pride at $45 per share, a price which Revlon reasonably concluded was grossly inadequate. Lazard Freres had so advised the directors, and had also informed them that Pantry Pride was a small, highly leveraged company bent on a "bust-up" takeover by using "junk bond" financing to buy Revlon cheaply, sell the acquired assets to pay the debts incurred, and retain

erate are identical, while the objects of their protection are different. See Hinsey, Business Judgment and the American Law Institute's Corporate Governance Project: The Rule, the Doctrine and the Reality, 52 Geo.Wash.L.Rev. 609, 611–13 (1984). In the transactional justification cases, where the doctrine is said to apply, our decisions have not observed the distinction in such terminology. See Polk v. Good & Texaco, Del.Supr., ___ A.2d ___, ___ (1986); Moran v. Household International, Inc., Del.Supr., 500 A.2d 1346, 1356 (1985); Unocal Corp. v. Mesa Petroleum Co., Del.Supr., 493 A.2d 946, 953–55 (1985); Rosenblatt v. Getty Oil Co., Del.Supr., 493 A.2d 929, 943 (1985). Under the circumstances we do not alter our earlier practice of referring only to the business judgment rule, although in trans-

actional justification matters such reference may be understood to embrace the concept of the doctrine.

11. The relevant provision of Section 122 is:

Every corporation created under this chapter shall have power to:

(13) Make contracts, including contracts of guaranty and suretyship, incur liabilities, borrow money at such rates of interest as the corporation may determine, issue its notes, bonds and other obligations, and secure any of its obligations by mortgage, pledge or other encumbrance of all or any of its property, franchises and income, . . .". 8 Del.C. § 122(13). . . .

the profit for itself.[12] In adopting the Plan, the board protected the shareholders from a hostile takeover at a price below the company's intrinsic value, while retaining sufficient flexibility to address any proposal deemed to be in the stockholders' best interests.

To that extent the board acted in good faith and upon reasonable investigation. Under the circumstances it cannot be said that the Rights Plan as employed was unreasonable, considering the threat posed. Indeed, the Plan was a factor in causing Pantry Pride to raise its bids from a low of $42 to an eventual high of $58. At the time of its adoption the Rights Plan afforded a measure of protection consistent with the directors' fiduciary duty in facing a takeover threat perceived as detrimental to corporate interests. *Unocal,* 493 A.2d at 954–55. Far from being a "show-stopper," as the plaintiffs had contended in *Moran,* the measure spurred the bidding to new heights, a proper result of its implementation. See *Moran,* 500 A.2d at 1354, 1356–67.

Although we consider adoption of the Plan to have been valid under the circumstances, its continued usefulness was rendered moot by the directors' actions on October 3 and October 12. At the October 3 meeting the board redeemed the Rights conditioned upon consummation of a merger with Forstmann, but further acknowledged that they would also be redeemed to facilitate any more favorable offer. On October 12, the board unanimously passed a resolution redeeming the Rights in connection with any cash proposal of $57.25 or more per share. Because all the pertinent offers eventually equalled or surpassed that amount, the Rights clearly were no longer any impediment in the contest for Revlon. This mooted any question of their propriety under *Moran* or *Unocal.*

C.

The second defensive measure adopted by Revlon to thwart a Pantry Pride takeover was the company's own exchange offer for 10 million of its shares. The directors' general broad powers to manage the business and affairs of the corporation are augmented by the specific authority conferred under 8 Del.C. § 160(a), permitting the company to deal in its own stock. *Unocal,* 493 A.2d at 953–54; *Cheff v. Mathes,* 41 Del.Supr. 494, 199 A.2d 548, 554 (1964); *Kors v. Carey,* 39 Del.Ch. 47, 158 A.2d 136, 140 (1960). However, when exercising that power in an effort to forestall a hostile takeover, the board's actions are strictly held to the fiduciary standards outlined in *Unocal.* These standards require the directors to determine the best interests of the corporation and its stockholders, and impose an enhanced duty to abjure any action that is motivated by considerations other than a good faith concern for such interests. *Unocal,* 493 A.2d at 954–55; see *Bennett v. Propp,* 41 Del.Supr. 14, 187 A.2d 405, 409 (1962).

---

12. As we noted in *Moran,* a "bust-up" takeover generally refers to a situation in which one seeks to finance an acquisition by selling off pieces of the acquired company, presumably at a substantial profit. See *Moran,* 500 A.2d at 1349, n. 4.

The Revlon directors concluded that Pantry Pride's $47.50 offer was grossly inadequate. In that regard the board acted in good faith, and on an informed basis, with reasonable grounds to believe that there existed a harmful threat to the corporate enterprise. The adoption of a defensive measure, reasonable in relation to the threat posed, was proper and fully accorded with the powers, duties, and responsibilities conferred upon directors under our law. *Unocal,* 493 A.2d at 954; Pogostin v. Rice, 480 A.2d at 627.

D.

However, when Pantry Pride increased its offer to $50 per share, and then to $53, it became apparent to all that the break-up of the company was inevitable. The Revlon board's authorization permitting management to negotiate a merger or buyout with a third party was a recognition that the company was for sale. The duty of the board had thus changed from the preservation of Revlon as a corporate entity to the maximization of the company's value at a sale for the stockholders' benefit. This significantly altered the board's responsibilities under the *Unocal* standards. It no longer faced threats to corporate policy and effectiveness, or to the stockholders' interests, from a grossly inadequate bid. The whole question of defensive measures became moot. The directors' role changed from defenders of the corporate bastion to auctioneers charged with getting the best price for the stockholders at a sale of the company.

III.

This brings us to the lock-up with Forstmann and its emphasis on shoring up the sagging market value of the Notes in the face of threatened litigation by their holders. Such a focus was inconsistent with the changed concept of the directors' responsibilities at this stage of the developments. The impending waiver of the Notes covenants had caused the value of the Notes to fall, and the board was aware of the noteholders' ire as well as their subsequent threats of suit. The directors thus made support of the Notes an integral part of the company's dealings with Forstmann, even though their primary responsibility at this stage was to the equity owners.

The original threat posed by Pantry Pride—the break-up of the company—had become a reality which even the directors embraced. Selective dealing to fend off a hostile but determined bidder was no longer a proper objective. Instead, obtaining the highest price for the benefit of the stockholders should have been the central theme guiding director action. Thus, the Revlon board could not make the requisite showing of good faith by preferring the noteholders and ignoring its duty of loyalty to the shareholders. The rights of the former already were fixed by contract. Wolfensohn v. Madison Fund, Inc., Del.Supr., 253 A.2d 72, 75 (1969); Harff v. Kerkorian, Del. Ch., 324 A.2d 215 (1974). The noteholders required no further protection, and when the Revlon board entered into an auction-ending lock-up agreement with Forstmann on the basis of impermissible considerations at the expense of the shareholders, the directors breached their primary duty of loyalty.

The Revlon board argued that it acted in good faith in protecting the noteholders because *Unocal* permits consideration of other corporate constituencies. Although such considerations may be permissible, there are fundamental limitations upon that prerogative. A board may have regard for various constituencies in discharging its responsibilities, provided there are rationally related benefits accruing to the stockholders. *Unocal,* 493 A.2d at 955. However, such concern for non-stockholder interests is inappropriate when an auction among active bidders is in progress, and the object no longer is to protect or maintain the corporate enterprise but to sell it to the highest bidder.

Revlon also contended that by Gilbert v. El Paso Co., Del.Ch., 490 A.2d 1050, 1054–55 (1984), it had contractual and good faith obligations to consider the noteholders. However, any such duties are limited to the principle that one may not interfere with contractual relationships by improper actions. Here, the rights of the noteholders were fixed by agreement, and there is nothing of substance to suggest that any of those terms were violated. The Notes covenants specifically contemplated a waiver to permit sale of the company at a fair price. The Notes were accepted by the holders on that basis, including the risk of an adverse market effect stemming from a waiver. Thus, nothing remained for Revlon to legitimately protect, and no rationally related benefit thereby accrued to the stockholders. Under such circumstances we must conclude that the merger agreement with Forstmann was unreasonable in relation to the threat posed.

A lock-up is not *per se* illegal under Delaware law. Its use has been approved in an earlier case. Thompson v. Enstar Corp., Del.Ch. (1984). Such options can entice other bidders to enter a contest for control of the corporation, creating an auction for the company and maximizing shareholder profit. Current economic conditions in the takeover market are such that a "white knight" like Forstmann might only enter the bidding for the target company if it receives some form of compensation to cover the risks and costs involved. Note, Corporations–Mergers—"Lock-up" Enjoined Under Section 14(e) of Securities Exchange Act—Mobil Corp. v. Marathon Oil Co., 669 F.2d 366 (6th Cir.1981), 12 Seton Hall L.Rev. 881, 892 (1982). However, while those lock-ups which draw bidders into the battle benefit shareholders, similar measures which end an active auction and foreclose further bidding operate to the shareholders' detriment. Note, Lock-up Options: Toward a State Law Standard, 96 Harv.L.Rev. 1068, 1081 (1983).[14]

Recently, the United States Court of Appeals for the Second Circuit invalidated a lock-up on fiduciary duty grounds similar to those

---

14. For further discussion of the benefits and detriments of lock-up options, also see: Nelson, Mobil Corp. v. Marathon Oil Co.—The Decision and Its Implications for Future Tender Offers, 7 Corp.L.Rev. 233, 265–68 (1984); Note, Swallowing the Key to Lock-up Options: Mobil Corp. v. Marathon Oil Co., 14 U.Tol.L.Rev. 1055, 1081–83 (1983).

here.[15]   Hanson Trust PLC, et al. v. ML SCM Acquisition Inc., et al., 781 F.2d 264 (2nd Cir.1986).   Citing Thompson v. Enstar Corp., supra, with approval, the court stated:

> In this regard, we are especially mindful that some lock-up options may be beneficial to the shareholders, such as those that induce a bidder to compete for control of a corporation, while others may be harmful, such as those that effectively preclude bidders from competing with the optionee bidder.   781 F.2d at 274.

In *Hanson Trust,* the bidder, Hanson, sought control of SCM by a hostile cash tender offer.   SCM management joined with Merrill Lynch to propose a leveraged buy-out of the company at a higher price, and Hanson in turn increased its offer.   Then, despite very little improvement in its subsequent bid, the management group sought a lock-up option to purchase SCM's two main assets at a substantial discount.   The SCM directors granted the lock-up without adequate information as to the size of the discount or the effect the transaction would have on the company.   Their action effectively ended a competitive bidding situation.   The Hanson Court invalidated the lock-up because the directors failed to fully inform themselves about the value of a transaction in which management had a strong self-interest.   "In short, the Board appears to have failed to ensure that negotiations for alternative bids were conducted by those whose only loyalty was to the shareholders."   Id. at 277.

The Forstmann option had a similar destructive effect on the auction process.   Forstmann had already been drawn into the contest on a preferred basis, so the result of the lock-up was not to foster bidding, but to destroy it.   The board's stated reasons for approving the transaction were: (1) better financing, (2) noteholder protection, and (3) higher price.   As the Court of Chancery found, and we agree, any distinctions between the rival bidders' methods of financing the proposal were nominal at best, and such a consideration has little or no significance in a cash offer for any and all shares.   The principal object, contrary to the board's duty of care, appears to have been protection of the noteholders over the shareholders' interests.

While Forstmann's $57.25 offer was objectively higher than Pantry Pride's $56.25 bid, the margin of superiority is less when the Forstmann price is adjusted for the time value of money.   In reality, the Revlon board ended the auction in return for very little actual improvement in the final bid.   The principal benefit went to the directors, who avoided personal liability to a class of creditors to whom the board owed no further duty under the circumstances.   Thus, when a board ends an intense bidding contest on an insubstan-

---

15.   The federal courts generally have declined to enjoin lock-up options despite arguments that lock-ups constitute impermissible "manipulative" conduct forbidden by Section 14(e) of the Williams Act [15 U.S.C. § 78n(e)].   See Buffalo Forge Co. v. Ogden Corp., 717 F.2d 757 (2nd Cir.1983), cert. denied, 464 U.S. 1018, 104 S.Ct. 550, 78 L.Ed.2d 724 (1983); Data Probe Acquisition Corp. v. Datatab, Inc., 722 F.2d 1 (2nd Cir.1983); cert. denied 465 U.S. 1052, 104 S.Ct. 1326, 79 L.Ed.2d 722 (1984); but see Mobil Corp. v. Marathon Oil Co., 669 F.2d 366 (6th Cir.1981).   The cases are all federal in nature and were not decided on state law grounds.

tial basis, and where a significant by-product of that action is to protect the directors against a perceived threat of personal liability for consequences stemming from the adoption of previous defensive measures, the action cannot withstand the enhanced scrutiny which *Unocal* requires of director conduct. See *Unocal,* 493 A.2d at 954–55.

In addition to the lock-up option, the Court of Chancery enjoined the no-shop provision as part of the attempt to foreclose further bidding by Pantry Pride. MacAndrews & Forbes Holdings, Inc. v. Revlon, Inc., 501 A.2d at 1251. The no-shop provision, like the lock-up option, while not *per se* illegal, is impermissible under the *Unocal* standards when a board's primary duty becomes that of an auctioneer responsible for selling the company to the highest bidder. The agreement to negotiate only with Forstmann ended rather than intensified the board's involvement in the bidding contest.

It is ironic that the parties even considered a no-shop agreement when Revlon had dealt preferentially, and almost exclusively, with Forstmann throughout the contest. After the directors authorized management to negotiate with other parties, Forstmann was given every negotiating advantage that Pantry Pride had been denied: cooperation from management, access to financial data, and the exclusive opportunity to present merger proposals directly to the board of directors. Favoritism for a white knight to the total exclusion of a hostile bidder might be justifiable when the latter's offer adversely affects shareholder interests, but when bidders make relatively similar offers, or dissolution of the company becomes inevitable, the directors cannot fulfill their enhanced *Unocal* duties by playing favorites with the contending factions. Market forces must be allowed to operate freely to bring the target's shareholders the best price available for their equity.[16] Thus, as the trial court ruled, the shareholders' interests necessitated that the board remain free to negotiate in the fulfillment of that duty.

The court below similarly enjoined the payment of the cancellation fee, pending a resolution of the merits, because the fee was part of the overall plan to thwart Pantry Pride's efforts. We find no abuse of discretion in that ruling.

IV.

Having concluded that Pantry Pride has shown a reasonable probability of success on the merits, we address the issue of irreparable harm. The Court of Chancery ruled that unless the lock-up and other aspects of the agreement were enjoined, Pantry Pride's opportunity to bid for Revlon was lost. The court also held that the need for both bidders to compete in the marketplace outweighed any injury to Forstmann. Given the complexity of the proposed transaction between Revlon and Forstmann, the obstacles to Pantry Pride obtaining

---

16. By this we do not embrace the "passivity" thesis rejected in *Unocal.* See 493 A.2d at 954–55, nn. 8–10. The directors' role remains an active one, changed only in the respect that they are charged with the duty of selling the company at the highest price attainable for the stockholders' benefit.

a meaningful legal remedy are immense. We are satisfied that the plaintiff has shown the need for an injunction to protect it from irreparable harm, which need outweighs any harm to the defendants.

V.

In conclusion, the Revlon board was confronted with a situation not uncommon in the current wave of corporate takeovers. A hostile and determined bidder sought the company at a price the board was convinced was inadequate. The initial defensive tactics worked to the benefit of the shareholders, and thus the board was able to sustain its *Unocal* burdens in justifying those measures. However, in granting an asset option lock-up to Forstmann, we must conclude that under all the circumstances the directors allowed considerations other than the maximization of shareholder profit to affect their judgment, and followed a course that ended the auction for Revlon, absent court intervention, to the ultimate detriment of its shareholders. No such defensive measure can be sustained when it represents a breach of the directors' fundamental duty of care. See Smith v. Van Gorkom, Del. Supr., 488 A.2d 858, 874 (1985). In that context the board's action is not entitled to the deference accorded it by the business judgment rule. The measures were properly enjoined. The decision of the Court of Chancery, therefore, is

AFFIRMED.

CAL. CORP. CODE § 1203

[See Statutory Supplement]

NOTE ON CTS CORPORATION v. DYNAMICS CORPORATION OF AMERICA

A number of states have adopted statutes regulating tender offers. These statutes are of various types, but most are intended to make tender offers more difficult. In Edgar v. MITE Corp., 457 U.S. 624, 102 S.Ct. 2629, 73 L.Ed.2d 269 (1982) a plurality of the Supreme Court struck down, as unconstitutional, one type of state tender-offer statute. However, in CTS Corporation v. Dynamics Corporation of America, ___ U.S. ___, 107 S.Ct. 1637, 95 L.Ed.2d 67 (1987), the Supreme Court distinguished *MITE* and upheld another type of statute, which had been adopted by Indiana. The Court described the Indiana statute as follows:

. . . The Act applies only to "issuing public corporations." The term "corporation" includes only businesses incorporated in Indiana. See § 23–1–20–5. An "issuing public corporation" is defined as:

"a corporation that has:

"(1) one hundred (100) or more shareholders;

"(2) its principal place of business, its principal office, or substantial assets within Indiana; and

"(3) either:

"(A) more than ten percent (10%) of its shareholders resident in Indiana;

"(B) more than ten percent (10%) of its shares owned by Indiana residents; or

"(C) ten thousand (10,000) shareholders resident in Indiana." § 23–1–42–4(a).

The Act focuses on the acquisition of "control shares" in an issuing public corporation. Under the Act, an entity acquires "control shares" whenever it acquires shares that, but for the operation of the Act, would bring its voting power in the corporation to or above any of three thresholds: 20%, 33⅓, or 50%. § 23–1–42–1. An entity that acquires control shares does not necessarily acquire voting rights. Rather, it gains those rights only "to the extent granted by resolution approved by the shareholders of the issuing public corporation." § 23–1–42–9(a). Section 9 requires a majority vote of all disinterested shareholders holding each class of stock for passage of such a resolution. § 23–1–42–9(b). The practical effect of this requirement is to condition acquisition of control of a corporation on approval of a majority of the pre-existing disinterested shareholders.

The shareholders decide whether to confer rights on the control shares at the next regularly scheduled meeting of the shareholders, or at a specially scheduled meeting. The acquiror can require management of the corporation to hold such a special meeting within 50 days if it files an "acquiring person statement," requests the meeting, and agrees to pay the expenses of the meeting. See § 23–1–42–7. If the shareholders do not vote to restore voting rights to the shares, the corporation may redeem the control shares from the acquiror at fair market value, but it is not required to do so. § 23–1–42–10(b). Similarly, if the acquiror does not file an acquiring person statement with the corporation, the corporation may, if its bylaws or articles of incorporation so provide, redeem the shares at any time after 60 days after the acquiror's last acquisition. § 23–1–42–10(a).

The Court first held that the Indiana Act was not preempted by the Williams Act:

. . . [T]he overriding concern of the MITE plurality was that the Illinois statute considered in that case operated to favor management against offerors, to the detriment of shareholders. By contrast, the statute now before the Court protects the independent shareholder against both of the contending parties. Thus, the Act furthers a basic purpose of the Williams Act,

" 'plac[ing] investors on an equal footing with the takeover bidder,' " Piper v. Chris–Craft Industries, 430 U.S., at 30 (quoting the Senate Report accompanying the Williams Act, S.Rep. No. 550, 90th Cong., 1st Sess., 4 (1967)).

The Indiana Act, operates on the assumption, implicit in the Williams Act, that independent shareholders faced with tender offers often are at a disadvantage. By allowing such shareholders to vote as a group, the Act protects them from the coercive aspects of some tender offers. If, for example, shareholders believe that a successful tender offer will be followed by a purchase of nontendering shares at a depressed price, individual shareholders may tender their shares—even if they doubt the tender offer is in the corporation's best interest—to protect themselves from being forced to sell their shares at a depressed price. . . . In such a situation under the Indiana Act, the shareholders as a group, acting in the corporation's best interest, could reject the offer, although individual shareholders might be inclined to accept it. The desire of the Indiana Legislature to protect shareholders of Indiana corporations from this type of coercive offer does not conflict with the Williams Act. Rather, it furthers the federal policy of investor protection.

In implementing its goal, the Indiana Act avoids the problems the plurality discussed in MITE. Unlike the MITE statute, the Indiana Act does not give either management or the offeror an advantage in communicating with the shareholders about the impending offer. The Act also does not impose an indefinite delay on tender offers. Nothing in the Act prohibits an offeror from consummating an offer on the 20th business day, the earliest day permitted under applicable federal regulations, see 17 CFR § 240.14e–1(a) (1986). Nor does the Act allow the state government to interpose its views of fairness between willing buyers and sellers of shares of the target company. Rather, the Act allows *shareholders* to evaluate the fairness of the offer collectively. . . .

The Court of Appeals based its finding of pre-emption on its view that the practical effect of the Indiana Act is to delay consummation of tender offers until 50 days after the commencement of the offer. 794 F.2d, at 263. As did the Court of Appeals, Dynamics reasons that no rational offeror will purchase shares until it gains assurance that those shares will carry voting rights. Because it is possible that voting rights will not be conferred until a shareholder meeting 50 days after commencement of the offer, Dynamics concludes that the Act imposes a 50–day delay. This, it argues, conflicts with the shorter 20–business-day period established by the SEC as the minimum period for which a tender offer may be held open. 17 CFR § 240.14e–1 (1986). We find the alleged conflict illusory.

The Act does not impose an absolute 50–day delay on tender offers, nor does it preclude an offeror from purchasing shares as soon as federal law permits. If the offeror fears an adverse shareholder vote under the Act, it can make a conditional tender offer, offering to accept shares on the condition that the shares receive voting rights within a certain period of time. The Williams Act permits tender offers to be conditioned on the offeror's subsequently obtaining regulatory approval. . . . There is no reason to doubt that this type of conditional tender offer would be legitimate as well.

Even assuming that the Indiana Act imposes some additional delay, nothing in MITE suggested that *any* delay imposed by state regulation, however short, would create a conflict with the Williams Act. The plurality argued only that the offeror should "be free to go forward without *unreasonable* delay." 457 U.S., at 639 (emphasis added). In that case, the Court was confronted with the potential for indefinite delay and presented with no persuasive reason why some deadline could not be established. By contrast, the Indiana Act provides that full voting rights will be vested—if this eventually is to occur—within 50 days after commencement of the offer. This period is within the 60–day maximum period Congress established for tender offers in 15 U.S.C. § 78n(d)(5). We cannot say that a delay within that congressionally determined period is unreasonable.

The Court then held that the Indiana Act did not violate the Commerce Clause:

The Court of Appeals . . . [held that the Indiana Act was unconstitutional because of its] potential to hinder tender offers. We think the Court of Appeals failed to appreciate the significance for Commerce Clause analysis of the fact that state regulation of corporate governance is regulation of entities whose very existence and attributes are a product of state law. . . . Every State in this country has enacted laws regulating corporate governance. By prohibiting certain transactions, and regulating others, such laws necessarily affect certain aspects of interstate commerce. This necessarily is true with respect to corporations with shareholders in States other than the State of incorporation. . . .

It thus is an accepted part of the business landscape in this country for States to create corporations, to prescribe their powers, and to define the rights that are acquired by purchasing their shares. A State has an interest in promoting stable relationships among parties involved in the corporations it charters, as well as in ensuring that investors in such corporations have an effective voice in corporate affairs. . . .

Dynamics' argument that the Act is unconstitutional ultimately rests on its contention that the Act will limit the number of successful tender offers. There is little evidence that this will occur. But even if true, this result would not substantially affect our Commerce Clause analysis. We reiterate that this Act does not prohibit any entity—resident or nonresident—from offering to purchase, or from purchasing, shares in Indiana corporations, or from attempting thereby to gain control. It only provides regulatory procedures designed for the better protection of the corporations' shareholders. We have rejected the "notion that the Commerce Clause protects the particular structure or methods of operation in a . . . market." Exxon Corp. v. Governor of Maryland, 437 U.S., at 127. The very commodity that is traded in the securities market is one whose characteristics are defined by state law. Similarly, the very commodity that is traded in the "market for corporate control"—the corporation—is one that owes its existence and attributes to state law. Indiana need not define these commodities as other States do; it need only provide that residents and nonresidents have equal access to them. This Indiana has done. Accordingly, even if the Act should decrease the number of successful tender offers for Indiana corporations, this would not offend the Commerce Clause.

DEL. GEN. CORP. LAW § 203

[See Statutory Supplement]

SECTION 3. RECAPITALIZATIONS—THE ELIMINATION OF ACCRUED DIVIDENDS

A recapitalization is a material readjustment in the relative rights, preferences, and privileges of a corporation's various classes of stock.[1] Most recapitalizations center on a drastic change in the rights of preferred shareholders, and in particular on their right to accrued but unpaid dividends. "Typically, the corporation is unable to pay these dividends in cash and will be unable to do so in the foreseeable future. The main purpose of the reclassification plan is to eliminate this obstacle to future financing by the corporation, by putting the reclassified preferred stock on a current basis and eliminating the right to these accrued dividends."[2] During the Depression huge arrearages had piled up on preferred stock dividends. Though not debt, these arrearages nevertheless represented a first claim upon earnings. A wave of recapitalizations took place in the late 1930's and the 1940's, as the economy showed signs of improvement and emergence from the Depression and management could look forward to the possibility of paying dividends once again. Since in most instances the directors were still elected by the common stock, the immediate issue was how a distribution could be made to the common in the face of prior claims of the preferred. This was the genesis of the wave of recapitalizations. (Another reason often given for recapitalizations is that large

---

1. A recapitalization differs from a reorganization under the Bankruptcy Act, in that it involves only persons who, as shareholders, normally have no right to receive payment prior to corporate liquidation.

Dodd, Fair and Equitable Recapitalizations, 55 Harv.L.Rev. 780, at 782 (1942).

2. 2 H. Marsh, Marsh's California Corporation Law and Practice 407, 413 (1987).

arrearages impair credit and impede desirable financing.[3] There is some doubt, however, whether *debt* financing would usually be hindered by the claims of preferred, which would be subordinate to the debt.) Whatever the explanation, as Dewing has said, "When stripped of all inconsequential verbiage, [a] proposed capital readjustment is invariably of benefit to the common shareholders as it brings the common stock nearer to the payment of dividends. Invariably the plan favors the common shareholder in contrast to the preferred."[4]

BOVE v. THE COMMUNITY HOTEL CORP. OF NEWPORT, RHODE ISLAND

Supreme Court of Rhode Island, 1969.
105 R.I. 36, 249 A.2d 89.

JOSLIN, Justice. This civil action was brought in the superior court to enjoin a proposed merger of The Community Hotel Corporation of Newport, Rhode Island, a defendant herein, into Newport Hotel Corp. Both corporations were organized under the general corporation law of this state and are hereinafter referred to respectively as "Community Hotel" and "Newport." No oral testimony was presented and a trial justice sitting without a jury decided the case on the facts appearing in the exhibits and as assented to by the parties in the pretrial order. The case is here on the plaintiffs' appeal from a judgment denying injunctive relief and dismissing the action.

Community Hotel was incorporated on October 21, 1924, for the stated purpose of erecting, maintaining, operating, managing and leasing hotels; and it commenced operations in 1927 with the opening of the Viking Hotel in Newport. Its authorized capital stock consists of 6,000 shares of $100 par value six per cent prior preference cumulative preferred stock, and 6,000 shares of no par common stock of which 2,106 shares are issued and outstanding. The plaintiffs as well as the individual defendants are holders and owners of preferred stock, plaintiffs having acquired their holdings of approximately 900 shares not later than 1930. At the time this suit was commenced, dividends on the 4,335 then-issued and outstanding preferred shares had accrued, but had not been declared, for approximately 24 years, and totalled about $645,000 or $148.75 per share.

Newport was organized at the instance and request of the board of directors of Community Hotel solely for the purpose of effectuating the merger which is the subject matter of this action. Its authorized capital stock consists of 80,000 shares of common stock, par value $1.00, of which only one share has been issued, and that to Community Hotel for a consideration of $10.

The essentials of the merger plan call for Community Hotel to merge into Newport, which will then become the surviving corporation. Although previously without assets, Newport will, if the contemplated merger is effectuated, acquire the sole ownership of all the

3. See Latty, Fairness—The Focal Point in Preferred Stock Arrearage Elimination, 29 Va.L.Rev. 1, at 12 (1942).

4. 2 A. Dewing, Financial Policy of Corporations 1195 (5th ed. 1953).

property and assets now owned by Community Hotel. The plan also calls for the outstanding shares of Community Hotel's capital stock to be converted into shares of the capital stock of Newport upon the following basis: Each outstanding share of the constituent corporation's preferred stock, together with all accrued dividends thereon, will be changed and converted into five shares of the $1.00 par value common stock of the surviving corporation; and each share of the constituent corporation's no par common stock will be changed and converted into one share of the common stock, $1.00 par value, of the surviving corporation.

Consistent with the requirements of G.L.1956, § 7–5–3, the merger will become effective only if the plan receives the affirmative votes of the stockholders of each of the corporations representing at least two-thirds of the shares of each class of its capital stock. For the purpose of obtaining the required approval, notice was given to both common and preferred stockholders of Community Hotel that a special meeting would be held for the purpose of considering and voting upon the proposed merger. Before the scheduled meeting date arrived, this action was commenced and the meeting was postponed to a future time and place. So far as the record before us indicates, it has not yet been held.

The plaintiffs argue that the primary, and indeed, the only purpose of the proposed merger is to eliminate the priorities of the preferred stock with less than the unanimous consent of its holders. Assuming that premise, a preliminary matter for our consideration concerns the merger of a parent corporation into a wholly-owned subsidiary created for the sole purpose of achieving a recapitalization which will eliminate the parent's preferred stock and the dividends accumulated thereon, and whether such a merger qualifies within the contemplation of the statute permitting any two or more corporations to merge into a single corporation.

It is true, of course, that to accomplish the proposed recapitalization by amending Community Hotel's articles of association under relevant provisions of the general corporation law [2] would require the unanimous vote of the preferred shareholders, whereas under the merger statute, only a two-thirds vote of those stockholders will be needed. Concededly, unanimity of the preferred stockholders is unobtainable in this case, and plaintiffs argue, therefore, that to permit the less restrictive provisions of the merger statute to be used to accomplish indirectly what otherwise would be incapable of being accomplished directly by the more stringent amendment procedures of

2. Section 7–2–18, as amended, provides that a corporation may ". . . from time to time when and as desired amend its articles of association . . ." and § 7–2–19, as amended, provides that "Unless otherwise provided in the articles of association, every such amendment shall require the affirmative vote of the following proportion of the stockholders, passed at a meeting duly called for the purpose:

"(a) . . .

"(b) Where the amendment diminishes the stipulated rate of dividends on any class of stock or the stipulated amount to be paid thereon in case of call or liquidation, the unanimous vote of the stockholders of such class and the vote of a majority in interest of all other stockholders entitled to vote."

the general corporation law is tantamount to sanctioning a circumvention or perversion of that law.

The question, however, is not whether recapitalization by the merger route is a subterfuge, but whether a merger which is designed for the sole purpose of cancelling the rights of preferred stockholders with the consent of less than all has been authorized by the legislature. The controlling statute is § 7–5–2. Its language is clear, all-embracing and unqualified. It authorizes any two or more business corporations *which were or might have been organized* under the general corporation law to merge into a single corporation; and it provides that the merger agreement shall prescribe ". . . the terms and conditions of consolidation or merger, the mode of carrying the same into effect . . . *as well as the manner of converting the shares of each of the constituent corporations into shares or other securities of the corporation resulting from or surviving such consolidation or merger,* with such other details and provisions as are deemed necessary." [3] (italics ours) Nothing in that language even suggests that the legislature intended to make *underlying purpose* a standard for determining permissibility. Indeed, the contrary is apparent since the very breadth of the language selected presupposes a complete lack of concern with whether the merger is designed to further the mutual interests of two existing and nonaffiliated corporations or whether alternatively it is purposed solely upon effecting a substantial change in an existing corporation's capital structure.

Moreover, that a possible effect of corporate action under the merger statute is not possible, or is even forbidden, under another section of the general corporation law is of no import, it being settled that the several sections of that law may have independent legal significance, and that the validity of corporate action taken pursuant to one section is not necessarily dependent upon its being valid under another. Hariton v. Arco Electronics, Inc., 40 Del.Ch. 326, 182 A.2d 22, aff'd, 41 Del.Ch. 74, 188 A.2d 123; Langfelder v. Universal Laboratories, Inc., D.C., 68 F.Supp. 209, aff'd, 3 Cir., 163 F.2d 804.

We hold, therefore, that nothing within the purview of our statute forbids a merger between a parent and a subsidiary corporation even under circumstances where the merger device has been resorted to solely for the purpose of obviating the necessity for the unanimous vote which would otherwise be required in order to cancel the priorities of preferred shareholders. Federal United Corp. v. Havender, supra; Hottenstein v. York Ice Machinery Corp., 3 Cir., 136 F.2d 944; 7 Fletcher, Cyclopedia of Corporations, chap. 43, § 3696.1, page 892.

A more basic problem, narrowed so as to bring it within the factual context of this case, is whether the right of a holder of cumulative preferred stock to dividend arrearages and other preferences may be cancelled by a statutory merger. That precise problem

---

3. The quoted provision is substantially identical to the Delaware merger statute (Del.Rev.Code (1935) C. 65, § 2091) construed in Federal United Corp. v. Havender, 24 Del.Ch. 318, 11 A.2d 331, infra pp. 93–94.

has not heretofore been before this court, but elsewhere there is a considerable body of law on the subject. There is no need to discuss all of the authorities. For illustrative purposes it is sufficient that we refer principally to cases involving Delaware corporations. That state is important as a state of incorporation, and the decisions of its courts on the precise problem are not only referred to and relied on by the parties, but are generally considered to be the leading ones in the field.

The earliest case in point of time is Keller v. Wilson & Co., 21 Del.Ch. 391, 190 A. 115 (1936). Wilson & Company was formed and its stock was issued in 1925 and the law then in effect protected against charter amendments which might destroy a preferred shareholder's right to accumulated dividends. In 1927 that law was amended so as to permit such destruction, and thereafter the stockholders of Wilson & Company, by the required majorities, voted to cancel the dividends which had by then accrued on its preferred stock. In invalidating that action the rationale of the Delaware court was that the right of a holder of a corporation's cumulative preferred stock to eventual payment of dividend arrearages was a fixed contractual right, that it was a property right in the nature of a debt, that it was vested, and that it could not be destroyed by corporate action taken under legislative authority subsequently conferred, without the consent of all of the shareholders.

Consolidated Film Industries, Inc. v. Johnson, 22 Del.Ch. 407, 197 A. 489 (1937), decided a year later, was an almost precisely similar case. The only difference was that Consolidated Film Industries, Inc. was not created until after the adoption of the 1927 amendment, whereas in the earlier case the statutory amendment upon which Wilson & Company purported to act postdated both its creation and the issuance of its stock. Notwithstanding the *Keller* rationale that an investor should be entitled to rely upon the law in existence at the time the preferred stock was issued, the court in this case was ". . . unable to discover a difference in principle between the two cases." In refusing to allow the proposed reclassification, it reasoned that a shareholder's fixed contractual right to unpaid dividends is of such dignity that it cannot be diminished or eliminated retrospectively even if the authorizing legislation precedes the issuance of its stock.*

* The opinion seems to overstate the *Johnson* case, which was based in substantial part on statutory interpretation: "[The plaintiff] was bound to know that the language of the amendment of 1927 was broad enough to permit the corporation to change the character of the stock in which he was willing to invest his money, into a stock of another kind in which, perhaps, he would not invest, and he assumed the risk of the exercise of the power of amendment by the corporation. But . . . [h]e was not informed that the exercise of the power not only would change the character of his stock and the rights incident thereto in the future, but also, by retrospection, would cancel his fixed, contractual right to dividends accrued through time, and which, as against common shareholders, he was entitled by virtue of his contract to have paid before distribution of earnings among them. He, therefore, was justified in the belief that he would be protected in his right to cumulative dividends accrued through time up to the time when, by corporate action, the status of his shares should be changed . . .

"The language of the amended section is clear and unambiguous. It authorized the amendment of charters. There is nothing in the language to suggest that the section,

Two years elapsed before Federal United Corp. v. Havender, supra, was decided. The issue was substantially the same as that in the two cases which preceded. The dissenting stockholders had argued, as might have been expected, that the proposed corporate action, even though styled a "merger," was in effect a *Keller* type recapitalization and was entitled to no different treatment. Notwithstanding that argument, the court did not refer to the preferred stockholder's right as "vested" or as "a property right in the nature of a debt." Neither did it reject the use of *Keller*-type nomenclature as creating "confusion" or as "substitutes for reason and analysis" which are the characterizations used respectively in Davison v. Parke, Austin & Lipscomb, Inc., 285 N.Y. 500, 509, 35 N.E.2d 618, 622; Meck, Accrued Dividends on Cumulative Preferred Stocks; The Legal Doctrine, 55 Harv.L.Rev. 7, 76. Instead, it talked about the extent of the corporate power under the merger statute; and it held that the statute in existence when Federal United Corp. was organized had in effect been written into its charter, and that its preferred shareholders had thereby been advised and informed that their rights to accrued dividends might be extinguished by corporate action taken pursuant thereto.

Faced with a question of corporate action adjusting preferred stock dividends, and required to apply Delaware law under Erie R.R. v. Tompkins, 304 U.S. 64, 58 Sup.Ct. 817, 82 L.Ed. 1188, it is understandable that a federal court in Hottenstein v. York Ice Machinery Corp., 3 Cir., 136 F.2d 944, 950, found *Keller, Johnson* and *Havender* irreconcilable and said,

> "If it is fair to say that the decision of the Supreme Court of Delaware in the Keller case astonished the corporate world, it is just to state that the decision of the Supreme Court in Havender astounded it, for shorn of rationalization the decision constitutes a repudiation of principles enunciated in the Keller case and in Consolidated Film Industries v. Johnson, supra." at 950.[4]

With Keller's back thus broken, *Hottenstein* went on to say that under Delaware law a parent corporation may merge with a wholly-owned inactive subsidiary pursuant to a plan cancelling preferred stock and the rights of holders thereof to unpaid accumulated dividends and substituting in lieu thereof stock of the surviving corporation.

as amended, was intended to have a retrospective operation." (Footnote by ed.)

4. To the same effect the court in Western Foundry Co. v. Wicker, 403 Ill. 260, said at 277, 85 N.E.2d 722 at 730:

"Thus, what was formerly regarded as an almost inviolable vested property right was now considered a mere defeasible right, subject to cancellation by merger by reason of the consent of the preferred shareholders granted at the time the stock was originally issued. There being little or no difference between a recapitalization by corporate amendment and recapitalization by merger of a parent corporation with a wholly-owned subsidiary, the present status of the *Keller* case is obscure. While not expressly overruled, the theory of the *Keller* case was entirely repudiated. Consequently, as an authority for the proposition that the power to change the 'rights' of preferred stock does not include the right to cancel unpaid cumulative dividends, Keller v. Wilson & Co. is highly questionable."

Only four years intervened between *Keller* and *Havender,* but that was long enough for Delaware to have discarded "vested rights" as the test for determining the power of a corporation to eliminate a shareholder's right to preferred stock dividend accumulation, and to have adopted in its stead a standard calling for judicial inquiry into whether the proposed interference with a preferred stockholder's contract has been authorized by the legislature. The *Havender* approach is the one to which we subscribe as being the sounder, and it has support in the authorities. Davison v. Parke, Austin & Lipscomb, Inc., supra; Langfelder v. Union Laboratories, Inc., 3 Cir., 163 F.2d 804; Western Foundry Co. v. Wicker, supra, note 4; Anderson v. International Minerals & Chemical Corp., 295 N.Y. 343, 67 N.E.2d 573; Hubbard v. Jones Laughlin Steel Corp., D.C., 42 F.Supp. 432; Donohue v. Heuser, 239 S.W.2d 238 (Ky.).

The plaintiffs do not suggest, other than as they may have argued that this particular merger is a subterfuge, that our merger statute will not permit in any circumstances a merger for the sole reason that it affects accrued, but undeclared, preferred stock dividends. Rather do they argue that what should control is the date of the enactment of the enabling legislation, and they point out that in *Havender,* Federal United Corp. was organized and its stock was issued subsequent to the adoption of the statute authorizing mergers, whereas in this case the corporate creation and the stock issue preceded adoption of such a statute. That distinguishing feature brings into question what limitations, if any, exist to a state's authority under the reserved power to permit by subsequent legislation corporate acts which affect the preferential rights of a stockholder. More specifically, it raises the problem of whether subsequent legislation is repugnant to the federal and state constitutional prohibitions against the passage of laws impairing the obligations of contracts, because it permits elimination of accumulated preferred dividends by a lesser vote than was required under the law in existence at the time of the incorporation and when the stock was issued.

The mere mention of the constitutional prohibitions against such laws calls to mind Trustees of Dartmouth College v. Woodward, 17 U.S. 518, 4 Wheaton 518, 4 L.Ed. 629, where the decision was that a private corporation charter granted by the state is a contract protected under the constitution against repeal, amendment or alteration by subsequent legislation. Of equal significance in the field of corporation law is Mr. Justice Story's concurring opinion wherein he suggested that application of the impairment clause upon acts of incorporation might be avoided if a state legislature, coincident with granting a corporate charter, reserved as a part of that contract the right of amendment or repeal. With such a reservation, he said, any subsequent amendment or repeal would be pursuant, rather than repugnant, to the terms of the contract and would not therefore impair its obligation.

Our own legislature [5] was quick to heed Story's advice, and in the early part of the 19th century, when corporations were customarily

---

5.   State v. Brown & Sharpe Mfg. Co., 18 R.I. 16, 25 A. 246, 17 L.R.A. 856.

created by special act, the power to alter, amend, or revoke was written directly into each charter. Later, when the practice changed and corporations, instead of being created by special enactment, were incorporated under the general corporation law, the power to amend and repeal was reserved in an act of general application, and since at least as far back as 1844 the corporation law has read in substance as it does today viz., " . . . The charter or articles of association of every corporation hereafter created may be amended or repealed at the will of the general assembly." Section 7–1–13.

The language in which the reserved power is customarily stated is not, however, self-explaining, and the extent of the legislative authority under it has frequently been a source of difficulty. Recognizing that problem, but not answering it, the United States Supreme Court said in a frequently quoted passage:

> "The authority of a state under the so-called reserve power is wide; but it is not unlimited. The corporate charter may be repealed or amended, and, within limits not now necessary to define, the interrelations of state, corporation and stockholders may be changed; but neither vested property rights nor the obligation of contracts of third persons may be destroyed or impaired." Coombes v. Getz, 285 U.S. 434, 441–442, 52 S.Ct. 435, 436, 76 L.Ed. 866, 871.

* * *

The problem is not novel in this court. In State v. Brown & Sharpe Mfg. Co., we said that the reservation of the power to alter or amend does not confer upon the state arbitrary control over the rights and property belonging to a body of corporators. Additionally, relying on Shields v. Ohio, 95 U.S. 319, 24 L.Ed. 357, we adopted as a "just and proper" rule that amendments or alterations proposed under the power, if they are to satisfy the constitutional requirement, must be reasonable, must be in good faith, and must not be inconsistent with the scope and object of the act of incorporation.

The plaintiffs go further than Brown & Sharpe Mfg. Co., supra . . . [T]hey insist that any legislation, if enacted subsequent to the creation of a corporation and the issuance of its preferred stock, may not be a source of authority for corporate action which deprives a holder of his stock or of its preferential rights or of the dividends accrued thereon. An attempt to do so, they say, constitutes an unconstitutional exercise of the reserved power. On this issue, as on most others in this case, the authorities are not in accord.

On the one side, there is a body of law which speaks of the threefold nature of the stockholder's contract and, while agreeable to an exercise of the reserved power affecting only the contractual relationship between the state and the corporation, rejects as unconstitutional any exercise which affects the relationship between the stockholder and the corporation or between the stockholders inter sese. Wheatley v. A.I. Root Co., 147 Ohio St. 127, 69 N.E.2d 187; Schaad v. Hotel Easton Co., 369 Pa. 486, 87 A.2d 227. Under this view, subsequent legislation purporting to permit a corporate act to cancel accrued preferred dividends would obviously be an improper exercise of the power inasmuch as the essence of a preferred stockholder's contract is its definition of his relationship with the corporation and with the other stockholders vis-à-vis such matters as the distribution of the profits of the enterprise or the division of its capital and surplus account in the event of liquidation.

The other side of the argument considers that the question is primarily one of statutory construction and that so long as the statute authorizes the corporate action, it should make no difference whether its enactment preceded or postdated the birth of the corporation or the issuance of its stock.[7]   The basis for this viewpoint is that the terms of the preferred stockholder's contractual relationship are not restricted to the specifics inscribed on the stock certificate, but include also the stipulations contained in the charter or articles of association as well as the pertinent provisions of the general corporation law.   One of those provisions is, of course, the reserved power; and so long as it is a part of the preferred shareholder's contract, any subsequent legislation enacted pursuant to it, even though it may amend the contract's original terms, will not impair its obligation in the constitutional sense.   It is as if the stock certificate were inscribed with the legend "All of the terms and conditions hereof may be changed by the legislature acting pursuant to the power it has reserved in G.L. 1956, § 7–1–13."

Speaking to this question, it has been said that "It is no more unconstitutional to permit the Legislature, under the reserved power, to authorize a corporation to abolish dividends which have accrued in the past, than it is to authorize a corporation to abolish dividends which may accrue in the future.   There is a difference in degree, but not one of kind.   In both cases there is interference with a contractual relationship between stockholders and the corporation or between the stockholders inter sese.   But this the Legislature is permitted to do, certainly under the reserved power in the Constitution and in the General Corporation Law, to alter or amend the charters of corporations. . . ."   McNulty v. W. & J. Sloane, 184 Misc. 835, 845, 54 N.Y.S.2d 253, 263.

* * *

On the basis of our own precedents we conclude that the merger legislation, notwithstanding its effect on the rights of its stockholders, did not necessarily constitute an improper exercise of the right of amendment reserved merely because it was subsequent.

In addition to arguing that the proposed plan suffers from a constitutional infirmity, plaintiffs also contend that it is unfair and inequitable to them, and that its consummation should, therefore, be enjoined.   By that assertion they raise the problem of whether equity should heed the request of a dissenting stockholder and intervene to

7.   This, in substance was the basis for the decision in Consolidated Film Industries, Inc. v. Johnson, supra . . . The corporation there, as distinguished from the one in Keller v. Wilson & Co., supra . . . was created subsequent to the amendment which permitted recapitalization.   Nonetheless, the court was ". . . unable to discover a difference in principle between the two cases."

prevent a merger notwithstanding that it has received the vote [8] of the designated proportions of the various classes of stock of the constituent corporations.

In looking to the authorities for assistance on this question, we avoided those involving recapitalization by charter amendment where a dissident's only remedy against allegedly unfair treatment was in equity. In those situations the authorities generally permit equitable intervention to protect against unfair or inequitable treatment. Kamena v. Janssen Dairy Corp., 133 N.J.Eq. 214, 31 A.2d 200, aff'd, 134 N.J.Eq. 359, 35 A.2d 894. They are founded on the concept that otherwise there might be confiscation without recompense. The same rationale, however, is not available in the case of a merger, because there the dissenting stockholders usually can find a measure of protection in the statutory procedures giving them the option to compel the corporation to purchase their shares at an appraised value. This is a significant difference and is ample reason for considering the two situations as raising separate and distinct issues. Anderson v. International Minerals & Chemical Corp., supra.

This case involves a merger, not a recapitalization by charter amendment, and in this state the legislature, looking to the possibility that there might be those who would not be agreeable to the proposed merger, provided a means whereby a dissatisfied stockholder might demand and the corporation be compelled to pay the fair value of his securities. G.L.1956, §§ 7–5–8 through 7–5–16 inclusive. Our inquiry then is to the effect of that remedy upon plaintiff's right to challenge the proposed merger on the ground that it is unfair and inequitable because it dictates what shall be their proportionate interests in the corporate assets. Once again there is no agreement among the authorities. Vorenberg, "Exclusiveness of the Dissenting Stockholder's Appraisal Right," 77 Harv.L.Rev. 1189. See also Annot. 162 A.L.R. 1237, 1250. Some authorities appear to say that the statutory remedy of appraisal is exclusive. Beloff v. Consolidated Edison Co., 300 N.Y. 11, 87 N.E.2d 561; Hubbard v. Jones & Laughlin Steel Corp., D.C., 42 F.Supp. 432. Others say that it may be disregarded and that equity may intervene if the minority is treated oppressively or unfairly, Barnett v. Philadelphia Market Co., 218 Pa. 649, 67 A. 912; May v. Midwest Refining Co., 1 Cir., 121 F.2d 431, cert. den. 314 U.S. 668, 62 S.Ct. 129, 86 L.Ed. 534, or if the merger is tainted with fraud or illegality, Adams v. United States Distributing Corp., 184 Va. 134, 147, 34 S.E.2d 244, 250, 162 A.L.R. 1227; Porges v. Vadsco Sales Corp., 27 Del.Ch. 127, 32 A.2d 148. To these differing views must also be added the divergence of opinion on whether those in control or those dissenting must bear the burden of establishing that the plan meets whatever the required standard may be. Vorenberg, supra; 77 Harv.L.Rev. 1189, 1210–1215.

---

8. For the purposes of this proceeding we have accepted the implied assumption of all of the parties that the proposed merger will receive the required vote and we have not sua sponte suggested that the suit might more properly have awaited that eventuality.

In this case we do not choose as between the varying views, nor is there any need for us to do so. Even were we to accept that view which is most favorable to plaintiffs we still would not be able to find that they have been either unfairly or inequitably treated. The record insofar as it relates to the unfairness issue is at best sparse. In substance it consists of the corporation's balance sheet as of September 1967, together with supporting schedules. That statement uses book, rather than the appraised, values, and neither it nor any other evidentiary matter in any way indicates, except as the same may be reflected in the surplus account, the corporation's earning history or its prospects for profitable operations in the future.

Going to the figures we find a capital and surplus account of $669,948 of which $453,000 is allocable to the 4,530 issued and outstanding shares of $100 par value preferred stock and the balance of $216,948 to surplus. Obviously, a realization of the book value of the assets in the event of liquidation forced or otherwise, would not only leave nothing for the common stockholders, but would not even suffice to pay the preferred shareholders the par value of their stock plus the accrued dividends of $645,000.

If we were to follow a rule of absolute priority, any proposal which would give anything to common stockholders without first providing for full payment of stated value plus dividend accruals would be unfair to the preferred shareholders. It could be argued that the proposal in this case violates that rule because an exchange of one share of Community Hotel's preferred stock for five shares of Newport's common stock would give the preferred shareholders securities worth less than the amount of their liquidation preference rights while at the same time the one to one exchange ratio on the common would enrich Community Hotel's common stockholders by allowing them to participate in its surplus.

An inherent fallacy in applying the rule of absolute priority to the circumstances of this case, however, is its assumption that assets would be liquidated and that nothing more than their book value will be realized. But Community Hotel is not in liquidation. Instead it is a going concern which, because of its present capitalization, cannot obtain the modern debt-financing needed to meet threatened competition. Moreover, management, in the call of the meeting at which it was intended to consider and vote on the plan, said that the proposed recapitalization plan was conceived only ". . . after careful consideration by your Board of Directors and a review of the relative values of the preferred and common stocks by the independent public accountants of the Corporation. The exchange ratio of five new common shares for each share of the existing preferred stock was determined on the basis of the book and market values of the preferred and the inherent value of the unpaid preferred dividends." Those assertions are contained in a document admitted as an exhibit and they have testimonial value.

When the varying considerations—both balance sheet figures and management's assertions—are taken into account, we are unable to conclude, at least at this stage of the proceedings, that the proposed plan is unfair and inequitable, particularly because plaintiffs as dissidents may avail themselves of the opportunity to receive the fair market value of their securities under the appraisal methods prescribed in § 7–5–8 through § 7–5–16 inclusive.

The plaintiffs argue that due consideration will not be given to their dividend accruals under the appraisal. We do not agree. Jeffrey v. American Screw Co., 98 R.I. 286, 201 A.2d 146, requires that the securities of a dissident invoking the statute must be appraised by a person "versed in the intricacies of corporate finance." Such a person will find when he looks to *Jeffrey* for guidance that the evaluation process requires him to consider ". . . all relevant value factors including market value, book value, asset value, and other intrinsic factors probative of value." Certainly, unpaid dividend arrearages fall within that directive and are a relevant factor to be considered in arriving at the full and fair cash value of the plaintiffs' preferred stock. While we make no decision one way or the other on the exclusiveness of appraisal as a remedy for a dissident, we do decide that its availability is an element or a circumstance which equity should weigh before intervening. When that is done in this case, we find no ground for intervention.

For the reasons stated, the judgment appealed from is affirmed.

———

Chapter XII

CORPORATE DISTRIBUTIONS

Conventionally, a corporation distributes funds to its shareholders in one of two ways: by paying a dividend, or by repurchasing a portion of its stock. Corporate law and (in a less elaborate way) the law of creditors' remedies have traditionally set limits on such distributions through the use of various financial tests. This chapter will begin with financial limitations imposed on the payment of dividends, and then turn to the subject of repurchases.[1]

SECTION 1. DIVIDENDS

(a) INTRODUCTION

D. KEHL, CORPORATE DIVIDENDS
14-21 (1941).

With the liability of corporate stockholders . . . limited to the amount of capital subscribed . . . it soon became apparent that the original capital should be permanently devoted to the needs of the corporation as at least a partial substitute for the unlimited personal liability existing in individual enterprise.

If the creation of a capital fund was not to defeat its purpose, safeguards against its withdrawal by repayment to shareholders in the guise of dividends, or otherwise, were indispensable. Historically, the principal objective of dividend law has therefore been the preservation of a minimum of assets as a safeguard in assuring the payment of creditors' claims. . . .

A second purpose in dividend regulation, sometimes neglected by overemphasis on protection of the creditor, is that of assuring continuous maintenance of capital in order that the enterprise may function for the purposes contemplated by stockholders. . . . The purpose of the stockholder is a capital investment, and although he expects dividends, he expects them from profits. When they are paid from capital, it should be an exceptional distribution which he has authorized. . . . Permitting a return of capital in the guise of supposed profit distributions is unfair also to subsequent stockholders, who are

---

1. In American corporation law, a purchase by a corporation of its own stock is conventionally referred to as a "repurchase." The term is used in the sense "to regain by purchase," rather than in its other sense, "to buy again."

entitled to expect that past dividends have been paid from profits and not capital. . . .

A third objective in dividend regulation is the establishment of a system of corporate accounting which will give directors, creditors, and stockholders a fair estimate of the corporation's financial position. Indeed, the declaration of dividends is as much an accounting question as it is a legal problem. . . .

In addition to the immediate interest of creditors and stockholders in dividend regulations, there is also a broader public interest. Present-day economic activity revolves in very large part around corporations.

INTRODUCTORY NOTE

The law of dividends is ultimately controlled by statute. Most dividend statutes incorporate one or more of the following four tests:

(i) An *insolvency* test, based on the corporation's actual financial condition, in terms of either its ability to pay its debts as they mature, or whether its assets exceed its liabilities.

(ii) A *balance-sheet* test, based on whether the corporation's assets exceed its liabilities plus its capital.

(iii) A *nimble-dividend* test, based on the corporation's current profits.

(iv) An *earned-surplus* test, based on the corporation's accumulated profits.

The traditional dividend statutes, which are still numerically dominant, center on the concepts of legal capital and surplus. Modern statutes break away from those concepts. Sections 1(c)–(f) of this Chapter concern the traditional statutes. The focus in these Sections will be on the New York statute (as an illustration of a "balance-sheet" statute); the Pennsylvania statute (as an illustration of an "earned surplus" statute, reflecting, in this respect, the old Model Act); and the Delaware statute. Thereafter, three leading modern statutes will be introduced in Section (h): California, the Revised Model Business Corporation Act, and Minnesota.

Because of the important role given to the concept of legal capital in the traditional statutes, it is useful to say a word here about that subject. Shares of stock are often assigned a *par value*. At one time, par value was an economically meaningful concept, because stock was characteristically issued—that is, sold by the corporation—at a price equal to its par value. Today, however, par value is usually unrelated to issue price, except in the case of preferred stock. Stock that carries a par value that is much lower than its issue price is called *low par* stock. Stock that has no par value is called *no par* stock. A corporation's *legal capital* or *stated capital* consists of (i) the total par value of all issued shares; (ii) that portion of the issue price of no par stock that the board allocates to legal or stated capital when the stock is issued;

and (iii) any amounts later transferred to legal or stated capital by the board.

The following accounting materials will be referred to in this Chapter: Accounting Series Releases, issued by the SEC; Accounting Research Bulletins, issued by the Committee on Accounting Procedure of the American Institute of Certified Public Accountants; Opinions issued by the Accounting Principles Board; and Statements issued by the Financial Accounting Standards Board. These will be cited as ASR's, ARB's, APB's, and FASB's, respectively.

It is conventional to put dividend questions in terms of whether dividends can be paid "from" or "out of" certain "funds," such as earnings or surplus. This chapter will employ the conventional terminology, but its limits should be kept in mind. The terminology implies that corporations set aside pools of cash from which dividends are withdrawn. In fact, the "funds" in question are not pools of cash, but financial measurements which appear on the right-hand (liability) side of the balance sheet. Under double-entry bookkeeping, the payment of a dividend in cash or property normally reduces two balance sheet accounts: one on the left-hand (asset) side, representing the cash or property actually paid out, and one on the right-hand side, representing the owners' interest in the corporation. The terms "from" and "out of" mean only that immediately before the dividend is paid the balance in the appropriate right-hand-side account must equal or exceed the amount of the dividend.

(b) THE INSOLVENCY TEST

N.Y. BUS. CORP. LAW §§ 102(a)(8), 510(a), (b)

[See Statutory Supplement]

UNIFORM FRAUDULENT TRANSFER ACT §§ 1, 2, 4, 5

[See Statutory Supplement]

BANKRUPTCY REFORM ACT OF 1978, 11 U.S.C. §§ 101(31), 548(a)

[See Statutory Supplement]

BACKGROUND NOTE ON THE INSOLVENCY TEST

1. In Massachusetts, insolvency is the only statutory test for dividends. See Mass. § 61. In many of the remaining states, dividend statutes such as N.Y.Bus.Corp.Law § 510 explicitly incorporate an insolvency standard.[1]

Questions: Do UFTA §§ 4 and 5 apply to dividends in a state like New York, which has an insolvency test built into its dividend statute? In a state like Delaware, which does not?[2]

2. There are two broad definitions of the term "insolvency." The definition embodied in N.Y.Bus.Corp.Law § 102(8) is known as the equity meaning, since it was the test generally applied by the equity courts, which had jurisdiction over insolvent estates before the enactment of the bankruptcy statute. The definition embodied in the Bankruptcy Reform Act, 11 U.S.C.A. § 101(29), is known as the bankruptcy meaning.[3] "The difference between these two conceptions can be very great. Solvency in the equity sense is concerned with liquidity; a debtor may be able to cope with his bills as they roll in month by month even though the market value of all his assets is only a fraction of the aggregate of his liabilities maturing over time in the future. The emphasis of the bankruptcy sense of solvency is upon liquidation; a debtor might not be sufficiently liquid to meet his current obligations but still hold unliquid resources having a value far

1. The payment of a dividend when a corporation is insolvent may also be illegal as a matter of common law, either on the theory of common law fraudulent conveyance, or on the theory that the assets of an insolvent corporation are a trust fund for creditors. See, e.g., Wood v. National City Bank, 24 F.2d 661, 663 (2d Cir.1928); Powers v. Heggie, 268 Mass. 233, 167 N.E. 314, 317 (1929); D. Kehl, Corporate Dividends 36 (1941).

2. See United States v. 58th Street Plaza Theatre, Inc., 287 F.Supp. 475 (S.D.N.Y. 1968); Powers v. Heggie, 268 Mass. 233, 167 N.E. 314 (1929); Clark, The Duties of the Corporate Debtor to its Creditors, 90 Harv.L.Rev. 505, 554–60 (1977); Kummert, The Financial Provisions of the New Washington Business Corporation Act, pt. II, 42 Wash.L.Rev. 119, 130–31 (1966); cf. Steph v. Branch, 255 F.Supp. 526 (E.D.Okl.1966), aff'd 389 F.2d 233 (10th Cir.1968).

Cal.Corp.Code § 506(d), which governs the liability of shareholders who have received improper dividends, explicitly provides that "[n]othing contained in this section affects any liability which any shareholder may have under [the Uniform Fraudulent Conveyance Act]." The Official Comment to Rev.Model Bus.Corp. Act § 6.40, which governs distributions to shareholders, states that "[t]he revised Model Business Corporation Act establishes the validity of distributions from the corporate law standpoint under section 6.40 and determines the potential liability of directors for improper distributions under sections 8.30 and 8.33. The federal Bankruptcy Act and state federal conveyance statutes, on the other hand, are designed to enable the trustee or other representative to recapture for the benefit of creditors funds distributed to others in some circumstances. In light of these diverse purposes, it was not thought necessary to make the tests of section 6.40 identical to the tests for insolvency under these various statutes."

3. Prior to the Bankruptcy Reform Act of 1978, whether a debtor could be put into involuntary bankruptcy turned in large part on whether it was insolvent in the bankruptcy sense. Under the 1978 Act, the test for involuntary bankruptcy turns principally on whether the debtor is insolvent in the equity sense. See 11 U.S.C.A. § 303(h). However, once a debtor has been put into bankruptcy, the trustee's right to avoid a pre-bankruptcy transfer as "fraudulent" turns principally on whether at the time of the transfer the debtor was insolvent in the bankruptcy sense. See 11 U.S. C.A. §§ 101(26), 548, supra.

The bankruptcy meaning of insolvency is itself susceptible to different nuances, as may be seen by comparing 11 U.S.C.A. § 101(26) with UFTA § 2(a).

in excess of the total of his obligations." B. Manning, Legal Capital 60 (2d ed. 1981). To put this differently, insolvency in the equity sense is based on cash flow; insolvency in the bankruptcy sense is based on market value.

3. In considering the relationship among the bankruptcy statute, the UFTA, and corporate dividend statutes like N.Y.Bus.Corp.Law § 510, two points must be kept in mind: (i) The three kinds of statutes may impose different *substantive rules,* because they may use the term "insolvency" in different senses. (ii) Even where the statutes impose the same substantive rule, they may involve different *remedies.* The latter issue will be considered at length in Sections 1(i) and (j), infra. To oversimplify somewhat, as regards dividends the corporate statutes are aimed primarily (although not exclusively) at the responsibility and liability of the board. In contrast, the UFTA and the bankruptcy statute are aimed primarily (although not exclusively) at permitting a creditors' representative to recapture improper distributions from the transferees, i.e., the shareholders.

(c) THE BALANCE SHEET TEST

NOTE ON BALANCE SHEET ACCOUNTING

A *balance sheet* is a financial statement that shows the financial condition of an enterprise at a given time. The left-hand side of a balance sheet shows assets; the right-hand side shows the sources from which the assets were derived. Sources, in turn, are separated into two further categories: *liabilities,* consisting of funds from "outside" sources, principally debtors of various kinds, and *net worth* or *equity,* consisting of funds or property derived from "inside" sources—what the owners have contributed to the business.

Every transaction engaged in by a business affects at least two items on the balance sheet, and the entries to reflect a transaction are always offsetting. Accordingly, recognition of a transaction may change the *totals* on the left- and right-hand sides, but does not upset their equality. For example, if a corporation purchases a machine in exchange for its $5000 note, the asset Equipment on the left-hand side, and the liability Notes Payable on the right-hand side, are both increased by $5000.[1] When the note is paid, the asset Cash on the

---

1. In practice, the balance sheet is not changed every time a transaction occurs. Instead, transactions are "posted" or entered in individual accounts (such as Cash, Equipment, or Notes Payable) known as "T-accounts," whose net balance is eventually "closed" or transferred to the balance sheet. By accounting convention, every transaction gives rise to equal left- and right-hand entries in the T-accounts. (For assets, an increase is posted on the lefthand side of a T-account and a decrease is posted on the righthand side. For liabilities, the procedure is reversed.) This convention forms the basis of the system called "double-entry bookkeeping."

Excellent introductions to the basic mechanics of modern accounting can be found in D. Herwitz, Materials on Accounting for Lawyers 1–83 (1980), and T. Fiflis, H. Kripke & P. Foster, Accounting for

left-hand side, and the liability Notes Payable on the right-hand side are both decreased by $5000. If the machine is purchased for cash, the asset Cash on the left-hand side is decreased by $5000 and the asset Equipment on the left-hand side is increased by $5000.

Corporate accounting differs from accounting for proprietorships and partnerships primarily in the way equity is treated. In the sole proprietorship and the partnership, equity is normally a fairly simple account. In the corporation, however, equity is divided into Stated Capital and Surplus, and Surplus is redivided into a number of further accounts.

Stated Capital (or Capital Stock) consists of the total par value of issued stock that has par value, or, if issued stock has no par value, the total amount allocated to capital by the board. To illustrate, if 10 shares of $100 par value common stock are issued for $1,000 in cash, the balance sheet entries would be:

Cash	$1,000	
Stated Capital		$1,000 [2]

The two most important Surplus accounts are Earned Surplus and Paid-in Surplus. Earned Surplus consists of internally generated profits that are reinvested in the business. Paid-in Surplus consists of the consideration paid to the corporation for par value stock in excess of the par value, or the consideration paid for no-par shares in excess of the amount allocated to Stated Capital. Thus if 10 shares of $100 par stock are issued for $1,500, the entries might be:

Cash	$1,500	
Stated Capital		$1,000
Paid-in Surplus		500

Other Surplus accounts will be considered elsewhere in this chapter.

In recent years, accountants have tended to substitute descriptive nomenclature for the traditional Surplus terminology. Thus Earned Surplus is given a title such as Retained Income, Retained Earnings, or Accumulated Earnings, and Paid-in Surplus is given a title such as Capital Contributed for Shares in Excess of Par or Stated Value. However, the new titles do not work a difference in substance, and courts, legislators, and lawyers have continued to use the old terminology.

RANDALL v. BAILEY

Supreme Court of New York, Trial Term, N.Y. Co., 1940.
23 N.Y.S.2d 173, aff'd 288 N.Y. 280, 43 N.E.2d 43 (1942).

Action by C. Walter Randall, as trustee of the Bush Terminal Company, debtor, against Frank Bailey and others to recover on

Business Lawyers 1–35 (3d ed. 1984). The text notes in this chapter draw heavily on these two books in dealing with accounting issues.

2. When there are separate classes of stock outstanding, a separate Stated Capital account is maintained for each class.

behalf of the debtor the amount of dividends declared and paid by defendants, former directors of the debtor. Defendants filed motions for judgment at the close of the whole case.

Motions granted and entry of judgment directed for defendants.

WALTER, Justice. A trustee of Bush Terminal Company, appointed in a proceeding under Section 77B of the Bankruptcy Act, 11 U.S.C.A. § 207, here sues former directors of that company to recover on its behalf the amount of dividends declared and paid between November 22, 1928, and May 2, 1932, aggregating $3,639,058.06. At the times of the declarations and payments, the company's books concededly showed a surplus which ranged from not less than $4,378,554.83 on December 31, 1927, down to not less than $2,199,486.77 on April 30, 1932. The plaintiff claims, however, that in fact there was no surplus, that the capital was actually impaired to an amount greater than the amount of the dividends, and that the directors consequently are personally liable to the corporation for the amount thereof under Section 58 of the Stock Corporation Law. Defendants claim that there was no impairment of capital and that the surplus was actually greater than the amount which plaintiff concedes as the amounts shown by the books.

The claims of the plaintiff, although branching out to a multitude of items, are basically reducible to four:

1. It was improper to "write-up" the land values above cost and thereby take unrealized appreciation into account.

2. It was improper not to "write-down" to actual value the cost of investments in and advances to subsidiaries and thereby fail to take unrealized depreciation into account.

3. It was improper to include as an asset an item of so-called good will, which the company carried at $3,000,000. . . .

I discuss first the item of good will.

On March 6, 1902, shortly after its organization, the Bush Terminal Company entered into a contract with Irving T. Bush, who owned or controlled Bush Company, Ltd., which was then conducting a terminal enterprise in Brooklyn, and either under that contract or some arrangement constituting in effect a modification of it or a waiver of strict performance thereof, Bush Terminal Company issued $2,000,000 face amount of bonds and $3,000,000 par value of stock and received in addition to certain services of Irving T. Bush a large tract of land nearly contiguous to that owned by Bush Company, Ltd., and equipped with piers and warehouses, and other terminal facilities, and a lease by Bush Company, Ltd., of two of the piers. The $3,000,000 of stock was not entered upon the books of the company until December, 1905, and then, under the same date, there was entered on the asset side of the ledger an item of good will in the same amount. It does not appear that that was done pursuant to any formal action of the board of directors fixing $3,000,000 as the value of any good will, but it does appear that the directors did in fact sanction the fixing of that value on such item.

Plaintiff stresses the fact that the company itself received the proceeds of the $2,000,000 of bonds and itself expended such proceeds in acquiring the land and erecting the piers and warehouses and other terminal facilities, and contends that it necessarily follows that the only possible asset which the company can be regarded as having received for the $3,000,000 of stock is the services of Mr. Bush for about two or three years. I think that is too narrow a view. Bush Company, Ltd., was an existing company which unquestionably had a good will of some value. Mr. Bush controlled that company. He also had an option to purchase the nearly contiguous land above-mentioned. In 1904 Bush Terminal Company acquired the assets of Bush Company, Ltd.

The result thus was that between the time of its organization in 1902 and the end of 1905 there had been assembled under the single ownership of Bush Terminal Company the existing plant and business of Bush Company, Ltd., and nearly contiguous land which Mr. Bush had permitted it to acquire at the price at which he had it under option, and additional piers and warehouses and other terminal facilities, and the whole thereof, at least so far as appears, were being profitably operated. Such profitable operation then continued for a long period of years, and consecutively, year in and year out, for a period of over twenty years the item of $3,000,000 for good will was set forth upon the company's balance sheets and reported to stockholders with the approval of successive boards of directors.

Directors obviously cannot create assets by fiat, and I do not go so far as to say that, even as against the company and in favor of directors, assets can be created by laches, acquiescence, or estoppel, but whatever may now be thought of the wisdom or business judgment displayed in valuing at $3,000,000 in 1905 what the company received for the $3,000,000 of stock, I do not think that anything has been shown respecting the history of the company from its organization in 1902 to November 22, 1928, or to May 2, 1932, which warrants a finding that during the period here in question, 1928 to 1932, there did not inhere in the assembled and established plant and facilities and going business an element of value in addition to physical assets which the directors were justified in valuing at $3,000,000.

The term "good will" is generally used as indicating that element of value which inheres in the fixed and favorable consideration of customers arising from an established and well-known and well-conducted business, and in an enterprise of this sort, enjoying no legal monopoly, and not a public utility in a legal sense, that element of value indisputably is property for which stock may be issued, and in the absence of fraud the judgment of the directors as to its value is controlling. . . . It also is recognized that, apart from good will in that sense, there is what in the public utility rate cases is called "going concern value", by which is meant that element of value which inheres in an assembled and established plant, doing business and earning money, over one not thus advanced, and such element of value is treated as property which must be considered in determining the base upon which the utility is entitled to earn a return . . . and I can perceive no reason why such "going concern value" should not be recognized here as well as in a utility rate case. . . . [T]he evidence abundantly establishes that what happened here was that an unused waterfront and adjoining uplands aggregating over 200 acres were assembled and converted into a great terminal, with piers, warehouses, lofts, railroads, and other shipping and transportation facilities, to which both industry and shipping were attracted as a result of diligent and in some instances ingenious efforts, and which enjoyed an international reputation for the excellence of the services rendered through assembled facilities and a trained personnel. I consequently hold this item allowable.

I next turn to the subject of unrealized appreciation and depreciation.

Until 1915 the company's land was carried upon its books at cost. In 1915 the land was written up to 80% of the amount at which it was then assessed for taxation, and in 1918 it was written up to the exact amount at which it was then so assessed. Those two write-ups totalled $7,211,791.72, and the result was that during the period here in question the land was carried on the books at $8,737,949.02, whereas its actual cost was $1,526,157.30. Plaintiff claims that the entire $7,211,791.72 should be eliminated because it represents merely unrealized appreciation, and dividends cannot be declared or paid on the basis of mere unrealized appreciation in fixed assets irrespective of how sound the estimate thereof may be. That obviously and concededly is another way of saying that for dividend purposes fixed assets must be computed at cost, not value, and plaintiff here plants himself upon that position, even to the point of contending that evidence of value is immaterial and not admissible. If that contention be sound, the company indisputably had a deficit at all the times here involved in an amount exceeding the dividends here in question. The importance of the question so presented, both to this case and to corporations and corporate directors in general, is thus apparent, and it is, I think, surprising that upon a question so important to and so often occurring in the realm of business there is, not only no decision which can be said to be directly in point, but, also, no discussion in text-book or law magazine which does much more than pose the question without answering it. Even in Halsbury's Laws of England, 2d Ed., Vol. 5, p. 393, note (f), published in 1932, it is stated that the question has not been decided.

It is to be emphasized at the outset that the question is not one of sound economics, or of what is sound business judgment or financial policy or of proper accounting practice, or even what the law ought to be. My views of the business acumen or financial sagacity of these directors, as well as my views as to what the legislature ought to permit or prohibit, are entirely immaterial. The question I have to decide is whether or not an existing statute has been violated. The problem is one of statutory construction.

The words of the statute, as it existed during the period here involved, are: "No stock corporation shall declare or pay any dividend which shall impair its capital or capital stock, nor while its capital or capital stock is impaired, nor shall any such corporation declare or pay any dividend or make any distribution of assets to any of its stockholders, whether upon a reduction of the number of its shares or of its capital or capital stock, unless the value of its assets remaining after the payment of such dividend, or after such distribution of assets, as the case may be, shall be at least equal to the aggregate amount of its debts and liabilities including capital or capital stock as the case may be." Stock Corporation Law, § 58, as enacted by Laws 1923, c. 787.

If the part of the statute containing the words "unless the value of its assets" etc. is to be read as relating back to the beginning of the section, the lack of merit in plaintiff's contention is apparent, for the statute would then read: "No stock corporation shall declare or pay any dividend . . . unless the value of its assets remaining after the payment of such dividend . . . shall be at least equal to the aggregate amount of its debts and liabilities including capital or capital stock as the case may be." I think there is much to be said in support of the view that that is what was intended, but nevertheless the structure of the statute is such as to make that reading grammatically impossible, and I hence prefer to base my decision upon the assumption that the controlling words of the statute are merely these: "No stock corporation shall declare or pay any dividend which shall impair its capital or capital stock, nor while its capital or capital stock is impaired."

Before one can determine whether or not capital or capital stock has been impaired, one must determine what is capital or capital stock. The words to be construed thus are words which have varied and different meanings and express radically different concepts in different connections. Capital means one thing to an economist, or, perhaps more accurately, different things to different economists, and it has still different meanings to accountants and to business men. It even means different things in different statutes. To determine its meaning in this statute it thus is essential, I think, to consider the history of the statute and what our courts have said respecting the statute's predecessors.

[As delineated in the Court of Appeals opinion (discussed below) the history was as follows: In 1825, the Legislature enacted a statute which provided that "it shall not be lawful for the directors or managers of any incorporated company in this state to make dividends, excepting from the surplus profits arising from the business of such corporation; and it shall not be lawful for the directors of any such company to divide, withdraw, or in any way pay to the stockholders, or any of them, any part of the capital stock of such company, or to reduce the said capital stock, without the consent of the legislature. . . ." This provision was in effect until 1890, when the legislature enacted a statute which provided that "[t]he capital stock of a stock corporation shall be deemed impaired when the value of its property and assets after deducting the amount of its debts and liabilities, shall be less than the amount of its paid up capital stock. No dividends shall be declared or paid by any stock corporation, except from the surplus profits of its business, nor when its capital stock is or will be impaired thereby, and no such corporation shall divide or withdraw or in any way pay to its stockholders, or any of them, any part of its property and assets, so as to reduce the value thereof after deducting the amount of its debts below the amount of its capital stock, or reduce its capital stock except in the manner prescribed by law." In 1892, the legislature returned to the pattern and most of the language of the 1825 statute. In 1912 the Legislature authorized the issuance of stock without par value, and provided that no corporation that had issued such stock "shall declare any dividend which shall reduce the amount of its capital below the amount stated in the certificate as the amount of capital with which the corporation will carry on business." In 1921, this section was amended to read, "No such corporation shall declare or pay any dividend which shall reduce the amount of its stated capital."]

. . . . At the time the revision of 1923 was undertaken there thus were upon the statute books two provisions upon the subject of unauthorized dividends, one which related to corporations having no-par stock and which was expressed in terms of reducing stated capital, and another which related to other corporations and which was expressed in terms of surplus profits. In the Stock Corporation Law of 1923 the heading of the prohibiting section became simply "Dividends" and as already noted, all reference to surplus or to profits or to surplus profits was omitted.

It thus appears that after using the surplus and surplus profits terminology for practically a hundred years the legislature completely abandoned it, and I think that is quite significant as indicating a conscious intent to get away from the idea of profits earned as a result of completed transactions as the sole source of dividends. I do not say that the legislature thereby changed the existing law. On the contrary, I think that the terms capital and capital stock as used in the earlier statutes had been construed by the courts in such a way that the terms surplus and surplus profits as used therein necessarily meant any accretion or accumulation over and above debts and the liability to stockholders, and that the legislature of 1923 recognized and adopted that construction and omitted any reference to surplus or surplus profits for the very reason that by some persons those words were believed to convey the idea of and to be confined to an accumulation of net earnings resulting from completed transactions and for the express purpose of so clarifying the statute as to prevent the precise claim which plaintiff now here presses. I briefly mention the cases which lead me to that conclusion. . . .

Those statements by our highest court seem to me to make it entirely plain that the terms capital and capital stock in these statutes mean an amount, i.e., a value, of property up to the limit of the number of dollars specified as the par value of paid-up issued shares (or as the stated value of no-par shares), and that when the amount, i.e., the value, of the company's property exceeds that number of dollars the excess, whether "contributed by the stockholders or otherwise obtained" is surplus or surplus profits and may be distributed as dividends until the point is reached where such dividends "deplete the assets," i.e., the value of the assets, "below the sum," i.e. below the number of dollars, specified as the par or stated value of the paid-up issued shares. In other words, the capital or capital stock referred to in these statutes is the sum of the liability to stockholders, and any value which the corporation's property has in addition to that sum is surplus. And I cannot doubt that the words "otherwise obtained" and "accumulated," as used by the court in the cases just mentioned, include an appreciation in the value of property purchased whether realized or unrealized. . . .

In summary, I think that it cannot be said that there is a single case in this State which actually decides that unrealized appreciation cannot be taken into consideration, or stated in different words, that cost and not value must be used in determining whether or not there exists a surplus out of which dividends can be paid. I think, further, that such a holding would run directly counter to the meaning of the terms capital and capital stock as fixed by decisions of the Court of Appeals construing the earlier statutes, and that such construction of those terms must be deemed to have been adopted by the legislature in enacting the statute here involved. See Matter of Scheftel's Estate, 275 N.Y. 135, 141, 9 N.E.2d 809. I thus obviously cannot follow decisions to the contrary in other States or any contrary views of economists or accountants. If the policy of the law be bad it is for the legislature to change it.

Throughout the period in question the company carried upon its books as assets its investments in and advances to its subsidiaries at their face value, i.e., at the cost thereof, and despite his insistence that unrealized appreciation of one asset cannot be taken into consideration, the plaintiff yet insists that these investments and advances must be written down to the value thereof as shown by the books of the subsidiaries, even though the subsidiaries are still carrying on business, and, further, that those books shall be what he calls "properly adjusted", so as to cause them to show the actual value of the stock of and claims against those subsidiaries. He thus, as it seems to me, takes the inconsistent position that while unrealized appreciation cannot be considered, unrealized depreciation nevertheless must be. Defendants, also, take the equally inconsistent position that while unrealized appreciation must be considered, unrealized depreciation need not be. I am of the opinion that the same reasons which show that unrealized appreciation must be considered are equally cogent in showing that unrealized depreciation likewise must be considered. In other words, the test being whether or not the value of the assets exceeds the debts and the liability to stockholders, all assets must be taken at their actual value.

I see no cause for alarm over the fact that this view requires directors to make a determination of the value of the assets at each dividend declaration. On the contrary, I think that is exactly what the law always has contemplated that directors should do. That does not mean that the books themselves necessarily must be altered by write-ups or write-downs at each dividend period, or that formal appraisals must be obtained from professional appraisers or even made by the directors themselves. That is obviously impossible in the case of corporations of any considerable size. But it is not impossible nor unfeasible for directors to consider whether the cost of assets continues over a long period of years to reflect their fair value, and the law does require that directors should really direct in the very important matter of really determining at each dividend declaration whether or not the value of the assets is such as to justify a dividend, rather than do what one director here testified that he did, viz. "accept the company's figures." The directors are the ones who should determine the figures by carefully considering values, and it was for the very purpose of compelling them to perform that duty that the statute imposes upon them a personal responsibility for declaring and paying dividends when the value of the assets is not sufficient to justify them. What directors must do is to exercise an informed judgment of their own, and the amount of information which they should obtain, and the sources from which they should obtain it, will of course depend upon the circumstances of each particular case. . . . If directors have blindly or complacently accepted either cost or any other arbitrary figures as indicative of value, they have not exercised either discretion or judgment and no court is required to act as if they had. When directors have in fact exercised an informed judgment with respect to the value of the company's assets, the courts obviously will be exceedingly slow to override that judgment, and clear and convincing evidence will be required to justify a finding that such judgment was not in accordance with the facts. In the last analysis, however, the issue, in any case in which it is claimed that dividends have been paid out of capital, is the value of the assets and the amount of the liabilities to creditors and stockholders at the times the dividends were declared and paid.

Upon the evidence in this case I find that the directors here did in fact exercise an informed judgment with respect to the value of the good will, the value of the land of the company, and the value of the improvements thereon, and also with respect to the value of the land and improvements thereon which were owned by the subsidiaries, Bush Terminal Buildings Company and Bush Terminal Railroad Company, and that they believed and determined that the good will was worth $3,000,000 and that such land and improvements were worth several millions of dollars more than the amounts at which they were carried on the books. At least one of the directors was thoroughly versed in real estate values by reason of long and extensive experience in buying and selling and in recommending mortgage loans on real estate and was personally and thoroughly familiar with the properties and business of all the companies just named, and of the development thereof, from the time of the organization of the company, and no one could criticise any other director for relying upon his knowledge and judgment as to the value thereof, or for basing a judgment thereon. His knowledge and judgment probably were as safe and sound a guide as any formal appraisal that could have been obtained. At least one other of the directors likewise had a thorough familiarity with these properties and business from the inception of their developments.

I find that there was not the same exercise of informed judgment with respect to the value of the investments in and advances to subsidiaries. To a very large extent the value of the investments in and advances to Bush Terminal Buildings Company and Bush Terminal Railroad Company were affected by the value of the land and improvements owned by those companies, as to which I have just found that there was an exercise of an informed judgment; but on the whole I find that the directors accepted the cost of the investments in and advances to all the subsidiaries, as the same were recorded upon the books, without in fact considering the extent to which such recorded costs reflected their true values at the times of the declaration and payment of the dividends here in controversy.

. . . [As to] the amounts which the plaintiff claims should be deducted from the book figures in order to reduce those investments and advances to actual values. . . . I find it unnecessary to determine to what precise extent the deductions claimed should be made, because I find ample evidence to sustain and justify the judgment of the directors that the value of the land and improvements exceeded the sum at which they were carried on the books by an amount sufficient to show a surplus greater than the amount of the dividends even if all the deductions so claimed by the plaintiff were allowed in full. . . .

Now turning to the land, the land which was carried on the books throughout the period in question at $8,737,949.02 was assessed for taxation at $11,863,000 in each of the years 1927 to 1932, and buildings which were carried on the books at $8,183,945.61 in 1927, $8,415,024 in 1928, $8,449,253.54 in 1929, $8,423,116.40 in 1930, and $8,395,108.40 in 1931, were assessed at $9,413,500 in 1927, $9,471,500 in 1928, $10,488,500 in 1929 and $10,497,000 in 1930 and 1931. Tax assessments in this City and other cities of this State repeatedly have been recognized as competent evidence upon the question of value . . . and I think it not uncommon for business men to act upon them, within reasonable limits, as a rough and ready indication of value.

With respect to these particular assessments the company instituted certiorari proceedings, and in its petitions and supporting affidavits it claimed that the assessments should be reduced far below the amount at which the properties were carried on its books. Those certiorari proceedings were pending unheard and undetermined when plaintiff was appointed receiver in April 1933. He and his then co-receiver, who afterwards were appointed as trustees, then entered into a compromise with the City of New York. . . . If the amounts requested in the company's certiorari proceedings be accepted as showing true values and plaintiff's other claims be allowed, deficits exceeding the amount of the dividends result (Exhibit 131). If the amounts fixed pursuant to the plaintiff's compromise be accepted as showing true values, and plaintiff's other claims be allowed, surpluses exceeding the amount of the dividends result (Exhibit BB). Each party thus in turn urges an acceptance of the other set of figures. Plaintiff says his compromise did not represent his judgment of values, or the judgment of any appraiser engaged by him, but merely the best compromise he could get from the City authorities. . . . That very circumstance, however, of itself imports a rather general recognition of the fact that a trial would not have resulted in a fixing of values at very much, if any, below the compromise figure, and I think that, at least in the absence of some extraordinary circumstance not here appearing, the figures at which the City and the taxpayer have agreed to compromise existing controversies with respect to the amount at which property should be assessed for taxation, fairly and justly may be taken as indicating the fair value of such property, and I here so find. Such figures are here also fully sustained by the testimony of a competent appraiser who here testified for defendants. It is also worthy of note that an engineering expert engaged by plaintiff to fix a value upon the properties and business as a whole accepted assessed valuations of land as at least one basis for his conclusions, and that no real estate appraiser has here attempted to fix a value of the land at lesser figures.

Each side has submitted an elaborate and detailed appraisal by an engineering appraiser of high repute. Each such appraiser has undertaken to find reproduction cost and also to arrive at a valuation by the method of capitalizing earnings, or a valuation supported by income, as it is expressed by one of them. Their views as to reproduction cost are not widely divergent despite the fact that they arrive at their conclusions upon that point by quite different methods, and under the view of either the surplus, i.e., the excess of asset value over liabilities to creditors and stockholders, at all times here in question, was substantially greater than the dividends paid. It is only when they come to arrive at a valuation by the method of capitalizing earnings that the views of these appraisers assume sharp contrast. According to defendants' appraiser the earnings support a value not greatly different from what he finds to be the reproduction cost less depreciation. According to plaintiff's appraiser the earnings fail to support a value equal to the liabilities to creditors and stockholders.

To point out the differences in detail would unduly expand this opinion, already disappointingly lengthy. It is sufficient, I think, to say that I find that plaintiff's appraiser (1) has made unjustified deductions in computing the net income before depreciation, (2) has deducted excessive amounts for repairs and maintenance and depreciation, and (3) has been unjustifiably conservative in capitalizing his assumed net earnings at too high a rate, or, in other words, in assuming that no one would be willing to invest in expectation of a lower rate of return than he has fixed. Comparatively slight differences in the assumptions made upon these three points (and it is to be emphasized that they are all merely assumptions and opinions) make an enormous difference in the result, and while I hold that directors may not impair capital and then free themselves from the resulting liability by saying that they did it in good faith, evidence more cogent than that which has been supplied is necessary to produce a conviction that a willing buyer and a willing seller would not have agreed upon a much higher price than is indicated by this particular appraiser's assumptions. Plaintiff submitted, also, another valuation by another appraiser based entirely upon a capitalization of earnings and reaching a valuation far below the valuation arrived at by plaintiff's expert already mentioned. I think it entitled to no weight whatever. Its fundamental postulates are, first, that no real estate ever is worth what it costs, and, second, that no one would buy a going business having large real estate holdings among its fixed assets except on the basis of being assured of a net return of ten per cent upon the investment. I conclude that the earnings support a value substantially as found by defendants' engineering appraiser.

It actually is unnecessary to go that far. Taking the land and improvements at the values fixed as a result of plaintiff's own compromise with the City's taxing authorities, taking the investments in and advances to subsidiaries at the values fixed by plaintiff's own witnesses as the same are tabulated on Exhibit 165, taking the good will at $3,000,000 and taking the other items of assets which have not been questioned at the values at which they appear on Exhibit 50 (each of which things I find it proper to do) gives a total of assets far in excess of all liabilities to creditors and stockholders.

In summary, therefore, after considering all the evidence, I find that at the times these dividends were declared and paid the value of the assets exceeded the total liabilities to creditors and stockholders by an amount in excess of the total dividends, and that there accordingly was no impairment of capital or capital stock. . . .

Defendants' motions for judgment at the close of the whole case are granted, and I direct the entry of judgment for defendants, with separate bills of costs to those appearing by separate attorneys.

QUESTIONS

(1) How is the value of fixed assets to be measured under Randall v. Bailey: Reproduction cost? Investment value, derived through the capitalization of earning power? Liquidation value? In Mountain State Steel Foundries v. Commissioner, 284 F.2d 737 (4th Cir.1960), construing a West Virginia statute which provided that a corporation could not purchase its own stock if the purchase would impair capital, the court stated, "At least until the highest court of West Virginia should otherwise decide, we think for our collateral purpose the statute should be construed as prohibiting the purchase of its own stock if the use of its funds for the purpose would deplete the realizable value of its assets to a point below the total of its liabilities and capital. . . . If we are to look to actual values in applying the statute, the spirit of the statute requires that they be conservatively determined. Opinion evidence of appreciation should be received with skepticism if insolvency ensues. . . ." 284 F.2d at 741–742. See also In re Kettle Fried Chicken, 513 F.2d 807 (6th Cir.1975);

Baxter v. Lancer Industries, Inc., 213 F.Supp. 92 (E.D.N.Y.1963), appeal dism'd 324 F.2d 286 (2d Cir.).

(2) So long as Bush Terminal remained a going concern, of what significance would it be that the reproduction cost of the Terminal had increased above original cost, if the relative earning power of the enterprise was maintained?

N.Y. BUS. CORP. LAW §§ 102, 506, 510, 717

[See Statutory Supplement]

The above provisions were part of a revision of the New York Business Corporation Law adopted in 1961. According to the Joint Legislative Committee's Explanatory Memorandum on [the] Business Corporation Law, "There is no basic change in the present law that permits dividends . . . to be paid out of any surplus, including unrealized appreciation of assets (§ 510)." Joint Legislative Committee to Study Revision of Corporation Laws, Fifth Interim Report, [Leg. Doc. No. 12], App. C, at 62 (1961). See generally Stanger, Accounting Concepts and the Standard for Declaration and Payment of Dividends under the New York Business Corporation Law, N.Y. Law J., Dec. 9, 1965, at 1, col. 4.

DEL. GEN. CORP. LAW §§ 141(e), 154, 170

[See Statutory Supplement]

(d) THE CURRENT EARNINGS TEST: NIMBLE DIVIDENDS

DEL. GEN. CORP. LAW § 170

[See Statutory Supplement]

Dividends payable out of current profits have been termed "nimble dividends"—a phrase originated by Professor Baker. Note, 62 Harv.L.Rev. 130 (1948). Directors must be "nimble" by declaring dividends before the close of the relevant period or within a short time thereafter. In effect, such dividends are distributions out of capital, in the sense that they can be paid in the face of a capital deficit.

MORRIS v. STANDARD GAS & ELECTRIC CO.
Court of Chancery of Delaware, 1949.
31 Del.Ch. 20, 63 A.2d 577.

[Defendant, a public-utility holding company incorporated in Delaware, declared a quarterly dividend in 1948 on two issues of senior preferred. Plaintiff, a holder of junior preferred, sought to enjoin the payment as violating Del. § 34(b), which provided as follows:

> The directors . . . shall have power to declare and pay dividends . . . either (a) out of its net assets in excess of its capital . . . or (b), in case there shall be no such excess, out of its net profits for the fiscal year then current and/or the preceding fiscal year; provided, however, that . . . [the balance of § 34(b) was virtually identical to the second sentence of present § 170(a)].

[No dividend had been paid since 1934, and there were heavy arrearages on all classes of preferred. It was conceded by the corporation that the power to pay the dividend had to be found under the nimble-dividend provision, and it was conceded by the plaintiff that the corporation had current earnings sufficient to cover the dividend. Plaintiff claimed, however, that the dividend did not pass the test in what is now the second sentence of § 170(a). The evidence showed that before declaring the dividend, the board had the corporation's assets appraised by an established firm "to determine whether . . . the assets less the liabilities exceeded $88,500,000 [which] was the approximate total of the aggregate capital represented by the . . . preferred, plus the sum required to pay a quarterly dividend on the prior preference stock." The report concluded that net assets had a fair value substantially in excess of that figure. A further report to the same effect was furnished to the board by the Vice President and Treasurer.]

SEITZ, Vice Chancellor. . . .

The problem is one of valuation which is surpassed in difficulty only in the domestic relations law. The numerous and varied standards applied in the legal, accounting and business fields have mapped a wavering course for one required to resolve a substantial problem of valuation. Here the governing statute has declared that the capital must—roughly speaking—be valued at its dollar equivalent before a dividend can be declared out of net profits for a designated period. This duty falls to the directors. What legal standard will be applied in determining whether the directors have valued the corporate assets in a manner deemed sufficient to comply with the requirements of Section 34(b)? . . .

. . . [The plaintiff] took the position that nothing short of an actual appraisal of the assets in the underlying companies whose stock was owned by the defendant would be sufficient. . . .

Initially, of course, reasonable men can differ as to what constitutes an appraisal. If by an appraisal plaintiff means that all the assets had to be viewed and evaluated separately by the directors or experts in a manner similar to a valuation for purposes of a reorganization of the type currently popular at least in the utility field, then I conclude that the statute imposes no such requirement on the directors as a prerequisite to the employment of the power granted in Section 34(b). In large companies, especially those such as the defendant, an appraisal of the type suggested by plaintiff would mean that as a practical matter the provisions of Section 34(b) would be unavailable. . . . I prefer the view expressed in [Randall v. Bailey]:

"I see no cause for alarm over the fact that this view [taking assets at actual value] requires directors to make a determination of the value of the assets at each dividend declaration. On the contrary, I think that is exactly what the law always has contemplated that directors should do. That does not mean that the books themselves necessarily must be altered by write-ups or write-downs at each dividend period, or that formal appraisals must be obtained from professional appraisers or even made by the directors themselves. That is obviously impossible in the case of corporations of any considerable size."

In concluding that a formal appraisal of the type mentioned is not required, I do not mean to imply that the directors are not under a duty to evaluate the assets on the basis of acceptable data and by standards which they are entitled to believe reasonably reflect present "values." It is not practical to attempt to lay down a rigid rule as to what constitutes proper evidence of value for the consideration of directors in declaring a dividend under Section 34(b). The factors considered and the emphasis given will depend upon the case presented. . . .

Plaintiff's case comes down to a disagreement with the directors as to value under circumstances where the directors took great care to obtain data on the point in issue, and exercised an informed judgment on the matter. In such a situation, I am persuaded that this court cannot substitute either plaintiff's or its own opinion of value for that reached by the directors where there is no charge of fraud or bad faith. As stated, the process of valuation called for by Section 34(b) of necessity permits of no one objective standard of value. Having in mind its function, the directors must be given reasonable latitude in ascertaining value. Such being the case, I conclude that the action of the directors in determining that the net assets were worth at least the aggregate amount of the capital represented by the issued and outstanding stock of all classes having preference upon the distribution of assets cannot be disturbed on the showing here made. Consequently, plaintiff is not entitled to a preliminary injunction restraining the payment of the dividend.

An order accordingly will be advised on notice.

———

(e) THE EARNED SURPLUS TEST

PA. §§ 1002, 1702

§ 1002. Definitions

* * *

(3) "Capital Surplus" means capital contributed for or assigned to shares in excess of the stated capital applicable thereto (whether as a result of original issue of shares at amounts in excess of their par or stated value, reduction in par or stated value after issuance, transactions by the corporation in its own shares, or otherwise) . . . and amounts of surplus arising from revaluation of or unrealized appreciation in assets. . . .

(7) "Earned Surplus" means the entire surplus of a corporation other than its capital surplus . . . .

(11) "Net Assets" means the amount by which the total assets of a corporation exceed the total liabilities of the corporation excluding stated capital and surplus. . . .

(20) "Stated Capital" means [the sum of the par value of all shares then issued having a par value, the consideration received for all shares then issued without par value, except such part thereof as may have been allocated to surplus, and such other amounts as may have been transferred to stated capital]. . . .

(23) "Surplus" means the excess of the net assets of a corporation over its stated capital.

§ 1702. Dividends

A. The board of directors of a business corporation may, from time to time, declare and the corporation may pay dividends on its outstanding shares in cash or property . . . except when the corporation is insolvent or when the payment thereof would render the corporation insolvent or when the declaration or payment thereof would be contrary to any restriction contained in its articles, but—

(1) Dividends may be declared and paid in cash or property only out of unreserved and unrestricted earned surplus of the corporation except as otherwise provided in this section;

(2) No dividend shall be paid which would reduce the remaining net assets of the corporation below the aggregate preferential amount payable in the event of voluntary liquidation to the holders of shares having preferential rights to the assets of the corporation in the event of liquidation. . . .

NOTE ON THE EARNED SURPLUS TEST

The earned surplus test for dividends is closely identified with the Model Act, although the Revised Model Business Corporation Act drops the earned surplus test. (See Section 1(h), infra.) The Pennsylvania statute is generally based on the old Model Act approach. However, while Pa. § 1002(7) uses an indirect approach to define earned surplus, under the old Model Act (and many other statutes) earned surplus is defined directly, as "the portion of . . . surplus . . . equal to the balance of . . . net profits, income, gains and losses from the date of incorporation . . . after deducting subsequent distributions to shareholders and transfers to stated capital and capital surplus made out of earned surplus." William Hackney comments as follows on the two approaches:

> In attempting to formulate statutory language limiting dividends to income, two distinct approaches were found possible.
>
> One is, like the capital-impairment restriction, a balance-sheet test. The surplus of net assets in excess of capital is obtained and then analyzed and any which is not paid-in or other capital surplus is deemed accumulated income.
>
> The second approach . . . is to take the balance of all the corporate income statements to date and deduct dividends and other transfers therefrom, with the remainder being earned surplus.
>
> The Model Act definition, it seems, utilizes the aggregate-income-statement method of arriving at earned surplus. It does not use the balance sheet as a source of reference but directs one to take the balance of net profits, income, gains and losses over a period of time. The Model Act's adoption of the American Institute of Accountants' definition of earned surplus argues strongly that just as accounting today is mainly concerned with the fairest possible presentation of period net income, regarding the balance sheet merely as a connecting link between successive income statements, so earned surplus as used in the act is intended to signify a composite income statement from the year of inception and not simply a balance-sheet increase in net assets.[1]
>
> . . . The Pennsylvania approach avoids the impossible task of defining earned surplus in terms of the income statement satisfactory to accountants and also consistent with the traditional legal approach; rather, the amendments attempt to "back into the concept by a process of elimination." The method of computation is to obtain the balance-sheet surplus of net assets in excess of stated capital, which is then analyzed, and any which is not paid-in or other capital surplus is deemed earned surplus.[2]

Despite the difference in approaches, the principal draftsman of the Pennsylvania amendments concluded that generally speaking earned surplus had the same meaning under both tests. Mulford, Corporate Distributions to Shareholders and other Amendments to the Penn-

1. Hackney, The Financial Provisions of the Model Business Corporations Act, 70 Harv.L.Rev. 1357, 1365–66 (1957).

2. Hackney, The Pennsylvania Business Corporation Law Amendments, 19 U.Pitt. L.Rev. 51, 69–70 (1957).

sylvania Business Corporation Law, 106 U.Pa.L.Rev. 536, 542 (1958).

(f) CAPITAL SURPLUS

(1) Introduction

N. Y. BUS. CORP. LAW §§ 102, 510, 520

[See Statutory Supplement]

DEL. GEN. CORP. LAW §§ 154, 170

[See Statutory Supplement]

PA. §§ 1002, 1702, 1703

§ 1002. Definitions

[See Section 1(e), supra]

§ 1702. Dividends

A. [See Section 1(e), supra]

B. The board of directors of a business corporation may also, from time to time, distribute to the holders of its outstanding shares having a cumulative preferential right to receive dividends, in discharge of their cumulative dividend rights, dividends payable in cash out of the unrestricted capital surplus of the corporation, if at the time the corporation has no earned surplus and is not insolvent and would not thereby be rendered insolvent. Each such distribution when made shall be identified as a payment . . . out of capital surplus.

§ 1703. Distributions in Partial Liquidation

The board of directors of a business corporation may, from time to time, distribute to its shareholders, in partial liquidation, out of unrestricted capital surplus of the corporation a portion of its assets, in cash or property, subject to the following provisions:

(1) No such distribution shall be made at a time when the corporation is insolvent or when such distribution would render the corporation insolvent;

(2) No such distribution shall be made unless such distribution shall have been authorized by the prior affirmative vote obtained within one year of such distribution of the holders of at least a

majority of the outstanding shares of each class whether or not entitled to vote thereon by the provisions of its articles;

(3) No such distribution shall be made to the holders of any class of shares unless all cumulative dividends accrued on all classes of shares entitled to preferential dividends prior to dividends on the shares to the holders of which such distribution is to be made shall have been fully paid;

(4) No such distribution shall be made to the holders of any class of shares which would reduce the remaining net assets of the corporation below the aggregate preferential amount payable in event of voluntary liquidation to the holders of shares having preferential rights to the assets of the corporation in the event of liquidation;

(5) Each such distribution, when made, shall be identified as a distribution in partial liquidation. . . . *

Broadly speaking, capital surplus is that portion of surplus which is derived from sources other than corporate earnings, such as amounts paid for stock in excess of par value. (For a more elaborate definition, see Pa. § 1002(3), supra.) In theory, the permissibility of dividends out of capital surplus marks the major difference between the balance sheet and earned surplus tests: Under a balance sheet test dividends can be paid out of capital surplus unless specifically prohibited. In contrast, under an earned surplus test dividends can be paid out of capital surplus only if specifically permitted. In practice, however, balance sheet statutes often contain provisions giving special treatment to dividends out of capital surplus, while earned surplus statutes often contain provisions permitting dividends out of capital surplus. N.Y. § 510(c) is an example of the former type of provision; Pa. §§ 1702(B), 1703 are examples of the latter.

The most important types of capital surplus are paid-in, reduction, and revaluation surplus. Paid-in surplus is the amount by which the price of newly issued stock exceeds that portion of the price which is allocated to stated capital. Reduction surplus is the amount by which stated capital is reduced through corporate action pursuant to statutory authority. Revaluation surplus is the unrealized appreciation in the value of fixed assets. The major problems raised by the various types of capital surplus will be considered in the sections that follow.

---

* Like some other statutory provisions that permit dividends out of capital surplus, particularly those in which the basic test is an earned surplus test, Pa. § 1703 employs the term "partial liquidation." However, provisions like § 1703 usually seem intended to cover dividends out of capital surplus whether or not the dividends are associated with liquidation of part of the corporation's business.

See generally M.A. Eisenberg, The Structure of the Corporation 262–66 (1976). (Footnote by ed.)

NOTE ON THE PROTECTION OF LIQUIDATION
PREFERENCES

Preferred stock normally carries an assets or liquidation preference which provides that on liquidation no assets can be distributed to junior shares until the preferred has been paid a designated amount—typically, the price at which the preferred was issued, or that amount plus accrued dividends. A central objective of dividend law should be to protect liquidation preferences by prohibiting dividends when the corporation's remaining net assets would be less than aggregate preferences. This objective is sometimes realized in full, sometimes hardly at all. At one extreme, some statutes, like Pennsylvania's, prohibit virtually all distributions which would "reduce the remaining net assets of the corporation below the aggregate preferential amount payable in the event of voluntary liquidation." Pa. §§ 1701(B)(5), 1702, 1703. See also, e.g., Cal.Corp.Code § 502. At another extreme is the Delaware statute, which affords protection to liquidation preferences only in connection with nimble and wasting-assets dividends, and even in those cases does not protect the preference as such, but instead protects only the "capital represented by" preferred shares with a liquidation preference—an amount that may be considerably less than the preference if the preferred is no par or low par.

Perched between these extremes are scattershot approaches like New York's. New York does not directly prohibit dividends that would impair liquidation preferences (except in the case of wasting-asset dividends, see N.Y.Bus.Corp.Law § 510(b))—but two provisions of the New York statute provide indirect (and incomplete) protection. First, N.Y.Bus.Corp.Law § 806(b)(3) provides that capital cannot be reduced by amendment of the certificate "unless after such reduction the stated capital exceeds the aggregate preferential amount payable upon involuntary liquidation . . . plus the par value of all other issued shares with par value." However, there are no counterpart protections when capital is reduced by techniques other than certificate amendment. (See N.Y.Bus.Corp.Law §§ 515, 516.) Second, N.Y.Bus.Corp.Law § 506(b) provides that when no-par preferred is issued, only that portion of the issue price in excess of the liquidation preference can be allocated to surplus. Since the liquidation preference often corresponds to the issue price, a provision like § 506(b) will normally force the corporation to allocate to capital an amount equal to the preference; and since dividends cannot be paid out of capital, the result is an indirect protection of the liquidation preference in the case of no-par preferred. However, there is no similar protection for low-par preferred. Thus if a corporation issues preferred with a price of $100, and a liquidation preference of $100, but a par value of only $10, the New York statute does not prohibit the corporation from allocating $90 per share to paid-in surplus rather than to stated capital. See A. Hoffman, Israels on Corporate Practice § 10.03 (4th ed. 1983); 2 S. White, New York Corporations ¶ 510.06 n. 37 (1978); T. Fiflis & H. Kripke & P. Foster, Accounting for Business Lawyers 430–31 (3d ed. 1984). Furthermore § 506(b) does not protect that part of a liquidation preference consisting of accrued but unpaid dividends.

---

(2) Paid–in Surplus

NOTE

1. Paid-in surplus is the excess of (i) the total purchase price of newly issued stock over (ii) that portion of the price allocated to stated capital. This type of surplus is a byproduct of the low par and no par phenomena, because it does not arise if stock is issued at par value.

2. In an economic sense paid-in surplus constitutes capital, since it is part of the shareholders' initial equity investment. Therefore, it is difficult to reconcile permission to pay dividends out of paid-in surplus with the creditor-protection purpose of dividend law, unless the statute limits such permission to corporations with some minimum degree of financial health. A few states do employ this kind of limitation. For example, R.I. § 7–1.1–41 provides that "No [distribution of capital surplus] shall be made . . . unless the fair value of the net assets of the corporation remaining after the distribution is at least equal to . . . [25%] of the total liabilities of the corporation." Similarly, N.C. § 55–50(e)(3), prohibits dividends on common out of capital surplus "if thereupon the present fair value of the assets of the corporation is less than twice the amount of its liabilities." Most statutes, however, have no comparable limitation.

3. Assuming creditor interests can be put aside, there seems to be no reason to prohibit dividends out of paid-in surplus if the corporation has only common stock outstanding. Even in that situation, however, the source of such dividends should be adequately disclosed, so that the shareholder is "given fair warning [that] his dividend check does not represent what he would normally expect it to be—i.e., a distribution of earnings—but is instead a return of his own or somebody else's capital." de Capriles, New York Business Corporation Law; Article 5—Corporate Finance, 11 Buff.L.Rev. 461, 471 (1962). A more difficult issue is whether dividends out of paid-in surplus should require shareholder approval, on the theory that shareholders do not expect the amounts paid for newly issued stock will be available for dividends at the will of the board even when the corporation has the earnings. Some statutes, like Pa. § 1703, do require shareholder approval. A few statutes pay lip-service to this principle by requiring shareholder approval unless the certificate otherwise provides.

4. Where a corporation has preferred outstanding the situation is much more complex. Four kinds of cases can arise:

Case 1: *Dividends Paid on Preferred Stock Out of Surplus Paid in by the Common.* This type of dividend seems unobjectionable, at least where it is paid during the period after the corporation has been organized but before it has earnings. Preferred stock is not totally unlike debt, and preferred shareholders, like creditors, may have a legitimate expectation that payments will ordinarily be made if the corporation is not in deep financial trouble and there is a legal source of dividends available. Moreover, payment of preferred dividends may advance the interest of common as well as preferred, since a default in preferred dividends is likely to cause a significant drop in the market value of both classes of stock.

Case 2: *Dividends Paid on Common Stock Out of Surplus Paid in by the Common.* This type of dividend should not be permitted, since the preferred shareholder is likely to have relied on the surplus paid in by the common as "a cushion which acts as an earnings base for dividends, a buffer to absorb losses which might otherwise precipitate bankruptcy, and a safeguard of his assets preference on dissolution." Hackney, The Financial Provisions of the Model Business Corporation Act, 70 Harv.L.Rev. 1357, 1402–03 (1957).

Case 3: *Dividends Paid on Common Stock Out of Surplus Paid in by the Preferred.* This type of dividend should also not be permitted, since preferred shareholders are hardly likely to expect the money they put in through the front door to be dropped out to common through the back.

Case 4: *Dividends Paid on Preferred Stock Out of Surplus Paid in by the Preferred.* This type of dividend should not be permitted in an earned-surplus jurisdiction, because it frees, for payment to common, earned surplus that might otherwise be exhausted in the payment of preferred dividends. (Of course, even if earned surplus is exhausted it might be possible to pay a dividend on common out of capital surplus, but this will not always be the case, due to restrictions on the use of capital surplus.)

The degree to which these four cases are covered by the statutes varies considerably. A few statutes explicitly prohibit the distribution of any paid-in surplus to common in a two-class context, except under tightly defined circumstances. See N.C. § 55–50. Most statutes, however fail to deal explicitly with the problem. Statutory provisions which require that an amount of the issue price equal to any preference must be allocated to capital may afford indirect protection. If the preference equals the issue price, these provisions will prevent the corporation from creating significant preferred paid-in surplus, and will thereby prevent Cases 3 and 4 from arising. Statutory provisions which prohibit dividends out of capital surplus if remaining net assets would be less than aggregate liquidation preferences may also afford indirect protection. (And wholly apart from statute, the problems in Cases 3 and 4 may not arise at all if par value approximates the issue price, or if appropriate protection is afforded by certificate provision.)

(3) Reduction Surplus

There are a great number of techniques for reducing capital, most of all of which can be grouped into three categories: (i) amendment of the certificate;* (ii) cancellation of reacquired shares; and (iii) transfers to surplus of stated capital in excess of the par value of issued shares. Frequently the statutory scheme for reducing capital is not well articulated, so that under any given statute it may not be completely clear which techniques are available, how they are to be exercised, and what if any protective limits are placed upon their exercise.

PA. §§ 1002, 1706, 1708, 1801, 1804, 1805

§ 1002. Definitions. . . .

(3) "Capital Surplus" [See Section 1(e) supra]

§ 1706. Reduction of Stated Capital Without Change in Share Structure

A reduction in the stated capital of a corporation which does not involve an exchange, reclassification, or cancellation of shares, or a reduction of the number of authorized shares of any class below the number of issued shares of that class, or a redemption and cancellation of shares may be effected [by a resolution of the board, proposing the reduction, which proposal] shall be adopted upon receiving the affirmative vote of the shareholders entitled to cast at least a majority of the votes which all shareholders are entitled to cast thereon, and if any class of shares is entitled to vote thereon as a class, the affirmative vote of the holders of at least a majority of the outstanding shares of each class entitled to vote as a class thereon.

§ 1708. Cancellation of Treasury Shares

Whenever any business corporation shall have acquired any treasury shares, it may, by resolution of its board of directors, cancel any or all such shares. In the case of shares which were not subject to redemption it may not do so without the prior affirmative vote obtained within one year of such cancellation of the holders of a

---

* Since the par value of a class of stock is not logically identical to the stated capital attributed to that class, it can be argued that a certificate amendment reducing either par value or the number of outstanding par value shares does not automatically reduce stated capital. See D. Herwitz, Business Planning 255–56 (temp. 2d ed. 1984); Ohio §§ 1701.30(A), (B)(1), 1701.69(A)(6), (7), (8). Nevertheless, most of the statutes seem to contemplate that such an amendment does automatically reduce the corporation's stated capital by the amount of any reduction in the total par value of outstanding shares. See, e.g., N.Y.Bus.Corp.Law §§ 801(b)(10), (11), 802, 805(a)(5); Ill.Atty.Gen'l Op. No. 766, 1935 A.G.O. 85, reprinted in D. Herwitz, supra, at 260. However, a certificate amendment reducing the number of outstanding no par shares will not reduce stated capital: "[S]hares of no par stock represent aliquot or proportionate parts of the capital, and when decreased in the same proportion, they represent the same aliquot or proportionate parts of capital." Radio Corp. of America v. Benson, 32 Del. 576, 128 A. 107 (1925).

majority of the outstanding shares of each class, whether or not entitled to vote thereon by the provisions of the articles of the corporation. Such corporation may apply to such cancellation an amount out of its stated capital and capital surplus which shall not be greater than that portion of the stated capital and capital surplus represented by or restricted by the purchase or redemption of such shares at the time of such cancellation and the stated capital and capital surplus of the corporation shall be reduced to this extent.

§ 1801. Amendment of Articles Authorized

A. A business corporation . . . may from time to time amend its articles for one or more of the following purposes. . . .

(4) To increase or diminish the number of shares which the corporation has authority to issue, or to reclassify the same by changing the number, par value, . . . preferences, . . . or other special rights of the shares, . . . or by changing shares with par value into shares without par value, . . . either with or without increasing or decreasing the number of shares. . . .

§ 1804. Shares Entitled to Vote on Amendments

. . . If a proposed amendment would (1) make any change in the preferences . . . or special or relative rights of the shares of any class adverse to such class, or (2) . . . decrease the par value of the shares of any class . . . the holders of the outstanding shares of such class shall be entitled to vote as a class on such amendment regardless of any limitations stated in the articles on the voting rights of such class. . . .

§ 1805. Adoption of Amendments by Shareholders

(A) . . . Unless the articles require a greater vote, the proposed amendment shall be adopted upon receiving the affirmative vote of the shareholders entitled to cast at least a majority of the votes which all shareholders are entitled to cast thereon, and if any class of shares is entitled to vote thereon as a class, the affirmative vote of the holders of at least a majority of the outstanding shares in each class of shares entitled to vote as a class thereon. . . .

DEL. GEN. CORP. LAW §§ 242(a)(3), 243, 244

[See Statutory Supplement]

BACKGROUND NOTE ON REDUCTION OF CAPITAL

1. A reduction of capital does not in itself impair the interests of any group protected by the dividend-regulation statutes. However, such a reduction creates a new surplus fund equal to the amount by which stated capital has been reduced. This fund is called reduction

surplus, and is a subcategory of capital surplus. Reduction surplus can be used in two ways: (i) It can be distributed to shareholders directly. (ii) It can be used to eliminate an earned surplus deficit, thereby freeing future earnings for distribution. The former alternative will be considered in this section; the latter, in the next.

2. The payment of dividends out of reduction surplus seems anomalous under either a balance sheet statute, in which the emphasis is placed on preservation of capital, or an earned surplus statute, in which the emphasis is placed on limiting dividends to earnings. Nevertheless, statutes of both types routinely permit such dividends on pretty much the same terms as dividends out of paid-in surplus, with no safeguards for creditors beyond those imposed by the insolvency test. The power to reduce capital therefore creates a gaping breach in the protective wall set up by dividend law as regards the interests of creditors.[1] Frequently, however, the statutes impose various protective devices to protect the interests of shareholders, although these protections are often spotty and incomplete:

(a) Shareholder Approval. Under some statutes (such as Pennsylvania), all significant techniques for reducing capital require shareholder approval. Under all statutes, a reduction of capital by certificate amendment requires such approval. However, many statutes allow the board to reduce capital without shareholder approval, by acquiring and cancelling nonredeemable stock or by transfering to surplus stated capital in excess of the par value of issued shares. See, e.g., N.Y.Bus.Corp.Law §§ 515, 516.

(b) Class Voting. Most statutes provide that the stated capital of a class cannot be reduced by certificate amendment unless the amendment is approved by that class, even if the class is otherwise nonvoting. See, e.g., Del.Gen.Corp.Law § 242(b); Pa. § 1804. Under N.Y. §§ 801(b)(10) and 804(a), a class vote is required for an amendment that would "reduce the par value of any authorized shares of any class" if the action "would adversely affect such holders." Brill v. Blakeley, 281 App.Div. 532, 120 N.Y.S.2d 713 (1953), aff'd on certified questions 308 N.Y. 951, 127 N.E.2d 96 (1955), indicates that a certificate amendment which reduces the par value of a class of preferred affects the class adversely within the meaning of these provisions.

(c) Appraisal Rights. Some statutes confer appraisal rights on dissenting preferred shareholders where preferred capital is reduced through certificate amendment. N.Y.Bus.Corp.Law § 806(b)(6) provides that "A holder of any adversely affected shares . . . shall . . . have the right to dissent and to receive payment for such shares, if the certificate of amendment . . . alters or abolishes any preferential right of such shares having preferences. . . ." Substantially the

1. Cf. Hackney, The Financial Provisions of the Model Business Corporation Act, 70 Harv.L.Rev. 1357, 1389 (1957): "The net result [of the old Model Act] is an apparent limitation of the funds available for dividends to earned surplus, but actually, in so far as real protection to creditors or preferred stockholders is concerned, there is a complete eradication of the concept of common capital as a cushion protecting the senior interests."

same provision was added to the Model Act in 1978. See Conard, Amendments of the Model Business Corporation Act Affecting Dissenters' Rights, 33 Bus.Law 2587, 2590–94 (1978). Such a statute may be interpreted to grant appraisal rights to dissenting preferred shareholders when preferred capital is reduced, and perhaps even when the capital of a *junior* class is reduced.

(d) Protection of Liquidation Preferences. Some statutes prohibit the reduction of stated capital through certain techniques unless, after the reduction, stated capital will exceed aggregate liquidation preferences plus the par value of all shares that do not carry a liquidation preference. See N.Y.Bus.Corp.Law §§ 516(b), 806(b)(3). But the same statutes may fail to apply this prohibition to all reduction techniques, or to prohibit a corporation from *initially* stating capital below liquidation preferences by issuing low par preferred. See Background Note on Paid-in Surplus, supra.

(e) Limits on Distributions of Reduction Surplus. Apart from limits on the reduction of capital itself, many statutes set limits on distributions out of the resulting reduction surplus, by defining such surplus as capital surplus and thereby triggering any limitations applicable to capital-surplus dividends. See, e.g., Pa. §§ 1002(3), 1702(B), 1703 [Sections 1(e), 1(f)(1), supra.].

---

(4) Revaluation Surplus

PA. §§ 1002, 1702

§ 1002. **Definitions**

    (3) "Capital Surplus" [See Section 1(e) supra.]

§ 1703. **Dividends in Partial Liquidation**

    [See Section (f)(1), supra.]

(g) CONTRACTUAL RESTRICTIONS ON THE PAYMENT OF DIVIDENDS

NOTE

1. It should be obvious by now that the dividend statutes provide little protection to creditors beyond that already afforded by the law of fraudulent conveyances. Involuntary creditors, trade creditors, and short-term lenders must normally take the protection of dividend law as they find it. Institutional lenders, however, who provide large amounts of money over a long period of time, have the power to impose contractual restrictions on dividends beyond the

weak limits imposed by corporation law, and normally do so. Similar restrictions are often extracted by underwriters in connection with bonds and preferred stock issued to the public. Indeed, as a practical matter, it may be said that the modern law of dividends is contractual rather than statutory. There are relatively few instances (except among recently formed companies) where at least some retained earnings do not appear on the balance sheets. Furthermore, corporation statutes are so liberal in allowing capital surplus to be created, either when stock is originally issued, through the use of no-par or low-par capitalization, or thereafter, through a reduction of capital, that resourceful counsel should be able to make a distribution legal even in the absence of retained earnings. Thus the real question is usually not whether a dividend is prohibited by statute, but whether it is prohibited by arrangements with lending institutions, or provisions agreed upon in connection with preferred stock financing.

2. Restrictions contained in long-term loan agreements are often known as negative covenants, because the borrowing corporation promises not to take particular actions while the loan is outstanding. Negative covenants concerning dividends, while often very complex and closely tailored to the particular situation, tend to fall into several basic patterns. Under the most common pattern, the borrowing corporation agrees that it will not make any distributions to shareholders unless the proposed distribution, plus all other distributions after a given "peg" date, would be less than earnings accumulated after the peg date plus the proceeds of new stock issues. The peg date is usually the beginning of the fiscal year in which the debt is issued. The thrust of such a covenant is to freeze net worth at the time of the loan, by permitting subsequent dividends only to the extent that net worth increases through accumulated earnings or new sales of new stock. (This type of provision may be supplemented by a covenant that working capital—current assets minus current liabilities—will not fall below a designated level, thereby helping to preserve the quality as well as the quantity of net worth.)

(h) NEW DEPARTURES

CAL. CORP. CODE §§ 114, 166, 500–502, 507

[See Statutory Supplement]

BACKGROUND NOTE ON CALIFORNIA'S DIVIDEND PROVISIONS

1. California's dividend provisions, enacted in 1977, mark a sweeping break with traditional dividend statutes. The ultimate foundation of most other statutes is a legal concept—stated capital. In

contrast, the ultimate foundation of the California statute is a set of economic realities: retained earnings, asset-liability ratios, liquidation preferences, and an insolvency test.

2. As originally adopted, § 500 provided that "in determining the amount of the assets of the corporation no appreciation in value not yet realized shall in any event be included, except with respect to readily marketable securities." The first part of this provision reflected generally accepted accounting principles; the second ran against those principles, which require marketable securities to be carried at lower of cost or market. Subsequently the statute was amended to delete the provision. Harold Marsh, the principal draftsman of the California Corporation Code, has explained the amendment as follows:

> The reason for this amendment was that generally accepted accounting principles do not in any event permit the write-up of the value of assets on the basis of appraised values, and it was thought that the exception relating to marketable securities might be too broad. . . . Therefore, it was decided simply to eliminate the entire provision and thereby require that the carrying value of all assets . . . be in conformity with generally accepted accounting principles under Section 114.

H. Marsh, Marsh's California Corporation Law § 13.10 (2d ed. 1987).

3. See generally H. Marsh, supra, §§ 13.1–13.30; Ackerman & Sterrett, California's New Approach to Dividends and Reacquisitions of Shares, 23 U.C.L.A.L.Rev. 1052 (1976); Dreyfuss, Distributions to Shareholders under the New California General Corporation Law, 9 Loy. of L.A.L.Rev. 839 (1976).

REV. MODEL BUS. CORP. ACT §§ 1.40(6), 6.40

[See Statutory Supplement]

MINN. BUS. CORP. ACT § 302A.551

Subdivision 1. When permitted. The board may authorize and cause the corporation to make a distribution only if the board determines, . . . that the corporation will be able to pay its debts in the ordinary course of business after making the distribution and the board does not know before the distribution is made that the determination was or has become erroneous, and the corporation may make the distribution if it is able to pay its debts in the ordinary course of business after making the distribution. . . . the corporation to make, distributions may be prohibited, limited, or restricted by, or the rights and priorities of persons to receive distributions may be established by, the articles or bylaws or an agreement. . . .

Subd. 4. Restrictions. (a) A distribution may be made to the holders of a class or series of shares only if:

(1) All amounts payable to the holders of shares having a preference for the payment of that kind of distribution are paid; and

(2) The payment of the distribution does not reduce the remaining net assets of the corporation below the aggregate preferential amount payable in the event of liquidation to the holders of shares having preferential rights, unless the distribution is made to those shareholders in the order and to the extent of their respective priorities. . . .

———

KUMMERT, STATE STATUTORY RESTRICTIONS ON FINANCIAL DISTRIBUTIONS BY CORPORATIONS TO SHAREHOLDERS (pt. II), 59 Wash.L.Rev. 185, 282–84 (1984). "[The California, Revised Model Business Corporations Act, and Minnesota approaches] have some remarkable similarities. All three proceed from a common assessment of the inadequacies of the concept of legal capital to abolish not only the statutory underpinnings of the concept (the notion of par value and accounting rules for consideration received for shares), but also the series of exceptions (nimble dividends, depletion dividends, and special repurchases of shares) and fictions (treasury shares) erected because of the existence of the concept. All three subject transfers of cash or property, or incurrences of indebtedness, by a corporation without consideration to its shareholders to a single set of restrictions, regardless of the form in which the transfer, or incurrence, occurs. All three address applications of the restrictions to such transfers, or incurrences, where the transferor, or obligor, is either the parent, or the subsidiary, of another corporation. Finally, drafters of each of the systems based their efforts on the premise that statutory systems founded on legal capital were essentially misleading insofar as they led creditors and senior security holders to believe that such systems operated to protect their interests.

"[D]espite these similarities, the three systems can be clearly distinguished on the basis of their respective responses to that possible misrepresentation. The California series attempts to rectify the misrepresentation by promulgating rules that will provide creditors and senior shareholders with the type of protection they *thought* they were getting from the legal capital system. On the other hand, the Amended Model Act and the Minnesota Act both attempt to rectify the misrepresentation by promulgating rules that will provide creditors and senior shareholders with the level of protection that the drafters preceived such groups *actually received* from the legal capital system. This variance in fundamental goals in turn produces the significant differences between the Acts on such issues as the relative freedom directors have and the status in the event of financial difficulty of debt issued on repurchase of shares."

———

(i) JUDICIAL REVIEW OF DIVIDEND POLICY

BERWALD v. MISSION DEVELOPMENT CO.

Supreme Court of Delaware, 1962.
40 Del.Ch. 509, 185 A.2d 480.

SOUTHERLAND, Chief Justice, and WOLCOTT and TERRY, JJ., sitting.

SOUTHERLAND, Chief Justice.

Plaintiffs, owners of 248 shares of the stock of Mission Development Corporation, brought suit to compel the liquidation of Mission and the distribution of its assets to its stockholders. Mission answered and filed a motion for summary judgment, based on affidavits and depositions. Plaintiffs tendered no contradictory proof. The Vice Chancellor granted the motion and the plaintiffs appeal.

The facts are as follows:

Defendant, Mission Development, is a holding company. Its sole significant asset is a block of nearly seven million shares of Tidewater Oil Company. Tidewater is a large integrated oil company, qualified to do business in all the States of the Union. It is controlled, through Mission Development and Getty Oil Company, by J. Paul Getty.

Mission Development was formed in 1948 for the purpose of acquiring a block of 1,416,693 shares of Tidewater common stock then owned by Mission Corporation, a Nevada corporation. Its avowed purpose was to invest only in Tidewater stock, and in furtherance of this purpose to acquire additional stock to fortify its position in Tidewater. Accordingly, Mission of Delaware issued to Mission of Nevada 2,833,386 shares of its common stock and received the block of Tidewater stock held by Mission. Appropriate orders under the Investment Company Act were obtained from the Securities and Exchange Commission. The shares of both Mission Development and Tidewater are listed on the New York Stock Exchange.

Mission of Delaware will be hereinafter referred to as "Mission".

From 1948 to 1951 Mission acquired an additional 1,050,420 shares of Tidewater. Thereafter, and by 1960, Mission's holdings of Tidewater, through a 100% stock dividend and annual stock dividends of five per cent, increased to 6,943,957 shares.

In 1954 Tidewater discontinued the payment of cash dividends, thus effecting a discontinuance of Mission's income. Mission, as above noted, received thereafter until 1960 an annual 5% stock dividend, but Mission's proportionate ownership of Tidewater was not thereby increased, and its management accordingly deemed it unwise to distribute the shares as a dividend, since to do so would have decreased its proportionate ownership of Tidewater.

As hereafter shown, Tidewater's discontinuance of cash dividends was prompted by the adoption in 1954 of a policy of corporate expansion and modernization. The use of its available cash for this purpose left it without funds for dividends.

Later in the same year, Tidewater proposed to its stockholders to exchange shares of its cumulative $1.20 preferred stock for shares of its common stock held by the stockholders. Getty Oil Company and Mission were excluded from this offer.

All of the foregoing facts were reported to Mission stockholders by letter of J. Paul Getty, President of the corporation, dated April 11, 1955.

We pause to note that some of the plaintiff's stock in Mission Development was bought in 1956 and 1959.

In 1960 Tidewater discontinued the practice of distributing stock dividends. In the same year it submitted to its stockholders an exchange offer similar to the one made in 1955, again excluding Getty Oil and Mission.

From September 1960 to and including August 1961 Getty Oil Company acquired 510,200 shares of Mission. Some of these were purchased off the market.

In November 1960 this suit was filed.

As above indicated, plaintiffs seek to compel a complete or partial liquidation of the defendant and the distribution of its assets, either through the medium of a winding-up receivership, or by means of a court order compelling the management to distribute or to offer to distribute, at least part of the Tidewater shares in exchange for Mission shares.

The extreme relief of receivership to wind up a solvent going business is rarely granted. To obtain it there must be a showing of imminent danger of great loss resulting from fraud or mismanagement. Hall v. John S. Isaacs, etc., Inc., Del.Ch., 163 A.2d 288, 293. Like caution is dictated in considering an application to compel a corporation to make a partial distribution.

Since no showing is made of fraud or mismanagement inflicting injury upon the corporation, what is the basis of plaintiff's case?

Plaintiff's argument proceeds as follows:

There is an inherent conflict of interest between the controlling stockholder of Mission, Mr. J. Paul Getty, and the minority stockholders. This arises out of the dividend policy of Tidewater. Because of high income taxes, Mr. Getty, it is said, is not interested in receiving dividends; he is interested in acquiring more shares of Tidewater. To achieve this end, it is charged, he has caused Tidewater to discontinue all dividends and to announce, in 1960, that no dividends could be expected for five years. The necessary effect of this policy, plaintiffs say, was to depress the market value of Mission shares, and enable Mr. Getty to buy more Mission shares at an artificially low price, at the expense of Mission's minority stockholders. This, plaintiffs charge, is just what he has done, as is proved by Getty Oil's purchases of stock in 1960 and 1961. Thus he and Mission have inflicted a serious wrong upon the minority stockholders.

It is quite true that in some cases the interests of a controlling stockholder and of the minority stockholders in respect of the receipt of dividends may conflict, because of the existence of very high income taxes. See Cases and Materials, Baker and Cary, p. 1375. And in some cases this may work hardship on the minority. But we find no such situation here.

It is plain that the whole argument based on a charge of conflict of interest rests upon the claim that Tidewater's dividend policy, and its public announcement of it, were designed to serve the selfish interest of Mr. Getty and not to further its own corporate interests. If the opposite is true—if Tidewater's policy was adopted in furtherance of its own corporate interest—then Mission's stockholders have not been subjected to an actionable wrong and have no complaint. The fact of Mr. Getty's purchase of Mission Development stock then becomes irrelevant.

What does the record show with respect to Tidewater's dividend policy?

In the ten years prior to 1953 Tidewater's expenditure for capital improvements did not exceed $41,100,000 in any one year. Shortly prior to 1954 Tidewater began to expand and modernize its facilities. In February 1955 it closed and subsequently sold its obsolete refinery at Bayonne, New Jersey, and built a new and modern refinery in New Castle County, Delaware at a cost in excess of $200,000,000. Also, it commenced and still continues the expansion and modernization of its refinery facilities at Avon, California, and the increase of its crude oil and natural gas resources. As of November 3, 1960, the budget for new capital projects to be begun in 1961 was $111,000,000.

It is unnecessary to elaborate the point. It is entirely clear from the facts set forth in the affidavits that Tidewater's cash has since 1960 been largely devoted to capital improvements and that, in the opinion of management, funds were not available for dividends. These facts are uncontradicted, and they constitute a refutation of the basic argument of plaintiffs that dividends were discontinued to enable J. Paul Getty to buy Mission stock at a depressed price.

Some point is sought to be made of the unusual action of the Tidewater management in announcing that dividends could not be expected for five years. As defendant's counsel says, this was done out of common fairness to its stockholders and to prospective purchasers of its stock.

It is earnestly argued that plaintiffs should be allowed to go to trial and adduce testimony on the issue of the selfish motives of the controlling stockholder. Plaintiffs say that they could show by expert testimony that the market price of Mission common was artificially depressed.

It is first to be noted that the record of market prices put in by the plaintiffs themselves fails to show any drop in prices coincident with or closely following the announcement of the cessation of dividends. Plaintiffs reply that this fact is meaningless because at that time the market was steadily going up, and say that expert testimony will establish this. The answer to this argument is that if plaintiffs had such proof they should have come forward with it. "In such a situation, a duty is cast upon the plaintiff to disclose evidence which will demonstrate the existence of a genuine issue of fact . . . if summary judgment . . . is to be denied." Frank C. Sparks Co. v. Huber Baking Co., 9 Terry 9, 48 Del. 9, 96 A.2d 456, 459.

There are other facts in this case that support the conclusion above indicated. The sole corporate purpose of Mission is and has been to hold Tidewater stock. Any investor in its shares could readily ascertain this fact. Because of this he knows, or should know, that he is buying for growth and not for income.

Some point is made of the exclusion of Mission from the exchange offers made by Tidewater to its stockholders in 1954 and 1960. Obviously, for Mission Development to have been included in the exchange would have defeated the very purpose of its corporate existence.

However the various arguments are put they come to this: Plaintiffs are in effect seeking to wind up the corporation, either wholly or partially, because it is doing exactly what it was lawfully organized to do.

We think the plaintiffs have failed to make a case.

The judgment below is affirmed.

SINCLAIR OIL CORP. v. LEVIEN

[See Chapter VIII, Section 6, supra]

SMITH v. ATLANTIC PROPERTIES, INC.

See Chapter VI, Section 6(a), supra

KUMMERT, STATE STATUTORY RESTRICTIONS ON FINANCIAL DISTRIBUTIONS BY CORPORATIONS TO SHAREHOLDERS (pt. I)
55 Wash.L.Rev. 359, 365–371, 376–379 (1980)

It is generally assumed that common shareholders seek to maximize their wealth and therefore desire corporate policies that maximize the value of the enterprise and its securities. A critical issue in determining such policies is whether the level of a corporation's dividend payout ratio (*i.e.*, dividends compared to earnings) has any long-run effect upon the value of a corporation's shares. Despite intense study for a number of years, the issue has not yet been definitively resolved.

A clear-cut answer can be obtained if one assumes that perfect capital markets exist in which all investors are rational, information is available to all at no cost, transactions are consummated instantaneously and without cost, new securities may be issued by a corporation without cost, no tax differential between dividends and capital gains exists, each corporation has a stated investment policy, and every investor is certain as to the future investments and profits of the corporation.[29] Under these conditions, shareholder wealth will not be affected by the dividend payout decision;[30] regardless of whether the corporation decides to finance its investments by retaining earnings or by selling new shares after it has distributed its earnings as dividends, total shareholder wealth will be the same.[31]

The effect of relaxing the perfect world assumptions is the subject of some dispute. The framers of the perfect world model argue that even if investors are uncertain as to the future investments and profits of the corporation, dividend policy will remain irrelevant as long as the other assumptions are unchanged because investors have no reason to differentiate between corporations with equal business risk on the basis of their retention ratios.[32] A number of other studies indicate, however, that changes in dividends have an effect upon share prices, apparently because the changes communicate unique information to investors about management's perception of the corporation's future profitability.[33] Other authors argue that investors' risk aversion will lead them to prefer current dividends for two different reasons. The first line of analysis notes that for many corporations dividends per share are stable over time as compared to the corporation's share price. Thus, it is argued that a risk averse investor will prefer a stable source of income to a fluctuating source. The second line of analysis argues that distant events are perceived by investors to present greater risk than near-future events, and that as a result a reduction of current dividends, even if connected with the prospect of increased future dividends, will reduce the corporation's share price because of the perceived increase in risk.

29. The assumptions are those of the seminal work on the effects of dividend policy on the value of a corporation, Miller & Modigliani, *Dividend Policy, Growth, and the Valuation of Shares,* 34 J.Business 411, 412 (1961). They define "perfect capital markets" as those in which no buyer or seller of securities is large enough to have an appreciable impact on price and in which securities are infinitely divisible. "Rational behavior" is defined as preferring more wealth to less and being indifferent to the form of increase in wealth. *Id.*

30. Even the principal proponent of the view that dividend payout affects valuations agrees that the level of payout is irrelevant under the stated assumptions. *See* Gordon, *Optimal Investment and Financing Policy,* 18 J.Finance 264, 265 (1963).

31. The Miller and Modigliani thesis also leads to the conclusion that shareholder wealth is unaffected by the corporation's

decision to finance investment opportunities through the use of debt. *See . . . .* V. Brudney & M. Chirelstein, Cases and Materials on Corporate Finance 438–42 (2d ed. 1979) (providing examples demonstrating that under the stated assumptions the total value of the corporation will be the same regardless of how investments are financed).

32. *See* Miller & Modigliani, *supra* note 29, at 428–29. Lewellen provides examples that demonstrate that if any differences in share prices developed between firms with the same business risk, but pursuing different retention policies, arbitrage would operate to equalize the prices. W. Lewellen, The Cost of Capital 54–57 (1969).

33. A number of empirical studies have concluded that dividend announcements convey information about future earning prospects that could not be obtained from past time series of future earnings. *. . . .*

Relaxation of the other perfect world assumptions leads to distinct preferences by various classes of investors for dividends or retained earnings. . . . The costs that a corporation would incur in connection with a new offering of shares should cause shareholders generally to prefer that the corporation retain earnings rather than distribute them and finance projects with the sale of new shares. This preference will be quite strong for shareholders in any corporation in which access to capital markets is impossible or in which transaction costs would be a large portion of the offering price. When the costs of transferring shares are considered, shareholders will have varying preferences depending on the particular shareholder's need for current funds and the size of any potential dividend. A shareholder who desires current income must, in the face of a corporate decision to retain all earnings, sell shares and pay the brokerage fee on such sale, which may be a sizeable percentage of a small sale. On the other hand, a shareholder who does not wish current income must, absent a dividend reinvestment program, pay brokerage fees to purchase shares with any dividend received. . . .

A corporation attempting to maximize shareholder wealth presumably would empirically determine the balance of shareholder preferences either directly or through a study of the relationship between share price and dividend payout for a sample of similar companies. It would then have to determine whether there is a generally preferred rate of payout for corporations, which if adopted by the subject corporation would increase the value of its shares. A number of empirical studies have been made on this question but they have produced conflicting results. The scope of these studies and their conflicting results suggest, however, that if excess demand for a particular dividend rate exists, it is unlikely that such demand is large or would be permanent. Thus, it would seem inappropriate for any corporation to attempt to shift from a payout policy determined optimal for its particular situation.

Corporations also appear to behave in a manner that is consistent with a belief that stable dividend payments will cause investors to place a higher value on the company's stock. A number of studies indicate that corporations adopt a long run target payout ratio, and that in any given year this payout ratio is applied to some measure of current performance to obtain the target levels for dividends. When current performance is improved over that of prior periods, dividends will be permitted to increase to the target level only if it is felt that the improved performance will be maintained. When current performance has declined compared to that of prior periods, the lag in the dividend adjustment is longer as companies appear reluctant to cut the current dividend. No comprehensive empirical study has yet demonstrated that a policy of dividend stability will lead to higher stock prices than those produced by other dividend policies, but such a policy does appear to satisfy a number of the investor preferences previously discussed. . . .

Although corporate law formally vests the power to formulate the distribution policy for a corporation in its board of directors, a number of recent studies indicate that the critical policymaking functions in most corporations are likely to be performed by the corporation's officers rather than its directors. That fact becomes significant in this context because of the possibility that management may pursue its own goals in formulating a distribution policy for the corporation, and that such goals may not be consistent with maximizing the value of the enterprise. Thus, some authors argue that managers may prefer to retain earnings for relatively unprofitable projects rather than pay them out as distributions because the reinvested funds may lead to advancement of existing managers, hiring of new managers, increased budgets for the growing divisions of the corporation, and other managerial emoluments. Another school of thought argues that managerial control does not result in behavior contrary to shareholder interests for at least three reasons: first, managers will be forced to use the equity capital market for additional funds necessary for expansion, and competition in that market will ensure value-maximizing behavior by the corporation; second, stock options, shares of the corporation owned directly, and insider trading will give managers an incentive to serve shareholder interests; and third, management's fear of takeovers will promote value maximization. Each of these arguments has been rebutted by proponents of the first school of thought. They argue that: (1) a very substantial number of corporations manage to avoid the disciplining influences of the securities or money markets, (2) stock options, shares, and insider trading do not provide the necessary incentive because the required causal connection between an executive's performance and the profitability of the corporation cannot be established in most corporations; and (3) the market for corporate control appears to be highly imperfect and thus management may exercise substantial discretion before a takeover is attempted. Unfortunately, the empirical studies on the question thus far have not produced a definitive answer.

V. BRUDNEY & M. CHIRELSTEIN, CASES AND MATERIALS ON CORPORATE FINANCE 496–97 (3d ed. 1987). "Entirely apart from their more or less direct economic role in relation to retained earnings, dividends are said to have a signaling effect on investors—increase in dividends is said to signal management's favorable expectations about the future profitability of the firm; decrease to signal unfavorable expectations.

"According to Asquith and Mullins, Signalling with Dividends, Repurchases and Equity Issues, pp. 15–16 (1984) (Research Paper 75th Anniversary Colloquium Series Harvard Business School), who conclude that dividend changes have significant informational content:

" 'There are reasons for the efficacy of dividends as signals. Dividend announcements are backed by hard, cold cash. The firm must generate this cash internally or convince the capital markets to supply it. Alternative communications may lack the credibility that comes from saying it with cash. Investors may suspect that statements from management are backed by the ghostwriting of well paid public relations specialists. They may feel that financial statements have been skillfully massaged by the financial staff. In addition, dividend decisions tend to be future oriented as opposed to accounting statements which document past performance.

" 'Besides credibility, dividends also have the advantage of simplicity and visibility. Many other announcements are, at the same time, complex and detailed in focus. They require time and expertise to decipher. In contrast, few investors fail to notice and understand a check in the mail. An empty mailbox is also easily interpreted. As simple numerical signals, dividends facilitate comparative analysis unlike statements by management which may be difficult to calibrate. Simplicity is especially advantageous for investors holding many firms' shares to achieve the benefits of diversification. Further, dividend signals convey information without releasing sensitive details which may be useful to competitors.' "

NOTE

Although directors have discretion whether to *declare* a dividend, once the dividend has been validly declared and announced it assumes the status of a debt which may not be rescinded, and which the shareholder may sue to recover.

NOTE ON DODGE v. FORD MOTOR CO.

One of the most famous of all cases involving judicial review of dividend policy—indeed, one of the most famous of all corporation law cases—is Dodge v. Ford Motor Co., 204 Mich. 459, 170 N.W. 668 (1919), referred to in Miller v. Magline. The case is unusual both in its result—judicial compulsion of an extremely large dividend—and in its early consideration of the issue (or at least one aspect of the issue) that is now known as corporate social responsibility.

Ford had been incorporated in 1903 with a capital of $150,000, and in 1908 the capital was increased to $2 million. Henry Ford owned 58% of Ford's stock and controlled the board; the two Dodge brothers owned 10%, and five other shareholders owned the balance. From 1908 on, Ford Motor had paid a regular annual dividend of $1.2 million, and between December 1911 and October 1915 it paid special dividends totaling $41 million. At the close of its July 31, 1916, fiscal year, Henry Ford, who controlled the board, declared it to be the settled policy of the company not to pay in the future any special dividends, but to put back into the business for the future all of the earnings of the company, other than the regular dividend of $1.2 million. "My ambition," declared Mr. Ford, "is to employ still more men; to spread the benefits of this industrial system to the greatest possible number, to help them build up their lives and their homes. To do this, we are putting the greatest share of our profits back into the business." At the time of the announcement, Ford Motor had a surplus of $112 million, including $52.5 million in cash and $1.3 million in municipal bonds. The Dodge brothers then brought an action, whose objects included compelling a dividend equal to 75% of the accumulated cash surplus, and restraining a proposed expansion of Ford Motor's facilities. The trial court ordered Ford Motor to declare a dividend of $19.3 million—equal to half its cash surplus as of July 31, 1916, minus special dividends paid between the time the complaint was filed and July 31, 1917. The Michigan Supreme Court affirmed this portion of the trial court's decree:

> When plaintiffs made their complaint and demand for further dividends the Ford Motor Company had concluded its most prosperous year of business. The demand for its cars at the price of the preceding year continued. It could make and could market in the year beginning August 1, 1916, more than 500,000 cars. Sales of parts and repairs would necessarily increase. The cost of materials was likely to advance, and perhaps the price of labor, but it reasonably might have expected a profit for the year of upwards of $60,000,000. . . . Considering [the facts of this case] a refusal to declare and pay further dividends appears to be not an exercise of discretion on the part of the directors, but an arbitrary refusal to do what the circumstances required to be done. These facts and others call upon the directors to justify their action, or failure or refusal to act. In justification, the defendants have offered testimony tending to prove, and which does prove, the following facts. [Ford Motor had a general policy to reduce the price of its cars every year while maintaining or improving quality. In June 1915, it adopted a general plan under which it would double productive capacity and also erect a smelter. In furtherance of this plan, the price of cars was not reduced for the year beginning August 1, 1915, so that a large surplus could be accumulated to pay for the expansion. Even without expansion, Ford Motor could have produced 600,000 cars in the year beginning August 1, 1916, and sold them for $440 each. However, the policy of reducing prices called for the cars to be sold at $360 each, a difference of $48 million.]

> The plan, as affecting the profits of the business for the year beginning August 1, 1916, and thereafter, calls for a reduction in the selling price of the cars. . . . In short, the plan does not call for and is not intended to produce immediately a more profitable business but a less profitable one; not only less profitable than formerly but less profitable than it is admitted it might be made. The apparent immediate effect will be to diminish the value of shares and the returns to shareholders.

> It is the contention of plaintiffs that the apparent effect of the plan is intended . . . to continue the corporation henceforth as a semieleemosynary institution and not as a business institution. In support of this contention they point to the attitude and to the expressions of Mr. Henry Ford. . . .

The record, and especially the testimony of Mr. Ford, convinces that he has to some extent the attitude towards shareholders of one who has dispensed and distributed to them large gains and that they should be content to take what he chooses to give. His testimony creates the impression, also, that he thinks the Ford Motor Company has made too much money, has had too large profits, and that although large profits might be still earned, a sharing of them with the public, by reducing the price of the output of the company, ought to be undertaken. We have no doubt that certain sentiments, philanthropic and altruistic, creditable to Mr. Ford, had large influence in determining the policy to be pursued by the Ford Motor Company—the policy which has been herein referred to.

It is said by his counsel that—

"Although a manufacturing corporation cannot engage in humanitarian works as its principal business, the fact that it is organized for profit does not prevent the existence of implied powers to carry on with humanitarian motives such charitable works as are incidental to the main business of the corporation." . . .

The difference between an incidental humanitarian expenditure of corporate funds for the benefit of the employees, like the building of a hospital for their use and the employment of agencies for the betterment of their condition, and a general purpose and plan to benefit mankind at the expense of others, is obvious. There should be no confusion (of which there is evidence) of the duties which Mr. Ford conceives that he and the stockholders owe to the general public and the duties which in law he and his codirectors owe to protesting, minority stockholders. A business corporation is organized and carried on primarily for the profit of the stockholders. The powers of the directors are to be employed for that end. The discretion of directors is to be exercised in the choice of means to attain that end and does not extend to a change in the end itself, to the reduction of profits or to the nondistribution of profits among stockholders in order to devote them to other purposes.

. . . As we have pointed out, and the proposition does not require argument to sustain it, it is not within the lawful powers of a board of directors to shape and conduct the affairs of a corporation for the merely incidental benefit of shareholders and for the primary purpose of benefiting others, and no one will contend that if the avowed purpose of the defendant directors was to sacrifice the interests of shareholders it would not be the duty of the courts to interfere.

We are not, however, persuaded that we should interfere with the proposed expansion of the business of the Ford Motor Company. In view of the fact that the selling price of products may be increased at any time, the ultimate results of the larger business cannot be certainly estimated. The judges are not business experts. . . . We are not satisfied that the alleged motives of the directors, in so far as they are reflected in the conduct of the business, menace the interests of shareholders. It is enough to say, perhaps, that the court of equity is at all times open to complaining shareholders having a just grievance. . . .

SECTION 2. THE REPURCHASE BY A CORPORATION OF ITS OWN STOCK

(a) INTRODUCTION

1. There are a number of reasons—some proper and some not—why a corporation may engage in the repurchase of its own stock. Among the most significant are: supporting the market for the stock; increasing the asset value or earnings per share of remaining stock; enabling the corporation to satisfy stock options, or make acquisitions, without heavily diluting earnings per share; fulfilling a buy-sell agreement on the death of a shareholder; eliminating fractional shares; preventing stock from being transferred to an unwelcome outsider; eliminating a dissident shareholder; reducing the proportion of stock held by the public, so as to shore up the position of those in control; sopping up excess corporate cash and driving up the market price of the stock, so as to make a takeover less attractive; drying up the market for publicly held stock, so as to put pressure on minority shareholders to sell their shares; complying with provisions for appraisal rights; reducing or eliminating an issue of preferred stock that carries an unfavorable dividend rate; changing the capital structure by increasing the debt-equity ratio.

2. As late as 1936 there were American cases following the English rule established by Trevor v. Whitworth, 12 App.Cas. 409 (H.L.1887), and putting into question whether a corporation had power to purchase its own stock. Pace v. Pace Bros. Co., 91 Utah 132, 59 P.2d 1 (1936). Today this question has been made obsolete by statute. Exercise of the repurchase power does, however, remain subject to the fiduciary obligation of directors and controlling shareholders and questions under the Williams Act. Most important for present purposes, the power to purchase own stock, like the power to pay dividends, is subject to financial limitations. At an early period, these limitations were minimal: A corporation was permitted to repurchase its own stock if the repurchase did not render the corporation insolvent, was made "in good faith," and was "without prejudice to the rights of other stockholders or creditors." Under this approach, the fact that a repurchase impaired capital would not in itself render the repurchase invalid or unenforceable. See Herwitz, Installment Repurchase of Stock: Surplus Limitations, 79 Harv.L.Rev. 303, 305 (1965); W. Cary, Cases and Materials on Corporations 1595–96 (4th ed. 1969); Note, Stock Repurchase Abuses and the No

Prejudice Rule, 59 Yale L.J. 1177 (1950). As the power developed, however, the no-prejudice doctrine was replaced by statutory rules assimilating repurchases to dividends. Indeed, in terms of the volume of current cases, the financial limitations imposed on repurchases is a much livelier issue than the financial limitations imposed on dividends.

(b) FINANCIAL LIMITATIONS

N.Y. BUS. CORP. LAW §§ 513, 515, 517

[See Statutory Supplement]

DEL. GEN. CORP. LAW § 160(a)

[See Statutory Supplement]

PA. §§ 1002, 1701, 1708

§ 1002. Definitions

* * *

(20) "Stated Capital" [See Section 1(e), supra]

(24) "Treasury Shares" means shares of a business corporation which have been issued, have been subsequently acquired by and belong to the corporation otherwise than in a fiduciary capacity, and have not, either by reason of the acquisition or thereafter, been cancelled. Treasury shares shall be deemed to be "issued" shares but not "outstanding" shares.

* * *

(27) "Unrestricted" means not restricted by section [1701(E)] of this act.

§ 1701. Right of Corporation to Acquire Its Own Shares

* * *

B. Purchases . . . by a business corporation of its own shares . . . shall not be made except:

(1) In the case of shares which are not subject to redemption—

(i) to the extent of the aggregate of (a) its unrestricted and unreserved earned surplus and (b) as much of its unrestricted capital surplus as has been made available for such purpose by the prior affirmative vote obtained within one year of such purchase of the shareholders of each class entitled to cast at least a majority of the votes which all shareholders of such class are entitled to cast thereon, whether or not entitled to vote thereon by the provisions of the articles. . . .

(4) When it is not insolvent and would not by such purchase . . . be rendered insolvent, and

(5) When such purchase . . . would not reduce the remaining net assets of the corporation below the aggregate preferential amount payable in the event of voluntary liquidation to the holders of shares having rights to the assets of the corporation in the event of liquidation prior or equal to the rights of the holders of the shares . . . purchased. . . .

E. To the extent that earned surplus or capital surplus is used as the measure of a business corporation's right to purchase . . . its own shares, such surplus shall be restricted until the removal of the restriction as hereinafter provided. To the extent that stated capital is so used, surplus thereafter acquired shall be restricted until the removal of the restriction as hereinafter provided. Upon the disposition of any such shares, the restriction shall be removed to the extent of the consideration received therefor, and upon the cancellation thereof to the extent of its stated capital and capital surplus reduced thereby, and any remaining surplus restricted by the purchase thereof shall be eliminated. . . .

§ 1708. Cancellation of Treasury Shares

Whenever any business corporation shall have acquired any treasury shares, it may, by resolution of its board of directors [and approval of the shareholders], cancel any or all of such shares. . . . Such corporation may apply to such cancellation an amount out of its stated capital and capital surplus which shall not be greater than that portion of the stated capital and capital surplus represented by or restricted by the purchase or redemption of such shares at the time of such cancellation, and the stated capital and capital surplus of the corporation shall be reduced to this extent.

REV. MODEL BUS. CORP. ACT § 6.31(a)

[See Statutory Supplement]

CAL. CORP. CODE § 510(a)

[See Statutory Supplement]

NOTE ON FINANCIAL LIMITATIONS AND CONSEQUENCES OF A REPURCHASE BY A CORPORATION OF ITS OWN STOCK

When a corporation purchases shares of its own stock, corporate assets flow out to shareholders. Accordingly, from the perspective of creditors a repurchase of stock is economically indistinguishable from a dividend on stock, and from the perspective of preferred a repurchase of common is economically indistinguishable from a dividend on common. Ideally, therefore, repurchases should be treated like dividends for legal purposes. The California statute and the Revised Model Business Corporation Act do just that, by treating repurchases and dividends together under the heading of "distributions." Most other statutes go a long way toward that end, by providing that (with specified exceptions) a corporation can expend funds to purchase its own stock only if it could pay a dividend in the same amount. However, the treatment of repurchases and dividends is not fully parallel under most statutes, since a dividend irreversibly decreases surplus, while a repurchase may not. This is because under most statutes repurchased stock is known as "Treasury Stock"—i.e., stock held in the corporation's own treasury—and retains the status of issued stock until it is cancelled or disposed of. The rationale of this treatment is that repurchased shares resemble an asset, since they can be resold. (Indeed, at one time treasury stock was frequently shown on the asset side of the balance sheet.[1]) This rationale might make a little sense if a corporation had no capacity to issue any shares unless it first repurchased shares already outstanding. In modern corporations, however, authorized shares normally far exceed issued shares, or can easily be made to do so by certificate amendment, so that a repurchase of its own stock normally enables a corporation to do nothing more than it could have done without the repurchase. Economically, therefore, repurchased shares are no more of an asset than authorized but unissued shares.

In recognition of this economic reality, both the new California statute and the Revised Model Business Corporation Act eliminate the concept of treasury stock, by providing that reacquired shares revert to the status of authorized but unissued stock.[2] The question remains, however, what is the impact of a repurchase on capital and surplus under the more typical statute. The answer to that question depends on several elements, including the terms of the applicable statute, and whether or not the corporation continues to hold the repurchased shares. The balance of this Note will illustrate the basic approaches to the problem by running variations on a basic hypothetical. In this hypothetical, it will be assumed that Corporation C has 1000 shares of $40 par value common outstanding, and that C's capital and surplus accounts are as follows:

(Table I)	Stated Capital	$40,000
	Capital Surplus	$40,000
	Earned Surplus	$20,000
	Equity	$100,000

We will examine first the effects of a repurchase, and next the effects of a cancellation of the repurchased shares. (For ease of exposition, this Note will deal only with par value stock. However, everything

1. ARB 43, ch. 1A and APB Op. No. 6 (1965) still provide that treasury stock may be shown as an asset "in some circumstances," but such a presentation would be highly questionable.

2. Cal. § 510(a); Rev. Model Bus. Corp. Act § 6.31(a).

said in this Note about par value is equally applicable to the stated value of no par stock.)

(1) Effect of the Initial Purchase. Assume first that C purchases 100 of its own $40 par value shares at $120 each, a total cost of $12,000. How must this purchase be accounted for as regards its effect on surplus and capital?

(a) Contraction of Capital technique. At one time, a repurchase of stock was accounted for by the Contraction of Capital technique (sometimes called the Par Value technique). Under this technique the par value of repurchased stock is deducted directly from Stated Capital. If the cost of the repurchased stock exceeds par value, the balance is deducted from Capital Surplus attributable to the repurchased shares (on either a tracing or pro rata basis), and any remaining balance is deducted from Earned Surplus. Thus if C repurchases 100 (10%) of its par value shares for $120 each, under the Contraction of Capital technique it would charge $4000 (100 × $40 par value) to Stated Capital; $4000 (10% of C's $40,000 Capital Surplus) to Capital Surplus; and $4000 (the balance of the purchase price) to Earned Surplus. C's capital and surplus accounts would then be as follows:

(Table II)	Stated Capital (including 100 treasury shares)	$36,000
	Capital Surplus	$36,000
	Earned Surplus	$16,000
	Equity	$88,000

The Contraction of Capital technique is still authorized by APB Op. No. 6 (1965), and accurately reflects the realities of a repurchase, since it treats a repurchase like a reduction of capital.[3] For that very reason, however, this technique is inconsistent with statutes that define stated capital in terms of issued shares, and treat treasury stock as still issued. Furthermore, under this technique a repurchase has no effect on surplus unless the purchase price exceeds par value. Therefore, the technique is also inconsistent with statutory provisions that require surplus to be reduced or restricted by the cost of repurchased stock.

(b) Cost technique. Both of these objections are met by the Cost technique (sometimes called the Unallocated Reduction technique), which is probably the most common modern method to account for a repurchase. Under this technique, the cost of repurchased shares is not deducted from specific capital and surplus accounts, but is instead shown as a floating charge against Equity. Thus if C purchases 100 shares of its common stock at $120 each, under the Cost technique C's balance sheet would continue to show Stated Capital, Capital Surplus, and Earned Surplus at their old amounts, but following these items there would be an unallocated offset of $12,000 Treasury Stock, so that C's capital and surplus accounts would read as follows:

---

3. It is also advocated as the preferred technique by the American Accounting Association (the academic counterpart of the AICPA). See American Accounting Association, Accounting and Reporting Standards for Corporate Financial Statements 7 (1957).

(Table III)	Stated Capital (including 100 treasury shares)		$40,000
	Capital Surplus		$40,000
	Earned Surplus ($12,000 restricted)		$20,000
	Treasury Stock	$12,000	
	Equity		$88,000

In effect, under the Cost technique the precise allocation of the cost of repurchased stock to particular capital and surplus accounts is suspended until the stock is either cancelled or disposed of.

The Cost technique is contemplated, although not explicitly provided for, by Pa. § 1701 and other statutes based on the old Model Act.[4] Under this type of statute, until the treasury stock is cancelled or otherwise disposed of, an amount of Earned Surplus (or Capital Surplus, if that was used as the measuring rod for the purchase) equal to the cost of the stock must be *restricted,* because pending cancellation or disposition of the stock that amount is no longer available for either dividends or further repurchases. Accordingly, while C's Earned Surplus account will remain at $20,000, a caption will show that $12,000 of that amount is restricted,[5] as in Table III.

(c) Reduction of Surplus technique. Still a third method of accounting for a repurchase is the Reduction of Surplus technique. Under this technique the entire cost of the repurchased shares is deducted from Surplus, following the dividend analogy. Under good accounting practice, Earned Surplus should normally be exhausted before Capital Surplus is resorted to. Thus after the purchase of 100 shares for $12,000, C's capital and surplus accounts would read as follows:

(Table IV)	Stated Capital (including 100 treasury shares)	$40,000
	Capital Surplus	$40,000
	Earned Surplus	$ 8,000
	Equity	$88,000

This technique is contemplated by the New York statute under § 513(a) (shares are repurchased "out of" surplus); § 515(c) (a repurchase does not affect stated capital); and § 517(a)(5) (if Earned Surplus was used to make the repurchase, it can be restored on resale).

---

4. These statutes typically define stated capital to include treasury stock, provide that nonredeemable shares may be purchased "to the extent of" rather than "out of" surplus, and provide that upon such a purchase, surplus will be restricted (rather than reduced). See Pa. §§ 1002(20), (24), 1701(B), (E).

5. See Hackney, The Pennsylvania Business Corporation Law Amendments, 19 U.Pitt.L.Rev. 51, 78–79 (1957); Mulford, Corporate Distributions to Shareholders and Other Amendments to the Pennsylvania Business Corporation Law, 106 U.Pa.L.Rev. 536, 552–54 (1958).

(c) INSTALLMENT REPURCHASES

As shown in the preceding Section, for purposes of financial regulation a repurchase by a corporation of its own stock can and should normally be treated like a dividend. There are, however, several important mechanical differences between a dividend and a repurchase, the most important of which are as follows: (i) A dividend is pro rata, while a repurchase may not be. (ii) Accordingly, a dividend treats all shareholders equally, while a repurchase may not. (iii) In the case of a dividend, the shareholder gives up nothing. In the case of a non pro rata repurchase, the shareholder gives up part or all of his relative share in the corporation's equity. (iv) A dividend usually involves a relatively small fraction of a corporation's equity and liquid assets. A repurchase may involve a very significant fraction of equity and liquid assets, particularly in a close corporation and sometimes even in a publicly held corporation. (v) Since dividends normally involve a relatively small fraction of equity and liquid assets, they are normally made payable almost immediately after being declared. In contrast, since repurchases often involve a very significant fraction of a corporation's equity and liquid assets, payment is often made in installments over a period of years.

The following material will examine some of the legal problems arising out of these differences.

NEIMARK v. MEL KRAMER SALES, INC.

Court of Appeals of Wisconsin, 1981.
102 Wis.2d 282, 306 N.W.2d 278.

Before DECKER, C.J., MOSER, P.J., and CANNON, J.

DECKER, Chief Judge.

This appeal questions whether the trial court erred in this shareholder's derivative action by ordering specific performance of a stock redemption agreement upon death of the principal shareholder of defendant corporation. We vacate the judgment and remand with directions.

Plaintiff seeks specific performance of an agreement for the redemption of stock owned by the late Mel Kramer (Kramer), founder and majority shareholder of Mel Kramer Sales, Inc. (MKS). MKS is a closely-held Wisconsin corporation engaged in the business of selling automotive parts and accessories. The interests of the shareholders are:

Shareholder	Number of Shares	Percentage
Mel Kramer/Estate of Mel Kramer	1,020	51
Delores Kramer	200	10
Jack Neimark	580	29
Jerome Sadowsky	200	10

Kramer died on December 5, 1976. On May 9, 1977, Delores Kramer, Kramer's widow, was appointed personal representative of his estate. Delores Kramer is president and a director of MKS. Jack Neimark is vice-president and a director. Directors David Gutkin and Sara Lee Begun are relatives of Delores Kramer.

On June 22, 1976, a stock redemption agreement was executed by MKS and its stockholders. The agreement requires MKS to purchase, and a deceased shareholder's estate to sell, all of the deceased shareholder's stock in MKS at $400 per share, less a specified credit.[1] The agreement also provided Delores Kramer with the option to sell her shares to MKS in the event of Kramer's death.

Under the agreement, Kramer's 1,020 shares were to be redeemed by MKS within thirty days after the appointment of his estate's personal representative, Delores Kramer, in the following manner. The redemption price of $408,000, less a specifically provided $50,000 credit, constituting a net price of $358,000, was to be paid in installments of $100,000 at the closing, and the balance in five consecutive annual installments. The first installment after the closing was to be $43,200, with four remaining installments of $53,700, plus interest at 6%. If Delores Kramer elected to redeem her shares, her stock was to be purchased at the same per-share price payable in two installments of $40,000, on the sixth and seventh anniversaries of the closing, plus interest at 6% after five years.

The agreement provided that the $100,000 payment for Kramer's shares was to be funded by a life insurance policy on Kramer's life. Upon Kramer's death, MKS received the $100,000 proceeds from the life insurance policy, and it was reflected in MKS's retained earnings as of December 31, 1976.

The agreement also provided that if MKS did not have sufficient surplus or retained earnings to purchase the deceased shareholder's stock, the parties would contribute the necessary capital to enable MKS to lawfully redeem the decedent's shares. It was also agreed that the parties would be entitled to specific performance of the agreement.

After Kramer's death, Delores Kramer indicated a reluctance to have MKS redeem the shares owned by her husband's estate. Neimark insisted that MKS redeem the estate's shares, and on May 23, 1977, the board of directors met to consider Neimark's demand.

---

1. The $50,000 credit was funded by a group life insurance policy paid to Kramer's beneficiary.

The MKS attorney who was the author of the stock redemption agreement was present at this meeting and explained to the board that redemption of the stock by MKS would violate sec. 180.385(1), Stats.[2] The board voted 3–1 not to purchase the Kramer estate's shares. Neimark, of course, cast the losing vote.

On November 30, 1978, Neimark commenced an action for specific performance of the 1976 agreement and alternatively, sought monetary damages. The first claim was derivative on behalf of MKS, pursuant to sec. 180.405, Stats.; the second claim was personal.

Subsequently, a third party offered to purchase the business for $1,000,000. Neimark conditioned his approval of the sale on the requirement that Delores Kramer and the Kramer estate receive proceeds equal only to the redemption price of the shares which was substantially less than the tendered per-share price. The defendants counterclaimed in Neimark's action and sought an order declaring that Neimark was entitled to receive only his ratable share of the proceeds of any sale of the business, which denied him the redemption agreement benefits. The trial court dismissed Neimark's personal claim, but ordered specific performance of the stock redemption agreement under the derivative claim. The counterclaim was dismissed.

Defendants present three issues for our consideration:

(1) did the failure to perform the stock redemption agreement cause injury to the corporation sufficient to provide a basis for the shareholder's derivative claim;

(2) did the trial court correctly conclude that MKS could lawfully redeem the estate's shares under secs. 180.385(1), 180.02(11), and 180.02(14), Stats.; and

(3) would specific performance of the redemption agreement be inequitable?

2. Section 180.385(1), Stats., provides:

180.385 Right of corporation to acquire and dispose of its own shares.

(1) Unless otherwise provided in the articles of incorporation, a corporation shall have the right to purchase, take, receive, or otherwise acquire, hold, own, pledge, transfer, or otherwise dispose of its own shares; provided that no such acquisition, directly or indirectly, of its own shares for a consideration other than it own shares of equal or subordinate rank shall be made unless all of the following conditions are met:

(a) At the time of such acquisition the corporation is not and would not thereby be rendered insolvent;

(b) The net assets of the corporation remaining after such acquisition would be not less than the aggregate preferential amount payable in the event of voluntary liquidation to the holders of shares having preferential rights to the assets of the corporation in the event of liquidation; and

(c) 1. Such acquisition is authorized by the articles of incorporation or by the affirmative vote or the written consent of the holders of at least a majority of the outstanding shares of the same class and of each class entitled to equal or prior rank in the distribution of assets in the event of voluntary liquidation; or

2. Such acquisition is authorized by the board of directors and the corporation has unreserved and unrestricted earned surplus equal to the cost of such shares. . . . .

I. INJURY OR WRONG TO MKS

A fundamental requirement of a stockholder's derivative action is an injury or wrong to the corporation. *Shelstad v. Cook,* 77 Wis.2d 547, 553, 253 N.W.2d 517, 521 (1977); *Rose v. Schantz,* 56 Wis.2d 222, 229, 201 N.W.2d 593, 598 (1972). In the context of this case, we view the existence of injury or wrong to MKS as a question of mixed fact and law. The trial court found that the failure of MKS to perform its agreement to redeem the Mel Kramer stock constituted an injury to MKS, because such conduct neglected to take advantage of a $50,000 credit upon the purchase price of the stock, and hazarded the prospect of acquisition of the stock by outsiders. We observe that such omission also sacrificed the utilization of the financial advantage to MKS of acquisition of the stock over a five-year period at a low interest rate.

The trial court's findings are basically grounded upon the terms of the stock redemption agreement. Since that evidence is undisputed and not in conflict with other evidence, we need not accord special deference to those findings. Nonetheless, we are in complete agreement with the trial court's conclusion that failure to perform the agreement resulted in economic injury to the corporation.

II. LAWFULNESS OF REDEMPTION, SECS. 180.385(1) and 180.02(11) and (14), STATS.

Section 180.385(1), Stats., prohibits, *inter alia,* acquisition by a corporation of its own stock if the corporation would thereby be rendered insolvent. "Insolvent" is defined in sec. 180.02(14) as the "inability of a corporation to pay its debts as they become due in the usual course of its business." The purpose of prohibiting own stock acquisition by a corporation if it would thereby be rendered insolvent is to protect the creditors, preferred security holders,[4] and in some cases, common stockholders whose stock is not acquired, from director action which would strip funds from the corporation and create a distributive preference to the stockholder whose stock is acquired.

In the context of this case, we view the question of whether MKS would be rendered insolvent by performance of the stock redemption agreement as a mixed question of law and fact. To the extent that the evidence with respect to factual matters is in conflict, we defer to the factual determination by the trial court unless we find it contrary to the great weight and clear preponderance of the evidence. *Zapuchlak v. Hucal,* 82 Wis.2d 184, 192, 262 N.W.2d 514, 518 (1978).

The trial court's finding of fact, that performance of the stock redemption agreement would not render the corporation insolvent, is supported by ample evidence, and is not contrary to the great weight and clear preponderance of the evidence. The evidence establishes the fact that the corporation had the ability to pay its debts as they became due. In arriving at that conclusion, the trial court is not

---

4. There are no holders of preferred security interests in MKS.

restricted to analyzing the cash and cash-equivalent assets of the corporation. The flow of cash to maintain solvency can be generated by a multitude of means other than cash generated solely from sales.

In this case, MKS had a $275,000 line of credit with a local bank. Its annual financial statements for 1976, 1977, and 1978, and the May 31, 1979, financial statement, disclose no inability of MKS to pay its debts as they became due if the redemption agreement had been performed.

Upon Kramer's death, it became the obligation of MKS to redeem his stock, provided the corporation could comply with sec. 180.385(1), Stats., with respect to solvency. We agree with the trial court's finding of fact that it could. To the extent that the finding also constitutes a conclusion of law, we also agree.

Contrary to the English rule, American courts at common law generally permit a corporation to acquire its own shares.[5] The American rule has undergone harsh criticism because of the opportunity it affords to prefer selected stockholder/sellers and strip funds from the corporation to the disadvantage of preferred security interest holders, other common stockholders, and creditors. The rule sought protection for those persons by vaguely requiring that the purchase be "without prejudice" to their interests. *Steven v. Hale-Haas Corp.,* 249 Wis. 205, 231, 23 N.W.2d 620, 632 (1946); *Koeppler v. Crocker Chair Co.,* 200 Wis. 476, 480–81, 228 N.W. 130, 132 (1930). Additional statutory restrictions resulted and culminated in the two major restraints (for the purposes of this case): the purchase must be made out of earned surplus and cannot be made if insolvency, in the equity sense, is present or would result. "[I]nsolvency in the equity sense has always meant an inability of the debtor to pay his debts as they mature. Under the Bankruptcy Act it means an insufficiency of assets at a fair valuation to pay the debts." *Finn v. Meighan,* 325 U.S. 300, 303, 65 S.Ct. 1147, 1149, 89 L.Ed. 1624 (1945). The surplus and insolvency tests were incorporated in § 6 of the Model Business Corporation Act which formed the basis of the revision of the Wisconsin Business Corporation Law in the early 1950's. Section 180.385, Stats., adopts surplus and insolvency tests. Purchase of shares is permitted if: "At the time of such acquisition the coroporation is not and would not thereby be rendered insolvent." Sec. 180.385(1)(a), Stats.

The self-evident applicability of the insolvency test at the time of acquisition of the stock is not equally self-evident in the case of an installment purchase. Considerations of "corporate flexibility" in the acquisition of its stock for legitimate purposes, balanced by "protection for creditors," led the majority of American courts to apply the

---

5. The cases constituting the American majority rules we have referred to and applied are collected and analyzed in several scholarly and exhaustive treatments of the subject: Hartmann and Wilson, *Payment For Repurchased Shares Under The Texas Business Corporation Act,* 26 Sw.L.J. 725 (1972); Herwitz, *Installment Repur-* *chase of Stock: Surplus Limitations,* 79 Harv.L.Rev. 303 (1965); Kessler, *Share Repurchases Under Modern Corporation Laws,* 28 Fordham L.Rev. 637 (1959–60); Kummert, *The Financial Provisions of the New Washington Business Corporation Act, Part III,* 43 Wash.L.Rev. 337 (1967–68).

insolvency test contemporaneously with each installment payment. The Model Business Corporation Act § 6 has been amended to specifically so provide. Although that specific change has not been incorporated in sec. 180.385(1)(a), Stats., we agree with the reasoning of the majority of American courts that the protection of the corporation's creditors requires that the insolvency limitation be applied both at the time of purchase and when each installment payment is made pursuant to the purchase agreement. When the payment is actually made, the assets leave the corporation and concomitantly the loss of financial protection occurs. If insolvency results or would result, the purchase may constitute a fraudulent conveyance. In any event, the hazard of fraud to creditors is too great to permit the insolvency test to be applied at times remote to payment for the share repurchase.

Section 180.385(1)(a), Stats., recognized the problem inherent in the single application of the insolvency test and achieved flexibility by prohibiting a purchase resulting in a corporation that "is" insolvent or "would . . . be" rendered insolvent. Thus, flexibility is achieved by the statute in its application of the insolvency test to each purchase payment.

When applying the insolvency test at the stage of each payment for a stock repurchase to achieve creditor protection, consistency suggests that the amount of each payment, not the total purchase price, should be a component of the determination of solvency. The weight of authority has so applied the tests and we adopt that method of application. That method is in accord with the equity sense insolvency test expressly prescribed by secs. 180.02(11) and 180.385(1)(a), Stats.

Defendants have not demonstrated insolvency in the equity sense to the trial court or to us. Our review of the corporate financial statements in evidence discloses no arguable claim of insolvency in the equity sense. The only claim of MKS's insolvency made by defendants is premised upon a deduction of the total stock redemption purchase price from the corporate assets, thereby creating a balance sheet negative net worth, although the installment payments of the purchase price are spread over five years. We reject the argument because it applies a bankruptcy rather than equity insolvency test, and is contrary to secs. 180.02(11) and 180.385(1)(a), Stats.[6]

The second limitation upon the corporate repurchase of its stock pertinent to this case is the restriction that "the corporation has unreserved and unrestricted earned surplus equal to the cost of such shares." Sec. 180.385(1)(c)2., Stats.[7] In this respect, the Wisconsin Business Corporation Law generally follows its paradigm, the Model Business Corporation Act. Earned surplus is defined in sec.

6. The modernized corporation statutes of Maryland, North Carolina, and Texas apply a bankruptcy insolvency test in addition to an equity insolvency test.

7. We have assumed the applicability of this section because the corporation exe- cuted the agreement and this action seeks to compel the board of directors to perform the agreement. The agreement itself applies a corporate surplus test.

180.02(11).[8] In this case, the parties do not dispute the amount of earned surplus.

Our review of the record again establishes the following undisputed evidence with respect to paid-up capital stock, retained earnings, and total stockholders' equity.

	12/31 1976	12/31 1977	12/31 1978	5/31 1979
Paid-up Capital Stock	69,400	69,400	69,400	69,400
Retained Earnings	246,409	276,073	317,586	317,584
Current Earnings				31,575
Stockholders' Equity	315,809	345,473	386,986	418,559

We subtract projected payments pursuant to the stock redemption agreement.

Retained and Current Earnings Adjusted to Reflect Deducted Installment Payments	276,073	217,586	205,961
Installment Payments Without Interest [9]	100,000	43,200	53,700
Net Retained Earnings	176,073	174,386	152,261
Credit	50,000		

Historically, the statutory insolvency cutoff test evolved from the "no prejudice to creditors" rule. Dissatisfaction with the limited effectiveness of that test resulted in the formulation of the surplus cutoff test to be applied in conjunction with the insolvency cutoff test.

The same problem arose with the application of the surplus cutoff test that developed in applying the insolvency cutoff test: in the case of an installment purchase, should the surplus test be applied at the time of purchase or at the time cash payment is made? Most cases demonstrate little effort to distinguish between the methods of applying both tests and resolve the question by the easier and more convenient method of applying both tests in the same fashion.

For example, the effect of the Fourth Circuit Court of Appeals' holding in *Mountain State Steel Foundries, Inc. v. Commissioner,* 284 F.2d 737 (1960), was to treat an installment repurchase transaction as if each successive installment constituted an independent purchase transaction by applying the surplus test at the time of each payment. *In re Matthews Construction Co.,* 120 F.Supp. 818 (S.D.Cal.1954), also involved application of the surplus cutoff test and like *Mountain State,* indiscriminately applied the reasoning found in *Robinson v. Wangemann,* 75 F.2d 756 (5th Cir. 1935), that a contract of sale was executory until each payment was made in cash, and therefore applied the surplus cutoff test to each installment payment.

---

8. For the purpose of this case, earned surplus can be considered to be the retained earnings of the corporation.

9. We have not calculated interest on the unpaid balances because it does not significantly affect the determination of insolvency.

Professor Herwitz discusses a number of reasons for applying the surplus to the time of purchase rather than at each installment payment.[10] We agree with his view that the statutory surplus cutoff rule should be applied only once, and at the time of purchase, for the following reasons:

(1) unlike the equity insolvency test, a surplus test does not center upon current liabilities;

(2) unlike the application of the insolvency test, the surplus test is analogous to a purchase for cash and a loan of the unpaid cash price back to the corporation;

(3) installment application of the surplus test could bar performance of a valid obligation of the corporation to the selling stockholder but permit the corporation to disburse funds to current stockholders;

(4) the statutory requirement that surplus be restricted by such a purchase agreement could be frustrated by a construction that would require restriction only on an installment-by-installment basis and permit distributions to shareholders even though the surplus was insufficient to consummate the purchase agreement;

(5) in the manner described in (4), a limited amount of surplus could be used to justify the purchase of an unlimited amount of stock;

(6) when applied to installment payments, the surplus test could be continued indefinitely with current stockholders receiving distributions, putting the selling stockholder in limbo without the status of either creditor or stockholder;

(7) if a default in an installment is compelled by the surplus test, the selling stockholder could possibly obtain a windfall return of all of stock, including the part for which payment had already been made;

(8) a creditor with knowledge of the purchase agreement could be unprotected by installment application of the statutory surplus test limitation, *Atlanta & Walworth Butter & Cheese Ass'n v. Smith,* 141 Wis. 377, 123 N.W. 106 (1909);

(9) if interest has been deducted in computing corporate net income, application of the surplus test upon an installment basis to the interest on the purchase price is unsupportable because it would take interest into account twice;

(10) the unpaid selling stockholder is given no consideration, at least to the extent of undistributed surplus, over the other stockholders who are the beneficiaries of the stock purchase; and

(11) the application of the surplus cutoff test at the outset of an installment purchase would in no way hamper or alter the installment application of the equity insolvency test.

We consider it a futile exercise to attempt to ground our decision upon the subtleties and nuances of semantic lexicography in defining "purchase," "acquisition," and the other acquisitory words of transfer used in the statute. The above reasons persuade us that the application of the surplus cutoff test is required to be timed to the purchase

---

10. *See* note 5, *supra.*

rather than the payment of cash. Such a construction comports with the need for corporate flexibility in acquiring its own stock for legitimate purposes and the protection of creditors and holders of other securities of the corporation.

The Minnesota and Texas Supreme Courts, and the Ninth Circuit Court of Appeals, have taken similar views in *Tracy v. Perkins-Tracy Printing Co.,* 278 Minn. 159, 153 N.W.2d 241 (1967); *Williams v. Nevelow,* 513 S.W.2d 535 (Tex.1974); and *Walsh v. Paterna,* 537 F.2d 329 (9th Cir. 1976). Although differing state statutory formulations were involved, like Wisconsin's, the statutes do not specifically resolve the issues presented there or here.

Although it is apparent from the MKS financial statements that application of the surplus cutoff test upon an installment basis would not have precluded specific performance as ordered by the trial court, application of the test at the outset will preclude specific performance upon the basis of the facts as presented to us. However, we note that the stock redemption agreement provides:

> (f) *Insufficient Corporate Surplus.* If the Corporation does not have sufficient surplus or retained earnings to permit it to lawfully purchase all of such shares, each of the parties shall promptly take such measures as are required to reduce the capital of the Corporation or to take such other steps as may be necessary in order to enable the Corporation to lawfully purchase and pay for the Decedent's shares.

We vacate the judgment of the circuit court and remand for further proceedings consistent with this opinion. The circuit court is directed to apply the surplus cutoff test to the time of specific performance of the stock redemption agreement if it concludes that the evidence justifies specific performance. Because we adopt an application of the statute which has not heretofore been explicated, we think it fair to permit the parties to offer current financial data with respect to MKS and the ability of the parties to the redemption agreement to take the necessary steps to enable the corporation to lawfully purchase and pay for the redeemed stock. Such evidence will enable a current evaluation of the propriety of specific performance. In the event the trial court deems specific performance appropriate, it shall make the necessary findings and requirements with regard to providing sufficient earned surplus and assuring solvency as a condition to specific performance.

We reject the defendants' claim of applicability of the business judgment rule [11] to the facts of this case. That rule accords judicial deference to a business judgment but is generally applicable to acquisition of a corporation's own stock where the board of directors has authorized the acquisition without approval of the stockholders, unlike the present circumstance where all of the stockholders consented and bound themselves to the stock redemption agreement.

---

11. *See, e.g., Steven v. Hale-Haas Corp., supra,* 249 Wis. at 221, 23 N.W.2d at 628.

III. ALLEGED INEQUITY OF SPECIFIC PERFORMANCE OF THE REDEMPTION AGREEMENT

Defendant Delores Kramer claims that enforcement of the stock redemption agreement would be inequitable. We disagree. The requirement of adequate surplus at purchase will provide a restricted surplus account to the extent of the unpaid balance of the purchase price. It is true that she becomes a creditor of the corporation and is subject to the hazard of a business failure. She also received the benefit of a compelled market for her stock, had she *desired* to liquidate her interest in MKS. Her predecessor owner executed the agreement which expressly provided for specific performance. The transaction by its terms made the seller a creditor of the business. Obviously Mel Kramer thought the agreement fairly balanced the corporate obligation to acquire the stock with the owner's opportunity to liquidate an investment in a corporation whose majority stockholder and principal officer had died.

Judgment vacated and cause remanded for further proceedings consistent with this opinion.

BACKGROUND NOTE

1. *Neimark* represents the general rule governing installment payments when the corporation has become insolvent,[1] but a few cases look the other way. In Wolff v. Heidritter Lumber Co., 112 N.J.Eq. 34, 163 A. 140 (Ch.1932), the corporation had agreed to repurchase Poppenga's stock and pay the purchase price in installments. Poppenga was to transfer the shares upon final payment in full, but had the right to re-repurchase the shares "at any time during the continuance of this agreement." After approximately one-third of the installments had been paid the corporation became insolvent, and Poppenga filed a claim against the receivers to recover the balance due. Held, for Poppenga:

> Suppose a corporation with assets of $100,000, debts of $10,000, and outstanding capital stock of $10,000, held in equal amounts by ten stockholders. There could be no objection if that corporation, all stockholders consenting, should reduce its capital stock by purchasing from each stockholder one-half his holdings for $500 per share, since ample assets would be left to pay all creditors; likewise there could be no objection to such a purchase

1. See, e.g., McConnell v. Estate of Butler, 402 F.2d 362 (9th Cir.1968); In re Trimble Co., 339 F.2d 838 (3d Cir.1964), on subsequent appeal 479 F.2d 103 (3d Cir. 1973); Robinson v. Wangemann, 75 F.2d 756 (5th Cir. 1935); Boggs v. Fleming, 66 F.2d 859 (4th Cir.1933); Keith v. Kilmer, 261 Fed. 733 (1st Cir.1920), cert. denied 252 U.S. 578, 40 S.Ct. 344, 64 L.Ed. 725 (for later proceedings in this case involving claimant's right to recover if a surplus remained after the other creditors were paid, see 265 F. 268 (1st Cir.1920); Keith v. Kilmer, 272 Fed. 643 (1st Cir.1921), cert. denied 257 U.S. 639, 42 S.Ct. 51, 66 L.Ed. 410); In re Fechheimer Fishel Co., 212 Fed. 357, 129 C.C.A. 33 (2d Cir.1914), cert. denied 234 U.S. 760, 34 S.Ct. 777, 58 L.Ed. 1580; In re Peoples Loan & Investment Co., 316 F.Supp. 13 (W.D.Ark.1970).

from a single stockholder only, if the other stockholders all consented. And if such a purchase would be valid if the money were then and there paid out of the corporate treasury, it is not perceived why the purchase would be invalidated if the company instead of giving its check in payment gave its note or its other obligation for deferred payment. The contract would be complete; the corporate assets necessary to pay debts would be no differently affected; the corporation's creditors would have no greater right to complain. The stockholder would become a creditor, an unpaid creditor instead of a paid vendor; but the debt due him, being valid then, would not become invalid by reason of the company subsequently becoming insolvent before the date of the debt's maturity. . . .

. . . Both on reason and authority the conclusion seems inescapable that a corporation may . . . instead of paying cash [for its shares], issue its obligation payable at a future date, and that the vendor holding such obligation becomes forthwith a creditor, instead of a stockholder, of the company and entitled to rank equally with other creditors in the event of subsequent insolvency of the company, provided that at the time of the purchase the company has sufficient assets to pay its creditors in full and provided the purchase is not made in disregard of the equitable rights of other stockholders.

2. Some cases hold that the *surplus* test must be met when each installment is payable, Mountain States Steel Foundries, Inc. v. Commissioner, 284 F.2d 737 (4th Cir. 1960), or both when each installment is payable and when the agreement is made. For example, in McConnell v. Estate of Butler, 402 F.2d 362 (9th Cir.1968), the court stated, "[w]ith regard to a corporation repurchasing its own stock from its shareholders, there are two aspects to be considered. First, for the repurchasing agreement to be *valid* the corporation must have an earned surplus to pay for the stock *at the time when the agreement is made.* . . . Second, for the repurchasing agreement to be *enforceable,* the corporation must have an earned surplus *at the time payment is to be made.*" (Emphasis in original.) [2]

3. Kleinberg v. Schwartz, 87 N.J.Super. 216, 208 A.2d 803 (App.Div.), aff'd on opinion below 46 N.J. 2, 214 A.2d 313 (1965), held that installments could not be paid when the corporation lacked sufficient surplus. Thereafter, the New Jersey statute was amended to provide that "A corporation which has purchased its own shares out of surplus may defer payment for such shares over such period as may be agreed between it and the selling shareholder. The obligation so created shall constitute an ordinary debt of the corporation and the validity of any payment made upon the debt so created shall not be affected by the absence of surplus at the time of such payment." N.J. § 14A:7–16(6).

---

2. See also In re Belmetals Mfg. Co., 299 F.Supp. 1290 (N.D.Cal.1969), aff'd sub nom. Eranosian v. England, 437 F.2d 1355 (9th Cir.1971); Cutter Laboratories, Inc. v. Twining, 221 Cal.App.2d 302, 34 Cal.Rptr. 317 (1963); Goodman v. Global Industries, Inc., 80 Cal.App.2d 583, 182 P.2d 300 (1947).

According to the Commissioners' comments:

> Subsection (6) changes existing law as stated in Kleinberg v. Schwartz . . ., and returns to the older New Jersey point of view, expressed in Wolff v. Heidritter Lumber Co., . . . on the status of a former shareholder who has sold out to the corporation on the installment plan. The rejected rule has not been an effective protection for creditors generally, because of the ease with which stated capital may be reduced. It has therefore become a trap for the unwary where corporate procedure has been lax or a weapon for remaining shareholders who seek to avoid a buy-out agreement. In changing the rule, the Commission had in mind the urgent need of participants in a close corporation, whose liquidity may be inadequate for cash purchases, to be able to plan at long-range for their retirement or for their estates without being forced to liquidate the enterprise. Under subsection (6), if a purchase, otherwise lawful, is made out of surplus, any deferred payment obligation may be treated as an ordinary liability and surplus may be charged immediately. So long as the corporation is solvent at the time of payment, the state of the net worth accounts is irrelevant. The effect of insolvency upon the lawfulness of such a payment is considered by the Commission to be the same as in the case of any other debt of the corporation, subject to the application of settled equitable principles, and is not determined by this Act.

REV. MODEL BUS. CORP. ACT § 6.40(e)

[See Statutory Supplement]

CAL. CORP. CODE § 166

[See Statutory Supplement][1]

---

1. Under Cal. § 166, normally each installment under a repurchase agreement must meet the statutory financial tests when it is payable, but the repurchase agreement need not meet these tests when it is made. However, if the corporation issues a negotiable debt security (as defined in UCC § 8–102) in exchange for the repurchased stock, the repurchase agreement must meet the statutory financial tests when it is made, but the installments need not meet the tests when they are payable. According to the statute's principal draftsman, the rationale for the exception is that "[i]n recent years, many corporations have offered to exchange debentures for a certain number of shares of the outstanding common stock of the corporation . . . to give a greater leverage to those shareholders desiring to retain their common stock. It [is] impossible to know at the time of the issuance of such debentures whether. . . . [they] will meet the [statutory] tests at such maturity date. In the meantime, both the debentures and the stock will have been traded in the market and will possibly be in entirely different hands than the persons who owned those securities at the time of the exchange. In this situation, it was believed . . . that the tests should be applied at the date of the exchange so that the corporation could at that time determine whether or not the transaction was legal." 2 H. Marsh, Marsh's California Corporation Law § 13.15 (2d ed. 1987). See also Cal. § 511 ("a negotiable instrument issued by a corporation for the purchase or redemption of shares shall be enforceable by a holder in due course . . . without notice that it was issued for that purpose. . . .")

Chapter XIII

THE ISSUANCE OF SHARES

SECTION 1. SUBSCRIPTIONS FOR SHARES

A subscription agreement is an agreement between a corporation or a corporation to be formed (made on its behalf by incorporators, agents or trustees) and a subscriber, the corporation agreeing to create and to issue shares and the subscriber agreeing to pay for them. Since this is an agreement to issue new shares, it is to be distinguished from either a transaction which involves the transfer of existing, presently owned share interests, or an agreement to subscribe sometime in the future, or an underwriting agreement to place or take shares.[1] Under some modern statutes there is a requirement that the subscriptions (whether before or after incorporation) shall be in writing.[2] If there is a writing, care should be devoted to the drafting of a subscription agreement since carelessness may result in the unenforceability of the agreement. Drafting also may obviate the kind of undesirable judicial handling of litigation in this area which will be discussed presently.

As a practical matter, the law relating to subscriptions is of greatly diminished importance today, and current cases on the subject are rare. Though minimal subscriptions may still be required in some jurisdictions, and promoters may still enter into a subscription agreement at the inception of a business, companies generally are being financed through the outright sale of shares.

DEL. GEN. CORP. LAW §§ 165, 166

[See Statutory Supplement]

REV. MODEL BUS. CORP. ACT § 6.20

[See Statutory Supplement]

---

1. See Stevens, Corporations 385 (1949).

2. See N.Y. § 503(b); Del. § 166. It should be noted that a post-incorporation subscription agreement has been held to be a "sale" and thus within the statute of frauds and the corresponding provisions of the Uniform Commercial Code. See Cooper v. Vitraco, Inc., 320 F.Supp. 239 (D.Virgin Islands 1970).

SECTION 2.   PROMOTERS' LIABILITY—A CORPORATE CAUSE OF ACTION

NOTE ON PROMOTERS' LIABILITY TO THE CORPORATION FOR SALE OF PROPERTY TO THE CORPORATION AT AN INFLATED PRICE

Suppose a promoter sells property to a newly formed corporation, in exchange for stock in the corporation, at an overvalued price, and then, as part of his plan, causes the corporation to issue shares to the public at a price reflecting the overvaluation of its property. By hypothesis, the corporate balance sheet is inflated. Accordingly, each individual shareholder might sue at common law for the fraud on him. Prior to the securities acts, however, it was an important and disputed question whether the corporation could sue the promoter at common law, and thereby in effect recover, in a single action, for the wrong done to all the public shareholders. In Old Dominion Copper Mining & Smelting Co. v. Lewisohn, 210 U.S. 206, 28 S.Ct. 634, 52 L.Ed. 1025 (1908), the Supreme Court, in an opinion by Mr. Justice Holmes, held that the corporation could not bring suit, reasoning as follows: When the promoter sold the property to the corporation he was the sole shareholder. Therefore, all the shareholders at the time of the transaction had given their consent, so the corporation could not have sued at that point. The corporation's rights could not be increased by the subsequent enlargement of its membership. The majority rule, however, was represented by Old Dominion Copper Mining & Smelting Co. v. Bigelow, 203 Mass. 159, 89 N.E. 193 (1909), which held that the corporation could bring suit in such a case:

> . . . The fiduciary relation must in reason continue until the promoter has completely established according to his plan the being which he has undertaken to create. His liability must be commensurate with the scheme of promotion on which he has embarked. If the plan contemplates merely the organization of the corporation his duties may end there. But if the scheme is more ambitious and includes beside the incorporation, not only the conveyance to it of property but the procurement of a working capital in cash from the public, then the obligation of faithfulness stretches to the length of the plan. It would be a vain thing for the law to say that the promoter is a trustee subject to all the stringent liabilities which inhere in that character and at the same time say that, at any period during his trusteeship and long before an essential part of it was executed or his general duty as such ended, he could by changing for a moment the cloak of the promoter for that of director or stockholder, by his own act alone, absolve himself from all past, present or future liability in his capacity as promoter.

Today, the securities acts have rendered the issue almost moot. For one thing, it has been held that the corporation in such a case has an action under Rule 10b–5 even if it does not have an action under state law. See Miller v. San Sebastian Gold Mines, Inc., 540 F.2d 807 (5th Cir.1976). For another, the extensive disclosure requirements of the Securities Act of 1933 and the state Blue Sky laws, and the liabilities under those statutes, have severely limited the ability of a promoter to profit through a corporate sale of stock at a price based on an overvaluation of the property that the promoter transferred to the corporation.

SECTION 3. WATERED, BONUS, AND DISCOUNT SHARES—A LIABILITY WHICH CAN ALWAYS BE AVOIDED

As recently as the beginning of this century, shares of stock had to carry a par value. After 1850, it became quite usual for statutes to provide that shares might be issued for property or for services. Still, for the most part, the statutes were silent as to the legal consequences of an agreement on the part of the corporation to take less than par value in full discharge of the obligation of a subscriber or shareholder. Such agreements were frequently made, even though the medium of such payment as was made was money, and thus arose the institution of *"discount"* shares. In many other instances, where the medium of payment was property or services, overvaluations were used and the total par value of shares issued exceeded the true or fair value of the property or services, and thus arose the institution of *"watered"* shares. In a smaller number of cases, par value shares were simply issued for nothing, either given or promised, but purporting to be full paid, and thus arose the institution of *"bonus"* shares.

As a practical matter liability upon watered stock (including bonus and discount stock as well) has become much less significant by reason of two fairly recent developments: (1) the disclosure requirements of the Securities Act of 1933,[1] and (2) the developing use of no-par shares and, more recently, low-par shares. The problems of liability, however, are still of some concern in the case of old issues of securities and of small issues not subject to federal regulation, where the careless practitioner has failed to recognize the problem at all.

Watered stock liability can always be avoided by competent counsel far-sighted enough to use shares having a very low par.

---

1. These disclosure requirements have had a similar impact upon promoters' liability: see Section 2, supra. See also The Public Distribution of Securities, Chapter 13.

(a) TYPES OF CONSIDERATION FOR WHICH STOCK MAY BE VALIDLY ISSUED

DEL. GEN. CORP. LAW §§ 152, 153

[See Statutory Supplement]

REV. MODEL BUS. CORP. ACT §§ 6.20, 6.21, 6.22(a)

[See Statutory Supplement]

NOTE

According to Bonbright:[2]

"If the law were to recognize nothing but cash received as a valid consideration for a stock issue, problems of valuation would seldom arise under the laws against stock watering. In fact, however, Anglo–American corporation law permits the issuance of stock for other forms of property and for services. In the language of the New York statute, which is typical, 'No corporation shall issue either shares of stock or bonds, except for money, labor done or property actually received for the use and lawful purposes of such corporation.' Whenever promoters take advantage of this opportunity to issue stock either for property or for services, which they almost invariably do whenever they wish to indulge in stock watering, a problem of valuation arises."

An example of the New York attitude is contained in the case of Brown v. Watson[3] where the trustees in bankruptcy sued to recover the par value of stock allegedly issued without legal consideration. Here an engineer, having a lucrative practice and promising position, left his job to join a new company (a management consulting firm) and received as compensation, pursuant to a directors' resolution, Class A stock "which presently has no value." The lower court, though recognizing that an executory contract to perform services was invalid consideration, nevertheless emphasized that this was not only an undertaking to leave his employment, but also to enter new employment in a risk venture. It therefore concluded (124 N.Y.S.2d at 506): "This, it is true, was intangible, yet this decision to go with the corporation was very much in the nature of giving or bringing good will to the corporation as well as the special skills of these defendants, and as such was property within the contemplation of the act." The Appellate Division, however, brusquely swept aside the

---

2. Valuation of Property (1937) Vol. 2 at pp. 795–796. Bonbright's analysis is based on David L. Dodd, Stock Watering— The Judicial Valuation of Property for Stock Issue Purposes (N.Y.1930). See also 55 Harv.L.Rev. 1365 (1942); 37 A.L.R.2d 913 (1954).

3. 124 N.Y.S.2d 504 (S.Ct.Sp.T.1953), modified in part and rev'd in part 285 App. Div. 587, 139 N.Y.S.2d 628 (1st Dept.1955).

lower court in the following language (139 N.Y.S.2d at 630): "While it may be said that special knowledge, experience and contacts in a particular field is something of value, nevertheless, it may not be considered as 'property' within the meaning of Section 69. To broaden the section so as to include peculiar knowledge and experience as valid consideration for the issuance of stock would undermine present law. . . ." [4]

There has been some movement away from the strict rule. Mich. § 450.1315(1) now refers to services "performed or to be performed," and Virginia § 13.1–643 ("contracts for services to be performed") followed, on the theory that elimination of the ban on future services will provide more attractive inducements by a corporation to individuals possessing needed skills. See 61 Va.L.Rev. 1650, 1661 (1975).

(b) BASES OF LIABILITY

B. MANNING, A CONCISE TEXTBOOK ON LEGAL CAPITAL 46 (2d ed. 1981). "Justice Story in his landmark opinion in Wood v. Dummer [30 Fed.Cas. 435 (No. 17,944) (C.C.D.Me.1824)] said that shareholders are not permitted to take their assets out of a corporation, thus rendering the company insolvent, because the shareholders' equity (the 'capital stock') is in the nature of a 'trust fund' for creditors. Later creditors' lawyers and courts took up the term 'trust fund' and sought to build from it a basis for a judicial remedy requiring shareholders to pay assets into the corporation to the extent of the par value of their shares.

"Though one still hears occasional reference to the 'trust fund' theory, the idea spawns an inconsistent and unsatisfactory jumble of case law. . . .

"In 1892 the Supreme Court of Minnesota in Hospes v. Northwestern Mfg. & Car Co. boldly announced that the 'trust fund' theory was a shambles. . . ."

HOSPES v. NORTHWESTERN MFG. & CAR CO.

Supreme Court of Minnesota, 1892.
48 Minn. 174, 50 N.W. 1117, 15 L.R.A. 470.

MITCHELL, J. This appeal is from an order overruling a demurrer to the so-called "supplemental complaint" of the Minnesota Thresher Manufacturing Company. . . .

The Minnesota Thresher Manufacturing Company, a corporation organized in November, 1884, as creditor, became a party to the

---

4. Note that the good will of a business has been held to be "property" and therefore valid consideration for the issue of shares under the New York statute. See Washburn v. National Wall–Paper Co., 81 Fed. 17 (2d Cir.1897). See also Norton v. Digital Applications, Inc., 305 A.2d 656 (Del.Ch.1973).

sequestration proceeding, and proved its claims against the insolvent corporation. In October, 1889, in behalf of itself and all other creditors who have exhibited their claims, it filed this complaint against certain stockholders (these appellants) of the car company, in pursuance of an order of court allowing it to do so, and requiring those thus impleaded to appear and answer the complaint. The object is to recover from these stockholders the amount of certain stocks held by them, but alleged never to have been paid for. . . .

Briefly stated, the allegations of the complaint are that on May 10, 1882, Seymour, Sabin & Co. owned property of the value of several million dollars, and a business then supposed to be profitable. That, in order to continue and enlarge this business, the parties interested in Seymour, Sabin & Co., with others, organized the car company, to which was sold the greater part of the assets of Seymour, Sabin & Co., at a valuation of $2,267,000, in payment of which there were issued to Seymour, Sabin & Co. shares of the preferred stock of the car company of the par value of $2,267,000, it being then and there agreed by both parties that this stock was in full payment of the property thus purchased.

It is further alleged that the stockholders of Seymour, Sabin & Co., and the other persons who had agreed to become stockholders in the car company, were then desirous of issuing to themselves, and obtaining for their own benefit, a large amount of common stock of the car company, "without paying therefor, and without incurring any liability thereon or to pay therefor;" and for that purpose, and "in order to evade and set at naught the laws of this state," they caused Seymour, Sabin & Co. to subscribe for and agree to take common stock of the car company of the par value of $1,500,000. That Seymour, Sabin & Co. thereupon subscribed for that amount of the common stock, but never paid therefor any consideration whatever, either in money or property. . . . That it was . . . given by the car company and received by these parties entirely "gratuitously." The car company was, at this time, free from debt, but afterwards became indebted to various persons for about $3,000,000.

The thresher company, incorporated after the insolvency and receivership of the car company, for the purpose of securing possession of its assets, property, and business, and therewith engaging in and continuing the same kind of manufacturing, prior to October 27, 1887, purchased and became the owner of unsecured claims against the car company, "bona fide, and for a valuable consideration," to the aggregate amount of $1,703,000. As creditor, standing on the purchase of these debts, which were contracted after the issue of this "bonus" stock, the thresher company files this complaint to recover the par value of the stock as never having been paid for. . . .

. . . The thresher company . . . plants itself upon the so-called "trust fund" doctrine. . . .

The phrase that "the capital of a corporation constitutes a trust fund for the benefit of creditors" is misleading. [Ed.: Discussion of the "trust fund" doctrine is omitted.]

Another proposition which we think must be sound is that creditors cannot recover on the ground of contract when the corporation could not. Their right to recover in such cases must rest on the ground that the acts of the stockholders with reference to the corporate capital constitutes a fraud on their rights. We have here a case where the contract between the corporation and the takers of the shares was specific that the shares should not be paid for. Therefore, unlike many of the cases cited, there is no ground for implying a promise to pay for them. The parties have explicitly agreed that there shall be no such implication, by agreeing that the stock shall not be paid for.

It is well settled that an equity in favor of a creditor does not arise absolutely and in every case to have the holder of "bonus" stock pay for it contrary to his actual contract with the corporation. Thus no such equity exists in favor of one whose debt was contracted prior to the issue, since he could not have trusted the company upon the faith of such stock. . . . It does not exist in favor of a subsequent creditor who has dealt with the corporation with full knowledge of the arrangement by which the "bonus" stock was issued, for a man cannot be defrauded by that which he knows when he acts. First Nat. Bank v. Gustin, etc., Mining Co., supra. It has also been held not to exist where stock has been issued and turned out at its full market value to pay corporate debts. Clark v. Bever, supra. The same has been held to be the case where an active corporation, whose original capital has been impaired, for the purpose of recuperating itself issues new stock, and sells it on the market for the best price obtainable, but for less than par (Handley v. Stutz, supra); although it is difficult to perceive, in the absence of a statute authorizing such a thing, (of which every one dealing with the corporations is bound to take notice) any difference between the original stock of a new corporation and additional stock issued by a "going concern."

It is difficult, if not impossible, to explain or reconcile these cases upon the "trust-fund" doctrine, or, in the light of them, to predicate the liability of the stockholder upon that doctrine.

But by putting it upon the ground of fraud, and applying the old and familiar rules of law on that subject to the peculiar nature of a corporation and the relation which its stockholders bear to it and to the public, we have at once rational and logical ground on which to stand. The capital of a corporation is the basis of its credit. It is a substitute for the individual liability of those who own its stock. People deal with it and give it credit on the faith of it. They have a right to assume that it has paid-in capital to the amount which it represents itself as having; and if they give it credit on the faith of that representation, and if the representation is false, it is a fraud upon them; and, in case the corporation becomes insolvent, the law, upon the plainest principles of common justice, says to the delinquent stockholder, "Make that representation good by paying for your stock."

It certainly cannot require the invention of any new doctrine in order to enforce so familiar a rule of equity. It is the misrepresentation of fact in stating the amount of capital to be greater than it really is that is the true basis of the liability of the stockholder in such cases; and it follows that it is only those creditors who have relied, or who can fairly be presumed to have relied, upon the professed amount of capital, in whose favor the law will recognize and enforce an equity against the holders of "bonus" stock. This furnishes a rational and uniform rule, to which familiar principles are easily applied, and which frees the subject from many of the difficulties and apparent inconsistencies into which the "trust-fund" doctrine has involved it; and we think that, even when the trust-fund doctrine has been invoked, the decision in almost every well-considered case is readily referable to such a rule.

It is urged, however, that, if fraud be the basis of the stockholders' liability in such cases, the creditor should affirmatively allege that he believed that the bonus stock had been paid for, and represented so much actual capital, and that he gave credit to the corporation on the faith of it; and it is also argued that, while there may be a presumption to that effect in the case of a subsequent creditor, this is a mere presumption of fact, and that in pleadings no presumptions of fact are indulged in.

This position is very plausible, and at first sight would seem to have much force; but we think it is unsound. Certainly any such rule of pleading or proof would work very inequitably in practice. Inasmuch as the capital of a corporation is the basis of its credit, its financial standing and reputation in the community has its source in, and is founded upon, the amount of its professed and supposed capital, and every one who deals with it does so upon the faith of that standing and reputation, although, as a matter of fact, he may have no personal knowledge of the amount of its professed capital, and in a majority of cases knows nothing about the shares of stock held by any particular stockholder, or, if so, what was paid for them.

Hence, in a suit by such creditor against the holders of "bonus" stock, he could not truthfully allege, and could not affirmatively prove, that he believed that the defendants' stock had been paid for, and that he gave the corporation credit on the faith of it, although, as a matter of fact, he actually gave the credit on the faith of the financial standing of the corporation, which was based upon its apparent and professed amount of capital. The misrepresentation as to the amount of capital would operate as a fraud on such a creditor as fully and effectually as if he had personal knowledge of the existence of the defendants' stock, and believed it to have been paid for when he gave the credit. For this reason, among others, we think that all that it is necessary to allege or prove in that regard is that the plaintiff is a subsequent creditor; and that, if the fact was that he dealt with the corporation with knowledge of the arrangement by which the "bonus" stock was issued, this is a matter of defense. Gogebic Inv. Co. v. Iron Chief Min. Co., 78 Wis. 427, 47 N.W. 726. Counsel cites Fogg v. Blair, supra, to the proposition that the complaint should have stated that this stock had some value; but that case is not in point, for the plaintiff there was a prior creditor; and, as his debt could not have been contracted on the faith of stock not then issued, he could only maintain his action, if at all, by alleging that the corporation parted with something of value. . . .

Order reversed.

NOTE ON ADOPTION AND CONTENT OF "HOLDING OUT" THEORY OF LIABILITY

In *Hospes*, Justice Mitchell took the problem out from under the trust fund doctrine, and voiced it in terms of tort, or representation. He thereby sought to avoid the difficulties concerning (a) a trust which did not exist and for which there was at least trouble in finding a present res where by hypothesis none had ever been created, and concerning (b) a contract where the only contract was that there was no more to be paid.

The analytical background thus newly put forward by Justice Mitchell was widely approved and adopted. Even where there were statutes of various kinds, especially statutes relating to proceedings by or for creditors against shareholders as to unpaid portions of their holdings, the holding out theory was freely read into these statutes in cases where the challenged shares had purported to be fully paid, and there was no contract basis upon which to sustain the creditors' proceeding. The result seems to be that, except in a few states, the doctrine of the *Hospes* case governs the creditor cases.

The approach taken by the *Hospes* opinion has been severely criticized by Ballantine, Stockholders' Liability in Minnesota, 7 Minn. L.Rev. 79, at 89 (1922):

> It is submitted that the constructive fraud doctrine, as laid down in the Hospes case and the subsequent Minnesota cases, is no more sound or satisfactory as a basis for the stockholders' liability than the trust fund doctrine. In the first place the stockholder, by accepting a certificate of watered stock doesn't make any actual representation to the creditor that he has paid for the stock in full and it seems difficult to convict him of having participated in any. As a general thing the creditor doesn't know how much of the authorized capital stock has been actually issued.

> In the second place it seems a pure fiction to say, as Morawetz and many courts have said, that the amount of capital stock is fixed for the purpose of obtaining commercial credit by indicating to the community what security has been provided for those who deal with the corporation. . . .

> Various writers on non-par stock have clearly pointed out that in a business reality the amount of outstanding stock purporting to be fully paid up affects the question of corporate credit very little, if at all. The time has gone by, if it ever existed,

when creditors rely on the professed capitalization rather than upon the real financial condition in extending credit.

The fictitious basis of this fraud doctrine clearly appears when we find that the supposed reliance of the creditor is *presumed* and that public policy requires that the fact whether a particular creditor did or did not trust the corporation on that basis should not be inquired into. It is apparent from this that the rule is really based upon reasons of convenience, public policy, and practical justice and that the supposed fraud is fraud in law or imaginary fraud rather than actual fraud. In other words it is merely a name for something else. . . .

BING CROSBY MINUTE MAID CORP. v. EATON

Supreme Court of California, 1956.
46 Cal.2d 484, 297 P.2d 5.

SHENK, Justice. The plaintiff appeals from an order granting a new trial after judgment in its favor. The defendant appeals from the judgment.

As a judgment creditor of a corporation the plaintiff brought this action against a shareholder of the corporation to recover the difference between the par value of stock issued to him and the fair value of the consideration he paid for the stock. At the conclusion of the trial, the court, sitting without a jury, made findings of fact and conclusions of law and entered judgment for the plaintiff. In support of his motion for a new trial the defendant assigned certain alleged defects in the findings as errors of law.

The defendant formed a corporation to acquire his going frozen foods business. The Commissioner of Corporations issued a permit authorizing the corporation to sell and issue not more than 4,500 shares of $10 par value stock to the defendant and other named individuals in consideration of the transfer of the business. The permit provided that 1,022 shares be deposited in escrow and not be transferred without the written consent of the Commissioner, and that the escrowed shares not be sold or issued until the prospective shareholders named in the permit waived certain rights to dividends and to participation in any distribution of assets.

The defendant transferred his business to the corporation. The corporation placed 1,022 shares in escrow in his name pursuant to the provisions of the permit. The remaining 3,478 shares were issued outright to the defendant and after three years were transferred to the other persons named in the permit. Although the 1,022 shares were listed on the corporate records as held by the defendant (accompanied by the notation "escrowed"), they were never released from escrow. The corporation had financial difficulties and executed an assignment of its assets for the benefit of creditors to a credit association. The plaintiff recovered a judgment against the corporation for $21,246.42. A writ of execution on the judgment was returned unsatisfied.

The trial court found that the value to the corporation of the consideration from the defendant was $34,780.83; that 4,500 shares of stock having a par value of $10 each were issued to the defendant and he became the owner of those shares; that subsequent to the issue of the shares the corporation purchased merchandise from the plaintiff and has not yet paid for all of it; that some $15,000 of the judgment the plaintiff recovered from the corporation remains unsatisfied, and that the corporation is insolvent.

The judgment for the plaintiff was for $10,219.17—approximately the par value of the 1,022 shares of stock placed in escrow. The judgment was based on the trial court's conclusion that the defendant was liable for the difference between the par value of the 4,500 shares and the value of the consideration the defendant paid for them.

The plaintiff contends that the trial court's findings of fact were supported by the evidence and required a judgment in its favor, and therefore that it was error to grant a new trial. The defendant contends that the order granting a new trial was proper because (1) the finding that he was the owner of 4,500 shares was unsupported by the evidence, and (2) the trial court failed to make a finding on a material issue raised by his answer.

In this state a shareholder is ordinarily not personally liable for the debts of the corporation; he undertakes only the risk that his shares may become worthless. See repeal of Cal.Const. art. XII, § 3, at general election, Nov. 4, 1930; repeal of former Civ.Code section 322, Stats.1931, ch. 257, p. 444; Kaysser v. McNaughton, 6 Cal.2d 248, 251–255, 57 P.2d 927. There are, however, certain exceptions to this rule of limited liability. For example, a subscriber to shares who pays in only part of what he agreed to pay is liable to creditors for the balance. Corp.Code, §§ 1300, 1306. Although the trial court in the present case found that the defendant had agreed to pay par value for the 4,500 shares registered in his name, the record on appeal discloses no evidence supporting this finding. Therefore, the defendant's liability cannot be predicated upon the theory that a subscribing shareholder is liable for the full consideration agreed to be paid for the shares.

The plaintiff seeks to base its recovery on the only other exception to the limited liability rule that the record could support, namely, liability for holding watered stock, which is stock issued in return for properties or services worth less than its par value. Accordingly, this case calls for an analysis of the rights of a creditor of an insolvent corporation against a holder of watered stock. Holders of watered stock are generally held liable to the corporation's creditors for the difference between the par value of the stock and the amount paid in.

The defendant's first contention is that because of the escrow he never became an owner of the 1,022 shares and that he therefore never acquired such title to the 1,022 shares as would enable a creditor to proceed against him for their par value. Section 25508 of the Corporations Code authorizes the Commissioner of Corporations to require that shares be placed in escrow. This authority has frequently been exercised for the protection of the public. . . .

. . . [T]he escrow did not affect the rights of future creditors and it would appear that despite the escrow the defendant acquired sufficient title to the 1,022 shares to permit the plaintiff to proceed against him for their par value.

The defendant's second contention is that the trial court failed to make a finding on a material issue raised by his answer.

The liability of a holder of watered stock has been based on one of two theories: the misrepresentation theory or the statutory obligation theory. The misrepresentation theory is the one accepted in most jurisdictions. The courts view the issue of watered stock as a misrepresentation of the corporation's capital. Creditors who rely on this misrepresentation are entitled to recover the "water" from the holders of the watered shares. . . .

Statutes expressly prohibiting watered stock are commonplace today. See statutes collected in 11 Fletcher, Cyclopedia of the Law of Private Corporations, rev. and perm. ed. 1932, sec. 5209. In some jurisdictions where they have been enacted, the statutory obligation theory has been applied. See cases collected in 7 A.L.R. 983–986; Dodd and Baker, Cases and Materials on Corporations, 2d ed. 1951, p. 795, n. 7. Under that theory the holder of watered stock is held responsible to creditors whether or not they have relied on an overvaluation of corporate capital.

In his answer the defendant alleged that in extending credit to the corporation the plaintiff did not rely on the par value of the shares issued, but only on independent investigation and reports as to the corporation's current cash position, its physical assets and its business experience. At the trial the plaintiff's district manager admitted that during the period when the plaintiff extended credit to the corporation, (1) the district manager believed that the original capital of the corporation amounted to only $25,000, and (2) the only financial statement of the corporation that the plaintiff ever saw showed a capital stock account of less than $33,000. These admissions would be sufficient to support a finding that the plaintiff did not rely on any misrepresentation arising out of the issuance of watered stock. The court made no finding on the issue of reliance. If the misrepresentation theory prevails in California, that issue was material and the defendant was entitled to a finding thereon. Code Civ.Proc. § 632; see Edgar v. Hitch, 46 Cal.2d 309, 312, 294 P.2d 3, 5. If the statutory obligation theory prevails, the fact that the plaintiff did not rely on any misrepresentation arising out of the issuance of watered stock is irrelevant and accordingly a finding on the issue of reliance would be surpulsage.

It is therefore necessary to determine which theory prevails in this state. The plaintiff concedes that before the enactment of section 1110 of the Corporations Code (originally Civ.Code, § 299) in 1931, the misrepresentation theory was the only one available to creditors seeking to recover from holders of watered stock. See Clark v.

Tompkins, 205 Cal. 373, 270 P. 946; Spencer v. Anderson, 193 Cal. 1, 6, 222 P. 355, 35 A.L.R. 822; Rhode v. Dock–Hop Co., 184 Cal. 367, 194 P. 11, 12 A.L.R. 437. However, he contends that the enactment of that section reflected a legislative intent to impose on the holders of watered stock a statutory obligation to creditors to make good the "water." Section 1110 provides that "The value of the consideration to be received by a corporation for the issue of shares having par value shall be at least equal to the par value thereof, except that: (a) A corporation may issue par value shares, as fully paid up, at less than par, if the board of directors determines that such shares cannot be sold at par. . . ." The statute does not expressly impose an obligation to creditors. Most jurisdictions having similar statutes have applied the misrepresentation theory obviously on the ground that creditors are sufficiently protected against stock watering schemes under that theory. . . . In view of the cases in this state prior to 1931 adopting the misrepresentation theory, it is reasonable to assume that the Legislature would have used clear language expressing an intent to broaden the basis of liability of holders of watered stock had it entertained such an intention. In this state the liability of a holder of watered stock may only be based on the misrepresentation theory.

The plaintiff contends that even under the misrepresentation theory a creditor's reliance on the misrepresentation arising out of the issuance of watered stock should be conclusively presumed. This contention is without substantial merit. If it should prevail, the misrepresentation theory and the statutory obligation theory would be essentially identical. This court has held that under the misrepresentation theory a person who extended credit to a corporation (1) before the watered stock was issued, Clark v. Tompkins, supra, 205 Cal. 373, 270 P. 946, or (2) with full knowledge that watered stock was outstanding . . . cannot recover from the holders of the watered stock. These decisions indicate that under the misrepresentation theory reliance by the creditor is a prerequisite to the liability of a holder of watered stock. The trial court was therefore justified in ordering a new trial because of the absence of a finding on that issue. It is unnecessary to further consider the defendant's appeal from the judgment.

The order granting the new trial is affirmed. The appeal from the judgment is dismissed.

GIBSON, C.J., and CARTER, TRAYNOR, SCHAUER, SPENCE and McCOMB, JJ., concur.

(c) VALUATION OF PROPERTY AND SERVICES

1. After having considered what constitutes valid consideration under the statute, and the alternative theories of liability, there is the further problem of determining the value of the property received as of the time when the stock was issued. Most of the cases today center

around the interpretation of a provision like that of Delaware § 152, cited earlier, "In the absence of actual fraud in the transaction, the judgment of the directors as to the value of such consideration shall be conclusive."

2. In the earlier cases there were said to be two rules governing the valuation upon which stock of a corporation may be issued as fully paid: 1) the true value rule and 2) the good faith test. Clinton Mining & Mineral Co. v. Jamison, 256 Fed. 577 (3d Cir.1919). It is doubtful whether the former has any vitality today.

The "good faith" or "absence of fraud" (or "of bad faith") rule is adopted in many states as a standard by which to test the defensibility of a valuation of property or services for which shares are given. In many statutes, this rule is confirmed by the "absence of fraud" or "of actual fraud" clause referred to above (see Del. § 152). Under this test, there is divergency in results and also in approved charges to juries. In some cases, actual intent to defraud (usually as an intent directed towards creditors) is required or emphasized.

In other cases, the required good faith, or at least absence of bad faith, is given a more intimate and direct connection with the task of appraising the property or services. An objective test is often applied, with allowance for errors of judgment (particularly so, since the subject-matter frequently has no readily ascertainable market value). The view seems to be that the legislature has entrusted semi-official power to directors in making appraisals for this purpose, and that therefore they owe an allegiance to the "law" in exercising them. Accordingly, conscious overvaluation is sufficient to condemn the transaction, without reference to intent to defraud creditors or even investors. Elyton Land Co. v. Birmingham Warehouse & Elevator Co., 92 Ala. 407, 9 So. 129, 12 L.R.A. 307 (1890); Whitlock v. Alexander, 160 N.C. 465, 469, 473, 76 S.E. 538, 540, 541 (1912) (here, as in many cases, conscious overvaluation is turned into "fraud," or at least sufficient fraud to condemn the transaction in a creditor case). This is extended. Gross overvaluation, objectively judged, is evidence of conscious overvaluation, and, unless satisfactorily explained, becomes "conclusive" evidence, and lays the foundation to condemn the transaction. See Boynton v. Andrews, 63 N.Y. 93, 96 (1875); Douglass v. Ireland, 73 N.Y. 100, 104 (1878); Lake Superior Iron Co. v. Drexel, 90 N.Y. 87 (1882).

SECTION 4. PAR AND NO PAR—A VESTIGIAL CONCEPT

See the Introductory Note in Chapter XII, Section 1(a).

SECTION 5. PREEMPTIVE RIGHTS AND FIDUCIARY DUTIES: NEW ISSUES OF SHARES

(a) PREEMPTIVE RIGHTS AND EQUITABLE REMEDIES

INTRODUCTORY NOTE

As noted in the preceding Section, corporations may be formed under modern statutes with an amount of authorized stock largely in excess of that which they intend to obtain through the immediate issue of shares. The power to issue additional shares at a later date is usually possessed by the board of directors. Both where the newly issued shares are part of those originally authorized and where they are part of those authorized by an amendment of the certificate, an individual shareholder may attempt to establish the proposition that the power to increase the capital, whether by issue of additional authorized shares or by increasing the number of shares authorized, does not include the power to issue them without affording existing shareholders an opportunity to subscribe to their proportionate part of the increase. The right to be given such an opportunity is commonly called the preemptive right.

STOKES v. CONTINENTAL TRUST CO.
Court of Appeals of New York, 1906.
186 N.Y. 285, 78 N.E. 1090.

Appeal from an order of the Appellate Division of the Supreme Court in the first judicial department, entered January 4, 1905, reversing a judgment in favor of plaintiff entered upon a decision of the court on trial at Special Term and granting a new trial.

This action was brought by a stockholder to compel his corporation to issue to him at par such a proportion of an increase made in its capital stock as the number of shares held by him before such increase bore to the number of all the shares originally issued, and in case such additional shares could not be delivered to him for his damages in the premises.

The defendant is a domestic banking corporation in the city of New York, organized in 1890, with a capital stock of $500,000, consisting of 5000 shares of the par value of $100 each. The plaintiff was one of the original stockholders and still owns all the stock issued to him at the date of organization, together with enough more acquired since to make 221 shares in all. On the 29th of January, 1902, the defendant had a surplus of $1,048,450.94, which made the book value of the stock at that time $309.69 per share. On the 2nd of January, 1902, Blair & Company, a strong and influential firm of private bankers in the city of New York, made the following proposition to the defendant: "If your stockholders at the special meeting to be called for January 29th, 1902, vote to increase your capital stock from $500,000 to $1,000,000 you may deliver the additional stock to us as soon as issued at $450 per share ($100 par value) for ourselves and our associates, it being understood that we may nominate ten of the 21 trustees to be elected at the adjourned annual meeting of stockholders."

The directors of the defendant promptly met and duly authorized a special meeting of the stockholders to be called to meet on January 29th, 1902, for the purpose of voting upon the proposed increase of stock and the acceptance of the offer to purchase the same. Upon due notice a meeting of the stockholders was held accordingly, more than a majority attending either in person or by proxy. A resolution to increase the stock was adopted by the vote of 4197 shares, all that were cast. Thereupon the plaintiff demanded from the defendant the right to subscribe for 221 shares of the new stock at par, and offered to pay immediately for the same, which demand was refused. A resolution directing a sale to Blair & Company at $450 a share was then adopted by a vote of 3596 shares to 241. The plaintiff voted for the first resolution but against the last, and before the adoption of the latter he protested against the proposed sale of his proportionate share of the stock and again demanded the right to subscribe and pay for the same, but the demand was refused.

On the 30th of January, 1902, the stock was increased, and on the same day was sold to Blair & Company at the price named. Although the plaintiff formally renewed his demand for 221 shares of the new stock at par and tendered payment therefor, it was refused upon the ground that the stock had already been issued to Blair & Company. Owing in part to the offer of Blair & Company, which had become known to the public, the market price of the stock had increased from $450 a share in September, 1901, to $550 in January, 1902, and at the time of the trial, in April, 1904, it was worth $700 per share.

Prior to the special meeting of the stockholders, by authority of the board of directors a circular letter was sent to each stockholder, including the plaintiff, giving notice of the proposition made by Blair & Company and recommending that it be accepted. Thereupon the plaintiff notified the defendant that he wished to subscribe for his proportionate share of the new stock, if issued, and at no time did he waive his right to subscribe for the same. Before the special meeting, he had not been definitely notified by the defendant that he could not receive his proportionate part of the increase, but was informed that his proposition would "be taken under consideration."

After finding these facts in substance, the trial court found, as conclusions of law, that the plaintiff had the right to subscribe for such proportion of the increase, as his holdings bore to all the stock before the increase was made; that the stockholders, directors and officers of the defendant had no power to deprive him of that right, and that he was entitled to recover the difference between the market value of 221 shares on the 30th of January, 1902 and the par value thereof, or the sum of $99,450, together with interest from said date. The judgment entered accordingly was reversed by the Appellate Division, and the plaintiff appealed to this court, giving the usual stipulation for judgment absolute in case the order of reversal should be affirmed.

VANN, J. . . . [T]he question presented for decision is whether according to the facts found the plaintiff had the legal right to subscribe for and take the same number of shares of the new stock that he held of the old.

The subject is not regulated by statute and the question presented has never been directly passed upon by this court, and only to a limited extent has it been considered by courts in this state. (Miller v. Illinois Central R.R. Co., 24 Barb. 312; Matter of Wheeler, 2 Abb. Pr.(N.S.) 361; Currie v. White, 45 N.Y. 822.) . . .

In other jurisdictions the decisions support the claim of the plaintiff with the exception of Ohio Insurance Co. v. Nunnemacher (15 Ind. 294) which turned on the language of the charter. The leading authority is Gray v. Portland Bank, decided in 1807 and reported in 3 Mass. 364. . . .

This decision has stood unquestioned for nearly a hundred years and has been followed generally by courts of the highest standing. It is the foundation of the rule upon the subject that prevails, almost without exception, throughout the entire country. . . .

If the right claimed by the plaintiff was a right of property belonging to him as a stockholder he could not be deprived of it by the joint action of the other stockholders and of all the directors and officers of the corporation.

What is the nature of the right acquired by a stockholder through the ownership of shares of stock? What rights can he assert against the will of a majority of the stockholders and all the officers and directors? While he does not own and cannot dispose of any specific property of the corporation, yet he and his associates own the corporation itself, its charter, franchises and all rights conferred thereby, including the right to increase the stock. He has an inherent right to his proportionate share of any dividend declared, or of any surplus arising upon dissolution, and he can prevent waste or misappropriation of the property of the corporation by those in control. Finally, he has the right to vote for directors and upon all propositions subject by law to the control of the stockholders, and this is his supreme right and main protection. Stockholders have no direct voice in transacting the corporate business, but through their right to vote they can select those to whom the law intrusts the power of management and control.

A corporation is somewhat like a partnership, if one were possible, conducted wholly by agents where the copartners have power to appoint the agents, but are not responsible for their acts. The power to manage its affairs resides in the directors, who are its agents, but the power to elect directors resides in the stockholders. This right to vote for directors and upon propositions to increase the stock or mortgage the assets, is about all the power the stockholder has. So long as the management is honest, within the corporate powers and involves no waste, the stockholder cannot interfere, even if the administration is feeble and unsatisfactory, but must correct such evils through their power to elect other directors. Hence, the power of the individual stockholder to vote in proportion to the number of his shares, is vital and cannot be cut off or curtailed by the action of all the other stockholders even with the co-operation of the directors and officers.

In the case before us the new stock came into existence through the exercise of a right belonging wholly to the stockholders. As the right to increase the stock belonged to them, the stock when increased belonged to them also, as it was issued for money and not for property or for some purpose other than the sale thereof for money. By the increase of stock the voting power of the plaintiff was reduced one-half, and while he consented to the increase he did not consent to the disposition of the new stock by a sale thereof to Blair & Company at less than its market value, nor by sale to any person in any way except by an allotment to the stockholders. The increase and sale involved the transfer of rights belonging to the stockholders as part of their investment. The issue of new stock and the sale thereof to Blair & Company was not only a transfer to them of one-half the voting power of the old stockholders, but also of an equitable right to one-half the surplus which belonged to them. In other words, it was a partial division of the property of the old stockholders.

The right to increase stock is not an asset of the corporation any more than the original stock when it was issued pursuant to subscription. . . . The corporation has no rights hostile to those of the stockholders, but is the trustee for all including the minority. The new stock issued by the defendant under the permission of the statute did not belong to it, but was held by it the same as the original stock when first issued was held in trust for the stockholders. It has the same voting power as the old, share for share. The stockholders decided to enlarge their holdings, not by increasing the amount of each share, but by increasing the number of shares. The new stock belonged to the stockholders as an inherent right by virtue of their being stockholders, to be shared in proportion upon paying its par value or the value per share fixed by vote of a majority of the stockholders, or ascertained by a sale at public auction.

While the corporation could not compel the plaintiff to take new shares at any price since they were issued for money and not for property, it could not lawfully dispose of those shares without giving him a chance to get his proportion at the same price that outsiders got theirs. He had an inchoate right to one share of the new stock for each share owned by him of the old stock, provided he was ready to pay the price fixed by the stockholders. If so situated that he could not take it himself, he was entitled to sell the right to one who could, as is frequently done. Even this gives an advantage to capital, but capital necessarily has some advantage. Of course, there is a distinction when the new stock is issued in payment for property, but that is not this case. The stock in question was issued to be sold for money and was sold for money only. A majority of the stockholders, as part of their power to increase the stock, may attach reasonable conditions to the disposition thereof, such as the requirement that every old stockholder electing to take new stock shall pay a fixed price therefor, not less than par, however, owing to the limitation of the statute. They may also provide for a sale in parcels or bulk at public auction, when every stockholder can bid the same as strangers. They cannot, however, dispose of it to strangers against the protest of any stockholder who insists that he has a right to his proportion. Otherwise the majority could deprive the minority of their proportionate power in the election of directors and of their proportionate right to share in the surplus, each of which is an inherent, preemptive and vested right of property. It is inviolable and can neither be taken away nor lessened without consent, or a waiver implying consent.

The plaintiff had power, before the increase of stock, to vote on 221 shares of stock, out of a total of 5000, at any meeting held by the stockholders for any purpose. By the action of the majority, taken against his will and protest, he now has only one-half the voting power that he had before, because the number of shares has been doubled while he still owns but 221. This touches him as a stockholder in such a way as to deprive him of a right of property. Blair & Company acquired virtual control, while he and the other stockholders lost it. We are not discussing equities, but legal rights, for this is an action at law, and the plaintiff was deprived of a strictly legal right. . . .

We are thus led to lay down the rule that a stockholder has an inherent right to a proportionate share of new stock issued for money only and not to purchase property for the purposes of the corporation or to effect a consolidation, and while he can waive that right, he cannot be deprived of it without his consent except when the stock is issued at a fixed price not less than par and he is given the right to take at that price in proportion to his holding, or in some other equitable way that will enable him to protect his interest by acting on his own judgment and using his own resources. This rule is just to all and tends to prevent the tyranny of majorities which needs restraint, as well as virtual attempts to blackmail by small minorities, which should be prevented.

The remaining question is whether the plaintiff waived his rights by failing to do what he ought to have done, or by doing something he ought not to have done. He demanded his share of the new stock at par, instead of at the price fixed by the stockholders, for the authorization to sell at $450 a share was virtually fixing the price of the stock. He did more than this, however, for he not only voted against the proposition to sell to Blair & Company at $450, but as the court expressly found, he "protested against the proposed sale of his proportionate share of the stock and again demanded the right to subscribe and pay for the same which demands were again refused," and "the resolution was carried notwithstanding such protest and demands." Thus he protested against the sale of his share before the price was fixed, for the same resolution fixed the price and directed the sale, which was promptly carried into effect. If he had not attended the meeting, called upon due notice to do precisely what was done, perhaps he would have waived his rights, but he attended the meeting and before the price was fixed demanded the right to subscribe for 221 shares at par and offered to pay for the same immediately. It is true that after the price was fixed he did not offer to take his share at that price, but he did not acquiesce in the sale of his proportion to Blair & Company, and unless he acquiesced the sale as to him was without right. He was under no obligation to put the corporation in default by making a demand. The ordinary doctrine of demand, tender and refusal has no application to this case. The plaintiff had made no contract. He had not promised to do anything. No duty of performance rested upon him. He had an absolute right to the new stock in proportion to his holding of the old and he gave notice that he wanted it. It was his property and could not be disposed of without his consent. He did not consent. He protested in due time, and the sale was made in defiance of his protest. While in connection with his protest he demanded the right to subscribe at par, that demand was entirely proper when made, because the price had not then been fixed. After the price was fixed it was the duty of the defendant to offer him his proportion at that price, for it had notice that he had not acquiesced in the proposed sale of his share, but wanted it himself. The directors were under the legal obligation to give him an opportunity to purchase at the price fixed before they could sell his property to a third party, even with the approval of a large majority of the stockholders. If he had remained silent and had made no request or protest he would have waived his rights, but after he had given notice that he wanted his part and had protested against the sale thereof, the defendant was bound to offer it to him at the price fixed by the stockholders. By selling to strangers without thus offering to sell to him, the defendant wrongfully deprived him of his property and is liable for such damages as he actually sustained.

The learned trial court, however, did not measure the damages according to law. The plaintiff was not entitled to the difference between the par value of the new stock and the market value thereof, for the stockholders had the right to fix the price at which the stock should be sold. They fixed the price at $450 a share, and for the failure of the defendant to offer the plaintiff his share at that price we hold it liable in damages. His actual loss, therefore, is $100 per share, or the difference between $450, the price that he would have been obliged to pay had he been permitted to purchase, and the market value on the day of sale, which was $550. This conclusion requires a reversal of the judgment rendered by the Appellate Division and a modification of that rendered by the trial court.

* * *

HAIGHT, J. (dissenting). I agree that the rule that we should adopt is that a stockholder in a corporation has an inherent right to purchase a proportionate share of new stock issued for money only, and not to purchase property necessary for the purposes of the corporation or to effect a consolidation. While he can waive that right he cannot be deprived of it without his consent, except by sale at a fixed price at or above par, in which he may buy at that price in proportion to his holding or in some other equitable way that will enable him to protect his interest by acting on his own judgment and using his own resources. I, however, differ with Judge Vann as to his conclusions as to the rights of the plaintiff herein. Under the findings of the trial court the plaintiff demanded that his share of the new stock should be issued to him at par, or $100 per share, instead of $450 per share, the price offered by Blair & Company and the price fixed at the stockholders' meeting at which the new stock was authorized to be sold. This demand was made after the passage of the resolution authorizing the increase of the capital stock of the defendant company and before the passage of the resolution authorizing a sale of the new stock to Blair & Company at the price specified. After the passage of the second resolution he objected to the sale of his proportionate share of the new stock to Blair & Company and again demanded that it be issued to him, and the following day he made a legal tender for the amount of his portion of the new stock at $100 per share. There is no finding of fact or evidence in the record showing that he was ever ready or willing to pay $450 per share for the stock. He knew that Blair & Company represented Marshall Field and others at Chicago, great dry goods merchants, and that they had made a written offer to purchase the new stock of the company provided the stockholders would authorize an increase of its capital stock from five hundred thousand to a million dollars. He knew that the trustees of the company had called a special meeting of the stockholders for the purpose of considering the offer so made by Blair & Company. He knew that the increased capitalization proposed was for the purpose of enlarging the business of the company and bringing into its management the gentlemen referred to. There is no pretense that any of the stockholders would have voted for an increase of the capital stock otherwise than for the purpose of accepting the offer of Blair & Company. All were evidently desirous of interesting the gentlemen referred to it in the company, and by securing their business and deposits increase the earnings of the company. This the trustees carefully considered, and in their notice calling the special meeting of the stockholders distinctly recommended the acceptance of the offer.

What, then, was the legal effect of the plaintiff's demand and tender? To my mind it was simply an attempt to make something out of his associates, to get for $100 per share the stock which Blair & Company had offered to purchase for $450 per share; and that it was the equivalent of a refusal to pay $450 per share, and its effect is to waive his right to procure the stock by paying that amount. An acceptance of his offer would have been most unjust to the remaining stockholders. It would not only have deprived them of the additional sum of $350 per share, which had been offered for the stock, but it would have defeated the object and purpose for which the meeting was called, for it was well understood that Blair & Company would not accept less than the whole issue of the new stock. But this is not all. It appears that prior to the offer of Blair & Company the stock of the company had never been sold above $450 per share; that thereafter the stock rapidly advanced until the day of the completion of the sale on the 30th of January, when its market value was $550 per share; but this, under the stipulation of facts, was caused by the rumor and subsequent announcement and consummation of the proposition for the increase of the stock and the sale of such increase to Blair & Company and their associates. It is now proposed to give the plaintiff as damages such increase in the market value of the stock, even though such value was based upon the understanding that Blair & Company were to become stockholders in the corporation, which the acceptance of plaintiff's offer would have prevented. This, to my mind, should not be done. I, therefore, favor an affirmance.

CULLEN, Ch. J., WERNER and HISCOCK, JJ., concur with VANN, J.; Willard BARTLETT, J., concurs with HAIGHT, J.; O'BRIEN, J., absent.

Ordered accordingly.

DEL. GEN. CORP. LAW § 102(b)(3)

[See Statutory Supplement]

REV. MODEL BUS. CORP. ACT § 6.30

[See Statutory Supplement]

NEW YORK BUS. CORP. LAW § 622

[See Statutory Supplement]

NOTE ON PREEMPTIVE RIGHTS

1. The preemptive right does not exist where the shares are issued for property. Meredith v. New Jersey Zinc & Iron Co., 55 N.J.Eq. 211, 37 A. 539 (Ch.1897), aff'd 56 N.J.Eq. 454, 41 A. 1116 (Err. & App.) (shares issued for purchase of mines).

2. In the consideration of preemptive rights, inquiry should be raised whether different policy objectives should govern in the case of the publicly-held corporation as distinguished from the closely-held concern.

(a) *With respect to the publicly held company,* the tendency among modern corporations is to have not only an ample reservoir of authorized shares, but also to ensure that preemptive rights do not interfere with their issuance by the board of directors. They are vanishing from the scene.

In its proxy statement dated February 27, 1975, American Telephone and Telegraph Company said (pp. 9–10):

> Preemptive rights originated at a time when corporations were small and had only a relatively few shareholders. Underlying the origin was a need to preserve the shareholder's proportionate interest and voting rights against possible dilution through disproportionate sales of additional shares to other more favored purchasers. Today, wherever a broad base of corporate ownership exists, this purpose has lost its significance. In the case of AT & T, there are approximately 3,000,000 common shareholders, and the largest single individual shareholder's interest is less than one fiftieth of one percent.

> . . . [I]n the future in order to maintain a sound capital structure, a significant proportion of new capital requirements must be obtained from the sale of equity securities.

> Therefore, your Directors believe elimination of mandatory preemptive rights will permit a more orderly issuance and attraction of equity capital in such specific amounts as may be required from time to time. It will permit tailoring to market conditions the particular type of equity security sold, the size of the offering and the method of sale—all to the benefit of both shareholders and customers.

Ballantine and Sterling,[1] referring to the California statute, said:

> The abrogation of preemptive rights under the California law, . . . may seem to play directly into the hands of manipulators and promoters. . . .

> It is believed, however, that these charges are not well founded. It seems a wise policy as a general rule to give the directors wide authority not only in the conduct of the business itself, but also in the procedure for obtaining new capital, as by arrangements with underwriting and banking concerns as to stock issues. The preemptive right to a first offering of a new issue of shares may operate as a hindrance to legitimate financing. . . .

(b) *With respect to closely-held concerns,* O'Neal[2] points out totally different policy considerations:

> ". . . [P]reemptive rights in a closely held corporation usually should not only be preserved but should be extended and strengthened [and] . . . made applicable to stock issued for property as well as for money. . . .

> "Most of the considerations that justify the elimination of preemptive rights in public corporations do not apply to closely held corporations, at least not to those with simple share structures. . . . Preemptive rights are needed in a closely held corporation to protect the shareholder's proportionate interest in

---

1. California Corporation Laws (1949) p. 142.

2. Adapted from O'Neal, Molding the Corporate Form to Particular Business

Practices: Optional Charter Clauses, 10 Vand.L.Rev. 1, at 41 (1956).

control, dividends and surplus. . . . [which] is likely to be proportionately greater than the individual interest of a shareholder in a public issue corporation. Usually the proportionate interest of . . . [the latter] is insignificant to begin with, and therefore an increase in stock makes little difference to him; and if it does, he can buy additional shares on the market.

Control is more important to a shareholder in a closely held corporation . . . because . . . [it] means employment. . . . Issuance of new stock to some shareholders but not to others may throw out of balance an otherwise carefully formulated plan distributing control among the various participants.

A final reason for maintaining preemptive rights in a closely held corporation is that its growth is likely to be due largely to the energy and personality of its shareholders. Therefore they should be in a position to purchase new issues of the corporation's stock and thus share in its expansion and prosperity.

(b) THE TRANSITION FROM PREEMPTIVE RIGHTS TO FIDUCIARY DUTY

ROSS TRANSPORT, INC. v. CROTHERS
Court of Appeals of Maryland, 1946.
185 Md. 573, 45 A.2d 267.

MARBURY, Chief Judge. This is a derivative suit by a stockholder of a Maryland corporation, acting on his own behalf as well as for other stockholders who might join and be made parties, brought after demand had been made on the corporation to institute such a proceeding, which demand was neglected and refused. The original plaintiff was Charles T. Crothers, and he was subsequently joined by another stockholder, his brother Edmund W. Crothers, who was made an additional party plaintiff by order of court. The defendants (appellants here) are the corporation, Ross Transport, Inc., Wallace Williams, F. DuPont Thomson, James W. Hughes and William B. Ross, directors, and Elizabeth B. Williams, Lois Williams Young and Corrine Williams, stockholders. The purpose of the suit is to set aside the issuance of 40 shares of stock to Elizabeth B. Williams, 100 shares of stock to Corrine Williams, 100 shares of stock to Lois Williams Young and 125 shares of stock to William B. Ross. The defendants all answered, testimony was taken and the court passed a decree granting the relief prayed, and directing the four stockholders named to repay to the corporation the dividends received by them on the stock declared to be illegally issued, and ordered cancelled. From this decree, all the defendants appealed.

It appears from the record that the corporation was organized on January 19, 1942 to operate a fleet of buses to transport employees of Triumph Explosives, Inc. to and from its plant at Elkton, Maryland.

The incorporators were Wallace Williams, William B. Ross and Gervase R. Sinclair who later died. These three and F. DuPont Thomson and James W. Hughes were the directors. At the organization meeting of the directors, Williams was named as President and Ross as General Manager. The authorized stock was 5000 shares of no par value. At the organization meeting a resolution was passed authorizing the sale of this stock at $20 a share, and providing that stock to the value of $30,000 be offered for sale. This limited the stock to be issued to 1500 shares. The stock records of the company showed the original subscriptions to stock, all in March and April 1942, to be as follows:

March 25th—	To	Wallace Williams	50	shares
"	"	Wallace Williams, Jr.	100	"
"	"	Elizabeth B. Williams	200	"
"	"	Edmund W. Crothers	100	"
"	"	William B. Ross	25	"
"	"	James W. Hughes	150	"
April 2nd	"	F. DuPont Thomson	150	"
"	"	Bessie F. Whitelaw	10	"
April 20th	"	Charles T. Crothers	50	"
April 27th	"	Gervase R. Sinclair	50	"
"	"	Jean W. Sinclair	150	"
		Total	1035	

In the latter part of July 1942, after the death of Mr. Sinclair, Charles T. Crothers purchased the Sinclair stock, 200 shares, at $20 and 5% interest from the date of issuance. This did not, of course, increase the amount of stock outstanding. On August 26, 1942, the stock complained of was issued to the wife and daughters of Wallace Williams and to William B. Ross, totaling 365 shares in all, and increasing the outstanding stock to 1400 shares. All of this stock was issued at the set price of $20.00 a share. The stock issued to the Williams family was paid by Mr. Williams' check for $4800. Mr. Ross paid the company $2500 for his stock.

As a result of these purchases by Williams and Ross the stock books showed that the Williams family had 590 shares, Ross had 150 shares, Hughes had 150 shares, Thomson had 150 shares, Whitelaw had 10 shares, Edmund W. Crothers had 100 shares and Charles T. Crothers had 250 shares. Williams and Ross, therefore, had the controlling interest in the company. Mr. Williams testified that all of the stock in the company was sold by him personally under the directors' resolution. He said that all the stock in dispute was definitely promised in the beginning, except 40 shares to Mrs. Williams. This, he said, he put in to round out an even 1400 shares, holding back 100 shares which he thought Hughes or Thomson might like to take. He never called any other directors meeting to authorize any of the sales made after the original subscriptions and none of the other stockholders were given an opportunity to buy. He told Mr. Ross and Mr. Hughes how he was going to divide it. Mr. Ross did not testify.

The sale of this additional stock to a director and to the family of the president and director without any further authority than the original resolution, and without opportunity to buy given to other stockholders, is sought to be justified on the ground that it was originally planned, and that the money was needed to purchase additional buses at a cost of about $16,000. The facts, however, show no such need. The company was an immediate financial success. It was engaged in a special business, of which it had a monopoly, and in which it could not help making money so long as Triumph Explosives continued to operate its large plant, employing the workmen the Transport Corporation hauled. The loan of $3000 by Triumph Explosives, made in March, was paid in June. The record shows the following figures during the first five months of its existence:

Surplus above liabilities and invested capital	Outstanding obligations on conditional sales contract	Cash Bank balance
April 25	$ 8,459.77	$50,372.22	$ 9,092.65
May 23	13,295.38	45,712.34	13,811.80
June 21	20,214.53	42,144.63	14,154.62
July 19	26,414.74	31,154.69	12,842.81
Aug. 16	25,057.73	28,997.68	8,970.83

On August 7th, the directors authorized salary payments dating back to February 1, 1942, $3915 to Mr. Williams, $2875 to Mr. Ross and $2025 to Mr. Hughes who was Secretary and Treasurer of the company which had started business a few months before with a paid in capital of $20,700, and which had bought its operating equipment, i.e. the buses, on conditional sales contracts, and had borrowed $3000 to pay for its licenses. Prosperity continued. On November 27, 1942, a dividend of $5 a share was declared. On December 17, 1942, one of $15 (called a return of capital, but not authorized by the stockholders, Code, Article 23, Sec. 32). On the same date, another dividend of $5 a share was declared payable June 30, 1943. The defendants, Williams and Ross, who were operating the company, knew on August 26, 1942, that they were about to receive large sums in dividends in addition to the salaries they were getting. The benefit of these dividends would not only increase the value of the stock, but the first two would pay back all the subscribers had invested, leaving any future earnings and distributions pure profit. Under these circumstances, they took the opportunity they thought they had to increase their investment, and in fact received in December the full amount they invested in August, leaving them with the additional stock on which to receive such further dividends as were obviously in sight.

The appellants contend that the company was not in the claimed good financial condition in August, because no allowance had been made for income and profits taxes. But if we reduce the book surplus of $25,000 on August 16, 1942, by allowing for a 40% tax (the limit unless the earnings increased), we still find the company with a net surplus of $15,000, 75% of the original investment. The stock had no "market value," but it must be obvious that it was worth much more than $20 a share on August 26th.

The appellees give two reasons for their contention that the stock sales of August 26th were void: First, because they deprive them and the other original stockholders of their pre-emptive rights to purchase a proportionate amount of the remaining shares, and, second, because, in selling to themselves and their nominees, Williams and Ross have abused their trust as officers and directors. They claim to be injured in two ways. Their voting powers have been proportionately lessened, and the control of the company has passed to Williams and Ross. And the amount paid in dividends has to be divided among 365 more shares of stock to the consequent financial loss of the holders of the original shares.

Before discussing these legal questions, the outline of the case may be completed by quoting from the appellants' brief certain facts about the plaintiffs (appellees) which appellants claim are pertinent. The original plaintiff, Charles T. Crothers, was an employee of the corporation as well as a stockholder. Edmund W. Crothers had no position in the corporation, but he furnished it part of the buses that were bought at the inception of the business. The appellants' brief states:

"The 365 shares complained of were issued on August 26th, 1942. Charles T. Crothers learned of the fact two or three weeks thereafter; and his brother, Edmund W. Crothers learned about it three or four weeks after said Stock was issued. Charles T. Crothers understood from the first that the Sale of 1,500 Shares had been authorized; and no one had ever represented to him that no more than 1,035 Shares would be issued. In July, 1942, Charles T. Crothers refused to turn over half of the Sinclair Stock, then purchased by him, to Ross, and assigned for his reason the fact that Ross could buy more Stock from the Corporation; and he also attempted to buy the remaining 100 of the authorized 1,500 Shares for himself. On February 1st, 1943, at a Meeting of Stockholders, Charles T. Crothers was elected a Director and served for one year. At that Meeting the Treasurer's Report was accepted on a motion seconded by Edmund W. Crothers. At that Meeting of the Stockholders a Resolution was adopted, expressing to the Management and Employees the appreciation of the Stockholders for the manner in which the operation of the Corporation had been conducted during the previous year. The minutes show that Edmund W. Crothers seconded this Resolution. Charles T. Crothers was then present, and testified that he does not know whether he voted for this Resolution, but he did not object to it. Edmund W. Crothers testified that he did not second the Resolution of Approbation and that he objected to the Minutes on the following year (after this suit was instituted by his brother, but before he, Edmund W. Crothers, had become a party thereto), and that he assigned as his reason for his protest that he was just reserving his decision. On September 13th, 1943,

Charles T. Crothers, then a Director, seconded and voted for the Declaration of a Dividend on all 1,400 Shares of Stock. No protest was made to the Corporation about the issuance of the 365 Shares until a letter of protest was written by counsel for Charles T. Crothers on October 27th, 1943, which was after he had been 'fired,' to use his own words, by the Corporation, in October, 1943. Charles T. Crothers, by his own testimony, never made any objection to the 365 Shares complained of having been issued at any meeting of the Corporation."

Charles T. Crothers testified that he protested to Mr. Hughes and to Mr. Thomson shortly after he learned of the stock issues of August 26th. Mr. Hughes said he was told by Mr. Thomson in "the latter part of the summer, or the early summer of 1942" that Edmund Crothers had spoken to him about it. Edmund Crothers said he got in touch with Mr. Thomson when he learned of the transaction, and also talked to Mr. Hughes, and at one time had "quite a little argument" with Mr. Williams and the latter said "Wouldn't you do it, if you could get away with it." Charles Crothers gave as a reason for not bringing up the matter at a directors meeting "They were just a matter of form. Mr. Williams was the boss of the company. He owned the company."

The doctrine known as the pre-emptive right of shareholders is a judicial interpretation of general principles of corporation law. Existing stockholders are the owners of the business, and are entitled to have that ownership continued in the same proportion. Therefore, when additional stock is issued, those already having shares, are held to have the first right to buy the new stock in proportion to their holdings. This doctrine was first promulgated in 1807 in the case of Gray v. Portland Bank, 3 Mass. 364, 3 Am.Dec. 156. At that time, corporations were small and closely held, much like the one before us in this case. But in the succeeding years, corporations grew and expanded. New capital was frequently required. New properties had to be acquired for which it was desirable to issue stock. Companies merged, and new stock in the consolidation was issued. Stock was issued for services. Different kinds of stock were authorized— preferred without voting power but with prior dividend rights— preferred with the right to convert into common—several classes of both common and preferred with different rights. Some stock had voting rights. Other stock did not. Bonds were issued, convertible into stock. All of these changes in the corporate structure made it impossible always to follow the simple doctrines earlier decided. Exceptions grew, and were noted in the decisions.

Only one of these exceptions is involved in the present case. It has been held that pre-emptive rights do not exist where the stock about to be issued is part of the original issue. This exception is based upon the fact that the original subscribers took their stock on the implied understanding that the incorporators could complete the sale of remaining stock to obtain the capital thought necessary to start the business. But this gives rise to an exception to the exception, where conditions have changed since the original issue. The stock sold the Williams family and Ross was part of the original issue, and it is claimed by the appellants that it comes within the exception, and the appellees and the other stockholders have no pre-emptive rights. . . . The appellees, on the other hand, contend, and the chancellors found, that changed conditions made it unnecessary to use the remaining unsold stock to obtain capital, and pre-emptive rights exist in it just as they would exist in newly authorized stock. Hammer v. Werner, 239 App.Div. 38, 265 N.Y.S. 172; Dunlay v. Avenue etc. Co., 253 N.Y. 274, 170 N.E. 917; 43 Harvard L.Rev. 586, 602–603.

It is unnecessary for us to decide which of these two conflicting points of view applies to this case, because another controlling consideration enters. The doctrine of pre-emptive right is not affected by the identity of the purchasers of the issued stock. What it is concerned with is who did not get it. But when officers and directors sell to themselves, and thereby gain an advantage, both in value and in voting power, another situation arises, which it does not require the assertion of a pre-emptive right to deal with.

It has long been the law in this State that trustees cannot purchase at their own sale, and trustees, in this sense, include directors of corporations. . . . "The transaction may not be ipso facto void, but it is not necessary to establish that there has been actual fraud or imposition practiced by the party holding the confidential or fiduciary relation;—the onus of proof being upon him to establish the perfect fairness, adequacy, and equity of the transaction; and that too by proof entirely independent of the instrument under which he may claim." This last quotation indicates that such a transaction is not absolutely voided at the option of the interested parties, but shifts the burden of proof upon the directors to establish its fairness. . . .

It is not necessary for us to determine in this case whether the sale of stock to the Williams family and Ross is voidable merely upon the application of some of the other stockholders, or whether proof of such sale merely makes it necessary for these appellants to show the complete equity of the transaction. If we take the latter view, which is that most favorable to these appellants, we must hold that the burden placed upon the two directors has not been met. They have not shown that the company needed the money so badly and was in such a financial condition that the sale of the additional stock to themselves was the only way the money could be obtained. On the contrary, the corporation appears to have been in a very good financial condition. It is probable that any necessary financing of any buses could easily have been arranged through some financial institution, and Williams and Ross benefited greatly by their action in selling the stock to themselves. Nor is there any corroboration of Williams' statement that it was all arranged in the beginning, who was to get this additional stock. None of the other incorporators or directors were called to testify about this, and Ross himself, as we have noted, did not testify at all. We conclude, therefore, that the sale must be set aside as a constructive fraud upon the other stockholders. . . .

The decree will be affirmed.

Decree affirmed with costs.

NOTE ON ISSUES FOR INADEQUATE PRICE OR FOR CONTROL: FIDUCIARY DUTY WHETHER OR NOT PREEMPTIVE RIGHT EXISTS

As indicated in the Ross case, supra, even where no preemptive right exists, it is improper for the directors to issue the shares for the purpose of perpetuating their control, and it is also improper to issue them for an inadequate price, particularly where the issue is to themselves or to persons closely associated with them.[1]

Schwartz v. Marien, 37 N.Y.2d 487, 373 N.Y.S.2d 122, 335 N.E.2d 334 (1975), develops the theme that regardless of the preemptive rights, fiduciary principles will be strictly applied in the case of a closely held corporation. There all the outstanding stock (150 shares) had been owned equally by three persons; one died and his shares were purchased by the corporation and kept in the treasury. Following the death of Marien his fifty shares were held by his widow and his sons. Just prior to the death of the third founder, Dietrich, there were four members of the Board, namely Dietrich, his daughter Schwartz, and two Mariens. At a special meeting the two Mariens succeeded in electing a third to fill the Dietrich vacancy and with no word of explanation voted to sell five shares of stock held in the treasury, one to each of them and two shares to long-time corporate employees. In this way their stock holdings provided a majority (53 of 105 shares) and assured control to the Marien family. After her complaints were ignored plaintiff-appellant Schwartz called a special meeting (which proved futile) and instituted the present action alleging conspiracy and fraud on the part of the defendants to deprive the Dietrich estate of its 50% ownership. The New York Court of Appeals concluded that there was sufficient evidence in the record to raise issues of fact and said, (335 N.E.2d at 337) "While it is conceded that pre-emptive rights as such do not attach to treasury stock . . ., members of a corporate board of directors nevertheless, owe a fiduciary responsibility to the shareholders. . . .," adding further that "even where statutes or articles of incorporation have abolished the stockholders' preemptive rights, there is still a fiduciary principle which protects the shareholders." In this case the court concluded that "disturbance of equality of stock ownership in a corporation closely held for several years by the members of two families calls for special justification in the corporate interest; not only must it be shown that it was sought to achieve a bona fide independent business objective, but as well that such objective could not have

---

1. See also Schwab v. Schwab–Wilson Machine Corp., Ltd., 13 Cal.App.2d 1, 55 P.2d 1268 (1936); Essex v. Essex, 141 Mich. 200, 104 N.W. 622 (1905); Elliott v. Baker, 194 Mass. 518, 80 N.E. 450 (1907); Chris- man et al. v. Avil's, Inc., et al., 80 D. & C. 395 (Pa.C.P.1951); Canada Southern Oils, Ltd. v. Manabi Exploration Co., Inc., 33 Del.Ch. 537, 96 A.2d 810 (1953); Johnson v. Duensing, 340 S.W.2d 758 (Mo.App.1960).

been accomplished substantially as effectively by other means. . . ."
(at 338).

NOTE ON THE FIDUCIARY OBLIGATION AND THE DILUTION POTENTIAL WHERE RIGHTS ARE OFFERED IN CLOSELY HELD CONCERNS

In Katzowitz v. Sidler, 24 N.Y.2d 512, 301 N.Y.S.2d 470, 249 N.E.2d 359 (1969), the problem was similar but the facts were substantially different from those in Hyman v. Velsicol. Again there were three parties involved. Katzowitz, the plaintiff, was a director and stockholder of a close corporation and engaged in several corporate ventures with two other men over a period of twenty-five years, sharing on an equal basis. A conflict flared in the open in 1956, at which time the two others joined forces to oust Katzowitz from any role in managing the corporations. However, they entered into a stipulation to the effect that they were "equal shareholders and each of said parties now owns the same number of shares . . . and that such shares of stock shall continue to be in full force and effect."

The business relationship established by this stipulation was fully complied with but the two controlling shareholders approached Katzowitz with regard to the purchase of his interest in one of the companies known as Sulburn. Sulburn was indebted to each stockholder to the extent of $2,500 for fees and commissions and the two in control wanted the corporation to use the money to lend to another company which all three men owned. They therefore called a meeting of the board to propose that additional Sulburn securities be offered at $100 per share, "the total par value which shall equal the total sum of the fees and commissions now owing by the Corporation to its directors." The offer was to be made to the stockholders in accordance with their respective pre-emptive rights, but the offering price of the securities was $1/18$ of the present book value of the stock. The two controlling parties purchased their full complement of shares but Katzowitz refused to do so. Shortly thereafter, the principal asset of Sulburn was destroyed and the company was dissolved. Upon dissolution, the two controlling shareholders each received more than $18,000 while Katzowitz received roughly $3,000. The lower court reasoned that Katzowitz waived his right to purchase the stock by failing to exercise his pre-emptive right or to take steps to prevent the sale of the stock. He sought only to obtain his aliquot share (namely one-third) upon the liquidation. Despite the holding of the lowest court with respect to waiver, the Court of Appeals found as follows (249 N.E.2d at 363–4): "Normally a stockholder is protected from the loss of his equity from dilution even though the stock is being offered at less than fair value because the shareholder receives rights. . . . If he exercises he has protected his interest, and if not, he can sell the rights, thereby compensating himself for the dilution. . . .

"When new shares are issued, however, at prices far below fair value in a closed corporation . . ., existing stockholders who do not want to invest or do not have the capacity to invest additional funds, can have their equity interest in the corporations diluted to the vanishing point . . .

"The protection afforded by stock rights is illusory in close corporations. Even if a buyer could be found for the rights, they would have to be sold at an inadequate price."

Under these circumstances the court decided that "the corporation's directors must show that the issuing price falls within some range which can be justified on the basis of valid business reason" and concluded further that "the corollary of a stockholder's right to maintain his proportionate equity in a corporation by purchasing additional shares is the right not to purchase additional shares without being confronted with dilution of his existing equity if no valid business justification exists for the dilution. Under these circumstances the additional offering of securities must be condemned because the directors in establishing the sale price did not fix it with reference to financial considerations . . ., but rather as an oppressive device which failed to account for the legitimate interests of the corporation and its shareholders."

See also Browning v. C & C Plywood Corp., 248 Or. 574, 434 P.2d 339 (1967); Steven v. Hale–Haas Co., 249 Wis. 205, 23 N.W.2d 620 (1945); Bennett v. Breuil Petroleum Corp., 99 A.2d 236 (Del.Ch.1953) (". . . [P]laintiff has the right not to purchase as well as the right to purchase. But his right not to purchase is seriously impaired if the stock is worth substantially more than its issuing price. Any other purchase at that price obviously dilutes his interest and impairs the value of his original holdings. . . ."). But see Hyman v. Velsicol Corp., 342 Ill.App. 489, 97 N.E.2d 122 (1951); Bellows v. Porter, 201 F.2d 429 (8th Cir.1953); Maguire v. Osborne, 388 Pa. 121, 130 A.2d 157 (1957); Tallant v. Executive Equities, Inc., 232 Ga. 807, 209 S.E.2d 159 (1974).

––––––––

Chapter XIV

THE PUBLIC DISTRIBUTION OF SECURITIES

SECTION 1. INTRODUCTION

(a) SECURITIES ACT TERMINOLOGY

SECURITIES ACT §§ 2(1), 2(4), 2(10), 2(11), 2(12);
SECURITIES ACT RULE 405

[See Statutory Supplement]

NOTE ON SECURITIES ACT TERMINOLOGY

The purpose of this chapter is to provide an introduction to the law concerning the public distribution of securities, which is governed principally by the Securities Act of 1933 and (to a lesser extent) by state Blue Sky laws. It is useful to begin by introducing some of the terminology employed in the Securities Act, particularly because the Act defines many key terms in a way that differs from ordinary business usage. Bear in mind that the following discussion is very broad. Many of the terms that are briefly discussed below will be considered in much greater depth later in this Chapter, and certain exceptions to the Securities Act's definitions are omitted at this stage for purposes of clarity.

Security. In ordinary usage, a "security" is a corporate stock or bond. Under section 2(1) of the Securities Act, however, the term security is defined to include "any note, stock, . . . bond, debenture, evidence of indebtedness, certificate of interest or participation in any profit-sharing agreement, investment contract, . . . or, in general, any interest or instrument commonly known as a 'security'."

Issuer. For most practical purposes, an "issuer" is a corporation that issues (that is, sells) its own stock or bonds. This usage is reflected in section 2(4) of the Securities Act, which defines "issuer" to mean "every person who issues or proposes to issue any security." Under section 2(11) of the Securities Act, however, for certain purposes the term issuer includes "an issuer, any person directly or indirectly controlling or controlled by the issuer, or any person under direct or indirect common control with the issuer."

937

Controlling person. Under Securities Act Rule 405, "[t]he term 'control' (including the terms 'controlling,' 'controlled by' and 'under common control with') means the possession, direct or indirect, of the power to direct or cause the direction of the management and policies of a person, whether through the ownership of voting securities, by contract, or otherwise."

Underwriter. In ordinary usage, an "underwriter" is a firm that markets securities on behalf of an issuer or controlling person. Under section 2(11) of the Securities Act, however, the term underwriter is defined to include "any person who has purchased from an issuer with a view to, or offers or sells for an issuer in connection with, the distribution of any security."

Dealer. In ordinary usage, a "dealer" is a person who buys and sells securities on his own behalf, taking title to the securities until sale. Under section 2(12) of the Securities Act, however, a dealer is defined as "any person who engages either for all or part of his time, directly or indirectly, as agent, broker, or principal, in the business of offering, buying, selling, or otherwise dealing or trading in securities issued by another person."

Broker. In ordinary usage, a "broker" is a person who buys and sells securities on behalf of others, never taking title to the securities. This usage is reflected in section 3(4) of the Securities Exchange Act of 1934, which defines a broker as "any person engaged in the business of effecting transactions in securities for the account of others." Under section 2(12) of the Securities Act, however, the term dealer is defined to include brokers.

Registration statement. The Securities Act requires that under certain circumstances securities must be registered with the Securities and Exchange Commission before they can be sold. To register securities under the Act it is necessary to file a registration statement that sets forth certain business and financial information concerning the issuer and the securities.

Prospectus. In ordinary usage, a prospectus is a document, prepared for distribution to the investment community and the public, that describes the issuer, the securities that are proposed to be sold, and the terms of the offering. Under section 2(10) of the Securities Act, however, a prospectus is defined much more broadly as "any prospectus, notice, circular, advertisement, letter, or communication, written or by radio or television, which offers any security for sale or confirms the sale of any security."

———

The balance of Section 1 consists of overviews of the securities markets, the underwriting process, and the Securities Act. Thereafter, this Chapter examines the following questions:

What constitutes a security? (Section 2)

What constitutes a sale or offer to sell securities? (Section 3)

What sales or offers to sell securities require registration? (Section 4)

What are the obligations of issuers, controlling persons, and underwriters when registration is required? (Section 5)

What are the liabilities for violating these obligations? (Section 6)

Caveat: The law governing the public distribution of securities is extremely intricate. The purpose of this Chapter is to examine the structure of the Securities Act and the most important concepts and rules in this area. Many details and some qualifications are left to coverage in Securities Regulation courses.

(b) AN OVERVIEW OF THE SECURITIES MARKETS

SELIGMAN, THE FUTURE OF THE NATIONAL MARKET SYSTEM

See Chapter V, Section 2(b), supra.

(c) AN OVERVIEW OF THE UNDERWRITING PROCESS

L. LOSS, FUNDAMENTALS OF SECURITIES REGULATION 75–86

2d ed. 1988.

A. DISTRIBUTION TECHNIQUES

The registration and prospectus provisions of the Securities Act of 1933 can be understood—and their effectiveness evaluated—only on the background of the techniques by which securities are distributed in the United States. With a healthy obeisance in honor of the still new "shelf registration" technique, there are three basic types of so-called underwriting that are in common use, sometimes with variations.

1. STRICT OR "OLD–FASHIONED" UNDERWRITING

Under the traditional English system of distribution—which is no longer common in that country—the issuer did not sell to an investment banking house for resale to the public, either directly or through a group of dealers. Instead a designated "issuing house" advertised the issue and received applications and subscriptions from the public on the issuer's behalf after an announced date. When sufficient applications had been received, an announcement was made that "the lists are closed," and the issuer proceeded to allot the securities directly to the applicants or subscribers, using various methods of proration in the event of an oversubscription. Securities firms normally subscribed to new issues not for their own accounts with a view to resale at a profit, but only as brokers for the accounts of their customers. Before the public offering was thus made, the issue was "underwritten" in order to ensure that the company would obtain the amount of funds it required.

This was underwriting in the strict insurance sense. For a fee or premium, the underwriter agreed to take up whatever portion of the issue was not purchased by the public within a specified time. And, just as insurance companies frequently reinsure large underwritings with other companies in order to distribute the risk, so the initial underwriter often protected himself by agreements with sub-underwriters, to which the issuer was not a party. The typical underwriting syndicate was not limited to investment bankers or so-called issuing houses. It included or might consist entirely of insurance companies or investment trusts or other institutions, or even large individual investors, who thus obtained large blocks of securities at less than the issue price. Accordingly, the underwriters planned to hold for investment any securities they might be required to take. Even the issuing houses that found themselves required to take up unsubscribed portions of issues were included to hold them temporarily until they found a buyer on favorable terms, instead of trying to resell them immediately, at a loss if necessary, as underwriters generally do in this country when issues get "sticky."

This method of distribution is called in the United States "strict" or "old-fashioned" or "standby" underwriting. It is seldom if ever used here except in connection with offerings to existing stockholders by means of warrants or rights. . . .

2. FIRM–COMMITMENT UNDERWRITING

"Firm-commitment" underwriting is not technically underwriting in the classic insurance sense. But its purpose and effect are much the same in that it assures the issuer of a specified amount of money at a certain time (subject frequently to specified conditions precedent in the underwriting contract) and shifts the risk of the market (at least in part) to the investment bankers. Traditionally the issuer would simply sell the entire issue outright to a group of securities firms, represented by one or several "managers" or "principal underwriters" or "representatives"; they in turn would sell at a price differential to a larger "selling group" of dealers; and they would sell at another differential to the public. In a very limited sense the process is comparable to the merchandising of beans or automobiles or baby rattles. The issuer is the manufacturer of the securities; the members of the underwriting group are the wholesalers; and the members of the selling group are the retailers. But it is not quite so simple. Except in the case of open-end investment companies, securities of particular issuers are distributed not continually but once in a long time, and then in a large batch. And the securities market is quite a different animal from the market for canned beans.

Before the Securities Act of 1933—particularly during the period of tremendous industrial and business expansion that began roughly in 1900—the procedure underwent an elaborate development. The risk of handling the increasingly large securities offerings of the Nation's industrial units had to be spread, and methods had to be developed to merchandise the securities among the ever-growing numbers of investors spread across the continent.

Jay Cooke is credited with having introduced the "underwriting syndicate" into this country in the sale of a $2 million bond issue by the Pennsylvania Railroad in 1870. By the turn of the century it was common in the case of large offerings for a single investment banker to do the "origination"—that is, carry on the preliminary negotiations with the issuer, make the investigations deemed necessary, and then purchase the issue from the issuer. The banker was chosen (and still is to a large extent except when the law requires competitive bidding) on the basis of his past relationships with the issuer and his past performance. The "origination" stage was followed by the process of "syndication": In order to spread the commitment, the originating banker would immediately sell the issue to a small "original purchase group." And that group would in turn sell to a larger "banking group"; or the members of the latter group might occupy the status of "old-fashioned underwriters." The originating banker would become a member of the purchase group; the members of that group would likewise become members of the banking group; and the originating banker would manage both groups. When the issue was not too large, the intermediate group might be omitted. In either event, the two or three steps followed each other very closely. The function of both groups was to spread the risk—although the process also permitted the originating banker to make participations available on favorable terms to large distributors, to those firms that had reciprocated in the past or might do so in the future, to those he might count on in less favorable times, and to those suggested by the issuer. In any event, these groups were not designed primarily to do the actual distributing; often the members of the groups were not organized for retailing purposes. The public sale would be effected, for the account of whichever group last bought the issue, by the manager (the originating banker) through an organization of employees and agents, which would sometimes include those members of the purchase and banking groups who were geared for retail distribution.

With the increase in the number and size of securities issues during World War I, as well as the development of coast-to-coast telephone and wire systems, both groups tended to grow in membership and, in order to facilitate the actual mechanics of distribution, it became customary to add still another step to the elaborate process: Instead of the originating banker's selling through agents and employees, a much larger and more dispersed "selling group" or "selling syndicate" would take the issue from the banking group; those members of the earlier group or groups with distributive facilities would join this new group; and it, too, would be managed by the originating banker. These developments also tended to speed up the distribution process and shorten the lives of the several groups.

The passage of the Securities Act of 1933, as well as the new federal securities transfer taxes that were imposed in 1932 [later repealed], made for a simplification of this system. Under the statute only negotiations between the issuer and "underwriters" are permitted before the filing of the registration statement. Until then the securities may not be offered to the public or even to dealers who are not "underwriters" within the statutory definition. And until the actual effective date of the registration statement, no sales or contracts may be made except with underwriters. This, in practice, means that today the interval between the signing of the underwriting contract and the effectiveness of the registration statement, during which whoever is committed to purchase at a fixed price cannot legally shift his liability against a decline in a frequently volatile market, has been reduced to an hour or two. One result of this has been the development of the "market out" clause in the underwriting contract. Although the use of this clause is by no means universal and in practice it is not considered "cricket" to take advantage of it, it typically provides that the manager of the underwriting group (or the representatives of the group) may terminate the agreement if before the date of public offering (or before the date of the closing or settlement between underwriters and issuer) the issuer or any subsidiary sustains a material adverse change, or trading in the securities is suspended, or minimum or maximum prices or government restrictions on securities trading are put into effect, or a general banking moratorium is declared, or in the judgment of the managing underwriter (or, alternatively, the representatives of the underwriters or a majority in interests of the several underwriters) material changes in "general economic, political, or financial conditions" or the effect of international conditions on financial markets in the United States make it impracticable or inadvisable to market the securities at specified public offering price. This clause is much broader than the traditional *force majeure* provision.

Another result of the Securities Act and the former transfer taxes has been a tendency to reduce the number of transfers between groups and to enlarge the number of "underwriters" who bear the initial risk. In effect, the originating banker and the purchase and banking groups have all been combined into a single "underwriting syndicate or group."

It is difficult to generalize about the practice today, because it may vary substantially from issue to issue. Each of the prominent banking houses tends to develop variations of its own. Nevertheless, certain patterns are familiar. Quite early the underwriter, specifically negativing any obligation, gives the issuer sufficient assurance, either orally or by a "letter of intent" to warrant the issuer's going ahead with the extensive work and expenses that are necessary. The single underwriting group is then created by a contract among its members (usually called the "agreement among purchasers" or the "agreement among underwriters") whereby they agree to be represented in their negotiations with the issuer by one or two or three of their number, whom it is currently the style to call merely the "representatives of the underwriters." It is the latter who, as successors to the old originating bankers, take the initiative and run the show. Through them all the underwriters enter into a "purchase contract" directly with the issuer. In order to limit exposure under § 11 of the 1933 Act, the liability of each underwriter to the issuer is several rather than joint. The trend has been toward larger underwriting groups, whose members are more and more able to do their own distributing. For that reason, and because of the tremendous expansion of the retail capability of many of the underwriting houses, there has also been a tendency to deemphasize formal "selling groups."

Typically the underwriters authorize their representatives to reserve out of the syndicate account (the "pot") whatever amount of the issue the latter choose for sale to selling-group dealers—sometimes termed simply "selected dealers"—as well as institutional investors. The dealers are usually selected by the representatives, or in any event approved by them if suggested by other members of the underwriting group. The degree of formality that surrounds the organization of the selling group (if there is one) or the selection of the "selected dealers" depends largely on the predilections of the representatives. Usually the dealers sign some sort of uniform "dealer offering letter" that is sent to them by the representatives.

The method of determining the [participations] of the several underwriters is by no means fixed. How much a particular house gets is apt to depend on its prestige, its capital, its distributing capacity, its geographical location, whether it has any special outlets (perhaps connections with large pension funds or the like), and frequently the issuer's wishes. The participation of a given house is not necessarily related to the amount it can distribute. Some houses join the group primarily as underwriters, with a view to making a profit out of assuming their shares of the risk, and they may give up most or all of their participations for sale by the representatives, for their account, to institutions and dealers. In other words, the amount reserved for such sale is not always prorated among the accounts of all the underwriters. Sometimes it is, but sometimes each member of the group indicates to the representatives what proportion of its share it would like to have for its own retail distribution. The portion that particular houses thus distribute at retail usually varies between 25 and 75 percent. Those underwriters who want more for their own retail distribution become "selected dealers." Not infrequently, too, the representatives reserve the right, in checking on the progress of the distribution, to take securities away from those underwriters that are slow and allocate them to members of the selling group whose distribution has been more successful. In any event the representatives are obligated under the "agreement among purchasers" to notify each underwriter, on or before the public offering date, of the amount of its securities that has not been reserved for offering to institutions and dealers, so that the several underwriters will know how much they have to distribute. . . .

[A recent trend] will bear watching . . . .

. . . The entire syndication procedure may be going the way of the elaborate pre-1933 system. Although 98 percent of common stock issues (measured in dollars) were syndicated as recently as 1981, by 1985 more than 30 percent were sold entirely by the managing underwriters. With 50–85 percent of even a syndicated deal going to institutional investors in the light of the increasing institutionalization of the market, syndication does not buy much extra distribution. . . .

3. BEST–EFFORTS UNDERWRITING

Companies that are not well established are not apt to find an underwriter that will give a firm commitment and assume the risk of distribution. Of necessity, therefore, they customarily distribute their securities through firms that merely undertake to use their best efforts. Paradoxically, this type of distribution is also preferred on occasion by companies that are so well established that they can do without any underwriting commitment, thus saving on cost of distribution. The securities house, instead of *buying* the issue *from* the company and reselling it as principal, *sells* it *for* the company as agent; and its compensation takes the form of an agent's commission rather than a merchant's or dealer's profit. There may still be a selling group to help in the merchandising. But its members likewise do not buy from the issuer; they are subagents. This, of course, is not really underwriting; it is simply merchandising. . . .

(d) AN OVERVIEW OF THE SECURITIES ACT

SECURITIES AND EXCHANGE COMMISSION, THE WORK OF THE SEC 5–8

1986.

Securities Act of 1933

This "truth in securities" law has two basic objectives:

- To require that investors be provided with material information concerning securities offered for public sale; and
- To prevent misrepresentation, deceit, and other fraud in the sale of securities.

A primary means of accomplishing these objectives is disclosure of financial information by registering securities. Securities subject to registration are most corporate debt and equity securities. Government (state and Federal) and mortgage-related debt are not. Certain securities qualify for exemptions from registration provisions; these exemptions are discussed below.

PURPOSE OF REGISTRATION

Registration is intended to provide adequate and accurate disclosure of material facts concerning the company and the securities it proposes to sell. Thus, investors may make a realistic appraisal of the merits of the securities and then exercise informed judgment in determining whether or not to purchase them.

Registration requires, but does not guarantee, the accuracy of the facts represented in the registration statement and prospectus. However, the law does prohibit false and misleading statements under penalty of fine, imprisonment, or both. And, investors who purchase securities and suffer losses have important recovery rights under the law if they can prove that there was incomplete or inaccurate disclosure of material facts in the registration statement or prospectus. If such misstatements are proven, the following could be liable for investor losses sustained in the securities purchase: the issuing company, its responsible directors and officers, the underwriters, controlling interests, the sellers of the securities, and others. These rights must be asserted in an appropriate Federal or state court (not before the Commission, which has no power to award damages).

Registration of securities does not preclude the sale of stock in risky, poorly managed, or unprofitable companies. Nor does the Commission approve or disapprove securities on their merits; it is unlawful to represent otherwise in the sale of securities. The only standard which must be met when registering securities is adequate and accurate disclosure of required material facts concerning the company and the securities it proposes to sell. The fairness of the terms, the issuing company's prospects for successful operation, and other factors affecting the merits of investing in the securities (whether price, promoters' or underwriters' profits, or otherwise) have no bearing on the question of whether or not securities may be registered.

THE REGISTRATION PROCESS

To facilitate registration by different types of companies, the Commission has special forms. These vary in their disclosure requirements but generally provide essential facts while minimizing the burden and expense of complying with the law. In general, registration forms call for disclosure of information such as:

- Description of the registrant's properties and business;
- Description of the significant provisions of the security to be offered for sale and its relationship to the registrant's other capital securities;
- Information about the management of the registrant; and
- Financial statements certified by independent public accountants.

Registration statements and prospectuses on securities become public immediately upon filing with the Commission. After the registration statement is filed, securities may be offered orally or by certain summaries of the information in the registration statement as permitted by Commission rules. However, it is unlawful to sell the securities until the effective date. The act provides that most registration statements shall become effective on the 20th day after filing (or on the 20th day after filing the last amendment). At its discretion, the Commission may advance the effective date if deemed appropriate considering the interests of investors and the public, the adequacy of publicly available information, and the ease with which the facts about the new offering can be disseminated and understood.

Registration statements are examined for compliance with disclosure requirements. If a statement appears to be materially incomplete or inaccurate, the registrant usually is informed by letter and given an opportunity to file correcting or clarifying amendments. The Commission, however, has authority to refuse or suspend the effectiveness of any registration statement if it finds that material representations are misleading, inaccurate, or incomplete.

The Commission may conclude that material deficiencies in some registration statements appear to stem from a deliberate attempt to conceal or mislead, or that the deficiencies do not lend themselves to correction through the informal letter process. In these cases, the Commission may decide that it is in the public interest to conduct a hearing to develop the facts by evidence. This determines if a "stop order" should be issued to refuse or suspend effectiveness of the statement. The Commission may issue stop orders after the sale of securities has been commenced or completed. A stop order is not a permanent bar to the effectiveness of the registration statement or to the sale of the securities. If amendments are filed correcting the statement in accordance with the stop order decision, the order must be lifted and the statement declared effective.

Although losses which may have been suffered in the purchase of securities are not restored to investors by the stop order, the Commission's order precludes future public sales. Also, the decision and the evidence on which it is based may serve to notify investors of their rights and aid them in their own recovery suits.

EXEMPTIONS FROM REGISTRATION

In general, registration requirements apply to securities of both domestic and foreign issuers, and to securities of foreign governments (or their instrumentalities) sold in domestic securities markets. There are, however, certain exemptions. Among these are:

- Private offerings to a limited number of persons or institutions who have access to the kind of information that registration would disclose and who do not propose to redistribute the securities;
- Offerings restricted to residents of the state in which the issuing company is organized and doing business;
- Securities of municipal, state, Federal, and other governmental instrumentalities as well as charitable institutions, banks, and carriers subject to the Interstate Commerce Act;

- Offerings not exceeding certain specified amounts made in compliance with regulations of the Commission; and
- Offerings of "small business investment companies" made in accordance with rules and regulations of the Commission.

Whether or not the securities are exempt from registration, antifraud provisions apply to all sales of securities involving interstate commerce or the mails.

Among the special exemptions from the registration requirement, the "small issue exemption" was adopted by Congress primarily as an aid to small business. The law provides that offerings of securities under $5 million may be exempted from registration, subject to conditions the Commission prescribes to protect investors. The Commission's Regulation A permits certain domestic and Canadian companies to make exempt offerings. A similar regulation is available for offerings under $500,000 by small business investment companies licensed by the Small Business Administration. The Commission's Regulation D permits certain companies to make exempt offerings under $500,000 with only minimal Federal restrictions; more extensive disclosure requirements and other conditions apply for offerings exceeding that amount but less than $5 million.

Exemptions are available when certain specified conditions are met. These conditions include the prior filing of a notification with the appropriate SEC regional office and the use of an offering circular containing certain basic information in the sale of the securities.

SECTION 2. WHAT CONSTITUTES A "SECURITY"

NOTE ON THE MEANING OF "SECURITY"

Section 2(1) of the Securities Act provides that the term "security" means

any note, stock, treasury stock, bond, debenture, evidence of indebtedness, certificate of interest or participation in any profit-sharing agreement, collateral-trust certificate, preorganization certificate or subscription, transferable share, investment contract, voting-trust certificate, certificate of deposit for a security, fractional undivided interest in oil, gas, or other mineral rights, any put, call, straddle, option, or privilege on any security, certificate of deposit, or group or index of securities (including any interest therein or based on the value thereof), or any put, call straddle, option, or privilege entered into on a national securities exchange relating to foreign currency, or, in general, any interest or instrument commonly known as a "security," or any certificate of interest or participation in, temporary or interim certificate for, receipt for, guarantee of, or warrant or right to subscribe to or purchase, any of the foregoing.

Obviously, this definition is extraordinarily broad.

Included within the scope of "security" are such standard documents as stocks and bonds. Also included are instruments of a more variable character designated by such descriptive terms as "investment contract" and "in general, any interest or instrument commonly known as a 'security.'" In particular, the term "investment contract" has been viewed by the courts as a "catch-all" phrase designed to encompass novel devices which serve the same purpose as a security.

The first major case dealing with the scope of Section 2(1) was SEC v. C.M. Joiner Leasing Corp., 320 U.S. 344, 64 S.Ct. 120, 88 L.Ed. 88 (1943). In pursuance of a plan to finance the drilling of oil wells, lessees of large tracts engaged in a campaign to sell assignments of leaseholds and represented to potential purchasers that test oil wells would be drilled. The promotional literature emphasized the potential return to the purchaser upon the drilling of a successful well. In holding that the transactions involved securities within the meaning of Section 2(1), even though under Texas law the leaseholds conveyed interests in land, the Supreme Court noted that

> In the Securities Act the term "security" was defined to include by name or description many documents in which there is common trading for speculation or investment. Some, such as notes, bonds, and stocks, are pretty much standardized and the name alone carries well-settled meaning. Others are of more variable character and were necessarily designated by more descriptive terms, such as "transferable share," "investment contract," and "in general any interest or instrument commonly known as a security." We cannot read out of the statute these general descriptive designations merely because more specific ones have been used to reach some kinds of documents. Instruments may be included within any of these definitions, as a matter of law, if on their face they answer to the name or description. However, the reach of the Act does not stop with the obvious and commonplace. Novel, uncommon, or irregular devices, whatever they appear to be, are also reached if it be proved as matter of fact that they were widely offered or dealt in under terms or courses of dealing which established their character in commerce as "investment contracts," or as "any interest or instrument commonly known as a 'security.'"

320 U.S. at 351, 64 S.Ct. at 123.

Three years later, in SEC v. W.J. Howey Co., 328 U.S. 293, 66 S.Ct. 1100, 90 L.Ed. 1244 (1946), the Supreme Court, in an attempt to clarify the *Joiner* holding, established a definition of "investment contract" that has come to be generally accepted:

> [A]n investment contract for purposes of the Securities Act means a contract, transaction or scheme whereby a person invests his money in a common enterprise and is led to expect profits solely from the efforts of the promoter or a third party. . . .

Id. at 298–99, 66 S.Ct. at 1103, 90 L.Ed. at 1249. In *Howey,* a Florida corporation owning a large citrus grove offered prospective purchasers a land sales contract for small parcels of orchard land along with a service contract for harvesting and marketing the fruit. The purchasers' tracts were jointly cultivated, and the company sold the produce, distributing to the purchasers a portion of the profits based on the acreage they owned. The purchasers had no legal right of entry on the land to market the crop, and had no right to specific fruit. The Supreme Court held that, in effect, the transactions involved the offering of an opportunity to contribute money and share in the profits of a large citrus fruit enterprise managed and partly owned by W.J. Howey Co. The land sales contracts served as a convenient method of determining the investors' allocable shares of the profits, but the resulting transfers of rights in land were viewed by the Court as "purely incidental" to the profit-seeking business venture:

> . . . The investors provide the capital and share in the earnings and profits; the promoters manage, control and operate the enterprise. It follows that the arrangements whereby the investors' interests are made manifest involve investment contracts, regardless of the legal terminology in which such contracts are clothed. . . .

Id. at 300.

Subsequent cases have generally relied on the *Howey* characterization of an "investment contract." However, more recent decisions added important refinements to the *Howey* test.

(i) "Solely" from the Efforts of Others. In SEC v. Glenn W. Turner Enterprises, Inc., 474 F.2d 476 (9th Cir.1973), cert. denied 414 U.S. 821, 94 S.Ct. 117, 38 L.Ed.2d 53, the court held that a pyramid selling scheme constituted investment contracts notwithstanding the fact that the investors themselves participated in the operation of the enterprise. The scheme involved the sale of self-improvement contracts by Dare to be Great, Inc., a subsidiary of Glenn W. Turner Enterprises, which primarily offered the buyer the opportunity of earning commissions on the sale of such contracts to others.

The defendants' main contention was that the buyers of the self-improvement contracts did not expect profits *"solely"* from the efforts of others, but were required to exert some efforts of their own in order to realize a return on their initial cash outlay. Thus, defendants argued that the pyramid selling scheme did not involve "investment contracts" within the meaning of Section 2(1) as interpreted by the court's decision in *Howey.* In rejecting defendants' argument, the Ninth Circuit commented that:

> For purposes of the present case, the sticking point in the *Howey* definition is the word "solely", a qualification which of course exactly fitted the circumstances in *Howey.* All the other elements of the *Howey* test have been met here. There is an

investment of money, a common enterprise,[3] and the expectation of profits to come from the efforts of others. . . .

> We hold, however, that in light of the remedial nature of the legislation, the statutory policy of affording broad protection to the public, and the Supreme Court's admonitions that the definition of securities should be a flexible one, the word "solely" should not be read as a strict or literal limitation on the definition of an investment contract, but rather must be construed realistically, so as to include within the definition those schemes which involve in substance, if not form, securities.

Id. at 481–82. Since literal adherence to the *Howey* test could allow circumvention by a requirement that the buyer contribute a modicum of effort, *id.* at 482, the court looked to a realistic test focusing on "whether the efforts made by those other than the investor are the undeniably significant ones, those essential managerial efforts which affect the failure or success of the enterprise." Id. at 482. Since the buyers in *Glenn W. Turner* were in essence obtaining shares in the proceeds of the selling efforts of Dare, and the success of the enterprise was dependent upon the "essential managerial efforts" of Dare, the court found that the *Howey* test had been satisfied.*

(ii) "Common Enterprise." In SEC v. Continental Commodities Corp., 497 F.2d 516 (5th Cir.1974), the court focused on the requirement of a "common enterprise" under the *Howey* definition. Continental Commodities, the defendant, was a commodities brokerage firm which sold to its customers options guaranteeing them the right to purchase specified commodities futures contracts at a stated price for a specified period of time. The district court concluded that the *Howey* requirement of a common enterprise was not satisfied, since each individual invested in different options and there was no pro-rata sharing of the profits. The court of appeals reversed, saying:

> . . . [W]e cannot accept the district court's view that Continental Commodities did not function as a common enterprise because it invested in different options on commodities futures for some investors than it did for others. . . .

> Rather . . . the critical inquiry is confined to whether the fortuity of the investments collectively is essentially dependent upon promoter expertise. . . .

---

3. A common enterprise is one in which the fortunes of the investor are interwoven with and dependent upon the efforts and success of those seeking the investment or of third parties.

* The Supreme Court has so far declined to express any view on the *Glenn W. Turner* reading of this element of the *Howey* test. *See* United Hous. Found., Inc. v. Forman, 421 U.S. 837, 852 n.16, 95 S.Ct. 2051, 2060 n.16, 44 L.Ed.2d 621, 632 n.16 (1975). Other circuits, however, generally follow *Glenn W. Turner.* See, e.g., Baurer v. Planning Group, Inc., 669 F.2d 770, 778–79 (D.C. Cir. 1981); SEC v. Aqua-Sonic Prods.

Corp., 687 F.2d 577, 581 (2d Cir. 1982), cert. denied 459 U.S. 1086; Lino v. City Investing Co., 487 F.2d 689, 692 (3d Cir. 1973); Youmans v. Simon, 791 F.2d 341, 445–46 (5th Cir. 1986); Davis v. Avco Fin. Servs., Inc., 739 F.2d 1057, 1063 (6th Cir. 1984) (also involving the Dare to be Great, Inc., scheme) cert. denied 470 U.S. 1005, 105 S.Ct. 1359, 84 L.Ed.2d 381 (1985); Miller v. Central Chincilla Group, Inc., 494 F.2d 414, 416–17 (8th Cir. 1974); McCown v. Heidler, 527 F.2d 204, 211 (10th Cir. 1975). But see Villeneuve v. Advanced Business Concepts Corp., 698 F.2d 1121, 1124–25 (11th Cir. 1983), rehearing granted, 698 F.2d 1127.

Id. at 522. Since the court of appeals found that Continental's customers relied on Continental's guidance for the success of their investments, the requisite commonality existed in the "essential fact that the success of the trading enterprise as a whole and customer investments individually is contingent upon the sagacious investment counselling of Continental Commodities." Id. at 522–23. Thus the options were "investment contracts" and therefore securities for purposes of the Securities Acts.

Another variation on the theme of commonality is demonstrated by SEC v. Haffenden–Rimar Int'l, Inc., 496 F.2d 1192 (4th Cir. 1974), which involved a scheme for financing Scotch whiskey inventory through the aging period. Defendant Haffenden–Rimar sold Scotch whiskey to customers, the selection of which would be made by Haffenden–Rimar out of its balanced inventory. The whiskey would then be aged in casks in a warehouse, and a warehouse receipt would be issued to the purchaser. Haffenden–Rimar would repurchase the whiskey for blending when it had aged sufficiently. The sales were promoted on the basis of an annual return of 20–25% on the buyer's investment. The warehouse receipts, demonstrative of the purchaser's interest in the whiskey, were held to be securities, and the requisite commonality was found to exist in the managerial skills and expertise provided by Haffenden–Rimar in the selection and aging process.

(iii) Expectation of Profits—Interests in Apartments. United Housing Foundation, Inc. v. Forman, 421 U.S. 837, 95 S.Ct. 2051, 44 L.Ed.2d 621 (1975), involved the purchase of shares of "stock" in a nonprofit cooperative housing corporation (Co-op City) by tenants in order to obtain the right to lease apartments in the complex. Each tenant was required to buy shares of stock in the cooperative for each room desired, and upon termination of occupancy, to offer his stock to the cooperative at the initial selling price. Thus, the stock was tied inextricably to the apartment, and no profit could be realized upon its resale.

The Supreme Court noted that the basic principle that had guided all of the Court's decisions determining the scope of the definition of "security" was that " 'form should be disregarded for substance and the emphasis should be on economic reality,' " quoting Tcherepnin v. Knight, 389 U.S. 332, 336, 88 S.Ct. 548, 553, 19 L.Ed.2d 564 (1967) (involving the application of the federal securities laws to withdrawable capital shares in an Illinois savings and loan association). The Court thereby rejected any suggestion of a "literal approach" to defining a security, remarking that the language in *Joiner* (quoted supra) was intended only to indicate that most instruments bearing traditional titles enumerated in Section 2(1) were likely to be covered by the securities laws. Although the shares in Co-op City were called "stock," the Court recognized that they did not have any of the characteristics "that in our commercial world fall within the ordinary concept of a security," especially in that the shares lacked "the most common feature of stock: the right to receive 'dividends contingent upon an apportionment of profits.' " Id. at 851. Thus, the Court held that such shares of stock were not "securities," but in effect a recoverable deposit, since the sole purpose of acquiring the shares was to enable the purchaser to occupy an apartment in Co-op City.

(iv) Outer Limits of the Definition of a Security—Interests in Pension Plans. Two important Supreme Court cases, International Brotherhood of Teamsters v. Daniel and Marine Bank v. Weaver, indicate some outer limits of the definition of a security. In International Brotherhood of Teamsters v. Daniel, 439 U.S. 551, 99 S.Ct. 790, 58 L.Ed.2d 808 (1979), the Supreme Court held that an employee's interest in a noncontributory compulsory pension plan did not constitute a "security." In that case a member of the Teamsters had been denied pension benefits because of a seven month hiatus in his work record. The pension plan required twenty years of continuous service in order to be eligible for benefits. The employee sued the Teamsters, his union local, and a trustee of the fund, alleging violations of § 10(b) and Rule 10b–5 of the 1934 Act and § 17(a) of the 1933 Act.

The Court began its analysis by examining the statutory language, noting that neither Act's definition of "security" referred to pension plans of any type. The Court then turned to the respondent's claim that an employee's interest in a plan was an "investment contract." The Court reiterated the *Howey* definition of an investment contract and proceeded to analyze the Teamster pension plan at issue to determine whether it involved an "investment of money" and an "expectation of profit from a common enterprise."

Under the plan the employees made no contributions themselves. The Court stated that any "investment" made in the plan by an employee by permitting part of his compensation from his employer to take the form of a deferred pension benefit was "a relatively insignificant part of an employee's total and indivisible compensation package." The Court said that since an employee surrenders his labor "as a whole" it was "only in the most abstract sense" that an employee exchanged part of his labor in return for the possible benefits. The Court concluded, "Looking at the economic realities, it seems clear that an employee is selling his labor to obtain a livelihood, not making an investment" for the future.

Turning to the second element of the *Howey* definition, the Court found that the plan involved no expectation of profits from a common enterprise. Although the pension fund depended to some extent on earnings from its assets, which in turn depended upon the efforts of the pension fund's managers, the Court said that a far larger portion of a pension fund's income comes from employer contributions, an income source that did not depend on the skill or efforts of the fund's managers.*

---

* The Court also said that the lesser importance of investment earnings to a pension fund was diminished still further by the fact that "substantial preconditions to vesting," rather than the financial success of the fund, were the principal barrier's to a particular employee's realization of benefits. Therefore, the Court concluded, the possibility of participating in a pension plan's asset earnings was too speculative and insubstantial to bring the entire pension fund within the Securities Acts (439 U.S. at 562, 99 S.Ct. at 797–8).

The Court's opinion focused on the compulsory, noncontributory aspects of the pension plan at issue in the *Daniel* case. This raises the question whether the rationale in *Daniel* should apply to noncompulsory or contributory plans where the employee's decision to participate is a conscious one and the plan cannot be characterized an insignificant part of an employee's "indivisible" compensation package.

In Marine Bank v. Weaver, 455 U.S. 551, 102 S.Ct. 1220, 71 L.Ed.2d 409 (1982), the Supreme Court held that a bank certificate of deposit was not a "security" under section 3(a)(10), because extensive banking regulation, together with federal insurance, virtually eliminated any risk to the holder of such a certificate:

> . . . In our view . . . there is an important difference between a bank certificate of deposit and other long-term debt obligations. This certificate of deposit was issued by a federally regulated bank which is subject to the comprehensive set of regulations governing the banking industry. Deposits in federally regulated banks are protected by the reserve, reporting, and inspection requirements of the federal banking laws; advertising relating to the interest paid on deposits is also regulated. In addition, deposits are insured by the Federal Deposit Insurance Corporation. . . .

> We see, therefore, important differences between a certificate of deposit purchased from a federally regulated bank and other long-term debt obligations. The Court of Appeals failed to give appropriate weight to the important fact that the purchaser of a certificate of deposit is virtually guaranteed payment in full, whereas the holder of an ordinary long-term debt obligation assumes the risk of the borrower's insolvency. The definition of "security" in the 1934 Act provides that an instrument which seems to fall within the broad sweep of the Act is not to be considered a security if the context otherwise requires. It is unnecessary to subject issuers of bank certificates of deposit to liability under the antifraud provisions of the federal securities laws since the holders of bank certificates of deposit are abundantly protected under the federal banking laws. . . .

SECTION 3. WHAT CONSTITUTES A "SALE" AND AN "OFFER TO SELL"

SECURITIES ACT §§ 2(3), 3(a)(9);
SECURITIES ACT RULE 145

[See Statutory Supplement]

NOTE ON THE MEANING OF "SALE" AND "OFFER TO SELL"

The term "sale" or "sell" is defined in section 2(3) of the Securities Act to include "every contract of sale or disposition of a security or interest in a security, for value." The term "offer to sell," "offer for sale," or "offer" is defined to include "every attempt or offer to dispose of, or solicitation of an offer to buy, a security or interest in a security, for value." The use of the word "includes" rather than "means" emphasizes the breadth of these definitions, and the courts have also interpreted the terms broadly "to include ingenious methods employed to obtain money from members of the public to finance ventures." S.E.C. v. Addison, 194 F.Supp. 709, 722 (N.D. Tex.1961)

A transfer of securities need not be voluntary to be a sale under the Securities Act. For example, most mergers and stock-for-assets combinations, and certain reclassifications, are sales under Rule 145.

Section 3(a)(9) of the Securities Act provides that "the provisions of this title shall not apply to. . . . any security exchanged by the issuer with its existing security holders exclusively where no commission or other remuneration is paid or given directly or indirectly for soliciting such exchange." There is an overlap between section 3(a)(9) and Rule 145, because both cover reclassifications. The SEC's position is that Rule 145 is applicable only if no exemption is available, so that if section 3(a)(9) is applicable to a reclassification, Rule 145 is not. See Securities Act Release No. 5463.

Rule 145 does not cover business combinations achieved through a stock-for-stock exchange. However, such an exchange is clearly a sale, and is not covered by Rule 145 only because Rule 145 was adopted to reverse a prior SEC interpretation under which mergers and other stock-for-assets transactions were not deemed to be sales. This interpretation had not affected stock-for-stock exchange offers, which therefore did not need to be covered by Rule 145.

———

SECTION 4. THE REQUIREMENT OF REGISTRATION

———

(a) THE BROAD SWEEP OF SECTION 5

———

SECURITIES ACT §§ 2(10), 5

[See Statutory Supplement]

———

NOTE ON SECTION 5

The structure of the Securities Act is exceptionally intricate. The key provision is section 5. Section 5(a) provides:

> Unless a registration statement is in effect as to a security, it shall be unlawful for any person, directly or indirectly—
>
> (1) to make use of any means or instruments of transportation or communication in interstate commerce or of the mails to sell such security through the use or medium of any prospectus or otherwise; or
>
> (2) to carry or cause to be carried through the mails or in interstate commerce, by any means or instruments of transportation, any such security for the purpose of sale or for delivery after sale.

Section 5(c) provides:

> It shall be unlawful for any person, directly or indirectly, to make use of any means or instruments of transportation or communication in interstate commerce or of the mails to offer to sell or offer to buy through the use or medium of any prospectus or otherwise any security, unless a registration statement has been filed as to such security. . . .

Section 2(10) defines a "prospectus" to mean "any prospectus, notice, circular, advertisement, letter, or communication, written or by radio or television, which offers any security for sale or confirms the sale of any security," subject to certain exceptions. Putting section 2(10) together with section 5(a) and (c), if any person proposes to sell a security by any means of communication in interstate commerce or by mail, or sends a security through the mail for purposes of sale, or offers to buy or sell a security by a letter, the security must be registered, unless an exemption applies. On its face, therefore, section 5 prohibits virtually every sale of securities, no matter how trivial and no matter who the seller, unless the securities are registered under the Act. Other provisions of the Act, however, carve out a variety of exemptions for large classes of securities and transactions. By virtue of the exemptions, these securities and transactions do not require registration despite the sweeping language of section 5. The balance of this Section will consider exemptions based on the number and character of the offerees, on the size of the offering, on the intrastate nature of an offering, and on the absence of an issuer, underwriter, or dealer.

———

(b) PRIVATE PLACEMENTS

SECURITIES ACT § 4(2)

4. The provisions of section 5 shall not apply to . . .

(2) transactions by an issuer not involving any public offering.

S.E.C. v. RALSTON PURINA CO.

Supreme Court of the United States, 1953.
346 U.S. 119, 73 S.Ct. 981, 97 L.Ed. 1494.

Mr. Justice CLARK delivered the opinion of the Court.

Section 4(1) of the Securities Act of 1933 exempts "transactions by an issuer not involving any public offering" [1] from the registration requirements of § 5. We must decide whether Ralston Purina's offerings of treasury stock to its "key employees" are within this exemption. On a complaint brought by the Commission under § 20(b) of the Act seeking to enjoin respondent's unregistered offerings, the District Court held the exemption applicable and dismissed the suit. The Court of Appeals affirmed. The question has arisen many times since the Act was passed; an apparent need to define the scope of the private offering exemption prompted certiorari. 345 U.S. 903, 73 S.Ct. 643.

Ralston Purina manufactures and distributes various feed and cereal products. Its processing and distribution facilities are scattered throughout the United States and Canada, staffed by some 7,000 employees. At least since 1911 the company has had a policy of encouraging stock ownership among its employees; more particularly, since 1942 it has made authorized but unissued common shares available to some of them. Between 1947 and 1951, the period covered by the record in this case, Ralston Purina sold nearly $2,000,000 of stock to employees without registration and in so doing made use of the mails.

In each of these years, a corporate resolution authorized the sale of common stock "to employees . . . who shall, without any solicitation by the Company or its officers or employees, inquire of any of them as to how to purchase common stock of Ralston Purina Company." A memorandum sent to branch and store managers after the resolution was adopted, advised that "The only employees to whom this stock will be available will be those who take the initiative and are interested in buying stock at present market prices." Among those responding to these offers were employees with the duties of artist, bakeshop foreman, chow loading foreman, clerical assistant,

---

1. 48 Stat. 77, as amended, 48 Stat. 906, 15 U.S.C. § 77d, 15 U.S.C.A. § 77d. [Ed. This is now § 4(2).]

copywriter, electrician, stock clerk, mill office clerk, order credit trainee, production trainee, stenographer, and veterinarian. The buyers lived in over fifty widely separated communities scattered from Garland, Texas, to Nashua, New Hampshire and Visalia, California. The lowest salary bracket of those purchasing was $2,700 in 1949, $2,435 in 1950 and $3,107 in 1951. The record shows that in 1947, 243 employees bought stock, 20 in 1948, 414 in 1949, 411 in 1950, and the 1951 offer, interrupted by this litigation, produced 165 applications to purchase. No records were kept of those to whom the offers were made; the estimated number in 1951 was 500.

The company bottoms its exemption claim on the classification of all offerees as "key employees" in its organization. Its position on trial was that "A key employee . . . is not confined to an organization chart. It would include an individual who is eligible for promotion, an individual who especially influences others or who advises others, a person whom the employees look to in some special way, an individual, of course, who carries some special responsibility, who is sympathetic to management and who is ambitious and who the management feels is likely to be promoted to a greater responsibility." That an offering to all of its employees would be public is conceded.

The Securities Act nowhere defines the scope of § 4(1)'s private offering exemption. Nor is the legislative history of much help in staking out its boundaries. The problem was first dealt with in § 4(1) of the House Bill, H.R. 5480, 73d Cong., 1st Sess., which exempted "transactions by an issuer not with or through an underwriter; . . ." The bill, as reported by the House Committee, added "and not involving any public offering." H.R.Rep. No. 85, 73d Cong., 1st Sess. 1. This was thought to be one of those transactions "where there is no practical need for [the bill's] application or where the public benefits are too remote." Id., at 5.[5] The exemption as thus delimited became law.[6] It assumed its present shape with the deletion of "not with or through an underwriter" by § 203(a) of the Securities Exchange Act of 1934, 48 Stat. 906, a change regarded as the elimination of superfluous language. H.R.Rep. No. 1838, 73d Cong., 2d Sess. 41.

Decisions under comparable exemptions in the English Companies Acts and state "blue sky" laws, the statutory antecedents of federal securities legislation, have made one thing clear—to be public, an offer need not be open to the whole world. In Securities and Exchange Comm'n v. Sunbeam Gold Mines Co., 95 F.2d 699 (9th

---

5. " * * * the bill does not affect transactions beyond the need of public protection in order to prevent recurrences of demonstrated abuses." Id., at 7. In a somewhat different tenor, the report spoke of this as an exemption of "transactions by an issuer unless made by or through an underwriter so as to permit an issuer to make a specific or an isolated sale of its securities to a particular person, but insisting that if a sale of the issuer's securities should be made generally to the public that that transaction shall come within the purview of the Act." Id., at 15, 16.

6. The only subsequent reference was an oblique one in the statement of the House Managers on the Conference Report: "Sales of stock to stockholders become subject to the act unless the stockholders are so small in number that the sale to them does not constitute a public offering." H.R.Rep. No. 152, 73d Cong., 1st Sess. 25.

Cir. 1938), this point was made in dealing with an offering to the stockholders of two corporations about to be merged. Judge Denman observed that:

> "In its broadest meaning the term 'public' distinguishes the populace at large from groups of individual members of the public segregated because of some common interest or characteristic. Yet such a distinction is inadequate for practical purposes; manifestly, an offering of securities to all redheaded men, to all residents of Chicago or San Francisco, to all existing stockholders of the General Motors Corporation or the American Telephone & Telegraph Company, is no less 'public', in every realistic sense of the word, than an unrestricted offering to the world at large. Such an offering, though not open to everyone who may choose to apply, is none the less 'public' in character, for the means used to select the particular individuals to whom the offering is to be made bear no sensible relation to the purposes for which the selection is made. . . . To determine the distinction between 'public' and 'private' in any particular context, it is essential to examine the circumstances under which the distinction is sought to be established and to consider the purposes sought to be achieved by such distinction." 95 F.2d at 701.

The courts below purported to apply this test. The District Court held, in the language of the *Sunbeam* decision, that "The purpose of the selection bears a 'sensible relation' to the class chosen," finding that "The sole purpose of the 'selection' is to keep part stock ownership of the business within the operating personnel of the business and to spread ownership throughout all departments and activities of the business." The Court of Appeals treated the case as involving "an offering, without solicitation, of common stock to a selected group of key employees of the issuer, most of whom are already stockholders when the offering is made, with the sole purpose of enabling them to secure a proprietary interest in the company or to increase the interest already held by them."

Exemption from the registration requirements of the Securities Act is the question. The design of the statute is to protect investors by promoting full disclosure of information thought necessary to informed investment decisions. The natural way to interpret the private offering exemption is in light of the statutory purpose. Since exempt transactions are those as to which "there is no practical need for [the bill's] application," the applicability of § 4(1) should turn on whether the particular class of persons affected need the protection of the Act. An offering to those who are shown to be able to fend for themselves is a transaction "not involving any public offering."

The Commission would have us go one step further and hold that "an offering to a substantial number of the public" is not exempt under § 4(1). We are advised that "whatever the special circumstances, the Commission has consistently interpreted the exemption as being inapplicable when a large number of offerees is involved." But the statute would seem to apply to a "public offering" whether to few or many.[11] It may well be that offerings to a substantial number of persons would rarely be exempt. Indeed nothing prevents the commission, in enforcing the statute, from using some kind of numerical test in deciding when to investigate particular exemption claims. But there is no warrant for superimposing a quantity limit on private offerings as a matter of statutory interpretation.

The exemption, as we construe it, does not deprive corporate employees, as a class, of the safeguards of the Act. We agree that some employee offerings may come within § 4(1), e.g., one made to executive personnel who because of their position have access to the same kind of information that the act would make available in the form of a registration statement. Absent such a showing of special circumstances, employees are just as much members of the investing "public" as any of their neighbors in the community. Although we do not rely on it, the rejection in 1934 of an amendment which would have specifically exempted employee stock offerings supports this conclusion. The House Managers, commenting on the Conference Report, said that "the participants in employees' stock-investment plans may be in as great need of the protection afforded by availability of information concerning the issuer for which they work as are most other members of the public." H.R.Rep. No. 1838, 73d Cong., 2d Sess. 41.

Keeping in mind the broadly remedial purposes of federal securities legislation, imposition of the burden of proof on an issuer who would plead the exemption seems to us fair and reasonable. Schlemmer v. Buffalo, R. & P.R. Co., 1907, 205 U.S. 1, 10, 27 S.Ct. 407, 408, 51 L.Ed. 681. Agreeing, the court below thought the burden met primarily because of the respondent's purpose in singling out its key employees for stock offerings. But once it is seen that the exemption question turns on the knowledge of the offerees, the issuer's motives, laudable though they may be, fade into irrelevance. The focus of inquiry should be on the need of the offerees for the protections afforded by registration. The employees here were not shown to have access to the kind of information which registration would disclose. The obvious opportunities for pressure and imposition make it advisable that they be entitled to compliance with § 5.

Reversed.

The CHIEF JUSTICE and Mr. Justice BURTON dissent.

Mr. Justice JACKSON took no part in the consideration or decision of this case.

---

11. See Viscount Sumner's frequently quoted dictum in Nash v. Lynde, " 'The public' . . . is of course a general word. No particular numbers are prescribed. Anything from two to infinity may serve: perhaps even one, if he is intended to be the first of a series of subscribers, but makes further proceedings needless by himself subscribing the whole." [1929] A.C. 158, 169.

(c) LIMITED OFFERINGS

SECURITIES ACT §§ 2(15), 3(b), 4(2), 4(6)
SECURITIES ACT RULE 215; REGULATION D
(RULES 501–506)

[See Statutory Supplement]

D. RATNER, SECURITIES REGULATION IN A
NUTSHELL 58–63

3d ed. 1988.

SA § 3(b) authorizes the SEC, "by rules and regulations," to exempt offerings, not exceeding a specified dollar amount, when it finds that registration is not necessary "by reason of the small amount involved or the limited character of the public offering." The dollar limit has been periodically raised by Congress from its initial level of $100,000, the most recent increase coming in 1980 and raising the limit from $2 million to the present level of $5 million. Under this authority, the Commission has adopted a number of rules providing exemptions for certain specialized kinds of offerings, as well as the general exemption in Regulation A. . . .

Also in 1980, Congress added a new § 4(6) to the 1933 Act, exempting any offering of not more than $5 million made solely to "accredited investors" (defined to include specified types of institutions and other classes of investors that the SEC might specify by rule).

These developments set the stage for the coordination of the private offering and small offering exemptions in a new Regulation D. . . .

In 1982, the Commission took a major step in simplifying and coordinating the exemptions for limited offerings by . . . [adopting] Regulation D, composed of Rules 501 through 506.

Definitions. Rule 501 defines the terms used in Regulation D. The most important of these is the term "accredited investor," which is defined to include (1) any bank, insurance company, investment company, or employee benefit plan, (2) any business development company, (3) any charitable or educational institution with assets of more than $5 million, (4) any director, executive officer or general partner of the issuer, (5) any person who purchases at least $150,000 of the securities being offered, provided the purchase does not exceed 20% of his net worth, (6) any person with a net worth of more than $1 million, and (7) any person with an annual income of more than $200,000.

Rule 502 sets forth certain conditions applicable to all offerings under Regulation D. . . .

Information. If an issuer sells securities under Rule 504 or to accredited investors only, there are no specific requirements for furnishing information to offerees or purchasers. If securities are sold to non-accredited purchasers under Rule 505 or 506, the following information must be furnished to all purchasers:

If the issuer is not registered under the 1934 Act, the information that would be contained in a registration statement on Form S–18 or, if the offering exceeds $5 million, the information that would be contained in a registration statement on the form the issuer would be entitled to use.

If the issuer is registered under the 1934 Act, its most recent annual report to shareholders and proxy statement, or the information contained in its most recent annual report to the Commission, plus specified updating and supplemental information.

Manner of Offering and Limitations on Resale. No general solicitation or general offering is permitted. Securities sold pursuant to Regulation D are considered to have been purchased in a non-public offering and cannot be resold without registration unless an exemption is available under § 4(1) or Rule 144. . . . The issuer must take certain specified precautions to insure that the purchasers do not make resales. . . .

Rule 504. Under Rule 504, an issuer can sell an aggregate of $500,000 of securities in any twelve-month period to any number of purchasers, accredited or non-accredited, with no requirements for furnishing of any information to the purchasers. If the offering is made only in states where it must be registered under state law and a disclosure document delivered to purchasers before the sale, the Rule 502 restrictions on the manner of offering and resales by purchasers do not apply. The exemption is available to all issuers except investment companies and companies registered under the 1934 Act.

Rule 505. Under Rule 505, an issuer can sell up to $5 million of securities in any 12–month period to any number of accredited investors and up to 35 other purchasers. If there are any non-accredited purchasers, the information prescribed by Rule 502 must be furnished to all purchasers. The exemption is available to any issuer other than an investment company or an issuer that would be disqualified by Rule 252 from using Regulation A. . . .

Rule 506. Under Rule 506, an issuer can sell an unlimited amount of securities to any number of accredited investors and up to 35 other purchasers. Prior to the sale, the issuer must reasonably believe that each non-accredited purchaser, or his "purchaser representative" (a term defined in Rule 501) has such knowledge or experience in financial and business matters that he is capable of evaluating the merits and risks of the prospective investment. If there are any non-accredited purchasers, the information prescribed by Rule 502 must be furnished to all purchasers. The exemption is available to all issuers.

Offerings complying with the terms of Rule 504 or 505 are deemed to be exempt under SA § 3(b); offerings pursuant to Rule

506, since they may exceed $5 million, cannot be exempt under § 3(b) and are considered to be non-public offerings under § 4(2). Rule 506 is not the exclusive means of making a non-public offering; the Preliminary Note to Regulation D states specifically that failure to satisfy all the terms and conditions of Rule 506 shall not raise any presumption that the exemption provided by § 4(2) is not available.

In 1987, the SEC proposed amendments to Regulation D which would (1) extend the definition of "accredited investor" to include savings institutions, broker-dealers and certain other categories, (2) increase the offering limit under Rule 504 to $1 million, (3) permit general solicitation in more offerings under Rule 504, and (4) extend the disqualifications found in Rule 505 to offerings under Rule 506. SA Rel. 6683.

Section 4(6). The Commission in 1982 also adopted a new Rule 215, defining the term "accredited investor" for purposes of § 4(6) to include the various categories of purchasers listed in Rule 501. Section 4(6) is thus an alternative exemption for an offering of up to $5 million made solely to accredited investors.

NOTE ON THE SIGNIFICANCE OF EXEMPTIONS

It's important to keep in mind that a provision exempting securities from registration under section 5 does not necessarily mean that a seller or offeror of those securities is not required to provide the buyers with information. Some exemptions explicitly require the seller to provide information very much like that required in a registration statement. For example, Regulation A (discussed below in Section (e)) requires an elaborate Offering Circular, and Regulation D requires the provision of registration-like information in certain cases. Other exemptions implicitly require the provision of information. For example, a distribution is unlikely to qualify as a private placement unless the offerees have had access to the kind of information that would have been disclosed under a registration statement. Accordingly, when sales are made under section 4(2) or Rule 506 through investment bankers, the issuer typically supplies an information statement that provides prospectus-like disclosure.

If an offeror of securities has to provide information comparable to that in a registration statement, what is the benefit of an exemption? First, *comparable* information may cost less to assemble and provide than the full information required in a registration statement. Second, an information statement may not require clearance by the SEC, as does a registration statement. Third, certain liability provisions of the Securities Act are keyed into registration, and therefore do not apply to an information statement. See Section 7, infra.

(d) THE INTRASTATE EXEMPTION

SECURITIES ACT § 3(a)(11); SECURITIES ACT RULE 147

[See Statutory Supplement]

SECURITIES ACT RELEASE NO. 4434 (1961)

SECTION 3(a)(11) EXEMPTIONS FOR LOCAL OFFERINGS . . .

General Nature of Exemption

Section 3(a)(11), as amended in 1954, exempts from the registration and prospectus requirements of the Act:

> Any security which is a part of an issue offered and sold only to persons resident within a single State or Territory, where the issuer of such security is a person resident and doing business within, or, if a corporation, incorporated by and doing business within, such State or Territory.

The legislative history of the Securities Act clearly shows that this exemption was designed to apply only to local financing that may practicably be consummated in its entirety within the state or territory in which the issuer is both incorporated and doing business. As appears from the legislative history, by amendment to the Act in 1934, this exemption was removed from section 5(c) and inserted in section 3, relating to "Exempted Securities," in order to relieve dealers of an unintended restriction on trading activity. This amendment was not intended to detract from its essential character as a transaction exemption. . . .

Doing Business Within the State

In view of the local character of the section 3(a)(11) exemption, the requirement that the issuer be doing business in the state can only be satisfied by the performance of substantial operational activities in the state of incorporation. The doing business requirement is not met by functions in the particular state such as bookkeeping, stock record and similar activities or by offering securities in the state. . . .

Residence Within the State

Section 3(a)(11) requires that the entire issue be confined to a single state in which the issuer, the offerees and the purchasers are residents. Mere presence in the state is not sufficient to constitute residence as in the case of military personnel at a military post. S.E.C. v. Capital Funds, Inc. No. A46–60, D.Alaska, 1960. The mere obtaining of formal representations of residence and agreements not to resell to nonresidents or agreements that sales are void if the purchaser is a nonresident should not be relied upon without more as establishing the availability of the exemption. . . .

NOTE ON THE INTRASTATE EXEMPTION

1. Under section 3(a)(11), all offerees (not merely all purchasers) must be residents of the state in question. An offer to even one nonresident makes the exemption unavailable, even if the offeree decides not to buy.

2. Section 3(a)(11) is restricted to cases where the corporation is both doing business *and* incorporated in the relevant state. Corporations incorporated in Delaware therefore cannot make use of the exemption unless they are doing business in Delaware and restrict the offer to Delaware residents.

3. Rule 147 offers a safe harbor for determining whether the requirements of section 3(a)(11) are satisfied, but it is not exclusive. An issuer may show that it satisfied section 3(a)(11) even though it failed to satisfy Rule 147.

(e) REGULATION A

SECURITIES ACT § 3(b); SECURITIES ACT REG. A [RULES 251–263]

[See Statutory Supplement]

SONSINI, REGULATION A, 16 REVIEW SEC. REG. 781

1983.

Regulation A is the body of rules the SEC designed pursuant to section 3(b) to provide a general exemption for issuances of up to $1,500,000. Specifically, it exempts from registration: (i) offerings by issuers, certain estates, or affiliates up to $1,500,000, provided that the aggregate offering price of securities offered or sold on behalf of any one affiliate, other than an estate, does not exceed $100,000; and (ii) offerings by persons other than the issuer or its affiliates, up to $100,000, provided that the aggregate offering price of securities offered or sold on behalf of all such other persons does not exceed $300,000. Notwithstanding the above limitations, the aggregate offering price of securities offered or sold on behalf of any estate may not exceed $500,000. As with other exemptions, regulation A only provides an exemption from the registration requirements and not from the antifraud provisions of the Securities Act. . . .

PRACTICAL ASPECTS OF REGULATION A

The most practical use of regulation A is for the offer and sale of securities by nonreporting ("privately held") issuers. Such offerings usually occur under employee stock option and purchase plans. These plans typically provide for a rather broad distribution of securities among the employee group. Because the plans usually involve a continuing offering, i.e., the continuous grant of stock options or the sale of shares under stock purchase plans, sooner or later the issuer faces a greater difficulty in perfecting an exemption under the Securities Act for the transactions. As the employee group broadens and deepens within the organization to middle and lower management personnel, the issuer can no longer rely on many of the conditions that must be satisfied under the private placement exemptions. Similarly, because many employees will reside in jurisdictions other than those where the issuer is incorporated and doing business, the intrastate offering exemption under section 3(a)(11) and rule 147 of the Securities Act will be unavailable. Also, privately held issuers will often find it inappropriate to file a registration statement under the Securities Act to cover its transactions under employee stock benefit plans. The cost of registration may be high, and the issuer may not be able to satisfy certain disclosure requirements, such as those regarding financial statements. Therefore, the exemption offered by regulation A may prove most beneficial in these employee stock benefit plans. The burden of disclosure is less than under the standard registration statement forms, particularly with respect to certified financial statements. . . . The cost of perfecting the exemption under the regulation will usually be less than for the preparation, filing, and policing of a registration statement. In addition, the scope of the required disclosure under the offering circular may be well suited for an offering of securities to an employee group who, by definition, are familiar with the business of the issuer. . . .

(f) TRANSACTIONS NOT INVOLVING AN ISSUER, UNDERWRITER, OR DEALER

SECURITIES ACT §§ 2(11), 4(1), 4(3)

[See Statutory Supplement]

INTRODUCTORY NOTE

Section 4(1) of the Securities Act provides that "The provisions of section 5 shall not apply to . . . transactions by any person other than an issuer, underwriter, or dealer." Requiring registration for *issuer* transactions is fairly straightforward, and section 4(3) exempts most transactions by *dealers*. Accordingly, the difficult problems under § 4(1) concern the meaning of the term "underwriter."

The paradigm case of an underwriter is an investment professional who distributes stock on behalf of an issuer. Section 2(11), however, defines "underwriter" so as to pick up transactions that don't look anything like that paradigm:

> The term "underwriter" means any person who has purchased from an issuer with a view to, or offers or sells for an issuer in connection with, the distribution of any security, or participates or has a direct or indirect participation in any such undertaking, or participates or has a participation in the direct or indirect underwriting of any such undertaking; but such term shall not include a person whose interest is limited to a commission from an underwriter or dealer not in excess of the usual and customary distributors' or sellers' commission. As used in this paragraph the term "issuer" shall include, in addition to an issuer, any person directly or indirectly controlling or controlled by the issuer, or any person under direct or indirect common control with the issuer.

This balance of this Section will focus on the meaning and implications of three terms in section (2)(11): (i) "offers or sells for an issuer in connection with . . . the distribution of any security"; (ii) "any person directly or indirectly controlling . . . the issuer"; and (iii) "purchased from an issuer with a view to . . . the distribution of any security."

---

1. "Offers or sells for an issuer in connection with . . . the distribution of any security"

NOTE ON SEC v. CHINESE BENEVOLENT ASS'N

The language in § 2(11), "offers or sells for an issuer in connection with . . . the distribution of any security," picks up the paradigm case of an investment banker distributing securities on an issuer's behalf. This language has also been broadly construed to encompass other situations. Perhaps the most notable case is SEC v. Chinese Consolidated Benevolent Ass'n., 120 F.2d 738 (2d Cir.1941), cert. denied, 314 U.S. 618, 62 S.Ct. 106, 86 L.Ed. 497. There, persons loyal to the Republic of China, who sold Chinese government bonds in the United States without recompense at the beginning of World War II, were held to be underwriters, within the meaning of section 2(11), and therefore subject to the registration requirements of the Securities Act. The court said:

> Under section 4(1) the defendant is not exempt from registration requirements if it is "an underwriter". The court below reasons that it is not to be regarded as an underwriter since it does not sell or solicit offers to buy "for an issuer in connection with, the distribution" of securities.

In other words, it seems to have been held that only solicitation authorized by the issuer in connection with the distribution of the Chinese bonds would satisfy the definition of underwriter contained in Section 2(11) and that defendant's activities were never for the Chinese government but only for the purchasers of the bonds. Though the defendant solicited the orders, obtained the cash from the purchasers and caused both to be forwarded so as to procure the bonds, it is nevertheless contended that its acts could not have been for the Chinese government because it had no contractual arrangement or even understanding with the latter. But the aim of the Securities Act is to have information available for investors. This objective will be defeated if buying orders can be solicited which result in uninformed and improvident purchasers. It can make no difference as regards the policy of the act whether an issuer has solicited orders through an agent, or has merely taken advantage of the services of a person interested for patriotic reasons in securing offers to buy. The aim of the issuer is to promote the distribution of the securities, and of the Securities Act is to protect the public by requiring that it be furnished with adequate information upon which to make investments. Accordingly the words "[sell] for an issuer in connection with the distribution of any security" ought to be read as covering continual solicitations, such as the defendant was engaged in, which normally would result in a distribution of issues of unregistered securities within the United States. Here a series of events were set in motion by the solicitation of offers to buy which culminated in a distribution that was initiated by the defendant. We hold that the defendant acted as an underwriter.

120 F.2d at 740–41.

––––––––––

2. "Any person directly or indirectly controlling the issuer"; What constitutes a "distribution"

––––––––––

NOTE ON OFFERS OR SALES FOR CONTROLLING PERSONS

Under the last sentence of section 2(11), a person is an "underwriter" if he offers or sells securities for a person who *controls* the issuer, "in connection with . . . the distribution of any security." This rule is particularly important in cases where brokers or dealers sell stock, without registration, on behalf of a controlling person. The applicability of this rule is often complicated by the issue whether a particular sale on behalf of a controlling person is a "distribution."

In In the Matter of Ira Haupt & Co., 23 S.E.C. 589 (1946), Ira Haupt & Company, a brokerage firm, sold approximately 93,000 shares of the unregistered common stock of Park & Tilford, Inc. for the accounts of David A. Schulte and a corporation and trust controlled by him. The sales were made in small lots over the course of approximately six months pursuant to Schulte's instructions to sell 200-share blocks from his personal holdings at "59 and every quarter up," and up to 73,000 shares for the trust "at $80 per share or better." The price of the stock rose sharply from $57 to $98 per share during this period because of the announcement that a whiskey dividend would be distributed in kind to the shareholders of Park & Tilford. (It should be borne in mind that a dividend in liquor was especially welcome during the wartime shortage.) Schulte was aware of the planned dividend at the time he placed his order to sell with Ira Haupt.

The Schulte interests initially held over 90 percent of the common stock of Park & Tilford, and it was therefore conceded that they controlled Park & Tilford. It was thus clear that Ira Haupt was selling the securities for a person "controlling the issuer" as contemplated by the last sentence of section 2(11). Ira Haupt nevertheless denied that it was a statutory underwriter for purposes of the transactions, claiming that such sales were not effected "in connection with . . . the distribution of any security."

At the outset, the Commission noted that although the term "distribution" is not defined in the Act, it had previously been held to comprise "the entire process by which in the course of a public offering the block of securities is dispersed and ultimately comes to rest in the hands of the investing public." The Commission further remarked:

> We find no validity in the argument that a predetermination of the precise number of shares which are to be publicly dispersed is an essential element of a distribution. Nor do we think that a "distribution" loses its character as such merely because the extent of the offering may depend on certain conditions such as the market price. . . . Such offerings are not any less a "distribution" merely because their precise extent cannot be predetermined.

Ira Haupt claimed that it was not aware of the distribution intended by the Schulte interests. The Commission concluded that this claim conflicted with the facts:

> . . . The record shows that respondent [Ira Haupt] was informed of the extent of Schulte's holdings and of his plan to sell 200 share blocks "at 59 and every quarter up." And, in the case of the Trust, respondent received its express authorization to sell up to 73,000 shares "at $80 per share or better" and affirmatively undertook to sell this block subject only to the contingency that the market reach the specified figure. . . .
>
> At the time of the first discussion with Schulte, respondent knew that the Schulte orders were to be placed after an announcement of a possible liquor dividend which was expected to create greatly increased market activity and a sharp rise in price

and that the stated purpose of these orders was "to have an orderly market." . . . The only reasonable conclusion that could have been reached by respondent was that it was intended that a large block would be sold. This is, of course, what actually happened. . . .

The Commission concluded that

 . . . respondent was selling for the Schulte interests, controlling shareholders of Park & Tilford, in connection with the distribution of their holdings in the stock and was, therefore, an "underwriter" within the meaning of the Act.

Thus, the exemption of section 4(1) was not applicable to the transactions.

3. "Any person who has purchased from an issuer with a view to . . . distribution"

NOTE ON GILLIGAN, WILL & CO. v. S.E.C.

Section 2(11) includes within the term "underwriter" a person "who has purchased from an issuer with a view to . . . distribution." Even a person who is not an underwriter in the normal usage of that term may be a statutory underwriter under this provision. Assume that A has purchased securities from an issuer. If A purchased the securities with the intent to offer or resell them through a distribution—as opposed to having purchased with an "investment intent"—he is an underwriter under section 2(11) and therefore cannot claim the section 4(1) exemption from registration. The classic case is that in which A has purchased unregistered securities under the private-placement exemption and then turns around and reoffers the securities to a number of buyers. In Gilligan, Will & Co. v. S.E.C., 267 F.2d 461 (2d Cir. 1959), cert. denied 361 U.S. 896, 80 S.Ct. 200, 4 L.Ed. 2d 152, Gilligan, a partner in Gilligan, Will, purchased $100,000 of a $3,000,000 private placement of Crowell–Collier convertible debentures for his own account, representing that he purchased for investment. Notwithstanding these representations, Gilligan quickly sold $45,000 of the debentures to Louis Alter, made offers to two other potential purchasers, selling $5,000 of debentures to one of them, and placed the remaining debentures in a Gilligan, Will trading account. Ten months later, Gilligan, Alter, and the Gilligan, Will firm converted their debentures into common stock and sold the stock at a profit on the American Stock Exchange. Gilligan and Alter later subscribed to an additional $200,000 of debentures, which they similarly converted to common stock. Gilligan, Will also was active in selling $200,000 of the debentures to a mutual fund, and as a result of this transaction other parties received warrants to purchase Crowell–Collier stock.

Gilligan and Gilligan, Will argued that since the conversion and sales occurred more than ten months after the purchase of the debentures, the Commission was bound to find that the debentures so converted had been held for investment, and were not purchased with a view to distribution. In answer to this contention the court noted that

> . . . Petitioners concede that if such sales were intended at the time of purchase, the debentures would not then have been held as investments; but [they argue] that the stipulation reveals that the sales were undertaken only after a change of the issuer's circumstances as a result of which petitioners, acting as prudent investors, thought it wise to sell. The catalytic circumstances were the failure, noted by Gilligan, of Crowell–Collier to increase its advertising space as he had anticipated it would. We agree with the Commission that in the circumstances here presented the intention to retain the debentures only if Crowell–Collier continued to operate profitably was equivalent to a "purchase . . . with a view to . . . distribution" within the statutory definition of underwriters in § 2(11). To hold otherwise would be to permit a dealer who speculatively purchases an unregistered security in the hope that the financially weak issuer had, as is stipulated here, "turned the corner," to unload on the unadvised public what he later determines to be an unsound investment without the disclosure sought by the securities laws, although it is in precisely such circumstances that disclosure is most necessary and desirable. . . .

NOTE ON EXEMPTED SECURITIES

The exemptions considered in this Section relate to types of *transactions,* and for the most part provide an exemption only from section 5. The Securities Act also exempts certain types of *securities* from the provisions of *the entire Act.* These exemptions are to be found in sections 3(a)(1)–(a)(8). They include U.S. government, state, and municipal securities (section 3(a)(2)), certain short-term paper (section 3(a)(3)), and bankruptcy trustee certificates (section 3(a)(7)).

SECTION 5. MECHANICS OF REGISTRATION

NOTE ON THE MECHANICS OF REGISTRATION

Assuming that securities must be registered, the registration process is begun by filing with the SEC a registration statement on the applicable form. The basic forms are S–1, S–2, and S–3, but there are many other forms for special situations.

In general, the registration statement must describe such matters as the characteristics of the securities; the character and size of the business enterprise; its capital structure, financial history, and earnings; underwriters' commissions; the names of persons who participate in the direction, management, or control of the business; their security holdings and remuneration, including options; payments to promoters made within two years or intended to be made in the near future; acquisitions of property not in the ordinary course of business, and the interests of directors, officers, and principal stockholders therein; pending or threatened legal proceedings; and the purpose to which the proceeds of the offering are to be applied. The registration statement must include the issuer's financial statements, certified by independent accountants.

The Commission is empowered to prevent the sale of securities to the public on the basis of statements that contain inaccurate or incomplete information. The Staff of the Division of Corporate Finance usually notifies the registrant, by an informal letter of comment, of respects in which the registration statement apparently fails to conform to these requirements. The registrant is afforded an opportunity to file an amendment before the statement becomes effective. However, in certain cases, such as where the deficiencies in a registration statement appear to stem from careless disregard of applicable requirements or a deliberate attempt to conceal or mislead, the Commission either institutes an investigation to determine whether "stop-order" proceedings should be instituted or immediately issues such an order.

The minimum period between the time of filing the registration statement and the time it may become effective is twenty days. This waiting period is designed to provide investors with an opportunity to become familiar with the proposed offering. Information disclosed in the registration statements is disseminated during the waiting period by means of the preliminary prospectus, which presents in summary form the more important of the required disclosures.

SECURITIES ACT FORMS S-1, S-2, AND S-3

[See Statutory Supplement]

NOTE ON THE INTEGRATION OF DISCLOSURE UNDER THE 1933 AND 1934 ACTS

Within recent years, the content of the registration forms has been dramatically affected by the concept of integration. The Securities Exchange Act of 1934 requires *periodic disclosure* by issuers whose stock is registered under that Act. For example, such issuers must file an annual 10–K report, which includes financial statements and various other information; must annually distribute a proxy statement, or the equivalent, containing information on such matters as remuneration of directors and officers and conflict-of-interest transactions; and must file timely 8–K reports whenever certain material events have occurred. In contrast, the Securities Act of 1933 requires only *transactional disclosure*—that is, disclosure only in connection with specific public distributions. Until the late 1970's, the disclosure schemes of the two Acts proceeded on separate courses. At that time, however, the Commission undertook a program of integrating the two disclosure schemes. Partly, this was accomplished by a uniform Regulation, S–K, which provides equivalent definitions and disclosure requirements for comparable issues under the two Acts. Partly, it was accomplished by stratifying issuers into three classes, and reducing the amount of disclosure required in registration statements under the 1933 Act filed for issuers that are already making periodic disclosure under the 1934 Act, and issuers as to whom a great deal of information is likely to be publicly available even apart from the 1934 Act's disclosure requirements.

———

SECURITIES ACT RELEASE NO. 6235 (1980)
[REGISTRATION FORMS]

* * *

SUMMARY: The Commission is publishing for comment three proposed new forms to be used to register offerings of securities under the Securities Act of 1933. This action represents another major step in the Commission's efforts to integrate the disclosure systems under the various federal securities laws and to simplify and streamline the disclosure requirements imposed under those systems. The three new forms proposed today would constitute the basic disclosure document format for most Securities Act registration, with different levels of disclosure and delivery requirements applicable for different levels of companies registering offerings of securities. . . .

I. Integration

The Commission's integration program involves a comprehensive evaluation of the disclosure policies and procedures underlying the Securities Act of 1933 and the Securities Exchange Act of 1934 with a view toward integrating the information systems under those Acts so that investors and the marketplace are provided meaningful, nonduplicative information periodically and when securities are sold to the public, while the costs of compliance for public companies are decreased.

The shape of the program will be influenced by the answers to two fundamental questions:

(1) What information is material to investment decisions in the context of public offerings of securities; and

(2) Under what circumstances and in what form should such material information be disseminated and made available by

companies making public offerings of securities to the various participants in the capital market system?

The task of identifying what information is material to investment and voting decisions is a continuing one in the field of securities regulation. Integration, as a concept, involves a conclusion as to equivalency between transactional (Securities Act) and periodic (Exchange Act) reporting. If a subject matter is material information (other than a description of the transaction itself), then it will be material both in the distribution of securities and to the trading markets. Moreover, requirements governing the description of such subject matters should be the same for both purposes. As an example, if a management's discussion of the financial statements is important for transactions involving distributions, then it would also be equally important for an informed trading market. Thus, both prospectuses and periodic reports should take this information into account. Also, the requirements for its content should be essentially the same. This principle of equivalency has led to the development and expansion of Regulation S–K, a technical device designed to state in one place uniform requirements which both Securities Act and Exchange Act items incorporate by reference. . . .

Integration consists, however, of more than just the notion of equivalency of reportable material information under both Acts. It involves answers to the second question posed above: Under what circumstances and to whom should this information be made available? Equivalency alone might be read to suggest that all the information contained, for example, in a Form 10–K should also be reiterated in all prospectuses.

However, the concept of integration also proceeds from the observation that information is regularly being furnished to the market through periodic reports under the Exchange Act. This information is evaluated by professional analysts and other sophisticated users, is available to the financial press and is obtainable by any other person who seeks it for free or at nominal cost. To the extent that the market accordingly acts efficiently, and this information is adequately reflected in the price of a registrant's outstanding securities, there seems little need to reiterate this information in a prospectus in the context of a distribution. The fact of market availability of information for sophisticated users also allows the exploration of other values in addition to cost reductions afforded through non-duplication: in particular, readability and effective communication in specific contexts. . . .

A. *Background* . . .

1. *The Law*

The Securities Act and the Exchange Act were enacted as separate legislation and in response to different needs. The Securities Act was intended to prevent frauds in the sale of securities by providing full and fair disclosure in the context of public offerings of securities. The Exchange Act was enacted to regulate brokers and dealers and securities markets. The disclosure framework of the Exchange Act contemplated in 1934 pertained primarily to classes of securities traded on stock exchanges. While both statutes were designed to provide disclosure to investors and the marketplace, the framework of the Securities Act was transaction oriented, i.e., the focus was upon the public offering of securities by any company. The framework of the Exchange Act was status oriented, i.e., the focus was upon issuers with a class of securities listed and traded on an exchange. Also, the two frameworks operated independently. Information required in the Securities Act context was not modified because of the existence of Exchange Act reporting and was only triggered by public offerings at varying times.

While the disparate orientations of the two statutes still exist, the gap between the disclosure frameworks has significantly narrowed since 1934. In 1936, Section 15(d) was added to the Exchange Act to provide that under certain circumstances the continuous reporting system would apply to unlisted companies with respect to classes of their securities for which a registration statement had become effective under the Securities Act. Thus, Section 15(d) expanded investor protection under the Exchange Act to the over-the-counter market, but only on a fragmentary basis.

The disparity between Exchange Act disclosure requirements for listed and unlisted classes of securities was not resolved until the passage of the Securities Acts Amendments of 1964 which brought many more companies into the continuous reporting system of the Exchange Act. With the passage of Section 15(d) and the 1964 amendments, all issuers of a certain size and issuers with certain characteristics selling securities to the public pursuant to an effective registration statement were subjected to the registration and reporting obligations of the Exchange Act. It is estimated that over 9,000 companies are now required to file periodic reports under the Exchange Act.

These amendments not only closed a gap under the Exchange Act, but also narrowed the gap between the disclosure framework under the Securities Act—information concerning the issuer and the transaction given only in the context of the public offering—and that under the Exchange Act—continuous disclosure about the issuer. Milton Cohen, a principal advocate of the concept of integration, opined that the disclosure frameworks under the Acts would have been quite different—and perhaps more congruent—if they "had been enacted in opposite order, or had been enacted as a single, integrated statute—that is, if the starting point had been a statutory scheme of continuous disclosures covering issuers of actively traded securities and the question of special disclosure in connection with public offerings had then been faced in this setting." In large part, the Commission's efforts will attempt to redress this legislative anomaly by establishing an integrated system of disclosure which will provide investor protection both in public offerings and in the securities markets, at a minimum burden to public companies.

2. *Nature of the Securities Markets*

The basic issues relating to Securities Act disclosure, i.e., the type of information that should be available and the dissemination of that information, must also be considered in light of the composition of today's markets. The participants in the markets, and therefore the users of the information made available to the markets, are varied and have correspondingly varied needs. They include the professional analyst, the institutional investor, the financial press, and the individual investor.

The professional analysts, widespread throughout the country, constantly digest and synthesize market and company-specific information. These professionals use, and often implore the Commission to require, increasingly complex and sophisticated information. The influx of institutional investors, and their financial advisors, also contributes to the constituency for technical but important statistical data. To a large extent, these professionals act as essential conduits in the flow of information to the ordinary investor and as intermediaries acting on behalf of participants in collective investment media.

In addition, this country has a uniquely active and responsive financial press which facilitates the broad dissemination of highly timely and material company-oriented information to a vast readership. The information needs of the individual investor must be considered in this context, recognizing that information reaches the individual investor through both direct and indirect routes.

It is incumbent upon the Commission to consider the entire community of users of company information in developing the proposed system and its model information package and to maintain a balance between the needs of the more and less sophisticated users. . . .

SECURITIES ACT RELEASE NO. 6331 (1981)
[REGISTRATION FORMS]

*   *   *

SUMMARY: The Commission is republishing for public comment three proposed forms to be used to register offerings of securities under the Securities Act of 1933. The three proposed forms would constitute the basic framework for registration statements under the Securities Act, with different levels of disclosure and delivery requirements applicable for different levels of companies registering offerings of securities. Republication of these and related proposals is intended to afford the public an opportunity to consider in a comprehensive manner the various elements of the Commission's integrated disclosure system. This action is a significant part of the Commission's program to integrate the disclosure systems under the various Federal securities laws and to simplify and improve the disclosure requirements imposed under these systems. . . .

II. Overview

Under the proposed registration statement framework, registrants would be classified into three categories: (1) companies which are widely followed by professional analysts; (2) companies which have been subject to the periodic reporting system of the Exchange Act for three or more years, but which are not widely followed; and (3) companies which have been in the Exchange Act reporting system for less than three years. The first category would be eligible to use proposed Form S–3, which relies on incorporation by reference of Exchange Act reports and contains minimal disclosure in the prospectus. This form is predicated on the Commission's belief that the market operates efficiently for these companies, i.e., that the disclosure in Exchange Act reports and other communications by the registrant, such as press releases, has already been disseminated and accounted for by the market place. The second category would be eligible for Form S–2, which represents a combination of incorporation by reference of Exchange Act reports and presentation in the prospectus or in an annual report to security holders of certain information. The third category would use Form S–1, which requires complete disclosure of information in the prospectus and does not permit incorporation by reference. . . .

Proposed Form S–3 recognizes the applicability of the efficient market theory to the registration statement framework with respect to those registrants which usually provide high quality corporate reports, including Exchange Act reports, and whose corporate information is broadly disseminated, because such companies are widely followed by professional analysts and investors in the market place. Because these registrants are widely followed, the disclosure set forth in the prospectus may appropriately be limited, without the loss of investor protection, to information concerning the offering and material facts which have not been disclosed previously. The abbreviated disclosure is made possible by the use of incorporation by reference of the registrant's Exchange Act information into the prospectus. Because of the abbreviated disclosure, the utility of proposed Form S–3 is limited to widely followed companies. . . . The proposed float requirement is designed to correlate the use of abbreviated Form S–3 to widely followed registrants.

. . . [P]roposed Form S–2 is designed for improved readability by streamlining disclosure requirements and allowing certain disclosure obligations to be satisfied either through the delivery of the annual report to security holders or by presentation of comparable updated information in the prospectus. More specifically, the financial statements, management's discussion and analysis and the brief business description required by proposed Form S–2 are identical to those already presented in the annual report to security holders. . . .

Finally, proposed Form S–1 . . . would be used to register securities when no other form is authorized or prescribed and would be used by companies in the Exchange Act reporting system for less than three years, such as new issuers. To ensure that adequate information concerning these registrants is readily available to investors, proposed Form S–1 requires delivery of a more lengthy and comprehensive prospectus than either proposed Form S–2 or Form S–3. . . .

III. Synopsis . . .

A. *Eligibility Rules for Use of Forms S–3, S–2 and S–1* . . .

1. *Form S–3*

The eligibility requirements for use of Form S–3 are broken down into two classifications, "Registrant Requirements" and "Transaction Requirements." A registrant first must meet the Registrant Requirements (which are identical for Forms S–3 and S–2) and then must meet at least one of the Transaction Requirements before it can use Form S–3.

a. *Registrant Requirements*

The first three Registrant Requirements are quite similar to those . . . in existing Form S–7. The first requires that the registrant be organized under the laws of the United States, its various states or territories, and have its principal business operations located there. The second requires that the registrant have a class of securities registered pursuant to Section 12(b) or 12(g) of the Exchange Act or be required to file reports pursuant to Section 15(d) of that Act. The third requires that the registrant have filed all the information required by Sections 13, 14 or 15(d) of the Exchange Act for at least 36 months and have been timely in such filings for the preceding 12 months. These requirements are necessary because the operation of an efficient market for a security depends on such information being made public promptly and its inclusion in filings made under the Exchange Act helps ensure its accuracy. . . .

b. *Transaction Requirements*

. . . If a registrant, which meets the eligibility requirements, meets the conditions of any one of the Transaction Requirements, it may use Form S–3 for the covered transaction.

i. *Primary and Secondary Offerings*

The first requirement proposes that, in order to use Form S–3 for primary and secondary offerings, an issuer must have a minimum of $150 million in aggregate value of voting stock held by non-affiliates (hereinafter referred to as "float"). This test was designed to make the Form available for such offerings only to those issuers which are actively and widely followed in the securities markets. . . .

ii. *Investment Grade Debt Securities*

Under the second Transaction Requirement any registrant which meets the Registrant Requirements, even one which does not meet the float criteria, would be able to register certain high grade non-convertible debt securities, defined as "investment grade debt securities," on Form S–3. This proposal reflects . . . the Commission's position that with respect to offerings of high quality debt issues a detailed prospectus is unnecessary since such securities are generally purchased on the basis of interest rates and security ratings. . . .

The proposed Form would define an "investment grade debt security" as a non-convertible debt security which, at the time the registration statement becomes effective, is rated in one of the top four corporate bond categories by at least one nationally recognized statistical rating organization. The proposed use of the top four categories is consistent with the Commission's current use of securities ratings and with the categories used by the rating organizations themselves, i.e., Standard & Poor's Corporation, Moody's Investor Service and Fitch Investors Service, Inc. . . .

2. *Form S–2*

As mentioned above, the Registrant Requirements of Form S–3 also constitute virtually the entire eligibility requirements for the use of Form S–2. . . . The Commission believes that the streamlined nature of the Form S–2 prospectus, while much more complete than that of Form S–3, still should be supplemented by the availability of a complete and current three year series of Exchange Act reports. Accordingly, it has retained the Exchange Act eligibility criteria which also are used for Form S–3. . . .

3. *Form S–1*

. . . [T]his more comprehensive form must be used by first time filers and others who have only been filing reports for a short period of time. . . .

c. *Disclosure Provisions*

In proposed Forms S–1, S–2 and S–3, the Commission has developed a Securities Act registration system which identifies the information material to investment decisions in the context of all public offerings and then determines in what form and to whom issuers must disseminate such information. The material information will be required to be part of all Securities Act registration statements, regardless of the form used, through incorporation by reference in some cases. Differences among the forms primarily involve dissemination, i.e., the extent to which the required information must be presented in the prospectus, or may be presented in other documents delivered with the prospectus and incorporated by reference, or may be simply incorporated by reference from information contained in the Exchange Act continuous reporting system.

Generally, it is the issuer-oriented part of the information material to a public offering, as opposed to the transaction-specific information, which, depending on the form available, may be satisfied otherwise than through full prospectus presentation. This information includes the basic package of information about the issuer which the Commission believes is material to investment decisions in all contexts and thus is also required to be presented in annual reports to the Commission on Form 10–K and in annual reports to security holders. Information about the offering will not have been reported on in any other disclosure document or otherwise have been publicly disseminated and thus will be required to be presented in all cases. . . .

2. *Incorporation by Reference*

The technique of incorporation by reference of Exchange Act disclosure documents is central to the integrated Securities Act registration system represented by proposed Forms S–1, S–2 and S–3. Proposed Form S–3 relies on incorporation by reference to replace prospectus presentation of information about the issuer of the securities being registered. Proposed Form S–2 uses incorporation by reference to allow streamlining of the prospectus presentation of issuer-specific information. Proposed Form S–1 uses no incorporation by reference and instead requires full disclosure about the issuer of the securities to be presented in the prospectus. . . .

3. *Disclosure Requirements by Form*

a. *Form S–3*

Proposed Form S–3 provides the shortest form for Securities Act registration. The prospectus would be required to present [certain] items calling for information about the offering. . . .

Information concerning the registrant would be incorporated by reference from Exchange Act reports, which would be available to investors on request. The documents required to be incorporated are the latest annual report on Form 10–K and all other reports filed pursuant to Section 13(a) or 15(d) of the Exchange Act since the end of the fiscal year covered by the Form 10–K, including all Section 13(d) or 15(d) reports filed subsequent to effectiveness of the registration statement and prior to termination of the offering. Unless there has been a material change in the registrant's affairs which has not been reported in an Exchange Act filing, the prospectus would not be required to present any information concerning the registrant. . . .

b. *Form S–2*

Proposed Form S–2 provides a simplified form for registration by certain registrants. While it requires delivery of information about the registrant in addition to delivery of the same information about the offering as required by Form S–3, proposed Form S–2 significantly streamlines the registrant-specific disclosure by making the required level of disclosure delivered to investors that of the annual report to security holders pursuant to Rule 14a–3 rather than that of the annual report on Form 10–K. Required information about the registrant includes the basic information package components (market price and dividend data, selected financial data, financial statements and management's discussion and analysis) and such other items (brief descriptions of business, segments, supplementary financial information) as are required to be included in the annual report to security holders pursuant to Rule 14a–3. Moreover, registrants are granted the option of providing this information either by presenting it in the prospectus or by delivering the latest annual report to security holders along with the prospectus. Finally, the registrant's latest annual report on Form 10–K and periodic reports on Form 10–Q and Form 8–K must be incorporated by reference into the prospectus, and made available upon request, to round out the information provided about the registrant. . . .

If the Form S–2 registrant elects the alternative of delivering its annual report, it must incorporate certain information in that document by reference and describe in the prospectus any material changes in its affairs since the end of the latest fiscal year reported in the delivered annual report. In addition, it must provide updating information but may avoid duplication of previously reported quarterly information because updating may be accomplished by any one of three means: (1) including in the prospectus such financial and other information as would be required to be reported in a report on Form 10–Q; (2) delivering a copy of the latest Form 10–Q with the prospectus and annual report; (3) delivering a copy of the latest informal quarterly report to shareholders if such report contained the same required information. . . .

c. *Form S–1*

Proposed Form S–1 presents a simple format. Full disclosure of all material information about the offering and the registrant is required to be presented in the prospectus itself. No incorporation by reference to any Exchange Act documents is allowed. Proposed Form S–1 looks entirely to Regulation S–K for its non-financial substantive disclosure provisions. First, like proposed Forms S–2 and S–3, proposed Form S–1 requires prospectus presentation of the offering-oriented items of § 229.500 of Regulation S–K and the description of securities (proposed Item 202 of Regulation S–K). In addition, the proposed Form S–1 prospectus must include the same information about the registrant as is required to be reported in an annual report on Form 10–K. This information includes, in addition to the basic information package with respect to the registrant, the full Regulation S–K descriptions of business, properties and legal proceedings as well as the Regulation S–K disclosures with respect to management and security holders. . . .

NOTE ON REGISTRATION FORMS

As adopted, Forms S–1 and S–2 reflected no major changes from the proposal in Release No. 6331. Form S–3, however, was revised in several important respects. The Commission adopted the proposed $150–million–float and high-grade-debt transaction requirements, but added two others: (i) the issuance of securities by companies with a $100 million float and 3 million share annual trading volume, and (ii) the issuance of high-grade non-convertible preferred. See Securities Act Release No. 6383 (1982).

SECTION 6. DUTIES AND PROHIBITIONS WHEN A SECURITY IS IN REGISTRATION

INTRODUCTORY NOTE

Assuming that a registration statement must be filed, the issuer, underwriter, and broker-dealers come under a variety of duties and prohibitions. To analyze these duties and prohibitions, it is necessary to separately consider three time periods. First, the period before registration (the "prefiling period"). Second, the period between the time the registration statement is filed and the time it becomes effective (the "waiting period"). Third, the period after the registration statement becomes effective (the "post-effective period").

SECURITIES ACT RELEASE NO. 4697 (1964)

OFFERS AND SALES OF SECURITIES BY UNDERWRITERS AND DEALERS

In view of recent comments in the press concerning the rights and obligations of, and limitations on, dealers in connection with distributions of registered securities, the Commission takes this opportunity to explain the operation of section 5 of the Securities Act of 1933 with particular reference to the limitations upon, and responsibilities of, underwriters and dealers in the offer and sale of an issue of securities prior to and after the filing of a registration statement.

The discussion below assumes that the offering is not exempt from the registration requirements of the Act and, unless otherwise stated, that the mails or facilities of interstate or foreign commerce are used.

The Period Before the Filing of a Registration Statement

Section 5 of the Securities Act prohibits both offers to sell and offers to buy a security before a registration statement is filed. Section 2(3) of the Act, however, exempts preliminary negotiations or agreements between the issuer or other person on whose behalf the distribution is to be made and any underwriter or among underwriters. Thus, negotiation of the financing can proceed during this period but neither the issuer nor the underwriter may offer the security either to investors or to dealers, and dealers are prohibited from offering to buy the securities during this period.[1] Consequently, not only may no steps be taken to form a selling group but also dealers may not seek inclusion in the selling group prior to the filing.

It should be borne in mind that publicity about an issuer, its securities or the proposed offering prior to the filing of a registration statement may constitute an illegal offer to sell. Thus, announcement of the underwriter's identity should be avoided during this period. Experience shows that such announcements are very likely to lead to illegal offers to buy. This subject will not be further discussed in this release since it has been extensively considered elsewhere.[2]

These principles, however, are not intended to restrict the normal communications between an issuer and its stockholders or the announcement to the public generally of information with respect to important business and financial developments. Such announcements are required in the listing agreements used by stock exchanges, and the Commission is sensitive to the importance of encouraging this type of communication. In recognition of this requirement of certain stock exchanges, the Commission adopted Rule 135, which permits a brief announcement of proposed rights offerings, proposed exchange offerings, and proposed offerings to employees as not constituting an offer of a security for the purposes of section 5 of the Act.

The Period After the Filing and Before the Effective Date

After the registration statement is filed, and before its effective date, offers to sell the securities are permitted but no written offer may be made except by means of a statutory prospectus. For this purpose the statutory prospectus includes the preliminary prospectus provided for in Rule 433 as well as the summary prospectus provided for in Rules 434 and 434A. In addition the so-called "tombstone" advertisement permitted by Rule 134 may be used.

During the period after the filing of a registration statement, the freedom of an underwriter or dealer expecting to participate in the distribution, to communicate with his customers is limited only by the antifraud provisions of the Securities Act and the Securities Exchange Act, and by the fact that written offering material other than a statutory prospectus or tombstone advertisement may not be used. In

---

1. The reason for this provision was stated in the House Report on the bill as originally enacted as follows:

   ". . . Otherwise, the underwriter . . . could accept them in the order of their priority and thus bring pressure upon dealers, who wish to avail themselves of a particular security offering, to rush their orders to buy without adequate consideration of the nature of the security being offered." H.R.Report No. 85, 73rd Cong., 1st Sess. (1933), p. 11.

2. See Securities Act Release No. 3844 (1957); Carl M. Loeb, Rhoades & Co., 38 S.E.C. 843 (1959); First Maine Corporation, 38 S.E.C. 882 (1959).

other words, during this period "free writing" is illegal. The dealer, therefore, can orally solicit indications of interest or offers to buy and may discuss the securities with his customers and advise them whether or not in his opinion the securities are desirable or suitable for them. In this connection a dealer proposing to discuss an issue of securities with his customers should obtain copies of the preliminary prospectus in order to have a reliable source of information. This is particularly important where he proposes to recommend the securities, or where information concerning them has not been generally available. The corollary of the dealer's obligation to secure the copy is the obligation of the issuer and managing underwriters to make it readily available. Rule 460 provides that as a condition to acceleration of the effective date of a registration statement, the Commission will consider whether the persons making the offering have taken reasonable steps to make the information contained in the registration statement available to dealers who may participate in the distribution.

It is a principal purpose of the so-called "waiting period" between the filing date and the effective date to enable dealers and, through them, investors to become acquainted with the information contained in the registration statement and to arrive at an unhurried decision concerning the merits of the securities. Consistently with this purpose, no contracts of sale can be made during this period, the purchase price may not be paid or received and offers to buy may be cancelled.

The Period After the Effective Date

When the registration statement becomes effective oral offerings may continue and sales may be made and consummated. A copy of the final statutory prospectus must be delivered in connection with any written offer or confirmation or upon delivery of the security, whichever first occurs. Supplemental sales literature ("free writing") may be used if it is accompanied or preceded by a prospectus. However, care must be taken to see that all such material is at the time of use not false or misleading under the standards of section 17(a) of the Act. If the offering continues over an extended period, the prospectus should be current under the standards of section 10(a)(3). All dealers trading in the registered security must continue to employ the prospectus for the period referred to in section 4.

SECURITIES ACT §§ 2(3), 5

[See Statutory Supplement]

NOTE ON THE PRE-FILING PERIOD

Under section 5(a) of the 1933 Act:

Unless a registration statement is in effect as to a security, it shall be unlawful for any person, directly or indirectly—(1) to make use of any means or instruments of transportation or communication in interstate commerce or of the mails to sell such security through the use or medium of any prospectus or otherwise; or (2) to carry or cause to be carried through the mails or in interstate commerce, by any means or instruments of transportation, any such security for the purpose of sale or for delivery after sale.

Under section 5(c):

It shall be unlawful for any person, directly or indirectly, to make use of any means or instruments of transportation or communication in interstate commerce or of the mails to offer to sell or offer to buy through the use or medium of any prospectus or otherwise any security, unless a registration statement has been filed as to such security. . . .

Under section 2(3):

The term "sale" or "sell" shall include every contract of sale or disposition of a security or interest in a security, for value. The term "offer to sell", "offer for sale", or "offer" shall include every attempt or offer to dispose of, or solicitation of an offer to buy, a security or interest in a security, for value.

There is an important exception to section 2(3):

The terms defined in [§ 2(3)] and the term "offer to buy" as used in subsection (c) of section 5 shall not include preliminary negotiations or agreements between an issuer . . . and any underwriter or among underwriters who are or are to be in privity of contract with an issuer. . . .

Putting together §§ 5(a), 5(c), and 2(3), neither a sale nor an oral or written offer to sell securities to be registered may be made during the prefiling period, except for preliminary negotiations between the issuer and the underwriter and between underwriters. The prohibition against offers in the prefiling period extends not only to formal offers, but to "gun-jumping"—unusual publicity by the issuer or a prospective underwriter that is in effect a preliminary step in the selling effort. On the other hand, if a corporation is already publicly held, blocking the normal flow of information would adversely affect the integrity of the market for the securities that are already outstanding. The cases and rules governing the prefiling period attempt to reconcile the undesirability of gun-jumping and the desirability of maintaining the normal flow of information.

———

SECURITIES ACT RELEASE NO. 5180 (1971)

GUIDELINES FOR THE RELEASE OF INFORMATION BY ISSUERS WHOSE SECURITIES ARE IN REGISTRATION

The Commission today took note of situations when issuers whose securities are "in registration" [1] may have refused to answer legitimate inquiries from stockholders, financial analysts, the press or other persons concerning the company or some aspect of its business. The Commission hereby emphasizes that there is no basis in the securities acts or in any policy of the Commission which would justify the practice of non-disclosure of *factual* information by a publicly held company on the grounds that it has securities in registration under the Securities Act of 1933 ("Act"). Neither a company in registration nor its representatives should instigate publicity for the purpose of facilitating the sale of securities in a proposed offering. . . .

. . . It has been asserted that the increasing obligations and incentives of corporations to make timely disclosures concerning their affairs creates a possible conflict with statutory restrictions on publication of information concerning a company which has securities in registration. As the Commission has stated in previously issued releases this conflict may be more apparent than real. Disclosure of factual information in response to inquiries or resulting from a duty to make prompt disclosure under the antifraud provisions of the securities acts or the timely disclosure policies of self-regulatory organizations, at a time when a registered offering of securities is contemplated or in process, can and should be effected in a manner which will not unduly influence the proposed offering.

Statutory Requirements

In order for issuers and their representatives to avoid problems in responding to inquiries, it is essential that such persons be familiar with the statutory requirements governing this area. Generally speaking, Section 5(c) of the Act makes it unlawful for any person directly or indirectly to make use of any means or instruments of interstate commerce or of the mails *to offer to sell* a security unless a registration statement has been filed with the Commission as to such security. Questions arise from time to time because many persons do not realize that the phrase "offer to sell" is broadly defined by the Act and has been liberally construed by the courts and Commission. For example, the publication of information and statements, and publicity efforts, made in advance of a proposed financing which have the effect of conditioning the public mind or arousing public interest in the issuer or in its securities constitutes an offer in violation of the Act. The

---

1. "In registration" is used herein to refer to the entire process of registration, at least from the time an issuer reaches an understanding with the broker-dealer which is to act as managing underwriter prior to the filing of a registration statement and the period of 40 to 90 days during which dealers must deliver a prospectus.

same holds true with respect to publication of information which is part of a selling effort between the filing date and the effective date of a registration statement. . . .

Guidelines

The Commission strongly suggests that all issuers establish internal procedures designed to avoid problems relating to the release of corporate information when in registration. As stated above, issuers and their representatives should not initiate publicity when in registration, but should nevertheless respond to legitimate inquiries for factual information about the company's financial condition and business operations. Further, care should be exercised so that, for example, predictions, projections, forecasts, estimates and opinions concerning value are not given with respect to such things, among other, as sales and earnings and value of the issuer's securities.

It has been suggested that the Commission promulgate an all inclusive list of permissible and prohibited activities in this area. This is not feasible for the reason that determinations are based upon the particular facts of each case. However, the Commission as a matter of policy encourages the flow of factual information to shareholders and the investing public. Issuers in this regard should:

1. Continue to advertise products and services.

2. Continue to send out customary quarterly, annual and other periodic reports to stockholders.

3. Continue to publish proxy statements and send out dividend notices.

4. Continue to make announcements to the press with respect to factual business and financial developments; *i.e.*, receipt of a contract, the settlement of a strike, the opening of a plant, or similar events of interest to the community in which the business operates.

5. Answer unsolicited telephone inquiries from stockholders, financial analysts, the press and others concerning factual information.

6. Observe an "open door" policy in responding to unsolicited inquiries concerning factual matters from securities analysts, financial analysts, security holders, and participants in the communications field who have a legitimate interest in the corporation's affairs.

7. Continue to hold stockholder meetings as scheduled and to answer shareholders' inquiries at stockholder meetings relating to factual matters.

In order to curtail problems in this area, issuers in this regard should avoid:

1. Issuance of forecasts, projections, or predictions relating but not limited to revenues, income, or earnings per share.

2. Publishing opinions concerning values.

In the event a company publicly releases material information concerning new corporate developments during the period that a registration statement is pending, the registration statement should be amended at or prior to the time the information is released. If this is not done and such information is publicly released through inadvertance, the pending registration statement should be promptly amended to reflect such information. . . .

SECTION 7. LIABILITIES UNDER THE SECURITIES ACT

SECURITIES ACT §§ 11, 12, 17; SECURITIES ACT RULES 175, 176

[See Statutory Supplement]

NOTE ON LIABILITIES UNDER THE SECURITIES ACT

The Securities Act contains four basic liability provisions: Sections 11, 12(1), 12(2), and 17(a).

1. *Section 17(a).* Section 17(a) is a general antifraud provision, which applies to any offer or sale of securities, and is not keyed into registration:

Sec. 17.   (a) It shall be unlawful for any person in the offer or sale of any securities by the use of any means or instruments of transportation or communication in interstate commerce or by the use of the mails, directly or indirectly—

(1) to employ any device, scheme, or artifice to defraud, or

(2) to obtain money or property by means of any untrue statement of a material fact or any omission to state a material fact necessary in order to make the statements made, in the light of the circumstances under which they were made, not misleading, or

(3) to engage in any transaction, practice, or course of business which operates or would operate as a fraud or deceit upon the purchaser.

Section 17(a) is highly comparable to Rule 10b–5, because the latter was modeled on the former. However, Rule 10b–5 applies to both sellers and buyers, while section 17(a) applies only to sellers. On the other hand, section 17(a) applies to an "offer" while Rule 10b–5 does not.

Section 17(a) does explicitly provide for liability in favor of injured buyers, and there is a split of authority on whether a private action should be implied under this section. See Note, Actions Under Section 17(a) of the 1933 Act, R. Jennings & H. Marsh, Securities Regulation—Cases and Materials (6th ed. 1987). The Supreme Court has held that scienter is a necessary element of a violation of section 17(a)(1), but not of sections 17(a)(2) or 17(a)(3). Aaron v. S.E.C., 446 U.S. 680, 100 S.Ct. 227, 64 L.Ed.2d 611 (1980).

2. *Section 12(2).* Section 12(2), like section 17(a), is a general antifraud provision that is not keyed into registration. Unlike section 17(a), section 12(2) explicitly provides for liability to injured buyers:

> Sec. 12. Any person who—. . . .
>
> (2) offers or sells a security . . . by the use of any means or instruments of transportation or communication in interstate commerce or of the mails, by means of a prospectus or oral communication, which includes an untrue statement of a material fact or omits to state a material fact necessary in order to make the statements, in the light of the circumstances under which they were made, not misleading (the purchaser not knowing of such untruth or omission), and who shall not sustain the burden of proof that he did not know, and in the exercise of reasonable care could not have known, of such untruth or omission,
>
> shall be liable to the person purchasing such security from him, who may sue either at law or in equity in any court of competent jurisdiction, to recover the consideration paid for such security with interest thereon, less the amount of any income received thereon, upon the tender of such security, or for damages if he no longer owns the security.

3. *Section 12(1).* Unlike sections 17(a) and 12(2), section 12(1) is keyed into registration:

> Sec. 12. Any person who—
>
> (1) offers or sells a security in violation of section 5
>
> . . .
>
> shall be liable to the person purchasing such security from him, who may sue either at law or in equity in any court of competent jurisdiction, to recover the consideration paid for such security with interest thereon, less the amount of any income received thereon, upon the tender of such security, or for damages if he no longer owns the security.

Notice that:

(i) Under both sections 12(1) and 12(2), privity is required— that is, a person who wrongfully sells an unregistered security is liable only to his buyer.

(ii) Under both sections 12(1) and 12(2), the buyer's recovery is limited to the return of the purchase price (with interest, but minus the amount of any income received), unless he has resold the security. If the buyer has resold the security, he is entitled to "damages," which is construed to mean the difference between the price he paid for the security and the price at which he resold the security.

(iii) Under both sections 12(1) and 12(2), there is no requirement that the plaintiffs have relied on the misstatement or omission. Johns Hopkins Univ. v. Hutton, 422 F.2d 1124, 1129 (4th Cir.1970).

(iv) Under section 12(1), it's irrelevant whether the seller made any false statements or omitted to state material facts; the buyer need only show that the security was sold in violation of section 5. In contrast, under section 12(2) the buyer must show a false statement or material omission. However, the buyer need not show that the seller was at fault. Once the buyer shows that an omission was material, or that a material statement was false, the seller has the burden of showing that he did not know and "in the exercise of reasonable care could not have known" of the untruth or omission. In effect, therefore, section 12(2) imposes a negligence standard but puts the burden of proof on the seller to prove he was not negligent.

4. *Section 11.* Section 11, like section 12(1), is keyed into registration. Omitting certain qualifications, section 11 provides:

> Sec. 11. (a) In case any part of the registration statement, when such part became effective, contained an untrue statement of a material fact or omitted to state a material fact required to be stated therein or necessary to make the statements therein not misleading, any person acquiring such security (unless it is proved that at the time of such acquisition he knew of such untruth or omission) may, either at law or in equity, in any court of competent jurisdiction, sue—
>
> > (1) every person who signed the registration statement;
> >
> > (2) every person who was a director of . . . the issuer at the time of the filing of the part of the registration statement with respect to which his liability is asserted; . . .
> >
> > (4) every accountant, engineer, or appraiser, or any person whose profession gives authority to a statement made by him, who has with his consent been named as having prepared or certified any part of the registration statement, or as having prepared or certified any report or valuation which is used in connection with the registration statement, with respect to the statement in such registration statement, report, or valuation, which purports to have been prepared or certified by him;
> >
> > (5) every underwriter with respect to such security. . . .
>
> (b) Notwithstanding the provisions of subsection (a) no person, other than the issuer, shall be liable as provided therein who shall sustain the burden of proof. . . .
>
> > (3) that (A) as regards any part of the registration statement not purporting to be made on the authority of

an expert, . . . he had, after reasonable investigation, reasonable ground to believe and did believe, at the time such part of the registration statement became effective, that the statements therein were true and that there was no omission to state a material fact required to be stated therein or necessary to make the statements therein not misleading; and (B) as regards any part of the registration statement purporting to be made upon his authority as an expert, . . . (i) he had, after reasonable investigation, reasonable ground to believe, at the time such part of the registration statement became effective, that the statements therein were true and that there was no omission to state a material fact required to be stated therein or necessary to make the statements therein not misleading, or (ii) such part of the registration statement did not fairly represent his statement as an expert; and (C) as regards any part of the registration statement purporting to be made on the authority of an expert (other than himself) . . . he had no reasonable ground to believe and did not believe, at the time such part of the registration statement became effective, that the statements therein were untrue or that there was an omission to state a material fact required to be stated therein or necessary to make the statements therein not misleading, or that such part of the registration statement did not fairly represent the statement of the expert or was not a fair copy of or extract from the report or valuation of the expert . . . .

(c) In determining, for purposes of paragraph (3) of subsection (b) of this section, what constitutes reasonable investigation and reasonable ground for belief, the standard of reasonableness shall be that required of a prudent man in the management of his own property. . . .

(e) The suit authorized under subsection (a) may be to recover such damages as shall represent the difference between the amount paid for the security (not exceeding the price at which the security was offered to the public) and (1) the value thereof as of the time such suit was brought, or (2) the price at which such security shall have been disposed of in the market before suit, or (3) the price at which such security shall have been disposed of after suit but before judgment if such damages shall be less than the damages representing the difference between the amount paid for the security (not exceeding the price at which the security was offered to the public) and the value thereof as of the time such suit was brought: Provided, that if the defendant proves that any portion or all of such damages represents other than the depreciation in value of such security resulting from such part of the registration statement, with respect to which his liability is asserted, not being true or omitting to state a material fact required to be stated therein or necessary to make the statements therein not misleading, such portion of or all such damages shall not be recoverable. . . .

Note that under section 11:

(i) Liability is limited to false statements in the registration statement.

(ii) The buyer normally doesn't have to show that he relied on the false statements.[1]

(iii) Damages are limited under the complicated scheme set forth in subsection (e).

(iv) The issuer is strictly liable—liable without fault. Any other nonexpert defendant is liable if, but only if, as to the nonexpertised portions "he had, after reasonable investigation, reasonable ground to believe" that the relevant statements were true and that there were no material omissions, and as to the expertised portions, "he had no reasonable ground to believe" that the statements made by the expert were untrue or contained material omissions. This is known as the due diligence defense. Thus section 11, like section 12(2), adopts a negligence standard with the burden of proof on the defendants. However, there is a difference in the formulations of the negligence standards in sections 11 and 12(2), and it is not clear whether this means that there are differences in the investigation required to satisfy the defendant's burden of proof under the two sections. See Sanders v. John Nuveen & Co., Inc., 619 F.2d 1222 (7th Cir.1980), cert. denied 450 U.S. 1005, 101 S.Ct. 1719, 68 L.Ed.2d 210 (1981) (opinion of Powell, dissenting from denial of certiorari).

The express remedy provided in section 11 does not preclude a buyer from bringing suit under Rule 10b–5 on the basis of misrepresentations or omissions in a registration statement. Herman & MacLean v. Huddleston, 459 U.S. 375, 103 S.Ct. 683, 74 L.Ed.2d 548 (1983).

———

NOTE ON ESCOTT v. BARCHRIS CONST. CORP.

Escott v. BarChris Const. Corp., 283 F.Supp. 643 (S.D.N.Y. 1968) is the leading case on what constitutes due diligence under section 11. The following passages from that case address the liability of several of the directors of BarChris in connection with a public issue of convertible debentures pursuant to a registration statement.

———

Russo

Russo was, to all intents and purposes, the chief executive officer of BarChris. He was a member of the executive committee. He was

---

1. If a security is acquired after the issuer has published a financial statement for the twelve-month period beginning at the date of the registration statement, the plaintiff's right of recovery is conditioned upon proof of reliance.

familiar with all aspects of the business. He was personally in charge of dealings with the factors. He acted on BarChris's behalf in making the financing agreements with Talcott and he handled the negotiations with Talcott in the spring of 1961. He talked with customers about their delinquencies.

Russo prepared the list of jobs which went into the backlog figure. He knew the status of those jobs. In addition to being chief executive officer of BarChris, he was a director of T-Bowl International, Inc., and the principals in St. Ann's were his friends.

It was Russo who arranged for the temporary increase in Bar-Chris's cash in banks on December 31, 1960, a transaction which borders on the fraudulent. He was thoroughly aware of BarChris's stringent financial condition in May 1961. He had personally advanced large sums to BarChris of which $175,000 remained unpaid as of May 16.

In short, Russo knew all the relevant facts. He could not have believed that there were no untrue statements or material omissions in the prospectus. Russo has no due diligence defenses.

Vitolo and Pugliese

They were the founders of the business who stuck with it to the end. Vitolo was president and Pugliese was vice president. Despite their titles, their field of responsibility in the administration of Bar-Chris's affairs during the period in question seems to have been less all-embracing than Russo's. Pugliese in particular appears to have limited his activities to supervising the actual construction work.

Vitolo and Pugliese are each men of limited education. It is not hard to believe that for them the prospectus was difficult reading, if indeed they read it at all.

But whether it was or not is irrelevant. The liability of a director who signs a registration statement does not depend upon whether or not he read it or, if he did, whether or not he understood what he was reading.

And in any case, Vitolo and Pugliese were not as naive as they claim to be. They were members of BarChris's executive committee. At meetings of that committee BarChris's affairs were discussed at length. They must have known what was going on. Certainly they knew of the inadequacy of cash in 1961. They knew of their own large advances to the company which remained unpaid. They knew that they had agreed not to deposit their checks until the financing proceeds were received. They knew and intended that part of the proceeds were to be used to pay their own loans.

All in all, the position of Vitolo and Pugliese is not sigificantly different, for present purposes, from Russo's. They could not have believed that the registration statement was wholly true and that no material facts had been omitted. And in any case, there is nothing to show that they made any investigation of anything which they may not have known about or understood. They have not proved their due diligence defenses.

Kircher

Kircher was treasurer of BarChris and its chief financial officer. He is a certified public accountant and an intelligent man. He was thoroughly familiar with BarChris's financial affairs. He knew the terms of BarChris's agreements with Talcott. He knew of the customers' delinquency problem. He participated actively with Russo in May 1961 in the successful effort to hold Talcott off until the financing proceeds came in. He knew how the financing proceeds were to be applied and he saw to it that they were so applied. He arranged the officers' loans and he knew all the facts concerning them.

Moreover, as a member of the executive committee, Kircher was kept informed as to those branches of the business of which he did not have direct charge. He knew about the operation of alleys, present and prospective. He knew that Capitol was included in 1960 sales and that Bridge and Yonkers were included in first quarter 1961 sales despite the fact that they were not sold. Kircher knew of the infirmities in customers' contracts included in the backlog figure. Indeed, at a later date, he specifically criticized Russo's handling of the T–Bowl situation. In brief, Kircher knew all the relevant facts.

Kircher worked on the preparation of the registration statement. He conferred with Grant and on occasion with Ballard. He supplied information to them about the company's business. He read the prospectus and understood it. He knew what it said and what it did not say.

Kircher's contention is that he had never before dealt with a registration statement, that he did not know what it should contain, and that he relied wholly on Grant, Ballard and Peat, Marwick to guide him. He claims that it was their fault, not his, if there was anything wrong with it. He says that all the facts were recorded in BarChris's books where these "experts" could have seen them if they had looked. He says that he truthfully answered all their questions. In effect, he says that if they did not know enough to ask the right questions and to give him the proper instructions, that is not his responsibility.

There is an issue of credibility here. In fact, Kircher was not frank in dealing with Grant and Ballard. He withheld information from them. But even if he had told them all the facts, this would not have constituted the due diligence contemplated by the statute. Knowing the facts, Kircher had reason to believe that the expertised portion of the prospectus, i.e., the 1960 figures, was in part incorrect. He could not shut his eyes to the facts and rely on Peat, Marwick for that portion.

As to the rest of the prospectus, knowing the facts, he did not have a reasonable ground to believe it to be true. On the contrary, he must have known that in part it was untrue. Under these circumstances, he was not entitled to sit back and place the blame on the lawyers for not advising him about it.

Kircher has not proved his due diligence defenses. . . .

Auslander

Auslander was an "outside" director, i.e., one who was not an officer of BarChris. He was chairman of the board of Valley Stream National Bank in Valley Stream, Long Island. In February 1961 Vitolo asked him to become a director of BarChris. Vitolo gave him an enthusiastic account of BarChris's progress and prospects. As an inducement, Vitolo said that when BarChris received the proceeds of a forthcoming issue of securities, it would deposit $1,000,000 in Auslander's bank.[18]

In February and early March 1961, before accepting Vitolo's invitation, Auslander made some investigation of BarChris. He obtained Dun & Bradstreet reports which contained sales and earnings figures for periods earlier than December 31, 1960. He caused inquiry to be made of certain of BarChris's banks and was advised that they regarded BarChris favorably. He was informed that inquiry of Talcott had also produced a favorable response.

On March 3, 1961, Auslander indicated his willingness to accept a place on the board. Shortly thereafter, on March 14, Kircher sent him a copy of BarChris's annual report for 1960. Auslander observed that BarChris's auditors were Peat, Marwick. They were also the auditors for the Valley Stream National Bank. He thought well of them.

Auslander was elected a director on April 17, 1961. The registration statement in its original form had already been filed, of course without his signature. On May 10, 1961, he signed a signature page for the first amendment to the registration statement which was filed on May 11, 1961. This was a separate sheet without any document attached. Auslander did not know that it was a signature page for a registration statement. He vaguely understood that it was something "for the SEC."

Auslander attended a meeting of BarChris's directors on May 15, 1961. At that meeting he, along with the other directors, signed the signature sheet for the second amendment which constituted the registration statement in its final form. Again, this was only a separate sheet without any document attached. Auslander never saw a copy of the registration statement in its final form.

At the May 15 directors' meeting, however, Auslander did realize that what he was signing was a signature sheet to a registration statement. This was the first time that he had appreciated that fact. A copy of the registration statement in its earlier form as amended on

---

18. After BarChris received the financing proceeds, it deposited in the Valley Stream National Bank not $1,000,000, but $150,000 in a checking account and $150,000 in a six-months' time deposit. The checking account was reduced to approximately $12,000 within a few weeks.

May 11, 1961 was passed around at the meeting. Auslander glanced at it briefly. He did not read it thoroughly.

At the May 15 meeting, Russo and Vitolo stated that everything was in order and that the prospectus was correct. Auslander believed this statement.

In considering Auslander's due diligence defenses, a distinction is to be drawn between the expertised and non-expertised portions of the prospectus. As to the former, Auslander knew that Peat, Marwick had audited the 1960 figures. He believed them to be correct because he had confidence in Peat, Marwick. He had no reasonable ground to believe otherwise.

As to the non-expertised portions, however, Auslander is in a different position. He seems to have been under the impression that Peat, Marwick was responsible for all the figures. This impression was not correct, as he would have realized if he had read the prospectus carefully. Auslander made no investigation of the accuracy of the prospectus. He relied on the assurance of Vitolo and Russo, and upon the information he had received in answer to his inquiries back in February and early March. These inquiries were general ones, in the nature of a credit check. The information which he received in answer to them was also general, without specific reference to the statements in the prospectus, which was not prepared until some time thereafter.

It is true that Auslander became a director on the eve of the financing. He had little opportunity to familiarize himself with the company's affairs. The question is whether, under such circumstances, Auslander did enough to establish his due diligence defense with respect to the non-expertised portions of the prospectus.

Although there is a dearth of authority under Section 11 on this point, an English case under the analogous Companies Act is of some value. In Adams v. Thrift, [1915] 1 Ch. 557, aff'd, [1915] 2 Ch. 21, it was held that a director who knew nothing about the prospectus and did not even read it, but who relied on the statement of the company's managing director that it was "all right," was liable for its untrue statements. See also In the Matter of Interstate Hosiery Mills, Inc., 4 S.E.C. 706 (1939).

Section 11 imposes liability in the first instance upon a director, no matter how new he is. He is presumed to know his responsibility when he becomes a director. He can escape liability only by using that reasonable care to investigate the facts which a prudent man would employ in the management of his own property. In my opinion, a prudent man would not act in an important matter without any knowledge of the relevant facts, in sole reliance upon representations of persons who are comparative strangers and upon general information which does not purport to cover the particular case. To say that such minimal conduct measures up to the statutory standard would, to all intents and purposes, absolve new directors from responsibility merely because they are new. This is not a sensible construction of Section 11, when one bears in mind its fundamental purpose of requiring full and truthful disclosure for the protection of investors.

I find and conclude that Auslander has not established his due diligence defense with respect to the misstatements and omissions in those portions of the prospectus other than the audited 1960 figures.
. . .

Grant

Grant became a director of BarChris in October 1960. His law firm was counsel to BarChris in matters pertaining to the registration of securities. Grant drafted the registration statement for the stock issue in 1959 and for the warrants in January 1961. He also drafted the registration statement for the debentures. In the preliminary division of work between him and Ballard, the underwriters' counsel, Grant took initial responsibility for preparing the registration statement, while Ballard devoted his efforts in the first instance to preparing the indenture.

Grant is sued as a director and as a signer of the registration statement. This is not an action against him for malpractice in his capacity as a lawyer. Nevertheless, in considering Grant's due diligence defenses, the unique position which he occupied cannot be disregarded. As the director most directly concerned with writing the registration statement and assuring its accuracy, more was required of him in the way of reasonable investigation than could fairly be expected of a director who had no connection with this work.

There is no valid basis for plaintiffs' accusation that Grant knew that the prospectus was false in some respects and incomplete and misleading in others. Having seen him testify at length, I am satisfied as to his integrity. I find that Grant honestly believed that the registration statement was true and that no material facts had been omitted from it.

In this belief he was mistaken, and the fact is that for all his work, he never discovered any of the errors or omissions which have been recounted at length in this opinion, with the single exception of Capitol Lanes. He knew that BarChris had not sold this alley and intended to operate it, but he appears to have been under the erroneous impression that Peat, Marwick had knowingly sanctioned its inclusion in sales because of the allegedly temporary nature of the operation.

Grant contends that a finding that he did not make a reasonable investigation would be equivalent to a holding that a lawyer for an issuing company, in order to show due diligence, must make an independent audit of the figures supplied to him by his client. I do not consider this to be a realistic statement of the issue. There were errors and omissions here which could have been detected without an audit. The question is whether, despite his failure to detect them, Grant made a reasonable effort to that end.

Much of this registration statement is a scissors and paste-pot job. Grant lifted large portions from the earlier prospectuses, modifying them in some instances to the extent that he considered necessary. But BarChris's affairs had changed for the worse by May 1961. Statements that were accurate in January were no longer accurate in May. Grant never discovered this. He accepted the assurances of Kircher and Russo that any change which might have occurred had been for the better, rather than the contrary.

It is claimed that a lawyer is entitled to rely on the statements of his client and that to require him to verify their accuracy would set an unreasonably high standard. This is too broad a generalization. It is all a matter of degree. To require an audit would obviously be unreasonable. On the other hand, to require a check of matters easily verifiable is not unreasonable. Even honest clients can make mistakes. The statute imposes liability for untrue statements regardless of whether they are intentionally untrue. The way to prevent mistakes is to test oral information by examining the original written record.

There were things which Grant could readily have checked which he did not check. For example, he was unaware of the provisions of the agreements between BarChris and Talcott. He never read them. Thus, he did not know, although he readily could have ascertained, that BarChris's contingent liability on Type B leaseback arrangements was 100 per cent, not 25 per cent. He did not appreciate that if BarChris defaulted in repurchasing delinquent customers' notes upon Talcott's demand, Talcott could accelerate all the customer paper in its hands, which amounted to over $3,000,000.

As to the backlog figure, Grant appreciated that scheduled unfilled orders on the company's books meant firm commitments, but he never asked to see the contracts which, according to the prospectus, added up to $6,905,000. Thus, he did not know that this figure was overstated by some $4,490,000.

Grant was unaware of the fact that BarChris was about to operate Bridge and Yonkers. He did not read the minutes of those subsidiaries which would have revealed that fact to him. On the subject of minutes, Grant knew that minutes of certain meetings of the BarChris executive committee held in 1961 had not been written up. Kircher, who had acted as secretary at those meetings, had complete notes of them. Kircher told Grant that there was no point in writing up the minutes because the matters discussed at those meetings were purely routine. Grant did not insist that the minutes be written up, nor did he look at Kircher's notes. If he had, he would have learned that on February 27, 1961 there was an extended discussion in the executive committee meeting about customers' delinquencies, that on March 8, 1961 the committee had discussed the pros and cons of alley operation by BarChris, that on March 18, 1961 the committee was informed that BarChris was constructing or about to begin constructing twelve alleys for which it had no contracts, and that on May 13, 1961 Dreyfuss, one of the worst delinquents, had filed a petition in Chapter X.

Grant knew that there had been loans from officers to BarChris in the past because that subject had been mentioned in the 1959 and January 1961 prospectuses. In March Grant prepared a questionnaire to be answered by officers and directors for the purpose of obtaining information to be used in the prospectus. The questionnaire did not inquire expressly about the existence of officers' loans. At approximately the same time, Grant prepared another questionnaire in order to obtain information on proxy statements for the annual stockholders' meeting. This questionnaire asked each officer to state whether he was indebted to BarChris, but it did not ask whether BarChris was indebted to him.

Despite the inadequacy of these written questionnaires, Grant did, on March 16, 1961, orally inquire as to whether any officers' loans were outstanding. He was assured by Russo, Vitolo and Pugliese that all such loans had been repaid. Grant did not ask again. He was unaware of the new loans in April. He did know, however, that, at Kircher's request, a provision was inserted in the indenture which gave loans from individuals priority over the debentures. Kircher's insistence on this clause did not arouse his suspicions.

It is only fair to say that Grant was given to understand by Kircher that there were no new officers' loans and that there would not be any before May 16. It is still a close question, however, whether, under all the circumstances, Grant should have investigated further, perhaps by asking Peat, Marwick, in the course of its S–1 review, to look at the books on this particular point. I believe that a careful man would have checked.

There is more to the subject of due diligence than this, particularly with respect to the application of proceeds and customers' delinquencies.

The application of proceeds language in the prospectus was drafted by Kircher back in January. It may well have expressed his intent at that time, but his intent, and that of the other principal officers of BarChris, was very different in May. Grant did not appreciate that the earlier language was no longer appropriate. He never learned of the situation which the company faced in May. He knew that BarChris was short of cash, but he had no idea how short. He did not know that BarChris was withholding delivery of checks already drawn and signed because there was not enough money in the bank to pay them. He did not know that the officers of the company intended to use immediately approximately one-third of the financing proceeds in a manner not disclosed in the prospectus, including approximately $1,000,000 in paying old debts.

In this connection, mention should be made of a fact which has previously been referred to only in passing. The "negative cash balance" in BarChris's Lafayette National Bank account in May 1961 included a check dated April 10, 1961 to the order of Grant's firm, Perkins, Daniels, McCormack & Collins, in the amount of $8,711. This check was not deposited by Perkins, Daniels until June 1, after the financing proceeds had been received by BarChris. Of course, if

Grant had knowingly withheld deposit of this check until that time, he would be in a position similar to Russo, Vitolo and Pugliese. I do not believe, however, that that was the case. I find that the check was not delivered by BarChris to Perkins, Daniels until shortly before June 1.

This incident is worthy of mention, however, for another reason. The prospectus stated on page 10 that Perkins, Daniels had "received fees aggregating $13,000" from BarChris. This check for $8,711 was one of those fees. It had not been received by Perkins, Daniels prior to May 16. Grant was unaware of this. In approving this erroneous statement in the prospectus, he did not consult his own bookkeeper to ascertain whether it was correct. Kircher told him that the bill had been paid and Grant took his word for it. If he had inquired and had found that this representation was untrue, this discovery might well have led him to a realization of the true state of BarChris's finances in May 1961.

As far as customers' delinquencies are concerned, although Grant discussed this with Kircher, he again accepted the assurances of Kircher and Russo that no serious problem existed. He did not examine the records as to delinquencies, although BarChris maintained such a record. Any inquiry on his part of Talcott or an examination of BarChris's correspondence with Talcott in April and May 1961 would have apprised him of the true facts. It would have led him to appreciate that the statement in this prospectus, carried over from earlier prospectuses, to the effect that since 1955 BarChris had been required to repurchase less than one-half of one per cent of discounted customers' notes could no longer properly be made without further explanation.

Grant was entitled to rely on Peat, Marwick for the 1960 figures. He had no reasonable ground to believe them to be inaccurate. But the matters which I have mentioned were not within the expertised portion of the prospectus. As to this, Grant, was obliged to make a reasonable investigation. I am forced to find that he did not make one. After making all due allowances for the fact that BarChris's officers misled him, there are too many instances in which Grant failed to make an inquiry which he could easily have made which, if pursued, would have put him on his guard. In my opinion, this finding on the evidence in this case does not establish an unreasonably high standard in other cases for company counsel who are also directors. Each case must rest on its own facts. I conclude that Grant has not established his due diligence defenses except as to the audited 1960 figures.

SECTION 8. BLUE SKY LAWS

NOTE ON BLUE SKY LAWS

Prior to the entry of the federal government into the field of securities regulation in 1933, almost all of the states had adopted statutes designed to protect the public from "speculative schemes which have no more basis than so many feet of 'blue sky.'"[1] Since section 18 of the 1933 Act provides that "Nothing in this title shall affect the jurisdiction of the securities commission (or any agency or office performing like functions) of any State . . . over any securities or any person," state and federal regulation have continued side by side.

At the present time, all states have blue sky laws in effect. These laws are of major significance, partly because many securities offerings are not registered under the federal Securities Act by virtue of exemptions, and partly because many of the blue-sky laws go beyond the disclosure requirements of the Securities Act.

The state statutes vary tremendously in coverage, approach and impact. Three basic methods of regulation are employed, which are sometimes referred to as the fraud, dealer-registration, and securities-registration methods. The vast majority of the states have adopted all three methods to varying extents, but the methods are embodied in different forms, and standards and procedures vary widely from state to state.

1. *The fraud method.* The fraud method simply makes certain practices, usually described by some form of the word "fraud," grounds for criminal prosecution, suspension of trading, or both. The blue sky administrator normally has broad investigatory powers, but those powers are unlikely to be exercised in the absence of complaint or suspicious circumstances. Probably for this reason, the fraud method is not thought to be sufficient in itself.

2. *The dealer-registration method.* The dealer-registration method requires dealers (including issuers, brokers, and salesmen) to register as a prerequisite to trading in securities within a state's borders. The amount, detail, and nature of the information that must be submitted varies widely. In a majority of states, registration may be denied or revoked for cause, and the administrator sometimes has considerable discretion in determining whether a dealer shall be permitted to do business within the state.

3. *The securities-registration method.* The securities-registration method prohibits dealing in an issue of securities until the issue has been qualified under the statutory standard in accordance with the statutory procedure. This method is sometimes referred to as "merit regulation," because, in contrast to registration under the Securities Act, the blue sky administrator can deny registration on the ground that the securities issue lacks merit, even though full disclosure has been made. The standards adopted and the procedures prescribed exhibit considerable variation from state to state. In general, the standards and procedures are aimed at unseasoned speculative securities being offered to the general public.

1. Hall v. Geiger–Jones Co., 242 U.S. 539, 550, 37 S.Ct. 217, 220–221, 61 L.Ed. 480, 489 (1917).

Three basic types of approaches fall within the securities-registration or merit-regulation method.

Under the *qualifying* approach, trading in non-exempt securities is permitted only following an affirmative administrative determination that the issue meets a designated statutory standard, such as "fair, just and equitable." More specific standards are usually imposed on the qualification of particularly unsafe issues. Thus "in practically all of the states, promotion stock, 'cheap stock,' and options are limited to stated percentages, or amounts which the administrators may deem reasonable." Mofsky, Blue Sky Restrictions on New Business Promotions, 169 Duke L.J. 273. Also, "39 states . . . requires escrow arrangements [for the promotional shares]." Id.

Under the *notification* approach, which is often available for seasoned securities, registration by notification becomes effective after a designated period unless the administrator moves to block it.

The *coordination* approach is similar to the notification approach, but is available only for issues registered under the federal Securities Act. The information submitted to the administrator basically consists of copies of the material filed with the SEC. The state registration "becomes effective at the moment the federal registration statement becomes effective," in the absence of adverse action by the administrator.

The potential for automatic effectiveness under the notification and coordination approaches does not mean that securities offerings will avoid merit review. During the waiting period, the administrator can and often does review an offering in light of the applicable merit criteria.

The bewildering variety of blue sky laws has led to attempts standardization. A Uniform Securities Act, drafted by Professor Loss, was adopted by the National Conference of Commissioners on Uniform State Laws in the 1950's and subsequently adopted by about three-fourths of the states, with varying degrees of amendment. At their 1985 annual meeting, the Commissioners approved a revised act, the Uniform Securities Act (1985). See Titus, Uniform Securities Act (1985), 19 Review of Securities & Commodities Regulation 81 (1986).

*

INDEX

References are to Pages

1003

†